The Prentice Hall Dictionary

of Culinary Arts

Second Edition

STEVEN LABENSKY

GAYE G. INGRAM

SARAH R. LABENSKY

ILLUSTRATIONS BY WILLIAM E. INGRAM

PEARSON

Prentice
Hall

Upper Saddle River, NJ 07458

Exectutive Editor: Vernon R. Anthony
Editorial Assistant: Beth Dyke
Director of Production & Manufacturing: Bruce Johnson
Managing Editor: Mary Carnis
Manufacturing Buyer: Cathleen Petersen
Creative Design Director: Cheryl Asherman
Cover Design Coordinator: Miguel Ortiz
Cover Design: Anthony Gemmellaro
Senior Marketing Manager: Ryan DeGrote
Senior Marketing Coordinator: Elizabeth Farrell
Marketing Assistant: Les Roberts
Composition: Carlisle Pubishers Services

Pearson Prentice Hall™ is a trademark of Pearson Education, Inc.
Pearson® is a registered trademark of Pearson plc
Prentice Hall® is a registered trademark of Pearson Education, Inc.

Pearson Education LTD.
Pearson Education Singapore, Pte. Ltd
Pearson Education, Canada, Ltd
Pearson Education–Japan
Pearson Education Australia PTY, Limited
Pearson Education North Asia Ltd
Pearson Educaçion de Mexico, S.A. de C.V.
Pearson Education Malaysia, Pte. Ltd

10   9   8   14 13 12

ISBN 0-13-171673-5

Contents

A Note from the Authors

One term not included in this dictionary is **culinary arts.** It is a phrase that means different things to different people and we could neither find nor devise any definition that captured all of its nuances. In the final analysis, however, we realized that it is this compendium of more than 25,000 entries on topics such as ingredients, preparation methods, restaurant management, wine and wine-making, cooking equipment, food history, food safety and sanitation, nutrition, prepared dishes and many more that truly defines culinary arts.

To assist you in using this dictionary, we note several rules that we followed in its preparation:

- If sources provided multiple, verified spellings for a term (including transliterations), we included alternative or variant spellings, listing the most commonly used one first.

- We tried to be faithful to the use of accent marks, characters and capitalization rules as found in the original (if written in the Latin alphabet) or most commonly approved source; often, other writers are not and many of the terms found here may appear elsewhere with the appropriate accents or capitalization omitted or altered.

- Pronunciations are given in a sounded-out phonetic form rather than with the standard phonetic alphabet with diacritical marks. This was done for the sake of practicality and usability. For languages that do not use the Latin alphabet, the transliteration is often the phonetic pronunciation as well (ex., Arabic).

- Where a geographic origin or time period is given, we did so with the understanding that such a designation identified the principal indigenous source of time period and that the specific ingredient, dish or the like may be available in other areas and eras.

Nothing found in this book, save this note, is the original creation of the authors. As with all reference books, it is a compilation derived from sources new and old, formally published and casually discussed. To paraphrase H. L. Mencken's preface to his *The American Language,* Supplement II (New York: Alfred A. Knopf, 1923):

> *We are not trained in linguistic science, and can thus claim no profundity for this book. It represents gatherings, not of experts in linguistics, but simply of teachers, cooks, and gourmets interested in language, and if there appears in it any virtue at all it is with the homely virtue of diligence.*

Errors and omissions are regrettable, but inevitable. We welcome comments and corrections, additions and explanations from users.

We wish to thank William Ingram for his superb illustrations and assistance throughout this project and Andrew W. Ingram for sharing his expertise in beer-making. We also wish to thank Neil Marquardt, our editor at Prentice Hall, for his guidance and patience, as well as Maurizio Cristiani of *Another Language* and Barry Karrh for their assistance with translations and pronunciations. Finally, we are indebted to our families and friends for their input and support during this project.

STEVEN LABENSKY
GAYE G. INGRAM
SARAH R. LABENSKY

AAC American Academy of Chefs.

Aal (all) German for eel.

aam (ah-ah'm) Hindi for mango.

aardappel (AHR-dahp-pul) Dutch for potato.

aardbeien (AHR-bay-uh) Dutch for strawberry.

Aarey (ah-ah-ree) A firm, rindless Indian cheese made from water buffalo's milk; it has a slightly nutty flavor and evenly distributed small, round holes.

aataa (ah-ah-tah-ah) Hindi for whole wheat flour.

abacate (ah-bah-KA-ta) Portuguese for avocado.

abacates com mel (ah-bah-KA-tas kon mehl) A dish from the Cape Verde Islands consisting of avocados drizzled with honey.

abacaxi (ah-bah-kah-SHEE) Portuguese for pineapple; also known as ananás.

abaisse (ah-bess) French for a thin bottom crust; a rolled-out pastry or biscuit.

abalone (a-buh-LOH-nee) A group of gastropod mollusks found in warm seas worldwide, generally having a brownish-gray ear-shaped shell with an average length of 6 in. (17.7 cm), a large adductor muscle that fills the entire shell opening and an ivory flesh with a chewy texture and mild flavor; they are usually available canned or fresh; significant varieties include the black, ormer, pink, red and southern green abalones.

abats (ah-baht) French for offal.

abbacchio (ah-BAHK-ee-yoh) Italian for baby lamb.

abbacchio al forno (ah-BAHK-ee-yoh al four-no) An Italian dish of roasted baby lamb seasoned with rosemary.

abbey beer A Belgian style of bottle-conditioned beer traditionally brewed in Trappist abbeys; generally, it is a strong, full-bodied, top-fermenting ale.

abboccato (ah-bo-KAH-toe) 1. Italian for semisweet or semidry. 2. When referring to an Italian wine, the meaning is drier than dolce (sweet) and sweeter than secco (dry) and asciutto (very dry).

Abbott's Bitters The proprietary name of an all-purpose bitters used for beverages.

ABC laws *See* alcoholic beverage control laws.

Abendbrot (ah-behn-brot) German for evening bread and used to describe a light supper.

Abendessen (AH-bent-ss-en) German for dinner.

abenkwan A Ghanaian soup made with palm oil, onions, tomatoes, okra, eggplant, and fish or crab.

Aberdeen Angus (a-behr-deen) A breed of black hornless steer, originally bred in Scotland and now raised in the United States as the principal beef steer; also known as Angus and Black Angus.

Aberdeen sausage A long Scottish sausage made from beef, bacon fat, oatmeal and seasonings.

Aberlour The proprietary name of a single malt Scotch whisky; it is full bodied and aromatic with a mellow, lingering aftertaste.

abish (ah-bish) A mixture of ground beef flavored with ginger, onions, garlic and tomatoes used as stuffing for unripened papaya, bell peppers or potatoes in Ethiopian cuisine.

abóbora (ah-BAW-boh-rah) A large pumpkinlike squash with an orange flesh; used principally in Portuguese soups.

abon (ah-bon) Fried sweetened and spiced flakes of poultry, beef, pork, fish or shellfish used as a garnish for Chinese and Indonesian rice dishes.

Abondance (ah-bone-DAHNCE) A semifirm cow's milk cheese from France's Savoie region; it has a creamy-brown natural brushed rind; a light yellow interior; and a buttery, fruity, nutty flavor; it is an excellent melting cheese.

above the line Promotional expenses associated with advertising in a particular medium.

aboyeur (ah-boh-yer) At a food services operation following the brigade system, it is the person who accepts orders from the dining room, relays them to the various station chefs and reviews the dishes before service; also known as the expediter.

abrestir An Icelandic dish of coagulated beestings milk served with thick cream, sugar and cinnamon.

abricot (ah-bree-COH) French for apricot.

Abricotine (ah-bree-COH-teen) The proprietary name of a French apricot liqueur.

abrikoos (ahb-ri-KOS) Dutch for apricot.

abrikos (ah-bree-KO-s) Russian for apricot.

abrow ne kokosi (ah-bro na koh-koh-see) A Ghanaian dish consisting of dried corn simmered with coconut milk and coconut flesh; also known as afiko.

abrow ne nkate A Ghanaian dish consisting of dried corn simmered with groundnuts or peanuts.

Abruzzese (ah-BROOZ-dzee) An Italian preparation method associated with Italy's Abruzzi region; the dishes are characterized by the generous use of very hot chiles.

absinthe (AHB-senth) An alcoholic beverage distilled from oil of wormwood, balm, mint, hyssop, fennel, star anise and a high-proof brandy; it has a light yellow-green color, has a pronounced licorice flavor and is banned in many countries because of its high alcohol content and the toxic effects of wormwood; it is usually consumed diluted with water. *See* Pernod.

Absinthe Suissesse A cocktail made with absinthe, Pernod or Herbsainte, egg white, heavy cream, orgeat syrup and ice mixed in a blender and served in an old-fashioned glass.

absolute alcohol Clinically pure ethyl alcohol (200 proof or 100%); it is used as a baseline for comparing the alcohol content of beverages.

absorbent packing Using absorbing materials in a package to take up any liquid that may leak from the packed container holding the liquids.

absorption 1. The incorporation of a liquid into a solid or of a gas into a liquid or solid. 2. The process by which products of digestion such as monosaccharides are passed through the walls of the small intestines into the blood to be carried to other parts of the body.

abura (AH-boo-rah) Japanese for oil.

aburage (ah-boo-rah-GAY) Japanese for fried bean curd. *See* bean curd, cotton.

abura-kiri (ah-boo-rah-kee-ree) Shallow Japanese pans fitted with a rack; they are designed to quickly drain oil from cooked foods.

aburu (AH-boo-roo) Japanese for to roast.

Abyssinian gooseberry A small fruit native to East Africa; it has a delicate orange color, a minimal amount of flesh and a flavor reminiscent of apricots.

AC *See* average check.

aca (A-ka) A Peruvian maize beer; the recipe has been in use for more than 2200 years.

acacia (AH-kay-sha) A food additive derived from trees of the genus *Acacia* and used as an emulsifier, stabilizer, thickener, flavoring agent, flavoring adjuvant and/or formulation aid in processed foods such as beverages, chewing gum, confections, dairy products, fats and snack foods; also known as arabic and gum arabic.

acacia honey A pale, clear honey with a delicate scent made principally from acacia blossoms in China, France, Canada, Hungary, Italy, Romania and elsewhere; it is one of the few honeys that does not crystallize with age.

acar; atjar (ah-car; at-jar) Indonesian spiced, cooked vegetables, usually cabbage with vinegar and chiles.

acarajé; acarage (ah-cah-raw-ha) Brazilian black-eyed pea fritters flavored with dried shrimp, fried in dendê oil and served with a sauce made from dried shrimp, onions, chiles, ginger and dendê oil.

acarne (ah-karhn) French for sea bream.

acceptance sampling A method of receiving fungible goods in which a few randomly selected items are examined and the lot is rejected or accepted based on this random examination.

accidental food additive *See* incidental food additive.

acciuga (ah-CHOO-gah) Italian for the Mediterranean anchovy; also known as alice.

account A record in which the current status (balance) of each type of asset, liability, owner's equity, sale and expense is maintained.

accounts payable Debts to suppliers of goods or services (creditors).

accounts receivable Amounts due from customers or guests (debtors).

ace in the hole *See* hobo egg.

aceite (ah-SAY-tay) Spanish for oil.

aceite de oliva (ah-SAY-tay day oh-lee-vah) A marketing designation for medium-grade Spanish cooking oil produced from a blend of refined and cold-pressed olive oils.

aceite de oliva virgen (ah-SAY tay day oh-lee-vah veer-jan) A marketing designation for high quality cold-pressed Spanish olive oil.

aceite de oliva virgen extra (ah-SAY -tay day oh-lee-vah veer-jan ex-trah) A marketing designation for the finest cold-pressed Spanish olive oil.

aceituna (ah-say-TOO-nah) Spanish for olive.

acepipes (a-se-PEE-peesh) Portuguese for hors d'oeuvre.

acerbic (ah-SER-bec) A wine-tasting term for a bitter, tart, coarse or astringent flavor caused by fermenting unripened grapes.

acerola (ah-see-ROLL-ah) A bright red cherry-sized fruit that grows on shrubs (*Malpighia punicifolia*) in the West Indies; it has three pits, a juicy flesh, a moderately acidic, raspberry-like flavor and is eaten fresh or used in preserves and pies; also known as Barbados cherry and West Indian cherry.

acescent (uh-SEHS-uhnt) 1. Turning sour or tending to turn sour. 2. Slightly sour. 3. A wine-tasting term for a vinegary aroma and flavor; caused by aerobic bacterial spoilage, a slight acescence is sometimes desirable in a port or a red table wine that has been well-aged in a wooden cask.

acesulfame-K; acesulfame potassium (a-seh-SUHL-faym-K) A noncaloric artificial sweetener approximately 200 times sweeter than sugar; it is used in processed foods such as beverages, confections, sugar substitutes, dairy products and dry bases for puddings.

acetal (ah-see-thal) A food additive with a nutlike flavor used as a flavoring agent and/or adjuvant.

acetanisole A food additive with a hawthornlike aroma used as a flavoring agent.

acetate of lime *See* calcium acetate.

acetic acid (a-SEE-tik) 1. An organic acid naturally occurring in plant and animal tissues. 2. The essential constituent of vinegar. 3. A food additive used as a pickling and curing agent, flavoring agent, flavoring adjuvant, pH control agent and/or vehicle in processed foods such as salad dressings and prepared sauces; also known as ethanoic acid. 4. A colorless, volatile acid found in wines; if an excessive amount develops, it will turn the wine to vinegar. *See* volatile acidity.

aceto (ah-CHEH-toh) Italian for vinegar.

aceto Balsamico (ah-CHEH-toh bahl-sah-MEH-coh) Italian for balsamic vinegar.

acetone peroxide A food additive used as a dough conditioner and/or flour aging and bleaching agent.

acetosa (ah-cheh-TOH-sha) Italian for sorrel.

acetylated monoglyceride A food additive used as an emulsifier, a protective coating for meat products, nuts and fruits (to improve their appearance, texture and shelf life) and an aerating agent in cake shortening and whipped products.

Achaea (ah-KEY-ah) A grape-growing and wine-producing region in Greece located along the southern coast of the Gulf of Corinth; it produces both red and white wines.

achar (aah-chaar) Spicy or sweet pickled and salted Indian relishes.

achara (ah-chah-rah) A Filipino relish of pickled fruits or vegetables garnished with grated green papaya or pickled cabbage.

achiote seeds (ah-chee-OH-tay) The seeds of the annatto tree, native to South America; the pulp surrounding the seeds is used as a yellow-to-red coloring agent for butter, cheese, margarine and smoked fish (it also adds a slightly musky flavor); also known as annatto and arnatto.

acid 1. Any substance that releases hydrogen ions in a watery solution; acids have a pH of less than 7, react with metals to form salts and neutralize bases. 2. A tasting term for a food or beverage with a pleasantly tart or tangy flavor; it can be a defect if too pronounced, however.

acid–base balance The mechanisms maintaining the proper equilibrium of acidity and alkalinity of the body's fluids (generally a pH of 7.35–7.45).

acidic 1. A sharp, sour or tart flavor. 2. A wine-tasting term for a sharp, sour flavor caused by an abnormally high acid content.

acidophilus cheese (ass-ceh-DOHF-eh-lus) A soft cheese made in the Mediterranean region from milk and the bacteria used for acidophilus milk; it has a white, creamy interior and a sharp, tart flavor.

acidophilus milk Milk cultured with *Lactobacillus acidophilus,* bacteria that consume lactose and produce lactic acid in the process (which sometimes causes a sour flavor); acidophilus milk and products made from it are used by people who are lactose intolerant.

acidulants Acidic food additives used as flavoring agents, preservatives, coagulating agents and the like.

acidulated water Water mixed with a small amount of lemon juice or vinegar and used to prevent the discoloration of fruits and vegetables caused by acidulation.

acidulation The browning of cut fruit caused by the reaction of an enzyme (polyphenoloxidase) with the phenolic com-

pounds present in these fruits; this browning is often mistakenly attributed to an exposure to oxygen; also known as enzymatic browning.

acini di pepe (ah-CHEE-nee dee PEE-pee) Italian for peppercorns and used to describe rice-shaped pasta.

Ackerbeere (ah-kuh-bear) German for dewberry.

acma (ahk-mah) A buttery Turkish yeast roll.

aconitic acid A food additive derived from members of the plant family Ranunculaceae and used as a flavoring agent and/or adjuvant.

açordas (ah-sor-dass) Portuguese soups made from broth, bread and sometimes olive oil, garlic, cilantro and eggs.

acorn The fruit of the oak tree (genus *Quercus*), it is shaped like a teardrop; some varieties are edible (but have a woody texture) and are eaten raw, roasted or roasted and ground into a flour or coffee substitute.

acorn curd *See* totori muk.

acorn squash A small- to medium-sized acorn-shaped winter squash with an orange-streaked dark green fluted shell (orange, yellow and creamy white varieties are also available), a pale orange flesh, a large seed cavity and a slightly sweet, nutty flavor.

acorn squash

acqua (AHK-kwah) Italian for water.

acrid 1. A sharp or biting flavor or aroma; pungent. 2. A wine-tasting term for a harsh, bitter aroma or flavor.

acrolein A bitter, volatile chemical produced from overheating fats.

acrospire The embryonic plant growing inside a grain's husk during germination.

active dry yeast A dehydrated granular form of yeast; a lack of moisture causes the yeast cells to become dormant, thus extending the product's shelf life. *See* yeast.

Acton, Eliza (Brit., 1799–1859) Author of *Modern Cookery for Private Families* (1845); intended as a text for British housewives during the first half of the 19th century, its recipes are clear with well-organized directions.

actual cost pricing Pricing an item based on the item's actual costs; in the food services industry, this price includes the cost of the raw ingredients, labor costs and operating costs.

açúcar (a-SOO-kar) Portuguese for sugar.

acute A tasting term, especially for wine and cheese, for a strongly or sharply defined aroma or flavor.

acute disease A disease that has a rapid onset, severe symptoms and a short course. *See* chronic disease.

Adam's ale Slang used in soda fountains for water.

adana (ah-da-nah) A Turkish soup consisting of beef stock and small meat-filled dumplings, garnished with yogurt, fresh thyme and mint.

adas (ah-dass) Arabic for lentils.

additive *See* food additive.

addled A traditional North American term for rotten or spoiled food.

adductor A mollusk's single muscle, it extends from one valve (shell) through the flesh to the other valve; when it is relaxed, the shell is open; in many mollusks, such as abalone, it is the principal edible part.

ade A slightly tart beverage made of sugar (or other sweetener), water and a citrus juice such as lemon (for lemonade), lime (for limeade) or orange (for orangeade); it is served chilled in a tall glass, usually with ice.

adega (ah-DE-ja) Portuguese for winery.

Adelaide Hills A grape-growing and wine-producing region in South Australia; the principal grape grown is a cool-climate Chardonnay that is used for both still and sparkling wines.

Ädelost (ah-dell-ohst) A Swedish and Finnish cheese made from whole cow's milk; it has a soft to semisoft paste, soft rind and greenish-blue veining.

adequacy In the nutrition context, the consumption of food and drink in amounts sufficient for a balanced diet. *See* moderation *and* variety.

adipic acid A food additive used as a flavoring agent, leavening agent and/or pH control agent in processed foods such as beverages, gravies, fats, frozen dairy desserts, gelatins and snack foods; also known as hexanedioic acid.

adipocytes Fat cells.

adjunct; adjunct grains Any fermentable ingredient, other than malted barley, added to a beer's mash as a source of sugar.

adjust To taste a dish and add salt, freshly ground black pepper or other seasonings, if necessary.

admiral sauce *See* amiral, sauce.

adobado (ah-doh-BAA-doh) 1. A Mexican and Latin American chile, garlic and herb marinade used to season meat. 2. Spanish for marinated and generally used to describe marinated beef. 3. A Filipino cooking method in which pieces of meat and garlic are browned and then broth and vinegar are added as a sauce before serving.

adobe bread (ah-doh-bee) A yeast-leavened bread made by the Pueblo Indians of the American Southwest; it is traditionally flavored with nuts or seeds and baked in a beehive-shaped oven.

adobo (ah-DOH-bo) A Filipino dish consisting of meat, fish or vegetables seasoned with garlic, vinegar, soy sauce, pepper and coconut milk.

adobo sauce (ah-DOH-bo) A Mexican seasoning paste or sauce made from ground chiles, herbs and vinegar.

adrak (add-rack) Hindi for fresh ginger root or green ginger; also known as sonth.

Adriatic fig A green-skinned, white-fleshed fig.

adulterate To make a substance impure by adding foreign, undesirous or inferior matter.

Advocaat; Advokatt (ad-voh-KAHT) A Dutch liqueur made from egg, brandy and sugar; it is thick and creamy with a yellow-beige color and a flavor similar to that of eggnog.

adzuki; azuki (ah-ZOO-kee; AH-zoo-kee) A small, somewhat square red bean of Asian origin (*Vigna angularis*); popular in Japanese cuisine either sugar coated or made into a sweet paste that is used to make sweets.

aeble (EHB-lerr) Danish for apple.

aebleskiver; ebleskiver (eh-bleh-SKEE-vor) 1. A Danish puffed cake or doughnut made in a specially designed pan with indentations for individually frying each cake; the cake is usually served as a breakfast treat with powdered sugar and strawberry jam. 2. Danish for doughnut.

aebleskiver pan (eh-bleh-SKEE-vor) A cast-iron pan with seven rounded 2.25-in.-wide indentations used for making aebleskiver.

aeg (ehg) Danish for egg.

aegir, sauce (ahg-rah) A French compound sauce made from a hollandaise flavored with dry or prepared mustard.

ae mono (ah-e moh-noh) Japanese for dressed foods, usually saladlike dishes served chilled.

aenjera *See* injera.

aerate 1. To dissolve air in a liquid or to expose a liquid to air. 2. To add air to a food (e.g., sifting flour or beating egg whites).

aerating agent; aerating gas *See* propellant.

aerobic bacteria; aerobes *See* bacteria, aerobic.

aerobic exercise Steady nonstop activities that require a steady oxygen intake and use the large muscle groups (e.g., jogging, swimming and biking). *See* anaerobic exercise.

afarseq (ah-fah-ah-sec) Hebrew for peach.

affetare (haf-fet-tarae) Italian for to slice.

affiné (ah-feen-nay) French term for a washed-rind cheese.

affumicato (ahf-foo-mee-KAA-toh) Italian for smoked.

afifsuke-nori (af-fee-sue-kee-noh-ree) Japanese for sheets of nori brushed with soy sauce.

afiko *See* abrow ne kokosi.

aflatoxin A toxin produced by molds and sometimes found on peanuts, cottonseed and corn.

African aubergines Any of a large group of plants grown in Africa, including the gnagnan and diakhatous; their fruit are slightly bitter and are eaten cooked.

African oil palm A palm (*Elaeis guinensis*) grown in western Africa; its red fruit yields a yellow oil used for cooking.

Afri-Koko A chocolate-coconut cordial made in Sierra Leone.

after-hours club An establishment open after bars are closed; some are open to members only and sell alcoholic beverages.

afternoon tea *See* tea, afternoon.

aftersmell An odor or aroma that lingers after a food or beverage has been swallowed.

aftertaste The sensation that remains in the mouth after swallowing or expectorating (spitting) a sampled food or beverage. *See* finish.

agar–agar; agar A food additive extracted from red algae and used as a flavoring agent, stabilizer and/or thickener in Asian foods and processed foods such as baked goods, baking mixes, frozen desserts, jellies, custards and confections; also known as Japanese gelatin and kanten.

agar-agar noodles Fine strips of agar-agar gelatin; used in Asian, particularly Chinese, cuisines.

agarico deliziosa (ha-ga-re-co da-li-tsio-sah) Italian for milky cap mushroom.

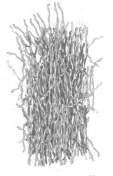

agar-agar noodles

agarico ostreato (ha-ga-re-co os-tra-ha-to) Italian for oyster mushroom.

agarico violetto (ha-ga-re-co ve-o-let-to) Italian for blewit.

agas (ah-gas) Hebrew for pear.

agave (ah-GAH-vee) A family of succulents native to the American Southwest, Central America and northern South America; the thick, pointed, flat leaves, which are sometimes poisonous if eaten raw, have a sweet, mild flavor when cooked.

agé (ah-gay) Japanese for deep-fry.

agé; agé puff (ah-gay) A hollow pouch or puff of deep-fried tofu, usually sold dried and used in Japanese cuisines; also known as aburage, deep-fried tofu puff and deep-fried tofu pouch.

aged meat Meat stored under specific temperature and humidity conditions to increase tenderness and flavor. *See* dry aging *and* wet aging.

agemono (AH-gay-mo-no) Japanese for fried foods.

ägg (ehg) Swedish for egg.

agglomerated cork A cork made from scraps of used corks glued together; also known as a composition cork or particle cork.

aging 1. The period during which freshly killed meat is allowed to rest so that the effects of rigor mortis dissipate. 2. The period during which freshly milled flour is allowed to rest so that it will whiten and produce less sticky doughs; this process can be accelerated chemically. 3. The period during which a cheese mellows and matures under specific temperature, humidity and other conditions; also known as curing. 4. The period during which wine, brandy, whiskey, certain beers and other alcoholic beverages are stored in oak barrels or stainless steel or glass tanks so that the slow, complex changes that add body, aroma and flavor characteristics can occur. 5. The period during which cigars are stored under humidified conditions to facilitate subtle mellowing.

aging agent A food additive used to accelerate the aging, maturing or ripening of processed foods such as flour or cheese; also known as a maturing agent or ripening agent.

agiter (ah-ghe-tay) French for to stir.

aglio (AH-l'yoh) Italian for garlic.

aglio e olio (AH-l'yoh a AW-loyh) Italian for garlic and oil, a dressing that is usually used on pasta.

agneau (ahn-YOH) French for lamb.

agnello (ahn-NYEHL-loa) Italian for lamb.

agnello arrosto (ahn-NYEHL-loa ah-roos-toh) Italian for roast lamb.

agnolotti (ahn-nyoa-LOT-tee) Crescent-shaped Italian ravioli.

agoni (ha-go-ne) Small freshwater flatfish found in Italy's Lake Como; they have a smoky flavor and are either cooked in oil and then marinated in a wild thyme–flavored vinegar or salted and dried; also known as sardina.

Agrafa (aah-yraa-pha) A Greek Gruyère-style cheese made from ewe's milk.

agrafe (ah-grahf) A clip used to secure the temporary cork in a bottle of sparkling wine during the secondary fermentation; it is now generally replaced with the less expensive crown cap.

agreeable A tasting term, especially for wine, for a well-defined, satisfying flavor and/or aroma.

agriao (ah-gree-ah-co) Portuguese for watercress.

agrio (ah-gree-oh) Spanish for sour.

agrodolce (aw-gro-DOLE-chay) Italian for a sweet–sour sauce.

água (AH-gwa) Portuguese for water.

agua (AH-gwa) Spanish for water.

aguacate (ah-gwa-KAH-tay) 1. Spanish for avocado. 2. A small variety of avocado that grows wild in the American Southwest.

aguamiel (AH-gwah-meel) The sticky, sweet sap from the agave plant, known in Mexico as the maguey and in the United States as the century plant; it is used to make tequila and mezcal.

aguardiente (ah-gwahr-DEHN-tay) 1. Spanish for brandy. 2. Any of a variety of high-alcohol-content, brandylike distilled spirits produced in Spain, South America, Mexico and the American Southwest.

aguardiente de cana (ah-gwahr-DEHN-tay day can-yeh) Aguardiente made from sugarcane or molasses; it is bottled without aging or rectification.

aguardiente UVA (ah-gwahr-DEHN-tay) Aguardiente made from grapes; it is bottled without aging or rectification.

agurk (ah-GOORK) Norwegian for cucumber.

ahi (ah-hee) Hawaiian for yellowfin tuna.

ahipa *See* jícama.

ahiru (AH-hee-ru) Japanese for duck.

ahjeen (aah-jhenn'h) Arabic for dough.

ahole (ah-hoh-lay) A saltwater fish found off Hawaii; it has large eyes and a silvery skin; the young fish is known as aholehole.

aholehole (ah-hoh-lay-hoh-lay) *See* ahole.

ahsal (aah-salh) Arabic for honey.

ahseer il limoon (aah-sheer ell la-moon) Arabic for lemon juice.

ahtapot (ah-taw-pot) Turkish for squid.

ahumado (ah-hoo-MAA-doh) Spanish for smoked.

ahuyama *See* calabaza.

ai ferri (aye FEH-ree) Italian term used to refer to any food that is cooked over a fire, such as on an outdoor grill or in an open hearth.

aiglefin (ah-ghil-fahn) French for haddock.

aigre (ay-gruh) French for sour, tart or bitter.

aigre-doux (ay-greh-DOO) French for the combined flavors of sour (aigre) and sweet (doux) (e.g., a sauce made with vinegar and sugar).

aiguillette (eh-gew-ee-ley) 1. A French cut of poultry (especially duck); it is a long, narrow slice of flesh taken from either side of the breastbone. 2. A French cut of the beef carcass; it is similar to rump round roast; also known as pièce de boeuf and pointe de culotte.

ail (ahy) French for garlic.

Ailsa Craig tomato A variety of large, spherical, red-skinned, juicy, flavorful tomato.

aïoli (ay-OH-lee) A garlic mayonnaise made in France's Provence region; it is used as a condiment or sauce.

aïoli à la Turque (ay-oh-LEE ah lah tewrk) A French sauce made from garlic and white bread soaked in milk, pressed through a sieve, blended with egg yolks and vinegar and then beaten with oil.

aipo (IE-poh) Portuguese for celery.

air curing The process of drying freshly picked tobacco in open-air covered barns to concentrate tobacco flavors and dissipate unwanted chemicals. *See* heat curing.

Airelle (ay-rehl) An eau-de-vie made from the red mountain cranberry. *See* Myrtille.

airelle rouge (ay-rehl rooj) French for cranberry.

Airén (ah'y-rain) A white wine grape grown throughout central Spain and used to make a white wine that is often distilled into brandy or used as a blending grape to lighten red wines.

airline bottle *See* nip.

airline breast A boneless chicken breast with the first wing bone attached.

airlock A one-way valve that allows carbon dioxide to escape from a beer fermentor and prevents air and contaminants from entering.

airspace Empty space between a liquid and its container's top.

aisu-kur-imu (I-su-koo-ri-moo) Japanese for ice cream.

aitch bone (H bohn) Part of a quadruped's pelvic bone; also known as the edge bone.

aji (ah-jee) Japanese for flavor.

aji (AH-khee) 1. A long, thin, tapering chile with thin flesh and a very hot, tropical fruit flavor; it has a green or red color when fresh and is yellow when dried and known as aji mirasol. 2. The common name used in Latin America to describe various members of the chile family *Capsicum baccatum.*

ajiaca (a-hee-a-ka) A Spanish meat and potato stew.

ajiaco (a-hee-a-koh) A Cuban stew made with pork, beef, yucca, taro, yam, sweet potatoes, calabaza, corn, chayotes and plantains and flavored with chiles, garlic and lime juice.

ajiaco bogatano (a-hee-a-koh bo-ga-tah-no) A Colombian soup made of chicken, potatoes and corn, flavored with onions, bay leaf, cumin seeds and thyme, and garnished with capers and avocado.

aji de gallina (a-hee day ga-jee-nah) A Peruvian dish consisting of chicken flavored with jalapeño, allspice, cumin and peanuts and garnished with boiled potatoes, hard-boiled eggs and olives.

aji dulce (AH-khee DOOL-seh) A small, elongated, wide-shouldered, fresh chile with a green, yellow, orange or red skin and a very fruity, hot flavor.

aji mirasol (AH-khee meh-rah-sohl) *See* aji.

aji-no-moto (ah-JEE-no-MO-toh) Japanese for monosodium glutamate.

aji-shioyaki (ah-jee-shi-o-ya-kee) A Japanese cooking method in which the food, usually fish or shellfish, is thickly coated with coarse salt before grilling or broiling; the salt forms a crust and does not render the foods too salty tasting.

ajo (AH-ho) Spanish for garlic.

ajonjoli (ah-hohn-hoh) Spanish for sesame seeds.

ajouter (ah-zhu-tay) French for to add (as in adding an ingredient).

ajowan seeds; ajwain seeds (aj-waa-an) Small greenish-brown seeds with a strong thymelike flavor used in Indian cuisines; also known as bishop's weed seeds and omum.

ajwi (AHJ-wee) Arabic for dates.

akagai (ah-kah-gah-ee) Japanese for the ark shell.

akami (ah-kah-mee) Japanese for the lean red flesh found near the spine of a tuna (maguro); it is used for sushi and sashimi. *See* chutoro *and* otoro.

aka miso (ah-kah me-soh) Japanese for dark bean paste.

akara (ah-cah-raw) Fritters made of white beans flavored with chiles and deep-fried in palm oil; traditionally made in West Africa (especially Nigeria and Mali) and now part of African-American cuisine.

akara awon (ah-cah-raw ah-won) Fritters made of white beans and okra.

akebia (AH-kee-be-ah) The fruit of a climbing shrub native to China, Korea and Japan; the banana-shaped fruit grows in clusters and has a gray-blue to purple skin, semitransparent white flesh, many black seeds and a mild flavor (both skin and flesh are edible).

akee (AH-kee) *See* genipa.

akee and saltfish A Jamaican dish of sautéed salted fish, onions, bacon, sweet peppers and tomatoes mixed with akee and flavored with basil and oregano.

å koke Norwegian for to boil.

aku (AH-ku) Hawaiian for skipjack tuna.

akule (ah-KOO-lay) A fish found off Hawaii; it is usually salted and dried; also known as bigeye scad.

akvavit *See* aquavit.

al (ahl) Italian for to the, at the or on the; used in relation to a food, it generally designates a style of preparation or presentation.

à la (ah lah) French for in the manner or style of; used in relation to a food, it designates a style of preparation or presentation.

à la carte (ah lah kart) 1. A menu on which each food and beverage is listed and priced separately. 2. Foods cooked to order, as opposed to foods cooked in advance and held for later service.

alae salt *See* Hawaiian salt.

à la king (ah lah KING) An American dish consisting of diced foods, usually chicken or turkey, in a cream sauce flavored with pimientos, mushrooms, green peppers and sometimes sherry.

Alameda (ah-lah-MEH-dah) A grape-growing and wine-producing county in northern California; the principal grapes grown are Chardonnay, Sauvignon Blanc, Sémillon and Gray Riesling as well as Cabernet Sauvignon and Petite Sirah.

à la mode (ah lah MOHD) 1. French for in the fashion or manner of. 2. In the United States, a dessert item topped with a scoop of ice cream.

alanin 1. An amino acid. 2. A food additive used as a nutrient source to significantly improve the biological quality of the total protein in a food containing naturally occurring protein.

Alaska cod *See* sablefish.

Alaskan halibut *See* Pacific halibut.

Alaskan king crab *See* king crab.

Alaskan pollock *See* pollock, Alaskan.

Alaskan Sweetheart potato A red-skinned potato with a pinkish, waxy flesh.

alati (ah-lah-tee) Greek for salt.

à la trompe d'Albanga A variety of squash with a long, thin, curved shape, a green-blushed, yellow skin and a pale, slightly sweet flesh.

albacora (ahl-bah-koh-rah) Portuguese for yellowfin tuna.

albacore French for yellowfin tuna.

albacore tuna (ahl-bah-kor) A variety of tuna found off Mexico and along the U.S. West Coast; it has a steely blue skin that becomes silvery on the belly, white flesh and an average market weight of 10–60 lb. (4.5–27 kg); it is often used for canning; also known as a longfin tuna.

albaricoque (al-bah-ri-koh-keh) Spanish for apricot.

Albariño (ahl-bah-REE-n'yoh) A white wine grape grown in Spain; it produces a fresh, crisp, light-bodied wine.

al batheeth (al baht-ehrt) A Middle Eastern sweet consisting of chopped dates mixed with coarse flour and samn.

albedo The fluffy white layer of a citrus rind; it has a bitter flavor. *See* zest.

albergo (ahl-behr-goh) Italian for hotel.

Albert, sauce (al-BAIR) A French compound sauce made from a velouté flavored with horseradish and mustard; it is usually served with beef.

albicocca (hal-bee-cock-kah) Italian for apricot.

albóndiga (ahl-BON-dee-gah) 1. Spanish for meatball. 2. A Mexican and Spanish dish of spicy meatballs, usually in a tomato sauce. *See* sopa de albóndigas.

alboni (al-bo-ne) An Italian brown sauce made from stock, grilled pine nuts and red currant jelly; it is usually served with venison.

Albuféra, sauce (ahl-bew-fay-rah) A French compound sauce made from a suprême sauce flavored with a meat glaze and finished with pimiento butter.

albukhara (ahl-boo-kah-rah) A plum native to the Caucasus Mountains; it has a light yellow color, firm flesh and sweet, slightly sour flavor.

albumen (al-BYOO-mehn) The clear portion of the egg used as the nutrient source for the developing chick, constituting approximately two-thirds of its internal mass and containing most of its protein and riboflavin; sometimes used in fresh or dried form as a fining or clarifying agent or whipped for general baking and cooking; also known as egg white.

albumin One of a group of simple proteins found in many plants and most animals; soluble in cold water and concentrated salt solutions and coagulates when heated; found in blood as serum albumin, in milk as lactalbumin and in egg whites as ovalbumin.

albumin cheese *See* Ricotta *and* whey cheese.

alcachofa (al-ka-CHOH-fa) Spanish for artichoke.

alcachofra (al-kah-shoh-frah) Portuguese for artichoke.

Alcamo (AHL-cah-mo) A dry white wine produced in the western part of Sicily from the local Catarratto grape.

alcaparras (ahl-kah-PAH-rrahs) Portuguese and Spanish for capers.

alcaporado (ahl-cah-poh-rah-doh) A spicy Cuban beef stew seasoned with olives and raisins.

alcaravea (ahl-cah-rah-vay-ah) Spanish for caraway seeds.

al carbon (ahl kar-bohn) Spanish (particularly in Mexico and Latin America) for a food cooked over coals or over an open grill.

alchermes (al-KEHR-mess) A bright red, spicy Italian liqueur; flavored with flowers and colored with cochineal, it is used to color and flavor desserts.

alcide sauce (ahl-seed) A French white wine sauce garnished with sweated shallots and horseradish.

Alcobaca (al-koh-bah-kuh) A firm Portuguese cheese made from ewe's milk; it has a white paste with a smooth consistency and a thin dry rind with patches of bloom.

alcohol 1. Popular term for ethyl alcohol. *See* ethyl alcohol. 2. An intoxicating beverage containing ethyl alcohol.

alcohol by volume The percentage of alcohol per metric volume of beer, wine or distilled spirits; also known as percentage of alcohol by volume.

alcohol by weight The percentage weight of alcohol per metric volume of beer, wine or distilled spirits (e.g., 6% alcohol by weight equals 6 g of alcohol per 100 cl of beer).

alcohol content The amount of alcohol in a beverage; federal regulations require that alcoholic beverages intended for retail sale be labeled with their alcohol content in proof and percentage of alcohol by volume.

alcoholic 1. A person who suffers from alcoholism. 2. A wine-tasting term for a burning or biting sensation caused by too much alcohol in relation to the wine's body and weight.

alcoholic beverage Any potable liquid containing 0.5–80% ethyl alcohol by volume.

alcoholic beverage control laws; ABC laws A general term for federal, state or local laws principally regulating the sale (as opposed to the manufacture) of alcoholic beverages.

alcoholism A disease condition resulting, in part, from the chronic, habitual and/or excessive consumption of alcoholic beverages.

alcool (AHL-kool) Italian for alcohol.

álcool (al-kohl) French and Portuguese for alcohol.

álcool blanc (al-kohl blahn) A French term for white or clear distilled spirits, usually brandies distilled from fruits other than grapes; also known as virgin brandy.

al dente (al DEN-tay) Italian for to the tooth and used to describe a food, usually pasta, that is cooked only until it gives a slight resistance when one bites into it; the food is neither soft nor overdone.

alderman's walk A British cut of the venison or lamb carcass; it is the longest, finest slice from the haunch.

ale 1. A fermented malt beverage or style of beer made with a top-fermenting yeast and brewed at 60–70°F (16–20°C); it is often lower in carbonation and darker in color than lager beer. 2. Historically, any nonhopped malt beverage.

Aleatico (ah-leh-AH-tee-co) A grape grown in Italy and Chile and used for a sweet red wine with a flavor reminiscent of Muscat.

ale barrel English for a barrel that contains 32 imperial gallons (146.47 l).

aleconner; ale conner (eiyl-CAH-ner) The old English title for a person who inspected public houses for fraud and tested (often by tasting) ale to determine its authenticity.

alecost *See* costmary.

Ale Flip A cocktail made of ale, raw egg and crushed ice.

alembic (AH-lamb-bik) A large copper vessel with an onion-shaped top traditionally used for the double distillation of Cognac and other brandies.

alembic brandy A brandy such as Cognac or Armagnac made from grapes distilled in an alembic.

Alentejo; Alemtejo; (ah-leyn-tay-joo) A soft Portuguese cheese made from ewe's milk with goat's or cow's milk sometimes added; it is cylindrical in shape and ripened for several weeks.

aleppo (a-leep-po) A coarsely ground red pepper used for its fragrance and flavor in Arabic cuisines.

alewife; ale wife 1. A member of the herring family found in the Atlantic Ocean off North America; it has a silvery skin, a strong flavor and a market weight of 0.25–1 lb. (100–450 g); it is usually available smoked or pickled. 2. In medieval England, a woman who brewed ale or maintained a tavern.

Alexander Valley A grape-growing and wine-producing region in northern Sonoma County, California; the principal grapes grown are Chardonnay, Cabernet Sauvignon, Merlot, Gewürztraminer, Johannisberg Riesling and Zinfandel.

Alexandra mayonnaise A French mayonnaise sauce prepared with hard-cooked egg yolks, seasoned with dry mustard and garnished with chervil.

Alexandra, sauce A French compound sauce made from a suprême sauce flavored with truffle essence.

alfabeto (ahl-fah-BEH-toh) Italian for alphabet and used to describe pastina in the shape of letters.

alface (ahl-FAH-say) Portuguese for lettuce.

alfajores (ahl-fah-HOA-rehs) 1. A Spanish pastry made with honey and cornmeal. 2. A South American pastry in which two flaky dough circles are sandwiched together with a cinnamon-flavored milk custard filling.

alfalfa (al-FAL-fuh) A plant (*Medicago sativa*) important for use as hay or animal fodder; also known as lucerne.

alfalfa honey A thick, creamy yellow honey principally made from alfalfa blossoms; popular in the United States, it is sometimes used for blending.

alfalfa sprouts Germinated alfalfa seeds; they have small, soft seeds and fine, slightly crunchy pale white to green sprouts and are used in sandwiches and salads.

alfonso Large, purple olives grown in Italy.

al forno (ahl FOHR-no) Italian term for a food that is baked or roasted in an oven.

al fresco (al FREHS-koh) Italian for in the open and used to describe a meal or other social event taken outdoors.

algae; alga Any of numerous chlorophyll-containing plants of the phylum Thallophyta; ranging in size from single cells to large multicelled organisms, they grow in freshwater and saltwater, on or in other organisms or in soil and are generally rich in nutrients.

algae, brown A food additive derived from various seaweeds harvested from northern Atlantic and Pacific Ocean waters and used as a flavor enhancer in processed spices, seasonings and flavorings.

algae, dried A nutrient supplement rich in vitamins and protein and believed by some to prevent cancer, curb the appetite and ease the symptoms of menopause.

algae, red A food additive derived from various seaweeds harvested from northern Pacific Ocean waters and used as a flavor enhancer in spices and packaged seasonings.

algarroba beer (al-ga-rr-OH-buh beeyr) Beer brewed in South and Central America from ripe carob beans or mesquite beans.

Algarve (al-garv) A grape-growing and wine-producing district along the coast of Portugal; it is known for red, white and rosé wines as well as an aperitif wine similar to dry sherry.

Algerian sauce *See* algérienne, sauce.

algérienne, sauce (al-JE-reh-en) A French compound sauce made from a tomato sauce garnished with julienne of sautéed green and red sweet peppers; also known as Algerian sauce.

algin; alginic acid A food additive derived from certain brown kelp and used as an emulsifier, stabilizer and/or thickener in processed foods such as soups and soup mixes.

Alhambra (a-lahn-bra) 1. A French garnish for meats; it consists of sautéed artichoke hearts, red or green bell peppers and tomatoes. 2. A French salad of beetroot, celery, artichoke hearts and lettuce dressed with mayonnaise.

alho (ah-YOH) Portuguese for garlic.

alho-poro (ah-lyoo-poh-roo) Portuguese for leek.

alice *See* acciuga.

Aligoté (ah-le-go-TAY) A white wine grape grown in France's Burgundy region as well as in central Europe and California; the wine produced from this grape is generally undistinguished and short-lived.

alimentari (ah-lee-men-TAH-ree) An Italian grocery store, especially a small, family-owned operation.

alimentary canal; alimentary tract The digestive tube from the mouth to the anus; the principal units are the mouth, esophagus, stomach, small intestine and large intestine. *See* digestive system.

alimentation The process of nourishing the body; it includes ingestion, mastication, swallowing, digestion, absorption and assimilation.

aliño criollo (ahl-lee-n'yoh cree-ohl-yoh) Spanish for Creole-style seasonings and used to describe a Venezuelan seasoning blend of garlic salt, cumin, ground achiote seeds, black pepper, oregano and sweet paprika.

aliolo (ah-lee-oh-loh) Spanish aïoli.

alkali A substance, such as baking soda, used in the bakeshop to neutralize acids and act as a leavening agent in cakes and breads. *See* base.

alkalized cocoa Cocoa powder ground from beans treated with an alkali solution (usually potassium carbonate) to raise their pH; this powder is milder, less acidic and darker than untreated cocoa; also known as Dutch-processed cocoa. *See* cocoa powder.

alkaloid A number of bitter organic substances with alkaline properties found in certain foods, principally plants.

alkohol (al-coe-hol) Norwegian for alcohol.

Alkohol (al-coh-hol) German for alcohol.

alky Slang for an alcoholic.

alla (AHL-lah) Italian for as done by, in, for or with; when used in relation to a food, it generally designates a style of preparation or presentation, especially a sauce or topping.

all-blue potato A variety of purple potato.

allemande, sauce (ah-leh-MAHND) A French compound sauce made from a velouté thickened with egg yolks and heavy cream and flavored with lemon juice; also known as German sauce.

all-grain beer A beer made from a mash of adjunct grains such as corn or rice and malted barley (as opposed to malt extract or malt extract and malted barley).

alliance, sauce (ah-leh-hanss) A French compound sauce made from a hollandaise flavored with tarragon vinegar, white wine, cayenne and white pepper and garnished with chervil.

allicin The odor-producing substance in garlic; some consider it effective in inhibiting bacterial growth and strengthening the immune system.

alligator A reptile found in the swampy areas of the American Gulf states that grows as long as 19 ft.; the flesh from its body has a pinkish color, a slightly tough texture and a strong flavor, and its tail flesh is either white, tender and reminiscent of veal or dark and very tough.

alligator pear *See* avocado.

alliin A substance in garlic that converts to allicin when garlic is chopped or crushed.

Allium (ahl-leh-uhm) Any of a variety of members of the genus *Allium* and members of the lily family; grown worldwide, they are usually highly aromatic and flavorful, with an edible bulbous base and edible flat, grasslike green leaves (e.g., onion, shallot, garlic and leek).

all-malt whisky *See* single-malt Scotch whisky.

allòro (ahl-LOH-roa) Italian for bay leaf.

all-purpose flour White wheat flour blended to contain a moderate amount of protein; it is used for a wide range of general baking and cooking, especially in nonprofessional kitchens and is available bleached (either chemically or naturally) or unbleached (they may be used interchangeably).

all-purpose potato *See* white potato, round.

allspice A member of the pimento family (*Pimenta officinalis*) and native to tropical regions in the Western Hemisphere; the plant has leathery leaves, white flowers and small, brown berries that are used as a spice; when ground, the berries have a flavor reminiscent of a mixture of cinnamon, clove, nutmeg, ginger and pepper; also known as Jamaican pepper.

allumette (al-yoo-MEHT) 1. A thin strip of puff pastry topped with a sweet or savory mixture (e.g., royal icing or flavored butter) and served as an hors d'oeuvre or petit four. 2. Foods (especially potatoes) cut into a matchstick shape of approximately $1/8 \times 1/8 \times 1$–2 in. ($0.3 \times 0.3 \times 2.5$–5 cm).

Allura® red AC *See* FD&C Red #40.

allyl anthranilate A food additive with a winelike aroma used as a flavoring agent in beverages and candies.

allyl caproate and allyl hexanoate Food additives with a pineapple-like aroma used as flavoring agents or adjuvants.

allyl cinnamate A food additive with a cherrylike aroma used as a flavoring agent in baked goods and candies.

allyl compounds A group of food additives containing an allyl group and used as flavoring agents and/or adjuvants.

allyl isothiocyanate A food additive with a pungent aroma used as a flavoring agent in mustard and horseradish; also known as mustard oil.

allyl isovalerate and allyl octanoate Food additives with a fruity aroma used as flavoring agents in beverages, ice creams, baked goods, candies and other desserts.

allyl mercaptan A food additive with a garlic aroma used as a flavoring agent in condiments and baked goods.

allyl nonanoate A food additive with a fruity-cognac aroma used as a melon or pineapple flavoring agent in beverages, ice creams and candies.

allyl phenoxyacetate and allyl sorbate A food additive with a very pronounced fruity aroma used as a quince or pineapple flavoring agent in beverages and candies.

allyl phenylacetate A food additive with a banana–honey aroma used as a flavoring agent in baked goods and candies.

alma Hungarian apple brandy.

almeja (al-may-ha) Spanish for clam.

almendra (ahl-MEHN-drah) Spanish for almond.

almendrado (ahl-mehn-dray-doh) A Mexican almond-flavored dessert of beaten egg whites bound with gelatin and served with a creamy custard sauce; it is often tinted the colors of the Mexican flag.

almendras garrapinadas (al-MEN-dra ga-rah-PA-nah-duz) A Spanish snack of toasted almonds caramelized in sugar and honey; it is prepared especially for festivals and celebrations.

almoço (al-moh-soo) Portuguese for lunch.

almond The nut of the almond tree (*Prunus amygdalus*), native to the Mediterranean region and now cultivated in California; the nut has a pitted, lozenge-shaped, tan shell, a pale yellow–ivory center surrounded by a thin brown covering and a distinctive flavor and aroma; it is available blanched, variously sliced and/or flavored and in paste form; also known as the sweet almond. *See* bitter almond oil.

almond bean curd An Asian dessert made with sweetened milk gelatin or soybean milk flavored with almond essence.

almond butter *See* beurre d'amandes.

almond cream A mixture of finely ground almonds, butter, eggs, sugar and flour used primarily as a filling in tarts and pastries; also known as frangipane.

almond extract A concentrated flavoring made from bitter almond oil and alcohol that is widely used in pastries and baked goods.

almondine *See* amandine.

almond meal; almond flour A fine powder made from ground almonds and sugar and used in desserts and pastries.

almond milk The almond-flavored liquid remaining after almonds are pounded to a paste with water and then strained.

almond oil A pale oil obtained by pressing sweet almonds; it has a clean, fairly neutral flavor and is used in baking and for confections, especially for oiling baking tins.

almond paste A pliable paste made of ground blanched almonds, sugar and glucose or egg whites and used in pastries as a flavoring and for decorative work; it is similar to marizipan but coarser, darker and less sweet.

almond syrup A syrup made from almonds and used as a sweetener and flavoring agent, especially in cocktails and desserts; also known as orgeat and sirop d'amandes.

almuerzo (al-moo-air-tzoe) Spanish for lunch.

aloco (ahl-loh-coh) A West African street food or treat consisting of slices of a firm, ripe plantain fried in palm oil. *See* dodo-ikire.

aloo (ah-lou) Hindi for potato.

alose (ah-loz) French for shad.

Aloxe-Corton (ah-loks-cor-tawn) A wine-producing village of the Côte d'Or, in France's Burgundy region; the red wines come exclusively from Pinot Noir and the white wines from Chardonnay.

aloyau (ah-lo-yo) French for sirloin.

alpha acid A soft, sticky resin found in hops and responsible for a beer's bitterness; it is measured as a percentage of the total weight of the hop cone.

alpha acid unit (AAU) A measurement of the potential bitterness of hops, expressed by their percentage of alpha acid; 1 oz. of 1% alpha hops contains 1 AAU.

alpha-amylase A food additive used to convert some starches in bread dough to sugar and dextrose.

alpha-carotene *See* carotene, alpha-, beta- and gamma-.

alphatocopherol *See* vitamin E.

Alphonso mango A variety of mango grown in India; it is particularly flavorful.

Alpin (al-pah) A Mont d'Or–style cheese made in France's Alpine region.

Alpine strawberry 1. A strawberry variety native to central Europe north of the Alps; the small fruit have a tapered, conical shape and an intense flavor. 2. An imprecisely used term to describe any wild strawberry.

Alsace (AL-zass) One of France's six principal grape-growing and wine-producing regions; located in northeast France, the major grapes grown are Riesling, Gewürztraminer, Sylvaner and Pinot Blanc and, to a lesser degree, Pinot Gris, Muscat and Pinot Noir; these generally very dry, assertive wines are sold in tall green bottles with sloping shoulders called flutes.

alsacienne, à l' (al-zah-SYEHN) French for a style of cooking that reflects Alsace's German heritage; it usually refers to a meat braised with sauerkraut, potatoes and sausage.

al sangue (ahl SAHN-g'weh) Italian for bloody and used to describe the degree of doneness for meat that is very rare.

Alsterwasser *See* shandy.

altaïskaja A variety of large, long, pear-shaped squash with a yellow flesh and a light green skin with dark green streaks.

Altbier (ALT-beer) A copper-colored, bitter German beer made with a top-fermenting yeast and a high barley and hops content.

Altenburger (ahl-ten-burger) A soft German cheese made from goat's milk or goat's and cow's milk with a white mold, a creamy, smooth interior and a rich flavor.

Altesse (ahl-tess) A white wine grape grown in the Savoie region of France; it produces a crisp, dry wine.

Althorp Crasanne pear A variety of Seckle pear with a brown-spotted, yellow skin, a firm flesh and a sweet, spicy flavor.

Alto Adige (AHL-toe AH-dee-jay) A grape-growing and wine-producing area in the northernmost part of Italy; the principal red grapes are the native Schiava and Lagrein and Pinot Nero, Cabernet and Merlot; white grape varieties include Chardonnay, Pinot Bianco, Pinot Grigio, Sylvaner, Müller-Thurgau and Traminer.

Alto Douro (AHL-toe DOO-roe) The classical region of port wine production in northern Portugal.

alto-zukuri (al-to-zoo-koo-re) A Japanese sashimi cut known as thread cut; it produces narrow slivers of fish from thin fillets, which are usually served in little mounds on a plate.

Altura (al-TUR-ah) Arabica coffee beans grown in Mexico; the beverage is lively and light, with a delicate, nutty flavor.

alubia (ah-LOO-bee-ah) Spanish for green bean.

alum (AL-uhm) Crystals of potassium aluminum sulfate formerly used as a crisping agent when canning pickles.

aluminum A metal used for cookware, cooking utensils, flatware, service items, storage items and other tools or equipment used in the kitchen; lightweight and a good conductor of heat, aluminum cookware is often coated with nickel, stainless steel or nonstick plastic.

aluminum ammonium sulfate A food additive used as a neutralizing agent and pH control agent in baking powders.

aluminum calcium silicate A food additive used as an anticaking agent.

aluminum foil *See* foil.

aluminum nicotinate A food additive used as a nutrient supplement (niacin), especially for those with special dietary needs.

aluminum sodium sulfate A food additive used as a buffer, neutralizing agent and firming agent.

aluminum sulfate A food additive used as a firming agent in pickles and processed vegetables and as a processing aid in baked goods, gelatin and puddings.

amabile (ah-MAH-bee-lay) An Italian term used to describe a semisweet wine.

Amador (AHM-uh-dor) A grape-growing and wine-producing region located in the foothills of the Sierra Nevada Mountains, California; the principal grapes grown are Zinfandel and Sauvignon Blanc and, to a lesser degree, Chardonnay, Cabernet Sauvignon and Chenin Blanc.

ama-ebi (ah-mah-ee-bee) Japanese for a variety of shrimp with a delicate, sweet flavor; also known as sweet shrimp.

amai (ah-MAH-ee) Japanese for sweet.

amala *See* Oka.

amalgamer (ah-maal-gah-mehr) French for to mix, blend or combine (referring to ingredients).

amande (ah-mahn) French for almond.

amandine (AH-mahn-deen; ah-mahn-DEEN) French term for a dish garnished with almonds; also incorrectly known as almondine.

amar al-din (ah-mar al-dean) An Egyptian beverage made by cooking apricot paste with water and flavoring it with mint.

amaranth (AM-ah-ranth) 1. A vegetable (genus *Amaranthus*) with green- or maroon-centered purple leaves; the leaves have a slightly sweet flavor and are used like spinach in Caribbean and Chinese cuisines; also known as callaloo (especially in the Caribbean), Chinese spinach and een choy. 2. A flour ground from the seeds of the amaranth plant.

amaretti (am-ah-REHT-tee) Crisp, airy Italian macaroons made with bitter almond or apricot kernel paste.

amarettini (am-ah-REHT-teen-ee) Miniature amaretti.

Amaretto (am-ah-REHT-toh) An Italian amber-colored liqueur with an almondlike flavor, although it is actually flavored with apricot kernels; it was originally made in Saronno and called Amaretto di Saronno.

amaro (ha-ma-roh) Italian for bitter.

Amarone (ah-mah-ROE-neh) A dry, aged red wine from Italy's Valpolicella district made from specially ripened grapes (Corvina Veronese) that are affected by *Botrytis cinera;* it is aged in casks for several years and sometimes gives a slightly sweet impression on the palate.

amatista (ahm-ah-tees-tah) A small, wide-shouldered, tapering chile with a rounded end; it has a purple color, a thick flesh and a sweet, earthy flavor; it is often pickled and used as a garnish.

amatriciana, all' (ah-mah-tree-chee-AH-nah, ahl) An Italian pasta dish served with a sauce made with pancetta, onion, chiles, tomato and cheese.

amazake; amasake (ah-MAH-zah-kee) A thick, fermented liquid made from cooked rice and koji starter; it is used as a beverage or flavoring ingredient in Japanese cuisine; also known as rice milk.

amazu (AH-mah-zoo) Japanese for sweet-and-sour sauce.

amazu shoga (AH-mah-zoo SHO-gah) Japanese for pink pickled ginger.

ambarella (ahm-bah-rehl-lah) A tree fruit (*Spondias dulcis*) native to the Society Islands in the South Pacific and related to the golden apple; the egg-sized fruit grows in clusters and has a grayish-orange skin, a yellowish pulp, several seeds, a pungent aroma and a slightly sour flavor reminiscent of an apple or pineapple.

ambassador cake A sponge cake flavored with Grand Marnier, filled with pastry cream and candied fruit and decorated with almond paste.

Ambassador walnut A variety of English walnut; its plump nuts are particularly flavorful.

ambassadrice, sauce (ahn-bas-sa-DRESSE) A French compound sauce made from a suprême sauce garnished with puréed poached chicken breast and finished with whipped cream.

amber acid *See* succinic acid.

ambergris *See* amber gum.

amber gum A waxy secretion from sperm whales used to enhance or fix seasonings and fragrances; also known as ambergris.

Amboise (ahm-bwahz) A grape-growing and wine-producing town on the Loire River in France; the principal grapes grown are Chenin Blanc, Malbec (locally known as Cot), Gamay and Cabernet Franc; the wines are fresh and fruity.

Ambrosia 1. A 19th-century salad or dessert made of fresh grated coconut and fresh fruit, especially oranges; popular in the American South. 2. A cocktail made of lemon juice, brandy, applejack, Cointreau and sparkling wine. 3. In Greek and Roman mythology, it refers to the food of the gods.

amburghese (am-burr-geh-sah) Italian for hamburger.

amchur; amchoor (AHM-choor) A powder made from dried, raw mangoes; it has a tangy flavor and is used as a spice, principally in Indian cuisines.

amdoe (ahm-dah) A Tibetan steamed dumpling filled with ground pork flavored with cumin, nutmeg and ginger.

ame (ah-me) A Japanese sweet jelly made from millet; it is used in confections and fish dishes.

amêijoas (ah-may-ho-ahs) Portuguese for venus-shell clams.

amêijoas à bulhao pato (ah-may-ho-ahs ah boo-yam-oh pah-toe) A Portuguese petisco dish consisting of mussels cooked in a stock with garlic, cilantro, lemon juice and pepper.

ameixa (a-MAY-shash) Portuguese for plum.

amelioration The addition of water and/or pure dried sugar, liquid sugar or invert sugar syrup to grape juice or wine during fermentation to adjust the acid level; allowed in the eastern United States, this process is prohibited elsewhere. *See* chaptalization *and* gallisation.

amêndoa (ah-MEN-doh-ah) Portuguese for almond.

amendolm (ah-man-dolm) Portuguese for peanut.

americainé, à l' (a-may-ree-KEHN) 1. A French dish (especially lobster) prepared with a spicy sauce of tomatoes, olive oil, onions, brandy and wine. 2. A French garnish for fish consisting of thin slices of lobster tail and americainé sauce.

americainé, mayonnaise à l' (ah-mair-ee-KANE) A French mayonnaise sauce blended with puréed lobster meat.

americainé, sauce (a-may-ree-KEHN) A spicy French sauce made of tomatoes, olive oil, onions, brandy and wine.

American beach plum *See* plum, American beach.

American bison *See* buffalo.

American breakfast A breakfast of juice, eggs, meat (bacon, sausages or ham), toast or pastries and coffee; sometimes hash browns, grits, pancakes and/or cereal are offered.

American Brick *See* Brick.

American brown ale *See* brown ale.

American cantaloupe *See* cantaloupe, American.

American Cheddar *See* Cheddar, American.

American cheese An imprecisely used term for any of a group of natural cheeses made in the United States, including Cheddar, Cheddar-style cheeses, Colby, granular cheeses, washed-curd cheeses, Brick, Monterey Jack and others.

American cheese, processed Any of the group of U.S. cheeses made with emulsifiers to increase smoothness and pasteurized milk to increase storage life; 51% of the final weight must be cheese.

American cranberry *See* cranberry.

American cress *See* land cress.

American eel *See* eel, American.

American fifth *See* fifth.

American garlic A medium-sized garlic bulb with a creamy-white outer covering and a strong flavor.

American leg of lamb A fabricated cut of the lamb primal; the center cut; also known as a center leg roast.

American lobster *See* Maine lobster.

American Market Selection (AMS) *See* candela.

Americano (ah-meh-ree-KAH-no) 1. A cocktail made of Campari, Italian sweet vermouth, lemon peel and a splash of soda; originated in Italy, the French version also contains red wine. 2. A French bittersweet vermouth.

American oysters; American cupped oysters *See* Atlantic oysters.

American persimmon *See* persimmon, American.

American plaice *See* plaice, American.

American plan (AP) A daily hotel rate that includes three full meals and a room; also known as full American plan and full board and pension. *See* modified American plan (MAP).

American pollock *See* pollock, American.

American roast *See* roast, city.

American service A style of service in which a waiter takes the order and brings the food to the table; the food is placed on dishes (i.e., plated) in the kitchen.

American shad *See* shad, American.

American snapper; American red snapper *See* red snapper.

American sturgeon caviar Roe from sturgeon harvested in the coastal waters of the American Northwest and the Tennessee River; it is generally considered inferior to Russian and Iranian caviars.

Amer Picon (ah-mehr pee-kohn) An orange-flavored French bitter usually mixed with water and sweetened with a dash of grenadine and served as an aperitif.

amethyst deceiver A small, delicate woodland mushroom (*Laccaria amethystea*) with a lilac-colored stem and cap, a hard, gummy texture and a mild flavor.

amfissa (ahm-fee-saw) A round black Greek olive with a nutty, sweet flavor.

amine group A nitrogen-containing organic compound used to form amino acids.

aminoacetic acid *See* glycine.

amino acids The building blocks of protein; every amino acid is composed of an amine group, an acid group and a distinctive side chain; approximately 20 are necessary for humans, approximately 8 of which are essential and must be obtained through diet.

amioca *See* waxy starch.

amiral, sauce (a-me-herl) A French white wine sauce garnished with lemon zest and capers and finished with anchovy butter; also known as admiral sauce.

Amish Paste An heirloom variety of medium-sized tomato with a bright red color and an outstanding flavor; it is used for sauces, canning and slicing fresh.

ammogghio (ah-MOH-gee-yoh) An Italian mixture of olive oil, garlic and herbs used as a topping, especially on fish.

ammonia 1. A colorless, pungent, poisonous water-soluble gaseous compound; used for refrigeration and in chemical products, including cleaning agents. 2. A toxic by-product of the body's breakdown of proteins; it is converted to urea and excreted in the urine.

ammoniated A cheese-tasting term for the ammonia-like aroma or flavor of an overly ripe cheese with a bloomy rind, such as a Brie or Camembert.

ammonium alginate A food additive derived from certain brown kelp and used as a stabilizer and/or thickener in processed foods such as confections, dairy products, gelatins, fats, sauces and jams.

ammonium bicarbonate A leavener that is a precursor of baking powder and baking soda; it must be ground to a powder before use; also known as carbonate of ammonia, hartshorn, and powdered baking ammonia.

ammonium carbonate, ammonium bicarbonate and ammonium chloride Food additives used as dough conditioners, leavening agents and/or pH control agents in processed foods such as baked goods.

ammonium hydroxide A food additive used as a surface-finishing agent, leavening agent and/or pH control agent in processed foods such as baked goods.

ammonium persulfate A food additive used as a bleaching agent for food starch.

ammonium phosphate, monobasic and dibasic A food additive used as a dough conditioner and pH control agent.

ammonium saccharin *See* saccharin.

ammonium sulfate A food additive used as a dough conditioner and firming agent.

ammonium sulfite A food additive used as a processing aid in caramel.

amoeba; ameba A genus of protozoa found in soil and water.

amoebiasis A disease caused by ingesting amoeba such as *Entamoeba histolytica;* symptoms include dysentery.

amontillado (ah-mon-tee-YAH-do) A type of sherry; it is dry, with a nutty flavor and has a pale to light gold color and a full body.

amoricaine, à l' (ah-more-ree-cane, ah-l') A French preparation for lobster in the Breton style (the ancient name for Brittany); the sliced lobster is sautéed in olive oil with tomatoes.

amorini (ah-mah-REE-nee) Italian for little cupids and used to describe pastina in the shape of small cupids.

amoroso (ah-mo-ROE-so) A term that traditionally described a somewhat sweet, velvety oloroso.

Amos black currant A variety of black currants; they are relatively large and juicy.

ampelography (am-peh-LAW-gra-fee) The study and classification of vines and grapes.

amphetamines Any of a group of psychologically and physically addicting prescription drugs that stimulate the nervous system and depress the appetite; they are sometimes used in medically supervised reduction diets; also known as speed.

amphora (ahm-fo-rah) An ancient earthenware container of Mediterranean origin used to hold wine or oil; it usually had two handles and a pointed end.

amradeen (ahm-raw-din) Thin sheets of sun-dried apricots used in Arabic cuisines, often in sweet-and-sour sauces.

AMS *See* candela.

amuse-gueule (ah-muz-gull) French for appetizer.

amygdalota (am-meeg-dah-low-tah) A Greek confection of small almond balls flavored with orange blossom water or rosewater.

amylase A class of enzymes that convert starches to fermentable sugars. *See* malt enzymes.

amylcinnamaldehyde A food additive with a jasmine aroma used as a flavoring agent or adjuvant.

amyl compounds A group of food additives containing an amyl group and sometimes derived from fruit oils; they are used as flavoring agents and/or adjuvants.

an (ahn) A Japanese sweetened paste of ground adzuki; it is available in smooth (koshi-an) and crunchy (tsubushi-an) forms.

anaaras (ah-nah-rahs) Hindi for pineapple.

anabolism The constructive phase of metabolism during which a cell takes from the blood a simple substance necessary for growth or repair and converts it into the more complex living cellular material. *See* catabolism.

anada (a-nah-dah) A Spanish term for vintage wine.

anadama bread (ah-nah-dah-mah) A colonial American yeast bread flavored with cornmeal and molasses.

anadromous A fish that migrates from a saltwater habitat to spawn in freshwater.

anaerobic bacteria; anaerobes *See* bacteria, anaerobic.

anaerobic exercise Physical activities that require short bursts of energy. *See* aerobic exercise.

anago (ahn-ah-go) Japanese for conger eel.

Anaheim chile (AN-uh-hym) A long, tapered chile with a pale to medium bright green color, relatively thick flesh and mild, vegetal flavor; it is available fresh, canned or roasted but not dried and is named for the California city where it was first grown commercially; also known as the California chile and long green chile.

analcolico (ah-nahl-KOL-lee-koh) Italian for a nonalcoholic drink.

ananas (ah-nah-nahs) Arabic, Dutch, French, Hebrew, Italian, Norwegian, Potuguese, Russian and Swedish for pineapple.

Ananas (ah-nah-nass) German for pineapple.

ananasnaja (ah-nah-nass-nah-tah) A variety of large kiwi grown in Russia; the fruit has a particularly spicy, sweet flavor.

Anasazi (ah-nah-sah-zee) An heirloom variety of bean that was cultivated by the ancient peoples in what is now New Mexico and Arizona; it has a dark wine red color spotted with white.

Anbaugebiet (ahn-BAO-geh-beet) The German term for the region (there are 11) whose wines are entitled to Qualitätswein or Qualitätswein mit Prädikat status; the appropriate regional name must appear on the label of any good-quality wine. *See* Bereich, Grosslage *and* Einzellage.

ancho (ahn-cho) A dried poblano with broad shoulders tapering to a rounded end; the chile has a brick red to dark mahogany color, wrinkled flesh and relatively mild, fruity flavor with overtones of coffee, licorice, tobacco and raisin.

anchoa (ahn-CHO-ahss) Spanish for anchovy.

anchoïade (anh-shwah) A dish from France's Provence region made from puréed anchovies mixed with crushed garlic and olive oil; it is served on toast or with raw vegetables.

anchois, sauce aux (ahn-SHWAH) A French white wine sauce beaten with anchovy butter and garnished with diced anchovy fillets; also known as anchovy sauce.

anchovy A member of the herring family found in the Mediterranean Sea and off southern Europe; it has a long snout, a large mouth and a blue-green skin that becomes silvery

anchovy

on the sides and belly; it ranges in length from 5 to 9 in. (12 to 22 cm); usually available pickled or salted.

anchovy butter *See* beurre d'anchois.

anchovy paste Pounded anchovies mixed with vinegar and spices and usually sold in a tube.

anchovy sauce *See* anchois, sauce aux.

ancienne, sauce (ahn-see-yen) A French compound sauce made from hollandaise and garnished with diced gherkins, sautéed mushrooms and truffles.

Ancient Age Distillery One of the 12 remaining U.S. whiskey distilleries; located in Frankfort, Kentucky, and founded c. 1869, its products include Ancient Age, Eagle Rare, Benchmark, Blanton's Single Barrel and Handcock's Reserve bourbons.

ancient eggs *See* hundred-year-old eggs.

and (ung) Norwegian for duck.

andalouse, à l' (ahn-dah-LOOZ, ah l') A French preparation method associated with the cuisine of Spain's Andalusia region; the dishes (usually large joints of meat) are characterized by a garnish of tomatoes, peppers, rice, eggplant and sometimes chipolatas.

andalouse, sauce (ahn-dah-LOOZ) A French compound sauce made from a velouté and tomato purée.

andalouse mayonnaise (ahn-dah-LOOZ) A French mayonnaise sauce made with mayonnaise flavored with tomato purée and pimiento.

Andalusia (ahn-day-lusha) A grape-growing and wine-producing region in southern Spain; it is known for sherry, Málaga and Montilla.

andé (ahn-DA) Hindi for egg.

Anderson Valley A grape-growing and wine-producing area in Mendocino County, California; principal grapes grown for still white wines are Gewürztraminer and Johannisberg Riesling and for méthode champenoise sparkling wines Chardonnay and Pinot Noir.

andijvie (ahn-DAY-vee) Dutch for endive.

andithia (an-dee-thia) Greek for endive.

andouille sausage (an-DOO-ee; ahn-DWEE) A spicy smoked pork sausage (made with neck and stomach meat); originally from France, it is now a hallmark of Cajun cuisine.

andouillette sausage (ahn-dwee-YET) A small andouille sausage; it is usually cooked but not smoked.

añejo (ahn-YEH-hoh) Spanish for aged; used in reference to distilled spirits such as tequila and rum.

añejo tequila (ahn-YEH-hoh tuh-KEE-lah) A tequila aged for at least 1 year in a government-sealed oak barrel. *See* reposado tequila.

anelli (ha-neh-lee) Italian for rings and used to describe pasta rings, usually used in soups.

anellini (ah-NEH-lee-ni) Italian for little rings and used to describe small pasta rings, usually used in soups.

anellini rigati (ah-NEH-lee-ni ree-gah-tee) Italian for gears and used to describe grooved rings of pasta, usually used in soups.

anelli

Anesone (ah-neh-SOH-neh) A clear, colorless Italian liqueur with an anise–licorice flavor and a high alcohol content.

aneth (ah-neht) French for dill.

aneto (ah-NEH-toh) Italian for dill.

angel biscuit A light, fluffy biscuit leavened with yeast, baking powder and baking soda; the dough must be refrigerated overnight before baking and can be kept refrigerated for several days and baked as needed.

angel food cake A light, airy cake made without egg yolks or other fats; its structure is based on the air whipped into the egg whites; it is typically baked in a tube pan.

angelica (an-JEHL-ih-cah) An herb of the parsley family (*Angelica archangelica*) with pale green, celerylike stalks; it is used to flavor liqueurs and sweet wines; the stalks are often candied and used to decorate desserts.

Angelica (an-gee-LEEK-cah) A mixture of grape juice and high-proof brandy produced in California.

Angeliquor An African-American term for wine made from the angelica plant.

angel pie A cream pie, usually lemon, prepared in a baked meringue pie shell.

angel's hair squash *See* Siamese gourd.

angel shark *See* shark.

angels on horseback An hors d'oeuvre of shucked oysters wrapped in bacon, broiled and served on buttered toast points.

angel's share 1. The quantity of wine or distilled spirits lost through evaporation, seepage or other processes during aging or storage. 2. An amount of food, too small to keep, left on a plate after dining.

Angel's Tit A cocktail made of crème de cacao, maraschino liqueur and cream; served in a pony glass and garnished with a maraschino cherry.

Anghelu Ruju (AHN-jeh-loo ROO-yoo) A sweet, red, fortified wine produced on the island of Sardinia from semi-dried Cannonau grapes.

anginάres (ahn-gee-nah-res) Greek for artichokes.

anglaise, à l' (ahn-GLEHZ, ah l') French preparation methods associated with English cuisine; the vegetables are poached or boiled and served plain or with chopped parsley and butter or the principal ingredient is coated in bread crumbs and pan-fried.

angler fish; anglerfish *See* monkfish.

angoor (ahn-gore) Hindi for grape.

Angostura Bitters (ang-uh-STOOR-ah) An aromatic bitters made in Trinidad.

angouria (ahn-goo-rhia) Greek for cucumbers.

anguila (an-goo-ee-lah) Spanish for eel.

anguille (ahn-gee) French for eel.

angular A wine-tasting term for a wine with a bitter or tart flavor and a stiff or hard body.

anguria A plant native to the West Indies; it produces a small, spiny, green fruit with a squashlike flavor; the fruit is peeled, steamed and eaten like a vegetable.

Angus *See* Aberdeen Angus.

anhydrite *See* calcium sulfate.

anhydrous milkfat *See* butter oil.

anice (AH-nes) Italian for aniseed.

anijs (ah-nee-j) Dutch for anise.

animal crackers Small crisp cookies shaped like various circus animals and packaged in a small box decorated like a circus train.

animal fat Any fat taken directly from an animal (e.g., chicken fat) or a fat processed from such fat (e.g., suet and lard) or other animal product (e.g., butter).

animal husbandry The business, science and practice of raising domesticated animals, usually for food.

animal starch *See* glycogen.

animelle (ah-nee-MEHL-lay) Italian for sweetbreads.

animelles (ah-neh-may-yay) 1. French for sweetbreads. 2. The general French culinary term for animal testicles.

anion *See* ion.

anis (ah-nee) French for anise.

Anis (AH-nees) German for aniseed.

anisakiasis A disease caused by ingesting larvae of the nematode worm family Anisakidae; common sources include undercooked fish organs and fish taken from contaminated waters; symptoms include intestinal colic, fever and abscesses.

anise (AN-ihs) 1. A small annual member of the parsley family (*Pimpinella anisum*) native to the eastern Mediterranean region; it has bright green leaves with a mild licorice flavor that are sometimes used as an herb or in salads. 2. Greek for aniseed.

aniseeds; anise seeds The tiny, gray-green egg-shaped seeds of the anise plant; their distinctive, licorice flavor is used to flavor sweet and savory dishes as well as alcoholic and nonalcoholic beverages.

anise pepper *See* Szechwan pepper.

anisette (ann-ei-set) A clear, colorless licorice-flavored French liqueur made from aniseeds; it turns milky white when mixed with water.

anisole A food additive used as an aromatic agent; it has a pleasant, perfumelike scent.

anisyl butyrate A food additive used as a flavor enhancer to intensify the vanilla flavor in ice cream, candy and baked goods.

anisyl formate A food additive with a floral aroma used as a berry flavoring agent in beverages, candies and baked goods.

anisyl propionate A food additive used as a flavor enhancer, especially for vanilla and fruit flavors such as plum and quince.

anitho (ah-nee-thoh) Greek for dill.

anitra (AH-nee-trah) Italian for duck.

anitra selvatica (AH-nee-trah sell-vah-tee-kah) Italian for wild duck.

anitroccolo (AH-nee-troc-co-loh) Italian for duckling.

anjan (an-chan) The blue flower of a plant native to Thailand; the extract is used to color foods such as water chestnuts.

anjeer (ahn-geer) Hindi for fig.

Anjou; Anjou-Saumer (ohn-joo) A grape-growing and wine-producing district in France's Loire Valley known for white wines made from Chenin Blanc grapes and red wines made from Cabernet Franc grapes; Rosé d'Anjou and Cabernet d'Anjou are the principal appellations.

Anjou pear (OHN-zhoo) The principal winter pear of North America; it has a broad, lopsided shape, a russet-marked, yellowish-green skin, a firm flesh and a sweet, succulent flavor; it can be eaten out of hand or cooked; also known as beurre d'Anjou.

anjovis (ann-sno-vees) Swedish for anchovy.

an kaké (AHN kah-kay) Japanese for a sauced food.

ankerstock (ahn-ker-stok) A Scottish sweet bread made with rye flour and flavored with spices and raisins.

ankimo (AHN-ki-mo) A Japanese dish of cooked monkfish liver served in slices, resembling foie gras.

Annabel Special A cocktail made of Benedictine, dry vermouth and lime juice.

Annapolis Valley A grape-growing and wine-producing region in southern Nova Scotia, Canada, best known for its ice wine and for full-bodied red wines, such as Maréchal Foch, and German-style Rieslings and Seyval Blanc; the area is also known for fruit wines made from apples, cranberries and blueberries.

Anna potatoes *See* pommes Anna.

Anna Russian An heirloom variety of large tomato with a distinctive pink-red color, a heart shape, a juicy pulp and an excellent flavor.

annatto; arnatto (uh-NAH-toh) *See* achiote seeds.

annatto extract A food additive used as a coloring agent, principally in cheese making; also known as bixin.

annatto lard Lard studded with annatto seeds, cooked until the fat turns a bright red, then strained and the seeds discarded; it is used in Filipino cooking.

Annette potatoes *See* pommes Annette.

annual A plant that completes its life cycle within one year.

annular ring *See* annulus.

annulus The skirtlike remnant of the partial veil after the spores have been released; it surrounds the upper stem of certain mushrooms; also known as an annular ring.

anon braich Scots Gaelic term for single malt; it appears on certain Scotch whisky labels.

anorexia nervosa An eating disorder characterized by a severe self-imposed restriction on food intake; generally found in young women, it can lead to severe weight loss (15% or more of normal body weight) and even death.

anoxomer A food additive used as an antioxidant and preservative.

anpan (AHM-pan) A Japanese yeast roll with a sweet red bean filling.

Anschovis (ahn-SHO-fiz) German for anchovies.

anterior At or toward the front of an object or place. *See* posterior.

anthocyanin The grape pigment that gives a red wine its color; a young wine's purple-red color is the result of fairly unstable anthocyanin molecules, which, as they age, join with tannins to give the older wine a ruby red color.

antibe mayonnaise (ahn-teeb) A French mayonnaise sauce blended with tomato purée and anchovy paste and garnished with tarragon.

antibiotic Any of a variety of natural or synthetic substances that inhibit the growth of or destroy microorganisms; used to treat some infectious conditions and diseases.

anticaking agent A type of food additive used to prevent caking, lumping or agglomeration in finely powdered or crystalline processed foods; also known as a free-flow agent.

anticuchos (antee-ku-chohs) A Peruvian dish of charbroiled beef hearts on a skewer; the cubes of heart are marinated in hot chiles, herbs and vinegar, grilled and served with a chile sauce.

antifogmatic A colonial American term for most any alcoholic beverage consumed in the morning to counteract the effects of dampness or fog.

Antigua (han-tee-gwah) Arabica coffee beans grown in Guatamala's Antigua region; the beverage is mild, with a good acidity and aroma.

antimicrobial agent A type of food additive that acts as a preservative by preventing the growth of microorganisms such as bacteria and molds.

Antin, sauce d' (dahn-tahn) A French compound sauce made from a Madeira sauce flavored with dry white wine and garnished with mushrooms, truffles and fine herbs.

antioxidant 1. A substance that prevents or inhibits oxidation of other compounds by being oxidized itself. 2. A compound that reduces or prevents free radical tissue damage otherwise associated with premature aging or a degenerative disease such as heart disease or cancer. 3. A type of food additive that acts as a preservative by retarding deterioration, rancidity or discoloration resulting from oxidation; it is used principally in processed foods such as fats and those containing artificial colorings.

antipasto (ahn-tee-PAHS-toe) Italian for before pasta and used to describe hot or cold appetizers, usually simple foods such as cheeses, sausages, olives, marinated vegetables or the like.

antiseptic An organic or inorganic chemical substance used to interfere with or inhibit the growth of some microorganisms, particularly bacteria; some antiseptic compounds can be applied to human tissue to help fight infections.

antojito (ahn-toh-HEE-toh) Spanish for little whim and used to describe any appetizer. *See* tapas.

anus The outlet at the end of the rectum where digestive wastes are eliminated.

anzu (AHN-zu) Japanese for apricot.

AOC *See* Appellation d'Origine Contrôlée.

Aom Atic An Israeli red, dry Burgundy-style wine.

aonegi (ah-oh-neh-gee) Japanese for green onion.

ao nori (an-O NO-ree) Green flakes of seaweed used as a flavoring in Japanese cuisine.

aoyagi *See* bakagai.

ao-yose (ah-oh-yo-seh) A green coloring obtained from spinach leaves; it is used in Japanese cuisines to color savory and sweet foods, including confections.

AP *See* American plan *and* as-purchased.

Apalachicola oyster (ah-pah-lah-chee-KOH-lah) A variety of Atlantic oyster found in the Gulf of Mexico and off the Florida coast.

apaz onion An edible wild onion found in the United States; it has a flavor similar to that of a pearl onion.

apee A soft, sour cream–based sugar cookie created in Philadelphia during the 19th century.

apel'sin (ah-pyeel-'SEE-in) Russian for orange.

aperitif (ah-pair-ee-TEEF) Any beverage, usually alcoholic, consumed before a meal to whet the appetite. *See* digestif.

Apfel (AH-pferl) German for apple.

Apfelmus (AH-pfel-mus) German for applesauce.

Apfelsaft (AH-pfel-zaft) German for apple juice.

Apfelschnapps (AH-pherl-sch-NOPZ) German for apple schnapps.

Apfelstrudel (AH-pfel-shtroo-derl) German for apple strudel.

Apfelwein (AH-pfel-vine) German for apple wine and used to describe a beverage made from fermented apples; it has a low alcohol content and a sour flavor.

aphrodisiac (ahf-roh-DE-ze-ahk) A food or drink believed to arouse sexual desires.

api A very small, western European, traditional apple with a red-blushed, yellow skin, a crisp flesh and a slightly sour flavor.

apiana (ah-pee-ah-nah) An ancient Roman wine made from the Muscat grape.

api étoile (ah-pee eh-twol) A small, western European, traditional apple with a yellow and red blush skin and a distinctive shape (its cross section resembles a five-pointed star with rounded points); also known as carré d'hiver, pentagone and pomme d'étoile.

api noire (ah-pee nwahr) A large, western European traditional apple with a dark reddish-brown skin and a white flesh.

apio (AH-pyoh) Spanish for celery and celeriac.

aplet A firm but chewy confection made with reduced apple juice, gelatin and nuts. *See* cotlet.

à point (ah PWAH) 1. A steak cooked to the medium stage. 2. French for a food cooked to the perfect degree of doneness.

apotoyiwa (ah-poe-toe-he-wah) A round earthenware vessel used for cooking and storage in West Africa (especially Ghana).

appa (aap-pa) A bowl-shaped rice pancake leavened with the sap of the coconut palm and usually eaten for breakfast in Sri Lanka and southern India; also known as a hopper and, when formed from fine strings of dough, a string hopper.

Appaloosa An heirloom variety of black and white or red and white bean native to the American Southwest.

appareil (ah-par-e-ll) A mixture of different elements used in the preparation of a dish (e.g., chicken croquette mixture).

appearance A wine-tasting term referring to a wine's clarity (as opposed to color); a good appearance is clear and free of suspended particles.

appel (ah-pell) Dutch and Swedish for apple.

Appellation Contrôlée (ah-pel-ah-s'yawn cawn-trol-lay) *See* Appellation d'Origine Contrôlée.

Appellation d'Origine Contrôlée (AOC) (ah-pel-ah-s'yawn daw-ree-JEEN cawn-trol-lay) French laws regulating a producer's use of labeling terms describing a wine's geographic origin (region, village or vineyard), quality and grape variety as well as regulating the minimum amount of alcohol that the wine must contain and the maximum production permitted per acre. Some of these laws and similar ones also apply to French cheeses. *See* Vin Délimités de Qualité Supérieure, vin de pays *and* vin de table.

Appellation d'Origin Simple *See* vin de pays.

appelpannekoek *See* pannekoeken.

appelsin (ah-perl-SSEEN) Norwegian for orange.

Appenzeller (A-pent-seller) 1. A firm cheese made in Switzerland's Appenzell canton usually from skimmed cow's milk; it has a delicate, somewhat fruity flavor, a straw-colored interior with tiny holes and a yellow rind; it is soaked in cider and/or white wine and spices. 2. A southern German (Bavaria and Baden) version of the Swiss cheese.

appetite The psychologically compelling desire to eat; it is usually experienced as a pleasant sensation associated with seeing, smelling or thinking of food. *See* hunger.

Appetitost (app-eh-teet-ohst) A Danish cheese made from soured buttermilk.

appetizer 1. Finger food served before the meal to whet the appetite; the term is often used synonymously with the term hors d'oeuvre. 2. The first course of a meal, usually small portions of hot or cold foods intended to whet the appetite; also known as a starter.

appetizer wine A term used improperly to describe a wine served before a meal; correctly called an aperitif.

apple A pome fruit (*Malus pumila*) with generally firm flesh that can range in flavor from sweet to tart; it is encased in a thin skin, which can range in color from yellow to green to red; apples can be eaten out of hand, cooked or used for juice and are grown in temperate regions worldwide and available all year, particularly during the fall.

Apple Blow Fizz A cocktail made of sugar syrup, lemon juice, egg white, club soda and applejack or Calvados.

apple brandy A brandy distilled from a mash of cider apples and usually aged in oak casks before blending and bottling. *See* applejack.

apple brown betty A colonial American baked pudding made with layers of fruit, spices, sugar and bread crumbs.

apple butter A thick brown spread made by slowly cooking apples, sugar, spices and cider.

apple charlotte A pastry made by lining a mold with buttered bread, then filling it with spiced, sautéed apples. *See* charlotte mold.

apple dumpling A dessert made by wrapping an apple in sweet pastry dough and baking it.

apple float *See* apple snow.

applejack 1. An alcoholic beverage made by grinding and pressing apples, fermenting the juice into cider and then distilling it; also known as apple brandy. 2. A sweet apple syrup. 3. An apple turnover.

apple juice The natural, unsweetened juice pressed from apples; it is pasteurized and may be partially or completely filtered.

apple of love *See* winter cherry.

apple pandowdy A deep-dish dessert made with a mixture of sliced apples, spices and sugar, topped with biscuit batter and baked.

applesauce A cooked purée of apples, sugar and sometimes spices; it can be smooth or chunky.

apple schnitz Dried apple slices used in Pennsylvania German cooking for dishes such as schnitz and knepp.

apple slicer; apple corer A tool used to cut and core fruits such as apples and pears; when pressed over the fruit, the wires or blades attached to the frame section the fruit while the corer at the hub separates out the core. *See* corer.

apple slicer/corer

apple snow A creamy dessert made by combining applesauce, sugar and whipped egg whites; it was popular during the early 20th century; also known as an apple float.

apple wine A wine made from sweet cider that has been chaptalized and allowed to ferment.

apprentice *See* commis.

approved coffee measure A measuring spoon developed by the Coffee Brewing Institute to measure two level tablespoons; also known as a coffee scoop.

apre (ah-prue) 1. French for harsh. 2. A wine-tasting term for a harsh, young red wine with a high tannin content.

apribottiglia (ah-pree-boh-TEEL-yah) Italian for a bottle opener.

apricot A small stone fruit (*Prunus armeniaca*) with a thin, velvety, pale yellow to deep burnt orange skin, a meaty golden cream to bright orange flesh and an almond-shaped pit; it is highly perishable, with a peak season during June and July; the pit's kernel is used to flavor alcoholic beverages and confections.

apricot

apricot, dried Dried, pitted, unpeeled apricot halves.

aprikose (ahp-ree-KOAZ-zern) Swedish for apricot.

Aprikose (ah-pri-KKOOSS) German for apricot.

aprikots (ah-pri-koots) Norwegian for apricots.

Apry (AP-ree) Apricot brandy.

Apulia (ah-POO-l'yah) A grape-growing and wine-producing region in southeast Italy; most of the wine, which is used for blending, has a deep color, a high alcohol content and a low level of acid.

AQ A menu term meaning as quoted, generally referring to the price of an expensive item (e.g., lobster); the server quotes the price.

aqua ardens Latin for burned water and used to describe alcohol.

aquafarming; aquaculture The business, science and practice of raising large quantities of fish and shellfish in tanks, ponds or ocean pens, usually for food.

aquavit; akvavit (ah-kar-VEET) A clear Scandinavian alcoholic beverage distilled from potatoes or grain and flavored with caraway seeds, cardamom and orange and lemon peels.

aqua vitae; aqua vita Latin for water of life; used to describe clear, distilled brandy.

arabaci corbasi (ar-bah-che shor-bas) A Turkish chicken soup with small, diamond-shaped dumplings and flavored with lemon juice.

arabic *See* acacia.

arabica coffee beans (ah-RAB-ie-kah) A species of coffee beans (*Coffea arabia*) grown around the world in high-altitude tropical and subtropical regions with plentiful rainfall; the most important species commercially, they are used for fine, richly flavored and aromatic beverages. *See* robusta coffee beans.

arabinogalactan A food additive derived from western larch wood and used as an emulsifier, stabilizer, binder and/or thickener in processed foods such as oils, sweeteners, flavor bases, dressings and pudding mixes.

arachide (ah-RAH-kee-day) Italian for peanuts.

arachide (ah-rah-szwid) French for peanut when it is used for oil.

arachidonic acid 1. An essential polyunsaturated fatty acid found in fish and plant oils; an omega-6 fatty acid. 2. A food additive used as a nutrient supplement.

Aragackij (ah-rah-gah-key-gee) An Armenian cheese made from ewe's and goat's milks; it has a thin, dark greenish-blue rind and a firm interior.

aragosta (ah-rah-GOS-sth) Italian for spiny lobster.

arak; arrack; arrak (ar-ruck) Any of various spirits distilled in the Middle East, Southeast Asia and the Far East from fermented coconut palm sap or a rice and molasses mash.

arakhis (ah-raw-kiss) Russian for peanut.

Arak Punsch *See* Swedish punsch.

arame (ah-rah-meh) Dried, shredded seaweed with a greenish-brown color and a mild, delicate flavor; it is used as flavoring in Japanese cuisines.

aram sandwich (A-rhum; EHR-uhm) A sandwich made from softened lavosh spread with a filling and rolled jelly-roll style, refrigerated and sliced into 1-in. pieces for service.

arancia (ah-RAHN-chah) Italian for orange.

arancini (ah-rahn-CHEE-nee) A Sicilian dish of rice and meat formed into balls.

arándano (a-ran-dah-noh) Spanish for blueberry.

arándano agrio (a-ran-dah-noh ahg-ree-koh) Spanish for cranberry.

araq (ar-rah-key) A Middle Eastern anise-flavored liqueur.

Arawatta A dry white wine made in South Australia's Barossa Valley from the Riesling grape.

arbequine (ahr-bah-key-nah) Small, spherical, tannish-pink olives from Spain.

arbi (AHR-bee) A starchy root vegetable native to India.

Arbois (ahr-bwah) A grape-growing and wine-producing district in eastern France; red and rosé wines are produced from Poulsard, Trousseau and Pinot Noir grapes and dry white wines are produced from Savagin and Chardonnay grapes.

Arborea (ahr-BOH-ree-yah) Wines made from either Sangiovese or Trebbiano grapes grown near the Arborea plains near Sardinia, Italy.

arborio rice (ar-BOH-ree-oh) An ovoid, short-grain rice with a hard core, white color and mild flavor; it becomes creamy when cooked and is used for risotto.

Arbroath smokies A Scottish dish consisting of small haddock that are gutted but not split, salted and smoked and then broiled just before serving.

Arbuckle's (AHR-buck-uhls) A slang term for coffee popular in the American Old West.

arbufas (ahr-BOO-fahs) A Sardinian gingerbread made with honey, raisins, nuts and cinnamon.

arbutus A small tree (*Arbutus unedo*) grown in the Mediterranean region; its small red berries have an acidic flavor and are generally used as garnish; also known as a tree strawberry.

archangel *See* white deadnettle.

archiduc, sauce (ahr-schwe-dehk) A French compound sauce made from a suprême sauce finished with a champagne reduction.

architectural food A style of presentation in which foods are arranged on a plate to emphasize height and visual interest; these constructions are sometimes very elaborate, consisting of multiple foods, and are often difficult to eat.

Arctic bramble A variety of Japanese wineberry with small fruit that have a red-amber color and a flavor reminiscent of pineapple; also known as crimson bramble.

Arctic char A freshwater fish found in northern Europe, Canada and the northern United States; related to the brook trout (but not a true trout); it has an average market weight of 1 lb. (450 g) and a white to red flesh with a delicate flavor; also known as omble.

ardei iute (ahr-da-e you-ta) Romanian for chile.

Ardennes ham A lean ham from Belgium's Ardennes region; it is brine cured and then cold smoked with beech or oak chips and juniper and thyme twigs.

ardent spirits An archaic term for distilled spirits.

area chef At a large hotel, conference center or the like, the person responsible for a particular facility or function.

areca nut The small fruit of the areca palm native to Southeast Asia; it has a mottled brown skin and a pleasantly astringent flavor; also imprecisely known as a betel nut.

arengo (ah-REHN-goh) A bulk red wine made from Barbera grapes in Italy's Piedmont region.

arenque (ah-REHN-kayss) Spanish for herring.

arepas (ah-ray-pass) A Colombian and Venezuelan staple made from flour ground from a very starchy cooked corn, mixed with water and salt and cooked quickly on a griddle.

Argenteuil (ar-zhawn-TEW-ee) A French preparation method used to describe a dish with a sauce or garnish of asparagus tips or purée.

arginine 1. An amino acid. 2. A food additive used as a nutrient source to significantly improve the biological quality of the total protein in a food containing naturally occurring protein.

argol The tartar (potassium bitartrate) that a maturing wine deposits on the barrel staves; this precipitate is used to make cream of tartar.

Argyll (ahr-gyle) A British carving dish that has indentations to catch and serve the juices from meat, game or poultry.

arhar dal (ahr-har dahl) Hindi for lentils. *See* pigeon pea.

ariboflavinosis A disease caused by a deficiency of vitamin B_2; symptoms include cracks at the corner of the mouth, hypersensitivity to light, skin rash and magenta tongue.

aril The lacy outer covering of some seeds (e.g., nutmeg).

aringa (ah-REENG-gah) Italian for herring.

arista (ah-REES-tah) 1. Italian for roasted loin of pork, usually with the bone in. 2. An Italian dish consisting of roasted boneless pork roast flavored with rosemary or fennel, garlic and olive oil.

ark shells A family of bivalves including Noah's ark and generally found in the eastern Atlantic Ocean and Mediterranean Sea; both valves are an identical rectangular, trapezoidal or oval shape, and the flesh, eaten raw, has a tough, chewy texture.

arlesienne, sauce (ahrl-ehs-yehng) A French compound sauce made from a béarnaise flavored with tomato purée and anchovy paste and garnished with diced tomatoes.

armadillo (ahr-mah-DEHL-lo) A large family of mammals of which one variety, the three-banded armadillo, is edible; native to South America, its small body and head are encased in a plating of small bony scales and its flesh is often used for sausage.

Armagnac (ar-manh-yak) A French brandy produced principally in Gers (southeast of Bordeaux) from white wine grapes; distilled and redistilled in one continuous operation and aged in black oak barrels, it has a dry, smooth flavor, a pungent bouquet and an amber color.

armand, d' (ar-mahnd, d') A French garnish consisting of soufflé potatoes, a red wine sauce, and chopped, sautéed goose liver and truffles; it is generally used for meats.

arm chops *See* blade chops.

Armenian cucumber A very long, sometimes slightly coiled, ridged slicing cucumber with dark green skin, a pale green flesh, a mellow, sweet flavor and edible seeds.

Armenian wax pepper An elongated sweet pepper with a yellow skin and a mild, sweet flavor; used pickled or fresh.

armilaria (ar-mee-lah-ree-ah) Spanish for honey mushroom.

armillaire (ahr-me-lair) French for honey mushroom.

arm roast 1. A subprimal cut from the beef primal chuck; somewhat tough, it is available with or without the bone. 2. A subprimal cut from the veal primal shoulder; usually available deboned, rolled and tied. 3. A subprimal cut of the pork primal shoulder; it is a moderately tender, flavorful roast.

arm steak A fabricated cut from the beef primal chuck; it is cut from the arm roast and available with or without the bone.

Arneis (ahr-NAY'Z) An Italian grape variety grown, in limited quantities, in Italy's Piedmont region; it produces an excellent dry white wine.

arni (ah-rnee) A Greek dish of lamb rubbed with salt, pepper and lemon and roasted on a spit over an open fire.

arni kléftiko (ah-rnee kleff-tea-koh) A Greek dish of lamb cooked in greaseproof paper with peas, carrots, tomatoes and potatoes.

aroma 1. Fragrance or odor. 2. In a young wine, the fruity odors related to the grape variety. *See* bouquet.

aromatic A food, usually an herb, spice or vegetable, added to a preparation primarily to enhance its aroma and secondarily its flavor.

aromatic hops *See* noble hops.

aromatic rice Rice with a perfumy, nutlike aroma and flavor (e.g., basmati, jasmine and Texmati).

aromatized wine A fortified wine in which various aromatic flowers, herbs and/or spices have been steeped to infuse aromas and flavors into the wine (e.g., vermouth).

arrabbiata (HAR-rah-bee-ah-tah) An Italian tomato sauce flavored with herbs, cayenne pepper, spicy sausage bits and bacon.

arracacha (ah-rah-cah-chah) A root vegetable (*Arracacia xanthoohiza*) native to northern South America; the brown-skinned cylindrical root has an off-white flesh with a potato-like texture and a vaguely sweet flavor.

Arran Pilot potato A popular variety of medium-sized, brown-skinned potato grown in the United States.

arroba (ah-RO-bah) A Spanish measure of approximately 16 liters or just over 4 U.S. gallons and equivalent to 25 lb. of grapes.

arrope (ah-ROH-pay) An unfermented grape juice concentrate (reduced to one-fifth its original volume) added to sherry for color and sweetness. *See* sancocho.

arroser (ah-roh-say) French for to baste or moisten.

arrosto (ahr-ROA-stoa) Italian for to roast.

arrowhead A small tuberous vegetable (*Sagittaria sinensis*) resembling a lily bulb, with smooth, beige skin, thin brown, layered leaves and a bland, slightly sweet flavor used as a starch in Chinese and Japanese cuisines; also known as kuwai (Japan) and tsee goo (China).

arrowroot A starchy white powder made from the underground stems of a tropical plant, generally used as a thickener; it is flavorless and becomes clear when cooked.

arrowroot vermicelli Brittle, thin, white Asian noodles made from arrowroot flour; usually sold in bundles and used in soups.

arroz (ah-ROHS) Portuguese and Spanish for rice.

arroz con costra (ar-ROHS con coss-trah) A Spanish dish consisting of rice and meat flavored with tomatoes, saffron, butifarra negra and white wine and topped with an egg crust.

arroz con leche (ar-ROHS con leh-tchay) Spanish for rice pudding.

arroz con pollo (ar-ROHS kon PO-yo) A Spanish and Mexican dish of sautéed chicken simmered with tomatoes, stock, saffron, sherry, rice and seasonings.

arroz de viuva (ar-ROHS day vee-eu-vah) A Brazilian dessert of rice cooked with milk, vanilla bean and sugar; it can be served at room temperature or chilled.

arroz marillo (ar-ROHS mahree-yoh) A Cuban dish consisting of rice flavored with saffron; also known as yellow rice.

arroz negro (ar-ROHS nae-gro) A Spanish dish consisting of rice blackened with octopus ink and flavored with garlic, tomatoes and parsley.

arsella (ahr-SEH-lah) Italian for mussel.

ärt (aer) Swedish for pea.

artesian-well water *See* water, artesian well.

artichaut (arti-cho) French for artichoke.

artichoke, common The large flowerhead of a plant of the thistle family (*Cynara scolymus*); it has tough, gray-green, petal-shaped leaves with soft flesh (which is eaten cooked) underneath, a furry choke (that is discarded) and a tender center (called the heart and that is also eaten, usually cooked or pickled); also known as a globe artichoke.

artichoke

artichoke, purple A variety of small artichoke with purple-green leaves; it can be eaten raw if very young.

artic wine Slang for straight whiskey.

artificial color *See* coloring agent.

artificial fat A fat substitute such as sucrose polyester; generally indigestible, it contributes few if any calories to the diet.

artificial flavor *See* flavor, artificial.

artificial sweetener A sugar substitute such as aspartame, cyclamate or saccharin; used as a food additive in processed foods or for individual use, has few if any calories and little if any nutritional value; also known as a synthetic sweetener.

Artillery Punch A punch made of rye, bourbon or whiskey, dry red wine, strong tea, dark Jamaican rum, orange juice, brandy, gin, lemon juice, Benedictine and sugar syrup; garnished with lemon peel.

artisanal (ar-TEE-shun-al) A craftsmanlike approach to bread making in which the baker's skill and intuition and the quality of raw ingredients are given the highest priorities.

artisjokk (ah-ti-SHOKK) Norwegian for artichoke.

aru (aa-ROO) Hindi for peach.

arugula (ah-ROO-guh-lah) A leaf vegetable (*Eruca sativa*) with dark green, spiky, dandelion-like leaves and a strong, spicy, peppery flavor; used in salads; also known as rocket, rucola and rugula.

arukoru (ah-roo-koh-roo) Japanese for alcohol.

AS *See* as-served.

Asadero (ah-sahr-DARE-oh) A semifirm Mexican cheese made from whole milk; it has a white color and a mild flavor and melts easily; also known as Oaxaca.

asado (ah-SAH-doh) 1. Spanish for to roast. 2. A Filipino cooking method in which meat is simmered in soy sauce with bay leaves, onions, tomato and peppercorns.

asado criolla (ah-sah-doh cree-ol-yah) An Argentine barbecue, traditionally featuring grilled sausages, a spit-roasted side of beef or pork, kid or suckling pig and grilled organ meats.

asafetida; asafoetida (ah-sah-FEH-teh-dah) A pale brown resin made from the sap of a giant fennel-like plant native to India and Iran; it has a garlicky flavor and a fetid aroma; available powdered or in lump form, it is used (sparingly) as a flavoring in Indian and Middle Eastern cuisines; also known as devil's dung.

asagohan (AH-sah-go-hahn) Japanese for breakfast; also known as choshoku.

asakusa nori (ah-SAH-koo-sah NOH-ree) Thin dark sheets of dried seaweed; used as a flavoring and sushi wrapper in Japanese cuisine.

asali (ah-saw-lee) An East African alcoholic beverage made from fermented honey.

asali ya nyuki (ah-saw-lee yah nyoo-key) Swahili for honey.

asam gelugor; asam jawa (ah-sum ge-loo-gore; ah-sum jah-wah) Dried slices of tamarind used as a flavoring in Malaysian and Nonya cuisines.

asam pedas (as-sum peh-das) An Indonesian cooking method in which fish or meat is cooked in a very spicy, sour sauce.

asari (ah-SAH-ree) A clam native to Japanese coastal waters.

Asbach Uralt (as-bah ou-halt) A German brandy, similar to Cognac.

asciutto (ah-shoo-toe) 1. Italian for very dry. 2. When referring to an Italian wine, the meaning is drier than secco (dry), abboccato (semidry) and dolce (sweet).

ascorbic acid A food additive used as a nutrient supplement as well as a preservative and antioxidant in foods such as processed meat, processed potato products and breakfast foods; it is sometimes used in the form of sodium ascorbate, isoascorbic acid, erythorbic acid or sodium erythorbate. *See* vitamin C.

ascorbyl palmitate A food additive used as a preservative.

Ascot A short, slender cigar with a 30–36 ring and a 3- to 5-in. length.

asfor The light orange stamens of the safflower; they are used to color rice in eastern Mediterranean cuisines.

ash The mineral substance remaining after burning organic matter; it is used to measure the inorganic salts that were in the substance that was burned.

ash bread A cornbread, typically wrapped in cabbage leaves, baked in the ashes left in a fireplace; also known as corn pone. *See* hoecake.

Ashley bread A bread similar to spoon bread but made with rice flour; probably created in South Carolina.

Asiago (AH-zee-AH-goa) A hard northern Italian grana cheese made from cow's milk; it has a pungent flavor and a grayish-white interior; when cured for 6 months or more, it is used for grating and cooking.

Asiago di Taglio (AH-zee-AH-goa dee tah-jo) An Asiago aged for not more than 60 days and used as a table cheese.

Asian eggplant *See* eggplant, Asian.

Asian pear A fruit ranging in size and color from large and golden brown to small and green; it has a juicy, crunchy, firm, granular texture and a sweet flavor; also known as a Chinese pear.

Asian radish *See* daikon.

å skiver Norwegian for to slice.

A. Smith Bowman Distillery One of the 12 remaining U.S. whiskey distilleries; located in Fredericksburg, Virginia, and founded in 1935, it produces Virginia Gentleman Bourbon, also known as Virginia Whiskey.

asopao (ah-soh-pah-oh) A Puerto Rican stew made with rice and fish, poultry or meat.

asparagas (ahs-paa-raa-ghas) Swahili for asparagus.

asparago (ha-spah-rah-goh) Italian for asparagus.

asparagus (ah-SPAR-ah-gus) A member of the lily family (*Asparagus officinalis*) with an erect stalk and small, scale-like leaves along the stalk, capped by a ruffle of small leaves; a young stalk is tender, with a slightly pungent, bitter flavor, an apple green color and a purple-tinged tip; it becomes tougher as it ages.

asparagus, white A very pale yellowish-green asparagus with a milder flavor than green asparagus; the asparagus is regularly reburied as the stalk grows, which retards the development of chlorophyll.

asparagus bean *See* yard-long bean.

asparagus pea *See* winged bean.

asparagus peeler A tool used to remove a fine outer layer of the stalk, allowing the stalk to cook in the same time as the tip.

asparagus steamer An assemblage consisting of two tall pots; the inner pot has a perforated bottom and holds the asparagus upright; the assemblage is partially filled with water so that the stalks are simmered while the tips are steamed.

asparagus steamer

asparges (as-SPAHR-ggerss) Norwegian for asparagus.

aspargo (ahs-par-goo) Portuguese for asparagus.

aspartame A food additive used as a synthetic sweetener in sugar substitutes and processed foods such as soft drinks, frozen desserts, refrigerated puddings and dried pudding bases; created by linking together two amino acids (aspartic acid and phenylalanine), it is 200 times sweeter than sucrose; it is registered under the name NutraSweet.

aspartic acid 1. An amino acid. 2. A food additive used as a nutrient source to significantly improve the biological quality of the total protein in a food containing naturally occurring protein.

asperges (ahs-spehr-rez) French for asparagus.

Aspergillus A group of molds used to inoculate beans and grains to make koji and as a starter for many Japanese fermented foods.

Aspergillus-derived enzymes Enzymes derived from the fungus genus *Aspergillus* and used as food additive processing aids.

asperulé (as-per-RHUL) French for woodruff.

aspic A clear savory jelly made from clarified meat, fish or vegetable stock and gelatin; it is used to glaze cold foods. *See* hure.

aspic cutters Small metal cutters in various shapes (similar to cookie cutters); used to cut aspic, truffles, hard-boiled egg whites, tomato skins and the like into decorative designs.

aspic mold A 1½-in.-(3.8-cm) deep, oval, flair-sided, stainless steel mold with a capacity of 4 oz. (113.4 g); it is used for single servings of foods such as eggs in aspic; also known as an oval dariole. *See* timbale mold.

aspic mold

aspic terrine *See* brawn.

Asprino (ah-SPREE-noh) A dry, light Italian wine produced north of Naples.

as-purchased (AP) The condition or cost (price) of an item as it is purchased or received from the supplier. *See* edible portion *and* yield.

assa (ah-sah) Ethiopian for fish.

assafir (ah-saw-fir) Tiny game birds fried whole in Lebanese cuisine.

assaisonné (ah-say-zoh-NAY) French for seasoned or seasoned with.

assaisonner (ah-say-sohn-nay) French for to season.

Assam (ahs-SAHN) Brittle leaves of black tea from the Assam region in northern India; the beverage has a reddish color and a brisk, strong flavor ideal for breakfast when served with milk.

Assam golden tips A black tea from India's Assam region made from leaf buds; the beverage is deeply aromatic and full bodied without any bitterness.

assar (ah-ssar) Portuguese for to roast.

assemblage (ah-SAHM-blahj) French for assembly and used to describe a wine or brandy blended from wines made from different grape varieties, fermentation vats and/or vineyard plots.

assertive A tasting term for a food or beverage's pronounced or characteristic flavor or aroma.

as-served (AS) The weight or size of a product as sold or served after processing or cooking.

asset Anything of value owned by a business.

assiette (ahs-zjet) French for plate.

assiette anglaise (ahs-zjet ahn-glez) A French dish consisting of assorted cold meats such as sliced ham, beef and tongue.

assimilation The process by which the products of digestion are converted to the chemical substances of body tissues; the constructive phase of anabolism.

assistant *See* demi-chef.

astakó (ah-staa-koh) Greek for lobster.

astice (ah-STEE-cheh) A large lobster caught off the coast of Sardinia.

Asti Spumante (AH-stee spoo-MAHN-teh) A sweet, white sparkling wine made by the Charmat process in the town of Asti, Piedmont, Italy.

astri (as-tree) Italian for stars and used to describe pastina in the shape of small stars.

astringent (ah-STREHN-gent) A tasting term for a wine, usually a young red wine, that makes the mouth pucker because of excessive tannin.

asure; ashure A sweet Middle Eastern soup made with whole grains, legumes, dried fruits and nuts; it is said to have been the last meal served on Noah's ark.

asuriana (ah-soo-ree-ah-nah) A Spanish blood sausage made with cow's blood, bacon and onions.

aszú (ah-soo) Hungarian term for the noble rot.

ata (ah-tah) A Nigerian chile sauce; it consists of onions, garlic, tomatoes, chiles, thyme and a Madras-style curry powder.

atalanti royal A round Greek olive of variable size and with a color ranging from light to dark brown to red; usually slit, salt brine cured and kept in a vinegar and oil mixture.

atap chee *See* palm nut.

ate (ah-tay) A Latin American and Middle Eastern sweetened fruit paste, usually quince or guava, served alone as a dessert or with cheese.

atemoya (a-teh-MOH-ee-yah) A hybrid fruit of the cherimoya and sweetsop and grown in Florida; it has a tough, sage green skin covered with short, petal-like configurations similar to those of a globe artichoke, a cream-colored pulp with large black seeds and a flavor reminiscent of mango and vanilla.

atesino (ah-the-ZEE-noh) An Italian wine term used to describe a wine produced along the Adige River in the Trentino–Alto Adige region.

athole brose; atholl brose (AH-thohl broz) A Scottish beverage made of whisky, oatmeal and honey; it is bottled and stored for two days before use.

atjar (at-jar) 1. South African pickled vegetables. 2. A South African pickling marinade; similar to achars, it usually consists of anchovies, garlic, fenugreek, turmeric, chiles and a Madras-style curry powder.

Atlantic clams Any of several varieties of clams found along the U.S. East Coast; they are generally classified as Atlantic hard-shell clams and Atlantic soft-shell clams.

Atlantic cod *See* cod, Atlantic.

Atlantic croaker *See* croaker.

Atlantic deep sea scallop *See* sea scallop.

Atlantic halibut A variety of halibut found off the East Coast of the United States and Canada; it has a lean white flesh with a sweet, mild flavor and a firm texture; also known as eastern halibut.

Atlantic hard-shell clams Atlantic clams with hard, blue-gray shells and a chewy meat that is not as sweet as that of other varieties; also known as quahogs; significant varieties include cherrystone clams, chowder clams, littleneck clams and topneck clams.

Atlantic mackerel A fish found in the Atlantic Ocean from the mid-Atlantic states of the United States to New England; it has a brilliant multihued coloration and two dozen or so wavy dark bands, a high fat content, a dark flesh, an average weight of 0.5–2.5 lb. (225–1140 g), and an assertive flavor; also known as Boston mackerel.

Atlantic oysters Any of several varieties of oysters found along the U.S. East Coast; generally, they have round, flat, dark gray shells, a grayish flesh with a soft texture and a briny flavor (the flavor and color often vary depending on the oyster's origin); many Atlantic oysters are named for their place of origin (e.g., Chesapeake Bay oysters and Long Island oysters); also known as American oysters, American cupped oysters and eastern oysters.

Atlantic salmon The most commercially important salmon species, aquafarmed extensively off Canada, Iceland, Ireland, Scotland and Norway (wild fish are rarely available); it has a grayish-brown skin with scattered black spots that becomes silvery and then white on the belly, a moist pink flesh, a high fat content, a delicate flavor and an average weight of 5–15 lb. (2.3–6.7 kg); it is often marketed with the fish's origin added to the name (e.g., Norwegian Atlantic salmon and Shetland Atlantic salmon).

Atlantic soft-shell clams Atlantic clams with thin, brittle shells that do not close completely because of the clam's protruding black-tipped siphon; they have a tender, sweet flesh; significant varieties include Ipswich clams, steamer clams and longneck clams.

atole (ah-TOH-leh) An ancient Mexican thick beverage consisting of masa, water or milk, crushed fruit and sugar or honey; it is served hot or at room temperature.

atoshi-buta (at-to-she-bu-ta) A Japanese wooden drop lid.

atsu (AHT-su) Japanese for thick.

atsuagé (at-su-ah-gue) Japanese tofu cutlets pressed free of water and deep-fried, steamed or baked.

atsui (aht-SU-ee) Japanese for hot.

atta (at-taa) A finely milled whole wheat flour used for various unleavened Indian breads such as chapati and paratha.

Atta Boy A cocktail made of gin, dry vermouth and grenadine and garnished with a twist of lemon.

Attakiska vodka A dry vodka made in Anchorage, Alaska, from the pristine waters of ancient glaciers.

attenuation In beer making, the reduction in the wort's specific gravity because of fermentation; it is a measure of the amount of dissolved solids that have been converted to alcohol and carbon dioxide.

attereau (ah-tehr-row) A French metal skewer on which sweet or savory foods are threaded, dredged in bread crumbs and deep-fried.

Attica (AH-tee-kah) A grape-growing region near Athens, Greece; most of the production is made into Retsina.

attieké; atsieke A fermented starch used in the cuisine of the Ivory Coast.

atum (a-TOOM) Portuguese for tuna.

atún (ah-TOON) Spanish for tuna.

atún amarillo Spanish (particularly in Mexico and Chile) for yellowfin tuna.

atún fresco con judias en escabeche (ah-too phray-skoe con hoo-dee-ahs en es-cah-bay-chae) A Spanish tapas of fresh tuna with white beans in a marinade.

a'u (AH-u) Hawaiian for any member of the marlin family.

aubergine (oh-berr-yeen) British and French for eggplant.

Aubergine (oh-berr-yeen) German for eggplant.

au bleu (oh BLEUH) A French term indicating that the fish was prepared immediately after it was killed.

auctioning Slang for when a server, who has the ordered food with him or her, asks all of the patrons at a table who ordered what dish and then serves accordingly.

Auflauf (AUF-law-oof) German for soufflé; it can be sweet or savory.

Aufschnitten (ah-oof-shnee-ten) German cold cuts; a variety of sliced cold meats and sausages sold in delicatessens.

au gratin (oh GRAH-tan) A French term referring to a dish with a browned topping of bread crumbs and/or grated cheese; also known as gratinée.

Augsburger Würst (aus-ber-ger verst) A sausage traditionally made in Augsburg, Germany, from pork and bacon fat, seasoned with cloves, nutmeg, salt and pepper and lightly smoked; served hot after poaching.

au jus (oh zhew) A French term for roasted meats, poultry or game served with their natural, unthickened juices.

au lait (oh lay) French for served with milk.

aumlet A traditional North American term for an omelette.

aumonières de pommes (oh-mohn-yair duh pomz) French apple turnovers; they are made with apples flavored with Calvados, wrapped in crêpes and tied with a strip of glazed leek leaf.

au naturel (oh nah-teur-EHL) A French term indicating that the food is served in its natural state; not cooked or altered in any fashion.

Aurora; Aurore (aw-ROAR-ah) A French-American hybrid grape widely planted in New York's Finger Lakes district and used for white table wine and sparkling wine.

aurore, à la (oh-ROHR, ah lah) A name given to some French dishes containing tomato purée, especially egg and chicken dishes coated with sauce aurore.

aurore, sauce (oh-ROHR) A French compound sauce made from a velouté with tomato purée.

Ausbruch (ow's-brook) A term used for sweet white Austrian wine made from grapes affected by the noble rot.

au sec (oh sek) A French term referring to something cooked until nearly dry.

Aus Eigenem Lesegut (ow's AH'Y-gennem lay-zeh-goot) A German wine term for "grower's own harvest," the equivalent of estate bottled.

Auslese (OUSE-lay-zuh) German for selected picking; a labeling term applied to rich, elegant, sweet dessert wines made from selected bunches of grapes containing a minimum of 20–24% natural grape sugar. *See* Qualitätswein mit Prädikat (QmP).

austere A wine-tasting term for a hard, dry wine that lacks richness and requires aging.

Austern (AUS-tern) German for oysters.

Austernseitling (AUS-tern-zit-ling) German for oyster mushroom.

Australian bramble A variety of Japanese wineberry with small, pinkish-red, juicy fruit.

Australian icing *See* rolled fondant.

autoclave (aw-toe-klah-veh) Italian name for the Charmat process.

autolysis A reaction that occurs when wine is aged on the lees; the yeast cells decompose, releasing amino acids into the wine that add flavor and aroma, thus enriching the wine's texture and complexity.

automatic bar A machine that dispenses a predetermined portion (i.e., controlled quantity) of a distilled spirit.

autumn olive The small orange or red berry of a shrub native to Asia and popular in southeastern Europe; it is used like a currant, fresh or dried.

aux champignons (oh sham-pee-nyohn) A French term indicating that the dish was prepared with mushrooms.

aux croutons (oh kroo-toh'n) French term indicating that the dish is served with croutons (bread cut in small dice and fried in butter).

Auxerrois (awk-sehr-WAH) 1. A white wine grape grown in France's Alsace region. 2. The local name for the red Malbec grape grown in the Cahors, a district east of Bordeaux. *See* Malbec.

avanzi (ah-VAHN-zee) Italian for leftovers.

Avdat Red A dry red Israeli wine.

Avdat White A dry light white Israeli wine.

avela (ah-veh-lah) Portuguese for hazelnut.

aveline (ah-vay-leen) French for filbert.

avella (ah-VELL-lah) Italian for hazelnut.

avellana (ahb-hay-LYAH-nahss) Spanish for hazelnut.

avena (ha-vae-nah) Italian and Spanish for oats and used to describe pastina in the shape of small dimpled disks.

average check (AC); average cover The dollar amount of food and/or beverage sales divided by the total number of checks.

average sales per seat A restaurant's sales for a specific period divided by its seating capacity.

average weighted cost The cost of a single unit when various quantities are purchased at different prices.

avga (ah-vgaá) Greek for egg.

avgolémono (ahv-goh-LEH-moh-noh) A Greek soup and sauce made from chicken broth, egg yolks and lemon juice (rice is added to the soup).

Aviation A cocktail made of gin, lemon juice, maraschino liqueur and apricot brandy.

avignonnaise, sauce (ah-vee-nyon-aze) A French compound sauce made from a béchamel flavored with garlic, seasoned with grated Parmesan, finished with an egg yolk liaison and garnished with parsley.

avocado (a-voh-CAH-doh) A tropical fruit (*Persea americana*) with a single large pit, spherical to pear shaped; it has a smooth to rough-textured green to purplish skin and yellow to green flesh with a buttery texture and a high unsaturated fat content; it is generally used like a vegetable and consumed raw; also known as an alligator pear and vegetable marrow.

avocado

avocado leaf The leaf of the avocado tree; toasted, it is used like a bay leaf in Mexican cuisines.

avocado oil A colorless, viscous oil obtained by pressing an avocado's pit; odorless, it has a neutral flavor and is principally used for salad dressings.

avocat (ah-voh-cah) French for avocado.

Avocatobirne (avo-cah-toh-beer-neh) German for avocado.

avoine (ah-vowan) French for oats.

avoirdupois weight A system for measuring weight based on a pound of 16 oz. and an ounce of 16 drams.

Aw *See* water activity.

awabi (ah-wah-beh) A variety of abalone found near Japan; it has an ivory flesh with a chewy texture and a mild flavor.

awamori (ah-wah-moh-reh) A high-alcohol-content spirit distilled from rice, made in Okinawa, Japan.

Awenda bread (AH-wen-dah) A quick bread made with hominy grits and cornmeal; named for an Indian settlement near Charleston, South Carolina.

awirma mashwiya An Egyptian dish consisting of baked pearl onions.

awwam (a-oo-ahn)A Lebanese dessert consisting of balls of deep-fried yeast dough dipped in a honey syrup flavored with rosewater and lemon.

ayer (ay-yer) Yiddish for eggs.

ayna (ah-e-nah) Turkish for spider crab.

ayran (a-e-ran) A Turkish beverage made from yogurt, water, heavy cream, salt and ice.

ayskrimu (ah-ee-skree-moo) Swahili for ice cream.

ayu (AH-you) Japanese for trout; also known as masu.

azafrán (ah-thah-FRAHN) Spanish for saffron.

azaroles (ah-zah-roh-lez) The fruit of the Mediterranean or Neopolitan medlar (a hawthorn); these large berries have a red, orange or yellow skin, a pasty flesh and an applelike flavor and can be eaten or used for a liqueur.

Azeitao (ah-ZAY-tah-oh) A Portuguese ewe's milk cheese, curdled with thistle.

azeite (a-ZAYT) Portuguese for oil.

azeitona (ah-ZAY-toh-nah) Portuguese for olive.

azeitona de mesa (ah-ZAY-toh-nah day meh-zah) Portuguese sweet olives eaten as a snack, either marinated or stuffed.

azienda agricola (ha-zee-en-dah ha-gree-co-lah) Italian for vineyard and winery.

azijn (ah-ZEYN) Dutch for vinegar.

azodicarbonamide A food additive used as a dough conditioner and/or flour aging and bleaching agent in processed foods such as baked goods.

azúcar (ah-THOO-kahr) Spanish for granulated sugar.

azuki *See* adzuki

Azul A blue cheese made in Latin America and Denmark from pasteurized cow's milk; it has a dense, greenish-blue–veined interior and a strong flavor.

baak choy (bahk CHOY) *See* bok choy.

baat gok (baht kok) Chinese for star anise.

baamieh (bam-yeh) Arabic for okra.

baba; baba au rhum (BAH-bah; BAH-bah oh rum) A light, rich Polish yeast cake studded with raisins and soaked in rum syrup; it is traditionally baked in individual cylindrical molds, giving the finished product a mushroom shape. *See* savarin.

babaco (BAH-bah-ko) A very long tropical fruit (*Carica pentagona*) native to South America with a star-shaped cross section, a soft, green skin that turns yellow when ripe, a juicy, pale apricot-colored flesh, few seeds and a slightly acidic flavor reminiscent of strawberries with hints of papaya and pineapple; also known as a chamburo.

baba ghanoush; baba ghanouj; baba ghannouj (bah-bah gha-NOOSH) A Middle Eastern dish of puréed eggplant, olive oil, tahini, lemon juice and garlic and garnished with chopped mint, pomegranate seeds or chopped pistachios; it is served as a dip or spread, usually with pita; also known as mutabbal.

babassu oil (bah-bahs-soo) The oil obtained from the Brazilian babassu palm; similar to coconut oil, it is used in vegetable fat–based products.

babeurre (bah-buhr) French for buttermilk.

babeurre (bah-bear-ray) An Algerian beverage consisting of milk and yogurt.

babi ketjap (bah-be ket-up) A Dutch East Indian dish of pork strips simmered with onions in diluted soy sauce and served with rice as part of a rijsttafel.

babka (bahb-kah) A Jewish, Russian and Polish dessert consisting of a rich yeast dough made with many eggs and sweet butter, flavored with citrus peel and studded with raisins; sometimes cocoa or a cinnamon–sugar syrup is added. *See* shikkereh babka.

babovka (bah-bove-kah) A tall round Czech cake made of alternating layers of chocolate and vanilla batters; the batters are flavored with nuts and rum.

baby 1. A marketing term for a small, whole cheese traditionally made in a large wheel, round or other shape. 2. A quarter bottle with a capacity of 1 imperial gill (0.1355 l); used for beer.

Baby All Blue potato A variety of a small, long, thin potato with a lavender-blue flesh.

baby back ribs A fabricated cut of the pork primal loin; it is a slab of ribs weighing 1.75 lb. (792 g) or less.

baby beef *See* calf.

baby boar A wild boar slaughtered when younger than 6 months; its reddish-pink flesh has a more delicate flavor and more tender texture than that of the mature wild boar. *See* wild boar.

Baby Bon *See* Bonbel.

baby clam *See* Manila clam.

baby eggplant *See* eggplant, Italian.

baby lamb The meat of a sheep slaughtered when it is 6–8 weeks old; the meat is very tender, with a mild, delicate flavor. *See* lamb, mutton *and* spring lamb.

Baby Ruth The proprietary name for a candy bar consisting of a chewy caramel and peanut center coated with milk chocolate.

baby vegetables A marketing term used to describe small vegetables that are picked young or are hybrids grown to be small; they are generally sweeter and more tender than the mature vegetables and add to the appearance of the plate.

bac à glace (back ah glass) A brine bath in which a Champagne or sparkling wine bottle's neck is frozen before degorgement.

bacalao (bah-kah-LAH-oh) Salt cod used in Spanish and South American cuisines.

bacalhau (bah-cah-LAW-oo) Salt cod used in Portuguese and Brazilian cuisines.

bacalhau com natas (bah-cah-LAW-oo com nah-tahs) A Portuguese dish consisting of dried cod and potatoes in a cream sauce.

bacalhau gomes sa (bah-cah-LAW-oo goh-man sah) An Angolan dish consisting of salted codfish and potatoes flavored with bay leaves, onions, pepper and oregano and garnished with olives and eggs.

Bacardi Cocktail A cocktail made of lime juice, sugar, grenadine and Barcardi light rum.

baccalà (bak-kah-LAH) Italian for dried salt codfish.

bacchanal (bak-ah-nahl) A drunken and riotous celebration.

Bacchus The Roman god of wine and of an orgiastic religion celebrating the power and fertility of nature. *See* Dionysus.

bachelor's button A small cookie topped with a maraschino cherry.

Bachforelle (bahk-fo-REH-el) German for brook trout.

Bachkrebs (bahk-krebt) German for crayfish.

baci (BAH-chee) Italian for kisses and used to describe small, round, chocolate-coated hazelnut candies made by the Perugina candy company.

bacilli *See* bacteria.

back 1. A portion of the veal carcass that contains the rib and loin primals in one piece. 2. A portion of the lamb carcass that contains the rack and loin primals in one piece. *See* spine.

back bacon *See* bacon, Canadian.

back bar The area behind the bar; it is generally used to display merchandise, hold the cash register and store supplies.

backbone An articulated series of small bones (vertebrae) connected by ligaments; it forms the supporting axis of the body and begins at the bottom of the skull, runs through the median dorsal part of the body and ends at the tail; also known as the spine.

backdaag Pennsylvania Dutch word for baking day, the one day each week, usually Friday, set aside for this activity.

backen (bah-ken) German for to bake.

Bäckerei (bay-ka-rye) German for bakery.

Backhühn (bahk-who-hun) A German dish of chicken rolled in bread crumbs and fried.

Backobst (bahk-obst) German for dried fruit.

Backofen (bahk-often) German for oven.

back of the house The areas of a restaurant, hotel or the like not open to the public; they are generally office and work areas such as the kitchen and other food preparation areas, storerooms, receiving docks, laundries, and so on. *See* front of the house.

Backpflaume (BAHK-pflauma) German for prune.

Backpulver (bahk-pull-ver) German for baking powder.

backribs A fabricated cut of the pork primal loin; it consists of the ribs cut from the anterior end; also known as country-style spareribs.

backstrap The elastic connective tissue found in the neck region of the beef, veal or lamb carcass; also known as yellow ligament.

back waiter The person at a restaurant responsible for clearing plates, refilling water and bread, crumbing the table and other tasks; also known as busperson, busser, commis de rang, demi-chef de rang and dining room attendant.

backward A wine-tasting term for a wine that needs additional bottle aging.

bacon A fabricated cut of the pork carcass, cut from the sides and belly; consisting of fat interspersed with strands of meat, it is salted and/or smoked and available sliced or in a slab.

bacon, Canadian A fabricated cut of the primal pork loin; it is a lean, boneless pork loin roast that is smoked; known as back bacon in Canada.

bacon, regular sliced Bacon sliced to a width of approximately 1/16 in.

bacon, thick sliced Bacon sliced to a width of approximately 1/8 in.; there are 10–14 slices per pound.

bacon, thin sliced Bacon sliced to a width of approximately 1/32 in.; there are 28–32 slices per pound; also known as hotel bacon and restaurant bacon.

bacon bits Small chips of preserved and dried bacon.

bacon bits, artificial Small pieces of a bacon-flavored product, sometimes made from soy or other vegetable proteins.

bacteria Any of the numerous species of microorganisms within the class Schizomycetes; there are three principal forms: spherical or ovoid (called cocci, which are incapable of movement), rod shaped (called bacilli) and spiral or corkscrew shaped (called spirilla if rigid and spirochetes if flexible); various bacteria play significant roles in putrefaction, fermentation, disease, digestion and so on, and they are generally very sensitive to temperature, moisture and pH levels. *See* lag phase, log phase *and* decline phase.

bacteria, aerobic Bacteria that need oxygen to survive; also known as aerobes.

bacteria, anaerobic Bacteria that can survive in the absence of oxygen; also known as anaerobes.

bacteria, facultative Bacteria that can survive with or without oxygen, although most show a preference for oxygen; most pathogenic bacteria are facultative; also known as facultative anaerobes.

bacteria, obligate anaerobic Bacteria that grow only in the absence of oxygen; also known as obligate anaerobes.

bactericide An agent capable of killing one or more species of bacteria.

badaam (bah-dahm) Hindi for almond or hazelnut.

badaami (bah-dah-ha-me) An Indian preparation method in which meat or chicken is cooked with ground almonds and spices.

Badacsonyi (bah-dah-t'CHON-yee) A Hungarian apellation of origin named after an extinct volcano; white wines are produced here from the native grapes Kéknyelü, Szürkebarat and Furmit.

badam (bah-dam) A South African dish consisting of a chicken baked with almonds and pistachios and seasoned with cloves, cardamom, coconut, cinnamon, poppy seeds, cumin, ginger, garlic and chiles.

BADD The organization Bartenders Against Drunk Drivers.

bade (bah-da) Small, fried doughnut-shaped Indian bean dumplings.

badian *See* star anise.

Badisch Rotgold (BAH-dish rote-gold) A rosé wine produced in the German region of Baden from the Ruländer (Pinot Gris) and the Spätburgunder (Pinot Noir) grapes, which are pressed and fermented together.

bael The fruit of a tree (*Aegle marmelos*) that grows wild in northern India and Southeast Asia; related to the citrus family, it resembles a grayish-yellow orange with a thin, hard rind and a gummy, yellow pulp with many seeds, a refreshing flavor and a strong, pleasant aroma.

baga Elderberry juice formerly used to add color to some ports.

bagatelle (bag-a-tel) A French strawberry cake composed of genoise cake split and filled with diplomat cream and fresh strawberries and topped with a thin layer of pale green marzipan; also known as le Fraisier.

bagel A dense, doughnut-shaped Jewish yeast roll; it is cooked in boiling water, then baked, which gives the rolls a shiny glaze and chewy texture.

bagel, egg A bagel made with eggs, which makes the dough lighter.

bagel, water The chewier, traditional form of the bagel.

bagel chips Thinly sliced stale bagels seasoned with garlic, salt, herbs and/or cheese.

bagel dog A boiled hot dog baked in bagel dough.

bagel with shmear A split bagel, toasted or not, with a dab of something, usually a condiment, cream cheese or butter, spread on it.

bagged cookie *See* spritz cookie.

baghar (bah-ghaar) An Indian spice-perfumed butter used for flavoring dal, yogurt salads, vegetables, relishes and some meat and poultry preparations.

bagna cauda (BAHN-yah COW-dah) Italian for hot bath and used to describe a dipping sauce made of olive oil, butter, garlic and anchovies and served with raw vegetables.

bagna cauda pot A tall glazed earthenware pot used for bagna cauda and often available with a burner.

bagno-maria (bah-nho-mah-ree-ah) Italian for a bain-marie.

bagnum (BAH-n'yoom) A dish of fresh anchovies cooked in tomato sauce; a specialty of the fishermen near Liguria, Italy.

bagoong (bo-go-ong) A Filipino fermented paste made from shrimp or fish; has a salty flavor and is used as a condiment.

bag-out A bakeshop term meaning to press a product out of a pastry bag onto a baking pan in the desired form or shape.

Bagozzo (bah-go-tzo) A hard Italian grana cheese made from cow's milk; it has a yellow interior, a surface often colored red and a sharp, strong flavor; also known as Bresciano.

baguette (bag-EHT) 1. A long, thin loaf of French bread with a hard, crisp crust and an airy, chewy interior. 2. An air-dried, salami-like French sausage shaped like a baguette. *See* French stick.

baguette pan A metal baking pan made of two or more long half-cylinders joined together side by side; the metal may be perforated to allow better air circulation; it is used for proofing and baking yeast breads; also known as a French bread pan.

baguette pan

baguettes (bag-EHTZ) French for chopsticks.

baharat (bah-hah-raht) Arabic for spice and used to describe a Middle Eastern flavoring blend that generally consists of peppercorns, coriander, cinnamon, cloves, cumin, cardamom, nutmeg and paprika.

Bahia navel orange A common market variety of navel orange.

bahmi goreng (bah-me go-rang) An Indonesian dish consisting of noodles cooked with foods such as shrimp or other shellfish, meat, chicken, eggs, onions, chiles, garlic, cucumber, peanuts and seasonings.

bái cài (bah-ee cah-ee) Chinese for bok choy.

baid maslouk A Middle Eastern dish consisting of hard-boiled eggs; they are often colored for special occasions.

baies de genièvre (bay duh jen-yavhr) French for juniper berries.

bai horapa (bah-e ho-rah-pah) Thai for sweet basil leaf.

bai karee (bah-e kah-ree) Thai for curry leaf.

báiländi (bah-ee-lahn-dee) Chinese for brandy.

Bailey's Irish Cream An Irish liqueur made with Irish whiskey, cream and cocoa.

bai mian (bahee mee-ahn) Fresh eggless Chinese noodles.

baingan (bah-en-gahn) Hindi for eggplant.

bain marie (bane mah-ree) 1. A hot water bath used to cook foods gently or to keep cooked foods hot; also known as a water bath. 2. A container for holding foods in a hot water bath.

bái putáojiu (bah-ee poo-tah-jeu) Chinese for white wine.

bai zhi ma (bah-ee shee mah) Chinese for white sesame seeds. *See* hei zhi ma.

ba jiao (bah gee-an-ho) Chinese for star anise.

bakagai (bah-kah-gah-ee) A variety of clam native to Japan; it has a rounded, light tan shell and a sweet flesh; it is used for sushi; also known as aoyagi.

bakara; bakari (bah-kah-rah; bah-kah-ree) Hindi for goat.

bake A Caribbean breadlike biscuit made with coconut milk and cooked on a griddle or in a frying pan.

bake-apple berry; bakeapple *See* cloudberry.

bake blind A technique for baking an unfilled pastry or tart shell; the shaped dough is weighted down with dry beans or pie weights, then baked completely before being filled.

bake cup A pleated paper or foil cup used to line a muffin or cupcake pan; the cup holds the batter, facilitating release of the baked product.

baked A wine-tasting term for a warm, toasty or roasted aroma and flavor created by fermenting extremely ripe grapes grown in a hot climate.

baked Alaska A dessert composed of liqueur-soaked sponge cake topped with a mound or half-sphere of ice cream, all of which is coated with sweetened meringue and browned just before service.

baked flour *See* brown flour.

bake-off 1. To finish baking a frozen dough or partially baked product. 2. A bakeshop operation that relies on frozen doughs or partially baked products supplied from a central bakery or purchased from a manufacturer. 3. A contest, usually amateur, for making baked goods.

baker *See* potato, mealy.

bakeri (bah-keh-ree) Norwegian for bakery.

bakers Deep round, oval or rectangular dishes without handles; used for casseroles, puddings and baking fruits and vegetables (if metal, they can also be used for roasting); they are available in ceramic, earthenware, metal and glass and in capacities of 1 pt. to 4 qt.

baker's bread cutter A tool used to cut crisp-crusted bread; it has a 10-in.-long and 3.5-in.-deep blade attached to a wooden platform; a slot in the platform receives the cutting edge; also known as a bistro knife.

bakers' cheese; baker's cheese A white cheese made from skim milk, similar to cottage cheese but softer, more homogeneous and more acidic; rarely available retail, it is used commercially for baked goods such as cheesecakes and pastries.

Baker's Joy The proprietary name of a combined vegetable oil and flour spray used to help release baked goods from their pans.

baker's knife A knife with a thin, 12-in. blade, a round, blunt tip and fine, closely spaced teeth; it is used for cutting delicate cakes and crisp pastries. *See* confectioners' knife.

baker's knife

baker's peel *See* peel.

baker's rack A portable metal rack designed to hold numerous sheet pans or hotel pans; it is used for moving pans of food quickly from one work area to another; also known as a speed rack.

baker's scale *See* balance scale.

bakers' yeast extract A food additive used as an emulsifier and thickener in salad dressings.

bakers' yeast glycan A food additive used as an emulsifier in processed foods such as dressings, frozen desserts, sour cream products, cheese products and snack dips.

bakers' yeast protein A food additive used as a nutrient supplement.

bakery section One of the principal work sections of a food services facility; it typically contains a baking station, a dessert station and a frozen dessert station.

bake sale An event at which baked goods are sold to raise money for a charitable cause. *See* ice cream social.

bakeware Utensils used in baking, such as bread pans and molds, cake pans and molds, baking sheets, cake rings, ramekins, flan rings, muffin tins, pie pans, quiche dishes, tart forms and the like.

bakewell tart; bakewell pudding A tart consisting of a layer of jam, preserved fruit or candied peel overlaid with a mixture of sugar, eggs and butter and baked with or without a pastry crust; also known as transparent pudding.

baking A dry-heat cooking method that heats food by surrounding it with hot, dry air in a closed environment; the term is usually used with reference to cooking breads, pastries, vegetables, fruits and fish. *See* roasting.

baking ammonia Ammonium bicarbonate; a chemical leavening agent sometimes used in cookies or crackers.

baking chocolate Pure chocolate liquor (although an emulsifier is sometimes added); also known as bitter or unsweetened chocolate.

baking powder A mixture of sodium bicarbonate and one or more acids, generally cream of tartar and/or sodium aluminum sulfate, used to leaven baked goods; it releases carbon dioxide gas if moisture is present in a formula.

baking powder, double-acting Baking powder that releases some carbon dioxide gas upon contact with moisture; more gas is released when heat is applied.

baking powder, single-acting Baking powder that releases carbon dioxide gas in the presence of moisture only.

baking sheet A firm, flat sheet of metal, usually aluminum, with low, straight sides, on which items are placed for baking.

baking soda Sodium bicarbonate, an alkaline compound that releases carbon dioxide gas when combined with an acid and moisture; it is used to leaven baked goods.

baking stone A heavy round or rectangular ceramic or stone plate used in lieu of a baking sheet for pizza and breads; also known as a pizza stone.

baking tile A thick, unglazed quarry tile, usually 8–12-in. square; used like a baking stone.

baklava (BAAK-lah-vah) A Middle Eastern sweet pastry made with buttered phyllo dough layered with

baking tile

honey, nuts and spices, usually cut into diamond-shaped pieces after baking.

baklazany (bahk-lah-zah-ni) Polish for eggplant.

baklazhan (bahk-lah-zhan) Russian for eggplant.

bakpoeder (bahk-pa-derr) Dutch for baking powder.

bakpulver (bahk-pull-verr) Swedish for baking powder.

bakudai (bah-koo-dah-i) A type of bean or pea used in Japanese cuisines to garnish sashimi and vinegared salads.

bakverk (baak-vark) Norwegian for pastry.

balachan; blachan (BAH-lah-chan) A flavoring used in Southeast Asian cuisines made from salted, mashed, fermented shrimp, sardines and other small fish; available in powder or cake form.

balachaung (bar-la-chah-ung) A strongly flavored Burmese dish of fried, dried shrimp, usually served as an accompaniment.

balanced; well balanced 1. Being in harmonious or proper arrangement, adjustment or proportion, as in a diet, meal, menu or plate presentation. 2. A wine-tasting term for a wine whose components (i.e., sugar, fruit, tannin, acid, alcohol, wood and so on) are evident, but none dominate and all are in harmony. *See* unbalanced.

balance scale A scale with two trays; one holds the item to be weighed and weights are placed on the other until the two trays are counterbalanced; weights can be in the metric, U.S. or imperial system; also known as a baker's scale.

balderdash A 17th-century slang term for an objectionable, jumbled mix of drinks such as beer and wine.

bald face Slang for inferior liquor.

Baldwin apple An apple (*Malus pumila*) from New York state and the vicinity; it has a mottled red skin streaked with yellow, a crisp texture and a mildly sweet–tart flavor and is a good, all-purpose apple.

bales Bundles of fermented tobacco leaves packed in a tough palm tree sheath and covered with burlap; tobacco is usually aged and transported in bales.

baligi *See* kilic.

balila (bah-lee-lah) A Middle Eastern meza, snack or street food of boiled chickpeas or broad beans; also known as leblabi.

Balling A saccharometer (hydrometer) used to measure the amount of fermentable sugars in a mash used for brewing or distillation; measured in degrees also called Balling. *See* Plato.

balloon whisk A large whisk used for whipping egg whites; its looped wires create a nearly spherical outline.

ballotine (bahl-lo-teen) A charcuterie item similar to a galantine; it is usually made by stuffing a deboned poultry leg with a forcemeat and then poaching or braising it.

ballpark mustard *See* mustard, American.

Balmoral Stirrup Cup A cocktail made of Scotch, Cointreau and Angostura bitters.

balloon whisk

baloney *See* bologna.

balsam A West Indian banana-flavored liqueur.

balsam apple *See* margosa.

balsamella (bal-sah-MEHL-ah) Italian for béchamel sauce.

balsamic vinegar (bahl-sah-mek) A dark, mellow Italian vinegar with a sweet–sour flavor; it is made from concentrated grape juice fermented and aged for 15–20 years in a series of wooden casks.

balsam pear *See* bitter melon.

balsam Peru oil A food additive extracted from the Peruvian balsam; it has a sweet balsamic aroma and is used as a flavoring agent and adjuvant.

Balthazar (bahl-THAH-zahr) An oversized Champagne or sparkling wine bottle holding 16 750-ml bottles (approximately 13 qt. or 416 fl. oz.).

balushahi (bah-lou-shah-he) An East Indian pastry consisting of sweet dough deep-fried in clarified butter, then dipped in sugar syrup.

balut (ba-loot) A Filipino delicacy consisting of a duck egg containing a partially developed embryo; it is usually dyed a bright fuchsia color.

balyk (bah-leak) A Russian hors d'oeuvre consisting of the dried back of the sevruga sturgeon sliced paper thin and served with a glass of vodka.

bambara; bambara groundnut (bahm-bah-raw) A groundnut (*Voandzeia subterranea*) native to Africa and often mistakenly considered a variety of the American peanut; its beanlike seeds are used fried, boiled, ground into flour or pressed for oil in many West and Central African cuisines.

bamboo flour Crushed bamboo seeds; it is used in Chinese cuisines as a thickener.

bamboo juice Slang for alcoholic beverages, first used by members of the U.S. Air Force stationed in the South Pacific during the Korean War.

bamboo leaves The long, narrow leaves of certain types of bamboo; used as wrappers for grilled, boiled or steamed foods, they impart a subtle flavor.

bamboo salt A salty substance found inside bamboo stems; it is used principally in China for medicinal purposes but also for culinary purposes.

bamboo shoots The ivory-colored edible shoots of a species of bamboo plant (*Bambusa vulgaris*); they are cut while the shoots are young and tender and have a woody appearance and fibrous texture; available fresh and canned and used in many Asian cuisines.

bamboo steamer An assemblage of two loosely slat-bottomed bamboo rounds with one lid; used to steam foods, the stacked baskets sit above boiling water in a wok and are available in diameters of 4–11 in.

bambouche (bahm-boosch) Slang used in the American South and Cajun country for a drinking spree.

ba mee (bah me) Thai for egg noodle.

bamia (bah-meh-ah) An Egyptian stew consisting of lamb, okra, tomatoes and onions flavored with lemon juice, coriander and garlic.

bamia masloukah (bah-meh-ah mahs-loo-kah) An Egyptian dish consisting of okra simmered with onions and flavored with lemon juice.

bamies (bah-mi-esh) Greek for okra.

bammie (BA-mi) A round, flat Carribbean bread made from the grated root of the cassava plant.

bamya (BAM-ya) Turkish for okra.

banadoura (ba-na-doo-rah) Arabic for tomatoes.

banan (bann-ahn) Russian and Norwegian for banana; also known as ananas.

banana The berry of a large tropical herb (especially *Musa paradisiaca sapientum*); the fruit grows in clusters (hands) and is long and curving with a brown-stained yellow skin (it is harvested while still green), a slightly sticky, floury, off-white pulp and a distinctive sweet flavor and aroma. *See* plantain.

banana Spanish for banana; also known as plátano.

banana chile A long, yellow-green chile with a mild flavor; used in salads, stuffed or pickled.

banana cream pie A single flaky pie crust filled with a mixture of custard and thinly sliced bananas, usually topped with meringue or whipped cream.

banana fish *See* bonefish.

banana flowers The compact, purple, pointed heads at the tip of a forming bunch of bananas; they are used in Southeast Asian cuisines as a vegetable and garnish.

banana leaves The large, flat, dark green leaves of the banana plant; used in Central and South American and African cuisines to wrap foods during cooking, they impart a delicate flavor to the foods and help keep them moist.

banana oyster Any of several varieties of elongated oysters used only in commercially prepared soups and stews.

banana passion fruit *See* curuba.

banana pudding A dessert from the American South consisting of vanilla custard layered with bananas and vanilla wafers and served chilled.

bananas Foster A dessert created by Brennan's Restaurant in New Orleans consisting of a sliced banana quickly sautéed in butter, rum, sugar and banana liqueur, then flambéed and served over vanilla ice cream.

banana split A dessert made from a banana cut in half lengthwise, then topped with ice cream, sweet syrups and whipped cream and garnished with chopped nuts or other toppings.

banane (bah-NAA-nah) Italian for banana.

Banane (bah-NAA-nah) German for banana.

banane (bah-nahn) French for banana.

Banbury cake; Banbury tart An oval-shaped British cake made of flaky pastry dough filled with dried fruit and spices; a speciality of Banbury, England.

Bancha (bahn-CHAH) A green tea made from roasted leaves; it has a flavor reminiscent of hay.

band A colorful paper ring identifying a cigar's maker; it is usually placed near the cigar's head.

B & B *See* Benedictine and Brandy.

ban de vendange (bahn duh vahn-danj) The official ceremony announcing the start of the grape harvest in France.

band gobhee (bahnd goh-bee) Hindi for cabbage.

bandiera, la (bahn-dee-YAH-rah, lah) Any Italian dish made with ingredients in the color of the Italian flag: red, white and green.

Bandol (bahn-dohl) A grape-growing and wine-producing area along the Mediterranean coast of France; most of the wine is red and rosé, and the principal grapes are Mourvèdre, Grenache and Cinsault; the wines must be aged in wood a minimum of 18 months.

bang (bahng) An East Indian fermented beverage made from hemp leaves and twigs infused in water.

bang chung; bang tet (bahng choong; bahng tat) A savory, Vietnamese glutinous rice cake filled with seasoned pork and ground mung beans, wrapped in a banana leaf and steamed; it is usually served at the lunar new year (Tet) celebration.

banger A British sausage traditionally made from ground pork and bread crumbs; a beef banger is also available.

banh mi (ben me) Vietnamese for French bread and used to describe submarine sandwiches of cold cuts on French-style rolls; when served as a cold-cut plate with bread on the side, it is called banh mi dia.

banh pho (ben fo) White rice stick noodles used in Vietnamese soup–noodle dishes.

banh trang (ben train) Thin, round, semitransparent, hard, dry rice-paper crêpes used after moistening to wrap Vietnamese spring rolls.

banh troi (ben troy) A Vietnamese dessert consisting of a ball of sweet bean paste encased in rice flour dough, boiled and then simmered in a syrup of fresh ginger and sugar; it is garnished with toasted sesame seeds and served in a warm sauce.

banh uot (ben ouk) Fresh rice papers used in Vietnamese cuisine to wrap grilled or barbecued meats and salad.

banilia (vaa-nee-lah) Greek for vanilla.

banira (bah-NEE-rah) Japanese for vanilla.

bánitsa (bah-nee-tsah) A Bulgarian tart made with paper-thin pastry similar to phyllo; fillings include nuts and cream or cheese and spinach.

bank An amount of money advanced to an employee to make change; also known as a float.

banker's sauce *See* banquière sauce.

banku (bahn-koo) 1. A Ghanaian dish consisting of dumplings made from ground fermented corn. 2. A West African dish consisting of a thick cornmeal porridge, sometimes flavored with chiles.

bannaan (bah-nah-ahn) Dutch for banana.

banneton (BAN-tahn) A French woven basket in which bread is allowed to rise before being baked; it is sometimes lined with cloth.

banneton

bannock (BAN-nuhk) A traditional Scottish sweet bread made with oats and barley and cooked on a griddle.

Banon (ba-NOHN) A soft to semisoft French cheese traditionally made from goat's milk (or sometimes ewe's milk, with a factory-produced cow's milk version available); it has a white creamy or chalky interior and a mild lemony or herbal flavor; it is aged in chestnut leaves and sometimes washed in Cognac or marc.

banquet (bahn-qwet) An elaborate and often ceremonious meal attended by many guests, sometimes in honor of a person or occasion.

banquet chef The person responsible for planning and preparing the food for an event such as a banquet or other large gathering.

banquet event order (BEO) The written confirmation of details for a special meal or event.

banquet facilities; banqueting facilities A room or other facility at a hotel, restaurant, conference center or the like used for banquets and other large gatherings.

banquet manager The person responsible for planning and arranging large gatherings at a hotel or other facility.

banquet section One of the principal work sections of a food services facility; it typically contains a steam cooking station, a roasting station and a holding area.

banquière, sauce (bahn-kehr) A French compound sauce made from a suprême sauce blended with tomato purée and veal glaze, finished with Madeira and butter and garnished with truffles; also known as banker's sauce.

bansan (BAHN-sahn) Japanese for dinner.

banshu somen (BAHN-shoo SO-meh) Japanese noodles made from wheat flour.

bantinjan bil saneeyee (beh-d'ten-jahn bel sah-nay-ah) A Middle Eastern dish of eggplant stuffed with hashwa; also known as sheikh il mihshee (Syria).

Banyuls (bahn-yulz) A French vin de liqueur comparable to a light, tawny port and used as an aperitif or dessert wine.

bao (bo) Slightly sweet, yeast-risen, steamed Chinese wheat buns with various fillings such as Chinese sausage, chicken with vegetables and salted duck egg, date and sweet bean paste and barbecued pork. *See* dim sum.

baobab (ba-OH-bahb) 1. The gourdlike fruit of a tree (*Adansonia digitata*) native to the tropical areas of central Africa; it has a whitish-yellow pulp that contains tartaric acid and is used as a food and flavoring ingredient; also known as monkey bread. 2. The leaves of this tree, which are eaten like a vegetable.

bap 1. A soft, white yeast roll traditionally eaten for breakfast in Scotland and England. 2. A soft, white yeast roll used for sandwiches, especially in Ireland.

Baptist cake A doughnutlike cake made with a ball of leavened dough that is immersed (baptized) in hot fat for deep-frying; especially popular in the New England region of the United States during the 1930s.

Baptist punch A punch made without alcoholic beverages.

baqdounis (bahk-DOO-ness) Arabic for parsley.

baqli (BAHK-lee) An Arabic eggplant purée flavored with sesame.

bar 1. A commercial establishment or area within an establishment where beverages, generally alcoholic, are sold and served by the drink to customers; also known as a cocktail lounge or taproom. 2. The counter at which one stands or sits to be served food and/or drink. 3. French for a type of perch.

bara brith (baa-rah breeth) Welsh speckled bread made with currants, raisins and spices; traditionally prepared for holidays and harvest festivals.

barack palinka (bah-rack pah-lean-kah) Austrian and Hungarian apricot brandy.

baraf (bah-rahf) Hindi for ice.

barafu (bah-rah-foo) Swahili for ice.

bara-jheenga (bah-rah-jene-gah) Hindi for lobster; also known as golda jheengari.

bar and grill A commercial establishment serving alcoholic beverages and foods (usually simple fare).

bara nimbu *See* nimboo.

baranina (bah-rah-nynah) Polish for lamb.

bárány (BAA-raan) Hungarian for lamb.

baraquille (bah-rah-key-ye) A French hors d'oeuvre consisting of a triangular puff pastry case filled with game bird fillets, truffles, mushrooms, sweetbreads and foie gras, bound with a Madeira-flavored allemande sauce.

barashek (bah-RAH-shash) Russian for lamb.

barazek (bar-raah-zeek) Middle Eastern cookies flavored with sesame seeds.

barbabiètola (bahr-bah-B'YEH-toh-lah) Italian for beetroot.

Barbacarlo (bar-ba-CAR-lo) A lightly sparkling red wine produced in the Lombardy region of Italy from various grape varieties such as Bonarda, Barbera and Croatina.

bar back A bartender's apprentice or helper who replenishes ice and other supplies, prepares drink garnishes, cleans the bar area and generally assists in all but the final presentation of drinks and the collection of moneys.

barbacoa (bahr-bah-KOH-ah) A Mexican and Latin American dish of chile-marinated braised beef; it was originally cooked wrapped in maguey leaves, but now it is steamed in banana leaves or simply braised.

Barbados cherry *See* acerola.

Barbados gooseberry The edible fruit of a cactus (*Pereskia aculeata*) native to the West Indies; it is small and spherical with a yellow to red color and a tart flavor.

barbagliata (bahr-bah-L'YAH-tah) An Italian beverage made with cocoa and espresso; it is served hot or cold.

Barbaresco (bar-bah-RESS-co) A wine made from the Nebbiolo grape in the Piedmont region of Italy; it must be aged a minimum of two years, one in wood.

barbary fig; barbary pear; barberry fig *See* prickly pear.

barbecue; barbeque; bar-b-q *v.* To cook foods over the dry heat created by this equipment. *n.* 1. A brazier fitted with a grill and sometimes a spit; it uses coals, hardwoods, gas or electricity as a heat source. 2. The foods, usually meat or poultry, cooked with this equipment and frequently coated with a tangy tomato- or vinegar-based sauce. 3. An informal meal or party, particularly in the United States, where such foods are cooked and served outdoors. *See* picnic.

barbecue brush A long-handled basting brush used for basting foods cooked on a grill or under a broiler. *See* basting brush.

barbecue mop *See* basting mop.

barbecue sauce An American sauce traditionally made with tomatoes, onion, mustard, garlic, brown sugar and vinegar; it is used to baste barbecued meats and poultry.

barbels Long, slender feelers growing from the jaw of certain fish (e.g., catfish).

Barbera (bar-BEARE-ah) A red wine grape widely planted in Italy's Piedmont region; it produces a tannic wine.

Barberey (bar-bae-ray) A Camembert-style cheese made in France's Champagne region and cured in ashes; also known as Fromage de Troyes.

Barberone (bar-beh-ROE-neh) An unofficial name used on labels of inexpensive California red wines; these wines tend to be full bodied and slightly sweet.

barberry; berberis; berberry An ovoid berry (*Berberis vulgaris*) grown in Europe and New England; the unripened green berries are pickled and used like capers and the ripened berries, with a red skin and tart flavor, are used in preserves, syrups and baked goods; also known as a mahonias or Oregon grape.

bar brands The proprietary liquors (i.e., not generic or house brands) served at an establishment.

barbuda (bar-boo-dah) Spanish for shaggy mane mushroom.

barbue (bahr-boo) French for brill.

Barcelona hazelnut A variety of hazelnuts; they are very large and easily cracked.

bar clam *See* surf clam.

bar code *See* Universal Product Code.

bar cookie A type of cookie made by baking the batter or dough in a sheet pan, then cutting it into individual serving–sized bars or squares.

barding fat A thin sheet of fatback used to wrap meats to be roasted or braised to keep them moist and prevent certain parts (such as the breasts of poultry) from overcooking.

Bardolino (bar-doe-LEE-no) A light red wine produced in Italy's Veneto region and best consumed within 2–5 years from harvest; the rosé version is known as Chiaretto.

Barentrank (ba-run-trank) A German alcoholic beverage distilled from potatoes and flavored with honey.

barfi (bar-fee) An East Indian fudgelike candy made with sweetened milk and almonds or pistachio nuts.

bar fly; barfly Slang for someone who idles away time drinking alcoholic beverages at a bar.

barg (bahrg) A Persian (Iranian) dish of thin meat strips that are marinated, threaded onto skewers, and grilled.

barhopping American slang for visiting several bars in one night; similar to the British term pub crawling.

baridi (bah-ree-dee) Swahili for cold.

barigoule, à la (bah-ree-goo-lay, ah lah) A French dish consisting of artichokes stuffed with mushrooms and bacon, braised in white wine and served with a reduction of the cooking liquid.

barista (bahr-RIH-stah) Hindi for the crisp fried onion shreds used in Moslem cooking.

bark A flat, irregularly shaped chocolate candy, usually containing nuts or fruit.

barkeeper *See* bartender.

Bar-le-Duc (bar-luh-DOOK) A French preserve traditionally made from white currants whose seeds were removed by hand; it is now made with red and white currants as well as other fruits, such as gooseberries and strawberries.

barley A small, spherical grain grown worldwide and usually pearled to remove its outer husk; the white grain has a slightly sweet, nutty, earthy flavor, chewy texture and high starch content; also known as pearl barley.

barley beer An alcoholic beverage prepared from barley and enjoyed by the ancient Greeks.

barley broth *See* Scotch broth.

barley flour Ground barley; used for baking (principally scones) and as a thickener for milk-based soups and sauces.

barley sugar 1. A confection made by heating white sugar to the melting point, at which point it forms small grains resembling barley. 2. A hard lemon-flavored candy made from barley water.

barley tea *See* mugi cha *and* poricha.

barley water 1. A drink made by boiling barley in water and cooling it to room temperature; it is typically consumed with meals in Korea. 2. A British lemon- or orange-flavored drink similar to a lemon or orange squash. 3. A slightly fermented beverage made by steeping barley in water.

barley wine An English term for a dark, strong ale.

barm *v.* To add yeast to wort. *n.* 1. The foam or froth atop fermenting beer. 2. The froth or foam atop a glass of beer; also known as a head. *See* foam.

barmaid A cocktail waitress or female bartender.

bar manager The person responsible for directing, organizing, forecasting and controlling all aspects of a beverage department or bar.

barm brack; barmbrack (BAHRM brak) An Irish yeast bread containing raisins and candied fruit peel.

barnyardy A tasting term for a food's (e.g., cheese) or beverage's (e.g., wine) earthy or goaty aromas or flavors reminiscent of a stable or barnyard; not necessarily intended to convey a negative impression.

Barolo (bah-ROH-lo) A red wine made from the Nebbiolo grape in the Piedmont region of Italy; it is a full-bodied, richly textured, complex and long-lived wine with a distinctive bouquet and taste.

baron 1. In the United States, a single section of the lamb carcass containing both hindquarters (legs and loin). 2. In the United States, an imprecisely used term to describe any of a variety of large subprimal cuts of beef used for roasting (e.g., steamship round). 3. In France, a single section of the lamb or mutton carcass containing the saddle and two legs. 4. In Great Britain, a single section of the beef carcass containing both primal sirloins.

baron d'agneau (bah-rohn dahn-YOH) A French cut of the lamb carcass; the top end of the leg.

Baron Solemacher A variety of Alpine strawberry; the fruit are relatively large.

Barossa Valley A grape-growing and wine-producing region in the state of South Australia; the principal grapes grown are Rhine Riesling, Shiraz, Grenache, Cabernet Sauvignon and Chardonnay.

barquette (bahr-KEHT) A small boat-shaped pastry shell used for appetizers or desserts; the dough may be sweet or savory.

barquette mold A boat-shaped tartlet mold with plain or fluted sides.

barracuda (bair-ah-COO-dah) *See* Pacific barracuda.

barquette mold

barrel 1. A cylindrical wooden container with slightly bulging sides made of staves hooped together with flat parallel ends; a standard barrel holds 31.5 U.S. gallons or 105 dry quarts. 2. The wooden, glass or stainless steel container in which wine, beer or a distilled spirit is stored, aged and sometimes shipped.

barrel aging The process of mellowing a wine or distilled spirit by storing it in a wooden barrel; over time, the product develops certain characteristics and also extracts components from the wood such as the tannin, which contributes to its body and flavor.

barrel fermentation A process used to make some white wines; the must ferments in an oak barrel instead of a temperature-controlled stainless steel vat to extract tannins, pigments, aromas and flavors from the wood.

barrel house An English commercial establishment that serves primarily beer and ale.

barrica (bah-rree-kah) A Spanish oak cask used to age wines; it holds 225 l.

barriga de freira (ba-xiga de frejra) Portuguese for nun's belly and used to describe a candy made with sugar, butter, eggs and bread crumbs.

barrique (bar-reek) A French oak barrel used to age wine; it holds approximately 230 l.

barrista (bar-RES-ta) A person who makes espresso and coffee drinks to order, especially at a coffee house.

barro (BAH-ro) A Spanish word that refers to clay soil, used in connection with the sherry-producing vineyards near Jerez de la Frontera; wines produced from this soil do not have the finesse of those produced from chalky soil.

barroom A room or establishment whose main feature is a bar used to sell and dispense alcoholic beverages; also known as a saloon or taproom.

bar round A subprimal cut of the beef primal round; it is a tied, boneless rump roast.

Barsac (bar-sack) A sweet white wine made from overly ripe grapes affected by the noble rot; produced in Barsac, in France's Sauternes district, it has a fruity, delicate flavor with a relatively high level of acid; also known imprecisely as Sauternes.

bar spoon A long-handled spoon used by a bartender to stir mixed drinks.

bar sugar A superfine sugar that dissolves quickly; it is used principally as an ingredient in cocktails.

bar syrup *See* simple syrup.

barszcz (bahr-sh-ch) A general category of Polish soups; the principal flavoring is pickled beetroot.

bartender The person in charge of a bar; he or she mixes and makes the drinks, serves customers at the bar and collects money; also known as a barkeeper, mixologist and tapman.

Bartlett pear A large, bell-shaped pear with a smooth, red-blushed yellow-green skin (there are also red- and green-skinned varieties), a tender texture and a sweet, somewhat musky flavor; also known as a Williams pear (especially in Great Britain).

Barton Distillery One of the 12 remaining U.S. whiskey distilleries; located in Bardstown, Kentucky, and founded as the Tom Moore distillery c. 1889, its products include Very Old Barton, Ten High and Tom Moore bourbons.

bas (baa) 1. French for low. 2. A geographic designation for a French grape-growing and wine-producing region with a low altitude (it does not denote quality). *See* haut.

basal metabolic rate The rate at which the body uses energy to support its basal metabolism; referred to as BMR.

basal metabolism The amount of energy needed to maintain life when the body is at digestive, physical and emotional rest.

basboosa (bahs-boo-sah) An Egyptian semolina cake flavored with rosewater and lemon syrup.

base Any substance that combines with hydrogen ions; bases have a pH value above 7 and neutralize acids to form a salt; also known as an alkali.

baseball steak *See* bucket steak.

base cost The cost of the basic ingredients of a drink or dish, not including labor or an allocation of overhead.

basi (ba-see) A Filipino alcoholic beverage fermented from sugarcane and flavored with herbs.

basic forcemeat *See* forcemeat, basic.

basic permit Document issued under the Federal Alcohol Administration Act authorizing the recipient to engage in the activities specified at the location stated; these permits are required for importers, domestic producers, blenders and wholesalers of alcoholic beverages. *See* liquor license.

basil (BAY-zihl; BA-zihl) An herb (*Ocimum basilicum*) and member of the mint family; it has soft, shiny light green leaves, small white flowers and a strong, pungent peppery flavor reminiscent of licorice and cloves (other varieties are available with flavors reminiscent of foods such as

basil

cinnamon, garlic, lemon and chocolate); available fresh and dried; also known as sweet basil. *See* opal basil.

basilic (bah-see-leek) French for basil.

basilico (bah-ZEE-lee-koh) Italian and Spanish for basil.

Basilikum (bah-see-lee-kum) German for basil.

basin A deep or shallow, open, rounded vessel used for holding liquids.

basket weave A cake-decorating technique in which frosting is piped onto a cake to look as if it consists of interlaced double ribbons, a pattern similar to that of a woven basket.

baskoot (bahs-KOOT) Arabic for biscuit or cookie.

basmati (bahs-MAT-tee) An aged, aromatic long-grain rice grown in the Himalayan foothills; it has a creamy yellow color, a distinctive sweet, nutty aroma and a delicate flavor.

basquaise (bas-kaz) An oval-shaped bottle, traditionally used for Armagnac.

basquaise, à la (bas-kaz, ah lah) 1. A French preparation method associated with the cuisine of the Basque; the dishes are characterized by the use of tomatoes, sweet peppers, garlic and often Bayonne ham. 2. A French garnish for large cuts of meat; it consists of Bayonne ham, mushrooms and pommes Anna.

bass 1. An imprecisely used term for several unrelated spiny-finned fish, including various freshwater sunfish such as the largemouth bass, saltwater corvina and aquafarmed hybrid striped bass. 2. A family of saltwater fish, including the black sea bass and striped bass.

black bass

bassine (bah-seen) A French hemispherical copper bowl used for beating egg whites.

bassine à friture (bah-seen ah free-tuhr) French for deep-fryer.

bastable pot An iron pot with an 18- to 20-in. diameter, a lid, handles and three short legs; used in Ireland for cooking stews and roasts sitting in or suspended by chains over a turf (peat) fire and for baking breads by placing burning turf on the lid top.

Bastard A sweet white wine from the Iberian Peninsula, popular in Elizabethan England, and made from the Bastardo grape in Madeira.

bastard saffron *See* safflower.

bastard steak A fabricated cut of the beef carcass; it consists of the odd-shaped ends trimmed from other fabricated cuts, such as a T-bone.

bastela; bastila *See* b'steeya.

baster *See* bulb baster.

basting Moistening foods during cooking (usually roasting, broiling or grilling) with melted fat, pan drippings, a sauce or other liquids to prevent drying and to add flavor.

basting brush A brush with natural or fine nylon bristles and a 10- to 12-in. handle; it is used for basting foods cooked on the stove top or in the oven. *See* barbecue brush.

basting mop A tool consisting of a loose tangle of cotton ropes attached to a handle; it is used to baste meats, especially during grilling; also known as barbecue mop and sauce mop.

bastirma (bous-teer-mah) A Middle Eastern dish consisting of dried spiced beef.

basto (BAH'SS-toe) A Spanish wine term meaning coarse or common that is applied to sherry of low quality.

bastoncini (bah-ston-chee-nee) Italian for chopsticks.

basturma (bous-tour-mah) An Armenian ham seasoned with garlic and cayenne.

bata (BAH-tah) Japanese for butter.

bata (bah-tah) Swahili for duck.

bata mzinga (bah-tah mzeen-gah) Swahili for turkey.

bâtarde (bah-tahr) A French white roux made with water bound with egg yolks and flavored with butter and lemon juice; also known as a butter sauce and usually served with vegetables and boiled fish.

Bâtard-Montrachet (bah-tar-mon-rah-shay) A vineyard in France's Burgundy region known for its wines made from the Chardonnay grape; the wines have a pale gold color, a high alcohol content and a comparatively dry flavor with a fine bouquet.

batata (ba-TA-tash) Portuguese for potato.

batata dulce *See* sweet potato, white.

Batavia arak A rich, pungent, aromatic Indonesian rum made from malted rice and molasses; it is barrel aged.

Batavian endive *See* escarole.

bata wa bukini (bah-tah wah boo-key-nee) Swahili for goose.

BATF *See* Bureau of Alcohol, Tobacco, and Firearms.

Bath bun A sweet yeast bun filled with currants and candied fruit and coated with sugar; it originated in the town of Bath, England.

Bath chap A British dish consisting of the smoked or pickled lower portion of the cheeks of a long-jawed hog; it is usually boiled and then eaten cold.

Bath Oliver A plain, round, unsweetend biscuit or cracker, usually served with cheese; created in Bath, England, by William Oliver (1695–1764).

bath towel Slang for tripe.

bathtub gin Alcohol mixed with herbs (traditionally in a bathtub), strained, and sold illegally during Prohibition.

Batida de Limão A South American (particularly Brazilian) cocktail made of lime or lemon juice, confectioners' sugar and Cachaça.

batinjaan; batinjan (bat-t'hin-jahn) Arabic for eggplant.

baton lele (bah-tohn la-la) A small branch of a tree with several shoots used as a whisk in Africa; also known as a twirl stick.

batonnet (bah-toh-nah) Foods cut into a matchstick shape of approximately 1/4 × 1/4 × 2–2 1/2 in. (0.6 × 0.6 × 5–6 cm).

battak (baht-tack) Hindi for duck.

Battenberg A rectilinear cake popular during the Victorian era; it is composed of pink and white (or yellow) genoise arranged in a checkerboard pattern, held together with apricot jam and wrapped in marzipan.

batter *v.* To dip a food into a batter before cooking. *n.* 1. A semiliquid mixture containing flour or other starch used to make cakes and breads; gluten development is minimized and the liquid forms the continuous medium in which other ingredients are disbursed; it generally contains more fat, sugar and liquids than a dough. *See* dough. 2. A semi-liquid mixture of liquid and starch used to coat foods for deep-frying.

batter bowl A mix-and-measure bowl, usually of 2-qt. capacity, with a handle, spout and liquid measures marked on the side; it is used for whipping cream or egg whites and is available in glass or plastic.

batter cakes *See* corn cakes.

batterie de cuisine (bat-TREE duh kwih-ZEEN) A French term for the cooking equipment and utensils necessary to equip a kitchen. *See* mise en place.

battuto (bah-TOO-toa) An Italian soup or stew flavored with onions, carrots, celery, parsley and garlic sautéed in butter; this mixture is added to broth and vegetables for the soup or vegetables, meat or fish for the stew; also known as sofritto.

batu giling; batu lesong (ba-tu gear-ling) A granite slab and roller used in Malaysia and Indonesia to grind large quantities of spices or other wet or dry seasonings.

batzi (baht-zee) Swiss for apple brandy.

baudroie (boa-drwah) French for monkfish.

Bauernklösse (bawern-kloos-suh) German dumplings made from oatmeal and potatoes and flavored with bacon, onions and herbs; they are generally baked and served with a gravy and vegetables.

Bauernschmaus (bawern-chmaoss) An Austrian dish consisting of pork loin chops, bacon and sausages cooked in beer with sauerkraut, onions and grated potatoes and seasoned with cumin seeds and garlic; typically served with bread crumb dumplings.

Bauernsuppe (bah-who-ner-sou-pay) A German peasant soup of vegetables, legumes and bacon.

Baumé (bo-may) 1. A hydrometer (saccharometer) used to measure the sugar content of grape juice or wine, especially sherry and port. 2. A scale for expressing the specific gravity of a liquid. 3. A method (scale) of measuring the density of sugar syrups.

Baumé scale *See* hydrometer.

Baumkuchen (baum-KU-zon) A traditional German Christmas cake composed of many thin rings or layers coated with chocolate glaze; it is designed to resemble a tree trunk.

baunilha (bow-nee-lyah) Portuguese for vanilla.

Bavarian; Bavarian cream A molded, chilled dessert consisting of an egg custard thickened with gelatin and lightened with whipped cream; it can be flavored with fruit, liquor, chocolate and the like.

Bavarian Blue A semisoft southern German blue cheese made from cow's milk; it has a creamy texture, an ivory-colored interior flecked with blue mold, a soft, white rind and a spicy flavor.

bavarois (bah-vah-wah) French for Bavarian.

bavaroise, sauce (bah-vah-wase) A French compound sauce made from a hollandaise beaten with crayfish butter and garnished with diced crayfish tails.

bavette (bah-ve-tae) Italian for steel castings and used to describe thin, oval ribbons of pasta.

bavettine (bah-ve-tee-nae) Very narrow bavette.

bavosa lupa (bah-VOA-sah loo-pah) Italian for wolffish.

bay A small tree of the laurel family (*Laurus nobilis*), native to Asia; it produces firm leaves that are shiny on top and dull beneath; used as an herb, the leaves impart a lemon–nutmeg flavor and are usually removed from whatever food they are used to flavor before the item is eaten.

bay leaves

bayd (bah-eed) Arabic for egg.

baymee (bah-mee-ah) Arabic for okra.

Bayonne ham (bah-yohn) *See* jambon de Bayonne.

bayou blue Whiskey made illegally in Louisiana's bayous and backwoods country during Prohibition.

bay rum leaves The leaves of the bay rum tree (*Pimenta acris*); they have a lemony flavor and are used in Creole cuisine.

bay rum seeds The seeds of the bay rum tree; they have a flavor similar to that of allspice and are used in Creole cuisine; also known as malaqueta.

bay salt *See* rock salt.

bay scallop A cold water scallop with a meat averaging 0.5 in. (1.27 cm) in diameter; its tender white meat is more succulent than that of the sea scallop.

bazant (bah-shant) Polish for pheasant.

BBQ ribs Barbecued beef, veal, lamb or pork ribs.

beach clam *See* surf clam.

beach plum A small wild plum (*Prunus maritima*) that grows along the Atlantic coast; it has dark purple skin and flesh and a tart, slightly bitter grapelike flavor; used for jams and jellies and as a condiment for meats.

bead border A border of piped frosting that resembles a string of beads; depending on application speed and pressure, the border can be a series of hemispherical beads or teardrops.

beading The bubbles that form on top of bottled whiskey when the bottle is shaken; large bubbles indicate a high proof.

beads The bubbles in a sparkling wine; the smaller the beads and the longer they take to rise, the better the wine's quality; also known as pinpoint bubbles.

beak The hinged, narrow end of the oyster shell.

beam balance scale A scale with a removable tray to hold the item to be weighed; weights are adjusted along a bar connected to the tray until the weights and bar are counterbalanced by the tray and item; it can be calibrated in the metric, U.S. or imperial system.

bean cake *See* dòufù.

bean curd A soft, cream-colored custard or gel-like product made from dried soybeans that have been soaked, puréed and boiled with water, then mixed with a coagulant, causing it to form curds; after the water is pressed out, it is usually cut into small squares and stored in cold water; it readily absorbs the flavors of other foods and sauces; also known as dòufù (China) and tofu (Japan).

bean curd, black A gray-black spongelike curd made from a tuber, similar in appearance to bean curd, and used in Japanese cuisines; also known as konnayaku.

bean curd, cotton A variety of bean curd with a firm texture and an irregular surface pattern achieved by straining the coagulated liquid through a semifine cloth and then pressing the curds; also known as aburage and momem tofu (Japan).

bean curd, silk A variety of bean curd with a soft, delicate texture and a smooth surface pattern achieved by straining the coagulated liquid through a fine mesh and allowing the strained curds to settle without pressing; also known as kinugoshi (Japan) and shui dòufù (China).

bean curd brains Lightly coagulated bean curd that has a lumpy appearance and a creamy gray color; used in vegetarian cooking, stuffings, braised dishes and soups.

bean curd cheese *See* dòufù-ru.

bean curd noodles Thick, creamy-yellow strips of bean curd with a chewy texture.

bean curd sheets *See* yuba.

bean curd skin noodles Narrow strips of the firm skin that sets over bean curd as it gels; used in Chinese and other Asian cuisines in vegetarian dishes.

beanery A small, inexpensive restaurant such as a diner.

bean jelly A slightly rubbery, neutral-flavored jelly made from mung beans, powdered rice or buckwheat; used as an ingredient in Chinese dishes (it readily absorbs other flavors) or eaten as a snack.

bean paste, red sweet A sweet purée of Chinese red beans, used as a pudding or a pastry filling.

bean paste, yellow A salty, pungent soybean paste used as a flavoring in Chinese cuisines.

bean pot An earthenware pot with a deep, bulbous body, a narrow mouth and a lid; the bowed sides expand the cooking surface and the narrow mouth minimizes moisture loss; available in 2- to 6-qt. capacities.

bean pot

beans 1. Any of various legumes (mostly from the genus *Phaseolus*) with a double-seamed pod containing a single row of seeds (sometimes also called beans); some are used for their edible pods, others for shelling fresh and still others for their dried seeds. 2. The ovoid or kidney-shaped dried seeds of legumes. *See* lentils, peas *and* pulses.

beans, dried Any of several varieties of seeds or peas left in the bean pod until mature and then shelled and dried.

beans, fresh Any of several varieties of beans that are picked when immature; the entire pod (except for the stem) is consumed (e.g., green beans and snow peas).

beans, shelling Any of several varieties of beans that are grown principally for the edible seeds inside the pod (the tough pod usually is not eaten); includes the green garden pea.

bean sprouts The tender, young shoots of germinated beans (seeds) such as mung beans, alfalfa seeds, soybeans and wheat berries.

bean threads; bean thread vermicelli; bean vermicelli *See* cellophane noodles.

bean thread vermicelli Extruded noodles made from mung bean flour and water; used dried in Asian soups and braised dishes.

bearberry The small, red fruit of a tree grown in mountainous regions worldwide; it has a mild flavor when cooked; also known as bear's grape. *See* cranberry.

beard The hairy-looking gills of bivalves such as oysters and mussels; it is found at the open end of the shells opposite the hinge.

Beard, James (Am., 1903–1985) A highly esteemed food writer and respected cooking teacher; he authored numerous books, including *Theory and Practice of Good Cooking, Beard on Bread* and *James Beard's American Cookery;* his former home and cooking school in Greenwich Village, New York City, now houses the James Beard Foundation, which supports and promotes American cuisine.

béarnaise, sauce (bair-NAYZ) A French sauce made with a reduction of vinegar, wine, tarragon, peppercorns and shallots and finished with egg yolks and butter.

bear's grape *See* bearberry.

beat To mix by stirring rapidly and vigorously in a circular motion.

beaten biscuit A hard, crisp biscuit made by beating the dough vigorously for as long as half an hour; it originated in the American South during the 1800s.

beating A mixing method in which foods are agitated vigorously to incorporate air or develop gluten; a spoon or electric mixer with a paddle attachment is used.

Beaufort (bo-for) A Gruyère-style cheese made in France's Savoy and Dauphine regions from cow's milk; it has a firm, ivory interior with a natural crust and a sweet, nutty flavor; also known as Gruyère de Beaufort.

Beauharnais, à la (boh-are-nay, ah-lah) A French garnish for tender cuts of beef (e.g., tournedos) consisting of stuffed mushrooms and quartered artichoke hearts.

Beaujolais (bo-jo-lay) 1. A district in southern Burgundy, France, known for its Gamay grapes. 2. A light, fruity red wine made from the Gamay grape; usually served at cellar temperature rather than room temperature; most are best consumed young.

Beaujolais Cru (bo-jo-lay crew) Ten villages in the northern Beaujolais region that produce wines using their own individual appellations; generally the highest-quality, most long-lived and most expensive Beaujolais.

Beaujolais Nouveau; Beaujolais Primeur (bo-jo-lay noo-vo) A Beaujolais released within a few weeks of harvest, traditionally the third Thursday in November, and best consumed within 2–3 months of bottling.

Beaujolais-Villages (bo-jo-lay vee-lagh) A blend of wines from the 39 communes in Beaujolais; it has more body and flavor than an ordinary Beaujolais.

Beaumont (bo-moh'n) A Saint-Paulin–style cheese made from pasteurized cow's milk in France's Haute-Savoie region, it has a yellow rind and interior, a supple texture and a mild, creamy flavor; factory produced, its wrapper is stamped with Girod.

Beaune (bone) The French town known as the center of the Burgundian wine trade.

Beaunois (bo-n'wah) A rarely used name for the Chardonnay grape.

beautiful bean *See* navy bean.

beauty A fabricated cut of the beef primal rib; it is the first steak cut from the rib before the bone or with the bone removed.

Beauty of Bath A rare, old-fashioned British apple with a bright pink and green skin and a sharp, sweet flavor.

bebida (beh-bee-dah) Portuguese and Spanish for beverage.

béchamel sauce (bay-shah-mell) A French leading sauce made by thickening milk with a white roux and adding seasonings; also known as a cream sauce and a white sauce.

Becherovka (bah-cha-rove-kah) A bitter herb schnapps served at the Karlsbad spa (Czech Republic); also known as the 13th thermal bath of Karlsbad.

beckenoff (beck-en-hoff) A dish from France's Alsace region consisting of layers of sliced lean and fat pork, lamb, onions and potatoes moistened with white wine and slow cooked in a casserole.

bécsiszelet (bew-zul-tah) A Hungarian dish of fried breaded veal cutlets.

Beda (beh-dah) An Egyptian cheese made from water buffalo's or cow's milk, either whole or partially skimmed; eaten fresh; it is rindless, dense and white.

bed and breakfast A small- to medium-sized inn, sometimes located in the owner's home; generally a bedroom (with or without a private bath) and breakfast are the only amenities available. *See* continental plan *and* en suite.

bee balm *See* bergamot.

beechnut; beech nut A small, three-angled nut of the beech tree (genus *Fagus*); it has a slightly astringent flavor, similar to that of a chestnut or hazelnut, that improves with roasting; it is used roasted and ground like coffee or ground as animal feed.

beechnut oil; beech nut oil An oil obtained from the beechnut; it has a distinctive, pleasant flavor.

beech tree Its fruits can be crushed for oil or roasted and ground and prepared like coffee.

beechwheat *See* buckwheat.

beechwood aging During kräusening, the period when beechwood chips or slats are immersed into a tank of beer to attract impurities and help clarify the beer; the beechwood does not impart flavor.

beef The meat of bovines (e.g., cows, steers and bulls) slaughtered when older than 1 year; generally, it has a dark red color, a rich flavor, interior marbling, external fat and a firm to tender texture. *See* calf, natural beef *and* veal.

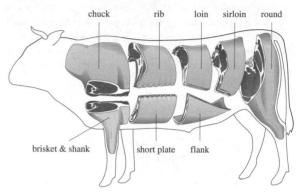

beef
(American primals)

beef, diced A commercial standard for chunks of beef cut from any portion of the carcass except the heel and shank: 75% of it must be the equivalent of a 0.75- to 1.5-in. (19- to 38-mm) cube, and surface or seam fat shall not exceed 0.5 in. (13 mm) in thickness.

beef, ground Beef ground from muscles found in various primals, but principally the chuck, short plate and sirloin; also known as hamburger and minced beef (especially in Europe).

beef, stewing A commercial standard for chunks of beef cut from any portion of the carcass except the heel and shank: 85% of it must be the equivalent of a 0.75- to 1.5-in. (19- to 38-mm) cube, and surface or seam fat shall not exceed 0.25 in. (6 mm) in thickness.

beef à la mode *See* boeuf à la mode.

beefalo A cross between American bison (buffalo) and cattle; the meat is dark red, lean and somewhat more strongly flavored and sweeter than beef.

beefalo, pure-bred A beefalo that is three-eighths bison and five-eighths domesticated beef animal (typically Hereford, Angus and/or Charolais).

beef bones A commercial standard for chunks of the cattle's shank, femur and humerus bones; they do not exceed 8 in. (203 mm) in length, and marrow is exposed on one end.

beefburger *See* hamburger.

beef carcass The cleaned carcass of a steer; split down the backbone into bilateral halves; each half is then split between rib numbers 12 and 13 into a forequarter and a hindquarter.

beef extract A strong beef stock reduced by evaporation to a thick, dark brown, salty paste and used as a flavoring.

beef filet *See* filet mignon.

beef forequarter Either bilateral half of the front portion of the beef carcass; it contains the chuck, brisket and shank, rib and short plate primals.

beef hindquarter Either bilateral half of the rear portion of the beef carcass; it contains the short loin, flank, sirloin and round primals.

beef jerky Thin strips of beef, traditionally dried in the sun and often lightly salted; they have a chewy, tough texture and a salty flavor.

Beefmaster An Italian variety of large red beefsteak tomato with a solid, meaty interior.

beef olives A British dish of slices of lean beef stuffed with bread crumbs, herbs and onions bound with egg and then braised with root vegetables.

beef on weck A western New York state sandwich consisting of thinly sliced roast beef on a kummelweck and garnished with horseradish.

beef primals The eight principal sections of the beef carcass: the chuck, brisket and shank, rib, short plate, short loin, flank, sirloin and round; each side of beef contains one of each primal.

beef quality grades *See* USDA quality grades, prime, choice, select, standard, commercial, utility, cutter *and* canner.

beef rib Any subprimal or fabricated cut from the beef primal rib with the bones intact.

beef ribs *See* short ribs.

beef short ribs A fabricated cut consisting of the ends of the rib bones from the beef primal rib (they are trimmed off to fabricate the rib roast).

beef side A matched forequarter and hindquarter of the beef carcass.

Beefsteak German for beef steak.

beefsteak mushroom A mushroom (*Fistulina hapatica*) that grows on trees, resembles a beefsteak, tongue or liver and has a good, meaty texture and flavor; also known as an ox tongue mushroom.

beefsteak tomato 1. A large, bright red tomato with a slightly squat, elliptical shape and juicy flesh with many seeds; good for eating raw or cooked; also known as the common market tomato and slicing tomato. 2. An imprecisely used term for any of several varieties of large, slightly squat, red-skinned tomatoes.

beef stroganoff *See* stroganoff.

beef tartare (tar-tar) Raw ground or chopped beef served with a raw egg yolk and garnished with chopped onions, capers and parsley.

beef tea A concentrated beef broth traditionally fed to persons unable to eat solid foods.

Beef Wellington *See* filet de boeuf Wellington.

beef yield grades *See* USDA yield grades.

Beenleigh Blue A semisoft to firm blue-veined cheese made in Devon, England, from unpasteurized ewe's milk; it has a smooth texture and clean, sharp, nutty flavor.

beer 1. Any of a large class of alcoholic beverages made by fermenting sugars derived from grains and often flavored with hops. 2. Any of various carbonated and/or slightly fermented alcoholic and nonalcoholic beverages flavored with roots. 3. The fermented mash of malted grains used to distill whiskey; also known as wash.

beer and skittles English slang for drinks and enjoyment.

beer bash; beer blast; beer bust A party, usually for young people, where the principal beverage is beer served from a keg.

beer-brewing process The process by which beer is made; typically: (1) barley is malted and then cracked into grist; (2) the grist is mixed with hot water to form the mash; (3) the malt enzymes in the mash convert the grain starches into sugar, forming the liquid wort; (4) the draff or spent grains are sparged to recover any remaining extractable materials, which are added to the wort; (5) the wort is filtered and boiled with hops, which impart a bitter flavor and characteristic aroma; (6) yeast is added to the cooled wort to begin fermentation; (7) when the desired alcohol level is reached through fermentation, the wort is considered green beer; (8) the green beer is fined to increase clarity and conditioned to increase carbonation by either kräusening or lagering (aging); and (9) the beer is bottled or kegged.

Beer Buster A cocktail made of ice cold vodka, Tabasco sauce and ice cold beer or ale; served in a chilled beer mug.

Beeren (BEAR-ern) German for berries.

Beerenauslese (BEAR-en-ouse-LAY-zuh) German for selected berry picking and used as a labeling term for a very sweet white wine made from individually selected grapes (the grapes chosen are sometimes affected by the noble rot). *See* Qualitätswein mit Prädikat.

beer engine A pumplike tap used to draw beer from a keg or cask.

beer garden A pub or other commercial establishment where beer is served; traditionally in a garden, courtyard or outdoor covered area.

beer list An establishment's beer menu.

beer standard The parts of the beer system visible above the counter, including the tap, faucet, drain and stainless steel housing.

beer system A mechanical system designed for the efficient service of draft beer at a bar; it consists of a keg of beer, carbon dioxide tank, regulator, beer box, beer lines and beer standard; also known as a draft beer system.

beer up Slang for drinking a great deal of beer.

beestings; beistyn The first liquid a cow gives after birthing; yellow and thick, it is thinned with plain milk and used for custards, puddings and tarts.

beeswax (yellow and white) Food additives derived from honeybee honeycombs and used as a lubricant, flavoring agent and/or adjuvant in processed foods such as confections and candies.

bee sweetin' Traditional American term for honey.

beeswing (BEEZ-wehng) A light, translucent sediment found floating in very old bottles of port and once prized as a guarantor of age; named for the pattern it creates.

beet A large, bulbous edible root with an edible leafy green top (*Beta vulgaris*); its color is typically garnet red but can range from pinkish-white to deep red; also known as beetroot (especially in Great Britain), garden beet and red beet.

beetberry The small, red, mulberry-like fruit of a weed similar to Fat Hen and Good King Henry.

Beetensuppe (bee-ten-sou-pay) German for borscht.

beet extract A food additive derived from the beet; it has a bright red color and is used as a coloring agent in yogurt, candies and desserts.

beetgreen *See* spinach beet.

beetroot British for beet.

beggar's apple *See* clochard.

beggar's purse An appetizer consisting of a small crêpe topped with a savory filling; the edges are pulled up in pleats to form a sack and tied with a chive.

begonia The flowers and leaves of this plant, native to South America (genus *Begonia*), have a mild flavor and are used as a garnish in South American cuisines.

behind the stick Slang for working the beer taps at a bar.

beignet (ben-YEA) French for fritter and used to describe a crisp, puffy, deep-fried, New Orleans pastry similar to a doughnut.

Beijing kao ya (bay-ging kah-o ya) Chinese for Peking duck.

beijos de anjo (bah-he-os da ah-nee-oh) A Brazilian dessert of egg yolks and stiffly beaten egg whites, baked until set and then poached in a sugar syrup flavored with vanilla and cloves.

Beilagen (by-la-ghen) German for side dishes.

bein (behn) Norwegian for bone.

beistyn *See* beestings.

bejinhos de coco (ba-gee-nyos da coh-coh) A Brazilian confection made from sweetened condensed milk and freshly grated coconut, cooked, shaped into balls and rolled in confectioners' sugar.

bekon (BAY-kone) Japanese for bacon.

Belegtes Brote (be-LAYK-tes broat) German for open-faced sandwiches, usually consisting of rye bread and sausages.

Belgian Blue Bull A large-framed breed of beef cattle; its meat has a superior flavor and texture and relatively low fat and cholesterol contents.

Belgian coffee Coffee served with a square of chocolate that is dropped into the coffee to melt.

Belgian endive (EN-dyv; AHN-deev) A member of the chicory family grown in Belgium; it has a long, cigar-shaped head of compact, pointed leaves; the leaves have a creamy color with yellow tips and fringes (a purple-tipped variety is also available) and a slightly bitter flavor; also known as French endive (if grown in France) and witloof.

Belgian waffle A thick waffle made with very large, deep grids or pockets, usually served with fruit and whipped cream, especially for dessert.

belicoso A medium-sized cigar with a 48 ring, a 6-in. length and a pointed head.

belicoso, petite A cigar with a 40 ring, a 5-in. length and a pointed head.

belimbing (beh-lim-bing) A small ovoid fruit (*Averrhoa bilimbi*) related to the carambola with a light green, slightly rough skin and a sour flavor; used in Asian cuisines.

belimbing asam (beh-lim-bing ah-sahm) A cylindrical fruit (*Averrhoa bilimbi*) native to Malaysia; it has a smooth, yellowish-green skin and a juicy flesh with an acidic flavor; used in Southeast Asian cuisines for pickles or in stews.

Bella Milano *See* Milano.

belle du bois (bel duh bwah) A large, western European traditional apple with a yellow skin with orange and green blush and a sweet, mealy flesh; also known as Louis XVIII, reinette des danois and rio.

belle fille de l'Indre (bel fil duh l'ohn-dra) A small, western European traditional apple with a bright yellow skin with a red blush and a sweet, juicy flesh.

Bellelay A semisoft Swiss Trappist cheese made from whole cow's milk; it has an ivory interior, a brownish rind and a tangy flavor; also known as Tête de Moine or Monk's Head.

belles de Nazelles A large western European traditional apple with a yellow-orange blushed skin.

Bellini (beh-lee-nee) 1. A cocktail made of puréed white peaches, lemon juice, dry Italian spumante and grenadine. 2. A cocktail made of sparkling wine and peach brandy or peach liquor.

bell of knuckle A subprimal cut from the beef primal round; generally lean, flavorful and tough.

bell pepper A large fresh sweet pepper with a bell-like shape, thick juicy flesh, a mild sweet flavor and available in various colors, including green (the most common), red (a green bell pepper that has been allowed to ripen), white, brown, purple, yellow and orange; also known as green pepper, sweet bell pepper and sweet pepper.

belly 1. A primal cut of the pork carcass located just above the primal loin; consists of the spareribs and a large amount of fat with streaks of lean meat (the latter is usually cured and smoked for bacon); also known as pork belly and primal side belly. 2. The general name for the underside of a fish or quadruped.

bellyfish *See* monkfish.

belly of pork A British cut of the pork carcass; it is comparable to spareribs.

belly wash 1. Slang for a soft drink; originated with loggers. 2. A Jamaican lemonade.

Belon (bay-lohn) 1. An oyster from France's Belon River region, it has a round, flat, brownish-green shell with a length of 1.5–3.5 in. (3.8–8.8 cm), a slim body and a slightly metallic flavor. 2. An imprecisely used marketing term for any of several European flat oyster varieties found along the New England coast.

Bel Paese (bell pah-AYZ-eh) A mild, soft, creamy Italian cheese made from cow's milk; it has an edible brownish-gray rind, a pale yellow interior and a fruity flavor; if made in Italy, the wrapper has a map of Italy; if made in the United States, it has a map of the Western Hemisphere.

belt Slang for a quickly consumed serving of an alcoholic beverage (e.g., whiskey), usually straight.

beluga (buh-LOO-guh) Caviar harvested from the largest species of sturgeon; the large eggs are dark gray, well-separated and fragile.

Belvedere A short, slender cigar with a 30–36 ring and a 3- to 5-in. length.

Bembel *See* Ebbelwoi.

bench A bakeshop term to describe the worktable, usually wooden, where products (bread doughs) are made.

bench scraper A handheld rectangular tool, typically 6 × 3 in., with a stainless steel blade and a rolled handle on one long side; used for cleaning and scraping surfaces.

ben cotto (bain KOT-toa) Italian for well done, usually referring to meat, particularly steak.

bend an elbow Slang for drinking an alcoholic beverage, usually whiskey.

Ben Davis A large apple with a yellow and red marbled skin and little flavor.

bender Slang for a drunken spree.

Benedictine A light brown liqueur made from herbs, honey, dried fruit skins and brandy; the secret recipe was developed in 1510 at a French Benedictine abbey.

Benedictine and Brandy (B & B) A drier version of Benedictine, made by mixing it with brandy.

bengali gram (ban-gah-lee gram) A brownish, wrinkled chickpea used in Indian cuisines.

bengali rice (ben-gah-lee) A short-grain white rice with a superior flavor, grown in the eastern India state of West Bengal.

Bengal Lancer's Punch A punch made of sparkling wine, dry red wine, gold Barbados rum, curaçao, lime juice, pineapple juice, orange juice and orgeat; garnished with lime slices.

bengjuang *See* jícama.

Benin wine A Nigerian spirit distilled from palm sap.

béni shoga (beh-nee shoh-gah) Japanese for red pickled ginger.

benitade (bee-nee-tah-da) A Japanese garnish of red sprouts with short stems and two petals or leaves, usually used in a clump.

benjamin *See* benzoin.

Ben Lear cranberry A cranberry variety with a deep red skin.

Ben Lomond currants; Ben More currants; Ben Sarek currants Varieties of black currants.

benne seeds *See* sesame seeds.

benne seed wafers Thin, crisp wafers from the American South; they are made of flour, shortening, roasted benne seeds and cayenne pepper, usually served with cocktails.

bento; bento box (BEHN-to) A Japanese metal or lacquered wooden box divided into compartments used to store small dishes that hold all of the components of an individual meal, usually lunch.

bentonite 1. A food additive derived from the clay of the same name and used as a processing aid. 2. A clay used as a fining agent for wine and beer; large deposits exist in Wyoming.

bentoo no tomo (behn-too noh toh-moh) A Japanese flavoring compound made from dried fish, salt, soy sauce, seaweed and monosodium glutamate.

benzaldehyde A group of food additives with a bitter, almondlike flavor and aroma used as flavoring agents and/or adjuvants.

benzoic acid; benzenecarboxylic acid A food additive naturally occurring in certain foods including cranberries, prunes and cinnamon; used as a preservative (antimicrobial agent), especially in acidic foods such as pickles, fruit juices and carbonated beverages.

benzoin A food additive used as a flavoring agent for its almondlike flavor; also called benjamin.

benzoyl peroxide A food additive used as a bleaching agent for flour and some cheeses.

benzyl butyrate A food additive with a fruity flavor and aroma; used as a flavoring agent and/or adjuvant.

benzyl propionate A food additive with a sweet, fruity aroma used as a flavoring agent.

BEO Food industry slang for a banquet event order.

beolas (ba-oh-lass) A Jewish fritter made from matzo meal; it is fried, sprinkled with ground cinnamon, sugar, lemon peel and water, and then broiled and eaten cold.

beor Old English for beer.

berberé (behr-beh-ra) An Ethiopian spice blend generally consisting of garlic, red pepper, cardamom, coriander and fenugreek as well as other spices; often used in stews and soups.

berberecho (ber-ber-a-tcho) Spanish for cockle.

berberis; berberry *See* barberry.

berbero (behr-behr-oh) Italian for barberry.

Berbesbeere (behr-bess-bear-reh) German for barberry.

berbigao (bar-be-gah-oh) Portuguese for a heart-shaped cockle; it is often served spiced as a petisco.

Berchoux, sauce (bear-choh) A French compound sauce made from an allemande sauce with cream and finished with herb butter.

Bercy, sauce A French compound sauce made from a fish velouté with shallots, white wine, fish stock and seasonings; usually served with fish.

Bercy butter (bair-SEE; BUR-see) A French sauce made from white wine, shallots, butter, marrow, lemon juice, parsley, salt and pepper and served with broiled or grilled meats or fish; also known as shallot butter.

Bereich (beh-REY'sh) German for area or district and used to describe the principal subdivisions within an Anbaugebiet; the wines are not identified by vineyards, only by the district.

berenjena (behr-ehn-HEH-nah) Spanish for eggplant.

Bergader (beh-gahr-dar) A soft German cheese made from cow's milk; it has blue-green veins, a smooth texture and a wrinkled, dark brown rind.

bergamot (BER-gah-mot) A member of the mint family (*Monarda didyma*); it has slightly toothed, dark green leaves with a citrusy flavor and the scent of bergamot oranges; the leaves are used in tisanes; also known as bee balm.

Bergamot A German brandy-based liqueur flavored with bergamot.

bergamot orange A small, slightly pear-shaped orange (*Citrus bergamia*) with a very acidic flesh; the peel, which is sometimes candied, yields an oil used in perfumes and to flavor candies and Earl Gray tea.

Bergkäse (berg-KAY-zer) A group of mountain cheeses made from cow's milk in Bavaria, Germany; most have rinds with traces of dark, dry mold or a moist bloom, springy interiors and widely scattered holes.

beriberi (berri-berri) A disease caused by a deficiency of vitamin B_1; symptoms include cardiac irregularities, pain, weakness, mental confusion and depression.

beringela (bay-reen-ZHEN-lah) Portuguese for eggplant.

berlam (bare-lahm) Turkish for hake.

Berliner (behr-LEE-ner) A yeast-leavened doughnut without the center hole, it is usually filled with a fruit mixture.

Berliner Weisse (behgh-LEE-ner VAY-se) A very pale top-fermented wheat beer brewed in northern Germany, particularly near Berlin; it is lightly hopped and has a low alcohol content.

Bermuda onion A large onion with a golden yellow outer layer, an ivory flesh and a moderately strong, pungent flavor.

Bermuda plan A daily hotel rate that includes a full American breakfast and a room.

Berner platte (BEHR-nerr PLAH-ter) A Swiss dish consisting of beef slices and sauerkraut layered with chopped pig's feet, flavored with white wine and topped with fried bacon and onions; it is cooked slowly and often served with sausages and potatoes.

Bernheim Distillery One of the 12 remaining U.S. whiskey distilleries; located in Louisville, Kentucky, and founded in the early 1890s, it produces both regular bourbons (distilled from rye), such as Old Charter and I. W. Harper, and wheated bourbons, such as W. L. Weller, Old Fitzgerald, Rebel Yell and Kentucky Tavern.

berry 1. A cereal grain's seed. 2. An imprecisely used term to describe any small, juicy fruit that grows on a vine or bush and generally has a thin skin, multiple small to tiny seeds and a sweet flavor. 3. A fruit with seeds embedded in the pulp (e.g., banana, grape or tomato). 4. A crustacean's egg.

berry, in A term applied to fish eggs in roe and to the hen lobster carrying eggs.

berrylike A wine-tasting term for an aroma reminiscent of blackberries, cherries, raspberries, strawberries or other berries.

berry wine A wine fermented from berries.

Berta's Special A cocktail made of tequila, sugar syrup or honey, egg white, orange bitters, club soda and lime juice; it is served in a Collins glass and garnished with a lime slice.

bertiche (behr-tee-ka) Italian for perch.

besan (bah-sahn) Channa dhal ground to a fine, pale yellow flour; it is used in Indian cuisines.

besciamella (bay-chee-MAYL-lah) Italian for béchamel.

besi (bae-see) 1. A generic term for several varieties of French pears with juicy white flesh, including besi d'héry, besi de caissoy and besi de la motte. 2. A dish of salted, fried cow's meat made in France's Jura region.

bessenoep (bess-en-ep) A Belgian soup flavored with red currant juice and sugar, garnished with vermicelli and thickened with potato flour.

best end of neck; best end 1. A British cut of the veal carcass that corresponds to the animal's ribs; sold on the bone for roasting or further fabricated into cutlets. 2. A British cut of the lamb carcass that includes the rib joint between the middle neck and loin; equivalent to the American rack of lamb. *See* middle neck, scrag *and* scrag end of neck.

beta acid A soft, bitter hop resin that is harsher than alpha acid and almost insoluble at a wort's normal pH value.

beta-apo-8'-carotenal A food additive with a light to dark orange hue used as a coloring agent, especially in cheese and cheese products.

beta-carotene 1. A nutrient supplement and food additive that, as an antioxidant, is believed to lower the risk of cancer. 2. Naturally occurring in spinach and other dark green leafy vegetables, a food additive and provitamin A used as a nutrient supplement and coloring agent in processed foods such as cake mixes, flour and shortenings. *See* carotene, alpha-, beta- *and* gamma-.

beta-jio (be-tah-gee-oh) A Japanese preparation method that requires foods to be dredged in salt at least 1 hour before they are rinsed and cooked.

betel leaf The heart-shaped leaf of the *Piper betle,* often treated with lime and used to make betel quid.

betel nut The small fruit of the areca palm (*Areca catechu*) native to the Philippines and Sumatra; it has a mottled brown skin and a pleasantly astringent flavor; the nut is chewed, but not swallowed, and is used as a breath sweetener and digestion aid.

betel quid A digestive aid and breath sweetener made from a paste of areca nut flavored with cardamom and cinnamon and spread on the leaf of the betel tree; also known as a sirih.

beterraba (beh-teh-rrah-bah) Portuguese for beetroot.

Betsy Ross A cocktail made of brandy, port, sugar syrup, egg yolk, curaçao and Angostura bitters; it is garnished with nutmeg.

betterave (bet-TRAHV) French for beetroot.

Better Boy tomato A variety of red-skinned beefsteak tomato.

bettola (BEH-toh-lah) Italian for a tavern.

betty A colonial American dessert consisting of a baked pudding made with layers of sweetened fruit and buttered bread crumbs; the most familiar is the apple brown betty, made with apples and brown sugar.

Between the Sheets A cocktail made of light rum, brandy, Cointreau and lemon juice.

beurre (burr) French for butter.

beurre blanc (burr BLANHK) French for white butter and used to describe an emulsified butter sauce made from shallots, white wine and butter; also known as butter sauce.

beurre Bosc (burr BAWSK) *See* Bosc pear.

beurre Chivry (burr she-VREE) A compound butter made with shallots, tarragon, chives and burnet.

beurre Colbert; Colbert butter (kohl-BAIR) Unsalted butter mixed with a meat glaze and tarragon.

beurre composé (burr com-poh-ZAY) French for compound butter.

beurre d'amandes (burr dah-mahnd) Toasted almonds mixed with unsalted butter and a pinch of salt and pepper; used in baked goods; also known as almond butter.

beurre d'anchois (burr don-SHWAH) Unsalted butter mixed with anchovy fillets and lemon juice; used for canapés and as a flavoring for certain fish sauces; also known as anchovy butter.

beurre d'Anjou *See* Anjou pear.

beurre d'écrevisses (burr day-cruh-VEESE) A compound butter flavored with crayfish essence, crayfish tail meat, salt and pepper; used for canapés and as a flavoring; also known as crayfish butter.

beurre hareng (burr ah-ran) A compound butter made with fresh herring.

beurre homard (burr oh-mar) A compound butter made with lobster.

beurre manie (burr man-yay) French for kneaded butter and used to describe a mix of equal weights of flour and whole butter; it is whisked into a sauce just before service for quick thickening and added sheen and flavor.

beurre marchand de vin (burr mah-shon duh van) A French compound butter made by reducing red wine, shallots and demi-glaze au sec, then blending it into softened butter with parsley and lemon juice; usually served with steak. *See* marchand de vin, sauce.

beurre mâtre'd (burr may-traw-DEE) A French compound butter made with lemon juice and chopped parsley; served with grilled meats, either melted or in solid rounds or slices.

beurre noir (burr NWAR) French for black butter and used to describe whole butter cooked until dark brown (not black); it is sometimes flavored with vinegar or lemon juice, capers and parsley and served over fish, eggs and vegetables.

beurre noisette (burr nwah-ZEHT) French for brown butter and used to describe butter cooked until it is a light hazelnut (noisette) color; it is flavored and used in much the same manner as beurre noir.

beurre piémontaise (burr pyay-mohn-tez) *See* piédmont butter.

beurre raifort (burr rah-for) A compound butter made with horseradish.

beurre rouge (burr rooge) 1. An emulsified butter sauce made from red wine, butter and shallots. 2. A compound butter made with shellfish coral.

Beuschel (ba-hoo-shell) German for lights (lungs).

bevanda (bay-vahn-dah) Italian for beverage.

beverage A general term for any consumable alcoholic or nonalcoholic liquid, especially if it is processed in some fashion. *See* drink.

beverage alcohol A term preferred by the spirits industry to refer to all alcoholic beverages as a group, whether distilled spirits, beer or wine.

beverage control The system used to track and control beverage products from purchase through receipt, storage, use or sale.

beverage cost The total cost of a beverage, including the costs of ingredients, waste, overproduction and pilferage; also known as the standard beverage cost.

beverage cost percentage The costs incurred for each dollar of beverages sold; it is expressed as a percentage of sales.

beverage cost percentage pricing Pricing a beverage based on the total beverage costs; it is calculated by dividing the cost per portion by the beverage cost percentage.

beverage issue report A periodic listing of all bottles or other containers of alcoholic beverages released from storage for use at the bar or other areas of a food services facility; the report helps with inventory control.

beverage manager The person responsible for supervising and setting policies for all divisions (alcoholic and nonalcoholic) of a beverage department, including development of a beverage menu, wine list and so on; it is sometimes combined with the position of food manager.

beverage operation The department or other division of a hotel, large restaurant or other facility responsible for the purchase, storage, distribution and sale of all beverages, including alcoholic beverages.

beverage sales Total revenue from beverage sales over a given or projected time period; the number can also be total revenues from a particular category or type of beverages, such as beer and wine.

beverage section One of the principal work sections of a food services facility; it typically contains a hot beverage station, a cold beverage station and an alcoholic beverage station.

beverage transfers The wholesale cost of beverages, both alcoholic and nonalcoholic, used by a hospitality or food services facility in a department other than the bar; the cost is used to determine expenses and revenues related to these other departments.

beyaz peynirli (beiz pa-ner-lie) A Turkish pastry roll filled with feta or kasseri and served hot as a meze.

beyin köftesi (bah-hin kof-tah-see) A Turkish hors d'oeuvre of calf's brain fritters.

beyin salatasi (bi-an sal-a-tas) A Turkish salad made from sheep's brains simmered with onions and vinegar, dressed with olive oil and lemon juice and garnished with olives.

bezelyeli havuçlu patates yemegi (be-za-lee-ah-lee ha-voo-klue pah-tah-tess ye-ma-gee) A Turkish hors d'oeuvre of mixed vegetables, such as potatoes, peas and carrots.

Bgug Panir (goog pah-near) An Armenian cheese made from skimmed ewe's milk and flavored with herbs; also known as Daralag.

BHA *See* butylated hydroxyanisole.

bhain *See* lotus root.

bhajias (bha-ji-aa) *See* pakoras.

bhara (bah-raw) Hindi for stuffed.

bharaat (bhur-aat) A sweet spice mix consisting of allspice, cinnamon, nutmeg and cloves; it is used to flavor rice dishes in Middle Eastern cuisines.

bharta (bhur-taa) 1. An Indian cooking method that describes a dish, typically one made with vegetables, that has been cooked and puréed. 2. An Indian dish of smoked eggplant fried with onion, tomatoes and herbs.

bhatoora (bah-to-raw) An Indian dish of leavened dough made of yogurt, potatoes and white flour, rolled into circles and deep-fried.

bher (ba-hr) Hindi for lamb.

bheshaj (ba-shy) Hindi for herbs.

bhindee (been-dee) Hindi for okra.

bhona (bow-nah) Hindi for fried.

bhone piaz ke lachee (bow-nah pee-ahz ka lah-chee) Crisp fried onion shreds used in Indian cuisines as a garnish, especially for rice dishes.

BHT *See* butylated hydroxytoluene.

bhuna (boo-mah) The Indian technique of sautéing and stirring meats as they cook until spices cling to the meat and any liquid evaporates.

bialy (bee-AH-lee) A round, flat, chewy Jewish yeast roll similar to a bagel but with an indentation instead of a hole.

bianco (b'yahn-co) Italian for white.

bianco carta (b'yahn-co KAHR-tah) Italian for white paper and used to describe an extremely light-colored white wine.

Bianco della Lega (b'YAHN-co deh-lah LEB-gah) A dry white wine from the Chianti Classico region of Tuscany made from the Trebbiano and Malvasia grapes.

bian dòu (bien doh) Chinese for beans.

bibb lettuce A variety of butterhead lettuce with soft, pliable green leaves that have a buttery texture and flavor and are smaller and darker than Boston lettuce leaves; also known as limestone lettuce.

bibiere Latin for beer.

bibim bob (be-beem bop) A Korean dish of rice mixed with vegetables and beef and served with a hot sauce.

bibim naengmyun (be-beem nang-myan) A Korean dish of cold noodles mixed with vegetables and beef and served with a hot sauce.

bibingka (bee-bing-ka) 1. A Filipino dough made from rice flour and water and used to make fresh or dried noodles, wrappers, dumplings and snacks. 2. A Filipino dish consisting of a flat rice pancake cooked in a special earthenware dish and topped with an egg, crumbled white cheese and sugar.

bibinka A Filipino confection made of glutinous rice, flour, brown sugar, coconut and milk and baked in a ti leaf; it is traditionally served at Christmas, New Year and other festivals.

Biblia con Pisco (be-blee-ah con pea-sko) A Bolivian eggnoglike beverage flavored with Pisco.

bicarbonate of soda *See* baking soda.

bicerin (bee-cheh-REEN) 1. Italian for a small beverage glass or cup with a metal handle. 2. A hot beverage of cocoa, milk and coffee popular in Italy's Piedmont region.

bicochos borrachos (bee-coh-chos bow-raw-choss) A Spanish sponge cake sprinkled with wine and cinnamon.

bidia (be-de-ah) A Zairian dish consisting of a thick cornmeal porridge, sometimes flavored with chiles.

bidos (be-doss) A Norwegian ragoût of reindeer meat, onions and potatoes cooked in a meat broth and flavored with cloves, bay leaves and a dash of vinegar.

bien asado (byen ah-sah-doh) Spanish for well done, usually referring to steak.

bien cuit (be-en KWEE) French for well done, usually referring to steak.

biennial A plant that completes its life cycle in two years; it grows during the first year and produces flowers and fruit during the second year.

Bier (beegh) Dutch and German for beer.

bière (be-yair) French for beer.

bière de garde (be-yair de gaghd) 1. French for any beer that has been aged for a long period of time. 2. An amber-colored, top-fermented beer from northern France; it is aged for long periods in casks, then bottled in bottles similar to those used for sparkling wines.

bière de mars (be-yair de maghs) French for March beer; a specialty beer from France, it is brewed in March with barley harvested the preceding August.

biere douce (be-yair dooze) A Creole beer made in Louisiana from pineapple skins, sugar, rice and water.

Biergarten (beer gart-ehn) A German beer garden.

Bierkäse *See* Weisslacker.

bieslook (BEES-lock) Dutch for chive.

bieten (BEE-ten) Dutch for beetroot.

bietola (bee-ay-TOA-lah) Italian for Swiss chard.

biètoline (bee-ay-toa-LEE-nay) *See* erbetté.

bife (bee-fay) Portuguese for beefsteak.

biff (bif) Norwegian and Swedish for beefsteak.

bifstek (beef-steak) Russian for beefsteak.

biftec al horno (beef-teck ahl ohr-noh) A Uruguayan dish of beef seasoned with garlic, chiles and cayenne and braised with tomatoes and beef broth.

bifteck (beef-tehk) French for beefsteak.

biftéki (beef-tah-kee) Greek meatballs.

biftik à la Montevideo (beef-tick ah lah mon-tae-vee-dae-oh) A French dish of beefsteak browned in oil with onions, garlic and chiles and baked with onions and tomatoes.

bifun (bee-foon) Light, transparent Chinese noodles made from rice flour and potato starch.

bifuteki (bee-FOO-teh-kee) Japanese for beefsteak.

big A wine-tasting term for a wine with a greater-than-average alcohol content, body and flavor but without much distinction; it provides an intense feeling on the palate.

biga (BEE-gah) An aged dough made with yeast or sour dough; used in Italy; it is a type of sourdough starter.

bigarade (bee-gah-RAHD) French for bitter orange.

bigarade, sauce (bee-gah-RAHD) A French compound sauce made with beef stock, duck drippings, orange juice, lemon juice, blanched orange peel and, sometimes, curaçao; traditionally made with bitter oranges but now made with sweet oranges, it is usually served with roast duck; also known as orange sauce.

bigarreau cherry A medium-sized, light to medium red cherry with a sweet flavor; also known as burlat cherry.

bigarro (bee-gah-roe) Spanish for periwinkle.

Big Beef tomato A variety of red-skinned beefsteak tomato.

Big Boy tomato A variety of red-skinned beefsteak tomato.

bigeye scad *See* akule.

Big huckleberry A huckleberry variety; the blue-skinned fruit are relatively large and flavorful.

bignay A tree found in Southeast Asia and Australia; its large purple berries grow in clusters; too acidic to eat fresh, they are used for preserves; also known as Chinese laurel, currant tree and salamander tree.

bigoli (BEE-goh-lee) A spaghetti-shaped whole wheat pasta made in northeastern Italy.

bigos (BEE-gohs) A Polish dish of alternating layers of sauerkraut and cooked meats simmered in bouillon; served with small grilled sausages; also known as hunter's stew.

bihoon; beehoon; bihun; bijon (bee-hoon) A fine, extruded, creamy-colored Filipino noodle made from a dough of rice flour and water.

bijol (bee-joh-el) Ground achiato seeds used in Caribbean cuisines to add a yellow color and a delicate fragrance to rice.

biko (bee-koh) A Filipino dessert made from glutinous rice, coconut milk and sugar that is poured into molds lined with banana leaves and served with a brown coconut milk curd.

bilateral Symmetrical halves arranged along a central axis.

bilberry *See* huckleberry.

bile A liver secretion stored in the gallbladder; once in the small intestine, it helps digest fats by acting as an emulsifier and moves food by stimulating peristalsis.

bile duct The passage through which bile travels from the gallbladder to the duodenum.

bill The thin end of an oyster shell.

billings A variety of small, green carambola; it is generally used for preserves.

billy An Australian term for a tin container used to boil water for tea.

billy by; billi-bi (bill-e bee) A French soup made from mussels cooked in white wine, onions, parsley and fish stock; the soup is served hot or cold with fresh cream, and the mussels are served separately.

biltong (BILL-tong) Strips of cured, air-dried beef or game; finer than beef jerky, it is used in South African cuisines.

bin 1. A storage rack on which wine bottles are laid on their side so that the wine is in contact with the cork; this prevents the cork from drying out, shrinking and allowing air to come into contact with the wine. 2. A box or enclosed space used to store dry goods such as grains.

bin card A card used in a beverage storeroom showing the bin number and stock on hand for each beverage item; it is a form of perpetual inventory.

bind 1. To thicken a hot liquid by stirring in eggs, flour and butter, cornstarch, cheese, cream or other ingredients. 2. To cause different foods to more or less adhere to one another, usually by mixing them with beaten eggs, milk, water, flour, oil, mayonnaise or other dressing.

bindae duk (bin-day tuck) A Korean dish of tofu garnished with pork.

binder 1. An ingredient or combination of ingredients used to thicken or hold a mixture together. 2. A leaf of tough, coarse tobacco that holds a cigar's filler in place; the binder is usually covered by a leaf of wrapper tobacco.

Bindner fleisch *See* Bündenfleisch.

bing (beeng) Chinese for ice.

bing (ping) Thai for to bake, roast or toast; it often refers to foods cooked in the oven, over a fire or by other dry-cooking methods.

Bing cherry A sweet cherry with a deep garnet, almost black color, smooth glossy skin, firm dark red flesh and sweet flavor.

binge A large intake of food, often high caloric, over a short period of time.

bingjiling (beeng-gee-lyn) Chinese for ice cream.

binnaga (been-nah-gah) Japanese for albacore.

binning Storing bottled wine in a bin while the wine ages.

Bintje (been-te-ah) A variety of hardy, high-yield potato with a golden-brown skin and yellow flesh; generally grown in northern Europe.

bioavailability The rate and extent to which a nutrient from food and the same nutrient taken as a supplement will be absorbed by the body.

bioengineered foods A process in which a gene or group of genes is extracted from the DNA of one plant or animal and spliced into that of another, generally to improve the appearance, texture and flavor of shipped- and shelf-stable foods or to develop insect- and disease-resistant strains; also known as genetically engineered foods.

bioflavonoids Substances in food that supply no recognized nutritional needs; some bioflavonoids are referred to by their proponents as vitamin P.

biological contaminant; biological hazard *See* hazard, biological.

biological value of proteins (BV) A measure of protein quality based on a determination of how well the protein supports the body's retention of nitrogen; a food's BV is scored against a reference protein (egg protein) of 100.

bior (bee-or) Hebrew for beer.

biotin A water-soluble vitamin used for metabolizing fatty acids and amino acids; present in many foods, significant sources include liver, kidney, milk, egg yolk, soy flour and yeast; formerly known as vitamin H.

biova (bee-OH-vah) A large loaf of lard bread from the Piedmont region of Italy.

bir Indonesian for beer.

bira (biera) Bulgarian and Turkish for beer.

birch A food additive derived from the birch tree (principally the sap) used as a flavoring and sweetening agent.

birch beer A sweetened, carbonated soft drink flavored with the sap of the black birch tree (genus *Betula*).

bird 1. A whole fowl, such as a turkey, chicken or duck. 2. *See* paupiette.

bird cherry *See* mazzard.

bird chile A small, fiery hot chile used in Caribbean cuisines for pickles and condiments.

bird fig *See* bluggoe fig.

bird's beak knife A paring knife with a curved blade used for cutting curved surfaces or tournéeing vegetables; also known as a tournée knife.

bird's beak knife

Birdseye, Clarence (Am., 1886–1956) An American scientist who pioneered the use of freezing as a method of food preservation; his work led to quick deep-freezing as we know it today, and the company he founded remains one of the largest processors of frozen food.

bird's nest Very thinly sliced potatoes deep-fried in a cup-shaped basket to form a nest; usually filled with vegetables for service.

bird's nest pudding A dessert from the New England region of the United States; it is made with fruit (usually apples), a crust and some type of sauce; also known as crow's nest pudding.

bird's nest soup A Chinese soup made from the nest of a salangane, a type of swallow; the birds feed on a gelatinous seaweed, and their salivary glands secrete a gelatinous saliva used for their nests; the nests are soaked overnight until transparent and are then used for soup.

biribia (bee-ree-bee-ah) A medium-sized ovoid fruit (*Rollinia mucosa*) native to tropical regions in South America; it has a creamy-yellow skin, a white or cream-colored juicy flesh and a sweet, pleasant flavor.

biringani (be-ring-ah-nee) Swahili for eggplant.

biriyani; biryani (beh-ree-YON-nee) An East Indian pilaf dish, usually made with chicken and flavored with cardamom, cloves, cinnamon and saffron and garnished with almonds and raisins.

Birne (BEER-ner) German for pear.

birra (bee-rah) Italian for beer.

birre (bee-rah) Albanian for beer.

birria (be-ree-ah) A Mexican and Latin American dish in which goat is braised, roasted and served with its braising liquid.

biru (BEE-roo) Japanese for beer.

biryani (beer-yah-nee) A South African dish consisting of layers of chicken, lentils, potatoes and hard-boiled eggs flavored with ginger, garlic, turmeric, cinnamon, cardamom, chiles, cumin, mint, coriander and yogurt and simmered or baked in an earthenware pot.

bisbas (bees-bahs) A very spicy Yemenite flavoring or condiment made from various hot chiles, salt, olive oil and tomatoes. *See* harissa *and* shatta.

bisbe; biscot (bees-bae; bees-kot) A large blood sausage from Spain's Catalonia region; it is made with meat, tongue and pig's offal.

Bischofsbrot (bee-shof-brott) An Austrian cake containing dried fruit and chocolate bits.

biscocho (bees-ko-cho) A thickening agent for Filipino meat sauces made from crumbled, oven- or sun-dried bread.

biscotte (bees-kott) French for rusk or biscuit.

biscotti (bee-skawt-tee) Italian for slices from a twice-baked flattened cookie loaf.

biscotti di Savoia *See* savoiardi.

biscotto (bee-SKAWT-toh) Italian for twice-baked; usually refers to a dry cookie.

biscuit (bees-kwee) 1. One of various types of French sponge cake, such as biscuit de Savoie or biscuit à la cuilliere. 2. French for cookie.

biscuit (BEHS-kitt) 1. A small, flaky quick bread leavened with baking soda or baking powder for a light, tender texture; the dough is rolled out and cut into circles or dropped from a spoon. 2. A thin, flat British cookie or cracker.

biscuit à la cuilliere (bees-kwee ah lah cwee-yehr) French for ladyfingers.

biscuit de Savoie (biss-kwee duh sah-wahr) A French sponge cake from Savoy; it is baked in a brioche pan.

biscuit method A mixing method used to make biscuits, scones and flaky doughs; involves cutting cold fat into flour and other dry ingredients before liquid is added.

biscuit shooter Cowboy slang for a waitress.

Bishop A hot beverage made from port, sugar and an orange studded with cloves.

bishop's bread A sweet quick bread made with dried fruit; created on the U.S. western frontier during the 19th century, where it was served to traveling clergy.

bishop's weed seeds *See* ajowan seeds.

bisket-to (bee-KET-to) Japanese for cookies; also known as kukki.

Biskote (bee-SKOT-teh) German for ladyfingers.

biskuti (bis-koo-tea) Swahili for cookies.

biskviti (bees-quit-ee) Russian for cookies; also called pechenie.

biskvitov (beesh-vee-tovv) Russian for corkscrew.

Bismarckheringe (BEHZ-mawrk-HEH-renj) German for Bismarck herring.

Bismarck herring A herring fillet cured in vinegar, salt, onions and sugar.

bisque (beesk) A thick French cream soup made of puréed fish, shellfish, poultry, meat or vegetables and traditionally thickened with rice.

bisque ice cream High-butter-fat-content ice cream with dried macaroons or sponge cake crumbs.

bistec (bees-TAYK) Spanish for beefsteak.

bistecca (bee-STAKE-ah) Italian for beefsteak.

bistecca alla Fiorentina (bee-STAKE-ah al-lah fee-or-en-tine-ah) An Italian dish of a broiled or grilled steak seasoned with olive oil and lemon.

bistecca alla pizzaiola (bee-STAKE-ah al-lah pee-tsa-ee-oh-la) An Italian dish of beefsteak sautéed in olive oil and served in a sauce of tomatoes, garlic and oregano.

bisteeya *See* b'steeya.

bistort, common A perennial herb (*Polygonaceae bistorta*) with a snakelike rhizome, an erect, unbranched stem, slender pointed leaves and pink flowers arranged in a dense terminal spike; the rhizome is used for medicinal purposes or eaten after soaking and roasting, and the young leaves are used in salads or cooked like spinach; also known as snakeroot.

bistro (BEES-troh) A small, casual cafe, usually serving relatively simple food and wine.

bistro knife *See* baker's bread cutter.

biswa tulsi (bees-vah tool-see) Hindi for sweet basil, the common market variety.

bita smietana (bee-tah sh-myeh-tah-nah) A Polish dish of sour cream whipped with sugar flavored with vanilla beans; usually served with rice and soft fruit.

bitki (beet-kee) Polish and Russian meatballs made with beef, fried onions and milk-soaked bread crumbs; they are floured, broiled or fried and served with sour cream and potatoes.

bittara appa (beh-ta-rah aa-up-pa) A Sri Lankan breakfast dish consisting of string hoppers cooked with a whole egg broken into the center. *See* appa.

bitter 1. A harsh, relatively disagreeable acrid flavor. 2. A wine-tasting term for a sharp, unpleasant flavor caused by excessive tannin levels or other factors. 3. A British amber-colored, heavily hopped, dry (rather than bitter), cask-conditioned ale; usually served on draft. 4. A beer-tasting term for a sharp, slightly sour flavor caused by excessive hops.

bitter almond oil An oil extracted from bitter almond seeds that contains traces of lethal prussic acid; processed bitter almond oil is used as a flavoring ingredient in extracts, liqueurs and orgeat but is illegal in the United States.

bitterballen (bee-teht-BAHL-lehn) A Dutch dish consisting of meatballs flavored with Worcestershire sauce, onions, parsley and nutmeg and cooked with a thick white sauce, coated with bread crumbs, deep-fried and served hot with mustard.

bitter chocolate *See* baking chocolate.

bittering hops 1. Hops used to add bitterness, but not aroma or flavor, to beer. 2. Hop varieties with high alpha acid content bred for this purpose.

bitter leaf A leafy plant with a bitter flavor; used like spinach in Nigerian cuisine.

bitter melon A long, cylindrical, bumpy-skinned fruit native to China and used like a vegetable; it has a yellow-green skin, a silvery-green flesh, brown seeds and a delicate, mild flavor; it becomes bitter and turns yellow-orange as it ages; also known as a balsam pear.

bitter orange *See* Seville orange.

bitters A liquid made by distillation and infusion using herbs, spices and aromatics blended with a spirit base (usually rum); it is used as an aperitif, digestif, cocktail ingredient and home remedy for fevers and other ills.

bittersweet chocolate Chocolate containing minimal amounts of sugar and at least 35% chocolate liquor; eaten as a candy or used in pastries and confections. *See* chocolate-making process.

bivalves A general category of mollusks characterized by a soft body contained within two bilateral shells attached at a single hinge by a muscle; includes clams, cockles, mussels, oysters and scallops.

biwa (bee-wah) Japanese for loquat.

bixin *See* annatto.

biyar (bee-jar) Hindi for beer.

Biza (bee-tza) A cheese made without rennet by Iraqi herdsman from skimmed ewe's milk and flavored with onions and garlic; also known as Fajy.

bizari (be-tza-ree) Swahili for curry.

bizcochitos (bees-koh-chee-tohs) Mexican anise-flavored cookies topped with sugar and cinnamon.

biznaga (bees-na-ga) Bland and sweet candied cactus (*Echniocactus grandis*) pods; used in Mexican cuisines for their bland flavor in meat stuffings, or, if sweetened, in desserts and sweet tamales.

blachan *See* balachan.

black abalone A variety of abalone found along the U.S. West Coast; it has a large, smooth, ovoid blackish shell and an ivory flesh with a chewy texture and mild flavor.

Black Amber plum A variety of Japanese plum; the large fruit have a dark purple, almost black skin, a firm, amber-colored flesh and a sweet flavor.

Black and Tan 1. A layered mixture of equal amounts of stout (on the top) and pale ale (on the bottom). 2. In Ireland, a layered mixture of equal amounts of stout (on the top) and a sparkling white wine (on the bottom). *See* Black Velvet.

black and white 1. A soda fountain concoction mixing chocolate and vanilla flavors, such as a chocolate soda with vanilla ice cream, a chocolate milk shake with vanilla ice cream or a vanilla ice cream sundae and chocolate sauce. 2. Black coffee with a container of cream on the side.

black and whites Restaurant slang for a waiter's tuxedo.

Black Angus *See* Aberdeen Angus.

blackback flounder A member of the flounder family found in the Atlantic Ocean from Georgia to Canada; it has a dark brownish-black skin on top, a firm white flesh, a delicate flavor and an average weight of 1–2 lb. (450–900 g); also known as a winter flounder. *See* lemon sole.

black bean A relatively large, dried bean with black skin, a cream-colored flesh and a sweet flavor; also called a turtle bean.

Black Beauty eggplant A variety of very large, purple-skinned Western eggplant.

blackberry A large shiny berry (*Rubus fruticosus*) with a deep purple, almost black color and a sweet flavor; also known as a bramble berry.

black Betty A 19th-century term for a bottle of whiskey passed among special occasion guests.

black bile *See* humors.

black bottom pie A rich custard pie made with a layer of dark chocolate custard on the bottom topped with a layer of white rum custard.

black bread A dark European-style peasant bread made with dark rye, molasses, cocoa, coffee and dark toasted bread crumbs.

black bryony (bree-ohn-nee) A plant (*Tamus commus*) whose young, slender asparagus-like shoots are eaten boiled in French cuisine (the shoots become poisonous as the plant ages); also known as repounsous (France).

black buffalo fish *See* buffalo fish.

black bun A traditional Scottish New Year's cake made of dried and candied fruit and spices enclosed in a rich pastry crust.

black butter *See* beurre noir.

black cake; black fruitcake A very dark, spicy fruitcake made with molasses; also known as English fruitcake.

blackcap 1. A variety of Japanese wineberry grown in the American Northwest; the small fruit have a purple-black color and a sweet flavor. 2. An imprecise term for any of a variety of purple- or black-colored raspberries; also known as a black raspberry.

black cod *See* sablefish.

black cow 1. Slang for an ice cream soda made with vanilla ice cream and some type of dark soda, such as root beer, chocolate soda or sarsaparilla. 2. Diner slang for chocolate milk.

black crappie *See* crappie.

black croaker *See* drum.

black cumin *See* nigella.

black currants *See* currants.

black currant syrup A sweetened syrup made from black currants and used as a flavoring agent in beverages and desserts; also known as sirop de cassis.

Black Death Vodka A Belgian vodka made entirely from sugar beets, based on an Icelandic recipe.

black drink A drink prepared by U.S. Gulf states Indians from the leaves of the *Ilex cassine;* used as a purification medicine, it sometimes induces a nervous state of mind; also known as yaupon by the Catawba Indians, saai-lupuputski by the Creeks and black tea or Carolina tea by English settlers and colonists.

black drum *See* drum.

black egg A variety of small, ovoid, dark-skinned Asian eggplant.

black elder The small, red-black berries of this tree (genus *Sambucus*), which grows in France, are used for syrup; its flowers are fermented in wine and served as a confection.

blackened A Cajun cooking method in which food, usually meat or fish, is rubbed with a spice mixture and cooked in a very hot cast-iron skillet, giving the food an extra-crisp crust.

black-eyed pea The seed of a member of the pea family (*Vigna sinensis*) native to China; it is small and beige, with a black circular eye on the curved edge, and used in American southern and Chinese cuisines; also known as a cow-pea (it was first planted in the United States as fodder). *See* yellow-eyed pea.

blackfish A fish found in the Pacific Ocean and used in Chinese cuisines; it has a lean flesh, a delicate flavor and many fine bones; also known as black trout and Chinese steelhead.

Black Forest ham A German smoked boneless ham with a blackened skin; traditionally, the color came from smoking the ham with resin-containing woods; also achieved by dipping the ham in cow's blood or soaking it in a caramel solution.

black forest mushroom *See* shiitake.

Black Forest torte A dessert made by layering Kirsch-soaked chocolate genoise with sour cherries and sweetened whipped cream.

black grouper A variety of Atlantic grouper found from Florida to Brazil; it has a blackish-brown skin with pale stripes, an average market weight of 10–20 lb. (4.3–8.6 kg) and a mild flavor.

black hake *See* hake.

Black Hawk raspberry A raspberry variety; the fruit are purplish-black, firm, juicy and flavorful.

Black Ischia fig A particularly flavorful and meaty variety of dark-skinned fig.

Black Krim A Russian variety of tomato that has a deep red, shiny skin, heavy green shoulders, a reddish-green flesh and a sweet, rich flavor.

black loganberry A variety of loganberry grown in New Zealand.

black malt Malted barley that has been roasted for a long time at a high temperature; it has a near black color and adds a bittersweet flavor to beer brewed from it.

black Mission fig A variety of fig with blue-black skin and crimson flesh.

blackmouth salmon *See* chinook salmon.

black mullet *See* mullet.

black mustard An annual herb of the cabbage family (*Brassica nigra*) with an erect, branched stem and yellow flowers; the seeds are ground as a spice; native to Europe and Asia, it is used as a condiment and for medicinal purposes.

black peppercorn *See* peppercorn, black.

Black Persian mulberry A variety of black mulberry with long, sweet, black-skinned fruit.

Black Plum An heirloom variety of a cherry tomato with an elongated shape, a deep mahogany to brown color and an excellent flavor.

Black Prince A Russian variety of small tomato that has a deep, garnet-red skin, a juicy green flesh and a rich, sweet flavor.

black pudding An Irish blood sausage. *See* blood sausage.

black raspberry *See* blackcap *and* thimbleberry.

black rice 1. A rice, grown in Indonesia and the Philippines, with a long black grain and a nutty flavor; often used in puddings and cakes. 2. Unpolished rice.

black rooster *See* gallo nero.

Black Russian A cocktail made of vodka and a coffee-flavored liqueur, such as Kahlua, served over ice.

Black Russian Bear A cocktail made of vodka, dark créme de cacao and heavy cream.

black salsify (SAL-sih-fee) *See* scorzonera.

black salt A salt with small quantities of other minerals; it has a reddish-gray color and a flavor similar to slightly sour, salty mineral water.

Black Satin Thornless blackberry A blackberry variety; the fruit are relatively large and sweet.

black sea bass A true bass found in the Atlantic Ocean from Cape Cod to North Carolina; it has a smoky gray to dusky brown skin, a firm, white, flaky flesh, a delicate, mild flavor and an average weight of 1.5 lb. (680 g); also known as a rock sea bass. *See* giant sea bass.

black sole *See* sole, Dover.

Black Tartarian cherry A variety of sweet cherry; the fruit has a dark red to purplish skin, a thick, tender flesh and a rich flavor.

black tea One of the three principal types of tea; the leaves are rolled and fully fermented before being heated and dried; the beverage is generally a dark reddish-brown color with a strong, full flavor. *See* green tea, oolong tea *and* black drink.

Blackthorn A cocktail made of Irish whiskey, dry vermouth, Pernod and Angostura bitters.

blackthorn plum *See* sloeberry.

blacktip shark *See* shark.

black trout *See* blackfish.

Black Velvet A drink made from equal amounts of stout and sparkling wine. *See* Black and Tan.

black vinegar A dark, mild, slightly sweet vinegar made from glutinous rice or sorghum; its flavor ranges from smoky to wine-yeasty.

black walnut A native American nut (*Juglans nigra*) with a very hard black shell, a strong, slightly bitter flavor and a high fat content; it is not as popular as the English walnut. *See* white walnut.

bladder 1. The sac that holds urine until it is eliminated. 2. A membranous bag from animals (usually pigs) sometimes used to hold foods during cooking.

bladder cherry *See* winter cherry.

bladder wrack A tropical plant with long clusters of green, white, red or black grapelike fruit; its juice has a sour flavor and can be eaten fresh or fermented into a winelike beverage.

blade *See* knife blade.

bladebone The scapula; the principal bone in the shoulder. *See* chuck.

blade chops A fabricated cut of the pork primal Boston butt and the lamb primal shoulder; it is tough and contains a large percentage of bone; also known as arm chops.

blade meat A subprimal cut of the beef primal rib; it is the lean flesh overlying the rib eye and ribs; also known as cap meat, deckle meat, false meat, rib lifter meat and wedge meat.

blade roast; blade pot roast A subprimal cut of the beef primal chuck; generally lean, tough and flavorful.

blade steak 1. A fabricated cut of the beef primal chuck; it is a relatively tough steak. 2. A fabricated cut of the pork primal Boston butt; it is a relatively tender steak.

bladselleir (blahd-sell-ayr) Danish for celery.

blaff A Caribbean fish stew seasoned with onions, chile and lemon juice and served over rice.

blakhan (blah-kahn) A strong and pungent Indonesian shrimp paste.

blanc de blanc (blanh duh blanh) 1. White wine made from white grapes. 2. In France's Champagne district, it refers to a light-bodied, delicate Champagne made entirely from Chardonnay grapes.

blanc de noirs (blanh duh n'wahr) 1. White wine made from black grapes. 2. A sparkling wine or Champagne made almost entirely from Pinot Noir grapes.

Blanc Fume (blahn foo-may) *See* Sauvignon Blanc.

blanching Cooking a food very briefly and partially in boiling water or hot fat; generally used to assist preparation (e.g., loosen peels), as part of a combination cooking method, to remove undesirable flavors or to prepare food for freezing.

blanching pot An assemblage of two pots: a smaller pot with perforated sides and bottom and a larger pot that holds the cooking liquid; food is placed in the smaller pot, which is submerged in the larger one; once the food is cooked, the inner pot is removed and the liquid drains away.

blancmange (BLAHNG-mahnzh) A French milk pudding or custard, usually flavored with almonds.

bland A tasting term for a food that is flat, dull and lacks flavor and/or finesse.

bland diet A hospital diet in which the food is seasoned with a minimum of salt but no other seasonings and portion size is carefully controlled.

blanket letter A Dutch Christmas cookie made in the shape of a letter of the alphabet.

blanquette (blahn-KEHT) A French white stew made with veal, lamb or chicken, mushrooms and small white onions; the meat is not browned and is cooked in a white stock; the dish is finished with egg yolk and cream.

blanquette d'agneau (blahn-KEHT dan-yoh) A French stew of lamb and vegetables; it is garnished with mushrooms and onions and served in a cream sauce.

Blanquette de Limoux (blahn-KEHT duh lee-moo) The most celebrated sparkling wine produced in the south of France; it is made from the Mauzac grape using traditional methods.

blanquette de veau (blahn-KEHT duh voh) A French stew of veal; it is garnished with mushrooms and onions and served in a cream sauce.

Blarney (blahr-nee) An Irish Emmental-style cheese made from cow's milk; it has a mild, buttery flavor and a bright yellow interior with numerous eyes; sold in red paraffin–coated wheels.

blaskjell (blahs-shell) Norwegian for mussel.

blast frozen Food frozen rapidly at extremely low temperatures (−10°F [−23.3°C] or lower) while air circulates around the item at high velocity.

blatjang A spiced, vinegar-based condiment used with some Cape Malay dishes.

Blatterteig (blatter-tig) German for puff pastry.

Blaubeeren (blaw-bear-ren) German for blueberries.

Blauer Limberger *See* Blaufrankisch.

Blaufrankisch (blaw-FRAHN-keesh) A grape widely planted in Austria and used to produce a light, acidic red wine; it is also cultivated in Germany, where it is known as Blauer Limberger.

Blaukraut (blaw-krowt) German for red cabbage; also known as Rotkohl and Rotkraut.

Blauschimmelkäse (blaw-she-mehl-kaize) German for blue cheese.

blé (blay) French for wheat.

bleached flour Flour that has been whitened by removing the yellow pigment; flour can be bleached through aging or by adding bleaching and oxidizing agents.

bleaching agent A type of food additive used to whiten processed foods such as flour or cheese to improve appearance.

bleeding A bakeshop term used to describe a dough (unbaked) that has been cut and left unsealed at the cut, thus permitting air and gas to escape.

blend *v.* 1. To mix two or more ingredients together until uniformly combined. 2. To combine different varieties or grades of an item to obtain a mixture of a particular character, quality and/or consistancy. *n.* A mixture of two or more flavors or other attributes.

blended bourbon Bourbon containing not less than 51% straight bourbon.

blended light whiskey; light whiskey Whiskey containing less than 20% straight whiskey.

blended rye A rye produced by combining two or more straight ryes; at least 20% of the final product must be from a single straight rye.

blended Scotch A Scotch whisky produced by combining malt whiskys (usually 20–50% of the final product) with grain whiskys; it is smoother, better balanced and of more uniform quality than a single-malt whisky.

blended whiskey 1. A mixture of at least 20% straight whiskey and varying amounts of neutral spirits or light whiskeys (its proof is adjusted with distilled water) or whiskeys distilled during different distillation periods; generally has a lighter flavor and body than a straight whiskey. *See* straight whiskey. 2. A whiskey blended from two or more straight whiskeys; at least 20% of the product must be from a single straight whiskey.

blender An appliance used to chop, blend, purée or liquefy foods; has a tall narrow container, usually with a lid and handle, that sits on top of a driveshaft and has a four-pronged rotating blade at its bottom. *See* immersion blender *and* vertical cutter/mixer (VCM).

blending 1. A mixing method in which two or more ingredients are combined just until they are evenly distributed; a spoon, rubber spatula, whisk or electric mixer with its paddle attachment is used. 2. Mixing two or more wines made from different grape varieties, vineyards and/or vintages; they should have different or complementary characteristics to achieve a more uniform quality. 3. Using an electric blender to incorporate ingredients into a cocktail. 4. Combining various tobaccos to achieve a consistent desired flavor and strength of a cigar.

blending fork A large fork with sharp blades on the backs of the tines; used for incorporating fat into flour.

blending fork

Blenheim apricot An apricot variety; the fruit are of a medium to large size with an orange-yellow skin and flesh and a sweet flavor.

Blenheim Orange A large pippin apple; it has a dull yellow and red skin, crisp flesh and a slightly acidic flavor; popular in early 19th-century England.

blenny (BLEN-ee) A group of scaleless freshwater or saltwater fish (the body is covered with a mucous membrane); it has an average market length of 4–6 in. (10–15 cm) and white flesh with a mild flavor.

blé noir (blay nwahr) *See* sarrasin.

blessed thistle An annual herb (*Cnicus benedictus*) with a branched, spreading, hairy stem, toothed hairy leaves and a single yellow flower; the stem and leaves are used to make bitter liqueurs and for medicinal purposes, the tender young shoots are eaten like artichokes and the leaves are added to salads.

bleu (bluh) *See* very rare.

Bleu; Fromage Bleu (bleuh; froh-MAHZ bleuh) 1. A French term for a group of Roquefort-style blue-veined cheeses made in France's Roquefort region from milk other than ewe's milk. 2. A French term for blue-veined cheeses made elsewhere in France regardless of the kind of milk used. *See* blue cheese.

bleu cheese *See* blue cheese.

Bleu d'Auvergne (blur d'oa-veh-awng-yeh) A creamy blue cheese made in France's Auvergne region; it has a pale ivory interior with dark blue marbling and a clean, sharp flavor.

Bleu de Bresse (bleuh dah bres-say) A creamy French blue cheese made from cow's milk; it has a whitish interior with blue streaks or splotches and a slightly spicy flavor.

Bleu de Cantal *See* Cantal.

Bleu de Haut Jura (bleuh dah oat giv-raw) A hard blue cheese made in France's Jura Mountains region from cow's milk; it has an ivory interior with blue streaks and a tangy, savory, relatively mild flavor; local varieties include Bleu de Gex and Bleu de Septmoncel.

Bleu des Causses (bluh duh KOSE) A French cow's milk cheese with a rindless, salty exterior, a bone-white, blue-veined, moist, slightly crumbly interior and a strong flavor and aroma.

blewit A wild mushroom (*Clitocybe nuda*) particularly popular in Great Britain; it has a lilac-colored stem and cap and a subtle, fresh flavor; also known as a woodblewit.

blinchiki s tvorogom (bleen-che-kee sa tva-rah-gome) A Russian dish consisting of pancakes cooked on one side and filled with a mixture of tvorog (curds), eggs, sugar, lemon peel, butter and sultanas, then folded and fried; served with meat or eaten instead of cheese.

blinde vinken (BLIN-duh VING-kuh) A Dutch dish of veal cutlets stuffed with a hard-boiled egg, fried onions and parsley or ground veal mixed with egg and bread crumbs; the cutlets are browned and then simmered with lemon slices and water.

blind pig *See* blind tiger.

blind receiving The receipt of goods that are either unaccompanied by an invoice or accompanied by an invoice that does not identify quantity, weight, quality and/or price; the receiver must count, weigh, examine, record and/or otherwise inspect each item.

blind tasting A method of evaluating foods or beverages (both alcoholic and nonalcoholic) without knowing the product's name, place of origin, principal or distinguishing ingredients or other identifying information.

blind tiger; blind pig Slang for an establishment selling illegally made spirits during Prohibition.

blini (blee-nee) Leavened Russian pancakes made from a buckwheat and wheat flour batter; they are usually served as hors d'oeuvre with sour cream and caviar or smoked fish; singular is blin.

blini pan A shallow pan with a heavy bottom, sloping sides and a smooth surface; used to make blini with a 3.75-in. diameter. *See* crêpe pan.

blini pan

blintz A very thin, tender Jewish pancake filled with fruit and/or cheese, then baked or sautéed.

bloater A salted and smoked herring.

bloater paste Baked, pounded bloaters mixed with butter and used as a condiment.

bloemkool (BLOOM-kohl) Dutch for cauliflower.

blomkål (BLOOM-koal) Norwegian for cauliflower.

blond de veau (blon duh voh) A concentrated veal broth used in French cuisine for soups and sauces; it forms a jelly when cold and is used for a chaud froid or any sauce that should set when chilled.

blond de volaille (blon duh voh-LIE) A concentrated chicken broth used in French cuisine for soups and sauces and for braising vegetables; it forms a jelly when cold and is used for a chaud froid or any sauce that should set when chilled.

Blonde d'Aquitaine (blon dah-quee-tahn) A breed of beef cattle with golden skin originally from southwestern France; its meat is generally lean.

blondir (blohn-dee) French for to cook lightly in fat.

blond sauce *See* velouté, sauce.

blood 1. The fluid that circulates through the heart, arteries, veins and capillaries of mammals, birds and fish, carrying nourishment, oxygen, heat, vitamins and other essential chemical substances; principally composed of a fluid medium (plasma) with red and white corpuscles (blood cells) and platelets. *See* humors. 2. The blood of certain animals is used to make black pudding and to thicken dishes called civet.

blood alcohol level The amount of alcohol found in the human body at a given time; it reflects the amount of alcohol a person has consumed and is expressed as a percentage of the alcohol in the blood by volume.

blood cholesterol Cholesterol found in the bloodstream; the measure of blood cholesterol level is used as an indicator of a person's risk for cardiovascular disease.

blood orange A medium-sized orange with a red or red-streaked white flesh (the color reflects a pigment, anthocyanin, not normally present in citrus); it has a sweet flavor that is less tart than that of a typical orange.

blood sausage; blood pudding A black-colored sausage generally made from hog's blood, bread crumbs, suet and oatmeal; sometimes rice is added; usually available as large links; also known as black pudding.

blood sugar *See* glucose.

Bloody Bull A cocktail made of tomato juice, vodka, lemon juice, Tabasco sauce, Worcestershire sauce, white pepper and beef bouillon, broth or consommé.

Bloody Mary A cocktail made of tomato juice, vodka, spices, seasonings and sometimes lemon juice; it is served over ice with a celery stalk swizzle stick. *See* Virgin Mary.

bloom 1. A dull gray film or grayish-whitish streaks that sometimes appear on chocolate if the cocoa butter separates; the chocolate's flavor and cooking properties are not affected; also known as chocolate bloom and fat bloom. 2. A measure of gelatin's strength. 3. The process of softening gelatin in a cool liquid before it is dissolved.

bloomy rind The white downy rind that develops on certain surface-ripened cheeses such as Brie and some chevres; it is formed by spraying the cheese's surface with spores of *Penicillium candidum* mold during curing.

blowby; blow-off A single-stage home beer-brewing method utilizing a plastic tube with one end inserted into a carboy and the other end submerged into a pail of sterile water so that any unwanted residue is expelled while air is prevented from coming into contact with the fermenting beer.

blown sugar A boiled mixture of sucrose, glucose and tartaric acid colored and shaped using an air pump; used to make decorative objects (e.g., fruits) and containers.

blue agave tequila; 100% blue agave tequila A tequila made from only the fermented and distilled juices of the blue agave (a variety of maguey); it must meet certain Mexican governmental standards.

blueback *See* lake herring.

blueback salmon *See* sockeye salmon.

blueberry A small berry (*Vaccinium corymbosum*) native to North America; it has a smooth skin, a blue to blue-black color, a juicy light gray-blue flesh and a sweet flavor; it is eaten raw, used in baked goods or made into jams and jellies.

blueberry, high-bush Any of a variety of large cultivated blueberry; also known as swamp blueberry.

blueberry, low-bush Any of a variety of small wild blueberry; also known as early blueberry.

Blue Blazer A cocktail made of Scotch whisky and honey; at service time, it is ignited to form a blue blaze that is passed back and forth from one mug to another.

Blue Cap Chimay *See* Chimay.

blue cheese 1. A generic term for any cheese containing visible blue-green molds that contribute a characteristic tart, sharp flavor and aroma; also known as a blue-veined cheese or bleu cheese. 2. A group of Roquefort-style cheeses made in the United States and Canada from cow's or goat's milk rather than ewe's milk and injected with molds that form blue-green veins; also known as blue mold cheese or blue-veined cheese.

blue cheese dressing A salad dressing made with a blue-veined cheese (other than Roquefort), heavy cream or sour cream, lemon juice, chives, Worcestershire sauce and Tabasco sauce. *See* Roquefort dressing.

Blue Cheshire *See* Cheshire.

blue cod *See* lingcod *and* pollock, American.

blue crab A variety of crab found in the Atlantic Ocean off the U.S. East Coast and the coast of Europe from France to Denmark as well as in the Gulf of Mexico; it has blue claws and an oval, dark blue-green hard shell, an average market diameter of 4–7 in. (10–18 cm) and a rich, sweet flavor; available in hard and soft shells, it accounts for most of the crab consumed in the United States and is sometimes referred to simply as crab. *See* buckram, peeler crab *and* various listings under crab.

bluefin tuna A variety of tuna found in the Pacific and Atlantic Oceans off North America; it has a deep blue-green skin, an ivory pink flesh, a rich flavor and an average market weight of 15–80 lb. (6.8–36 kg); used for sashimi.

bluefish A saltwater fish; it has a blue-green skin on top that fades to silver on the belly, an average market weight of 3–6 lb. (1.4–2.7 kg), high fat content and dark flesh with a delicate flavor; also known as a blue runner.

Bluefort A factory-made Canadian blue cheese.

bluegill; bluegill crappie A freshwater fish and member of the sunfish family found throughout the United States; it has a black spot on the dorsal fin, a blue-black ear flap and an average market weight of 0.5 lb. (225 g).

blue meat Slang for meat from an unweaned calf.

blue mold cheese; blue-veined cheese *See* blue cheese.

Blue Mountain Arabica coffee beans grown in Jamaica's Blue Mountain region; the beverage is mild, smooth and expensive.

blue mussel A variety of mussels found wild along the U.S. East Coast and aquafarmed on both coasts; it has a dark blue, elongated ovoid shell, orangish-yellow plump meat with a firm texture and a sweet flavor (the meat of a wild blue mussel is much smaller than that of a cultivated blue mussel).

blue no. 1 *See* coloring agent.

blue plate special A menu term, generally at an inexpensive restaurant, for the day's special; it is usually an entire meal (appetizer or soup, entrée, dessert and beverage).

bluepoint oyster; blue point oyster 1. An Atlantic oyster found in Long Island's Great South Bay; it has a squarish shell with a length of 5–6 in. (12–15 cm) and a plump flesh. 2. An imprecisely used term for any medium-sized Atlantic oyster.

blue potato *See* purple potato.

blue quail A variety of quail found in the American Southwest.

blue runner *See* bluefish.

Blue Shropshire A firm cheese made in Leicestershire, England, from pasteurized cow's milk; it has a blue-veined interior, a speckled brown rind and a mild, savory flavor.

blue vinney; blue vinny A hard, dry English cheese made from partly skimmed cow's milk with an ivory interior streaked with mottled blue veins, a crusty brownish rind, a sharp sour flavor and a strong aftertaste; also known as Dorset and Dorset Blue.

bluggoe fig (blue-goh-ah) A variety of bananas grown in the Caribbean; the fruit has a reddish-purple color and is used like a vegetable; also known as a bird fig.

Blumenkohl (BLOO-mern-kohl) German for cauliflower.

blush wine 1. A slightly sweet, light-bodied white wine made from black grapes such as Zinfandel, Pinot Noir or Cabernet Sauvignon; its color ranges from pale salmon to pink. 2. A wine blended from red and white wines; also known as a light rosé.

blutig (blue-teeg) German for undercooked and used to describe meat cooked too rare.

Blutwürst (BLOOT-voorst) A German blood sausage made from hog's blood, pork, pork fat and seasonings; it has a dark brown color and is cooked and smoked.

BMR *See* basal metabolic rate.

Boal *See* Bual.

boar An uncastrated male swine. *See* pig, sow *and* wild boar.

boardinghouse meat Slang for meat from an unweaned calf.

Bobby Burns A cocktail made of Scotch whisky, sweet vermouth and Benedictine.

bobi Russian for beans.

bobici (boh-BEE-chee) An Italian soup containing beans, corn, potatoes and ham.

bobotee An American puddinglike dish of milk, bread crumbs, onions, almonds and hot sauce.

bobotie (BOH-boh-tee) A South African meat pie consisting of soaked bread, milk, onions, minced cooked lamb and almonds flavored with garlic, curry powder, tamarind liquid, lemon leaves and bay leaves; it is served with rice and chutney.

bob veal; bobby Meat from calves slaughtered when very young (usually less than 21 days old); it has a lean, light pink flesh, a very delicate flavor and an extremely tender texture. *See* beef *and* calf.

bobwhite A variety of quail found in the eastern United States.

bocaccio (boh-kah-chee-oh) A member of the rockfish family found off the U.S. West Coast and western Canada; it has a red-flushed light green to dark brown skin, often with black spots, a market length of 34 in. (85 cm) and a firm, white flesh with a mild flavor.

bocadillo (bow-kah-dee-loh) Spanish for sandwich.

bócài (baw-tsai) Chinese for spinach.

bocconcini (buh-CON-chee-ny) 1. An Italian dish consisting of slices of veal, ham and Gruyère rolled together, fried and served with tomato sauce. 2. Italian for small mouthfuls and used to describe short, grooved tubes of pasta. 3. Fresh mozzarella cheese shaped into small balls, about 1 in. in diameter.

boccone squadrista (boh-ko-nae squah-dree-stah) An Italian dish consisting of fish cooked between slices of apple, sprinkled with rum and flamed for service.

böcek (bean-check) Turkish for crayfish.

bo cha dum (bow chah duhm) A Vietnamese dish of ground beef, clear noodles and tree ear mushrooms formed into a large ball and steamed.

bock beer (bok) A dark, sweet, full-bodied lager beer traditionally brewed during the spring in Germany.

Bocksbeutel (BAWKS-boy-tel) A squat, flat-sided flagon in which Franconian white wines (Steinwein) and other German wines are traditionally bottled; the bottle is presumably named for its resemblance to a goat's scrotum.

boczek (boh-chehk) Polish for spare ribs.

bode (boh-duh) Portuguese for a male goat.

bodega (bo-DAY-gah) 1. A Spanish ground-level wine warehouse or winery. 2. Spanish for a small grocery store.

Bodengeschmack (boh-dan-ghesh-mack) German wine-tasting term for earthy.

body 1. A tasting term used to describe the feel or weight of a food on the palate or the feel of a food to the touch; it can be firm, springy, supple, elastic, runny, grainy and so on. 2. A tasting term used to describe the feel and weight of a beverage on the palate; it can range from a full body to a light body (watery). 3. The consistency of something. 4. The entire physical structure of an organism. 5. The torso or trunk of an animal. 6. *See* strength.

bodying agent *See* thickening agents.

boeren jongens; boren jongens (BORE-en yohn-gans) A Dutch–American beverage made from whiskey and raisins, traditionally served at Christmas.

Boerenkaas (BORE-en-kahss) 1. A Dutch cow's milk cheese; semifirm to rock hard with a natural burnished golden rind and beige-yellow interior, it has a rich, sharp, complex flavor and a nutty aroma; also known as Farmer's Gouda. 2. Dutch for farmer cheese; the term is stamped on Gouda cheeses made on farms in the dairy region of Gouda, Holland.

boeuf (buhf) French for beef.

boeuf à la ficelle (buhf ah lah fee-seel-lae) French for beef on a thread and used to describe a beef filet tied with string to resemble a rolled roast; the string is tied to a wooden spoon that is used to suspend the meat over a saucepan, where it is immersed in a vegetable broth and boiled until done; it is served with sea salt, pepper, mustard and gherkins.

boeuf à la mode (buhf ah lah mod) A French beef stew with vegetables.

boeuf bourguignon (buhf bor-geen-yohn) A French dish of beef braised in red wine and garnished with onions and mushrooms.

bofu (boo-who) A Japanese garnish for sushi and sashimi consisting of the red stems of young parsnips split lengthwise into quarters and curled in ice water.

boga (bow-gah) Swahili for pumpkin.

bogavante (bow-gah-ban-tae) Spanish for a large-clawed lobster.

bogbean A perennial herb (*Menyanthese trifoliata*) with a thick rhizome, trifoliate leaves and numerous five-lobed white or pinkish flowers; the bitter-tasting leaves were traditionally used for making beer and for herbal cigarettes; also known as buckbean.

bogobe (boh-goh-bee) A staple of Botswana cuisine, it is a thick cornmeal porridge, sometimes flavored with chiles.

Bohea (bo-hee) 1. Originally, one of the highest grades of Chinese black tea. 2. Now, the lowest-quality Chinese black tea made from the season's last crop of leaves.

bòhetáng (boh-ha-tang) Chinese for mint.

Bohnen (BOA-nern) German for beans (a generic term that includes a large variety of fresh, canned and dried beans).

Bohnenkraut (BOA-nern-krowt) German for summer savory.

boi (boy) Portuguese for ox.

boil; boiling *v.* To cook by boiling. *n.* 1. A moist-heat cooking method that uses convection to transfer heat from a hot (approximately 212° F [100° C]) liquid to the food submerged in it; the turbulent waters and higher temperatures cook foods more quickly than do poaching and simmering. 2. The first step in brewing beer after mashing and sparing when the hops are added and the wort is bittered.

boil, full rolling Large bubbles rise and break on the surface of the heated liquid so rapidly that vigorous stirring does not interfere.

boil, steady Medium-sized to large bubbles rise regularly to the surface of the heated liquid and break there, but reduced bubbling occurs when the liquid is stirred.

boil down To reduce or concentrate a liquid by heating it until the desired amount of moisture is removed through evaporation.

boiled candy A candy made by boiling sugar, butter and a flavoring, usually peppermint.

boiled custard 1. An egg and milk custard cooked on the stove top rather than baked in the oven. 2. A beverage from the American South made from an egg and milk custard, similar to eggnog.

boiled dinner *See* New England boiled dinner.

boiled dressing A type of mayonnaise made by cooking salt, mustard, sugar, cayenne, flour, egg, milk, butter and vinegar until thickened; it is then strained and cooled.

boiled icing *See* Italian meringue.

boiled-whey cheese A cheese made from whey that is cooked slowly to impart a caramel flavor to the finished product. *See* whey cheese.

boiler The container used for boiling either clarified wort or cooked mash for brewing or distilling; more specifically called a still, kettle, evaporator or cooker.

Boilermaker A straight shot of a distilled spirit (traditionally whiskey) either followed by a beer chaser or poured into a glass of beer.

boiler onion A small, tender onion with a white outer layer, a white flesh and a mild flavor; usually creamed or used in casseroles, soups and stews.

boiling firepot *See* Mongolian hot pot.

boiling fowl *See* chicken, stewing.

boiling meat A fabricated cut from the beef primal short plate; it is quite fatty.

boiling point The temperature at which a liquid reaches a boil; the boiling point varies depending on the specific gravity of the substance and the altitude.

ALTITUDE	BOILING POINT OF WATER	
Sea level	212° F	100° C
2,000 feet	208° F	98° C
5,000 feet	203° F	95° C
7,500 feet	198° F	92° C
10,000 feet	194° F	90° C

boiling potato *See* red potato, white potato, round *and* potato, waxy.

boil to a height Boiling to the point of candying or crystallizing.

boisson (bwa-sohn) French for a beverage.

boîte nature (bwoh-tay nah-tur) French for natural box and used to describe a cedar cigar box.

bok choy A member of the cabbage family native to southern China; it has long, wide, white, crunchy stalks with tender, smooth-edged, dark green leaves; it is used raw, pickled or cooked; also known as baak choy, Chinese mustard, Chinese white mustard cabbage, celery mustard, pak choi and white mustard cabbage.

Bola (BOH-lah) An Edam-style Portuguese cheese made from cow's milk.

bolacha (boh-LAH-shah) Portuguese for cookies.

bolar A subprimal cut of the beef primal chuck; it is a tough, very lean roast.

bolchi (bohl-chee) A Cuban dish consisting of a marinated pot roast filled with hard-boiled eggs.

bolet (boh-lay) French for boletus.

bolete A wild mushroom (*Boletus edulis*) with a large bulbous stem, a broad bun-shaped cap, a brownish-tan color, a smooth, meaty texture and a pungent, woodsy flavor and aroma; more commonly available dried in the United States.

boletus (boh-le-tus) A genus of wild mushrooms with fleshy caps and stems, ranging in color from white to dark brown; significant varieties include the bolete, cèpe and porcini.

boli-bopa (boh-lee-boh-pah) A Nigerian street food or snack of grilled plantains, cut in cubes and mixed with salted peanuts.

bolinhos de amêndoa (bow-lee-nyos day ah-men-doe-ah) A small Portuguese almond cake.

bolinhos de bacalhau (bow-lee-nyos duh bah-kah-lyeown) A Brazilian dish of deep-fried salt cod and potato fritters flavored with cilantro, green onions, nutmeg and paprika.

bolitas (boh-LEE-tah) Spanish for fritter.

bollabouche; billabusse; bollebuysjes (boh-lah-boo-sha) Tiny puffed Dutch pancakes fried in a special pan with indentations.

boller (boal-er) Danish for dumpling.

bollire (bowl-lee-rae) Italian for to boil.

bollito (bo-lee-to) 1. An Italian dish consisting of a variety of boiled meats, such as calf's head, turkey, beef, veal and/or pork sausages served with green beans and other vegetables. 2. A variety of bean; it is related to the pinto bean, but smaller.

bollitos (boh-yee-TOHS) A Cuban dish consisting of a mixture of black-eyed peas and garlic rolled into balls and deep-fried.

bolo (BOH-loh) Portuguese for cake.

bolo de coco (BOH-loh day coe-coe) A small Portuguese coconut cake.

bologna (bah-LOW-nyah; bah-LOW-nee) A large, highly seasoned sausage made from pork, beef and veal; named for Bologna, Italy (although the Italian sausage associated with that city is mortadella), it is available cooked and usually served cold; also known as baloney.

bolognese (boh-loh-nay-see) An Italian meat sauce for pasta made from ground meat, tomatoes, celery, carrots and bacon and seasoned with garlic, herbs and olive oil; also known as ragù and sugo.

bolognese, alla (boh-loh-nay-see, ahl-lah) Italian term for a food garnished with a tomato and cheese sauce.

bolo rei (BOH-loh ray) Portuguese for king's cake and used to describe a Christmas cake made with a yeast dough and dried fruits and nuts.

bolster The thick band of steel on a forged knife blade; part of the blade, it runs along the heel and up onto the spine; also known as the shoulder.

boluó (baw-luo) Chinese for pineapple.

bomba (bom-bha) A variety of rice grown in the Mediterranean region; particularly Spain; it is nearly round, with a creamy texture after cooking and is generally used for paella.

bombardier ale An English ale with a distinctive rich copper color and a robust, bitter flavor.

Bombay A cocktail made of brandy, dry vermouth, sweet vermouth, curaçao and Pernod; garnished with an orange slice.

Bombay duck A pungent dried, salty fish used in India to flavor curry dishes or crisp fried and eaten as a snack.

Bombay gin An aromatic, dry gin distilled and bottled in London.

Bombay Sapphire gin An extremely dry, aromatic and flavorful superpremium dry gin with a high alcohol content.

bombe; bombe glacée (baum) A French dessert consisting of layers of ice cream and sherbet packed into a round or spherical mold, frozen, then unmolded and decorated for service.

bomber A long-necked beer bottle containing 22 fl. oz.

Bom Petisco (bon peh-tish-coo) A semisoft Portuguese cow's milk cheese.

bon appétit (boh nah-pay-TEE) French for good appetite, meaning I wish you a good meal, hearty appetite or enjoy your meal.

Bonarda (boh-NAHR-dah) A red wine grape grown in Italy's Lombardy and Piedmont regions.

Bonbel (bahn-BEHL) A Saint-Paulin–style cheese made worldwide; it has a pale ivory color, semisoft, buttery texture and a mild flavor; sold in paraffin-coated rounds; a small version is known as Baby Bon.

bonbon (bohn-bohn) 1. A small piece of candy, usually chocolate-coated fondant. 2. French for any bite-sized candy, confection or sweetmeat.

bon chretien (bohn krae-tee-en) French for Bartlett pear.

bondard; bonde; bondon (bohn-dar) Derived from the French for bung and used to describe the small corklike shape of numerous small, soft, double and triple cream cheeses of Normandy and Picardy.

bondiola (bohn-dee-OH-lah) An Italian sausage made with pork and beef and flavored with red wine; it is cooked and may also be smoked.

Bondon (bahn-dahn) A small, fresh French Neufchâtel-style cheese made from whole cow's milk.

Bondost (bohn-ohst) A semisoft Swedish farm cheese (also produced in Wisconsin) made from raw or pasteurized cow's milk and sometimes flavored with cumin or caraway seeds.

bone *v.* To remove a bone from a cut of meat, poultry or fish. *n.* Any of numerous structures forming a vertebrate's skeleton; they are composed of cartilaginous substances and calcareous salts; larger bones have a soft, fatty substance in their center known as marrow.

bone china A white translucent ceramic ware developed in England and made from kaolin, china stone and bone ash fired at an intermediate temperature; can be decorated and is used for fine dishes and serving pieces.

boned; boneless A cut of meat from which the bone has been removed. *See* bone-in.

bone dish A crescent-shaped dish used for fish bones; part of each place setting, it was popular in the United States during the late 1800s and early 1900s.

bonefish A game fish found off Florida; it has a silvery color; also known as banana fish and ladyfish.

bone-in A cut of meat containing the bone. *See* boned.

bone-in brisket A subprimal cut of the beef primal brisket and shank; part of the animal's breast, it is quite fatty.

boneless cross-cut shank A fabricated cut of the beef primal brisket and shank; cut from the foreshank with the bone removed, it has many connective tissues and a high collagen content; used for stock.

boneless riblifter A fabricated cut from the beef primal rib; it is a tender, end-cut rib steak.

boneless rib roast A subprimal cut of the beef primal short loin; it is tender and flavorful and can be fabricated into strip loin steaks.

boneless shoulder roast A subprimal cut of the beef primal chuck; it is tough and flavorful and is sometimes fabricated into boneless shoulder steaks.

boneless strip steak *See* strip loin steak.

boneless veal strip loin A fabricated cut of the veal primal loin; this tender cut is the loin eye muscle removed from the bones.

bone marrow *See* marrow.

bone meal A nutrient supplement derived from bones and intended to supply calcium and other minerals.

bo nhung dam (bow nyoohg dahm) A Vietnamese dish of thinly sliced beef cooked at the table in a vinegar broth.

boniato (bou-nee-AH-toh) *See* sweet potato, white.

boning knife A knife used to separate meat from bones; there are two types: one has a rigid blade 5–7-in. long, and the other has a longer, thinner blade that can be rigid or flexible.

boning knives

bonito (boh-NEE-toa) A variety of tuna found in the western Pacific Ocean; it has a moderate to high fat content, a strong flavor and a weight that generally does not exceed 25 lb. (11.3 kg); often used in Japanese cuisine.

bonne femme; bonne-femme, à la (bun fam) French for good wife and used to describe dishes prepared in a simple, homey, rustic manner and usually served in the dish in which they were cooked (e.g., a casserole).

bonner (BUR-err) Norwegian for beans.

bonnethead shark *See* shark.

bonnyclabber *See* clabber.

bontemps (bohn-tahn) A small wooden bowl used in France's Bordeaux region to beat the egg whites used for fining; it is also the emblem of the French wine fraternity Commanderie des Bontemps du Médoc et des Graves.

bontemps, sauce (bohn-tahn) A French compound sauce made from a velouté flavored with a reduction of onion, paprika, mustard and cider and finished with butter.

bootlegger A person who makes or sells illegal whiskey or other spirits.

boova shenkel (BOO-vah SHEHN-kehl) A Pennsylvania Dutch dish of beef stew with potato dumplings.

booze Slang for whiskey; derived from E. G. Booz, a grocer who bought bourbon whiskey by the barrel and then bottled and sold it.

boqollo (boh-ko-low) Ethiopian for corn.

boquerón (boe-que-rhon) Spanish for fresh anchovies.

borage (BOHR-ihj) An herb (*Borago officinalis*) native to Europe, with downy blue-green leaves and blue flowers; the leaves have a slight cucumber flavor and are used for tisanes and as a flavoring for vegetables, and the flowers are used in salads and for tisanes.

børd (bohr-deh) Norwegian for table.

Bordeaux (bohr-DOH) 1. One of France's six principal grape-growing and wine-producing regions; it is located in southwest France. 2. A French prepared mustard made from black or brown mustard seeds, sugar, vinegar and herbs (principally tarragon); it has a mild aromatic flavor and a dark brown color.

Bordeaux, red Red wines from Bordeaux; the principal grapes used are Cabernet Sauvignon, Cabernet Franc and Merlot and to a lesser extent Malbec and Petit Verdot.

Bordeaux, white White wines from Bordeaux; the principal grapes used are Sauvignon Blanc and Sémillon and to a lesser extent Muscadelle, Colombard and Ugni Blanc.

bordeaux bottle A wine bottle with a tall cylindrical body, high shoulders and a short neck that holds 750 ml (25.4 fl. oz.); it originated in Bordeaux, France; generally green glass is used for red wines and clear glass for white wines. *See* burgundy bottle *and* flute bottle.

Bordeaux mixture *See* bouillie bordelaise.

Bordeaux sauce *See* bordelaise, sauce.

bordelaise, à la (bohr-dl-AYZ, ah lah) French for in the style of Bordeaux and used to describe dishes using ingredients such as bone marrow, shallots and wine (both red and white).

bordelaise, sauce A French compound sauce made from a demi-glaze flavored with red wine, herbs and shallots; cooked, diced marrow is added before serving; also known as Bordeaux sauce.

border mold A doughnut-shaped mold with a large interior void; it is used to mold food that will be used as a border around a second food that will sit in the interior well.

borecole A variety of kale that grows to 6 ft. (2 m) or more in height; also known as palm tree cabbage.

borek; bourek, burek (BOOR-ehk) Any of various Turkish fried or baked appetizers made from layers of very thin wheat dough filled with a sweet or savory (especially cheese) mixture.

Borelli (boh-rae-lee) A small Italian cheese made from water buffalo's milk.

borjú (BAWR-yoo) Hungarian for veal.

borlotto (boar-LOT-to) A plump, oval-shaped dried bean native to Italy; it has a thin, pink to pale brown maroon-streaked skin and a bitter flavor.

borneol A food additive derived from camphor; it has a burning, mintlike flavor and is used as a flavoring agent.

bornholmsk biksemad (bore-noll-msk beak-sah-mad) A Danish herring dish consisting of bloaters mixed with fried onions, boiled potatoes, gherkins and tomatoes; it is traditionally eaten hot from the skillet.

Borovicka (bor-roh-vee-kah) A Czech and Slovak juniper brandy with a flavor similar to that of gin.

borowik (boh-roh-veek) Polish for bolete.

borracha, salsa (boh-rah-tchah) A Mexican salsa made with poblanos, orange juice, onion and tequila.

borrel (boh-ral) Dutch for schnapps.

borscht; borsch; borschok (BOHR-sht; BOHR-sh) A Polish and Russian soup made with fresh beets, shredded cabbage and/or other vegetables, with or without meat; it is served hot or cold and garnished with sour cream.

bosanski lonac (bow-san-ski low-nuts) A Bosnian casserole made from pork, beef, lamb, onions, sweet peppers, eggplant, tomatoes and other vegetables flavored with herbs, spices and white wine.

boscaiolo, alla (boss-kye-OH-loh, AH-lah) Italian for woodsman's style and used to describe a pasta sauce made with mushrooms, tomatoes and fried eggplant.

Bosc pear (bawsk) An all-purpose winter pear with a long, tapering neck, dark gold skin overlaid with russet, a tender, juicy, slightly gritty texture and a sweet, buttery flavor; also known as beurre Bosc.

Boston baked beans An American dish of navy or pea beans, salt pork, molasses and brown sugar baked in a beanpot or casserole.

Boston bean *See* navy bean.

Boston bluefish *See* pollock, American.

Boston brown bread A dark, sweet steamed bread made with rye and wheat flour, cornmeal and molasses.

Boston butt A primal cut of the pork carcass; located just above the primal pork shoulder, it consists of a portion of the bladebone and is very meaty and tender; used for roasts and steaks; also known as butt and shoulder butt. *See* cottage ham.

Boston clam chowder *See* chowder; also known as New England clam chowder.

Boston cooler A black cow ice cream soda made with vanilla ice cream and root beer soda.

Boston cracker A large, thin biscuit or cracker with a plain but slightly sweet flavor; served with cheese.

Boston cream pie A traditional American cake made of two layers of sponge cake filled with vanilla custard and topped with chocolate glaze.

Boston cut A subprimal cut of the beef primal chuck; it is a tough, flavorful roast with a bone.

Boston fish chowder A soup associated with Boston and consisting of onions, green pepper, celery, fish and potatoes cooked in fish stock and milk, flavored with cayenne and herbs and garnished with flaked cod or other fish.

Boston hake *See* hake.

Boston lettuce A variety of butterhead lettuce with soft, pliable pale green leaves that have a buttery texture and flavor and are larger and paler than bibb lettuce leaves.

Boston mackerel *See* Atlantic mackerel.

Boston russet apple An early cultivated apple in the United States; it has a red-brown skin and a sweet, juicy, white flesh.

bota (boh-tay) 1. Spanish for butt or cask. 2. A Spanish leather wine pouch, usually made of goat skin.

botano (bow-tah-noh) Mexican and Latin American appetizers or foods usually consumed with alcoholic beverages.

boti kabob (boh-tee kah-bahb) An Indian dish consisting of boneless pieces of meat, marinated, skewered and grilled.

bot khoai tay (bot ko-away thay) Very fine potato flour used as a binder for meat mixtures in Vietnamese cuisine.

botoko *See* ramontchi.

botrytis cinerea (bo-trie-tiss sin-eh-ray-ah) The mold on wine grapes that gives rise to the noble rot and the gray rot. *See* noble rot *and* gray rot.

botrytized A description of the sweet wines made from grapes affected by the noble rot.

bottatrice (boh-tah-tree-tche) Italian for burbot.

botte (BOH-tee) Italian for a large oak cask used for aging wine.

bottle *v.* To place a liquid in a bottle. *n.* 1. A container of various shapes and capacities, usually made of glass or plastic, without handles and with a narrow neck that is closed with a plug (cork), screw top or cap; principally used to hold liquids. 2. The quantity that a bottle holds. 3. Slang for a drinking problem (i.e., his problem is the bottle).

bottle, oversized wine *See* wine bottle, oversized.

bottle, standard wine *See* wine bottle, standard.

bottle aging The development of a beer or still wine while in its bottle; during this period, the products become softer and richer, and complex aromas and flavors are created.

bottle club An after-hours social club where alcohol is sold legally.

bottle coding A number or other code placed on a bottle when it leaves the storeroom for the bar to assist with inventory control.

bottle conditioning The secondary fermentation and maturation of a beer or sparkling wine while in its bottle; during this period, complex aromas, flavors and effervescence are created.

bottled in bond A whiskey labeling term indicating that the contents are 100 proof, at least 4 years old, produced by a single distiller in one distilling season and stored in a bonded warehouse under government supervision until taxed and shipped to the retailer; it is a means of aging whiskey without having to pay tax on it until it is ready for sale.

bottled water *See* water, bottled.

bottle fermentation The secondary fermentation in the production of a sparkling wine; it can be induced in the bottle by adding liqueur de tirage.

bottle fermented 1. A description of all sparkling wines produced by the méthode champenoise. 2. A description of a sparkling wine made with a secondary fermentation in the bottle or by the transfer method.

bottle gourd *See* dudi.

bottlescrew A colonial American name for a corkscrew.

bottle sickness A condition causing a wine to have a flat, lifeless flavor just after bottling; a sound wine will recover after a few weeks.

bottle stink An unpleasant odor that emanates from an old bottle of wine (the wine is generally still good); it usually dissipates quickly.

bottom fermenting beer *See* lager.

bottom fermenting yeast A yeast used in brewing beer such as a lager; it converts sugars to alcohol and carbon dioxide at 37–49°F (2.7–9.4°C); it flocculates late in fermentation and sinks to the bottom of the fermentor.

Bottom Line A cocktail made of vodka, Rose's lime juice and tonic water; it is served in a Collins glass and garnished with a lime slice.

bottom round A subprimal cut of the beef primal round; it is the muscle found along the leg bone on the outside side of the animal's leg and sometimes includes the eye round; fairly tender and flavorful, it is sometimes fabricated into steaks; also known as the outside round.

bottoms *See* lees.

bottom sirloin A subprimal cut of the beef primal round; it is the end of the sirloin tip muscle.

bottom sirloin butt steak; bottom butt steak A fabricated cut of the beef primal sirloin nearest the round; it is somewhat tough.

Bottoms up! A toast suggesting that the glass's entire contents be drunk quickly, usually in one gulp.

botulism An extremely severe form of food poisoning that can lead to paralysis and even death; it is caused by ingesting toxins created by the bacteria *Clostridium botulinum*. *See* Clostridium botulinum.

botvinya (boht-vee-nyah) A Russian cold soup made of puréed sorrel and young beet tops mixed with kvass, sugar and fruits (e.g., cranberries, apples and strawberries) and garnished with cucumber, dill, fennel and tarragon; usually served with small pieces of salmon or sturgeon and grated horseradish.

bouchée (boo-SHAY) French for mouthful and used to describe a small round puff pastry container usually filled with a hot savory mixture.

boucher (boo-cher) 1. French for butcher. 2. At a food services operation following the brigade system, it is the person responsible for butchering all meats and poultry.

boucherie (boo-cher-ree) 1. French for butcher shop. 2. A daylong Cajun event held when hogs are slaughtered and every edible part is prepared for use.

bouchon (boo-shon) French for cork.

boudin blanc (boo-dahn blahnk) 1. French for white sausage and used to describe a sausage made with poultry, veal, pork or rabbit mixed with bread crumbs. 2. A Louisianian sausage made from pork shoulder, rice and onions.

boudin noir (boo-dahn nwahr) French for black sausage and used to describe a sausage made with blood and pork fat, onions and cream; also known as black pudding.

bouillabaisse (BOOL-yuh-BAYZ) A thin stew traditionally made in France's Provence region from a variety of fish and shellfish, olive oil and tomatoes, flavored with white wine, garlic, herbs and saffron and served over thick slices of bread.

bouillie bordelaise (boo-yae bohr-dae-laze) A fungicide spray used against grapevine diseases such as mildew; it is made from copper sulfate and slaked lime; also known as Bordeaux mixture.

bouillir (boo-yeer) French for to boil.

bouillon (BOOL-yahn) French for broth and used to describe a stock made by cooking meat, poultry, fish or vegetables in water; the solids are removed before the broth is used in soups or sauces or as a poaching medium.

bouillon cube A concentrated cube of dehydrated beef, chicken or vegetable stock; it is also available in granular form; both must be dissolved in a hot liquid.

bouillon spoon A spoon with a deep, rounded bowl used for eating bouillon or other clear soups.

boula; boula boula An American soup originally from the Seychelles; a turtle soup mixed with puréed green peas, flavored with sherry, topped with whipped cream and quickly browned.

bouillon spoon

boulanger (bu-layn-jhaj) At a food services operation following the brigade system, it is the person responsible for all breads and baked dough containers for other menu items; also known as the bread baker.

boulangère, à la (bu-lahn-jehr, ah lah) A French preparation method for meat (especially lamb) in which the meat is roasted in a pan on a bed of potatoes and onions.

boulangerie (bu-lahn-jher-ree) French for bakery.

boule de neige (bool duh nejg) French for the common mushroom.

Boulette d'Avesnes (boo-lett dah-ven) A small, conical cheese made in northern France from buttermilk; the curds are kneaded with parsley, tarragon and paprika and then aged; the cheese is soft, with a red rind and a spicy flavor.

Bounce A beverage popular in colonial America; it was made by combining rum or brandy with fruit, sugar, spices and water and then fermented for several weeks.

bounceberry *See* cranberry.

bouncer A person who removes unwanted patrons from an eating or drinking establishment.

bound salad A salad composed of cooked meats, poultry, fish, shellfish, pasta or potatoes combined with a dressing.

bouquet (boo-kay) The complex odors that a mature wine develops in the bottle; it is caused primarily by the interaction of alcohols and acids. *See* aroma.

Bouquet des Moines (boo-kay day mowan) A Belgian cow's milk cheese; it has a smooth, even texture, a delicate flavor and a golden-brown rind with white patches.

bouquet garni (boo-kay gar-nee) A French seasoning blend of fresh herbs and vegetables tied in a bundle with twine and used to flavor stocks, sauces, soups and stews; a standard bouquet garni consists of parsley stems, celery, thyme, leeks and carrots. *See* nouet, sachet *and* touffe.

bouquetière (boo-kuh-tyehr) French for a garnish (bouquet) of carefully cut and arranged fresh vegetables.

bouquetière, à la (boo-kuh-tyehr, ah lah) 1. A dish that is garnished with bouquets of vegetables of different colors. 2. A dish garnished with a macédoine of vegetables bound with a béchamel sauce.

bourbon An American straight whiskey distilled from a fermented grain mash made with a minimum of 51% corn; it is aged in new charred white oak barrels (which impart color, flavor and aroma) for at least 2 years and bottled between 80 and 125 proof; also known as straight bourbon. *See* blended bourbon.

bourbon and branch A traditional term for a drink of bourbon and water. *See* branch water.

bourbon ball A small, round uncooked candy made with bourbon whiskey; the alcohol content remains in the finished product.

Bourbon biscuit An oblong chocolate-flavored cookie with a chocolate cream filling, supposedly named after the Bourbon family, which ruled France from 1272 to 1792.

Bourbon Cobbler A cocktail made of bourbon, Southern Comfort, lemon juice, peach brandy, sugar syrup and club soda; garnished with a peach slice.

Bourbon Daisy A cocktail made of bourbon, lemon juice, grenadine, Southern Comfort and club soda; garnished with an orange slice or pineapple chunk.

Bourbon Milk Punch A cocktail made of milk, bourbon, vanilla extract and honey or sugar syrup; garnished with nutmeg.

bourdurella A variety of cultivated strawberry; it resembles a wild strawberry in flavor and size.

bourekia (boo-reh-khia) A Greek meze of phyllo pastry stuffed with any of a variety of savory fillings (e.g., meat, cream cheese and spinach) and fried.

Bourgain (boor-gan) A fresh, very soft French Neufchâtel-style cheese made from cow's milk; it has a low fat content, a high percentage of moisture and no salt; it is generally consumed locally.

bourguignonne, à la (bohr-ghee-n'yohn, ah lah) A French preparation method associated with the cuisine of the Burgundy region; the dishes are characterized by braising meats with red wine and usually garnishing them with mushrooms, small onions and bacon.

bourguignonne, sauce A French compound sauce made from a demi-glaze cooked with red wine and bacon and flavored with onions, shallots, parsley, thyme and bay leaf; also known as Burgundy sauce.

bourride (boo-REED) A fish stew made in France's Provence region; after cooking, the liquid is removed and the stew is bound with aïoli.

Boursault (boor-SOH) A French triple cream cheese; has a soft, white rind and a very rich, slightly nutty flavor; it is sold in small paper-wrapped cylinders.

Boursin (boor-SAHN) A triple cream cheese made from cow's milk in factories worldwide; it has a white color, no rind and a spreadable texture; it is often flavored with pepper, herbs or garlic and packaged in foil-wrapped cylinders.

bourtheto (boo-rthéh-too) A spicy dish from Corfu consisting of baked fish with sliced onions and tomatoes and seasoned with cayenne pepper.

bouteille (bo-TAY-yah) French for bottle.

boutique wine A wine produced in a limited quantity by a boutique winery; usually of fine quality.

boutique winery Wineries (usually in the United States or Australia) of modest size and production; they usually grow only a few grape varieties (if more than one) and generally make good-quality wines.

bouza (BOO-za) Arabic for ice cream.

bovine Pertaining to members of the oxen family, including bulls, calves, cows, heifers, stags and steers.

bowara (boh-wah-rah) Zimbabwean for pumpkin leaves; they are used fresh, dried or cooked in stews.

bowl 1. A round vessel used for preparing and serving foods, especially those with a liquid or semiliquid texture. 2. The concave (from the front) portion of a spoon attached to the handle. 3. The part of a glass or goblet that rests on a stem or foot and holds the liquid.

Bowle (boh-oh-lah) German cold wine punch.

bowl knife A spatula or flexible, dull-edged knife used to scrape the batter or dough from the sides of a bowl.

bowl of red *See* chili con carne.

bowl scraper A palm-sized, wedgelike plastic tool with a curved edge to help it conform to concave surfaces; it is used to remove and transfer the last bits of food from a bowl or board to a bowl, board, pastry bag or other receptacle; also known as a scraper.

bowties Bowtie-shaped pasta. *See* farfalle.

box *See* case.

Box A mild German cheese made from cow's milk, flavored with caraway seeds and similar to American Brick cheese; also known as Hohenburg; soft Box cheese is made of equal volumes of whole and skimmed milk; firm Box is made from whole milk.

box grater Four flat graters, generally of different degrees of coarseness, joined to form a box, usually with a handle on top.

box huckleberry *See* juniper berry.

box oyster An Atlantic oyster found in Long Island's Gardiner's Bay; it has a squarish shell with a length of 5–6 in. (12.7–15.2 cm) and a large body.

box pressure The degree of pressure applied to cigars packed in boxes; cigars should retain their round shape when packed (i.e., they are round packed); too much pressure causes the cigars to assume a slightly square shape (square packed).

box grater

boxty; broxty (BOX-tee) An Irish dish consisting of a thick potato and wheat flour pancake cut into wedges and cooked on a griddle.

Boyne raspberry A raspberry variety; the fruit are large, red and intensely flavored.

boysenberry A blackberry and raspberry hybrid named for its progenitor, Rudolph Boysen; shaped like a raspberry, it has a purple-red color and a rich, sweet, tart flavor.

boza (BO-za) A Turkish fermented-grain drink usually made from millet.

bozbash (bors-bash) A Russian soup made from boiled mutton and garnished with peas, potatoes, apples, tomatoes and fried onions.

bozzoli (boh-ZOH-lee) Italian for cocoon and used to describe small cocoonlike shapes of pasta.

Bra A hard Italian cheese made from partly skimmed cow's milk; it has a compact texture, whitish interior and sharp, salty flavor.

braai (brah-ee) A South African barbecue.

bracelet A cut of the lamb carcass that contains the primal rack with the connecting breast section.

Brachetto (bra-KEH-toe) An Italian wine grape cultivated in the Piedmont region; it produces a light red wine that can be slightly sweet and fizzy.

braciola (brah-chee-OHL-lah) 1. Italian for escallop. 2. An Italian dish consisting of a sautéed veal scallop with a sauce made from Marsala and pan drippings. 3. Italian for a slice or chop of meat, often stuffed.

braciole (brash-shee-OH-lay) Italian pasta cases filled with a meat stuffing.

bracken; brake A fern (*Pteridium aquilinum*); its young unopened leaves are edible and have a smoky flavor; its roots are boiled and served with a vinaigrette; also known as fiddlehead fern.

brackish 1. Slightly salty; briny. 2. A beer-tasting term for a salty flavor.

Braeburn A variety of apple with a red-blushed green skin, a crisp, juicy flesh and a tart–sweet flavor.

Brägenwurst (bra-ghen-voorst) A long thin German sausage made of pig's brains, oats, flour and onions.

brains The soft, convoluted mass of gray and white matter found in the cranium of vertebrates that controls mental and physical activities; as a variety meat, sheep and pig brains are best.

braising (bray-zeng) A combination cooking method in which foods are first browned in hot fat, then covered and slowly cooked in a small amount of liquid over low heat; braising uses a combination of simmering and steaming to transfer heat from a liquid (conduction) and the air (convection) to the foods.

bramata (brah-MAH-tah) Finely ground Italian cornmeal.

bramble berry *See* blackberry.

bramble jelly An English jelly made from crab apples and blackberries.

Brambling Cross (braem-bling kras) A variety of hops grown in the United Kingdom.

bran The tough, outer covering of the endosperm of various types of grain kernels; it has a high fiber and vitamin B content and is usually removed during milling; used to enrich baked goods and as a cereal and nutrient supplement.

branch celery *See* celery.

branch lettuce *See* saxifrage.

branch water Pure, clean water from a tiny stream (called a branch).

brandade (brahn-DAHD) A dish from France's Provence region consisting of a purée of salt cod, olive oil and milk served on croutons rubbed with garlic and garnished with black truffles.

brandi (bran-dee) Swahili for brandy.

Brandkrapferlsuppe (brahnd-krap-fairl-sup-pay) An Austrian beef broth garnished with fried profiteroles.

brand name 1. The name that a manufacturer, distributor or retailer gives a specific food, beverage or other item to distinguish it from similar goods; a brand name is often protected under intellectual property laws and may be accompanied by a similarly protected sign, mark or logo. 2. A grade or quality of meat determined by a packer or processor rather than the USDA; also known as a packer brand name.

brandy A spirit distilled from grape wine or the fermented juice of other fruits with a minimum proof of 60 and usually aged in an oak cask; its color, flavor and aroma depend on the wine or fermented juice used and the length of time it ages in the cask. *See* Cognac.

Brandy Alexander A cocktail made of brandy, cream and a chocolate liqueur, usually served after dinner. *See* Panama.

brandy butter An English hard sauce made with butter, sugar and brandy; served cold with hot Christmas pudding and other steamed puddings. *See* hard sauce.

Brandy Cooler A cocktail made of brandy, pineapple syrup or sugar syrup and curaçao, maraschino liqueur or peach liqueur; garnished with an orange slice and maraschino cherry.

Brandy Crusta A cocktail made of brandy, lemon juice, maraschino liqueur, Angostura bitters and superfine sugar; served in a wine glass lined with an orange or lemon peel spiral and garnished with a maraschino cherry.

Brandy Daisy A cocktail made of brandy, sugar syrup, lemon juice, club soda, Pernod or maraschino liqueur and raspberry syrup or grenadine; served in a chilled wine glass and garnished with an orange slice, pineapple chunk and maraschino cherry.

Brandy Fix A cocktail made of brandy, sugar syrup, water and lemon juice.

Brandy Flip A cocktail made of brandy, cream, sugar syrup and egg; served in a chilled wine glass and garnished with nutmeg.

brandy glass; brandy snifter *See* snifter.

Brandy Milk Punch A cocktail made of milk, brandy and sugar syrup; garnished with nutmeg.

brandy papers Parchment or writing papers soaked in brandy and traditionally used to cover jars and crocks to preserve their contents.

Brandy Sangaree A cocktail made of brandy, superfine sugar and water; garnished with nutmeg.

brandy snap A thin, crisp cookie usually flavored with brandy, spices and molasses.

brandy warmer A metal cradle used to hold a brandy glass at an angle over a heat source (usually a candle); the glass is slowly rotated to warm the brandy gently.

brandywine The traditional name for brandy.

Brandywine An heirloom tomato variety with a deep pink skin, a red flesh and a sweet, spicy flavor.

Brandza (bran-zah) A Romanian cheese made from ewe's milk and aged in brine; it has a whitish color, a rich, salty flavor and a texture ranging from soft to firm.

bran muffin A muffin that contains a large amount of bran and, often, raisins.

brannigan Slang for a drinking spree.

Branntwein (brant-vine) German for brandy; also known as Kognak.

Branston Pickle Relish The proprietary name of an English condiment made of carrots, rutabaga, cauliflower, zucchini, dates and tomatoes; usually served with cheese, cold meats and open-faced sandwiches.

branzino (brahn-ZEE-noh) Italian for sea bass.

brasato (brah-SAH-toh) Italian for braised.

brasciuoli (brash-shee-OH-lay) A dish from Naples, Italy, consisting of veal stuffed with meat, garlic, onions, raisins, pine nuts and cheese.

Bras d'Or An Atlantic oyster found off Cape Breton, Nova Scotia; it has a curved shell and a flat body.

brasserie (BRAHS-uhr-ee) A restaurant where beer, wine, cider and other drinks are served; the limited menu usually offers simple, hardy foods.

Brassica *See* cabbages.

brat (braht) Slang for Bratwurst.

Bratapfel (braht-ah-pferl) German for baked apple.

braten (braht-ern) German for to roast or braise; roasted or braised.

Brathering (bra-tah-reng) A German dish consisting of grilled or floured and fried herring pickled in a boiled vinegar marinade.

Bratklops (braht-klops) German for rissole, usually served with sauerkraut in Germany.

Bratwurst (BRAHT-wurst; BRAHT-vurst) A fresh German sausage made from pork and veal, seasoned with ginger, nutmeg and coriander or caraway seeds.

Braunschweiger (BROWN-shwi-ger) A soft, spreadable German smoked sausage made from pork liver enriched with eggs and milk.

Brave Bull A cocktail made of white tequila and Kahlua; garnished with a twist of lemon.

brawn 1. A charcuterie item made from simmered meats packed into a terrine and covered with aspic; also known as an aspic terrine. 2. An English dish of boiled, boned, jellied and potted pig's head; served cold; also known as headcheese.

Brawn (brahvn) German for headcheese.

brawny A wine-tasting term for a muscular (usually young) red wine with a relatively high tannin and alcohol content.

brazier; braiser A pan designed for braising; it is usually round with two handles and a tight-fitting lid; also known as a rondeau.

Brazil cherry *See* grumichama.

Brazilian Robusta coffee beans grown in Brazil and usually used to make instant coffee.

Brazilian arrowroot *See* cassava.

Brazilian malagueta (mah-lah-gwee-tah) A small, tapered fresh chile with a thin, light to medium green flesh and a very hot, vegetal flavor.

Brazilian roast *See* roast, Brazilian.

Brazil nut A seed of an Amazon jungle tree (*Bertholettia excelsa*); the white, richly flavored and high-fat nut is encased in a very hard, dark brown triangular shell; the seeds grow in a cluster inside a hard, globular pod; also known as a creamnut, para, paranut and savory nut.

bread *v.* To coat a food with flour, beaten eggs and bread crumbs or cracker crumbs before cooking. *n.* A food baked from a dough or batter made with flour or meal, water or other liquids and a leavener.

bread and butter 1. Slang for the finest center-cut chuck steaks. 2. The essential sustaining element of something (e.g., catering was the bread and butter of her business).

bread-and-butter pickles Sweet pickles made from sliced cucumbers cured with onions, mustard seeds and celery seeds.

bread and butter plate A plate, 5–6 in. in diameter, used for individual servings of bread and butter; also known as a butter plate.

bread baker *See* boulanger.

bread bowl A round loaf of bread; the top is sliced off, the center hollowed out and the crust and remaining interior is used as a bowl for soups, stews or the like, with the bowl being consumed as part of the meal.

bread crumbs Small bits of bread used as a coating for fried foods or as a topping; they can be made from most breads and are sometimes seasoned with herbs and/or spices.

bread crumbs, dry Commercially prepared bread crumbs or oven-dried fresh bread crumbs; they are more uniform and crisper than fresh bread crumbs and provide a smoother, denser coating.

bread crumbs, fresh Crumbs obtained by processing fresh bread in a food processor; they are softer and give more texture to breaded foods than do dry bread crumbs.

bread flour A strong flour, usually made from hard winter wheat and containing 11–13% protein; used for making yeast-leavened breads.

breadfruit A large spherical fruit of a tropical tree related to the fig family (*Artocarpus communis*) and grown in the South Pacific, India and West Indies; it has a bumpy green skin, a cream-colored flesh with the texture of fresh bread, and a bland flavor; baked, grilled, fried or boiled, it is served as a sweet or savory dish.

breading 1. A coating of bread or cracker crumbs, cornmeal or other dry meal applied to foods that will typically be deep-fried or pan-fried. 2. The process of applying this coating.

bread knife A long, moderately rigid knife with a wave-cut edge similar to a serrated edge; used to slice baked goods; its blade ranges in length from 8 to 10 in. and has a blunt tip.

bread knife

bread machine An electrical, computer-driven machine that mixes, kneads, proofs and bakes bread; a blade in the cannister base mixes and kneads the dough and a heating coil bakes the bread.

bread-making process The process by which most yeast breads are made; typically (1) the ingredients are scaled or weighed; (2) the dough is mixed and kneaded; (3) the dough is allowed to ferment; (4) the dough is punched down; (5) the dough is divided into portions; (6) the portions are rounded and shaped; (7) the shaped portions of dough are proofed; and (8) the products are baked, cooled and stored.

breadnut The fruit of a tree (*Brosimum alicastrum*) grown in the Caribbean and Central America; it is generally roasted and ground for flour; also known as Maya breadnut.

bread pudding A baked dessert made with cubes or slices of bread soaked in a mixture of eggs, milk, sugar and flavorings.

bread sauce An English sauce of bread crumbs and onion-flavored milk seasoned with cayenne and nutmeg and finished with cream; traditionally served with boiled beef, game, roasted poultry and large joints of meat.

bread stick A long, thin stick of yeast bread, usually crispy and garnished with seeds or herbs.

break The coagulation and precipitation of proteins during the boiling and cooling of the wort used to make beer. *See* hot break *and* cold break.

break-even point The point at which costs equal revenues and profits and losses are zero.

breakfast cream *See* cream, light.

breakfast steak A fabricated cut of the beef primal chuck; a thin, moderately tender steak.

breakfast tea *See* English breakfast tea *and* Irish breakfast tea.

bream 1. In Europe, a common freshwater fish and member of the carp family. 2. An imprecisely used name for a variety of freshwater sunfish caught in the United States for sport. *See* sea bream.

breast 1. The portion of the beef carcass containing the primal short plate and brisket (with or without the shank). 2. A subprimal section of the veal primal foreshank and breast; it is the flavorful breast, which has a high percentage of connective tissue and is often ground, cubed or rolled and stuffed. 3. A primal section of the lamb carcass; it is located beneath the primal rack and contains the rib tips, breast and foreshank. 4. The fleshy white meat part of the body between the neck and abdomen on poultry.

breathe To aerate a red wine by pouring it from the bottle into a clean container (a carafe or glass) and allowing it to stand for a period of time before it is consumed.

bredie (bra-dee) A South African stew, usually of lamb or mutton with one or two dominant vegetables such as tomatoes, pumpkin or green beans.

breed A wine-tasting term for an elegant, refined wine of great distinction.

Brei (bri) German for a purée or porridge.

Bréjauda (bray-jo-dah) A French soup made from brown stock, cabbage and bacon; red wine is added to the last few spoonfuls left in the plate, and this is known as charbrol.

brek; brik (brehk) A Tunisian deep-fried turnover filled with a spicy meat or fish mixture often bound with egg; served with harissa.

brem bali (brem ba-li) A sweet-tasting, pink-colored Indonesian rice wine made from fermented glutinous rice.

Bremer Küchenragout (breh-mer KOOK-hern-rah-goo) A German dish of meat and vegetables in a rich cream sauce.

bresaola (brehsh-ay-OH-lah) An Italian dried, salted beef filet that has aged for 2 months; it is usually sliced thin and served as antipasto.

Bresciano *See* Bagozza.

Bresse (bress) A region in France famous for its poultry.

Bresse mayonnaise A French sauce made from a Spanish mayonnaise flavored with Madeira and orange juice, seasoned with cayenne pepper and finished with puréed, sautéed chicken livers.

bretonne, à la (breh-TAWN, ah lah) A French garnish (for mutton and lamb) of puréed white haricot (navy) beans with a sauce bretonne.

bretonne, sauce 1. A French sauce for fish or chicken: a white wine sauce finished with cream and garnished with julienne of celery, leeks, mushrooms and onions. 2. For meat: a French compound sauce of demi-glaze flavored with a reduction of white wine and shallots, tomato purée, butter and parsley.

Breton sauce *See* bretonne, sauce.

bretzel au flan (brat-zel oh flahn) French for pretzel with filling and used to describe a puff pastry pretzel filled with vanilla custard.

brew *v.* 1. To make tea or coffee by boiling or steeping the tea leaves or coffee grounds in water. 2. To make beer. *See* beer-brewing process. *n.* Slang for beer, especially draught.

brewers' yeast *Saccharomyces cerevisiae;* a cultured yeast used for brewing beer; also used as a nutritional supplement.

brewery 1. A building that houses the apparatus used to make, store and age beer. 2. An establishment that makes and sells beer.

brewing salt A blend of Epsom salts, gypsum, noniodized salt and other minerals added to water considered too soft for brewing beer.

brewis (breh-wis) A Welsh teakettle broth traditionally made from oat husks boiled with bacon fat, salt and pepper; bread crusts and butter are sometimes substituted.

brew kettle The vessel in which the wort is boiled and to which the hops are added during beer brewing.

brew pub A commercial establishment that brews its own beer for sales on and off premises; it typically also serves food.

brewster During the Middle Ages in England, a title given to the female family member responsible for brewing beer, ale and/or mead at home.

Brezel (BRET-sehl) A large soft German pretzel.

briami (bree-ah-me) Greek baked vegetables. *See* ladera.

briary (BRI-uh-ree) A wine-tasting term for a wine that is aggressive rather than spicy.

brichetti (brick-que-tee) Italian for bricks and used to describe small rectangular pasta.

briciole (bree-tcho-lae) Italian for bread crumbs.

brick The red-brown color often found in both well-aged, mature red wines and slightly old ones.

Brick A semisoft, sweet-curd American cheese made from cow's milk; it has a pale yellow color, irregular holes and a mild earthy, slightly nutty flavor when young, becoming more pungent as it ages; sold in brick-shaped loaves it slices well without crumbling; also known as American Brick.

Brickbat A firm cheese made in Wiltshire, England, from cow's milk and cream.

brick tea Tea leaves that are steamed and pressed into a brick; originally made for easy transportation, now prized for their attractive embossed designs.

bridge mix An assortment of candies or nuts, often coated with chocolate, served at social events such as bridge parties.

Brie (bree) A soft, creamy French cheese made from cow's milk; it has a pale ivory-gold color, a soft, leathery white rind and a delicate, somewhat nutty flavor; rind-ripened, it can develop an ammonia odor if overly ripe; traditionally named after its place of origin.

brie d'amateur (bree da'mah-tuhr) A cheese-tasting term for a Brie that is past its prime; it is strongly flavored and gray colored.

Brie de Meaux (bree dah moe) *See* Meaux.

Brie de Melun (bree dah mae-lohn) *See* Melun.

brigade A system of staffing a kitchen so that each worker is assigned a set of specific tasks; these tasks are often related by cooking method, equipment or type of foods being produced; also known as a kitchen brigade.

bright 1. A wine-tasting term for a wine that is free of suspended particles. 2. A description of the wine when it begins to clarify naturally shortly after fermentation ceases.

brik (breek) *See* brek.

brill *See* petrale sole.

Brillat-Savarin (bree-yath-sah-vah-ren) A French triple cream cheese made from pasteurized cow's milk in small, flat disks; it has a downy white rind and a rich, buttery, creamy flavor.

Brillat-Savarin, Jean-Anthelme (Fr., 1755–1826) A magistrate and gastronome and the author of *Physiologie du goût* (*Physiology of Taste,* 1825), which contains his observations on dining, food preparation and the science of cuisine; several classical French preparations carry his name.

brilliant A wine-tasting term for a wine with a perfectly clear appearance; the wine is neither hazy nor cloudy.

brilliant blue FCF *See* FD&C Blue #1.

Brin d'Amour; Brindamour (BRAN dah-MORE) A soft French ewe's or goat's milk cheese; its crust is coated with dried rosemary, powdered thyme, coriander seeds, juniper berries and, sometimes, tiny, whole red chiles; its interior can range from snow-white, creamy, moist and soft to bone-white and almost runny; also known as Fleur du Maquis.

brine 1. A salt and water solution. 2. *See* washed-rind cheese.

bringan (breen-gahn) Hindi for eggplant.

bringebær (BRING-er-bahr) Norwegian for raspberry.

bringukollar (bring-oo-kuhl-ahr) An Icelandic dish of a breast of lamb soured with pickling brine.

brining A method of curing, preserving and/or flavoring certain foods such as meats, fish, vegetables and cheese by immersing them in brine or injecting brine into them; also known as pickling. *See* pickle.

brining solution A very salty marinade (generally 20% salinity) used to preserve and/or flavor certain foods; it can be flavored with sugar, herbs and spices.

Brinza; Bryndza (BRIHN-zah) A goat's or ewe's milk cheese made throughout the Carpathian Mountain regions of central Europe; often aged in brine.

brio (prio) Thai for sour.

brioche (bree-ohsh) A light, tender French yeast bread enriched with eggs and butter.

brioche a tête (bree-ohsh ah tet) Brioche shaped in a round, fluted mold and topped with a small ball of dough, which creates a topknot or head after baking.

brioche pan A round, fluted metal baking pan with flared sides, available in many sizes; used for baking traditionally shaped brioche and for molding custards and Bavarians.

brioche pan

brioli (bree-oh-lee) A Corsican dish of chestnut meal prepared like polenta and served with milk or cream.

briouats (bree-oh-ats) Moroccan warka pastry triangles; they can be sweet (e.g., filled with blanched almonds, cinnamon, sugar, orange blossom water and butter and then immersed in honey before serving) or savory (e.g., filled with ground beef, harissa and spices).

brique (breek) French for brick and used to describe brick-shaped French cheeses; briquette is used to describe small brick-shaped cheeses.

brisk A wine-tasting term for a moderately acidic, crisp, refreshing wine.

brisket (bres-khet) A fabricated cut of the beef primal brisket and foreshank; it is the animal's breast; available boneless, it is tough and flavorful.

brisket, deckle-off A brisket with the layer of hard fat removed from the inside surface.

brisket, flat cut A very flavorful brisket with minimal fat.

brisket, point cut A fattier and less flavorful brisket.

brisket and shank A primal section of the beef carcass; it is under the primal chuck and includes such flavorful, moderately tough subprimal or fabricated cuts as the brisket and foreshank.

brisling; brisling sardine A young or small sprat packed in oil.

Bristol Cream A blended sherry marketed by a British firm, Harveys of Bristol; the most popular sherry sold in the United States.

Bristol oyster An Atlantic oyster found off South Bristol, Maine; it has a round shell with an average length of 2.5 in. (6.3 cm) and a plump body.

British gallon A unit of measurement for volume in the imperial system; it is 160 fl. oz.; also known as an imperial gallon.

brittle A flat, irregularly shaped candy made by mixing nuts into caramelized sugar.

briwat (bree-what) A Tunisian confection made from almond paste, rice and honey.

Brix (briks) 1. A hydrometer (saccharometer) used to measure the sugar content of unfermented grape juice or must and as a means to determine the probable alcoholic content of the finished wine; measured in degrees also called Brix. 2. A system used to measure the density and concentration of sugar in a solution. 3. A system used to measure the concentration of sugar in a fruit; typically a fruit, such as a peach, with a Brix of 12–17 is sweet to very sweet.

broa (broah) A yeast-leavened Portuguese cornbread made with finely ground corn flour and olive oil.

broad bean *See* fava bean.

brocca (BROH-kah) An Italian earthenware jug used as a wine carafe.

Broccio; Brocciu; Brouse (bro-tcho) A ricotta-style Corsican cheese made from soured goat's or ewe's milk or the whey from other cheeses, such as Venaco; it is unsalted and eaten fresh.

broccoflower (BROH-koh-flowr) A light green cauliflower that is a cross between broccoli and cauliflower, with a milder flavor than either vegetable.

broccoli (BROH-klee) Italian for cabbage sprout and used to describe a member of the cabbage family (*Brassica oleracea*) with a tight cluster (called a curd) of emerald green florets on top of a stout, paler green edible stalk with dark green leaves.

broccoli, sprouting *See* calabrese.

broccoli raab (BROH-klee RAH-ahb) *See* rape.

broche (brosh) French term for a wooden or metal skewer used to suspend and turn meat or poultry as it roasts.

broche, à la (brosh, ah lah) French for in the style of a brochette; an item cooked and served on a skewer.

brochet (broh-shay) French for the fish pike.

brochette (broh-SHEHT) French for skewer.

brochette, en (broh-sheht, ahn) A food (usually meat) threaded onto a skewer and grilled or broiled.

brochette meat Cubes of beef, veal, lamb or pork to be put on a skewer; they are usually marinated and then broiled or grilled; also known as cube meat and kabob meat.

brochettes (bro-shettz) Skewers, either small hors d'oeuvre or large entrée size, threaded with meat, poultry, fish, shellfish and/or vegetables and grilled, broiled or baked; sometimes served with a dipping sauce.

brocoletti di rape *See* rape.

brocoli (broc-coa-lay) French for broccoli.

Brocotta *See* Ricotta.

bróculo (broh-coo-low) Portuguese for broccoli.

brød (brur) Norwegian for bread.

brodet (broh-day) A Balkan stew made with fish, onions and shrimp, flavored with tomato purée, wine vinegar and red wine and garnished with parsley, garlic and lemon peel.

brodetto (bro-DET-toe) A thick Italian fish or meat soup flavored with garlic, onions, parsley, tomatoes, bay leaves and wine or wine vinegar.

brodo (BROH-doh) Italian for broth.

brødsmuler (broad-me-oo-lerr) Norwegian for bread crumbs.

Broglie, sauce (bro-glee) A French compound sauce made from a Madeira sauce flavored with mushrooms and garnished with diced ham.

broiler Cooking equipment in which the heat source (gas or electric) is located above the rack used to hold the food; it is generally enclosed and can be combined with an oven.

broiler; broiler chicken *See* chicken, broiler-fryer.

broiler-fryer duck; broiler-fryer duckling *See* duck, broiler-fryer.

broiler pan An assemblage consisting of a 1.5-in.-deep drip pan with a slotted tray insert; the slots channel rendered fats to the drip pan to reduce smoking and splattering.

broiling A dry-heat cooking method in which foods are cooked by heat radiating from an overhead source. *See* grilling.

broken case A case received from a distributor that contains different brands of the same alcoholic beverage or different types of alcoholic beverages.

broken case room A locked storeroom where opened cases of alcoholic beverages are kept.

broken pekoe Broken pekoe tea leaves, generally used for quick brewing. *See* pekoe.

Broken Spur A cocktail made of gin, white port, sweet vermouth, anisette and an egg yolk.

Brokkoli (brok-koh-lee) German for broccoli.

bromated flour A white flour to which potassium bromate has been added.

Brombeere (brohm-bear-eh) German for blackberry.

bromelin (BROH-meh-lin) An enzyme found in pineapples and used as a meat tenderizer.

brominated vegetable oil (BVO) A vegetable oil whose density has been increased to that of water by adding bromine; often used as a food additive to stabilize fruit drinks.

Bronte (BRAWN-tay) An English herbal liqueur made of fruits and spices; also known as Yorkshire liqueur.

Bronx Cocktail 1. A cocktail made of gin, orange juice and dry vermouth. 2. A cocktail made of gin, orange juice, and dry and sweet vermouth.

brood A seed oyster 1–3 years old and ready to spawn.

broodje (BROHT-yus) A Dutch white bread roll or bun used to serve a variety of foods.

brookie Slang for brook trout.

brooklime A wild green with a slightly bitter flavor found near North American and northern European streams and marshes.

Brooklyn cake A light, white cake made with beaten egg whites, sugar, lemon juice and cornstarch; popular in the late 19th century.

brook trout A freshwater trout found in eastern North America, Argentina and Europe; it has a dark olive skin that pales on the sides and becomes reddish on the belly, with red spots outlined in pale blue, a white flaky flesh (wild brook trout has a pale yellow or orange flesh), a delicate flavor

and an average weight of 1 lb. (450 g); also known as a speckled trout.

broom straws Fresh, clean straw used to make brooms or the topmost (and clean) pieces removed from a broom; they are used to separate two pie crusts that are baked in the same pan before the filling is added and to test cakes and quick breads for doneness.

broonie (BROO-nee) A British oatmeal gingerbread cookie.

Bröschen (broh-shan) German for sweetbreads.

brose (broz) 1. A Scottish porridge made from oatmeal. 2. A Scottish soup thickened with oatmeal.

brosse (bross) French term for cheeses that are brushed during ripening.

Brot (broat) German for bread.

Brötchen (broat-ken) German for rolls.

broth A flavorful liquid obtained from the long simmering of meats and/or vegetables.

Brotkrume (broat-krum) German for bread crumbs.

Brotzeit (broat-zah-it) A German snack, often eaten about 11:00 A.M. or 4:00 P.M.; it usually consists of beer and bread, cold cuts or pretzels.

brouillé (broo-ye) French for scrambled.

Brouilly (brew-yee) A grape-growing and wine-producing district in France's Beaujolais region; the wines are generally fruity, supple and full flavored.

brown To caramelize the surface sugars of a food by applying heat, invariably through a dry-heat cooking method.

brown ale A dark brown ale with a malty bouquet, a bittersweet flavor, a light to medium body and a relatively low alcohol content; made in the United States, Great Britain, Belgium and Canada; also known as American brown ale.

brown and serve A term used to describe a product (usually bread) that is cooked to doneness but not browned; browning is done just before service.

brown bag *v.* To bring such a meal to the workplace or other site. *n.* A meal made and packed at home and taken elsewhere to eat, usually to the workplace.

brown bagging A practice of allowing customers in an unlicensed or occasionally licensed establishment to bring in their own bottles of alcoholic beverages to be consumed on the premises; a corkage or setup fee is often charged.

brown bean A plump ovoid-shaped bean with a brown skin and lighter brown flesh; used in northern European and Scandinavian cuisines; also known as the Dutch brown bean.

brown flour White flour baked to a brownish color on a baking sheet in the oven or "bubbled" with fat before the liquid is added when making gravy or sauce; this is done to take away the raw taste; also known as baked flour.

brown goods A liquor industry term describing brown-colored distilled spirits such as bourbon and Scotch. *See* white goods.

brownie A cakelike bar cookie, usually made with chocolate and garnished with nuts.

browning 1. The change in a red wine's color from ruby-purple to ruby with brown edges, caused by aging; once the wine has completed browning, it is fully mature and not likely to improve. 2. The change in a food's appearance as its surface sugars caramelize through the application of heat, invariably through a dry-heat cooking method. *See* caramelization.

brown malt vinegar *See* malt vinegar.

brown rice A form of processed rice with only the tough outer husk removed; the retained bran gives the rice a light tan color, a nutlike flavor and a chewy texture; it is available in long-, medium- and short-grain forms.

brown roast *See* roast, city.

brown sauce A French leading sauce made with a rich, brown meat stock to which a brown roux and mirepoix are added, followed by a tomato purée; also known as espagnole sauce and Spanish sauce.

brown sherry A type of sherry with a very sweet, nutty flavor, dark brown color and full body.

brown slab sugar Layered, semirefined sugar, usually of two tones of brown, compressed into flat slabs and cut into 6-in. (15-cm) fingers.

brown stew A stew in which the meat is first browned in hot fat.

brown stock A richly colored stock made of chicken, veal, beef or game bones and vegetables, all of which are caramelized before they are simmered in water with seasonings.

brown sugar Soft, refined sugar with a coating of molasses; can be dark or light, coarse or fine.

brown trout A freshwater trout found in North America and Europe; it has a golden-brown to olive skin with large black or brown spots and small orange-red spots, an average market weight of 1–2 lb. (450–900 g), a white to pale orange flaky flesh and a delicate flavor.

brown Turkey fig A particularly meaty and flavorful pear-shaped fig with a skin color that ranges from violet to brown.

brown venus clams Any of several varieties of venus clams found off western Europe and in the Mediterranean Sea; they have a thick, brown, smooth, shiny shell with an average length of 3–5 in. (7.6–12.7 cm) and sweet meat; also known as smooth venus clams.

brown water Australian slang for beer.

brown wine A white wine with a deeper-than-normal color.

broyage (broo-ah-yah-ja) Swiss for a flat disk of baked meringue containing nuts.

BRT A designation for meat that is boned, rolled and tied (or netted).

Bruder Basil A smoked cheese made in Germany's Bavaria region from pasteurized cow's milk; it has a yellow interior, a mahogany-brown rind, a firm texture with small holes and a light smoky flavor.

brughair (BROO-er) Ancient Gaelic term for a brewer.

Bruhe (BREW-ehr) German for broth.

bruise 1. To crush a food partially, especially an herb, to release its flavor. 2. To crush or injure a food, causing discoloration or softening.

bruised beer Beer that has been cooled, allowed to return to room temperature and then recooled; this causes a loss of quality and carbonation.

brukselka (brook-sel-kah) Polish for Brussels sprouts.

brûlé (broo-LAY) French for burned and used to describe the browning of a food by means of direct, intense heat.

brunch A meal taken, usually leisurely, between 11 A.M. and 3 P.M.; a combination of breakfast and lunch, it usually offers breakfast foods and almost anything else.

brune kager (broo-nay kah-gher) A Danish Christmas cookie flavored with dark corn syrup, brown sugar, spices and lemon peel and decorated with blanched almonds.

Brunello di Montalcino (broo-NELL-o dee mon-tahlt'CHEE-no) A deep-colored, intense, tannic and long-lived Italian wine made from the Brunello grape in Italy's Tuscany region; it cannot be released until 4 years after harvest and must have spent a minimum of 3 1/2 years in wood.

brun lapskaus (broon lapp-skoys) A Norwegian stew made with beef, potatoes and other vegetables.

Brunnenkresse (broo-nen-KRE-seh) German for watercress.

brunoise (broo-nwaz) 1. Foods cut into approximately 1/8-in. (3-mm) cubes. *See* paysanne. 2. Foods garnished with vegetables cut in this manner.

Brunswick fig *See* magnolia fig.

Brunswick stew A stew associated with Brunswick County, Virginia; originally made with squirrel and onions; today, it is generally made with rabbit or chicken and vegetables such as corn, okra, lima beans, tomatoes and onions.

bruschetta (broo-SKEH-tah) 1. An Italian appetizer of toasted bread slices rubbed with garlic and drizzled with olive oil and sometimes topped with tomatoes and basil; served warm. 2. In the United States, any of a variety of appetizers made from toasted bread drizzled with olive oil and topped with olives, tomatoes, cheese or other ingredients.

brush To apply a liquid with a pastry brush to the surface of a food to baste or glaze the item.

brushing The process of applying a liquid such as brine, beer, wine or brandy to the surface of a washed-rind cheese during curing to keep the rind moist.

brussels lof (BROOS-suls lawf) Dutch for Belgian endive.

Brussels sprouts A member of the cabbage family (*Brassica oleracea*) developed in Belgium; the small, spherical heads of tightly packed yellow-green leaves grow along a long, tapering stalk.

brut (broot) A very, very dry Champagne or sparkling wine, drier than one labeled extra dry; contains 0.8–1.5% sugar. *See* demi-sec, extra dry *and* sec.

brut nature *See* nature.

brutti ma buoni (BROO-tee mah B'WHO-nee) Italian for ugly but good and used to describe a meringue cookie made with hazelnuts or almonds.

bruxelloise, à la (broo-csa'-l'wahz) A French garnish for small joints of meat consisting of stewed Brussels sprouts, chicory and potatoes.

Bryndza *See* Brinza.

brzoskwinie (bshoh-sk-fee-nyeh) Polish for peaches.

b'steeya; bisteeya; bastela, bastila and pastilla (bs-TEE-yah) A Moroccan dish of phyllo dough filled with shredded pigeon or chicken, almonds and spices; baked and sprinkled with confectioners' sugar and cinnamon.

Bual; Boal (boh-ahl) 1. A white wine grape grown on the island of Madeira. 2. A Madeira wine made from this grape; of the four Madeira styles, it is the medium sweet style.

bubble and squeak A British dish of mashed potatoes, chopped cabbage and, traditionally, boiled beef, mixed together and fried.

bubbly Slang for sparkling wine.

bublanina (boo-lah-nee-nah) A Czech sponge cake flavored with pitted cherries or plums and sprinkled with vanilla-flavored sugar while still warm.

bucati (boo-CAH-tee) Italian for with a hole and used to describe certain hollow or pierced pasta.

bucatini (boo-cah-TEE-nee) Very thin, short, straight, hollow Italian pasta.

buccellato (book-chahl-LAH-toa) 1. A Sicilian ring-shaped cake containing dried fruit and spices. 2. A raisin and anise-flavored cake typically presented to children on their confirmation day in Italy's Tuscany region.

Bucelas (boo-SEL-as) A dry Portuguese white wine that is often wood aged.

bûche de Noël (boosh dah noh-ehl) French for Yule log and used to describe a traditional Christmas cake made with genoise and buttercream, shaped and decorated to resemble a log.

Bucheron (BOOSH-rawn) A tangy but mild French goat's milk cheese; it has a soft, white interior and usually comes in logs with a white rind or covered in black ash.

buck 1. Fermented mash used to make moonshine. 2. A male deer, antelope or rabbit.

Buck A type of cocktail made of liquor, a carbonated beverage and sometimes lemon juice. *See* Gin Buck.

buckbean *See* bogbean.

bucket candy Slang for small candies such as gumdrops, bonbons and sugar drops that are sold in bulk from large buckets.

bucket glass A short, squat cylindrical glass ranging in size from 12 to 15 fl. oz.; used for double mixed drinks and cocktails on the rocks; also known as a double old-fashioned glass.

bucket of blood Slang originating in Montana for a tough and rowdy saloon.

bucket steak A fabricated cut of the beef primal round; cut from the side of the round, it has an oval shape and is moderately tender; also known as a baseball steak.

buckeye A candy made by dipping small balls of a creamy peanut butter mixture in melted chocolate; popular in Ohio, the Buckeye State.

buckle An old-fashioned, deep-dish, fruit dessert made with a layer of cake batter that rises to the top as the dish bakes, forming a crisp crust.

buckram A blue crab whose soft shell has toughened but has not yet become hard.

buckwheat; buckwheat groat (BUHK-wheht grot) Neither a wheat nor a grain, it is the hulled and slightly crushed triangular seed (called a groat) of a plant related to the rhubarb; used like rice; also known as beechwheat, saracen corn, sarrasin and sarrazin. *See* kasha.

buckwheat flour Ground buckwheat; it has a dark color with darker speckles and a strong flavor.

buckwheat crêpe *See* galette.

buckwheat honey A thick, reddish-brown, strongly flavored honey, traditionally coarse and granulated; made principally from buckwheat blossoms in North America and Europe; also available in a clear form.

bucky dough A bakeshop term used to describe dough that is hard to handle.

budin (boo-din) Spanish for pudding.

budino (boo-DEE-noe) Italian for pudding.

budo (boo-DOH) Japanese for grapes.

budoshu (boo-DOH-shoo) Japanese for red wine.

bue (BOO-eh) Italian for beef; also known as manzo.

bue allo spiedo (boo-ae ah-low spee-ae-doh) An Italian dish of beef cooked on skewers.

buey (boo-ee) Spanish for ox.

bufala (BOO-fah-lah) Italian for water buffalo; it is used as a work animal and for producing the milk used in mozzarella.

buffalo The meat of the American bison (also known as buffalo); it has a deep red color, coarse texture and strong, sweet flavor. *See* beefalo.

buffalo berry The berry of a wild bushy tree (*Shepherdia argentea*) native to the northern American Midwestern states; the small red or yellow berry has an acidic flavor and is used for preserves or as a sauce for buffalo meat; also known as a Nebraska currant.

buffalo chopper An appliance used to process moderate to large amounts of food such as bread crumbs or onions; food is placed in a large bowl that rotates beneath a hood where curved blades chop it; can also be fitted as a slicer/shredder or meat grinder; also known as a food chopper.

buffalo cod *See* lingcod.

buffalo fish A fish found in the Mississippi River and Great Lakes; it has a dull brown to olive skin with a white ventral side, an average market weight of 8–10 lb. (3.6–4.5 kg), a moderate amount of fat and a firm texture; significant varieties include the black, prairie, rooter, smallmouth and suckermouth buffalo fish.

buffalo's milk *See* milk, water buffalo's.

Buffalo wings 1. Deep-fried chicken wings served with a spicy red sauce and blue cheese dressing as an appetizer or finger food; they originated in the Anchor Bar in Buffalo, New York. 2. A term used imprecisely to describe any variety of seasoned chicken wings (e.g., teriyaki) served as an appetizer or finger food.

buffer; buffering agent A substance added to a solution to neutralize the acids and/or bases while maintaining the solution's original acidity or alkalinity.

buffet 1. A meal or social event at which persons help themselves to foods arranged on a table or other surface; seating is not always provided. 2. A sideboard table from which foods are served or kept during a meal.

buffet service restaurant; buffet service-style restaurant A restaurant or institutional dining room offering buffet service and charging by the meal. *See* cafeteria.

bug juice 1. Cowboy slang for whiskey. 2. Slang for noncarbonated and typically fruit-flavored soft drinks.

bugnes (buny') A French fritter made of rolled dough that is then fried.

bulb baster A tool used to baste meat, poultry and fish; the basting liquid is drawn into the hollow body by suction created by squeezing the bulb at the other end; available with a hollow, needlelike attachment for injecting the basting liquid into food.

Bulgarian mayonnaise; mayonnaise Bulgare (bulgahr) A French mayonnaise sauce blended with puréed tomato sauce and garnished with diced celery root that was poached in lemon and white wine.

bulgogi (bul-go-gy) A circular and slightly conical Korean metal hot plate used over a tabletop heat source.

bulgur; bulgar; bulghur; bulghur wheat (BUHL-guhr) A wheat berry that has had the bran removed; it is then steamed, dried and ground into various degrees of coarseness; it has a nutlike flavor and texture and a uniform golden-brown color; it is used for salads, stews or cooked like rice. *See* tabbouleh.

bulimarexia An eating disorder combining binge-and-purge behavior with periods of self-induced starvation.

bulimia An eating disorder characterized by binge eating followed by purging.

bulk buying Purchasing products in quantity, usually at a lower as-purchased price per unit; also known as discount purchasing and quantity purchasing.

bulking *See* fermentation.

bulking agent *See* thickening agent.

bulk process *See* Charmat process.

bulk wine An inexpensive wine, usually a blend, of no discernible quality or character; it is generally marketed under the name of the producer or distributor (as opposed to the vintner) or with a general reference to the geographic area where the grapes were grown (e.g., mountain red).

bulla (BU-la) A Jamaican flat cake made from flour and heavy dark sugar; bulla and avocado is a traditional Jamaican snack.

bullabesa (boo-lahn-bah-saw) A fish stew from Spain's Catalonia region.

bullace A wild plum (*Prunus instititia*) native to Europe; it is small and spherical, with a very dark purple-blue to black skin.

bull cheese A 19th-century slang term for strips of dried buffalo meat.

bullet A lobster (usually a Maine lobster) with no claws.

bullhead catfish *See* catfish, bullhead.

bullhorn pepper A long, curved fresh yellow pepper with a mild flavor.

Bullion (BUL-yen) A variety of very bitter hops grown in England and the American Northwest.

bullock's heart *See* cherimoya.

bulls Male cattle, usually not raised to be eaten, although bulls younger than 2 years are sometimes slaughtered for their meat.

bull's eye A large, round English peppermint.

Bull Shot A cocktail made of beef consommé or bouillon, vodka and seasonings, served in a double old-fashioned glass.

bully beef British slang (especially during World War II) for pressed and canned salted, spiced beef.

bulve (bull-vay) Lithuanian for potato.

bumper A glass or cup filled to the brim with an alcoholic beverage; an old English toast is to drink to a bumper.

bun Any of a variety of small, round yeast rolls; can be sweet or savory.

bun Vietnamese for rice vermicelli; it is used in Vietnamese cuisine in a variety of manners, from soups to accompaniments for grilled meats.

bunch grape *See* pigeon grape.

bunch onions *See* scallions.

Bündenfleisch (BEWND-ner-flysh) A Swiss method of serving air-dried beef; it is scraped into very thin wafers and dressed with oil and vinegar and served as an hors d'oeuvre; also known as Bindnerfleisch or Bündnerteller.

bundled cigars Cigars, usually of lesser quality and expense, sold in plastic wrap packs of 10 or 25 (instead of an 8-9-8 box).

Bündnerteller *See* Bündenfleisch.

Bündnerwurst (BEWND-ner-verst) A Swiss sausage made from pork and bacon, seasoned with cloves and pepper, stuffed into a calf's bladder and smoked; it is boiled and served hot or cold.

Bundt pan A tube pan with curved, fluted sides and used for baking cakes and quick breads.

bung A cork, wood or silicon plug or stopper that seals the bunghole of a cask or barrel.

bunghole The hole in a barrel or cask where liquid is added or extracted.

Bundt pan

bunna (boo-nah) Ethiopian for coffee.

buñuelo (boo-NWAT-loh) A light, hollow Spanish pastry that is deep-fried and dusted with cinnamon sugar.

buon appetito! (bw'ohn ah-peh-TEE-toh) Italian for good appetite and used as an invitation to begin eating.

buraki (boo-ran-kee) Polish for beetroot.

burande (boo-RAHN) Japanese for brandy.

Burbank potato A variety of russet potato grown in California.

burbot A freshwater cod found in the United States and Europe; it has a mottled brown skin with a white underbelly, a white, tender flesh that is slightly fattier than the saltwater varieties and a delicate flavor.

burdock A slender root vegetable (*Arctium lappa*) with a rusty brown skin, grayish-white flesh, crisp texture and sweet, earthy flavor; it grows wild in the United States and Europe and is cultivated in Japan, where it is known as gobo.

Bureau of Alcohol, Tobacco, and Firearms (BATF) The U.S. Treasury Department bureau regulating, among other activities, the labeling, transportation and sale of alcoholic beverages.

burek *See* borek.

burger *See* hamburger.

burghul (burr-groll) Arabic for bulgur.

burgoo 1. A thick stew from the American South; it is made from pork, chicken, lamb, veal, beef, potatoes, onions, cabbage, carrots, corn, lima beans and okra. 2. An oatmeal porridge served to English sailors as early as 1750.

Burgos (BOOR-gous) A firm Spanish cheese made from cow's, goat's or ewe's milk; it has a white color, no rind and no holes; often aged in brine.

Burgundy (boor-guhn-dee) 1. One of France's six principal grape-growing and wine-producing regions, located in southeast France. 2. The red or white wine produced in this region.

Burgundy, red The red wines produced in Burgundy, principally from Gamay and Pinot Noir grapes; the wines mature quickly and are generally dry and full bodied, with a tannin content less harsh than that in a Bordeaux.

Burgundy, white The white wines produced in Burgundy; the wines, made from the Chardonnay grape, are generally dry and full bodied.

burgundy bottle A wine bottle with a tall cylindrical body, sloping shoulders and a moderately long neck holding 750 ml (25.4 fl. oz.); originating in Burgundy, France; generally green glass is used for both red and white wines. *See* bordeaux bottle *and* flute bottle.

Burgundy sauce *See* bourguignonne, sauce.

Burgundy snail *See* escargot de Bourgogne.

buriti (boo-ree-tee) A pear-shaped fruit (*Mauritia flexuosa*) native to Brazil; it has a red, scaly skin, a white, segmented flesh and a slightly sour flavor.

burlat cherry *See* bigarreau cherry.

Burmeister A soft, ripened, Brick-style cheese made in Wisconsin from cow's milk.

burned drink *See* short drink.

burner A device that produces heat from gas, electricity or other fuels; it can be arranged with other burners on a stove top or be portable, sometimes with a built-in fuel source such as propane.

burnet (BUR-niht) An herb (*Poterium sanguisorba*) with tiny-toothed, bright green leaves and a sharp, nutty, cucumber-like flavor; the leaves are used in salads and soups or cooked as a vegetable; also known as salad burnet.

burnt china An archaic name for porcelain.

burong dalag (boo-wrong da-lag) A Filipino delicacy made from a mudfish that has been preserved by layering it with salt, soft boiled rice and a food coloring in an earthenware pot for several days, it is then sautéed with tomatoes, onions and garlic.

burrida (bee-REED-dah) A northern Italian stew made with fish, tomatoes and mushrooms flavored with pine nuts, celery, Spanish saffron and parsley.

burrito; burro (bur-EE-toh) A Mexican and American Southwest dish consisting of a large flour tortilla folded and rolled around a savory filling of chorizo, chicken, machaca, refried beans or the like and garnished with lettuce, sour cream, cheese, tomato, guacamole and so on. *See* wrap.

burro (BOOR-roa) Italian for butter.

burro banana A variety of banana grown in Mexico; it has a flat, boxy shape and a tangy lemon–banana flavor; also known as a chunky banana.

burtugal (bur-too-gal) Arabic for orange.

Burundian Arabica coffee beans grown in Burundi; the beverage is rich and pleasantly acidic with a medium to full body.

Bury A type of simnel cake made from a sweet dough enriched with candied orange peel, dried fruits and spices; the dough is rolled into a thin round and decorated with almonds placed in the shape of a cross.

busecca (BOO-zayk-KAH) A thick northern Italian tripe soup served with grated Parmesan and fried bread rubbed with garlic.

bushel A unit of volume measurement in the American and imperial systems; approximately 2150 cu. in. or 4 pecks.

bush pumpkin A variety of small, flat, ribbed squash with a bright white skin, a yellow flesh and a flavor reminiscent of artichoke hearts.

busil (baas-sahl) Arabic for onion.

busser; busperson *See* back waiter.

buster A blue crab at a stage midway between a soft and hard shell; it is battered and deep-fried in Louisianian cuisine.

buta (boo-TAH) Japanese for pork.

butcher *v.* To slaughter and dress or fabricate animals for consumption. *n.* The person who does one and/or the other.

butcher knife A knife with a rigid 6- to 14-in. blade that curves upward in a 25-degree angle at the tip; it is used for fabricating raw meat;  also known as a scimitar.

butcher knife

butcher's cleaver *See* cleaver.

butcher's steel *See* steel.

butcher's twine A narrow, strong string generally made of cotton or linen, used to truss poultry, tie roasts and so on.

buterbrod (boo-tar-broad) Russian for sandwich.

butifarra (boo-teh-FAH-rah) A sausage from Spain's Catalonia region made from lean and fatty pork, seasoned with garlic, oregano, cloves, cinnamon and hot pepper.

butifarra blanca (boo-teh-FAH-rah blahn-kah) A sausage from Spain's Catalonia region; it is made from chopped pork, tripe and fat.

butifarra negra (boo-teh-FAH-rah nae-graw) A small, dark, well-seasoned blood sausage from Spain's Catalonia region.

butler service; butlered hors d'oeuvre The presentation by service staff of hors d'oeuvre, carried on trays, to guests; also known as passed hors d'oeuvre.

butler's pantry A small room or pantry located between the dining room and the kitchen; used for serving and storing china, crystal and the like.

butt 1. The sirloin end (as opposed to the short loin end) of a beef primal loin. *See* Boston butt. 2. The upper end of a ham (opposite the narrow shank end); also known as the rump. 3. The traditional standard cask or barrel used for aging and shipping sherry; it holds 500 l (approximately 132 U.S. gallons). 4. The rear end of a knife handle.

butter A fatty substance produced by agitating or churning cream; it contains at least 80% milkfat, not more than 16% water and 2–4% milk solids; it melts into a liquid at approximately 98°F (38°C) and reaches the smoke point at 260°F (127°C); used as a cooking medium, ingredient and topping.

Butter (BOO-er) German for butter.

butter, clarified Purified butterfat; the butter is melted and the water and milk solids are removed; also known as drawn butter.

butter, concentrated A high-fat butter (96% milkfat content) made by removing moisture and milk solids from the milk before it is made into butter.

butter, dairy Freshly prepared unsalted butter.

butter, drawn *See* butter, clarified.

butter, salted Butter with up to 2.5% salt added; salt changes the flavor and extends the keeping qualities.

butter, sour cream Butter made from sour cream.

butter, sweet cream Butter made from pasteurized cream and usually lightly salted; this is the type of butter principally sold in the United States.

butter, whey Butter made from the cream remaining after the whey is drained from the curds during cheese making.

butter, whipped Butter with air incorporated into it to increase volume and spreadability (it also becomes rancid more quickly).

butter bean *See* lima bean.

butter clam A small Pacific hard-shell clam found in Puget Sound; it has a sweet, buttery flavor.

buttercream A light, smooth, fluffy frosting of sugar, fat and flavorings with egg yolks or whipped egg whites sometimes added; there are three principal kinds: simple, Italian and French.

buttercrunch lettuce *See* lettuce, butterhead.

buttercup squash A moderately large, wide, squat turban squash with a blue-gray turban and a dark green shell; it has an orange-colored flesh and a flavor reminiscent of a sweet potato.

butter curler A tool with a curved serrated blade; used to produce a shell-like curl of butter by dragging the knife across the butter.

butterfat *See* milkfat.

butterfish A fish found off the northeast coast of the United States; it has a silvery skin, average market weight of 1.5 lb. (675 g), high fat content, rich,  sweet flavor and fine texture; also known as dollarfish and harvest fish.

butter curler

butter-flavored granules A low-calorie product made by removing the fat and water from butter extract; it is reconstituted by blending with a liquid or being sprinkled directly on food.

butterflied A market form for fish; the fish is pan dressed, boned and opened flat like a book; the two sides remain attached by the back or belly skin.

butterfly To split food, such as boneless meat, fish or shrimp, nearly in half lengthwise, leaving the halves hinged on one side so that the item spreads open like a book; used to increase surface area and speed cooking.

butterhead lettuce *See* lettuce, butterhead.

Butterkäse (BOOT-er-KAIZ-er) A German and Austrian soft cheese made from cow's milk; it has a yellow interior with no holes, a thin rind lightly covered with mold and a mild, buttery flavor.

butter knife A small knife used to serve butter at the table.

butter lettuce *See* lettuce, butterhead.

butter melter A short, round, tin-lined copper pot with a spout and available in 2- to 9-oz. capacities; used for melting butter; also known as a spouted saucepan.

Buttermilch (BOO-tur-milc) German for buttermilk.

buttermilk 1. Fresh, pasteurized skim or low-fat cow's milk cultured (soured) with *Streptococcus lactis* bacteria; also known as cultured buttermilk. 2. Traditionally, the liquid remaining after the cream was churned into butter.

Buttermilk A soft, fresh English cheese made from buttermilk curds; similar to cottage cheese but with an ivory color and a finer grain.

buttermilk, dried The powder form of buttermilk; often used as a food additive in dry mixes, desserts, soups and sauces.

butter mold A mold used to form softened butter into an attractive shape or to imprint a design on its surface.

butter muslin A British term for cheesecloth.

Butternockerlsuppe (boo-tah-nock-erl-zup-pa) An Austrian beef soup garnished with small dumplings.

butternut *See* white walnut.

butternut squash A large, elongated pear-shaped squash (*Caryoka nuciferum*) with a smooth yellow to butterscotch-colored shell, an orange flesh and a sweet, nutty flavor.

butter oil The clarified fat portion of milk, cream or butter obtained by removing the product's nonfat constituents; also known as anhydrous milkfat.

butter paddles Two ridged wooden paddles used to make decorative butter balls; the butter is placed between the paddles and rotated lightly until it forms a small ball.

butter pat 1. A small piece of butter intended as an individual serving. 2. A small dish, 2–3-in. in diameter, designed to hold butter at the dinner table; it is part of each place setting.

butter plate *See* bread and butter plate.

butter sauce *See* bâtarde and beurre blanc.

butterscotch 1. A flavor derived from brown sugar and butter, used for cookies, candies, sauces and the like. 2. A hard candy with the flavor of butterscotch.

butter spreader A small dull-edged knife with a moderately broad blade used by a diner to spread butter; it is often placed on the bread plate at each setting.

butter steak A fabricated cut of the beef primal chuck; it has a grainy texture and is relatively tender.

butter steam A method of cooking in butter or margarine in a closed container; also known as sweating.

butter tart A Canadian dessert made with a sweet pastry shell and filled with a vanilla-flavored buttery filling sweetened with brown sugar and raisins.

Butterteig (BOO-ter-taik) German for puff pastry.

butter the size of an egg A traditional measure of volume for butter; approximately 1/4 cup (2 oz).

butter the size of a walnut A traditional measure of volume for butter; approximately 2 tablespoons (1 oz.).

buttery 1. A wine-tasting term for an aroma and sometimes flavor reminiscent of butter; often found in Chardonnays. 2. A larder or pantry used to store provisions.

buttock steak *See* topside.

button An immature stage of growth of a capped mushroom when the cap has not yet expanded.

button mushroom *See* common store mushroom.

Buttons up! A toast based on a Scandinavian custom of drinking as many toasts as there were buttons on a man's dress coat at a formal gathering.

butt tenderloin The larger portion of the tenderloin found in the beef primal sirloin; it is used to fabricate châteaubriand. *See* short tenderloin.

butyl acetate and butyl heptanoate Food additives with a strong fruity aroma used as flavoring agents.

butylated hydroxyanisole (BHA) A food additive used as an antioxidant and preservative in dried or dehydrated foods and in processed foods such as breakfast cereals and snack foods.

butylated hydroxytoluene (BHT) A food additive used as an antioxidant and preservative in dried and dehydrated foods and in processed foods such as oils and breakfast cereals.

butyl butyryllactate A food additive with a cooked-butter aroma used as a flavoring agent in baked goods and candies.

butylparaben A food additive used as a preservative.

butyric acid A food additive derived from butter; it has a somewhat objectionable aroma and is used as an acidulant in soy milk–type beverages.

buyback A complimentary drink given to a customer who has already bought three or four.

buza (boo-zah) An Egyptian alcoholic beverage distilled from dates.

búzios (boo-zee-ohs) Portuguese for whelks.

BV *See* biological value of proteins.

BVD A cocktail made of Dubonnet or Byrrh, dry vermouth and light rum; garnished with a twist of orange.

BVO *See* brominated vegetable oil.

byefstroganov (beef-stroh-gah-noff) Russian for beef stroganoff.

byelii greeb (bee-am-lee gra-ahb) Russian for bolete.

BYO Slang abbreviation for bring your own whatever (lunch, bottle, chair and so on) to an event.

BYOB Slang abbreviation for bring your own bottle, beer, or booze, meaning that guests should bring their own beverages, usually alcoholic.

Byrrh (bihr) A French aromatized red wine flavored with herbs and quinine.

Byrrh Cassis (bihr kah-SEES) A cocktail made of Byrrh, crème de cassis and club soda; served in a chilled wine glass.

bythot (bah-dedh) Arabic for eggs.

bzar (bz-ahr) A North African masala with sweet and hot spices such as cinnamon, red pepper, cloves, turmeric, ginger, black pepper and cumin.

caballa (cah-bah-yah) Spanish for mackerel.

cabbage, green The common market cabbage (*Brassica olercaea*) with a large, firm, spherical head of tightly packed pale green waxy leaves; flat and conical heads are also available; also known as the common cabbage.

cabbage, red A variety of the green cabbage with dark red-purple waxy leaves; a red cabbage is usually smaller than a green cabbage, with tougher, slightly more bitter leaves.

cabbage, white A variety of the green cabbage with creamy white waxy leaves; also known as a drumhead cabbage and Dutch cabbage.

cabbages 1. Vegetables of the *Brassica* family; generally quick-growing, cool-weather crops used for their heads (e.g., red cabbage), flowers (e.g., cauliflower), stalks and leaves (e.g., bok choy), and leaves (e.g., kale). 2. More specifically, various members of the *Brassica* family used for their heads.

cabbage turnip *See* kohlrabi.

Cabecou (CAB-bay-koo) A ewe's or sheep's milk cheese from southwestern France; rindless, it has a soft, creamy white interior with a sweet flavor when young and a hard, brown interior with an acrid and unpleasantly goaty flavor when aged; the small flat disks are usually wrapped in chestnut leaves.

Cabernet d' Anjou *See* Cabernet Franc.

Cabernet Franc (cab-air-nay frahn) 1. A red wine grape grown extensively in Bordeaux, France. 2. A wine made from this grape, similar to a Cabernet Sauvignon; it has a herbaceous, minty aroma and a flavor reminiscent of green olives; it is the major red grape in France's Loire Valley, where it is used to produce red wines and the popular rosé known as Cabernet d'Anjou.

Cabernet Sauvignon (cab-air-nay so-vee-n'yohn) 1. The premier red wine grape of Bordeaux, France, California, Australia and many other wine-producing areas; sometimes referred to as the noblest of all red wine grape varieties. 2. A red wine made from this grape; generally tannic when young, it ages slowly, producing a complex, rich mature wine.

cabidela (kah-be-da-law) A Portuguese dish of chicken cooked in butter, parsley, aniseed, bay leaves, tomatoes and red wine and served with rice.

cabillaud (kah-bee-yoa) French for cod.

Caboc A soft double cream cheese made in the Scottish Highlands from cow's cream (and without rennet); it has a delicate, creamy flavor and is rolled in toasted oatmeal, resulting in a crunchy exterior covering a soft, rich interior.

cabra (KAH-brah) Portuguese and Spanish for goat.

Cabrales (kah-BRAH-layss) A firm Spanish cheese traditionally made from goat's milk but may contain cow's or ewe's milk; it has an ivory color with blue-brown veins and a pungent flavor.

cabras cegas (cah-brass sah-gas) Portuguese for a very small, rare variety of crab with a delicate flavor.

cabrilla (cah-bree-yah) Spanish for sea bass.

cabrito (kah-BREE-toh) Portuguese and Spanish for a kid (baby goat).

cacahuates (cah-cah-oo-ah-tess) Spanish for peanuts.

cacahuète (cah-cah-weet) French for peanut.

caçao (cah-cah-oo) Portuguese for a type of small shark; it is an important ingredient in fish stews.

cacao (kah-KAH-oh) The dried and partly fermented seed of the cacao tree (*Theobroma cacao*) grown in tropical regions of the Western Hemisphere; it is used principally in the preparation of cocoa, chocolate and cocoa butter.

caca-poule (cau-cau-poo-la) A small spherical fruit (*Diospyros digina*) native to the Caribbean region; it has a yellowish-brown skin and a sweet, brownish flesh; also imprecisely known as sapote.

cacciatore, à la (ka-cha-TOH-reh) An Italian preparation method for meats, usually chicken, stewed with tomatoes, onions, mushrooms and various herbs and spices and sometimes wine (e.g., chicken cacciatore).

cachaca (cah-chaw-kuh) A dry Brazilian rum distilled from sugarcane.

cachous Small scented tablets used to sweeten the breath; popular in England during the late 1800s.

Cacietto (kah-CH'YEH-toh) A firm Italian cheese made from cow's milk; it has a pale yellow-ivory color and a slightly tangy flavor; it is hand molded into small pear shapes.

cacik (ka-chick) A Turkish salad made with cucumbers, yogurt, fresh mint and dill; served cold as a salad or soup.

Caciocavallo (kah-choh-kuh-VAH-loh) An Italian pasta filata cheese usually made from cow's milk or a mixture of cow's and ewe's milks; it has a mild, delicate flavor when young; after aging 6–12 months, its flavor sharpens and it is used as a grating cheese; it has a white to pale straw yellow interior with a thin, smooth, straw-colored rind and is shaped like a spindle, with one bulbous end and the other elongated with a small ball at the top.

cacio e pepe (KAH-ch'yoh eh PEH-peh) An Italian dish of spaghetti tossed with Pecorino and freshly ground black pepper.

Caciofiore (kah-chah-oh-fee-OR-ay) A soft Italian Caciotta-style cheese made from ewe's and/or goat's milk (sometimes cow's milk is added); tinted yellow with saffron, it has a delicate, buttery flavor.

Caciotta (ca-chee-oh-tah) A semisoft Italian farm cheese made from ewe's and/or goat's milks (sometimes cow's milk is added); it has a pale yellow interior and a flavor that ranges from sweet to mildly piquant.

cactus candy A confection made from the sweet pulp of certain cacti.

cactus pear *See* prickly pear.

ca dai (kah dah-he) Round Thai eggplants ranging in size from that of a pea to that of a grapefruit and in color from white to green, purple, yellow and red; mild ones are eaten raw and green ones, which are very bitter, are used in sauces and curries in Thailand and Laos.

Caen, à la mode de (cah-an, ah lah mohd duh) A French preparation method for foods such as tripe, which are braised with onions, carrots, leeks and blanched ox feet and flavored with herbs, garlic, brandy and white wine; they are usually cooked in a marmite.

Caerphilly (kar-FIHL-ee) A semisoft cheese traditionally made in Wales and now made in Somerset, England, from fresh cow's milk; it has a fresh, tart flavor and a smooth, crumbly, white interior.

Caesar salad (SEE-zar) A salad created in Mexico; it consists of greens, traditionally romaine lettuce, tossed with a garlic vinaigrette flavored with Worcestershire sauce, lemon juice, coddled eggs and sometimes anchovies and garnished with croutons and grated Parmesan.

ca fe (cafay) Thai for coffee.

cafe (kah-FAY) A small, informal and inexpensive restaurant or coffee house (Americanization of the French term *café*).

café (ka-FAY) 1. French for coffee. 2. A small, informal and inexpensive restaurant or coffee house.

café (kah-fay) Norwegian, Portuguese and Spanish for cafe (restaurant).

café (kah-FEH) Portuguese and Spanish for coffee.

Cafe German for cafe (restaurant).

Café Amaretto A hot beverage made of black coffee, amaretto, cloves, sugar, orange zest, lemon zest and cinnamon sticks.

café au lait (ka-FAY oh LAY) A French beverage of equal parts hot, strong coffee and hot milk.

café brûlot (ka-FAY broo-LOW) A traditional New Orleans drink of dark coffee and brandy; it is flavored with citrus rind and usually served flaming.

café Carioca (kah-FEH ca-ree-O-ca) A Portuguese beverage of coffee diluted with hot water.

café com leite Portuguese for coffee with milk.

café complet (ka-FAY kom-play) A traditional French breakfast consisting of a croissant, butter, jam and coffee or café au lait.

café con leche (kah-FEH kohn LEH-cheh) Spanish for coffee with milk.

café continental A beverage of hot coffee mixed with coriander, sugar and warmed sweet red wine; served in a mug garnished with a quartered slice of orange.

café de olla A Mexican beverage of coffee flavored with cloves, cinnamon and brown sugar.

Café Diable (ka-fay dee-ah-blae) A hot beverage made of black coffee, Cognac, Cointreau, curaçao, cloves, coffee beans and cinnamon sticks.

café double (ka-FAY dewbl) A French beverage of double-strength coffee.

café filtre (ka-FAY filt'r) Coffee made by pouring hot water through ground coffee beans held in a filtering device fitted over a cup or pot.

café frappé (ka-FAY frah-pay) French for iced coffee.

café noir (ka-FAY nwahr) French for black coffee.

Café Normande (ka-FAY nohr-mahnd) A French beverage of coffee and Calvados; served hot.

Café Royale (ka-FAY roi-yahl) A hot beverage made of black coffee, bourbon and sugar.

café-simples (kah-fay-SEE-plesh) Portuguese for black coffee.

café society The swirl of socialites, celebrities and other fashionable types who frequent chic nightclubs, resorts, restaurants, fashionable events and the like.

cafeteria A restaurant or institutional dining room that offers buffet service and that charges by the dish. *See* buffet service restaurant.

cafeteria round Any of a variety of subprimal cuts of the beef primal round; they are large roasts, with or without bones, generally carved on a buffet line.

cafetiére (ka-fay-tee-yair) A coffeemaker consisting of a glass pot fitted with a plunger covered in a fine wire mesh; coffee grounds and hot water are added to the pot, allowed to brew and then the plunger is pushed down, trapping the grounds; the coffee then rises through the mesh; also known as an infusion coffeepot and plunger coffeepot.

caffè (kahf-AY) 1. Italian for coffee. 2. Italian for an informal and inexpensive restaurant or coffee house.

cafetiére

caffè Americano (kahf-AY a-mer-i-CAH-no) An Italian beverage made from approximately one-fourth espresso and three-fourths hot water.

caffè corretto (kahf-AY cohr-ett-toh) An Italian beverage made from espresso laced with a small amount of brandy or liqueur; usually served in a small cup.

caffeine (kaf-feen) An odorless, bitter-tasting alkaloid found in cacao beans, coffee beans, cola nuts, tea leaves and other plants; acts as a stimulant on the central nervous system and as a diuretic.

caffè latte (kahf-AY LAH-tay) 1. An Italian beverage made from one-third or less espresso and two-thirds or more steamed milk, sometimes served with a dollop of foam on top; usually served in a tall glass. 2. Italian for coffee with milk.

caffè mocha (kahf-AY MO-kah) A beverage made from chocolate syrup, one-third espresso and approximately two-thirds steamed milk; it is topped with whipped cream sprinkled with cocoa powder; usually served in a tall glass.

caffè nero (kahf-AY NAY-roa) Italian for black coffee.

caffeol (kah-fay-ol) A fragrant oil produced by roasting coffee beans; it gives coffee its characteristic aroma and flavor.

caffè ristretto (kahf-AY ree-strai-toh) An Italian beverage made from 1 oz. of coffee and 1 oz. of water; one of the most concentrated and strongest of espresso drinks; usually served in a small cup.

caffuts (kah-fuh) French for cheese balls.

Cahors (cah-or) A red wine produced in southwest France near Bordeaux; the principal grape is Malbec.

càidanr (kah-e-dahn-r) Chinese for menu.

caife (KA-fee) Irish for coffee.

càihua (kah-he-wah) Chinese for cauliflower.

cai juan (cah-ee jew-ahn) Chinese for egg roll.

caille (CAH-yuh) French for quail.

Caillebotte (caie-butt) A fresh French cheese made from cow's milk; it is white, rich and popular in Brittany, where it is often served with fruit.

cainito *See* star apple.

Caipirinha (Cah-e-pee-ree-nya) A South American (particularly Brazilian) cocktail made of cachaça, lime chunks and confectioners' sugar.

cajan; cajen *See* pigeon pea.

cajeta (kah-HEH-tah) 1. A Mexican caramel sauce made from goat's milk. 2. A Mexican dessert made from fruit or milk cooked with sugar until thick.

cajuada (Cah-joo-ah-dah) A West African alcoholic beverage made from fermented cashew nuts.

Cajun cooking A style of cooking associated with the descendants of French Acadians from Nova Scotia now living in Louisiana; it combines the cuisines of France and the American South, producing hardy dishes typically containing spices, filé powder, onions, green pepper, celery and a dark roux. *See* Creole cooking.

Cajun Martini A cocktail made of vodka (usually pepper flavored) and dry vermouth; garnished with a jalapeño.

Cajun popcorn An appetizer of spicy shelled, battered and deep-fried crawfish or shrimp.

cake In the United States, it includes a broad range of pastries, including layer cakes, coffee cakes and gateaux; it can refer to almost anything that is baked, tender, sweet and sometimes frosted.

cake breaker A long-toothed metal comb with 3.5-in.-long (8.8-cm-long) metal teeth attached to an offset handle; used to cut angel food and chiffon cakes.

cake circle Variously sized circles of corrugated cardboard placed underneath a cake or cake layer for support and stability.

cake comb A small, flat triangle or rectangle of hard plastic or stainless steel with dull serrated edges used for marking a design or pattern into the frosting on a cake; also known as an icing comb or a pastry comb.

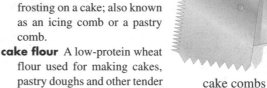
cake combs

cake flour A low-protein wheat flour used for making cakes, pastry doughs and other tender baked goods.

cake fork *See* salad fork.

cake knife A knife with a flat, spadelike 6-in.-long (15.2-cm-long) blade with fine cutting teeth; used to portion and serve cakes and pies and also for lifting and serving the portions.

cake knife

cake lifter; cake stencil A flat, round (approximately 9-in. diameter) utensil with a design in the center and a wedge-shaped handle; it is used (1) to lift and move cake layers for icing and assembly and (2) as a stencil when confectioners' sugar or cocoa is sprinkled over the cake.

cake marker A metal or plastic utensil shaped like a bicycle wheel and used to score the top of a cake into equal wedge-shaped slices.

cake pans Variously shaped and sized containers for baking cake batter.

cake strip A heat-resistant strip of metallic fabric wrapped around the outside of a cake pan to maintain an even temperature during baking.

cake tester A long, thin metal wire with a small ring or handle; it (or a clean broom straw) is used to test a cake for doneness.

cala *See* picnic ham.

calabacita (kah-lah-bah-SEE-tah) Spanish for zucchini.

calabash (KAH-lah-bahsh) 1. A variety of passion fruit (*Passiflora maliformis*) native to Central America and the Caribbean region; it has an apple shape, a thin yellowish-brown skin that can be leathery and flexible or hard and brittle, a grayish or orange-yellow juicy flesh and a pleasant, fragrant flavor. 2. In American southern cuisine, a style of breaded or battered fried fish; named for the seacoast town of Calabash, North Carolina.

calabaza (kah-lah-BAH-tha) 1. A very large, spherical or slightly pear-shaped squash with a fine-grained orange-colored flesh and a flavor similar to that of a pumpkin but moister and sweeter; also known as abobora, ahuyama, cra-paudback, Cuban squash, giraumon, toadback, West Indian pumpkin and zapallo. 2. Spanish for pumpkin.

calabrese (cah-la-brae-sae) A variety of broccoli native to Calabria, Italy; it has large, densely packed blue-green florets and a delicate flavor; also known as green or purple sprouting broccoli.

calamansi A small citrus fruit (*Citrus madurensis*) native to the Philippines; it has a slightly ovoid shape, an orange rind and a very tart flavor and is used in Filipino cuisine principally for its juice.

calamar (kal-ah-mahr) Spanish for squid.

calamares rellenos (kal-ah-mahr-reys ree-an'yohs) A Spanish tapas of stuffed squid; the saclike body is often filled with chopped meat, ham or mushrooms.

calamari (kah-lah-MAA-ree) Italian for squid.

calamata *See* kalamata.

calamondin A very small citrus fruit with a flattened, spherical shape, a thin yellow-orange rind and a slightly sour flavor; native to the Philippines, it is the natural cross product of a kumquat and wild mandarin orange.

calapash The flesh adjoining the upper turtle shell. *See* calipee.

calas (KAH-lahs) A New Orleans pastry made by frying patties of a sweet batter containing cooked rice.

calasparra (cah-las-par-rah) A fine Spanish rice; it is the only controlled denomination of origin rice in Europe and is sold in small cotton sacks.

calciferol *See* vitamin D.

calcium 1. A major mineral used principally to form bones and teeth and to ensure proper nerve conduction, blood clotting and muscle contraction and relaxation; significant sources include dairy products, sardines, beans and bean curd, cauliflower, chard, kale, some citrus fruits, legumes and calcium-fortified foods. 2. A food additive used as a nutrient supplement.

calcium acetate A food additive used as a firming agent, pH control agent, stabilizer and/or thickener in processed foods such as cheeses, baked goods, gelatins, fillings, syrups and toppings; also known as acetate of lime and vinegar salts.

calcium alginate A food additive derived from certain brown kelp and used as a stabilizer and/or thickener in baked goods, fats, gelatins, jams and alcoholic beverages.

calcium ascorbate A food additive used as a preservative and antioxidant.

calcium bromate A food additive used as a bleaching and aging agent for flour.

calcium carbonate *See* ground limestone.

calcium chloride A food additive used as an anticaking agent, drying agent, antimicrobial agent, curing or pickling agent, firming agent (especially in canned foods), flavor enhancer, nutrient supplement, pH control agent, stabilizer, thickener and/or texturizer in processed foods such as beverages, condiments and fruit products.

calcium citrate A food additive used as a firming agent in processed vegetables and to improve the baking properties of flour.

calcium cyclamate A food additive used as a nonnutritive sweetener in soft drinks and processed foods, especially those that are intended to be low in sodium.

calcium disodium ethylenediaminetetraacetate; calcium disodium EDTA A food additive used as a preservative, sequestrant, color stabilizer, flavor stabilizer and/or texture stabilizer in processed foods such as canned cooked shellfish, dressings and distilled alcoholic beverages.

calcium gluconate A food additive used as a firming agent, stabilizer, thickener and/or texturizer in processed foods such as baked goods, dairy products, sugar substitutes and gelatins.

calcium glycerophosphate A food additive used as a nutrient supplement in processed foods such as gelatins, puddings and fillings.

calcium hydrate and calcium hydroxide Food additives used to promote dispersion of ingredients in sauces and similar products; also known as hydrated lime and slaked lime.

calcium iodate A food additive used as a dough conditioner.

calcium lactate A food additive used as a firming agent, flavor enhancer, flavoring agent, flavoring adjuvant, leavening agent, nutrient supplement, stabilizer, thickener and/or preservative in processed foods such as baked goods.

calcium lactobionate A food additive used as a firming agent in processed foods such as dry pudding mixes.

calcium oxide A food additive used as an anticaking agent, firming agent and nutrient supplement; also known as lime and quicklime.

calcium pantothenate A food additive used as a nutrient supplement.

calcium pectinate A food additive obtained from citrus fruit and apples; it is used as a gel coating for meat products and to form food gels.

calcium peroxide A food additive used as a dough conditioner.

calcium phosphate A food additive used as a leavening agent in baked goods.

calcium phosphate monobasic and calcium biphosphate *See* monocalcium phosphate.

calcium propionate A food additive used as an antimicrobial agent in processed foods such as baked goods, cheeses, gelatins, jams and jellies.

calcium saccharin *See* saccharin.

calcium silicate A food additive used as an anticaking agent in processed foods such as salt.

calcium sorbate A food additive used as a preservative in a variety of processed foods.

calcium stearate A food additive used as an anticaking agent, flavoring agent, flavoring adjuvant, lubricant, release agent, stabilizer and/or thickener in processed foods such as baked goods.

calcium stearoyl-2-lactylate A food additive used as a dough conditioner for yeast-leavened products and as a whipping agent.

calcium stearyl lactylate A food additive used as a dough conditioner or whipping agent for egg whites.

calcium sulfate A food additive used as an anticaking agent, coloring agent, coloring adjuvant, dough conditioner, drying agent, firming agent, leavening agent, stabilizer and/or thickener in processed foods such as baked goods, confections, gelatins and grain products; also known as plaster of paris, gypsum and anhydrite.

caldana (kahl-DAH-nah) A small Italian oven used for proofing breads.

Caldaro (CABL-dah-ro) An Italian red wine produced in the Alto Adige region from the native Schiva grape.

caldeirada (KAHL-day-RAH-dah) A Portuguese stew made with octopus, squid, prawns, shrimps and lobster and flavored with onions and bay leaf.

caldera (KAHL-deh-rah) Spanish for kettle or cauldron.

caldillo (cah-dee-yoh) A light Spanish broth.

caldillo de congrio (cah-dee-yoh day kohn-gree-oh) A Chilean stewlike dish made from congrio, tomatoes, potatoes and fish stock and flavored with garlic, bay leaf, lemon peel, oregano and cilantro.

caldo (KAHL-doa) Italian for hot.

caldo (KAHL-doh) Portuguese and Spanish for broth.

caldo de camarâo A soup from the Cape Verde Islands consisting of shrimp cooked with green (unripened) bananas, onions and potatoes and flavored with chiles and tomatoes.

caldo gallego (kal-doh gah-jay-goh) A thick Spanish meat and vegetable stew.

caldos (KAHL-dohs) Portuguese for soups made with a clear broth.

caldo verde (KAHL-doh VAIR-deh) A Portuguese soup made with kale, cabbages, onions, sliced potatoes, linguiça sausage and olive oil.

caldron; cauldron A heavy cast-iron or cast-aluminum casserole or kettle with a rounded bottom and straight sides.

calendula (cah-len-duh-lah) A plant (*Calendula officinalis*) with bright yellow-orange flowers that are used as a garnish or as a yellow food coloring; also known as pot marigold.

calf Meat from cattle slaughtered when 5–10 months old; it has a grayish-red color, some marbling and external fat and a less delicate flavor than that of veal. *See* beef, bob veal *and* veal.

calf's foot jelly An aspic made from the collagen extracted by boiling calves' feet; it is seasoned with wine and spices.

Calia ham A subprimal cut of the pork primal shoulder; it is a relatively tender roast.

Calibogus; Calibougas (kahl-ee-boh-gahs) A beverage made of rum, spruce beer and molasses.

Calichal (ke-lee-CHAL) A Mexican drink made with one part beer to four parts pulque.

calico bass *See* crappie.

calico bean *See* lima bean.

calico scallop A variety of very small scallops found in warm waters off the U.S. East Coast and Gulf coast; it has a red and white speckled shell and tender, sweet white meat.

caliente (kahl-LEEN-tah) Spanish for hot.

California chile *See* Anaheim chile.

California chile, dried *See* New Mexico green chile, dried *and* New Mexico red chile, dried.

California corvina; California corbina *See* drum.

California Dover sole *See* English sole.

California halibut A variety of flounder found off the U.S. West Coast; it has an average market weight of 12 lb. (5.4 kg), lean white flesh, a sweet, mild flavor and a firm texture.

California ham *See* picnic ham.

California horse mackerel *See* jack mackerel.

California Jack *See* Monterey Jack.

California long white potato *See* white potato, long.

California mayonnaise Heavy cream blended with ketchup and seasoned with Worcestershire sauce, Tabasco, paprika and lemon juice.

California menu A single menu listing breakfast, lunch and dinner foods, all of which are available all day.

California roast A fabricated cut of the beef primal chuck; it is a semiboneless, moderately tough, center-cut chuck roast.

California roll A form of sushi made for the American palate; it consists of avocado, crabmeat, cucumber and other ingredients wrapped in vinegared rice and bound by nori.

calimyrna fig (kahl-eh-MURN-a) A large squat fig with a green skin, white flesh and sweet flavor.

calipee The flesh adjoining a turtle's lower shell. *See* calapash.

Calisay (cah-lee-sah-e) A beverage from Spain's Catalonia region made from cinchona.

calisson (kahl-lee-shon) A traditional diamond-shaped confection from the south of France flavored with ground almonds, candied fruits and orange flower water and topped with royal icing.

callaloo; calaloo; calalou; calalu; callilu (CA-la-lu) 1. The very large leaves of plants native to the Caribbean region; they have a flavor similar to that of spinach. *See* dasheen. 2. A Caribbean stew made with callaloo, crab, pork and okra.

calliope coffee A simple gelatin dessert made with strong coffee; it is molded in individual servings and garnished with whipped cream; popular on Mississippi River showboats in the early 20th century.

call liquor A brand name liquor specified by a customer.

callos (KAH-lyoass) Spanish for tripe.

calmar A rare, small squid found in the Mediterranean Sea and Atlantic Ocean off of Portugal.

calonche; colonche (kahl-lohn-chay) An alcoholic beverage made from the fermented juice of certain cacti.

Caloric Punsch *See* Swedish Punsch.

Calorie; calorie 1. A Calorie or kilocalorie (also written as kcalorie, kcal or Cal.) is the amount of heat necessary to raise the temperature of 1 kg of water 1°C. 2. A calorie is a unit of heat used to measure the energy-producing value of foods (1 g of pure carbohydrate or 1 g of pure protein has 4 kcal; 1 g of pure fat has 9 kcal, and 1 g of alcohol has approximately 7 kcal); calorie is frequently and inappropriately used instead of Calorie. *See* joule.

calorie control The limitation on the intake of energy; a principle of many reduction diet plans.

calories The FDA term identifying the total number of calories each serving of a product contains. *See* Calorie; calorie.

calories from fat The FDA term identifying the calories from fat each serving of a product contains.

calories per gram The FDA information reminding consumers that carbohydrates and proteins have 4 calories per gram and fat has 9 calories per gram.

calpis (call-peas) A sweet syrup usually flavored with orange or grape and used to make Japanese soft drinks.

calrose rice A white rice with a high starch content; it becomes slightly sticky when cooked.

calsones (kahl-sow-ness) A Sephardic stuffed noodle, similar to cheese ravioli.

Calvados (KAL-vah-dohs) An apple brandy made in Calvados, Normandy, France; distilled from a mash of cider apples, it is aged in oak casks for 3–10 years before blending and bottling.

calvaille du roi (kal-vah-yay duh rwah) A small, western European traditional apple with a yellow-orange skin, a firm texture and a sour flavor.

calves Young cows or bulls. *See* veal *and* calf.

calves' feet; calf's foot The ankle and hoof of a calf; a variety meat used for stocks and gelatins.

calves' liver; calf's liver The large-lobed organ of a calf; it has a dark reddish-brown color, a tender texture and a strong flavor.

calzone (kal-ZOH-nay) 1. An Italian–American dish made with pizza dough shaped like a large turnover and stuffed with various meats, vegetables and cheeses; it is deep-fried or baked. 2. A Mexican sugar cookie.

camaranga Carambola jam.

camarão (kah-mah-row) Portuguese for shrimp.

camarão de coco (kah-mah-roh day koh-koh) A Mozambican dish consisting of shrimp simmered in coconut milk flavored with chiles, garlic, cumin and tomatoes and served over rice.

camarão grelhado piri piri (cah-mah-rah-oh gre-lha-doe pe-ree pe-ree) A Mozambican dish consisting of shrimp marinated in hot bird chiles, piri piri, garlic and lemon juice and then grilled.

camarero (kah-mah-ray-roh) Spanish for waiter.

camaroes de costa (cah-mah-roe-es day cos-tah) Portuguese for a type of small shrimp.

camaróne (kah-mah-ROH-neh) Spanish for shrimp; also known as gamba.

camaron rebosado A Filipino dish of shelled shrimp (with tail on) dipped in a batter and deep-fried.

cambric tea A beverage of hot water, milk, sugar and a dash of tea, given to children to make them feel like a part of a social gathering.

Cambridge A soft English cheese made from whole cow's milk; it has a salty, fresh flavor and should be eaten fresh.

Cambridge sauce; Cambridge mayonnaise An English sauce similar to mayonnaise and used as a cold sauce for cold meat or fish dishes; it is made from oil and vinegar dripped into pounded hard-cooked egg yolks, capers, anchovies, chervil, tarragon, chives and cayenne.

Camellia sinensis A woody plant, usually pruned to a flat-topped shrub, whose young shoots, unopened leaf buds and leaves are used to make tea; it is grown in warm, wet, subtropical and tropical climates at various elevations worldwide; the finer teas tend to come from plants grown at higher altitudes, and the choicest selections are the terminal bud with its two adjacent leaves.

camel's milk *See* milk, camel's.

Camembert (kam-uhn-BAIR) A soft, creamy French cheese made from cow's milk; it has a creamy texture, a pale ivory-gold color and a whitish-gray, yellow-flecked rind; when perfectly ripe, it oozes thickly, and when overly ripe, it is runny and bitter, with a strong ammonia odor.

Camembert, Fiva An Icelandic camembert-style cheese.

Camembert, Latrobe Valley An Australian camembert-style cheese.

Camembert de Normandie (kam-uhn-BAIR duh nor-mahn-DEE) A French cow's milk cheese made from pasteurized and unpasteurized milk; the unpasteurized version has a bloomy rind with a slight beige mottling, a straw-colored interior and a strong flavor reminiscent of mushroom, garlic and truffle; the pasteurized version has a bloomy rind with reddish mottling and a mild flavor with a slight mushroomy aroma; both are sold in small disks in wooden or cardboard boxes.

Camembert Fermier (kam-uhn-BAIR fehr-meh-yair) Farmhouse Camembert principally made in France's Normandy region from the rich milk of Norman cows.

Camembert Suisse (kam-uhn-BAIR sou-ees) A Swiss camembert-style cheese.

Camerani, sauce (cah-mae-rah-nee) A French compound sauce made from a Madeira sauce garnished with minced black truffle.

cameriere (cah-mah-R'YEH-reh) Italian for waiter.

Cameroun Robusta coffee beans grown in Cameroon.

cami A hybrid of the tangerine and pomelo; it has a smooth, orange rind with a knob at the stem end, a sweet–sour flavor and no seeds.

Camosun A semisoft American cheese made from cow's milk; it has an open texture and a flavor similar to that of Colby.

camote (cah-MOH-tay) *See* sweet potato, white.

campagnola, alla (kahm-pah-N'YOH-lah, AH-lah) Italian for country style and used to describe a preparation method in which the principal ingredient is served with tomatoes and onions.

Campari (kahm-PAH-ree) An Italian bitters with an astringent, bittersweet flavor and red color; a sweet variety is also available.

Campari and Soda A cocktail made from Campari and soda water.

Campbeltown Scotch A Scotch-producing area in southwest Scotland; the Scotch generally has a very full body and a very smoky flavor and aroma.

campden tablet A potassium metabisulfite tablet sometimes added to must or wine as a sterilizing agent and antioxidant.

camper 1. Slang for a person who stays at the bar all night (as in camping out). 2. Slang for a restaurant patron who continues to stay long after the bill is paid.

camphene A food additive used as a synthetic flavoring.

Campidano (cahm-pee-dah-noe) The primary grape-growing and wine-making area of Sardinia; the principal grapes grown include the Malvasi, Moscato and Nuragus.

Campylobacter jejuni A species of bacteria that causes gastroenteritis (called campylobacteriosis); the bacteria is transmitted through contaminated raw milk.

caña (CAHN-yah) 1. The sugarcane from which molasses is derived. 2. A small, slender, straight-sided glass with a heavy bottom used for drinking Manzanilla, particularly in southern Spain; the shape is reminiscent of a venencia.

caña de lomo *See* lomo embuchado.

Canadian bacon *See* bacon, Canadian.

Canadian whisky Made in Canada, a whisky distilled from a mash of corn, rye, wheat and barley and aged for 6–8 years in oak casks; it has a light body, a slightly pale color and a mellow flavor.

Canadice grapes A variety of seedless Concord table grapes; the fruit have a red skin and a particularly fine flavor.

canaigre (kahn-neh-gruh) An herb (*Rumex hymenosepalus*) native to the American Southwest with long green leaves and a reddish stem; its tuberous roots are roasted and ground into flour in Native American cuisines.

Canaiolo (cah-nah-YOH-lo) A red wine grape grown in Italy's Tuscany and Umbria regions; it is often blended with Sangiovese to soften and round out the latter's tannic astringency.

cananga oil A food additive derived from the flowers of a tree of the Anonacea family; it has a strong, somewhat harsh floral aroma and is used as a flavoring agent.

canapé (KAN-uh-pay; KAN-uh-pee) An hors d'oeuvre consisting of toasted or untoasted bread cut into a shape (sliced vegetables such as cucumbers are also used) and typically topped with a spread (e.g., butter or cream cheese) and one or more savory garnishes (e.g., foie gras or sausage).

canard (kah-NARD; kah-NAR) French for duck.

canard à la presse (kah-nar ah lah press) A French dish consisting of a roasted duck served with a sauce made from the mashed liver, juices extracted from the carcass in a duck press, Cognac and wine; the legs are grilled and served as a second course; also known as pressed duck.

canari (cah-nah-ree) An earthenware vessel used to make stews and for baking in West Africa, particularly the Ivory Coast.

Canary Island banana A variety of banana; it is shorter, more flavorful and more delicate than the common banana; also known as the Chinese banana and dwarf banana.

Canary wines Wines from Spain's Canary Islands, particularly popular during England's Elizabethan era.

cancellation system A system used to indicate that a drink recorded on a guest's check has been served; the system usually requires the bartender or server to tear or mark the check, punch a hole in the stub or the like.

cancha (kahn-cha) Toasted corn; traditionally served over a ceviche in Peruvian cuisine.

candela A type of cigar wrapper made from flue-cured tobacco; the light greenish-brown wrapper adds little flavor to the cigar; also known as American Market Selection (AMS), double claro and jade.

candelilla wax A food additive derived from the candelilla plant and used as a lubricant and/or surface-finishing agent in processed foods such as confections and candies.

candied fruit Fruit that is crystallized in sugar.

candle, taper A long, slender, cylindrical mass of wax or tallow with a wick of linen or cotton threads used to give light or sometimes scented (citronella) to repel insects.

candle, votive A short, squat cylindrical mass of wax with a wick of linen or cotton threads used to give light or as a heat source for warming foods.

candlefish; candlelight fish *See* eulachon.

candlenut A spherical, oily nut (*Aleurites moluccana*) with a creamy yellow color and similar in texture and flavor to the macadamia; cultivated in Indonesia, the Philippines and other Pacific Islands and generally used crushed to provide flavor and texture to savory dishes.

candling A method of determining a wine's clarity by holding the bottle horizontally in front of a light source, allowing the light to penetrate the bottle and illuminate any sediment.

candy *v.* 1. To preserve or coat a fruit, flower or other food with sugar or heavy sugar syrup. 2. To cook a food such as carrots or sweet potatoes in sugar and butter, or in syrup, so as to give it a sweet, glossy coating. *n.* Any of a large variety of sweet confections made principally from sugar and flavorings.

candy apple; candied apple An apple immersed in a red sugar syrup that forms a hard, candylike coating on the fruit; usually served on a stick.

candy bar A sweet packaged food, often shaped into a rectangular bar, containing nuts, jellies, coconut, caramel, fondant, nougat, peanut butter and/or other flavorings and often coated with chocolate.

candy cane beet *See* chiogga.

candy coffee beans Commercially produced candies with the shape and flavor of coffee beans; used to decorate desserts, pastries and confections.

candy dipper *See* chocolate dipping fork.

candy dish A small shallow bowl, often footed, used to serve candies, nuts or other sweetmeats. *See* dessert server.

candy hearts Small heart-shaped candies made from sugar paste dyed various colors, usually imprinted with a Valentine's Day message; also known as conversation hearts.

cane beer A sweet–sour beer made from the skimmings of sugarcane syrup (i.e., the froth that rises to the top when sugarcane is boiled).

cane corn Slang for whiskey made from corn and sugarcane.

canederli (ka-NEE-dehr-lee) Large Italian dumplings stuffed with smoked bacon and served with a tomato sauce.

cane fruit *See* strawberry tree.

canela (kah-NEH-lah) Portuguese and Spanish for cinnamon.

canelle knife *See* stripper.

Canestrato Rigato *See* Incanestrato.

cane syrup A thick, sweet syrup; it is the result of an intermediate step in the sugarcane-refining process when the syrup is reduced.

caneton (kan-eh-TOHN) French for duckling.

caneton à la bigrade *See* caneton à l'orange.

caneton à l'orange (ka-nuh-tohn ah lo-rahnzh) A French dish consisting of a roast duckling served with an orange-flavored sauce and garnished with fresh orange slices; also known as caneton à la bigrade and duck à l'orange.

cangrejo (kahn-GREH-khoa) Spanish for crab.

canistel (kah-NEHS-stuhl) A long, egg-shaped fruit (*Pouteria campechiana*) native to Central America and the Caribbean region; it has a shiny lemon to orange-yellow skin when ripe, a firm orange flesh that becomes softer toward the center and a flavor reminiscent of a baked sweet potato.

canister A cylindrical or rectangular container with a close-fitting removable lid, usually of metal or plastic; used for holding dry products such as tea, flour or sugar.

canja (cahn-gee-ah) Portuguese for chicken broth.

canjin (cahn-gin) Chinese for napkin.

canna The tuber of this popular flower (genus *Canna*) is ground and used as a flour and thickening agent in West Indian soups and sauces; also known as Indian shot.

canneberge (can-berj) French for cranberry.

canned cheese A cheese-making process in which the curds are pressed and then sealed in a can for aging and eventual sale; the canning eliminates the moisture and weight loss usually associated with the aging process.

canned ham *See* ham, canned.

canneler (can-lay) French for to flute and used to indicate that the edges of a pastry shell or similar item should be fluted or that a fruit or vegetable should be cut with an implement that leaves a fluted edge.

cannella (kahn-NEHL-lah) Italian for cinnamon.

cannelle (kahn-eh-LEE) Italian for small reeds or pipes and used to describe large, hollow pasta.

cannelle (kahn-nehl) French for cinnamon.

cannellini (kan-eh-LEE-nee) Large, elongated kidney-shaped beans grown in Italy; they have a creamy white color and are used in soups and salads; also known as white kidney beans.

cannelloni (kahn-eh-LONE-ee) Italian for large reeds and used to describe large, hollow tubes of pasta; they are usually boiled, stuffed with meat, fish or chicken and then baked and served with a sauce and grated cheese.

cannelloni

canner The lowest USDA quality grade for beef; the meat is not for retail sale and is used primarily in processed or canned products.

canning A food preservation method; a food is sealed in a metal or glass container that is then subjected to high temperatures to destroy microorganisms that cause spoilage (it also cooks the foods slightly); the sealed environment also eliminates oxidation and retards decomposition.

canning, open-kettle Preserving food by cooking it in an uncovered saucepan and packing it, usually while hot, in a hot, sterilized jar, which is then sealed, cooled and stored.

canning, pressure Processing sealed jars of food under pressure at 240°F (115°C) (at sea level to 2000 ft. [600 m] above; adjustments must be made at higher altitudes); this method is necessary for low-acid food to destroy bacteria that can cause spoilage and food poisoning, including botulism.

canning, water bath Processing certain acidic and/or sweet foods to destroy bacteria, enzymes, molds and yeasts that can cause spoilage; filled, sealed jars are boiled (or simmered) for specific lengths of time in water deep enough to cover them by an inch or so at top and bottom.

cannoli (kan-OH-lee) An Italian pastry composed of a deep-fried tube of sweet pastry dough filled with sweetened ricotta studded with candied fruit, chocolate or pistachio nuts.

cannoli form (kan-OH-lee forhm) A 4- to 6-in.-long aluminum or tinned steel tube with a diameter of 5/8 to 1 in.; it is used to shape cannoli by wrapping the dough around the form before frying it.

Cannonau (cah-noh-NAH-oh) An Italian red-wine grape cultivated in Sardinia; it produces wines that may be dry or sweet, natural or fortified, as well as some rosés.

cannonball guava A large green guava with a dark ring around it; its yellow-pink flesh is sweet and its seeds are edible.

canola oil (kan-OH-luh) An oil made in Canada from rape-seeds; it is relatively low in saturated fats, contains omega-3 fatty acids and has a bland, neutral flavor suitable for cooking and other uses.

can opener, crank A hand tool used to open tin cans; a sharp cutting wheel is clamped over the rim of the can, then a hand crank is turned, causing the wheel to puncture the can and bend down the cut edge around the perimeter of the lid.

can opener, manual A tool used to open tin cans, lift off crown caps, and uncork bottles; the tip of the short blade punctures the can; then, with a rocking motion, it rips around the perimeter of the lid; it usually has a hook that lifts crown caps and a coiled wire worm to uncork bottles.

can opener, table-mounted A table-mounted tool with a long arm to which is attached a sharp blade that pierces the can; a hand crank turned against the blade cuts the can lid.

canopy management The science and practice of growing and training grapevines.

Canquillote (koh-kee-yaht) A cheese made in eastern France from skimmed cow's milk; after the curds are fermented, water, salt, eggs and butter are mixed with the curds, which are then molded into various shapes.

Cantabria (kan-tah-bree-ah) A mild, semifirm Spanish cheese made from cow's milk.

Cantal (cahn-tah) A firm cheese made in France's Cantal region from cow's milk; it has a yellow color and piquant flavor; so-called "accidental" internal molds occasionally form, and the cheese is then known as Bleu de Cantal.

cantaloupe (KAN-teh-lohp) Named for Cantalupo, Italy, where it was first grown in Europe; it is a small, spherical melon (*Cucumis melo*) with a rough surface that is fissured into segments, it has a pale green to orange flesh with a sweet flavor and a central cavity with many small seeds. *See* Charentais melon *and* Ogen.

cantaloupe, American (KAN-teh-lohp) A muskmelon with a raised netting over a smooth grayish-beige skin, a pale orange flesh, a large seed cavity with many seeds and a sweet, refreshing, distinctive flavor; also known as a netted melon or nutmeg melon.

canterela (kan-tay-ray-lah) Spanish for chanterelle.

cantharides The dried, powdered form of a brilliant green blister beetle (*Cantharis vesicatoria*) considered by some to be an aphrodisiac and used in various North African cuisines as a flavoring; also known as Spanish fly.

canthaxanthin A food additive derived from several different plants or animals and used as a pink to red coloring agent.

cantina (cahn-TEE-nah) 1. Italian for cellar, winery or bar. 2. Spanish for bar. 3. A saloon, usually in the American Southwest or with a Southwestern theme.

cantina sociale (cahn-TEE-nah so-shah-LEH) An Italian cooperative wine cellar.

Canton noodles Chinese noodles made from wheat flour, duck eggs, salt and vegetable oil.

cantucci (kahn-TOO-chee) Almond-flavored cookies from Italy's Tuscany region; they are usually eaten with wine.

canvasback duck A wild duck found in North America; it has a distinctive, rich flavor.

cao-mei (tsao-may) Chinese for strawberry.

cap Grape residue (skins, pips and stems) that float to the top of the must during red wine fermentation. 2. The top of a mushroom and usually the spore-bearing part; also known as a pileus. 3. The flat metal covering on a bottle; also known as a crown cap. 4. The tobacco leaf covering the head of a premium cigar; it prevents the wrapper from unraveling and increases mouth feel; also known as the flag.

capão (kah-PAHNG) Portuguese for capon.

capeado (kah-peh-ah-doh) Spanish for dipped in batter and fried.

Cape Cod; Cape Codder A cocktail made of cranberry juice, vodka, sugar syrup and lime juice; served in a chilled double old-fashioned glass.

Cape Fear pecan A pecan variety; the nuts are flavorful and easily cracked.

cape gooseberry A cherry-sized fruit (*Physalis peruviana*) native to South America; enclosed in a thin, papery, cream-colored husk, it has a thin, waxy yellow-green to orange skin, many seeds and a pleasant, distinctive flavor; eaten raw or used in baked goods and jams; also imprecisely known as a ground-cherry or winter cherry.

capelli d'angelo (kahp-PAYL-lee dahn-GEHL-o) Italian for angel's hair and used to describe very thin, long, cylindrical strands of pasta, usually used in soups.

capellini (kahp-payl-LEE-nee) Italian for fine hair and used to describe extremely fine spaghetti.

capelvenere (cah-pel-va-nah-rae) Italian for maidenhair fern and used to describe very fine strands of pasta used in soups.

capers The unopened flower buds of a shrub (*Capparis spinosa*) native to the Mediterranean region; after curing in salted white vinegar, the buds develop a sharp, salty–sour flavor and are used as a flavoring and condiment. *See* nonpareils.

caper sauce An English sauce made from capers, butter, flour and the juices from the roasted meat with which it is served.

capillary; capillaire A syrup of maidenhair fern, water and sugar; it is traditionally combined with cold water to make a refreshing drink.

capirotada (kahpeh-roh-tah-dah) A Mexican bread pudding made with raisins, caramelized sugar and cheese; it is typically served during Lent.

capital cut steak A fabricated cut of the beef primal rib; it is a bone-in rib steak.

capiteux (cah-pee-tuh) A French term meaning heady and applied to a wine that has a high alcohol content.

capitolade (kah-pee-toh-lahd) A French ragout made with cooked meat leftovers, particularly chicken, that are stewed until they disintegrate.

capitone (kah-pee-TOE-nay) A large eel used in Italian cuisine.

cap meat *See* blade meat.

capocollo (kah-poa-KOAL-loa) A flavorful cured ham from Parma, Italy.

capocuoco (cah-poe-cou-oh-coe) Italian for chef; also known as cuoco.

capon A rooster castrated before it is 8 weeks old and fattened and slaughtered before it is 10 months old; it has a market weight of 4–10 lb. (1.8–4.5 kg), a soft, smooth skin, a high proportion of light to dark meat, a relatively high fat content and juicy, tender, well-flavored flesh.

caponata (kap-oh-NAH-tah) A Sicilian dish of cooked eggplant, onions, tomatoes, anchovies, olives and pine nuts flavored with capers and vinegar and served at room temperature as a salad, side dish or relish.

cappelletti (kahp-PAYL-et-ee) Italian for little hats and used to describe small dumplings in the shape of a peaked hat; traditionally served on Christmas day.

cappelli di prete (kahp-PAYL-lee de pray-tee) Italian for priests' hats and used to describe pasta in the shape of a priest's hat (a tortellini with a pointed edge sticking up).

cappelli pagliaccio (kahp-PAYL-lee pah-glee-ACH-chee-oh) Italian for clowns' hats and used to describe pasta in the shape of a clown's hat (triangular tortellini).

capperi (KAH-peh-ree) Italian for capers.

cappone (ca-PONY) Italian for capon.

cappuccino (kahp-uh-CHEE-noh) An Italian beverage made from equal parts espresso, steamed milk and foamed milk, sometimes dusted with sweetened cocoa powder or cinnamon; usually served in a large cup.

capra (kah-prah) Italian for goat.

câpres (kah-PREH) French for capers.

capretto (kah-PREH-toa) Italian for a kid (baby goat).

Caprini (kah-PREE-nee) A fresh, soft, unripened, rindless ewe's or cow's milk cheese from Italy's Piedmont and Lombardy regions; it has a snow-white, moist interior and a sweet-cream flavor.

Caprino Romano (kah-preh-noh roh-MAH-noh) A goat's milk Romano.

capriole (kah-preh-oh-lay) Italian for salted capers.

caprylic acid A naturally occurring fatty acid; a food additive used as a flavoring agent and/or adjuvant in processed foods such as baked goods, cheeses, fats, frozen dairy desserts, gelatins and snack foods; also known as octanoic acid.

capsaicin (kap-say-ee-zin) A compound found in the placental ribs (the interior white veining to which the seeds are attached) of a chile (genus *Capsicum*) and responsible for the chile's hot flavor.

capsicum (KAP-sih-cuhm) *See* chile *and* pepper.

capsule The aluminum, lead or plastic cover placed over the cork of a wine bottle to secure closure and improve appearance.

capsuni (cap-soo-nee) Romanian for strawberry.

captain The person at a fine dining restaurant responsible for explaining the menu to guests and taking their orders as well as any table-side preparations; also known as chef d'étage.

capuchin (cap-eu-chene) A variety of nasturtium grown in Europe; its yellow, orange or rust blossoms have a mild cresslike flavor and are used as a garnish and in salads; also known as Indian cress, Jesuit cress and Peruvian cress.

caque (kak) A large basket traditionally used in France to carry grapes from the vineyard to the press.

caquelon (kak-lohn) A French and Swiss cheese fondue pot.

caqui (kah-kee) Spanish for date plum.

caracois (cah-rah-coe-is) A Portuguese petisco dish of small spicy snails flavored with piri-piri, pepper, garlic, onions and herbs in oil.

caracol (cah-rah-col) Spanish and Portuguese for an edible land or sea snail.

carafe (kah-RAHF) A glass container used to serve wine (generally young, inexpensive wine), coffee, water or other beverages at the table; usually in liter and half-liter sizes and generally without a lid, cork or other stopper. *See* decanter.

caraguejo *See* navalheira.

carambola (kair-ahm-BOH-lah) A fruit (*Averrhoea corambola*) native to Asia; it has a moderately long body with five prominent ridges running its length that create a star-shaped cross section; the fruit has a waxy orange-yellow skin, a crisp, juicy, yellow flesh and a sweet to tart flavor; used in sweet and savory dishes, as a garnish, or in chutneys; also known as star fruit and Chinese star fruit.

caramel 1. A substance produced by cooking sugar until it becomes a thick, dark liquid; its color ranges from golden to dark brown, and it is used for coloring and flavoring desserts, candies, sweet and savory sauces, and other foods. 2. A firm, chewy candy made with sugar, butter, corn syrup and milk or cream.

caramel coloring A light brown coloring agent added to foods (e.g., baked goods and prepared sauces) and beverages (e.g., whiskey, brandy and soft drinks).

caramelization The process of cooking sugars; the browning of sugar enhances the flavor and appearance of foods.

caramelize To heat sugar to very high temperatures, usually 310–360°F (153–182°C); this causes the sugar to brown and develop a full, rich, intense flavor.

caramel malt Green malt kiln dried at a relatively low temperature; it has a reddish-gold color and adds body and a caramel, almost sweet, flavor to beer brewed from it; also known as crystal malt.

caramelo (kah-rah-MAY-loo) Spanish for candy.

caramel ruler; caramel bar A stainless steel or chromed steel bar (0.5 × 0.5 × 20–30 in.) used to hold a caramel, chocolate or fondant mixture while it cools; also known as a chocolate ruler or chocolate bar.

caramel sauce A dessert sauce made from caramelized sugar diluted with water, milk or cream.

caranguejo (kah-rehn-GAY-zhoh) Portuguese for crab.

caraotas negras (kah-rah-oh-tas nay-gras) A Venezuelan dish of black beans mixed with onions, garlic, chiles and cumin; also known as caviar crillo.

carapace The hard outer covering of a shellfish.

cara pulcra (cah-rah pool-cra) A Peruvian dish made with papa seca, pork and ground peanuts and flavored with onions, garlic, cumin and aji.

caraway An herb and member of the parsley family (*Carum carvi*); the fleshy root is eaten as a vegetable, and the feathery leaves are used in salads or as garnish.

caraway mint *See* rau la tia to.

caraway seeds The small, crescent-shaped brown seeds of the caraway plant; they have a nutty, peppery, aniselike flavor and are used to flavor baked goods, savory dishes and the liqueur Kümmel.

carbohydrates A class of organic nutrients, including sugars, glycogen, starches, dextrin and cellulose, that contain only carbon, hydrogen and oxygen; occurring naturally in plants and milk, they are used by the body principally for energy.

carbo-load Slang used by athletes to describe the practice of eating large amounts of food rich in carbohydrates before an athletic event or strenuous exercise.

carbon A nonmetallic element that, along with oxygen and hydrogen, is the characteristic constituent of organic matter; it occurs in pure form as diamonds and graphite and in impure form as charcoal.

carbonada (kahr-boh-NAH-doh) Any of several South American stewlike dishes baked in a casserole.

carbonada criolla (car-boh-NAH-dah cree-ohl-yah) An Argentinean stewlike dish made with beef, onions, chiles, garlic, tomatoes, sweet potatoes, white potatoes, white beans, apples, squash, corn and apricots.

carbonada en zapallo (car-bo-nah-dah en tza-pah-yoh) An Argentinean dish consisting of a veal, sweet potato, corn and potato stew served in a baked pumpkin.

carbonade (car-bohn-ahd) 1. Meat that has been browned until it has a crust and is then cooked in a liquid (braised). 2. An Italian stew made with beef and red wine.

carbonara, alla (kar-boh-NAH-rah, ah-la) An Italian dish of pasta, usually spaghetti, with a sauce of eggs, cream, Parmesan and bits of cooked bacon.

carbonated ammonia A leavening agent made of ammonia and carbonic acid.

carbonated beverage A beverage that does not contain alcohol; it is effervescent (mechanically induced) and usually flavored, sweetened and/or colored; also known imprecisely as a soft drink.

carbonated water *See* water, carbonated.

carbonated wine A sparkling wine made from a still wine infused with carbon dioxide (as opposed to a sparkling wine made by the méthode champenoise or the Charmat process); the bubbles, which are large and coarse, quickly lose their sparkle.

carbonate of ammonia *See* ammonium bicarbonate.

carbonation The process or effect of dissolving carbon dioxide in a liquid to create or increase effervescence.

carbon dioxide 1. A colorless, odorless gas formed from the combustion of carbonaceous materials, the fermentation process or found in natural springs. *See* fermentation *and* carbonation. 2. A food additive used as a leavening agent in processed foods such as baked goods, as an aerating agent and/or propellant in processed foods such as beverages and whipped cream, and as a processing aid.

carbonic maceration A wine-making process in which whole grape clusters are sealed in a fermentor filled with carbon dioxide so that a complex fermentation takes place within the berries, resulting in minimal tannin and volatile acid development; the juice is then pressed and conventionally fermented, producing light-bodied, less alcoholic, fruity wines consumable a few weeks after fermentation (e.g., the French Beaujolais Nouveau wines); also known as whole-berry fermentation.

carbonnade à la flamande (kar-bohn-AHD ah lah flah-MAHND) A thick Belgian beef stew flavored with beer, bacon, onions and brown sugar.

carbon steel An alloy of carbon and iron used for knife blades; easily sharpened, it corrodes and discolors easily. *See* stainless steel *and* high-carbon stainless steel.

carboxymethylcellulose (CMC) A food additive (gum) used as a thickener, stabilizer, binder and the like in dressings, ice creams, baked goods, sauces and puddings.

carboy A large glass bottle with a narrow opening at the top; sometimes used as a fermentor in home beer brewing.

carcass The cleaned, dressed body of a slaughtered animal; it contains both forequarters and hindquarters.

carcinia *See* ma-dun.

carcinogen (car-SIN-oh-jen) A substance that tends to produce or incite a cancer.

carcinogenic Causing cancer.

carciofo (car-CHAW-foe) Italian for artichoke.

cardamom (KAR-duh-muhm) A member of the ginger family (*Elettaria cardamomum*); its long, light green or brown pods contain a seed that has a strong, lemony flavor with notes of camphor and a pleasantly pungent aroma; available in the pod, whole or ground and used principally in Indian and Middle Eastern cuisines.

cardeiro (car-dee-eh-row) Portuguese for lamb.

Cardhu The proprietary name of a single-malt Scotch whisky; it has a mellow, malt, sweet flavor with a lingering aftertaste; it is particularly suitable as a digestif.

cardi (car-dee) Italian for cardoons.

cardinal (kahr-dee-nahl) The culinary approximation of the color scarlet; it is usually obtained naturally from the coral of the hen lobster.

Cardinale (kahr-dee-nahl) A cocktail made of crème de cassis and red wine.

cardinale, sauce (kahr-dee-NAHL) A French compound sauce made from a béchamel flavored with fish stock and truffle essence, seasoned with cayenne pepper, and finished with lobster butter.

carding; to card Slang for checking a prospective patron's identification to determine if he or she is of legal drinking age before serving or selling the person any alcoholic beverages; also known as ID'ing.

cardiovascular endurance The cardiovascular system's ability to sustain oxygen delivery to the muscles over time.

cardo A thistle used in Portugal to curdle the ewe's milk used to make certain cheeses.

cardoon (kahr-DOON) Closely related to the globe artichoke, this vegetable (*Cynara cardunculu*) is composed of stalks that grow in bunches; the silver-gray stalks are long, flat and wide with notched sides and a fuzzy texture; they are boiled, baked and braised in French, Italian and Spanish cuisines.

carel A small, western European traditional apple with a bright yellow skin, a crisp flesh and an intense aroma.

Carême, Marie-Antoine (Antonin) (Fr., 1783–1833) A chef and pastry cook acknowledged as the master of French grande cuisine. He worked his way up from the streets of Paris to become one of the most famous chefs of all time, ultimately employed by Tsar Alexander I of Russia, the Prince Regent of England, Talleyrand and Baron de Rothschild. He authored several texts on the culinary arts, primarily *L'Art de la Cuisine,* and instituted the system for sauce classification still in use today.

cari (kah-ree) Spanish for curry.

Caribbean cabbage *See* taro.

Caribbean coffee A beverage of hot coffee and rum.

Caribbean lobsterette *See* prawn.

Caribe potato A variety of purple potato.

caribou A large antlered member of the reindeer family; a game animal, its fatty meat, known as venison, is not particularly flavorful.

Carignan (cah-ree-n'yahn) A red wine grape grown in France, California, South America and Spain; it is the principal variety grown in Israel; generally used for table wines; also known as Cariñena and Mazuelo.

Carignan, sauce A French compound sauce made from a demi-glaze flavored with tomatoes and finished with Málaga or port.

caril (kah-reel) Portuguese for curry.

Cariñena *See* Carignan.

carissa A fruit from a low, thorny bush native to southern Africa (*Carissa macrocarpa*); the small spherical fruit has a scarlet skin with dark red streaks, white-flecked red flesh, thin brown seeds, a granular texture, and a slightly sharp, acidic flavor; also known as a natal plum.

Carmignano (kahr-mee-N'YAH-noh) A DOCG red wine from Italy's Tuscany region; it is made with Sangiovese and, sometimes, Cabernet Sauvignon grapes.

carmine (kahr-meen) *See* cochineal.

carnatz (car-nutz) A Romanian dish of croquettes formed from boiled or roasted beef and pork seasoned with marjoram and paprika; they are coated with bread crumbs, deep-fried and served with a tomato sauce.

carnauba wax A food additive derived from the Brazilian wax palm and used as an anticaking agent, surface-finishing agent, lubricant and/or release agent in processed foods such as baked goods and mixes, fruit juices, gravies and confections.

carne (KAHR-neh) Italian, Portuguese and Spanish for meat.

carne asada (KAHR-neh ah-SAH-dah) Spanish for grilled meat.

carne de porco (KAHR-neh duh POR-koo) Portuguese for pork.

carne de res (KAHR-neh day rehs) Spanish for beef.

carne guisado (KAHR-neh gee-sa-doh) A Guatemalan pork stew flavored with bay leaves, thyme, jalapeños, cinnamon and nutmeg, cooked in sour orange juice and tomatoes and thickened with bread crumbs.

carneiro (car-na-e-row) Portuguese for mutton.

carne picada (KAHR-neh peh-cah-dah) A Mexican dish consisting of small pieces of beef quickly sautéed and simmered with onions and green chiles, usually served in warm flour tortillas.

carnero (kahr-neh-roh) Spanish for lamb.

carne seca (KAHR-neh seh-kah) Sun-dried and salted beef used in Mexican and Latin American cuisines.

carnitas (kahr-NEE-tahz) Mexican for little meats and used to describe a dish of small shreds of browned pork, usually eaten with salsa or used as a filling for tacos and burritos.

carnivore (kahr-neh-voor) An animal that eats only or primarily meat.

carob (KAIR-uhb) The edible pulp of the long, leathery pods of an evergreen tree of the pea family (*Ceratonia siliqua*) native to the Middle East; the pulp has a chocolate-like flavor and is usually dried, roasted and ground to a powder and used to flavor candy and baked goods or as a chocolate substitute; also known as St. John's bread and locust bean.

carob bean gum *See* locust bean gum.

Carolina tea *See* black drink.

caroline (kah-o-leen) A small French pâte à choux stuffed with a meat purée or pâté and coated with chaud-froid; served as an hors d'oeuvre or garnish.

carota (kah-RAW-tah) Italian for carrot.

carotene, alpha-, beta- and gamma- 1. A substance found in plants and used by the body as a vitamin A provitamin. 2. A group of yellow to orange pigments found in plants. 3. A food additive used as a yellow or orange food coloring. 4. Especially beta-carotene, a nutrient supplement and food additive that, as an antioxidant, is believed to lower the risk of cancer.

carotenoid A naturally occurring pigment that predominates in red and yellow vegetables such as carrots and red peppers.

carotte (kah-rot) French for carrot.

carp A freshwater fish found in Asia, Europe and North America; generally has an olive green skin that becomes more yellow on the belly, an average market weight of 2–8 lb. (0.9–3.6 kg), and a lean, firm flesh that sometimes has a muddy flavor.

carpaccio (kahr-PAH-chee-oh) An Italian dish of thinly sliced raw beef drizzled with olive oil and lemon juice, garnished with capers and sometimes onions, and served as an appetizer.

carpano (kar-pan-noh) A sweet Italian vermouth with a bitter aftertaste.

carpe (kahrp) French for carp.

carpel *See* pip.

carpetbag steak A thick beef steak with a pocket cut into it; the pocket is stuffed with seasoned oysters and the meat is grilled.

carrageenan; carrageen (KAHR-ah-ghee-nahn) A food additive derived from a red algae (also called Irish sea moss) and used as an emulsifier, stabilizer and/or thickener in processed foods such as beers and ice creams, to control ice crystal growth in frozen products, and as a clarifying agent in beverages; also known as chondrus extract.

carré (kar-ray) 1. A French cut of the pork carcass; it consists of the foreribs and can be roasted whole or divided into chops. 2. French for square and used to describe square, flat cheeses.

carré d'agneau (kar-ray dahn-yo) French for rack of lamb.

Carré de l'Est (kar-ray duh-lest) A square, flat French camembert-style cheese made from raw or pasteurized whole cow's milk; it has a more pungent flavor than Camembert.

carré d'hiver (kar-ray dee-vehr) *See* api étoile.

Carré Frais (kar-ray fray) A fresh French Neufchâtel-style cheese made from a rich milk and cream mixture, salted, and coagulated with rennet.

carrettiera, alla (kah-reh-tee-EH-rah, AH-lah) Italian for trucker's style and used to describe a pasta sauce made with browned parsley, onions, garlic, anchovies, capers and bread crumbs.

carrier A person (or other animal) who harbors a pathogenic organism and is potentially capable of spreading it to other humans or animals; a carrier usually appears not to have any discernible signs or symptoms of the disease.

carrot A member of the parsley family (*Daucus carota*); it has lacy green foliage, an edible orange taproot with a mild, sweet flavor and crisp texture, and a tapering shape; it comes in a variety of sizes; also known as an underground cherry.

carrot oil A food additive used as a yellow food coloring.

carrot powder *See* xoi gat.

carrottes (kar-rhetz) French for tiny, sweet carrots.

Carrowgarry A cheese made from cow's milk in a convent in Roscommon, Ireland; it has a pale yellow color, a mild flavor and a semifirm texture.

carryout *See* takeout; take home.

carryover cooking The cooking that occurs after a food is removed from a heat source; it is accomplished by the residual heat remaining in the food.

carta (kahr-tah) Italian for menu; also known as lista.

carta da musica (KAHR-tah dah MOO-zee-kah) Thin, fragile, unleavened sheets of bread made from semolina; a specialty of Sardinia.

carte (kart) French for menu; also known as menu.

cartilage A tough, whitish elastic connective tissue that helps give structure to an animal's body; also known as gristle.

cartòccio (car-toh-CHEE-oh) An Italian preparation method for fish; the fish and a battuto are sealed in oiled paper and baked.

carton *See* case.

carubin *See* locust bean gum.

caruru (kah-roo-roo) A Brazilian stew made from okra, dried shrimp, fresh shrimp, dende oil, onions, cashews, peanut butter, ginger and malagueta and thickened with manioc flour.

carvacrol A food additive with a spicy, pungent aroma used as a flavoring agent.

carve To slice cooked meat or poultry into portions.

carvi (karvi) French for caraway.

carving fork A two-pronged fork with a hand guard. *See* two-pronged fork.

carving knife A knife with a long slender blade used to slice cooked meat; it can

carving fork

have a beveled edge (used for carving a ham) or be more rounded (which adds strength); also known as a meat carver.

carving station The area of a buffet where freshly roasted meats are carved to order; the station is usually a free-standing table with a heat lamp to keep the meats warm.

casaba (kah-SAH-bah) A large, spherical winter melon (a muskmelon) native to Turkey; it has a thick yellow rind with deep, rough furrows that wrinkle at the pointed end, an ivory-colored flesh, and a mild cucumber-like flavor.

casabe (cah-sah-bey) Dry flat cakes made from grated cassava roots and used for various Caribbean dishes.

casalinga, alla (kah-sah-LEEN-'gah, AH-lah) Italian for housewife style or homemade and used to generally describe peasant or country cooking.

Casanova, à la (cah-sah-noh-vah, ah lah) A French garnish for fish consisting of oysters and mussels in a white wine sauce sprinkled with truffle slices.

Casanova mayonnaise A French mayonnaise sauce garnished with hard-cooked egg yolks, tarragon and truffles.

casareccie (cah-sah-rae-tche-ay) Small, twisted pasta from Sicily.

cascabel (KAHS-kah-behl) A small, dried, spherical chile with a thick reddish-brown flesh and a medium hot, slightly acidic flavor.

Cascade A variety of hops grown in the American Northwest.

case 1. A cardboard or wooden box used to hold and/or transport goods. 2. A container used for bottles of wine, beer or other beverages; a standard case holds a dozen 750-ml bottles, two dozen 12-fl. oz. cans, or 9 l or 2.4 U.S. gallons; also known as a carton or box.

casein (kay-seen) 1. A milk protein containing all essential amino acids. 2. The principal milk protein that solidifies milk into cheese; this solidification is facilitated by the action of rennet.

caseinates A group of food additives used as protein supplements, emulsifiers, water binders and whipping aids in processed meats, whipped toppings, coffee whiteners, egg substitutes and diet foods.

case price The wholesale price per case of beverage or food items, as opposed to the price per unit contained within the case, which is usually higher.

cash bar A social function at which guests pay for their own drinks; also known as a no-host bar.

Cashel Blue A farm cheese made in County Tipperary, Ireland, from unpasteurized cow's milk; it has a brownish rind, a creamy interior, and blue-green veining.

cashew A sweet, butter-flavored, kidney-shaped nut with a high fat content; it grows at the end of the cashew apple in three layers of shell, one of which contains a toxic brown oil.

cashew apple A pear-shaped fruit (actually a stalk) from a tree (*Anacardium occidentale*) native to Central and South America; it has a yellow-orange skin and tart, astringent flavor and is used for making vinegar, liqueurs and wine; the cashew nut grows on the outside of the apple at its base; also known as darkassou.

cashier's bank The cash available at the start of a shift necessary to make change for customers; also known as opening cash.

casing The outer covering or membrane of a sausage; it holds the forcemeat or other fillings; a casing can be made from animal intestines, collagen or artificial materials.

cask A wooden (usually oak), barrel-like container with round or oval ends used to store, mature and sometimes transport beer, wine or distilled spirits; it is generally larger than a standard-sized barrel.

cask-conditioned ale *See* real ale.

cassabanana; casabanana (cah-sah-bah-nah-nah) A fruit (*Sicana odorifera*) native to Central America; it resembles a large, thick cucumber with a smooth, shiny skin that can be red, purple or black; it has a yellow or orange flesh and a melonlike flavor and aroma; it can be eaten raw, made into jam, or used in sweet and savory dishes; also known as coroa, curuba, musk cucumber and sikana.

cassareep (KAS-sah-reep) A syrupy condiment used regularly in West Indian cuisine; it is made by boiling the bitter juice of the cassava plant with brown sugar and spices.

cassata (kas-SAA-tah) A Sicilian dessert for which a mold is lined with liqueur-soaked chocolate sponge cake, then filled with ricotta, candied fruit and chocolate shavings; the dessert is chilled, unmolded and decorated with marzipan and whipped cream.

cassatedde (kah-sah-THE-deh) A Sicilian sweet turnover filled with ricotta, fried and coated with honey.

cassava; cassava root (cah-SAH-vah) A large, long starchy root (*Manihot utilissima*) with a tough brown skin and crisp white flesh; a staple of South American and African cuisines and used to make tapioca; also known as Brazilian arrowroot, manioc and yuca.

cassava flour *See* tapioca.

cassava meal Sun-dried and grated cassava.

casserole 1. Any of a variety of baked dishes made with meat, poultry, fish, shellfish, pasta and/or vegetables, bound with a sauce and often topped with bread crumbs, cheese or the like. 2. The deep dish, usually with two handles and a tight-fitting lid and made of ceramic or glass, used to bake and serve these foods.

casserole braising A method for cooking poultry and meats in a close-fitting covered casserole; also known as en cocotte; casserole braising can be carried out with fat alone (poêler) or with a small amount of liquid (étuver).

casseruola bassa (ka-se-rou-oh-lah bah-sah) Italian for brazier.

cassia (KAH-see-uh; KASH-uh) A spice that is the inner bark of the branches of a small evergreen tree (*Cinnamomum cassia*); it has a darker red-brown color, coarser texture and stronger, less subtle and slightly more bitter flavor than its close relative, cinnamon, and is often sold as cinnamon; it is also known as Chinese cinnamon. *See* cinnamon.

cassia blossom wine *See* kweilin gui hua jiu.

cassis *See* crème de cassis.

cassonade (cas-sohn-ahd) French for brown (unrefined) sugar.

cassoulet (ka-soo-LAY) A French stew of white beans, sausages, pork or lamb and preserved goose or duck flavored with a bouquet garni and an onion studded with cloves and garlic.

castagna (kah-STAH-n'yah) Italian for chestnut.

castana (kah-STA-nah) Spanish for chestnut.

castanha (kah-STAN-nya) Portuguese for sweet chestnuts.

Castelan sauce; castellane, sauce (cas-tay-lan) A French compound sauce made from a Madeira sauce flavored with tomatoes and garnished with diced bell peppers and ham; usually served with lamb or beef medallions, garnished with diced, sautéed tomatoes, potato croquettes and fried onion rings.

Castelmagno (kah-stehl-MAH-n'yoh) A mild gorgonzola-style cheese made in Italy's Piedmont region from cow's milk; has a yellow-white interior with bluish-green veining and a mild flavor when young that becomes stronger as it ages.

caster A small glass, ceramic or metal bottle with a perforated top used for sprinkling sugar, pepper, dry mustard or other dry seasonings or ingredients on food.

caster set A set of casters, each intended to hold a different seasoning, held on a tray and used at the table.

cast iron An alloy of iron, carbon, and other elements; depending on the composition, it can be soft and strong or hard and brittle. *See* ironware.

castor oil A food additive used as a release and antisticking agent for hard candy and a component of protective coatings for vitamin and mineral tablets.

castor sugar; caster sugar *See* superfine sugar.

castrato (kah-STRA-doh) Italian for a castrated sheep.

catabolism The destructive phase of metabolism during which complex substances are converted into simpler ones, often with the release of energy. *See* anabolism.

catalan (ka-tah-lahn) French for milky cap mushroom.

catalane, à la (kah-tah-lon, ah lah) French for in the style of Catalonia (Spain) and used to describe certain meat garnishes (e.g., beef is garnished with diced eggplant and rice pilaf and chicken and lamb are garnished with tomatoes, chipolata and olives).

Catalane, sauce (kah-tahl-ahn) A French compound sauce made from a Madeira sauce, seasoned with garlic, mustard, tomato and cayenne; it is typically served with sautéed beef medallions on a base of sliced, sautéed eggplant and garnished with large mushroom caps stuffed with risotto.

catalyst A substance causing or accelerating a chemical change in another substance or substances without itself being affected permanently by the process.

cataplana (kah-tah-plah-nah) A Portuguese copper pan with two handles and a hinged lid; used to steam and serve shellfish and vegetables.

catarina (cah-tah-reh-nah) A small, dried, garnet-colored chile shaped like a teardrop or bullet; it has a medium hot, crisp flavor.

Catarratto (cah-tah-RAH-toe) A white wine grape

cataplana

grown in Italy (especially Sicily) and used to make Marsala.

Catawba (ca-TAW-ba) 1. An American grape (*Vitis labrusca*) grown principally in New York state; it has a pronounced and very sweet grape flavor. 2. The still or sparkling white wine made from this grape.

catch *v.* To broil or grill a food until its edges burn or scorch. *n.* A quantity of fish, usually all those caught during a specific period.

catchup; catsup *See* ketchup.

caterer A person or entity that supplies foods, beverages, service items, personnel and/or almost anything else nec-

essary for a social event at the caterer's own facility or elsewhere.

catering director The person at a hotel, restaurant or comparable facility who solicits, promotes and arranges for social events such as parties, meetings and the like to be held on or off premises with food, beverages and service equipment and personnel supplied by the facility.

catfish A freshwater fish found in southern and midwestern American lakes and rivers and extensively aquafarmed; it has long barbels, a scaleless brownish skin, a pure white, slightly fatty flesh, a firm texture, and a mild, sweet flavor. *See* hogfish.

catfish, bullhead A small catfish with an average weight of 1 lb. (450 g).

catfish, channel The common catfish; it has a deeply forked tail, a relatively small head, small irregular spots on a tough, inedible skin, and an average weight of 2–5 lb. (1–2.2 kg). *See* fiddler.

catfish tender A subprimal cut of the beef primal chuck; it is a somewhat tough, front-cut chuck roast.

cathartics Strong laxative agents; also known as purgatives.

cation *See* ion.

cat's claw A nutrient supplement made from the bark of an Amazon rain forest thorny vine and believed by some to help individuals with asthma, ulcer, and cancer.

cats' tongues Long, thin, slightly sweet cookies; also known as langues de chat.

cattle The collective name for all domesticated oxen (genus *Bos*), including bulls, calves, cows, heifers, stags and steers.

Cattley guava A small red guava with a white flesh and a berrylike flavor.

Caucasian wingnut The nut of a tree native to the Caucasus; it has semicircular wings.

caudalie (coh-dah-lee) A French wine-tasting term for the length of time that a wine's aftertaste lingers in the mouth; 1 caudalie equals 1 second of persistence.

caudle (KAHU-dahl) A hot drink made of wine or beer mixed with eggs, bread, sugar and spices; usually consumed for alleged medicinal purposes.

cauled A process in which a liquid, usually stock, is heated to just below the boiling point, when scum forms.

caul fat The fatty membrane that lines the abdominal cavity of hogs and sheep; this thin, lacy, weblike net is used to wrap forcemeats and melts rapidly when cooked, thereby basting the item.

cauliflower A member of the cabbage family (*Brassica oleracea*); it has a head (called a curd) of tightly packed white florets (a purple variety is also available) partially covered with large, waxy, pale green leaves on a white-green stalk; some varieties have a purple or greenish tinge.

cauliflower fungus A very large, cream-colored wild mushroom (*Sparassis crispa*) with a brittle, waxlike flesh and a pleasant smell.

causa (cah-who-sah) A Peruvian dish of potatoes mashed with onion, dried chiles and oil, molded into a dome, and garnished with hard-boiled eggs, olives, cheese, shrimp, avocado and corn on the cob.

caustic potash *See* potassium hydroxide.

cava (cah-vah) 1. Spanish sparkling wine made by the méthode champenoise. *See* granvas. 2. Spanish for cellar. 3. Greek for a high-quality table wine.

cavaliére, sauce (cah-vah-lee-yair) A French compound sauce made from a demi-glaze flavored with tomatoes, seasoned with mustard and tarragon vinegar, and garnished with capers and diced sour gherkins.

cavallo (kah-VAH-loh) Italian for horse meat.

cavatappi (kah-vah-tap-pee) Italian for corkscrew.

cavatelli (kah-vah-tel-ee) Long, crinkle-edged shells of Italian pasta.

cave (cah'v) French for an underground storage area for wine.

caveach A British dish of fried, pickled fish.

caveau (kah-vo) A French wine-tasting cellar open to the public.

cave cooperative French for wine cooperative.

caviale (kah-vee-AH-lay) Italian for caviar.

caviar (kav-ee-AHR) 1. The salted roe of the sturgeon; the small spheres have a crisp texture that should pop in the mouth and have a pleasantly salty flavor; available fresh or pasteurized in tins and jars. *See* beluga, malossol, osetra *and* sevruga. 2. An improperly and imprecisely used term to describe the roe of fish such as whitefish, lumpfish, salmon, herring, pike and perch.

caviar, pasteurized Caviar that is heated and placed in airtight jars; it has a long shelf life, although some flavor is lost.

caviar, pressed A processed caviar made from osetra and sevruga roes; it has a spreadable, jamlike consistency.

caviar crillo *See* caraotas negras.

caviste (cah'v-est) French for wine cellar man or master cellarer.

cavolfiore (kah-voal-fee-OA-ray) Italian for cauliflower.

cavolo (KAA-voa-loa) Italian for cabbage.

cavolo rosso (KAA-vole-oh roo-so) Italian for red cabbage.

cavolo verde (KAA-vole-oh vair-day) Italian for green cabbage.

cawl (kah-ool) Welsh for soup.

çay (sah-e) Turkish for tea.

cayenne; cayenne pepper (KI-yen; KAY-yen) 1. A hot, pungent, peppery powder blended from various ground, dried hot chiles and salt; it has a bright orange-red color and fine texture; also known as red pepper. 2. A dried, thin, short chile with a bright red color, thin flesh and hot, tart, acidic flavor; usually used ground.

cazuela (kah-SWEH-lah) 1. A shallow, rustic unglazed earthenware casserole with a glazed interior and no cover; used in traditional and rural Spanish cuisines. 2. The stew cooked in such a dish.

cazuela de pavo (kah-SWEH-lah day pah-voh) A Chilean

cazuela

dish of turkey marinated in garlic, wine and orange juice and braised in a cazuela with onions, tomatoes, bay leaf, chiles and the marinade.

CC Certified Culinarian; it is the entry-level certification offered by the American Culinary Federation.

CCC Certified Chef de Cuisine.

CCE Certified Culinary Educator.

CCK *See* cholecystokinin.

CCP Certified Culinary Professional.

CDC *See* Centers for Disease Control and Prevention.

çebiç (cheh-chi) 1. A Turkish dish of spit-roasted whole kid or lamb. 2. A daylong Turkish party; it begins with breakfast, and çebiç is served at noon.

cebola (sah-boh-lah) Portuguese for onion.

cebolina Portuguese for shallot.

cebolla (theh-BOH-lah) Spanish for onion.

cebollita (theh-BOH-leh-tah) Spanish for green onion.

Cebreiro (seh-BRAIR-oh) A Spanish cow's milk cheese made in the shape of a soufflé; it has a sour, bitter flavor, a buttery aroma, and a beige crust with a white and yellow interior.

Cebrero (theh-BREH-tou) A Spanish cheese with a creamy, blue-veined interior, a yellow rind, and a sharp flavor.

cebulka (tze-boal-kah) Polish for shallot.

CEC Certified Executive Chef.

ceci (cheh-chee) Italian for chickpeas.

cecina (say-see-nah) Air-dried beef that has been salted, marinated and sometimes smoked; a specialty of Spain's León region.

cecum The first portion of the large intestine.

cedary A wine-tasting term for the characteristic cedarlike aroma associated with red wines aged in oak casks; it is often found in the red wines of Bordeaux, France, and Rioja, Spain.

cédrat (sa-drah) French for citron.

cedro (tchae-droh) Italian for citron.

céleri (sal-ree) French for celery.

celeriac (seh-LER-ee-ak) A small to medium-sized, brown, knobby vegetable (*Apium graveolens*) that is the root of a specially bred celery plant; it has a flavor reminiscent of celery and parsley and is eaten raw or cooked; also known as celery knob and celery root.

céleri bâtard *See* lovage.

celery (SELL-ree) Developed in 16th-century Italy, this vegetable (*Apium graveolens*) grows in bunches of long, stringy, curved stalks or ribs surrounding a tender heart; it can be eaten raw, cooked or used as a flavoring; there are two principal celery varieties: Pascal (which is pale green) and golden (which is creamy white); also known as branch celery.

celery knob *See* celeriac.

celery mustard *See* bok choy.

celery root *See* celeriac.

celery salt A seasoning blend of ground celery seeds (lovage) and salt.

celery seeds The seeds of the herb lovage; they are small and brown and are used in pickling and as a flavoring.

celeste fig A medium-sized pear-shaped fig with a purple skin and a pinkish flesh.

cell The smallest unit in which independent life can exist; living things are either single cells or organisms composed of cells.

cellar 1. A place to store wine; although not necessarily underground, it should be cool, dark and vibration free; also known as a wine cellar. 2. A wine collection.

cellar *See* saltcellar.

cellared and bottled by A labeling term for a wine that was purchased from another winery but blended and bottled at the designated winery.

cellar temperature The temperature of a wine cellar, it is generally cool, approximately 55–60°F (12.8–15.6°C), although it can fluctuate from 45 to 70°F (7.2 to 21.1°C).

cellophane noodles Relatively clear Asian noodles made from a dough of mung bean flour and water; they have a slippery-soft texture when cooked; also known as translucent noodles, transparent noodles, shining noodles, silver noodles, bean threads and bean vermicelli.

cell salts A mineral supplement prepared from healthy, living cells and of no recognized nutritional significance.

cellulose 1. A polysaccharide occurring naturally in the cell walls of plants; as dietary fiber, it provides no nutritional value, because it is not absorbed during digestion. 2. A food additive derived from plants and used as a thickener and/or texturizer in processed foods such as baked goods, especially reduced-calorie breads.

Celsius A temperature scale with 0° as the freezing point of water and 100° as its boiling point; to convert to Fahrenheit, multiply the Celsius figure by 9, divide by 5, and add 32; also known as centigrade.

celtuce (cehl-TUSS) A hybrid lettuce with celerylike stalks and moderate-sized tender leaves with a celerylike flavor.

cena (tchae-nah) Italian and Spanish for dinner.

cenci (CHEN-chee) Italian for rags and tatters and used to describe pastries made from thinly rolled strips of sweet rum- or brandy-flavored dough tied into knots, deep-fried and sprinkled with confectioners' sugar while still warm.

Cendrat (sen-drat) A large goat's milk cheese with a creamy consistency and a characteristic flavor from Spain's Catalonia region.

cendré (sun-drae) French term for cheeses ripened in ashes (vegetable ash gives them a bluish hue); they are usually made in wine-producing regions.

cenoura (seh-NOH-rah) Portuguese for carrot.

centaury, common An annual or biennial herb (*Cenaurium erythraea*) with an erect stem, slender, narrow leaves and bright rose-red, funnel-shaped flowers; the stems are used medicinally and to make bitter herbal wines and liqueurs.

centeio (sen-tyu) Portuguese for rye.

centeno (sen-tay-noh) Spanish for rye.

center cut 1. A fabricated or subprimal cut of beef, veal, lamb or pork taken from the interior of a subprimal or primal cut; the outer edges or ends of the larger cut are removed to create a more desirable portion from which more uniform and attractive smaller cuts are produced. 2. The cut that divides a ham into the rump (butt) and shank halves. *See* wheel.

center-cut chuck steaks Fabricated cuts of the beef primal chuck; they are steaks cut from the center of the primal chuck and are flavorful and meaty.

center-cut steak A fabricated cut of the beef primal round; it is a tender, very lean round steak.

center leg roast *See* American leg of lamb.

center loin chop; center-cut rib chop A fabricated cut of the pork primal loin; a chop cut from the center of the loin.

Centers for Disease Control and Prevention (CDC) Part of the U.S. Department of Health and Human Services; its principal function is to track illnesses, including those caused by foodborne pathogens.

center slice ham A fabricated cut of the pork primal fresh ham; it is an oval slice of ham containing a small round bone and cut from an area approximately 1 in. (2.54 cm) on either side of the center cut.

centi- *See* metric system.

centigrade *See* Celsius.

Central Coast A large grape-growing and wine-producing region covering all California coastal counties from San Francisco to Los Angeles (Alameda, Contra Costa, Santa Clara, Santa Cruz, Monterey, San Benito, San Luis Obispo and Santa Barbara); the principal grapes grown are Pinot Noir, Johannisberg Riesling, Zinfandel, Cabernet Sauvignon, Chenin Blanc, Sauvignon Blanc and Pinot Blanc.

century eggs *See* hundred-year-old eggs.

century plant *See* maguey.

cep (sehp) French for the individual vine or vinestock.

cépage (seh-pahj) French for the variety of grapevine.

cèpe (sehp) French for bolete.

cephalopods (SEHF-uh-luh-pods) A general category of mollusks characterized by elongated muscular arms, often with suckers, a distinct head with well-developed eyes and a beak-shaped jaw, a saclike, fin-bearing mantle, an ink sac, and a thin internal shell called a pen or cuttlebone; significant varieties include the cuttlefish, octopus and squid.

ceramics Hard, sometimes brittle, materials made from clay and similar materials treated by heat and often glazed; ceramics, which include earthenware, porcelain and stoneware and are used for cookware, bakeware, dinnerware and serviceware, conduct heat evenly, retain temperatures well and, depending on the glaze, if any, are generally nonreactive with acids and bases.

Cerasuolo (cheh-rah-SWAW-loh) Italian for a cherry-hued rosé wine.

cerdena (serr-day-nah) Spanish for sardine.

cerdo (serr-doh) Spanish for pork.

cerdo con frutas (serr-doh kon froo-tas) A Venezuelan dish of pork chops baked with apricots, raisins, ground almonds and orange juice, flavored with ginger, cinnamon, nutmeg, and allspice, and garnished with avocado.

cereal 1. Any gramineous plant yielding an edible grain such as wheat, rye, oats, rice or corn. 2. A term used imprecisely to describe any such plant, as well as a plant yielding an edible seed such as buckwheat. 3. These grains and seeds. 4. Processed foods such as breakfast cereals made from these grains and seeds.

cereal beer *See* nonalcoholic malt beverage.

cereal bowl A moderately deep bowl, usually without a rim, used for breakfast cereals, soup and the like.

cereal cream *See* cream, cereal.

cereja (say-RAY-zhah) Portuguese for cherry.

cereza (se-ray-sah) Spanish for cherry.

cereza de Jamaica (se-ray-sah day jah-may-kah) Spanish for Barbados cherry.

cerfeuil (sehr-fuhy) French for chervil.

cerfoglio (tchaer-foe-io) Italian for chervil.

ceriman (SEHR-uh-muhn) *See* monstera.

cerise (suh-reez) French for cherry.

cerise des Antilles (suh-reez da-san-tee-yea) French for Barbados cherry.

certified When used in connection with a food additive, it means that the food additive has been approved by the FDA.

certified milk *See* milk, certified.

Certosa (sehr-toh-suh) A variety of Italian monastery liqueurs reminiscent of Chartreuse.

cerveja (sehr-vay-hah) Portuguese for beer.

cervelas (sehr-veh-la) A French sausage available in large and small sizes; traditionally made with hog brains, now made from pork meat and fat, seasoned with garlic; also known as saucisse de Paris or saucisson de Paris.

cervelat (SIR-vuh-lat) A style of French sausages made from chopped pork and/or beef, seasoned with herbs, spices and other flavorings such as garlic or mustard; they are preserved by curing, drying and smoking and have a semidry to moist, soft texture.

Cervelatwürst (SEHR-veh-layt-voost) A spreadable, highly spiced, smoked German sausage made from pork and beef filets.

Cervellata (cher-veh-LAH-tah) A Milanese sausage made with pigs' brains and flavored with saffron.

cervelles (sehr-vehlz) French for brains, usually calves' brains.

cerveza (sehr-vay-saa) Spanish for beer.

cerviche; cebiche *See* seviche.

cèrvo (CHEH-voa) Italian for game venison.

cestino di frutta (cheh-stee-noh dee FROO-tah) Italian for fruit basket.

cetriolo (chay-tree-o-loa) Italian for cucumber.

ceun chai (kern chai) Thai for celery.

ceviche *See* seviche.

cevizli ay (sah-vees-lee a-e) Turkish croissants with a sultana and walnut filling.

Ceylon A Sri Lankan black pekoe tea; the beverage has a golden color, full flavor, and delicate fragrance; ideal for serving iced, because it does not become cloudy when cold.

Ceylon cinnamon *See* cinnamon.

Ceylon gooseberry *See* ketembilla.

CF *See* conversion factor.

chá (shah) Portuguese for tea.

chá (tsah) 1. Chinese for tea. 2. Chinese for simmering a food in a large quantity of water. *See* chu.

cha; char; chia British slang for tea; the name is derived from the Mandarin Chinese word for tea: chá.

chaar magaz (tcha-aha mah-gatz) A paste made from ground melon, pumpkin, squash and watermelon seeds; it is used as a thickener and flavoring in Indian curries.

chaay (tcha-ee) Hindi for tea.

Chabichou (cha-be-shoe) A soft French cheese made from goat's milk; it has an assertive, tangy flavor and chalky white interior; it is sold in a cone shape with a bluish-gray rind or as a log with a white rind.

Chablais (shah-b'lay) A wine district in eastern Switzerland that is planted with the Chasselas grape; the wines are all white and fairly full bodied; they rank among the best Swiss wines.

Chablis (shah-blee) 1. A white Burgundy wine made from Chardonnay grapes and named for the village and surrounding area in northern Burgundy, France, where it is produced; generally dry, it has a pale straw color and can be thin and tart or rich and full. 2. In the United States and Australia, a sometimes imprecisely used term to describe any inexpensive and not necessarily dry white wine. *See* French Colombard.

chaclét (sha-klat) Hindi for chocolate.

chafing dish A dish used to warm or cook foods; it consists of a container with a heat source (candle, solid fuel or electric element) directly beneath it; the container can be an assemblage similar to a bain marie; also known as réchaud, which is French for reheat.

chafing dish

chagal (sha-gal) Hindi for goat.

chai (chie) Russian for tea.

chai (shay) A ground- or aboveground-level warehouse used for storing wine in France, principally in Bordeaux.

chai (tcha-ee) Swahili for tea.

chain The side muscle of a tenderloin.

chakhokhbili (chah-kok-bee-lee) A Russian dish of chicken or lamb simmered with onions and tomatoes flavored with vinegar, stock, bay leaf and other seasonings; it is served with peeled, sliced tomatoes and lemon slices and garnished with parsley.

chakin (cha-ken) A Japanese form of sushi; thin sheets of omelet are filled with a seasoned rice mixture and shaped into rolls or balls.

chakko (tcha-koe) Hindi for knife.

chakla (tcha-klah) A marble or wooden board used for rolling bread in India.

chakleti (tcha-ka-tee) Swahili for chocolate.

chakula (tcha-koo-lah) Swahili for food.

chakula cha asubuhi (tcha-koo-lah cha ah-soo-bah-he) Swahili for breakfast.

chakula cha jioni (tcha-koo-lah cha gio-nee) Swahili for dinner.

chakula cha mchana (tcha-koo-lah cha mah-cah-nah) Swahili for lunch.

chalada fakya (sha-law-dah fah-key-ah) An Algerian salad of citrus fruit, melons, banana and apples dressed with orange juice, lemon juice, sugar, orange water, vanilla and cinnamon.

chalada felfel (sha-law-dah fell-fell) An Algerian salad of grilled bell peppers and tomatoes dressed with lemon juice, olive oil, cumin, parsley and black pepper.

chalaza; chalaza cord (kuh-LAY-zah) *pl.* chalazae. A thick, twisted strand of egg white anchoring the yolk in place; neither an imperfection nor part of an embryo; the more prominent the cord, the fresher the egg.

chalkboard menu A large sign, usually positioned at the front of a food services facility, announcing one or more special items.

chalky A cheese-tasting term for a very white or very smooth and fine-grained cheese, usually a goat cheese; a positive attribute, the term does not refer to flavor.

challah; hallah (HKAH-lah; HAH-la) A tender, rich Jewish yeast bread usually made with butter and honey and shaped into a braided loaf.

challah knaidel (khah-la knayd-dhul) A Jewish dumpling made from dried challah crumbs.

chalni (tchal-knee) Hindi for strainer, sieve or sifter.

chalote (shah-LOU-tah) Spanish for shallot.

chalupa (chah-LOO-pah) Corn tortilla dough formed into the shape of a boat and fried; it is used in Mexican cuisine filled with shredded beef, pork, chicken, vegetables or cheese.

chamak (cha-muk) An Indian cooking technique of searing the surface of a food in hot ghee.

chamanju (cha-mahn-joo) A Japanese confection consisting of sweet bean paste formed into balls, encased in a wheat flour dough and steamed; traditionally served with afternoon tea.

chambering The process by which a pocket inside an oyster's shell that is started by water, a worm or a grain of sand is sealed off with a chalky substance the oyster produces; the foreign substance putrefies and releases a strong odor, indicating that the oyster may be bad.

Chambertin (shahm-bair-tan) A famous vineyard in France's Burgundy Côte d'Or region; it produces a powerful, long-lived red wine from the Pinot Noir grape.

Chambéry (sham-ba-ree) A light French vermouth that is delicate and aromatic; traditionally served straight.

Chambord (sham-bor) A plum-colored, sweet French liqueur with a black raspberry flavor.

Chambourcin (sham-boor-san) A French–American hybrid grape widely planted in France's Loire Valley and in the eastern United States; it produces a good-quality red wine.

Chambraise (shahm-braze) A light French vermouth flavored with the juice of wild Alpine strawberries.

chambrer (shahm-bray) To bring a cellar-temperature red wine gradually to room temperature.

chamburo *See* babaco.

chamira (chah-mee-rah) A North African flour and water broth fermented with vinegar and added to soups.

chammach (tcha-mah-k) Hindi for spoon.

chamomile; camomile (KAM-uh-meel) A perennial plant (*Chamaemelum nobile*) with daisylike flower heads that are used for a tisane that calms the stomach and has a faint aroma reminiscent of lemon and pineapple.

champ An Irish dish of mashed potatoes combined with green onions and butter.

Champagne (cham-PANE-ya) 1. A sparkling wine from France's Champagne region made by the méthode champenoise using only three grape varieties: Chardonnay, Pinot Noir and Pinot Meunier. 2. The district in northeast France where this sparkling wine is made. 3. A term inappropriately applied to any sparkling wine other than that produced in Champagne.

champagne, sauce au 1. A French compound sauce made from a béchamel flavored with shallots and Champagne and finished with butter. 2. A French compound sauce made from a demi-glaze flavored with shallots, herbs and wine and finished with butter and Cognac.

champagne cider A cider that has undergone a secondary fermentation in the bottle, much like a sparkling wine; it has a sweet, strong apple flavor and a mild effervescence.

Champagne Cocktail A cocktail made of a sugar cube, orange bitters and Champagne; it is served in a chilled champagne flute and garnished with a twist of lemon.

Champagne Cooler A cocktail made of brandy, Cointreau and Champagne; it is served in a chilled squall glass or wine glass and garnished with a mint sprig.

champagne coupe *See* champagne saucer.

Champagne Cup A cocktail made of Champagne, brandy, orange and lemon slices, cucumber peel and borage; it is served over ice.

champagne grapes A variety of very small, purplish-black or reddish-brown grapes with a very sweet flavor; used for garnish and snacking and not for wine.

champagne loquat A variety of loquat with a golden skin and a white flesh.

champagne mustard *See* Florida mustard.

Champagne Punch A punch made of sparkling wine, club soda, Cognac, maraschino liqueur, curaçao and sugar syrup.

champagne saucer A stemmed glass with a flattened, shallow bowl ranging in size from 3 to 10 fl. oz.; traditionally used to serve sparkling wine, it is no longer generally used, because too great a surface area of wine is exposed to the air, thus allowing the effervescence to escape too rapidly; also known as a saucer, saucer glass or coupe.

champagne tulip A stemmed glass with an elongated V-shaped or tulip-shaped bowl ranging in size from 6 to 10 fl. oz.; developed by French Champagne producers, it is recommended for serving sparkling wines because it helps trap the effervescence.

champagne
tulip

champagne vinegar A vinegar with a pale color and a mild flavor; it is used for making salad dressings.

champignon (sham-peen-yawn) 1. A domed hand tool usually made of wood and resembling a mushroom; it is used to purée fruit, vegetables, fish and poultry through a tamis. 2. French for the common store mushroom.

champigñon (sham-PEE-nyohn) Spanish for mushroom; also known as seta.

champignon de Paris (sham-PEE-nyohn dah pah-ree) French for the common field mushroom.

Champigons (sahm-peen-yawn) German for mushrooms; also known as Pilze.

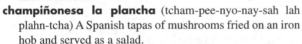

champignon

champiñonesa la plancha (tcham-pee-nyo-nay-sah lah plahn-tcha) A Spanish tapas of mushrooms fried on an iron hob and served as a salad.

champurrado (sham-puhr-rah-doh) A kind of atole made with roasted blue cornmeal and chocolate.

chamuças (sham-oo-sas) Deep-fried triangular Portuguese pastries consisting of a thin, crispy layer of dough filled with ground chicken or other meat, seasoned with curry, piri-piri and mint.

chanakhi (sha-nah-key) A stew made in the Republic of Georgia from lamb or mutton, potatoes, onions, green beans, tomatoes and eggplant.

Chanchamayo (tchan-tcha-maw-yoh) Arabica coffee beans grown in Peru; considered the best Peruvian coffee beans, the beverage is mildly acidic with a good flavor.

Chandler walnut A variety of English walnut; the large nuts have a light-colored meat.

chanfaina (tchan-pha-ee-nah) A Spanish stew made from kid offal, head and feet with artichokes, chard, lettuce and peas.

chang A Tibetan beer usually made from barley, but rice, wheat, corn, oats and millet are sometimes used.

chang fun (tchang foon) Chinese for steamed rice flour sheets rolled around a filling of beef, shrimp or barbecued pork.

channa (chaa-naa) 1. Hindi for dried chickpeas or garbanzos. 2. An Indian dish consisting of cooked chickpeas and spices.

channa dal (chaa-naa dahl) Yellow split peas used in Indian cuisines. *See* besan *and* pigeon pea.

channel bass *See* redfish.

channel catfish *See* catfish, channel.

channeled whelk A variety of whelk found in the Gulf of Mexico and along the U.S. East Coast; it has a thin, irregularly channeled, brownish shell with an average size of 6 in. (15.2 cm) and a lean, very tough, and flavorful flesh; also known as the pear whelk.

channel fat Fat located over the vertebrae on the inside of the pork primal loin and the beef chuck and rib primals.

Channel Island milk A rich milk with 4% milkfat; it is produced by Guernsey and Jersey cows on the Channel Islands.

chanoyu (cha-no-yu) The traditional Japanese tea ceremony.

Chantelle (shan-tell) A ripened Bel Paese–style cheese made in the United States and Canada from whole cow's milk; it has a mild flavor, an open texture, and a smooth, waxy body.

chantepleure (shahn-tuh-pluhr) The spigot of a wine barrel, usually made of boxwood; it squeaks when opened and thus sings (Fr: *chante*) as the wine pours out (i.e., weeps [Fr: *pleure*]).

chanterelle (shan-tuh-REHL) A trumpet-shaped wild mushroom (*Cantharellus cibarius*) found in North America and Europe; it has a ruffled-edge cap, a yellow-orange color, a smooth, slightly chewy texture, a distinctive fruity, nutty flavor, and a clean, earthy aroma; several closely related species are sold under the same name.

chanterelle commune (shan-te-rell co-mun) French for chanterelle.

Chantilly (shan-TIHL-lee; shahn-tee-YEE) 1. A general category of hot and cold emulsified French sauces to which whipped cream is added; the sauces are also known as mousselines. 2. Lightly sweetened whipped cream sometimes flavored with vanilla and used as a dessert topping.

Chantilly; Chantilly cream (shahn-tee-YEE) *See* crème Chantilly.

Chantilly, sauce (shahn-tee-YEE) A French compound sauce made from a suprême with unsweetened whipped heavy cream folded in; usually served with poached chicken or veal sweetbreads.

Chantilly mayonnaise A French mayonnaise sauce flavored with lemon juice and blended with unsweetened whipped cream.

chao (chow) Chinese for stir-frying.

chao mein; chow mein (chow MAYN) 1. Chinese fried noodles. 2. A Chinese–American dish of chicken, shrimp, beef and/or pork stir-fried with vegetables such as bean sprouts, mushrooms, water chestnuts, bamboo shoots and onions and served over noodles.

Chaource (shah-oorceh) A soft, camembert-style cheese made in France's Champagne region from whole cow's milk; it has a fruity, rich flavor.

chapati; chapatti (chah-PAH-tee) An Indian pancakelike unleavened bread made from whole wheat dough and cooked on a griddle.

chapati flour (chah-PAH-tee) Finely ground whole wheat flour used to make chapatis.

chapeau (shah-poe) French for cap. *See* cap.

chapelure (cha-plur) French for bread crumbs.

chapon (shah-POHN) A bread crust rubbed with garlic and used to garnish a salad or a thin soup or to rub inside a bowl to impart a slight garlic flavor to its contents (e.g., salad greens).

chaptalization (shap-tally-zah-see-awn) The addition of sugar or concentrated grape juice to the must before or during fermentation to increase the resulting wine's alcohol content (it does not add sweetness and is usually used in poor vintage years); the practice is prohibited in California and Italy. *See* amelioration.

char *See* lake trout.

character A tasting term for the distinctive and unmistakable qualities of a food (e.g., cheese) or beverage (e.g., wine) based on factors such as ingredients, geographical origin, and production methods.

Charante (shah-ron't) A wine district north of Bordeaux that is planted with the Ugni Blanc grape; the low-alcohol white wine is light and acid and is distilled to make Cognac.

charcoal A porous black residue of partially burned organic matter, particularly wood; once ignited, it puts forth a steady heat and is used for cooking, especially grilling.

charcuterie (shahr-COO-tuhr-ree; shar-coo-tuhr-EE) 1. The production of pâtés, terrines, galantines, sausages, crépinettes and similar foods. 2. The shop where such foods are made and/or sold. 3. Originally referred only to products produced from pork.

charcutière, sauce (shahr-COO-tee-aihr) A French compound sauce made from a sauce Robert garnished with a julienne of sour gherkins.

chard 1. A general term for the leafstalk of leafy green vegetables; also known as midrib. 2. A member of the beet family (*Beta vulgaris,* var. *cicla*); it has crinkly dark green leaves and silvery, celerylike stalks; the leaves are prepared like spinach and have a similar tart flavor, and the stalks are prepared like asparagus and have a tart, somewhat bitter flavor; also known as Swiss chard. *See* rhubarb chard.

chard cabbage *See* napa cabbage.

Chardonnay (shar-doh-nay) 1. Considered by some the finest white wine grape, it is planted worldwide and used for the great French white Burgundies and sparkling wines; sometimes called Pinot Chardonnay, even though not a member of the Pinot family. 2. White wines made from this grape; they range from clean, crisp and with a hint of fruit to rich and complex. 3. A sparkling white wine made from this grape.

Charentais melon (shahr-ahng-tehs) A French variety of cantaloupe; it has a yellow-green ribbed skin and a sweet, fragrant, orange flesh; it is spherical rather than ovoid.

charger 1. A large flat plate placed under a dinner plate on which foods are rarely placed; also known as a service plate. 2. A large flat plate used for food, usually carefully composed presentations and architectural foods. 3. A large flat platter used for carrying and serving meats.

Charleston Gray watermelon A watermelon variety; the fruit have a long, ovoid shape, a light green skin and a crisp red flesh.

charlotte (SHAR-loht) A French dessert in which a mold is lined with ladyfingers, sponge cake or bread, then filled with Bavarian cream and/or fruit, chilled, and unmolded for service.

charlotte mold A deep, pail-shaped cylindrical mold with a small handle on each side, usually made of tinned steel; used for molding desserts.

Charlotte potato A variety of medium-sized potato with a smooth, golden skin and a deep yellow flesh; generally grown in western Europe.

charlotte mold

charlotte russe A French dessert consisting of a charlotte made with strawberries and whipped cream.

Charmat process A sparkling wine-making process during which the second fermentation takes place in a tank rather than in the bottle; also known as bulk process, tank fermentation, cuvé close, autoclave and granvas. *See* méthode champenoise *and* vinification.

charmoula; chermoula (skar-moo-lah) A thick, spicy ragoût of onions, raisins, carrots and celery flavored with ras al-hanout, bay leaf, dried rose petals, vinegar and shallots; served hot or cold as a sauce for grilled meats in various Arabic cuisines.

charni (tchar-nee) Hindi for chutney.

Charolais (shar-roh-lay) A breed of cattle originally from France that yield very high quality lean beef.

charoli nut (cha-roh-lee) A small, round, subtly flavored nut used to garnish East Indian sweetmeats; also known as chironju (India).

charoset (ha-row-set) A Jewish dish made from apples, nuts and raisins flavored with cinnamon and bound with red wine; part of the Passover seder.

charred A food prepared on a hot grill or cooking surface; the food's surface is usually well cooked, with a roasted, caramelized flavor, while the interior is rare.

charring 1. The process of searing the outside of a food, usually on a hot grill or cooking surface. 2. The process of burning the inside of a barrel that will be used for wine, whiskey, brandy, or other distilled spirits; this helps color, mellow and age the barrel's contents.

Chartreuse (shar-trooz) A French liqueur made from brandy and flavored with a secret combination of herbs; yellow Chartreuse is sweeter and less alcoholic than the original and better known green Chartreuse.

chaser The beverage consumed immediately after a different beverage was swallowed (e.g., a glass of beer following a shot of whiskey); usually both beverages contain alcohol.

cha siu bau (tcha see-yoo bah-who) A Chinese dumpling of barbecued pork in a soft wheat bun.

chasni (chaa-sh-nee) A sweet syrup used in Indian cooking to glaze the top of food to be grilled, roasted or cooked in a tandoor oven.

chasnidarh (chaa-sh-nee-daar) An Indian preparation method referring to a dish with a sweet–sour flavor, usually achieved by steeping the food in chasni.

chasoba (CHA-so-bah) Japanese soba noodles made with green tea.

Chasselas (shah'ss-lah) A white wine grape grown in France, Germany and Switzerland; there are many subvarieties, including Gutedel (Germany) and Fendant and Dorin (Switzerland).

chasseur (shah-SUR) French for hunter and used to describe a dish of sautéed chicken, veal, beef or game served with a brown sauce flavored with shallots and white wine and garnished with mushrooms.

chat (chaat) 1. An Indian dish made with vegetables, fruits and spices, eaten cold as a snack or appetizer. 2. General term for India's many and varied snack foods.

chataignier (sha-tain-yey) A small, western European traditional apple with a gray-spotted, yellow skin with red flush and streaks and a white, juicy flesh; also known as a martrange and maltranche.

Château (shah-toe) When used in reference to French wines, especially those of Bordeaux, it is synonymous with vineyard or wine estate.

château bottled A French label term indicating that the wine, especially a Bordeaux, was bottled on the property indicated and produced by the vineyard owner indicated.

châteaubriand (sha-toh-bree-AHN) 1. A fabricated cut of the tenderloin muscle from the beef short loin and sirloin primals; it is cut from the thick end of the muscle generally found in the sirloin primal and is very tender and flavorful. 2. A thick slice of filet of beef tenderloin grilled and traditionally served with château potatoes or soufflé potatoes and béarnaise sauce.

châteaubriand, sauce A French sauce traditionally used for a grilled châteaubriand aux pommes (now sauce béarnaise is more frequently used); a compound sauce made from a demi-glaze flavored with white wine, shallots and tarragon and finished with cayenne and lemon juice.

Château Chalon (shah-toe shah-LAWN) A hamlet in France's Jura district that produces vin jaune (yellow wine) from the Sauvignon Blanc grape; as it matures in the cask, a flor forms over the wine, imparting a flavor and aroma similar to that of sherry.

Château d'Yquem (shah-toe dee-kem) A famous vineyard in Bordeaux known for its Sauternes, luscious, sweet wines made from grapes affected with the noble rot.

Châteauneuf-du-Pape (shah-toe-nuff-doo-pahp) A red wine from France's Rhône region made from Grenache, Syrah, Mourvedre and Cinsault.

château potatoes *See* pommes château.

Château Richon A semidry, golden, Sauternes-type Israeli wine.

cha thai A Thai iced tea made of ground tea leaves, vanilla, roasted corn and orange food coloring; it is brewed several times and then mixed with sugar and milk.

Chatham oyster An Atlantic oyster found off Chatham, Cape Cod; it has a fat body and bland flavor.

chatini (tcha-tee-nee) Swahili for chutney.

chat masala (chaat ma-sa-la) A masala consisting of ground asafetida, mint, ginger, ajowan, cayenne, black salt, mango powder, cumin and dried pomegranate seeds and used to season Indian vegetable salads.

chatti (chat-tee) An unglazed clay cooking pot used in Sri Lanka and India for cooking curries, rice and dal; the porous surface of the pot absorbs the oils from spices and helps to develop the flavor of the dish.

Chauce Gris (choss gree) *See* Gray Riesling.

chaud (shoh) French for hot.

chaudeau (chaw-doe) A Polish sweet sauce.

chaud-froid (shoh-FRWAH) French for a dish prepared hot and served cold; usually refers to meat, poultry or game covered with a brown or white sauce, glazed with aspic, and garnished with cut vegetables set in the aspic.

chaudin A Cajun dish of ground pork combined with vegetables and seasoned rice and packed into a pig's stomach and baked or steamed; it is sliced and eaten warm or cold.

chaudron (shoh-drohn) A small French cauldron, usually made of copper, used to make confit d'oie and confit de porc.

chauffe (show-fa'y) The first distillation in Cognac making.

Chaumes (shom) A semisoft French cheese made from cow's milk; it has an assertive, tangy flavor, a deep orange-colored, washed rind, and a pale yellow interior with numerous small holes.

chaunk gobhi (tcha-oonk goh-be) Hindi for Brussels sprout.

chaurice (shoh-reeze) A Cajun and Creole pork sausage containing fresh vegetables and seasoned with powdered chiles.

chausson aux pommes (show-son oh pomz) A French apple turnover made with puff pastry.

chavetta (cha-va-tah) A crescent-shaped knife used by cigar makers to cut the leaf, pack the filler into the cigar, and shape the cigar; also known as a tuck.

chawa A long, curved, tapering pepper with a yellow flesh and sweet, mild flavor.

chawal (chaa-waal) Hindi for rice.

chawan (cha-waan) A round porcelain or ceramic cup about 2 in. (5 cm) in height and diameter, without a handle, used for drinking tea in Japan; a taller version, usually with a lid, is used as a cooking pot for egg custard.

chayote (chy-OH-tay) A squashlike, pear-shaped fruit (*Sechium edule*) native to Central America; used like a vegetable, it has a pale green furrowed or slightly lumpy skin, a white-green flesh, a single seed, and a bland, somewhat starchy, cucumber-like flavor; also known as mirliton (especially in Louisiana) and vegetable pear.

chaza (tcha-zah) Swahili for oyster.

chazi (tcha-zee) Chinese for fork.

che Various Vietnamese sweet drinks and puddinglike desserts.

cheater *See* shot glass.

chebureki (che-boo-ra-key) Small deep-fried Russian turnovers stuffed with lamb or mutton, onions and rice seasoned with dill and parsley.

check *See* guest check.

checkerberry *See* wintergreen.

checkout 1. The process of calculating and receiving payment from a guest for his or her hotel accommodations. 2. A hotel room that has been vacated and needs to be cleaned for the next occupant.

Cheddar, American A firm cheese made from whole cow's milk (generally pasteurized) produced principally in Wisconsin, New York and Vermont; its color ranges from white to orange and its flavor from mild to very sharp.

Cheddar, English A firm cheese made from whole cow's milk (raw or pasteurized) and named for the village of Cheddar in Somersetshire, England; its color ranges from nearly white to yellow or orange and its flavor from mild to sharp.

Cheddar, goat's milk An American Cheddar made from goat's milk; it has a white color and the rich and faintly sweet character of goat's milk.

Cheddar, New York *See* Herkimer.

Cheddar, Vermont A Cheddar cheese made in Vermont; it has a light yellow to yellow-orange color and a rich, sharp, assertive flavor.

cheddaring process An alternative to the milling step in cheese making; the dense curds are stacked on top of each other to squeeze out the whey and force the fine filaments of milk protein closer together, giving the final cheese (usually called Cheddar) a more solid texture. *See* cheese-making process.

Cheedam A semifirm Australian cheese made from cow's milk through a process that combines aspects of Cheddar and Edam cheese-making techniques; it has a pale interior and a mild flavor.

cheegay (chee-gye) A thin, souplike Korean stew used for cooking many types of ingredients, such as crab, fish and bean curd.

cheeks The tender fleshy muscles located beneath the eyes and between the ears and nose (or snout) of a mammal; veal and hog cheeks are often consumed; also known as jowls.

cheena chatti (chen-na chat-ti) A Sri Lankan woklike pan used for cooking bread and pancakes, especially appa.

cheenee Hindi for sugar.

cheese Dairy products made from milk curds separated from the whey; numerous varieties are found worldwide.

cheese, fat content of The fat content of a cheese's dry matter; a few cheeses have a fat content of 10% or less, most have a fat content of 45–50%, double cream cheeses have a fat content of 60%, and triple cream cheeses have a fat content of at least 72%.

cheese balls Mashed cheese mixed with herbs and/or other flavorings and reshaped into balls; the balls are then sometimes coated in herbs, nuts or other garnishes; usually served as an hors d'oeuvre.

cheesecake A rich, smooth dessert made by blending cream cheese, cottage cheese or ricotta with sugar, eggs and other flavorings, then baking; usually prepared in a springform pan dusted with cookie crumbs or ground nuts; the baked dessert is often topped with sour cream or fruit.

cheesecloth A loosely woven cotton gauze used for straining stocks and sauces and wrapping poultry and fish for poaching.

cheese culture Bacteria used in the coagulation of casein during cheese making.

cheese cutter *See* double-handled cheese cutter.

cheese fondue pot A small, deep, bulbous pot traditionally made of glazed earthenware and used for fondue.

cheese grater A grater with a slightly convex, relatively fine grating surface attached to a handle; used for grating hard cheeses such as Parmesan directly over food.

cheese grater

cheese knife *See* Gorgonzola knife, hard cheese knife, Parmesan knife *and* tomato knife.

cheese-making process The process by which cheese is made; typically (1) milk is warmed and a lactic starter bacteria added to alter the milk's acidity; (2) rennet is added to coagulate the milk into curds and whey; (3) the whey is drained away and the curds are cut and cooked, resulting in dense curds; (4) the dense curds are milled into curd granules; (5) the curds are salted and pressed to remove any additional whey, the resulting product being called green cheese; (6) mold or bacteria is added and the cheese is allowed to ripen and age. *See* cheddaring process *and* ripening.

cheese plane A spade-shaped utensil with a single slot; the cutting edge, on the front side of the slot, is

cheese plane

parallel to and just below the flat blade and tilts upward at a 25-degree angle; cheese is sliced by pulling the plane across it; the edge cuts the cheese, and the slice is lifted through the slot to rest on the plane's top.

cheese powder A dry form of cheese used in instant soups, dry sauces and snack foods.

cheeses, firm A general category of cheeses (e.g., Cheddar and Emmental) that are aged and firm (but not brittle or hard), have an open or closed texture, a moisture content of 30–40%, and a flavor ranging from mild to very sharp; also known as semifirm or semihard cheeses.

cheeses, fresh A general category of cheeses (e.g., cottage cheese, cream cheese, Neufchâtel, feta and mozzarella) that are uncooked, unripened and highly perishable with a creamy texture, a mild, tart, tangy flavor and a moisture content of 40–80%; also known as unripened cheeses.

cheeses, hard A general category of cheeses (e.g., Asiago and Parmigiano-Reggiano) that are aged for an extended period and generally used for grating; they have a hard, dense texture, a moisture content of approximately 30%, and a sharp, tangy flavor; also known as cured cheeses.

cheeses, semisoft A general category of cheeses that have a semisoft, smooth, sliceable texture and a moisture content of 40–50%; includes cheeses with a mild buttery flavor (e.g., Gouda and Havarti) and blue cheeses (e.g., Gorgonzola and Roquefort).

cheeses, soft A general category of cheeses with thin skins, creamy centers and a moisture content of 50–75%; when young, they are firm and have little flavor; as they mature they become softer (even runny) and more flavorful (e.g., Bel Paese, Brie and Camembert; double and triple cream cheeses).

cheese sauce A Welsh sauce made by adding cheese to a white sauce; it is served with boiled or au gratin leeks.

cheese steak An American sandwich consisting of a French or Italian roll topped with thinly sliced, sautéed beef and onions and melted cheese; also known as a Philadelphia cheese steak.

cheese wire A long, thin wire with handles at each end used to cut a round of cheese into wedges.

chef 1. French for chief or head. 2. Short for chef de cuisine. 3. A title of respect given to a person skilled in food preparation and usually in charge of a professional kitchen; he or she is generally responsible for planning menus, ordering foodstuffs, training and supervising cooks and other personnel, and preparing food.

cheese wire

chef de rang (chef duh rhang) *See* front waiter.

chef de salle (chef duh sal) *See* headwaiter.

chef d'étage (chef day tahj) *See* captain.

chef de vin (chef duh van) *See* wine steward.

chef du cuisine At a food services operation, the person responsible for all kitchen operations, developing menu items, and setting the kitchen's tone and tempo. *See* chef *and* executive chef.

chef du culture (chef duh kul-tuhr) French for a vineyard manager.

chef potato *See* white potato, round.

chefs de partie (chef duh par-tee) *See* station chefs.

chef's fork *See* two-pronged fork.

chef's knife An all-purpose knife used for slicing, chopping and mincing; its rigid 8- to 14-in.-long blade is wide at the heel, tapering to a point; also known as a French knife.

chef's knife

chef's salad A salad of tossed greens topped with julienne of cold meat (usually ham, chicken and/or turkey) and cheese and sliced vegetables and hard-boiled eggs; it is topped with a dressing; often served as an entrée.

chelating agent A substance that surrounds or combines with another substance to prevent or promote activity, movement or chemical processes.

Chelsea buns Square, spicy yeast rolls filled with fruit and coated with sugar; created at the Chelsea Bun House and popular in London during the late 17th and early 18th centuries.

chemical contaminant; chemical hazard *See* hazard, chemical.

chemical leavening agents Chemicals added to batters and doughs to assist leavening through the production of carbon dioxide released as the result of chemical reactions between acids and bases. *See* baking powder *and* baking soda.

chemical scoring A measure of protein quality based on a comparison of the protein's chemically determined amino acid composition with human amino acid requirements.

chemise; en chemise (she-meez; ahn she-meez) 1. The cloth towel used by servers to wipe the neck of a wine bottle after each pouring. 2. The cloth towel used to pat dry a bottle of wine or sparkling wine after it is removed from an ice bucket; it is placed around the bottle.

chemise, en To wrap a food in pastry or to coat a food with aspic or sauce.

chemiser (shi-meez-ai) French for to coat.

chemsha (chem-shaw) Swahili for boil.

Chenas (sheh-nass) A Beaujolais cru; the wine is relatively sturdy and long-lived.

cheng (chang) Chinese for steaming.

Chenin Blanc (sheh-nan blahn) 1. A white wine grape grown predominantly in California, France's Loire Valley and South Africa; also known as Steen (in South Africa). 2. A white wine made from this grape; it can range from clean, crisp and fruity to rich, sweet and honeyed.

chenna; chhana; chhena (CHAY-nah) A fresh, fine-grained Indian cheese made from soured cow's milk; in India it is used for making milk sweets.

cherbourg (shehr-borg) A French beef consommé flavored with Madeira wine and garnished with julienne of mushrooms and truffles, poached egg and ham quenelles.

cherbourg, sauce (shehr-borg) A French compound sauce made from a béchamel finished with crayfish butter and garnished with crayfish tails.

chereshnya (VEESH-nyee) Russian for cherry.

cherimoya (chair-uh-MOY-ah) The egg-shaped fruit of a small tropical tree (Annona cherimola); it has a rough green skin that turns blackish-brown when the fruit is ripe, a yellowish-white segmented flesh, a custardlike though somewhat granular texture, and a flavor reminiscent of pineapple, mango and strawberry; also imprecisely known as a custard apple or sweetsop.

Cheri-Suisse A Swiss liqueur flavored with chocolate and cherries.

cherne (sher-nay) Portuguese for grouper.

Cherokee Purple A large heirloom tomato variety with a dusky pink skin, a flattened spherical shape, and a full flavor.

cheroot A small cigar; traditionally smoked using a decorative holder.

cherries jubilee A dessert made by topping vanilla ice cream with dark, pitted cherries that were sautéed with sugar and Kirsch or brandy; the cherry mixture is often flamed table side.

cherry 1. A small stone fruit from a tree (genus Prunus) grown in temperate climates worldwide; there are two principal types: sour and sweet; both types are generally available fresh, dried, canned and frozen. 2. The ripe red berry of the coffee plant; a coffee bean is the seed within the cherry.

cherry, sour Any of a variety of cherries (Prunus cerasus) with a skin and flesh color varying from light to dark red and an acidic, tart flavor; they are usually cooked with sugar and used as a pie or pastry filling; also known as a tart cherry.

cherry, sweet Any of a variety of cherries (Prunus avium) that are spherical to heart shaped, with a skin and flesh color varying from pale yellow to dark red, a juicy flesh and a sweet flavor; they are eaten fresh, candied or in baked goods.

Cherrybarb A cocktail made of brandy and sugar.

Cherry Herring See Peter Herring.

cherry pitter See pitter.

cherry plum See mirabelle and plum, cherry.

Cherry Red rhubarb A rhubarb variety that is sweeter than most other varieties.

cherry snapper See tilapia.

cherrystone clam; cherrystone quahog An Atlantic hard-shell clam that is under 3 in. (7.6 cm) across the shell; the shells are tannish gray, and the chewy meat has a mild flavor.

cherry tomato 1. A small spherical tomato with a bright red or yellow skin; the yellow-skinned variety has a less acidic and blander flavor than the red-skinned variety. 2. An imprecisely used term for any of several varieties of small, spherical tomatoes.

chervil (cher-vil) An herb and member of the parsley family (Anthriscus cerefolium) native to Russia; it has dark green, curly leaves that have a parsleylike flavor with overtones of anise and are generally used fresh.

Cheshire A firm English cheese made from cow's milk; it has a mild, slightly salty flavor (the result of salt deposits in the cows' pastures), a compressed, oily center, and an oily rind; there are three varieties: red (dyed with annatto), white (actually a pale yellow), and blue (blue veined and marketed as Blue Cheshire).

chesnok (ches-nock) Russian for garlic.

chess pie A dessert from the American South consisting of a flaky pie shell filled with a sweet custard made from sugar, eggs, butter and small amounts of vinegar and cornmeal or flour; when baked, the filling becomes dense and translucent, with a thin, crisp, crusty top.

Chester blackberry A blackberry variety with a particularly sweet flavor.

chestnut The nut of the sweet chestnut tree (Castanea sativa); edible when cooked, it has a dark brown outer shell, a bitter inner skin, and a high starch content; it is used in savory and sweet dishes.

chestnut flour Dried and ground chestnuts.

chestnut pan A shallow frying pan with a perforated bottom used to roast chestnuts; designed to permit some contact between the food and the heat source (usually a flame).

chestnut pan

chestnut pumpkin A variety of medium-sized spherical squash with a bumpy, yellow-orange skin, a slightly flattened appearance, and a flavor reminiscent of chestnuts.

cheung fun (cha-oong foon) A Chinese rice flour roll filled with barbecued pork, shrimp or beef and topped with scallion oil.

cheung guen (cha-oong goo-ehn) A Chinese spring roll.

Chevaliers du Tastevin (sheh-val-yay duh tat-van) A French wine fraternity founded in 1934 to promote the wines of Burgundy; named for the shallow silver tasting cup still used in the region.

cheveux d'ange (cha-voh danj) French for angel hair pasta.

chèvre (SHEHV-ruh) 1. French for goat. 2. Any French goat's milk cheese; usually pure white with a tart flavor, their textures can range from soft, moist and creamy to dry, firm and crumbly and their shapes from small to medium-sized cones, cylinders, disks or pyramids left ungarnished or covered with black ash, leaves, herbs or pepper.

chevrette (shev-reht) French for chanterelle.

chevreuil (shev-ROY) French for venison.

Chevrier (sheh-v'ree-yay) *See* Sémillon.

chevrotin (sheh-vroh-teen) A category of cheeses made in France's Alpine region from goat's milk; the cheeses are generally dried and firm with a smooth surface and a tangy flavor.

chewing gum A flavored, rubbery substance often made from chicle; it is chewed and should not be swallowed.

chewy 1. A food that is difficult to chew completely because it is tough, sticky or gummy. 2. A wine-tasting term for a rich, full-bodied, slightly alcoholic, and very strongly flavored wine.

Chex The proprietary name of a breakfast cereal made from corn, wheat or rice; the puffed cereal squares have many small holes on the surface.

Chex party mix A savory snack of Chex brand cereals mixed with nuts and flavored with Worcestershire sauce and butter.

Cheyenne pecan A pecan variety; the nuts are flavorful and easily cracked.

chi (tchee) Chinese for eat.

chia *See* lake trout.

Chianti (k'yahn-tee) A red wine made in Tuscany, Italy, principally from Sangiovese grapes mixed with small amounts of Canaiolo grapes and the white Malvasia grapes; the young wines are refreshing and tart, and the older wines aged in wooden casks are richer and more complex.

Chianti Classico (k'yahn-tee clah-see-co) A red wine made from grapes grown in an area between Florence and Siena, Tuscany; it is a particularly rich, complex Chianti.

Chianti Riserva (k'yahn-tee ree-sehr-vah) A Chianti aged for at least 3 years, but not necessarily in wooden casks.

chiao-tzu (jiao-zi) Chinese pan-fried dumplings filled with various chopped meats or vegetables, served boiled or steamed; also known as pot stickers.

Chiaretto (k'yah-REH-toe) *See* Bardolino.

Chiboust cream (she-boo) A vanilla pastry cream lightened with Italian meringue; gelatin is sometimes added to the cream for stability; used in French pastries as a filling (e.g., gâteau St. Honoré).

Chicago A cocktail made of brandy, Champagne, superfine sugar and Angostura bitters; garnished with a lemon wedge.

Chicago deep-dish pizza *See* pizza, deep-dish.

chicha (CHEE-chah) A corn-based beer made by the ancient Incas.

chicharrón; cicharón (chee-chah-RROHN) Mexican pork cracklings that are fried twice at different temperatures, causing them to balloon into honeycombed puffs.

chicken One of the principal kinds of poultry recognized by the USDA includes any of several varieties of common domestic fowl used for food as well as egg production; it has both light and dark meat and relatively little fat.

chicken, broiler-fryer A chicken slaughtered when 13 weeks old; it has a soft, smooth-textured skin, a relatively lean flesh, a flexible breastbone, and an average market weight of 3.5 lb. (1.5 kg).

chicken, free-range A chicken allowed greater access to the area outside the coop and usually raised on a special diet made without additives; it is generally slaughtered when 9–10 weeks old and marketed with head and feet attached; the average market weight is 4.5–5 lb. (2–2.3 kg).

chicken, roaster A chicken slaughtered when 3–5 months old; it has a smooth-textured skin, tender flesh, a less flexible breastbone than that of a broiler, and an average market weight of 3.5–5 lb. (1.5–2 kg).

chicken, stewing A chicken slaughtered when 10–18 months old; a mature bird, it has a nonflexible breastbone, a flavorful but less tender flesh, and an average market weight of 2.5–8 lb. (1.1–3.6 kg); also known as a stewing hen and boiling fowl.

chicken à la king An American dish of diced chicken (or turkey) in a cream sauce with pimientos, mushrooms, green peppers and sometimes sherry.

chicken cacciatore *See* cacciatore, à la.

chicken classes Significant chicken classes are the game hen, broiler-fryer chicken, roaster chicken, capon and stewing chicken.

chicken-fried steak A dish from the American South and Midwest; it consists of a thin, tenderized steak dipped into a milk–egg mixture and seasoned flour, then pan-fried; it is usually served with country gravy.

chicken fry steak A fabricated cut of the beef primal round; it is cut from the top round and somewhat tough.

chicken grape *See* frost grape.

chicken Kiev (kee-EHV) A dish consisting of a boned chicken breast wrapped around a piece of herbed butter, breaded, and deep-fried.

chicken liver The small twin-lobed liver of a chicken; it has a reddish-brown color, a soft, crumbly texture and a delicate flavor.

chicken lobster A marketing term for a 1-lb. (455-g) lobster. *See* deuce, heavy chicken, heavy select, jumbo, quarter, select *and* small jumbo.

chicken long rice A Hawaiian souplike preparation consisting of mung bean threads and chicken flavored with ginger and green onions; it is often served at a luau.

chickennat (tchee-kan-nat) A Ugandan stew consisting of chicken and groundnuts or peanuts flavored with pepper, onions and parsley.

chicken of the wood mushroom A wild mushroom (*Laetiporus sulphureus*) with a red-orange cap that is bright yellow underneath; it has a somewhat stringy, chewy texture and a mild flavor.

chicken paprikash *See* paprikás csirke.

chicken salad An American salad of cooked chicken garnished with celery, onions, grapes and/or other items and bound with a mayonnaise dressing.

chicken steak *See* chuck tender.

chicken Tetrazzini (teh-trah-ZEE-nee) An Italian dish consisting of spaghetti and julienne of chicken bound with a sherry and Parmesan sauce, topped with bread crumbs and/or Parmesan and baked; originally made with swan; turkey can be substituted for the chicken.

chickpea; chick-pea A somewhat spherical, irregular-shaped, pealike seed of a plant (*Licer arieinum*) native to the Mediterranean region; it has a buff color, a firm texture, and a nutty flavor; used in Mediterranean and Middle Eastern cuisines in soups, stews and salads, it is also roasted and eaten as a snack; also known as ceci and garbanzo bean.

chickweed A wild green that grows in temperate climates worldwide; it is a tender vegetable that goes well with rich meats.

chicle A masticatory substance naturally occurring in the sapodilla tree and used as a chewing gum base.

chicorée frisée (CHIHK-or-ree free-zay) *See* frisée.

chicory A plant (*Cichorium intybus*) with long silvery white, tightly folded leaves and a slightly bitter flavor; also imprecisely known as endive (especially in France and the United States). *See* Belgian endive, endive, radicchio *and* succory.

chicos Dried kernels of corn used in Native American and Southwestern stews; also known as parched corn.

chidini famigliola buona (key-dee-nee fahm-e-gle-oh-la bw'ohn-ah) Italian for honey mushroom.

chien (tchee-an) Chinese for shallow frying.

chiffon A sweet cream or custard thickened with gelatin and lightened with stiffly whipped egg whites.

chiffonade (chef-fon-nahd) *v.* To finely slice or shred leafy vegetables or herbs. *n.* Finely cut leafy vegetables or herbs often used as a garnish or bedding.

chiffon cake A light, moist, airy cake made with oil, usually flavored with lemon or orange, and baked in a large tube pan.

chiffon pie A dessert traditionally made with a crumb crust and filled with a fluffy, delicately flavored filling made by adding flavorings and whipped egg whites to an egg yolk base (sometimes gelatin is added as a stabilizer).

chiftele (keyf-taele) Romanian for meatballs.

chijun (key-joon) Chinese for hedgehog mushroom.

chikkus *See* sapodilla.

chikuwa (chi-koo-wa) A kamaboko formed around a bamboo stem and then steamed.

chilaca (chee-LAH-kah) A thin, long, curved fresh chile with a dark brown color and medium hot flavor; usually available dried and called pasilla or negro.

chilaquiles (chee-lah-KEE-lehs) A Mexican dish consisting of tortilla strips sautéed with foods such as chiles, chorizo, beef or chicken and cheese; sometimes layered like lasagna and baked.

chilcostle A thin, elongated, tapering dried chile with a splotchy red-orange skin, a thin flesh, and a dry, citrusy, medium hot flavor.

Child, Julia (Am., 1912–) An American trained in French cooking; she is best known for teaching Americans about French cuisine through her public television show, *The French Chef,* begun in 1963, and her many books, including *Mastering the Art of French Cooking, Volumes I and II* (1961, 1970), *From Julia Child's Kitchen* (1975), and *The Way to Cook* (1989).

children's menu A menu whose items and design appeal to children; the portions are generally small and are priced accordingly; available at many family restaurants.

chile; chile pepper; hot pepper The fruit of various plants of the Capsicum family; a chile can have a mild to fiery hot flavor (caused by the capsaicin in the pepper's placental ribs) with undertones of various fruits or spices; a fresh chile is usually yellow, orange, green or red, and its shape can range from thin, elongated and tapering to conical to nearly spherical; a dried chile, which is sometimes referred to by a different name than its fresh version, is usually more strongly flavored and darker colored. *See* pepper *and* sweet pepper.

Chilean hot sauce *See* pebre.

Chilean Pine strawberry A variety of June-bearing strawberry whose large fruits have a flavor reminiscent of pineapples; most modern strawberries are a hybrid of Chilean Pine and Scarlet Virginian strawberries. *See* Scarlet Virginian strawberry.

chile bean sauce *See* hot black bean sauce.

chile caribe *See* Fresno chile.

chile cera *See* Fresno chile.

chile Colorado *See* New Mexico red chile, dried.

chile con queso (CHIH-lee kon KAY-soh) A Mexican dip of melted cheese flavored with green chiles and served with tortilla chips or raw vegetables.

chile flakes Coarsely crushed dried chiles whose flavor and color depend on the chiles used; also known as crushed chiles.

Chile nut *See* monkey puzzle.

chile oil A vegetable oil in which hot red chiles have been steeped to impart flavor and color; used as a cooking medium and flavoring in Asian cuisines.

chile paste; chile paste with garlic A paste made from fermented fava beans, flour, red chiles and sometimes garlic; used as a flavoring in Chinese cuisines. *See* Szechwan chile sauce.

chile powder Pure ground dried chiles; depending on the variety used, its flavor can range from sweet and mild to pungent and extremely hot and its color from yellow-orange to red to dark brown; used as a flavoring. *See* chilli.

chile rellenos (CHEE-leh rreh-YEH-nohs) A Mexican dish of mild roasted chiles stuffed with cheese, dipped in an egg batter and fried.

chili A stewlike dish flavored with chiles. *See* chile *and* chilli.

chili con carne (CHIL-ee kohn KAHR-nay) A Mexican stewlike dish of ground or diced meat, usually beef, flavored with onions, tomatoes, chiles and chilli powder; if beans are added, it is known as chili con carne with beans; also known as chili or a bowl of red.

chili dog A frankfurter smothered with a spicy beef chili and often garnished with grated cheese and/or chopped onions.

chilled A food that has been refrigerated, usually at temperatures of 30–40°F (−1 to +4°C).

chill haze *See* cloudy.

chilli; chilli powder A commercial blend of herbs and spices such as oregano, cumin, garlic, dried chiles and other ingredients; its flavor and color vary depending on the manufacturer; it is used in American southwestern and Mexican cuisines.

chilli sauce; chili sauce A spicy, ketchuplike sauce made from tomatoes, chiles or chile powder, onions, green peppers, vinegar, sugar and spices.

chilorio (che-loh-ree-oh) A Mexican dish consisting of shredded pork with chiles and spices.

chilpachole (che-pah-choh-le) A Mexican spicy shellfish stew, popular in Veracruz.

chilte A masticatory substance of vegetable origin used as a chewing gum base.

chiltepe A short, curved, tapering dried chile with a thin flesh, a bright orange-red color, and a searingly hot flavor.

chiltepin; chiltecpin *See* tepín.

Chimay (chee-may) A Belgian monastery known for its beers of the same name; Red Cap is copper colored and very smooth, White Cap is amber colored with a delicate bitterness, and Blue Cap is a dark, fruity, strong, full-bodied beer with a thick creamy head.

chimichanga (chee-mee-CHAN-gah) A dish from the American Southwest consisting of a deep-fried burrito, which can be filled with a sweet or savory mixture such as apples or shredded pork; depending on the filling, it can be garnished with confectioners' sugar or sour cream, salsa, pico de gallo, guacamole and shredded cheese.

chimichurri (chee-mee-choo-rree) A thick Argentinean herb sauce made with olive oil, vinegar and finely chopped parsley, oregano, onion and garlic, it is usually served with grilled meats.

china 1. Plates, bowls and cups made of porcelain. 2. An imprecisely used term to describe plates, bowls and cups made from materials other than porcelain, such as plastic, earthenware, metal and the like.

china cap A conical metal strainer with a perforated metal body; used for straining stocks and sauces and, with a pestle, to purée soft foods. *See* chinois.

China Caravan A blend of Chinese keemum teas; the beverage has a distinctive, smooth flavor and is usually served with lemon.

China-Martini The proprietary name of a syrupy Italian liqueur with a bitter, quinine flavor.

China rose tea A blend of Chinese black tea and freshly cut rose petals; the beverage has a heavy rose scent.

chinchin A Nigerian dish consisting of loops of deep-fried dough flavored with sugar, nutmeg and orange rind; they are sometimes brightly colored.

chine (chyn) *v.* To sever the backbone during butchering. *n.* 1. The backbone or spine of an animal. 2. A subprimal cut of a beef, veal, lamb, pork or game carcass containing a portion of the backbone with some adjoining flesh.

Chinese anise *See* star anise.

Chinese artichoke *See* chorogi.

Chinese banana *See* Canary Island banana.

Chinese black beans *See* fermented black beans.

Chinese broccoli *See* gaai laan.

Chinese cabbage *See* napa cabbage.

Chinese cheese; Chinese white cheese *See* dòufù-ru.

Chinese chives *See* chives, garlic.

Chinese cinnamon *See* cassia.

Chinese cleaver A smaller, medium-weight cleaver used to chop and trim foods; also known as a kitchen cleaver. *See* cleaver.

Chinese cleaver

Chinese cucumber *See* tea melon.

Chinese date An olive-sized fruit (*Zizyphus jujuba*) with a leathery red, off-white or black skin, a yellow flesh and a prunelike flavor; it is usually stewed with a sweetener and used in sweet and savory dishes or eaten as a snack; also known as Chinese jujube, jujube and red date.

Chinese dumplings *See* pot stickers.

Chinese five-spice powder A spice blend generally consisting of ground cloves, fennel seeds, star anise, cinnamon and Szechwan pepper; used in Chinese and Vietnamese cuisines.

Chinese flat cabbage *See* tsai goo choi.

Chinese flowering cabbage *See* choy sum.

Chinese gooseberry *See* kiwi.

Chinese jujube *See* Chinese date.

Chinese kale *See* gaai laan.

Chinese keyes A member of the ginger family, its brown, multipronged root has a distinctive aroma and sweet flavor; it is used in Thai and Indonesian curries and pickles.

Chinese ladle A ladle with a broad, shallow, 4-oz. bowl and a long handle; the disklike face of the bowl is used for turning or transferring food in and from a wok.

Chinese lantern A plant (*Physalis alkekengi*) commonly grown for decorative purposes; its small red berries have a slight acidic flavor and are used for preserves and in sauces. *See* winter cherry.

Chinese laurel *See* bignay.

Chinese leaf *See* po tsai.

Chinese melon *See* tea melon.

Chinese mixed pickle Vegetables such as carrots, green peppers and cucumbers flavored with ginger, mustards and chiles and pickled in vinegar, sugar and salt; used as a condiment in Chinese cuisines for cold meats, fried foods and fermented eggs and as an ingredient in sweet-and-sour dishes.

Chinese mustard *See* bok choy.

Chinese mustard cabbage *See* gai choy.

Chinese olive *See* pili.

Chinese parsley *See* cilantro.

Chinese pear *See* Asian pear.

Chinese pepper *See* Szechwan pepper.

Chinese pickle; Chinese pickled cucumber *See* tea melon, pickled.

Chinese plum A fruit (*Prunus armeniaca, P. mume*) native to China; it is similar to an apricot, with a reddish-gold skin and a sweet flavor.

Chinese red cheese Pressed red bean curds fermented in rice wine with spices and salt until the curds are brick red and very pungent; used to flavor pork or as a side dish served with rice; also known as red bean curd cheese, spiced red bean curd or southern (China) cheese.

Chinese restaurant syndrome A medical condition characterized by headaches, neck or chest pains, hot flashes and/or heart palpitations; thought by victims to be caused by consuming foods containing the flavor enhancer monosodium glutamate (MSG).

Chinese sausage *See* lop chong.

Chinese snow pea *See* snow pea.

Chinese spinach *See* amaranth.

Chinese star fruit *See* carambola.

Chinese steelhead *See* blackfish.

Chinese water spinach *See* ung choy.

Chinese white mustard cabbage *See* bok choy.

Chinese wisteria The buds of this plant's (*Wisteria sinesis*) blue flowers are eaten like a vegetable in Chinese cuisines.

chingri (shin-gree) Hindi for shrimp.

chinois (sheen-WAH) A conical metal strainer with a very fine mesh; it is used for straining stocks and sauces. *See* china cap.

chinois

Chinook A variety of hops grown in the United States.

chinook salmon Salmon found in the Pacific Ocean from northern California to Alaska; it has a greenish skin that becomes silvery on the sides and belly, a mouth with a black interior, a high fat content, a red-orange to pale pink, large-flaked flesh, a rich flavor and an average weight of 5–30 lb. (2.3–13.6 kg); it is often marketed with the fish's spawning river added to the name (e.g., Columbia chinook salmon, Yukon chinook salmon); also known as blackmouth salmon and king salmon.

chiocciolo (kee-yoh-chee-OH-loh) 1. Italian for snail. 2. Short, ribbed, snail-shaped Italian pasta.

chiogga A beet with concentric red and white rings; also known as a candy cane beet.

chiorro (chee-oh-rroh) A dish from Spain's Basque region consisting of a cooked fish placed on a large crouton and garnished with a sauce of onions, garlic and tomatoes flavored with mace, paprika, cayenne and red wine.

chip 1. A small fragment of a food used as an ingredient (e.g., chocolate). 2. An archaic name for a thick, irregular slice of fruit or fruit peel preserved in sugar.

chipirones (chee-ree-roh-nays) Spanish for small squid. *See* chocos.

chipolata (shee-po-LAH-tah) A small Italian sausage made from pork flavored with thyme, chives, coriander, cloves and sometimes red pepper.

chipolatas, à la (shee-po-lah-tahs, ah-lah) A French method of garnishing foods with small pork sausages.

chipotle (chih-POHT-lay) A dried, smoked jalapeño; this medium-sized chile has a dull tan to dark brown color with a wrinkled skin and a smoky, slightly sweet, relatively mild flavor with undertones of tobacco and chocolate.

chipped beef Wafer-thin slices of beef that is smoked, salted and dried; also known as dried beef.

chipped beef on toast Chipped beef served in a white sauce over toast.

chippy British slang for a fish-and-chips shop.

chips 1. Any of a variety of small, thinly sliced deep-fried foods such as potatoes or tortillas; usually eaten as snacks, often with a dip. 2. British for French fries.

chiqueter (shee-kwee-teh) French for to flute the rim or edge of a pastry dough.

chiquibul A masticatory substance of vegetable origin used as a chewing gum base.

chiquihuite (chee-kee-WEE-teh) A Mexican basket of woven reed grass lined with a cloth and used to hold tortillas.

chirashi-zushi (chee-RAH-shee SOO-shee) Japanese for scattered sushi and used to describe a type of sushi made by arranging cooked or raw fish, shellfish and sometimes vegetables on loosely packed zushi; it is often served in a bowl.

chirinabe (chree-ree-NAH-beh) A Japanese dish consisting of pieces of fish (cod or sea bass), tofu and vegetables that are cooked in a simmering broth by an individual diner at the table.

chironju *See* charoli nut.

chirorija An orange and pomelo citrus hybrid.

Chiroubles (shee-roob'l) A Beaujolais cru; its red wines are fruity, elegant and appealing.

chispe e feijão branco (chis-puh ee fay-jeown brun-koo) A Portuguese dish of white beans cooked with a pig's foot, pork and carrots and flavored with garlic, aniseed and parsley.

chitarra (key-tah-rah) A guitarlike Italian tool used to cut pasta by rolling the dough against (or over) the tool's steel wires.

chitterlings; chitlins; chitlings The small intestines of freshly slaughtered hogs; cleaned and simmered for soups, battered and fried, or used as sausage casings.

chiu hwa (tchee-oo har) A Chinese blend of small, dried chrysanthemum blossoms and black or green tea; similar to jasmine tea, it is sweetened with rock candy and served with a pastry after a meal; also known as chrysanthemum tea.

chives An herb and member of the onion family (*Allium schoenprasum*), with long, slender, hollow, green stems and purple flowers; the stems have a mild, onionlike flavor and are generally used fresh, although dried, chopped chives are available.

chives, garlic An herb and member of the onion family (*Allium tuberosum*), with solid stems that have a garliclike flavor and are broader, coarser and flatter than regular chives; generally used fresh, although dried garlic chives are available; also known as Chinese chives, flowering chives, kuchai and oriental garlic.

chives

Chivry, sauce (she-VREE) A French compound sauce made from a chicken velouté flavored with white wine, shallots, tarragon and chervil and finished with Chivry butter; usually served with eggs and poached or sautéed poultry. *See* beurre Chivry.

chix A lobster (usually a Maine lobster) weighing less than 1 lb. (450 g).

chizu (chee-zoo) Japanese for cheese.

chlodnik (CHLAHD-nihk) A Polish soup made with beets, onions, cucumbers, herbs and sometimes veal; it is served cold and garnished with sour cream.

chlorinated hydrocarbons A group of chemical solvents used in the direct contact method of decaffeinating coffee; they are suspected of being carcinogenic.

chlorine A major mineral principally used as an electrolyte and a component of hydrochloric acid, which is essential for proper digestion; significant sources include salt, soy sauce and many processed foods.

chlorine and chlorine dioxide Food additives used as aging and bleaching agents for flour.

chloropentafluoroethane A food additive used as a propellant and aerating agent.

chlorophyll The pigment in plants that aids photosynthesis; its color ranges from green to bluish black.

cho The triangular block of raw fish (especially maguro) from which sushi and sashimi slices are cut.

chobek and pergulakan (choh-bek and per-gull-a-kan) An Indonesian clay mortar and pestle.

choclo (choh-cloh) Small chunks of corn on the cob added to soups and stews in South American cuisines.

choco (tcho-koh) Portuguese for cuttlefish; they are often served in their own ink.

chocoholic Slang term for someone addicted to or with a strong preference for chocolate.

chocolat (chohk-o-lah) French for chocolate.

chocolate Roasted, ground, refined cacao beans used as a flavoring, confection or beverage. *See* chocolate-making process.

chocolate, white A confection made of cocoa butter, sugar and flavorings; it does not contain cocoa solids.

chocolate bloom *See* bloom.

chocolate dipping fork A wooden-handled utensil with a stainless steel oval or round bowl, a wire spiral or grid, or long tines; each shape is used for dipping a particular shape or type of candy into melted chocolate; also known as a candy dipper or truffle dipper.

chocolate liquor; chocolate mass The product formed during the first stage of the chocolate-making process; it results from crushing or grinding cocoa nibs before the sugar or flavorings are added; also known as cocoa liquor. *See* chocolate-making process.

chocolate-making process The process by which chocolate is made; typically (1) large pods containing cocoa beans are harvested from the tropical cacao tree; (2) the beans are scraped out of the pods and allowed to ferment; (3) the fermented beans are dried in the sun and then packed and shipped to manufacturers; (4) at the factory, the beans are blended and roasted to create the desired flavors and aromas; (5) they are crushed and the shells (husks) are removed; (6) the cleaned cocoa kernels, known as nibs, are milled into a thick paste, known as chocolate liquor or mass, which is distributed as unsweetened chocolate; (7) the chocolate mass may be refined further by pressing it to remove the cocoa butter, leaving dry cocoa powder; (8) cocoa butter, sugar, milk solids, vanilla and other flavorings can be added to the chocolate mass to produce various types of chocolate: bittersweet, semisweet or milk (white chocolate is produced from cocoa butter, sugar and flavorings, without cocoa solids); (9) after the flavorings are added, the mixture is blended and milled until smooth; (10) some manufacturers refine the blended chocolate further through conching, which results in a velvetlike texture and added stability; (11) the finished chocolate is poured into molds to harden, then wrapped and shipped to purchasers.

chocolate milk A beverage generally made of whole, pasteurized, homogenized milk with 1.5–2% liquid chocolate and sometimes a sweetener.

chocolate mill A wooden stick with an enlarged end used to whip or beat chocolate to a froth.

chocolate mold A plastic or metal mold, available in a variety of shapes and sizes, used for molding chocolate candies; a shallow mold is used for solid molding and a two-part mold is used for hollow molding and filled chocolates.

chocolate plastic; chocolate modeling paste A pliable decorating paste with the texture of marzipan; made from a mixture of chocolate and corn syrup.

chocolate ruler; chocolate bar *See* caramel ruler.

chocolate syrup A pourable mixture of chocolate and cream or butter; it is often sweetened and flavored with an extract or liqueur and used to garnish pastries and desserts.

chocolate truffle A rich, creamy candy made by coating a ball of chocolate ganache with tempered chocolate, cocoa powder, confectioners' sugar, chopped nuts or the like.

chocolate velvet cake A very rich, dense, fudgelike chocolate cake created by pastry chef Albert Kumin at the Four Seasons restaurant in 1959.

Chocolat Suisse (chohk-o-lah swesse) A chocolate-flavored Swiss liqueur; the bottles contain small chocolate squares.

chocos (SHOU-koos) Spanish for large squid. *See* chipirones.

Choctaw pecan A pecan variety; the nuts are flavorful and easily cracked.

choice The second-highest (USDA) quality grade designation for beef, veal and lamb; the most commonly used grade; it is well marbled (but less so than prime) and will produce a tender and juicy product.

choi-sam A member of the cabbage family native to China; it has long, dark green leaves, green stems and a slight mustard flavor.

Chokalu (choh-koh-loo) A semisweet, chocolate Mexican liqueur.

choke *See* artichoke, common.

chokeberry The fruit of an ornamental shrub (genus *Aronia*); inedible raw, it can be cooked with sugar for preserves.

chokecherry Any of several varieties of wild sour cherries (*Prunus virginiana*) native to North America; the skin, which is red when immature, blackens as it ripens, and the dark red flesh has an astringent flavor; used for making preserves.

chokoreto (choh-KOH-reh-toh) Japanese for chocolate.

cholecalciferol *See* vitamin D.

cholecystokinin (CCK) A hormone secreted into the blood from the intestine; it signals the brain to create a feeling of satiety.

cholent; cholend (chkoll-ent) A Jewish one-dish braised meal consisting of meat (usually beef or tongue), a grain (typically pearl barley) and vegetables (carrots, onions, potatoes and the like) flavored with schmaltz, garlic, thyme and paprika.

cholera (khol-ah-rah) An acute infection involving the entire small bowel and characterized by profuse watery diarrhea and vomiting; sometimes fatal, it is caused by consuming water or food contaminated with the bacterium *Vibrio cholerae*. *See* Vibrio cholerae.

cholesterol (koh-LESS-ter-all) A sterol found in animal foods and manufactured by the body to assist in the formation of certain hormones, vitamin D and cell membranes; excess cholesterol in the blood has been linked to cardiovascular disease. *See* HDL cholesterol *and* LDL cholesterol.

cholic acid A food additive with a bitter flavor and sweetish aftertaste used as an emulsifying agent in egg whites.

choline A substance sometimes grouped with the vitamin B complex, although not an actual vitamin; found in egg yolks, beef liver and grains, it is water soluble and assists nerve functions and fat metabolism.

chompoo *See* pink rose apple.

chomwa (chom-oo-ah) Swahili for smoked.

chondrus extract *See* carrageenan.

chongos (chon-goss) A Spanish custard or pudding flavored with lemon and cinnamon.

chooree (chhoo-ree) Hindi for knife.

chop *v.* To cut food into small pieces; uniformity of size and shape is neither necessary nor feasible. *n.* A fabricated cut of meat including part of the rib.

chop che (jop chee) A Korean stir-fry of clear noodles, beef and assorted vegetables; the Korean version of chow mein.

chopsticks A pair of slender sticks, usually cylindrical and sometimes slightly pointed, made of metal, ivory, plastic, wood or other materials that are held between the thumb and fingers of one hand and used to move food during cooking or from a service item to the mouth; used principally in Asian countries such as China, Japan and Korea.

chop suey (chop soo-ee) A Chinese–American dish of stir-fried beef, pork, chicken and/or shrimp and vegetables such as bean sprouts, mushrooms, water chestnuts, bamboo shoots and onions in a starchy sauce served over rice.

choquinhos (tcho-key-nyos) Portuguese for small cuttlefish; they are often served as petiscos.

choquinhos fritos com tinta (tcho-key-nyos free-tos com tin-tah) A Portuguese petisco dish of small squid fried in their ink.

chorba (chore-bah) Bulgarian for soup.

chorba dess (chor-bah dess) An Algerian lentil soup garnished with potatoes, carrots and onions and flavored with coriander.

chorba hamra (chor-bah hahm-rah) A spicy Algerian vegetable soup.

choriho (cho-ree-ho) Japanese for recipe.

chorizo (chor-EE-zoh; chor-EE-soh) 1. A Mexican sausage made from fresh pork, seasoned with garlic and powdered chiles; usually cooked without the casing. 2. A Spanish sausage made from smoked pork, seasoned with garlic and powdered chiles; it is usually cooked without the casing.

chorizo de Bilba (chor-ee-zoh day bill-bah) A Spanish sausage used as a flavoring ingredient.

chorogi (cho-RO-ghee) A hairy plant native to China and Japan (*Stachys affinis*); the tuber, which looks like a string of large, whitish beads, has a sweet, nutty flavor and can be eaten raw or cooked; also known as a Chinese artichoke, Japanese artichoke and knotroot.

Choron, sauce (show-RAWHN) A French compound sauce made from a béarnaise tinted red with tomato purée.

choshoku *See* asagohan.

chota piaz (ycho-tah pea-az) Hindi for shallot.

chotoo jheen-gar (tcho-to gin-gaur) Hindi for large shrimp or prawns. *See* jheenga; jhneengari.

chou (shoo) French for cabbage.

Chouao (tcho-who-ah-oh) An area in Venezuela reputed to grow some of the world's finest cocoa beans.

chou coco; chou glouglou; chou palmiste *See* hearts of palm.

choucroute (shoo-CROOT) A dish made in France's Alsace region from cabbage cooked with goose fat, onions, juniper berries and white wine.

choucroute à l'ancienne (shoo-CROOT ah lan-see-ahn) A French dish consisting of sauerkraut prepared in the traditional way with carrots and onions; it is flavored with peppercorns, caraway seeds, garlic, cloves, juniper berries, bay leaves and thyme and served with sausages and smoked loin of pork; a specialty of Alsace.

choucroute fork A 2.5-in.-wide fork with four sharp tines and a slight dip at the prong–handle juncture to prevent juices from being transferred from the pot to the platter; the tines are used to separate strands from their mass.

choucroute garni Choucroute garnished with potatoes and smoked pork, pork sausages, ham or goose.

chou farci (shoh fahr-cee) French for stuffed cabbage.

chou-fleur (shoo-FLERR) French for cauliflower.

chou-rave (shoo-rav) French for kohlrabi.

chouriço (shoh-REE-soh) A Portuguese smoked sausage made from pork meat and fat, seasoned with white pepper, garlic, paprika and white wine.

choux de bruxelles (shoo duh brew-SELL) French for Brussels sprouts.

choux pastry (shoo paste-re) A classic French pastry dough used for making éclairs, cream puffs and the like; this sticky, pastelike dough is made with boiling water and/or milk, butter, flour and eggs, first cooked on the stove top, then baked in an oven; the resulting products have a hard, crisp exterior and a nearly hollow interior; also known as pâte à choux.

chow-chow; chowchow 1. A mixed vegetable and pickle relish flavored with mustard. 2. Originally, orange peel and ginger in a heavy syrup; used as a condiment in Chinese cuisines.

chowder A hearty soup made from fish, shellfish and/or vegetables, usually containing milk and potatoes and often thickened with roux.

chowder clam; chowder quahog An Atlantic hard-shell clam; it usually measures more than 4 in. (7.6 cm) across the tannish-gray shell and has a very chewy and tough, pinkish-tan meat; usually minced for chowders and soups.

chow fun (tcha-oo foon) A Chinese dish of flat fresh rice flour noodles stir-fried with other ingredients.

chow mein; chao mein 1. Chinese for fried noodles. 2. A Chinese–American stir-fry dish of poultry, shrimp and/or meat with vegetables such as bean sprouts, mushrooms, water chestnuts, bamboo shoots and green onions served over fried noodles.

choy sum; choysum A member of the cabbage family; it has yellow flowers and dark green leaves; when steamed it is crisp and tender with a delicate flavor; also known as Chinese flowering cabbage.

chrane (kra-nay) A Jewish preserve made from cooked beets flavored with horseradish, malt vinegar and sugar.

chremslach (kreem-slack) A Jewish dish consisting of small balls of matzo meal dough stuffed with preserved fruits and nuts bound with honey and then fried and garnished with almonds and honey or sugar.

Christmas melon *See* Santa Claus melon.

Christmas mushroom *See* enoki.

Christmas pudding An English steamed pudding made of suet, dried fruits and spices, usually flamed with brandy and decorated with holly.

christophene (crees-toh-fen) French for chayote.

Christópsomo (hree-stoph-posh-moh) A Greek Christmas bread enriched with eggs and flavored with anise; the dough is shaped into large round loaves and decorated with the design of an early Christian cross.

christorra (cree-STORE-raw) A chorizo from Spain's Basque region; it is usually deep-fried or boiled.

chromium A trace mineral used principally to assist in metabolizing glucose; significant sources include meat, dairy products, whole grain cereals and fats.

chromium picolinate A chemical substance believed by some to burn fat, build lean muscle tissues, and reduce food cravings.

chronic disease A disease that progresses slowly, if at all. *See* acute disease.

chrysanthemum greens The green leafy portions of a chrysanthemum variety; they are generally picked before the plant blooms and have a slightly bitter flavor.

chrysanthemum tea *See* chiu hwa.

chu (choo) Chinese for simmering a food in a small amount of water. *See* chá.

chub A member of the whitefish family found in American midwestern lakes; it has a very soft flesh and an average market weight of 0.6–2.5 lb. (0.15–1.1 kg); often smoked.

chuck A primal section of the beef carcass; it is the shoulder and contains some of the backbone, five rib bones, bladebone, arm bone and much connective tissue; it includes such flavorful but often tough subprimal or fabricated cuts as the clod, cross-rib pot roast and chuck short ribs and is used for cubed steaks and ground beef; also known as the bladebone (especially in Great Britain) and shoulder.

chuck, ground Beef ground from the various small muscles found in the primal chuck.

chuck filet A subprimal cut of the beef primal chuck; cut from the center, it is somewhat tough.

chuck roast A fabricated cut of the beef primal chuck; it is a somewhat tough but flavorful roast cut from the shoulder.

chuck short ribs A fabricated cut of the beef primal chuck; they are the tips of the first five ribs.

chuck tender A subprimal cut of the beef primal chuck; somewhat tough and lean with a streak of gristle in its center; it is fabricated into small steaks (with the gristle left in) or the gristle is removed for a tied roast; also known as chicken steak, Jewish tender, mock tender and Scotch tender.

chuck wagon A ranch wagon converted into a kitchen on wheels and used as a place to prepare and cook meals for cowboys on cattle drives; it is fitted at the rear with a box of compartments (chuckbox) used to hold supplies and utensils.

chuck wagon steak A fabricated cut of the beef primal chuck; it is somewhat tough, flavorful, boneless and round.

chufa *See* tiger nut.

chúfáng (chou-fan) Chinese for kitchen.

chug; chug-a-lug Slang for swallowing a drink without pausing between gulps.

chui (tchoo-he) A green that grows wild in the Korean mountains; it has a flavor similar to spinach and watercress and is used in soups.

chukandar (choo-kahn-dahr) Hindi for red beet.

chukar partridge *See* partridge.

chuka soba (CHOO-koo soh-bah) Thin yellow Japanese soba noodles; generally used for soups and salads.

chuleta (choo-LEH-tah) Spanish for cutlet or chop.

chu miso (CHOO mee-soh) A moderately thick Japanese bean paste.

chump A British cut of the lamb, pork and veal carcass; it is the hind end of the loin before it becomes the top of the leg.

chump chop A British cut of the lamb, pork and veal carcass; it is a chop cut from the chump. *See* loin chop.

chum salmon A variety of salmon found in Washington's Puget Sound and off the west coasts of Canada and southern Alaska; it has a metallic blue skin with a slight purplish sheen that becomes silvery on the sides and belly, a lean, yellow to white flesh, a poor flavor, and an average market weight of 5–10 lb. (2.3–4.5 kg); also known as dog salmon and keta salmon.

chumvi (choom-vee) Swahili for salt.

chun (tchooh) Chinese for plunging a food rapidly into and out of hot oil.

chungwa (choon-goo-aw) Swahili for orange.

chun juan (tchoon jew-ahn) Chinese for spring roll.

chunked and formed A meat product consisting of chunks of beef, veal, lamb or pork that have been massaged, ground or diced and then formed into the desired shape.

chunked and formed ham *See* ham, sectioned and formed.

chunk-style honey Honey with pieces of the honeycomb included; also known as comb honey.

chunky banana *See* burro banana.

chuno (choo-noh) Spanish (especially in South America) for dried vegetables, generally tubers and especially potatoes.

chuoi chien (tchoo-no-he che-an) A Vietnamese dessert of bananas stuffed with a sweet filling such as pistachio or hazelnut paste, dipped in a batter, deep-fried, and dusted with confectioners' sugar; the dessert is sometimes flamed.

chupa-chupa A fruit (*Quararibea cordata*) native to Peru and Colombia; it has a long, ovoid shape with a flavor reminiscent of an apricot and mango.

chupe (choo-pay) A South American term for a thick, savory stew made with ingredients such as potatoes, tomatoes, corn, milk or a soft cheese, eggs and other ingredients.

chupe de camarones (choo-pay day kam-ah-roe-ness) A Peruvian chupe made with shrimp, tomatoes, potatoes, corn and peas flavored with garlic, pepper, chiles, cilantro and oregano.

chupe de guatitas (choo-pay day goo-ah-tea-tass) A Chilean tripe stew.

chura (choo-raw) A soft Tibetan cow's milk cheese.

chura kampo (choo-raw kham-poh) Dried chura loenpa.

chura loenpa (choo-raw loh-ahn-pah) A cottage cheese–style Tibetan cheese.

Churchill A moderately sized cigar with a 47 or 48 ring and approximately 7-in. length (they can be as short as 6 in. and as long as 8 in.); named for Winston Churchill.

church key Slang for a bottle opener, usually used in connection with a bottle of beer.

churn *v.* To agitate cream or milk so that the fat separates from the liquid, forming a solid (butter). *n.* The vessel in which milk or cream is agitated to make butter or ice cream.

church key

churn beater A tool with a spring tightly coiled into a conical shape; it is used to agitate thin batters in a small container.

churrasco a gaucha (choo-raw-scoe ah gah-oo-chah) A Brazilian barbecue.

churro (choo-roa) A deep-fried Mexican pastry similar to a doughnut; it is flavored with cinnamon and rolled in a cinnamon–sugar mixture while hot.

churn beater

chúshi (tchu-she) Chinese for chef.

chushoku (choo-shoh-kuh) Japanese for lunch.

chutney From the Hindi chatni, it is a condiment made from fruit, vinegar, sugar and spices; its texture can range from smooth to chunky and its flavor from mild to hot.

chutoro (choo-toh-roh) Japanese for the somewhat fatty flesh found at the belly near the tail and back of a tuna (maguro); it is used for sushi and sashimi. *See* akami *and* otoro.

chylomicrons A lipoprotein made by the intestines; it transports lipids through the lymph and blood.

chyme The nearly liquid mixture of partially digested food and digestive secretions found in the stomach and small intestine during the digestive process.

ciabatta (ch'yah-BAH-tah) Italian for slipper and used to describe a slipper-shaped loaf of bread.

ciastka (chy-ah-stka) Polish for cookies.

ciasto (chy-ah-sto) Polish for dough.

ciaudedda (CHOW-deh-DAH) An Italian dish of braised artichokes stuffed with potatoes, fava beans, salt pork and onions.

cibo (chee-boh) Italian for food.

ciboulette (cee-boo-layt) French for chives.

cicely, sweet cicely A fragrant herb of the parsley family; it has anise-flavored leaves and seeds.

cicharón See chicharrón.

cider Pressed apple juice; it is used to make sweet cider, hard cider, vinegar and applejack.

cider apple Any of a variety of apples whose fruit have a somewhat bitter, astringent flavor; generally used to make cider.

cider mill 1. A machine that releases the juice from an apple by applying pressure. 2. The building where cider is made.

cider vinegar A vinegar made by fermenting pure apple juice into hard cider and then exposing it to the air; clear, it has a pale brown color and a strong, somewhat harsh flavor.

cidery A beer-tasting term for an undesirable aroma or flavor caused by bacterial infestation.

cidra (see-drah) Spanish for citron.

cielecina (chy-eh-lehn-chy-nah) Polish for veal.

ccigala (see-gah-lah) Spanish for spiny lobster.

cigale (chi-gah-lay) Arabic for sea ant; it is usually grilled.

cigallas (see-GAh-yass) A Spanish tapas of langoustes brushed with olive oil and broiled on an iron hob.

cigar A compact roll of tobacco prepared for smoking; there are three basic parts to a cigar: filler, binder and wrapper (including the flag).

cigar, fat A cigar with a 50 or greater ring (i.e., a diameter of 50/64ths of an in. or more).

cigar, handmade A cigar made from tobacco picked, sorted, and bundled by hand and then rolled by individuals (rollers); cigars made by hand tend to be of better quality than those that are machine made.

cigar, machine-made A cigar made from tobacco picked by a machine and then rolled by a machine; often the filler used is short filler or tobacco scraps.

cigar, thin A cigar with a 38 or less ring (i.e., a diameter of 38/64ths of an in. or less).

cigar bar An establishment where patrons can buy and smoke cigars; usually drinks are also sold.

cigar boxes Hinged boxes used for cigars (usually distributed by manufacturers in 8-9-8 packages); traditionally made from cedar, but paper-covered cardboard and basswood boxes are also available. See bundled cigars.

cigar club An establishment where patrons (members) can buy, smoke and store cigars; usually drinks are also provided or sold.

cigar-friendly bar; cigar-friendly restaurant A drinking and/or dining establishment that tolerates or even encourages cigar smoking.

cigarillo A small cigar, generally not much larger than a cigarette; it is made from cigar leaf tobacco, but because it is so small, it contains short filler to promote even burning.

ciger (gig-ar) Turkish for liver.

çig köfte (sig kof-ta) A Turkish hors d'oeuvre of raw ground meat with hot spices.

cilantro (thee-LAHN-troh) The dark green, lacy leaves of the cilantro plant (*Coriandrum sativum*); used as an herb, they have a sharp, tangy, fresh flavor and aroma and are used fresh in Mexican, South American and Asian cuisines; also known as Chinese parsley. See coriander.

çilbir (seal-beer) A Turkish dish of poached eggs in yogurt garnished with butter and flavored with paprika and cayenne.

ciliegia (chee-L'YEH-j'yah) Italian for cherry.

cilindrati (chee-leen-drah-tee) Italian croissants made from a very thin bread dough that has been rolled out repeatedly before being formed into rolls.

cima ripièno (chee-mah ree-PEE-nah) A northern Italian dish of veal breast stuffed with veal brains, sweetbreads, chopped veal, eggs, artichoke hearts and green peas, flavored with Parmesan and marjoram, boiled, and served cold.

cinchona Any of several trees of the genus *Chincona* native to the Andes; their bark yields quinine.

Ciney (see-nae) The proprietary name of a Belgian monastery beer that is dark and slightly sweet.

cinghiale (cheen-G'YAH-leh) Italian for wild boar.

cinnamic acid A food additive derived from cinnamon and used as a flavoring agent.

cinnamon A spice that is the inner bark of the branches of a small evergreen tree (*Cinnamonum zeylanicum*) native to Sri Lanka and India; it has an orange-brown color and a sweet, distinctive flavor and aroma; usually sold in rolled-up sticks (quills) or ground, it is used for sweet and savory dishes and as a garnish; also known as Ceylon cinnamon. See cassia.

cinnamon roast See roast, cinnamon.

cinnamyl anthranilate A food additive with a fruity, balsamic aroma used as a flavoring agent.

cinnamyl compounds Food additives that contain a cinnamyl group and are used as flavoring agents and/or adjuvants for their piquant, sharp flavor.

cinnamyl isobutyrate A food additive with a dry, fruity aroma used as a flavoring agent in baked goods and candies.

Cinsaut; Cinsault (san-so) 1. A red wine grape principally grown in Europe, Lebanon and South Africa; also known as Hermitage (especially in South Africa). 2. A full-bodied, deep-colored wine made from this grape.

cioccolata (choak-koa-LAA-tah) Italian for chocolate.

cioppino (chuh-PEE-noh) An Italian or Italian–American stew made with tomatoes and a variety of fish and shellfish.

cipolla (chee-POL-lah) Italian for onion.

cipollini (chilp-oh-LEE-nee) The bulbs of the grape hyacinth (genus *Muscari*); they resemble small onions and have a mild, onionlike flavor; cooked like a vegetable in Italian cuisine.

çipura (sea-poo-raw) Turkish for gilthead.

cirnat (cheer-naht) Romanian for sausage.

Cirò (CHEER-oh) A DOC-rated wine from Italy's Calabria region; it is usually a red wine, but a youthful rosé and a white wine are also produced.

ciruela (thee-RWAY-lah) Spanish for plum.

cisco (sis-co) *See* lake herring.

ciseler (see-sah-lay) 1. French for to cut, specifically to cut foods into julienne. 2. French for to score, as in slashing a whole fish to speed cooking.

ciste An Irish term meaning cake and used to describe the crackling or skin of a roast.

cistern 1. A vessel used to hold bottles (especially wine) in cold water; traditionally placed on the floor near the sideboard in a dining room. 2. A vessel used to hold a large supply of punch or other alcoholic or nonalcoholic beverage; traditionally placed on a sideboard or other serving table. 3. A vessel used to hold water or other liquids, especially a tank to hold rainwater.

citral A food additive derived from lemon and lemon grass oil; it has a citrus aroma and is used as a flavoring agent in baked goods, candies and ice creams.

citral and citronellyl compounds Food additives that contain a citral or a citronellyl group and are used as flavoring agents and/or adjuvants for their lemon- or orangelike flavors, especially in baked goods, candies and ice creams.

citrange An orange and lemon citrus hybrid.

citrangiquat An orange and kumquat citrus hybrid.

citric acid A food additive used as a pH control agent, sequestrant, preservative and/or antioxidant in processed foods such as beverages and canned fruits.

citroen (see-TROO-nuh) Dutch for lemon.

citroen sap (see-TROO-nuh sop) Dutch for lemon juice.

citron (cee-troa) Danish, French and Swedish for lemon.

citron (SIHT-ron) A citrus fruit (*Citrus medica*) native to China; approximately the size of a lemon, it has a dry pulp and a thick, lumpy, yellow-green skin that is candied and used in baking.

citronella A tropical perennial grass (*Cymbopogon nardus*); it has a strong, lemony aroma and is used as a flavoring and in salads; the oil is used as an insect repellent.

citronella grass *See* lemon grass.

citronellal A food additive with an intense lemon, citronella, and rose aroma used as a flavoring agent.

citronellyl propionate A food additive with a light rose and fruit aroma used as a flavoring agent in baked goods, candies, beverages and ice creams.

citron vert (cee-troa vehr) French for lime.

citrus; citrus fruits Members of the genus *Citrus*; grown on trees and shrubs in tropical and temperate climates worldwide, these fruits generally have a thick rind, most of which is a fluffy, bitter white layer (albedo) with a thin exterior layer of skin (zest) that can be green, yellow, orange or pinkish; the flesh is segmented and has an acidic flavor ranging from sweet to very tart.

citrus fruit wine; citrus wine A wine produced by fermenting citrus fruit; citrus must, citrus brandy and/or alcohol are sometimes added.

citrus oil A food additive obtained by pressing citrus rinds; it is used as a flavoring agent, especially in beverages.

citrus red no. 2 A food additive used as a red or yellow-red coloring agent.

citrus stripper *See* stripper.

citrusy A wine-tasting term for a wine, usually white, with characteristics similar to those of citrus fruits, such as a high acidity and tart flavor.

citrus zester *See* zester.

city chicken Veal cubes served on kabobs.

city roast *See* roast, city.

ciuperci (chee-oopr-chee) Romanian for mushrooms.

civet (SIHV-iht) 1. A French stew of any furred animal, especially rabbit, squirrel or hare, with onions and larding bacon, cooked with red wine and thickened with the animal's blood. 2. A fixative derived from glandular secretions of the African civet cat.

civet fruit *See* durian.

cizbiz; cizbiz kofte (chiz-biz; chiz-biz kof-ta) Grilled Turkish meatballs made of minced lamb, onions, parsley and thyme.

clabber Naturally soured and curdled unpasteurized whole milk that is thin enough to drink; it can separate into a very white semifirm liquid on the bottom and a layer of yellow cream on top; very sour, it is often eaten in the American South with sugar or black pepper and cream.

clabber; bonnyclabber To curdle.

clafouti (kla-foo-tee) A rustic French dessert tart made with fruit, usually dark sweet cherries, baked in an egg custard.

Claiborne, Craig (Am., 1920–) Food writer and restaurant reviewer for the *New York Times* and author of *The New York Times Cookbook*; his recipes introduced international fare to novice cooks, and his reviews taught readers how to respect and critique every kind of dining establishment.

clairet (cleh-ray) 1. An old French term for a rather light red wine of Bordeaux. 2. A light red wine made in France's Bordeaux region; the wine, which has little tannin and a deep rose color, resembles a full-bodied rosé and is usually served chilled.

Clamart, à la (clah-mahr, ah lah) A French garnish consisting of whole or puréed green peas.

clambake A social gathering where the food, usually clams, lobsters, crabs, chicken, corn, potatoes and sweet potatoes, is cooked in a pit lined with heated rocks and covered with seaweed.

clam chowder, Manhattan A clam chowder made with tomatoes.

clam chowder, New England A clam chowder made with cream or milk; also known as Boston clam chowder.

clam knife A small knife used to open clams; it has a rigid blade and a round tip.

clams A large group of bi- valve mollusks found in coastal saltwaters world- wide; they have hard or soft, beige, gray, blue or brown shells and juicy, of- ten chewy, pinkish-tan to

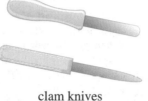

clam knives

gray meat with a mild to sweet flavor. *See* Atlantic clams *and* Pacific clams.

clams casino An American dish of clams served hot on the half shell with a topping of seasoned butter and crisp bacon.

Clapp Favorite A broad-based pear; it has a dull yellowish-green skin with some russeting and a granular flesh.

clapshot (KLAHP-shoat) A dish from the Orkney Islands consisting of mashed boiled potatoes and turnips flavored with chives and bacon fat.

claret (KALHR-eht) 1. In the United States and continental Europe, a light, red table wine made from any red wine grapes grown anywhere. 2. In England, a red wine from France's Bordeaux region.

clarete (clah-REH-teh) Spanish for any red wine that is light in body and color.

Clare Valley A grape-growing and wine-producing area north of Adelaide in the state of South Australia; the principal grapes grown are Rhine Riesling, Cabernet Sauvignon and Chardonnay.

clarification The process of transforming a broth into a clear consommé by trapping impurities with a clearmeat.

clarified butter *See* butter, clarified.

clarify To clear a cloudy liquid by removing the suspended particles and sediment.

clarifying chips Small, thin pieces of wood used to help clarify beer during a secondary fermentation. *See* beechwood aging.

clarity A beer- and wine-tasting term for the brilliance or absence of haze in the product.

claro A type of cigar wrapper; the tobacco has a light brown or tan color, a slight oily sheen, and a delicate, smooth flavor; also known as a natural wrapper.

clary An herb (*Salvia sclarea*) used principally for medicinal purposes; the dull, gray, furry leaves have a slight sage flavor and are used in salads.

clary sage The essential oil of clary; it is used to flavor vermouth and liqueurs; also known as Muscatel oil.

classed growth English for cru classé.

classes The subdivision of poultry kinds based on the bird's age and tenderness.

classic cuisine; classical cuisine A late-19th- and early-20th-century refinement and simplification of French grande cuisine; it relies on the thorough exploration of culinary principles and techniques and emphasizes the refined preparation and presentation of superb ingredients.

Classification of 1855 The first French classification of fine wines, conducted at the Paris Exhibition of 1855; used initially to set prices (considered an indication of quality) for the wines of two Bordeaux districts (Médoc and Sauternes).

classimo (clah-see-moe) Italian labeling term for all sparkling wines produced by the méthode champenoise as of the release of the 1991 vintage.

clavelin (clah'v-lan) A short, stumpy bottle used in France's Jura district for vin jaunes.

Claville blanche d'hiver (cla-vee blahn-sha dee-vair) A large apple native to France; it has a golden skin and a juicy, aromatic flesh.

clavo (KLAH-boh) Spanish for clove.

clawed lobster *See* Maine lobster.

clay A natural earthy substance that is pliable when wet and used to make ceramics.

claytonia *See* miner's lettuce.

clay chicken pot An unglazed clay casserole with a lid; it is soaked in cold water before use; when heated, the steam from the wet clay helps cook the food.

clean In a food safety context, to remove visible dirt and soil from an object or environment. *See* sanitize *and* sterilize.

clean; clean tasting A wine-tasting term for a palatable, refreshing, agreeable wine with no off-aromas or off-flavors.

cleaning agent A preparation such as a detergent or soap used for removing dirt, grease or the like.

clear liquid diet A hospital diet in which the food is appropriately seasoned with salt and other seasonings but no solid foods are allowed; also known as a liquid diet.

clearmeat A mixture of egg whites, ground meat, an acidic product and other ingredients; used to clarify a broth.

clear soups Unthickened soups, including broths, consommés and broth-based soups.

cleaver A large, heavy, almost rectangular knife with a relatively flat cutting edge; unbalanced to add momentum to the stroke, it is used to split cartilage and bone; also known as a butcher's cleaver. *See* Chinese cleaver.

clementine A small, spherical citrus fruit that is a hybrid of the tangerine and the Seville orange; it has an orange-red rind, a seedless, juicy flesh, and a sweet flavor.

clemenvilla A clementine and tangelo citrus hybrid.

Clemson Spineless okra A popular variety of okra.

climat (clee-mah) A French wine term used to refer to the climate or environmental conditions of a specific vineyard (usually one in Burgundy); used like the American term microclimate.

clingstone A general description for a fruit that has flesh that adheres to its pit. *See* freestone.

clinkers Slang for biscuits, usually stale, used for dunking in milk, coffee or tea.

clip *See* knife point.

clip-on A separate sheet or card attached to a menu identifying one or more specials.

clochard A small, western European traditional apple with a bumpy, dark yellow skin; also known as a beggar's apple.

cloche (klosh) 1. A convex dish cover with a knob or handle on top, usually of stainless steel or silver-plated metal; used to keep food hot, especially in restaurants. 2. An unglazed ceramic baking dish with a high domed cover used for baking crisp, crusty breads.

cloche, sous (klosh, soo) French for under bell, usually of glass or metal.

clod A subprimal cut of the beef primal chuck; it contains the large outside muscle system above the elbow; lean, tough and flavorful, it is often fabricated into steaks and roasts; also known as the shoulder clod.

cloning A horticultural technique of propagation from a single source; the resulting plants, called clones, are identical to the source; the technique has recently been applied to livestock, where the source of the second animal is a single cell from the original.

clos (cloh) French for a walled or enclosed vineyard.

close A cheese-tasting term for a cheese with a smooth, dense interior that has no holes. *See* open.

closed A wine-tasting term for a wine (usually a young one) that is not showing its potential; additional aging may cure the problem.

closed cup mushroom A stage in the growth of a cultivated mushroom when the membrane breaks but the gills are not yet visible and the cap is still milky white.

closed date A production code that a manufacturer, distributor or retailer stamps on a food product's label to monitor distribution and ensure quality. *See* open date.

closed pit A barbecue cooking pit or style of cooking in which the meat is cooked in an enclosed space using heat and smoke from a fire. *See* open pit.

closed side The right side of a beef carcass. *See* open side.

close trim To remove more external fat from beef, veal, lamb or pork than is ordinarily required by commercial specifications.

Clostridium botulinum A species of bacteria that causes botulism; common sources include cooked foods (e.g., rice, smoked fish and canned foods, especially vegetables) held for an extended period at warm temperatures with limited oxygen.

Clostridium perfringens A species of bacteria that causes food poisoning; common sources include reheated meats, sauces, stews and casseroles.

clotted cream A thickened cream made from unpasteurized milk that is gently heated until a semisolid layer of cream forms on the surface; after cooling the thickened cream is removed and can be spread or spooned, often onto a scone or other baked good; also known as Devonshire cream or Devon cream.

cloudberry A wild berry (*Rubus chamaemorous*) found in Scandinavia, Canada and New England; resembling a raspberry, it has an amber color and a tart flavor and is used principally for jams; also known as bake-apple berry, mountain berry and yellow berry.

cloud ear mushroom A mushroom (*Auricularia polytricha* and *A. auricula*) that grows on tree stumps in China; it has a shallow oval cup, a slightly crunchy texture and a bland flavor and is generally available only in dried form; also known as Jew's ear mushroom, tree ear mushroom and wood ear mushroom.

clou de girofle (klue duh gee-roe-flay) French for clove, the spice.

cloudy 1. A wine-tasting term for a low-alcohol-content wine in which some albuminous substances refuse to settle; the term does not apply to a wine that has thrown a sediment. *See* hazy. 2. A beer-tasting term for the temporary hazy condition of a beer stored at temperatures below 34°F (1.1°C) for a long period; also known as chill haze.

clove 1. A spice that is the dried, unopened flower bud of a tropical evergreen tree (*Eugenia aromatica*); it has a reddish-brown color, a nail shape and an extremely pungent, sweet, astringent flavor; available whole or powdered. 2. A segment of a bulb, such as garlic. 3. A British unit of weight for goods such as cheese; equal to 8 lb. (3.5 kg).

Clover Club A cocktail made of gin, lime juice, grenadine and egg white.

clover honey A thick, light-colored, full-flavored, all-purpose honey principally made from clover blossoms and popular in North America and Europe.

cloverleaf roll A soft yeast roll made by placing three small balls of dough in a muffin cup to rise together, resulting in a roll shaped like a three-leaf clover.

cloying A wine-tasting term for an overly sweet, unbalanced, flabby wine with little acidity.

club car *See* lounge car.

club cheese *See* cold-pack cheese.

club sandwich; clubhouse sandwich A double-layer sandwich of toasted or untoasted bread, chicken or turkey, lettuce, tomato and bacon.

club soda *See* seltzer water.

club steak A fabricated cut of the beef primal short loin; this tender cut contains an L-shaped section of the backbone and a portion of loin eye muscle but none of the tenderloin. *See* shell steak, T-bone steak *and* porterhouse steak.

club steak, boneless A club steak without the bone.

club steak, center-cut A center-cut club steak.

cluck and grunt Cowboy slang for eggs and bacon.

Cluster A variety of hops grown in the United States.

CMC Certified Master Chef; it is the highest level of certification offered by the American Culinary Federation.

CMC *See* carboxymethylcellulose.

CMPC Certified Master Pastry Chef; it is the highest level of certification offered to pastry chefs by the American Culinary Federation.

coachman *See* Fiaker.

coagulation The irreversible transformation of proteins from a liquid or semiliquid state to a drier, solid state; usually accomplished through the application of heat.

Coalhada (koh-ah-lyah-duh) A fresh Brazilian cheese made from cow's milk; it has a creamy texture and a mild flavor and is usually eaten with an abundance of sugar.

coalpot A piece of cooking equipment used in the Caribbean region; it consists of a large brown clay pot up to 18 in. (45 cm) high and 10–12 in. (25–30 cm) in diameter; the wide, deep bowl with holes bored in the bottom forms the top of a broad, hollow column, partly open on one side near the base and broadened at the bottom to provide stability; a fire is started in the bowl, and cooking takes place inside on pans or a grill.

coarse 1. Composed of relatively large parts or particles; not fine in texture. 2. A wine-tasting term for a rough-textured wine that may have too high an alcohol content or a wine lacking finesse. 3. A beer-tasting term for an overly hopped, bitter beer.

coarsely chop To cut food into small pieces, about 3/16-in. (0.5-cm) square.

coarse salt *See* kosher salt.

coaster A napkin or small plate or mat placed under a glass or bottle to protect a table or other surface.

coat To cover a food (sometimes first dipped in a liquid such as eggs or milk) with an outer covering (coating) of bread crumbs, flour, dry seasonings or the like.

Coatapec (coe-ah-tah-peck) Arabica coffee beans grown in Mexico; considered one of the best Mexican varieties, the beverage is light and rich with a fine acidity.

coat a spoon A technique used to determine if a mixture such as a custard is done; it is done if the mixture clings to a spoon when held aloft and a line drawn across it does not disappear.

coating A layer of foods (e.g., flour, bread crumbs, batter or cornmeal) covering a principal ingredient; a coating is used to produce a crispy or caramelized surface, to protect the principal ingredient from a cooking medium, or to add flavors and texture.

cob; cobnut *See* filbert.

cobalamin *See* vitamin B_{12}.

cobalt A component of vitamin B_{12} and a trace mineral principally used to assist the nervous system and blood cell formation; significant sources include meat and dairy products.

coban (koh-bahn) 1. A dried, smoked pequin; this chile has a fiery hot flavor. 2. A Turkish salad of tomatoes, onions, cucumbers, green peppers, fresh mint and parsley dressed with lemon juice and olive oil.

Coban (koh-bahn) Arabica coffee beans grown in Guatemala's Coban region; the beverage is mild with a good acidity and aroma.

cobbler 1. A deep-dish fruit tart with a rich, sweet, biscuit-type dough covering the fruit. 2. A tall drink made of fruit and liquor, usually served in a goblet with shaved ice and garnished with fresh fruit and mint.

cobblerfish *See* pompano.

cobb salad A salad of chopped chicken or turkey, tomatoes, avocado, bacon, hard-boiled eggs, scallions, Cheddar and lettuce dressed with a vinaigrette and garnished with a blue cheese.

cocada (koa-KAH-dah) A Spanish sweet coconut custard.

cocalán (coe-cah-lahn) A honeylike syrup made in Chile from palm sap.

cocci (cox-cee) *See* bacteria.

cochineal; cochineal extract (kosh-ee-nel) A food additive obtained from the dried bodies of female cochineal insects and used as a food coloring; also known as carmine.

cochinillo (coe-chee-knee-yoh) Spanish for suckling pig.

cochinita pibil (koh-chee-nee-tah peh-bel) A Mexican and Latin American dish of Yucatecan-style pit-roasted young pig, now replaced by pork meat.

cochon (ko-shawng) French for pig.

cocido (koa-thee-dhoa) Spanish for cooked or boiled and used to describe a variety of soupy, stewlike dishes containing meats and vegetables, especially chickpeas.

cocido de fruta paso (coh-thee-dhoa da froo-tah pah-soh) A Colombian stew made from beef, onions, garlic, carrot, bell peppers and dried fruits, flavored with cinnamon, oregano and wine, and baked; served with rice.

cocido español (koa-thee-dhoa ay-spah-nyole) A thick Spanish soup of beef or chicken and assorted vegetables.

cocina (koh-see-nah) Spanish for kitchen.

cocinar (koh-si-nahr) Spanish for to cook.

cocinero (koh-se-nay-roh) Spanish for chef.

cock 1. The male of any bird. 2. A rooster.

cock-a-leekie; cockie leekie (kock-ah-LEE-ke) A Scottish soup made from an old cock or hen flavored with leeks, bacon, parsley, thyme, bay leaf and other seasonings and garnished with cooked prunes and leeks.

cockerel A young domestic cock.

cockles A family of bivalves with heart-shaped shells that measure 1 in. (2.5 cm) across; they have a long, finger-shaped foot, a gritty, chewy texture, and a mild flavor; also known as heart clams.

cockscomb; cock's comb The red, fleshy crest found on the head of male poultry; used in French cuisine as a garnish or as a savory tart filling.

cocktail 1. A drink made of one or more alcoholic beverages mixed with juice, soda or other ingredients and sometimes garnished with fruit; it is usually consumed before a meal or at a party; also known as a mixed drink. 2. A dish of cold foods, often bound or served with a dressing or sauce and generally served as an appetizer or dessert (e.g., shrimp cocktail and fruit cocktail).

cocktail avocado A variety of small avocado.

cocktail frank A frankfurter usually measuring 1–2 in. (2.54–5 cm) in length; often served as an hors d'oeuvre.

cocktail glass A stemmed glass with a bell-shaped or tapered bowl holding approximately 3 fl. oz.; used for straight-up cocktails, it should be chilled before use.

cocktail lounge See bar.

cocktail mix station An auxiliary bar equipped with an ice compartment and the appropriate ingredients for preparing cocktails.

cocktail napkin A small cloth or paper napkin given with a cocktail or other drink; used to wrap the glass to keep the hand dry or as a coaster.

cocktail party A social gathering typically held during the early evening; guests usually stand and are served alcoholic beverages and hors d'oeuvres.

cocktail sauce A sauce used for shellfish and as a condiment; made from ketchup or chile sauce mixed with horseradish, lemon juice and a hot red pepper sauce.

cocktail sherry An imprecise American term for a dry sherry, usually amontillado, as opposed to a very dry fino or manzanilla.

cocktail strainer A perforated stainless steel spoon or round strainer often surrounded by a flexible metal coil or wire spring; it has ears or grips that fit over the rim of a shaking glass and is used for straining cocktails containing fruit, pulp or ice.

cocktail tray A cork-lined, rimmed tray, usually circular or oval, used for serving drinks.

cocktail waitress; cocktail waiter A server at a bar.

coco (KOH-koh) Portuguese for coconut.

cocoa 1. A hot beverage made with cocoa, a sweetener and milk; also known as hot chocolate. 2. Chocolate that has had most of its fat removed, then is pulverized into a powder; used to flavor baked goods and sauces.

cocoa beans Seeds of the cacao tree. See cacao and chocolate-making process.

cocoa butter The cream-colored fat extracted from cocoa beans during the process of making cocoa powder; used to make bar chocolate, white chocolate and cosmetics. See chocolate-making process.

cocoa liquor See chocolate liquor.

cocoa mix A mixture of cocoa powder, dry milk and a sweetener; mixed with hot or cold water to make a chocolate-flavored beverage; also known as instant cocoa.

cocoa nibs Roasted, shelled cocoa bean kernels. See chocolate-making process.

cocoa powder A brown, unsweetened powder produced by crushing cocoa nibs and extracting most of the fat (cocoa butter); it is used as a flavoring; also known as unsweetened cocoa. See alkalized cocoa and chocolate-making process.

cocoa powder, Dutch process Cocoa powder that has been treated with an alkali to neutralize its natural acidity; it is darker and milder than a nonalkalized powder.

Coco Chanel A cocktail made of gin, heavy cream and Kahlua or Tia Maria.

cocomero (koa-KOA-may-roa) Italian for watermelon.

cocomoka (KOH-koh-moh-kah) A beverage combining coffee and cocoa powder, served hot or cold.

coconut The fruit of a tropical palm tree (Cocos nucifera); it has a hard, woody shell enclosed in a thick fibrous husk; the shell is lined with a hard white flesh, and the hollow center is filled with a sweet milky-white liquid.

coconut, dried The shredded or flaked flesh of the coconut; often sweetened; also known as copra.

coconut cream A coconut-flavored liquid made like coconut milk but with less water; the resulting liquid is thicker, creamier and more flavorful. See cream of coconut.

coconut dates See honey dates.

coconut juice; coconut water The slightly opaque liquid from a fresh coconut; sometimes known imprecisely as coconut milk.

coconut milk A coconut-flavored liquid made by pouring boiling water over shredded coconut; the mixture is cooled and the white liquid is strained.

coconut oil An oil obtained from the dried coconut; dense, white, buttery and high in saturated fats; it is used for cooking and in processed products such as candies, margarine, baked goods, soaps and cosmetics.

coconut syrup A nonalcoholic, sweetened syrup made from coconut meat and milk; used for preparing cocktails and as a flavoring agent in desserts.

coconut water The slightly opaque liquid contained within a fresh coconut.

cocoon An immature stage of growth of a mushroom when it is egg shaped and usually freshly emerged from the ground.

Cocoribe An American liqueur made from coconuts and light Virgin Islands rum.

cocotte (koh-KOT) French for casserole and used to describe a round or oval cooking pan with two handles and a tight-fitting lid; used for slow cooking dishes such as daubes and other braised dishes; it is available in a variety of materials and sizes. See en cocotte.

cocoyam See malanga.

cocozelle (kok-ah-ZEL-le) A variety of zucchini grown in Italy; these summer squash are very long and have a dark green skin with yellow and green stripes and an excellent flavor.

cocum A large, dark purple fruit with a large seed and sour flavor used in Indian cuisine to flavor fish dishes, curries, sherbets and cold drinks.

cod; codfish A large family of saltwater fish, including Atlantic cod, Pacific cod, pollock, haddock, whiting and hake; generally, they have a mild, delicate flavor, a lean, white flesh and a firm texture; they are available fresh, sun-dried, salted or smoked.

cod, Atlantic Cod found in the northern Atlantic Ocean; they have a silvery skin with rust-colored spots and an average market weight of 10 lb. (4.4 kg). *See* scrod.

cod, Atlantic

cod, Pacific Cod found in the northern Pacific Ocean; they have a dark gray or brown skin that fades to grayish-white on the belly, a very soft texture, and an average market weight of 5–10 lb. (2.2–4.5 kg); they are sometimes mistaken for rock cod or black cod, which are unrelated; also known as gray cod.

coddle To cook foods, usually eggs, slowly in a container set in a water bath.

cod fat A rough and irregularly shaped fatty deposit found in the scrotal region of steers.

codiniac (koh-den-ee-ack) An archaic name for quince marmalade.

Codlin A family of British cooking apples; generally elongated, with a pale green or yellow skin, sometimes with a reddish flush.

codorniz (koa-doarn-NEETH) Spanish for quail.

codorna (coh-dor-nee) Portuguese for quail.

coelho (koh-AYL-yoh) Portuguese for rabbit.

coenzyme Any of various small substances, many of which contain a B vitamin, that promote or assist an enzyme's activities.

coeur (kurr) French for heart.

coeur à la crème (kurr ah lah krehm) French for heart with cream and used to describe a dessert made by combining cream cheese with whipping cream or sour cream and molding the mixture in a wicker or cheesecloth-lined mold (usually heart shaped) to remove the whey or liquid; the cheese is unmolded and garnished with berries.

coeur à la crème mold A heart-shaped wicker basket or heart-shaped porcelain mold with holes in the bottom used to mold the dessert coeur à la crème; it is approximately 1 in. high and 3–7 in. in length and diameter.

coeur à la crème mold

Coeur de Bray A soft French cheese made from cow's milk; heart shaped, it has a white creamy interior and a bloomy white rind.

coeur de Bruxelles *See* pain à la grecque.

coeur de filet (cou-ere day fee-lay) A French cut of the beef carcass from the heart of the tenderloin; it is a porterhouse steak.

coffee 1. A dark brown, aromatic beverage made by brewing roasted and ground beans of the coffee plant (genus *Coffea*). 2. The beans of the coffee plant; of two general varieties, they are usually named for the geographical location where they are grown. *See* arabica coffee beans *and* robusta coffee beans. 3. A term used imprecisely to describe the beverage as generally consumed in the United States and made from approximately 2 level tablespoons of ground coffee per 6 fl. oz. of water.

coffee, decaffeinated 1. Coffee beans that have had the caffeine removed by the direct contact method or the Swiss water process. 2. The beverage made from such beans.

coffee, flavored A coffee that has acquired a particular flavor or aroma by tumbling the beans with one or more flavoring or aromatic oils; flavors include vanilla, chocolate, liqueurs, spices and nuts.

coffee beans, green Coffee beans (both arabica and robusta) in their raw state; when fresh from the berry, they are a light olive-tan; as they dry, they become pale yellow-orange.

coffee break A brief work stoppage during which workers refresh themselves by drinking coffee or other beverages, smoking and so on.

coffee cake; coffeecake A sweet, leavened, breadlike cake usually flavored with nuts, fruit or spices and topped with frosting, glaze or streusel; traditionally served for breakfast or brunch.

coffee can A British term for a straight-sided mug with a height and diameter of approximately 2 1/2 in.

Coffee Cooler A cocktail made of iced coffee, vodka, Kahlua and heavy cream; served in a chilled double old-fashioned glass and topped with coffee ice cream.

coffee cream *See* cream, light.

coffee-cup-full A traditional measure of volume; it is approximately 6 fl. oz.

coffee grinder A machine that grinds roasted coffee beans before brewing; it can be electric or manual, with the fineness of the grind usually dependent on the length of time the grinder operates; also known as a coffee mill.

coffee house An establishment where coffee and other refreshments (but usually not alcoholic beverages) are served.

coffee klatch; coffee klatsch A casual social gathering for coffee and conversation; also known as a kaffeeklatsch (Germany).

coffee milk 1. Coffee with hot milk. 2. A little coffee in a glass of milk.

coffee mill *See* coffee grinder.

coffeepot A metal, ceramic or glass vessel with a lid and a spout used for brewing and/or serving coffee.

coffee scoop *See* approved coffee measure.

coffee sugar crystals Topaz or rainbow-colored sugar candy crystals, similar to rock candy and used for sweetening coffee.

coffee syrup A coffee-flavored sweetened syrup used as a flavoring agent, principally in beverages.

coffee urn A large container often used in commercial settings to brew coffee by pumping hot water over the ground coffee beans.

coffee whitener A nondairy product used to whiten coffee; usually made from corn syrup, emulsifiers, vegetable fats, coloring agents, preservatives and artificial flavorings.

Coffey still A continuous still for distilling alcohol.

coffin 1. A pie crust. 2. The dish or mold in which a pie is baked.

Cognac (kohn-yahk) A brandy distilled from wines made from Folle Blanche, Saint-Emilion and Colombard grapes grown within France's Charente and Charente-Martime departments; it is distilled in a two-step process and aged in Limousin oak barrels, sometimes for as long as 50–55 years. *See* brandy.

cognac (kohn-yahk) French and Italian for brandy.

cogumelo (koh-goo-MEH-loh) Portuguese for mushrooms.

cohiba 1. Caribbean for tobacco, a derivative of the pre-Columbian term. 2. One of Cuba's best and most famous cigar brands.

coho salmon (koh-ho) A variety of salmon found in the Pacific Ocean from Oregon to Alaska; it has a metallic blue skin that fades to silver on the sides and belly with irregular black spotting, a black mouth with a white gum, a light to dark pink flesh, high fat content, a mild flavor, and an average market weight of 3–12 lb. (1.4–5.4 kg), although aquafarmed coho are usually 1 lb. (450 g); also known as a silver salmon.

coing (kwahn) French for quince.

Cointreau (KWAHN-troh) A clear, colorless, orange-flavored French liqueur.

col (kohl) Spanish for cabbage.

cola A sweet, carbonated soft drink flavored with a syrup made from an extract of coca leaves and cola (kola) nuts, caramel, sugar, acids and aromatic substances.

colache (koh-lah-chay) A Mexican dish consisting of onions, zucchini, tomatoes, sweet corn, garlic and green beans, flavored with sugar, salt and vinegar, and fried in bacon fat.

Cola de Lagarto Spanish for lizard's tail and used to describe a cocktail made of dry white wine, vodka or gin, lime juice, confectioners' sugar and crème de menthe served over ice.

colander A bowl-shaped utensil with many perforations and usually short legs; it is used to drain liquids from solids.

cola nuts; kola nuts The reddish, fragrant, nutlike seeds of the kola tree (*Cola acuminata* and *C. nitida*), native to tropical Africa and grown in the West Indies and South America; they contain caffeine and theobromine and are used as a principal flavoring ingredient in carbonated soft drinks.

colander

colasse *See* taro.

colazione (koh-lah-tsi-oh-nae) Italian for lunch.

Colbert, sauce (kohl-bair) A French compound sauce made from a demi-glaze flavored with butter, wine, shallots, lemon juice, nutmeg, tarragon, parsley and Madeira; often used for meats or game.

Colbert butter *See* beurre Colbert.

Colby (KOHL-bee) A firm American granular cheese made in Wisconsin from whole cow's milk; it has a yellow-orange color, a mild flavor, and an open texture; similar to English Cheddar.

colcannon (kuhl-CAN-uhn) An Irish dish of mashed potatoes and cooked cabbage mixed with butter and milk and flavored with chives and parsley.

Colchester oyster (KOAL-chuh-str) A variety of common European oyster found off Colchester, England; known as a Walflete oyster during Elizabethan times.

cold box 1. A large walk-in storage room for foods and beverages, kept at a temperature of 34–40°F (1.1–4.4°C). 2. A chilled room where Champagne and sparkling wines are disgorged.

cold break The coagulation and precipitation of proteins during the cooling of the wort during the beer-making process.

cold cuts Thin slices of various meats, such as ham, roast beef, salami and turkey, and sometimes cheeses, sliced and served cold, usually for a sandwich or salad.

Cold Duck 1. A mix of Champagne and a sparkling Burgundy wine; it has a light red color. 2. A pink sparkling wine made by either the Charmat process or méthode champenoise.

cold fermentation A process used to make some white wines; the juice ferments at temperatures below 55°F (12.7°C) to retain a greater measure of the grape's varietal character.

cold filtering A clarifying process in which wine or beer is stored at 25–30°F (−3.8–1.1°C); this causes the insoluble solids to precipitate.

cold flour A provision used by American soldiers on the Oregon Trail; it consisted of parched corn pounded into a coarse, polenta-like meal and mixed with sugar and cinnamon; it was eaten as is or cooked with water into a gruel.

cold one Slang for beer.

cold-pack cheese A cheese product made from one or more cheeses of the same or different varieties (typically Cheddar-style or Roquefort-style cheeses) finely ground and mixed without heating to a spreadable consistency; flavorings are sometimes added; also known as club cheese. *See* processed cheese.

cold pressed A method of extracting oil from olives without the use of heat; usually the first pressing.

cold smoker A smoker used to cold smoke foods; the heat source is separate from the food, with the smoke channeled to the food through a pipe to dissipate heat.

cold smoking A method of curing, preserving and/or flavoring certain foods by exposing them to smoke at temperatures of 50–85°F (10–29°C) for a prolonged period; such foods are usually not fully cooked, and many must be cooked before eating; most cold-smoked meats, fish, shellfish and poultry are first salt cured or brined and often are drier than hot smoked foods and have more concentrated flavors. *See* hot smoking.

cold-water tails Tails harvested from spiny lobsters caught off South Africa, Australia and New Zealand; available frozen, their flavor is superior to that of warm-water tails.

colère, en (koh-lehr, ahn) A French preparation for fish; the fish is cooked with its tail in its mouth, giving it an angry look; it is usually dipped in egg and bread crumbs, deep-fried, and served with a tomato sauce.

coleslaw; cole slaw A salad of Dutch origin made from shredded cabbage and sometimes onions, sweet peppers, pickles and/or bacon bound with a mayonnaise, vinaigrette or other dressing and sometimes flavored with herbs.

colewort An archaic generic name for members of the cabbage family.

colher (koh-lyer) Portuguese for spoon.

coliflor (ko-lee-FLOR) Spanish for cauliflower.

colin (coe-len) French for hake.

collagen A water-insoluble protein found in connective tissues such as skin, ligaments, tendons and cartilage; it yields gelatin when cooked with moist heat.

collard; collard greens; collards A member of the kale family, with dark green, paddlelike leaves that grow on tall, tough stalks; the leaves have a flavor reminiscent of cabbage and kale.

collared beef An English and Irish dish of beef (usually from the flank), rubbed with salt, parsley and allspice, rolled in a cloth, simmered and then pressed until cold; served cold and sometimes in aspic.

collared pork An Irish dish made from a salted pig's head simmered with onions, turnips, carrots, nutmeg, lemon rind and herbs; the peeled, sliced tongue is wrapped in cloth and placed between the two halves of the head and cooked again, the tongue is then pressed and served cold.

collé (coe-lay) French for with gelatin added.

collée, mayonnaise (koh-lee) A French mayonnaise sauce blended with liquefied meat aspic and used as a coating for cold foods.

coller To stiffen a food by adding dissolved gelatin.

collet (kho-lay) A French cut of the lamb carcass; it is the tough meat cut from the end of the neck near the shoulder.

Collins A cocktail base made of citrus juice, sugar syrup and soda water, served over ice in a Collins glass; the cocktail is called a Tom Collins if made with gin and a John Collins if made with vodka.

Collins glass A tall, cylindrical glass holding approximately 12 fl. oz.; used for long drinks such as a Tom Collins.

collop (KOHL-luhp) Archaic English or Scottish for a thick or thin slice of meat or offal. *See* minced collop.

colmenilla (col-man-ee-ah) Spanish for morel.

colocassi (koo-loo-kaa-see) A variety of taro native to Cyprus; the tuber is long, slender, and tapering with a rough brown skin.

Colombard (kohl-om-bar) *See* French Colombard.

Colombian Arabica coffee beans grown in the foothills of the Andes Mountains in Colombia; the beverage has a rich, mellow flavor.

Colombia Ñarino Supremo Arabica coffee beans grown in Colombia; the beverage is unusually full bodied, with a flavor slightly reminiscent of walnuts.

colombo 1. A gritty curry powder from the (French) Antilles; usually a blend of cassava flour and ground mustard seeds, turmeric, cloves, cumin, dried mango pulp, cinnamon, coriander and anise. 2. Any of a variety of meat and/or vegetable dishes made with this curry blend. 3. An African climbing plant whose roots are used to make a tonic and aperitif drinks.

colon The portion of the large intestine that extends from the cecum to the rectum and is divided into the ascending, transverse, descending and sigmoid (or pelvic) colons; it mixes the intestinal contents, absorbs water and completes the digestive processes begun in the small intestine.

colonche *See* calonche.

colony A group of microorganisms, especially bacteria, growing in one place. *See* culture.

Colony Club A cocktail made of gin, anisette and orange bitters.

color *v.* To change, enhance or otherwise alter the natural color of a food item through the use of other foods or food additives. *n.* A criterion for judging a wine's quality (i.e., a rosé should be pink with a hint of orange; a white can be straw, yellow or gold; and a red can have a hint of violet if young and amber if aged).

color, artificial *See* coloring agent.

color adjuvant; coloring adjuvant A type of food additive used to help maintain or remove color in a processed food.

colorado A type of cigar wrapper; the light brown or tan tobacco has a reddish tint, a smooth, oily surface and an exceptional flavor.

colorado claro A type of cigar wrapper; the brown tobacco has a dark reddish tint, an oily sheen, and a strong, slightly nutty flavor; also known as English Market Selection (EMS).

color chilena An oil seasoned with garlic and sweet paprika and used in Chilean cuisine.

color enhancer; coloring enhancer A type of food additive used to add, preserve or intensify the color or shading of a processed food.

coloring agent One of three dozen or so naturally occurring or synthetic food additives used to add, change or intensify color in a processed food; most coloring agents are known by their color and number (e.g., blue no. 1, yellow no. 5, and red nos. 3 and 40); also known as artificial color and food coloring. *See* pigment.

color stabilizer; coloring stabilizer A type of food additive used to maintain the color or shading of a processed food.

coltello (col-TELL-oh) Italian for knife.

columba; columba pasquale (koh-LOHM-bah pas-KWAH-leh) An Italian Easter cake in the shape of a dove made with a yeast-risen dough filled with candied fruit and topped with crystallized sugar and toasted almonds.

Columbia River smelt *See* eulachon.

Columbia Valley A grape-growing and wine-producing area in the south-central portion of the state of Washington.

column still *See* double column still.

Colwick An English slipcoat-style cheese made from cow's milk.

comal (koh-MAHL) A round, flat griddle used for cooking tortillas; made of unglazed earthenware (to be used over a fire) or metal (to be used on a stove top).

combava *See* sambal.

comb honey Liquid honey still in the comb, both of which are edible; also known as chunk-style honey.

combination cooking methods Cooking methods, principally braising and stewing, that employ both dry-heat and moist-heat procedures.

combination menu A menu that combines the pricing techniques of table d'hôte and à la carte menus; that is, some items are grouped together for a set price and other items are priced individually.

combine To mix two or more ingredients together until they do not separate.

come The stage during butter making when the milk begins to thicken, just before it turns into butter.

comer (coh-maer) Spanish and Portuguese for to eat.

Comet A variety of very bitter hops grown in the state of Washington.

comfits (kohm-fees) Pieces of fruit, nuts, seeds or spices dipped in a sugar syrup and then rolled in finely pounded granulated sugar.

comfrey (KOHM-free) An herb of the borage family (*Symphytum officinale*) with coarse stems and leaves and bell-shaped white, yellow or pinkish flowers; the leaves can be battered and fried and the flowers added to salads as garnish; also known as consound.

Comice pear (cuh-MEES) A broad, blunt pear with a greenish-yellow to red-blushed yellow skin, a juicy, smooth, firm texture, and a sweet flavor and aroma; also known as Doyenné du Comice (French for top of the show).

comida (koh-mee-dah) Portuguese and Spanish for food.

comino (koh-MEE-noh) *See* cumin.

Commandaria A sweet red or amber wine made in Cyprus from dried grapes; of ancient origin, it was originally known as Nama.

commercial The best of the lower USDA quality grades for beef; it is usually sold as ground beef.

comminuted Meat reduced in size by grinding, dicing or the like.

commis (kohm-ee) The apprentice at a food services operation following the brigade system.

commis de rang (kohm-ee duh rhang) *See* back waiter.

common A wine-tasting term for a wine that is clean and sound but without any distinguishing features.

common cabbage *See* cabbage, green.

common corn *See* corn.

common European oyster Any of several varieties of oysters; generally, they have a flat, smooth, almost circular shell with an average length of 2–5 in. (5.08–12.7 cm) and pale gray or green to tan flesh; their flavor varies depending on their origin, and many are named for their place of origin.

common field mushroom A wild mushroom (*Agaricus campetris*) found in open grassy areas during the summer and fall; closely related to the common store mushroom; also known as field mushroom and meadow mushroom.

common green market cucumber A long cylindrical slicing cucumber with a relatively thin, dark green skin, a pale white-green, juicy flesh with small, creamy, white, soft seeds and a refreshing, slightly astringent flavor.

common limpet A variety of limpet found in coastal areas of Europe from southern England to Spain; it has an orange-gray shell with alternating strong and weak ribs, an average length of 2.5 in. (6.3 cm), and a tough, flavorful flesh.

common market tomato *See* beefsteak tomato.

common meringue A mixture of stiffly beaten egg whites and granulated sugar; depending on its intended use, it may be soft (made with equal parts egg white and sugar) or hard (made with at least twice as much sugar as egg white).

common store mushroom The common, all-purpose market mushroom (*Agaricus brunnescens* and *A. bisporus*) cultivated worldwide; it has a pale, off-white, thick stem, a gently rounded, small- to medium-sized cap that is pale off-white when fresh and turns brown when bruised and gray with age, a mild, earthy flavor, and a dense, firm texture that softens when cooked; also known as button mushroom, white button mushroom, market mushroom, cream mushroom, Italian brown mushroom and Paris brown mushroom.

common sturgeon *See* lake sturgeon.

Communard (com-muh-nahr) A French aperitif of crème de cassis and a dry, fruity red wine.

comp Slang for giving a customer a free service or item.

complementary proteins Two or more plant foods that lack different essential amino acids, but paired together, they are the equivalent of a complete protein (e.g., soybeans and rice; legumes and cereal). *See* mutual supplementation.

complete protein A protein containing all of the essential amino acids in the correct proportions for human use; found in only a few animal foods (e.g., chicken eggs and milk) and generally lacking in plant foods.

complex A wine-tasting term for an interesting wine with a variety of subtle yet detectable aromas and flavors existing in harmony.

complex carbohydrates A group of carbohydrates with little to no flavor and various levels of solubility and digestibility; includes polysaccharides such as starches, dextrin, cellulose and glycogen, all of which are composed of long chains of sugars; generally found in vegetables, grains and some fruits.

composition cork *See* agglomerated cork.

composta di frutta (kohm-POH-stah dee FROO-tah) An Italian cooked mixture of fruit, usually one stewed with wine.

compote 1. Fresh or dried fruit cooked in a sugar syrup. 2. A deep, stemmed dish (usually glass or silver) used to hold candy, nuts or fruit; also known as a compotier.

compotier (KAHM-poht-tee-ay) *See* compote.

compound butter A mixture of softened whole butter and flavorings used as sauce or to flavor and color other sauces; also known as beurre composé.

compound sauces *See* small sauces.

compressed yeast A mixture of yeast and starch with a moisture content of approximately 70%; also referred to as fresh yeast. *See* yeast.

compulsive eating The feeling of an uncontrollable, overwhelming need to eat; the behavior is not based on hunger but on factors such as emotions, habits or the failure of the body's appetite-control mechanisms.

Comté; Comté Gruyère (kom-tee gru-yayr) A hard Gruyère-style cheese made in France's Franche Comté region from cow's milk; it has an ivory to pale yellow interior, a golden yellow to brown rind, small- to medium-sized eyes and a fruity flavor; it is marketed in huge wheels; also known as Gruyère de Comté.

coñac (kohn-nyack) Spanish for brandy.

concassée (kon-kaas-SAY) Peeled, seeded and diced tomatoes.

concasser (kon-kaas) To pound or coarsely chop a food, usually tomatoes or parsley.

concentrate *v.* To remove moisture from a food, principally by boiling, drying or freeze-drying. *n.* 1. The resulting product; it can be dry or syrupy and usually has a rich, very full flavor and is used as a flavoring (e.g., demiglaze) or is rehydrated (e.g., coffee). 2. Grape juice reduced to a syrup and added to fermenting must to increase the alcohol content of the resulting wine and as an alternative to chaptalization.

concentrated A wine-tasting term for a rich, fruity wine of great depth and appeal.

concentrated butter *See* butter, concentrated.

concentrated milk Milk with a large portion of its water removed; presumably, this provides all the nutrients in a smaller volume.

conch A medium-sized to large gastropod mollusk found in the Caribbean Sea and off Florida; it has a peachy-pink spiral shell and a lean, smooth, and very firm, chewy flesh with a sweet–smoky flavor; also known as lambi (especially in the Caribbean).

concha (kon-chyah) Spanish for conch.

conchiglie (kon-KEE-lyay) Italian for conch shell and used to describe pasta shaped like ridged or smooth conch shells, traditionally served with meat sauces.

conchigliette (kon-key-yet-tae) Small conchiglie.

conching (KONCH-eng) One of the final stages in chocolate production; a process in which huge vats of melted chocolate are slowly stirred with rotating blades; this gives the chocolate a very smooth texture and removes excess moisture and volatile acids. *See* chocolate-making process.

concombre (koh-kawng-br) French for cucumber.

concombres, sauce aux (koh-kawng-br) A French compound sauce made from a velouté flavored with aniseed and garnished with parsley and julienne of fresh or pickled cucumbers.

Concord grape A grape native to North America (*Vitis labrusca*); it has a loose, blue-black skin, a pale green flesh and seeds, and a mild, sweet flavor; used principally for preserves and juice.

con crianza (kohn cree-AHN-zah) *See* crianza.

condementada (kohn-deh-mehn-tah-dah) Spanish for spicy. *See* picante.

condensed milk *See* milk, sweetened condensed.

condiment 1. Traditionally, any item added to a dish for flavor, including herbs, spices and vinegars; now also refers to cooked or prepared flavorings or accompaniments such as relishes, prepared mustards, ketchup, bottled sauces and pickles; unlike seasonings, condiments are typically added to a dish by the diner. *See* seasoning. 2. (kohn-day-mohn) French for chutney.

conditioning The process of developing carbon dioxide and clarity in a sparkling wine through aging or secondary fermentation in the bottle or cask and in a beer through aging, kräusening or lagering.

Condrieu (coh'n-dree-uh) A white wine from the Rhône Valley in France made from the Viognier grape; the wine is dry and rich and has a bouquet reminiscent of peaches and apricots.

conduction The transfer of heat from one item to another through direct contact (e.g., from a pot to a food).

conejo (koa-NAY-khoh) Spanish for rabbit.

conejo con mani (coh-na-ho con mah-nec) A Chilean dish of fried rabbit served with a peanut sauce.

Coney Island 1. A hot dog covered with relish, mustard, ketchup and sauerkraut; more rarely, a hamburger garnished in the same fashion. 2. A white pork sausage.

confection A general term for any kind of candy or other sweet preparation (e.g., ice cream or fruit preserves).

confectioner The person who makes or sells confections.

confectioners' foil Brightly colored, pliable foil used to wrap candies, individual pastries or pieces of cake for an attractive presentation.

confectioners' knife A knife with a 10-in. blade, a round, blunt tip and a widely spaced wave cut edge; the blade cants upward 5°, making it more comfortable for slicing; used for cutting candies, fruit jellies or baked meringues.

confectioners' knife

confectioners' sugar Refined sugar ground into a fine, white, easily dissolved powder; also known as powdered sugar and 10X sugar.

confectionery; confectionary 1. A general category of candies, sweets and other food products based on sugar. 2. The art, techniques and processes for producing them as well as the place where they are produced or sold. 3. The place where they are produced or sold.

confectionery coating *See* summer coating.

confectionery fat A fat that is hard at room temperature and soft at body temperature, such as hydrogenated coconut oil or cocoa butter; it is used primarily in baked goods.

confeitaria *See* padaria.

conference pear A winter pear particularly popular in Great Britain; it has a long, thin shape, a russet skin and a sweet flavor.

confiserie (kawng-fee-ser-ree) French for confectionery or candy.

confiseur (kawng-fee-sewr) At a food services operation following the brigade system, the person responsible for all candies, petit fours and similar items.

confit (kohn-FEE) A method of preserving meats, especially poultry, associated with southwestern France; the meat is cooked in its own fat and stored in a pot covered with the same fat.

confitura (kon-fee-tuu-rah) Spanish for jam; also known as mermelada.

confiture (kwang-fee-tewr) French for jam, jelly, marmalade or fruit preserves.

confiture d'épine-vinette (kohn-fee-tour dae-pee-nay vennet) A French barberry jam.

confiture pan *See* preserving pan.

conformation The proportion of meat to bone and the general shape of the carcass; a basis for determining quality and yield.

congeal To change from a liquid to a solid state; to become set, firm or rigid, usually by chilling.

congee (kohn-gee) An Asian (particularly Chinese) watery rice porridge.

congeners Chemical substances other than alcohol that provide the flavor, aftereffects, and other physiological effects or characteristics unique to various alcoholic beverages.

conger eel A very large scaleless, saltwater, eel-shaped fish; it has little culinary significance.

congo pea *See* pigeon pea.

congrio (con-gree-oh) 1. A fish native to the Pacific Ocean off Chile; it has a firm flesh. 2. Spanish for conger eel.

congro (cohn-grow) Portuguese for sea eel; also known as safio.

conhaque (kon-nya-kuh) Portuguese for brandy.

conical pestle A snub-nosed wooden cone with a short handle used to press cooked or partially cooked foods through a chinois.

coniglio (koa-NEE-lyo) Italian for rabbit.

connective tissues Tissues found throughout an animal's body that hold together and support other tissues such as muscles.

Connover's Colossal asparagus A variety of particularly flavorful asparagus.

conpoy (kohn-poi) Amber-colored, dried discs of a type of sea scallop used as a flavoring in Chinese and other Asian cuisines.

conque (kongk) French for conch.

conserva picante (kon-sehr-vah pee-kan-tuh) Portuguese for chutney.

conserve A spread for baked goods made from fruits, nuts and sugar cooked until thick.

consolante (kohn-soh-lahn't) The French practice of giving an alcoholic beverage to the cooks while they work in the kitchen.

consommé (kwang-soh-may) 1. A rich stock or broth that has been clarified with a clearmeat. 2. French for soup and used to describe a clear, thin, flavorful broth. *See* potage *and* soupe.

Consort currants A variety of black currants; the fruit have a musky–sweet flavor.

Consorzio (kawn-SORD-zyoh) An Italian consortium or group of producers, such as those for certain wines or cheeses.

consound *See* comfrey.

Constania A grape-growing and wine-producing region of South Africa; the principal grapes grown are the Cabernet Sauvignon, Pinot Noir, Chardonnay and Sauvignon Blanc.

contaminant Something that contaminates. *See* hazard, biological; hazard, chemical; *and* hazard, physical.

contaminate In the food safety context, to render an object or environment impure or unsuitable by contact or mixture with unclean or unwanted matter.

contamination In the food safety context, the presence, generally unintentional, of harmful organisms or substances in food; the contamination hazards can be biological, chemical or physical. *See* direct contamination *and* cross-contamination.

Conti, à la (KON-tee) A French dish garnished with lentils (usually puréed) and sometimes bacon.

continental breakfast A breakfast of bread (e.g., toast, croissants, pastries or the like) and a beverage (e.g., coffee, tea, milk or juice).

continental plan A daily hotel rate that includes a continental breakfast and a room; also sometimes known as a bed and breakfast.

continental roast *See* roast, espresso.

continuous still A still with a continuous inflow of distilling liquid.

conto (KOHN-toh) Italian for the bill or check at a restaurant or hotel.

contorni (con-thor-nee) Italian for vegetables.

contre filet (kawgntr fee-leh) *See* faux filet.

controllable costs *See* variable costs.

controlled denomination of origin An industry or governmental system that limits the use of certain geographic or similar references when naming or referring to a food (particularly wines and cheeses); the references or names can be used only for items actually grown or produced in that area.

controls The processes and criteria for measuring job performance or product quality.

control state A state in which the government has part or full control over the distribution system for alcoholic beverages. *See* license state.

convection The transfer of heat caused by the natural movement of molecules in a fluid (air, water or fat) from a warmer area to a cooler one.

convection, mechanical Convection facilitated by the stirring of the molecules.

convection oven An oven in which the heat is circulated by an interior fan.

convenience food A processed food product; generally of three types: an item that is completely prepared and needs only to be used (e.g., peanut butter), an item that is completely prepared and needs only to be heated (e.g., a frozen pizza) or an item that requires some preparation but far less than that needed if made from scratch (e.g., a cake mix).

conversation hearts *See* candy hearts.

conversion factor (CF) A multiplier used to increase or decrease ingredient quantities and recipe yields.

converted rice Rice that is pressure-steamed and dried before milling to remove surface starch and help retain nutrients; it has a pale beige color and the same flavor as white rice; also known as parboiled rice.

coocoo; coo coo A Caribbean dish of steamed cornmeal and okra garnished with tomatoes, green pepper, parsley and other herbs.

cook *v.* To prepare foods. *n.* One who prepares foods for consumption by others.

cookbook A book of recipes, sometimes accompanied by social or historical commentary.

cooked cheese A cheese that is made by heating the milk to help solidify the curds.

cooked-curd cheese Cheese made from curds aged for 3–4 days that are heated (cooked) at 180°F (82.2°C) until

melted; the cheese is then poured into molds or other containers, covered and cooled; also known as cup cheese.

cooked syrup *See* sugar syrup *and* simple syrup.

cooker 1. A stove. 2. An apple used for cooking purposes (as opposed to being eaten raw).

cookery The art, practice or work of cooking.

cookie cutter A metal or plastic tool used to cut rolled-out doughs into various shapes.

cookie molds Wood, plastic, metal or ceramic molds, available in a huge variety of shapes and sizes, used to make decorative designs from cookie dough.

cookie press; cookie gun A tool consisting of a hollow tube fitted at one end with a decorative template or nozzle and at the other with a trigger for forcing soft cookie dough through the template to create the desired shape.

cookies Small, sweet, flat pastries, usually classified by preparation or makeup techniques as drop, icebox, bar, cutout, pressed and wafer.

cookie sheet A flat, firm sheet of metal, usually aluminum, with very low or open sides on which cookies, biscuits and other items are baked.

cookie stamp A small glass, plastic, wood or ceramic tool for pressing a pattern or design into the dough of individual cookies before baking.

cookie stamps

cooking The transfer of energy from a heat source to a food; this energy alters the food's molecular structure, changing its texture, flavor, aroma and appearance.

cooking banana *See* plantain.

cooking dates *See* honey dates.

cooking medium The air, fat, water or steam in which food is cooked.

cooking oil Any oil used as a cooking medium. *See* salad oil.

cooking surface The burners, griddle or other heated areas or platforms used for stove-top cooking.

cooking wine An inexpensive red, white or rosé wine, often with salt added, used for cooking and not as a beverage.

cook's spoon A long-handled spoon with a large bowl; its bowl can be solid (used for serving in the kitchen) or slotted (used for removing foods from a liquid).

cookware Any of a large variety of vessels and containers used on the stove top or in an oven to cook food or store it; they can be made of metal (e.g., copper, aluminum, stainless steel and cast iron), glass, ceramics or the like and include pots, pans, hotel pans and molds.

cool To allow a food to sit until it is no longer warm to the touch.

cool drink A South African cooler.

cooler 1. A long drink, usually based on fruit juices, with a low alcohol content. 2. A long drink, usually a mixture of white wine and fruit juice. 3. A device, container or room that cools or keeps food cool. *See* ice chest.

cooling rack A flat grid of closely spaced metal wires resting on small feet; used for cooling baked goods by allowing air to circulate around the food.

Coonawarra A grape-growing and wine-producing region in southeastern South Australia known for its dry red wines made from Shiraz and Cabernet Sauvignon grapes and white wines made from Chardonnay grapes; it is defined as an area of terra rosa soil about 3 km wide and 15 km long.

Coonawarra Boundary A grape-growing and wine-producing region on the fringes of the terra rosa soil of Australia's Coonawarra region; the grapes are grown in the gray soil surrounding the red and therefore cannot be identified as Coonawarra.

coon cheese An American Cheddar-style cheese aged at a higher-than-usual temperature and humidity; the surface is very dark, the body quite crumbly and the flavor particularly sharp and tangy.

coon oyster A small oyster found attached to tree roots along the southern U.S. East Coast; they are often eaten by raccoons when exposed at low tides.

coon perch *See* yellow perch.

cooperage (koo-pehr-rige) 1. The total number of wooden casks, vats or barrels used for storage in a given cellar, winery, brewery, distillery or the like. 2. An establishment where barrels are made.

cope *See* knife point.

copeaux en chocolat (coe-poe ahn show-coe-lah) French for chocolate shavings.

coperto (koh-PHER-toh) Italian for a cover charge in a restaurant; it is the amount added to the bill to cover the linens, bread and glassware.

copita (koh-PEE-tah) A tulip-shaped glass used for tasting and sampling sherry.

copolymer condensates of ethylene oxide and propylene oxide Food additives used as stabilizing agents in flavor concentrates, as dough conditioners in baked goods and in the dehairing of hogs and defeathering of poultry.

coppa (KOAP-pah) An Italian sausage made from pork loin marinated in garlic and red wine; it is braised, dried and eaten before it hardens.

copita

copper 1. A trace element used principally as an enzyme component and to assist the formation of collagen and hemoglobin; significant sources include meat and drinking water. 2. A metal used for cookware and an excellent conductor of heat; the cookware can be solid copper, copper lined with tin or copper sandwiched between layers of aluminum or stainless steel; also used for flatware and serviceware.

copper ale A dark, copper-colored, bitter ale with a winelike flavor and aroma.

copper bowl A round-bottomed, unlined copper bowl available in various sizes and usually used for whisking egg whites.

copper gluconate and copper sulfate Food additives used as nutrient supplements.

copra *See* coconut, dried.

coprin chevelu (koh-pren che-vae-lu) French for shaggy mane mushroom.

coprino chiomato (ca-pree-noh key-oh-ma-tao) Italian for shaggy mane mushroom.

coq au vin (kohk oh VAHN) A French dish of chicken, mushrooms, onions and bacon or salt pork cooked in red wine.

coqueret du Péron (ko-kah-ray duh pay-rohn) French for cape gooseberry.

coquille (koh-KEE) A French variety of mâche.

coquilles (koh-KEE) French for shells and used to describe a shell-shaped dish used for baking and serving foods such as fish in a white sauce.

coquilles Saint Jacques (koh-kee san zhahk) A French dish of scallops in a creamy wine sauce (sauce Mornay), topped with bread crumbs or cheese and browned; usually served in a scallop shell.

coral The roe (eggs) of a mollusk such as a scallop or a crustacean such as a lobster.

coralli (ko-rah-lee) Italian for coral and used to describe very small smooth or ribbed tubes of pasta, usually used in soups.

coratella (ko-rah-tae-lah) An Italian lamb and offal stew.

corba (kor-bah) Serbo-Croat and Turkish for soup.

Cordelier, sauce (kor-duh-lee-ay) A French compound sauce made from a Madeira sauce finished with goose liver purée and garnished with sliced black truffles; also known as Franciscan sauce.

cordero (coor-DEH-roh) Spanish for lamb.

cordero en ragout (cor-dah-roe an rah-goo) A Spanish lamb stew.

cordero lechal (kor-dah-roh leh-chal) Spanish for suckling lamb; one usually slaughtered at 3–4 weeks. *See* pastenco.

cordial (KOHR-dhuhl) *See* liqueur.

cordial glass A stemmed, tubular glass ranging in size from 1 to 3 fl. oz.; used for serving cordials or liqueurs neat as well as layered cordial drinks.

Cordial Médoc The proprietary name of a French liqueur with a brandy base and overtones of raspberry, orange, cacao and other flavorings.

cordon bleu (kor-dohn BLUH) 1. French for blue ribbon and used to describe the honor afforded chefs of great distinction. 2. A French dish consisting of thin boneless chicken breasts or veal scallops sandwiched around a thin slice of prosciutto or other ham and an emmenthal-style cheese, then breaded and sautéed.

Cordon Jaune (kor-dohn jhahn) French for yellow ribbon. *See* Grand Marnier.

Cordon Rouge (kor-dohn rooj) French for red ribbon. *See* Grand Marnier.

cordula (core-doo-lah) A Sardinian dish of roasted sheep's intestines rubbed with herbs and oil.

core *v.* To remove the central seeded area from a fruit. *n.* The center part of pomes (fruits from the family Rosaceae such as apples, pears and quince); sometimes tough and woody, it contains the fruit's small seeds (called pips).

cored A pome that has had its core removed.

cörek A rich, savory or slightly sweetened Turkish bread decorated with almonds, aniseed, poppy seeds and nigella seeds and glazed with saffron and eggs.

corer A short, sharp-ended metal cylinder set on a shaft attached to a handle; used to remove the core from fruits such as apples or to hollow vegetables for stuffing. *See* apple slicer, pineapple corer *and* zucchini corer.

corer

coriander (KOR-ee-an-der) The tiny yellow-tan ridged seeds of the cilantro plant (*Coriandrum sativum*); used as a spice, they have a flavor reminiscent of lemon, sage and caraway; they are available whole or ground and are used in Middle Eastern, Indian and Asian cuisines and pickling spice blends. *See* cilantro.

coriandre (ko-ree-ahndr) French for coriander.

coriandro (ko-ree-an-droh) Italian for coriander.

cork 1. The spongy tan bark of the *Quercus suber* (cork oak). 2. A bottle stopper carved from this material or formed from such bark granules bound with an adhesive.

corkage A restaurant's charge for opening, cooling (if necessary) and pouring a bottle of wine brought by a customer to the restaurant for his or her use.

cork puller A tool used to extract a cork from a bottle; it has two narrow, flat, flexible metal prongs, approximately 4–5 in. long, which are inserted on either side of the cork and twisted, embracing and removing the cork.

corkscrew A tool used to remove a cork from a bottle; the simplest is a spiral wire attached to a handle.

corky A wine-tasting term for an unpleasant earthy or moldy aroma and/or flavor caused by a flawed cork.

corn 1. A tall, annual plant native to the Western Hemisphere and producing white, yellow, blue or multicolored grains arranged on a cob; the grains (called kernels) are consumed as a vegetable when young and are available fresh, canned, frozen or dried and ground into cornmeal; also known as maize (especially in Great Britain), sweet corn and common corn. *See* hominy. 2. The edible seeds of other plants, especially wheat in England and oats in Scotland.

corn, dent Any of a variety of hardy, high-yield corn grown principally for fodder in the United States, although starch and oil are also extracted from it.

corn, flint Any of a variety of fast-ripening corn; this hardy corn is most similar to wild corn.

corn, flour Any of a variety of corn grown in Central and North America principally for flour.

corn, sweet Any of a variety of corn grown worldwide principally to be eaten on the cob or in loose form; the kernels can be white or yellow and are sweet and tender.

corn, waxy Any of a variety of corn whose kernels are covered with a waxy substance; it has a low starch and high sugar content and is used as a food additive in puddings and sauces; grown in Asia principally for flour.

corn bran A dry-milled product of high fiber content obtained from corn; used to increase the fiber content of baked goods or to thicken sauces and soups.

corn bread A quick bread made with cornmeal.

corn bread, hot water A batter of cornmeal and hot water dropped into deep hot fat and fried.

corn bread, light Traditional corn bread batter with a small amount of yeast to give the finished product rise; it is usually cooked on a griddle.

corn bread dressing A poultry stuffing made with crumbled corn bread, sausage, onions, celery and herbs.

corn cakes Small pancakelike cakes made from a batter of cornmeal and water or milk; also known as batter cakes.

corn dodgers; dodgers Deep-fried, boiled or baked corn cakes made from corn pone.

corn dog A frankfurter dipped in cornmeal batter and fried or baked; usually served on a stick.

corne (core-nay) French for pastry scraper.

corned Meat that has been cured in a brine solution.

corned beef Beef, usually a cut from the brisket or round, cured in a seasoned brine; it has a grayish-pink to rosy red color and a salty flavor; also known as salt beef.

corned beef hash *See* hash.

corned belly bacon *See* salt pork.

cornelian cherry; cornel A small, olive-shaped fruit (*Cornus mas*) with a long stone, a bright red color and a tart, slightly bitter flavor; used for preserves or pickled like olives; also known as dog cherry and Siberian cherry.

Cornelius keg (kor-NEEL-ee-yuhs kehg) A stainless steel canister with ball locks that holds from 2.5 to 5 gallons; used by home brewers for fermenting and serving beer.

Cornell A cocktail made of gin, Maraschino and egg white.

Cornell bread An enriched bread made with a high-protein flour; the formula, developed at Cornell University in the 1930s, adds small amounts of soy flour, nonfat dry milk powder and wheat germ to unbleached white flour.

corn endosperm A food additive used as a yellow food coloring.

corner plate A subprimal cut of the beef primal short plate; it includes portions of ribs numbers 6–8.

cornet (kohr-nay) 1. A French horn-shaped pastry filled with sweetened whipped cream. 2. An hors d'oeuvre or garnish consisting of a slice of meat rolled into a cone and filled, usually with a cream cheese– or butter-based spread.

corn flour 1. Finely ground cornmeal; it has a white or yellow color and is used as a breading or in combination with other flours. 2. In Great Britain, refers to both finely ground cornmeal and cornstarch. *See* cornstarch.

corn gluten The principal protein component of corn endosperm and a food additive used as a nutrient supplement.

Cornhusker A softer-bodied, moister Cheddar-style cheese made in Nebraska from cow's milk; it has a bland flavor and is marketed in loaves.

cornichon (KOR-nih-shohn; kor-nee-SHOHN) French for a tiny pickled gherkin cucumber; it is the traditional accompaniment to a meat pâté.

Cornish pasty *See* pasty.

cornmeal Dried, ground corn kernels (typically of a variety known as dent); it has a white, yellow or blue color, a gritty texture and a slightly sweet, starchy flavor and is available in three grinds (fine, medium and coarse); used in baking, as a coating for fried foods or cooked as polenta.

cornmeal, steel-ground Cornmeal ground by a process that removes the hull and germ.

cornmeal, water-ground Cornmeal ground by a process that preserves some of the hull and germ.

corn oil A pale yellow oil obtained from corn endosperms; it is odorless, almost flavorless and high in polyunsaturated fats and has a high smoke point; a good medium for frying and also used in baking, dressings and to make margarine.

cornouille (kor-newy') French for cornelian cherry.

corn pone An eggless cornmeal batter shaped into small ovals and fried or baked.

corn poppy *See* poppy, common.

corn salad *See* mâche.

corn silk The stigmas and styles that appear as a silky tuft or tassel at the tip of an ear of corn.

corn smut A bulb-shaped fungus (*Ustilago maydis*) that grows on ears of corn, causing them to swell and turn black; considered a delicacy, it has a sweet, smoky flavor similar to a cross between corn and mushrooms; also known as cuitlacoche.

cornstarch A dense, very fine, powdery flour made from ground corn endosperm and used as a thickening agent; also known as corn flour (especially in Great Britain).

cornstick pan A cast-iron baking pan with several decorative depressions resembling ears of corn; used for baking corn bread.

corn sugar *See* glucose.

corn sugar vinegar A food additive of fermented corn sugars used as an acidulant.

corn syrup A thick, sweet syrup derived from cornstarch and composed of dextrose and glucose; available as clear (light) or brown (dark), which has caramel flavor and color added.

corn syrup, fructose *See* fructose corn syrup.

corn syrup solids The dry form of corn syrup; used where the liquid syrup is impractical.

corn whiskey An American whiskey distilled from a mash made from a minimum of 80% corn; aged for at least 2 years in new or used charred oak barrels.

coroa *See* cassabanana.

corona 1. The classic-sized cigar with a 42 ring and a 5 1/2-in. length. 2. *See* tobacco plant.

corona, double 1. A well-sized cigar with a 49–52 ring and a 7 1/2- to 8-in. length; the large diameter provides a cooler smoke. 2. An imprecisely used term for a Churchill.

corona, petite A short cigar with a 40–42 ring and a 4 1/2- to 5-in. length.

corona extra; corona royale A slightly stubby cigar with a 44–46 ring and a 5 3/4-in. length.

corona grandes A well-sized cigar with a 44–46 ring and a 6- to 6 1/2-in. length.

corossol A Benin beverage made from soursops, milk, vanilla and sugar.

corporate restaurants Theme restaurants and family restaurants often owned or operated as chains and franchises; they generally emphasize marketing over food.

correct seasonings 1. To taste a food just before service and add seasonings, especially salt and freshly ground black pepper, if necessary. 2. To reduce a strong flavor by adding a liquid.

corrosion-resistant material In the food safety context, refers to any material that maintains its original surface characteristics under prolonged exposure to food, cleaning compounds and sanitizing solutions.

corrugated abalone *See* pink abalone.

cortar (kohr-tahr) Spanish for to slice and/or to cut.

cortar em fatias (kor-tahr ayn fah-tee-ah) Portuguese for to slice.

Cortese (cor-TEH-zeh) 1. A white wine grape grown principally in the southeastern area of Italy's Piedmont region. 2. A wine made from this grape; it has a pale color, light body and fresh flavor.

Cortina Cup A cocktail made of vodka, white crème de cacao, Sambuca and heavy cream.

cortinaire de Berkeley (kor-tee-nair duh berk-lee) French for shiitake.

Cortland apple A large apple native to North America; it has a yellow and red skin, a crisp flesh and a sweet but moderately acidic flavor; it browns only minimally when cut and is a good all-purpose apple.

corvina rellena (kohr-vee-nah ray-jay-nah) An Argentinean dish of a whole fish stuffed with onions, garlic, bread crumbs and hard-boiled eggs, flavored with cilantro, and baked and served with the pan juices.

Corvo (COR-vo) The proprietary name of well-made red and white wines produced near Palermo, Sicily.

Corynebacterium diphtheriae A species of bacteria that causes diphtheria; the bacteria are transmitted by infected food handlers or through ingestion of contaminated foods (especially milk) or water.

coryol (coe-REE-ohl) The small, tannish-yellow, nutlike fruit of a variety of palm grown in Chile.

còscia (KOAS-chee-ah) Italian for chicken leg or thigh.

cosciotto (koh-SH'YOH-toh) Italian for a leg of meat.

cosciotto di porcello la forno (koh-chee-oh-toh day pohr-chel-loh lah four-noh) An Italian dish consisting of the roasted leg of a very young pig.

cos lettuce *See* romaine lettuce.

Cossack Charge A cocktail made of vodka, Cognac and cherry brandy.

Cossack Coffee Grog A cocktail made of vodka, chilled black coffee, vanilla extract, cinnamon, chocolate ice cream and Kahlua, Tia Maria or crème de cacao; served in a chilled double old-fashioned glass.

cossack pineapple *See* ground-cherry.

cost The price paid to acquire or produce an item; also known as expense.

costa (KOH-stah) Italian for chop.

costard A now-extinct variety of large, flavorful apple native to Great Britain and one of the first apples to be distinguished by its own name; popular from at least the 13th century to the 17th century.

Costa Rican Any of a variety of arabica coffee beans grown in Costa Rica; the beverage is generally rich and sharp.

costata (KOH-stah-tah) Italian for rib steak or entrecôte.

cost controls All of an operation's processes used to control expenses in an attempt to increase profits.

costillar de cerdo asado a la pasas (cos-sti-yar da ser-dow ah-saw-doe ah-law pah-sas) A Peruvian dish consisting of a pork loin marinated in vermouth, aniseeds, cloves, allspice, ginger and brown sugar, sprinkled with bread crumbs and roasted in the marinade, butter, milk, cinnamon and raisins.

costmary (KOHS-mah-ree) An herb (*Chrysanthemum balsamita*) with a strong camphor, minty flavor and aroma; used to clear and preserve home-brewed ale and occasionally as a salad ingredient or garnish; also known as alecost.

cost of goods sold In the food services industry, the amount, at cost, of food items sold during a given period.

costoletta (koas-toe-LET-tah) Italian for a chop, either pork or veal.

Costoluto Genovese (cos-toe-LOO-toe JAY-no-va-say) An Italian heirloom tomato variety that is deeply ridged, with a red skin, a firm red flesh and a sweet flavor.

cost per portion The cost of one serving; calculated as the total recipe cost divided by the number of portions produced from that recipe.

cosy A fabric cover, usually knitted or quilted, used to cover a teapot to keep it warm.

Cot *See* Malbec.

côte (koat) French for rib and used to describe a cut from the ribs of a veal carcass; côtelettes premières are the four cutlets from the more desirable end of the neck nearest the loin, and côtelettes sécondes or découvertes are the four cutlets from the area nearest the shoulder.

Côte, La (koat, la) A grape-growing and wine-producing area in Switzerland; the principal grape grown is the Chasselas.

cotechino (coh-teh-KEE-noh) A large, soft Italian sausage made from pork rind and meat, seasoned with nutmeg, cloves and pepper.

côte de filet; côtelettes dans le filet (koat duh fee-lay; kot-ter-leht dahn luh fee-lay) A French cut of the lamb carcass; they are chops cut from the loin.

Côte d'Or (koat door) A grape-growing and wine-producing district in Burgundy, France, containing the greatest Burgundian vineyards; it is divided into two areas: Côte de Nuits in the north and Côte de Beaune in the south.

coteghino (ko-tae-gee-noh) A relatively large Italian sausage made of seasoned pork; it is cooked in an herbal broth and served hot.

côtelette (kot-ter-leht) French for cutlet. *See* côte.

Cotherstone (KOWTH-ehr-stohn) A blue-veined cheese made in Yorkshire, England, from unpasteurized Jersey cow's milk; it has an ivory interior and a slightly crumbly texture; also known as Yorkshire Stilton.

cotlet A firm but chewy confection made with cooked apricots, gelatin and nuts. *See* aplet.

cotogna (koa-TOA-nyah) Italian for quince.

cotriade (koh-tree-AHD) A soup from France's Brittany region made from fish (no shellfish), onions and potatoes and sometimes served over thick slices of bread.

cottage cheese A soft, fresh cheese made from skimmed cow's milk or reconstituted skimmed or nonfat dry cow's milk powders; it has a white color, a moist, large grain texture and a mild, slightly tart flavor; it cannot contain more than 80% moisture; available flavored or unflavored in three forms: small curd, medium curd and large curd; also known as curd cheese.

cottage cheese, creamed Cottage cheese with 4–8% added cream; available plain or flavored, it is highly perishable.

cottage fries; cottage fried potatoes *See* home fries.

cottage ham A fabricated cut of the Boston butt; it is smoked and usually boneless.

cottage pudding A plain cake topped with a warm, sweet, puddinglike sauce.

cotto (KOH-toh) Italian for cooked.

cotton candy A confection made by wrapping colored, flavored threads of spun sugar around a cardboard stick to create a puffy balloon of candy.

cottonseed oil A thick, colorless oil obtained from the seeds of the cotton plant (genus *Gossypium*); it is usually blended with other oils to make highly refined products sold as vegetable or cooking oil.

cotto salami (kot-TOE suh-LAH-mee) A large Italian sausage made from pork and beef, highly seasoned with garlic, black peppercorns and other spices; it is cured and air-dried.

Cotuit oyster An Atlantic oyster found off Cotuit, Cape Cod; it has a shell with an average length of 3 in. (7.6 cm), a plump body and a moderately salty flavor.

couche (koosh) French for a large piece of heavy linen or canvas that is dusted with flour and wrapped around yeast bread dough to help hold its shape during proofing.

coucou de Malines (KOO-KOO da mah-lee-na) A type of chicken raised in Belgium; it has a slaughter weight of 2.5–3 lb. (1.3–1.4 kg) and a delicately flavored, succulent flesh.

couennes de porc (kwan duh por) French for fresh pork rinds.

coulant (koo-LAHN) 1. French for flowing and used to describe Brie, Camembert and other soft cheeses, the interiors of which ooze from the rind at the appropriate temperature. 2. A wine-tasting term for a wine that is light, refreshing and easy to drink; it usually has low tannin and alcohol levels.

coulibiac (koo-lee-BYAHK) The French adaptation of a Russian dish, kulebiaka, which consists of a creamy mixture of salmon, rice, hard-cooked eggs, mushrooms, shallots and dill enclosed in a pastry envelope usually made with brioche dough; it can be large or small and served as a first course or a main course.

coulis (koo-lee) 1. A sauce made from a purée of vegetables or fruit; it may be hot or cold. 2. Traditionally, thickened meat juices used as a sauce.

Coulommiers (coo-loa-mee-a) A soft French Brie-style cheese made from cow's milk.

coumarone-indene resin A food additive used as a coating on fresh citrus fruit.

count 1. The number of individual items (e.g., four eggs). 2. An indication of the size of individual items bought in a given measurement of weight or volume (e.g., 15–18 count shrimp means that a pound of shrimp contains 15–18 individual shrimp, each weighing approximately 1 oz.).

Counter tomato A variety of large, spherical, red-skinned, flavorful tomato.

country captain A dish of chicken, onions, tomatoes, green pepper, celery, currants, parsley, curry powder and seasonings cooked in a covered skillet, served over rice and garnished with toasted almonds.

country gravy A gravy made from pan drippings, flour and milk; consistency can vary from thick to thin.

country ham *See* ham, country.

country-style forcemeat *See* forcemeat, country-style.

country-style ham; country-cured ham *See* ham, country-style.

country-style spareribs *See* backribs.

Count Stroganoff A cocktail made of vodka, white crème de cacao and lemon juice.

coup de feu (koo duh feh) 1. A French term used to describe a food that has been subjected to too high a heat and has blackened. 2. Kitchen slang for the hours spent preparing a meal.

coupé (coo-pay) A blended or diluted wine.

coupe (koop) 1. A glass or metal bowl sitting on a short stem and used to serve ice cream, fruit salad or similar foods. *See*

Champagne saucer. 2. A dessert of ice cream topped with fruit and whipped cream, usually served in a coupe dish.

coupette glass (koo-pet) A stemmed glass with a bowl that is small at the bottom and flares out at the top; ranging in size from 5 to 9 fl. oz., it is used for blended cocktails, cream or ice cream drinks and house specialty drinks.

coupler A plastic conical tube with a screw-on cover or nut; the conical piece is placed inside a pastry bag and a pastry tip is attached to the bag with the nut; used to allow pastry tips to be changed during decorating without emptying the pastry bag. *See* pastry bag *and* pastry tip.

couques fourrées (kook foo-ray) A French pastry made with squares of Danish pastry dough filled with almond cream or pastry cream and folded into a triangle.

courgette (koor-jhet) French for zucchini and the name used for it throughout Europe. *See* marrow squash.

courmi (kohr-mee) Ancient Gaelic term for ale.

couronne (kohr-rohn') French for crown or wreath and used to describe a loaf of French bread shaped like a crown or wreath.

couronne, en (coo-ron-nee) French for in the shape of a crown or ring.

court bouillon (kort boo-yon) Water simmered with vegetables, seasonings and an acidic product such as vinegar or wine; used for simmering or poaching fish, shellfish or vegetables.

Court pendu plat (kort pahn-du pla) A variety of small apples grown in France; they have a green skin with faint red stripes and a rich flavor.

Courvoisier Cognac (koar-vwah-see-ay) A Cognac made at France's Château Courvoisier from young Cognacs purchased from local distillers; they are then aged and bottled.

couscous (KOOS-koos) 1. Small, spherical bits of semolina dough that are rolled, dampened and coated with a finer wheat flour; a staple of the North African diet. 2. A North African dish composed of a meat and/or vegetable stew flavored with cumin and served over the cooked semolina.

couscousière (koos-koos-yair) A metal or earthenware assemblage of two bulbous pots; the top pot, which holds the couscous, has a perforated bottom and lid and sits on the lower pot, which holds the stew; the steam from the stew cooks the couscous.

couteau (koo-toh) French for knife.

couve (koh-vay) Portuguese for cabbage.

couve-flor (koh-vay floor) Portuguese for cauliflower.

couscousière

couve galega (koh-vay gah-leh-gah) A tall cabbage grown in Portugal's Galicia region.

couve portuguese (koh-vay por-too-gha-sha) A Portuguese cabbage used in cozido; its leaves are cooked and served with meat or fish.

couverture (koo-vay-tyoor) A high-quality chocolate with a minimum of 32% cocoa butter; very smooth and glossy, it is used for coating candies and truffles, molding and pastry making. *See* chocolate-making process.

couvrosse (koo-vross) French for oyster mushroom.

cover Slang for a paying customer at a food services facility; the number of covers equals the number of customers for any given meal or time period.

cover charge A fee, either added to the bill or taken at the door, to pay for entertainment, special seating arrangements or the like at a restaurant, bar or nightclub.

cover count The number of customers at a food services facility over a specific time period.

covered chicken fryer A deep frying pan, usually made of cast iron, with a short stubby handle and a domed lid; used for frying and braising.

covered-dish supper; covered-dish social A social event for which prepared foods are brought and shared with other guests; also known as a potluck supper.

cowa-mangosteen A variety of large mangosteen with an orange skin and a very tart flavor; it is usually used for preserves.

cowberry A member of the cranberry family (*Vaccinium vitis-ideae*); a red berry with a tart flavor, it grows wild in pastures in the northern United States and Canada; used for preserves; also known as a mountain cranberry and red whortleberry.

cowboy cocktail Slang for a straight shot of whiskey.

cowpea *See* black-eyed pea.

cows Female cattle after their first calving; raised in the United States principally for milk; in France, they are used for beef when no longer needed for milk.

cowslip A sweetly scented spring flower (*Primula veris*); it can be eaten fresh (usually with cream), crystallized in sugar as a confection or used to flavor wine, vinegar, mead or syrup.

cow's milk *See* milk, cow's.

Cox apple; Cox orange pippin apple A medium-sized spherical apple popular in Great Britain; it has a crisp texture, a sweet–tart flavor and a dull brown-green skin with faint red stripes as well as a red blush on one side.

cozer (koh-zehr) Portuguese for to cook.

cozida (kou-ZEE-dah) Portuguese for boiled and used to describe boiled fish or vegetables.

cozido à portuguesa (kou-ZEE-doh ah pohr-ta-gah-zah) A Portuguese meat stew made from brisket of beef, pork belly, pig's ears, chicken, chouriço, garlic sausages, cabbage and beans.

cozinha (koh-zee-nya) Portuguese for kitchen.

cozinheiro(a)-chefe (koh-zee-nyay-roo) Portuguese for chef.

cozze (COTS-say) Italian for mussels.

CPFM Certified Professional Food Manager.

C-ration A canned field ration used by the U.S. army.

crab Any of a large variety of crustaceans found in freshwaters and saltwaters worldwide; generally, they have a flat, round body with 10 legs, the front 2 being pinchers, and a pink-tinged white flesh with a sweet, succulent flavor; significant varieties include the blue, dungeness, king, snow and stone crabs. *See* blue crab.

crab, claw meat A market form of the blue crab; it consists of the brownish claw meat.

crab, flake and lump meat A market form of the blue crab; it is a combination of flake and lump meat.

crab, flake meat A market form of the blue crab; it consists of small pieces of meat from the body muscles.

crab, lump meat A market form of the blue crab; it consists of whole, relatively large chunks of meat from the large body muscles.

crab, soft-shell A blue crab harvested within 6 hours after molting; it has a soft, pliable, brownish-green shell and an average market width of 3.5 in. (8.75 cm); once cooked, the entire crab is eaten; it has a crunchy texture and a mild flavor; available fresh or frozen. *See* buckram *and* peeler crab.

crab apple; crabapple Any of a variety of small, hard apples (*Malus sylvestris*) with a deep red skin and a very tart flavor; used principally for preserves or spiced and canned for use as a condiment for pork and poultry or as a garnish.

crab boil A commercial spice blend used to flavor the liquid in which shellfish will be cooked; generally contains mustard seeds, peppercorns, bay leaves, allspice, ginger and chile flakes; also known as shrimp boil.

crab butter The fat found inside the back shell of a large crab; it has a yellow-white color and is used in sauces.

crab cake A mixture of lump crabmeat, bread crumbs, milk, egg, scallions and seasonings formed into small cakes and fried.

crab cracker A hinged utensil with a serrated surface near the pivot that gives added traction for holding the crab claw while it is being cracked.

crab cracker

crabe (krab) French for crab.

crabeye bean *See* pinto bean.

crab imperial An American dish of crabmeat bound with mayonnaise or a sherried cream sauce and placed in blue crab shells or scallop shells, sprinkled with bread crumbs or Parmesan and baked.

crab Louis (LOO-ee) A cold dish of crabmeat on a shredded lettuce bed, dressed with mayonnaise, chiles, cream, scallions, green pepper, lemon juice and seasonings and garnished with tomatoes and hard-boiled eggs.

cracked 1. A food broken into small pieces, usually not of uniform size and shape (e.g., cracked wheat or cracked ice). 2. An olive that has been lightly crushed but not pitted.

cracked wheat The whole wheat berry broken into coarse, medium or fine particles.

cracker A dry, thin, crisp baked product, usually savory.

cracker flour A soft wheat flour that does not absorb much moisture and does not need prolonged mixing.

Cracker Jack The proprietary name of a confection of candy-coated popcorn, peanuts and a prize sold in a red and white striped box decorated with a picture of Sailor Jack and Bingo, his black-eyed dog.

cracking A milling process in which grains are broken open.

cracklin' bread Cornbread with bits of cracklings scattered throughout.

crackling The slightly sparkling characteristic of a wine whose effervescence is natural, induced by bottling before fermentation is complete, or induced by carbonation; the effervescence is not produced by the méthode champenoise or Charmat process.

crackling rice A Chinese dish made from the scrapings of rice from the bottom of the rice cooker or pot; the scrapings are dried, then deep-fried, and often served with soup or a sauce.

cracklings; cracklin's The crisp pork rind after the fat has been rendered.

cracknel A light, crisp cracker with a curved or hollow shape.

Cracow sausages Polish sausages containing 80% pork, 10% bacon and 10% beef and flavored with garlic, pepper and caraway seeds.

cradle *See* wine cradle.

Cragganmore The proprietary name of a single-malt Scotch whisky; it is initially slightly sweet and malty then grassy and dry with a sharp aftertaste.

cranberry; craneberry A small red berry of a plant (genus *Viburnum*) with low, trailing vines that grows in American bogs; it has a tart flavor and is used for sauces, preserves, beverages and baked goods; also known as American cranberry, bounceberry and bearberry.

cranberry, European A small cranberry with a more acidic, tart flavor.

cranberry bean A kidney-shaped bean with a red-streaked, cream-colored skin and a nutty flavor; available fresh and dried; also known as a shell bean and shellout.

cranberry extract A food additive with a red color used as a color agent, especially in acidic foods such as beverages.

cranberry juice The juice made from the liquid constituent of cranberries; it can be sweetened or unsweetened.

cranshaw melon *See* crenshaw melon.

crap (crap) Romanian for carp.

crapaudback *See* calabaza.

crapaudine, à la (crah-poh-deen, ah lah) A French preparation method for poultry, especially small birds, that are trussed to look like toads, coated with bread crumbs, fried or broiled and served with a deviled sauce or sauce Robert.

crappie (CRAW-pee) A member of the sunfish family found in the Mississippi River and Great Lakes; it has an average market weight of 2–5 lb. (0.9–2.3 kg) and a soft, lean, white flesh with a bland flavor; principal varieties are the black crappie and white crappie; also known as calico bass, papermouth, speckled perch (especially in the American South) and strawberry bass.

crappit heids A Scottish dish consisting of simmered heads of haddock, traditionally stuffed with oatmeal, suet or butter and onions but now stuffed with crab, lobster, anchovies and bread crumbs.

crauti (krah-OO-tee) Italian for sauerkraut.

crawdad *See* crayfish.

crawfish *See* crayfish.

crayfish Any of several freshwater crustaceans found in North America; generally, they resemble small lobsters, with a brilliant red shell when cooked; they range in size from 3.5 to 7 in. (8 to 17.5 cm) and have lean, tender flesh (mostly in the tail) with a sweet flavor; also known as crawfish and crawdad (particularly in the American South).

crayfish

crayfish butter *See* beurre d'écrevisses.

cream 1. A component of milk with a milkfat content of at least 18%; it has a slight yellow to ivory color, is more viscous and richer tasting than milk, and can be whipped to a foam; it rises to the top of raw milk; as a commercial product, it must be pasteurized or ultrapasteurized and may be homogenized. 2. *See* creaming.

cream, cereal Cream with a milkfat content of 10.5–18%; also known as half and half.

cream, heavy whipping Cream with a milkfat content of 36–40%; pasteurized but rarely homogenized; it is used for thickening and enriching sauces and making ice cream; can be whipped to a foam and used as a dessert topping or folded into custards or mousses for flavor and lightness.

cream, imitation *See* coffee whitener.

cream, light Cream with a milkfat content of 18–30% and typically used for coffee, baked goods and soups; also known as breakfast cream, coffee cream and table cream.

cream, light whipping Cream with a milkfat content of 30–36%; used for thickening and enriching sauces and making ice cream; it can be whipped to a foam and used as a dessert topping or folded into custards or mousses for flavor and lightness.

cream, manufacturing; cream, manufacturers' A heavy cream packaged without pasteurization; it contains 40% milkfat and is thicker than regular cream; it is used in sauces and can attain a greater, more stable volume when whipped.

cream, pressurized whipping Cream with sugar, stabilizers, emulsifiers and other food additives added and sold under pressure in an aerosol can; used principally as a decorative topping.

cream, single The English term for light cream with a milkfat content of at least 18%; it is often poured over fruit, flans and puddings.

cream ale A sweet, honey- to golden-colored ale brewed in the United States; highly carbonated, with a rich foam and strong effervescence.

cream cheese A fresh, soft, mild, white cheese made from cow's cream or a mixture of cow's cream and milk (some goat's milk cream cheeses are available); used for baking, dips, dressings, confections and spreading on bread products; it must contain 33% milkfat and not more than 55% moisture and is available, sometimes flavored, in various-sized blocks or whipped.

cream cracker A crisp, unsweetened English biscuit usually eaten with cheese.

creamed cottage cheese *See* cottage cheese, creamed.

creamer 1. A small pitcher or jug for cream; usually used for service and not storage. 2. A substitute for cream (e.g., nondairy coffee creamer).

creamery 1. A room, building or establishment where milk and cream are processed and butter and cheese are produced. 2. A place where dairy products are sold.

cream filling A pie filling made of flavored pastry cream thickened with cornstarch.

cream horn A small pastry made by wrapping thin strips of puff pastry around a cone-shaped metal form and baking; the baked horn is then removed from the form and filled with whipped cream or custard.

cream horn mold A tapered, tinned-steel tube 6 in. long with a base diameter of 1–1 1/4 in.; used for making cream horns.

creaming A mixing method in which softened fat and sugar are combined vigorously to incorporate air; used for making some quick breads, cookies and high-fat cakes.

Cream Jack *See* Teleme Jack.

cream liqueur A beige-colored mixture of dairy cream and whiskey (usually Irish or Scotch).

cream mushroom *See* common store mushroom.

creamnut *See* Brazil nut.

cream of coconut The thicker, more flavorful liquid that rises to the top of coconut milk; it is available sweetened. *See* coconut cream.

cream of tartar Tartaric acid; a fine white powder derived from an acid found on the inside of wine barrels after fermentation; it is used to give volume and stability to beaten egg whites and to prevent sugar from crystallizing when making candy or frosting.

cream puff A small round shell made from choux pastry and filled with custard or whipped cream; served alone or as part of another dessert (e.g., gâteau St. Honore or croquembouche).

cream puff pastry *See* choux pastry.

creams Light, fluffy or creamy-textured desserts or dessert ingredients made with whipped cream or whipped egg whites (e.g., Bavarian creams, chiffons, mousses and crème Chantilly); also known as crèmes.

cream sauce *See* béchamel sauce.

cream sherry A type of sherry; it is sweet, with a rich, nutty flavor, a deep golden color and a full body.

cream soda A sweet, carbonated drink flavored with vanilla; originally made with soda water.

cream soups Thickened soups made from vegetables, poultry, fish and/or shellfish but not necessarily cream; the ingredients are often puréed.

cream tea *See* clotted cream.

Crécy (kray-cee) A French soup made from puréed carrots.

Crécy, à la (kray-cee, ah lah) 1. A French garnish consisting of julienne of carrots. 2. A French preparation method characterized by dishes containing carrots.

cree To boil any variety of grain into a porridge.

creir de vitel pane (cra-ir da vee-tell pah-nah) A Romanian dish of pancakes rolled around calf's brains, onions, parsley and eggs, dipped in egg and bread crumbs and deep-fried.

crema (KRAI-mah) 1. Spanish and Italian for cream (especially in northern Italy). *See* panna. 2. An Italian custard, creamed soup or flavor of ice cream. 3. The soft, golden froth that appears on a cup of freshly brewed espresso. 4. A Greek corn flour (cornstarch) pudding sometimes flavored with vanilla or tangerine peel and served chilled, garnished with cinnamon or nuts.

crema caramella (KRAI-mah KARA-mel-ah) Italian for crème caramel.

crema catalana (kra-mah cah-tah-lah-nah) A custard dessert from Spain's Catalonia region; it has a caramelized top and is flavored with cinnamon and lemon.

Crema Dania; Crema Danica (KREHM-uh DAHN-yuh; DAHN-uh-kuh) A double cream Danish cheese made from cow's milk; it has a white rind, a soft ivory interior and a rich flavor.

cremant (creh-mahn) A description of a mildly sparkling wine whose effervescence is not produced by the méthode champenoise or Charmat process; instead, it can occur naturally, be induced by bottling before fermentation is complete or infused by carbonation; the effervescence is less than that of a wine described as perlant and greater than that described as petillant.

crème; crèmes (krehm) French for cream. *See* creams.

Creme (kray-meh) German for cream.

crème anglaise; crème a l'anglaise (krehm ahn-GLEHZ; khrem ah lahn-GLEHZ) A rich, sweet French custard sauce made with eggs, sugar, vanilla and milk or cream; also known as vanilla custard sauce.

crème au beurre (ah burr) French for buttercream.

crème au beurre au lait (oh burr oh lay) A French buttercream made with pastry cream.

crème brûlée (broo-lay) French for burned cream and used to describe a rich custard topped with a crust of caramelized sugar.

crème caramel (kair-ah-MEHL) A French egg custard baked in a caramel-lined mold; the chilled custard is inverted and unmolded for service, creating its own caramel glaze and sauce; also known as flan in Spanish, crema caramella in Italian and crème renversée in French.

crème Chantilly; Chantilly cream (shan-tee) Heavy cream whipped to soft peaks and flavored with sugar and vanilla; used to garnish pastries or desserts or folded into cooled custard or pastry cream for fillings.

crème Chiboust (chee-boos) A pastry cream lightened by folding in Italian meringue.

crème d'abricots (dah-bree-KOH) A sweet, apricot-flavored liqueur.

crème d'amande (dah-MAHND) A pink, almond-flavored liqueur. *See* crème de noyaux.

crème d'ananas (dah-nah-NAHS) A pineapple-flavored liqueur.

crème de (krehm duh) French for cream of and used as part of the name of intensely sweet liqueurs; usually followed by the name of the principal flavoring ingredient.

crème de banane (bah-NAHN) A banana-flavored liqueur.

crème de cacao (kah-KAH-oh) A clear or brown liqueur flavored with cocoa beans and vanilla beans.

crème de cassis (cah-see'ss) A reddish-purple liqueur made from black currants.

crème de cerise (sair-EEZ) A cherry-flavored liqueur.

crème de fraises (frez) A clear, strawberry-flavored liqueur.

crème de framboises (frahm-bwahz) A clear, raspberry-flavored liqueur.

crème de menthe (menthe) A syrupy, mint-flavored liqueur; green, gold, red, blue and colorless varieties are available.

crème de noisette (nooa-zet) A hazelnut-flavored liqueur.

crème de noix (nwah) A walnut-flavored liqueur.

crème de noyaux (nwah-YOH) A bitter almond–flavored liqueur made from fruit stones; also called crème d'amande.

crème de rose A liqueur flavored with vanilla, spices and the essential oil of rose petals.

crème de vanille (vay-nay) A liqueur flavored primarily with Mexican vanilla beans.

crème fouetté (fweh-eht) French for whipped cream.

crème fraîche (krehm fraysh) A cultured cream product with a tart, tangy flavor similar to sour cream but thinner and richer; used in French cooking.

crème glacée (glahs-say) French for ice cream; also known as glace.

crème Parisienne (pah-ree-see-ehn) French term for whipped cream flavored with chocolate or chocolate ganache.

crème pâtissière (pah-tees-syehr) French for pastry cream. *See* pastry cream.

crème pralinée (prah-leh-nay) Pastry cream blended with powdered pralines and used as a filling in pastries and confections.

crème renversée (rehn-vehr-seh) A French custard baked over a layer of caramelized sugar and inverted for service.

Crème Yvette (e-vet) An American liqueur popular in Europe; it is flavored with the essential oil of violets.

Cremina (cra-meh-nah) A factory-made Italian cream cheese–style cheese; it is sold in foil-wrapped rectangles.

crenata (kray-nah-tah) Japanese for pine nut.

crenshaw melon; cranshaw melon A large ovoid to pear-shaped hybrid muskmelon with a netless, lightly ribbed rind, a golden-green color, a salmon-orange flesh and a strong spicy aroma.

Creole A soft, unripened, rich, and creamy cottage cheese–style cheese made in Louisiana from clabber and heavy cream.

Creole, à la (cree-ohl, ah lah) A French preparation method associated with Creole cuisine; the savory dishes are characterized by the use of rice, tomatoes, green pepper, onions and spices, and the sweet dishes are characterized by the use of rum, pineapples and vanilla.

Creole coffee Coffee brewed from ground coffee beans and chicory root; also known as New Orleans coffee.

Creole cooking A cuisine combining elements of French, Spanish and African cuisines and native to New Orleans, Louisiana; it is characterized by the use of butter, cream, green peppers, onions, celery, filé powder and tomatoes. *See* Cajun cooking.

Creole cream cheese A homemade soft cow's milk cheese; it is made by clabbering buttermilk with skim milk; after the mixture is drained, cream is poured over the curds; when ready to eat, the cream is mixed with the curds and topped with sugar and fruit or salt and pepper.

Creole mustard A hot, spicy mustard flavored with horseradish and made from brown mustard seeds that have been marinated in vinegar.

Creole sauce An American sauce consisting of onions, green and red peppers, celery, tomatoes and tomato paste, flavored with bay leaves.

Creole tomato A delicate, thin-skinned red tomato lightly streaked with yellow; it has a juicy flesh and a sweet flavor.

Creole water A West Indian liqueur flavored with mamey blossoms.

crêpe (krayp) A thin, delicate, unleavened griddle cake made with a very thin egg batter cooked in a very hot sauté pan; used in sweet and savory preparations.

crêpe pan A low pan with a heavy bottom, sloping sides and a smooth surface; it is sized by diameter of the crêpe made: 5–6 in. for dessert crêpes and 6–7 in. for entrée crêpes. *See* blini pan.

crêpe pan

crêpes au sucre (krayp oh soo-re) A French dish of crêpes sprinkled with sugar and lemon juice.

crêpes aux confitures (krayp oh kohn-fee-thur) A French dish of crêpes spread with jam and rolled up.

crêpes bretonnes (krayp bre-tohn) French crêpes made with buckwheat flour and rum.

crêpes fourrées (krayp four-reh) A French dish of crêpes filled with custard and raisins and other dried fruits that have been soaked in rum.

crêpes soufflées (krayp soo-flay) A French dish of crêpes filled with a soufflé, usually praliné, and then heated in the oven.

crêpes Suzette (kraypz sue-zeht) A dessert consisting of sweet crêpes sautéed in orange butter, then flamed with an orange liquor or brandy.

crêpes Suzette pan A stainless steel–lined copper pan used for table-side presentations; it has a flat, 12-in.-wide bottom and 1-in.-deep sides. *See* flambé pan, round.

crépinette (kray-pee-NEHT) A small, slightly flattened French sausage made from pork, lamb, veal or chicken; sometimes flavored with truffles; it is wrapped in caul rather than a casing.

Crescenza (krehz-CHAY-tsah) A Stracchino-style cheese made in Italy's Lombardy region from whole cow's milk; it has a soft, creamy texture, a yellowish interior and a mild, sweet flavor.

crescione (cray-SHOW-nay) 1. Italian for watercress. 2. Small crescent-shaped pasta used for garnishing soups.

crespelle (krehs-PEHL-lay) Thin Italian pancakes; they are either stacked with different savory or sweet fillings between the layers or filled and rolled like crêpes.

crespolini (krehs-poh-LEE-nee) An Italian dish consisting of pancakes rolled around chopped veal and ham bound with egg and grated cheese and baked in a tomato sauce.

cress Any of a variety of plants (*Lepidium sativum*) related to the cabbage family with small dark green leaves, thin stems and a delicate, slightly peppery flavor (e.g., watercress); used for salads.

cresson (krehs-sawng) French for watercress.

cressonière, mayonnaise (cray-sohn-n'yair) A French mayonnaise sauce flavored with watercress and usually served with soft-boiled or poached eggs.

creste di galli (crest-ae dee gah-lae) Italian for cockscombs and used to describe pasta shaped like a cockscomb; it is available in various sizes.

cresyl acetate A food additive with a strong, floral aroma used as a flavoring agent.

crevette (kruh-VEHT) French for shrimp.

crianza (cree-AHN-zah) Spanish labeling term referring to the aging of a wine in oak casks; con crianza or vino de crianza indicates that the wine has been aged in wood for at least 1 year; sin crianza indicates that it has been aged but not in wood.

Crimea Cooler A cocktail made of grapefruit juice, vodka, crème de cassis, and ginger ale; served in a chilled Collins glass and garnished with a mint sprig and orange spice.

crimini (kree-MEE-nee) Italian for various common store mushrooms.

crimp 1. To pinch or press together the edges of pastry dough using fingers, a fork or other utensil; the decorative edge seals the dough. 2. To cut gashes along both sides of a fresh fish; the fish is then soaked in ice water to firm the flesh and help the skin crisp when cooked.

crimper/cutter A hand tool with two crimping disks axle-set flush against either side of a cutting wheel; it can press, crimp and cut dough simultaneously; used for ravioli, empañadas, turnovers and other pastry doughs; also known as a doughspur.

crimper/cutter

crimson bramble *See* arctic bramble.

crisp *v.* To refresh vegetables such as carrots or celery by soaking them in ice water or baked goods such as crackers by heating them. *adj.* 1. A description of produce that is firm and fresh and not soft or wilted (e.g., an apple or lettuce leaf) or a baked good that is hard and brittle and not soft (e.g., a cracker). 2. A beer- and wine-tasting term for a product with a relatively high acid content and a light, clean, fresh flavor. *n.* A baked deep-dish fruit dessert made with a crumb or struesel topping; similar to a cobbler.

crispbread A thin, crisp, rectangular Scandinavian-style crackerlike bread traditionally made with rye flour but now often containing some wheat flour.

crispelle (crisp-EL-lae) An Italian dish consisting of small rounds of either pizza dough or salted bread fried in oil.

crisp head lettuce *See* lettuce, crisp head.

Crispin *See* Mutsu.

crisps British for potato chips. *See* game chips.

Criterion A variety of apple with a yellow skin, sometimes blushed with red, and a very sweet, firm, juicy flesh.

critical control point *See* Hazard Analysis Critical Control Points (HACCP).

croaker A member of the drum family found off the U.S. East Coast and in the Gulf of Mexico; it has a dark speckled skin, an average market weight of 0.5–2 lb. (225–900 g), and a lean flesh with a mild flavor; also known as Atlantic croaker, crocus, hardhead and king billy.

crocchette (kroa-KAYT-tay) Italian for croquettes.

crocette (kroa-khet) An Italian yeast bread made in the shape of a cross.

crockpot An electrical appliance that simmers food slowly for extended periods of time in a covered glass or ceramic pot.

crocus *See* croaker.

croissant (kwah-SAHN; kwah-SAHNT) A rich, buttery, crescent-shaped roll made with flaky yeast dough.

croissant cutter A hollow, rolling pin–shaped utensil

croissant cutter

with stainless steel triangular blades; when rolled across dough, it cuts out triangular shapes that are then rolled into croissants.

croissant dough A rolled-in or laminated dough made with yeast and large quantities of butter; used for making croissants and other pastries.

crookneck squash A summer squash with a long slender neck and bulbous body, a pale to deep yellow skin with a smooth to bumpy texture, a creamy yellow flesh, and a mild, delicate flavor; also known as yellow squash.

crop The gullet of birds; in grain-eating birds, it forms a pouch that can be stuffed.

cropadeu A Scottish dish consisting of an oatmeal dumpling stuffed with well-seasoned bits of haddock's liver; the dumpling is boiled and the liver dissolves into the dough.

croquant (kroa-kant) A crunchy, almond brittle candy.

croquante (krow-kahn't) 1. An elaborate centerpiece for a traditional grand French buffet; made with trellised bands of marzipan set on a pastry base; the marzipan top is filled with small rounds of pâte feuilletée, each with a preserved cherry in the middle. 2. A French confection consisting of a basket made of marzipan filled with ice cream.

croque au sel, à la (krok oh sell) A French term used to describe foods that are eaten raw with no seasonings other than salt (e.g., celery, nuts and small globe artichokes).

croque madame (krohk mah-dahm) A croque monsieur with a fried egg on top.

croquembouche (kroh-kuhm-BOOSH) French for crisp in the mouth and used to describe an elaborate dessert composed of small, custard-filled cream puffs that are coated with caramel and stacked into a tall pyramid; the outside is then decorated with spun sugar and sugar flowers; traditionally served at weddings.

croquembouche mold A tall stainless steel cone-shaped form used as a base for stacking the small cream puffs (profiteroles) used to make a croquembouche.

croque monsieur (krohk muhs-yur) A French ham and cheese sandwich cooked in a sandwich grilling iron.

croquetas (kroh-kee-tahs) A Spanish tapas of flour and bread crumb croquettes made with vegetables, egg, cheese, meat or fish.

croquette (kroh-keht) A food such as salmon or potatoes that has been puréed and/or bound with a thick sauce (e.g., béchamel), formed into small shapes, breaded and deep-fried.

cross-contamination In the food safety context, the transfer, typically by food handlers, of biological, chemical or physical contaminants to food while processing, preparing, cooking or serving it. *See* direct contamination.

cross-cut A fabricated cut of meat cut across the muscle grain or on the bias.

cross-cut shank A fabricated cut of the beef primal brisket and shank; it is cut from the shank; available with or without the bone and used for stewing.

crosse (kross) A French cut of the veal carcass; it is the heel end of the hind leg and used for stock.

cross rib roast; cross rib pot roast A subprimal cut of the beef primal chuck; it contains the large muscles on the exterior of the front ribs and is tough, flavorful, and available with or without the bone.

cross training *See* job rotation.

crostatina (kroa-stah-TEE-nah) Italian for tart.

crostini (kroh-STEE-nee) 1. Italian for little toasts and used to describe small, thin slices of toasted bread, usually brushed with olive oil. 2. Canapés of thin toasted bread with a savory topping. 3. Croutons used for soups or salads.

Crotonese (crow-toh-nae-sae) An Italian Pecorino-style cheese made from goat's and ewe's milks and flavored with pepper.

crottin (kroh-tinh) Any French goat's milk cheese shaped like a small flattened ball.

Crottin de Chavignol (kroh-tinh duh sha-vee-nyol) A French cheese made from goat's milk; it has a white rind splotched with brown, a chalky white interior, and a flavor that ranges from tangy when young to quite sharp as it ages.

Crouchen (croo-shen) A grape variety from southwest France that produces a white wine; the grape is known as Clare Riesling in Australia and Paarl or Cape Riesling in South Africa.

croustade (kroo-STAHD) An edible container used to hold creamed meat or vegetable mixtures (e.g., a thick stew); it can be a hollowed-out bread loaf or made from shaped and deep-fried pastry dough or puréed potatoes.

croûte, en (KROOT, ahn) A food (usually meat, poultry, fish or pâté) wrapped in pastry and baked.

crouton (KROO-tawn) 1. A small piece of bread, often seasoned, that has been toasted, grilled or fried; it is used as a garnish for soups or salads. 2. A small piece of aspic, usually in a decorative shape, used to garnish a cold dish.

Crowdie (KREW-dee) 1. A fresh double cream Scottish cheese made from cow's milk and fresh butter; it has a creamy, buttery flavor, a whitish-yellow creamy interior and a white mold rind. 2. A Scottish breakfast dish made of finely ground oatmeal and buttermilk.

crown cap A metal stopper whose edges are crimped over the mouth of the bottle; used for some soft drinks and other beverages as well as for sparkling wines during their secondary fermentation in the bottles.

crown gum A masticatory substance of vegetable origin used as a chewing gum base.

crown roast 1. A fabricated cut of the lamb primal rack; it is formed by tying the ribs in a circle (ribs up and fat inside); after roasting, the tips can be decorated with paper frills and the hollow center section filled with a stuffing. 2. A fabricated cut of the pork primal loin; similar to the lamb cut.

Crown Royal A superpremium Canadian whisky.

crow's nest pudding *See* bird's nest pudding.

cru (krew) 1. French for growth and used as a designation for a French vineyard: by implication, one of superior quality.

See cru classé, grand cru *and* premier cru. 2. French and Portuguese for raw.

cru classé (krew clah-say) French for classed growth and used as a designation of quality for wines from Bordeaux. *See* grand cru *and* premier cru.

crude fiber A laboratory measure of dietary fiber.

crudités (kroo-dee-TAY) Raw vegetables usually served as hors d'oeuvres accompanied by a dipping sauce.

crudo (KROO-doh) Spanish and Italian for raw.

cruet (krew-ay) French for a small jar with a lid used for making and storing vinaigrette dressing, vinegar or other liquids.

cruibeen Irish for pig's trotter (foot).

cruller (KRUHL-uhr) A Dutch doughnut-type pastry made from a twisted strip of deep-fried dough topped with sugar or a sugar glaze.

crumb *v.* To remove crumbs and other food debris from the table, usually between courses. *n.* 1. A small piece, especially of a bread or other food. 2. The texture of a food, especially breads or baked goods.

crumber A tool used for crumbing, such as a brush and tray or a long, thin metal trough with a scraping edge.

crumbly A tasting term for a food that has a tendency to fall apart or break into small pieces.

crummin; crumb-in Slang for corn bread crumbled up into a large glass of buttermilk or whole milk.

crumpet A small, thin, round, yeast-leavened British batter bread cooked on a griddle or stove top, similar to an English muffin.

crush *v.* 1. To reduce a food to its finest form (e.g., crumbs, paste or powder); it is often done with a mortar and pestle. 2. To smash an ingredient such as garlic or ginger with the side of a knife or cleaver to release their flavors or facilitate cooking. *n.* 1. The harvest of the grapes used for a wine; a term synonymous with harvest or vintage. 2. A type of soft drink, usually citrus flavored.

crushed chiles *See* chile flakes.

crust 1. The hardened outer layer of a food such as a bread or a casserole. 2. A pie or tart shell. 3. The sediment a wine (usually a red wine and especially a vintage port) deposits during bottle aging; sometimes referred to as deposit.

Crusta A sour cocktail served in a glass completely lined with an orange or lemon peel cut in a continuous strip; usually made with brandy, although any distilled spirit may be used.

crustacé (crus-tah-say) French for crustacean.

crustacean One of the principal classes of shellfish; they are characterized by a hard outer shell and jointed appendages; includes crabs, lobsters and shrimp. *See* mollusks.

crusted port A style of ruby port made from a blend of two or three vintages; it is aged in wood for approximately 4 years and then bottled; during bottle aging it throws a deposit or crust.

Crystal (KRIS-tel) A variety of hops grown in the United States.

crystal apple A traditional variety of slicing cucumber; it has an almost spherical shape and a prickly, dark green skin.

crystallization The process of forming sugar crystals.

crystallized flowers Flowers such as violets soaked in a thick sugar syrup heated to 220–224°F (32–36°C), drained and dried; sugar crystals are left on the flowers, and they are used to decorate baked goods and candies.

crystallized fruits Small fruits or segments of larger ones soaked in a thick sugar syrup heated to 220–224°F (32–36°C), drained and dried; sugar crystals are left on the fruits.

crystal malt *See* caramel malt.

crystal sugar Refined sugar processed into grains that are several times larger than those of granulated sugar; used for decorating cookies and other baked goods; also known as sanding sugar and pearl sugar.

CSC Certified Sous Chef.

cseresznye (sha-resh-nick) Hungarian cherry brandy.

csipetke (chi-pet-ke) Small pieces of thinly rolled egg noodle dough used for sweet and savory Hungarian dishes; also known as pinched noodles.

cú (chu) Chinese for vinegar.

Cuajada (koa-hah-dah) A soft Venezuelan cheese made from cow's milk; it has a creamy interior and is wrapped in banana leaves, which impart a mild vegetal flavor.

Cuarenta y Tes (kwa-ron-tah ee tess) The proprietary name of a Spanish brandy-based liqueur containing 43 ingredients and a vanilla-like flavor; also known as Licor 43.

cuaresmeño (kwah-res-meen-yoh) A Mexican chile similar to the jalapeño but rounder, hotter and less flavorful.

cuauhtemoc A Mexican dish of cooked dried black beans, puréed and lightly fried in oil with tomatoes, onions and garlic; eggs with the yolks unbroken are set on top and baked.

Cuba Libre A cocktail made of cola, rum and lime juice, served in a Collins glass and garnished with a lemon or lime wedge.

Cuban bread A hard-crusted white bread made with only flour, water, yeast, salt and sugar; slightly sweeter than traditional French bread, which it otherwise resembles.

Cubanelle pepper A long, tapered sweet pepper with a yellow or red color.

Cuban squash *See* calabaza.

Cuban style *See* heavy.

Cuban sweet potato *See* sweet potato, white.

cube To cut food into 0.5-in. (1.27-cm) squares; these chunks are generally larger than foods that are diced.

cubebs The small berries of a plant native to Indonesia (*Piper cubeba*); similar to black peppercorns but with a slightly bitter, aromatic flavor, they are used as flavorings in Moroccan and West African cuisines; also known as piment pays (Benin).

cubed steak A fabricated cut, typically from the beef chuck, round or flank primals; they are tough slices of meat that are tenderized by pounding and scoring the surface in a pattern of squares; also known as tenderized steak.

cubed veal steak A fabricated cut, typically from the veal primal shoulder.

cube meat *See* brochette meat.

cubes *See* brunoise *and* paysanne.

cubic foot A unit of volume measurement in the American and imperial systems; 1782 cu. in. equals 1 cu. ft.

cucchiaio (cook-key-ah-eeh-oh) Italian for spoon.

cuchara (koo-chaa-rah) Spanish for spoon.

cuchillo (koo-chee-jyo) Spanish for knife.

cucina (kuh chee-nah) Italian for kitchen.

cucinare (koo-chee-nah-rae) Italian for to cook.

cucumber The edible fleshy fruit of several varieties of a creeping plant (*Cucumis sativus*); most have a dark green skin and a creamy white to pale green flesh; generally divided into two categories: pickling and slicing.

cucumber-horned melon *See* kiwano.

cucumber

cucumbers, pickling Cucumbers such as the dill and gherkin; they have sharp black or white spines and a bitter, astringent flavor when raw; used for pickling.

cucumbers, slicing Cucumbers such as the burpless, English, lemon and common green market variety; they have a relatively thin skin, a juicy flesh, many soft, whitish seeds and a cool, astringent flavor.

Cucurbitaceae *See* gourd, melon, *and* squash.

Cuff and Buttons The original name for Southern Comfort; also known as White Tie and Tails.

cuillère (kwee-yair) French for spoon.

cuillère, à la (kwee-yair, ah lah) French for a method of brown-braising meats for a long period until they are so soft they can be served with a spoon.

cuire (kweehr) French for to cook.

cuisine (kwih-ZEEN) 1. French for the art of cookery. 2. French for kitchen. 3. The ingredients, seasonings, cooking procedures and styles attributable to a particular group of people; the group can be defined by geography, history, ethnicity, politics, culture or religion.

cuisine minceur (kwee-ZEEN man-SEUR) A style of cooking pioneered by the French chef Michel Guerard; it emphasizes healthful foods prepared in a light style without added cream or fats.

cuisseau (kwee-so) A French cut of the veal carcass; it is the cushion of veal; also known as noix.

cuisse de poulet (kwees duh poo-lay) A particularly flavorful variety of shallot; it has a long bulb.

cuisson (kwee-sohn) 1. French for cooking and used to connote culinary processes and details, especially cooking time. 2. The liquid used for shallow poaching.

cuissot (kwee-soh) French for a haunch of venison or boar.

cuitlacoche; huitlacoche (hweet-la-KO-chay) *See* corn smut.

cuka A mild colorless vinegar used in Indonesian cuisine.

cul *See* quasi.

culatello (koo-lah-TEHL-oh) An Italian ham that has been cured and soaked in wine during aging; it is lean, with a rosy red color and a delicate flavor.

culebra A cigar consisting of three intertwined cigars, each with a 34 ring and a 5- to 6-in. length; to smoke, the group is unwound and each cigar is smoked separately.

culinary (KUL-ah-nair-e; QUE-lynn-air-e) Of or relating to a kitchen or the activity of cooking.

cull *v.* To examine a group of fungible or nonfungible goods and select appropriate units. *n.* 1. A lobster, usually a Maine lobster, with only one claw. 2. The lowest USDA quality grade for lamb and veal; the meat is usually used for ground, canned or other processed products.

cullender Archaic term for a colander.

culotte de boeuf (koo-loht duh buff) 1. A fabricated cut of the beef primal sirloin; also known as a sirloin steak. 2. A French cut of the beef carcass; it is the end of the loin near the hipbone and usually cooked as a roast. 3. A British cut of the beef carcass; it is part of the rump (round) and is used for a rump roast or further fabricated into rump steaks.

cultivar A cultivated variety; in wine terms it refers to a vine selected for planting from wild varieties and hybrids; in some countries cultivar is preferred over the term grape variety.

culture A group or aggregation of microorganisms, especially bacteria; generally, the culture is intended for commercial or scientific use and is composed of descendants of a single such microorganism growing in a special medium conducive to growth. *See* colony.

cultured Used to describe any dairy product made from milk inoculated with certain bacteria or molds to achieve flavor, aroma and texture characteristics in the final product (e.g., buttermilk and blue cheese).

cultured buttermilk *See* buttermilk.

cultus cod *See* lingcod.

Cumberland raspberry A raspberry variety; the fruit are purplish-black, firm, juicy and flavorful.

Cumberland sauce An English sweet-and-sour sauce made from port, lemon and orange juice and zest and red currant jelly; usually served with duck, venison or other game.

cumin (KUH-mihn; KYOO-mihn) A spice that is the dried fruit (seed) of a plant in the parsley family (*Cuminum cyminum*), native to the Middle East and North Africa; the small crescent-shaped seeds have a powerful, earthy, nutty flavor and aroma and are available whole or ground in three colors (amber, white and black); used in Indian, Middle Eastern and Mexican cuisines; also known as comino.

cuminal A food additive used as a flavoring agent.

cuminic aldehyde A food additive with a strong, pungent aroma used as a flavoring agent.

cumin water *See* jira pani.

cuocere al forno (koo-oh-tchae-rae ahl four-noh) Italian for to bake.

cuoco *See* capocuoco.

cuore (KW'OH-reh) Italian for heart.

cup 1. A vessel with a handle; it rests on a saucer and is generally used for coffee or tea. 2. A unit of measurement in the U.S. system equal to 8 fl. oz. *See* measuring cups, dry; *and* measuring cups, liquid. 3. A punch-type beverage such as Sangria made of wine flavored with brandy, liqueurs, fresh fruits and/or herbs mixed in a pitcher with ice and served in a cup or glass.

cupcake A small individual-sized cake baked in a mold such as a muffin pan; usually frosted and decorated.

cup cheese A semisoft cheese made in the Pennsylvania German country from cow's milk and eggs; named for the white china cups used to take it to market. *See* cooked-curd cheese.

cup of java Slang for a cup of coffee.

cup of joe Slang for a cup of coffee.

cuppa British and Australian slang for a cup of tea.

cupping; cup testing The process of testing coffee beans to determine quality by smelling and tasting freshly ground beans mixed with hot water.

cuprous iodide A food additive used as a source of iodine in table salt.

cups *See* punch.

cupuaçu (coo-poo-ah-saw) A Brazilian rain forest tree whose pods contain seeds that are processed like cocoa beans to produce a mellow, bitter sweet chocolate with fruity undertones.

curaçao (KYEUR-uh-soh) A liqueur flavored with the dried peel of bitter oranges found on the Caribbean island of Curaçao; it can be colorless, pink, green or blue.

curd The edible flower head of various members of the cabbage family (e.g., broccoli and cauliflower).

curd cheese *See* cottage cheese.

curd granules *See* cheese-making process.

curdle The separation of milk or egg mixtures into liquid and solid components; generally caused by excessive heat, overcooking or the presence of acids.

curds The semisolid portion of coagulated milk (whey is the liquid portion); generally used for making cheese.

cure To preserve foods by drying, salting, pickling or smoking.

cured cheeses *See* cheeses, hard.

curing Any of several methods of processing foods, particularly meats and fish, to retard spoilage. *See* aging, drying, pickle, salt curing *and* smoking.

curing agent A type of food additive used to give a unique flavor (and sometimes color) to a processed food and to increase its shelf life; sometimes also known as a pickling agent.

curing salt A mixture of salt and sodium nitrite that inhibits bacterial growth; used as a preservative, often for charcuterie items.

curly endive *See* endive.

curly parsley *See* parsley.

Curnonsky The pen name of the French gastronome, journalist and food critic Maurice-Edmond Sailland (1872–1956); he founded the Academy of Gastronomes in 1928, wrote *Le France gastronomique* and a dozen cookery books, and encouraged the development of the modern restaurant.

currant gooseberry A gooseberry variety; the fruit are relatively small with a reddish skin and sweet–tart flavor.

currants 1. Dried Zante grapes; seedless, they resemble very small, dark raisins and are used in baked goods and for snacking. 2. The small berries of a prickly shrub (genus *Ribes*); grown in clusters like grapes, they have a tart flavor and can be black, red or golden (also known as white); black currants are used to make syrups, preserves and liqueurs (e.g., crème de cassis); red and golden currants are used in sauces, desserts, preserves (e.g., bar-le-duc) and sweet dishes.

currant tomato A tiny spherical tomato with a bright red or golden yellow color; used as a garnish.

currant tree *See* bignay.

curry 1. Any of several hot, spicy Indian meat and/or vegetable stewlike dishes; usually served with rice and side dishes such as chutney, nuts and coconut. 2. A general term used to imprecisely describe any of a wide variety of spicy, Asian, stewlike dishes.

curry leaf An herb (*Chalcas koenigii*) with bright, shiny green leaves resembling bay leaves (it should not be confused with the ornamental gray-leaved curry plant); the leaves, which impart a spicy, currylike flavor, are used in Indian and Southeast Asian cuisines.

curry paste A blend of ghee, curry powder, vinegar and other seasonings.

curry pot A terra-cotta pot with a curved base and a narrow, lipped neck used throughout Asia, especially in India, Indonesia and Malaysia, for cooking curries.

curry powder An American or European blend of spices associated with Indian cuisines; the flavor and color vary depending on the exact blend; typical ingredients include black pepper, cinnamon, cloves, coriander, cumin, ginger, mace and turmeric, with cardamom, tamarind, fennel seeds, fenugreek and/or chile powder sometimes added.

curry powder, Bombay style A distinctively sweet, moderately hot style of curry powder.

curry powder, Chinese style A distinctively hot, peppery style of curry powder.

curry powder, Madras style A distinctively pungent, hot style of curry powder.

curuba (coo-roo-bah) An elongated fruit (*Passiflora molissima*) native to South America; it has a soft, yellowish-green skin, an orange flesh and a slightly tart flavor similar to that of passion fruit; also known as banana passion fruit.

curuba di indio (coo-roo-bah dee en-dee-oh) A variety of passion fruit; it has a yellow skin and a particularly rich, sweet flavor.

cusa A small, long, light green zucchini used in Middle Eastern cuisines.

cu-san A climbing plant (*Pachyrhizus abgulatus*) native to Southeast Asia; its root is eaten raw or boiled; also known as pig peas.

cuscus dolce (KOOS-koos dole-CHAY) A Sicilian dish of couscous flavored with pistachios, almonds, cinnamon and almond oil; it is steamed, and then a sugar syrup is added; it is served mounded on a platter and sprinkled with grated chocolate and confectioners' sugar and garnished with candied fruit.

cuscuz de galinha (coos-coos duh gah-lee-nya) A Brazilian dish of cornmeal couscous steamed with meat, fish or shellfish and vegetables.

cush (koosh; kuhsh) 1. A sweetened, mushy cornmeal mixture that is fried in lard and served as a cereal with cream and sugar or cane syrup. 2. A cornmeal pancake from the American South. 3. A soup of cornmeal, milk, onions and seasonings popular in the American South. 4. The Gullah term for cornmeal mush.

cushaw (koo-SHAH) A large, ivory-colored crookneck squash with yellow-orange flesh and a bland flavor.

cushion of veal A British cut of the veal carcass just anterior to the rump end of the loin and used to cut lean scallops. *See* topside.

cusk A fish found off the New England region of the United States; it varies in color from a greenish-brown to pale yellow that becomes cream colored on the belly; it has an average market weight of 5–10 lb. (2.3–4.5 kg), a soft, white, lean flesh and a delicate flavor; also known as a deep-sea whitefish.

Cussy, sauce (cue-SEE) A French compound sauce made from a Madeira sauce finished with a poultry glaze.

custard Any liquid thickened by the coagulation of egg proteins; its consistency depends on the ratio of eggs to liquid and the type of liquid used; it can be baked in the oven in a bain marie, or on the stove top.

custard apple *See* cherimoya.

custard cup A small handleless ceramic cup with a 4- to 5-oz. capacity.

custard squash *See* pattypan squash.

custard tofu *See* kinugoshi.

cut *v.* To separate into pieces using a knife or scissors. *n.* An imprecise term for a piece of meat (usually a fabricated cut).

custard cup

cutability The quantity of usable meat that can be realized from a carcass; it is usually expressed as a percentage.

cut in A technique for combining solid fat with dry ingredients until the mixture resembles small crumbs; it is done with a pastry fork, pastry blender, two knives, fingers, a food processor or an electric mixer.

cutlet 1. A thin, tender cut of meat, usually lamb, pork or veal, taken from the leg or rib section. 2. Finely chopped meat, fish or poultry bound with a sauce or egg and formed into the shape of a cutlet; usually breaded and fried.

cutlet bat A utensil used to flatten meat, poultry and fish; there are two types: one has a flat, shovel-like blade and the other has a disk attached to a handle so that the pounding surface is parallel with the handle.

cutter 1. The second lowest USDA quality grade for beef; it is generally used in canned meat products, sausages and ground beef. 2. A device used to remove or puncture a cigar's cap to facilitate a smooth, even draw.

cutting *v.* 1. Reducing a food to smaller pieces. 2. A mixing method in which solid fat is incorporated into dry ingredients until only lumps of the desired size remain. *n.* A root, stem or leaf removed from a plant and used for propagation.

cutting and folding The process of repeatedly moving a spatula or spoon vertically through a mixture, lifting the ingredients and turning the ingredients over to achieve a uniform disbursement; often used in the context of adding beaten egg whites; also known as folding.

cutting board A flat surface of either wood or plastic (acrylic) on which food is cut, sliced or chopped.

cutting edge The sharpened edge of a knife. *See* serrated edge *and* wave cut edge.

cutting loss The unavoidable and unrecoverable loss of food during fabrication; the loss is usually the result of food particles sticking to the cutting board or the evaporation of liquids.

cuttlebone *See* cephalopods.

cuttlefish A cephalopod mollusk found in the Atlantic Ocean; it has a flattened, ovoid body extending into thin fins at the sides, black and white stripes on the top and a lighter coloring beneath; it can reach 25 in. (63.5 cm) in length and 12 in. (30.4 cm) in diameter; it has a tough, chewy texture and a mild flavor.

cuvage (coo-vahj) The duration of the cuvaison process, which varies depending on the kind or style of red wine being produced; also known as maceration.

cuvaison (coo-veh-zohn) The red wine-making process during which the grape juice and skins ferment together so that the resulting wine gains color, tannin, flavor and aroma from the skins.

cuvé (koo-vay) French for the vat used to ferment wines.

cuvé close *See* Charmat process.

cuvée (koo-vey) A specific lot or blend of a given wine; often associated with the wines of France's Champagne region.

cuvée speciale A deluxe Champagne, usually in a specially designed bottle.

cuvier (coo-v'yay) French for the part of a winery where the vats are located.

cuy (coo-ee) A Peruvian dish of fried guinea pig.

CWC Certified Working Chef.

cwikla (kwi-klah) A Polish sauce made from beetroot and horseradish and served with boiled meats.

cyanocobalamin *See* vitamin B$_{12}$.

cyathi (tchee-ah-tee) An ancient Roman cup that held the equivalent of a quarter of a liter.

cyclamate A nonnutritive (zero calories) artificial sweetener approximately 30 times as sweet as sugar; available in Canada, its use is restricted in the United States because of its possible carcinogenic properties.

cycle menu; cyclical menu A set of menus that change every day for a certain period and then repeat in the same order (e.g., on a 7-day cycle, the same menu is used every Monday).

cyclohexyl acetate, cyclohexyl butyrate, cyclohexyl cinnamate, cyclohexyl formate and cyclohexyl

propionate Food additives with a fruity aroma used as apple, apricot, banana, berry, peach or plum flavoring agents in beverages, baked goods, candies and ice creams.

cygne (sig-nah) A French swan-shaped pastry made with pâte à choux and filled with Chantilly cream.

cymling squash (SEHM-len) *See* pattypan squash.

cynaderki (see-nah-der-key) Polish for kidneys.

Cynar (tchee-nar) An Italian aromatized wine flavored with artichokes.

cysteine; cystine 1. An amino acid. 2. A food additive used as a nutrient source to significantly improve the biological quality of the total protein in a food containing naturally occurring protein.

cytherean apple *See* great hog plum.

czysciec bulwiasty (she-shak boo-lee-as-tea) Polish for Jerusalem artichokes.

daanti (dahn-tee) *See* imamdusta.

dab (dahb) 1. A small flatfish found in the Pacific Ocean from California to Alaska; it has an average market weight of 4–12 oz. (110–340 g), low fat content, and moist flesh with a delicate, sweet flavor; also known as a sanddab. *See* plaice, American. 2. A term used imprecisely to describe various flounders and other small flatfish.

dabbo (DAH-bow) Ethiopian for bread.

dabo kolo (DAH-bow KOH-low) An Ethiopian snack of dough flavored with berberé and baked in strips.

dac biet (duck bee-ek) Vietnamese for speciality of the house.

Dacca (daa-caa) An Indian cheese made from cow's milk; it is semisoft, lightly pressed and often smoked.

dacquoise (dah-kwahz) 1. A baked meringue made with ground nuts. 2. A French pastry made with layers of baked meringue filled with whipped cream or buttercream.

dadel (DAH-deh) Dutch for date.

dadler Norwegian for date.

daegee bool goki (dee-gee boll go-gee) A Korean dish of thinly sliced barbecued pork served with a spicy chile and soy sauce.

dago red *See* red ink.

Dagwood sandwich An extremely thick sandwich made with a variety of meats, cheese, condiments and lettuce; named for a comic strip character in "Blondie," Dagwood Bumstead.

dahchini (dah-tchee-nee) Hindi for cinnamon or cassia.

dahee (daa-hee) Hindi for yogurt.

dahlia root The tuberous root of the popular flower (genus *Dahlia*) is used in Mexican cuisines; boiled in salt water, it has a sweet flavor reminiscent of artichokes.

dahorp (dah-hore'p) A Balkan stew made with mutton, onions, rice and green peppers flavored with herbs and vinegar.

daidokoro (DAH-ee-DO-koh-roh) Japanese for kitchen; also known as kitchin.

daikon (DI-kon) A long, large cylindrical radish native to Asia; it has a creamy white or black skin, a juicy, crisp, white flesh and a sweet, slightly spicy, fresh flavor; it can be eaten raw or cooked; also known as Asian radish, rettiche and winter radish. *See* kaiware *and* radish, white.

daikon oroshi (dai-i-kon o-roh-shee) Finely grated white radish used as a marinade ingredient in Japanese cuisine.

daily production report In the food services industry, a list of items produced in the kitchen during a day.

daily report A daily record of costs and sales.

daily values Nutrition facts information approved by the U.S. Food and Drug Administration (FDA) that provides some basics of a balanced diet; it is used to help show how the particular food fits into such a daily diet.

Daiquiri (dak-ree) A cocktail traditionally made of rum, lime juice and sugar; sometimes puréed fruit (e.g., strawberries or bananas) are blended into the mix.

Daiquiri, frozen A Daiquiri blended with crushed ice.

dairy A room, building or establishment where milk is kept and butter and/or other dairy products such as cheese are made and sometimes sold.

dairy butter *See* butter, dairy.

dairy cheese An imprecisely used term suggesting or establishing that the particular cheese was mass-produced in a factory; also known as factory cheese. *See* farm cheese.

dairy cows; dairy cattle Breeds such as Brown Swiss, Guernsey, Jersey, Holstein-Friesian and others raised principally for their milk and not necessarily as a source of meat.

dairy products Cow's milk and foods made from cow's milk, such as butter, yogurt, sour cream and cheese; sometimes, other milks and products made from them are included (e.g., goat's milk cheese).

daisy A perennial herb (*Bellis perenis*) with white to pinkish flowers and slightly hairy leaves; the flower heads are used medicinally and in tisanes; the young leaves are used in salads and soups.

Daisy A cocktail made of fruit syrup (usually raspberry), lemon juice, seltzer and liquor served in a highball glass over cracked ice.

daizu (DAH-ee-zoo) Japanese for dried soybeans; they are used as a vegetable or made into products such as soy sauce, miso, tofu and the like.

dak bool goki (duch boll go-key) A Korean dish of thinly sliced chicken breast marinated in a spicy chile and soy sauce.

dakhar (DAH-kahr) A Senegalese beverage consisting of tamarind juice and sugar.

dal *See* dhal.

dalasini (dah-lah-sea-nee) Swahili for cinnamon.

dallah (dahl-lah) A metal pot with a handle, a hinged lid, and a long, downward pointing spout used to make coffee in the Arabian Peninsula.

Dallas cut chuck roast A subprimal cut of the beef primal chuck; it is a roast with the fat and bone removed.

dalle (dal) *See* darne.

Dalwhinnie The proprietary name of a single-malt Scotch whisky; it has a subtle malt flavor with a sweet, lingering aftertaste.

dà mahayu (dah mah-hah-you) Chinese for salmon.

damasco (dah-MAHSS-koh) Portuguese for apricot.

damassa (dah-mahs-sah) A Middle Eastern metal or earthenware pot used to cook lentils, dried beans and the like; it has a narrow neck and a bell-shaped bottom.

dambun nama (dahm-boon nah-mah) A Nigerian snack or street food consisting of beef simmered with pepper and ginger, then pounded or shredded and fried; it is sprinkled with ginger, pepper and salt.

Damietta; Domiati; Dumyat (dah-mch-ah-tah; doh-mc-ah-ta; do-me-at) A Middle Eastern (principally Egyptian) cheese made from whole or partly skimmed cow's or water buffalo's milk and usually pickled in brine; it has a soft texture with no holes, a white color, and mild, salty flavor when fresh that becomes more acidic when aged.

Dampfbier (dampf-beer) German for steam beer.

Dampfnudeln (dam-phoo-daln) German yeast dumplings sweetened and served with fruit.

damson plum *See* plum, damson.

dan (dahn) Chinese for egg.

Danablu A semisoft Danish blue cheese made from cow's milk; milder and less complex than other Roquefort-style cheeses, it can be sliced, spread and crumbled; also known as Danish Blue and Jutland Blue.

Danbo A Danish cheese made from cow's milk; it has a supple texture and mild flavor, and is sometimes seasoned with caraway seeds.

dancing shrimp *See* odori-ebi.

dancy orange A variety of mandarin orange; it is relatively small with a medium to dark orange rind.

dandelion A plant (*Taraxacum officinale*) with bright green jagged-edged leaves that have a slightly bitter, tangy flavor and are used in salads or cooked like spinach.

dandelion coffee A beverage made from the roasted and ground roots of the dandelion plant.

dandelion honey A honey made from dandelion blossoms.

dandelion wine A wine made from the fresh yellow flowers of the wild dandelion plant, citrus fruits and raisins.

dán-gao (dahn-gaho) Chinese for cake.

dang myun (tan myon) Korean dried vermicelli.

dang noi (tang noi) Thai for tapioca.

Danish agar *See* furcelleran.

Danish Blue *See* Danablu.

Danish caviar *See* lumpfish caviar.

Danish cutter *See* dough divider.

Danish dough whip A tool with a long wooden handle attached to a flat coiled wire whisk; used for combining batters and bread doughs.

Danish export cheese A Danish cheese made from skimmed cow's milk and buttermilk; intended for export, it is small, flat and cylindrical.

Danish lobster *See* prawn.

Danish pastry A breakfast pastry made with a sweet, buttery, flaky yeast dough filled with fruit, nuts or cheese and sometimes glazed.

Danish pastry dough; Danish dough A sweet rolled-in or laminated dough made with yeast and eggs; it is used for Danish pastries and sweet rolls.

Danish Port Salut *See* Esrom.

Danish Tilsit *See* Havarti.

dank A beer- and wine-tasting term for a moldy aroma reminiscent of a damp cellar.

dan mian (dahn me-ahn) Fresh Chinese egg noodles.

Danoise, sauce; Danish sauce (dan-whaz) A French compound sauce made from a béchamel blended with poached chicken purée, flavored with mushroom essence and garnished with chopped herbs.

dan ta (dahn tah) Chinese short-pastry tarts filled with a sweet, dense egg custard.

dao minu (dah-oh mih-nuh) *See* pea shoot; pea tendril.

daozi (dah-oh-zee) Chinese for knife.

daqleq (dah-clee'k) Arabic for flour.

Daralag (dahr-ah-lahg) *See* Bgug Panir.

darang (dah-rang) A Filipino preserved fish that has been dried and smoked but not salted; it develops a characteristic blood-red color.

darázsfészek (dah-rass-fay-shak) A Hungarian coffee cake made of individual pinwheels of yeast-leavened dough filled with walnuts, raisins, butter and sugar; it is usually broken into puffs rather than sliced.

Darb A cocktail made of gin, dry vermouth, apricot brandy, lemon juice and sugar syrup.

dariole (DAIR-ee-ohl; dah-ree-OHL) 1. A small, deep-sided mold used for pastries, cheese flans, babas, vegetable custards and rice pudding. 2. An item made in such a mold.

dariole, oval *See* aspic mold.

Darjeeling (dahr-jee-lehng) A large-leaf black tea grown on the Indian foothills of the Himalayas; the beverage has a rich flavor and a bouquet reminiscent of muscat grapes.

darkassou *See* cashew apple.

dark beer A full-bodied, deep-colored and creamy-tasting beer usually produced by adding roasted barley to the mash during the initial brewing stages.

dark meat The leg and thigh flesh of a chicken or turkey; it has a dark grayish-brown color when cooked and more connective tissue and fat than light meat; the darker color is the result of the increased myoglobin content in these frequently used muscles; other birds, such as duck or goose, are all dark meat.

dark roast; dark French roast *See* roast, French.

darne (dahrn) A French cut of fish, especially of a large roundfish such as salmon; it is a thick slice cut perpendicular to the backbone; also known as a dalle.

dartois (dahr-twah) A French pastry or hors d'oeuvre consisting of two sheets of puff pastry enclosing a sweet or savory filling; it is baked and cut crosswise into individual pieces.

daru (dah-roo) Hindi for an alcoholic beverage. *See* sharaab.

dash A traditional measure of volume; it refers to a small amount of a seasoning that is added to a dish by a quick, downward stroke of the hand and is approximately 1/16 or 1/8 teaspoon.

dasheen (da-SHEEN) A large, spherical root vegetable related to taro and grown in the southern United States and Caribbean region; the tuber has a brown skin, a gray-white starchy flesh and a nutty flavor when cooked; its large leaves, known as callaloo, have a delicate flavor and are cooked like spinach or used to wrap foods for cooking.

dashi (DAH-shee) A Japanese stock made with katsuobushi and dried kelp; it is used as a soup or flavoring.

dashi-no-moto (DAHshee-noh-MOH-toh) An instant form of dashi; it can be granulated, powdered, or concentrated.

date The fruit of a palm tree (*Phoenix dactylifera*) native to the Middle East and Mediterranean region; most varieties are long and ovoid (some are more spherical) with a thin, papery skin that is green and becomes yellow, golden brown, black or mahogany red when ripe; it has an extremely sweet flesh with a light brown color, a chewy texture and a single, long, narrow seed; eaten fresh or dried.

DATEM *See* diacetyl tartaric acid esters of mono- and diglycerides.

date plum A cherry-sized fruit (*Diospyros lotus*) related to the American persimmon; it has a yellowish-brown to blue-black skin color and a datelike flavor.

date sugar The coarse brown crystals obtained by pulverizing dehydrated dates.

dátil (DAH-teel) Spanish for date.

datte (datt) French for date.

Datteln (DAH-terln) German for dates.

dattero (DAH-tay-roa) Italian for date.

daube (doab) A French dish consisting of beef, red wine, vegetables and seasonings braised in a daubiére.

daubiére (doh-beh-yay) A medium-sized French covered pot with a deep, bulbous ceramic or metal body and a high-angled handle; used for daubes and other braised dishes; also known as a toupin.

Daumont, sauce (doe-MON) A French compound sauce made from a hollandaise flavored with oyster liqueur and garnished with diced mushrooms, truffles and oysters.

daubiére

daun kesom (da-woon kay-som) An herb (*Polygonum* sp.) with purple-tinged stems, long, slender, deep green leaves and a flavor similar to that of basil and mint; used in Indonesian fish and noodle dishes.

daun mangkok (da-woon mung-cock) An Indonesian shrub (*Polyscias scutellarium*) whose aromatic leaves are finely cut and mixed with grated coconut and used as a green vegetable; the large leaves are also used as platters and containers for food.

daun salam (da-woon sah-larm) A tree (*Eugenia polyantha*) native to Indonesia and Malaysia whose leaves are similar to bay leaves and are used as a flavoring.

dauphine, à la (doh-FEEN) 1. French for in the style of Dauphine and used to describe a method of preparing vegetables in the same manner as dauphine potatoes. 2. A joint of meat garnished with dauphine potatoes.

dauphine potatoes; pommes dauphine A French dish of puréed potatoes mixed with choux pastry, shaped into balls, and deep-fried.

dauphinoise, pommes à la (doh-feen-wahz) 1. A French method of preparing potatoes; the potatoes are cut into thin, round slices and placed in a gratin dish with garlic, butter and cream and baked. 2. A French method of preparing sliced potatoes by covering them with a mixture of eggs, milk and cream in a gratin dish and then topping them with grated cheese and baking.

dau phong rang (dow fong ran) Vietnamese for roasted peanuts; they are often used as a garnish or as a flavoring in sauces.

daurade (doa-rahd) *See* dorade.

Davis, Adelle (Am., 1904–1974) A dietitian and nutritionist, she popularized current concepts of nutrition; promoted vitamin supplements, organic produce, fertilized eggs, raw milk, whole grain breads, preservative-free foods, exercise and psychotherapy, and wrote *Let's Cook It Right, Let's Eat Right to Keep Fit, Let's Get Well,* and *Let's Have Healthy Children.*

dawa (dah-wah) A barley-type millet used in African cuisine.

dead soldier Slang for an empty beer bottle.

de agua (day ahg-wah) A long, thin, tapering chile with a thin red and green flesh and mild, vegetable flavor; often stuffed or used in soups and mole sauces.

de árbol (day ahr-bohl) An elongated, pointed, brick red, dried chile with a thin flesh and a very hot, smoky, tannic, and grassy flavor.

Death in the Afternoon A cocktail made of Pernod and sparkling wine; served in a chilled champagne flute.

deba-bōtchō (DAY-bah-BOAT-cho) A Japanese knife used to fillet fish; medium length, wide, and spear shaped, it is ground on only one side.

deba-bōtchō

debone To remove the bones from a cut of meat, fish or poultry.

debourbage (deh-boor-bahj) French for settling.

Debrõi   Hárslevelü (dah-BROO-yee   HARSH-leh-veh-LOO) A Hungarian semisweet white wine made from the Hárslevelü grape.

debudding Nipping off the flower buds that sprout from the top of many plants, including herbs and tobacco, to force the plant to expend additional energy to grow bigger, better leaves.

deca- *See* metric system.

decaf Slang for decaffeinated coffee.

decaffeinated coffee *See* coffee, decaffeinated.

decant To transfer a wine from its original bottle to another container without disturbing the sediment.

decanter The glass container into which wine is decanted before serving; it usually has a stopper and a capacity of 750 or 1500 ml. *See* carafe.

deci- *See* metric system.

Decio (da-chee-oh) An old Italian variety of small apple; it has an ivory and red skin, a crisp flesh and a refreshing flavor.

deckle meat *See* blade meat.

deck oven An oven containing separate shelves; the product can be baked in pans or directly on the solid shelves.

decline phase A period during which bacteria in a colony or culture die at an accelerated rate because of overcrowding and competition for food, space and moisture; also known as negative growth phase. *See* lag phase *and* log phase.

decoction 1. The process and result of extracting flavors or essences by boiling and reducing a liquid and food. 2. A style of mashing in which portions of the mash runoff are boiled and returned to the mash during beer brewing.

decompose To separate into constituent parts; to disintegrate; to rot. *See* putrefaction.

decorateur (deck-koh-rah-tuhr) At a food services operation following the brigade system, it is the person responsible for all showpieces and special cakes.

decoration The ornamenting of food for presentation; unlike a garnish, a decoration does not form an integral part of the dish; a decoration (e.g., sprigs of herbs or pieces of fruit) should echo flavors in the food itself.

decorator's icing *See* royal icing.

dee la (ti la) Thai for sesame seed.

deep A wine-tasting term for a rich, full-bodied and mouth-filling wine.

deep clean A thorough cleaning, including a maintenance upgrade, of hotel accommodations; usually done once or twice a year.

deep-dish A sweet or savory pie made in a deep pie dish or a shallow casserole and having only a top crust.

deep-dish pizza A pizza baked in a 1 to 2 in. deep, straight-sided pan; the crust is usually thick and chewy.

deep-freezing A method of preserving food by storing it at a temperature of −10 to 0°F (−40 to 18°C); flavors generally remain unimpaired even after several months of storage.

deep-fried tofu puff; deep-fried tofu pouch *See* agé.

deep fryer; deep-fat fryer 1. An appliance used to cook foods in hot fat; the fat is heated by an internal source controlled by a thermostat; it has a deep well to hold the fat and usually comes with baskets to hold and drain the foods. 2. A deep pot with two handles and slightly curving or sloping sides and a wide surface area; it is used to cook foods in hot fat, which is heated by the stove top on which the pot sits; it usually has a basket to hold and drain the foods.

deep-frying A dry-heat cooking method using convection to transfer heat to a food submerged in hot fat; foods to be deep-fried are usually first coated in a batter or breading.

deep-sea perch *See* ocean perch.

deep-sea whitefish *See* cusk.

deer *See* venison.

deerback pan *See* saddleback pan.

defective product A product that is (or should be) unmarketable because it or its container has deteriorated or been damaged or because it is missing labels or strip stamps.

defumado (duh-foo-mah-doo) Portuguese for smoked.

degchi (de-ghi) A handleless Indian cooking pot with straight sides and a heavy, flat base, usually of brass and tinned on the interior; it is used for cooking over a fire.

deghi mirch (deeg-hee meer-chee) Hindi for an Indian paprika made from mild Kashmiri pepper pods.

degla berida (da-glaw ba-ree-daw) The poorest marketing designation for dates; they are dry and mealy. *See* deglet-nour *and* ghars.

deglaze To swirl or stir a liquid (usually wine or stock) in a pan to dissolve cooked food particles remaining on the bottom; the resulting mixture often becomes the base for a sauce.

deglet-nour (da-glet noor) 1. The finest marketing designation for dates; they are soft and particularly sweet. *See* degla berida *and* ghars. 2. A variety of date palm.

dégorgement (day-gor-jeh-mahn) French for disgorging.

degré alcoolique (da-gra ahl-koh-leek) French for alcohol content, which is a degree expressed in percentage by volume.

degrease To skim the fat from the top of a liquid such as a sauce or stock.

dégustation menu (deh-gys-tah-ssyohn mehn-hu) A prix fixe menu consisting of numerous small courses specially chosen and prepared by the chef; also known as a tasting menu.

dehydrate To remove or lose water.

dehydrated Dried.

dehydrated beets A food additive used as a red coloring agent in foods such as baked goods, jams and jellies.

dehydrating *See* drying.

dehydration A loss of water from the body because of insufficient intake or excessive vomiting, sweating or diarrhea.

dehydroacetic acid A food additive used as a preservative.

déjeuner (day-zhoo-NAY) French for lunch.

Delaney clause A provision in The Food Drug and Cosmetic Act, Food Additive Amendment, stating that no substance known to cause cancer in humans or animals at any dosage level shall be added to foods.

de La Varenne *See* La Varenne, François Pierre.

Delaware grape A small grape native to the eastern United States; it has a tender, light red skin and a juicy, sweet flesh; used as a table grape and sometimes to make a sparkling wine.

delft Tin-glazed earthenware, usually white with a blue pattern; originally made in the Dutch city of Delft and now also made in England.

Delft A Dutch spiced Leyden-style cheese made from partly skimmed cow's milk.

delicata squash (dehl-ih-CAH-tah) A long, cylindrical winter squash; it has a pale yellow skin with green striations, yellow flesh, and a flavor reminiscent of sweet potato and butternut squash; also known as a sweet potato squash.

delicate A wine-tasting term for a light, subtle, fine, elegant wine, usually a white.

delicatessen; deli 1. A grocery store that specializes in cooked meats (e.g., pastrami and corned beef) and prepared foods (e.g., potato salads and pickles); traditionally, the foods were of Jewish cuisines, but other ethnic foods, especially Italian, are now included. 2. Such foods.

Delicious apple *See* Red Delicious apple *and* Golden Delicious apple.

delimited area An area or region whose name is given to the wine, distilled spirit, cheese, or other item produced within its specified boundaries.

della casa (DEH-lah KAH-sah) Italian for of the house and used to describe the dishes that are a restaurant's specialty.

Delmonico family (active 1835–1881) A Swiss-born family that built the first luxurious restaurant in New York; the menu was written in both French and English, and the original cuisine—part French and part regional American—was labeled Continental and included the Delmonico steak, avocado salad, lobster Newburg and baked Alaska.

Delmonico glass *See* juice glass.

Delmonico potatoes A 19th-century American dish of boiled, buttered potato balls sprinkled with lemon juice, parsley, salt and pepper.

Delmonico steak *See* strip loin steak.

deluxe 1. A designation for a European hotel of the finest quality, one with private baths and full services, including a dining room. 2. A designation for a top-grade American hotel, one that maintains a high standard of decor and service and has private baths, public rooms and full services.

demand The market's willingness and ability to purchase an item or service; there should be a balance between such willingness and ability and the price of the item or service.

Demerara rum A rum produced from sugarcane grown along the Demerara River in Guyana; it is the darkest, strongest and richest rum.

Demerara sugar A dry, coarse-textured raw cane sugar from Guyana.

demi; demie (DEH-mee) French for half (masculine and feminine forms).

demi-chef At a food services operation following the brigade system, it is the person responsible for assisting a chef de partie (station chef); also known as an assistant.

demi-chef de rang *See* back waiter.

demi-glace (deh-me-glass) French for half-glaze and used to describe a mixture of half brown stock and half brown sauce reduced by half.

demi-glaze (deh-me-glaz) The English spelling of demi-glace.

demijohn A large, squat, round bottle or jug, often covered in wicker; its capacity can range from 1 to 10 U.S. gallons or 5 to 50 750-ml bottles.

demineralized water *See* water, demineralized.

demi-pension (dee-mee-pawn-see-awn) A daily hotel rate that includes a room, breakfast and dinner.

demi-sec (deh-mee-seck) French for half dry; applied to sparkling wines or Champagne, it indicates a relatively sweet wine with 3.5–5% sugar. *See* brut, extra dry *and* sec.

demi-tasse (dehm-ee-tahs) 1. Strong, black coffee served after dinner; especially in France. 2. A small cup with a single handle; used for coffee.

demitasse (dehm-ee-tahss) A short, slender cigar with a 30–36 ring and a 3- to 5-in. length.

denatured alcohol Alcohol treated with an additive rendering it unfit for human consumption.

denatured protein A protein that has been treated with heat, acid, base, alcohol, heavy metal or other agent, causing it to lose some of its physical and/or chemical properties.

dendê (dha-n-dha) An oil obtained from a type of palm fruit; the oil is heavy, semisolid and bright orange and is used to add color, flavor and texture to Brazilian foods.

dénerver (day-nay-vay) French for to remove gristle, tendons, membranes and the like from meat.

deng (dang) Chinese for lamb.

dengaku (den-gah-koo) A Japanese cooking term for foods that are skewered, coated with a sweetened miso paste and grilled.

Denniston's Superb greengage A common variety of greengage; the fruit are relatively large and flavorful.

Denominación de Origen (DO) (deh-noh-mee-nah-th'yon deh oh-ree-hen) Spanish laws regulating wine production; they define factors such as district boundaries, permitted grape varieties, minimum alcohol content, and minimum aging requirements in wood and in the bottle.

Denominazióne di Origine Controllata (DOC) (deh-noh-mee-nah-t'zee-OH-nee dee oh-REE-jeen-eh contraw-LAH-tah) 1. Italian laws regulating wine production; they define factors such as geographic area of production, permitted grape varieties, minimum alcohol levels, maximum yield, and aging requirements; based on regional traditions, the laws now apply to approximately 250 production zones and 650 types of wine. 2. Italian laws regulating cheese production; they define factors such as geographic areas of production, types of milk, process of production, and so on; the laws now apply to only 26 or so cheeses.

Denominazióne di Origine Controllata e Garantita (DOCG) (deh-noh-mee-nah-t'zee-OH-nee deh oh-REE-jee-neh eh gah-rahn-tee-tah) Italian laws regulating wine production; they require wines to be made from specific grapes grown in specific geographic areas and require that the wines meet certain standards for flavor, aroma, alcohol content, acidity, and so on; DOCG designation is only awarded to wines of particular esteem; there are now approximately 18 such wines.

density The compactness of a substance; the degree of opacity of any translucent medium.

denuded Cuts of beef, veal, lamb or pork from which practically all of the surface or external fat has been removed; also known as peeled.

Denver omelet *See* western omelet.

Denver pot roast A subprimal cut of the beef primal round; it is the tough, well-trimmed heel of the round.

Denver ribs *See* lamb riblets.

Denver sandwich *See* western sandwich.

deoch an doris (dok en doris) Scottish and Irish Gaelic for drink at the door; a term for a parting drink.

dépecer (da-pa-sae) French for to cut up or carve.

deposit The sediment a wine forms during bottle aging; sometimes referred to as a crust.

dépouiller (da-pooh-ye) French for to skim the fat or scum from the surface of a liquid such as a sauce or stock.

depression cake A cake made with shortening, water and brown sugar instead of butter, eggs and milk; also known as a war cake.

depth A wine-tasting term for a wine with intense, full aroma or flavor attributes.

Depth Charge A drink made by dropping a shot glass filled with liquor (often bourbon) into a glass of beer; the object is to drain the glass and finish with the shot glass between the teeth.

Derby; Derbyshire A firm, sweet-curd cheese made in Derbyshire, England, from whole cow's milk; it has a pale golden orange interior that flakes when broken, a high moisture content, a natural or waxed rind, and a delicate, mild flavor; available flavored with sage.

Derby Pie The proprietary name of a very rich, single-crust, chocolate chip–pecan pie flavored with bourbon.

desayuno (deh-sah-YOO-noh) Spanish for breakfast.

Desdemona A pastry named for the Shakespearean character, it consists of small round biscuits similar to ladyfingers sandwiched together with a vanilla-flavored whipped cream, brushed with apricot glaze, and covered with a Kirsch-flavored fondant.

desem (DAY-zum) A type of sourdough made by storing a small ball of unleavened dough in a sack of flour for several days to develop natural yeasts.

deshebrar (da-sa-bra-r) Spanish for to shred.

desiccate 1. To dry thoroughly. 2. To preserve foods by removing virtually all moisture.

desiccated liver A nutrient supplement derived from dehydrated liver and intended to supply in concentrated form all the nutrients found in liver.

designated driver A person who is appointed or volunteers not to drink any alcohol so that he or she can safely drive others.

designer beef Light, natural beef.

Desirable pecan A pecan variety; the nuts are large and easily cracked.

desirable weight The weight range for height and body build associated with the lowest frequency of disease; also known as ideal weight.

desosser (day-zoh-say) French for to bone.

dessert (dess-ahrt) The last course of a meal; a sweet preparation, fruit or cheese is usually served.

dessert (dee-zerr) Russian for dessert.

dessert fork *See* salad fork.

dessert server A tiered assemblage of plates, usually china or glass, with a central supporting column; it is used to display and serve foods, usually desserts or foods for a tea; also known as a tea server or tiered candy dish.

dessert spoonful A traditional measure of volume; it is approximately 1½ teaspoons.

dessert wine A sweet wine served with dessert or after a meal; it includes those whose grapes were affected by the noble rot (e.g., Sauternes or Beerenauslese), wines made from dried or partially dried grapes and fortified wines (e.g., sherry or port).

destination inspection An inspection the buyer performs on receipt of goods to determine whether the goods shipped conform with purchase specifications.

destination resort A hotel offering its guests a full range of amenities, including dining facilities and activities, so that guests do not need to leave the site.

destination restaurant A fine dining restaurant frequented by some patrons only on special occasions.

détendre (deh-tahn-druh) A French culinary term meaning to soften a paste or mixture by adding an appropriate substance such as milk, stock or beaten eggs.

detergent 1. Any of a group of synthetic or organic liquid- or water-soluble cleaning agents that, unlike soap, are not prepared from fats. 2. A term used imprecisely for any cleaning agent, including soap.

detrempe (day-trup-eh) A paste made with flour and water during the first stage of preparing a pastry dough, especially rolled-in doughs.

deuce 1. Restaurant industry slang for a table for two; also known as a two-top. 2. A marketing term for a 1¾- to 2- lb.

(794- to 907-g) lobster; also known as a 2 pounder. *See* chicken lobster, heavy chicken, heavy select, jumbo, quarter, select *and* small jumbo.

Deutscher Sekt (doy-t'cher zekt) A Sekt made from grapes (especially Riesling) grown only in Germany.

Deutscher Tafelwein (doy-t'cher TAH-fel-vine) German for German table wine; wine labeled as such must contain only wine produced in Germany, whereas a wine labeled Tafelwein can contain non-German wine, provided that its origin is noted.

Deutsches Beefsteak (doy-t'chis) German for hamburger.

deveiner *See* shrimp deveiner.

deveining The process of removing a shrimp's digestive tract.

developing dough Mixing a dough to make it smoother (i.e., the proteins are properly hydrated and the gluten is stretched and relaxed); the dough is developed when it pulls away from the sides of the bowl.

Deventer koek (dah-van-ther koe-k) A sturdy, oblong-shaped Dutch cake made with rye flour and honey.

deviled beef bones An English dish consisting of the ribs left over from a roast beef, served in a spicy sauce flavored with curry powder and cayenne.

deviled egg plate A plate with several egg-shaped indentations and used for serving deviled eggs.

deviled eggs Hard-boiled eggs whose yolks are removed from the white, mashed, seasoned and bound with mayonnaise; the mixture is then returned to the white using a pastry tube or spoon.

deviled egg plate

devilfish *See* monkfish *and* octopus.

devil's claw *See* martynia.

devil's dung *See* asafetida.

devil's food cake A very rich, moist chocolate cake leavened with baking soda, which gives the cake a reddish-brown color.

devil's foot noodles *See* shirataki.

devils on horseback 1. In the United States, an appetizer of oysters wrapped in bacon, seasoned with red pepper or Tabasco sauce, broiled, and served on toast points. 2. In Great Britain, an appetizer of wine-poached prunes stuffed with a whole almond and mango chutney, wrapped in bacon, broiled, and served on toast points.

Devil's thumbprint *See* haddock.

devil's tongue *See* konnyaku.

Devon Garland A firm farm cheese made in Devon, England, from unpasteurized Jersey cow's milk and a vegetable-based rennet; it has a creamy yellow interior and a flaky texture and is flavored with herbs.

Devonshire cheese A soft, creamy cheese made by draining the whey from Devonshire cream (clotted cream).

Devonshire cream; Devon cream *See* clotted cream.

dewberry Any of a variety of blackberries (*Rubus caesius*) grown on trailing vines; the berry is smaller than an ordinary blackberry and has fewer and larger drupelets.

dextrans Food additives that are forms of glucose; they are used as sweeteners in confections.

dextrin 1. A polysaccharide formed by the breakdown of starch during digestion or by the action of heat or acid on a starch. 2. A virtually tasteless food additive derived from starchy vegetables and used as a stabilizer, thickener, surface-finishing agent and/or processing aid.

dextrins The unfermentable complex carbohydrates that contribute to a beer's terminal specific gravity and mouth feel.

dextrose 1. Glucose produced from cornstarch that has been treated with heat and acids or enzymes. *See* glucose. 2. A food additive used as a nutritive sweetener in processed foods such as beverages, particularly fruit juices, and as a binding agent in processed foods such as sausages.

dezato (day-ZAH-toh) Japanese for dessert.

dhal; dhall; dal (d'hahl) 1. Hindi for any of a large variety of dried and split pulses used in Indian cuisines. 2. An Indian dish made with such legumes, onions and spices. *See* pigeon pea *and* gram.

dhania (dah-nee-ah) Hindi for coriander.

dhansak (dhan-sak) A central-western Indian dish consisting of several types of lentils, cooked lamb, dhanska masala, cinnamon and cardamom; it is traditionally served with grilled kebabs and tart pickles.

dhansak masala (dhan-sak ma-saa-laa) A spice mixture of toasted coriander seeds and cumin seeds used to flavor dhansak.

dhwen-jang (dwen-jang) A thick, reddish-brown, salty Korean bean sauce similar to Chinese soybean paste and Japanese miso; used as a seasoning in many dishes; also known as Korean bean paste.

diabetic diet A hospital diet in which the food is appropriately seasoned with salt and other seasonings; portion size is carefully controlled, and sugar is excluded.

Diable, sauce (dee-AHB-luh) A French compound sauce made from a demi-glaze flavored with shallots, white wine, vinegar, herbs, dry mustard, black pepper and cayenne and garnished with parsley.

diablotin (dee-a-blow-tan) 1. French for a very thin, round slice of bread sprinkled with cheese and browned in the oven; it is used for garnishing soups. 2. A small spoon used to measure spices for cocktails.

diacetyl A food additive with a strong, pungent odor used as flavoring agent and/or adjuvant.

diacetyl tartaric acid esters of mono- and diglycerides (DATEM) Food additives used as emulsifiers, flavoring agents and/or adjuvants in processed foods such as baked goods and baking mixes, beverages, confections and fats.

diagonals Elongated or oval-shaped slices of cylindrical vegetables or fruits.

diagonal slicing A cutting method in which the food (often tough meat or hard vegetables) is sliced at an angle of approximately 60 degrees (i.e., not perpendicular to the cutting surface).

diakhatous (dee-ah-kah-toos) A plant grown in Africa; its yellow or green fruit has a firm white flesh with a slightly bitter flavor.

Diamond Head A cocktail made of pineapple juice, gin, curaçao and sweet vermouth.

diamond roast A subprimal cut of the beef primal round; it is a very lean, somewhat tender roast cut from the side of the round.

Diana, sauce (dee-AHN-ah) A French compound sauce made from a pepper sauce flavored with a game glaze, finished with heavy cream, and garnished with hard-cooked egg whites and black truffle; usually served with venison.

Diane, à la (dee-AHN, ah lah) A French preparation method for sautéed or broiled steak; the steak is garnished with Worcestershire sauce, cream and butter; variations include the addition of sherry, shallots, brandy and/or pâté.

diang (di-ang) Filipino sun-dried salted fish.

diastase An amylase enzyme that enhances the conversion of starches to sugars during brewing or distillation.

diavola (dee-A-vuh-lah) An Italian tomato sauce seasoned with paprika and cayenne pepper.

dibs (deebs) A Middle Eastern syrup made by boiling fruits (dates, raisins, carob beans and/or grapes) with water.

dibs rumman (deebs room-man) Hindi for pomegranate syrup.

dicalcium phosphate, anhydrous A food additive used as a dough conditioner and mineral supplement in baked goods and pastas.

dicalcium phosphate, dihydrate A food additive used as a bleaching agent in flour and as a dough conditioner and mineral supplement in baked goods and cereals.

dice v. To cut food into cubes. n. The cubes of cut food.

dice, large Cubes of approximately 5/8 in. (1.5 cm).

dice, medium Cubes of approximately 3/8 in. (9 mm).

dice, small Cubes of approximately 1/4 in. (6 mm).

diced beef See beef, diced.

Dick Smith Slang for a person who drinks alone or one who never buys a drink for people at the bar.

diente de perro chile A small, canine tooth–shaped, bright red, hot chile used in Guatemalan cuisine.

dieppoise, sauce (dee-ep-WAHZ) A French compound sauce made from a fish velouté finished with shrimp butter.

diet 1. The liquid and solid foods regularly consumed during the course of normal living. 2. A prescribed or planned allowance of certain foods for a particular purpose, such as a low-sodium diet for a person prone to high blood pressure. 3. A prescribed or planned program of eating and drinking sparingly in order to lose weight.

diet; dietetic A food-labeling term approved by the U.S. Food and Drug Administration (FDA) to describe a food that is either a low-calorie or a reduced-calorie food.

diet, balanced A diet with adequate energy-providing nutrients (carbohydrates and fats), tissue-building nutrients (proteins), inorganic chemicals (water and minerals), regulators and catalysts (vitamins), and other foods (dietary fiber) necessary to promote health.

diet, low-carbohydrate See low-carbohydrate diet.

diet, reduction A diet that reduces caloric intake sufficient for weight reduction; a sound reduction diet provides sufficient protein, minerals, carbohydrates, fats, vitamins, minerals, water and bulk to maintain health.

dietary fiber Carbohydrates such as cellulose, lignin and pectin that are resistant to digestion but nutritionally significant because they add bulk to the diet by absorbing large amounts of water and facilitate elimination by producing large stools; also known as roughage.

dietitian A person trained in nutrition, food science and diet planning who applies that knowledge and experience to regulating or advising on the dietary needs of the healthy and sick; a registered dietitian (R.D.) has met certain minimal educational standards and passed the American Dietetic Association's professional examination. See nutritionist.

diet pills See phenylpropanolamine.

diet spread A margarine product with 40% less fat and approximately half the calories of regular margarine; available whipped or in a squeeze bottle, it is generally used as a spread and not for cooking or baking.

diffa (DEE-fah) Moroccan for meal or feast.

diffusion The process by which a substance tends to spread itself evenly within the available space.

digester A 17th-century pressure cooker consisting of a container with a tightly fitting lid so that under pressure the contents could be raised to a high temperature; used principally to soften bones to make jelly for invalids.

digestif (dee-jess-teef) A beverage (usually a brandy or liqueur) consumed at the end of a meal and thought to aid digestion. See aperitif.

digestion The process by which food is mechanically and chemically broken down in the alimentary tract and converted into either absorbable substances used to sustain life (e.g., monosaccharides) or waste.

digestive biscuit A slightly sweet English biscuit made from wholemeal flour and sometimes covered with chocolate; also known as a sweetmeal biscuit.

digestive system All of the organs and glands directly associated with the ingestion and digestion of food; the principal units are the mouth, salivary glands, esophagus, stomach, liver, gallbladder, bile duct, pancreas, pancreatic duct, small intestine (including the duodenum, jejunum and ileum), large intestine (including the cecum, colon and rectum) and anus.

diglycerides Food additives used as emulsifiers in processed foods such as ice creams and peanut butter.

Dijon (deh-zjohn) A French prepared mustard made in the Dijon region from black or brown mustard seeds blended with salt, spices and white wine or verjuice; it has a clean, sharp, medium-hot flavor, a yellow-gray color and a creamy texture.

Dijon-style mustard; dijon mustard Any prepared mustard similar to Dijon but not made in that region.

dilauryl thiodipropionate A food additive used as a preservative.

dill An annual plant and a member of the parsley family (*Anethum graveolens*); the feathery leaves have a parsleylike flavor with overtones of anise and are used fresh or dried as an herb; the flat, oval, brown seeds have a slightly bitter, caraway-like flavor, also with overtones of anise, and are used as a spice.

dill

dille Dutch for dill.

dill pickles Preserved cucumbers; the preserving medium is usually strongly flavored with dill.

dill pickles, fermented The cucumbers are packed (fermented) in brine and seasonings.

dill pickles, sour The cucumbers are prepared in a fermented salt stock, then placed in a seasoned vinegar solution.

dill pickles, sweet The cucumbers are packed in brine, then drained and packed in a sugar syrup with vinegar.

dill pickles, unfermented The cucumbers are packed in brine, vinegar and seasonings.

dilute To reduce a mixture's strength or flavor by adding a liquid, usually water.

Dimbula A Sri Lankan black tea; the beverage has a golden color and a rich, mellow flavor and is served throughout the day, with or without milk.

dimethyl dicarbonate A food additive used as a preservative, principally in wine.

dimethylpolysiloxane A food additive used as an antifoaming agent and processing aid for wine, sugar, gelatin and gums.

dim sum; dem sum (dihm suhm) Cantonese for heart's delight and used to describe a variety of snacks such as steamed or fried dumplings, shrimp balls, spring rolls, steamed buns and Chinese pastries; they can be served any time of day.

dinde (dahnd) French for turkey hen.

dindon (dahn-dun) French for tom turkey.

dindonneau (dan-doh-noh) French for young turkey.

dîner (deh-na) French for dinner.

diner An inexpensive restaurant, usually serving homestyle breakfast, lunch and dinner foods and often designed to resemble a railroad dining car.

dinich (de-neech) Ethiopian for potato.

dining room attendant *See* back waiter.

dining room manager The person responsible for running the front of the house; duties include training service personnel, overseeing wine selections, working with the chef to design the menu, and arranging guest seating; also known as mâitre d'hotel or mâitre d'.

dinner 1. Traditionally, in the United States, the main meal of the day, which was served at noon. *See* supper. 2. The main meal of the day, usually served in the evening.

dinner fork A large fork with three or four tines; it is used at the table.

dinnerhouse A moderately priced, family-oriented restaurant with a casual atmosphere; often part of a chain or franchise, it offers traditional homestyle food or popular ethnic foods.

dinner knife A knife used at the table; it has a rigid blade with a sharp cutting edge, which is sometimes minimally serrated.

dinner napkin A square piece of fabric or paper used at the table for cleaning or wiping one's hands or mouth.

dinner pail; dinner bucket *See* lunch box.

dinner plate A large plate, approximately 10 in. in diameter, sometimes with a slightly indented center and a broad, slightly angled rim; used for the meal's main course.

dinnerware The china, flatware and glassware used at the table for eating. *See* serviceware.

dioctyl sodium sulfosuccinate A food additive used as an emulsifier and/or flavor enhancer in processed foods such as dry beverage and gelatin bases, sugar and cocoa products.

Dionysus The Greek god of wine and of an orgiastic religion celebrating the power and fertility of nature. *See* Bacchus.

diosmos (ntee-HO-smos) Greek for mint.

dip 1. A thick creamy sauce or condiment (served hot or cold) to accompany raw vegetables, crackers, processed snack foods such as potato chips or the like, especially as an hors d'oeuvre; usually made with a mayonnaise, sour cream or cream cheese base and flavorings. 2. Thai for raw, half cooked.

diples (dee-pless) A Greek confection of pastry bows fried in oil; they are topped with a honey syrup and sprinkled with finely chopped walnuts.

diplomat, sauce (de-plo-mah) A French compound sauce made with lobster butter and a sauce normandy, garnished with diced truffles and lobster.

diplomat cream A mixture of equal parts vanilla pastry cream and sweetened whipped cream.

diplomat pudding A British dessert made of liqueur-soaked ladyfingers or sponge cake layered with candied fruit, jam and custard.

dipotassium monophosphate and dipotassium phosphate Food additives used as emulsifiers in cheese and as pH control agents.

dipping fork A fork with two long thin tines used for spearing foods to be dipped in sugar, chocolate or the like.

direct contact method A method of removing caffeine from coffee beans by applying a chemical solvent (e.g., methylene chloride) or carbon dioxide gas (under high pressure and at a high temperature) to the beans; this removes the caffeine and the wax but not the flavoring agents; the chemical solvent is burned off during the roasting. *See* Swiss water method.

direct contamination In the food safety context, contamination of raw foods, or the plants or animals from which they come, in their natural settings or habitats by contaminants in the air, soil or water. *See* cross-contamination.

direct food additive *See* intentional food additive.

direct import The practice of a retailer purchasing directly from a supplier, bypassing a distributor; considered illegal or unethical under certain circumstances.

director A very large cigar with a 52–64 ring and an 8- to 10-in. length; the large diameter provides a cooler smoke.

direct purchases The practice of using items in a production area immediately after they are received without first checking them through a storeroom; this process is prone to employee pilferage.

Dirty Martini A cocktail made of gin, dry vermouth and a splash of brine from bottled olives, served straight-up or on the rocks, and garnished with an olive.

dirty rice A Cajun dish of rice cooked with chicken livers or gizzards and onions and flavored with bacon fat.

disaccharide A carbohydrate such as sucrose, lactose or maltose that is crystalline, sweet, soluble and digestible; composed of two sugar units, it will hydrolyze into its component simple sugars (monosaccharides); also known as a double sugar.

discount purchasing *See* bulk buying.

Discovery 1. An apple native to Great Britain; it has a bright crimson and green skin, a pink-tinged flesh, and a flavor with undertones of raspberries. 2. A medium-sized American apple with a scarlet skin, a creamy white flesh and a sweet flavor.

disease A pathological condition of the body that presents a particular group of clinical signs and symptoms that sets the condition apart as an abnormal state; it can be the result of heredity, infection, diet and/or the environment. *See* illness.

disgorging A final step in the méthode champenoise during which the sediment is removed from each bottle of sparkling wine before the dosage is added.

dishcloth *See* tea towel.

dish cross A low stand with adjustable crossing arms used for holding serving pieces at the table; there is often a lamp beneath to keep food warm.

disher *See* portion scoop.

dish mop A tool used for washing dishes; it usually has a head of fine, soft cotton threads attached to a short wooden handle.

dish cross

dishtowel *See* tea towel.

disinfect In the food safety context, to cleanse an object or environment of potentially pathogenic microorganisms.

disinfectant A cleaning agent used to remove or destroy potentially pathogenic microorganisms from or on an object or environment.

disinfest In the food safety context, to rid an object or environment of rodents, insects or the like.

disjoint To divide two bones (with flesh attached) at their joint (e.g., separating a chicken leg from the thigh).

disodium calcium ethylenediaminetetraacetate (EDTA) and disodium dihydrogen ethylenediamine tetraacetate (EDTA) Food additives used to prevent deterioration of color and texture and as sequestrants.

disodium ethylenediaminetetraacetate (EDTA) A food additive used as a preservative and color stabilizer in processed foods such as dressings and canned vegetables, especially beans and peas.

disodium guanylate A food additive used as a flavor enhancer in processed foods such as soups, canned meats and meat products and canned poultry and poultry products.

disodium inosinate A food additive used as a flavoring adjuvant and enhancer in processed foods such as ham, soups, canned chicken and chicken products.

disodium phosphate A food additive used as a protein stabilizer, emulsifier, buffer and mineral supplement.

disossare (de-soh-sar-rah) Italian for to bone.

dissolve To make a solution; to incorporate a gas, liquid or solid into a liquid.

distillation The separation of alcohol from a liquid (or, during the production of alcoholic beverages, from a fermented mash); it is accomplished by heating the liquid (the mash) to a gas that contains alcohol vapors; this steam is then condensed into the desired alcoholic liquid (beverage).

distillation process *See* distillation.

distilled monoglyceride A food additive used as an emulsifier.

distilled spirits Whiskey, rum, brandy, gin and other liquids created through the distillation process and containing ethyl alcohol; also known as spirits and more imprecisely and commonly known as liquor.

distilled vinegar *See* spirit vinegar.

distilled water *See* water, distilled.

distilled white vinegar A vinegar made from a grain alcohol mixture; clear and colorless, it has a rather harsh, biting flavor.

distillery 1. A building housing the apparatus used to distill, store and age spirits; also known as a still house. 2. The establishment making the distilled spirits.

distributor A business that purchases goods wholesale directly from suppliers or other middlemen and then sells the goods to retailers; a distributor sometimes repackages or relabels the goods.

distributor post-off The discount on the price of a case of alcoholic beverages a distributor sometimes offers a retailer.

ditali (dee-TAH-lee) Italian for thimbles and used to describe small, short, curved pasta tubes.

ditalini (dee-TAH-lee-nee) Smaller ditali; traditionally used in minestrone.

ditali

dithotse (dee-toe-tsa) A South African snack consisting of roasted salted seeds from a pumpkin, butternut squash or calabaza.

diuretic A substance that increases the secretion of urine and decreases the amount of water in the body.

dividend Slang for the remains of a cocktail left in the shaker; the liquid is usually relatively tasteless and watery from melted ice.

Divine, sauce (de-vee-nay) A French compound sauce made from a hollandaise flavored with poultry glaze and finished with unsweetened whipped cream.

divinity A white, fudgelike candy made with whipped egg whites, sugar and chopped nuts or other flavorings. *See* seven-minute frosting.

Dixie A cocktail made of orange juice, gin, Pernod, dry vermouth and grenadine.

djaaj; djaj (d'har) Arabic for chicken.

djaj bil-qasbour (d'har bill-gas-boor) An Algerian dish consisting of chicken flavored with coriander, lemon juice, lemon leaves, garlic and saffron and braised with olives.

DL-alanine A food additive used as a sweetening enhancer.

D.N.D. Do not disturb.

DO *See* Denominación de Origen.

dobin mushi (doh-ben moo-shee) A Japanese clear soup, often flavored with fresh pine needles and cooked and served in a small teapot.

Dobostorte; Dobos torte (DOH-bohs-TOR-te) A German pastry composed of several very thin layers of sponge cake filled with chocolate or mocha buttercream and topped with caramel glaze.

DOC *See* Denominazióne di Origine Controllata.

doce (doe-sha) Portuguese for sweet.

DOCG *See* Denominazióne di Origine Controllata e Garantita.

docinhos de amendoim (doh-che-nyos day amen-doh-him) Brazilian sweet peanut cakes made with roasted peanuts, grated coconut, sugar and eggs; the mixture is cooked, cooled, and cut into squares that are rolled in confectioners' sugar and garnished with roasted peanuts.

docker A tool used to pierce small holes in pastry dough; it resembles a small paint roller, with numerous short spikes.

dock glass A short-stemmed glass with an elongated, tulip-shaped bowl holding 2–3 fl. oz.; it

docker

is used for tasting ports and also known as a port glass.

docking Pricking small holes in an unbaked dough or crust to allow steam to escape and prevent the dough from rising when baked.

dodgers *See* corn dodgers.

dodine de canard (doh-deen duh kanard) 1. A French duck stew flavored with onions, herbs and red wine. 2. A galantine of duck.

dodo-ikire (doh-dohe-key-ra) A Nigerian street food or treat consisting of slices of a soft, overripened plantain fried in palm oil. *See* aloco.

doenjang chigae (the-eyn-jong chi-que) A Korean stew of vegetables, tofu and shellfish (especially clams).

Dofino *See* Havarti.

dog cherry *See* cornelian cherry.

dogfish; dogfish shark *See* shark.

doghouse *See* Siberia.

dögme (dog-meh) Wheat flour made from grains that have been soaked in water, dried and pounded; used principally for pilaf in Turkish cuisine.

dögme pilav (dog-meh polo) A Turkish dish of pilaf made from pounded ripe wheat.

dog salmon *See* chum salmon.

Dog's Nose A cocktail made with hot beer, gin and sugar.

doily An ornamental paper or fine fabric napkin used to decorate plates, especially for desserts, or to distinguish different items (e.g., decaffeinated coffee from regular coffee).

dolce (dole-shay) 1. Italian for sweet, as in sweet tasting. 2. When referring to an Italian wine, means sweeter than abboccato (semidry), secco (dry) and asciutto (very dry). *See* amabile.

Dolcetto (dohl-CHET-oh) 1. A red wine grape grown in Italy's Piedmont region. 2. The wine made from this grape; it is dry with soft, lush, supple qualities.

dolci (DOAL-chee) Italian for sweets or desserts.

Dôle (dole) A red wine made in the Swiss canton of Valais from the Pinot Noir and Gamay grapes; the wine resembles a light Burgundy.

dollarfish *See* butterfish.

dollop An imprecise measure of volume for a soft food such as whipped cream or mashed potatoes; it can be approximately the mounded amount contained on a teaspoon or tablespoon.

dolly mix An English assortment of small sweets in various shapes, colors and flavors.

Dolly Varden An anadromous trout found in the northern Pacific Ocean from California to Alaska and Japan to Korea; it has an olive skin with pink, orange or yellow spots, a yellow to orange, flaky flesh, and a delicate flavor and can weigh up to 20 lb. (9 kg).

dolma (dol-MAH) Any of a variety of fruits (e.g., apples), vegetables (e.g., squashes and peppers) or leaves (e.g., grape and cabbage) stuffed with a savory filling and braised or baked; served hot or cold, as an appetizer or entrée, in Mediterranean cuisines.

dolo (DO-low) An African beer made from fermented millet; although it is not hopped, it is flavored with a variety of bitter plants.

dolomite A nutrient (calcium magnesium carbonate) derived from limestone and marble and used as a food additive nutrient supplement.

dolphin 1. A marine mammal; it is illegal to catch or sell a dolphin for food. 2. An imprecisely used term for the saltwater fish known as a dolphinfish.

dolphinfish A saltwater fish found in tropical waters; it has a silvery, iridescent skin, an off-white to pink flesh, a firm texture, a moderately high fat content, a sweet flavor, and an average market weight of 5–15 lb. (2.7–6.8 kg); also known as mahi mahi (Hawaiian) and dorado (Spanish). *See* pampano.

dom (tom) Thai for to boil or cook in water.

domaine (doe-mehn) French for estate; in Burgundy, it refers to all the vineyards comprising a single property (even if located in different villages); in other regions of France, it refers to a single vineyard.

Domäne (doh-MAY-nuh) German for domain or estate; it is used to indicate a state-owned and/or state-managed vineyard.

domates (ntoo-maa-tees) Greek for tomatoes.

domatesli karnsnik kizartma (doh-mah-tess-lee kar-sneak-key czart-mah) A Turkish hors d'oeuvre of fried vegetables in a tomato sauce.

dómatiz (toh-mah-tez) Turkish for tomato.

Dombito tomato A variety of large, spherical, red-skinned, juicy, flavorful tomato.

domestic Dover sole A member of the flounder family found off the U.S. West Coast; it is often afflicted with a parasite that causes the flesh to become slimy and gelatinous.

Domiati *See* Damietta.

dominant meat The meat, fish, shellfish, poultry or vegetable that gives a forcemeat its name and essential flavor.

Dom Perignon (dom peh-ree-n'yawn) 1. The 17th-century cellar master at the Abbey d'Hautviller, popularly credited with inventing Champagne (all he actually discovered was that blending grapes from different vineyards improved the quality of the sparkling wine produced the following spring). 2. The finest and most expensive sparkling wine produced by Moët and Chandon.

Dona A French variety of medium-sized tomato with a deep red skin, a smooth, slightly flattened shape and an excellent ratio of acid to sugar.

donburi (don-boor-ree) A Japanese meal in a bowl consisting of rice with a wide range of topping choices.

dong (dohng) Thai for pickle.

dong gu (dong goo) Chinese for mushrooms.

dongpa (dong-pah) A Tibetan drink made from fermented and aged millet mixed with hot water.

dong sun (dong soon) Chinese for winter bamboo shoots.

donut *See* doughnut.

donzela (don-zeh-lah) Portuguese for burbot.

doodh; doohdh (dood) Hindi for milk.

doodhi lokhi (dood-hee lohk-he) *See* dudi.

doogh (dooke) Persian for a palate-cleansing yogurt and soda water drink flavored with dried mint.

doon (doon) Thai for to steam; usually done in a woven cane basket or perforated metal container over a wok or a pot of simmering water.

dopahar kaa khaanaa (dough-pah'r kah kah-nah) Hindi for lunch.

dopamine A neurotransmitter and hormone that helps regulate mood and food intake.

dope 1. Slang for gravy, probably derived from the Dutch sauce doop. 2. Slang, especially in the American South, for cola drinks because of the slightly stimulating effects of the caffeine.

do piaaza (do pi-aa-jaa) Chopped onions allowed to cook to a purée and used to add a sweet flavor to Indian curries.

Doppelbock (DOHP-pel-BOHK) A very strong, dark lager beer made in Bavaria, Germany, and served during the winter.

Doppelrahmstufe (dohpl-rham-stuf-fa) An official category of German cheeses consisting of double cream cheeses (those with a milkfat content of 60–85%).

Doppltes Beefsteak (dopple-tess bif-stek) A German cut of the beef carcass; it is comparable to châteaubriand.

dorade (doh-rahd) French for any of the breams or porgies; also known as daurade.

dorado (doh-rah-doh) *See* dolphinfish.

dorato (doh-RAH-toh) Italian for an ingredient that has been dipped in egg batter and fried to a golden color.

dorée (do-ray) French for John Dory or Saint-Pierre.

Dorin *See* Chasselas.

dormant A dish that remains on the table throughout a meal, such as a centerpiece.

doro (doe-roe) Ethiopian for chicken.

Dorobouski; Dorogoboukski (da-roh-boo-schki) A soft Russian cheese made from cow's milk; it has a soft whitish rind, a piquant flavor, and a slight ammonia smell and is sold as small cubes.

doro wat; doro wot' (doe-roe oo-at) An Ethiopian chicken stew flavored with garlic, berberé, nit'rk'ibé and tomatoes, served with hard-boiled eggs and eaten with injera.

Dorsch (dorsch) German for cod.

Dorset; Dorset Blue *See* blue vinney.

Dortmunder (dort-muhn-dar) A golden beer with high levels of hops and malt and of a style associated with Dortmund, Germany; it is drier and less effervescent than typical German pale lagers.

dosa (do-sah) A pancakelike bread made in southern India from ground lentils and flavored with coriander, cumin, black peppercorns and fenugreek; traditionally served with a thin vegetable curry flavored with sambar masala.

dosage (doe-sahj) A mixture of sugar and wine added to sparkling wine after disgorging and before final corking to determine the finished wine's sweetness; also known as liqueur d'expedition.

dot To place small pieces of an ingredient, usually butter, over the surface of a food.

Dotter (dough-ter) A cheese made in Nuremberg, Germany, from skimmed cow's milk and egg yolks.

double-acting baking powder A chemical leavening agent that releases carbon dioxide gas when moistened and again when heated. *See* baking powder.

double boiler An assemblage used to cook heat-sensitive foods such as sauces, chocolate or custards; one pot sits partway down a second pot; simmering water in the bottom pot gently heats the top pot's contents; also known as a double saucepan.

Double Brandy Flip A cocktail made of brandy, apricot brandy, sugar syrup and egg; garnished with nutmeg.

double claro *See* candela.

double column still A still consisting of two cylindrical columns fitted with a system of interconnecting tubes; the alcoholic liquid is fed into the tubes, where it is distilled, redistilled and removed in a highly concentrated and purified form.

double corona *See* corona, double.

double cream; double crème A description for a cow's milk cheese enriched with cream and having a minimum milkfat content of 60%; fresh or aged, it generally has a soft, creamy texture and a mild, slightly sweet flavor; usually made as small wheels.

double crust A pie, cobbler or other pastry prepared with both a top and bottom layer of dough. *See* crust.

double-frying process A moist-heat cooking method in which a food (e.g., potatoes) is first deep-fried at one temperature and then deep-fried again at a higher temperature, causing the food to puff up.

Double Gloucester *See* Gloucester, Double.

double-handled cheese cutter A utensil used for cutting large, firm cheeses (e.g., Gruyère or Cheddar); it consists of a single 11- to 12-in.-long blade with offset handles on both ends.

double-handled cheese cutter

double maduro *See* maduro maduro.

double magnum An oversized still or sparkling wine bottle holding the equivalent of four 750-ml bottles or 3 liters (approximately 101 fl. oz.). *See* Jeroboam.

double old-fashioned glass *See* bucket glass.

double rack *See* rib.

double saucepan *See* double boiler.

double sugar *See* disaccharide.

doubloon *See* shiitake.

douce (doos) French for sweet.

doucereux (doos-roo) French for cloying.

dou ch (doo tchee) Small, dried, salted Chinese black beans.

dòufù (doh-foo) Firmly pressed Chinese-style tofu; also known as bean cake.

dòufù-bok (doh-foo-bock) Deep-fried hollow cubes of Chinese-style tofu; also known as hollow agé cubes.

dòufù-kan (doh-foo-khan) A small cake of firmly pressed Chinese-style tofu.

dòufù-ru (doh-foo-roo) A Chinese-style fermented tofu cube in brine; it can be red or white; also known as bean curd cheese, Chinese cheese, Chinese white cheese (if white) and fuyu.

dough A mixture of flour and other ingredients used in baking and often stiff enough to cut into shapes; it has a low moisture content and gluten forms the continuous medium into which other ingredients are embedded; it generally has less fat, sugar and liquid than a batter. *See* batter.

dough conditioner; dough strengthener A type of food additive used to modify a dough's starch and gluten content to produce a more stable product, increase loaf volume and/or prevent loss of leavening.

dough cutter; dough scraper A thin, rectangular piece of unsharpened stainless steel topped with a wooden or plastic handle; used to cut portions of dough, to clean wooden worktables, and to lift or move foods; also known as a bench scraper.

dough cutter/scraper

dough divider A stainless steel tool composed of several cutting wheels attached to metal bars on an expandable, accordion-like frame; used to cut several evenly sized strips of dough at once; also known as a Danish cutter or an expandable pastry cutter.

dough gods Cowboy slang for biscuits.

doughnut; donut A small round or ring-shaped cake of sweet, leavened dough that is deep-fried, often coated with glaze, sugar or frosting and sometimes filled.

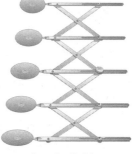
dough divider

doughnut cutter A utensil made of two 1-in.-high rings; the smaller one is centered inside the larger one, and the utensil is held together with a U-shaped handle; sometimes the inner ring is detachable; it is used to cut doughnuts from dough.

doughnut peach A variety of squat, round peach with a concave center.

doughnut screen A screenlike or gridded utensil used to lift doughnuts from the cooking fat or to keep them under the fat's surface during cooking.

doughspur A scalloped wheel with a handle, used for decorating pastry; also known as a crimper/cutter.

dough wrangler Cowboy slang for a cook.

Douglas Fairbanks A cocktail made of gin, lemon juice, apricot brandy, sugar syrup and egg white.

dou jiang (doo gee-hang) Chinese for soybean milk.

dourada (doo-rah-dah) Portuguese for gilthead.

Douro (DOO-roh) A grape-growing and wine-producing region of Portugal; famous for Port, it also produces dry red table wines made from grapes from the Touriga and Tinta families.

doute (doo-ta) A Senegalese kinkéliba tisane.

doux (doo) 1. French for sweet. 2. A Champagne or sparkling wine containing at least 5% sugar.

Doux de Montagne (doo duh mahn-tahn-yuh) A semisoft French cheese made from cow's milk; it has a mellow, sweet, fruity flavor, a pale yellow interior with irregular holes, and a dark rind; also known as Pain de Pyrenees.

Dover sole *See* sole, Dover.

dovi (doe-vee) A Zimbabwean stew made from chicken, onions and groundnuts or peanuts, flavored with chiles and garlic, and served with boiled bowara.

Downing mulberry A variety of black mulberry with long, sweet, black-skinned fruit.

Doyenné du Comice (doh-enn du cuh-MEES) *See* Comice pear.

dozen Twelve.

draff The spent grains left in the lauter tun after the malt's starches have been converted to sugars during brewing or distillation.

draft beer; draught beer Unpasteurized beer sold in a 1-gallon or larger container; the beer is drawn off for service through a tap or spigot.

draft beer system *See* beer system.

dragées (dra-zhay) 1. Tiny silver or gold balls made of sugar and used to decorate cookies and pastries. 2. Candied almonds with a hard sugar coating.

dragoncello (drah-goan-CHAYL-lo) Italian for tarragon; also known as serpentaria.

dragon's eye *See* longan.

Dragoon Punch A punch made of sparkling wine, ale, porter, amontillado sherry, brandy, sugar and lemon slices.

drain *v.* 1. To allow a liquid to withdraw from, pour out of or pour off an item, sometimes with the use of a strainer or colander. 2. To blot fat from a food. *n.* A device facilitating or channeling the withdrawing liquid.

dram; drachm 1. An archaic term for a drink of liquor. 2. A traditional apothecary weight; about 3/4 teaspoon or 0.12 oz.

Drambuie (drahm-BOO-ee) A Scottish amber-colored liqueur made from fine old Highland malt Scotch whisky, heather honey and herbs.

dram shop An archaic term for a bar.

dram shop act; dram shop law A law under which a bar, liquor store, host or any other person or entity providing alcoholic beverages to someone who appears to be intoxicated can be held legally responsible for part or all of any injuries or damages caused by that person while intoxicated.

draw 1. To eviscerate (i.e., remove the entrails from) game, poultry, fish or the like. 2. To clarify a mixture, as in drawn butter.

draw The intake of cigar smoke.

drawn A market form for fish in which the viscera is removed.

drawn butter *See* butter, clarified.

draw one Slang for pouring a beer.

dredger A can-shaped container with a perforated top used for sprinkling dry condiments at the table or for sifting cocoa powder or confectioners' sugar onto pasteries or confections in the kitchen.

dredging Coating a food with flour or finely ground crumbs; usually done before sautéing or frying or as the first step of the standardized breading procedure.

dregs *See* lees.

dresil (dra-scal) A Tibetan dessert consisting of white rice flavored with brown sugar, nuts, raisins and butter.

dress 1. To prepare game, foul or fish for cooking by eviscerating, plucking, trussing, cleaning, scaling and so on. 2. To add a vinaigrette or other salad dressing to a salad. 3. To set and decorate a table or room for a festive occasion. 4. To add an unexpected touch to a dish or meal.

dresser 1. A sideboard or table in the kitchen used for dressing foods. 2. A small side table used for serving foods.

dressing 1. A sauce, usually cold, used on salads. 2. Another name for poultry stuffing. *See* stuffing.

dried beef *See* chipped beef.

dried fruit Fruit from which most of the moisture has been removed through a natural or artificial dehydration process (final moisture content is 15–20%); this concentrates sweetness and alters (usually strengthening) the flavor; dried fruit usually has four to five times the calories by weight as fresh fruit and can be stored for 1 year; eaten as a snack or used in baked goods, sweet dishes and savory dishes, either as is or reconstituted with a liquid.

dried milk; dry milk powder A product made from whole milk from which the water has been extracted, leaving the milkfat and milk solids in a dried, powdery form.

dried milk, nonfat; dry milk powder, nonfat A product made from skim milk from which the water has been extracted, leaving the milk solids in a dried, powdery form.

dried red fermented rice *See* hongqu.

dried scallops Amber-colored, heavily salted discs of dried scallops used to add flavor to vegetable dishes, soups and congees in Asian cuisines.

dried shrimp roe Small reddish, salty grains used as a condiment for mildly flavored Japanese dishes.

drikkevarer (deerk-ka-vah-rare) Norwegian for beverage.

drink *v.* 1. To consume a liquid. 2. To consume an alcoholic beverage. *n.* 1. Any liquid that is swallowed to quench thirst, for nourishment or for enjoyment. 2. A beverage containing alcohol.

drink box The plastic or waxed-cardboard container in which a beverage, usually a juice product, is sold; also known as a juice box.

drinking straw A rigid or flexible paper or plastic tube used for sipping and/or mixing beverages.

drinking water *See* water, drinking.

drink list A menu of common and speciality drinks offered by an establishment; sometimes brand names are identified.

drip pan A shallow pan used in a smoker to catch dripping fat or basting runoff.

drippings The melted fat and juices released when meat is roasted; used as a flavoring, a sauce, a gravy base or a cooking medium; also known as pan drippings.

drizzle To pour a liquid in a very fine stream over a food or plate.

drob de miel (drobb da me-l) A Romanian dish of simmered calf's stomach stuffed with lamb's liver, lungs and heart and flavored with onions and herbs.

droo (droo) A Tunisian dish consisting of a millet porridge flavored with hazelnuts, almonds, pistachios, sesame seeds and confectioners' sugar.

drop batter A batter that is too thick to pour; it is dropped from a spoon in portions or mounds.

drop cookie A cookie made by dropping spoonfuls of soft dough onto a baking sheet.

drop lid A lid that is smaller than the pot; it is placed directly on the food being cooked to help prevent delicate foods from losing their shape or falling apart.

drozhzhi (droe-sha-shak) Russian for yeast.

druer (drew-er) Norwegian for grapes.

drum Any of a large variety of fish named because of the drumming or croaking sounds they make during mating; found in temperate Atlantic and Pacific Ocean waters, principally off North America; they generally have a low fat content, a firm white flesh, and a market weight of 1–30 lb. (0.9–13.5 kg); significant varieties include the Atlantic croaker, black croaker, black drum, California corvina, hardhead, kingfish, redfish, sea trout, spot and white sea bass.

drumhead cabbage *See* cabbage, white.

drum sieve A utensil used for puréeing foods; a mushroom-shaped pestle pushes food through the sieve's mesh, which is held in a wooden ring and can be fine or coarse and made from wire, horsehair or nylon; also known as a tamis.

drum sieve

drumstick 1. The lower portion of a poultry leg, including the bone, meat, fat layer and skin. 2. *See* winged bean.

drunk The condition of being intoxicated with alcohol.

drunken crabs Shanghai hairy crabs preserved in spices and wine.

drupelets Small, individual sections of a fruit, each with its own seed; as a group, they comprise the entire fruit (e.g., a raspberry).

drupes Members of the genus *Prunus,* many of which are native to China but now grow in temperate climates world-

wide; these fruits (e.g., apricots and peaches) generally have a thin skin (called an epicarp), a soft, juicy, sweet flesh (called a mesocarp), and a single woody pit (called a stone); also known as stone fruits.

druva (drew-vah) Swedish for grape.

dry 1. A tasting term for an alcoholic beverage, except Champagne or sparkling wine, that retains very little if any detectable sugar; there is little to no sensation of sweetness on the palate (e.g., red Bordeaux). *See* semidry, semisweet *and* sweet. 2. A Champagne or sparkling wine that is medium sweet.

dry aging The process of storing meat under specific temperature and humidity conditions for up to 6 weeks to increase tenderness and flavor; it is the start of the natural decomposition process and can result in significant moisture loss. *See* wet aging.

dry beer A beer that is drier to the taste than most other beers and leaves little to no aftertaste; it is usually made by extracting as much sugar as possible from the mash during the cooking process and then fermenting it for an additional 7 days.

dry county A county in which the sale of alcoholic beverages is limited to private clubs or prohibited entirely.

dry cured Meat or fish preserved by rubbing the food with salt (seasonings are often also applied); also known as salted.

dry curing A method of curing meat or fish by packing it in salt and seasonings.

dry goose *See* fitless cock.

dry-heat cooking methods Cooking methods, principally broiling, grilling, roasting or baking, sautéing, pan-frying and deep-frying, that use air or fat to transfer heat through conduction and convection; dry-heat cooking methods allow surface sugars to caramelize. *See* moist-heat cooking methods.

dry hopping A step late in the fermentation process when hops are added for aroma and flavor without significantly increasing a beer's bitterness.

dry ice The proprietary name of a form of crystallized carbon dioxide used as a coolant; it passes directly from a solid to a gas at $-109.3°F$ $(-78.5°C)$, absorbing a great deal of energy.

drying A method of preserving foods by dramatically reducing their moisture content, either naturally or by mechanical means; drying usually changes the food's texture, appearance and flavor; also known as dehydrating.

drying agent A type of food additive with a moisture-absorbing ability; used to prevent sogginess and to maintain a low moisture environment for, and improve the texture of, various processed foods.

drying out A wine-tasting term for an old wine that is beginning to lose its flavor.

Dry Jack Aged Monterey Jack cheese; it has a yellow color, a firm texture and a sharp flavor; typically used as a grating cheese.

Dry Mahoney A cocktail made of bourbon and dry vermouth garnished with a twist of lemon peel.

dry malt extract Malt extract in a dry powder form made by mashing malted barley with warm water, then concentrating and dehydrating it; used for brewing beer.

dry matter All of the components of a cheese except moisture (water); it includes proteins, milkfat, milk sugars and minerals.

dry measuring cups *See* measuring cups, dry.

dry mustard *See* mustard, ground.

drynaki (dri-nah-key) A Belorussian and Russian dish consisting of potato pancakes fried in pork fat and served with pork fat and sour cream.

dry quart A unit of volume measurement in the American and imperial systems; approximately 67.2 cu. in.

dry roasting A dry-heat cooking method that heats food by surrounding it with hot air, usually in a closed environment and with little or no moisture or fat added.

Dry Sack A medium-sweet sherry.

dry storage A storeroom or storage area where nonrefrigerated goods are stored; it can be an environment offering some control over temperature, humidity and/or light.

dry stout The Irish version of stout; it is slightly more bitter than an English stout.

dry vermouth *See* vermouth, dry.

Dubarry, à la; du Barry, à la (doo-bah-ree) A French dish prepared or garnished with cauliflower.

dubbel (DU-bel) A sweet, fruity, amber-colored Belgian ale.

Dublin Bay prawn *See* prawn.

Dublin coddle An Irish dish consisting of layers of slowly cooked onions, potatoes, bacon and sausages.

Dublin lawyer An Irish dish consisting of lobster meat flamed with Irish whiskey, mixed with cream and returned to the shell for service.

Dubonnet; Dubonnet rouge (doo-bo-nay) A French aperitif made from red wine and flavored with quinine and bitter herbs, usually served over ice with a squeeze of lemon.

Dubonnet blanc A drier white version made from white wine.

Dubonnet Cocktail A cocktail made of gin and Dubonnet rouge; served in a chilled old-fashioned glass with a twist of lemon peel.

Dubonnet Fizz A cocktail made of Dubonnet rouge, vodka and club soda; garnished with a twist of lemon.

duchesse, à la (duh-shees, ah lah) 1. A French preparation method in which various dishes are garnished, surrounded or served with duchess potatoes. 2. In pastry, refers to certain preparations containing almonds.

duchesse, sauce; duchess, sauce (duh-shees) A French compound sauce made from a béchamel finished with butter and garnished with julienne of pickled tongue and mushrooms.

duchess potatoes; pommes duchesse (duh-shees) A purée of cooked potatoes, butter and egg yolks, seasoned with salt, pepper and nutmeg; it can be eaten as is or used to prepare several classic potato dishes.

Duchilly hazelnut A variety of large, long hazelnuts.

duck 1. One of the principal kinds of poultry recognized by the USDA; any of several varieties of domesticated webfooted swimming birds used for food; it has a high percentage of bone and fat to meat, a fatty skin, no light meat, and a rich flavor; significant varieties include the Long Island duck and muscovy duck. 2. African-American slang for an alcoholic beverage.

duck, broiler-fryer; duckling, broiler-fryer A duck slaughtered before it is 8 weeks old; it has a soft bill and windpipe, an average market weight of 3.5–5 lb. (1.5–1.8 kg) and very tender flesh.

duck, mature A duck slaughtered at 6 months or older; it has a hard bill and windpipe, an average market weight of 4–6 lb. (1.8–2.5 kg) and tough flesh.

duck, roaster; duckling, roaster A duck slaughtered before it is 16 weeks old; it has an easily dented windpipe, an average market weight of 4–6 lb. (1.8–2.5 kg) and a tender flesh with a rich flavor.

duck, wild Any of several varieties of duck that have not been domesticated; generally, their flesh is darker than that of a domesticated duck and has a denser texture and a nuttier, gamier flavor; significant varieties include the mallard, teal and widgeon.

duck à l'orange *See* caneton à l'orange.

duck classes Significant duck classes are the broiler-fryer duckling, roaster duckling and mature duck.

duckling A young duck.

duck liver *See* foie gras.

duck press A device used to extract the juices from a cooked duck carcass; used in French cuisine for preparations such as pressed duck.

duck sauce A thick, sweet-and-sour Chinese sauce made from plums, apricots, sugar and seasonings; served with duck, pork or spareribs; also known as plum sauce.

dudevan (doo-do-vahn) Hebrew for cherry.

dudi (doo-dee) A variety of edible gourds with a pale green hard shell that is sometimes slightly fluted, a creamy yellow-green flesh, and a mild flavor reminiscent of cucumbers; also known as bottle gourd, doodhi lokhi, lokhi and woo lo gwa.

duck press

dudong *See* manatee.

Duel (dool) A soft, aged Austrian cheese made from cow's milk; sold in small square blocks.

duff 1. A steamed pudding containing fruit; traditionally boiled in a cloth bag. 2. Archaic English for dough.

dügan çorbas (dun-gan SHOR-bas) A Turkish wedding soup made from stock thickened with flour, flavored with lemon juice, and garnished with egg yolks, paprika and butter.

duika (doo-e-kah) The mangolike fruit of a tree native to central Africa; its seeds are used in cooking; also known as a wild mango.

duivekater (doo-ee-veh-kah-terr) A large, flat Dutch bread shaped like a shinbone or diamond, sometimes flavored with raisins or currants.

du jour (doo-zhoor) French for of the day and used to introduce a menu item that is a special for a particular day, such as a soup.

duk (dook) A Korean rice cake shaped into a log, sliced, and served in broth with meat and vegetables or coated with soybean flour, fried, and dipped in honey.

dukka; dukkah (DOO-kah) An Egyptian spice paste consisting of ground toasted nuts and seeds, usually hazelnuts and chickpeas, flavored with pepper, coriander, cumin and sesame seeds; it is often used as part of a snack: bread is dipped in olive oil and then the spice paste.

duku A fruit (*Lansium domesticum*) native to Southeast Asia; the medium-sized spherical fruit grows in clusters and has a tannish-gray skin, a white segmented juicy flesh and a sweet–sour flavor.

dulce (DOOL'th-eh) 1. Spanish for sweet. 2. A sweetening agent added to certain sherries at bottling. 3. A very sweet Spanish confection made with sugar and cream.

dülger (dool-gher) Turkish for John Dory.

dull 1. A tasting term for a food that lacks distinction and character. 2. A wine-tasting term for a wine that may be full bodied and have other qualities but lacks distinction and character.

dulse A coarse, red seaweed found on the rocky coasts of the North Atlantic; it is dried and eaten as is or fried or toasted in Scottish cuisine; it has a salty, tangy flavor.

dum (dum) An Indian cooking method in which a pot's lid is sealed with a dough strip and the foods are cooked gently in the sealed environment.

Dumas, Alexandre (Fr., 1802–1870) A prolific dramatist and novelist and the author of the *Grand Dictionaire de Cuisine,* which is considered to be more picturesque than accurate.

dumb A wine-tasting term for a closed wine that has not developed sufficiently to show any character.

dump cake A cake made by combining and mixing all the ingredients in the pan in which the batter is baked.

dumpling 1. A dessert made by covering a piece of fruit or fruit mixture with sweet dough and baking. 2. A dessert consisting of a small mound of sweet dough poached in a sweet sauce, usually served with cream. 3. Any of a variety of small starchy products made from doughs or batters; they can be plain or filled with a savory mixture and simmered, steamed or fried.

Dumyat See Damietta.

dùn (dang) A Chinese cooking method in which foods are braised in their own juices (seasoned or plain) over high heat or slowly over low heat in a tightly covered casserole; also known as wei.

Dunant, sauce; Dunand, sauce (dew-nahn) A French compound sauce made from a hollandaise flavored with truffle essence and langoustine (or lobster) butter and finished with unsweetened whipped cream.

Dundee cake A Scottish fruitcake made with candied citrus, currants, almonds and spices; the top is completely covered with blanched almonds.

Dundee Marmalade The proprietary name of a dark, rich orange marmalade, originally made in Dundee, Scotland.

dunder The lees of cane juice; used to promote fermentation for the distillation of rum.

dundu (doon-doo) A Nigerian dish consisting of fried yams served with an onion paste flavored with chiles.

dungeness crab A variety of crab found in the Pacific Ocean from Alaska to Mexico; only males can be sold legally; it has a flattened body, a reddish-brown, spotted, hard shell, small, short legs, an average market width of 5.25–6.5 in. (14.3–16 cm), and a white flesh with a delicate, sweet flavor.

dunghill fowl Archaic slang for barnyard poultry such as chickens (as opposed to wild or game birds).

dunkel (DUNE-kul) 1. German for dark, as in color. 2. A description of a dark-colored German beer. *See* hell.

Dunlop (DUHN-loap) A semisoft to firm Scottish cheese made from cow's milk; it has an ivory color and mild flavor when young that becomes sharper with age.

dünsten (doon-stan) German for to steam or to stew.

Dunsyre Blue A semisoft to firm cheese made in Lanarkshire, Scotland, from unpasteurized cow's milk; it has a creamy white interior with vertical blue veins and a mild, tangy flavor.

duodenum The first portion of the small intestine, extending from the stomach to the jejunum; the site where bile, pancreatic juice and intestinal juices mix with the acid and food that have just passed through the stomach (known as chyme).

duogong *See* manatee.

dupe Slang for duplicate and used to describe the portion of a multipart form given to the bar or kitchen (also known as the soft copy) recording a customer's drink or food order; the other portion (known as a hard copy) is given to the customer.

duqqa (doo-kah) A Middle Eastern flavoring blend consisting of roasted coriander seeds, roasted peanuts, sumac, roasted chickpeas, dried mint, roasted sesame seeds and sometimes dried or roasted lentils and salt; the mixture is ground into a crumbly (not oily) texture.

durazno (doo-RAHS-soh) *See* melocotón.

Durbanville A grape-growing and wine-producing region in South Africa located in the rolling hills northeast of Cape Town; it is best known for red wines produced from Cabernet Sauvignon and Pinot Noir grapes.

durian (DOOR-ee-uhn) A very large fruit (*Durio zibethinus*) native to Southeast Asia; it has a brown-green spiked shell, a yellow-white flesh, a rich, custardlike texture, a slightly sweet flavor, and an overwhelmingly foul aroma; also known as civet fruit.

durometer A device used to test a fruit's firmness.

durondeau pear (duh-ron-doh) A variety of pear; the fruit has a rust-blushed green and yellow skin, an ivory flesh, and a sweet flavor.

durum wheat A very hard wheat with high glutenin and gliadin contents; usually ground into semolina, which is used to make pasta.

dusky shark *See* shark.

dust *v.* To coat a food or utensil lightly with a powdery substance such as flour or confectioners' sugar. *n.* The smallest size of broken tea leaves or tea particles; generally used in tea bags. *See* orange fannings *and* fannings.

dusting flour Flour sprinkled on a workbench or other surface to prevent dough from sticking to the surface when being rolled or formed.

Dutch brown bean *See* brown bean.

Dutch cabbage *See* cabbage, white.

Dutch chile; Dutch pepper A long, slightly curved, tapering fresh chile with a bright red color, a thick flesh, and a sweet, hot flavor.

Dutch courage 1. Slang for the false courage induced by alcohol. 2. Slang for gin imported from the Netherlands.

Dutch gin *See* Genever.

Dutch medlar A variety of large medlar.

Dutch oven A large kettle, typically made of cast iron, with a tight-fitting lid; used for stewing or braising.

Dutch-processed cocoa *See* alkalized cocoa.

Dutch sauce *See* hollandaise.

duvec (jew-vitch) Serbo-Croat for casserole and used to describe a Balkan casserole of meat (usually pork or lamb) cooked with onions, potatoes, rice, tomatoes, green peppers and/or other vegetables, seasoned with paprika and herbs.

Duvel The proprietary name of a Belgian beer with a strong golden color and a lingering aftertaste.

duxelles (dook-SEHL; deu-SEHL) A French garnish or stuffing mixture made from chopped mushrooms, onions and shallots sautéed in butter.

duxelles, sauce à la (dook-SEHL) A French compound sauce made from a demi-glaze flavored with puréed mushrooms, shallots and onions simmered in white wine; tomato purée is then added, and it is finished with butter and parsley.

dwarf banana *See* Canary Island banana.

dwarf coconut A variety of small coconut grown in Malaysia; also known as nyiur-gading.

dwarf elderberries The small, red-skinned berries of this mountain tree (genus *Sambucus*) grow in tight clusters; the berries have a slightly bitter flavor and are used for preserves.

dynia (di-nyah) Polish for pumpkin.

dynya; dyna (DI-nyah) Russian for melon.

dyrejøtt (deyr-shut) Norwegian for game venison.

dyrekølle (deyr-shu-le) Danish for venison.

dyrlægens natmad (deer-la'gans-nat-mahd) A Danish smørrebrød dish of salted, boiled beef on liver pâté with meat gelatin and onion rings.

dyspepsia coffee A mixture of equal parts ground coffee and cornmeal moistened with molasses, browned in the oven and used as one would use ground coffee; considered a cure for indigestion.

dziczyzna (dzy-lhi-znah) Polish for game.

é Chinese for goose.

E *See* Extra.

Earl Grey A mixture of Indian and Sri Lankan black teas, flavored with oil of bergamot; the beverage has a delicate flavor and is served without milk or lemon.

early-bird special A discount offered on goods or services purchased at a time earlier than typically associated with them or before they are typically in demand (e.g., a dinner served at 4:00 P.M.).

early blueberry *See* blueberry, low-bush.

Early Cluster A variety of hops grown in the state of Washington.

Early Girl tomato A variety of medium-sized beefsteak tomato with a bright crimson color, a meaty, firm texture, and a blemish-resistant skin.

Early Golden apricot An apricot variety; the fruit are medium sized, with a yellow-orange skin, a whitish-yellow flesh, and a sweet flavor.

Early Harvest A light, crisp white wine (usually Californian) made from grapes picked with a maximum of 20° Brix or approximately 20% sugar. *See* Late Harvest.

Early Richmond cherry A sour cherry with a bright red skin.

Early Rivers nectarine A variety of nectarine; the fruit have a red-blushed yellow skin and a good flavor.

Early Sulphur gooseberries A variety of gooseberries; the flavorful fruit have a golden yellow skin.

Early Times Distillery One of the 12 remaining U.S. whiskey distilleries; located in Louisville, Kentucky, and founded c. 1860, its products include Early Times Old Style Kentucky Whiskey and Old Forester bourbon.

earth almond *See* tiger nut.

earthenware Any of a variety of vessels or containers used for cooking, service or storage that are made of low-fired clays that are slightly porous and are usually glazed (at least on the interior); they tend not to conduct heat well, but once hot, they will retain the heat.

earthnut *See* peanut.

earthy 1. A cheese-tasting term for a hearty, assertive, rustic flavor and/or aroma of a cheese, usually a monastery cheese or one made from ewe's or goat's milk; an excessively earthy flavor can be undesirable. 2. A coffee-tasting term used to describe a somewhat spicy flavor reminiscent of the rich soil in which the coffee trees are grown. 3. A wine-tasting term for the rich, clean, soil-like aroma and/or flavor that certain soils impart to grapes and the wines made from them.

easily cleanable In the food safety context, any utensil or piece of equipment that is readily accessible and of such material and design that residue can be removed completely by normal cleaning methods.

eastern halibut *See* Atlantic halibut.

eastern oysters *See* Atlantic oysters.

eastern red cedar A variety of juniper that produces particularly flavorful berries.

eastern whitefish *See* whitefish.

East Kent Goldings A variety of hops grown in England.

East meets West *See* fusion cuisine.

eau (oh) French for water.

eau-de-vie (oh-duh-VEE) French for water of life and used to generally describe distilled spirits made from grape wine or fermented fruits.

eau-de-vie de marc (oh-duh-VEE duh mar) *See* marc.

eau-de-vie de poire (oh-duh-VEE duh pwahr) A colorless pear brandy distilled from the Williams pear.

eau parfumée (oh par-foo-may) A Moroccan beverage made by capturing the scent of burning gum arabic (a vessel is placed over smoldering gum arabic ashes) and then pouring water and orange-flavored water into the vessel.

Ebbelwoi (eb-bell-voh-ee) German apple wine from Sachsenhausen (in Frankfurt); it has an acerbic, dry flavor with an alcohol content of 5.5%; it is served from stoneware pitchers, known as Bembel, into ribbed glasses with wooden lids.

ebi (eh-BEE) Japanese for shrimp, prawn or lobster.

Eβstäbchen (ess-tah-chen) German for chopsticks.

ebulliometer (eh-bu-lee-A-muh-der) A device for measuring the alcohol content of a liquid.

Eccles cake An individual-sized, dome-shaped British cake made with puff pastry or short crust pastry and filled with currants, dried fruit, sugar and spices; traditionally served for afternoon tea.

échalote (ee-shah-lot) French for shallot.

echicharos (a-che-cha-ross) Mexican for peas.

échine (a-cheen) A French cut of the pork carcass; it is the top part of the shoulder and the equivalent of the butt.

éclair (ay-clahr) An oblong, finger-shaped French pastry made with choux dough, filled with pastry cream and topped with icing or glaze.

éclair paste A soft dough that produces hollow baked products with crisp exteriors (e.g., éclairs, cream puffs and savory products); also known as pâte à choux.

éclair plaque A flat rectangular metal pan with 12 1- × 3-in. shallow indentations used to form éclairs, ladyfingers and langues de chat.

E. coli *See* Escherichia coli.

economy class 1. A designation for a European hotel of modest standards with few, if any, private baths; also known as tourist class. 2. A designation for an American hotel of modest quality with few, if any, private baths and very limited services; also known as tourist class.

écossaise, sauce (a-koss-saze) A French compound sauce made from a béchamel blended with hard-boiled egg yolks and garnished with julienne of hard-boiled eggs; also known as Scotch sauce.

écrevisse (ay-cruh-VEESS) French for crayfish.

Ecuadoran Robusta coffee beans grown in Ecuador; the beverage is generally neither interesting nor full flavored.

eda (a-dah) Russian for food.

Edam (EE-duhm) A semisoft to firm Dutch sweet-curd cheese made from cow's milk; it has a pale yellow interior and a mild, slightly salty flavor; it is usually shaped as a slightly flattened ball and, if intended for export, is colored red, rubbed with oil, and wrapped in a transparent material; also known as Katzenkopf and Manbollen.

eda mame (eh-DAH mah-meh) Japanese for fresh soybeans.

Edam, American An American Edam, covered with red paraffin or other tightly adhering red coating.

eddik (EHD-dik) Norwegian for vinegar.

eddike (EHDH-egger) Dutch for vinegar.

eddo A small, spherical variety of taro native to the Caribbean region.

Edefaule (eh-dell-foy-luh) German term for the noble rot.

Edelpilzkäse (a-dehl-pe-kaizah) A firm German cheese made from cow's milk; it has a white interior with dark blue veins, a crumbly texture, and a particularly strong moldy or fruity flavor; usually served as a dessert cheese.

edes *See* Szamorodni

edge bone *See* aitch bone.

edible portion (EP) The amount of a food item available for consumption after trimming or fabrication. *See* as-purchased *and* yield.

Edomae-zushi (ah-DOE-may-zhoo-she) *See* nigiri-zushi.

EDTA *See* ethylenediaminetetraacetate.

eel A variety of anadromous fish with an elongated, snakelike shape, pointed snout, and large mouth; colors range from gray to olive to black; generally, it has a fatty flesh with a firm texture and a rich, sweet flavor.

eel, American An eel found in rivers and bays along North America's northern East Coast; also known as a silver eel.

eel, baby A young eel, usually available during the spring; it has a tender texture and a sweet flavor and is served with garlic and red peppers in Spanish cuisine.

eel, European An eel found in European waters; it has a dark gray to olive skin and gelatinous flesh.

een choy *See* amaranth.

effervescence Small bubbles released in a liquid, creating a sparkling sensation on the palate.

efterratter (AYF-terr-reht) Swedish for dessert, sweet or pudding course.

e-fu Relatively flat, yellow-colored Chinese noodles made from eggs and wheat flour.

egg The ovoid, hard-shelled reproductive body produced by a bird, consisting principally of a yolk and albumen; it is a good source of protein, iron, sulfur and vitamins A, B, D and E, but also relatively high in cholesterol.

egg, bantam An egg from a breed of small chicken; about half the size of a regular chicken egg, but with the same characteristics.

egg, chicken An egg with a white to brown shell, a bright yellow yolk, and an egg white that is generally colorless with streaks of white when raw, turning milky white when cooked.

egg, duck An egg with an off-white shell and a richer flavor than a chicken's egg; when boiled, the white turns bluish and the yolk turns red-orange.

egg, goose An egg with a white shell; it is four to five times larger than a chicken egg and has a somewhat richer flavor.

egg, guinea fowl An egg with an ivory shell flecked with brown; it has a more delicate flavor than that of a chicken egg.

egg, gull An egg with light to dark brown blotches and of various small sizes; it has a slightly fishy flavor.

egg, ostrich An egg with a thick, ivory-colored shell; it can be 20 times as large as a chicken egg.

egg, partridge A small egg with a white, buff or olive shell and a mild flavor.

egg, pheasant A small egg with a white, buff or olive shell and a mild flavor.

egg, quail A small egg with a speckled brown shell and a rich flavor.

egg, turkey A large egg with a brown shell and a delicate flavor.

egg, turtle An egg with a buff or speckled soft shell and a mild, rich flavor.

egg-and-bread-crumb A method of dipping food into beaten egg and then into bread crumbs before frying it to give it a crisp coating.

egg bagel *See* bagel, egg.

egg barley *See* farfel.

egg beater *See* rotary egg beater.

egg bread A yeast bread enriched with eggs, such as brioche or challah. *See* spoon bread.

egg cheese A Finnish cheese made from fresh cow's milk and 2–12 eggs per quart of milk.

egg coffee Coffee to which an egg had been added during preparation (boiling); the egg helps precipitate the coffee grounds.

egg cook Slang for a food service facility's breakfast cook.

egg cream A soda fountain concoction consisting of chocolate syrup, milk and seltzer; there is no egg or cream in an egg cream, but if properly made, a foamy, egg white–like head forms on top of the drink.

egg custard A dessert made with eggs, sugar and vanilla, usually baked in individual molds or cups.

egg foo yong; egg foo yung A Chinese–American dish of eggs mixed with garnishes (e.g., bean sprouts, scallions, water chestnuts, pork, chicken and/or shrimp) and pan-fried; usually served with a thick sauce.

egg grades A grading system developed by the U.S. Department of Agriculture (USDA) and based on a chicken egg's exterior and interior qualities, not size; grade AA is the highest, followed by grades A and B.

egg grades, grade A The shell is clean, normal shaped, and unbroken; when first broken, the egg spreads slightly; it has a clear, reasonably firm albumen with prominent chalazae and a firm, fairly high yolk.

egg grades, grade AA The shell is clean, normal shaped, and unbroken; when first broken, the egg's spread remains compact; it has a clear, thick albumen with prominent chalazae and a firm, centered yolk.

egg grades, grade B The shell may be slightly stained or misshapened; when first broken, the egg spreads over a wide area; it has a clear, watery albumen and an enlarged, flattened yolk.

eggnog A rich beverage made of eggs, cream or milk, sugar, spices and spirits (usually rum, brandy or whiskey). *See* nog.

egg noodles *See* noodles.

egg piercer A tool with a sharp steel pin, usually spring mounted, used to make a tiny hole in the large end of the egg; this prevents cracking by slowly releasing the air inside.

eggplant A member of the nightshade family (*Solanum melongena*), its fruit is used like a vegetable; the fruit has a dense, khaki-colored flesh with a rather bland but sometimes bitter flavor that absorbs other flavors during cooking; also known as a guinea squash.

eggplant

eggplant, Asian Any of a variety of eggplants that are generally small with soft flesh and are either spherical or long and thin, with skin colors ranging from creamy white to yellow to deep purple; also known as a garden egg (especially in Africa), oriental eggplant and Japanese eggplant.

eggplant, Italian A variety of eggplant that looks like a miniature Western eggplant; also known as a baby eggplant.

eggplant, Western A variety of eggplant shaped like a large plump pear with a shiny lavender to purple-black skin.

eggplant caviar A dip or spread of thick, puréed roasted eggplant, onion, olive oil and seasonings.

egg poacher, immersible A small, footed utensil with a long handle and perforated oval bowl used to hold an egg while it is immersed in lightly vinegared simmering water.

egg roll A deep-fried Chinese pastry made from a thin flour and water dough wrapper folded around a savory filling of vegetables and sometimes meat. *See* spring roll.

egg roll skins Wafer-thin sheets of dough made from flour, eggs and salt and used to wrap fillings; available in squares or circles and used in Chinese and other Asian cuisines. *See* lumpia wrappers.

egg poacher

egg salad A salad of hard-boiled eggs, celery and onions bound with mayonnaise and flavored with cayenne.

eggs Benedict A brunch dish consisting of an English muffin topped with ham or Canadian bacon, a poached egg and hollandaise sauce.

egg separator A small cuplike vessel with a slot running midway around the perimeter; the egg white slides through the slot, leaving the yolk in the cup.

eggshell An egg's hard, brittle outer covering; composed of calcium carbonate, its color is determined by species and breed and has no effect on quality, flavor or nutrition.

eggs Hussarde (oo-sard) A brunch dish consisting of an English muffin topped with ham, a poached egg and a red wine sauce.

egg slicer A utensil with a hinged upper portion tautly strung with stainless steel wires and a base with an oval depression with slats that correspond to the wires; an egg is placed in the base and the top portion is brought down, cutting the egg into even slices.

eggs Minsk *See* yaitsa po-minski.

eggs Sardou (sahr-DOO) A brunch dish consisting of an artichoke heart topped with anchovy fillets, a poached egg and hollandaise sauce, sprinkled with chopped ham and garnished with a truffle slice.

egg slicer

egg substitute A liquid product usually made of egg white, food starch, corn oil, skim milk powder, artificial coloring and other additives; it does not contain cholesterol and is generally used like real eggs.

egg timer An hourglass that drains in 3 minutes, the time necessary to soft boil an egg.

egg wash A mixture of beaten eggs (whole eggs, yolks or whites) and a liquid, usually milk or water, used to coat doughs before baking to add sheen.

egg white *See* albumen.

egg yolk *See* yolk.

egrappoir (ay-gra-pwahr) French for stemmer; a device used to remove the stems from wine grapes, thus reducing the tannin in the wine.

Egri Bikaver (urh-ridge beek-lahol) Hungarian for bull's blood and used to describe a full-bodied red wine made from Kadarka grapes.

egusi (a-goo-sea) The small, pale, flat seeds of an African watermelon; they are eaten as a snack or ground and mixed to a paste and used to thicken stews and soups.

Egyptian lentils *See* lentils, Egyptian.

Egyptian rice A short-grain, round, semiglutinous rice used for puddings and stuffed vegetables in North African cuisines.

Ehrenfelser (AIR-en-fel-zer) A new German grape variety that is a cross of Riesling and Sylvaner with characteristics of the Riesling.

eider duck (igh-der) A duck chiefly prized for the down on its breast; although its flesh is rarely eaten, its eggs are a delicacy in Icelandic and Scandinavian cuisines.

Eier (IGH-err) German for egg.

Eiercreme (IGH-err-krem) German for custard.

eieren (AY-uh-ruh) Dutch for eggs.

8-9-8 package A 3-layered box of 25 cigars (9 in the middle and 8 on the top and bottom). *See* bundled cigars.

eight-precious pudding; eight treasures *See* pa-pao-fan.

86 Restaurant slang for being out of something, especially a beverage or menu item.

einbren (AIN-bern) Hebrew for thickening and usually used to describe flour or matzo meal used to thicken a gravy, soup or the like.

eingelegte (ihn-gae-leg-tah) German for pickled or preserved.

Eingemacht (ihn-ghae-mak-t) German pickles and/or preserves.

Einkorn (ain-corn) German for one grain and used to describe a variety of coarse-grain wheat cultivated in regions of central Europe with poor soil; also known as German wheat.

Einspanner (ihn-spahn-ner) German for hitch and used to describe a Viennese coffee drink of black coffee in a glass with whipped cream, sprinkled with chocolate powder.

Eintopf (ihn-toff) German for a one-dish meal; it usually contains both meats and vegetables.

Einzellage (AY'n-t'sel-lah-guh) German for a single vineyard and used to identify the origin of a Qualitätswein or Qualitätswein mit Prädikat wine (the village name often precedes the vineyard name).

Eis (eyess) German for ice and ice cream.

Eisbein (IGHS-bighn) A German dish of boiled, pickled shank of pork, served with boiled potatoes and sauerkraut.

Eisbock (ice-bok) An extra strong German bock beer made by freezing the beer then thawing it and drawing off the water, thus concentrating the flavor and alcohol content.

Eiswein (ice-vine) A labeling term for a sweet German wine made from perfectly ripe grapes that are partially frozen while on the vine (the freeze more than doubles the sugar in the unfrozen juice). *See* Qualitätswein mit Prädikat *and* icewine.

eja (eh-hah) A Brazilian dish of snapper marinated in lemon juice, malagueta chiles and dried shrimp and then fried; the thickened marinade is used as the sauce.

Ekte Gjetost (eck-tuh YEHT-ohst) A Norwegian and Swedish Gjetost cheese made from goat's milk.

elaichi (a-lay-chi) Hindi for cardamom.

elastin A protein found in connective tissues, particularly ligaments and tendons, that does not dissolve when cooked; it often appears as the white or silver covering on meats known as silverskin.

Elberta peach A variety of freestone peach with a red-blushed, yellow skin, a pinkish-yellow flesh, and a sweet flavor.

elbow macaroni Small semicircular tubes of pasta.

elderberry The fruit of the elder tree (*Sambucus canadensis*), which grows throughout the northern hemisphere; it has a purple-black skin and a very tart flavor; used for preserves, pies and wine; the berry contains a poisonous alkaloid that is destroyed during cooking.

elderberry wine A wine, usually produced at home, made from the berries and flowers of the elder tree; it has a flavor similar to that of muscatel.

elderflower The flower of the elder tree; it has white petals, which are used as a flavoring in preserves and fritters or as a garnish.

election cake A leavened fruitcake flavored with spices and sherry; traditionally baked to celebrate election day, especially in New England.

electrolytes Substances such as sodium, potassium and chlorine salts that, when dissolved, separate into ions capable of conducting an electrical charge; the body uses these substances to help transmit nerve impulses and maintain a normal fluid balance inside and outside the cells as well as a proper acid–base balance within the body.

electronic scale A scale that weighs objects according to the degree an internal spring is depressed when the object is placed on a tray above the spring; the weight is displayed on a digital readout that can be finely calibrated in the metric, U.S., or imperial system; electronic scales are often used as portion scales. *See* spring scale.

elegant A wine-tasting term for a well-balanced, graceful wine of breed and finesse.

elephant apple *See* wood apple.

elephant ear 1. A Midwest American deep-fried yeast dough confection; the dough is shaped into a large disk, deep-fried, and sprinkled with confectioners' sugar or cinnamon sugar while hot. 2. *See* palmier.

elephant garlic A member of the leek family; the very large cloves have a white outer layer, a pinkish-white interior and a mild garlicky flavor.

elevage (eh-lay-vahj) The art, science and practice of maturing wines.

elévage en fût (eh-lay-vahj ahn fuot) French for maturation in wooden casks; it is usually used to describe fruit brandies, not all of which are matured in wooden casks.

elevener Slang from the American South for a person who waits until midmorning before having his or her first drink of an alcoholic beverage.

Elijah Craig 1. Proprietary name for a Kentucky bourbon produced by the Heaven Hill distillery. 2. The Baptist preacher erroneously credited with founding the Kentucky bourbon industry, c. 1789.

Elisen (e-lee-zehn) A German gingerbread leavened with whipped egg whites.

elixir (ee-lick-sur) An archaic French term for liqueur.

ellies (eh-lee-es) Greek for olives.

elongated clam A variety of giant clam found in the Red Sea and Indian Ocean; it measures 5–8 in. (12.7–20.2 cm) across the shell.

elongated wine British term for a wine diluted with water to reduce the alcohol content for excise duty purposes.

El Salvadoran Arabica coffee beans grown in El Salvador; the beverage has a mild body and a light flavor.

Elstar apple A small apple with a red-blushed or red-spotted yellow skin, a firm yellowish flesh and a sharp flavor.

embers The smoldering coal or ash of a dying fire; the pieces of burning wood or coal usually glow with heat without producing a flame.

emblic A fruit (*Phyllanthus emblica*) native to tropical regions of Asia; it has a light green skin that becomes ivory-tan or dull yellow-green to red when ripe and has a crisp, juicy flesh.

embutido (ehm-boo-tee-doh) A Filipino dish consisting of ground pork stuffed with ham, pickles, eggs and raisins.

ementa (eh-men-tah) Portuguese for menu.

Emerald okra A variety of smooth-skinned okra with a dark green skin.

Emerald Riesling 1. A white wine grape developed in California by crossing the Riesling and Muscadelle grapes. 2. A white wine made from this grape; it is usually used as a blending wine but sometimes sold as a semidry varietal wine.

emetics Agents that cause vomiting.

Emiliano (ee-mee-lee-YAH-noh) A grana cheese made in Italy's Emilia region from cow's milk; it has a light yellow interior, a dark, oiled surface, a granular texture and a flavor that ranges from mild to rather sharp; used for grating.

émincé (ay-mahnss-say) French for chopped into small pieces; minced.

emince (eh-manss) A small, thin, boneless fabricated cut of meat.

Emmental; Emmentaler (EM-en-tahler) A firm cheese made in Switzerland's Emme River Valley from cow's milk; it has an ivory-gold color, medium-sized to large eyes, a natural light brown rind and a nutty, sweet flavor; sold in large wheels stamped with the word Switzerland on the rind like spokes; also commonly known as Swiss in the United States and Emmenthal in France. *See* Gruyère.

Emmenthal *See* Emmental.

emmer A very old form of wheat grown in Switzerland and southern Germany.

emotional eating Eating in response to feelings such as depression, anxiety, stress or anger and not because of hunger.

empadas (en-pah-dush) Brazilian version of empanaditas.

empadinhas (em-pah-deen-nyash) Brazilian version of empañadas.

empañadas (ehm-pah-NAH-dah) Deep-fried turnovers of various sizes, usually filled with meat, vegetables or a sweet filling; they are part of many South and Central American cuisines.

empañadas a la criolla (ehn-pah-NAH-dahs ah lah cree-oh-lah) Chilean turnovers stuffed with beef, raisins, olives and chiles and flavored with cumin, parsley and cilantro.

empanaditas Small empañadas.

empandita (em-pahn-dee-taw) A Spanish turnover; the type of filling is indicated by the turnover's shape.

Emperor grape An ovoid grape grown in California; it has a pale red to purple-red skin and a mild-flavored flesh with scattered seeds.

empregado (en-pruh-gah-doo) Portuguese for waiter.

empress sauce *See* impératrice, sauce.

empty calories Calories derived from foods such as alcoholic beverages, sugar and candies; so named because although these foods may be high in calories, they lack essential vitamins, minerals and amino acids; also known as foods of low nutrient density.

EMS *See* colorado claro.

emu A large flightless bird native to Australia; smaller than an ostrich, its meat is similar: lean and purple, turning brown when cooked and with a flavor similar to that of lean beef. *See* ostrich *and* rhea.

emulsification The process by which generally unmixable liquids, such as oil and water, are forced into a uniform distribution.

emulsifier; emulsifying agent A type of food additive used to aid emulsification (i.e., to create a uniform dispersion) as well as improve and/or preserve homogeneity and stability in processed foods.

emulsion 1. A uniform mixture of two unmixable liquids, often temporary (e.g., oil in water). 2. A flavoring oil, such as those from citrus fruits, mixed into water with the aid of emulsifiers.

enameled cast iron Cast iron coated with enamel to provide a protective coating and decrease surface tension; its use for cookware is prohibited in certain areas because the enamel surface chips easily, allowing a place for bacteria to grow and providing an opportunity for enamel chips to be ingested. *See* ironware.

enamelware Cast-iron or steel cookware that has been coated with enamel to prevent rusting.

en bordure (ahn bohr-dur') French for in a border and used to describe food prepared with a border of duchesse potatoes.

enchido Portuguese for stuffed.

enchilada (en-chuh-LAH-dah; en-chee-LAH-tha) A Mexican dish consisting of a soft corn tortilla wrapped around fish, shellfish, poultry, meat or cheese and topped with a tomato-based salsa, cheese, guacamole and/or sour cream; enchiladas are also served stacked, topped with a fried egg.

enchilada style A manner of garnishing Mexican foods such as burritos with a tomato-based salsa, cheese, guacamole and/or sour cream.

en cocotte (ahn koh-KOT) French for cooked in a casserole.

en croûte *See* croûte, en.

end cut A fabricated or subprimal cut of beef, veal, lamb or pork taken from the ends of a subprimal or primal cut; it consists of the outer edges or ends of the larger cut and usually produces smaller cuts that lack uniformity of appearance.

end cut pork chop A fabricated cut of the pork primal loin; it is a chop from either end of the loin (as opposed to the center) and is generally tough.

endive (ehn-deeve; ahn-deeve) 1. A plant (*Cichorium endivia*) with curly dark green leaves and a slightly bitter flavor; also known as curly endive and imprecisely known as chicory (especially in France and the United States). *See* chicory, escarole *and* frisée. 2. A term used imprecisely in the United States to describe Belgian endive.

endive, smooth A variety of endive with a pale heart, broad smooth leaves and a milder flavor than other endives.

endivia (en-dee-vee-ah) Italian for endive or curly-leafed lettuce.

Endivie German for endive (the green curly-leaf variety).

endocarp The part of a fleshy fruit that contains the seeds. *See* epicarp *and* mesocarp.

endo-mame (en-DOH-mah-meh) Japanese for peas.

endorphins Chemical substances produced in the brain that create pleasurable responses and reduce pain sensations.

endosperm The interior and largest portion of a cereal kernel; it has a high protein and starch content and is the part principally used for milled products.

end-to-end A meat-purchasing specification requesting that the butcher provide all the cuts made from the primal or subprimal.

energy The capacity of a system to do work; the body converts the chemical energy in nutrients (measured in calories) to mechanical, electrical, heat or other forms of energy.

Engadine nut torte A Swiss tartlike cake consisting of a pastry shell filled with a mixture of cream, honey and walnuts caramelized in sugar and topped with a layer of pastry.

Engelswurz (en-gulz-voors) German for angelica.

English breakfast A hearty breakfast consisting of eggs, meat (sausage, bacon, ham and/or fish), broiled tomatoes, mushrooms, baked goods, jam, fruit or juice and tea or coffee.

English breakfast tea A blend of several Indian and Sri Lankan black teas; the robust beverage is more full flavored and richly colored than one made from any single black tea.

English Cheddar *See* Cheddar, English.

English chop A fabricated cut of the veal primal loin and the lamb primal loin; it contains part of the kidney; also known as a kidney chop.

English cucumber; English seedless cucumber A long, virtually seedless cucumber with a mild flavor and dark green skin; also known as a hothouse cucumber.

English cut roast A subprimal cut of the beef primal chuck; it is tough and flavorful and has the bones intact.

English dairy cheese A hard English Cheddar-style cheese made from cow's milk; it is used principally for cooking.

English fruitcake *See* black cake.

English Market Selection (EMS) *See* colorado claro.

English monkey An American dish made from bread crumbs, milk, butter, tomatoes and cheese poured over crackers.

English Morello cherry *See* Morello cherry.

English muffin A thin, round bread made with yeast dough and baked on a griddle, usually split and toasted for service.

English peas *See* green garden peas.

English sole A member of the flounder family found off the U.S. West Coast; it has a brownish-gray skin, a white flesh, a mild flavor, and an average market weight of 0.75 lb. (340 g); also known as lemon sole and California Dover sole.

English walnut A nut (*Juglans regia*) with a hard, wrinkled, tan shell enclosing two double-lobed sections; it has a sweet flavor and is used for snacking, in sweet and savory dishes, and for obtaining oil; also known as the Persian walnut. *See* black walnut.

English wheat *See* froment renfle.

English whole grain mustard A hot, pungent mustard made from whole mustard seeds, white wine, allspice and black pepper.

enguias (en-goo-yass) Portuguese for eels.

enguias de escabeche (en-goo-yass day es-kah-bah-cha) A Portuguese petisco dish consisting of small eels fried in a well-seasoned marinade and served with fried onion rings.

enkephalos (een-kee-phaa-los) Greek for brains.

Ennis hazelnut A hazelnut variety; the nuts have a superior flavor.

enoki; enokitake; enokidake (en-oh-kee; en-oh-kee-TAH-kee) A mushroom (*Flammulina velutipes*) native to Japan but now cultivated in the United States; grown in clumps, the mushroom has a long, thin stem, a tiny white or pale orange cap, a crunchy texture and a mild, almost fruity flavor; it is usually eaten raw or used as a garnish (heat tends to toughen it); also known as Christmas mushroom, velvet stem mushroom and winter mushroom.

enologist; oenologist (ee-nahl-oh-jist) *See* winemaker.

enology; oenology (ee-NAHL-uh-jee) The art and science of wine production from harvest to vinification to bottling.

enophile; oenophile (EE-nuh-file) A wine connoisseur.

enoteca (eh-no-TEK-kah) An Italian establishment where patrons can sample and buy wine.

en papillote (ahn pah-pee-yoa) *See* papillote, en.

enquial (en-quee-ahl) Ethiopian for egg.

enrich To thicken or enhance a sauce by adding butter, egg yolks or cream just before service.

enriched Subject to U.S. Food and Drug Administration (FDA) regulations, a processed grain or cereal product such as bread, flour or rice to which specific vitamins (riboflavin, niacin and thiamine) and iron have been added during processing, either to replace nutrients lost during processing or to supplement naturally occurring ones. *See* fortified.

enriched bleached flour Flour that has been whitened to remove yellow pigments and fortified with vitamins and minerals.

enricher An ingredient such as cream, sour cream or a liaison added to a sauce to give it more flavor.

enrobe To coat a candy or pastry with chocolate, sugar or fondant, usually by pouring rather than dipping.

ensalada (een-sah-LAH-tah) Spanish for salad.

ensalada del salmón marinada (een-sah-LAH-tah del sau-mon mah-reh-nah-dah) A Spanish tapas of marinated salmon served on a variety of lettuce leaves.

ensalata mixta (een-sah-LAH-tah meex-tah) A Spanish tapas salad of lettuce, tomatoes, olives and tuna fish.

en sauce (ahn suas) French for a method of braising fish fillets and converting the braising liquid into a sauce, using various processes.

ensopado de borrego (en-sow-paw-doe day poh-ra-go) A Portuguese dish of lamb ragoût served over sourdough bread.

en suite (ahn sweet) A British term describing a bed and breakfast accommodation of a bedroom with an attached private bathroom.

Entamoeba histolytica A species of parasitic amoeba that causes amoebic dysentery (called amoebiasis) when found in the human intestinal tract; common sources include contaminated water and food.

Ente (EHN-ter) German for duck.

Entenbrust (EHN-ter-broost) German for duck breast.

entercuisse (ahn-tar-kwis-sae) French for the second joint or thigh of poultry and game birds.

en tirage (ahn tee-rahj) A description of a sparkling wine during the secondary fermentation.

entosensal (en-tos-sen-sal) Filipino for caul fat.

entrada (een-traa-tha) A Greek dish consisting of simmered meat, usually beef, and vegetables such as onions, carrots, celery, tomatoes and potatoes.

entrails The internal organs contained within the trunk of an animal; includes the liver, intestines, stomach, kidneys and so on.

entrecôte (ahn-treh-KOHT) French for between the ribs and used to describe a French cut of the beef carcass that is the flesh between the 9th and 11th ribs; it is the classic French steak.

entrée (ahng-tray) 1. In the United States, the main dish of a meal and often consisting of meat, poultry, fish or shellfish accompanied by a starch and/or vegetable. 2. In many European countries, the first course.

entremesas (ehn-treh-MAY-sehs) Spanish for appetizers.

entremetier (ehm-tray-mee-tee-ay) At a food services operation following the brigade system, the person responsible for the combined functions of the potager and legumier.

entremets (ehm-tray-mais) The course served after the roast at a classic cuisine-style banquet; usually composed of vegetables, fruits, fritters or sweets.

enzian (en-zee-ahn) A Scandinavian distilled spirit made from the long roots of the yellow mountain gentian plant; it is quite bitter and is usually served icy cold after dinner.

enzymatic browning *See* acidulation.

enzyme Any of various protein substances that act as a catalyst for chemical changes in organic substances.

enzyme-modified fats Food additives derived from fats processed with enzymes and used as flavoring agents and/or adjuvants.

E.P. *See* edible portion *and* European plan.

épaule (ay-pahl) French for a shoulder cut of meat.

épaule braisée ménagère (ay-pahl brah-see meh-nagh-yair) A French dish consisting of lamb shoulder stuffed with sausage meat and braised in white wine with onions, carrots and potatoes.

epazote (eh-pah-soh-teh) An herb (*Chenopodium ambrosiodes*) native to the Americas with a kerosene-like aroma and a wild, strong flavor; it is used fresh in Mexican and American Southwestern cuisines and used dried for a beverage; also known as stinkweed and wormweed.

épergne (ay-pern-yah) An elaborate center dish or ornament used for the dinner table; it typically has multiple arms to hold small plates of fruit, sweetmeats or desserts.

éperlan (ah-pair-lahn) French for smelt.

epi (ay-pee) 1. French for an ear of wheat. 2. A yeast dough baguette that is shaped to resemble a stalk of wheat.

epicarp The outer part or skin of a fleshy fruit of the genus *Prunus*. *See* endocarp *and* mesocarp.

épice (ay-pis) French for spice.

épices fines (ay-pis feen) French for fine spices and used to describe a spice and herb blend that generally includes white pepper, allspice, mace, nutmeg, rosemary, sage, bay leaves, cloves, cinnamon and marjoram.

epicure (EHP-ih-kyoor) One who cultivates the knowledge and appreciation of fine foods and wines.

Epicurus A Greek philosopher who espoused the pursuit of happiness (or the avoidance of pain and disturbance); this philosophy has often been interpreted as praising an indulgence in luxury and sensual pleasures.

épigramme (ay-pee-grahm) A French dish of two slices of lamb (usually a slice from the breast and a cutlet or chop) cooked, dipped in egg and bread crumbs and grilled or fried.

épinard (ay-pee-NAHR) French for spinach.

épine-vinette (a-peen-vee-net) French for barberry.

eple (EHP-ler) Norwegian for apple.

éplucher (a-pluh-shae) French for to peel.

Époisses (ay-pwass) A soft cheese made in Burgundy, France, from cow's milk; it has a smooth, creamy interior, a pleasant flavor and a slightly orange crust that is washed with the local white wine or marc.

éponger (ay-ponh-jhay) French for sponge and referring to the process of draining foods cooked in water or oil.

Epsom salts A processed form of gypsum.

equity 1. The original investment in a business plus any retained earnings. 2. Assets minus liabilities.

erba (AIR-bay) Italian for herb.

erba cipollina (her-bah chee-poll-een-nah) Italian for chives.

erbetté (ehr-BEHR-tah) A vegetable native to Italy with a small, spear-shaped green leaf on a slim, green, tender stalk; it has a slightly bitter, tart flavor; also known as bìetoline.

Erbsen (EHRP-senn) German for peas, usually dried.

Erdapfel (EHRD-ah-pfel) German for potato; also known as Kartoffel.

Erdbeeren (EHRT-bay-ren) German for strawberries.

Erdnuβ German for peanut.

ergogenic To increase work; a food-labeling term (not approved by the FDA) intended to suggest that the particular food or supplement provides energy.

ergosterol, irradiated A food additive used to fortify milk with vitamin D.

eritadenine A substance found in shiitakes that is believed to lower blood cholesterol levels.

ersatz food A substitute food; a food product created to resemble or substitute for a natural food (e.g., a hamburger made from textured plant protein).

erter (AE-terr) Norwegian for peas.

erva (ehr-vah) Portuguese for herb.

ervilha (ehr-VEEL-yah) Portuguese for pea.

Ervy (er-vee) A soft, rich, Camembert-style cheese made in France's Champagne region.

erwtjes (EHR-tyus) Dutch for pea.

eryngo; eringo Candied aromatic sea holly root (*Etyngium maritimum*); thought to be an aphrodisiac.

erythorbic acid *See* ascorbic acid.

erythrosine *See* FD&C Red #3.

Erzeugerabfüllung (AIR-t'zoo-gher-AHB-foo-lung) German wine-labeling term for bottled by the proprietor; similar in concept to estate bottled, but it can also be used by cooperative cellars.

ESB *See* extra special bitter.

escabèche (es-keh-BEHSH) A Spanish dish of poached or fried fish soaked in a spicy marinade and served chilled.

escalibada (es-cah-lee-bah-dah) A dish from Spain's Catalonia region consisting of mixed vegetables, such as sweet peppers, eggplants, tomatoes and onions, grilled over charcoal.

escalivada (ess-cah-leh-vah-dah) A Spanish dish of oven-cooked vegetables such as eggplant, peppers, tomatoes and onions flavored with garlic and wine vinegar.

escallop (eh-SKAH-laph) To bake foods (e.g., potatoes or fish) with a sauce topped with bread crumbs.

escalope (eh-SKAL-oph) A French term for a thin scallop of meat.

escalope de veau (eh-SKAL-oph duh voh) French for a thin slice of veal and used to describe a slice that has been flattened and usually dredged in flour before sautéing.

escargot (ays-skahr-go) French for snail.

escargot achatine A large snail weighing up to 1 lb. (500 g) bred in Asia and imported from China; chunks of its flesh are sometimes put in Burgundy snail shells and marketed simply as escargot.

escargot de Bourgogne (ays-skahr-go day boor-gone-yay) A land snail from France's Burgundy region; it has a dull, yellowish-brown shell, a market length of 1.75 in. (4.1 cm), and a mottled grayish-tan flesh with a rich flavor and firm, tender texture; also known as the Burgundy snail.

escargot fork A small slender fork with two very sharp tines; used to extract the snail from its shell or simply to eat the snail if served on a dish; also known as a snail fork.

escargot fork

escargot petit-gris (ays-skahr-go peh-te-GREE) A snail found in southern Europe; it has a yellow-flecked white shell, an average market length of less than 1 in. (2.5 cm), and a brownish-gray flesh with a more delicate flavor than that of the larger escargot de Bourgogne.

escargot plate A plate with indentions to hold snail shells (usually 6 or 12) during baking and service; also known as a snail plate.

escargots bourguignonne (eays-skahr-go boorg-ee-enyun) A French dish of snails served hot in their shells or ceramic cups and cooked in butter flavored with shallots, garlic and parsley.

escargot plate

escargot tongs Spring-operated tongs used to hold a snail shell while extracting the meat; they are opened by applying pressure on the handles; also known as snail tongs.

escarole (es-kah-roll) An endive with broader, paler, less curly leaves and a less bitter flavor; also known as Batavian endive.

Escherichia coli (E. coli) A species of bacteria that causes acute diarrheal disease; the bacteria are transmitted by infected food handlers and through ingestion of contaminated foods (especially milk) or water.

Escoffier (es-kohf-fyay) A cocktail made of Calvados, Cointreau, Dubonnet rouge and Angostura bitters; garnished with a maraschino cherry.

Escoffier, Auguste (Fr., 1846–1935) A chef known for refining and defining French cuisine and dining during the late 19th century; he operated dining rooms for the finest hotels in Europe, including the Savoy and the Carlton in London and the Place Vendôme in Paris, and authored several culinary texts, including *Ma Cuisine* (1934) and a treatise for professional chefs, *Le Guide Culinaire* (1903).

eshkolit (as-koe-lit) Hebrew for grapefruit.

esophagus The muscular tube that, by means of peristalsis, passes swallowed food from the mouth to the stomach.

espadarte (ess-pah-dhare-ta) Portuguese for swordfish.

espadarte fumado (ess-pah-dhare-ta fu-mah-toh) A Portuguese petisco dish of thin-sliced smoked swordfish.

espadon (es-pah-doan) French for swordfish.

espagnole, mayonnaise á l' (ess-spah-noyl) A French mayonnaise sauce flavored with garlic, mustard and paprika and garnished with ham; also known as Spanish mayonnaise.

espagnole, sauce (ess-spah-noyl) A French leading sauce made of brown stock, mirepoix and tomatoes and thickened by brown roux; it is often used to produce a demiglaze; also known as brown sauce and Spanish sauce.

esparguetes (esh-pahr-geh-tish) Portuguese for spaghetti.

espárrago (ehs-PAHRR-ah-goh) Spanish for asparagus.

especia (es-pay-syal) Spanish for spice.

especiaria (esh-peh-syah-ah-ree-ah) Portuguese for spice.

espinacas (ehs-prr-NAH-kahs) Spanish for spinach.

espinacas con passas y piñones (ehs-prr-NAH-kahs con pah-SAHS e pin-YOHN-nez) A Spanish dish consisting of spinach cooked with raisins and pine nuts.

espinafre (ess-pee-NAH-fray) Portuguese for spinach.

espresso (ess-PRESS-o) 1. An Italian coffee-brewing method in which hot water is forced through finely ground and packed coffee (usually very dark roasted beans) under high pressure; the resulting beverage is thick, strong, rich and smooth, not bitter or acidic. 2. The resulting beverage; it is usually served in a small cup or used as an ingredient in other coffee drinks.

Espresso An Italian liqueur made from Illy coffee; also known as Illy Coffee Liqueur.

espresso con panna (ess-PRESS-o cone PA-na) An Italian beverage of espresso marked with a dollop of whipped cream; usually served in a small cup.

espresso cup A small cup with a handle and a capacity of approximately 1.5 fl. oz.

espresso lungo (ess-press-o loon-go) An Italian beverage of espresso made with almost twice as much water as a regular espresso; popular in the United States.

espresso machiatto (ess-PRESS-o mock-e-AH-toe) An Italian beverage of espresso marked with a dollop of steamed milk; usually served in a small cup.

espresso maker An hourglass-shaped assemblage used to make espresso; the base is filled with water and the center basket with finely ground coffee; heat forces the steam and boiling water through a central vent and across the coffee grounds; the finished espresso is then received in the top container.

espresso maker

espresso powder A powder made from dried roasted espresso beans; it is used to give a rich coffee flavor and aroma to pastries, desserts and confections.

espresso roast *See* roast, espresso.

espumante (esh-poo-mun-teh) Portuguese for a sparkling wine.

espumoso (ess-poo-MOH-soh) Spanish for sparkling, especially as applied to a sparkling wine such as a cava or granvas.

esqueixada (es-que-es-saw-dah) A tapas from Spain's Catalonia region; it consists of a dried salt cod salad with fresh pepper, tomato and onion.

Esrom (EHS-rom) A Port du Salut–style cheese made in Esrom, Denmark, from pasteurized cow's milk; it has a thin, yellow-brown rind, a pale yellow interior and a mild flavor; also known as Danish Port Salut.

essen (assen) German for to eat.

essence 1. A concentrated liquid usually made from an herb, spice or flower and used as a flavoring or aromatic. 2. French for the concentrated stock or extract of a flavorful ingredient (e.g., mushroom, truffle, celery or leek); it can be used as a sauce (sometimes either finished with butter or emulsified as a vinaigrette) or as a flavoring ingredient for classic sauces.

Essencia An extremely sweet style of Hungarian Tokay.

essential amino acids Amino acids that cannot be synthesized in the body at all or in amounts sufficient to maintain health and must be supplied by the diet; generally recognized as essential for a normal adult are histidine, isoleucine, leucine, lysine, methionine, cysteine, phenylalanine, tyrosine, threonine, tryptophan and valine; arginine is considered essential for infants and children but not adults, and some nutritionists consider tyrosine and cysteine nonessential. *See* complete proteins.

essential fatty acids Unsaturated fatty acids (linoleic, linolenic and arachidonic) that cannot be synthesized in the body in amounts sufficient to maintain health and must be supplied by the diet (principally from fish oils and certain vegetable oils such as corn and peanut).

essential nutrients Nutrients such as minerals, many vitamins and certain amino acids the body cannot synthesize at all or in amounts sufficient to meet its needs; necessary for growth and health, they must be obtained through the diet.

essential oils The volatile oils that give plants their distinctive fragrances; these oils, usually composed of esters, can be extracted or distilled from some flowers, leaves, seeds, resins or roots and used as aromatics and flavorings in cooking (e.g., peppermint oil and citrus oil) and the production of alcoholic beverages.

Essig (EHS-sikh) German for vinegar.

est' (esst) Russian for to eat. *See* kushat'.

establishment number The numerical designation for a meatpacking or meat-processing plant that complies with all requirements for federal inspection; it appears on the inspection stamp.

éstaminet (eh-sta-mee-NEY) A Belgian café or bistro.

estate bottled A wine-labeling term indicating that the wine was bottled on the property where it was produced by the vineyard owner; this guarantees a wine's origin but not quality.

esters Volatile compounds formed by combining acids and alcohol; many have flowery, fruity or spicy aromas and are used to add aroma and flavors to foods, especially fermented products such as beer and wine.

Est! Est! Est! di Montefiascone (EHST EHST EHST dee mawn-teh-fyahs-KAW-neh) A light, dry white wine made from the Trebbiano and Malvasia grapes in Italy's Lake Bolsena region.

estilo de; estilo al (es-tea-low day; es-tea-low ahl) Spanish for in the style of.

Estiman potato A variety of medium-sized potato with a light brown skin and yellow flesh; generally grown in the northeastern United States.

estimated costs The costs (expenses) that a business expects to incur over a given period; generally based on prior performance or industry standards.

estimated sales The sales that a business expects to make over a given period; generally based on prior performance or industry standards.

estofado (ehs-toh-FAH-doh) 1. A Filipino dish of meat simmered with vinegar, sugar and spices. 2. Spanish for braised meat or meat cooked in a casserole.

Estomacal-Bonet (es-toh-mah-cal-bow-net) A Spanish liqueur similar to Izzara.

estouffade (ehs-toh-fhad) 1. A French stew in which the pieces of meat are first browned in fat before moistening, usually with white or red wine. 2. A concentrated brown stock made with both beef and veal; the term is rarely used in this sense in modern kitchens.

estragao (esh-trah-geow) Portuguese for tarragon.

estragon (ehst-rah-gah-nohn) Russian for tarragon.

estragon; Estragon (ess-trah-GON) French, German (with a capital e), Norwegian, Spanish and Swedish for tarragon.

estragon, sauce à l' (ess-trah-GON, ah-l') A French compound sauce made from a demi-glaze flavored with shallots and tarragon and garnished with tarragon; also known as tarragon sauce.

estufa (esh-TOO-fah) Portuguese for hothouse; and used to describe the heated cellar where casks of Madeira are baked.

esturgeon (es-tuhr-joahn) French for sturgeon.

esturion (es-too-ryon) Spanish for sturgeon.

eta (ah-tah) A flat-ended wooden tool used for mashing foods in West Africa (especially Ghana).

étamine (eh-tay-meen) A French cloth used for straining stocks, sauces and the like.

ethanoic acid *See* acetic acid.

Ethiopian Mocha *See* Moka.

ethnic cuisine Generally, the cuisine of a group of people having a common cultural heritage, as opposed to the cuisine of a group of people bound together by geographical or political factors.

ethoxylated mono- and diglycerides Food additives used as emulsifiers in processed foods such as cakes and cake mixes, icings and icing mixes, frozen desserts and dairy substitutes for coffee.

ethoxyquin A food additive used as an antioxidant, preservative and/or color stabilizer in processed foods such as dried chile products.

ethyl acetate A chemical solvent used in the direct contact method of decaffeinating coffee.

ethyl acetate, ethyl butyrate and ethyl caproate Food additives with fruitlike flavors and aromas used as flavoring agents and/or adjuvants.

ethyl alcohol (ETOH) A colorless, volatile, flammable, water-miscible liquid with an etherlike aroma and a burning flavor produced by the yeast fermentation of certain carbohydrates; the intoxicating component of alcoholic beverages; also known as alcohol, fermentation alcohol, grain alcohol, pure alcohol, spirits and spirits of wine.

ethyl cellulose A food additive used in the manufacture of vitamin preparations and as a flavor stabilizer in processed foods such as artificial flavors.

ethyl crotonate A food additive with a sharp, winelike aroma used as a flavoring agent.

ethyl oxyhydrate *See* rum ether.

ethylenediaminetetraacetate (EDTA) A food additive used as a preservative in processed foods such as mayonnaise and dressings.

ethylene gas A colorless, odorless hydrocarbon gas naturally emitted from fruits and fruit-vegetables; it encourages ripening.

ethylene oxide polymer A food additive used as a foam stabilizer in fermented malt beverages.

ethylenesuccinic acid *See* succinic acid.

ethyl formate A food additive used as a flavoring agent in processed foods such as baked goods, frozen dairy desserts and confections; also known as ethyl methanoate.

ethyl isobutyrate A food additive with a dry, fruity aroma used as a flavoring agent in candies, baked goods and beverages.

ethyl lactate A food additive with a sherrylike aroma used as a flavoring agent in beverages.

ethyl maltol A food additive with a distinctive sweet, fruity aroma used as a flavoring agent.

ethyl methanoate *See* ethyl formate.

ethyl-methyl-phenyl-glycidate A food additive with a strawberry-like aroma used as a flavoring agent in candies, beverages and ice creams.

ethyl nonanoate A food additive with a fruity, Cognaclike aroma used as a flavoring agent in alcoholic beverages, ice creams and candies.

ethyl propionate A food additive with a rumlike aroma used as a flavoring agent in beverages, candies and baked goods.

ethyl sorbate A food additive with a fruity aroma used as a pineapple, papaya and passion fruit flavoring agent in ice creams, beverages, candies and baked goods.

ethyl vanillin A food additive with a strong vanilla-like aroma used as a flavoring agent.

étouffée (eh-too-fay) French for smothered and used to describe a stewed dish cooked with little or no liquid in a tightly closed pot; usually served over white rice.

Ettinger avocado A large, pear-shaped avocado with a shiny green skin and green-yellow flesh; it is soft when ripe.

etto A standard unit of measure in Italy; it is equal to 100 g (3.3 oz.).

étuver; étouffer (eh-too-vay) A French term describing how a food is to be covered while it is being cooked; in most recipes, the term implies that the food is to be cooked in a very small amount of liquid, but it could also mean that the food is to be cooked in a covered container. *See* casserole braising.

eucalyptus 1. Any of numerous trees of the genus *Eucalyptus,* native to Australia; the leaves yield an oil with a distinctive sharp aroma used for candies and medicines. 2. A wine-tasting term for the aroma reminiscent of the evergreen species; it is found in some California Cabernet Sauvignon and Pinot Noir wines.

eugenyl acetate, eugenyl benzoate, eugenyl formate and eugenyl methyl ether Food additives with a spicy flavor used as flavoring agents and/or adjuvants.

eulachon A variety of smelt found in the Pacific Ocean from Alaska to California; it has a silvery body with olive green markings, an average market length of 12 in. (30.4 cm), a very high fat content, and a rich flavor; a significant market variety is the Columbia River smelt; also known as candlefish or candlelight fish (Native Americans used dried smelts with a bark wick as a source of light).

Eureka lemon A common variety of lemon.

European eel *See* eel, European.

European flat oyster *See* Belon.

European lentils *See* lentils, French.

European oak A general term given to barrels used in the wine trade made from oak trees (genus *Quercus*) grown principally in France and the Balkans.

European plaice *See* plaice, European.

European plan (EP) A daily hotel rate for a room; no meals are included.

European roast *See* roast, European.

European tomato knife *See* tomato knife.

evaporated milk *See* milk, evaporated.

evaporated skim milk *See* milk, evaporated skim.

evaporation The process by which heated water molecules move faster and faster until the water turns to gas (steam) and vaporizes; evaporation is responsible for the drying of foods during cooking.

Eva's Purple Ball An heirloom tomato with a pinkish-purple skin, a spherical shape, a juicy interior and a sweet flavor.

everything bagel A bagel topped with sesame seeds, poppy seeds, coarse salt, garlic and onion flakes.

eviscerate *See* draw.

Evora (a voh-raw) A firm, tart Portuguese ewe's milk cheese.

ewe's milk *See* milk, ewe's.

ewe's milk cheeses Cheeses made from ewe's milk; they typically have a white to pale yellow color, a firm to hard texture and a sharp, pungent flavor; many are aged.

excise tax The tax levied by the U.S. government on the alcohol content by volume of distilled spirits, malt beverages and wine.

executive chef At a large food services operation, the person responsible for coordinating and directing kitchen activities, developing menu items, educating dining room staff, purchasing food and equipment and so on.

exercise Bodily exertion or the performance of muscle activities, voluntary or otherwise, especially to maintain or improve fitness. *See* aerobic exercise *and* anaerobic exercise.

exotic A coffee-tasting term used to describe an unusual aroma or flavor such as those reminiscent of flowers, berries or sweet spices.

expandable pastry cutter *See* dough divider.

expandable steamer basket *See* steamer basket.

expediter *See* aboyeur.

expense The cost of assets or resources used or consumed to generate revenue.

expiration date A date stamped by a manufacturer, distributor or retailer on a food product's label indicating the last date on which the consumer should use it; the date is usually preceded by the phrase "use by."

Explorateur (ex-ploh-rah-tuhr) A triple cream cheese made in La Tretoire, France, from cow's milk; it contains 75% milkfat and has a bloomy white rind, an ivory interior and a delicate, rich flavor.

exterior fat *See* subcutaneous fat.

external cue theory The theory that some people eat in response to external factors such as the time of day or the aroma or sight of food rather than in response to the internal sensation of hunger.

extra A marketing designation for Spanish rice with a maximum of 4% broken grains. *See* primero.

Extra A labeling term for brandy, Cognac and Armagnac indicating a product of extremely high quality and that the youngest brandy used in the blend was at least 5 1/2 years old.

extract of malted barley and corn *See* malted cereal syrup.

extracts 1. Concentrated mixtures of ethyl alcohol and flavoring oils such as vanilla, lemon and almond. 2. Concentrated flavors obtained by distilling, steeping and/or pressing foods. 3. Sugars derived from malt during the mashing process in brewing and distillation. 4. Nonvolatile and nonsoluble substances in wine such as acids, tannins and pigments; to the taster, they indicate the presence of elements that add flavor and character.

extra dry A dry sparkling wine; sweeter than brut, it contains 1.2–2% sugar; also known imprecisely as extra brut. *See* brut, demi-sec *and* sec.

extra lean A food-labeling term approved by the FDA to describe meat, poultry, game, fish or shellfish that contains less than 5 g of fat, less than 2 g of saturated fat and less than 95 mg of cholesterol per serving or per 100 g.

Extra Old A label designation of a brandy's quality (the brandy must have aged for approximately 30 years in the cask); often written as XO.

extra special bitter (ESB) A style of beer that is malty, full bodied and rich in color.

extremeña (ex-trae-meen-yah) A Spanish blood sausage made with chopped meat, potatoes or pumpkin.

extrusion The process of forcing dough (e.g., pasta) through perforated plates to create various shapes.

eye round; eye of round A subprimal cut of the beef primal round; it is not attached to the leg bone and is flavorful and somewhat tough; it is sometimes combined with the bottom round for a roast or fabricated into steaks.

eyes The holes found in some cheeses; they are formed by gases released during aging.

eysines A variety of medium-sized, spherical squash with a white-spotted green skin.

Ezekiel mix A mixture of flours and grains based on a biblical formula found in Ezekiel 4:9; it usually contains wheat flour, barley, spelt, millet and ground lentils.

faarekød (fah-rah-cod) Danish for mutton.

Fabaceae The leguminous plant family that includes lentils, beans, peas, chickpeas and soybeans.

fabada asturiana (fah-BAH-dah as-tou-ree-ahn-nah) A Spanish peasant stew consisting of dried fava beans cooked slowly with salt pork, ham, sausages and onions.

fabricate To cut a large item into smaller portions; it often refers to the butchering of meat, poultry or fish.

fabricated cut A small cut of meat or an individual portion cut from a subprimal cut.

fabricated product A food item after trimming, boning, portioning and so on.

fabricated yield percentage The yield or edible portion of a food item expressed as a percentage of the amount of the item purchased.

faca (fah-kah) Portuguese for knife.

face round A subprimal cut of the beef primal round; cut from the side of the round, it is flavorful and somewhat tough.

factory cheese *See* dairy cheese.

facultative bacteria; facultative anaerobes *See* bacteria, facultative.

fad diets Popular reduction diets offering quick weight loss; often nutritionally unsound and sometimes dangerous, they frequently provide an early and temporary weight loss accomplished by metabolizing proteins from lean muscles and water loss.

faded A wine-tasting term for a flat, insipid wine or one that has lost its character, usually through age.

Fadennudeln (faden-nudelin) German for vermicelli; usually made into a sweet dish.

faggots (feh-go) 1. A northern English and Welsh dish consisting of a forcemeat made with pork offal, bread crumbs, onions and spices pressed into a large tin, covered with pig's caul, and baked or braised (if braised, the caul is omitted and the forcemeat is shaped into balls); served hot or cold. 2. Fresh herbs and spices tied together into a bundle.

fagiano (fah-JAA-noa) Italian for pheasant.

fagioli (fa-ZHOH-lee) Italian for beans, usually referring to white kidney beans.

fagiolini (fah-joa-LEE-nee) Italian for string beans.

Fahrenheit (FAIR-uhn-hyt) A temperature scale with 32° as the freezing point of water and 212° as its boiling point; to convert to Celsius, subtract 32 from the Fahrenheit, multiply by 5, and divide by 9.

faïence (fay-ahns) A type of white or patterned pottery used for tableware and traditionally made in Faenza, Italy; the earthenware is covered with a tin glaze so that the color is completely masked.

faiglan (fay-glahn) A round, spiraling yeast bread (often made with challah dough) and served on Jewish holidays, especially New Year's.

faire tomber à glace (fare thom-bay ah glass) French for the process of reducing a liquid, such as a stock or a sauce, until the sugars caramelize and separate from any fat contained in the liquid.

fairing A traditional term for foods, usually sweets or cakes such as gingerbread nuts, sold at British and American fairs.

fair water Archaic term for fresh water.

fairy bread A British snack consisting of slices of fresh bread spread with butter and coated with hundreds and thousands.

fairy ring mushroom A mushroom (*Marasimus oreades*) that grows in a ring on areas of short-cropped grass, especially in Europe, and has a mild flavor; with a slender stem and a round, flat cap, it appears similar to certain poisonous mushrooms; also known as faux mousseron.

faisán (feh-zahng) French for pheasant.

faisan (figh-SSAHN) Spanish for pheasant

faisão (fay-ZAHNG) Portuguese for pheasant.

Faiscre Grotha An Irish cream cheese–style cheese made from cow's milk.

fait tout (fay too) French for do all and used to describe a flare-sided saucepan.

fajita meat (fah-HEE-tuh) Extra lean, boneless meat or poultry cut into narrow, irregular strips, usually 1–3 in. (2.54–7.6 cm) long.

fajitas (fah-HEE-tuhs) A Mexican–American dish consisting of strips of skirt steak marinated in lime juice, oil, garlic and red pepper, and then grilled; the diner wraps the meat in a flour tortilla and garnishes it with items such as grilled onions and peppers, guacamole, pico de gallo, refried beans, sour cream and salsa; chicken, pork, fish and shellfish (usually shrimp) can be substituted.

Fajy *See* Biza.

fakheth lahum ghanum (fahk-heh'th lah'um gah-num) A Middle Eastern dish consisting of roast leg of lamb flavored with pepper, ginger, marjoram, sage and thyme.

faki (faa-khee) 1. Greek for brown lentils. 2. A Greek soup made from brown lentils and flavored with vinegar.

falafel; felafel (feh-LAH-fehl) Middle Eastern deep-fried balls of highly spiced, ground chickpeas; usually served in pita bread with a yogurt sauce or tahini.

Falerno (fah-LAIR-no) Red and white wines popular in ancient Rome.

falernum A flavoring syrup made from a simple syrup, lime juice, almonds, ginger and spices; used as a sweetener and flavoring ingredient for rum drinks.

Falscher Hase (FAHL-shur HAH-zuh) A German dish consisting of chopped beef, veal and pork mixed with eggs and flavored with onions, capers, lemon juice, butter and seasonings, shaped into a loaf, rolled in bread crumbs and baked in butter; the pan drippings are boiled with cream and poured over the loaf.

false edge *See* knife point.

false meat *See* blade meat.

false saffron *See* safflower.

false Solomon's seal *See* treacle berry.

false truffle *See* horn of plenty mushroom.

false wine Wine made from sources other than grapes; also known as second wine.

faluche (fah-loos-chay) A small, round Belgian bread that is cut open, spread with butter and sugar and heated in the oven before eating.

family 1. A botanical and zoological term to describe a group of related genera. 2. An imprecisely used term to describe a group of seemingly related plants or animals.

family restaurant A food service establishment specializing in menus and amenities that appeal to families; these amenities include children's menus, high chairs, booster seats, booths and inexpensive, often homestyle or popular ethnic foods.

fàn (fahn) Chinese for rice.

fanciest Formosa oolong An expensive Taiwanese oolong tea; the beverage has a peachy, nutty and slightly peppery flavor.

fancy 1. Fish that has been frozen previously. 2. A quality grade of fruits, especially canned or frozen.

F and B *See* food and beverage manager.

faneca (fah-nah-cah) Portuguese for a type of small cod.

fanesca (fah-ness-kah) A vegetable soup from Ecuador made with corn, rice, cabbage, squash, green beans, peas and peanuts and flavored with salt cod, garlic, onions, oregano, cumin and chiles; it is served with queso blanco.

fanguan (fahn-goo-ahn) Chinese for restaurant.

fanner basket A large flat basket used throughout much of Africa for winnowing grains.

fannings Moderate-sized particles of broken tea leaves. *See* orange fannings *and* dust.

fan shell scallop A variety of scallop found in the Mediterranean Sea; it has a white shell with a diameter of 4–5 in. (10.1–12.7 cm) and a tender, sweet, white meat.

fan si (fahn see) Chinese cellophane noodles.

får (fohr) Norwegian for mutton.

farambwaz (fah-ram-buass) Arabic for raspberry.

faraona (fah-rah-OA-nah) Italian for guinea fowl.

farareg *See* mumbar.

farasine (fah-rah-seen) Ribbon-shaped Italian pasta; the noodles are available in long blocks.

farawla (fa-rou-leh) Arabic for strawberry.

farayah A variety of long, bluish dates; the fruit have a particularly rich flavor.

far breton (fah bru-tohn) A French baked egg custard or flan with prunes or raisins.

farce (faahrs) French for stuffing and used to describe a forcemeat.

farci (far-SEE) 1. French for stuffed. 2. A French dish of cabbage stuffed with sausage meat, wrapped in cheesecloth and cooked in stock.

farcito (fah-CHEE-toa) Italian for stuffed.

fardh (far'dh) A variety of date popular in the Middle East.

fare The selection of food that is offered, usually at a restaurant.

farfalle (fah-FAHL-lay) 1. Italian for butterfly and used to describe bow-shaped pasta. 2. In the United States, pasta bows, usually made with an egg dough; also known as bowties.

farfalline; farfallette (far-fall-lee-nay) Small farfalle.

farfalloni (far-fall-oh-nee) Large farfalle.

farfalle

farfel (FAHR-fuhl) 1. Fresh egg noodle dough that is grated or minced and used in soups; also known as egg barley. 2. In Jewish cuisine, a food that is broken into small pieces (e.g., dried noodles). 3. A Jewish dish of small pieces or balls of lokshen dough; they are cooked like rice or noodles, or toasted.

farika (fah-RE-kah) Unripened cracked wheat; it is sometimes used as a replacement for rice in Middle Eastern cuisines.

farina (fah-REE-nah) 1. A fine flour made from a grain, roots or nuts; used chiefly for puddings or as a breakfast cereal. 2. A porridge made from such flour. 3. The purified middlings of hard wheat other than durum. 4. A fine wheat flour used like arrowroot or semolina. 5. A fine powder made from potatoes and used as a thickener. 6. Italian for flour.

farinaceous (fah-ree-nank-chay-ooz) A food consisting of or made from flour or meal.

farine (fah-reen) French for flour.

farinha (fah-REE-nyah) Portuguese for flour.

farin sukker (far-een suhk-ehr) Norwegian for granulated sugar.

farl (FAR-el) A Scottish oatmeal cake, usually thin and triangular, cut into quarters.

farm cheese; farmhouse cheese 1. A term used imprecisely to suggest or establish that the particular cheese was made on a farm (usually from unpasteurized milk) using traditional methods and not mass-produced in a factory. *See* dairy cheese. 2. A British cheese labeling term establishing that the cheese was made on a farm by expert cheese makers; it can be graded as Super Fine Grade Farmhouse, Fine Grade Farmhouse, and Graded and initialed MMB.

Farmer, Fannie (Am., 1857–1915) The author of *The Boston Cooking-School Cookbook* (1896), which later became known as *The Fannie Farmer Cookbook,* and culinary arts instructor; as an educator and author she stressed the accurate use of measurements and strived for a uniformity of results, thereby making cooking a science rather than a hit-or-miss affair.

farmer cheese; farmer's cheese 1. An American cottage cheese–style cheese made from whole or partly skimmed cow's milk; generally eaten fresh, it has a soft texture (but is firm enough to slice or crumble), a milky white appearance and a slightly tangy flavor; also known as pressed cheese. 2. A term used imprecisely to describe a basic, fresh cheese such as cottage cheese.

Farmer's Gouda *See* Boerenkaas.

farnesol A food additive derived from acacia flowers; it has a slightly floral aroma and flavor and is used as a flavoring agent.

faro (fah-ro) A lambic beer sweetened with sugar candy.

Faro (FAH-roh) A Denominazióne di Origine Controllata (DOC) red wine made in Sicily from Nerello Mascalese and other grapes.

farofa (fah-roh-fah) A Brazilian condiment (especially for beef) made with manioc flour, palm oil, onions and malagueta chiles.

farofia (fah-row-fee-ah) An Angolan dish consisting of fried cassava meal flavored with onions, palm oil and vinegar.

färserade (farr-sah-rah-da) Swedish for stuffed.

farseret (far-sa-rett) Danish for stuffed.

farshirovanniy (far-she-row-vah-nee) Russian for stuffed.

farsz (fah-rsh) Polish for stuffing.

fasan (fah-SAAN) Danish for pheasant.

Fasan (fah-ZARN) German for pheasant.

Faschierter Braten (fah-SHEER-ter BRAR-tern) An Austrian and German dish consisting of ground beef and pork mixed with bread crumbs, eggs and seasonings, shaped into a loaf and baked; a sauce is made from sour cream and the pan juices.

faseole A variety of haricot bean grown in the Mediterranean region.

Fasnacht; Fastnacht (FAAS-nakht) A Pennsylvania German diamond-shaped potato yeast dough that is deep-fried in pork fat; traditionally served with jam or molasses for breakfast on Shrove Tuesday.

fasol (fah-SSOL) Russian for beans.

fasola (fah-sol-lah) Polish for beans.

Fass (fah'ss) German for a wooden cask or barrel.

fassolada; fassolatha (faa-sho-lah-tha) A Greek soup made from dried beans, celery, carrots, onions and tomato purée, flavored with olive oil, parsley and seasonings.

fassolakia freska (faa-sho-lah-khia frees-kah) Greek for green beans.

fassoulia (fah-soo-lee-ah) Arabic for pulses.

fast food 1. Food dispensed quickly at a restaurant generally offering a limited menu of inexpensive items, many of which may not be particularly nutritious; the food can be eaten on premises, taken out or sometimes delivered. 2. Precooked or other processed food requiring minimal preparation at home. 3. *See* slow food.

fast green FCF *See* FD&C Green #3.

fasting The process of going without food so that the body must use stored nutrients for energy (first glycogen stored in the liver, then proteins stored in the lean muscles and finally fats); fasting is practiced for various dietary, religious and social reasons.

fasùl yahniya (fah-sool yah-nee-ha) A Bulgarian dish of dried white beans cooked with onions, red and green peppers and tomatoes.

fat A wine-tasting term for a rich, supple wine with low acidity. *See* fats.

fat, artificial *See* artificial fat.

fatayer (fah-tayh-erh) A Syrian meat pie (lamb or beef), usually flavored with yogurt and pine nuts and made open faced or closed.

fatayer jibnah (fah-tayh-erh geeb-nah) A muajeenot of phyllo dough filled with cheese.

fatayer sabaneq (fah-tayh-erh saw-bah-neck) A muajeenot of yeast-leavened dough filled with spinach flavored with sumac and lemon juice.

fatback The layer of fat that runs along a hog's back just below the skin and above the eye muscle; usually available unsmoked and unsalted; used for lard and lardons and to prepare charcuterie items. *See* salt pork.

fat bloom *See* bloom.

fat calories Calories derived from fats; 1 g of pure fat supplies 9 kilocalories; fat calories should not exceed 30% of a person's daily calories.

fat cells Cells used principally to store fat.

fat cigar *See* cigar, fat.

fatfold test A test of body fatness in which the thickness of a fold of skin on the back of the arm, below the shoulder blade, or at other places on the body is measured with a caliper; formerly known as the skinfold test.

fatia (fah-TEE-ah) Portuguese for a slice.

fatir mushaltet (fah-teyh-erh moo-shall-tat) An oily Egyptian bread with many fine layers.

fat mop *See* grease mop.

fat rascal A large scone, about 6 in. in diameter, made with candied citrus peel, candied cherries, spices and almonds and served split in half and buttered; a specialty of Yorkshire, England.

fats 1. A general term used to describe a class of organic nutrients that includes the lipid family of compounds: triglycerides (fats and oils), phospholipids and sterols. 2. Nutrients composed of glycerol and 3 units of fatty acid; they occur naturally in animals and some plants and are used principally in the body to store energy from food eaten in excess of need (1 g of fat delivers 2.25 times the calories delivered by 1 g of carbohydrates or protein). 3. Lipids that are solid at room temperature. 4. A general term for butter, lard, shortening, oil and margarine used as cooking media or ingredients.

fat-soluble vitamins *See* vitamins, fat-soluble.

fatta (fah-taw) A Middle Eastern dish consisting of a rich meat or chicken soup poured over bread (often shraak) and left to soak before being served; sometimes a layer of rice, puréed chickpeas and/or yogurt is spread on the bread before the soup is added. *See* thareed.

fattoria (fah-toh-REE-ah) Italian term for an estate, traditionally in Tuscany; when referring to wine, it implies, but does not guarantee, that the wine is estate bottled.

fattoush (fah-TOOSH) A Middle Eastern meza salad made with toasted bread, lettuce, spinach, scallions, cucumbers, tomatoes and bell peppers flavored with parsley and mint and dressed with lemon juice, olive oil, garlic and sumac.

fatty acids 1. A group of water-insoluble organic acids found in animals and certain plants that combine with glycerol to form triglycerides; they are classified as saturated or unsaturated (monounsaturated or polyunsaturated) based on the number of hydrogen atoms attached to the fatty acid's carbon chain (which has oxygen atoms at the end). 2. Food additives used as lubricants, binders and components of other food additives.

faux filet (foh fee-LAY) A French cut of the beef carcass; it is the eye of sirloin; also known as contre filet.

faux mousseron (foh moos-rohn) *See* fairy ring mushroom.

fava bean (FAH-vuh) A large, flat, kidney-shaped bean (*Vicia faba*) with a tough pale green skin when fresh that turns brown when dried; the skin is usually removed before cooking; the interior is light green when fresh and cream colored when dried; available fresh, dried or canned and used in Mediterranean and Middle Eastern cuisines; also known as a broad bean.

fava frita (fah-vah free-tah) Portuguese deep-fried fava beans spiced with piri-piri and eaten as a snack.

Favorita (fah-voh-REE-tah) 1. A white wine grape grown in Italy's Alba region. 2. The wine made from this grape; it is light and crisp.

fawakeh (fah-wha-kah) Arabic for fruits.

fazant (fah-ZAHNT) Dutch for pheasant.

fazole (fah-zoe-lay) Czech for bean.

fazolky (fah-zoll-key) Czech for green bean.

FDA *See* Food and Drug Administration.

FD&C Blue #1 A food additive used as a greenish-blue coloring agent in candies, baked goods, beverages and desserts; also known as brilliant blue FCF.

FD&C Blue #2 A food additive used as a dark blue coloring agent in candies, confections and baked goods; also known as indigotine.

FD&C Green #3 A food additive used as a bluish-green coloring agent in cereals, beverages and desserts; also known as fast green FCF.

FD&C Red #3 A food additive used as a bluish-pink coloring agent in candies, confections and cherry products; also known as erythrosine.

FD&C Red #40 A food additive used as a yellowish-red coloring agent in beverages, desserts, candies, confections, cereal and ice cream; also known as Allura® red AC.

FD&C Yellow #5 A food additive used as a lemon-yellow coloring agent in beverages, baked goods, desserts, candies, confections, cereal and ice cream; also known as tartrazine.

FD&C Yellow #6 A food additive used as a reddish-yellow coloring agent in beverages, baked goods, desserts, confections and ice cream; also known as sunset yellow FCF.

feathery Leaves that are divided into very fine segments.

fécula (FEHK-eul) The very finely ground, starchy powder obtained from potatoes, chestnuts, arrowroot, cassava and other vegetables; used for thickening soups and sauces; each product is usually identified by its source and called flour (e.g., potato flour).

fedelini (feh-duh-lee-nee) Italian for little faithful and used to describe the thinnest of spaghetti.

feed trough Cowboy slang for dining table.

fegatini (fay-gah-TEE-nee) An Italian tomato-based sauce containing chopped chicken livers.

fegato (fay-GAH-toa) Italian for calf's liver.

fegato alla veneziana (fay-GAH-toa allah v'net-zee-ah-nah) An Italian dish of calf's liver cooked with onions and white wine.

féi (fay) Chinese for fat.

Feige (FAIG-ahn) German for fig.

feijão (fay-zhah-oh) Portuguese for bean.

feijão preto (fay-zhah-oh preh-too) Portuguese for black bean.

feijão verde (fay-zhah-oh vehr-day) Portuguese for green bean.

feijoa (fay-YOH-ah; fay-JOH-ah) A small- to medium-sized fruit (genus *Psidium*) native to South America; it has an ovoid shape, a thin, green, bloom-covered skin sometimes blushed with red, a cream-colored, somewhat grainy flesh encasing a jellylike center with many tiny seeds, and a flavor reminiscent of pineapple and strawberry; also known as a guavasteen and pineapple guava.

feijoada (fay-JOH-dah) A Brazilian stew of smoked meats (especially pork), dried beef, chorizo and/or tongue with black beans and flavored with onions, garlic, tomatoes, chiles, oranges and herbs; it is served with rice and a hot pepper sauce with lime.

feints The end or tails of a run in a distillate; they contain a high percentage of alcohol and impurities and are set aside from the main body of the distillate to be redistilled later.

feit (fa-it) Norwegian for fat.

felafel *See* falafel.

Felix, sauce A French compound sauce made from a demiglaze flavored with lobster butter and finished with lemon juice.

fell The tough, thin membrane covering a carcass; it is just below the hide and consists of intermingled connective and fatty tissues.

fen (fan) Mandarin Chinese for fresh, flat rice noodles.

fenalår (FAY-nah-lawr) A Norwegian dish consisting of a leg of mutton, slightly salted, wind-dried and usually smoked.

Fenchel (fehn-chal) German for fennel.

Fendant (fahn-dahn) *See* Chasselas.

fengmi (phang-me) Chinese for honey.

fennel, common A perennial plant (*Foeniculum vulgare*) with feathery foliage and tiny flowers; the plant's oval, green-brown seeds have prominent ridges, short, hairlike fibers and a weak, aniselike flavor and aroma and are available whole and ground; used in baked goods and savory dishes in Italian and central European cuisines and to flavor alcoholic beverages.

fennel, Florence A perennial plant (*Foeniculum vulgare* var. *dulce*) with a broad, bulbous root, white to pale green celerylike stalks and bright green, feathery foliage; it has a flavor similar to but sweeter and more delicate than that of anise; the root is cooked like a vegetable, the foliage is used as a garnish or flavor enhancer and the stalks are used in salads or cooked; also known as finocchio and sweet fennel and known imprecisely as sweet anise.

fennel, Florence

fennel flower *See* nigella.

fennikel (fenn-ick-ell) Norwegian for fennel.

fenouil (FUH-nuj') French for fennel.

fenouillet (fuh-nujz-yay) A family of French pears; their flavor has undertones of aniseed.

fen pi (fan pee) Chinese for mung bean sheets.

fen si (fan see) Chinese for cellophane noodles made from dried mung beans.

fenugrec (fay-noo-greek) French for fenugreek.

fenugreek (FEHN-yoo-greek) A spice that is the seed of an aromatic plant of the pea family (*Trigonella foenumgracum*) native to the Mediterranean region; the pebble-shaped seeds have a pale orange color and a bittersweet, burned-sugar flavor and aftertaste; the seeds are available whole and ground and are used in Indian and Middle Eastern cuisines.

feqqas (fa-kass) Any of a number of classic Moroccan cookies; examples include (1) cream cheese pastry wrapped around a filling of sautéed peanuts, chilled, cut into rounds and baked and (2) crunchy, twice-baked cookies flavored with ground almonds, aniseeds, sesame seeds, golden raisins and orange flower water; they are often served with mint tea.

fer à glacer (fair ah glass-say) French for salamander; also known as pelle rouge and salamandre.

ferme; fermier (fehrm; fehrm-yay) French for farm and farmer, respectively, and used to describe a farm-produced cheese.

Ferme (fehrm) *See* Fromage à la Pie.

fermentation 1. The process by which yeast converts sugars to alcohol and carbon dioxide; this process is fundamental to the making of leavened breads, beers, wines and spirits. 2. The period that yeast bread dough is left to rise. 3. The process of souring milk with certain bacteria to create a specific dairy product (e.g., yogurt and sour cream). 4. The process by which air-cured tobacco leaves mature and release impurities; the leaves are placed in large piles and allowed to compost; also known as bulking and sweating.

fermentation, malolactic A second fermentation in some wines; malic acid is converted into lactic acid and carbon dioxide, which softens the wine and reduces acidity.

fermentation alcohol *See* ethyl alcohol.

fermentation lock A one-way valve on top of a closed fermentor that allows carbon dioxide to escape and prevents oxygen from entering.

fermented black beans Small black soybeans preserved in salt; they have a very salty, pungent flavor and are used in Chinese cuisines as a flavoring for meat and fish dishes; also known as Chinese black beans and salty black beans.

fermented dry Refers to a beer that has been fermented to a low specific gravity or until almost no residual sugar remains.

fermented eggs *See* hundred-year-old eggs.

fermented red rice Annatto seeds mixed with the lees from rice wine making; they are used for their yeasty flavor and red coloring properties in northern Chinese cuisine.

fermenter; fermentor An open or closed vessel used to hold the wort during beer fermentation.

fermière, à la (fayr-myayr, ah lah) 1. A French garnish for poultry and braised meats consisting of carrots, turnips, onions, potatoes and celery braised in butter and the meat's natural juices. 2. A French garnish consisting of small half-moon slices of carrots, celeriac, turnips and leeks simmered in butter and mixed with either a veal velouté or a white wine sauce.

fern bar Slang for a bar (with or without attached dining area) decorated with hanging plants (especially ferns), oak, brass and Tiffany-style glass, popular during the 1980s.

fernet (fer-net) An aromatic Italian bitters used for beverages, especially as a digestif; a well-known brand is Fernet Branca.

Fernet Branca (fer-net bran-kah) The proprietary name of a bitter aperitif flavored with cinchona bark, gentian, rhubarb, calamus, angelica, myrrh, chamomile and peppermint; sometimes used as a remedy for stomachaches or hangovers.

ferri, ai; ferri alla griglia (FEH-ree, ay; FEH-ree ah-lah GREEl'yah) Italian for grilled over an open fire.

ferric ammonium citrate A food additive used as a nutrient (iron) supplement.

ferric citrate A food additive used as a nutrient (iron) supplement.

ferric phosphate and ferric pyrophosphate Food additives used as nutrient (iron and phosphorus) supplements.

ferrous compounds Food additives containing iron and used as nutrient supplements.

ferrous gluconate A food additive used as a nutrient (iron) supplement and a red-brown coloring agent.

fersken (FAYRSK-nerr) Norwegian for peach.

ferver (fehr-vehr) Portuguese for to boil.

fesanjune (fa-saw-nee-who-na) A Middle Eastern dish consisting of chicken (peacock was originally used) flavored with pomegranate syrup, pomegranate juice, lemon juice, walnuts and sugar and garnished with pomegranate seeds and chopped walnuts; also known as yakhni baza.

fesenjan (fa-saw-nee-ann) A Persian (Iranian) meat or chicken stew (khoresh) flavored with crushed walnuts and concentrated sour pomegranate juice.

fesiekh (fa-sea-hech) An Arabic term for any dried fish or shellfish; they can be eaten as snacks (e.g., dried sardines), rehydrated in soups or stews (e.g., dried shark) or used as flavorings (e.g., dried shrimp) in Middle Eastern cuisines.

Festbier (fest-beer) A beer of any style or alcohol content made for a particular German festival such as Oktoberfest.

festy cock *See* fitless cock.

Feta (FEH-tah) 1. A soft Greek cheese made from ewe's milk (or occasionally goat's milk) and pickled in brine; it has a white color, a crumbly texture, and a salty, sour, tangy flavor. 2. A soft, white, flaky American feta-style cheese made from cow's milk and stored in brine.

Fett (fet) German for fat.

fetta (FAY-tah) Italian for a slice.

fettucce (feht-tuh-chee) The widest fettuccine.

fettuccelle (feht-tuh-CHEL-lee) Narrow fettuccine.

fettucce riccie (feht-tuh-chay ree-tchee-a) Italian for curly ribbons and used to describe a moderately narrow pasta ribbon with one ruffled edge, similar to Margherita.

fettuccine (feht-toot-CHEE-nee) Italian for small ribbons and used to describe thin, flat ribbons of pasta; sold as straight ribbons or loosely bent and curled.

fettuccine Alfredo (feht-tuh-CHEE-nee al-FRAY-doh) An Italian dish of fettuccine mixed with a rich sauce of butter, cream and Parmesan and sprinkled with black pepper.

feu doux (fer doo) French for gentle heat and used to describe an enameled cast-iron oval pot with a deeply in-

dented lid used for braising and available in capacities of 2.5–6 qt.; the lid's large encircling groove once held hot coals but now is used for iced water to condense internal steam quickly, causing the droplets to drip into the pot.

feuille de chêne (fuh-yuh duh cheen) French for oak leaf lettuce.

feuilletage (fuh-yuh-TAHZH) French for flaky and used to describe puff pastry or the process of making puff pastry. *See* mille-feuille *and* puff pastry.

feuillette (fuh-YET) 1. A wooden wine barrel traditionally used in France's Chablis region; it has a capacity of 136 liters. 2. A square-, rectangular-, or diamond-shaped puff pastry box that can be filled with a sweet or savory mixture.

few A food-labeling term approved by the U.S. Food and Drug Administration (FDA) to describe a food that can be eaten frequently without exceeding dietary guidelines for fat, saturated fat, cholesterol, sodium or calories.

fewer A food-labeling term approved by the U.S. Food and Drug Administration (FDA) to describe a nutritionally altered food that contains at least 25% fewer calories than the regular or reference (i.e., FDA standard) food.

fewer purveyor shopping The practice of purchasing more goods from fewer suppliers (as opposed to few goods from many suppliers).

Fiaker (fee-ah-kerr) 1. German for coachman and used to describe an Austrian goulash made with a small sausage, a fried egg and a pickle cut and spread out like a fan; the traditional "hold-me-over" meal for a coachman. 2. A Viennese coffee that is sweetened and served in a glass; also known as a coachman.

fiambre (fee-ahm-bray) Spanish for cold meats or cold cuts.

fiambre (FYAHM-brayss) Portuguese for cold cooked ham.

fiasco (vee-ASK-co) The hand-blown, round-bottomed bottle with a woven straw covering associated with Chianti; these bottles are now rarely used because of their expense.

fiasco

fiber A slender, threadlike structure or cell that combines with others to form animal tissues (such as muscles) or plant tissues (such as membranes). *See* dietary fiber.

ficelle (feh-cell) French for string and used to describe a very long, thin loaf of French bread with a high ratio of crust to interior.

ficelle, à la (feh-cell, ah lah) A French preparation method for a filet of beef; it is bound with twine, browned in the oven, and boiled in consommé.

fichi (FEE-key) Italian for figs.

fiddlehead fern An edible fern (*Pteridium aquilinium*); the young, tightly coiled, deep green fronds have a flavor reminiscent of asparagus and green beans; cooked like a vegetable or used in a salad; also known as bracken and ostrich fern.

fiddler A small channel catfish; it has an average weight of 1 lb. (450 g).

fide (fee-the) Very thin Greek egg noodles, often served in broths and soups.

fideos (fee-DHAY-oass) Very thin, spaghetti-like Spanish pasta, usually loosely coiled when packaged.

fidget pie; figet pie A Welsh dish of potatoes and apples layered with onions and unsmoked bacon, covered with a pastry crust, and baked.

field mushroom *See* common field mushroom.

field pea A variety of pea, either green or yellow, cultivated to be dried and not to require soaking before it is cooked; it usually splits into two small hemispherical disks along a natural seam; also known as a split pea.

field salad *See* mâche.

fiesta grande *See* margarita glass.

FIFO First in–first out; a system for using and valuing inventory, particularly perishable and semiperishable goods, in which the items are used in the order of their receipt; that is, items that are received first are used before subsequently received ones; also known as rotating stock.

fifth A bottle holding one-fifth of a gallon (25.4 fl. oz. or 750 ml) and typically used for the sale of wine or distilled spirits; also known as an American fifth.

fig A variety of oblong or pear-shaped fruits (*Ficus carica*) that grow in warm climates; generally, they have a thick, soft skin that is green, yellow, orange or purple, a tannish-purple flesh, a sweet flavor, and many tiny edible seeds; available fresh or dried.

figa (fee-gah) Russian for fig.

figado (FEE-gah-doh) Portuguese for liver.

figado oder iscas (fee-gah-doe oh-der ees-cass) A Portuguese petisco dish of thin slices of fried liver served cold on bread.

figaro, sauce (fee-gah-roh) A French compound sauce made from a hollandaise flavored with tomato purée and parsley; usually served with fish or poultry.

figatelli (fee-gah-tel-lee) Corsican sausage made from hog's liver.

figgy pudding An English dish made of dried figs stewed in wine and often served with a fish course during Lent.

fig leaves The dark green leaves of the fig tree; they are used in Mediterranean cuisines to wrap fish or poultry for grilling.

Fig Newton A square hollow cookie filled with fig jam; it was first machine produced in Massachusetts in 1891 and named after the town of Newton.

figo (fee-goh) Portuguese for fig.

figo com presunto (fee-go com pra-soon-toe) A Portuguese petisco dish of fresh figs served with cured ham.

figue (fig) French for fig.

fiken (fee-ken) Norwegian for fig.

filascetta (fee-las-cheh-tah) An Italian round, flat bread made from a yeast dough and sprinkled with fried onions and then baked.

filbert The nut of the cultivated hazel tree (genus *Corylus*); shaped like a smooth brown marble, it is a bit larger and less flavorful than its wild cousin, the hazelnut, and its bitter skin should be removed before using; a similar type of cultivated hazel tree nut is known in England as a cob, cobnut or Kentish cob. *See* hazelnut.

filé powder (fih-LAY; FEE-lay) The ground leaves of the sassafras tree; used in Cajun and Creole cuisines as a seasoning and thickener.

filet (fee-lay) *v.* To fabricate a boneless cut of meat. *n.* 1. A general term for a boneless cut of meat, usually one that is tender and flavorful; sometimes imprecisely spelled fillet. *See* fillet. 2. A French cut of the lamb carcass; it is the entire loin and is usually fabricated into chops known as côte de filet or côtelettes dans le filet. 3. A French cut of the pork carcass; it is cut from the center of the loin and has the kidney attached.

filet de boeuf rôti (fee-lay duh buff roe-TEE) French for roast filet of beef.

filet de boeuf Wellington (fee-lay duh buff well-eng-tohn) A dish of a roasted filet of beef coated with foie gras or duxelles and wrapped in pastry and baked.

filete de pescada (fee-la-ta day pess-cah-dah) A Portuguese petisco dish of deep-fried pieces of hake served cold with bread.

filetes (fee-leh-tess) Spanish for thinly cut filets of beef.

filetes empanados (fee-leh-tess em-paw-nah-doss) A Spanish dish consisting of veal filets dipped in egg and fried.

filet mignon (fee-lay me-NYON) A fabricated cut of the short end of the tenderloin found in the beef short loin and sirloin primals; it is cut from the center of the tenderloin and is lean, very tender, flavorful and larger than a tournedo; also known as a beef filet.

filet of beef *See* undercut.

filetto alla mignon (fee-LEHT-toa ah-lah me-NYON) Italian for filet mignon.

filful (fell-fehll) Arabic for pepper.

Filipino-style pot roast *See* mechado.

filled cheese A product made with vegetable fat.

filled milk A product made from either vegetable fat and skim milk or vegetable fat and nonfat dry milk reconstituted with water.

filler The tobacco leaves that comprise the bulk of a cigar and deliver most of the flavor; they are held in place by a binder and covered with a wrapper.

filler, long Long, hand-cut tobacco leaves; most handmade cigars are made with long filler.

filler, short Tobacco scraps used to fill the middle of a cigar; most machine-made cigars are short filled.

fillet (FIHL-eht) A British cut of the beef carcass; it is the short loin.

fillet (FILL-eh) *v.* To fabricate a boneless cut of fish. *n.* The side of a fish removed intact, boneless or semiboneless, with or without skin. *See* filet.

filleting knife A knife used to bone fish or thinly slice produce; its flexible blade is 6–7 in. long.

fillette (fee-yet) French for young girl and used informally in the Loire Valley and elsewhere to mean a half bottle of wine.

fillings Whiskey just after it is removed from the still.

filleting knife

filo (PHE-lo) *See* phyllo.

filter grind *See* grind, fine.

filtering The process of clarifying a wine or beer by passing it through filters made from cellulose fibers, diatomaceous earth or fine membranes.

filter method A coffee-brewing method; finely ground coffee is measured into a paper filter fitted into a plastic or china cone sitting on a pot or mug, hot water is slowly poured over the grounds, and the coffee drips into the receptacle, which can be kept warm over a low flame or on a hot plate.

final specific gravity In beer making, the specific gravity of the wort at the end of fermentation; also known as terminal specific gravity.

financier (fee-nahng-syehr) A French sponge cake made with ground almonds; traditionally rectangular and coated with sliced almonds; served as a petit four or individual pastry or used as part of a more elaborate pastry.

financière, sauce (fin-ahn-see-AIR) A French compound sauce made from a demi-glaze flavored with chicken stock, truffle essence and Sauternes or Madeira and garnished with truffles and mushrooms.

finanziera (fee-nahn-Z'YEH-rah) An ancient stewlike dish from Italy's Piedmont region; it consists of sweetbreads, mushrooms, truffles and sometimes cockscomb or calf's brains.

Fin de Bagnols (fehn duh bahn-yol) A particularly flavorful variety of French green beans.

fine 1. Consisting of minute particles, not coarse; very thin or slender. 2. An overused wine-tasting term; used appropriately, it describes a wine of inherent, unmistakable superior quality.

Fine Champagne Cognac A brandy made from grapes grown in the Petit or Grande Champagne areas of France's Cognac region.

fine de la maison (feen duh la mai-zohn) French for house brandy.

fines herbes (FEENZ erb) A seasoning blend used in French cuisine; it typically includes chervil, chives, parsley, tarragon and other herbs. *See* herbes à tortue.

finesse A wine-tasting term for a wine that has breed, class, subtlety and distinction; a wine that is well out of the ordinary.

finger bowl A small bowl of water, sometimes scented with lemon or a flower, used at the table to rinse one's fingers.

finger foods Small portions of foods or small foods comfortably eaten in one bite; usually served as hors d'oeuvre.

Finger Lakes A grape-growing and wine-producing region in west-central New York state; the principal grapes grown are native American (e.g., Catawba), French–American hybrids (e.g., Aurora) and vinifera species (e.g., Chardonnay and Johannisberg Riesling).

fingerlings Any of a variety of small, long, thin potatoes.

finger meat Slivers of meat found between the ribs of a beef, veal, lamb or pork carcass; also known as rib fingers.

finiki (FEE-nyee-kee) Russian for dates.

fining The process of clarifying a beer or wine by adding a fining agent.

fining agent A substance such as egg whites, bentonite, charcoal, gelatin or isinglass used for the fining of a beer or wine by inducing or facilitating the settling out of suspended particles; also known as a settling agent.

finish *v.* 1. To add butter to a sauce nearing completion to impart shine, flavor and richness. 2. To brown a food (often, one with bread crumbs, grated cheese or other topping) under an overhead heat source. 3. To complete the cooking of a food begun on the stove top by putting it in the oven. *n.* 1. A wine-tasting term for the sensation or final taste remaining in the mouth after swallowing or expectorating the wine; often described as long (i.e., lingering) or short (i.e., fleeting) finish. *See* aftertaste. 2. The proportion of fat to lean meat on a carcass or in a particular cut; a basis for determining yield and quality.

finkel (fing-kell) A Norwegian high-proof spirit distilled from potatoes.

finlabong (fin-lah-bong) Filipino for bamboo shoot.

finnan haddie; finnan haddock (FIHN-uhn HAD-ee) A partially boned, lightly salted, smoked haddock; named after the Scottish fishing village of Findon.

Finnish yellow potato A variety of white potato with a golden skin, a creamy flesh and a buttery flavor; also known as a yellow Finn potato.

finnlendskaia (fin-land-sky-ah) A Finnish garnish for beef broth; it consists of slices of a pancake made with sour cream and grated parsley root added to the batter; after it is fried, the pancake is sprinkled with grated cheese, bread crumbs and butter and then browned.

Finnoise, sauce; Finnish sauce (fenn-wahz) A French compound sauce made from a chicken velouté seasoned with paprika and garnished with a julienne of green peppers and herbs.

fino (fee-no) A type of sherry; it is very dry, with a slightly pungent flavor, a very pale gold color, and a medium body.

finocchio (fee-nok-kee-o) Italian for fennel. *See* fennel, Florence.

finocchiona (fee-nok-kee-OAN-ah) An Italian sausage flavored with fennel seeds.

Fiorano (fee-oh-RAH-no) The proprietary name for unusual red and white Italian wines produced south of Rome; the red is made from Merlot and Cabernet Sauvignon grapes, and the white is made from Malvasia di Candia.

Fior d'Alpe (FEE-oar dahlp) A clear, spicy Italian liqueur bottled with an herb sprig (juniper, mint, thyme, wild marjoram or hyssop), onto which excess sugar crystallizes.

Fior di Latte (FEE-oar day LAHT-tay) An Italian mozzarella-style cheese made from cow's milk (as opposed to water buffalo's milk) and sometimes shaped like a pear; also known as Scamorze.

Fiore Sardo (fee-OA-ray sahr-doa) A hard Italian cheese traditionally made in the mountains of Sardinia from ewe's and cow's milk (known as Pecorino Sardo if made only from ewe's milk); it has a white or yellow interior, a yellow crust and a sharp flavor; used as a table cheese when young and for grating when aged; also known as Sardo.

fiori di zucca (f'YOH-reh dee ZOO-kah) An Italian dish consisting of squash blossoms dipped in batter and fried.

fique (fee-que) French Caribbean for banana.

fire Slang for the order to begin cooking a dish.

fireweed *See* rosebay willowherb.

firik (fi-rek) Toasted unripened wheat berries used like rice or couscous in Turkish cuisine.

firik pilav (fi-rek poh-lov) A Turkish pilaf made with toasted unripened wheat.

firkin (fur-ken) 1. A small wooden vessel used to hold butter or cheese. 2. A British measure of volume equal to 0.25 barrel.

firm-ball stage A test for the density of sugar syrup: the point at which a drop of boiling sugar will form a firm but pliable ball when dropped in cold water; equivalent to approximately 248°F (120°C) on a candy thermometer.

firm cheeses *See* cheeses, firm.

firming agent A type of food additive used to keep fruits and vegetables firm during processing by precipitating residual pectin to prevent tissue collapse.

firni (FIHR-nee) An east Indian custard made with rice flour, almonds and milk.

first class 1. A designation for a European hotel of medium-range quality with private and semiprivate baths. 2. A designation for an American hotel of medium-range quality with private and semiprivate baths, public rooms and most services.

first courses *See* appetizers.

first growth English for premier cru.

first in–first out *See* FIFO.

Fisch (fish) German for fish.

fisduq (fuss-due'kah) Arabic for pistachio.

fish Any of thousands of species of aquatic vertebrates with fins for swimming and gills for breathing found in saltwater and freshwater worldwide; most are edible; fish are classified by bone structure as flatfish or round fish. *See* flatfish, round fish *and* shellfish.

fish and chips A British dish of deep-fried fish fillets and French fries, usually served with malt vinegar.

Fisher, M. F. K. (Am., 1908–1992) One of America's greatest food writers and the author of *Serve It Forth, Consider the Oyster, How to Cook a Wolf, The Gastronomical Me* and *An Alphabet for Gourmets,* as well as the translation of *The Physiology of Taste, or Meditations on Transcendental Gastronomy,* by Jean Anthelme Brillat-Savarin.

fish escovitch (es-ko-VEECH) A Caribbean dish of fish seasoned with red pepper, onions and vinegar and fried at a high temperature so that the skin crisps.

fish fingers *See* fish sticks.

fish fork A fork with three broad, flat tines used for eating fish.

fish grill A hinged wire frame approximating the shape of a fish and used to hold a fish during grilling; it has a handle and is available with folding feet to adjust the distance from the heat source.

Fish House Punch A punch made of brandy, peach liqueur, rum, sugar, lemon juice and water.

fish knife A knife with a short, very broad, saber-shaped blade with a notch near the handle (for removing bones) and a slightly angled top edge; used for eating fish.

fish lifter A slightly bowed metal spatula with a 6.5- × 4.5-in. perforated blade; the bow cradles the fish, and the perforations allow it to drain.

fish maw The bladderlike organ in a fish that acts like a decompression chamber.

fish paste A thick, dark brown paste made from mashed, dried fish and/or shellfish; sometimes chiles are added; used as a flavoring, it has a very salty flavor and a strong, pungent aroma.

fish poacher A long, narrow, metal pan with a perforated rack used to raise and lower the fish in one piece.

fish poacher

fish protein isolate A food additive derived from dried proteins of bony fish and used as a nutrient supplement.

fish quality grades U.S. Department of Commerce (USDC) grades for common fish packed under federal inspection; each species has its own grading criteria.

fish quality grades, grade A The top designation; the product is of top quality, with a good flavor and odor and practically free of blemishes.

fish quality grades, grade B The product is of good quality.

fish quality grades, grade C The product is of fair quality and is usually used for canned or processed products.

fish sauce A thin, dark brown liquid made from anchovy extract and salt; used as a flavoring, it has a very salty flavor and a strong, pungent aroma.

fish scaler A tool used to remove the scales from a fish; it has two rows of teeth and is drawn across the fish, removing the scales without tearing the flesh.

fish shears A pair of strong scissors with straight blades (one is thin, tapering and serrated, and the other is broad and has a rounded point); used to cut through fish fins, flesh and bones. *See* kitchen shears.

fish shears

fish station chef *See* poissonier.

fish sticks Fillet of fish that has been sliced into sticks approximately 1 in. (2.54 cm) wide, battered or rolled in bread crumbs, and fried or baked; usually available frozen; also known as fish fingers.

fish tea A Caribbean broth made from fish, green bananas and vegetables and seasoned with allspice and pepper.

fish tobermory A Scottish dish consisting of poached fish fillets served on a bed of spinach and topped with a cheese sauce and broiled until the cheese has melted.

fish velouté A velouté made from fish stock.

fisk (feesk) Danish, Norwegian and Swedish for fish.

fiskfilet med remoulade (feesk-fee-lit mead ray-moo-lahd) A Danish smørrebrød dish of fillets of breaded, deep-fried plaice on black bread garnished with rémoulade and lemon.

fitless cock A Scottish dish consisting of oatmeal, suet, onions and seasonings bound with an egg, shaped into the form of a fowl and boiled in a cloth like a dumpling (in the Highlands) or roasted in ashes (in the Lowlands); also known as dry goose and festy cock.

fitness The body's ability to meet demands; generally considered to include five factors (weight, flexibility, strength, muscle endurance and cardiovascular endurance); facilitated by exercise.

five-spice powder *See* Chinese five-spice powder *and* Tunisian five-spice powder.

Fix A cocktail made of fruit syrup (usually pineapple), lemon juice, seltzer and liquor served in a highball glass over cracked ice.

fixative An additive such as musk or amber gum used in a food to prevent the more volatile ingredients from evaporating too quickly.

fixed costs Costs that are generally constant or fixed (e.g., property taxes) and not subject to increase or decrease based on business volume; typically not subject to an operation's control; also known as noncontrollable costs. *See* variable costs.

Fizz A long drink (cocktail) made of liquor, sugar, lemon juice, soda water and other ingredients such as egg whites, liqueurs and cream; served over ice.

fjaderfa (fee-ah-derr-fah) Swedish for poultry.

fjerkrae (feer-krah-ah) Danish for poultry.

flabby A wine-tasting term for a wine that is too rich and heavy and lacks structure.

flaeske (flehsk) Danish for pork.

flag 1. A toothpick holding a cherry and orange slice, used as a cocktail garnish. 2. *See* cap.

flageolet (fla-zhoh-LAY) A small kidney-shaped bean cultivated in France; it has a pale green to creamy white color, is generally available dried or canned and is used as an accompaniment to lamb.

flagon (fla-ghon) 1. An ancient metal or pottery vessel with a handle and spout; used for drinking wine. 2. A large, bulbous, short-necked bottle.

flake *v.* To separate pieces of food (e.g., cooked fish) into small slivers. *n.* A small sliver.

flaked rice 1. White or brown rice that is rolled and crushed to produce lightweight flakes that are used principally for cereal. 2. Flattened and parboiled short-grain rice, often tinted green, and used in Asian puddings and other sweets.

flakes Processed adjunct grains added to the mash kettle without cooking when brewing beer.

flaki (flah-kee) Polish for tripe.

flamande, à la (flah-MAHND, ah lah) 1 A French term indicating that beer is an ingredient in the dish. 2. A French preparation method associated with Belgian cuisine; the dishes are characterized by a garnish of stuffed braised balls of green cabbage, glazed carrots and turnips, potatoes and sometimes diced salt pork and slices of sausages.

flamande, sauce; Flemish sauce (flamanhd) A French compound sauce made from a hollandaise seasoned with dry mustard and garnished with parsley.

flambé (flahm-bay) Foods served flaming; the flame is produced by igniting the brandy, rum or other alcoholic beverage poured on or incorporated into the item; also known as flamed.

flambé pan, oval An oval pan used for flaming and table-side preparation of dishes such as steak au poivre and steak Diane; made of aluminum-lined copper or silver-lined copper and available in sizes from 7.5 × 12 to 9 × 15 in.

flambé pan, round A round stainless steel–lined copper pan used for table-side presentations; it has a flat, 11-in.-wide round bottom and 1-in.-deep sides. *See* crêpes Suzette pan.

flamber (flahm-bay) To pour warmed spirits such as brandy, whiskey or rum over foods such as meat and game puddings, pancakes and fruit and then ignite it.

flambé trolley A small table on casters fitted with one or two burners (butane or spirit) and used in restaurants for flaming dishes table side. *See* guéridon.

flamed The American word for flambé.

flame seedless grapes A popular variety of red-skinned table grapes; the fruit have a crisp flesh and a sweet flavor; also known as red flame seedless grapes.

Flame Tokay A table grape grown in California; part of the crop is used to make a wine that is distilled into brandy.

flamusse (fla-moose) 1. A tart baked with a filling of Gruyère, cream and beaten egg yolks; made in France's Burgundy region. 2. An apple pudding similar to clafoutis; a speciality of Burgundy.

flan (flahn) 1. A shallow, open-faced French tart, usually filled with fruit or custard. 2. A custard baked over a layer of caramelized sugar and inverted for service. 3. Spanish for crème caramel.

flanchet (flan-shay) A French cut of the beef carcass; it is the flank.

flan de naranja (flahn day nah-raan-jga) A Spanish orange custard garnished with crystallized oranges.

flan de queso (flahn dee quee-soh) A Peruvian custard dessert made of cottage cheese, condensed milk, water and eggs, served with fresh or stewed fruit.

flank A primal section of the beef carcass; located beneath the loin and behind the short plate, it contains no bones, and the meat is flavorful but tough, with a good deal of fat and connective tissue; it produces fabricated cuts such as flank steak, London broil, the hanging tenderloin and ground beef.

flanken A fabricated cut of the beef primals short rib or plate; it is similar to the fabricated short ribs.

flanker Slang for a menu item made without all of the sugar or salt typically used for the product.

flank steak A fabricated cut of the beef primal flank; this tough, somewhat stringy cut is very flavorful.

flan ring A bottomless metal mold with straight sides; it is used for shaping pastry shells and tarts and is available in several shapes and sizes.

flan tin A tart pan with a removable bottom.

flan ring

flapjack Slang for pancake.

flare-sided saucepan *See* saucepan, flare-sided.

Flasche (FLAH-shuh) German for bottle.

flash frozen Food that has been frozen very rapidly using metal plates, extremely low temperatures or chemical solutions.

fläsk (flahsk) Swedish for pork.

flask A bottle-shaped container made of metal, glass or ceramics. *See* hip flask.

flat 1. A shallow basket, crate or other container in which produce is shipped to market. 2. A tasting term for a beer, sparkling wine, carbonated soft drink or other effervescent beverage that has lost its effervescence. 3. A tasting term for a food or beverage that is bland, dull or lacks the right degree of a characteristic flavor.

flatbread; flat bread A category of thin breads that may or may not be leavened, with textures ranging from chewy to crisp; these products tend to be more common in regional or ethnic cuisines (e.g., tortilla, pita bread, naan and focaccia).

flatbrød (FLAHT-brur) Scandinavian cracker breads; they are very thin and crisp and usually made with rye, barley and/or wheat flour.

flat case A case containing a standardized amount of any product.

flatfish A general category of fish characterized by asymmetrical, compressed bodies with both eyes on top of the heads and a dark top skin; they swim in a horizontal position and are generally found in deeper ocean waters (e.g. flounder, halibut and turbot). *See* round fish.

flat icing A simple icing made of water, confectioners' sugar and corn syrup and usually flavored with vanilla or lemon; it is white and glossy and is usually used as a glaze on baked goods such as Danish pastries; also known as plain water icing.

flatiron A subprimal cut of the beef primal chuck; it is a boneless roast divided in the middle.

flat-leaf parsley *See* Italian parsley.

flat slicing A cutting method in which the knife blade is held parallel to the ingredient (and the cutting surface) and the food is sliced horizontally from right to left; generally used with soft foods such as tofu and cold jellied meats.

flat top A cooking surface that is a single steel plate; it supplies even but less intensive heat than an open burner but is able to support heavier weights and makes a larger surface available for cooking. *See* griddle.

flatware Eating utensils such as forks, knives and spoons. *See* silverware.

flat whisk A long whisk used for quickly incorporating flour into melted butter; its looped wires lay in near parallel planes; also known as a roux whisk.

flauta (FLAUW-tah) A Mexican dish consisting of a corn tortilla rolled around a savory filling and deep-fried; often garnished with guacamole, sour cream and salsa.

flat whisk

flavonoids A group of more than 200 naturally occurring compounds (pigments) found in produce such as citrus, leafy vegetables (e.g., red cabbage), red onions, red beets and soybeans; they may have antioxidant capabilities.

flavor *v.* To add seasonings or other ingredients to a food or beverage to improve, change or add to the taste. *n.* 1. The distinctive taste of a food or beverage. 2. A quality of something that affects the sense of taste.

flavor, artificial A synthetic food additive that mimics a natural flavor and is used as a flavoring agent or flavor enhancer.

flavor adjuvant; flavoring adjuvant A type of food additive used to maintain or remove flavor in a processed food.

flavored coffee *See* coffee, flavored.

flavored oil An oil, typically olive or canola, that is flavored with the essential oil of a flavoring ingredient such as garlic, chile, lemon or basil; it is used for cooking or as a flavoring ingredient; also known as an infused oil.

flavored vinegar A vinegar, typically wine or distilled, that is flavored by steeping a flavoring ingredient such as raspberry or rosemary in it; it is used for cooking or as a flavoring ingredient. *See* herb vinegar *and* fruit vinegar.

flavor enhancer; flavoring enhancer A type of food additive used to add, preserve or intensify the flavor of a processed food without imparting its own flavor.

flavoring An item that adds a new flavor to a food and alters its natural flavors; flavorings include herbs, spices, vinegars and other condiments.

flavoring agent A type of food additive used to impart its own characteristic flavor to a processed food.

flavor stabilizer; flavoring stabilizer A type of food additive used to preserve or maintain the flavor (naturally occurring or added) of a food.

flax seeds The seeds of the flax plant (*Linum usitatissium*), an annual herb; the seeds are used for linseed oil and as a flavoring and garnish in Asian cuisines.

flead The inner membrane of a pig's stomach; it is a fine, thin lining full of pieces of pure lard; lard must be purified if taken from areas other than the flead.

Fleckerln (fleck-er-len) A variety of very small, square German and Austrian noodles used as a garnish in soups and also as an accompaniment to meat. *See* Schinkenfleckerln.

fleeting *See* finish.

Fleisch (flysh) German for meat.

Fleischbrühe (flysh-BREW-ah) German for meat broth.

fleischig (fly-schigg) Yiddish for meat, foods made of meat and meat products; one of the three categories of food under Jewish dietary laws (kosher). *See* kosher, milchig *and* pareve.

Flemish sauce *See* flamande, sauce.

flesh 1. When referring to fruits and vegetables, it is typically the edible area under the skin or other outer covering; also known as the pulp. 2. The muscles, fat and related tissues of an animal.

fleshy A wine-tasting term for a wine that is full bodied, with high alcohol, extract and glycerine contents.

flet (fleh) French for flounder.

flétan (flae-tah'n) French for halibut.

fleurde sel de Guerande Very rare and expensive sea salt from French salt basins just south of Brittany; its grey, mineral-laden crystals have a complex flavor, so it is used mainly as a garnish.

Fleur du Maquis (FLUR doo mah-KAY) *See* Brin d'Amour.

Fleurie (fluh-ree) A famous Beaujolais cru; the wines are fruity and fragrant.

fleuron (flew-rawng) A half-moon shape of puff pastry used to garnish entrées.

Fleurs d'Acacia (flewr da-kay-see-ah) An Alsatian eau-de-vie made from acacia flowers.

flexibility 1. Capable of being bent without breaking. 2. The body's ability to bend without injury; it depends on the con-

dition of the joints and the elasticity of the muscles, tendons and ligaments.

flinty A wine-tasting term for a bouquet reminiscent of two flints being rubbed together or struck with steel; often found in hard, dry, white wines such as French Chablis and Pouilly Fumé.

Flip A drink made of liquor or wine, sugar and eggs, blended until frothy; in colonial America and England, the ingredients were heated with a red-hot fireplace poker called a flip iron or flip dog.

flitch 1. A side of a hog, salted and cured. 2. A strip or steak cut from a fish, especially halibut.

float *v.* 1. To pour a shot of distilled spirits on top of a finished drink or coffee without stirring or mixing it in. 2. To pour or place a garnish on top of a food (e.g., soup) without stirring or mixing it in. *n.* 1. A scoop of ice cream in a carbonated beverage, such as root beer. 2. *See* bank.

floating island A dessert consisting of mounds of poached meringue floating in vanilla custard sauce; also known as oeufs à la neige and snow eggs.

flocan (flo-kohn) A French cornflakelike product used to garnish soups or make porridge.

flocculation The clumping together of yeast cells into large particles that settle out toward the end of fermentation during beer and wine making.

Flohkrebs (flock-krebz) German for prawns.

flommen tzimmes (flowm-mehm t'zim-mis) A slightly sweet Jewish pot roast; the beef is cooked with schmaltz, onions, prunes, carrots and honey.

flor (flore) A special yeast native to Spain's Jerez region and France's Jura district; dead yeast cells form a crust over the wines during aging (e.g., sherries and vins jaunes, respectively), imparting a distinctive aroma and flavor.

floral A wine-tasting term for a flowery bouquet; often found in fine white wines made from grapes grown in cool districts; also known as flowery.

Florence fennel *See* fennel, Florence.

florendine (flow-rehn-deen) An 18th-century English pie made from veal loin and kidneys, hard-boiled eggs, rice, currants, sugar, nutmeg, thyme and cream, covered with puff pastry and baked; 19th-century variations include oysters, anchovies, pork, lemon, shallots, mace, butter, consommé and white wine.

Florentina (FLOOR-en-teen-nah) 1. An Italian garnish associated with Florence; spinach is the principal ingredient. 2. An Italian cheese sauce garnished with spinach.

florentine (FLOOR-en-teen) A very thin, crisp cookie or candy made with honey, sugar, nuts and candied fruit; the underside of the cooled confection is usually coated with chocolate.

florentine, à la (FLOOR-en-teen, ah lah) A French preparation method associated with the cuisine of Florence, Italy; the dishes are characterized by a bed of spinach on which the principal ingredient, topped with a Mornay sauce and sometimes sprinkled with cheese and browned, is laid.

floret One of the closely clustered small flowers that comprise a composite flower or curd (e.g., broccoli or cauliflower).

Florian, à la (flo-ree-ahn, ah lah) A French garnish for slices of meat; it consists of braised lettuce, browned pearl onions, and carrots cut into ovals.

Florida Gulf oyster A variety of Atlantic oysters found in the Gulf of Mexico off Florida.

Florida lobsterette See prawn.

Florida mullet See mullet.

Florida mustard A mild mustard made in France's Champagne region and flavored with wine; also known as champagne mustard.

fløte (FLUR-ter) Norwegian for cream.

Flötost (fluht-ohst) A Norwegian Mysost-style cheese made from cow's milk; it has a relatively high percentage of fat.

flounder A large family of flatfish found in the coastal waters of the Atlantic Ocean, Gulf of Mexico and Pacific Ocean; generally, they have a brownish-gray skin, a lean, firm, pearly or pinkish-white flesh and a mild flavor; some are marketed as sole, and sometimes different varieties of flounder and sole are marketed under the same name; significant varieties include blackback flounder, English sole, fluke, gray sole, plaice, starry flounder and yellowfin flounder. See sole.

flounder

flour v. To cover or dust a food or utensil with flour. n. A powdery substance of varying degrees of fineness made by milling wheat, corn, rye or other grains or grinding dried vegetables (e.g., mushrooms), fruits (e.g., plantains) or nuts (e.g., chestnuts).

flour, strong Flour with a high protein content.

flour, weak Flour with a low protein content.

flour sifter See sifter.

flour-treating agents A category of food additives used to improve the color and/or baking qualities of milled flour; includes bleaching agents, aging agents and dough conditioners.

floutes (flute) Cork-shaped quenelles from France's Alsace region made from mashed potatoes, eggs, flour and nutmeg; poached, they are served with a beurre noisette mixed with bread crumbs.

flower cheeses A group of soft, aged English cheeses made from whole cow's milk with flower petals (typically rose or marigold petals) mixed in and often named for the particular flower; they generally have a delicate, floral aroma.

flowered tea A tea flavored with flowers.

flower former A trough used to hold flowers and leaves made from icing while they dry so as to give them a more natural curve.

flower head See head.

flowering chives See chives, garlic.

flowering kale See kale, ornamental.

flower mushroom See shiitake.

flower nail A small tool that consists of a metal or plastic nail-like stem topped with a platform; used in cake decorating to form three-dimensional flowers, arches or scrolls.

Flower of Kent A large apple grown in Great Britain and said to be the variety that inspired Sir Isaac Newton; it has a green skin.

flower nail

flowers, edible Flowers used as an ingredient (e.g., squash blossoms), a flavoring (e.g., pansies, nasturtiums, violas, roses and chive flowers) or an edible garnish (e.g., borage, lovage, lavender, chamomile, citrus, peach, plum and mimosa).

flowery See floral.

flowery white pekoe A Chinese white pekoe tea made from the unopened bud of the tea bush; the beverage has a rosy color and a gentle, sublime flavor.

floyeres (floh-ye-res) Greek almond-stuffed pastry rolls.

fl. oz. See fluid ounce.

flue-cured tobacco Tobacco cured in artificially heated barns; it is less flavorful than tobacco allowed to cure naturally in warm breezes.

fluff duffs Cowboy slang for fancy food.

fluffernutters Sandwiches made with sliced bread, peanut butter and marshmallow fluff.

fluid ounce (fl. oz.) A measure of liquid volume used in the U.S. system; 128 fl. oz. equals 1 U.S. gallon.

fluke 1. A member of the flounder family found in the Atlantic Ocean from the mid-Atlantic states to New England; it has a dark, spotted skin, a lean, white flesh, a sweet, mild flavor and an average market weight of 2–4 lb. (0.9–1.8 kg); also known as summer flounder. 2. A term used imprecisely to describe any young or small flounder found in the Atlantic Ocean.

flummery (FLUHM-muh-ree) 1. A British dessert that traditionally was a molded oatmeal or custard pudding. 2. In the United States, a dessert of simmered berries thickened with cornstarch and served cold with cream.

Flunder (FLUHN-der) German for smoked plaice and flounder.

flundra (fluhn-dra) Swedish for flounder.

fluoridated water See water, fluoridated.

fluorine A trace mineral principally used in forming bones and teeth and protecting teeth from decay; significant sources include cow's milk, egg yolks, tea, shellfish and fluoridated drinking water.

flute v. 1. To make a decorative pattern on the raised edge of a pie crust. 2. To carve grooves, slashes or other decorative markings into vegetables and fruits. n. 1. A stemmed glass with an elongated, V-shaped bowl; used for sparkling wines. *See* Champagne tulip. 2. A thin, slightly sweet, flute-shaped cookie served with ice cream, pudding or the like. 3. A long, thin loaf of French bread.

flute bottle A 750-ml (25.4-fl. oz.) wine bottle with a short, cylindrical body, long sloping shoulders, and a long neck; it originated in Germany's Moselle and Rhine regions; generally, brown glass is used for German wines and green glass for wines from France's Alsace region. *See* bordeaux bottle *and* burgundy bottle.

fluting knife A small knife with a wedge-shaped blade; used for making shallow decorative grooves, notches or cuts in various foods, especially produce.

fluting knife

FMP Foodservice Management Professional; it is the highest level of certification offered by the National Restaurant Association.

foam 1. The thick, creamy collar of gas bubbles that cling to the top of a glass of beer; it is approximately 25% beer. *See* barm. 2. The mass that forms when eggs and sugar are beaten together (e.g., in a sponge cake), before the flour is added.

foamed milk Milk that is heated with steam to approximately 150°F (65°C); air is incorporated while heating to create a light foam; it is used for cappuccino and other coffee drinks.

foam frosting *See* seven-minute frosting.

foaming The process of whipping eggs to incorporate air.

FOB Free on board or freight on board.

FOB shipping point A reference to the agreement between a buyer and seller that the costs of shipping the purchased goods from the seller (such as a manufacturer) to the buyer (such as a store) will be paid by the buyer.

FOB store A reference to the agreement between a buyer and seller that the costs of shipping the purchased goods from the seller (such as a manufacturer) to the buyer (such as a store) will be paid by the seller.

focaccia (foh-CAH-chee-ah) Italian flat bread leavened with yeast and flavored with olive oil and herbs; traditionally made with potato flour.

focused A tasting term for a product with clearly defined aromas and flavors.

fodder Coarse plant food for animals, generally consisting of the entire aboveground plant, including the leaves, stalks and grains.

fofas de bacalhau (FOU-fahsh duh bah-kah-lee-YAU) Small Portuguese fried balls of puréed salt cod.

foguete (fo-gha-tay) Portuguese pastries consisting of a deep-fried pastry tube filled with pineapple, cashews and raisins flavored with rosewater, often dipped in a sweet syrup and dusted with confectioners' sugar.

foie (fwah) French for liver.

foie gras (fwah grah) The enlarged liver of a duck or goose (the birds are methodically fattened through force-feeding

of a corn-based diet); it has two smooth, rounded lobes with a putty color and an extremely high fat content.

foie gras, canned Processed duck or goose foie gras; it can be a solid piece or small pieces compacted to form a block.

foie gras, duck The enlarged liver of a duck; it has a rich and somewhat winy flavor.

foie gras, goose The enlarged liver of a goose; it has a pale putty color and a delicate flavor.

foil; aluminum foil A thin, pliable sheet of aluminum; it is easily molded, conducts heat well, can withstand temperature extremes and is impervious to odors, moisture and air; used to cover foods for cooking and storage.

foil candy cup A small foil cup with fluted edges used to hold truffle creams and liquid candy mixtures; when the candy is set, the foil can be peeled away, leaving a fluted design on the sides of the candy.

foiolo (foh-eeh-oh-loh) Italian for tripe.

foku (foe-coo) Japanese for fork.

folacin A water-soluble vitamin essential for forming blood cells; susceptible to loss during cooking or food storage, significant sources include yeast, leafy green vegetables, legumes, seeds and liver; active forms are known as folic acid and folate.

folate *See* folacin.

fold *v.* To incorporate light, airy ingredients into heavier ingredients by gently moving them from the bottom up over the top in a circular motion. *n.* A measurement of the strength of vanilla extract.

folding *See* cutting and folding.

folic acid A food additive used as a nutrient supplement in processed foods such as breakfast cereals. *See* folacin.

Folle Blanche (fawl blahn'sh) A white wine grape grown in France and used to make Cognac; also known as Gros Plant.

fond (fahn) 1. French for stock. 2. French for bottom and used to describe the concentrated juices, drippings and bits of food left in pans after foods are roasted or sautéed; they are used to flavor sauces made directly in the pans in which the foods were cooked.

fondant (FAHN-dant) A sweet, thick, opaque sugar paste commonly used for glazing pastries (e.g., napoleons) or making candies. *See* rolled fondant.

fondant funnel A large, metal, cone-shaped utensil with a handle on the side, a small opening in the pointed end, and a trigger mechanism that controls the flow of the fondant, chocolate or sauce; it is used to create uniform-sized candies or sauce designs.

fond d'artichaut (fon d'ahr-tee-choh) French for artichoke heart.

fond lié (fahn lee-ay) *See* jus lié.

fondu (FON-du) A cheese that has been melted and blended with liquid or powdered milk, cream, butter, casein or whey and sometimes flavorings.

fondue (fahn-DOO) 1. Traditionally, a hot dish of melted cheeses (usually Emmental style) into which diners dip pieces of bread or other foods to be coated and consumed. 2. A hot preparation of other melted foods, such as chocolate, into which diners dip pieces of food to be coated and consumed. 3. A preparation of thinly sliced vegetables cooked slowly in butter over very low heat until reduced to a pulp; used as an ingredient or accompaniment.

fondue bourguignon (fahn-doo boor-GEEN-yon) A French fondue of beef cubes cooked in oil and served with a variety of sauces.

fondue fork A 9-in.-long fork with a metal shaft and tines and a color-coded handle; used for dipping foods in a fondue pot; two-tined forks with inset barbs are used to hold meat or fish, and three-tined barbless forks are used for bread.

fondue pot A bulbous pot with a broad base to provide adequate heat contact and a narrow top to keep hot oil from splattering; available in sizes from 1½ pt. to 2 qt.

fonduta (foan-DOO-tah) Italian for fondue.

Fontal (fon-tal) Italian Fontina-style cheeses made in regions other than Piedmont from cow's milk; the cheeses are softer and less distinctive than Fontina Val d'Aosta, and their flavors range from bland to sharp; sometimes referred to improperly as Fontina.

Fontina, American An American Fontina-style cheese made from whole cow's milk.

Fontina Val d'Aosta (fahn-TEE-nah val DAY-ohs-TA) A cooked, semisoft to firm cheese made in Italy's Piedmont region from whole ewe's milk; it has a dark golden brown rind stamped with purple, a pale yellow interior, and a mild, nutty flavor; when partly aged, it is used as a table cheese, and when fully aged, it is hard and used for grating.

food 1. Any plant or animal product that provides nourishment when ingested. 2. Any raw, cooked or processed edible substance.

food additive Any one of several thousand organic and inorganic, natural and synthetic substances not normally consumed as a food by itself and usually found (intentionally or incidentally) in processed (as opposed to whole) foods either as a component of the food or as an agent affecting a characteristic of the food such as flavor, texture, color or freshness; regulated by the U.S. Food and Drug Administration (FDA), an additive must be safe, effective and measurable in the final product; some additives are available for home use, and others are generally used only for commercial processing purposes. *See* incidental food additive *and* intentional food additive.

food and beverage department The division or department of a hotel, convention center or the like responsible for all of the establishment's food and beverage activities.

food and beverage manager The person responsible for all aspects of an establishment's food and beverage operation; known as the F and B.

Food and Drug Administration Part of the U.S. Department of Health and Human Services, its activities are directed at protecting the nation's health against impure and unsafe foods, drugs, cosmetics, medical devices and other products; it approves and regulates food additives, sets standards for food-labeling language, and carries out many of the provisions of The Food, Drug and Cosmetic Act of 1936, as amended.

food chopper *See* buffalo chopper.

food color; food coloring *See* coloring agent.

food-contact surface In the food safety context, the surface of any utensil or piece of equipment with which food normally comes in contact.

food cost formulas Various methods of calculating the cost of the menu items offered by a food services facility.

food cost percentage The costs incurred for each dollar of menu items sold; it is expressed as a percentage of sales.

food cost percentage pricing Pricing a menu item based on the total food costs; it is calculated by dividing the cost per portion by the food cost percentage.

food costs The costs of the materials (all of the foods) used in the fabrication of a menu item as well as overproduction, pilferage and waste; calculated as the total cost of all foods used during a specific period or as a cost of one particular portion or menu item; also known as the cost of goods sold and raw food costs.

food court An area in a shopping mall, stadium, office complex or other public facility housing one or more (but usually several) small refreshment stands or dining establishments, each offering a different menu (typically ethnic foods, salads, burgers, sandwiches and the like); diners typically purchase their foods and return to a central dining area, although some of the establishments may offer limited seating. *See* mall food.

food danger zone The temperature range of 40–140°F (5–60°C), which is most favorable for bacterial growth; also known as the temperature danger zone.

food guide pyramid; food pyramid Adopted by the U.S. Department of Agriculture (USDA) in 1992, it is a planning tool providing priorities and portions for daily food choices in a balanced diet; it generally emphasizes increased consumption of fruits, vegetables and grains and reduced consumption of fatty foods; at the pyramid's base are breads, cereals, rice and pasta (6–11 daily servings), next are fruits (2–4 servings) and vegetables (3–5 servings), then milk, yogurt and cheese (2–3 servings), then meat, poultry, fish, dry beans, eggs and nuts (2–3 servings), and at the top, fats, oils and sweets (to be eaten sparingly).

food mill A tool used to strain and purée foods si-

food mill

multaneously; it consists of a hopper with a hand-crank mechanism that forces the food through a perforated disk; most models have interchangeable disks with various-sized holes.

food poisoning 1. An illness resulting from the ingestion of foods containing poisonous substances (e.g., certain mushrooms) or foods contaminated with certain insecticides. 2. A term used imprecisely to describe an illness resulting from the ingestion of rancid or partially decomposed (putrefied) foods or foods containing pathogenic bacteria.

food processor An appliance used to purée, chop, grate, slice and shred foods; it consists of a bowl that sits atop a motorized driveshaft; an S-shaped blade on the bottom of the bowl processes food that can be fed into the bowl through an opening or tube on top; some models can be fitted as a juicer and/or pasta maker.

food sales Total revenue from food sales over a given or projected period; the number can also be total revenues from a particular category or type of food or menu item.

food service chemicals Chemicals such as pesticides, cleaning agents, polishes, abrasives and the like that are used for beneficial purposes in food preparation and service but that, if they remain on or come in contact with food, a dish or utensil, pose or may pose a danger when ingested.

foods of low nutrient density *See* empty calories.

food supplements *See* supplements.

food wine An American term for a wine that goes particularly well with food, as opposed to one more suitably consumed on its own.

foofoo; foufou; fufu; foutou An extremely thick porridge made from ground cassava, corn, rice and/or yams and a staple of Central and West African cuisines.

fool A British dessert made by folding puréed fruit (traditionally gooseberries) into whipped cream.

foon tiu mein *See* chow fun.

foot The end of the cigar that is lit. *See* head.

foot-long A foot-long frankfurter.

foo yong *See* egg foo yong.

Forbidden Fruit An American liqueur made from a shaddock (pomelo) steeped with brandy.

forcemeat A mixture of ground cooked or raw meats, fish, shellfish, poultry, vegetables and/or fruits combined with a binder, seasoned and emulsified with fat; it is the primary ingredient in charcuterie items such as pâtés, terrines, galantines and sausages; there are three principal styles: basic, countrystyle and mousseline.

forcemeat, basic A moderately fine forcemeat that is well seasoned, especially with pâté spice; most pâtés and terrines are made with a basic forcemeat.

forcemeat, countrystyle A coarsely ground forcemeat heavily seasoned with onions, garlic, pepper, juniper berries and bay leaves.

forcemeat, mousseline A light, delicate and airy forcemeat, usually made with fish or shellfish; egg whites and cream are often added to lighten and enrich the mixture. *See* mousse.

forchetta (for-CHEH-tah) Italian for fork.

Fordhook lima bean A plump bean with a slight kidney shape; it has a pale green color and is meatier and more flavorful than a lima bean.

forecast For a food services facility, an estimate or calculated guess of customer count and/or food and beverage sales.

foreigner's cheeks *See* jambosa.

forel (fah-REHL) Russian for trout.

Forelle (foh-REL-ea) German for trout.

forequarter 1. Either bilateral half of the front section of a beef carcass; it includes the entire rib, chuck, short plate, and brisket and shank primals. 2. Either bilateral half of the foresaddle of a veal carcass; it contains half of the shoulder, rib, and foreshank and breast primals. 3. Either bilateral half of the foresaddle of a lamb carcass; it contains half of the shoulder, breast and rack primals. 4. *See* hindquarter.

forequarter flank A British cut of the beef carcass; it is the equivalent of American short ribs.

foresaddle 1. The undivided forequarters (the front half) of a veal carcass; it includes the shoulder, rib and foreshank and breast primals. 2. The undivided forequarters (the front half) of a lamb carcass; it includes the shoulder, rack and breast primals. 3. *See* hindsaddle.

foreshank 1. A portion of the lower forelimb (below the knee) of a quadruped. 2. A fabricated cut of the beef primal brisket and foreshank; it is tough and flavorful and contains a large amount of connective tissue. 3. A fabricated cut of the veal primal foreshank and breast; it is similar to the beef cut. 4. A subprimal cut of the lamb primal breast; it is similar to the beef cut.

foreshank, ground Meat ground from the muscles along the beef foreshank; it is high in collagen and is used to clarify and flavor consommés.

foreshank and breast A primal section of the veal carcass; it is beneath the shoulder and rib primals and consists of cartilaginous tissue, rib bones, breast bones and shank bones, many of which are more cartilaginous than boney; the meat is generally flavorful but somewhat tough; significant fabricated cuts include the veal breast roast, foreshank and cubed and ground products.

foreshot The first crude spirit that appears from the still during whiskey production.

Forester A cocktail made of bourbon, cherry liqueur and lemon juice; garnished with a maraschino cherry.

forestière, à la (foh-reh-styehr, ah lah) A French preparation for small cuts of meat or vegetables; they are garnished with mushrooms, bacon and diced potatoes.

forest mushroom *See* slippery jack.

forged knife blade *See* knife blade, forged.

fork A utensil usually made of metal with two, three or four prongs (tines) on the end of a handle; used at the table and in the kitchen.

formaggi di pasta filata (fohr-MAH-jee day pahs-tah fee-laht-ah) A group of Italian cheeses made from pasta filata (e.g., mozzarella, Provolone, Caciocavallo and Incanestrato).

formaggini (fohr-MAH-gee-knee) An Italian term describing any of several kinds of small, Italian cheeses.

formaggio (fohr-MAH-jee-oh) Italian for cheese.

formaggio di capra (fohr-MAH-jee-oh dee cah-prah) Italian for goat's milk cheese.

formaggio pecorino (fohr-MAH-jee-oh peh-kuh-REE-noh) Italian for ewe's milk cheese.

formaggio vacchino (fohr-MAH-jee-oh vah-CHEE-noh) Italian for cow's milk cheese.

formic acid A food additive with a pungent aroma used as a flavoring agent.

Formosa Oolong An expensive Taiwanese oolong tea; the beverage has a pale yellow color and light peachy flavor and is best served without milk.

Formosa Pouchong A Taiwanese oolong tea; the leaves are scented with jasmine, gardenia or yulan blossoms; the beverage has a pale yellow color and delicate floral aroma and is best served without milk.

formula The bakeshop term for a recipe.

formula-fed veal *See* veal, milk-fed.

formulation aid A category of food additives used to promote or produce a desired texture or physical state in a processed food; includes binders, fillers, plasticizers and so on.

formula wine A wine other than a standard one, produced on bonded premises (not necessarily a winery) under an approved formula (e.g., vermouth).

forno (fohr-no) Italian and Portuguese for oven.

forno, al (FOR-no, ahl) Italian term used to describe an item baked in the oven.

forretter (FOR-reht-er) Norwegian for hors d'oeuvre or appetizer.

fortification The process of adding distilled spirits to a wine to stop fermentation, enhance keeping properties, increase the wine's alcohol content and/or strengthen its flavor and aroma; fortification creates a distinctive type of wine. *See* fortified wine.

fortified Refers to products such as milk, salt, sports drinks or other beverages to which, subject to U.S. Food and Drug Administration (FDA) regulations, vitamins (e.g., vitamins A and D in milk and vitamin C in sports drinks) and/or minerals (e.g., iodine in salt) have been added during processing to replace nutrients lost during processing, supplement naturally occurring nutrients or add nutrients not normally present in the food. *See* enriched.

fortified milk Milk with vitamins A and D added.

fortified skim milk Skim milk with vitamins A and D added.

fortified wine A wine that has had its alcohol content enhanced with brandy or rectified alcohol to create a distinctively new product such as port, sherry, Madeira or Marsala. *See* fortification.

fortune cookie A thin, crisp wafer cookie folded around a small strip of paper on which a message or fortune is printed; served in Chinese–American restaurants.

for two A menu term indicating that the item is prepared to serve and priced for two people.

forward A wine-tasting term for a wine that has revealed its character fully.

fouet (foo-ay) 1. A very thin, semidry French pork sausage seasoned with only salt and pepper. 2. French for whisk.

fougasse (foo-gahss) A rectangular, ladder-shaped bread from southern France, usually made with baguette dough and flavored with anchovies, olives, herbs or nuts.

four (foor) French for oven.

fourchette (four-cheht) French for fork.

four food groups A planning tool for a balanced daily diet adopted by the U.S. Department of Agriculture (USDA) in 1956 and superseded by the food pyramid; it divided foods into four groups—(1) milk and cheese, (2) meats and fish, (3) fruits and vegetables and (4) grains—and recommended four or more servings from the last two groups and two or more servings from the first two groups, with a maximum of 12 servings per day.

Fourme d'Ambert (furm d'am-bear) A French cheese made from cow's milk; it has a mottled gray rind, a white interior with deep blue veins and a sharp, tangy flavor.

Four Roses Distillery One of the 12 remaining U.S. whiskey distilleries; located in Lawrenceburg, Kentucky, and founded c. 1888, it became part of the Frankfort Distilling Company in 1902; its products include Four Roses straight bourbon and Four Roses blended whiskey.

four spices *See* quatre épices.

four-top Restaurant slang for a table that seats four people.

fowl Any edible wild or domesticated bird. *See* poultry.

fox grape A North American grape variety; the spherical fruit have a purplish-black skin and a musky flavor; also known as a plum grape or skunk grape.

foxy A tasting term used to describe a food or beverage with a musky, animal-like aroma.

Fra Diavolo (fra dee-AH-vo-lo) Italian for Brother Devil and used to describe a peppery or piquant dish.

fragola (FRAH-goh-lah) Italian for strawberry.

fragole all'aceto (FRAH-goh-leh ahl ah-chet-toh) An Italian dessert of wild strawberries marinated in balsamic vinegar.

fragole al vino (FRAH-goh-leh ahl vee-noh) An Italian dessert of wild strawberries served with sugar and wine, which is poured over the berries at the table.

fragrant A tasting term for an agreeable floral, fruity, vegetal, herbal or spicy aroma or bouquet.

frâiche (frehsh) French for fresh; also spelled *frais* (fray).

frais (fray) French for fresh or cool and used as a wine-labeling term to suggest that the wine should be served well chilled.

fraisage (fray-sawgh) A French technique of kneading dough by smearing it across the board with the heel of the hand, then reforming it into a ball.

fraise (frehz) 1. French for strawberry. 2. A brandy made in France's Alsace region from wild and cultivated strawberries.

Fraiser Valley A grape-growing and wine-producing region in Canada's British Columbia province; the principal grapes grown are Chardonnay and Pinot Blanc; the area is also known for fruit wines made from blueberries, raspberries and red and white currants.

fraises des bois (frehz duh bwah) Small, elongated wild strawberries grown in France; they have a light red skin, a juicy red flesh and a rich, sweet flavor.

Fraisier; le Fraisier (fray-zee-aihr) A French strawberry layer cake made with rectangular layers of genoise filled with a mousseline cream and sliced fresh strawberries; usually topped with a thin layer of pale pink or green marzipan; also known as bagatelle.

Framberry The proprietary name of a French raspberry liqueur.

framboesa (frahm-boh-theh-sah) Portuguese for raspberry.

framboise (frahm-bwahz) 1. French for raspberry. 2. A brandy made in France's Alsace region from wild raspberries. 3. A rasberry lambic beer.

frambozen (frahm-BO-zuh) 1. A Belgian raspberry lambic beer; it should be served chilled in champagne flutes; also known in French as framboise. 2. Dutch for raspberry.

frambuesa (frahm-BWAY-ssahss) Spanish for raspberry.

frame size The size of a person's skeleton and musculature.

Francaise, sauce; French sauce (frahn-saze) A French compound sauce made from beárnaise flavored with a fish glaze and tomato purée.

francese (fran-TCHAE-sae) An Italian dish in which the main ingredient (e.g., veal cutlet) is dipped in egg and flour and sautéed in butter and white wine.

Franciscan sauce *See* Cordelier, sauce.

Francois I, sauce (franz-wahz) A French white wine sauce finished with butter and garnished with diced tomatoes and mushrooms.

Frangelico (fran-JELL-ih-koh) A hazelnut-flavored liqueur.

frangipane (fran-juh-pahn) 1. An almond-flavored pastry cream used in the preparation of various desserts and cakes; also known as frangipane cream. 2. In classic French cookery, a pastry dough similar to pâte à choux.

frangipane cream *See* frangipane.

frango (FRAN-goo) Portuguese for young chicken.

frango de campo (FRAN-goh day kam-pho) Portuguese for free-range chicken.

frango grelhado pili pili (FRAN-goh grehl-hah-doh pee-lee pee-lee) An Angolan dish consisting of chicken marinated in lemon juice, peanut oil and pili pili and then grilled.

Franken (FRAHN-ken) An Anbaugebiet located along the Main River in southeast Germany; the wines are typically dry to semisweet, flowery and flavorful rather than delicate and are often sold in a Bocksbeutel.

Frankfort Distilling Company Founded in 1902 as a collection of small Kentucky whiskey distilleries, it was granted permission to produce whiskey for medicinal purposes during Prohibition; it was later sold to Seagram and Sons.

frankfurter; frank A smoked, seasoned, precooked sausage made from beef, pork, chicken and/or turkey, with or without a casing; it can contain up to 30% fat and 10% added water; the most common size is 6 in. (15.2 cm) in length; also known as a hot dog or a wiener.

Franschhoek A grape-growing and wine-producing region of South Africa; the town was settled in 1688 by French Huguenots, who brought wine-producing skills with them; it is known for high-quality dry white wines made from the Cabernet Sauvignon and Shiraz grapes; sparkling wines are also produced using the Methode Cap Classique.

frappé (fra-PAY) 1. Fruit juice or other flavored liquid frozen to a slushy consistency; it can be sweet or savory and served as a drink, appetizer or dessert. 2. French for very cold when used as a wine term. 3. A liqueur served over shaved ice. 4. Italian for milk shake.

frasca (FRAH-skah) A casual Italian restaurant, usually located near a winery.

Frascati (frahs-CAH-tee) A fresh, spicy, white wine produced near the central Italian village of Frascati; known as the traditional house wine of Roman trattorie.

Frascati, à la (FRAH-skah-tee, ah lah) A French garnish for beef; it consists of sliced foie gras, truffles, fluted mushroom caps and asparagus with a demi-glaze poured over the top.

frattaglie (frah-tah-yae) Italian for giblets.

freddo (FRAYD-do) Italian for cold.

free The food-labeling term approved by the U.S. Food and Drug Administration (FDA) and used to describe a food containing no or only physiologically inconsequential amounts of fat, saturated fat, cholesterol, sodium, sugar or calories.

freebie Slang for services or items given free of charge to a customer.

free-flow agent *See* anticaking agent.

free on board *See* FOB.

free pour The portion of distilled spirits poured from a bottle without the aid of a measuring device.

free radical A compound that can damage living tissue; free radicals, generally oxygen fragments, occur naturally in the body and are found in polluted air, radiation, tobacco smoke, ultraviolet sunlight and rancid fats.

free-range chicken *See* chicken, free-range.

free-range veal *See* veal, free-range.

free-run juice In wine making, the grape juice released by the sheer weight or pressure of the mass before the grape press is used; this juice is sometimes fermented separately or combined with press juice. *See* press juice.

freestone A general description for a fruit that has flesh that does not adhere to its pit. *See* clingstone.

freeze To subject food to a temperature below 32°F (0°C) so that the moisture in the food solidifies; used as a preservation method.

freeze-dried coffee granules or crystals Granules or crystals made from freshly brewed coffee that has been frozen into a slush before the water is evaporated; considered to produce a reconstituted beverage superior in flavor to instant coffee. *See* instant coffee.

freezer An insulated cabinet (reach-in) or room (walk-in) used to store foods at very low (below freezing) temperatures created by mechanical or chemical refrigeration. *See* refrigerator.

freezer burn The surface dehydration and discoloration of food that results from moisture loss at below freezing temperatures.

freight on board *See* FOB.

freloin A British cut of the pork carcass; it is the rib end of the loin.

french, to 1. To cut meat or vegetables into long, slender strips. 2. To remove the meat from the end of a chop or rib, thereby exposing the bone; also known as frenched.

French bread A crusty white yeast bread made with only flour, water, yeast and salt, usually shaped in a long, slender loaf.

French bread pan *See* baguette pan.

French buttercream A rich, creamy frosting made by whipping whole eggs or egg yolks into a thick foam with hot sugar syrup, then beating in softened butter and flavorings.

French Colombard (kohl-om-bar) 1. A white wine grape grown principally in California. 2. A white wine made from this grape; it has a pale color and a tart flavor; it is often blended with Chenin Blanc to make a California Chablis.

French doughnuts Doughnuts made from pâte à choux.

French dressing 1. A mixture of oil and vinegar, usually seasoned with salt and pepper and various herbs and garlic; also known as vinaigrette. 2. An American dressing that is creamy, tartly sweet and red-orange in color.

French drip pot A three-tiered coffeemaker; the upper container is filled with water, which drips through a middle container holding the coffee grounds; the coffee is then collected in the bottom container.

frenched A roast, rack or chop of meat, especially lamb, from which the excess fat has been removed, leaving the eye muscle intact, and all meat and connective tissue have been removed from the rib bone.

frenched green bean A green bean cut lengthwise into very narrow strips.

French endive *See* Belgian endive.

French-fried onions Large onion rings dipped in a batter and deep-fried in oil.

French fries Potatoes cut into matchstick shapes, soaked in cold water, dried, and deep-fried until crisp and golden brown. *See* shoestring potatoes, steak fries *and* straw potatoes.

French fry *See* deep-frying.

French fry cutter A tool used to cut a potato into sticks; the potato is forced through a metal cutting grid.

French green bean; French bean *See* haricot vert.

French Improved plum A variety of plum used mostly for prunes.

French knife *See* chef's knife.

French lentils *See* lentils, French.

French oak Oak (genus *Quercus*) cut from forests in France's Limousine, Never, Allies, Bourgogne, Trenches and Visages regions and used to make the barrels in which wine is aged and stored.

French pastry Any of a variety of small, fancy cakes and other pastries, usually in a single serving size.

French roast *See* roast, French.

French sauce *See* Francaise, sauce.

French service 1. Restaurant service in which one waiter (a captain) takes the order, does the table-side cooking, and brings the food and beverages while the back waiter serves bread and butter, crumbs the table, serves coffee and the like. 2. Restaurant service in which each item is separately served and placed on a customer's plate (as opposed to all items being plated in the kitchen).

French 75 A cocktail made of gin, lemon juice and brandy mixed with ice and strained into a champagne glass, which is then filled with Champagne.

French stick An English term for a long, thin loaf of French bread, commonly known as a baguette.

French toast A breakfast dish of bread dipped in egg and milk, sautéed in butter, sometimes garnished with fruit, and served with syrup or confectioners' sugar.

French vermouth *See* vermouth, dry.

French vinegar Archaic cookbook term for tarragon vinegar.

fresa (FRAY-ssahss) Spanish for strawberry.

fresca (FREHS-kah) Spanish for fresh.

fresco (FRAYZ-ko) Italian and Portuguese for fresh.

fresh 1. A food that has not been frozen. 2. A food that has been recently produced, such as a loaf of bread. 3. A food as grown or harvested; not canned, dried or processed and containing no preservatives. 4. A wine-tasting term for a clean, lively wine that has not lost its youthful charm.

fresh bean *See* beans, fresh.

fresh cheeses *See* cheeses, fresh.

freshening Rinsing salt-preserved butter or other foods in several changes of water to make them more palatable.

fresh-frozen A food that was frozen while still fresh.

fresh ham A primal section of the pork carcass; it is the hog's hind leg and contains the aitch, leg and hind shank bones and large muscles. *See* ham.

freshly brewed coffee Brewed coffee that is less than 1 hour old; a generally accepted standard in the food and beverage industry.

freshness date *See* open date.

freshwater drum *See* sheepshead.

fresh yeast *See* compressed yeast.

Fresno chile A short, conical fresh chile with a green color (that reddens when ripe), a thick flesh, and a sweet, hot flavor; named for the California city where it was first grown commercially; also known as chile caribe and chile cera.

friandises (free-yawn-DEEZ) French for confections served after a meal (e.g., truffles, mints or petit fours).

fricandelles; fricadelles (frick-ah-dell) A Belgian dish consisting of balls of minced pork, onions, bread crumbs, white wine, egg yolks and stiffly beaten egg whites, rolled in flour and fried, then poached in stock with potatoes; also used in les choesels.

fricandò (free-kahn-DOH) An Italian dish of veal that is larded, browned and then braised in marsala wine.

fricassée (FRIHK-uh-see) A French white stew in which the meat (usually chicken or veal) is cooked in fat but not browned before the liquid is added.

Fridatten (frid-DAH-tern) An Austrian garnish for soups consisting of a pancake cut into matchlike strips.

fried pies *See* hand pies.

fried rice A Chinese and Chinese–American dish of cold cooked rice seasoned with soy sauce and fried; egg, meat, shellfish, poultry and/or vegetable garnishes are usually added.

fries 1. The intestines of a pig or lamb. 2. The testicles of a pig, lamb, calf or bull. 3. Slang for French fries. 4. *See* fry.

Friesian milk (free-ZEE-ayn) Whole milk from a Friesian cow.

frijoles (free-HOH-lehs) Spanish (particularly in Mexico) for beans, including pink, black, kidney and pinto beans.

frijoles negros escabechados (free-HOH-lehs nay-gross es-caba-tcha-doss) A Peruvian dish of precooked black beans cooked (again) with ham, garlic, cumin and chile powder and garnished with hard-boiled eggs and olives.

frijoles refritos (free-HOH-lehs reh-FREE-tohs) Spanish for well-fried beans (often improperly translated as refried beans).

frikadellar (free-kah-DAYL-err) 1. Danish meatballs made with pork and beef and fried in butter. 2. Swedish meatballs made from veal, bread crumbs, herbs and egg white and simmered in sour cream or yogurt.

Frikadellen (free-kah-dell-ahn) German meatballs made of beef, bread crumbs and egg.

frikasse (free-kah-se) Norwegian for stew.

frill A fluted paper ornament slipped over protruding bones as a decoration; typically used on a crown roast of pork or lamb, lamb chop and leg of lamb.

fringe The end of an oyster opposite the hinge.

frío; frio (FREE-ah) Spanish and Portuguese for cold.

frire (free) French for to fry.

frisch (free-sch) German for fresh.

Frischkäse (free-scha-kaiz) A fresh, soft, German cream cheese made from cow's milk; it has a mild flavor.

Frisco Sour A cocktail made of whiskey, Benedictine, lemon juice, lime juice and grenadine; served in a whiskey sour glass and garnished with an orange slice.

frisée (free-zay) A variety of endive with yellowish-green curly leaves; also known as chicorée frisée.

frisk (freesk) Norwegian for fresh.

frit (free) French for fried.

fritangas (free-tahn-gas) Spanish for fried things and used to describe small fried foods or fritters eaten as antojitos in South and Central America.

fritar (free-tahr) Portuguese for fried.

fritas (FREE-tahs) Spanish for fritters and used to describe a dish consisting of chicken and ham cooked in a white sauce, then pressed between slices of stale bread, coated with beaten egg and deep-fried; served with lemon or tomato sauce.

fritelle (free-TEL-lah) Corsican snack food made by deep-frying a yeast-leavened dough flavored with chestnut flour, olive oil and fennel.

fritiert (free-tea-ert) German for fried.

frito (FREE-toh) Spanish for fried.

frittata (free-tah-ta) An open-faced omelet of Spanish–Italian heritage.

fritter A small, sweet or savory, deep-fried cake made by either combining chopped foods with a thick batter or dipping the food into the batter.

fritto (FREET-toh) Italian for fried.

fritto misto (FREET-toh MEES-toh) Italian for mixed fry or mixed fried and used to describe small pieces of meat or vegetables dipped in batter and deep-fried.

friturier (free-too-ree-ay) At a food services operation following the brigade system, the person responsible for all fried items; also known as the fry station chef.

frizzante (free-ZAHN-teh) The Italian equivalent of a slightly sparkling wine described as pétillant; the best known is Lambrusco.

frizzes (FRIHZ-ihs) Dry Italian sausages made from pork or beef, seasoned with garlic and anise; they have a squiggly shape and are available highly spiced (corded with a red string) or mild (corded with a blue string).

frizzle To deep-fry small pieces or slices of food (e.g., a soft tortilla) until they are crisp and curled.

frog An amphibian; its legs have an average market weight of 2–8 oz. (57–230 g) and a tender, lean flesh with an ivory-white color and a delicate flavor; significant varieties include the wild common frog and the farm-raised bullfrog.

frog-eye gravy *See* redeye gravy.

frogfish *See* monkfish.

Frogmore stew A dish from the American South consisting of crab, shrimp, corn on the cob, potatoes and sausage cooked in a spicy broth; also known as Low Country boil.

froid (fwah) French for cold.

froise An archaic English cooking term for a food, sometimes battered, that was fried.

frokost (fruh-kohst) Norwegian for breakfast.

frollini (froh-LEE-nee) A soft Italian butter cookie made with potato starch.

fromage (froh-MAJH) French for cheese.

Fromage à la Crème (froh-MAJH ah lah krem) A soft, simple French cheese made from cow's milk or a mixture of milk and cream; it has a rich, mild, slightly sweet flavor and should be eaten fresh.

Fromage à la Pie (froh-MAJH ah lah pee) A French cottage cheese–style or farmer cheese–style cheese made from whole or skimmed cow's milk; it has a soft texture, and white appearance and is generally eaten fresh; also known as Ferme, Maigre and Mou.

fromage a tàrtiner (froh-MAJH ah tahr-tee-nay) French for a melting cheese.

Fromage Blanc (froh-MAJH blahn) A French cream cheese–style cheese made from skimmed cow's milk; it has a very soft, almost liquid consistency; eaten fresh, usually with fruit and sugar added.

Fromage de Bourgogne (froh-MAJH duh boor-gohn-yah) A soft cheese made in France's Burgundy region from cow's milk; it has a white interior and mild flavor; sold in a loaf shape.

Fromage de Foin (froh-MAJH duh fwahn) A French Livarot-style cheese ripened on freshly cut hay, which imparts a characteristic aroma.

fromage de soja (froh-MAJH duh soh-jha) French for tofu.

fromage de tête (froh-MAJH duh tet) French for head-cheese.

Fromage de Troyes (froh-MAJH duh trwoa) *See* Barberey.

Fromage Fort (froh-MAJH four) A cooked cheese made in France from skim milk; after melting, the curds are pressed in cloth and grated fine; after ripening for several days, milk, butter, salt, pepper, wine or other flavorings are added and the cheese is ripened further.

froment renfle A variety of wheat grown in the Mediterranean region; it produces a flour with a low gluten-forming potential, which makes poor-quality breads; also known as English wheat.

from scratch; scratch To make an item, usually baked goods, from the raw ingredients, without using a mix or processed convenience products (other than items such as baking powder).

from the well *See* well drink.

front of the house The areas of a restaurant, hotel or the like open to the public or within public view, such as a lobby, bar, dining room or other public space. *See* back of the house.

front waiter The person at a restaurant responsible for ensuring that the tables are set properly for each course, foods are delivered properly to the proper tables and the guests' needs are met; also known as a chef de rang.

Froschsckenkel (FROSH-shehnkerl) German for frog's legs.

frost To coat or cover an item with frosting or icing.

frostfish *See* rainbow smelt.

frost grape A North American grape variety; the fruit have a dark purple skin and, after a frost, are generally used for home wine making; also known as a chicken grape or winter grape.

frosting 1. A sweet decorative coating used as a filling between the layers or as a coating over the top and sides of a cake; also known as icing. 2. Chilling a mug or glass in the freezer, with or without first wetting it; usually done for serving beer or straight-up cocktails.

froth Foam; a formation of tiny bubbles.

Frothee A product made from egg whites and other ingredients and used to make an airy, foamy head on certain cocktails.

Froupe A cocktail made of brandy, sweet vermouth and Benedictine.

frowy Archaic slang for stale or rancid.

Frucht (frukht) German for fruit; also known as Obst.

fructose 1. A monosaccharide occurring naturally in fruits and honey that is sweeter than table sugar; also known as levulose and fruit sugar. 2. A food additive used as a nutritive sweetener in processed foods such as beverages and candies.

fructose corn syrup A food additive used as a sweetener in beverages, canned fruit, frozen desserts and dairy drinks; also known as isomerized syrup and levulose-bearing syrup.

Frühstück (FRU-stook) 1. A small German Limburger-style cheese made from whole or partly skimmed cow's milk; marketed fresh or aged in a cylindrical shape wrapped in foil or parchment. 2. A Belgian cheese of similar description. 3. German for breakfast.

fruit (frwee) French for fruit.

fruitage A yield of fruit.

fruit a pain (frwee ah pan) French for breadfruit.

fruitarian One whose diet includes fruits, seeds and nuts but no vegetables, grains or animal products. *See* vegetarian.

fruit basket *See* gift basket.

fruit butter A sweet spread of fresh fruit flavored with sugar and spices and cooked until thick and smooth.

fruitcake A Christmas cake made with candied fruit, dried fruit and nuts bound with a relatively small amount of a dense, spicy batter.

fruit cocktail A chilled mix of various chopped fruits served as an appetizer; spices or liqueurs are sometimes added.

fruit leather Puréed fruit, sometimes with sugar or honey added, spread in a thin layer and dried; usually rolled and eaten as a snack.

fruit oils The essential oils found in certain fruit, especially the rind of citrus fruit; used as flavorings.

fruits The edible organs that develop from the ovary of flowering plants; they contain one or more seeds and are usually sweet and eaten as is or used as ingredients. *See* vegetable.

fruit salad A salad of various fresh, frozen and/or canned fruits; the natural fruit juices used for the dressing are sometimes flavored with a sweet liqueur and lemon juice.

fruit salad fruit *See* monstera.

fruits de mer (frwee duh MAIR) French for fruits of the sea and used to describe almost any combination of fish and/or shellfish.

fruit soup A soup made from puréed fruit and flavored with wine, milk or cream, spices and other flavorings; served hot or cold.

fruit sugar *See* fructose.

fruit syrup A blend of concentrated sugar syrup and fruit juice.

fruit-vegetables Foods such as avocados, eggplants, chiles and tomatoes that are botanically fruits but are most often prepared and served like vegetables.

fruit vinegar A flavored vinegar made by steeping whole or crushed fruit in a wine vinegar (the fruit is usually removed before use); typical fruits include raspberries, pears, black currants and strawberries.

fruity 1. A cheese-tasting term for the sweet, appealing flavor or aroma of a cheese, usually a monastery cheese or a firm mountain cheese. 2. A wine-tasting term for a wine with a pleasing aroma reminiscent of fresh, ripe fruit but not necessarily of grapes.

frukt (frewkt) Norwegian for fruit.

frukt (FROOK-ti) Russian for fruit.

frumenty (FROU-men-tee) Hulled wheat cooked in milk and sweetened.

frusta (FROO-stah) Italian for wire whisk.

fruta (froo-tah) Portuguese and Spanish for fruit.

frutsu jus (froot-soo jew-s) Japanese for juice; also known as juse.

frutta (FROOT-tah) Italian for fruit.

frutta di martorana (FROO-tah dee mahr-toh-RAH-nah) Italian candies made of marzipan molded into various fruit shapes.

frutti de mare (FROOT-tee dee MA-ray) Italian for fruits of the sea and used to describe almost any combination of fish and/or shellfish.

fry *v. See* frying. *n.* 1. An imprecisely used term for almost any fish when it is still young and not more than a few inches long. 2. A single French fry. 3. A social gathering at which foods are fried and eaten (e.g., a fish fry). 4. *See* fries.

fry bread A Native American (especially Navajo and Hopi) bread; it consists of thin rounds of plain dough that are deep-fried and served hot with sweet or savory toppings.

fryer; fryer chicken *See* chicken, broiler-fryer.

fryer-roaster turkey *See* turkey, fryer-roaster.

frying A dry-heat cooking method in which foods are cooked in hot fat; includes sautéing, stir-frying, pan-frying and deep-frying.

frying pan A round pan with a single long handle and low, sloping sides and used to pan-fry foods; available with a nonstick surface and in 8-, 10- and 12-in. diameters; also known as a skillet.

frying pan

frying pan, electric A frying pan, usually a 12-in. square and sometimes with a nonstick surface, with a built-in thermostatically controlled heat source.

fry station chef *See* friturier.

fu (foo) A dried wheat-gluten product; available in thin sheets or thick round cakes; mixed into soups and vegetable dishes as a protein supplement in Chinese cuisines.

fuchsia jelly A jelly made from the small, spherical or ovoid, purple fruits of the fuchsia.

fuder (foo-duh) A traditional oak cask from Germany's Moselle region with a capacity of 1000 liters (approximately 264 U.S. gallons).

fudge A semisoft candy made by cooking butter, sugar, cream and flavorings, especially chocolate, together to the soft-ball stage; nuts or other garnishes are often added.

Fuertes avocado (foo-ehr-TAY) An avocado with a relatively smooth, green skin.

fuet (foo-ah) A very thin Spanish sausage seasoned with pepper.

fufu *See* foofoo.

Fuggles A variety of hops grown in England and Oregon.

Fuji apple A medium-sized apple with a yellow, orange and red-streaked skin, a crisp, white flesh, and a sweet flavor.

fuki (foo-KEE) A rhubarblike vegetable native to Japan.

Fukien oolong An oolong tea from China's Fukien province; the beverage has a pale color and slightly fruity flavor.

fukko (foo-koe) Japanese for a large sea bass (suzuki); it is used for sushi and sashimi. *See* seigo.

fukurotake (foo-koo-roh-tah-kee) Japanese for straw mushroom.

ful (fuhl) Arabic for fava beans.

full American plan *See* American plan.

full board and pension *See* American plan.

full-bottle replacement A bar control practice in which bartenders are only given new, full bottles in return for completely empty ones.

full-cut round A fabricated cut of the beef primal round; it is a very lean, somewhat tough steak cut perpendicular to the bone and includes all of the muscles.

full pension (fuhl pohn-see-nyon) A daily hotel rate that includes a room and three full meals; the European equivalent of the American plan.

full rib roast *See* rib roast, full.

full roast *See* roast, French.

full rolling boil *See* boil, full rolling.

full tang *See* tang.

ful medames; ful imdammas (fool MAY-da-mez) 1. Small, plump broad beans (*Lathyrus sativus*) native to the Middle East; they have a light brown skin and nutty flavor; used in Egyptian and other Middle Eastern cuisines. 2. An Egyptian dish of these beans drizzled with olive oil and lemon.

fumarate A food additive used to strengthen dough that will be subjected to commercial bread-making machinery.

fumaric acid A food additive used as an acidulant and antioxidant in dry mixes and oil- or lard-based products.

fumé (foo-may) French for smoked.

Fumé Blanc (foo-may blahn) An American marketing term created by Robert Mondavi in the late 1960s for a crisp, dry California white wine made from the Sauvignon Blanc grape; used to distinguish this wine from the semisweet wine traditionally made from that grape.

fumet (fyoo-maht) A concentrated stock usually made from fish bones and/or shellfish shells and vegetables; used for sauces and soups.

fumo nero (foo-moh nay-roh) Italian for black smoke and used to describe the coating made of lamp black, burned umber and wine used to seal Parmesan.

fun (foon) Cantonese Chinese for fresh, flat rice noodles.

funa-gata (foo-nah-gat-tah) A portion of rice for nigiri-zushi shaped like an upside-down boat.

funcho (fuun-shoo) Portuguese for fennel.

fundido (fuhn-DEE-doh) Spanish for melted.

fun gau (foon gah-oo) A Chinese crescent-shaped dumpling of shrimp, pork, mushrooms and bamboo shoots in a wheat starch wrapper.

funge *See* oka.

funghi (FOON-ghee) Italian for mushrooms.

funghini (FOON-ghee-nee) Italian for little mushrooms and used to describe pastina in the shape of small mushroom caps.

fungible A description of goods, each of which is identical to, and freely exchangeable for, another (e.g., any one wine glass within a set of identical wine glasses).

fungicide A synthetic or naturally occurring substance used to kill fungi such as mushrooms and mold; used to protect a food crop, it can become an incidental food additive.

fungus *pl.* fungi. A division of plantlike organisms that lack chlorophyll and range in size from single-celled organisms to giant mushrooms; fungi, some of which are pathogenic, are found in the air, soil and water. *See* mold *and* yeast.

funnel A conical-shaped tool with a short, straight tube at the tip; used to transfer liquids into a narrow-mouthed container; some are equipped with strainers in the bottom to clear the liquid of small particles.

funnel, canning A wide-stemmed funnel designed to fit the necks of standard home canning (Mason) jars.

funnel cake A deep-fried Pennsylvania Dutch pastry made by pouring batter through a funnel into hot fat with a spiral motion; the fried dough is served with confectioners' sugar or honey.

furai (foo-rae) Japanese for to fry.

furcelleran A food additive refined from red seaweed and used as an emulsifier, stabilizer and/or thickener; also known as Danish agar.

Furmit (foor-mint) A white wine grape grown in Hungary; susceptible to the noble rot and often used for Tokay; if unaffected, it is used for a full-bodied dry white wine.

fursadi (foor-sah-dee) Swahili for raspberry.

fusilli (foo-SEEL-lee) Italian for twists and used to describe long, spiral-shaped pasta; usually served with thick sauces.

fusilli bucati (foo-SEEL-ee boo-cah-tee) Italian for twists with a hole and used to describe long spirals of pasta tubes.

fusion cuisine A style of cooking that draws on elements from European and Asian cuisines; generally, the application of Asian preparation techniques to European or American ingredients; also known as East meets West.

fusilli bucati

fusto (FOO-stoh) An Italian cask or barrel used to age wine.

fût (foo) French for barrel.

futari (foo-TAH-re) A Tanzanian dish consisting of pumpkin or other squash simmered with sweet potatoes and flavored with coconut milk, cinnamon, cloves and lemon juice.

futo-maki Thick-rolled maki-zushi. *See* hoso-maki.

fuwuyuan (phoo-who-huan) Chinese for waiter.

fuyu *See* persimmon, Japanese, *and* dòufù-ru.

Fuzzy Navel A cocktail made of peach schnapps and orange juice.

Fuzzy Pucker A cocktail made of peach schnapps and grapefruit juice.

fuzzy squash; fuzzy melon A large cylindrical squash native to China; it has a medium green skin covered with a hairlike fuzz, a cream-colored flesh, a moderately firm texture, and a bland flavor that absorbs flavors from other ingredients; also known as a hairy melon.

fylt (feelt) Norwegian for stuffed.

g *See* gram.

gaai laan (gah-ee lahn) A plant with white flowers, soft green leaves with a grayish-white bloom, and edible pale green tender stalks; also known as Chinese broccoli and Chinese kale.

gaaykaa gosht (ga-ah-khee gosht) Hindi for beef.

Gabel (gaa-berl) German for fork.

Gabelfrühstück (gaa-berl-FREW-shtewk) German for fork breakfast, indicating that hot foods such as eggs and ham will be served.

Gabiano (gah-bee-AH-no) A long-lived red wine made from the Barbera grape in Italy's Piedmont region.

gacho (GAH-cho) Japanese for goose.

gadeed (gah-dad) Thin slices of sun-dried meat, usually lamb or camel, used in North African and Middle Eastern cuisines; also known as gargoosh.

gado gado; gado-gado (GAH-doh GAH-doh) 1. An Indonesian dish consisting of raw and slightly cooked vegetables served with a spicy peanut sauce made with hot chiles and coconut milk. 2. The sauce itself.

Gaelic steak An Irish dish consisting of beefsteak cooked in butter in an iron skillet; shots of Irish whiskey and cream are added to the meat juices to form a sauce; it is traditionally served with cooked potatoes, fried onion rings, mushrooms and green vegetables.

gaeng (gah-hang) Thai for soup.

gaffel (gah-fell) Norwegian for fork.

gag A variety of Atlantic grouper.

gai (gee-ah) Thai for chicken.

gai choy; gai choi A leafy Chinese vegetable with long, green leaves, a long, pale green stalk and a strong mustard flavor; also known as Chinese mustard cabbage and swatow mustard.

gaika (GRYEHT-kah) Russian for nut. *See* orekh.

gai lae pet (gah-e la pet) Thai for poultry.

Gaiskäsli (gah-ees-kah-seal) A small, soft German or Swiss cheese made from goat's milk.

gajar (ga-har) Hindi for carrot.

gakkduki (gack-doo-kah) Korean-style pickled radish.

galactose A monosaccharide that combines with glucose to form the disaccharide lactose.

galaktoboúreko (gah-lack-toe-boo-ra-koh) A Greek confection of phyllo filled with vanilla cream.

galanga; galangal; galingale root (gah-LAHN-gah) The rhizome of a plant (*Alpina officinarum*) native to Southeast Asia; the rhizome has a reddish skin, an orange or whitish flesh, and a peppery, gingerlike flavor; used dried or fresh as a spice in Thai and Indonesian cuisines.

galantine (GAL-uhn-teen; gal-ahn-TEEN) A forcemeat of poultry, game, fish, shellfish or suckling pig, wrapped in the skin of the bird or animal, if available, and poached in an appropriate stock; usually served cold in aspic.

galantine mold A rectangular porcelain mold with slightly sloping sides and lug handles; the contents are served from the mold.

galapong (ga-lah-pong) A partially fermented dough made from ground rice and water; used in Filipino confections and sweet snacks.

galantine mold

galareta (gah-lah-reh-tah) Polish for jelly.

Galena (guh-LEE-hun) A very bitter variety of hops grown in the states of Idaho and Washington.

Galestro (gah-LESS-troe) A name used by Chianti producers for a light, dry white wine from Italy's Tuscany region made primarily from Trebbiano and Malvasia grapes; it must be fermented slowly and contain no more than 10.5% alcohol.

galette (gah-leht) 1. A round, flat, thin French cake made with puff pastry or a yeast-leavened dough, usually sprinkled with sugar before baking. 2. A thin, round cake made from potatoes or cereal grains; also known as a buckwheat crêpe in Normandy. 3. A small shortbread cookie.

gali (gah-lee) Chinese for curry.

galia melon A spherical melon with a netted skin, a brownish color and a moderately dark green flesh.

galinha (gah-LEE-nyah) Portuguese for chicken.

galinha de campo (gah-LEE-nyah day kam-poh) Portuguese for free-range hen.

gallbladder A saclike structure that stores and concentrates the bile secreted by the liver until it is discharged through the bile duct into the duodenum.

galletas (gah-jyay-tahs) Spanish for cookies.

Galliano (gal-LYAH-noh) *See* Liquore Galliano.

gallimaufry (gal-luh-MAW-free) 1. A medieval chicken stew flavored with bacon, verjuice, ginger, mustard and wine; originally French, it was brought to the British Isles by the Normans. 2. A dish with a mixture of ingredients (e.g., stew, ragoût or hash).

gallinaccio (gal-lee-nah-tchee-oh) Italian for chanterelle.

gallinaccio spinoso (gal-lee-nah-tchee-oh spee-noh-soh) Italian for hedgehog mushroom.

gallisation The addition of water and/or pure dried sugar, liquid sugar or invert sugar syrup to the grape juice or wine before fermentation to adjust the acid level. *See* amelioration *and* chaptalization.

gallon 1. An American unit of measurement equal to 128 fl. oz.; contains 8 pt. (16 fl. oz. each). 2. An English unit of measurement equal to 1.2 U.S. gallons, 10 lb., or 160 fl. oz.; contains 8 pt. (20 fl. oz. each); also known as the imperial gallon.

gallo nero (GAH-lo NEH-ro) The black rooster neck seal on Chianti Classico wine bottles used by members of the Chianti Classico Consorzio, a group of vintners adhering to self-imposed quality standards stricter than those of the DOC.

gallo nero

gallo pinto (gal-loh pen-toh) A Costa Rican dish of black beans flavored with bay leaf, cumin, oregano, garlic, onion, red pepper and hot chile sauce and served over rice.

gallopoulo (yah-io-poo-loh) Greek for turkey.

galo (gah-loh) Portuguese for cockerel.

galumblee (gah-lump-lee) Thai for cabbage.

galushkes (gal-oosh-keys) A Jewish dish consisting of a water, egg and flour dough that is forced through a colander or special sieve directly into boiling water.

galushki (gah-loosh-kee) Ukrainian flour dumplings made with sour cream; usually poached and served with butter or sour cream.

galuska (gah-lush-kah) Fresh, soft Hungarian egg dumplings cut into small squares and used as a garnish for stews and soups.

Gamay (gam-may) 1. A red wine grape grown in France's Beaujolais region. 2. A red wine made from this grape, generally known for its acidity and fruity characteristics.

gamba (gahm-bah) Portuguese for large shrimp.

gamba (GAHM-bah) *See* camaróne.

Gambel *See* quail, American.

gamber (gahm-BAY-ree) Spanish for crayfish.

gambero (gahm-BAY-roh) Italian for shrimp.

gambe secche (GAHM-bay she-shay) Italian for fairy ring mushroom.

game Wild mammals, birds or fish hunted for sport or food as well as the flesh of these animals; common game include deer, rabbit, hare, bear, boar, duck, goose, pheasant, quail and pigeon, many of which are also ranch raised and available commercially.

game chips British for potato chips that are served with game and poultry; when served with drinks or cocktails, they are called crisps.

game crumbs Dry bread crumbs fried in butter until golden and typically served with roasted feathered game.

game hen A young or immature progeny of Cornish chickens or of a Cornish chicken and White Rock chicken; slaughtered when 4–6 weeks old, it has an average market weight of 2 lb. (900 g), relatively little fat, and a fine flavor. *See* Rock Cornish game hen.

gamma-carotene *See* carotene, alpha-, beta- and gamma-.

gammel ost (gahm-mel oh'st) A Danish smørrebrød dish of a mature, spicy cheese on bread and butter garnished with pieces of aspic and sprinkled with rum.

Gammelöst (GAHM-mer-loost) A semisoft Norwegian cheese made from soured skim milk; it has a rather sharp, aromatic flavor, a brown rind and a brownish-yellow interior streaked with blue-green veins.

gammer *See* kishta.

gammon (GAHM-muhn) 1. A British dish of a cured hog's foreleg. 2. A British cut of the pork carcass; it is a thick slice taken from the top of the ham and sometimes smoked; also known as a ham steak.

gamy A tasting term for a food with a penetrating, musky aroma.

gān Chinese for liver.

ganache (ga-nosh) A rich blend of chocolate and heavy cream and, optionally, flavorings, used as a pastry or candy filling or as a frosting.

gandaria A small, mangolike tropical fruit (genus *Bouea*); it has a thin, yellow- or apricot-colored skin and yellow or orange flesh.

gandul *See* pigeon pea.

gánlan (gahn-lahn) Chinese for olive.

ganmo; ganmodoki (gahn-moh; gahn-moh-doh-kee) Deep-fried Japanese tofu patties or balls containing minced vegetables.

gan modoki (gahn moh-doh-kee) Japanese patties of mashed bean curd mixed with vegetables and spices and sold commercially as a vegetarian meal.

gans (khahns) Dutch for goose.

Gans (gahns) German for goose.

ganso (gan-soh) Portuguese for goose.

ganth gobhi (gahnt go-be) Hindi for kohlrabi.

ganzi (gahn-zee) Chinese for orange.

gao-yang-rou (gah-oo-young-row-who) Chinese for lamb.

Gaperon; Gapron (ga-pear-rohn) A semisoft French cheese made from skimmed cow's milk or buttermilk and heavily flavored with garlic; it has a rich, garlicky flavor and a dark rind with an ivory interior.

gar; garfish Any of a variety of freshwater fish found in North America with a long beak and large teeth; often smoked; also known as needlefish.

garam (gah-RAHM) Hindi for hot.

garambullos Small reddish berries from a cactus grown in Mexico; they are used in preserves or eaten dried like raisins.

garam masala (gah-RAHM mah-SAH-lah) A flavorful and aromatic blend of roasted and ground spices used in Indian cuisines (usually added toward the end of cooking or sprinkled on the food just before service); the blend usually contains peppercorns, cardamom, cinnamon, cloves, coriander, nutmeg, turmeric and/or fennel seeds; also known as a gorum moshla and masala.

garam masala, northern Indian style A masala that includes cumin, fenugreek, ginger, garlic and other spices.

garam masala, southern Indian style A masala that includes mustard seeds, tamarind, asafetida and other spices; generally mixed with vinegar, water or coconut milk to form a paste.

garbage disposal An electrical device, usually installed in a sink, with rotating blades that grind foods into very small particles that are then washed down the drain.

garbanzo bean (gar-BAHN-zoh) *See* chickpea.

garbanzos compuestos (garr-BAHN-zoes com-poo-es-tess) Toasted chickpeas sprinkled with dried chile flakes and served as a Central or South American snack or antojito.

garbure (gahr-bewr) A dish from France's Bearn region consisting of a soup made from carrots, potatoes, garlic, cabbage and green beans cooked with salt pork and preserved goose; the pork and goose are removed before service and browned with a topping of bread crumbs, cheese and butter and served after the soup.

garbure (gar-BOOR) A dish from Spain's Basque region consisting of a thick soup made from potatoes, cabbage, beans and pork, bacon or preserved goose.

garçon (gar-sohn) French for waiter.

garde manger (gahr mohn-zahj) 1. At a food services operation following the brigade system, the person responsible for the cold food preparations, including salads and salad dressings, cold appetizers, charcuterie items and similar dishes; also known as the pantry chef. 2. This category of foods. 3. The area in a kitchen where these foods are prepared; also known as the pantry.

garde-manger section One of the principal work sections of a food services facility; it typically contains a salad station, cold foods station, sandwich station and charcuterie station.

garden beet *See* beet.

garden cress A plant (*Lepidium sativum*) eaten raw as a seedling or sprout; it has a peppery flavor.

garden egg *See* eggplant, Asian.

Gardener's Delight tomato A variety of relatively small, spherical, red-skinned, flavorful tomato.

garden huckleberry A berry from a member of the nightshade family (genus *Solanum*); the smooth berry grows in a cluster and has a blue-black skin and a mild flavor reminiscent of a blueberry.

garden relish A relish made from tomatoes, celery, cucumber, green pepper and onion and dressed with olive oil and vinegar.

garfo (gahr-foo) Portuguese for fork.

Garganega (gahr-GAH-neh-gah) A white wine grape grown in Italy's Veneto region and blended with Trebbiano Toscano grapes to make Soave.

gargoosh *See* gadeed.

garhi yakhni (gaa-rhee yaa-kh-nee) A concentrated, gelatinous stock made from bones and meat; used in east Indian cuisine as a flavoring for rice dishes; also known as yakni.

gari; garri (GAH-ree) 1. A West African term for a coarse cassava powder made from grated, roasted cassava. 2. A stiff porridge made from this powder. 3. Sushi-shop slang for vinegared ginger; also known as béni shoga.

garibaldi (gah-ree-BAHL-dee) An Italian butter cookie studded with raisins.

Garibaldi, sauce (gar-ree-BALL-dee) A French compound sauce made from a demi-glaze seasoned with mustard, cayenne pepper and garlic and finished with anchovy butter.

garides; garithes (yah-ree-tha) Greek for shrimp.

garlic A member of the lily family (*Allium sativum*); the highly aromatic and strongly flavored edible bulb (called a head) is covered in a papery layer and is composed of several sections (called cloves), each of which is also covered with a papery membrane; used as a distinctive flavoring in cuisines around the world.

garlic

garlic bread Slices of French or Italian bread that are spread with garlic butter and toasted, broiled or grilled.

garlic butter Softened butter mixed with minced or crushed garlic; used as a cooking medium, flavoring or spread.

garlic chives *See* chives, garlic.

garlic flakes Bits or slices of dehydrated garlic; used as a seasoning, either dried or rehydrated; also known as instant garlic.

garlic juice; garlic extract The juice of pressed garlic cloves; used as a seasoning.

garlic powder Finely ground dehydrated garlic; used as a seasoning; also known as powdered garlic.

garlic press A tool used to press garlic cloves through a perforated grid to make a paste.

garlic press

garlic salt A blend of garlic powder, salt and an anticaking agent or humectant; used as a seasoning.

garmugia (gar-MOO-jah) An Italian stew made from beef, peas, onions and artichokes flavored with olive oil and garlic.

garnaal (kah-r-NAH-ahl) Dutch for small shrimp.

Garnacha (gahr-NAB-shah) Spanish for Grenache.

Garnele (gahr-NAY-le) German for shrimp.

garni (gahr-nee) French for garnished and used to describe a dish that includes vegetables and potato.

garnish *v.* To use food as an attractive decoration. *n.* 1. Food used as an attractive decoration. 2. A subsidiary food used to add flavor or character to the main ingredient in a dish (e.g., noodles in chicken noodle soup).

garniture (gahr-nih-TEUR) French for garnish and used to describe the various ingredients that blend with the foods and flavors of the main dish.

garrafeira (gah-rah-FAIR-ah) Portuguese for wine cellar; used as a labeling term to indicate that a red wine has been aged in wood for at least 2 years and in the bottle for 1 year or that a white wine has been aged in wood for at least 6 months and in the bottle for 6 months.

Garrotxa (gar-ROACH-uh) A Spanish goat's milk cheese with a gray rind and a white, tightly textured interior with a mild, nutty, herbal flavor with hints of thyme and rosemary.

garum (GAR-uhm) A condiment popular in ancient Rome; it was made by fermenting fish in brine with aromatic herbs and then mixing the resulting paste with pepper and oil or wine.

gås (goass) Danish, Norwegian and Swedish for goose.

Gascogne, sauce (gas-kon-ya) A French compound sauce made from a velouté flavored with a reduction of white wine and herbs and finished with a small amount of anchovy butter.

Gascoyne's Scarlet An apple native to Great Britain; it has a pale greenish-white skin with one large bright red area, a juicy flesh and little flavor.

gasperou *See* sheepshead.

gassy A cheese-tasting term for a spoiled or fermented odor; usually indicates that the cheese may be defective.

gastrique (gas-strek) Caramelized sugar deglazed with vinegar and used in fruit-flavored savory sauces (e.g., duck with orange sauce) and tomato-based sauces.

gastroenteritis Inflammation of the stomach and intestinal tract.

gastrointestinal tract The portion of the alimentary canal relating to the stomach and intestines. *See* digestive system.

gastronome (GAS-truh-nohm) 1. An epicure. 2. A Russian food store.

gastronome, sauce (GAS-truh-nohm) A French compound sauce made from a Madeira sauce flavored with a meat glaze, seasoned with cayenne pepper and finished with Champagne.

gastronomia (gah-stroh-noh-MEE-ah) An Italian food store, especially one specializing in delicacies and prepared foods.

gastronomy The art and science of eating well.

gastropods *See* univalves.

Gaststätte (gas-sthay-tte) German for restaurant.

gâteau (gah-toh) 1. French for cake. 2. In the United States, any cake-type dessert. 3. In France, various pastry items made with puff pastry, éclair paste, short dough or sweet dough.

gâteau de sirop (gah-TOH duh seh-roph) A Louisiana spice cake made with cane syrup, frosted with an icing of brown sugar and butter, and garnished with pecan halves.

gâteau l'opera (gah-TOH lo-pay-rah) A French pastry composed of three layers of almond genoise filled with coffee buttercream and ganache.

gâteau St. Honoré (gah-TOH san-tah-naw-RAY) A French pastry composed of a base of puff pastry topped with a ring of small choux puffs, attached to the base with caramelized sugar; the center is filled with Chiboust cream and cream Chantilly.

Gattinara (gah-tee-NAH-rah) A full-bodied DOCG red wine from Italy's Piedmont region; it is made from Nebbiolo grapes blended with Bonarda grapes.

gau (GAH-oo) A Chinese steamed rice cake made with coconut, flour and brown sugar, topped with sesame seeds and a red date and traditionally served at the lunar New Year celebration.

Gaucho A firm Argentinean cheese made from skimmed cow's milk; it has a buttery flavor and is sold in small wheels.

gau choy fa (gah-oo tcho-e pha) Chinese for garlic chives.

gaudes (goude) A French corn flour porridge; usually chilled and then sliced, fried in butter and served hot or cold.

gaufre de Bruxelles (goh-freh duh brew-sehl) A fluffy Belgian waffle made with beaten egg whites; it is eaten with sugar, whipped cream or chocolate.

gaufre de Liège (goh-freh duh lege) A small, sweet, square Belgian waffle flavored with vanilla, cinnamon and small pieces of sugar.

gaufres (goh-freh) French for waffles.

gaufrette (goh-FREHT) A thin, crisp fan-shaped French wafer, often served with ice cream.

gaufrette potatoes; gaufrette pommes de terre (goh-FREHT pohm duh tehr) A French dish of crisp, fried, latticed or waffle-cut potatoes.

Gavi (GAH-vee) A dry white wine made from the Cortese grape in Italy's Piedmont region.

Gaviota A large European plum with a reddish-yellow skin, a ruby-colored juicy flesh, and a sweet flavor.

gayette (gay-eht) A flat sausage made in France's Provence region from pork liver, bacon and garlic, wrapped in pork caul and baked; it is served cold.

Gay-Lussac A metric system for measuring the alcohol content of alcoholic beverages.

gazpacho (gahz-PAH-choh) A cold Spanish soup made of uncooked tomatoes, cucumbers, sweet peppers, onions, oil and vinegar and traditionally thickened with bread crumbs or slices of bread.

gazzosa (gah-ZOH-sah) An Italian carbonated lemon beverage.

Gbejna A soft Maltese cow's milk cheese now made in Australia; it has a white color and is delicately flavored; also available coated with peppercorns.

gean *See* mazzard.

Gebäck (ger-BAHK) German for cookies.

gebacken (ger-BAHKN) German for baked.

gebakte (geh-bach't) Yiddish for baked.

gebna; gibna A cheese made in the Middle East from water buffalo's, cow's, goat's or ewe's milk; usually made at home, it is white and should be eaten very fresh.

gebna makleyah (ghab-nah mah-kla-ya) An Egyptian appetizer of deep-fried cheese.

gebrotene (geh-bro-tin) Yiddish for roasted.

gebs (ghabs) Ethiopian for barley.

gedempte fleisch (geh-demph't fly'sch) A classic, country-style Jewish pot roast; the beef is cooked with onions, cloves, carrots, bell peppers, parsley, paprika and bay leaf and is typically served with horseradish.

geela masala bhoonana (gee-laa mah-sah-lah boo-nah-nah) An Indian garnish or ingredient consisting of fried onions, garlic and gingerroot.

geese *See* goose.

gefilte fish (geh-FIHL-teh) A Jewish dish of ground fish (usually carp, pike and/or whitefish) mixed with eggs, matzo meal and seasonings, shaped into balls and simmered in a vegetable or fish stock.

Geflügel (ger-FLEW-gerl) German for fowl or poultry.

gefüllt (ghe-fullt) German for filled or stuffed.

gefüllte helzel (ghe-full-tay hell-zal) A Jewish dish of a chicken or other poultry neck stuffed with chestnuts, onions and bread crumbs or flour and flavored with herbs and schmaltz.

Gehirnwurst (gay-heer'n-vurst) A German sausage made from hog brains and pork meat and fat, seasoned with mace, salt and pepper.

gehockte leber (geh-hoc't lee-ber) A Jewish dish of chopped chicken liver; it is flavored with schmaltz, onion, eggs and pepper.

gehoon (ga-hun) Hindi for wheat.

geit (yeht) Norwegian for goat.

gekochte (geh-kock't) Yiddish for cooked.

gelateria (jeh-LAH-tehr-e-a) Italian for an ice cream store or parlor.

gelatin; gelatine A colorless, odorless and flavorless mixture of proteins from animal bones, connective tissues and other parts as well as from certain algae (agar-agar); when dissolved in a hot liquid and then cooled, it forms a jelly-like substance that is used as a thickener and stabilizer in molded desserts, cold soups, chaud-froid creations and the like and as a fining agent in beer and wine.

gelatin, granulated A granular form of unflavored, unsweetened gelatin.

gelatin, leaf Paper-thin sheets of unflavored gelatin; also known as sheet gelatin.

gelatin, sheet *See* gelatin, leaf.

gelatinization The process by which starch granules are cooked; they absorb moisture when placed in a liquid and heated; as the moisture is absorbed, the product swells, softens and clarifies slightly.

gelatinized wheat starch *See* pregelatinized starch.

gelato (jah-laht-to) An Italian-style ice cream that is denser than American-style ice cream.

gelée (zhay-LAY) French for aspic.

geléia (ie-lay-ah) Portuguese for jam.

gellan gum A polysaccharide gum produced from *Pseudomonas elodea;* as a food additive, it is used as a stabilizer and/or thickener.

gellometer *See* bloom.

gelo (ZHAY-loh) Portuguese for ice.

gemelli (ge-mel-lee) Italian for twins and used to describe two short pieces of spaghetti twisted together like a rope; also known as twists Napoletani in the United States.

gem pan A pan designed to make miniature muffins.

Gemüse (ger-MEW-zer) German for vegetable.

gendarme (ghan-dahrm) 1. French slang for pickled herring. 2. A dry, very hard Swiss sausage.

gemelli

Generally Recognized As Safe List *See* GRAS List.

generic 1. A class or group of products with predominating common characteristics such as usage, origin, principal ingredients and so on. 2. A product (usually a house brand) that closely resembles a well-known brand name product.

generous A wine-tasting term for a wine that has a rich color and body as well as high alcohol and extract contents.

genetically engineered foods *See* bioengineered foods.

Genever; Genever gin A full-flavored gin with a malty flavor and aroma; made from a blend of malted barley, corn and rye that is then redistilled with juniper berries, caraway seeds and other botanicals; also known as Shiedam, Dutch gin and Holland gin.

gengibre (zhehn-ZHEE-bruh) Portuguese for ginger.

genièvre (zheh-neehv) 1. French for juniper berry. 2. A gin flavored with juniper berry.

genip; ginup (heh-NEEP) A cherry-sized tropical fruit (*Melicoccus bijugatus*); it has a slightly ovoid shape, a thick green skin, a gummy yellowish or orange-pink flesh, a single seed or two seeds flattened together, and a flavor reminiscent of grapes; also known as akee (especially in the Barbados), honeyberry, limoncillo, Spanish lime and mamoncillo and imprecisely known as genipa or genipap.

génmai cha (jehn-MAH-ee chah) A Japanese beverage made from green tea leaves and roasted rice kernels; it has a smoky aroma and flavor.

Genoa salami A large sausage from Genoa, Italy, made from pork and beef, highly seasoned with garlic, white peppercorns and other spices; it is cured and air-dried.

genoise (zhen-waahz) 1. A form of whipped-egg cake that uses whole eggs whipped with sugar. 2. A French sponge cake.

Genovese, salsa An Italian pasta sauce made from onions, carrots, tomatoes, dried mushrooms, celery and veal simmered in stock and white wine; sometimes strained.

gentian A plant (*Gentiana lutea*) with a thick rhizome, elliptical blue-green leaves, and showy, stalked, golden yellow flowers; the rhizome is used to make gentian brandy and bitter liqueurs and as a bitter flavoring agent; also known as great yellow gentian.

Gentiane An eau-de-vie made from gentian root.

Gentleman's Relish *See* patum peperium.

Genuine Parmigiano *See* Parmigiano-Reggiano.

genus *pl.* genera. A botanical and zoological term used to describe a group of closely related but distinct species; the genus is the first word in the scientific name; genera are grouped into families.

geoduck clam; gweduck clam (GOO-ee-duhk) A variety of Pacific clam with a soft shell; it can weigh as much as 10 lb. (4.5 kg) and has a large siphon; the tender meat has a rich, briny flavor and is used in Asian cuisines.

geophagy The practice of eating earthy substances such as clay or chalk.

George A. Dickel's Cascade Distillery One of the 12 remaining U.S. whiskey distilleries; located in Tullahoma, Tennessee, and founded c. 1881, it produces Dickel's Tennessee Sour Mash Whisky.

Georgian A black tea grown in the Republic of Georgia; the beverage has a full body and flavor and should be served strong and with lemon; also known as Russian tea.

Georgia Peach A cocktail made of vodka, peach-flavored brandy, peach preserves, lemon juice and chopped peaches; served in a chilled double old-fashioned glass.

gepregelte (geh-pree-geel't) Yiddish for sautéed.

geranium, scented Geranium (genera *Geranium* and *Pelargonium*) leaves that have scents reminiscent of fruits and other flavorings, such as oranges, lemons and roses; a syrup or liquid infused with the leaves is used to flavor custards, sugars, preserves and sorbets.

geranyl isovalerate A food additive with a fruity aroma used as an apple or pear flavoring agent in beverages, ice cream, candy and baked goods.

geräuchert (ger-ROT-khert) German for smoked.

Geräucherte Bratwürste (ger-ROY-khert brat-vursteh) A German sausage made from lean pork and bacon fat and seasoned with black pepper; it is smoked in its casing for approximately 1 week.

germ 1. An imprecise term used to describe any microorganism, especially pathogenic ones. 2. The smallest portion of a cereal kernel and the only portion containing fat.

German beer purity law *See* Reinheitsgebot.

German caviar *See* lumpfish caviar.

German chocolate; German's sweet chocolate Baking chocolate with sugar, milk and vanilla added.

German chocolate cake A rich, American-style layer cake made with sweet chocolate and filled with a cooked coconut-pecan frosting.

German potato salad A salad made with cooked potatoes, bacon, onions, celery and green pepper bound with a dressing of bacon fat, vinegar, seasonings and sometimes sugar; served hot, room temperature or cold.

German sauce *See* allemande, sauce.

German wheat *See* Einkorn.

germicide An agent capable of killing some kinds of microorganisms; used to protect crops or to sterilize food service areas, it can become an incidental food additive.

germination The process during which a seed, spore, bulb or the like begins to grow and develop into a plant; sprouting.

Géromé (gay-rohm-may) A soft Munster-style cheese made in the Vosges Mountain region of France and Switzerland from cow's milk with some goat's milk added; it has a strong, spicy flavor, an orange rind, and a yellow interior; also known as Munster Géromé.

geropiga (jeh-roh-PEE-gah) A very sweet port used for blending.

gerste; Gerste (chehrst) Dutch and German for barley.

Gervais (zhair-VAY) A Petit-Suisse cheese made from cow's milk.

geschabt (gha-shatt) German for ground, grated or scraped.

geschnitzeltes mit rösti (ger-SHNEH-tsert-terss mit roostee) A Swiss dish of chopped veal simmered in white wine and broth and served with rösti.

Geselchtes (gae-selk-tess) An Austrian snack of thick-cut bacon or other pork parts and crusty bread; it is usually served with Heurigen wine. *See* Heurigen.

gesztenye (guess-ta-nye) Hungarian for chestnut.

getost (yeht-ohst) Swedish for goat cheese.

Getränk German for a beverage.

Gewürztraminer (geh-VAIRTZ-tra-MEE-ner) 1. A white wine grape grown principally in France's Alsace region, Germany, Austria, Italy and California. 2. A white wine made from this grape; it has a perfumed aroma reminiscent of rose petals; the wine ranges from dry and flavorful to spicy.

ghagin fin (ghah-g'inn feen) Very small star- or coin-shaped pasta served with Maltese meat broths or vegetables soups.

ghameh (ga-MEHH) An Arabic dish of stuffed sheep's stomach.

ghanum (g'ran-nehmm) Arabic for lamb.

ghars The midlevel marketing designation for dates; they are semisoft and moderately sweet. *See* degla berida *and* deglet-nour.

ghatti A gum derived from the *Anogeissus latifolia* tree and used as a gum and stabilizer; also known as Indian gum.

ghee (gee) 1. Hindi for fat or buttermilk. 2. A form of clarified butter (after the moisture has evaporated, the milk solids are allowed to brown) originating in India but now mass-produced worldwide and used as an ingredient and cooking medium; it has a long shelf life, high smoke point and a nutty, caramel-like flavor; ghee flavored with ginger, peppercorns or cumin is available.

gherkin (gerr-ken) A small, dark green pickling cucumber; usually harvested before it ripens and pickled in vinegar.

ghiaccio (gee-AHT-choa) Italian for ice.

ghiotta (G'YOH-tah) 1. An Italian dish consisting of peppers, potatoes, zucchini and tomatoes cut into strips and baked. 2. Italian for glutton and used to describe a sauce made with pan drippings.

ghiveci (goy-vah-chee) A Romanian dish of sautéed vegetables (e.g., onions, eggplant, tomatoes, cabbage, peas, beans and green peppers) simmered with herbs and oil in a casserole and topped with fried onions and garlic.

ghoraiybah (go-ray-bah) A Middle Eastern shortbread cookie studded with almonds.

gialetti (jee-ah-LEH-tee) Cornmeal biscuits from Italy's Romagna region.

giambonette (jam-bow-nay-tay) Italian for little leg and used to describe a boned chicken leg and thigh stuffed with chicken, ham, bacon, spices and Parmesan, fried or braised in broth and served with a sauce.

gianduja (gyan-doo-hah) A blend of chocolate, usually milk chocolate, and hazelnuts; used for flavoring many Spanish and Mexican pastries.

giant clam A variety of clam found in the tropical waters of the western Pacific Ocean, particularly the South Sea; it can weigh as much as 110 lb. (49.8 kg) and has a large shell with prominent flutes.

giant garlic; giant leek *See* rocambole.

Giant Poha Berry A variety of large cape gooseberry grown in the United States and New Zealand.

giant scallop *See* sea scallop.

giant sea bass A member of the grouper family; it has a lean white flesh, a firm texture, and a mild to sweet flavor and can weigh as much as 550 lb. (249.4 kg); sometimes mistakenly called a sea bass or black sea bass; also known as a jewfish.

giant shells Large shell-shaped smooth or ridged pasta, usually served stuffed.

giant whelk *See* knobbed whelk.

giardiniera, alla (jahr-dee-N'YEHR-ah, AH-la) Italian for garden style and used to describe dishes served with vegetables.

gibberellic acid Along with its potassium salts, a food additive used in the malting of barley for the production of fermented malt beverages and distilled spirits.

gibelotte (jhee-beh-loat-teh) A French stew made from rabbit, onions, bacon and sometimes potatoes, flavored with herbs and red or white wine.

gibier (jhee-byay) French for game and used to refer to all wild animals or birds that are hunted for food.

giblets The edible internal organs of a bird; in the United States, these include the heart, liver and gizzard as well as the neck; in France, they also include the cockscomb and kidneys (testes).

Gibson A martini garnished with a small white onion.

gidnoom (git-NOOM) Russian for hedgehog mushroom.

gift basket A present of assorted cheeses, crackers, fruit, candies, muffins, nuts, packaged meats, still or sparkling wines and the like; the items, which are sometimes chosen thematically, are arranged in a basket that is usually then wrapped in plastic. *See* muffin.

gigante A very large cigar with a 52–64 ring and a 8- to 10-in. length; the large diameter provides a cooler smoke.

Gigantella strawberry A variety of very large (up to 3.5 in.), although not necessarily flavorful, strawberry.

gigantes plaki (gee-gan-tess plah-key) A Greek appetizer of baked butter beans.

gigot (jhee-GOH) French for leg of lamb or mutton.

gigot d'agneau (jhee-GOH dan-yoh) French for the shank end of the leg of lamb that is suitable for roasting.

gigot d'agneau boulangère (jhee-GOH dan-yoh boo-lahn-jehr) A French dish consisting of a leg of lamb studded with garlic cloves cooked in a casserole on top of sliced potatoes seasoned with shallots and rosemary.

gild To brush pastry or other foods with egg yolk so that the brushed surface will brown when cooked.

gilderne soup (ghil-der-nay) A Jewish chicken soup served on the 25th and 50th wedding anniversaries; the golden fat globules are left on top as an omen of further happiness.

Gilka (gheel-kah) A German kümmel.

gilka koutalioú (gee-l-kah coo-tah-lee-oh-oo) A Greek dessert of fruit preserved in syrup; it is usually served in a glikothiki.

gill 1. A unit of measurement in the imperial system; it is 0.25 pt. (5 fl. oz.). 2. In England, an informal unit of measurement equal to 0.5 pt. 3. A unit of measurement in the U.S. system; it is 0.25 pt. (4 fl. oz.). 4. A small medieval English glass.

gills 1. The organs on fish and shellfish used to obtain oxygen. *See* beard. 2. Thin curtains of membranes radially arranged under the caps of certain mushrooms and the area that usually bears spores; also known as lammellae.

gilthead; gilt-poll A saltwater fish related to the porgy and found in the Mediterranean Sea and temperate areas of the Atlantic Ocean; it has a bright gold crescent between the eyes and a delicate flavor; also known as a golden eyebrow fish.

Gimlet A cocktail made of gin and Rose's lime juice.

gin A clear spirit distilled from grain and flavored with juniper berries; it has a high alcohol content.

Gin and Bitters A cocktail made of gin and Angostura bitters; served in a chilled old-fashioned glass without ice; also known as Pink Gin.

Gin and It Slang for gin and Italian vermouth.

Gin and Tonic A cocktail made of gin and tonic water; served over ice and garnished with a slice of lime.

ginataan (ghe-nat-ahn) A Filipino term for cooking foods in coconut milk.

Gin Buck A cocktail made of gin, ginger ale and lemon juice; popular during Prohibition. *See* Buck.

Gin Cobbler A cocktail made of gin, orgeat syrup and club soda; garnished with an orange slice.

Gin Daisy A cocktail made of gin, lemon juice, club soda and raspberry syrup or grenadine; garnished with an orange peel.

ginebra (gee-na-vrah) Spanish for gin.

ginepro (jee-NEH-proa) Italian for juniper.

Gin Fizz A cocktail made of gin, sugar, soda water and lemon juice; garnished with a maraschino cherry.

gingelly (gin-jel-lee) Hindi for a light sesame oil.

gingembre (jheen-jhehm-breh) French for ginger.

ginger; gingerroot The gnarled, bumpy rhizome (called a hand) of a tall flowering tropical plant (*Zingerber officinale*) native to China; it has a tan skin, an ivory to greenish-yellow flesh, a peppery, fiery, slightly sweet flavor with notes of lemon and rosemary and a spicy, pungent aroma; used to flavor beverages and in sweet and savory dishes in Asian and Indian cuisines; available fresh, powdered, preserved in sugar, crystallized, candied or pickled.

ginger, green Fresh ginger.

ginger, pickled Ginger preserved in rice vinegar, brine or red wine; it has a pinkish color and a slightly spicy, sweet flavor; used in Asian cuisines.

ginger ale A sweetened carbonated beverage flavored with a ginger extract.

gingerbread A sweet cake or cookie flavored with ginger and other spices.

gingerbread nut A traditional hard ginger cookie.

ginger bud The fragrant, pink, edible buds of several types of ginger plants (*Phaeomeria sepciosa* and *Nicloaia atropurpurea*) used in Southeast Asian cuisines.

Ginger Champagne A mocktail made with club soda and ginger flavoring.

ginger grater A flat ceramic grater with rows of ceramic teeth used for grating ginger.

ginger nut A small, round ginger-flavored cookie.

ginger powder Dried ground ginger; it has a yellow color and a flavor that is spicier and not as sweet as fresh ginger; used in baked goods.

ginger grater

gingersnap A thin, crisp cookie flavored with ginger and molasses.

ginger tea A tisane made by boiling a small piece of ginger in water; considered a remedy for indigestion.

ginkgo nut The nut of a spherical, plum-sized, brown fruit of the Asian ginkgo tree (*Ginkgo biloba*); the olive-sized kernel turns pale green when cooked and is used in Asian cuisines; also known as maidenhair nut.

gin liqueur A liqueur for which gin is used as the distilled spirit base; the resulting liqueur has a predominant gin flavor.

Gin Milk Punch A cocktail made of milk, gin, sugar syrup, lemon juice, lime juice and club soda; garnished with a maraschino cherry.

gin mill Slang for bar or saloon.

ginnan (GEEN-nahn) Japanese for ginkgo nut.

Gin Rickey A cocktail made of gin, club soda and lime juice; served in a highball glass.

ginseng (JIHN-sing) A plant of the ivy family (*Panax ginseng*) native to China; the forked root is highly aromatic, with a flavor reminiscent of fennel, and is used in tisanes, as a flavoring for soups, and as a tonic believed by some to be an aphrodisiac and restorative.

ginseng, red Steamed ginseng dried over a fire; it has a reddish tint.

ginseng, white Sun-dried ginseng.

Gin Sling A cocktail made of gin, lemon juice, club soda and orgeat or sugar syrup.

Gin Sour A cocktail made of gin, lemon juice and sugar syrup; garnished with an orange slice and maraschino cherry; served in a chilled whiskey sour glass.

Ginza Mary A cocktail made of vodka, tomato juice, sake, lemon juice and Tabasco sauce.

giorno, del (johr-no, del) Italian menu term for speciality of the day.

giouvarlakia (yeh-oo-vah-reh-lah-kha) Greek meatballs; usually lamb or mutton, simmered in stock thickened with avgolémono.

Gipfels (gayp-fels) A type of croissant popular in Germany and Switzerland consisting of a triangle of dough rolled and stretched into a circular crescent; the dough has more and thinner layers than French-style croissants.

girasol *See* Jerusalem artichoke.

giraumon *See* calabaza.

giri (GEE-ree) Japanese for a cut or stroke of the knife.

giriama (ghe-ree-yah-mah) A Kenyan dish of fish cooked with tomatoes and flavored with coconut milk, garlic, onions, saffron, turmeric and cumin.

Girl Scout Cookies The proprietary name for a selection of packaged cookies sold annually by Girl Scouts to raise money for their organization.

girofles (gee-ro-fl) French for cloves.

girolle (jhee-rol-yah) French for chanterelle.

gizzard A bird's second stomach; it has a thick muscle used to grind food after it has been mixed with the gastric juices in the first stomach.

Gjetöst; Gietost; Getost; Getmesost (YEHT-ohst) A Norwegian and Swedish boiled whey cheese made from goat's milk with cow's milk sometimes added; it has a sweet, caramel-like flavor and can range in consistency from a spreadable paste to a hard cheese.

gjœr (yah-er) Norwegian for yeast.

glaçage (glah-sahlzhg) French for browning or glazing.

glace (glahs) 1. French for ice and ice cream. 2. French for the icing used on a cake.

glacé (glahs-say) French for glazed and used to describe both a fruit dipped in a syrup that hardens when cold and a cake with a shiny, sweet surface (icing).

glace de poisson (glahs duh pwah-sawng) A syrupy glaze made by reducing a fish stock; used to flavor sauces.

glace de viande (glahs duh vee-AHND) A dark brown, syrupy glaze made by reducing a brown stock; used to color and flavor sauces.

glace de volaille (glahs duh vo-lahy) A light brown, syrupy glaze made by reducing a chicken stock; used to color and flavor sauces.

glacé royale See royal glaze.

glacial acetic acid A food additive used as an acidic flavoring agent in salad dressings; an acidulant and a preservative.

glacier (glahs-ee-yay) At a food services operation following the brigade system, the person responsible for all chilled and frozen desserts.

glacier; glacière See sorbétière.

glacière (glahs-ee-yair) French for sugar dredger.

Gladpit A variety of large apple with a full flavor.

Glamorgan sausage (glah-MOHR-gun SAUS-ahg) A Welsh meatless sausage; a mixture of Caerphilly cheese and bread crumbs flavored with black pepper, dry mustard, minced onions and egg rolled into a log and fried.

gland A cell or group of cells (a structure) that manufactures a secretion used in some other part of the body.

glandless cotton A variety of cotton bred without certain glandlike structures that secrete a toxin; its protein-rich seeds are used as an additive in energy bars and for oil.

Glärnerkäse (glar-neh-kaize) A small, hard, German Sapsago-style cheese made from cow's milk; it has a sharp, pungent flavor, a pleasing aroma, and a light green color, all resulting from the melilot (clover) leaves added to the curd; used for grating.

glaserade ägg (glah-ser-ah-da ahahg) A Swedish dish of eggs in aspic.

glass 1. Any of a large class of materials made by fusing silicates and boric oxide, aluminum oxide or phosphorus oxide; the resulting product is generally hard, brittle and transparent or translucent; it is used for dinnerware, stemware, serviceware and cookware (especially microwavable and ovenproof products). 2. A glass, ceramic, plastic or metal vessel used for holding and drinking individual portions of a beverage, usually cold; handleless, it can be stemmed or footed.

glass, footed A glass with a bowl for holding liquids sitting on a short cylindrical column set on a base.

glass, stemmed A glass with a bowl for holding liquids sitting on a tall slender column set on a base.

glassato (GLAH-sah-toh) Italian for glazed.

glass cup measures See measuring cups, liquid.

glassful A traditional measure of volume (especially in Creole cuisine); it refers to the volume of a shot glass, approximately 1/4 cup.

glass rack A wooden or metal frame used to hold stemware, often above a bar or in a cabinet; suspended from the ceiling or the bottom of the shelf above, the rack consists of a series of parallel rods; the base of a glass is slid along the top of two rods, with the stem and bowl hanging below.

glasswort See marsh samphire.

Glayva (gla-VAH) A Scottish liqueur made from Scotch whisky, honey and a secret herb formula.

glaze v. To apply a shiny coating to a food. n. 1. Any shiny coating applied to a food or created by browning. 2. The dramatic reduction and concentration of a stock. 3. A thin, flavored coating poured or dripped onto a cake or pastry.

glazed 1. Food that has been dipped in water and then frozen; the ice forms a glaze that protects the item from freezer burn. 2. Food that has been coated with a glaze (e.g., glazed doughnut).

glazirovanniye sirki (glah-zee-row-vahn-nee-a seer-key) A Russian confection made of cream cheese, farmer's cheese, sugar, egg yolks, lemon zest and lemon juice, all wrapped in cheesecloth, drained overnight, formed into balls, chilled and dipped in melted chocolate.

Glen Deveron The proprietary name of a single-malt Scotch whisky; it is mild and light, with a full malt flavor and a dry aftertaste.

Glenfiddich The proprietary name of a single-malt Scotch whisky; it has a pale golden color, a well-balanced, fruity, sweet flavor, and a slightly malty aroma; it is particularly suitable as a digestif.

Glenlivet The proprietary name of a single-malt Scotch whisky; it has a flowery, fruity flavor reminiscent of peaches and vanilla.

Glen Mist A liqueur made from Scotch whisky.

Glen Moray The proprietary name of a single-malt Scotch whisky; it is light colored, with a malt flavor and clean aftertaste.

gliaden See gluten.

glikothiki (glee-ko-tea-key) A Greek serving piece; it is a silver bowl with spoons hanging from the sides; guests use the spoons to help themselves to the bowl's contents.

glister pudding A British steamed pudding made with marmalade and flavored with ginger.

globe artichoke See artichoke, common.

globe carrot A carrot with a light orange color and a squat conical to spherical shape.

glögg (gloog) A Swedish drink made of brandy or aquavit, wine, spices and other ingredients served warm with a cinnamon stick and garnished with almonds, raisins and orange peel.

Gloom Lifter A cocktail made of whiskey, brandy, raspberry liqueur, sugar syrup, egg white and lemon juice.

glop *See* gorp.

Gloucester; Single Gloucester (GLOSS-tuhr) A very firm cheese made in Gloucester, England, from cow's milk; it has a yellow color, a smooth, waxy texture, a red or brown surface, and a rich, mild flavor.

Gloucester, Double A Gloucester made with twice the milk and aged for a longer period than Single Gloucester; it has a creamy interior and a more mellow flavor.

glove The velvety feel of certain fruits (e.g., kiwi) or vegetables (e.g., fresh string beans).

glucocorticoids Hormones secreted by the adrenal cortex; they help convert protein into carbohydrates and regulate protein, carbohydrate and fat metabolism.

glucomannan A product derived from the konjac tuber used in Japanese cuisine and believed by some to have weight-controlling properties.

gluconic acid A food additive used as an acidulant, antioxidant and leavening agent.

glucono delta-lactone A food additive used as a curing and pickling agent, leavening agent and/or pH control agent.

glucose 1. A monosaccharide occurring naturally in fruits, some vegetables and honey with about half the sweetness of table sugar; used as the principal source of energy for most body functions; also known as dextrose, blood sugar, corn sugar and grape sugar. 2. A food additive used as a nutritive sweetener in processed foods such as confections and candies.

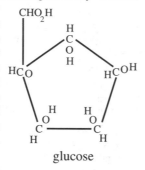

glucose

Glühwein (glew-vine) German for mulled wine.

Glumse (GLOOM-zuh) An eastern German cottage cheese–style cheese made from soured, skimmed cow's milk; milk or cream is usually added before the cheese is eaten.

glutamic acid *See* glutamine.

glutamic acid and glutamic acid hydrochloride Food additives used as salt substitutes.

glutamine 1. An amino acid. 2. A food additive used as a nutrient source to significantly improve the biological quality of the total protein in a food containing the naturally occurring protein. Also known as glutamic acid.

gluten An elastic-like network of proteins created when glutenin and gliadin (proteins found in wheat flour) are moistened and kneaded; it is this network that traps gases inside the batter or dough, causing it to rise.

gluten flour A flour made from hard wheat flour from which a large percentage of the starch has been removed; usually used for making bread for diabetic individuals and others who abstain from starch or to add protein to flours, such as rye, that do not produce gluten naturally.

glutenin *See* gluten.

glutinous rice Short- or medium-grain rice with a high starch content available in black (unpolished) and white varieties; used in Japanese and Chinese cuisines for sweet and savory dishes, in part because the rice, which has a slightly sweet flavor, sticks together when cooked, making it easier to eat with chopsticks; also known as sticky rice and sweet rice.

glutinous rice flour A fine white flour made from ground glutinous white rice; it is used in Asian cuisines to make the soft, chewy dough used for sweets, buns and dumplings.

glycerin; glycerine *See* glycerol.

glycerol 1. An organic alcohol that combines with three fatty acids to produce a triglyceride; also known as glycerin or glycerine. 2. A sweet, clear, syruplike liquid that is a by-product of the fermentation of wine; its presence enhances the wine's fattiness and softness. 3. A food additive derived from fats that is used as a sweetener, solvent and/or humectant in processed foods such as confections and candies.

glycerol ester of wood rosin A food additive used in beverages containing citrus oils.

glycerol monostearate A food additive used as a humectant in processed foods such as baked goods and mixes.

glyceryl-lacto esters of fatty acids Food additives derived from vegetable oils and used as emulsifiers and plasticizers.

glyceryl-lacto-stearate A food additive used as an emulsifier in cake mixes, chocolate coatings and whipped toppings.

glyceryl monolaurate A food additive used as an antimicrobial agent in baked goods, cheese products and whipped toppings.

glyceryl monooleate A food additive used as a flavoring agent and/or adjuvant in processed foods such as baked goods, baking mixes, meat products, beverages and candies.

glyceryl triacetate A food additive with a slightly fatty aroma used as a solvent and humectant.

glyceryl tristearate A food additive used as a crystallization accelerator in cocoa products, as a lubricant and release agent in baked goods and as a processing aid for fats.

glycine 1. An amino acid. 2. A food additive used as a nutrient source to significantly improve the biological quality of the total protein in a food containing the naturally occurring protein; also used to mask the bitter aftertaste of saccharin in beverages and as a stabilizer in fats; also known as aminoacetic acid.

glycogen A polysaccharide and the principal form for storing carbohydrates in the liver; when needed, it is converted into glucose for use as an energy source; it has little or no flavor and occurs naturally in significant quantities in liver, muscles, yeast and fungi; also known as animal starch.

glycyrrhizin A food additive derived from the licorice root and used as a flavoring agent in bacon and a sweetener in low-fat dessert products.

glyko (ylee-koh) Greek for jam or fruit preserve.

gnagnan (nyahn-yahn) A plant native to Africa; its small, red-orange fruit, which resemble peppercorns, have a slightly bitter flavor and are used as a condiment.

gnetum A tree native to Southeast Asia; its small fruit grow in bunches and have a dark red skin and edible seeds.

gnocchi (NYOH-kee) Italian for dumplings and used to describe irregularly shaped balls or small concave oval disks made from a dough of potatoes, flour, semolina flour, cornmeal and/or rice flour, with or without eggs; they are boiled or baked.

gnocchi alla romana (NYOH-kee al-lah roh-mah-nah) Italian gnocchi made with semolina, sprinkled with Parmesan and baked.

goa *See* winged bean.

goat Any of several varieties of horn-rimmed ruminants closely related to sheep and used for their flesh and milk; the meat is generally tough and strongly flavored. *See* kid.

goatfish A family of saltwater fish named for their two long chin barbels, which resemble goat whiskers; their skin ranges in color from brilliant yellow to rose red; their flesh is firm and lean, and they are found off the U.S. East Coast, Florida Keys and Hawaii.

goat's milk *See* milk, goat's.

goat's milk cheeses Cheeses made from goat's milk; usually pure white with an assertive, tangy, tart flavor; their texture can range from soft, moist and creamy to dry, firm and crumbly and their shape from small- to medium-sized cones, cylinders, disks or pyramids; they are left ungarnished or covered with black ash, leaves, herbs or pepper.

goblet 1. A stemmed drinking vessel with a base and bowl, usually made of glass or precious metal. 2. A method of pruning grapevines so that they take on the shape of a goblet.

gobo (goh-BOH) *See* burdock.

gobstopper A hard sweet English candy.

gocce d'or (got-chae doh-row) A golden plum grown around Venice, Italy.

gochian (go-chee-an) Black beehive-shaped mushrooms from India's Kashmir region, similar to French morels.

gochiso sama deshita (go-tchi-soe sah-mah da-she-tah) Japanese for I have been royally feasted; said after eating.

gochujang (go-choo-jang) A salty chili paste with a mild flavor used in Korean cuisines.

go-cup A New Orleans term for a paper or plastic cup used by bar patrons to hold their cocktails while they stroll outdoors, especially in the French Quarter.

goblet

goggle-eye bass *See* rock bass.

gogol mogol (go-gool moe-goal) The Russian version of the dessert zabaglione.

gogosari (goh-goh-sah-ree) Romanian for sweet pepper.

goguette A highly spiced flat French sausage made from pork.

gohan (GOH-hahn) Japanese cooked rice. *See* zushi.

goi (go-ee) Vietnamese for salad.

goi tom cang (go-ee tom kang) A Vietnamese salad of shrimp and cucumber.

golabki ze slodkiej kapusty (go-wo-pkee zeh swoh-t-kyey kah-poo-sti) A Polish dish of cabbage leaves rolled around seasoned rice and cooked in bouillon or a liquid of fermented rye.

golda jheengari (GOHL-da JEEN-ga-ree) *See* bara-jheenga.

gold beet A beet with a golden-yellow color and a flavor that is sweeter than that of a red beet; it can be eaten raw or cooked.

gold watermelon; golden watermelon *See* watermelon, yellow.

golden apple A small, yellow, egg-shaped fruit (*Spondias cytheria*) with a single seed; native to Polynesia, it has a sweet and slightly acidic flavor and is used for preserves and as an ingredient in savory dishes.

Golden Berry A variety of cape gooseberry grown in the United States and New Zealand.

golden buck A British dish of Welsh rarebit served with a poached egg on top. *See* Welsh rarebit.

Golden Cadillac A cocktail made of Galliano, white crème de cacao and heavy cream.

golden celery *See* celery.

Golden Chasselas *See* Palomino.

Golden Delicious apple An apple with a yellow to yellow-green skin, a juicy, crisp flesh and a rather bland flavor that is further lost when cooked; a good all-purpose apple that resists browning.

golden eyebrow fish *See* gilthead.

golden gin A dry gin with a light, golden color (the result of aging the gin in a wooden cask).

golden mantle oyster A Pacific oyster found off the U.S. West Coast from Washington to Vancouver; it has a long, ovoid shell and a plump flesh with a golden color.

golden needle *See* tiger lily bud.

golden nugget squash A small, pumpkin-shaped winter squash with a dull orange skin, an orange flesh and a sweet, slightly bland flavor.

golden oak *See* shiitake.

golden raisins Small seedless raisins with a pale gold color made from sultana grapes and used in confectionery and for table use; also known as white raisins and sultanas.

Golden Sunrise tomato A variety of medium-sized, spherical tomato with a yellow-orange skin and flesh.

golden syrup A light, sweet syrup with an amber color and a butterscotch flavor; it is a refined by-product of the sugar-refining process. *See* treacle.

golden thistle A thistle native to southern Europe (*Scolymus hispanicus*); it has a fleshy white root similar to that of salsify; also known as Spanish oyster plant.

Golden Transparent plum A variety of plum with a yellow skin and a very sweet flavor.

golden whitefish caviar Roe harvested from whitefish native to the northern U.S. Great Lakes; the small, golden eggs are very crisp.

Goldings A variety of hops grown in England.

gold leaf The pure metal beaten into a gossamer-thin square and sold in packages interleaved with tissue paper; edible in small quantities, it is used to decorate rice dishes in Indian cuisines, and desserts, confections and candies; also known as vark and varak. *See* skewings.

Goldmine nectarine A variety of nectarine; the fruit are relatively small, with a red-blushed white skin and a rich, sweet flavor.

gold powder 22- to 24-karat gold that is ground to dust and used to decorate desserts, pastries and confections.

Goldwasser (GOLT-vahs-sehr) A colorless, sweet German liqueur flavored with spices and dried orange peel; it contains flecks of gold leaf.

Golfin, sauce (goal-fahn) A French compound sauce made from a white wine sauce garnished with a julienne of gherkins and pickled tongue.

Golf Martini A cocktail made of gin, dry vermouth and Angostura bitters and garnished with a green olive.

golonka (go-lon-kah) A Polish dish consisting of a leg of pork roasted with root vegetables and flavored with caraway seeds, allspice and marjoram.

golubtses (goh-lube-t'seas) *See* prakkes.

goma (GOH-mah) Japanese for sesame seeds (used for seasoning and garnishing); white seeds are known as shiro goma, and black seeds are kuro goma.

goma abura (GOH-mah AH-boo-rah) Japanese for sesame oil.

gomashio; goma-shio (GOH-mah-SHEE-oh) Japanese for a mixture of sea salt and toasted black sesame seeds; used as a garnish and flavoring in Japanese cuisine.

gombo *See* okra.

gomen (go-mann) Ethiopian for collard green.

gomme A prepared simple syrup (sugar and water boiled with beaten egg whites to clarify the mixture) used as a sweetener in certain cocktails.

gomost (goom-ohst) A Norwegian dish of curdled milk eaten with salt or sugar.

Gomost (go-moost) A Norwegian cow's milk cheese with a buttery consistency.

gong yew chew Amber-colored, dried discs of a type of sea scallop used as a flavoring in Chinese and other Asian cuisines.

Gonyaulax A species of protozoa that causes food poisoning (called paralytic shellfish poisoning); symptoms include facial numbness, breathing difficulties, muscle weakness and sometimes partial paralysis; the typical source is contaminated shellfish found in red tidewaters.

goober; goober pea *See* peanut.

good A midlevel U.S. Department of Agriculture (USDA) quality grade for veal and lamb; this meat lacks the flavor and tenderness of the higher grades of prime and choice.

good health cheese *See* Holsteiner Gesundheitskäse.

good King Henry An herb and member of the spinach family native to England (*Chenopdium bonus henricus*); its leaves have a flavor reminiscent of asparagus and are used like spinach.

Good Manufacturing Practices (GMP) A series of U.S. Food and Drug Administration (FDA) regulations intended to increase food safety and sanitation by providing guidelines for the manufacturing, processing, packing and holding of foods.

good source of A food-labeling term approved by the U.S. Food and Drug Administration (FDA) to describe a food that contains 10–19% of the daily value per serving of the nutrient specified.

goodwill The value of an established business based on its name or reputation.

goody *See* spot.

Goo Goo Cluster The proprietary name for a candy composed of caramel, marshmallow and peanuts or pecans coated with chocolate.

goongoo *See* pigeon pea.

goop *See* gorp.

goose One of the principal kinds of poultry recognized by the U.S. Department of Agriculture (USDA); domesticated geese have very fatty skin and dark meat with a rich, buttery flavor.

goose, mature A goose slaughtered when older than 6 months; it has a hard windpipe, an average market weight of 10–16 lb. (4.5–7 kg), a very large amount of fat and a tough flesh.

goose, young A goose slaughtered when 6 months old or younger; it has an easily dented windpipe, an average market weight of 6–12 lb. (2.5–5.5 kg), a large amount of fat, a tender dark flesh and a rich, buttery flavor.

gooseberry A large berry (*Ribes grossularia*) originally grown in northern Europe; it has a smooth or furry green, yellow, red or white skin and a tart flavor; available dried or fresh and used in preserves and baked goods.

goose classes Significant goose classes are the young goose and mature goose.

goose fat Fat obtained from roasting a goose or rendering the fat; it is soft, flavorful and high in saturated fats.

goose feather brush A pastry brush made from several goose feathers sewn together; it is used for glazing delicate fruits and applying egg washes.

goosefish *See* monkfish.

goose liver *See* foie gras.

gooseneck A subprimal of the beef primal round; it is the whole bottom round trimmed for roasting or fabricated into steaks.

goose plum *See* plum, wild.

goose skirt A British cut of the beef carcass; it is the inner muscle of the belly wall attached to the rump.

goraka; gorka (goh-rah-kah) A medium-sized fruit (*Garcinia cambogia*) native to Sri Lanka; related to the carambola, it has a yellow or orange fluted skin and a tart flavor; used as a thickener, flavoring agent and souring agent in Sri Lankan cuisine, especially for fish dishes.

gorchitsa (gahr-CHYEE-tsi) Russian for mustard.

gordita (gohr-DEE-tah) Spanish for little fat one and used to describe a thick tortilla made of masa, lard and water, fried and then filled with ground pork or chorizo; it is topped with cheese, lettuce and the like.

gordo (gore-doe) Portuguese for fat.

goreng bawang (GO-rang bah-wang) Crisp fried onions used as a garnish in Indonesian and Thai cuisines.

gorenjski zelodec (go-ran-ya-ski jel-oo-ditz) A Balkan sausage made from a pig's stomach stuffed with meat from the head, cooked with salt, pepper and garlic; after cooking, it is pressed to remove excess liquid and then air-dried.

Gorgonzola (gohr-guhn-ZOH-lah) An Italian cheese made from cow's milk; it has an ivory interior streaked with blue-green veins and a slightly pungent flavor when young that grows stronger as it ages (it also becomes drier and more crumbly as it ages).

Gorgonzola Bianco (gohr-guhn-ZOH-lah BEE-ahn-coh) A fast-ripening Gorgonzola without the blue mold but with the same flavor and other characteristics of Gorgonzola; also known as White Gorgonzola, Gorgonzola Dolce and Pannerone.

Gorgonzda Dolce *See* Gorgonzola Bianco.

Gorgonzola knife A knife with a rigid, medium-length, broad, blunt-edged 6-in.-long blade; used to dig into a blue-veined cheese, splitting it apart along the veins.

Gornyi (gahr-n'ye-ee) A hard, granular Russian cheese made from cow's milk; it has a mild flavor and is generally used for cooking.

gorokh (gah-ROHK) Russian for peas.

gorp *v.* To eat noisily or greedily. *n.* A mix of nuts, raisins, seeds, dried fruit and oats used as an energy source by athletes; also known as glop and goop.

gorum moshla *See* garam masala.

goryachee (go-ree-ash-ee) Russian for hot.

gosht (gosht) Hindi for meat.

gossi A Senegalese dessert of rice cooked with milk, vanilla bean and sugar; it can be served at room temperature or chilled.

gostinitza (go-stee-ne-tzah) Russian for hotel.

gotovit' (go-toe-vitt) Russian for to cook.

Gouda (GOO-dah) A semisoft to firm Dutch sweet curd cheese made from cow's milk; it has a yellow interior and a mild, nutty flavor (it is sometimes flavored with cumin or other herbs and spices); marketed in large wheels with a yellow wax coating.

Gouda, Baby A small wheel of Gouda marketed with a red wax coating.

gouge à jambon (gough ah jahm-bohn) A tool with a strong backwardly arched metal trough and a wooden handle used to separate the flesh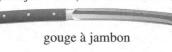

gouge à jambon

of the ham from the bone so that the bone can be extracted.

gougère (goo-ZHAIR) A savory round or ring-shaped choux pastry flavored with cheese (e.g., Gruyère, Comté or Emmental); it is a traditional accompaniment to wine tastings in France's Burgundy region.

gougsou (goog-soo) Long, thin wheat flour noodles used in Korean cold soups and stir-fries, which are often flavored with chile sauces.

goujon, en (goo-jhoh, ahn) French term for small fried strips of fish, such as sole.

goulash (GOO-lahsh) A Hungarian stew made with beef and vegetables and flavored with paprika; also known as Hungarian goulash.

gourd 1. The nonedible fruit of various plants of the gourd family (*Cucurbitaceae*); generally, they have a tough, hard shell that can be used as a utensil or storage unit once the flesh is removed and the shell is dried. *See* squash. 2. British for several edible squashes.

gourmand (goor-mahnd) A connoisseur of fine food and drink, often to excess.

Gourmandise (goor-mahn-DEEZ) A soft, creamy processed cheese product made from cow's milk and flavored with cherry juice or extract (in France, Kirsch is used); sold in small cakes or wedges, sometimes with a chopped-nut topping.

gourmet (goor-may) A connoisseur of fine food and drink.

gourmet, sauce A French compound sauce made from a demi-glaze, red wine and fish stock; it is flavored with lobster butter and garnished with diced lobster and truffles.

gourmet foods A term used imprecisely to denote foods of the highest quality, perfectly prepared and beautifully presented.

Gournay (gour-nay) A soft French Neufchâtel-style cheese made from cow's milk; it has a delicate, salty flavor; when it matures, it resembles a rustic Camembert and is usually sold wrapped in foil.

gouronopoulo (yoo-roo-noh-poo-loh) Greek for suckling pig.

goût (goo) French for taste.

goût de bois (goo duh bwah) French wine-tasting term for woody.

goût de bouchon (goo duh boo-shon) French wine-tasting term for corky.

goût de terrior (goo duh terh-wahr) French wine-tasting term for earthy.

goûter (goo-tay) 1. French for to taste. 2. French for a snack, similar to afternoon tea.

goutte d'encre (goot dahn'r) French for shaggy mane mushroom.

governo (goh-VAIR-no) An Italian wine-making technique in which a sugar-rich must made from dried grapes or a commercial grape concentrate is added to the wine to induce a second fermentation; the resulting wine, such as some Chianti, has a low acid content, a high alcohol content and a slight sparkle.

Governor's plum *See* ramontchi.

govyadina (gah-VYAH-dyee-nah) Russian for beef.

Goya (gaw-yah) An Argentinean Asiago-style cheese made from whole or partly skimmed cow's milk.

goyave (go-yahv) French for guava.

gözleme tatlisi (gohs-lah-mah that-lee-sea) A Turkish confection of rolled sheets of pastry fried in oil and soaked in a sugar syrup.

Gradeal Special A cocktail made of gin, light rum, sugar syrup and apricot brandy or apricot liqueur.

grades *See* USDA quality grades *and* USDA yield grades.

grading A series of voluntary programs offered by the U.S. Department of Agriculture (USDA) to designate a food's overall quality.

grafting A horticultural technique of inserting a bud, shoot or scion of one plant into the stem or rootstock of another plant in which it will continue to grow.

graham cracker A sweetened whole wheat cracker.

graham flour Coarsely milled whole wheat flour; named for Dr. Sylvester Graham (1794–1851), an American dietary reformer.

grain alcohol *See* ethyl alcohol.

grains 1. Grasses that bear edible seeds, including corn, rice and wheat. 2. The fruit (i.e., seed or kernel) of such grasses.

grains of paradise The small, reddish-brown seeds of this plant (*Aframomum melegueta*) are used as a spice in many West African cuisines; they have a pungent, peppery flavor; also known as melegueta pepper.

grain spirits Spirits distilled from a fermented mash of grains and stored in oak containers; unlike neutral spirits, they obtain certain characteristics from their wooden storage containers.

grain vinegar *See* spirit vinegar.

grain whiskey Whiskey made from unmalted grain and distilled in a patent still.

grainy A tasting term for a food with a gritty or mealy texture.

graisse *See* gras.

gram (g) The basic measure of weight in the metric system; 28.35 g equal 1 oz., and 1000 g (1 kg) equal 2.2 lb. (U.S.).

gram Hindi for any of a large variety of dried, whole pulses used in Indian cuisines. *See* dhal.

gramigna (grah-me-nha) Italian for weed and used to describe small, slightly curved, ridged tubes of pasta.

gram poo (gramm poe-ho) Thai for cloves.

grams per liter A unit of measurement similar to parts per thousand.

grana (GRAH-nah) A category of Italian cheeses that are usually aged; they have a hard, granular texture with very small eyes and a sharp flavor and are principally used for grating (e.g., Asiago, Lodigiano and Parmigiano-Reggiano).

grana (gra-nah) A sandy, red coloring used in salted eggs in the Philippines.

granada (grah-NAH-dah) Spanish for pomegranate.

granadiglia (grah-nah-dee-ya) Italian for passion fruit.

granadilla (gran-ah-DEE-yuh) The fruit of a member of the passion fruit family (genus *Passiflora*); it has a large, spherical shape, a smooth, brittle orange skin that is speckled with tiny white dots, a grayish flesh and seeds and a mildly sweet flavor.

Granatapfel (grah-nan-tah-fell) German for pomegranate.

granatina (grah-nah-TEE-nah) An Italian dish consisting of a mixture of ground beef, eggs and bread crumbs shaped into a patty, breaded with additional bread crumbs, and fried.

granchio (GRAN-kyoh) Italian for crab.

grand cru (grahn crew) French for great growth (a great vineyard) and used as a designation for the best vineyards in France's Burgundy, Chablis and Alsace regions as well as certain villages in Champagne. *See* cru *and* premier cru.

grand cru classé (grahn crew clah-say) French for great classed growth and used as a designation of the great vineyards in France's Bordeaux region.

Grande Champagne The premier grape-growing area of France's Cognac region; it has nothing to do with sparkling wine.

grande cuisine The rich, intricate and elaborate cuisine of the 18th- and 19th-century French aristocracy and upper classes; it was based on the rational identification, development and adoption of strict (and often very elaborate) culinary principles.

Grande Marque A French Champagne-producing firm.

Grand Gruyère (gran grew-yair) A Swiss herbal liqueur.

Grandjo (grun-joo) A sweet Portuguese white wine made from late-gathered grapes affected by the noble rot.

Grand Marnier (GRAN mahr-NYAY) An orange-flavored French liqueur made in two styles: Cordon Rouge (has a light amber color and is made from Cognac and aged for 18 months) and Cordon Jaune (a paler variety made with a lesser-quality brandy).

grand mère, à la (grahn mer, ah lah) French for in the grandmother's style and used to describe a dish, particularly a chicken casserole, served with pieces of bacon, glazed onions, sautéed mushrooms and fried potatoes.

Grand Passion A cocktail made of gin, passion fruit liqueur and Angostura bitters.

grand reserve A French labeling term for Armagnac or Cognac; it indicates that the youngest brandy used in the blend was at least 5.5 years old.

grandule *See* pigeon pea.

grand vin (gran van) French for the best or first wine of a particular winery.

granita (grah-nee-TAH) An Italian frozen mixture made with water, sugar and a flavoring such as fruit juice or wine; stirred frequently while freezing, it has a grainy texture.

granité (grah-nee-TAY) A French frozen mixture made with water, sugar and a flavoring such as fruit juice or wine; stirred frequently while freezing, it has a grainy texture.

graniteware Ironware covered with enamel speckled to resemble granite; used for cookware and dinnerware.

gran kongle; grankongle (grahn kon-geel) Norwegian for pine nuts.

Granny Smith apple Named for an Australian gardener, Maria Ann Smith, and originally grown in Australia, South Africa and New Zealand; a good all-purpose apple with a rich, almost emerald green skin, a tart, sweet flavor, and a firm flesh.

grano (gr-no) Italian for wheat.

granola A mix of grains, nuts and dried fruits, sometimes coated with oil and honey, eaten for breakfast or as a snack. *See* musli.

gran reserva (grahn reh-ZEHR-vah) A Spanish term used to denote the length of time a wine has aged; for red wine it indicates that the wine has been aged for at least 5 years, 2 of which have been in a wooden cask; for a white or rosé wine, it indicates that the wine was aged for at least 4 years, with 6 months in wood.

granturco (grahn-TOOR-coa) Italian for corn.

granular cheese A cheese made from raw or pasteurized cow's milk curds stirred until dry, then salted and pressed in hoops (e.g., Colby); also known as stirred-curd cheese.

granulated gelatin *See* gelatin, granulated.

granulated sugar Fine, white sucrose crystals, a general-purpose sweetener; also known as table sugar.

granvas (grahn-vah'ss) A Spanish term for sparkling wine made by the Charmat or bulk process. *See* cava.

grao (grah-oh) Portuguese for chickpea.

grao com bacalhau (grah-oh com bah-cahl-ah-oo) A Portuguese petisco salad of chickpeas, dried cod, onions, vinegar and oil.

grape color extract A food additive derived from Concord grapes and used as a red coloring agent.

grapefruit A tropical citrus fruit (*Citrus paradisi*) that is an 18th-century hybrid of the orange and pomelo; the relatively thin skin is yellow, and the juicy pulp has a distinctive flavor; available with seeds or seedless.

grapefruit, ruby A grapefruit with yellow-pink to brilliant ruby pulp; it has a sweeter flavor than the white grapefruit.

grapefruit, white A grapefruit with yellow-white pulp; it has a tarter flavor than the ruby grapefruit and is better for juicing.

grapefruit knife A small knife with a curved double-edged serrated blade used to section citrus fruit.

grape juice The liquid constituent of the grape; accounts for more than 85% of the fruit.

grape leaves The large dark green leaves of the grapevine; used in Mediterranean and Middle Eastern cuisines to wrap foods for cooking or as a garnish; available fresh or packed in brine; also known as vine leaves.

grape pie A dessert from the American South consisting of Concord grapes cooked with sugar and thickened with cornstarch and lemon juice and poured into a baked pie shell; when cool, it is garnished with whipped cream and fresh seeded grapes; also known as a jelly pie (especially in North Carolina).

grapes Smooth-skinned, juicy berries (with or without seeds) that grow in clusters; members of the genus *Vitis,* they are used for wine making, raisins and eating out of hand.

grapes, black Grapes with skin colors ranging from light red to purple-black; also known as red grapes.

grapes, red *See* grapes, black.

grapes, red wine Grapes generally used for making red wines; principal varietals grown in the United States include Cabernet Sauvignon, Merlot, Pinot Noir, Zinfandel, Gamay, Petite Sirah, Cabernet Franc, Maréchal Foch, Barbera and Syrah.

grapes, rosé Grapes generally used for making rosé wines; principal varietals grown in the United States include Cabernet, Grenache, Pinot Noir and Zinfandel.

grapes, white Grapes with skin colors ranging from pale yellow-green to light green.

grapes, white wine Grapes generally used for making white wines; principal varietals grown in the United States include Chardonnay, Riesling, Sauvignon Blanc, Chenin Blanc, Sémillon, Seyvel Blanc, Gewürztraminer, Pinot Blanc and French Colombard.

grape scissors A pair of scissors with long handles and 1- to 2-in.-long, snub-tipped blades, one of which is concave and the other straight; used to snip bunches of grapes from a cluster.

grape scissors

grape seed oil An oil obtained from grape seeds; it has a pale color, a delicate, neutral flavor and high smoke point and is used for frying and other culinary purposes.

grape skin extract A food additive used as a red or purple coloring agent.

grape stones Grape seeds.

grape sugar The natural sugar (primarily glucose) found in ripe grapes.

grape tomato A very small, ovoid tomato with a bright red or golden yellow color and a very sweet flavor.

grape variety; grape varietal The specific type of grape used to make a particular wine (e.g., Pinot Noir or Chardonnay).

grape wine Wine produced by the normal fermentation of the juice of ripe grapes with or without the addition of pure condensed grape must, grape brandy or alcohol after fermentation.

grapey A wine-tasting term for a wine, usually young, with a pronounced grape or fruity aroma and flavor.

grappa (GRAHP-pah) *See* marc.

gras; graisse (grah; grohss) 1. French for fat. 2. A French term for soft, full wines.

GRAS (Generally Recognized As Safe) List A list of food additives established by the U.S. Food and Drug Administration (FDA) generally recognized as safe throughout the scientific community.

grasa (grah-sah) Spanish for fat.

gras-double (grah-DOOB-luh) French for tripe.

graslök (grasse-luhk) Swedish for chives.

graslok (grass-lock) Norwegian for chives.

Grasshopper A cocktail made of crème de menthe, white crème de cacao and cream; usually served after dinner.

grasshopper pie A light, creamy pie flavored with green crème de menthe and white crème de cacao.

grasso (grass-oh) Italian for fat, especially meat fat.

grass pike *See* northern pike.

grass snake A snake prepared like eel in French cuisine; also known as hedge eel.

grassy 1. A tea-tasting term used to describe a tea that has a flavor and/or aroma reminiscent of freshly cut grass. 2. A wine-tasting term for certain white wines such as Sauvignon Blanc that have a vegetal, herbaceous aroma; a subtle amount adds character; a more pronounced aroma is less appealing.

grate To reduce food to small pieces by scraping it on a rough surface.

Gräte (gra-tah) German for fish bone.

grated cheese A hard, dry, low-milkfat cheese (e.g., a grana such as Parmigiano-Reggiano) ground to a coarse powder; often used as a condiment or topping.

grater A tool used to reduce hard foods to small pieces or long thin strips by passing the food over the sharp raised edges of various-sized holes or slits. *See* box grater, cheese grater, ginger grater, lemon grater, Mouli grater *and* nutmeg grater.

gratin, au (GRAW-ten, oh) A dish that is topped with cheese or bread crumbs and baked until browned; usually served in the baking dish.

gratin dish (GRAW-ten) A shallow oval or round metal or ceramic dish, generally with twin handles or a rim that extends on either side to form handles; it is used for preparing dishes that

gratin dish

are usually topped with cheese or bread crumbs and cooked in a hot oven; the food is served from the dish.

gratinée (grah-teen-nay) French for a dish that is topped with cheese, bread crumbs or sauce and browned in the oven or under a broiler.

gratinerad rom (grah-tea-na-rahd romm) A Swedish smörgåsbord dish of baked cod's roe; the roe is mixed with chives, beaten eggs and milk and baked in the oven.

gratin forcemeat A French forcemeat of chicken livers browned in pork fat and flavored with herbs; used as a spread for croutons or canapés or as a stuffing.

Gratte-Paille (grott-pie) A soft-ripened, double crème cow's milk French cheese; it has a beige-mottled, white, bloomy rind with a buttery texture and a raw-milk flavor.

grattons; gratterons A dish from southwestern France made from the remains of melted pork, goose or turkey fat or rinds; salted while hot and eaten cold as an hors d'oeuvre.

gratuity Money given voluntarily in return for or anticipation of service. *See* tips.

Gravenstein apple A large, slightly lopsided apple with a red-streaked green skin, a crisp, juicy flesh and a rather acidic flavor; it is good for applesauce and pies.

Graves (grahv) A principal grape-growing and wine-producing area within France's Bordeaux region; red wines are marketed with the vineyard or château name and are made from Cabernet Sauvignon, Cabernet Franc or Merlot grapes and are soft and ripe; white wines, marketed with the regional appellation, are made from Sauvignon Blanc and Sémillon grapes and are generally crisp, dry and acidic.

graviaks med rævesauce (grah-vee-aks med ra-vess-sass) A Danish smørrebrød dish of gravlax on white bread with mustard sauce.

gravlax (GRAHV-lahks) A Swedish dish of salmon cured in a sugar, salt and dill mixture, sliced thin and served on dark bread with a dill and mustard sauce.

gravy A sauce made from meat or poultry juices combined with a liquid (e.g., milk, broth or wine) and a thickening agent (e.g., flour or cornstarch).

gravy boat An elongated, boat-shaped pitcher used to serve gravy; it usually sits on a plate, which is sometimes attached, and has a ladle; also known as a sauceboat.

gravy boat

gravy browning A coloring agent used to darken sauces and gravies; usually made with caramelized sugar, salt and water.

gravy powder A blend of dehydrated meat extracts and thickening agents such as corn or wheat flour; used to thicken stews and soups.

gravy separator A clear plastic cup with a long spout set low in the cup; pan drippings are poured into the cup, the fat rises to the top, and the desirable underlying liquid can be poured off through the spout; generally available in 1.5- to 4-cup capacities.

gravy separator

gray bass *See* sheepshead.

gray cheese A cheese made in Austria's Tyrol region from soured skimmed cow's milk; it has a gray color and pleasant flavor.

gray cod *See* cod, Pacific.

gray mullet *See* mullet.

Gray Riesling 1. A misnamed white wine grape grown in California; not a true Riesling but rather a French grape known as Chaucé Gris. 2. The white wine made from this grape; it is soft, mild and neutral and is sometimes labeled Grey Riesling.

gray rot The undesirable deterioration of unripened grapes affected by the mold *Botrytis cinerea. See* noble rot.

gray sea trout *See* sea trout.

gray snapper *See* uku.

gray sole A member of the flounder family found in the Atlantic Ocean; it has a gray striped skin on top, an average market length of 25 in. (63.5 cm), and a white flesh with a fine flavor; also known as witch flounder.

grazing The practice of snacking or eating small portions of several foods or dishes, usually at a restaurant; also known as modular eating.

grease *v.* To rub fat or a fat substitute on the surface of a cooking utensil or item of cookware. *n.* Rendered animal fat, such as bacon, beef or chicken fat.

grease mop A small rag mop made with absorbent strips attached to a handle; brushed across the surface of soups or stocks, the strips absorb the floating fat; also known as a fat mop.

greaseproof paper *See* wax paper.

greasy spoon Slang for an inexpensive restaurant usually serving foods of low quality.

great hog plum A medium-sized, slightly ovoid fruit (*Spondias cytherea*) with a yellow skin and a stringy, sweet-flavored, peach-colored flesh; also known as a cytherean apple.

Great Lakes lettuce A variety of crisp head lettuce similar to iceberg.

Great Lakes trout *See* lake trout.

great Northern bean A large, flat, kidney-shaped white bean; it has a delicate flavor and is generally available dried. *See* white beans.

great scallop A variety of scallops found in the Atlantic Ocean from Norway to Africa; it has a red to reddish-brown shell with a violet luster, an average diameter of 5–6 in. (12.7–15.2 cm), and a tender, sweet white meat.

Great White An heirloom tomato variety with a pale yellow color, a meaty flesh and a mild, nonacidic, creamy flavor.

great yellow gentian *See* gentian.

grebenes; gribenes; gregen (greh-bah-nehz) A Jewish dish of the chicken fat and skin from the neck, thigh and rear fried with onions; the rendered fat is schmaltz, and the cracklings are eaten as a snack on toast or used for stuffings.

grecque, à la (greh-kew, ah lah) A French preparation method associated with Greek cuisine; the dishes are characterized by vegetables cooked in olive oil and lemon juice, served cold, or by a fish topped with a white wine sauce flavored with celery, fennel and coriander seeds.

greeb-shiitakye (gra-ab-she-tah-key-ah) Russian for shiitake.

Greek coffee *See* Turkish coffee.

green 1. A food that is not yet ripe (e.g., a green banana) or mature (e.g., green meat). 2. A wine-tasting term for a wine with a vegetal character, a green, leafy aroma, and a raw, tart, excessively acidic flavor; caused by fermenting unripened grapes; also known as stalky.

green back rashers Unsmoked bacon from the hog's back; it lacks the meaty streak found in belly bacon and is used in British cuisine.

green banana An unripened sweet yellow banana; before the starch is converted to sugar, the unripened banana can be used as a starchy vegetable in place of plantains or potatoes.

green Bartlett pear *See* Bartlett pear.

green bean A long, slender green pod that contains several small seeds; the entire crisp pod is edible; also known as a string bean (because of the fibrous string that runs down the side; modern varieties do not have this fiber), fresh bean and snap bean. *See* wax bean.

green beer Beer that has just finished fermenting; it is still cloudy and has not yet been conditioned.

green cabbage *See* cabbage, green.

green cheese Immature cheese. *See* cheese-making process.

green chile stew A Native American dish of lamb cooked with onions, tomatoes, garlic, roasted green chiles and pinto beans and flavored with oregano and cumin; generally served on fry bread and topped with chopped onions and grated cheese.

green coffee beans *See* coffee beans, green.

green congo pea *See* pigeon pea.

green crab A variety of crab found in the Atlantic Ocean from New Jersey to Maine; it has a dark green or yellow-mottled green shell and an average width of 3 in. (7 cm); more popular in Europe than in the United States, where they are often used as bait.

greengage 1. A small, spherical plumlike fruit (*Prunus italica*) with a greenish-yellow skin and flesh and a tangy–sweet flavor; also known as Reine Claude. 2. An imprecisely used term for any of a variety of yellow- or green-skinned plums.

green garden peas Common small green peas; also known as English peas.

green garlic A young garlic plant that has not yet formed a well-defined bulb; it has long green leaves and a small, soft bulb that is white, sometimes tinged with pink; the immature bulb has a subtle, mild garlicky flavor.

green goddess dressing A salad dressing made from mayonnaise, tarragon vinegar and anchovies, seasoned with parsley, chives, tarragon, scallions and garlic; also used as a sauce for fish or shellfish.

green gram *See* mung bean.

Green Hungarian 1. A white wine grape grown in California; sometimes used as a blending grape. 2. A pale white wine made from this grape.

greening 1. An oyster's greenish appearance that results from the oyster feeding on certain algaelike organisms. 2. Any of a variety of green-skinned apples.

green leaf lettuce A variety of leaf lettuce with bright green, ruffled-edge leaves, a tender texture and a mild flavor.

greenling *See* lingcod.

green lip abalone *See* smooth ear shell abalone.

greenlip mussel; greenshell mussel A variety of large mussels found off New Zealand and Southeast Asia (especially Thailand); it has an elongated ovoid, gray-blue shell with a distinctive green edge, a plump orangish-yellow meat with a firm texture and a sweet flavor.

green malt Malted barley that has sprouted and is kiln-dried to stop further growth.

green mango An unripe mango; it has a high pectin content and a sour flavor and is the basis for chutneys and pickles, especially in India.

green mealie soup A South African soup consisting of fresh corn flavored with thyme, mace, bay leaf, parsley and white wine.

green meat Freshly slaughtered meat that has not had sufficient time to age and develop tenderness and a full flavor.

green onions *See* scallions.

green pepper; green bell pepper *See* bell pepper.

green peppercorn *See* peppercorn, green.

green pills Nutrient supplements made from crushed, dehydrated vegetables; each pill contains nutrients approximately equal to those in a forkful of fresh vegetables.

greens 1. A general term for the green, leafy parts of various plants that are eaten raw or cooked. 2. Members of the cabbage family, such as kale, spinach and chard, that have edible leaves.

green salad A salad consisting of a variety of salad greens (e.g., lettuce, spinach, endive, chicory and arugula) often combined with garnishes such as croutons, cheese and bacon and dressed with a vinaigrette or mayonnaise-based dressing.

green sauce A mayonnaise-based sauce flavored with finely minced herbs (e.g., parsley, chives, tarragon and watercress) or spinach; also known as mayonnaise verte.

green tea One of the three principal types of tea; the leaves are steamed and dried but not fermented; the beverage is generally a greenish-yellow color with a slightly bitter flavor suggestive of the fresh leaf. *See* black tea *and* oolong tea.

green tobacco *See* young tobacco.

green turtle A variety of turtle found in warm Pacific Ocean waters; it has a smooth, olive-green shell and a whitish-green flesh that has a tough texture and a mild flavor similar to that of veal; used in Asian cuisines; also known as a sea turtle.

Green Zebra An heirloom tomato variety; the small spherical tomato has a bright amber-green skin with light green stripes and an excellent flavor.

grefrut (grye-frutt) Russian for grapefruit.

grelos (GRAY-loos) Portuguese for dandelion leaves.

Grelot aux noix (grae-low oh nwah) A small, hard, salami-like French sausage studded with nuts; a specialty of Savoy.

gremolada (greh-moa-LAH-dah) An aromatic garnish of chopped parsley, garlic and lemon zest used for osso buco.

Grenache (greh-nah'sh) 1. A red wine grape widely planted in California, southern France, Spain, Australia and South Africa; also known as Garnacha. 2. In the United States, a full-bodied rosé wine or blending wine made from this grape.

grenade (greh-nahd) French for pomegranate.

grenadille (groh-nah-dee) French for passion fruit.

grenadin (greh-nah-dihn) A French cut of the veal carcass; it is a small thick steak cut from the leg.

grenadine (GREN-a-deen) A sweet, thick red syrup made from pomegranates; used in cocktails or consumed diluted with water.

grenadine molasses *See* pomegranate syrup.

grenadins (gruh-nah-danz) A French dish consisting of slices of beef (grenadins de boeuf), chicken (grenadins de volaille) or veal (grenadins de veau) larded with pork fat and braised with vegetables and seasonings.

grenouille (gruh-noo-ee) French for frog.

grenouilles provençale (gruh-noo-ee pro-vahn-sahl) A French dish of frog legs sautéed in olive oil with garlic and parsley.

greshnevaia kasha (grash-na-vah-ya kah-shahw) A Russian dish of buckwheat groats with mushrooms and onions.

gresskar (gress-car) Norwegian for pumpkin.

gressløk (grehass-lurk) Norwegian for chives.

gretskiy orekh (grat-skee oh-rack) Russian for walnut.

gribee (grih-bee) Middle Eastern butter cookies flavored with rosewater.

gribenes *See* grebenes.

gribi (gree-BEE) Russian for mushrooms.

gribiche, sauce (gree-beesh) A cold French sauce based on a mayonnaise made with hard-cooked egg yolks instead of raw egg yolks and garnished with capers, herbs and julienne of hard-cooked egg whites; served with calf's head or fish.

griby v semtanie (gree-be v'sam-tam-nee-a) A Russian zakuski dish of mushrooms in sour cream that is sprinkled with cheese and browned in the oven.

griddle 1. A cooking surface similar to a flat top but made of thinner metal; foods are usually cooked directly on its surface. 2. A pan, usually made of cast aluminum or cast iron and sometimes with a nonstick coating, used to fry foods and available with a long handle or two hand grips.

griddle cake Any of a variety of breadlike products cooked on a flat griddle (e.g., pancakes).

griddle scraper A metal tool with a trapezoidal, beveled blade used to remove grease and food debris from a griddle.

griesciai (gree-shy) Lithuanian for parsnips.

griglia, alla (GREE-l'yah, AH-la) Italian for grilled.

grigliata mista (GREE-lee-ah-tah me-stah) Italian for mixed grill.

grigliata mista di pesce (GREE-lee-ah-tah me-stah day PEH-sheh) An Italian dish of mixed broiled fish.

Grignolino (gree-n'yoh-LEE-no) 1. A red wine grape grown in Italy's Piedmont region. 2. A wine made from this grape; it has a light body, a delicate flavor and a slightly orange color.

grill v. To cook on a grill. n. 1. Cooking equipment in which the heat source (gas, charcoal, hardwood or electric) is located beneath the rack on which the food is placed; it is generally not enclosed, although it can be covered. 2. A restaurant or room, where, in theory, only grilled foods are served. 3. A restaurant or room, usually in a large hotel, where the service is faster and the meals less elaborate than in the main dining room. 4. *See* mixed grill.

grillade (gree-YAHD) 1. A Creole dish of pounded round steak cooked with tomatoes and other vegetables, seasoned with thyme, parsley and cayenne pepper, and usually served with grits. 2. French for grilled foods, especially meats.

grillades de porc (gree-YAHD duh por) A French dish consisting of pork chops seasoned with salt, pepper and herbes de Provence and grilled, usually over vine twigs; it is served with broiled pork sausage.

grillardin (gree-yar-dahn) At a food services operation following the brigade system, it is the person responsible for all grilled items; also known as the grill station chef.

grillettes (gree-YEHT) Small pieces of fatty meat, usually duck or pork, grilled or fried until crisp.

grilling A dry-heat cooking method in which foods are cooked by heat radiating from a source located below the cooking surface; the heat can be generated by electricity or by burning gas, hardwood or hardwood charcoals. *See* broiling.

Grillo A white wine grape grown in Italy and used to make Marsala.

grill pan A round or rectangular pan with a ridged bottom, usually made of cast iron or anodized aluminum, and used to grill meats on a stove top.

grill pan

grill spatula

grill spatula A large offset metal spatula, sometimes perforated, used for turning or removing foods from a grill or other cooking surface.

grill station chef *See* grillardin.

grilse The young salmon when it first leaves the sea to spawn in fresh water. *See* smolt.

grimslich (greems-lick) A Jewish dish of fritters made from matzo meal.

grind v. To reduce an object to small particles, usually by pounding, crushing or milling. n. The size, texture or other characteristic of a ground object.

grind, coarse The largest grind of roasted coffee beans; used for making coffee by the pot method.

grind, espresso; grind, fine espresso A very fine grind of roasted coffee beans; used for making espresso.

grind, fine A small grind of roasted coffee beans; used for making coffee by the drip and filter methods; also known as filter grind.

grind, medium An intermediate-sized grind of roasted coffee beans; used for making coffee by the pot method or in cafétiéres, percolators and small espresso machines.

grind, powdered The finest grind of roasted coffee beans; used for strong Turkish coffees; also known as pulverized grind.

grinder 1. Any of a variety of manual or electrical devices used to reduce food to small particles of varying degrees by the action of rotating blades; also known as a mill. 2. *See* hero.

grinding A milling process during which the grains are reduced to a powder; the powder can be of different degrees of fineness or coarseness.

grip A wine-tasting term for a red wine with a strong character, a rich texture and a relatively high tannin content; the opposite of bland.

gris (gri) Norwegian for pork.

griskin British for a hog's backbone.

grissini (gruh-SEE-nee) Thin, crisp Italian breadsticks.

grist Milled malt or a combination of milled grains that, when mixed with hot water, form the mash for making beer.

gristle *See* cartilage.

grits Ground dried hominy; they have a bland flavor and a gritty texture; these tiny white granules are available in three grinds: fine, medium and coarse; also known as hominy grits.

groat 1. A grain kernel (e.g., oat and barley) that has had its husk removed. 2. The whole buckwheat kernel.

groente (KHROON-tuh) Dutch for vegetables.

Grog 1. A drink made of rum and water, sometimes flavored with spices and fruit. 2. A drink made of rum, a sweetener and boiling water, garnished with a slice of lemon.

Grolleau (groe-low) *See* Groslot.

grønnsaker (GRUHN-ssah-kerr) Norwegian and Swedish for vegetables.

grooved carpet shell A bivalve mollusk found in the Atlantic Ocean from Norway to Senegal; it has a large brown and yellow shell with a lattice pattern of ribs and stripes and an average market length of 1.5–3 in. (3.8–7.6 cm).

Gros-Blanquet (groh-blahn-ket) A pear grown in France; it has a greenish-yellow skin and a gritty texture.

groseille à maquereau (gro-zeh-yah ah mah-kar-roa) French for mackeral currant and used to describe the gooseberry.

groseille rouge (gro-zeh-yah rooj) French for red currant.

grosella blanca (groh-say-jya blan-kah) Spanish for gooseberry.

grosella colorada (groh-say-jya koh-loh-rah-dah) Spanish for red currant.

Gros Locard A medium-sized, western European traditional apple with a brown-spotted yellow skin, a white flesh and a very sweet flavor.

Groslot (gro-lo) A red wine grape grown in France's Loire Valley and used to make Rosé d'Anjou; also known as Grolleau.

Gros Plant (groh plahn) 1. A white wine grape grown in France; also known as Folle Blanche. 2. The wine made from this grape; it is light, fresh and tart.

gross A dozen dozen (144).

gros sel (groh sell) French for crystalline unrefined sea salt; it is grayish in color and has a rich flavor.

Grosser Brauner (gros-ser bro-ee-ner) German for big brown and used to describe Viennese coffee served in a large cup with a dash of milk.

Grosslage (GROSS-lah-guh) German for large vineyard and used to describe a large area containing more than one Einzellagen that produce wines of similar quality and character.

gross margin; gross profit Revenue less the immediate (as opposed to overhead) costs associated with the production of the goods sold; in the food services industry, the difference between the costs of food served and the dollars collected for food sales.

gross weight The weight of a container and its contents. *See* net weight.

G'röstl (grow-stl) An Austrian hash made from fried onion rings, fried cooked potatoes and sliced, cooked beef, seasoned with caraway seeds.

groszek (groh-shek) Polish for peas.

ground beef *See* beef, ground.

ground-cherry 1. A cherry-sized fruit (*Physalis pruinosa*) with a yellow skin and a sweet, tart flavor reminiscent of pineapple; also known as a cossack pineapple and strawberry tomato. 2. An imprecisely used name for the closely related cape gooseberry. *See* cape gooseberry.

groundhog *See* woodchuck.

ground lamb *See* lamb, ground.

ground limestone A food additive consisting generally of calcium carbonate from naturally occurring limestone and used as a flavor enhancer and flavoring agent in processed foods such as beverages, baked goods, confections, herbs and seasonings.

groundnut *See* bambara *and* peanut.

grounds 1. Small particles of roasted coffee beans used to make coffee; the smaller the grounds, the greater the amount of surface area exposed to the water during the coffee-making process. *See* grind. 2. The sediment at or from the bottom of a liquid.

ground veal *See* veal, ground.

grouper A family of saltwater fish found in temperate waters worldwide; generally, they have a lean, white flesh, a firm texture, a mild to sweet flavor and an average market weight of 5–20 lb. (2.2–8.8 kg), although some can be much larger.

grouper

grouper, Atlantic Atlantic Ocean grouper varieties include the yellowfin grouper, yellowmouth grouper, black grouper, red grouper, Nassau grouper and gag.

grouper, Pacific Pacific Ocean grouper varieties include the sea bass and spotted cabrilla.

grouper, red A common variety of Atlantic grouper found off Florida; it has dark bars on the head and body, sometimes with scattered spots, and an average market weight of 4–6 lb. (1.8–2.7 kg).

grouse (grahus) Any of a variety of game birds found in Europe, especially Great Britain, and similar to the quail, with an average weight of 1.5 lb. (700 g); the flesh is dark red with a rich, gamy flavor.

growlers Containers, usually with a capacity of 1 to 1 1/2 gallons, used to buy and transport beer from a pub or microbrewery.

growth *See* cru.

gruel A cereal, usually oatmeal, cooked with water or milk; it is usually thin and has little flavor.

grumichama (groo-me-cha-mah) The small fruit of a tree (*Eugenia brasilliensis*) native to Brazil; it has a soft flesh and a mild flavor; there are three principal varieties distinguished by skin color: dark red, vermilion and white; also known as the Brazil cherry.

Grüne Bohnen (grew-ner BOA-nern) German for green beans.

Grüner Veltliner (GROO-ner felt-LEE-ner) 1. A white wine grape grown in Austria. 2. The wine made from this grape; it is pale, light bodied and refreshing.

grunion (GRUHN-yuhn) A fish found along the southern California coast; it has a silvery skin, an average market weight of 3–6 oz. (85–170 g), a moderately fatty flesh and a rich flavor.

grunt 1. A fish found off Florida; it has a rich, sweet flesh. 2. A colonial American dessert made with fresh fruit topped with biscuit dough and steamed in a closed container; also known as slump.

grusha (GROO-shah) Russian for pear.

gruszki (groo-shkee) Polish for pears.

Grütswürst (GREWTZ-voorst) *See* Pinklewürst.

Gruviera; Groviera (groo-vee-YAIR-uh) An Italian Gruyère-style cheese made from cow's milk; it has a pale gold interior with scattered eyes and a mild, nutty, sweet flavor.

Gruyère (groo-YAIR) 1. A Swiss cheese, now also produced in France, made from cow's milk; it has a golden brown rind, a pale yellow interior, well-spaced very large holes, and a rich, sweet, nutty flavor. *See* Emmental. 2. A term used imprecisely, especially in France, for almost any cooked, compressed cheese sold in large rounds, including Emmental, Beaufort and Comté.

Gruyère de Beaufort (groo-yair duh bo-for) *See* Beaufort.

Gruyère de Comté *See* Comté.

grybai (gree-bah'e) Lithuanian for mushroom.

grzanki (gshah-n-kee) Polish for croutons.

guacamole (gwah-kah-MOH-lee; gwah-kah-MOH-leh) A Mexican dip, sauce or side dish made from mashed avocado flavored with lemon or lime juice and chiles; sometimes chopped tomatoes, green onion and cilantro are added.

guaiacol A precursor of vanillin.

guaiva (guava) Italian for guava.

guajillo (gwah-HEE-yoh) An elongated, tapering dried chile with a deep orange-red color and a brown tinge, a thin flesh, and a sweet, hot flavor with undertones of green tea.

guajolote (gwa-hoh-LOH-teh) Mexican for wild turkey.

guanabana *See* soursop.

Guanyin *See* Iron Goddess of Mercy.

guar 1. A drought-tolerant legume (*Cyanopsis psorallioides*) grown for forage and for its seeds, which produce a gum that is used as a thickening agent. 2. A water-soluble dietary fiber that can lower blood cholesterol levels by modest amounts.

guardanapo Portuguese for napkin.

guard of honor A lamb roast made by joining two trimmed racks so that they face each other, with the fat side facing out and the ribs pointing upward and interlocking.

guar gum A food additive derived from guar seeds and used as an emulsifier, stabilizer and/or thickener in processed foods such as baked goods, baking mixes, fats, sauces, milk products, fruit products and vegetable products.

guarnito (gwahr-NEE-toh) Italian for garnished.

guascas; huascas (goo-ass-cass) An herb (*Galinsoga parviflora lineo*) native to the Andes; it is available dried and ground into a green powder that has a faint, sweet, vegetal flavor; it is used to flavor South American stews.

Guatemalan Arabica coffee beans grown in Guatemala; the beverage has a mild flavor with good acidity.

guava A medium-sized tropical fruit (*Psidium guajave*); it has a spherical to plump pear shape, a smooth or rough greenish-white, yellow or red skin, a pale yellow to bright red flesh, small gritty seeds and an acidic, sweet flavor; eaten raw or used for preserves.

guava

guavasteen *See* feijoa.

Guave (goo-ahv) German for guava.

guayaba (goo-wa-yah-bah) Spanish for guava.

Gubbeen (goo-BEAN) An Irish raw cow's milk cheese; it has an orange, brine-washed rind with a strong aroma and a nutty, beefy flavor with a faint smoky undertone.

guchul pan (gu-jeol pan) A Korean appetizer consisting of tiny pancakes with eight different fillings (e.g., shredded omelet, vegetables or meat) served with a tart, salty sauce flavored with crushed sesame seeds; often served in a compartmentalized lacquered or porcelain tray; also known as nine varieties.

gudgeon A small fish with a large head, thick lips and a very delicate flesh found in European lakes and rivers; it is dipped in flour, fried until crisp and served as an hors d'oeuvre.

guedge (goo-ed-jay) Dried smoked fish used in Senegalese and other West African cuisines as a flavoring or ingredient.

guéridon (gha-ree-dawn) French for a pedestal table and used to describe a rolling cart used for preparing foods table side at a restaurant. *See* flambé trolley.

güero (GWEH-roh) A general name for any of a variety of fresh yellow chiles; usually those with a pale yellow color, an elongated, tapering shape and a medium to hot, slightly sweet flavor.

guest check 1. A form used by a food services facility to record all the food and/or beverages (with their prices) that a customer orders; it is tabulated and, with taxes and sometimes a gratuity added, presented to the customer for payment; also known as a check. 2. A form used by a hotel or the like to record the length of a guest's stay as well as all food, beverages and/or services charged to the room (i.e., account, with their prices) by the guest; it is tabulated and, with taxes added, presented to the guest for payment; also known as a check.

Gueuze; gueuze lambic (ghe-zay) A blend, usually of young and old lambic beers, that undergoes further fermentation and achieves some natural carbonation.

gueytoew (goo-hay-to-hav) Thai for noodles.

gugelhopf (GOO-gerl-hupf) *See* kugelhopf.

guillotine cut *See* straight cut.

guinataan (gi-na-tan) A Filipino cooking method in which ingredients are simmered in coconut milk.

guindilla (gheen-dehl-yah) A sweet, medium-hot Spanish chile.

guinea; guinea fowl One of the principal kinds of poultry recognized by the U.S. Department of Agriculture (USDA) and the domesticated descendant of a game bird; it has light and dark meat, very little fat, a tender texture and a strong flavor.

guinea, mature A guinea slaughtered when older than 3 months; it has a hard breastbone, an average market weight of 1–2 lb. (0.5–1 kg) and a tough flesh.

guinea, young A guinea slaughtered at 3 months; it has a flexible breastbone, an average market weight of 0.75–1.5 lb. (340–675 g) and a tender flesh.

guinea classes Significant guinea classes are the young guinea and mature guinea.

guinea squash Another name for eggplant.

guipí (goo-e-pee) Chinese for cinnamon.

guisado (ghee-SAH-doh) A Spanish stew of hare, rabbit, goose or pheasant flavored with bacon, herbs and wine; the cooking liquids are thickened with blood from the animal.

guisado (ghee-ZAH-doh) A Portuguese stew of poultry (chicken, goose or turkey) or game, tomatoes and onions; it is flavored with Port, garlic and herbs and sometimes garnished with raw eggs stirred into the sauce.

guisado de repollo (ghee-SAH-doh day reh-POH-loh) A Bolivian stew made from cabbage, onions, tomatoes, chiles and potatoes and flavored with cilantro.

guisantes (ghee-SAHN-tehs) Spanish for peas.

gulab jal (goo-lab jal) Hindi for rosewater.

gulab jamun (goo-lab jah-moon) An Indian dish consisting of a rich, condensed-milk, cheeselike ball that is fried and brushed with syrup containing rosewater and cardamom.

gulai (goo-lai) An Indonesian dish in which the ingredients are simmered in a large volume of liquid (either coconut milk or a sauce made sour by adding tamarind or pineapple), rempah and spices.

Gulasch (GOO-lahsh) An Austrian stew made from meat or poultry fried with onions and then simmered with paprika, tomato purée, marjoram, caraway seeds and vinegar (if veal is used, sour cream is added) and served with nockerln.

gulerød (GOOL-er-rurd) Danish for carrot.

gulrøtt (gool-roht) Norwegian for carrot.

gulyás (GOO-yaash) Hungarian for goulash.

gum 1. Any of various thick, sticky, glutinous discharges from plants that harden on exposure to air and are soluble in water or will form a viscous mass with water. 2. *See* chewing gum. 3. Food additives used as emulsifiers, thickeners, binders, stabilizers and/or bodying agents in processed foods.

gum arabic *See* acacia.

gumbo A Louisianan stewlike dish of meat, poultry and/or shellfish, okra, tomatoes and onions flavored with bay leaves, Worcestershire sauce and cayenne. *See* okra.

gum ghatti A food additive derived from a tree (*Anogeissus latifolia*) found in Indian and Sri Lankan forests and used as an emulsifier in processed foods such as beverages; also known as Indian gum.

gummi candy *See* Chinese date.

gummy A tasting term for a food with a (usually) undesirable gooey, sticky or tough texture.

gum paste A modeling paste made with confectioners' sugar, gum tragacanth, glucose, water and flavorings; used to make three-dimensional flowers and figures, especially for decorating cakes.

gum paste tools and cutters Plastic or metal tools used to shape and cut gum paste into various forms that can be assembled into flowers, structures or other designs.

gum tragacanth A food additive derived from a Middle Eastern thorny shrub (*Astragalus gummifer*) and used as an emulsifier, stabilizer and/or thickener in processed foods such as baked goods, baking mixes, condiments, fats, sauces, meat products and fruit products.

gum tree A tree native to South America (*Leguminosae* family); the pale yellow, sweet, mealy paste of its brown pods can be eaten raw, or cooked and then ground into a flour.

gung (goong) Thai for crustacean, prawn or lobster.

gungo pea *See* pigeon pea.

Gunner gooseberry A gooseberry variety; the relatively large fruit have a dark green skin and a strong flavor.

Gunpowder A Chinese green tea; the leaves are rolled into minuscule balls; the beverage has a pale straw color and a mild, fruity but slightly bitter flavor.

guojiàng (goo-oh-gee-young) Chinese for jam.

gurka (GEWR-kah) Swedish for cucumber.

Gurken (GOOR-kern) German for cucumbers.

gurnard A fish found in the warmer Atlantic Ocean waters and in the Mediterranean Sea; there are two principal varieties: a red gurnard (also known as a sea cuckoo and sometimes mistakenly sold as a red mullet) and the inferior yellow gurnard.

gurr cake An Irish bread cake made by lining a pan with pastry and topping it with a filling of stale bread, flour, brown sugar and dried mixed fruit, then covering it with another pastry sheet; after baking, the cake is sprinkled with sugar and cut into small squares.

gury (ghoo-re) A Russian dish consisting of a whole raw white cabbage soaked in brine with beetroots and red peppers; the pickled cabbage has a soft red color.

gus (goos) Russian for goose.

gusano The worm placed in bottles of mezcal as a marketing ploy.

guska (goos-kah) Serbo-Croat for goose.

gut To remove the viscera from animals.

Gutedel *See* Chasselas.

gútou (goo-to-hoo) Chinese for bone.

guts An animal's intestines.

gutui (goo-too-e) Romanian for quince.

gweduck clam *See* geoduck clam.

gyle (ga-el) Unfermented beer added to a finished stout or ale for conditioning.

gyoku (ghee-ho-koo) A thick, sweet Japanese omelet; it can be eaten as a starter (especially before sushi) or dessert. *See* ichinin-mae.

gyoz (gee-OH-zah) Japanese-style Chinese meat-filled grilled dumpling.

gypsum A soft common mineral (hydrous calcium sulfate) used as a fertilizer, fining agent and plaster of paris.

gyro (JEER-oh; ZHEER-oh; YEE-roh) A Greek dish consisting of spiced minced lamb molded around a spit and roasted vertically; it is sliced, folded in a pita, and topped with grilled onions, sweet peppers, tomatoes and a cucumber–yogurt sauce; marinated chicken is sometimes used instead of lamb.

gyropalette (jee-ro-pah-let) An automated riddling machine used in the production of sparkling wines; capable of riddling 4032 bottles at one time. *See* riddling rack.

gyuma (giu-mah) A Tibetan blood sausage made with rice, goat's or sheep's blood, wheat, barley, various animal organs and onions and flavored with pepper, caraway, chiles and shallots.

gyuniku (GYOO-nee-koo) Japanese for beef.

haar chee mein (hahr che ma-in) Long, slightly thick rods of Chinese noodles, usually made from a dough flavored with ingredients such as dried shrimp.

Haas avocado *See* Hass avocado.

haba (hah-vah) Spanish for fava or broad bean.

habañero (ah-bah-NEH-roh) A squat cylindrical chile with a dark green to orange skin that becomes red when mature and an exceptionally hot flavor; also available dried.

habash (HAH-bash) Arabic for turkey.

habas secas (hah-vas sae-caw) Spanish for dried beans.

haché (ah-she-ay) French for hashed; minced.

haché (hay-shay) A Dutch stew or hash made from onions and beef simmered with cloves, bay leaf, vinegar and Worcestershire sauce and served with cooked red cabbage and boiled potatoes.

hachée, sauce (ah-schay) A classic French sauce of chopped shallots and onions reduced in vinegar, mixed with demi-glace and tomato purée, and flavored with duxelles, capers, ham and parsley; it is usually served with roasted red meat or venison.

hachimitsu (hah-chee-mit-soo) Japanese for honey.

hachiya *See* persimmon, Japanese.

Hackbraten (HAHK-braa-tern) German for meat loaf.

haddee (hah-dee) Hindi for bone.

haddock A fish related to the cod, found in the north Atlantic Ocean from Cape Cod to Newfoundland; it has a dark lateral line and a black patch on the shoulder known as the Devil's thumbprint or St. Peter's

haddock

mark, a very lean, white flesh, a more delicate texture and stronger flavor than Atlantic cod, and an average market weight of 2–5 lb. (1–2.3 kg).

Haden mango A purple-colored mango with a sweet, orange-yellow flesh; it is grown in the United States.

haejangkook (hey-jong-cook) A Korean beef soup made with abundant bones, marrow and blood pudding that is thought to cure hangovers; some call it Korean menudo.

ha gau (ha gah-oo) A Chinese crescent-shaped shrimp dumpling in a wheat starch wrapper.

Hagebutte (ha-ghe-boo-tay) German for rose hip.

haggamuggie A Shetland Island fish haggis in which the stomach (muggie) of a large fish is filled with oatmeal and chopped fish liver, tied at both ends, and boiled in salted water.

haggis (HAG-ihs) A Scottish dish consisting of a stomach lining (usually from a sheep) stuffed with a mixture of liver, heart, lungs, onions, suet and oatmeal, seasoned with nutmeg and cayenne pepper, and then simmered. *See* paunch and pluck.

hagi (HAH-ghee) Japanese mochi formed into small flat cakes or balls, coated with puréed azuki beans or chestnuts, rolled in roasted ground nuts, sesame seeds or soybean flour, and baked.

Hahn (ha'nn) German for cock or rooster.

haiga-mai (hah-i-gah-mah-i) A Japanese rice with a nutty flavor; its grains are incompletely polished, leaving the germ intact.

hairy basil A type of basil with long, narrow, pale green leaves and sprigs that culminate in a red-tinged cluster of seed pods that, when dried, are soaked and used to add a lemony aroma and peppery flavor to beverages.

Hairy Buffalo A cocktail made from whatever remains on the mat or well after a bartender has fixed other orders; usually given gratis.

hairy eggplant *See* mauk.

hairy melon *See* fuzzy squash.

Haitian Arabica coffee beans grown in Haiti; the beverage has a rich, mildly sweet flavor.

hai xian jiang (hah-e shang ge-young) Chinese for hoisin sauce.

hajikami shoga (ha-ji-kar-mah show-ga) Japanese for blushing ginger and used to describe a garnish of pink-colored ginger shoots used for grilled foods.

hajikami su-zuké (ha-ji-kar-mah soo-zoo-kee) Whole young ginger, pickled and used as a garnish for grilled fish and sushi dishes in Japanese cuisine.

hákarl (HAH-karl) Icelandic smoked shark.

hake A variety of fish related to cod found in the Atlantic Ocean from southern Canada to North Carolina and in the Pacific Ocean along the U.S. West Coast; generally, they have an average market weight of 1–8 lb. (0.5–3.6 kg) and lean white flesh; significant varieties include the black hake, Boston hake, king hake, ling, mud hake and white hake.

hakka (hah-kah) Japanese for mint.

hakkebøf (HAHGG-er-burf) Danish for hamburgers.

hako-gata (hah-koh-gah-ta) A portion of rice for nigiri-zushi shaped like a rectangular box.

hakusai (HAH-kuh-sigh-ee) Japanese for napa cabbage.

hal (hall) Hungarian for fish.

halal (hah'laal) Meat slaughtered according to Islamic law.

halaszslé (hah-lash-lay) A Hungarian fish soup flavored with rose paprika and sweet paprika.

halawiyat (hah'lah-wee-yacht) Arabic for sweet pastries and desserts.

halbstück (hahlb-shtook) A traditional cask used in Germany's Rheingau region with a capacity of 600 L (approximately 158 U.S. gallons).

halbtrocken (hahlb-trock-en) German for half dry and used to describe semisweet wines.

Halb und Halb Schimmegespann (hahlb dond hahlb sheem-ma-ghae-spann) A bittersweet German liqueur flavored with oranges and herbs.

haldi (hal-dee) Hindi for turmeric.

haleeb (hah-leeb) Arabic for milk.

half-and-half 1. A mixture of equal parts light cream (with an 18% milkfat content) and milk (with a 3.5% milkfat content); it does not contain enough fat to whip into a foam. 2. An English drink of equal parts stout and ale.

half barrel *See* keg.

half-cut round steak A fabricated cut of the beef primal round; it is a top round steak cut in half.

half keg A container, usually used for beer, with a capacity of 7.75 U.S. gallons or 0.25 barrel.

hálfmánar (hahlf-mah-nahr) Icelandic crescent-shaped butter cookies flavored with cardamom and filled with fruit preserves or prune spread, sprinkled with crystal sugar, and baked; traditionally served during Christmas.

half-ware A 2- to 3-year-old oyster.

halibut A variety of flatfish found in the Pacific and Atlantic Oceans off North America; it has an average market weight of 10–60 lb. (4.5–27.2 kg) and tender, lean, white flesh with a mild flavor; significant varieties include Atlantic and Pacific halibut.

hallacas (ay-YAH-kahs) A Colombian and Venezuelan dish consisting of ground beef, pork or chicken mixed with ingredients such as cheese, olives or raisins; the mixture is then coated with a ground-corn dough, wrapped in banana leaves, and steamed.

hallah (HAH-lah) *See* challah.

halleeb (HA-leeb) Arabic for milk.

Hallimasch (ha-lee-mash) German for honey mushroom.

hallon (HAH-lon) Swedish for raspberry.

Hall's Hardy almond An almond variety; the nuts are particularly flavorful.

halo-halo (ha-low-ha-low) A Filipino milk shake that contains an assortment of ingredients, including strips of young coconut, jackfruit and sweet red beans.

Haloum; Haloumi; Halloumi; Halumi (hah-loom; haa-loo-mee) A semisoft to firm cheese made in Greece, Cyprus, Turkey and other parts of the eastern Mediterranean from ewe's, goat's or cow's milk and preserved in whey; it has a creamy, slightly salty flavor; after rinsing it is used for cooking.

halvah; halva (hahl-VAH; HAHL-val) A Middle Eastern confection made from ground sesame seeds and honey, sometimes flavored with nuts or chocolate.

ham 1. A subprimal or fabricated cut of the pork primal fresh ham, with or without bones; available fresh, cured or smoked. 2. A term imprecisely applied to certain subprimal cuts of the pork Boston butt or shoulder primals. *See* fresh ham.

ham, canned A boneless ham with no more than 7% of its weight the result of added water; usually cured but not smoked, packed in vacuum-sealed cans with gelatin added, and then cooked in the can.

ham, country A bone-in ham produced in rural areas of the Southeastern United States; dry-cured in salt, sodium nitrate, sugar and other seasonings, then smoked over hardwood and aged for up to 12 months; it has a salty, well-seasoned flavor and a firm texture.

ham, country-style; ham, country-cured A bone-in ham produced outside of rural areas of the Southeastern United States but in the same manner as a country ham.

ham, fresh *See* fresh ham.

ham, sectioned and formed; ham, chunked and formed A boneless ham; the muscles are torn apart, tenderized (and usually defatted), and then reassembled in a casing or mold.

ham, skinless-shankless A ham with the shank bone removed (the leg and aitch bones remain).

ham, smoked A ham that is smoked or has a smoky flavor imparted by liquid smoke.

ham, water-added A ham with up to 10% of its weight the result of water injected during the curing process; usually available with a smoke flavor.

hamaguri (ha-amh-goo-ree) Japanese for hard-shell clams.

hamam bil zaytun (hah-mamm beel zah-he-toon) A Middle Eastern dish consisting of pigeons cooked with olives and flavored with lemon juice, cinnamon, cloves, nutmeg, ginger, bay leaf and samn and served over rice.

Haman's ears Deep-fried, ear-shaped Jewish pastries served with sugar or honey at Purim.

hamantaschen (HAH-mahn-tah-shuhn) Small triangular Jewish pastries with a sweet filling of honey and poppy seeds, puréed prunes, apricots or nuts, usually served during Purim.

hambaga HAHM-bah-gah) Japanese for hamburger.

hamburger A patty made of ground beef; typically served on a bun and garnished with one or more condiments or foods, such as mustard, ketchup, cheese, bacon, and so on, and often identified by the items added (e.g., cheeseburger or bacon burger); also known as burger, beefburger and hamburger steak. *See* beef, ground.

hamburger bun A soft, round yeast roll, 3.5 to 4 in. in diameter; it may be made with regular or whole wheat flour and topped with sesame seeds, poppy seeds or toasted, chopped onions; usually used for hamburgers.

hamburger press A utensil used to form a round, flat ground meat patty; the bottom is a round mold of the appropriate height and depth and holds the meat; a plunger then presses the meat into the mold.

Hamburger rauchfleisch (HAM-boo-gar RAHOOSH-flaish) A German dish of smoked brisket of beef, boiled and served cold with grated horseradish.

hamburgerryg (HAHM-boo-rer-rewg) A Danish smoked loin of pork served hot with a horseradish cream sauce and caramelized potatoes.

Hamburg parsley *See* parsley root.

hamburguesa (am-boor-gay-sah) Spanish for hamburger.

hamed m'raked (hah-mad m'raw-ked) Fermented, pickled lemons used as a flavoring and condiment in North African cuisines.

ham hock The lower portion of a hog's hind leg, consisting of bone, flesh and connective tissue and usually available in 2- to 3-in. (5.08- to 7.6-cm) lengths, smoked, cured or fresh; used to flavor soups and cooked vegetables.

hamine (hah-meen-eh) An Egyptian dish of an egg boiled in its shell in a stew or soup to absorb that food's flavor.

hamira (hah-me-raw) Swahili for yeast.

Hammel (HAH-merl) German for mutton; also known as Hammelfleisch.

Hammelfleisch *See* Hammel.

hammer oyster An oyster found in the western Pacific Ocean and Indian Ocean; the shell has a hammer or ice pick shape and is 4–8 in. (10–20 cm) across.

hamoor (hah-moor) A small red snapper found in the Mediterranean Sea.

hamsi (hahm-sea) Turkish for anchovy.

ham steak A fabricated cut of the pork primal fresh ham; it is a center-cut slice that has been smoked and cured. *See* gammon.

hamu (HAH-moo) Japanese for ham.

ham with water and by-products A ham with water and bits of less desirable cuts of the pork carcass, pressed and formed; the percentage of by-products present must be stated on the label.

hana-gata (HAH-nah-GAH-tah) Japanese for flower shaped and used to describe a decorative cut for a food.

hànbaobaoc (han-ba-ho-ba-ho) Chinese for hamburger.

hand 1. A cluster of bananas. 2. A multipronged root or rhizome (e.g., ginger). 3. A bunch or bundle of leaves. 4. A British cut of the pork carcass; it is the foreleg and part of the shoulder and the equivalent of the picnic ham.

handai (HAHN-da-ee) A Japanese wooden tub used to mix rice with seasonings.

hand-formed cookies Cookies formed by hand into balls, logs, crescents or other shapes.

handful A traditional measure of weight or volume; it is approximately 1 oz. or 1 fl. oz.

Handkäse (hant-kaiz) A German and central European cheese made from soured cow's milk and traditionally shaped by hand; it has a gray rind, an ivory interior, and a very sharp, pungent flavor and odor.

handle *See* knife handle.

handmade cigar *See* cigar, handmade.

hand pies Small, hand-sized pies made with a biscuit or pie dough crust enclosing a filling of stewed dried fruit; they can be baked or fried; also known as fried pies.

hand shaker A mixing glass with a stainless steel container that fits over the top like a sleeve or cap; used for making cocktails that need to be shaken by hand. *See* mixing glass.

han gétsu-giri (HAHN geh-sue-GHEE-ree) Japanese for half-moon–shaped and used to describe a decorative cut for a food.

hanging tenderloin A fabricated cut of the beef primal flank not part of the tenderloin, it is somewhat tough but flavorful.

hanging weight The weight of a carcass or portion of a carcass before it is trimmed of any fat or bone.

Hangtown fry An omeletlike dish with oysters and bacon.

han namagashi (HAHN nah-mah-GAH-shee) A classification of wagashi; these Japanese confections are not as moist as namagashi. *See* higashi *and* namagashi.

hanpen (han-pen) A soft-textured kamaboko sold in squares or rounds and usually eaten as a snack, dipped in soy sauce.

hao gu (hah-o goo) Chinese for oyster mushroom.

hao wei jiang (hah-o oo-a-e gee-young) Chinese for oyster sauce.

happy hour A period of 1–3 hours after the business day generally ends and before dinner when people indulge in a cocktail or other beverage; bars usually discount drinks and offer complimentary food during this period.

Happy Marriage A beverage of equal parts coffee and hot chocolate.

hapukapsa salat (ha-pul-sta sah-lot) An Estonian salad of sauerkraut, apples and onions bound with sour cream and usually served with meat.

hapu'upu'u Hawaiian for grouper or sea bass.

hara piaz (hah-raw pee-ahz) Hindi for scallion.

hard A wine-tasting term for an austere wine or a tannic, astringent red wine.

hardalis (arr-dah-leas) Swahili for mustard.

hard-ball stage A test for the density of sugar syrup: the point at which a drop of boiling sugar forms a rigid ball when dropped in ice water; this is equivalent to 250–265°F (121–130°C) on a candy thermometer.

hard-boiled egg; hard-cooked egg An egg simmered in its shell until it reaches a hard consistency, usually 12–15 minutes. *See* soft-boiled egg.

hard cheese grater *See* cheese grater.

hard cheese knife A knife used to cut hard cheeses; the blade ranges in length from 4.5 to 12 in. and has a coped tip, flat cutting edge and etched sides (to prevent the cheese from sticking); its handle is usually offset.

hard cheese knife

hard cider Pressed apple juice fermented without additional sugar; it usually has a relatively low alcohol content and a limited shelf life.

hard copy *See* dupe.

hard-crack stage A test for the density of sugar syrup: the point at which a drop of boiling sugar will separate into brittle threads when placed in ice water; equivalent to 300–310°F (148–153°C) on a candy thermometer.

hard cure A preservation method for meat; the meat is packed in salt, and the salt slowly displaces the meat's moisture content.

hardfiskur (hardt-fees-kurr) An Icelandic dish of air-dried fish served with butter.

hardhead *See* drum.

hard liquor A term popularly applied to any distilled spirit containing at least 40% alcohol.

hard roe *See* roe.

hard roll *See* kaiser roll.

hard sauce A dessert sauce made from sugar and butter creamed until fluffy, then flavored with vanilla or a liquor such as brandy or rum; traditionally served with plum pudding; also known as brandy butter.

hard sausages *See* sausages, dried.

hardtack Hard, coarse unleavened bread traditionally used as army or navy rations because of its long shelf life; also known as a sailor's biscuit or sea biscuit.

hard water *See* water, hard.

hare Any of a variety of larger rabbits, usually not domesticated; generally, they have a lean, darkish flesh with a chewy texture and an earthy flavor.

hareng (ah-rahng) French for herring.

har gow (har go-who) Chinese steamed shrimp-filled dumplings with a slightly chewy, wheat starch and tapioca flour covering.

haricot bean (ahr-ee-ko) A general term for several beans native to North America and cultivated in Europe; includes the flageolet, red kidney bean and navy bean.

haricot blanc (ahr-ee-ko blanh) French for fresh or dried white kidney bean.

haricot rouge (ahr-ee-ko rooj) French for fresh or dried red kidney bean.

haricots (ahr-ee-ko) French for beans.

haricot vert (ahr-ee-ko ver) French for green bean and used to describe a young, very slender green bean with a dull green, tender pod and very small seeds; also known as a French green bean and French bean.

hari gobhi (hah-ree go-bee) Hindi for broccoli.

hari mirch; simla mirch (HAH-re me-rch; SEEM-law me-rch) Hindi for green pepper.

harina (ah-REE-nah) Spanish for flour.

harina enraizada (ah-REE-nah ehn-RAY-zah-dah) Flour made from sprouted wheat; because some of the starch is converted into sugar, it typically imparts a slight sweetness to products made from it.

harina para bollitos (ah-REE-nah pah-rah boh-lee-tohs) Cooked black-eyed peas, ground into a flour used to make fritters that are served as snacks and appetizers in South American and Caribbean cuisines.

harira (hah-REE-rah) A hearty North African (especially Moroccan) soup made with lamb, chicken, lentils and chickpeas and flavored with turmeric, cinnamon, coriander and a large amount of pepper; traditionally eaten to break a Ramadan fast.

harissa (hah-REE-suh) A hot, spicy North African condiment made from oil, chiles, garlic, cumin, coriander, caraway seeds and sometimes dried mint or verbena; served with couscous, soups and dried meat. *See* bisbas *and* shatta.

harmonious 1. An arrangement of foods, including garnishes, on a plate, platter or table so that there is a well-designed balance of shapes, colors and/or textures. 2. A wine-tasting term for a wine that has a well-balanced bouquet and flavor.

Harracher (hore-ach) A Hungarian Limburger-style cheese made from cow's milk.

Harrar; Harar Arabica coffee beans grown in the Harrar region of Ethiopia; the beverage, sometimes described as winy, has a strong, berrylike, earthy flavor, a full body and an excellent aroma.

harsh A wine-tasting term for a rough wine that is more severe than hard; the characteristic often disappears over time.

Hárslevelü (HARSH-leh-veh-LOO) A white wine grape grown in Hungary.

hartgekocht (har-gae-koct) German for hard boiled.

hartshorn *See* ammonium bicarbonate.

harusame (hah-roo-SAH-mee) Translucent Japanese noodles made from a dough of soybean powder and water.

Harvard beets A dish of beets cooked in a sauce of vinegar, sugar and butter thickened with cornstarch.

harvest *v.* To gather crops. *n.* 1. The time when ripened crops are gathered. 2. The crops so gathered. 3. *See* crush.

harvest fish *See* butterfish.

Harvey House; Harvey Restaurants A chain of eating establishments opened in railroad stations throughout the American Southwest during the late 1800s by Fredrick Henry Harvey (Brit., 1835–1901); these facilities were known as clean, civilized places run by well-groomed, well-respected waitresses known as Harvey Girls.

Harveys *See* Bristol Cream.

Harvey sauce One of the oldest English bottled sauces; made from anchovies, cayenne pepper, mushrooms, ketchup, juice from pickled walnuts, shallots, garlic and vinegar.

Harvey Wallbanger A cocktail made of vodka, Galliano and orange juice; served over ice cubes with Galliano floating on top.

Hase (HAA-zer) German for hare; also known as Kaninchen.

Haselnusse (HAA-zeri-news) German for hazelnut.

Hasenpfeffer (HAH-zuhn-fehf-uhr) A thick German stew of rabbit flavored with peppers, wine and vinegar, served with noodles and dumplings, and garnished with sour cream.

hash *v.* To cut food into very small, irregularly shaped pieces. *n.* A dish of chopped meat (usually roast beef and/or corned beef), potatoes, and sometimes green pepper, celery and onions; pan-fried and often served with a poached or fried egg on top.

hash browns; hash-browned potatoes Chopped or grated cooked potatoes (green peppers and onions are sometimes added), fried in fat, traditionally bacon fat, pressed into a cake, and fried on the other side.

hashi (hash-ee) Japanese for chopsticks; also known as ohashi.

hashwa; hashwa ghanum ma'snoober (hash-wah g'ran-nehmm mah-s'hoh-bar) A Middle Eastern stuffing consisting of ground lamb, rice and pine nuts; generally used with poultry.

haspir *See* safflower.

Hass avocado; Haas avocado An avocado with a dark green, almost black, pebbly skin.

hasselnötter (hahss-erl-nurt) Swedish for hazelnut.

hasselnøtter (hahss-ell-noe-ter) Norwegian for hazelnut.

hasty pudding A dish of cornmeal mush made with water or milk and sweetened with honey, maple syrup or molasses; it is served hot with milk or cream as a breakfast dish or dessert; also known as Indian pudding.

hasu (ha-sou) Japanese for lotus root and renkon.

hatcho-miso (hat-choo-mee-so) A granular, strongly flavored, dark, salty miso made principally from soybeans and used in soups and stewlike dishes.

hâtelet (ah-tuh-lay) A 17th-century French skewer with a narrow, silver-plated 8- to 10-in.-long shaft topped with a fleur-de-lis or other decoration and used to serve (not prepare) food in a stylish manner.

hâtelet

haunch The hindquarter of a game animal such as a deer; it consists of the leg and loin.

haupia A Hawaiian pudding of coconut milk, sugar and arrowroot, chilled until firm and cut into squares; it is often served at a luau.

Hauptgerichte (hah-oopt-gae-ree-ste) German for main course.

Hausfrauen Art (house-froh-en art) German for housewife's style and used to describe a dish made with sour cream and pickles.

hausgemacht (house-gmae-makt) German for homemade.

haut (oh) 1. French for high. 2. A geographic designation for a French grape-growing and wine-producing region with a high altitude (the term does not denote quality). *See* bas.

haute cuisine (OHT kwih-ZEEN; kwee-ZEEN) French for high cooking style and used to describe fine foods professionally and elegantly prepared in an appropriate manner.

Haut-Médoc (oh-meh-doc) The southern section of the Médoc area of France's Bordeaux region, famous for cru classes such as Saint-Estèphe, Pauillac, Saint-Julien and Margaux.

Havarti (hah-VAHR-tee) A semisoft Danish cheese made from cow's milk; it has a pale yellow interior with small irregular holes and a mild, tangy flavor that intensifies as it ages; also known as Danish Tilsit and Dofino.

haver-cake An obsolete northern English term for oatcake.

Haverford Hooker A cocktail made of orgeat syrup, vanilla ice cream, club soda and gin or vodka; garnished with a mint sprig.

havre (haarv-rer) Swedish for oats.

Havre, sauce (ahrve) A French white wine sauce flavored with mussel stock and garnished with mussels and shrimp.

haw; hawberry A small berry of a member of the hawthorn family (genus *Crataegus*); it has a dark red color and a tart flavor and is usually used with crab apples for preserves.

Hawaiian chile A thin, elongated fresh chile with a green color (that turns red when ripe) and an extremely hot flavor.

Hawaiian Orange Blossom A cocktail made of gin, orange juice, curaçao and pineapple juice; served in a chilled whiskey sour glass.

Hawaiian salt A sea salt with a mild flavor, coarse texture and reddish tint; also known as alae salt.

Hawkes Bay A large grape-growing and wine-producing region in New Zealand; it is a warm-climate area located on the east coast of the North Island; the pricipal grapes grown are Sauvignon Blanc and Chardonnay.

Hawkestone An English farm cheese made from goat's milk; it has a hard, orange rind and a rich, nutty flavor.

hawksbill turtle An aquatic tortoise; its eggs are considered a delicacy.

Haxen (haxe-ahn) A German dish of boiled ham hocks (also known as knuckle of pork) served with sauerkraut and mashed potatoes.

hay cutting A method of cutting in which one hand holds the knife handle and the other hand holds the back of the blade toward the end; the cutting is done either (1) with firm downward pressure to provide accuracy on difficult-to-cut foods such as crabs or meat with many small bones, or (2) in a seesaw fashion with the right and left ends of the knife going up and down alternately.

haydari (hah-e-dah-ree) A Turkish hors d'oeuvre of ewe's milk cheese mixed with herbs.

haymakers' punch *See* switchel.

Hayward kiwi A common variety of kiwi.

hazard, biological In the food safety context, a danger to the safety of food due to disease-causing microorganisms such as bacteria, molds, yeasts, viruses or fungi.

hazard, chemical In the food safety context, a danger to the safety of food caused by chemical substances, especially cleaning agents, pesticides, herbicides, fungicides and toxic metals. *See* residual chemicals *and* food service chemicals.

hazard, physical In the food safety context, a danger to the safety of food caused by particles such as glass chips, metal shavings, bits of wood or other foreign matter.

Hazard Analysis Critical Control Points (HACCP) (hass-up) A rigorous system of self-inspection intended to increase food safety by focusing on the flow of food through a food services facility; a critical control point is any step during the processing of food when a mistake can result in the transmission, growth or survival of a contaminant (usually pathogenic bacteria); the HACCP system evaluates the type and severity of the risk at each critical control point and identifies actions that can be taken to prevent or reduce each identified risk.

hazelnut The nut of the wild hazel tree (genus *Corylus*) found in the northern United States; shaped like a smooth brown marble, the nut has a rich, sweetish, distinctive flavor and is used (after the bitter brown skin is removed) in a variety of dishes, especially in baked goods and desserts containing chocolate or coffee flavors. *See* filbert.

hazelnut oil An oil obtained by pressing hazelnuts; it has a nutty-brown color, a full, nutty flavor, and a fragrant aroma; used principally in baked goods and salad dressings.

hazy A wine-tasting term for a relatively clear, but not brilliant, wine; the next stage is cloudy. *See* cloudy.

HDL *See* high-density lipoproteins.

HDL cholesterol Cholesterol packaged in high-density lipoproteins; it transports fats in the blood, and a high level of HDL cholesterol is associated with a reduced risk of cardiovascular disease. *See* LDL cholesterol.

head 1. The uppermost or forwardmost part of a vertebrate's body. 2. The dense grouping of flower buds on vegetables such as broccoli and cauliflower; also known as the flower head. 3. The entire garlic bulb. 4. The moderately loose to dense rosette of leaves on vegetables such as lettuce. 5. Slang for an individual patron (as in, charging $5.00 a head). 6. The end of the cigar that is smoked; it is often covered by a cap (especially if it is a handmade cigar). *See* foot. 7. *See* barm *and* foam.

headcheese A seasoned sausage made from meat picked from a calf's or hog's head; it is cooked in a gelatinous broth, molded, and served cold and thinly sliced.

head lettuce *See* lettuce, head.

headwaiter The person responsible for service throughout a restaurant or a section of a restaurant; in smaller operations, this role may be assumed by the maître d' or a captain; also known as a chef de salle.

heady A wine-tasting term for a wine with a high alcohol content or a sparkling wine with a persistent surface foam.

health food A popular and often misleading labeling term not approved by the U.S. Food and Drug Administration (FDA) but used to suggest that the particular food or groups of foods will promote health; generally used in connection with the marketing of natural or organic foods.

heart 1. A variety meat; generally tough, chewy and flavorful; lamb and calf hearts are often stuffed and braised; poultry hearts are used for stocks and stuffing. 2. The dense center of a leafy, stalky vegetable such as cabbage. 3. *See* artichoke, common.

heart bread *See* sweetbreads.

heartburn A burning chest pain caused by the reflux of the stomach's acidic contents into the lower esophagus; often associated with overeating, eating spicy foods, or drinking alcoholic beverages.

heart clams *See* cockles.

hearth The heated floor or baking surface of an oven.

hearth bread Any bread baked directly on the floor of the oven instead of in a pan.

hearts of palm The inner part of the stem of the tropical cabbage palm (family Palmaceae); it has an ivory color, many concentric layers, and a delicate flavor reminiscent of an artichoke; usually available canned (packed in water) and used in salads; also known as chou coco, chou glouglou, chou palmiste, palm hearts and swamp cabbage.

heartslet Archaic term for the heart and liver of an animal.

heat curing The process of aging or drying tobacco by using heat; heat-cured tobacco has less concentrated flavors than air-cured tobacco. *See* air curing.

heat diffuser

heat diffuser A metal grid, approximately 1 in. tall, placed on a stove top to raise a pot farther from the heat source to help maintain a very slow simmer.

heather honey A reddish-brown honey with a creamy texture similar to that of soft butter and a strong, distinctive flavor; it is principally made from heather blossoms.

heat lamp A specialized piece of equipment used (especially at banquets or off-premises

heat lamp

events) to keep food warm and to maintain the temperature of foods that might become soggy in a chafing dish (e.g., pizza or fried foods).

Heaven Hill Distillery One of the 12 remaining U.S. whiskey distilleries; located in Bardstown, Kentucky, and founded in 1935, its products include Evan Williams, Elijah Craig and Henry McKenna bourbons and Pikesville Rye Whiskey.

heavenly hash 1. A dessert made with whipped cream and vanilla wafer cookies. 2. A candy made with marshmallows and nuts and coated with chocolate.

heavy 1. A wine-tasting term for a full-bodied wine that lacks balance and distinction. 2. A cigar-tasting term for a very full, round, rich smoke; a cigar with a heavy smoke generally has a high nicotine and tar content; also known as Cuban style and imprecisely known as strong.

heavy chicken A marketing term for a 1- to 1 1/8-lb. (455- to 510-g) lobster. *See* chicken lobster, deuce, heavy select, jumbo, quarter, select *and* small jumbo.

heavy cream; heavy whipping cream *See* cream, heavy whipping.

heavy select A marketing term for a 2- to 2 1/4-lb. (0.907- to 1-kg) lobster. *See* chicken lobster, deuce, heavy chicken, jumbo, quarter, select *and* small jumbo.

heavy syrup A mixture of two parts sugar dissolved in one part water; used in beverages and sorbets and for moistening and flavoring sponge cakes.

hebi A spearfish found off Hawaii; it has an amber-colored flesh, a mild flavor, and an average market weight of 20–40 lb. (9–18 kg); usually cut into steaks.

hecho a mano (ha-choh au mah-noh) Spanish for handmade and used on a cigar box label to indicate that the products are handmade, invariably with long filler.

hecto- *See* metric system.

hedge eel *See* grass snake.

hedgehog mushroom A wild, creamy yellow mushroom (*Hydnum repandum*) with firm flesh and a succulent, tangy flavor; also known as a wood hedgehog mushroom.

hedgehog pudding Any of several boiled or baked puddings whose upper surface is stuck with slivered almonds.

hedonic Relating to the pursuit of happiness.

heel The rear edge of a knife blade; it extends below the bottom line of the handle.

heel; heel of round 1. A subprimal cut from the beef primal round; it is composed of the small muscle groups located in the lower round and adjacent to the femur; also known as horseshoe. 2. A subprimal cut from the veal primal leg.

heel end A subprimal cut of the beef primal round; it is a group of small muscles located in the lower portion of the outside round.

Hefe (HAY-fe) 1. German for yeast. 2. A German labeling term indicating that the beer has not been filtered or has sediment.

heifers Young cows or cows before their first calving; their flesh is darker, more flavorful and slightly tougher than veal.

heiko (hi-koe) A smooth, thick, dark brown shrimp paste used in Thai and Malaysian cuisines as a flavoring; also known as kapi leaw (Thai).

Heilbutt (hail-boot) German for halibut.

heimài (hei-mah-e) Chinese for rye.

Heimlich maneuver A first-aid procedure for choking victims; a sudden upward pressure is applied to the upper abdomen to force any foreign object from the windpipe.

heiss (hais) German for hot.

hei zhi ma (he-ee shee mah) Chinese black sesame seeds. *See* bai zhi ma.

heko (heh-koh) A mildly flavored, salty Filipino seasoning made by cooking bagoong with water.

helado (ay-LAH-dhoa) Spanish for ice cream.

helbon (heh-lmp-oon) An ancient Greek wine.

hel fisk i kapprock (hell feesk ee kap-rock) A Swedish dish of stuffed mackerel or trout baked in paper.

hell; helle (HEL-es) 1. German for light, as in color. 2. A description of a pale or golden German beer. *See* dunkel.

hellefisk (HEHL-ler-feesk) Norwegian for halibut.

helleflynder (HAYL-er-flew-nerr) Danish for halibut.

Helles Bier (HEH-lerss beer) German for light beer.

helping Slang for a serving or portion of food.

hemoglobin The iron-containing red pigment in red blood cells; it carries oxygen from the lungs to the tissues.

hen 1. The female of domesticated fowl, especially the chicken. 2. The female lobster.

hen clam *See* surf clam.

hen, stewing A mature hen slaughtered when older than 10 months; it has a good flavor, a slightly tough flesh, a non-flexible breastbone, and an average market weight of 2.5–8 lb. (1–3.5 kg).

Henne (han-nay) German for hen.

hen of the wood mushroom A large wild mushroom (*Grifola frondosa*) with a reddish-orange cap; it has a somewhat chewy texture and mild flavor; also known as ram's head mushroom.

Henry IV A classic French dish consisting of tournedos or kidneys, garnished with potatoes pont-neuf and béarnaise sauce.

Henry Morgan's Grog A cocktail made of whiskey, Pernod, heavy cream, Jamaican dark rum and nutmeg; served in a chilled old-fashioned glass and sprinkled with nutmeg.

hepatitis A A strain of the hepatitis virus that causes liver inflammation; common sources are infected food handlers, contaminated water and shellfish harvested from polluted waters.

heptanone compounds Food additives containing a heptanone group and used as a flavoring agent and/or adjuvant.

heptyl cinnamate A food additive with a hyacinth aroma used as a flavoring agent in candies, beverages and ice cream.

heptyl formate and heptyl isobutyrate Food additives with a fruity aroma used as flavoring agents in beverages, candies and baked goods.

heptyl paraben A food additive used as a preservative and antimicrobial agent.

herbaceous A wine-tasting term for the distinctive vegetal or herblike aroma of wines made from certain grape varieties, such as Sauvignon Blanc.

herbed cheese A cheese to which one or more herbs (e.g., dill) are added to the curds during the cheese-making process.

herbes (airbs) French for herbs.

herbes à tortue (airbs ah tore-tuh) An herb blend used in French cuisine; its basic components are basil, chervil, fennel, marjoram and savory. *See* fines herbes.

herbes de Provence (AIRBS duh proh-VAWNS) Traditionally associated with France's Provence region, it is a blend of dried herbs such as basil, thyme, sage, rosemary, summer savory, marjoram, fennel seeds and lavender.

herbicide A synthetic or naturally occurring substance used to kill plants, especially weeds; if used to protect a food crop, it can become an incidental food additive.

herbivore An animal that, by nature, eats only plant foods. *See* vegetarian.

herb mill A utensil used to mince herbs; it consists of a hopper with rotating blades that are turned by a crank.

herb patience dock *See* sorrel.

herbs Any of a large group of annual and perennial plants whose leaves, stems or flowers are used as a flavoring; usually available fresh and dried. *See* spices.

herb mill

Herbsainte An absinthe substitute similar to Pernod; made in New Orleans.

herb salt A seasoning blend of salt with various dehydrated herbs and vegetables.

herb tea; herbal tea *See* tisane.

herb vinegar A flavored vinegar made by steeping herbs in wine vinegar.

Hercules' bludgeon gourd The fruit of *Lagenaria vulgaris*, native to Africa, with a pale green skin, a pale flesh and a bland flavor; edible ones can be round (called a siphon squash), bottle shaped (pilgrim's squash) or pear shaped (powder squash).

Hereford A breed of beef cattle descended from 18th-century English stock; it efficiently converts grass to meat.

Heritage raspberry A raspberry variety with dark red berries.

Herkimer A Cheddar-style cheese made in Herkimer County, New York, from cow's milk; it has a white color, a dry, crumbly texture, and a sharp flavor.

Herman Midwestern colloquialism for a sweet sourdough starter made with sugar or honey; used for making sweet breads and coffee cakes.

hermetical seal An airtight closure of a casserole or container created to keep the steam inside the vessel during cooking; it can be made with a water and flour paste or bread dough applied around the juncture of the vessel and its lid.

hermit A colonial New England cookie made with spices, chopped fruit, nuts and brown sugar or molasses.

Hermitage (air-mee-tahj) *See* Cinsaut *and* Syrah.

hermit crab A small crab found in empty univalve shells; eaten deep-fried or sautéed.

hero; hero sandwich 1. A large sandwich consisting of a small loaf of French or Italian bread filled with cold cuts and garnished with tomatoes, lettuce, pickles and peppers; also known as grinder, hoagie, po'boy, and submarine sandwich. 2. Any large sandwich built on a small loaf of French or Italian bread and filled with hot or cold foods such as meatballs or tuna salad.

Herrgardsost (HAER-goar-oost) A Swedish Emmental-style factory cheese made from pasteurized cow's milk; it has a firm texture, a pale straw-colored interior with scattered small holes, a yellow wax rind and a delicate, nutty, sweet flavor.

herring A very large family of saltwater fish most often found in the northern Atlantic and Pacific Oceans; generally, they have a long body, a silvery-blue skin, a moderate-to-high fat content, a soft texture, a strong flavor, and an average weight of 8 oz. (226.8 g); usually available smoked, pickled or cured in brine. *See* sardine.

Hersbrucker (HEHRS-bruk-er) A variety of hops grown in the state of Washington.

Hervé (air-VAY) A soft Belgian Limburger-style cheese made from cow's milk; it has a pale yellow interior, a reddish-brown coating, and a strong, sharp flavor and aroma; sometimes flavored with herbs.

hervir (her-veer) Spanish for to boil.

hesperidin A food additive found in citrus pulp and used as a flavoring agent.

hétáo (ha-tah-oh) Chinese for walnut.

Het Pint A warm Scottish drink made by heating beer with nutmeg and sugar to which an egg is added; it is served in heated mugs.

Heung Peen (ha-eong pan) Chinese for fragrant petals and used to describe a black tea from Chinkiang province; the beverage is unusually fragrant.

Heurigen (HOY-ree-guhn) 1. Fresh, young Austrian wines. 2. Austrian establishments selling such wines.

Heurigenplatte (HOY-ree-guhn-plat) An Austrian snack of sausages, cold, sliced, pickled meats, cheeses, chopped onions, sour pickles and bread; it is served with Heurigen.

heuvo (WEH-voh) Spanish for egg.

hexanedioic acid *See* adipic acid.

hexyl compounds Food additives containing a hexyl group and used as a flavoring agent and/or adjuvant.

HFCS *See* high-fructose corn syrup.

hibachi (hih-BAH-chee) Japanese for fire pot and used to describe a small square, round or oblong container, usually of cast iron, made to hold fuel (usually charcoal); it has a grill that sits on top.

hibachi

Hican A hybrid of pecan and hickory; the nuts have a thin shell and a hickory nut–like flavor.

hickory nut The nut of any of several trees of the genus *Carya,* including the pecan; the common hickory nut has a very hard shell and a rich, buttery flavor and can be used instead of the thinner-shelled pecan.

hideg tlöételek (he-dag tloe-at-lake) Hungarian for cold hors d'oeuvre or appetizers.

hielo (YEH-loh) Spanish for ice.

hierbabuena (YAYR-bah-bwan-ah) Spanish for mint.

hierbas finas (YAYR-bahss FEE-nahss) Spanish for herbs.

hígado (EE-gah-doh) Spanish for liver.

higamugi (he-gah-moo-gee) Thin udon noodles.

hígardo (he-gahr-doe) Spanish for liver.

hígardo con vino (he-gahr-doe con vee-no) A Colombian dish of calf's liver marinated in red wine and then sautéed; it is served with a reduction of the marinade.

higashi (high-gah-she) A classification of wagashi; these Japanese confections are generally hard and include sweets such as candies and more savory crackers. *See* han namagashi *and* namagashi.

high 1. A tasting term for a fully ripened (aged) or overly ripened (aged), strong-smelling cheese or meat (especially game). 2. A food-labeling term approved by the U.S. Food and Drug Administration (FDA) to describe a food with 20% or more of the daily value of a desirable nutrient per serving.

high alpha hops A hops variety with a significant percentage of its weight (10% or more) attributable to alpha acid.

highball A long drink of liquor (usually whiskey) and water, soda water or a carbonated beverage, served over ice in a tall glass.

highball glass A tall cylindrical glass ranging in size from 5 to 10 fl. oz.; used for mixed drinks served on the rocks.

high-carbon stainless steel An alloy of carbon and stainless steel that will not rust or corrode; when used for a knife blade, it is easily sharpened and holds its edge. *See* carbon steel *and* stainless steel.

high-density lipoproteins (HDL) Small, dense lipoproteins that return cholesterol to the liver for dismantling.

high-fructose corn syrup (HFCS) A food additive used as a nutritive sweetener in processed foods such as candies and confections; generally contains 40–90% fructose.

high-gluten flour A term used imprecisely for wheat flour with a high protein content; this results in high gluten-forming potential. *See* gluten.

highlanders British shortbread cookies shaped into small, thick rounds. *See* shortbread.

Highland malt Scotch A Highland Scotch whisky made from only malt whisky with no grain whisky added.

Highland Park The proprietary name of a single-malt Scotch whisky; it has a red color and a rich, sweet, honey and malt flavor and aroma; it is particularly suitable as a digestif.

Highland Scotch A Scotch produced in the highlands of northern Scotland; it generally has a full body and a very smoky flavor, with vegetal or peaty notes.

High-Moisture Jack *See* Teleme Jack.

high ratio 1. A type of cake batter containing a large amount of sugar and liquid as well as an emulsified shortening and mixed using a special method. 2. A mixing method for such cakes (the liquid is added in two stages); also known as the two-stage method.

high-ratio cakes A form of creamed-fat cake that uses emulsified shortening and has a two-stage mixing method.

high tea *See* tea, high.

higo (EE-go) Spanish for fig.

higo chumbo (EE-go tchum-boe) Spanish for prickly pear.

hijiki; hiziki (hee-GEE-kee) A dark brown seaweed that turns black when dried; it has a spaghetti-like consistency and a strong flavor and is used as a flavoring and ingredient in Japanese cuisines.

hikari-mono (hi-kar-ree-moh-noh) Japanese for things that shine and used to describe small fish served with their scales removed but with the skin attached.

hilbeh (heel'beh) A spicy, slightly bitter Middle Eastern meza dip, spread or flavoring made from fenugreek, chiles, coriander, garlic, baharat, onions and tomatoes.

hillib (hill-ba) Somali for meat.

Himbeeren (HIM-bay-rerm) German for raspberries.

Himbergeist (him-bear-gheest) A German raspberry eau-de-vie.

Himmel und Erbe (him-mel oond her-bae) German for heaven and earth and used to describe a casserole of apples, potatoes, onions and sausage.

hind loin A British cut of the pork carcass; it contains the kidney and tenderloin.

hindquarter 1. Either bilateral half of the back section of a beef carcass; it includes the entire round, short loin, sirloin and flank primals as well as the kidneys. 2. Either bilateral half of the hindsaddle of a veal carcass; it contains half of the loin and leg primals. 3. Either bilateral half of the hindsaddle of a lamb carcass; it contains half of the loin and leg primals. 4. *See* forequarter.

hindsaddle 1. The undivided hindquarters (the rear half) of a veal carcass; it contains the loin and leg primals. 2. The undivided hindquarters of a lamb carcass; it contains the loin and leg primals and both kidneys. 3. *See* foresaddle.

hindshank A portion of the lower hindlimb (below the knee) of a quadruped. *See* shank.

hinner yoich (hine-ner yoy'ch) Yiddish for chicken soup; it is usually flavored with pepper, onions, carrots and celery and can be garnished with rice, matzo balls or noodles.

hinojo (ee-NOU-hoh) Spanish for fennel.

hip bone steak A fabricated cut of the beef primal sirloin; it is a steak cut from the center of the sirloin.

hip flask A container, usually metal, used to hold liquor and shaped to fit easily (and often surreptitiously) into a hip pocket.

Hippen paste; Hippen masse (hip-in MAHSS) A sweet wafer dough, often flavored with almonds; the batter is spread on a baking sheet, baked, then shaped while still hot to form decorations for pastries or containers for ice cream, custards or fruit.

Hippocras (he-PAH-kras) A highly spiced ancient Greek drink made of wine (sometimes soured), honey, cinnamon and other botanicals; allegedly first made by the Greek physician Hippocrates, it remained popular through the Middle Ages and is considered the forerunner of modern cordials and liqueurs; also known as hydromel.

hirame (hee-RAH-meh) A member of the flounder family found in saltwaters near Japan; it has a white, flaky flesh and a mild flavor.

hirankaa gosht (high-rann-kah-ah gosht) Hindi for venison or game.

hîratake (hee-rah-tah-kee) Japanese for oyster mushroom.

hira-zukuri (he-ra-zoo-koo-re) A Japanese slicing technique used for large fish fillets; the fish is cut into a rectangular block, then into slices or sticks that can be cubed.

hirino (heh-ree-no) Greek for pork or pig.

Hirsch (heersh) German for game venison.

his and hers Slang for any large beef steak suitable for two people.

histidine 1. An essential amino acid. 2. A food additive used as a nutrient source to significantly improve the biological quality of the total protein in a food containing the naturally occurring protein.

hitashi (hee-tah-shee) A Japanese dish of vegetables in clear broth.

hiya (hee-ya) Japanese for cold sake.

hiyamugi (hee-yah-MOO-gee) A thin Japanese wheat flour noodle usually served cold with a soy-based dipping sauce.

hiyashi (hee-YAH-shee) Japanese for chilled or cold.

hiyoko (hee-YOH-koh) Japanese for chicken; also known as niwatori.

hoagie *See* hero.

hoan tsie'u (ho-an tsee-oo) Chinese for yellow rice wine, referring to a type of sake.

hob A cooking surface built into the work surface of a kitchen and fitted with two to four gas or electric burners.

hobo egg A dish made from a piece of bread with a hole in its center; an egg is placed in the opening and the entire concoction is fried; also known as ace in the hole.

hochepot (osh-eh-poa) A French and Belgian stewlike dish consisting of layers of vegetables and meats, including pig's ears and feet.

hock 1. The lower portion of a mammal's leg, usually corresponding to the human ankle. 2. British term for German white wines, specifically those produced in the Rhine River region as opposed to the Moselle River region.

hoecake A cornmeal pancake cooked on a griddle; also known as a johnnycake.

Hoegaarden (he-gahr-den) The proprietary name of a Belgian wheat beer.

Hofkäse (hohf-kaiz) A Tilsit-style cheese made in Germany's Bavaria region from cow's milk.

hogfish A saltwater variety of catfish.

hogget British for yearling lamb.

hog jowl; hog's jowl A hog's cheek, usually cut into squares and then cured and smoked; fattier than bacon, it is used in much the same manner; also known as jowl bacon.

hog maw A hog's stomach, usually stuffed with a sausage mixture, simmered, and then baked.

hog plum 1. A small, plumlike fruit (*Spondias mombin*) native to the Southern United States and Caribbean region; it has a thin yellow-orange skin, a yellow-orange flesh and a single large seed; used for preserves. 2. *See* plum, wild.

hogs 1. The collective name for all domesticated swine (family Suidae), including pigs, sows and boars. 2. Domesticated swine weighing more than 120 lb. (54.4 kg) and raised for their flesh.

hogshead A cask or barrel of varying capacity, occasionally used for storing or shipping distilled spirits or beer.

Hohenburg *See* Box.

hoisin (HOY-sihn) A thick, reddish-brown, sweet-and-spicy sauce made from soybeans, garlic, chiles and various spices and used as a condiment and flavoring in Chinese cuisines; also known as Peking sauce, red vegetable sauce and ten-flavored sauce.

hói sìn jeung (oh-ee sin ja-oong) A thick, rich, dark brown Chinese sauce made from fermented soybeans, garlic, sugar and salt and used to flavor sauces and marinades.

hoja santa (OH-hah sahn-tah) A sassafras- or anise-flavored herb (*Piper auritum sanctum*) with large, heart-shaped, dark green leaves and long, thin, creamy-colored flowers; used with fish and in tamales and green moles in Mexican cuisines.

hojuelas de naranja (ho-who-a-lass da nah-ran-hah) A Colombian pastry made with a sweet pastry dough flavored with fresh orange juice; it is deep-fried and dusted with confectioners' sugar.

hokey-pokey 1. A crunchy, toffee candy bar from New Zealand and an ice cream containing pieces of such candy. 2. Archaic British for an inexpensive ice cream sold by street vendors.

Hokkaido (hoh-KA-ee-doh) A firm Japanese Cheddar-style cheese made from cow's milk; it has a yellow-orange color and a medium sharp flavor.

Holander (ho-lahn-der) German for elderberry.

holishkes (ho-lish-kees) A Jewish dish consisting of cabbage leaves rolled around seasoned beef and cooked in a tomato-based broth.

hollandaise; hollandaise, sauce (ohl-lahn-dez) A French leading sauce made from an emulsification of butter, egg yolks and flavorings (especially lemon juice); also known as Dutch sauce.

Holland gin *See* Genever.

hollandse koffietafel (hol-lahnd-sa koe-fee-tah-fell) A Dutch noontime meal consisting of a variety of sliced sausages, cold meats, breads, jams and sweet spreads with fresh fruit and coffee.

hollow A wine-tasting term for a wine that lacks depth and does not sustain the initial flavor.

hollow agé cubes *See* dòufù-bok.

hollow molding A chocolate or candy molding technique using a two-part hinged mold; the mold is opened and the inside of the entire mold is coated with the candy mixture or melted chocolate; after it sets, the candy or chocolate is removed and the halves are joined, forming a single, hollow unit. *See* solid molding.

holly berries The small, bright red berries of the holly tree (genus *Ilex*); they are sometimes used as a flavoring in alcoholic beverages.

Holstein (hol-steen) 1. A French preparation method for a veal escalope; it is breaded, pan-fried, and garnished with poached or fried egg, gherkins, beetroot, olives, capers, anchovies and lemon wedges. 2. A breed of large black and white dairy cattle that produce large quantities of relatively lowfat milk.

Holstein, sauce A French compound sauce made from a béchamel flavored with white wine and fish glaze, seasoned with nutmeg and bound with a liaison of egg yolks.

Holsteiner Gesundheitskäse (HOL-shtigh-nerr guh-szoon-tight-kaiz) A German cooked cheese made from soured cow's milk enriched with cream; called good health cheese, it is sometimes flavored with caraway seeds.

Holsteiner Maigerkäse (HOL-shtigh-nerr may-ger-kaiz) A German cooked cheese made from soured skimmed cow's milk and buttermilk; called skimmed milk cheese, it is sometimes flavored with caraway seeds.

Holsteiner Schnitzel (HOL-shtigh-nerr SHNIT-serl) A German veal cutlet that is breaded and fried and garnished with a fried egg and anchovy; also known as veal Holstein.

holushki (ho-loosh-key) Czech for noodles.

holy trinity The combination of chopped green peppers, onions and celery used in Creole cooking.

homard (oh-MAHR) French for lobster. *See* langouste *and* paquette.

homard à la crème (oh-MAHR ah lah khrem) A French dish consisting of lobster chunks sautèed in butter and covered in a cream sauce flavored with lemon and cayenne pepper.

homard à l'Américaine (oh-mahr-da la-may-ree-ken) A French dish consisting of a lobster sautéed in olive oil, then cooked in a sauce of tomatoes, garlic, onion, shallots, white wine, brandy, tarragon and parsley.

homard à la nage (oh-MAHR ah lah najg) A French dish consisting of a whole small lobster cooked in white wine stock.

homard au court bouillon (oh-MAHR oh kort boo-yon) A French dish consisting of a whole lobster cooked in a flavorful broth; it is usually served cold with mayonnaise.

home brew An alcoholic beverage (usually beer) made at home or with homemade equipment.

home brewing The practice of brewing beer at home for personal use and not for resale.

home fries; home-fried potatoes Slices of raw or boiled potatoes that are pan-fried, sometimes with onions and green peppers; also known as cottage fries.

homemade; home style A menu term indicating that the product has been prepared at the food services operation that is offering it for sale.

hominy Dried corn kernels from which the hull and germ have been removed by either mechanical methods or soaking the grains in hydrated lime or lye; the white or yellow kernels resemble popcorn and have a soft, chewy texture and a smoky–sour flavor. *See* grits.

hominy grits *See* grits.

homogenization The process by which milk is spun at very high speeds to break down the fat globules and produce a stable, uniform dispersion.

homogenized tobacco product Pulverized and reconstituted tobacco blended with natural binders; it is often used as a wrapper for cigarillos.

hom soi gok (hom soh-e goke) A Chinese sticky rice flour dumpling filled with minced pork, shrimp, bamboo shoots and black mushrooms.

höna (huh-na) Swedish for fowl.

Honduran Arabica coffee beans grown in Honduras; the beverage has a clean, lively flavor with a light to medium body.

hone (HOH-nay) Japanese for bone.

hone nuki (HOH-nay NOO-kee) Japanese tweezers used for deboning.

honey A sweet, usually viscous, liquid made by bees from flower nectar and stored in the cells of the hive for food; generally contains 17–20% water and 76–80% sucrose; consumed fresh or after processing, it is usually used as a nutritive sweetener.

honeybee Any of several social bees of the genus *Apis* (especially *A. mellifera*), widely domesticated as a source of honey and beeswax.

honeyberry *See* genip.

honeybun A flat, spiral-shaped yeast breakfast roll glazed with honey.

honeycomb A structure composed of rows of hexagon-shaped wax cells formed by bees in their hives to store honey, pollen and eggs.

honey dates A variety of dates grown in China; they have a hard, dark brown skin with fine ridges and a very sharp, narrow, pointed, hard seed; used in sweets, cakes and puddings; also known as coconut dates, palm dates and cooking dates.

honeydew melon A slightly ovoid, large muskmelon; it has a smooth, creamy-yellow rind with a pale green, juicy flesh and a sweet flavor.

honeyed A wine-tasting term for a wine with a honeylike aroma and flavor.

honey mushroom A long-stemmed, yellow mushroom (*Armillaria mellea*) that grows wild in large clusters on tree trunks; it has a robust, meaty, slightly astringent flavor and should always be cooked.

Honey Red Seedless watermelon A variety of small, red-fleshed, seedless watermelon.

honey wine *See* mead.

hóng chá (hon chah) Chinese for black tea.

hong dou sha (hon doo shah) Chinese for red bean paste.

hongo campesino (hon-goh cam-pay-see-noh) Spanish for the common store mushroom.

hongo con puas (hon-goh con pooh-as) Spanish for hedgehog mushroom.

hongo shii-take (hon-go she-tah-kee) Spanish for shiitake.

hóng pútáojiu (hong poo-tah-oh-jee-oo) Chinese for red wine.

hongqu (honk) Long-grain rice fermented with a red mold; the fermented rice is dried and powdered and used as a food coloring in Chinese cuisines; also considered to have medicinal applications; also known as dried red fermented rice.

hongroise, à la (ohng-wahz, ah lah) French for Hungarian style and used to describe a dish served with onions, sour cream, paprika and perhaps sweet bell pepper, cabbage or leeks.

Hongroise, sauce (ohng-wahz) A French compound sauce made from a velouté or tomato concentrate flavored with onions, paprika and white wine and finished with a Mornay sauce (if used with eggs), a fumet with butter (if for fish), a demi-glaze (if for meat), or additional velouté or suprême sauce (if for poultry).

hong zao (hong sah-oh) Chinese for jujubes.

Honig (HOA-nikh) German for honey.

Honigpilz (HOA-nikh-pils) German for honey mushroom.

honning (HON-ning) Norwegian for honey.

honor bar A system by which hotel guests are expected to record and pay for the food and beverages they consume from an in-room bar, refrigerator and/or storage area.

hooch 1. Slang for any inferior liquor. 2. A Canadian liquor brewed at home from sugar and sourdough.

hood; hood vent *See* vent.

hoop A tall ring used to form large cakes.

Hoosier cake A coarse-textured gingerbread cake, popular in Kentucky and Indiana during the mid-19th century.

Hopfenkäse (hop-fahn-kaiz) A semisoft German cheese made from cow's milk; flavored with caraway seeds and packed in casks between layers of hops to ripen; it has a zesty, spicy flavor.

hop pellets Ground hops compressed into pellets.

Hoppelpoppel (hoe-pahl-pop-pahl) A German dish of scrambled eggs with potatoes and bacon.

hopper *See* appa.

hopping john; hoppin' john A dish from the American South consisting of black-eyed peas cooked with a ham hock and served over white rice.

hop rate The ratio of hops to wort; it indicates the bitterness of the final beer.

hops The cones (flowers) of the female *Humulus lupulus* plant; principally used to impart a bitter flavor to beer.

horchata (oar-CHAH-tay) A Spanish and Mexican beverage made from almonds or pumpkin seeds; alcoholic and non-alcoholic versions are available.

horehound A downy-leaved member of the mint family (*Marrubium vulgare*); the juice extracted from its leaves has a slightly bitter flavor and is used to make horehound candy, cough syrup and lozenges.

horehound candy A hard sugar candy with a slightly bitter flavor.

horen-so (hoh-rehn-soh) Japanese for spinach.

horiatki salata (hoe-ree-at-kee sah-lah-tah) Greek for country salad; it consists of tomatoes, cucumber, green pepper, onion and Feta; it is dressed with oregano, thyme, black pepper, oil and vinegar and garnished with black olives.

Horlick's The proprietary name of a powder made from malted cereals and dried milk; it is used to make a beverage by adding milk.

hormok (hor-mock) A Thai custardlike mixture of minced fish or chicken, coconut milk, lime leaves and seasonings that is steamed either in clay cups or wrapped in banana leaves.

hormone An organic compound secreted by a specific organ, gland or other body part in response to conditions requiring chemical regulation at another specific site in the body.

hornazo (oar-nah-zoe) A Spanish pastry filled with a mixture of chorizo, ham, poultry and eggs.

hornear (oar-nae-r) Spanish for to bake.

horned turban A univalve conical shell mollusk found off the coasts of Korea and Japan; it has a golden brown, pointed shell with a row of bumps and an average market length of 3–4 in. (7.6–10 cm).

hornli (horn-lee) Small pasta in the shape of horns; used in Swiss cuisine.

horno (OAR-noh) Spanish for oven.

horn of plenty mushroom A funnel-shaped wild mushroom (*Craterellus cornucopioides*) found throughout Europe; it has a fluted edge, deep gills, a dark brown-gray to black color, a delicate texture and a rich, buttery flavor (especially if dried and then reconstituted); also known as false truffle and trumpet of death mushroom.

horoku (ho-roh-ku) A large Japanese earthenware plate with a fitted lid, used in the oven for baking.

hors d'oeuvre (ohr durv) *sing.* and *pl.;* Americanized *pl.* also hors d'oeuvres. A very small portion of a hot or cold food served before a meal to stimulate the appetite or at a social gathering in lieu of a meal.

horse mackerel *See* jack mackerel.

horse meat The flesh of a horse; it has a red color, a coarse texture and a slightly unpleasant, sweet flavor.

horse mushroom A large, white mushroom (*Agaricus arvensis*) that grows in open spaces during the fall and is similar to the common field mushroom but with a more concentrated, slight aniselike flavor.

horseradish A plant (*Armoracia rusticana*) with a large, white root that has a sharp, biting, spicy flavor; the root is peeled and grated and used as a condiment.

horseradish sauce An English sauce made from horseradish, vinegar, sugar, dry mustard, cream, salt and pepper; usually served with roast beef or fish.

horseshoe A subprimal cut of the beef primal round; the primal's heel end, it is somewhat tough and flavorful.

horse's neck A strip of lemon peel cut in a continuous spiral, used as a cocktail garnish.

Horse's Neck 1. A tall glass of ginger ale and ice served with lemon peel. 2. A cocktail made of ginger ale and bourbon, blended whiskey or gin, served with the lemon peel in a tall glass over ice. 3. A drink of moonshine and dry, hard cider.

horta (HÓH-rtah) Greek for green vegetables (e.g., cabbage) and salad greens (e.g., lettuce and dandelion).

hortelã (or-TAY-lah) Portuguese for mint.

hoshi-budo (hoh-shee-boo-doh) Japanese for raisin.

hoska (hos-kah) A Czech and Slovak holiday bread flavored with raisins, almonds and citron and shaped in a three-tier braid.

hoso-maki (hoh-so-mah-kee) Thin-rolled maki-zushi. *See* futo-maki.

hospital diets A variety of diets tailored to meet specific patient needs in an institutional setting such as a hospital or nursing home. *See* bland diet, clear liquid diet, diabetic diet, house diet, low-sodium diet *and* soft diet.

host bar; host's bar; hosted bar *See* open bar.

hostel (hahs-tel) An inexpensive lodging or shelter generally catering to students; facilities, which are sometimes carefully supervised, usually include communal bathrooms and dormitory sleeping; also known as a youth hostel.

host or hostess 1. The person responsible for reservations, seating guests and sometimes acting as cashier at a restaurant or other dining facility. 2. The person or entity responsible for a social event. 3. *See* parasites.

hosui A variety of nashi.

hot 1. Having or giving off heat. 2. Spicy or fiery; causing a burning sensation (which can be pleasurable) in the mouth. 3. A wine-tasting term for a highly alcoholic wine with a heady aroma and a fiery, burning finish.

hotategai (hoe-tah-ta-gee-ah) Japanese for scallop.

hot black bean sauce A paste of fermented soybeans and ground hot chiles used as a flavoring in Chinese cuisines; also known as chile bean sauce.

hot break The coagulation and precipitation of proteins during the boiling of the wort in the beer-making process.

Hot Bricks A drink made of whiskey, boiling water and a ball of butter; also known as Stirrups.

Hot Buttered Rum A cocktail made of hot rum, water, sugar, cloves, cinnamon and lemon peel; garnished with nutmeg and butter.

Hot Buttered Rum, Down East A cocktail made of hot apple cider, golden rum, brown sugar, cloves, cinnamon and lemon peel; garnished with nutmeg and butter.

hot chocolate *See* cocoa.

hotchpotch; hodgepodge Any of several American dishes based on European stewlike dishes made with layers of various meats and vegetables (particularly onions and potatoes).

hot closet An archaic term for a warming oven.

hot cross buns Round, sweet yeast rolls containing candied fruit or raisins and marked on top with a cross of white confectioners' sugar icing; traditionally served on Good Friday.

hot dog *See* frankfurter.

hôtel (oh-tel) French for hotel.

hotel A facility offering guests sleeping accommodations and often some dining or room service facilities.

hotel bacon *See* bacon, thin sliced.

hotel classes *See* deluxe, first class *and* economy class.

hotel garni A designation for a European hotel that serves breakfast but otherwise lacks dining facilities.

hoteli (ho-ta-le) Swahili for hotel.

hoteli y kula (ho-ta-le e koo-lah) Swahili for restaurant.

hotell (ho-tayl) Swedish and Norwegian for hotel.

hotel pan A rectangular stainless steel pan with a lip; it is designed to rest in a steam table or rack and is used to cook, drain, ice, store or serve foods; a full-sized pan is 12 × 20 in. with pans one-half, one-third, and so on of this size available; depth is standardized at 2-in. intervals (a 2-in.-deep pan is known as a 200 pan); also known as a steam table pan.

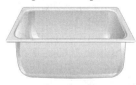

hotel pan

hotel rack *See* rack *and* veal hotel rack.

hotel steak A fabricated cut of the beef primal loin; it is a bone-in shell steak or boneless strip steak from the top of the loin.

hoteru (HOH-teh-roo) Japanese for hotel.

hot-foods section One of the principal work sections of a food services facility; it typically contains a broiler station, fry station, griddle station, sauté/sauce station and a holding area.

hot fudge A thick, rich sauce made with chocolate, butter, sugar and cream; served warm as an ice cream or dessert topping.

hothouse cucumber *See* English cucumber.

hot oven An oven set to a temperature of 400-450°F (204.4–232°C). *See* moderate oven *and* slow oven.

hot pack A canning term used to describe food that is precooked and packed into canning jars while still hot, sealed, and processed in a boiling water bath.

hot pepper *See* chile.

hot plate 1. An electrically heated lidded pan for cooking or warming food. 2. A tabletop cooking device with one or two electric or gas burners.

hotpot A British stewlike dish consisting of layers of vegetables, mutton, sheep's kidneys and sometimes oysters, topped with potatoes.

hot sauce A seasoning sauce, usually commercially made, containing chile peppers, salt and vinegar.

Hot Scotch A drink made of Scotch whisky and a small amount of hot water.

ho tsee (ho tsee) Chinese for dried oyster.

hot smoker, indoor A metal smoke box with a sliding cover; 15 × 11 × 3 in.; it sits on a single burner that heats a small amount of wood shavings in the bottom of the box whose fumes waft up and around a drip-pan insert with an inset rack holding the food.

hot smoking A method of curing, preserving and/or flavoring certain foods by exposing them to smoke at temperatures of 200–250°F (93–121°C); such foods are usually fully cooked after smoking; many hot-smoked meats, fish, shellfish and poultry are first salt-dried or brined. *See* cold smoking.

Hot Toddy A cocktail made of sugar syrup, boiling water, cinnamon, cloves, lemon, nutmeg and whiskey, brandy, rum, gin or vodka.

Hottentot fig The small, figlike fruit of a succulent native to Africa; it can be eaten raw, cooked, pickled or preserved.

hot water A colonial American term for distilled spirits.

hot water dish An assemblage used to keep food warm at the table, either as a serving piece or as part of a place setting; it consists of a covered plate set on a shallow bowl filled with hot water.

houblons (oo-blon) French for hops.

hour glass An hourglass-shaped glass ranging in size from 8 to 10 fl. oz.; used for beer.

house The management or ownership of a commercial establishment, as in "house rules" and "on the house."

house brand 1. The brands of alcohol that a bar uses for well drinks. 2. An otherwise generic product sold under the retailer's name. 3. A menu term indicating that a product has been prepared on the premises or by an outside purveyor according to the offering establishment's recipe or specifications.

house diet A hospital diet in which the food is appropriately seasoned with salt, pepper and other seasonings and served in standard portions; except for caloric intake, there are no restrictions on foods served; also known as a regular diet.

house wine The wine served by a restaurant or bar when no particular wine is specified; often served by the glass, carafe or half carafe with no identifying characteristics given other than grape variety; it can also be specially blended, bottled and labeled for the establishment.

Houx (oo) A French holly berry eau-de-vie.

hovezi maso (ho-vah-zee mah-soh) A Czech or Slovak beef stew made with root vegetables and garnished with pickled cucumbers.

Hovis 1. The proprietary name of a type of brown flour with added wheat germ. 2. The bread made from this flour.

Howgate Wonder A large cooking apple that disintegrates completely when cooked and has little flavor.

howtowdie A Scottish dish consisting of a braised chicken stuffed with bread crumbs, onion and parsley and served with a sauce made from the cooking stock, chicken livers and cream.

hreesi (hree-see) Arabic wheat porridge.

hrete (reh-te) Norwegian for wheat; also known as hvete.

HRI Hotels, restaurants and institutions; synonym for the food services industry.

HRM Home meal replacement.

hsan kyasan (sahn key-ah-sahn) Burmese dried rice vermicelli.

hsun (shoon) A Chinese term for smoking fish, duck or pork.

htamin lethoke (ta-min let-took) A Burmese dish of cooked rice and a variety of noodles mixed (by hand) with sauces and ingredients such as garlic, onions, roasted chickpea powder, chili powder, fish sauce and/or tamarind.

htapodi (htaa-po-thee) Greek for octopus.

huacatay An herb of the marigold family (genus *Tagetes*); it has a disagreeable, dank flavor and is used in Peruvian cuisine.

huachinango (who-ah-chee-nan-go) Spanish (particularly in Mexico) for red snapper.

hua hom (whoo-ah hom) Thai for onion.

hua jiao (whoo-ah gee-ah-oh) Chinese for Szechwan peppercorns.

huánggua (nwang-gwa) Chinese for cucumber.

huángyóu (nwang-yo) Chinese for butter.

huascas *See* guascas.

hua sheng (whoo-ah shang) Chinese for peanut.

hubalhal (huh-bahl-hahl) Arabic for cardamom.

hubaq (huh-bahk) *See* numname.

Hubbard squash A large winter squash with a very thick, bumpy shell, a green to orange color, a grainy, yellow-orange flesh, and a bland, mild flavor; also known as Ohio squash.

hubet il baraky (hah-baht el bar-rah-key) Arabic for caraway seed.

huckleberry A wild berry (*Vaccinium myrtillus*) native to North America; it has a thick dark blue skin, a blue flesh,

10 hard seeds in the center, and a mildly sweet flavor and is eaten raw or used in preserves and baked goods; it is sometimes confused with the blueberry, which has a thinner skin and many tiny seeds; also known as bilberry and whortleberry.

hueso (WEH-soh) Spanish for bone.

huevo (WEH-voh) Spanish for egg.

huevos a la flamenco (WEH-voh ah lah flaw-man-coe) A Spanish dish of eggs baked on a bed of peas, peppers, onions, tomatoes, ham and sausage.

huevos asturian (WEH-vos ahs-too-ree-ahn) A Spanish dish of scrambled eggs with eggplant, tomatoes and fava beans.

huevos pasados por agua (WEH-vos paw-saw-dohs pour AH-gwa) Spanish for soft-boiled eggs.

huevos Quimbos Colombian egg cookies made with egg yolks that are beaten until thick; the cookies are baked, cut into various shapes, and soaked in a sugar syrup flavored with rum.

huevos rancheros (WEH-vohs rahn-CHER-ohs) A Mexican dish of fried eggs set on a tortilla and covered with a tomato and chile salsa.

huevos revueltos (WEH-vos rah-voo-el-toss) Spanish for scrambled eggs.

Huguenot torte (hue-gah-knot tort) A dessert popular in Charleston, South Carolina, consisting of a baked apple and nut mixture; when cool, it is garnished with whipped cream and sprinkled with chopped nuts.

Huhn (hoon) German for chicken.

Hühnerbrust (hew-nerr-brust) German for chicken breast.

hui (who-he) Chinese for blending or cooking small bits of food together in a covered pot; the mixture is usually thickened before service.

huile (lweel) French for oil.

huile d'arachide (lweel dah-rah-szwid) French for peanut oil.

huile de colza (lweel duh kohl-zah) French for rapeseed oil.

huile de mais (lweel duh mays) French for corn oil.

huile de noisette (lweel duh nwah-ZEHT) French for hazelnut oil.

huile de noix (lweel duh nwah) French for walnut oil.

huile d'olive (lweel doll-eev) French for olive oil.

huitlacoche (hweet-la-KO-chay) *See* corn smut.

huître (weetr) French for oyster.

huíxiang (who-e shang) Chinese for fennel.

hújiao (who-jaw-oh) Chinese for pepper.

hull *v.* 1. To remove the hull (husk) from grains. 2. To remove the leafy portion of a strawberry found at the base of its stem and often adhering to the fruit. *n.* The general term for the outermost protective covering of a grain kernel or nut; its texture can range from hard and brittle to thin and papery. *See* husk.

hulled wheat Wheat with the hull removed; it has a creamy color, a plump shape and a soft texture; used in soups and as the principal ingredient in asure.

hulling A milling process in which the hull (husk) is removed from grains.

Hull Thornless blackberry A blackberry variety; the fruit are relatively large and sweet.

húluóbò (hoo-luo-bo) Chinese for carrots.

human's milk *See* milk, human's.

humble pie A 17th-century British dish of deer organs (e.g., liver, heart and kidney) cooked as a pie and fed to the servants.

humbug A boiled, striped, peppermint-flavored English candy.

humectant (hoo-meck-tant) A type of food additive that has hygroscopic abilities; used to promote moisture retention in a processed food to maintain or improve its texture and shelf life; also known as a moisture-retention agent.

humidor An enclosed container designed to keep cigars in a tropical environment (high humidity) to prevent them from drying out; it can be a tabletop box or a walk-in storage facility; ideal storage temperature is 70°F (21°C) with 70% humidity.

humitas con achiote (oo-mee-tas kon ah-chee-oh-tay) An Argentinean and Chilean dish of puréed corn flavored with achiote, chiles, onion, garlic and paprika, pan-fried, topped with cheese, and then wrapped in corn husks and steamed.

hummer (HOOM-merr) Danish, Swedish and Norwegian for lobster.

Hummer (HUM-merr) German for lobster.

hummingbird cake A moist layer cake made with pineapple and bananas and filled with a cream cheese frosting.

hummus (HOOM-uhs) A Middle Eastern sauce made from mashed chickpeas seasoned with lemon juice, garlic and olive or sesame oil; usually served as a dip.

hummus bi tahina (HOOM-uhs be tah-hee-nah) Hummus flavored with tahini.

humors The four elemental fluids of the human body—blood, phlegm, black bile, and yellow bile—believed by medieval Europeans to determine a person's physical and mental health; any imbalance of the four fluids was believed to cause a physical or emotional illness.

humpback salmon *See* pink salmon.

Humulus lupulus *See* hops.

humus; hummus (hum-muss) Arabic for chickpeas.

hundreds and thousands Small, brightly colored sugar candies used as decoration on cakes, trifle and cookies; also known as sprinkles. *See* jimmies.

hundred-year-old eggs Chinese preserved eggs; they are covered with lime, ashes and salt, buried in shallow holes for 100 days, and then eaten uncooked accompanied by soy sauce and minced ginger; also known as Ming Dynasty eggs, fermented eggs, ancient eggs and century eggs.

hung (hoong) Chinese for roasting or broiling meat.

Hungarian cherry pepper; Hungarian cherry chile A small, almost spherical chile with a deep red color, a thick flesh and mild to medium hot flavor; available fresh or dried.

Hungarian goulash *See* goulash.

Hungarian partridge *See* partridge.

Hungarian sweet pepper; Hungarian sweet chile An elongated, tapering pepper with a rounded end, a deep red color, a thick flesh and a sweet flavor. *See* paprika.

Hung Cha (hoong tcha) A tea from China's Fukein province; served in many Chinese restaurants in the United States, the beverage is generally mild and pale; it was the tea dumped during the Boston Tea Party.

hunger The sensation resulting from a lack of food and the compelling need to eat; generally experienced as weakness and an unpleasant sensation or even pain in the lower part of the chest. *See* appetite *and* external cue theory.

hünkâr begendi (hoo-nkahr ba-gen-de) A Greek and Turkish dish consisting of a lamb stew served over an eggplant purée and garnished with green pepper.

hunter's sauce A sauce that contains tomatoes, garlic, onions and mushrooms.

hunter's stew *See* bigos.

Hunter Valley A grape-growing and wine-producing region located in New South Wales, Australia; the principal grapes grown are the Shiraz, Sémillon (sometimes known as Hunter River Riesling), Chardonnay, Cabernet Sauvignon and Sauvignon Blanc.

Huntsman An English product consisting of layers of Double Gloucester cheese and Stilton cheese sandwiched together.

hun tun (hoon toon) Chinese for wonton wrappers.

huoji (hoo-gee) Chinese for turkey.

huo tui (hoo too-ee) Chinese for ham.

hupu (hoo-poo) Chinese for recipe.

hure (uhr) Meat, fish or vegetables presented in aspic in a terrine; served sliced or in an individual mold; sometimes called an aspic.

Hurricane A cocktail made of dark rum, passion fruit flavoring and citrus juices, served in a hurricane glass.

hurricane glass A footed glass that is bulbous at the bottom and tapers to a flaring cylinder at the top; holds approximately 22–24 fl. oz.; used for blended or frozen tropical drinks and specialty drinks such as the Hurricane.

hush puppy A deep-fried cornmeal dumpling flavored with onions, traditionally served with fried fish, especially in the American South.

husk The outermost protective covering found on most grains; usually a dry, thin, papery wrapper. *See* hull.

husk tomato *See* tomatillo.

hussaini kabab (hoo-sah-ee-nee kah-bahb) An Indian dish of ground meat shaped into thin sausages, stuffed with nuts and raisins, and pan-fried or broiled.

hu tieu uot Cassava noodles dyed bright colors; they have a chewy texture and bland flavor and are used in southeast Asian cuisines; also known as tapioca shreds.

hutspot (HUHTS-poht) A Dutch stewlike dish consisting of layers of beef, onions, potatoes and carrots.

Hutzelbrot (HOOT-serl-broat) German for a bread made with fruit.

hvete (va-ta) Norwegian for wheat; also known as hrete.

hvidkål (veet-kawl) Danish for white cabbage.

hvitløk (veet-luhk) Norwegian for garlic.

hvityin (vee-tin) Norwegian for white wine.

HVP *See* hydrolyzed vegetable protein.

hyacinth bean *See* lablab.

hybrid The offspring of plants or animals of different breeds, varieties, species or genera. *See* variety.

hybrid berries Berries that are the result of a cross between established or wild berry canes or roots.

hybrid menu A menu that combines features of a static menu with a cycle menu or a market menu of specials.

hydrate lime *See* calcium hydrate *and* calcium hydroxide.

hydrochloric acid 1. A slightly yellow corrosive liquid; used by the body for digestion. 2. A food additive used as a buffering or neutralizing agent.

hydrocolloids Gums.

hydrogenated fat Generally, a bland, white semisolid saturated fat (e.g., hard magarine) made from an unsaturated liquid oil.

hydrogenated sperm oil An indirect food additive derived from the fatty tissues of the sperm whale and used as a release agent or lubricating agent for bakery pans.

hydrogenation The process of hardening (solidifying or semisolidifying) an unsaturated fat by adding hydrogen at one or more points of unsaturation.

hydrogen peroxide A food additive used as an antimicrobial agent and/or oxidizing agent in processed foods such as dairy and egg products and as a flour bleaching and aging agent.

hydrogen peroxide solution An indirect food additive used to sterilize polymeric food-contact surfaces.

hydrogen sulfide A flammable, poisonous gas found in many mineral waters. *See* rotten-egg odor.

hydrolysis The chemical process by which a substance splits into simpler compounds by adding or taking up the elements of water (e.g., sucrose hydrolyzes into glucose and fructose).

hydrolyzable gallotannin *See* tannic acid.

hydrolyzed protein A protein treated with acids or enzymes to produce free amino acids and peptide chains.

hydrolyzed vegetable protein; hydrolyzed plant protein (HVP) A vegetable protein such as soybeans that has been chemically broken down into amino acids; it is used as a flavor enhancer in processed foods.

hydromel A mixture of honey and water that, after fermentation, becomes mead. *See* Hippocras.

hydrometer An instrument consisting of a sealed cylinder and weighted bulb that when placed in a liquid indicates its specific gravity by a comparison of the surface of the liquid with gradations on the instrument's emerging stem.

hydroponics The science of growing plants in a liquid nutrient solution rather than soil.

hydroxylated lecithin A food additive made from soybean lecithin treated with peroxide; it is used as an emulsifier and antioxidant in baked goods.

hydroxypropyl cellulose A food additive used as a binder and disintegrator in vitamin and/or mineral supplements.

hygrometer Any of various devices used to measure atmospheric humidity.

hygroscopic Having the property or characteristic of absorbing or attracting moisture from the air.

hyldebaer (HEWL-derr-bear) Danish for elderberry.

Hymettus honey (hye-mee-toos) A dark brown, aromatic honey with a dominant thyme flavor from Mount Hymettus in Greece.

hypogeous Growing underground.

hypovitaminosis A A disease caused by a deficiency of vitamin A; symptoms include anemia, night blindness, reduced growth in children, rough skin, rashes, dry eyes and respiratory and digestive system infections.

Hyson A Chinese green tea with long, twisted leaves of various ages; the beverage has a pale straw color and a mild, slightly bitter flavor.

hyssop An herb (*Hyssopus officinales*) with dark green leaves and deep blue or pink flowers; the leaves have a strong mint and licorice flavor and aroma and are used in salads and with fatty meats and fish.

Iago (E-ah-go) A small British pastry or petit four named for the villain in Shakespeare's *Othello;* composed of layers of sponge cake sandwiched with coffee buttercream and topped with coffee fondant.

iahnie (yah-nee-ah) A Romanian vegetable ragoût.

Ibores (ee-BORE-ace) A hard, dense Spanish goat's milk cheese with an orange rind and a distinctive flavor; also known as Sierra Ibores.

ibrik (I-brik) A small, long-handled Turkish pot with a bulbous bottom, narrow waist and flared top; used for Turkish coffee.

ice *v.* 1. To chill a glass or serving dish so that a coat of frost forms on its surface. 2. To spread frosting (icing) over the surface of a cake or cookie. *n.* 1. Frozen water; water freezes at 32°F (0°C). 2. A frozen mixture of water, sugar and a flavoring such as fruit juice or wine; stirred frequently while freezing; it has a grainy texture.

ice bath A mixture of ice and water used to chill a food or beverage rapidly.

ice beer A style of North American lager beer; it is conditioned at temperatures so cold that part of the water freezes into ice from which the beer is separated.

iceberg lettuce A variety of crisp head lettuce with a compact spherical head of pale green leaves that become whitish-yellow toward the center; developed in the United States at the end of the 19th century.

icebox cookie A type of cookie in which the dough is formed into a log and chilled, then sliced into rounds for baking; also known as a refrigerator cookie.

icebox pie A pie with a cookie-crumb crust and a creamy filling that is chilled or frozen until firm.

ice bucket 1. A bucket, usually plastic, metal or glass, often with a lid and sometimes insulated; used to hold ice needed for drinks. 2. A container in which wine is chilled and/or kept, usually at the table; also known as a wine bucket or wine cooler.

ice carving tools *See* ice chipper, ice pick *and* V-shaped ice chisel.

ice chest An insulated box used to keep foods cold. *See* cooler.

ice chipper A metal ice-carving tool resem-

ice chipper

bling a small rake; it has a 2-in.-wide band with six 1-in.-long spikes.

ice cream A rich, frozen dessert made with dairy products, sugar, eggs and various flavorings; the U.S. Department of Agriculture (USDA) requires products labeled ice cream to contain at least 10% milkfat and 20% milk solids.

ice cream cone 1. A wafer rolled into a cone and used to hold ice cream for eating; sometimes dipped in chocolate or other syrup and coated with nuts or the like. 2. A wafer cylinder used to hold ice cream. 3. The cone and ice cream.

ice cream fork A medium-sized fork with a bowl-shaped or blade-shaped end tipped with three short tines; used for eating ice cream.

ice cream freezer 1. An appliance used to make ice cream; the ingredients are sealed in a metal container equipped with a paddle, the container is placed in a tub of ice and salt, and the paddle is turned by hand or a motor until the mixture is set. 2. An ice cream maker with a layered container; the ingredients are placed in the cavity with a paddle that is turned by hand; there is a refrigerant between the layers, which, when chilled before using, sets the ingredients. 3. An electrical appliance that chills and churns the ice cream mixture.

ice cream parlor An establishment featuring ice cream and related desserts; they can be consumed on or off the premises.

ice cream salt *See* rock salt.

ice cream scoop A utensil used to remove ice cream from its container; it can be a simple trowel-like tool or have a bowl with a lever-operated blade to remove the bowl's contents; available in various sizes.

ice cream scoop

ice cream social A social event where ice cream is sold and consumed; often held to raise money for a charity. *See* bake sale.

ice cream soda A beverage made from soda water, flavored syrup and ice cream, sometimes topped with whipped cream.

ice cube Water frozen and formed into a cube, nugget or other shape.

iced coffee A beverage of coffee, a sweetener and milk or cream; served chilled with ice in a glass.

iced coffee Viennese A beverage made of iced coffee and light rum or brandy, topped with whipped cream.

iced tea Freshly brewed tea chilled and served with ice and sometimes flavored with a sweetener and/or lemon juice.

iced tea glass A tall cylindrical glass holding 12–14 fl. oz.

iced tea spoon A long-handled spoon used for stirring iced tea.

icefish *See* rainbow smelt.

Icelandic lobster *See* Norway lobster.

Iceland moss Not a moss but a shrublike lichen (*Cetraria islandica*) that grows principally in northern Europe and is used medicinally, dried and ground into flour for baking, or boiled and cooled to make a nutritious jelly.

Iceland scallop A variety of scallops found off Greenland and Iceland through the Arctic Ocean to Japan; the brownish-green shell has an average diameter of 4 in. (10.1 cm); the meat is tender, sweet and white.

ice machine; ice-making machine A freestanding commercial machine for making ice.

ice milk A frozen dessert made with dairy products, sugar, eggs and flavoring; similar to ice cream but made with less milkfat (3–6%), sugar (12–15%) and milk solids (11–14%).

ice pail *See* sorbétière.

ice pick An awl-like tool with a weighted handle and a strong, thin 5-in. shaft with a sharp point; it is used for chopping large blocks of ice.

ice plant A succulent plant (*Mesembrtanthemum crystallinum*), native to the Mediterranean region, whose leaves have a sour flavor and are sometimes eaten boiled.

ice scoop A metal or plastic scoop used to remove ice from an ice-making machine.

ice tongs Small tongs often with claw-shaped tips used to remove ice from an ice bucket.

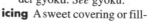
ice scoop

ice tub A shallow rubber or plastic tub used behind the bar for ice cubes and/or chilling containers (bottles and cans) of beer and other beverages for fast service.

ice water Very cold water, often with ice in it.

icewine Canadian term for a wine produced from partially frozen grapes, known in German as Eiswein. *See* Eiswein.

ichiban A variety of long, very slender Asian eggplant.

ichigo (ee-CHEE-goh) Japanese for strawberry.

ichijiku (he-sue-gee-kou) Japanese for fig.

ichinin-mae (he-she-nin-mah-a) Japanese for a serving for one and used to order gyoku. *See* gyoku.

ichiban

icing A sweet covering or filling such as buttercream or ganache; used for cakes and pastries; also known as frosting.

icing comb *See* cake comb.

icing stencil A flat plastic disk with words and/or designs cut out of it; it is pressed onto the cake top, leaving an indention that provides a pattern to be followed when squeezing icing from a pastry bag.

icing sugar British for confectioners' sugar.

icre (e-cra) Romanian for roe.

Ida Gold A variety of egg-shaped cherry tomato with an orange skin and an outstanding flavor.

Idaho potato A variety of russet potato grown in Idaho.

Idared (I-dah-red) A medium-sized American apple; a hybrid of a Jonathan and a Wagener, it has a red and yellow skin and a sweet, moderately acidic flavor.

ideal weight *See* desirable weight.

Idiazábal (ee-dee-ah-ZAH-bahl) A Spanish unpasteurized ewe's milk cheese with a hard, orange to rich walnut brown exterior and a yellowish-beige interior with many tiny holes; it has a rich, buttery, nutty flavor with overtones of smoke and balsam.

ID'ing *See* carding; to card.

idlis (id-lee) An east Indian dish of small, fluffy steamed breakfast cakes made from a dough of ground rice and fermented dal.

iepure (yah-roo-rah) Romanian for hare.

igname (ee-nyam) French for yam.

Igt A Bedouin goat's or ewe's milk cheese made from boiled soured curds flavored with herbs.

IGT *See* Indicazione geografica tipica.

iguama (E-goo-au-mah) Filipino for cu-san.

ijee (ee-ghee) A Syrian omelet.

ika (EE-kah) Japanese for squid or cuttlefish.

ika soba (EE-kah SOH-bah) A Japanese dish of squid cut into strips as fine as noodles and served chilled.

ikeleko (ee-ka-la-koh) A South African dish consisting of samp flavored with animal fat or butter and served with a meat entrée; also known as matutu and setampo.

ikijime (ee-kih-jee-me) Japanese for fish that are kept alive and killed shortly before preparation (especially when making sushi and sashimi). *See* nojime.

ikrá (ee-khra) Russian for caviar.

ikrá cherny (ee-khra churn-nee) Russian for black caviar.

ikrá crasney (ee-khra crasz-nee) Russian for red salmon roe.

ikura (ee-koo-ra) Japanese for the orange-red roe of salmon, which, when eaten, release a creamy textured, rich, concentrated, fish-flavored oil; often used as a sushi topping.

ilama A fruit (*Annona diversifolia*) native to Mexico; it has an elongated shape and a smooth or rough skin; there are two principal varieties: pink (has a magenta pink skin with a white bloom, a pink flesh and a flavor similar to a cherimoya) and green (has a green skin with a white bloom, a greenish flesh and a sweeter flavor reminiscent of a sugar apple).

il diplomatico (eel dep-loh-mah-tee-koh) An Italian pastry made by lining a loaf pan with slices of sponge cake soaked in rum and espresso, then filling the pan with chocolate mousse; the loaf is unmolded and coated with melted chocolate or chocolate ganache.

île flottante (eel floh-tahng) 1. French for floating island and used to describe a dessert composed of a single large mound of meringue floating in a pool of vanilla custard sauce. *See* floating island. 2. A French dessert composed of a liqueur-soaked sponge cake topped with jam, nuts and whipped cream that is served in a pool of custard sauce.

ileum The last portion of the small intestine, extending from the jejunum to the cecum, and the principal site of nutrient absorption.

Ilha (eel-yah) A firm cheese made from cow's milk in the Azores and exported to Portugal.

Illinois Ever-Bearing mulberry A variety of black mulberry with a sweet–tangy flavor.

illness A state of being sick; unlike a disease, an illness is highly individualized and personal. *See* disease.

Illy Coffee Liqueur *See* Espresso.

imam bayildi (AH-mahn by-yahl-deh) Turkish for the Imam fainted and used to describe a dish of roasted eggplant stuffed with tomatoes, garlic, onions, peppers and pine nuts; served cold.

imamdusta and daanti (i-maam-dus-taa and daan-ti) An Indian clay or enamel mortar and pestle.

imbir' (him-beer) Russian for ginger.

imbottigliato (im-boh-tee-l'YAH-toe) Italian for bottled.

imbottigliato all'origine Italian wine term that is the equivalent of estate bottled.

imbottito (eem-boh-TEE-toh) Italian for stuffed or filled.

imbu (eem-boo) A tree native to Brazil (*Spondias tuberosa*); it has a medium-sized ovoid fruit with greenish-yellow skin and a flavor reminiscent of a sweet orange; also known as an umbu.

imitation cheese A dense, rubbery, cheeselike food product made from dairy by-products and soy products mixed with emulsifiers, flavoring agents and enzymes; it tends to have little flavor other than salty.

imitation food A labeling term approved by the U.S. Food and Drug Administration (FDA) to describe a processed food that is intended to substitute for another food and is nutritionally inferior to the food being imitated (e.g., cheese and imitation cheese); although it may have fewer essential nutrients and often less flavor than the food it is intended to imitate, it usually has improved shelf life, cooking properties or other characteristics.

imitation milk A product made from several nondairy ingredients processed to a milklike appearance and flavor; the ingredients include vegetable fat, sodium caseinate (a protein product), soya solids, corn syrup, flavorings, stabilizers, emulsifiers and water.

imjadarra humra (im-jah-dar-rah hum-rah) A Lebanese soup of lentils and bulgur.

imli (him-lee) Hindi for tamarind.

immensa A very large cigar with a 52–64 ring and a 8- to 10-in. length; the large diameter provides a cooler smoke.

immersion blender A small, narrow, handheld blender with a rotary blade at one end; portable, it has variable speeds and can be immersed directly into a pot; whisk attachments are available.

impanare (eem-pah-NAH-reh) Italian for to coat with bread crumbs.

Imperator The common market carrot with a medium to dark orange color.

impératrice, a l' (ahn-pair-ah-TREES, ahl) French for empress and used to describe a variety of rich sweet or savory dishes with a rice base; the name is most commonly applied to a dessert made with rice, candied fruits and a Bavarian cream mixture.

impératrice, sauce; empress sauce (ahm-pair-ah-TRESS) A French compound sauce made from an allemande sauce flavored with truffle essence and chicken glaze and finished with unsweetened whipped cream.

Imperial 1. A Chinese green tea; an older version of Gunpowder, with larger, looser leaves; the beverage has a pale straw color and a mild, fruity, slightly bitter flavor. 2. An oversized wine bottle holding eight 750-ml bottles (approximately 205 fl. oz.); it has the same capacity as a Methuselah and is occasionally used in the Bordeaux region.

impériale, à l' (eem-pay-ree-ahl, ahl) A French garnish for fowl consisting of truffles, foie gras, mushrooms and cockscombs.

Impérial-Frischkäse (im-pee-ree-al freesh-kaiz) An Austrian cottage cheese–style cheese made from skimmed cow's milk.

imperial gallon *See* British gallon *and* gallon.

Imperial stout A strong, rich stout with a burned currant, almost tarlike flavor.

imperial system A measurement system used in Great Britain, Canada and other countries associated with the former British Empire; it uses pounds and ounces for weight and pints and fluid ounces for volume. *See* metric system *and* U.S. system.

Imp n' Arp A drink made from Imperial whiskey and Iron City beer (a beer associated with Pittsburgh).

impossible pie A dessert made with a mixture of eggs, milk, sugar, butter, coconut and a packaged biscuit mix that is baked in a pie tin; the mix settles to the bottom during baking, forming the crust.

IMPS/NAMP *See* NAMP/IMPS.

inab (een-ahb) Arabic for grape.

inaka-miso (ee-nah-kah-mee-so) A rich, red miso made with barley mold; it can be sweet or salty and is used in soups or braised dishes; also known as red miso and sendai-miso.

inamona A Hawaiian condiment of crushed kukui mixed with chiles and salt.

inari (EE-nahr-EE) Japanese for foods made with fried bean curd.

Incanestrato (een-kah-nehs-STRAH-toh) 1. An Italian pasta filata cheese made from ewe's milk or a mixture of ewe's and cow's milks; the curds are pressed into wicker molds or baskets; also known as Canestrato Rigato and Rigatello; when made from only ewe's milk, it is known as Pecorino Incanestrato. 2. An American version of this cheese made from cow's milk.

incense 1. An aromatic substance such as wood or a gum burned to produce a pleasant aroma. 2. The aroma so produced.

incidental food additive Any substance (food additive) inadvertently added to foods during growing, processing, preparing, packaging and storing; its use is generally regulated by the U.S. Food and Drug Administration (FDA), and the substance may not discernibly affect the flavor, aroma, nutritional value, color or other characteristic of the food; also known as an accidental or indirect food additive. *See* intentional food additive.

incomplete protein A protein lacking one or more of the essential amino acids; generally found in plant foods. *See* mutual supplementation.

indeyka; indeika (en-day-kuh) Russian for turkey.

Indian cress *See* nasturtium *and* capuchin.

Indian CTC Black tea leaves from India that are crushed, torn and curled in pellets that unfurl when brewed; commonly used to make powdered iced tea mixes.

Indian date *See* tamarind.

Indianerkrapfen (in-dee-ah-ner-krah-fan) An Austrian pastry consisting of a small, hollowed-out sponge cake filled with whipped cream and covered with a shiny chocolate glaze.

Indian fig; Indian pear *See* prickly pear.

Indian gooseberry The small, spherical yellow or green berry of the *Emblica offinicalis;* it has a very tart flavor and is usually made into jam or pickled.

Indian gum *See* gum ghatti.

Indian meal Another name for cornmeal.

Indian nut *See* pine nut.

Indian pudding *See* hasty pudding.

Indian rice Rice grown in India (e.g., basmati and patna).

Indian saffron *See* turmeric.

Indian shot *See* canna.

Indian sorrel *See* Jamaican sorrel.

Indian whiskey *See* trade whiskey.

India pale ale 1. A bitter ale with a hoppy aroma and flavor. 2. A style of ale originally brewed in England for shipment to British troops stationed in India during the 18th century; the high hop content acted as a preservative during shipping.

Indicazione geografica tipica (IGT) (in-dee-cah-zee-oh-na ja-oh-grah-phee-cah tee-pee-cah) The Italian category of officially classified wines that refers to whole provinces or large areas.

indienne, à l' (een-DYEHN, ahl) A French preparation method associated with Indian cuisines; the dishes are usually prepared with curry powder and served over rice.

indigenous A plant or animal native to the particular area.

indigotine *See* FD&C Blue #2.

indirect food additive *See* incidental food additive.

individually quick frozen (IQF) A preservation method in which each individual item of food (e.g., a slice of fruit, berry or fish) is rapidly frozen before packaging; IQF foods are not packaged with syrup or sauce.

Indonesian A light fragrant tea grown in Indonesia, used principally for blending.

Indonesian relish A pickle made from vegetables such as cabbage, onions, leeks, carrots and cucumbers; it has a mild flavor and is usually served with smoked fish.

induction cooking A cooking method that uses a special coil placed below the stove top's surface in combination with specially designed cookware to generate heat rapidly with an alternating magnetic field.

indyk (een-dik) Polish for turkey.

inebriated Intoxicated.

infectant *See* infection.

infection 1. The condition produced when pathogenic microorganisms (including viruses) invade tissues and multiply there, causing injurious effects. 2. In the food safety context, a type of bacterial illness caused by ingesting pathogenic bacteria (called infectants); the infectants, which cause the illness, can usually be destroyed by cooking foods containing the bacteria to a sufficiently high temperature, generally 165°F (74°C).

infestation The presence and multiplication of unwanted living organisms in a particular location.

infuse To steep a seasoning or food in a hot liquid until the liquid absorbs the item's flavor.

infused oil *See* flavored oil.

infusion coffeepot *See* cafetiére.

ingefær (inge-feh-rah) Norwegian for ginger.

ingefäer (I-nger-fae-rah) Swedish for ginger.

ingelegde vis (in-gel-leg-da viss) A South African dish of fish pickled in vinegar, turmeric, brown sugar and curry powder.

ingen (ENG-ghen) Japanese for string beans.

ingestion The process of taking food into the digestive system.

ingladsild (ing-lahd-sill) Norwegian for pickled herring.

Ingwer (INJ-vehr) German for ginger.

Ingwerbrot (INJ-vehr-broat) German for gingerbread.

inhaler *See* snifter.

inib (ein-na-bah) Arabic for grapes.

inihaw (ee-nee-how) A Filipino cooking method in which fish, poultry or skewered meats are grilled over a fire.

injected meat A cut of meat that has had a curing solution introduced throughout it by injection or pumping; also known as pumped meat.

injera; aenjera (in-jah-raw) An Ethiopian pancakelike bread, often made from teff.

inkfish *See* squid.

inky cap; ink cap A bell-shaped mushroom (*Coprinus atramentarius*) with a pale gray color.

inland whitefish *See* whitefish.

inn 1. Traditionally, an establishment that offers both lodging and refreshments. 2. A term used imprecisely for a restaurant, cocktail lounge or the like.

inorganic The class of elements or compounds not derived from plants or animals or based on carbon.

inositol A food additive derived from corn kernels and used as a nutrient supplement.

in-room bar A small refrigerator and storage cabinet in a hotel guest room stocked with snacks and beverages. *See* honor bar.

insahm cha (in-sam cha) A Korean tea made with ginseng root; it has an earthy, medicinal flavor and is highly regarded for its rejuvenating powers.

insalata (ihn-sah-LAH-tah) Italian for salad.

insalata frutti di mare (ihn-sah-LAH-tah frut-tee dee MAH-reh) Italian for seafood (fish and shellfish) salad.

in season A menu term indicating that the product is readily available in its fresh state.

insecticide A synthetic or naturally occurring substance used to kill insects; used to protect a human or animal food crop, it can become an incidental food additive.

inside chuck roll A subprimal cut of the beef primal chuck; it is a rolled center-cut chuck roast that is flavorful but tough.

inside round; inside top round *See* top round.

inspection mark of meat products The stamp found on a cut of meat indicating that it was inspected by the appropriate federal or state agency; the stamp bears the establishment number of the last processing site.

instant A processed food or a food from which water has been removed; it is ready to use or consume once rehydrated with the appropriate amount of hot or cold water or other liquid.

instant cocoa *See* cocoa mix.

instant coffee 1. A powdered soluble extract made by heat-drying freshly brewed coffee. *See* freeze-dried coffee granules or crystals. 2. The reconstituted beverage, usually hot, made from the extract.

instant garlic *See* garlic flakes.

instantized flour A readily pourable flour made by a milling or agglomerating procedure.

instant oats *See* oats, instant.

instant-read thermometer *See* thermometer, instant-read.

instant rice Fully cooked and flash-frozen rice; when rehydrated, it can lack flavor and be gritty; also known as quick-cooking rice.

instant tea 1. Soluble powder or granules made by heat-drying freshly brewed tea; sometimes flavored with sweeteners, lemon and/or other flavorings. 2. The reconstituted beverage, either hot or iced, made from the powder or granules.

Institute of Masters of Wine *See* Master of Wine.

institutional cook A cook who generally works with large quantities of prepackaged or prepared foods for a captive market such as a school or prison.

Institutional Meat Purchasing Specifications *See* NAMP/IMPS.

institutional roast *See* roast, cinnamon.

insulated carriers Equipment used to hold food at a constant temperature for a limited period of time by use of various insulating materials; they are often designed to hold hotel pans or sheet pans and are used when preparing for buffets or off-premise catering events; some are equipped with wheels and/or spigots for serving hot or cold beverages.

insulated carrier

insulation; insulating materials Materials that do not conduct heat, electricity or sound.

insulin A hormone secreted by the pancreas in response to high blood glucose levels; essential for the proper metabolism of glucose.

integrale (een-teh-GRAH-leh) An Italian term for a product (e.g., bread or pasta) made from whole wheat.

integrated pricing A method of pricing in which the price of any particular item bears some reasonable relationship to the price of any comparable item or the overall mix of items.

intentional food additive A substance (food additive) intentionally added to a food that becomes a component of the food; its use is generally regulated by the U.S. Food and Drug Administration (FDA) and the substance is intended to affect a characteristic such as nutrient content, flavor, texture, color or freshness or to assist processing; also known as a direct food additive. *See* incidental food additive.

interior The part of the cheese that is inside the rind or crust; also known as the paste.

interiores (in-ta-ree-oh-ress) Spanish for organ meats.

interlard *See* lard.

international unit *See* IU.

interval ownership *See* time-share ownership.

intestines 1. A variety meat, generally from cows, calves, lambs and hogs; long tubes of slightly translucent, somewhat elastic flesh with a bland flavor; used for casings or deep-fried as chittlings. 2. *See* large intestine *and* small intestine.

in the rough A lobster cooked whole and served in the shell, usually outdoors.

intoxicated The condition of being significantly and legally under the influence of excessive amounts of alcohol and considered incapable of complete control of one's actions.

intoxicating liquors The beverages subjected to Prohibition restraints; defined as any beverage containing 1% or more alcohol.

intoxication 1. A type of bacterial illness caused by ingesting toxin-producing bacteria; although the bacteria are themselves harmless, the toxins produced as a by-product of their life processes can be poisonous, and the toxins are usually not destroyed by cooking foods that contain them (although the bacteria will be destroyed). 2. The condition of being intoxicated.

invecchiato (in-veh-chee-YAH-toh) Italian for aged, as in wine or cheese.

inventory *v.* To count and record all assets. *n.* An asset of a business; an item owned by the business.

inventory, direct Assets such as the raw materials used to make the goods the business sells as well as any finished goods waiting to be sold.

inventory, indirect Assets such as the supplies that a business uses; they are not meant to be sold to customers.

inventory speculation The practice of buying more goods than currently needed in anticipation of an increase in their price.

inventory valuation The process of determining the value of inventory.

invert sugar Sucrose that has been broken down (i.e., inverted) into its two components, glucose and fructose, with the use of heat and acid; this inversion prevents crystallization and makes for smoother candies, frostings and confections.

invert sugar syrup A food additive used as a sweetener in soft drinks.

involto di carne (een-voul-TOH dee karn-ee) An Italian term indicating that a meat has been rolled around a stuffing.

Inzolia (in-zoe-lee-ah) A white wine grape grown in Italy and used to make Marsala.

iodine 1. A trace mineral principally used as a component of the thyroid hormone thyroxine that helps regulate growth, development and metabolic rate; significant sources include iodized salt, fish, shellfish and many plant foods. 2. A food additive used as a nutrient supplement, principally in table salt.

iodized salt Table salt (sodium chloride) containing potassium iodide, a source of the essential nutrient iodine.

iogurt (yo-goorth) Italian for yogurt.

iogurte (yo-goor-ta) Portuguese for yogurt.

ion An electrically charged atom or group of atoms formed by the loss of one or more electrons; a cation has a positive charge (e.g., sodium) and an anion has a negative charge (e.g., chloride).

IPA *See* India pale ale.

Ipswich clams An Atlantic soft-shell clam.

IQF *See* individually quick frozen.

irfa (hir-faw) An Egyptian beverage consisting of water heated with cinnamon and sugar and garnished with mukassaraat.

iri (EE-ree) Japanese for to roast.

iri nuka (EE-ree NOO-kah) Japanese dry-roasted rice bran.

irio (e-ree-oh) A Kenyan dish of stewed vegetables such as corn, beans, potatoes, lentils and spinach.

Irish breakfast A hearty breakfast consisting of eggs, meat (sausage, blood sausage, bacon, ham and/or fish), baked goods, jam, juice and tea or coffee.

Irish breakfast tea A blend of Indian Assam teas; the beverage is strong and robust.

Irish Canadian Sangaree A cocktail made of Canadian whisky, Irish Mist, orange juice and lemon juice; served in a chilled old-fashioned glass and dusted with nutmeg.

Irish Coffee A drink made of Irish whiskey, hot black coffee and sugar with a layer of cream floated on top.

Irish Fix A cocktail made of Irish whiskey, Irish Mist, lemon juice and pineapple syrup or pineapple juice, garnished with orange and lemon slices.

Irish Mist An Irish liqueur made from Irish whiskey and heather honey.

Irish moss A variety of seaweed; when dried and boiled, it yields a gelatinous cream-colored liquid that is then sweetened with condensed milk and flavored with nutmeg and vanilla; it is consumed as a beverage in the Caribbean.

Irish oats *See* oats, steel-cut.

Irish peach apple An ovoid apple with a thin golden skin and a flavor reminiscent of a peach.

Irish pease pudding An Irish dish of dried green or yellow peas cooked, mashed and mixed with egg and butter and sometimes flavored with Worcestershire sauce; often used as an accompaniment to pickled pork.

Irish potato A spherical, thin-skinned potato; principally used for boiling, frying and roasting.

Irish sea moss *See* carrageenan.

Irish soda bread A round, free-form bread made with baking soda and buttermilk, often flavored with currants and caraway seeds.

Irish stew An Irish stewlike dish of mutton layered with potatoes and onions, simmered, and served with pickled red cabbage.

Irish whiskey A triple-distilled whiskey made in Ireland from the same fermented grains Scots use to make Scotch whisky (the grains are not, however, smoke cured); it has a smooth, full body and a clean, malty flavor.

iron A trace mineral principally used for forming hemoglobin and myoglobin and to assist energy utilization; significant sources include red meat, fish, shellfish, eggs, legumes and dried fruits as well as foods to which iron has been added as a nutrient supplement.

iron ammonium citrate A food additive used as an anti-caking agent in processed foods such as flour.

iron-choline citrate complex A food additive used as a nutrient supplement.

Iron Goddess of Mercy A Chinese oolong tea named for the goddess Guanyin, patroness of would-be mothers; the beverage is copper colored, astringent and richly aromatic and considered a digestive aid.

iron oxide A food additive used as a red-brown coloring agent.

ironstone A hard white stoneware pottery developed during the 19th century as a less expensive alternative to bone china.

ironware Heavy, brittle cookware and utensils made from iron or cast iron, usually preseasoned or coated with enamel; the iron or cast iron distributes heat evenly and retains high temperatures well.

irradiation A preservation method used for certain fruits, vegetables, plant products and grains in which ionizing radiation sterilizes the food, slows ripening and prevents sprouting; irradiation has little effect on the food's texture, flavor or appearance.

ir sus (hir soos) An Egyptian licorice-flavored beverage.

is (eess) Danish, Norwegian and Swedish for ice.

iscas com elas (ees-cahs com ah-lass) A Portuguese dish consisting of marinated calf's liver usually served with potatoes and garnished with parsley.

Ischl tart (ISH-lehr) An Austrian pastry made with two buttery nut cookies sandwiched together with berry jam; the top cookie has a cut-out center so that the jam shows through; also known as a linzer cookie.

ise-ebi (EE-seh-EH-bee) Japanese for lobster.

Isigny A semisoft American cheese; it has an ivory color and a mildly pungent flavor.

isinglass A very pure form of gelatin made from a sturgeon's swimbladder and used principally as a fining agent.

iskembeci (is-kam-bah-tchee) Turkish restaurants that specialize in variety meat and tripe soup as well as asure.

iskrem (ice-cram) Norwegian for ice cream.

Islay Scotch (I-lay) A Scotch whisky produced in an area of southwest Scotland; the Scotch generally has a full body and a smoky, pungent flavor and aroma.

isleta bread (ees-LEH-tah) Pueblo Indian bread shaped like a bear's claw.

Ismail Bayaldi A classic French garnish consisting of sliced fried eggplant, tomatoes, rice pilaf and sauce portugaise.

isoamyl acetoacetate A food additive with a light aroma of green leaves and fruit, used as a flavoring agent in beverages and candies.

isoamyl butyrate, isoamyl formate and isoamyl hexamoate Food additives with fruity aromas used as flavoring agents in dessert gels and baked goods.

isoascorbic acid *See* ascorbic acid.

isobutyl acetate A food additive with a banana aroma used as a flavoring agent.

isobutyl cinnamate and isobutyl formate Food additives with fruity aromas used as flavoring agents in beverages, candies and baked goods.

isobutyric acid A food additive with a strong buttery aroma used as a flavoring agent.

isoflavones A group of naturally occurring plant chemicals that weakly mimic the effects of estrogen hormones in some parts of the body while acting as antihormones in others; some researchers believe that isoflavones, which are in soy, may help reduce cholesterol levels.

isoleucine 1. An essential amino acid. 2. A food additive used as a nutrient source to significantly improve the biological quality of the total protein in a food containing the naturally occurring protein.

isomerized syrup *See* fructose corn syrup.

isoproyl citrate A food additive used as an antioxidant in vegetable oils.

issai A variety of hairless kiwi.

issuing The process of releasing an item from a storage area to a production area.

istakoz (is-taw-kosh) Turkish for lobster.

istiridyá (stir-tee-gee) Turkish for oysters.

Istrian Smiling A cocktail made of gin, crème de cassis, Madarine Napoleon and tonic; served in a highball glass.

isungura (e-soon-goo-raw) Swahili for rabbit.

isuto (ee-SU-toh) Japanese for yeast.

ita-kamaboko (ee-tah-kah-mah-bow-ko) A kamaboko that is often grilled for a toasty flavor.

Italian bread An American term for a variety of chewy, hard-crusted yeast breads made with flour, water, yeast and salt.

Italian brown mushroom *See* common store mushroom.

Italian buttercream A creamy frosting made by beating softened butter into cooled Italian meringue; also known as meringue buttercream.

Italian dressing A salad dressing consisting of olive oil and wine vinegar or lemon juice and seasoned with oregano, basil, dill, garlic and fennel.

Italian eggplant *See* eggplant, Italian.

Italian garlic A garlic with a mauve-colored outer layer and a milder flavor than American garlic; also known as Mexican garlic.

Italian meringue A fluffy, shiny meringue made by slowly beating hot sugar syrup into whipped egg whites; when used as a cake frosting, known as boiled icing.

Italian parsley A variety of parsley (*Petroselinum neopolitanum*) with flat, darker green leaves and a stronger, coarser flavor than curly parsley; generally used fresh as a flavoring; also known as flat-leaf parsley. *See* parsley.

Italian parsley

Italian red onion *See* red onion, Italian.

Italian roast *See* roast, espresso.

Italian sausage A style of pork sausages seasoned with garlic and fennel seeds; available in medium-sized links, there are two principal types: hot (flavored with red chiles) and sweet (without the chiles).

Italian tomato *See* plum tomato.

Italian vermouth *See* vermouth, sweet.

Italico (ee-TAH-lee-koh) A group of semisoft Italian Bel Paese–style cheeses; they are quick ripening and have a smooth rind, a white to pale straw-yellow color, a dense, supple interior, and a mild, buttery, sweet flavor.

Italienne, sauce (ee-ṭahl-lee-een) 1. A French compound sauce made from a velouté flavored with shallots, parsley and mushrooms cooked in white wine. 2. A cold French sauce made from mayonnaise garnished with a purée of calf's brains and chopped fine herbs.

itamae (he-tam-mah-a) A Japanese sushi chef.

itame ni (eeh-TAH-meh nee) Japanese for sauté.

IU International Unit, a measure of quantity used for fat-soluble vitamins (A, D and E) and certain hormones, enzymes and biologics; the measurement is based on potency, not weight.

ivoire, sauce (ee-vwahr) A French compound sauce made from a suprême flavored with a white veal or chicken glaze; usually served with eggs, offal and poached or sautéed chicken; also known as Wladimir sauce.

iyan (he-yahn) A Nigerian porridge made from pounded yams.

Izarra (ee-zah-rah) A liqueur flavored with plants from the French Pyrenees; available in two forms: green (which has the higher alcohol content) and yellow.

izyum (he-suum) Russian for raisin.

J

ja (jah) A Chinese cooking method of deep-frying foods in a wok.

jaa-jar Hindi for carrot.

jabalí (khah-bhah-LEE) Spanish for wild boar.

jablok (jhah-blok) Russian for apple; also known as yabloko.

jaboticaba (zheh-buht-eh-KOHB-eh) A fruit (*Mycaria cauliflora*) grown in Brazil; the fruit is borne directly on the trunk, limbs and branches; the cherry-sized spherical fruit has a maroon or purple skin, a white to pinkish flesh, and a flavor reminiscent of a grape.

jabtka (yap-kah) Polish for apple.

jabuguito (khah-boo-ghee-toh) A Spanish chorizo sausage; it can be served raw or deep-fried.

Jack *See* Monterey Jack.

Jack Daniel Distillery One of the 12 remaining U.S. whiskey distilleries; located in Lynchburg, Tennessee, and founded in 1866, it produces the Jack Daniel's line of Tennessee sour mash whiskeys.

jackfish *See* ulua.

jackfruit; jakfruit A huge tree-borne fruit (*Artocarpus heterophyllus*) related to the breadfruit and grown in India and Asia; it has an ovoid shape with a spiny skin, a firm, thick flesh, and a flavor reminiscent of pineapple and banana; when green, it is used as a starchy vegetable, with both the flesh and the seeds being eaten; when ripened and sweeter, generally used as a dessert.

jackfruit stones The seeds of the jackfruit; they are cooked as a vegetable, roasted for a snack, or sliced into coconut milk to make a dessert in Indian and Southeast Asian cuisines.

jackknife clams *See* razor shell clams.

jack mackerel A fish found in the Pacific Ocean from Canada to Chile and a member of the jack family; it has a dark green back that becomes silvery below and an average market weight of 1–2.5 lb. (0.5–1.14 kg); it is generally used for canning or smoking; also known as horse mackerel and California horse mackerel.

Jack Rose A cocktail made of applejack, grenadine and lime or lemon juice.

Jacob's cattle An heirloom variety of bean; it is white and maroon with a somewhat sweet flavor.

Jacquère (jah-kair) 1. The principal white wine grape grown in France's Savoie region. 2. The wine made from this grape; it is fresh, light and dry.

jade *See* candela.

Jaffa orange A particularly large, flavorful, pulpy variety of navel orange; generally grown in Israel.

jagacida A dish from the Cape Verde Islands consisting of beans, rice and chouriço flavored with garlic, paprika, black pepper and bay leaves.

jagaimo (jah-EE-moh) Japanese for potato.

Jäger; Jäger Art (ya-gher; ya-gher art) German for hunter's style and used to describe a dish made with mushrooms and a wine sauce.

Jägermeister (YAG-er-mice-ter) A complex, aromatic German beverage made from 56 herbs, gentian, roots and fruits; served as an aperitif or digestif.

jaggery A coarse brown sugar made from the sap of the Palmyra palm (*Borassus flabellifer*) and used in Indian and Southeast Asian cuisines; also known as palm sugar.

jagging wheel A type of pastry wheel with a fluted cutting edge; also known as a pie jagger.

jagnje (yag-n'yay) Serbo-Croat for lamb.

jagging wheel

jaiba (hah-bah) Spanish (particularly in Mexico) for crab.

jaiphul (jah-ee-pool) Hindi for nutmeg.

jaja (yah-yah) Polish for egg.

jajtsa; jajtza (jhaj-tsah) Russian for egg; also known as yaytsa.

jake An alcoholic beverage made from Jamaican ginger; popular during Prohibition.

jalapeño (hah-lah-PEH-nyoh) A short, tapering chile with a thick flesh, a moderately hot, green vegetal flavor and a dark green color (a red version is also available; it is a green chile that has been allowed to ripen); available fresh or canned and named for the Mexican city of Jalapa. *See* chipotle *and* mora.

jalea (khah-LAY-ah) Spanish for jelly.

jalebi ka rang (ja-lai-bee kar rang) An artificial yellow food coloring used in India to color foods, especially sweet dishes.

jalebis (ja-lai-be) An east Indian confection of sweet batter piped into hot oil, deep-fried, and coated with a sugar syrup.

jallab (jah-lahb) A Middle Eastern sweet purple beverage made from berries and garnished with pine nuts.

jalouise (ZAH-luh-zee) A rectangular French pastry with a lattice top that allows the jam or fruit filling to show through.

jam A fruit gel made from fruit pulp and sugar.

Jamaican Coffee A cocktail made of Cognac, Tia Maria, dark Jamaican rum and hot black coffee; garnished with whipped cream, cinnamon and ground ginger.

Jamaican honeysuckle *See* water lemon.

Jamaican hot chile A short, tapering fresh chile with a thin flesh, a red color and a sweet, hot flavor.

Jamaican mango A dark, almost black, mango with a sweet, orange-yellow flesh grown in the Caribbean region.

Jamaican pepper *See* allspice.

Jamaican rum A rich, full-bodied and pungent dark rum made in Jamaica.

Jamaican sorrel A plant (*Hibiscus sabdariffa*) native to West Africa and popular in the West Indies; the large, red, fleshy calyx of the plant's flower has a sweet–sour flavor and is used for jams and to flavor a traditional Christmas drink; also known as Indian sorrel, red sorrel and roselle.

jamal (jah-mahl) Arabic for camel; its meat is sometimes consumed during the winter when sheep are too lean to butcher.

jambalaya (juhm-buh-LI-yah) A Creole dish of ham, shrimp, crayfish and/or sausage (usually chaurice) cooked with rice, tomatoes, green peppers, onions and seasonings.

jambe (zaham) French for leg, usually of meat.

jamberry 1. A cherry-sized fruit of a plant (*Physalis ixocarpa*) native to South America; it has a violet skin and is enclosed in a loose, papery husk; it is often used in salsa. 2. *See* tomatillo.

jambolan (jam-boh-lahn) A wild fruit (*Syzgium cumini*) native to India and Southeast Asia; it has a teardrop shape, a purple skin, a white or purple flesh, and an astringent flavor; also known as a Java plum.

jambon (zham-BOHN) 1. French for ham. 2. A French cut of the pork carcass; it consists of the muscles of the hind leg, usually with the bone in.

jambon cru fumé (zham-BOHN crew foo-may) A type of raw smoked ham from Alsace, the French Ardennes, the Jura, the Haut Savoie or Sancerre; it is smoked over vine sticks.

jambon cuit à l'os (zham-BOHN kwee't ah lohs) A French marketing designation for a whole ham that is cooked and then cut from the bone.

jambon cuit supérieur (zham-BOHN kwee't soo-pear-reh-er) A French marketing designation for a good quality ham that was not frozen before sale.

jambon de Bayonne (zham-BOHN duh bay-YOHN) A ham from Bayonne, France; it is rubbed with salt, saltpeter, sugar, pepper and aromatic herbs and dried for 4–6 months and then mildly smoked.

jambonneau (zhan-bun-NO) A French cut of the pork carcass; it is a portion of the foreleg or a knuckle from the foreleg or hind leg that is cured and pickled or salted.

jambon persille (zham-BOHN pair-see-YAY) A French dish consisting of strips or cubes of ham and parsley bound with a meat–wine gelatin.

jambon supérieur maison (zham-BOHN soo-pear-reh-er may-zohn) A French marketing designation for a cooked ham produced by the butcher and cut by him or her on the day of sale.

jambosa The bell-shaped fruit of a plant (*Eugenia javanica*) native to Indonesia; it has a pinkish-green skin and a white flesh with a tangy flavor; also known as foreigner's cheeks.

jameed (jah-meed) 1. A sun-dried, reconstituted yogurt used in Middle Eastern cuisines. 2. *See* labanah mackbouseh.

jammy; jamlike A wine-tasting term for a wine, usually red, with a concentrated grapey, fruity or berrylike flavor reminiscent of jam.

jamón (ah-MOHN) Spanish for ham.

jamonera (ah-MOHN-eh-rah) A wood or metal rack used in Spain for cutting wafer-thin slices of ham; the ham is placed on the rack with one of the flat sides facing up, the fat and rind are removed, and then slices are cut using a long, flexible knife.

jamu (JAH-moo) Japanese and Swahili for jam.

janhagel (eeahn-ghal) A Dutch almond cookie flavored with cinnamon and allspice and garnished with almond slices or halves.

jänis (YAE-niss) Finnish for hare.

Jansson's fresteise; Jansson's temptation A Swedish smörgåsbord dish consisting of potato and anchovy gratin.

jantaboon (yan-tah-boon) Thick, flat, rice flour noodles used in Thai cuisine.

jantar (jun-tahr) Portuguese for dinner.

jao-tze (yah-oh-tza) Chinese noodles similar to ravioli or dumplings.

Japanese abalone *See* Kamchatka abalone.

Japanese artichoke *See* chorogi.

Japanese Early Purple eggplant A variety of long, very slender, purple-skinned Asian eggplant.

Japanese eggplant *See* eggplant, Asian.

Japanese gelatin *See* agar-agar.

Japanese littleneck clam *See* Manila clam.

Japanese medlar *See* loquat.

Japanese oysters *See* Pacific oysters.

Japanese pickled radish Daikon radish pickled in soy sauce and sugar; used as a condiment, especially with fish, in Japanese cuisine; available in chunks, slices and shreds.

Japanese plum *See* plum, Japanese *and* loquat.

Japanese rice A short-grain, grayish-white variety of rice with oval, translucent grains; when cooked, it is moist, firm and sticky.

Japanese wineberry A plant (*Rubus phoenicolasius*) native to Japan and China; its small, raspberry-like fruit range in color from yellow-orange to bright red and have a sweet–tart flavor.

jap chae (jop che) A Korean dish of clear noodles garnished with pan-fried vegetables and beef.

japonaise (zhah-pawng-ayz) A French baked meringue containing ground hazelnuts or almonds.

jardinière, à la (jahr-duh-NIHR) A French term for dishes garnished with vegetables.

jaresh A very finely cracked wheat; it has a slightly nutty flavor and is used in Middle Eastern cuisines in stuffings.

Jargonelle (jar-go-nell) A pear grown in France with a distinctive aroma.

Jarlsberg (YAHRLZ-behrg) A Norwegian Emmental-style cheese made from cow's milk; it has a pale yellow interior with large holes and a delicate, sweet, nutty flavor.

jarret (zhar-RAY) 1. French for shin or knuckle. 2. A French cut of the veal carcass; it is the knuckle or shin and contains the leg bone with marrow and meat.

jars, Mason Glass containers with threaded necks made especially for home canning, pickling and preserving; they range in size from 4 oz. (1/2 cup) to 1/2 gallon; most brands use two-part self-sealing lids; tapered Mason jars, larger at the mouth than at the base, can be used for freezing and canning.

jar woo kwok (jar who koo-oek) Chinese deep-fried taro flour turnovers.

jasmine flowers The aromatic white to pale yellow flowers of several jasmine shrubs or vines (genus *Jasminum*) that can be used in fruit salads or as a flavoring for ice creams, sorbets and tisanes.

jasmine rice A young, tender rice with a strong flowerlike aroma and a delicate flavor; used in Thai and Vietnamese cuisines.

jasmine tea A blend of Chinese black and green teas scented with jasmine petals; the beverage is light and fragrant and best served without milk or lemon.

jaune de mulhouse A particularly flavorful variety of golden-skinned onion; it has a somewhat flattened shape.

Java (JAH-va) 1. Arabica coffee beans grown on the main island of Indonesia; the beverage is full bodied, with a strong, peppery flavor. 2. Slang for coffee.

javali (gia-vah-lee) Portuguese for boar.

java olive 1. An imprecisely used name for a type of pili nut. 2. A tree grown in Africa and Asia (*Sterculia foetida*); its dark brown, olive-sized seeds are roasted (the seeds are contained in a large, red, lobed pod).

Java plum *See* jambolan.

javitri (jah-ve-tree) Hindi for mace.

jawz al-hind (jaws ill-hind) Arabic for coconut.

Jbane (jib-nat) A Moroccan cheese made from goat's milk; it has a hard texture and a sharp flavor.

jeera (gee-rah) Hindi for cumin.

Jefferson, Thomas (Am., 1743–1826) America's third president, author of the Declaration of Independence, and America's first serious gourmet; he introduced America to the waffle iron, pasta maker, dumbwaiter, Parmesan, figs, anchovies, Dijon mustard, tarragon vinegar, vanilla, olive oil, pomegranates, Italian peaches and Italian rice, and his cultivation of native grapevines gave rise to Virginia's wine industry.

jejunum (jeh-JUNE-uhm) The middle portion of the small intestine, extending from the duodenum to the ileum.

jelebi (jah-lah-bee) A sweet east Indian deep-fried flour fritter made from a swirl of dough and flavored with syrup and rosewater.

jelenia (yeh-leh-nyah) Polish for venison.

jell To congeal.

Jell-O The proprietary name for a brand of flavored gelatin dessert.

jelly 1. A clear, shiny mixture of cooked fruit juice and sugar thickened with pectin; its texture is soft but firm enough to hold its shape when unmolded; used as a spread for bread or a glaze on pastries. 2. British for any gelatin dessert.

jelly bag A tightly woven cloth bag used for draining puréed fruit to make a clear jelly.

jelly beans Small, brightly colored ovoid candies with a chewy, gelatinous interior and a hard candy coating; available in many flavors and colors.

Jelly Belly The proprietary name for jelly bean candies made in dozens of unusual flavors. *See* jelly beans.

jelly glass A footed trumpet-shaped glass used to hold sweetened, jelled fruit juice; typically, it has two handles, although it can have one or none.

jellying agent *See* thickening agent.

jelly pie *See* grape pie.

jelly roll cake A thin sheet of sponge cake spread with jam, jelly or other fillings, then rolled up; the cake is cut crosswise into pinwheel slices.

jelly roll pan A rectangular baking sheet with 1-in.-deep sides; used for baking a thin cake.

jengibre (hen-hee-bray) Spanish for ginger.

Jenny Lind A French consommé made from game and garnished with strips of quail and mushrooms.

jelly roll pan

Jerez de la Frontera (heh-RETH duh lah fron-TEH-rah) The southern Spanish city considered the birthplace of sherry.

Jerez-Xérès-Scherris (heh-RETH-seh-REHS-shear-ris) Spain's delimited sherry-producing district, located in Spain's Andalusia region.

jerk *v.* 1. To cut meat into long strips and preserve them by sun-drying, oven-drying or smoke curing. 2. To make and serve ice cream and related products at a soda fountain. *n.* A Jamaican preparation method in which meats and poultry are marinated in herbs and spices, then cooked over a pimento (allspice) wood fire; commercial blends of jerk spices are available.

jerk wine An inexpensive and seldom-produced wine made by adding water to the pressed grape remains to extract additional juice, which is then fermented.

jerky Thin strips of meat, usually beef or turkey, dried in the sun or an oven; they typically have a salty flavor and a tough, chewy texture.

Jeroboam (jer-rue-BOW-uhm) 1. An oversized sparkling wine or still wine bottle holding four 750-ml bottles or 3 l (approximately 101 fl. oz.). *See* double magnum. 2. An oversized bottle used for Bordeaux wines; it holds 4.5 l or six 750-ml bottles (approximately 150 fl. oz.).

Jersey shallot A particularly flavorful variety of shallot; it has a spherical bulb.

Jerusalem artichoke Not related to the artichoke, this member of the sunflower family (*Helianthus tuberosus*) has a lumpy, multipronged, brown-skinned tuber that has a crunchy texture and a nutty, sweet flavor; it can be eaten raw, cooked or pickled; also known as a girasol and sunchoke.

jesiotr (yeh-syo-tr) Polish for sturgeon.

Jester An English dessert apple.

Jesuit cress *See* capuchin.

jets de houblons (zjah du'bl-owng) A French dish consisting of the top shoots and flowers of the hop plant.

Jewel raspberry A raspberry variety; the fruit are purplish-black and intensely flavored.

jewfish *See* giant sea bass.

Jewish filet; Jewish daube A fabricated cut of the beef primal chuck; it is a center-cut chuck roast that is flavorful but tough.

Jewish ravioli *See* kreplach.

Jewish tender *See* chuck tender.

Jew plum Jamaican for ambarella.

Jew's ear mushroom *See* cloud ear mushroom.

Jew's mallow *See* molokhia.

jhannaa (zhan-naa) A long-handled spoon with a perforated bowl used in India for forming batter into droplets over hot oil or boiling liquids.

jheenga; jhneengari (JEEN-gah; JEEN-ga-ree) Hindi for shrimp or prawn; also known as yerra.

jhol (j'hool) Hindi for curry.

ji (jee) Chinese for chicken.

jian (jee-ahn) Chinese for pan-frying marinated foods (sometimes coated in a batter or flour) over low heat.

jian dui (jee-ahn doo-ee) Chinese for deep-fried rice flour balls stuffed with sweet bean paste.

jiang (gee-hang) Chinese for gingerroot.

jiang yu (gee-hang ee-ou) Chinese for soy sauce.

jiaozi (gee-ah-oh-zee) Chinese for dumpling.

jibini (gee-be-nee) Swahili for cheese.

jibnah (jib-nah) Arabic for cheese.

jibnah makliya (jib-nah mah-kley-yah) A Middle Eastern meza of fried cheese garnished with olives.

jicama (HEE-kah-mah) A legume that grows underground as a tuber; this large, bulbous root vegetable has a brown skin, a white flesh, a crisp, crunchy texture, and a sweet, nutty flavor; peeled, it is eaten raw or cooked; also known as ahipa, Mexican potato and yam bean.

jidàn (gee-dahn) Chinese for egg.

jido denshi hon-gama (jee-doh DEHN-shee HOHN-goh-mah) Japanese for automatic rice cooker.

jièmo (gee-ah-moe) Chinese for mustard.

jien dui (gee-ahn doo-ee) A Chinese dim sum; it is a chewy, sweet sesame seed ball filled with red bean paste.

jiffy A fabricated cut of the beef primal flank; it is a thinly cut and/or cubed steak.

jigger 1. A standard 1.5-fl. oz. measure used for mixed drink recipes, usually for the amount of liquor; also known as a shot. 2. The glass, metal, plastic or ceramic vessel used to measure this amount. 3. A whiskey glass of this size.

jiko la kuokea (gee-koe law kwo-ka-ah) Swahili for oven.

jikoni (gee-koe-nee) Swahili for kitchen.

Jim Beam Distillery One of the 12 remaining U.S. whiskey distilleries; located in Clermont and Boston, Kentucky, its founding is traced to Jacob Beam, who began selling his Kentucky whiskey in 1795; its products include rye whiskeys and Old Taylor, Old Crow, Old Grand-Dad, Knob Creek, Baker's and Booker's bourbons.

jimmies Tiny chocolate or sugar candies sprinkled on desserts, ice cream or confections. *See* hundreds and thousands.

jin zhen (gin zen) Chinese for tiger lily buds.

jira The small seed from a sweet herb; it has a spicy flavor and is used in West Indies cuisine.

jirad *See* locust.

jira pani (jee-raa paa-nee) A tart, cumin-flavored beverage served in northern India; also known as cumin water.

jiru (GEE-roo) Japanese for soup.

ji tang (gee tang) Chinese for chicken soup.

jitomate (heh-toh-mah-te) Spanish (particularly in Mexico) for tomato.

jiu cai (gee-oo cah-ee) Chinese for chives.

jiujing (gee-ou-gee-ng) Chinese for alcohol.

jizar (jah-zahr) Arabic for carrot.

joban (jehb-nahn) Arabic for cheese.

job description; job specification A detailed summary of what a particular job entails, including the tasks that must be performed, when they must be performed and sometimes how they are to be performed.

jobfish *See* uku.

job rotation The practice of training employees for more than one job so that they can be shifted as needed; also known as cross-training.

Job's tear A plant (*Coix lacryma-Job*) native to India and similar to wild corn; it has small edible seeds (kernels) covered in a tough, inedible envelope.

Jochberg A cheese made in Austria's Tyrol region from a mixture of cow's and goat's milks; sold in very large rounds.

jockey box An underbar cooling system for draft beer.

Joe's special A popular breakfast or brunch dish from San Francisco; it consists of eggs scrambled with cooked, crumbled ground beef, onions, garlic, mushrooms and spinach.

Joghurt (YOA-goort) German for yogurt.

jogurt (yoh-guert) Serbo-Croat for yogurt.

Johannisberger *See* Sylvaner.

Johannisberg Riesling (yoh-HAHN-ihss-berk reece-ling) 1. The true Riesling wine grape grown in Germany; the name is used in California to distinguish this grape from other varieties that are not true Rieslings; also known as White Riesling (especially in Oregon and other states). 2. A white wine made from this grape; generally fruity, it can range from light and crisp to full bodied and rich.

John Collins *See* Collins.

John Dory A saltwater fish found off Europe; it has a distinctive round black spot outlined in yellow on each side of its body, a firm, flaky white flesh, and a delicate, mild flavor; also known as St. Peter's fish.

johnnycake 1. A griddle cake made of cornmeal, salt and boiling water or cold milk; also known as a hoecake. 2. A Caribbean breakfast food made from flour, water, salt and baking powder, shaped into balls and fried.

John Dory

johore jack A variety of small, particularly sweet, jackfruit.

join To make a seam, as in pinching dough together.

joint *v.* To sever a piece of meat at the joint; also disjoint. *n.* 1. In Great Britain, a large piece of meat for roasting. 2. Anatomically, the fixed or movable place or part where two bones or elements of a skeleton join.

Joinville, sauce (zhwen-veel) A French compound sauce made from a Normandy sauce with a coulis of crayfish, shrimps and sometimes truffles; served with fish, especially sole.

Jolie-fille, sauce (zhow-lee-fill) A French compound sauce made from a suprême garnished with hard-boiled egg yolks and parsley.

jollof rice A West African dish made of rice garnished with meat, poultry or fish.

Jonagold A large apple that is a hybrid of Jonathan and Golden Delicious; it is yellow with a red blush and a tart–sweet flavor.

Jonathan apple An all-purpose apple native to North America with a bright red skin, a tender flesh and a sweet–tart flavor.

Jonchée (gion-key) A group of fresh French cheeses sold in woven baskets; the cheeses are generally made of ewe's milk (particularly in Brittany and are infused with laurel) or goat's milk (in regions south of Brittany).

Jordan almond A large, plump almond sold plain or coated with a hard pastel candy coating.

jordbær (YOOR-baer) Norwegian for strawberry.

jordgubbar (YOORD-gew-ber) Swedish for strawberry.

jordnøtt (yord-not) Norwegian for peanut.

Joséphine de Malines (joe-sah-feen-yay duh mah-lee-nay) A pear grown in Belgium; it has a pink flesh and an aroma reminiscent of a hyacinth.

joshinko (jo-shee-nn-ko) A fine, white rice flour used for making taffylike Japanese sweets.

Josta currants A variety of large black currants.

josta fruit A hybrid of black currants and gooseberries.

jota (YOH-tah) An Italian soup made with polenta, beans, onions, fermented turnips, sage and cabbage.

joule A unit of work or energy used in the metric system instead of calories; 1 Calorie (kilocalorie) equals 4185.5 joules; 1 calorie equals 4.1855 joules.

joululimppu (you-loo-lim-poo) A Finnish Christmas bread made with a rye flour and potato yeast dough and flavored with molasses, aniseeds and currants.

joven abocado Labeling term used to indicate a gold tequila that has been briefly aged in barrels, sweetened and colored with caramel.

jowl bacon *See* hog jowl.

jowls *See* cheeks.

Juan-Les-Pins (joo-ahn-lay-pen) A cocktail made of gin, Dubonnet blanc, apricot brandy and lemon juice; garnished with a maraschino cherry.

ju-bako (joo-bah-koh) A Japanese box used for serving food.

Judasohr (jeu-dah-sore) German for cloud ear mushroom.

Judge Jr. A cocktail made of gin, light rum, lemon juice and grenadine.

judia (who-dee-ahn) Spanish for kidney bean.

jug 1. A large deep vessel with a handle and a narrow mouth and spout; used to hold liquids. 2. A small pitcher used for serving foods at the table (e.g., cream jug).

jugged A stew made from game, especially hare, cooked in a deep stoneware jug or casserole; sometimes some of the animal's blood is added to the cooking liquid.

jugo (KHOO-goa) Spanish for juice.

jugo de naranja (KHOO-goa da nah-ran-hah) Spanish for orange juice.

jug wine A wine, usually an inexpensive table wine of no particular character, sold in a large bottle such as a magnum or Jeroboam.

juice *v.* To extract the juice of a fruit or vegetable. *n.* 1. The liquid released or squeezed from any raw food, whether animal or vegetable, but particularly fruit. 2. The blood and other liquids that run from meat or poultry during cooking. 3. The liquid surrounding the flesh of certain shellfish, such as an oyster, when first opened; also known as liquor.

juice bar 1. An establishment that serves fruit and vegetable juices as well as foods believed to be particularly healthful. 2. A bar that serves only juice and other nonalcoholic beverages; it generally caters to teenagers.

juice box *See* drink box.

juice glass A short cylindrical glass ranging in size from 5 to 7 fl. oz.; used for juice, cocktails or sours with frothy heads; also known as a Delmonico glass.

juicer An electric or manual device used to extract juice from certain fruits and vegetables; a half fruit is placed onto its ridged cone and pressure is applied. *See* reamer.

juicer

jujube *See* Chinese date.

jujubes (JOO-joo-bees) Small fruit-flavored candies with a chewy, gelatinous texture; also known as gummi candies.

juku shta (jew-koo sh'tah) Japanese for ripe.

Julep 1. A cocktail made from gin, rum or a distilled spirit and sometimes flavored with citrus juice. 2. A cocktail made from bourbon, sugar and mint served with finely crushed ice; also known as a Mint Julep.

Jules Verne, à la A French garnish for meat consisting of potatoes and turnips filled with any of a variety of stuffings and then braised with mushrooms in butter.

Juliana tart A round, shallow French pastry made with a sweet dough topped with apricot marmalade or raspberry jam and almond paste or frangipane; the top is decorated with a lattice of puff pastry.

Julie mango A variety of particularly flavorful mango grown in India.

julienne (ju-lee-en) *v.* To cut a food into a julienne shape. *n.* 1. Foods cut into a matchstick shape of approximately 1/8 × 1/8 × 1/2 in. (0.3 × 0.3 × 2.5–5 cm). 2. A garnish of foods cut in such a shape.

jumble A colonial American cookie; it is a delicate, crisp, ring-shaped sugar cookie made with sour cream and flavored with rosewater.

jumbo A marketing term for a lobster weighing more than 2 1/2 lb. (1.2 kg). *See* chicken lobster, deuce, heavy chicken, heavy select, quarter, select *and* small jumbo.

Juneberry *See* shad bush.

junges Lamm (jun-guess lahm) German for young lamb.

jung-jong (jeong-jong) A clear, potent, sakelike beverage brewed in Korea from fermented rice.

juniper berry oil A food additive derived from juniper berries; it has a bitter flavor and a strong, piney aroma and is used as a flavoring agent.

juniper berry The dried, aromatic, blue-black berry of an evergreen bush (*Juniperus communis*); used to flavor gin and savory dishes (especially ones with game); also known as a box huckleberry.

Jun Jing (june geeng) Chinese for dragon well and used to describe a very fine green tea from Chinkiang province; the beverage is lightly colored and freshly flavored.

junket A type of British pudding made with milk, sugar and flavorings and set with rennet; it has a soft texture and is usually served well chilled with fresh fruit.

junk food A term applied imprecisely to foods such as processed snack foods and fast foods believed to be lacking in substantial nutritional value or to contain high amounts of fat, sugar and/or salt.

junzabeel (jen-zah-beel) Arabic for ginger.

Jupiter A cocktail made of gin, French vermouth, orange juice and Parfait Amour.

Juplier The proprietary name of a Belgian bottom-fermented blond beer with a slightly bitter, dry flavor.

Jura (joo-rah) A grape-growing and wine-producing region in eastern France near the Swiss border; known for vin jaune.

Jurade de Saint-Émilion (joo-rahd san't eh-mee-l'yon) A French fraternal organization formed in 1948 to celebrate and promote the wines of the Saint-Émilion district of Bordeaux.

jus (zhoo) 1. French for juice. 2. *See* au jus.

juse *See* frutsu jus.

jus lié (zhoo lee-ay) A sauce made by thickening brown stock with cornstarch or similar starch and often used like a demi-glaze, especially to produce small sauces; also known as fond lié.

Jutland Blue *See* Danablu.

juusto (YOOS-toa) Finnish for cheese.

juwar *See* sorghum.

jydske terninger (yewd-sheh tarn-ing-ar) A baked Danish sandwich made from short pastry filled with a thick mixture of chopped pork, onions and potatoes flavored with grated lemon peel and parsley and moistened with a gravy or white sauce.

kaa (kah) Swahili for crab.

kaag-pénch (koh-hag-pan-ch) Hindi for corkscrew.

kaak (kack) 1. A Middle Eastern bread baked to a crunchy hardness and flavored with mahleb and coated with sesame seeds; it is dunked in tea or milk and eaten for breakfast. 2. A Lebanese pastry of yeast-risen dough rolled into ropes, formed into rings, and baked; it is then dipped into a glaze of milk and sugar and often topped with sesame seeds. 3. *See* kaick.

kaaki (cah-key) A Tunisian pretzel-like street food.

kaali (KAA-li) Finnish for cabbage.

kaas (kahs) Dutch for cheese.

kaasdoop (KAHS-doop) A Dutch Gouda cheese fondue served with roasted or boiled potatoes.

kaatna (kah-at-nah) Hindi for to slice.

kaawi A variety of yam.

kabak (kay-bak) Turkish for zucchini.

kabanos (kah-bah-nos) A very thin Polish dried pork sausage.

kabayaki (KAH-bah-YAH-kee) Japanese for grilled eel.

kab el ghal (cab il gahl) A Moroccan crescent-shaped pastry made of sweet dough filled with a mixture of almonds, sugar and orange flower water; usually served with mint tea.

Kabeljau (kah-bell-jah-oo) German for cod.

Kabinett (kah-bee-NET) German wine-labeling term for dry wines with a relatively low alcohol content made from fully ripened grapes fermented without added sugar. *See* Qualitätswein mit Prädikat.

kabob *See* kebab.

kabob meat *See* brochette meat.

kabocha (kah-BOH-chah) 1. A medium to large winter squash; it has a dark green shell with lighter green streaks, a smooth, tender orange flesh, and a sweet flavor. 2. Japanese for pumpkin.

kabu (kah-buh) Japanese for turnip.

kabuli-channa (kaa-bu-lee-cha-naa) Hindi for yellow or creamy-colored chickpeas; they have a nutty flavor and hard texture.

kaccavia; kakavia (kah-kah-vhia) A Greek soup consisting of fish and/or shellfish simmered in a broth.

kacha (kah-tcha) Hindi for raw.

Kachkaval (koh-cha-kah-val) A hard cheese made in Hungary and the Balkan states from ewe's milk; it has a white to pale yellow interior, a salty flavor, and a pronounced aroma.

kaczka (kah-ch-kah) Polish for duck.

kadaifa *See* knafa.

Kadarka (CA-dar-ca) 1. A red wine grape grown in Hungary. 2. The wine made from this grape; it has a deep color, a full body and high tannin level.

kadayif (kah-dah-eef) 1. Thin pastalike strands of a Middle Eastern dough made with flour and water. 2. A pastry made with buttered layers of this dough filled with either chopped nuts or a creamy rice pudding and topped with a sweet syrup.

kaddoo (kahd-do) Hindi for pumpkin.

kadhai (kah-dah-ee) An Indian cooking utensil similar to a Chinese wok; it is used for frying food. *See* karahi.

kadhi (kah-dee) Indian dumplings made with chickpea flour and simmered in yogurt with spices and vegetables.

kadin budu (kah-dean boo-doo) A Turkish dish of beef and rice patties flavored with parsley, boiled, chilled, and then dipped in egg and fried.

kadin göbegi (kah-dean go-ba-gee) Turkish fritters made from a sweet pastry dough flavored with almond extract and rolled into balls with indented centers, then deep-fried, soaked in sugar syrup flavored with lemon, and served with whipped cream piped into the indentations.

Kadmon An Israeli Madeira-type wine that has a sweet flavor and amber color.

kadota fig A small, thick-skinned fig with a yellow-green skin.

kaernemaelk (KAYHR-nah-MEYLK) Danish for buttermilk.

kafé (kah-fay) Russian for coffee.

kafei (kay-fay) Chinese for cafe.

kafeiguanr (kah-fay-goo-ahn) Chinese for cafe.

kaffe (KAH-fay) Swedish and Norwegian for coffee.

Kaffee (kah-FAY) German for coffee.

kaffeeklatsch (kay-FAY-klah-ch) *See* coffee klatch.

Kaffeekuchen (kah-FAY-KOO-khern) German for coffee cake.

Kaffee mit Milch (kah-fay meet meelk) German for coffee with milch.

kaffe med melk (KAH-fay med melk) Norwegian for coffee with milk.

kaffir; kaffir corn; kafir; kafir corn A variety of African sorghum (*Sorghum bicolor*) grown in the American Midwest as a cereal grain and forage.

kaffir lime A citrus fruit (*Citrus hystrix*); the medium-sized fruit has a knobby dark green skin; the leaves look like a figure eight, with two leaves joined together base to tip; the sharply aromatic, citrus-flavored leaves and the fruit's rind are used as flavorings in Thai cuisine, and the leaves are used in Indonesian cuisine.

kafi (kah-fee) Hindi for cafe (restaurant).

kafir (kah-fir) 1. A fermented Middle Eastern beverage made with camel's milk and flavored with spices. 2. A small limelike citrus fruit; it is used dried as a flavoring in North African cuisines.

kager (KAA-err) Danish for pastry.

kagitta levrek (ka-ghe-tah lah-vrack) A Turkish dish of sea bass baked in paper with a sauce of onions, butter, tomatoes, cumin, cloves, bay leaf and mastic.

kahawa (kah-ha-wah) Swahili for coffee.

kahawa yenye maziwa (kah-ha-wah jan-ja mah-zee-wah) Swahili for coffee with milk.

kahfe (kah-fee) Hindi for coffee.

kahfe dudhke saath (kah-fee du-de-ka sa'w-at) Hindi for coffee with milk.

kahjur (kah-jour) Hindi for dates.

Kahlúa (kah-LOO-ah) A dark brown, coffee-flavored Mexican liqueur.

kai (phai) Thai for egg.

kai (kah-he) Japanese for shellfish.

kaick (kah'ck) 1. A Middle Eastern bread flavored with anise; often served as a snack with a sweet syrup flavored with orange blossom water. 2. *See* kaak.

kailkenny The Scottish version of colcannon.

kaïmaki (kai-mah-kee) A very thick, somewhat hard Greek cream or cream cheese–like dairy product; eaten fresh or used in cooking.

kai ruanmusai de jiuqizi (kah-ee roo-ahn-moo-sah-ee de jew-key-zee) Chinese for corkscrew.

kaiseki (kah-ee-SEH-kee) An elegant Japanese formal dinner.

kaiseki ryori (kah-ee-SEH-kee ryoh-ree) A formal Japanese meal consisting of a series of small, seasonal dishes.

Kaiserfleisch (KIGH-zerr-flighsh) An Austrian dish consisting of a rack of smoked pickled pork, boiled and served with sauerkraut and dumplings made with white bread or a purée of green split peas.

kaiser roll A large, round yeast roll with a crisp crust, used for making sandwiches or served as a breakfast roll; also known as a hard roll or Vienna roll.

kaiware The sprouts of a daikon radish; they are slender and have a silky texture, a white base that becomes greener toward the top, and a spicy flavor; used in Asian cuisines.

kaiwari daikon Japanese for daikon sprouts.

kaiwarina Sushi made with sprouts (e.g., daikon sprouts).

kajiki (KAH-jee-kee) A fish related to the Pacific blue marlin and found off Hawaii; it has a rough gray skin, a lean, amber-colored flesh that whitens when cooked, and a market weight of 80–300 lb. (36–135 kg).

Kajmak (KA-ee-muk) A Serbian cream cheese made from ewe's milk; it has a white or ivory color and a mild flavor when fresh that sharpens as it ages; also known as Serbian butter.

kajoo (kah-joo) Hindi for cashew nut.

kaka (KAA-kah) Swedish for cake.

kakavia (kah-kah-ve-ah) A Greek fish soup with tomatoes, carrots and potatoes and flavored with celery tops, bay leaves, dill and parsley.

kake (kah-ka) Norwegian for cake.

kaki (KAH-kee) Japanese for oyster.

kaki (kah-KEE) 1. Japanese for persimmon. 2. *See* persimmon.

kål (kawl) Norwegian for cabbage.

kala (KAH-laa) Finnish for fish.

kalafjory (kah-lah-fyo-ri) Polish for cauliflower.

kala jiri (kah-lah jee-ree) Hindi for black cumin but also used for nigella.

kalakukko (kah-lah-koo-koe) A Finnish dish consisting of fish and meat encased in pastry; a common example is a whole perch wrapped in fatty pork, flavored with dill, and enclosed in a rye flour pastry dough; it is then baked and eaten hot or cold with butter.

kalamansi (ka-la-man-see) A small, round lemon native to the Philippines, with a bright green skin, yellow flesh, and sour flavor; the juice is used in beverages, and the rind is candied and used as a garnish for desserts.

kalamansi calamondin *See* musk-lime.

kalamar (kah-lah-mahr) Turkish for cuttlefish.

kalamaria (kah-lah-mah-rhia) Greek for squid.

kalamata; calamata (kahl-uh-MAH-tuh) A large blue-black olive native to Greece; usually packed in olive oil or vinegar and slit to better absorb the marinade.

kala namak (kah-lah nah-maak) Hindi for black salt.

kalarepka (kah-lah-reh-pkah) Polish for kohlrabi.

Kalb (kahlp) German for veal.

Kalbsbraten (kahlp-braa-tern) German for roasted veal.

Kalbsbrust (KAHLP-brust) German for breast of veal.

Kalbsschnitzel (KAHLP-shnit-serl) German for a thin veal cutlet sautéed in butter.

kaldou (kall-doo) A Senegalese fish stew seasoned with onions, chiles, and lemon juice and served over rice.

kaldt (kahl) Norwegian for cold.

kale A member of the cabbage family (var. *acephala*) with curly leaves arranged in a loose bunch; the leaf colors, which depend on the variety, range from pale to deep green tinged with lavender, blue or purple to white shaded with pink, purple or green; although all are edible, the green varieties are better for cooking, and the more colorful varieties are better used for garnish.

kale, ornamental The more colorful varieties of kale that are used principally for garnish and decoration; also known as flowering kale and savoy.

kaléje (ka-le-jee) Hindi for liver.

kali mirch (ka-lee mirch) Hindi for black pepper.

kalk (kahlk) Swedish and Norwegian for lime.

kalkan (kahl-kahn) Turkish for turbot.

kalkoen (kal-KOON) Dutch for turkey.

kalkon (kal-KOONN) Swedish for turkey.

kalkun (kall-koon) Norwegian for turkey.

kallun (kall-oon) Danish for tripe.

kalt (kehlt) German for cold.

Kaltschale (KAHLT-shaaler) A German cold soup made from fruits and their juices and served for dessert.

kalvekjott (kall-ve-shut) Norwegian for veal.

kalvekod (kall-ve-shud) Danish for veal.

kalvkottlett (KALV-kot-LAHT) Swedish for veal cutlet.

kamaboko (KAH-mah-bow-ko) A firm, slightly rubbery cake or sausage of ground fish used as an ingredient in Japanese cuisine or served as is.

kamba (kahn-bah) Swahili for shrimp.

kamba mkubwa (kahm-bah koo-boo-ah) Swahili for lobster.

Kamchatka abalone A variety of abalone found along the Pacific Coast from California to southern Alaska and off Japan; it has a small oval shell and an ivory flesh with a chewy texture and mild flavor; also known as Japanese abalone.

kami-jio (kah-meh-gee-oh) A Japanese salting technique for sushi or sashimi; the fish is sandwiched between paper, with salt placed on top of and beneath the paper; the salt is drawn through the paper.

Kamikaze A cocktail made of citrus juices, vodka and Cointreau, garnished with a mint sprig.

kamin (kha-meen) Thai for turmeric.

kaminari (KAH-mee-NAH-ree) Japanese for lightning and used to describe a fancy curlicue cut for food.

kamoun (kah-moon) Arabic for cumin seed.

kampyo (kahm-pee-oh) Dried squash cubes used as a flavoring for Japanese soups.

kampyo-maki (kahm-pee-oh mah-key) A nori-maki made with kampyo.

kamut (kah-MOOT) A natural variety of high-protein wheat with very large kernels that have a nutty flavor; generally available only in processed foods (e.g., pasta and crackers).

kanafa (kah-naw-faw) A Middle Eastern sweet dough similar to a finely shredded phyllo and used for a pastry of the same name; the pastry can be filled with a thickened cream, nuts or cheese.

kanaka A metal (usually brass or silver) Egyptian coffeepot.

Kandeel A rich beverage similar to eggnog but made with wine instead of distilled spirits.

Kandy A black tea from Sri Lanka's Kandy region; the beverage is full bodied, with a strong flavor.

kanel (kah-NAYL) Norwegian for cinnamon.

kangkong (kung-kong) A plant native to the Philippines; its smooth green leaves have a mild, spinachlike flavor and a tender texture.

kani (KAH-nee) Japanese for crab.

kanin (kah-NEEN) Norwegian for rabbit.

Kaninchen (kah-NEEN-khern) German for rabbit.

kanom (kah-nom) Thai for cake or cookie.

kanom bang (kah-nom bahng) Thai for bread.

kanom mo kaeng (kah-nom moe kah-hang) Thai custard squares flavored with coconut and brown sugar that are baked, browned under the broiler, and topped with sautéed shallots.

Kansas City broil A fabricated cut of the beef primal chuck; it is a bone-in or boneless center-cut steak.

Kansas City steak A fabricated cut of the beef primal short loin; it is a well-trimmed porterhouse or T-bone steak.

Kansas City strip steak *See* strip loin steak.

kanta (kah-tah) Hindi for fork.

kanten (KAHN-tain) *See* agar-agar.

kantola A small squash with a bright green shell, a slightly sweet flesh, and edible seeds used in Indian, Chinese and Southeast Asian cuisines.

kao (kah-oh) Chinese for to roast.

kaoliang (kah-ho-lee-hang) 1. A Chinese grain similar to sorghum. 2. A clear, high-alcohol-content Chinese spirit distilled from that grain.

kao mao (ka-oh me-o) A Thai rice harvested when still slightly immature; with its husk intact, it is flattened and roasted and often used as a coating for fried foods.

kaong (ka'hong) *See* palm nut.

kaoxiang (kah-ho-shang) Chinese for oven.

kapakoti (kaa-paa-koo-tee) Greek for pot-roasting.

kapartsy (khah-parr't-sya) Russian for capers.

Kapaun (kah-POWN) German for capon.

Kaper (kah-perr) German for caper.

kapee (kah-pee-e) A sun-dried mixture of shrimp and salt used as a sauce in Thai cuisine.

kapers (KAH-pehrs) Danish and Norwegian for capers.

kapi (kah-pe) A fermented fish or shrimp paste used as a seasoning in Thai cuisine.

kapi leaw (ka-pe le-aw) *See* heiko.

kaplon (kah-pee-lon) Polish for capon.

kapostu (kah-poz-too) Latvian for cabbage.

káposzta (KAA-paw-sto) Hungarian for cabbage.

kappa maki (kah-pah mah-key) Japanese sushi (vinegared rice) filled with cucumber and rolled in seaweed.

kapr (kah'pr) Czech for carp.

kapusta (kah-POOS-tah) Russian and Polish for cabbage.

kapustnie kotlety (ka-poost-nee-a koe-tla-tea) A Russian dish known as cabbage cutlets; the cabbage is cut into quarters, boiled, dipped in egg and bread crumbs, and baked; served with sour cream and chopped parsley.

Kapuziner (kah-poo-tzee-nar) German for monk and used to describe a Viennese coffee served with lots of milk.

kara-age (kah-rah-ah-gue) A Japanese preparation method in which foods are dusted with flour and then deep-fried.

karahi (ka-ra-he) A heavy iron or brass pan used in India for deep-frying; similar to a Chinese wok, only deeper and with a thick, looped metal handle on each side. *See* kadhai.

karai (kah-RAH-ee) Japanese for spicy and salty.

karakot (kah-raw-kott) An Uzbek confection of stewed fruit mixed with sugar, ground almonds and vanilla, thickened with egg yolks and stiffly beaten egg whites, and baked; it is traditionally served sliced with lemon tea.

karanda A fruit from a low, thorny bush native to southern Asia (*Carissa congesta*); the small spherical fruit has a scarlet skin with dark red streaks, a white-flecked red flesh, thin brown seeds, a granular texture, and a slightly sharp, acidic flavor.

karaoloi (kaa-rah-oo-lee) Greek for snails.

karashi (kah-RAH-shee) A very strong dry Japanese mustard.

karaya gum A food additive derived from trees of the genus *Sterculia* and used as an emulsifier, stabilizer, thickener and/or formulation aid in processed foods such as candies and dairy products; also known as sterculia gum.

karczochy (kar-choh-hi) Polish for globe artichoke.

kare (KAH-ree) Japanese for curry.

karee (kah-ree) Thai for curry.

Kareish (kar-eish) An Egyptian Damietta-style cheese made from water buffalo's milk or skimmed cow's milk and aged in brine; it has a white color, no eyes and a mild, salty flavor when fresh that becomes more acidic as it ages.

kare-kare; kari kari (ka-re-ka-re) A Filipino stew made with oxtail, beef or tripe, eggplant, banana buds and other vegetables cooked in peanut sauce and thickened with ground toasted rice.

karela (kah-ra-law) A large, cylindrical melon with a bitter flavor; the Thai variety has a white skin and the Indian variety is darker.

kari (kah-ree) Russian for curry.

karides (kah-ri-dess) Turkish for shrimp.

karides güveci (kah-ri-dess goo-vah-tche) A Turkish hors d'oeuvre of shrimp cooked in a clay pot.

karidópita (kah-ree-doe-pee-tah) A Greek walnut cake soaked with brandy syrup.

karifurawa (KAH-ree-foo-RAH-wah) Japanese for cauliflower.

kari leaf The aromatic leaf of the kari plant; used in Indian cooking, especially in curries.

kari podi (kah-ree poe-dee) Hindi for curry powder.

karkadeh (kar-kah-da) An Egyptian beverage consisting of water flavored with roselle and sugar.

karmonadle (kar-moh-nah-dleh) A Polish dish of pork chops dipped in egg and bread crumbs and fried.

karnabahar köftesi (kar-nah-bah-har koff-ta-sea) A Turkish hors d'oeuvre of cauliflower fritters.

karni yarik (kar-nee yah-reek) A Turkish dish consisting of an eggplant stuffed with lamb, chopped eggplant and onions, covered with butter, and baked.

karnotzl (car-not'zil) A Romanian beef sausage flavored with garlic and either an herb and spice blend (allspice, thyme and cloves) or onions and paprika.

Karoo A grape-growing and wine-producing region of South Africa; this semiarid area is best known for its fortified wines, such as port and Muscatel, and for brandy; white wines made from the Chardonnay and Chenin Blanc grapes are also produced.

karoti (kah-row-tea) Swahili for carrot.

Karotten (kah-ROT-tern) German for carrots.

Karpfen (KAHR-pfern) German for carp.

karpouzi (car-poo-zee) Greek for watermelon.

karri (kah-ree) Norwegian for curry.

karringmelkbeskuit (kahr-ring-malk-bess-kwit) A very dry South African cookie used to dip in milk or coffee.

kartofel (kahr-TO-fyehl) Russian for potato.

Kartoffel (kahr-TOF-ferl) German for potato.

Kartoffelbrei (kahr-TOF-ferl-brigh) German mashed potatoes.

Kartoffelklösse (kahr-tof-fell-klos-say) German potato dumplings.

kartoffel knaidel (car-towf-fil knayd-dhul) A Jewish potato dumpling.

kartoffel kugel (car-towf-fil koo-gle) A potato kugel, usually flavored with onions.

Kartoffelpuffer (kahr-tof-fell-pooh-fair) German potato pancakes.

kartul (kar-tool) Estonian for potato.

karve (kahr-feh) Norwegian for caraway.

Kasar (ko-sar) A hard Turkish cheese made from ewe's milk; it has a smooth, dry rind, a dense white interior without eyes and a strong, pungent flavor.

Käse (kaiz) German for cheese.

Käseteller (kah-sell-tell-her) German for cheese plate.

Käsetorte (KAIZ-uh-tor-teh) German for cheesecake.

kasha (KAH-sha) The hulled, roasted buckwheat groat; it has a reddish-brown color with a strong, nutty, almost scorched flavor and a slightly sticky, chewy texture.

kashata na nazi (kah-shaw-tah nah nah-zee) A Ugandan candy of sugar, coconut and cinnamon cooked until firm and cut into squares; traditionally served as a snack.

kasha varnishkes (kah-sha var-nish-keys) A Jewish dish of kasha garnished with eggs noodles (in the United States, farfalle is used) and sautéed onions.

Kashkaval; Kachkaval; Katschkawalj (KASH-kah-vahl) A pasta filata cheese made in the Balkans from ewe's milk; it has a dry, supple rind, a white to ivory color and a salty flavor.

kashmiri masala (kash-mee-ree ma-saa-laa) A spice mixture consisting of cardamom, cumin seeds, peppercorns, cloves, cinnamon, nutmeg and mace; used in north Indian chicken and lamb dishes.

kashrus (kahsh-rut) *See* kosher.

Kaskawan (kass-kah-one) A Middle Eastern cow's milk cheese; it has a yellowish color, a firm texture and a sharp flavor.

Kasnudeln (kass-nood-lehn) A German dish consisting of noodles stuffed with a savory meat and cheese filling or a sweet filling of fruit and poppyseeds.

kasoori methi (kah-soo-ree mae-tee) Hindi for dry fenugreek leaves.

Kasseler Rippenspeer (kass-sah-laer ripp-ahn-speer) A German dish consisting of cured and smoked pork loin served on a bed of sauerkraut with mashed potatoes and apples or red cabbage and potato dumplings and a red wine–sour cream gravy.

Kasseri (kuh-SAIR-ee) A Greek cheese made from ewe's or goat's milk; it has a hard texture, a white interior and a salty flavor; grated or used for saganaki.

Kassier rib A fabricated cut of the pork primal loin; it is a smoked, bone-in loin.

kastana (kah-stah-nah) Greek for chestnuts.

Kastanie (kah-stan-ee) German for chestnut.

kasza (kah-shah) Polish for buckwheat.

kasztany (kash-tah-ni) Polish for chestnut.

kata doufu (kah-tah doo-foo) A firm, coarse type of tofu used in Chinese cuisines.

katafi *See* knafa.

kataifi (kah-tie-yeif-ee) *See* knafa.

katakuri (kah-tah-koo-ree) The roots of the dogtooth violet (*Erythronium dencanis*); they are dried and ground into a starch used as a thickener in Japanese cuisine.

katalu (gha-tah-lo) A Turkish dish of eggplants, green peppers, tomatoes, green beans and okra simmered in oil with garlic and parsley.

katch (kah-tch) Hindi for lamb.

katchupa *See* manchupa.

katei ryori (kah-te-e ree-yoh-ree) Japanese for home-style cooking.

Katenschinken (kah-ten-shen-kan) German for country smoked ham.

kati A traditional Chinese measurement of weight approximately 1 1/2 lb. (625 g), used today in vegetable markets.

katori (ka-to-ree) A small metal bowl used to hold liquid and semiliquid foods on a traditional Indian dinner plate. *See* thal.

katsikaki (kah-tsee-kaa-kee) Greek for kid.

katsu (KAH-tzu) Japanese for cutlet.

katsuo (kat-soo-oh) Japanese for bonito.

katsuobushi; katsuo-bushi (KAH-tzu-oh-boo-shi) Pink flakes of bonito tuna that are boiled, smoked and then sun-dried; used in Japanese cuisine as a garnish or in dashi.

katsura muki (KAH-tzu-rah moo-kee) Japanese for wide peel and used to describe a decorative cut for foods.

Katzenjammer (KAHT-sehn-jahmm-ehr) A German and Austrian dish consisting of thin slices of cold beef marinated in olive oil, vinegar and mustard, then mixed with mayonnaise, gherkins and potatoes; considered a cure for hangovers.

Katzenkopf *See* Edam.

ka'u orange A variety of orange grown in Hawaii; it has a brown skin, a juicy orange flesh and a sweet flavor.

kaura (kow-rah) Finnish for rolled oats.

kava A drink made in the South Sea Islands from the roots of a pepper plant (the roots are pounded, soaked in water, and strained); it has a peppery, soapy flavor and leaves the mouth and throat dry and numb.

kavurma *See* pilau.

kawaita (kah-WAH-ee-tah) Japanese for dry.

kayaku (KAH-yah-koo) Assorted foods used to garnish rice or noodles in Japan.

kaymak (ghay-mak) A very thick, dense cream made from water buffalo's milk and used in Turkish desserts and baked goods.

KBF asparagus A variety of particularly flavorful asparagus.

kcal; kcalorie *See* Calorie.

kebab; kabob (kah-BEHB; kuh-BOB) Minced meat or cubes of meat on a skewer, usually marinated before cooking and typically grilled. *See* shish kebab.

kebàp (kah-bap) Bulgarian for kebab.

kebeji (ka-ba-gee) Swahili for cabbage.

kebsa (kab-saw) A North African and Middle Eastern spice mixture, traditionally made with cardamom, cinnamon, cumin and red and black pepper.

kecap asin (ket-chup a-seen) A thick, salty, dark, soy-based sauce used in Indonesian cuisine for color and flavor.

kecap hitam (ket-chup he-tum) A sweet, dark soy sauce used in Malaysian cuisine as a seasoning and condiment.

kecap manis (ket-chup mah-nees) A dark, thick Indonesian soy sauce flavored with palm sugar, garlic, star anise and other spices.

kechapi *See* santol.

kedgeree; kegeree (kehj-uh-REE) 1. An Indian dish of rice, lentils and onions. 2. An English variation of the dish in which smoked fish, hard-boiled eggs and a cream sauce flavored with curry are added.

keema (kee-MAH) 1. Hindi for ground meat. 2. An east Indian gravy dish cooked with ground meat.

Keemum (key-moon) A black tea from China's Kiansi and Anwhei provinces; the beverage has a strong aroma and a rich, delicate flavor that is less astringent than most teas.

Keemun Hao Ya (key-moon ha-o eea) A black tea grown in China's Hao Ya mountains, a famous tea-growing region; the beverage is delicately flavored, with a slightly sweet aroma, and is sometimes used in blends such as English and Irish breakfast teas.

Kefalotiri (keh-fag-loo-tee-ree) A hard Greek cheese made from ewe's milk; it has a drab yellow interior, a tough rind, and a strong, sharp flavor; used for cooking.

kefir (ke-FEHR) *See* koumiss.

kefta (KEHF-tah) A central European dish consisting of patties of chopped beef, veal, poultry or game mixed with bacon and spices and sometimes bound with egg; the patties are floured and sautéed.

keftedes; keftethes; kephthethakia (kaf-ta-dess; kaf-ta-des; kaf-ta-tah-key-ya) Meatballs or rissoles popular throughout the Balkans and Middle East; made from meat, bread crumbs, onions, eggs and grated cheese and flavored with ouzo or lemon juice.

keg A metal, plastic or wooden container, usually used for beer, with a capacity of 15.5 U.S. gallons or half of a barrel; also known as a half barrel.

kejenou; kedjenou (kay-jay-nu) A stew from the Ivory Coast consisting of chicken or guinea hen, onions and tomatoes flavored with chiles, garlic, ginger and black pepper slowly cooked in a canari that has been sealed with a banana leaf; the dish is served with attiéké.

kék (kake) Hindi for cake.

kekada (ka-kah-dah) Hindi for crab.

keki (KEH-kee) Japanese and Swahili for cake.

keks (kaks) Russian for cake.

Keks (kaks) German for cookie or cracker.

kela (kah-lah) Hindi for banana.

Kellner (kell-nuhr) German for waiter.

Kellogg, John Harvey (Am., 1852–1943) While the superintendent of a sanatorium for dyspepsia (indigestion), he developed a precooked cereal product known as "granola." Later, he and his brother Will perfected a method of flaking, which they tried with wheat and then corn; cornflakes soon became the world's most well known breakfast cereal.

kelner Norwegian for waiter.

kelp Any large, brown to grayish-black seaweed of the family Laminariceae; often dried and used in Japanese and other Asian and Pacific Island cuisines.

kelsai onion A variety of very large (up to 6 lb.) onion.

kem (kam) Thai for salty.

Kent Goldings A variety of hops grown in England.

Kentish cob *See* filbert.

Kent oyster An Atlantic oyster found off Kent Island in the Chesapeake Bay; it has a 3-in. (7.6-cm) shell and a plump body.

Kentucky Cooler A cocktail made of bourbon, brandy, lemon juice, sugar syrup, club soda and Barbados rum; served in a chilled Collins glass with a float of rum.

Kentucky Hot Brown An open-face turkey sandwich covered with hot brown gravy and garnished with crisply fried bacon.

Kentucky jam cake A spice cake made with jam, usually blackberry, added to the batter and frosted with caramel icing; also known as a Tennessee jam cake.

Kentucky whiskey A bourbon-type whiskey distilled in Kentucky from corn and aged for at least 1 year in charred white oak barrels.

Kenyan 1. Arabica coffee beans grown in Kenya; the beverage is straightforward, with an appealing, rich flavor slightly reminiscent of black currants. 2. A black Kenyan tea; the beverage has a reddish color and a strong flavor.

keratin An extremely tough and water-insoluble protein found in hair, nails and horny tissues.

kermangi (kehr-mahn-gee) A type of basil native to Indonesia and Malaysia; it has a mild though distinctive flavor.

Kerman pistachios A variety of superior-quality pistachios.

kernel 1. The softer, usually edible part, contained within the shell of a nut or a stone of a fruit; also known as the meat. 2. The body of a seed within its husk or other outer covering. 3. A whole seed grain (e.g., wheat and corn).

kernel paste A mixture of ground apricot kernels and sugar used as a filling for baked goods.

kerry; kerrie (KEHR-ruh) Danish for curry and curry powder.

kervel (kerr-val) Dutch for chervil.

kesar (kah-sahr) Hindi for saffron; also known as zaffran.

kesong puti (ke-song poo-tee) A type of Filipino cottage cheese usually made in the home from water buffalo's milk.

keta salmon *See* chum salmon.

ketchup; catchup; catsup A spicy sauce or condiment; it is usually made with the juice of cooked fruits or vegetables such as tomatoes, walnuts and mangos as well as vinegar, sugar and spices; the name may be derived from the Chinese kê-tsiap, which means brine of pickled fish.

ketembilla A fruit (*Dovyalis hebecarpa*) native to Sri Lanka; it resembles a dark purple cherry covered with fine hairs, has an acidic flavor, and is used for making preserves; also known as a Ceylon gooseberry.

ketogenic diet A reduction diet high in proteins and low in carbohydrates; the diet causes the body to increase production of ketones, which can lead to ketosis and even death.

ketone; ketone body The substance resulting from the incomplete breakdown of fat for energy (fat is used when carbohydrates are unavailable).

ketosis The undesirable accumulation of ketones in the body; this increases the body's acidity, which causes headaches, nausea, fatigue and dizziness and increases the risk of cardiovascular disease; it can be fatal; ketosis is often the result of ketogenic or starvation diets.

kettle 1. A large metal pot with a lid and a wire loop handle, usually made of iron. 2. An imprecisely used term for a teakettle.

kettledrum The traditional British name for a large tea party.

Keule (coh-ee-lay) German for the leg of a carcass (e.g., leg of lamb).

kewra A flavoring extracted from the blossoms of a variety of screw pine (*Pandanus adoratissimus*); used in Indian and Sri Lankan sweet or rice dishes.

Key lime A small lime with a greenish-yellow skin and a very tart flavor; also known as the Mexican lime, West Indies lime and true lime.

Key lime pie A cream pie made with tart Key limes, usually in a graham cracker– or cookie-crumb crust and topped with whipped cream.

kg *See* kilogram.

kha (khaa) A large gingerroot native to Thailand; it has a whiter color than the common gingerroot; also known as galanga.

khaanaa (kahn-ah-ah) Hindi for eat or for food.

khachpuri (kahsh-poo-ree) Small cheese tarts sold by street vendors in the Republic of Georgia.

khadi (KA-dee) An alcoholic beverage made in Botswana from honey and berries; it is similar to mead.

khal (kal) A Nepalese stone mortar and pestle.

khamir (kha-meer) A natural yeast ferment (starter) made from flour and yogurt, used in India for leavening naans and various other soft breads.

khanom (khaa-nom) Thai liquid desserts, puddings and sweetmeats served throughout the day.

khanom chine (khaa-nom jeen) Thai bite-sized cooked rice noodles usually served with currylike dishes and spicy sauces.

khansama (kahn-SAH-ma) Hindi for cook or chef.

khao (ka-oo) Thai for rice.

khao chae (ka-oo chae) A Thai method of serving rice in ice water.

khao neow (ka-oo na-how) A high-gluten rice from Thailand; it is usually soaked and steamed.

khao niew (ka-oo nee-a-who) Thai for sticky rice.

khao pad (ka-oo pah'd) Thai for fried rice.

khao phoune (ka-oo poon) A Laotian breakfast dish consisting of rice vermicelli in a thick, creamy sauce of coconut milk with meat or fish.

khao pohd (ka-oo pohd) Thai for sweet corn.

khao soi (ka-oo soy) A northern Thai noodle dish in a creamy, soupy yellow curry, served with many condiments on the side.

khara (kah-rah) Hindi for plain (unelaborate) and used to describe a food made with few if any spices.

kharbuja (kahr-boo-jah) Hindi for melon.

khar-gosh Hindi for rabbit.

kharjoor (kha-joor) Hindi for dates.

kharoof mishshee (khar-oof mih'sh-shee) A Middle Eastern dish of roasted spring lamb stuffed with ground lamb, pine nuts and rice flavored with allspice and cinnamon.

khas-khas (kahs-kahs) Hindi for white poppy seeds.

khatte (kaht-tah) Hindi for sour.

khchaf (ch'chaff) An Algerian beverage flavored with sugar, raisins and cinnamon.

kheer (keer) Hindi for pudding, especially rice pudding.

kheera (kee-rah) Hindi for cucumber.

khleb (KHLYEH-b) Russian for bread.

khlebnie kroshki (khlyeh-b-nee-a krow-skee) Russian for bread crumbs.

khligh (klee-geh) A Moroccan Jewish dish consisting of braised beef shanks flavored with olive oil, parsley and salt.

khlodnik; kholodets (klod-neek; koe-low-dets) Any Russian cold soup.

khobaz; khoubz (khoh-bahz) 1. A soft, yeast-leavened Middle Eastern bread; small and round or oval, it puffs up while baking, forming a pocket convenient for holding other foods; imprecisely known as pita. 2. An inprecisely used term for any Middle Eastern bread.

khobaz arabee (khoh-bahz air-ra-bee) A thin, flat, round Middle Eastern wheat bread; before serving, the hard, brittle bread is often soaked in water and pieces are torn off by hand and used to wrap bits of food; also known as marquq.

khobaz smeek (khoh-bahz smeek) A yeast-leavened Middle Eastern bread baked in a skillet.

kholodnye (koh-loh-dn'yah) Russian for cold.

khoob (coob) A large melon grown in Iran; it has a netted orange skin, an orange flesh, and an aroma and flavor reminiscent of pineapple.

khourabia An Armenian crescent-shaped shortbread, sometimes made with ground walnuts, cinnamon and sugar.

khoya (koh-ee-ah) Hindi for milk cooked down to fudgelike consistency.

khren (kran) Russian for horseradish.

khumee (koom-ee) Hindi for mushrooms.

khuthra (khue't-drah) Arabic for vegetables.

khyaar; khyar (khi-yar) Arabic for cucumbers.

khyar ma'laban (key-yarr ma'lah-ben) A Middle Eastern salad of cucumbers and yogurt flavored with mint.

kibbeh; kibbi; kibbe (KIHB-beh; KIHB-bee) A Middle Eastern dish of ground meat (usually lamb) with bulgur wheat and seasonings, usually baked.

kibbeh makliya (key-ba ma-klee-hah) A Middle Eastern dish consisting of small, football-shaped balls of kibbeh stuffed with ground lamb and nuts and flavored with onions, cinnamon, parsley and allspice.

kibbeh niyah (key-ba nee-yah) Arabic for raw kibbeh.

kibble 1. To grind coarsely. 2. Coarsely ground meal or grain.

kibbled wheat Wheat whose grains have been coarsely ground; it is used in muesli and sprinkled on top of bread and rolls.

kichel (kich-hel) Yiddish for cookie.

kicker 1. A method of determining a drink's price by adding 5–10% to the base cost of the drink; this method eliminates the need to determine the cost of every ingredient. 2. A chemical added to the mash used for a beer or distilled spirit to accelerate the fermentation process.

kickshaw The traditional name for a fancy dish, usually something dainty, elegant and unsubstantial, such as a trifle.

kid A goat slaughtered when approximately 6 months old; the lean flesh has a tender texture and delicate flavor similar to that of lamb.

kidney 1. An organ that filters blood to remove waste material and forwards it to the bladder for excretion. 2. A variety meat; generally small with a reddish-brown color, a tender texture, and a strong flavor; beef and veal kidneys are multilobed; lamb and pork kidneys are single lobed.

kidney bean A medium-sized, kidney-shaped bean with a dark red skin, cream-colored firm flesh, and bland flavor; available fresh, dried and canned; also known as red kidney bean. *See* white kidney bean.

kidney chop *See* English chop.

kielbasa; kielbasy (kihl-BAH-sah) 1. A general term used for most Polish sausages. 2. A Polish sausage made from pork (with beef sometimes added) flavored with garlic; smoked, usually precooked, and sold in medium to large links; also known as Polish sausage.

kievskie kotlety (key-ah-skee koh-tla-tea) Russian for chicken Kiev.

kifir *See* kafir.

ki-ichigo (key-ee-che-go) Japanese for raspberry.

kijiko (key-gee-koh) Swahili for spoon.

kiku (kee-koo) An edible Japanese garnish of chrysanthemum flowers and leaves.

kikurage (kee-ku-ra-gue) Japanese for cloud ear mushroom.

kilawin (kee-la-win) A Filipino cooking method in which fish is soaked in vinegar and lime or kalamansi juice until it is transparent, then mixed with coconut milk, onions, ginger and tomato.

kilderkin An old English barrel holding 18 imperial gallons.

kilic (key-lich) Turkish for swordfish; also known as baligi.

Kilimanjaro Arabica coffee beans grown in Tanzania's Mount Kilimanjaro region; the beverage has a mellow flavor and slight acidity.

kill-devil An English colonial name for West Indian rum.

kiln An apparatus traditionally used to dry barley and other grains used for brewing or distilling and consisting of a mesh (which holds the grains) positioned over a fire; this apparatus is now generally replaced by large drums filled with the grains rotating over a heat source.

kilo- *See* metric system.

kilocalorie *See* Calorie.

kilogram (kg) A measure of weight in the metric system; 1 kg equals 1000 g or 2.2 lb.

kilojoule 1000 joules.

kim bob (gimm bap) A Korean dish consisting of vegetables, beef and rice rolled in seaweed.

kim chee; kimchi (gim-chee) A very spicy Korean pickled cabbage, usually napa cabbage; seasoned with garlic, chiles, green onions, ginger and other spices; also known as Korean cabbage pickle.

kinako (KEE-nah-koh) Japanese for soy flour.

kinds The categories of poultry recognized by the U.S. Department of Agriculture (USDA): chickens, ducks, geese, guineas, pigeons and turkeys.

king (king) Thai for ginger.

king, à la *See* à la king.

king billy *See* croaker.

King cake A briochelike cake topped with purple, green and yellow icing; a red bean or a small figurine is baked in the cake, promising good luck to the finder; popular in Louisiana during the carnival season before Mardi Gras.

king coconut A variety of coconut grown in Sri Lanka; its juice is extremely sweet.

king crab A variety of very large crab found off Alaska that can grow to 10 lb. (24.8 kg); it has an average market weight of 7 lb. (3.2 kg), a flesh that is white with red edges, and a sweet flavor and coarse texture; also known as Alaskan king crab.

King Edward potato A variety of potato with a golden skin and a slightly pink flesh; generally grown in Great Britain.

kingfish *See* drum *and* king mackerel.

king hake *See* hake.

king mackerel A member of the mackerel family found in the Atlantic Ocean from Florida to Massachusetts; it has a high fat content, a finely textured and flavorful flesh, and an average market weight of 5–25 lb. (2.3–11.3 kg); also known as a kingfish.

king orange A large orange grown in Florida; it has a somewhat flattened shape with a loose, rough, orange-colored skin, a juicy, pale orange flesh and a sweet–tart flavor.

king salmon *See* chinook salmon.

King's Peg A cocktail made of Cognac and dry sparkling wine; served in a chilled wine glass.

king steak *See* porterhouse steak.

kinkéliba (keen-kah-lee-bah) An herb native to West Africa; it has a slightly bitter flavor and is used dried in medicinal tisanes.

kinome (kih-noh-MAY) The leaves of the prickly ash tree (genus *Zanthoxylum*); they have a fresh, subtle, minty flavor and a tender texture and are used as a garnish in Japanese cuisine.

kinugoshi (kee-noo-GOH-she) A soft Japanese-style tofu; also known as custard tofu, silk tofu and soft tofu.

kinywaji (kee-nee-wah-gee) Swahili for beverage.

kip (kip) Dutch for fowl or hen.

kipfel (KEEP-fell) *See* rugalach.

kiping Filipino wafers made from a batter of rice flour tinted bright colors; they are steamed in a banana leaf and, when dry, deep-fried, dipped in a sweet syrup or coated with a thin coconut jam; for festivals, they are stitched together with thread and displayed.

kipper *v.* To cure, usually fish, by cleaning, salting and drying or smoking. *n.* A male salmon during or shortly after the spawning season.

kippered herring A herring that is butterflied, cured in brine, and cold smoked; it has a smoky, salty flavor and is usually given an artificial golden color.

kippered salmon 1. In the United States, a chunk, steak or fillet of salmon (usually chinook) soaked in brine, hot smoked, and dyed red. 2. In Europe, a split salmon soaked in brine and cold smoked. 3. *See* lox *and* smoked salmon.

kipyatit' (key-pea-ah-teet) Russian for to boil.

Kir (keer) An aperitif of crème de cassis and dry white wine.

kirby cucumber A small cucumber with a dull green skin that can be bumpy or ridged; used for pickling.

kiri (kee-ree) Japanese for cut.

kiriboshi daikon (kee-ree-BOW-shee DAH-ee-kone) A Japanese dish of shredded dried daikon, softened and braised.

kirimi (kee-REE-mee) Japanese for a slice.

Kir Royale (keer roy-al) An aperitif of crème de cassis and Champagne or other sparkling wine.

Kirsch (kersch) A clear cherry brandy; double distilled from small semisweet cherries gathered in Germany's Black Forest, France's Vosges region and areas of Switzerland; it has a characteristic bitter almond flavor that comes from the oils derived from the cherries' crushed stones; also known as Kirschwasser in Germany.

Kirschen (KEER-shern) German for cherries.

Kirschtorte (kersch tohr-ta) A Swiss cake composed of two hazelnut meringue layers and two layers of genoise that are alternated with a Kirsch-flavored buttercream; the sides are spread with buttercream and coated with toasted ground hazelnuts, and the top is heavily dusted with confectioners' sugar and decorated with green marzipan leaves and candied cherries; also known as Zugor Kirschtorte.

Kirschwasser (KERSCH-vass-er) *See* Kirsch.

kirsebær (KEER-sser-baer) Norwegian for cherry.

kishik (kisk-kah) A sun-dried, powdered mixture of yogurt and bulgur used as a thickener and starch in Middle Eastern cuisines.

kishimen (KEE-shee-mehn) Wide, thin udon.

kishk (keehk) Arabic for yogurt fermented with cracked wheat, dried and ground.

kishke; kishka (KIHSH-keh) A Jewish sausage made with beef, matzo meal, fat and onions, stuffed into a beef casing, steamed and roasted.

kishmish (kish-mish) Armenian for dried fruits.

kish-mish (kish-mish) Hindi for raisin.

kishta (key-sh'tah) A Middle Eastern clotted cream; it can be made with cow's, goat's, buffalo's, ewe's or camel's milk; also known as gammer.

kisir (key-sear) A Turkish salad of bulgur, tomatoes and peppers flavored with parsley, mint and hot paprika and dressed with olive oil and lemon juice.

kisk (key'sk) A Middle Eastern dish consisting of milk, yogurt and bulgur fermented and then cooked to a porridge-like consistency.

Kislav (kee-slav) A Russian spirit distilled from watermelons.

kissaten (KEE-sah-tehn) Japanese for cafe.

kissel (kee-SUHL) A Russian dessert made with a starch-thickened fruit purée (usually cranberries or another red berry); served warm or cold with custard sauce, cream or yogurt.

kisu (kee-soo) Swahili for knife.

kitambaa (key-tahm-bah-ah) Swahili for napkin.

kitchen The room or area containing cooking facilities or the area where food is prepared.

kitchen appliances Generally, mechanical devices used to prepare foods and includes items such as mixers, toasters, juicers, stoves and the like.

kitchen brigade *See* brigade.

kitchen cleaver *See* Chinese cleaver.

kitchen garden A small garden intended to supply produce for the kitchen.

kitchen shears A pair of strong scissors (one blade with a serrated edge) used to cut fish, poultry, meat and produce, crack nuts and remove packaging materials such as bottle caps; sometimes it has tabs to be used as a screwdriver or lever. *See* fish shears *and* poultry shears.

kitchen shears

kitchenware Generally, utensils used to prepare foods and includes items such as pots, pans, mixing bowls, ladles and the like.

kitcheri (kit-chae-ree) Hindi for kedgeree.

kitchin *See* daidokoro.

kited fillet A fish cut along the backbone and filleted but left attached at the belly.

kitfo leb leb (kit-foe leb leb) An Ethiopian dish consisting of minced beef flavored with chiles, ground cloves, cardamom, grains of paradise, black pepper, salt and minced onions and then very briefly cooked in nit'ir qibe; it is served very rare.

kiu (key-oo) An ancient Chinese beer.

kiwada (kee-wahd-dah) Japanese for yellowfin tuna.

kiwai A variety of kiwi grown in Europe; its fruit are small, with a smooth, fine, edible skin.

kiwano (kee-WAHN-noh) A fruit and member of the cucumber family (*Cucumis metuliferus*) native to New Zealand; it has a bright orange skin studded with little horns, many edible black seeds, and a bright green flesh that has a flavor reminiscent of mango and pineapple; also known as cucumber-horned melon.

kiwi; kiwi fruit; kiwifruit (KEE-wee) A small, barrel-shaped fruit (*Actinidia sinensis*) native to New Zealand; it has a greenish-brown skin covered with fuzz, a brilliant green flesh that becomes yellower toward the center, many small, edible black seeds, and a sweet–tart flavor; named for the flightless bird of New Zealand; also known as the Chinese gooseberry.

kizbara (KEHZ-bah-rah) Arabic for coriander.

kizibuo (key-zi-boo-oh) Swahili for corkscrew.

kizilcik (key-zee-lick) Turkish for cornelian cherry.

kjøkken (shuh-ken) Norwegian for kitchen.

kjokkensjef (shuh-ken-shahf) Norwegian for chef.

kjot (shuht) Icelandic for meat.

kjøtt (khurt) Norwegian for meat.

kkaetnip (KAT-nip) Korean sesame leaves; they are eaten fresh with rice or stuffed, battered and fried.

Klarer (klah-rear) The collective German word for all aromatic distillations of schnapps that are clear and colorless.

kleiner Brauner (kli-nerr bru-ner) German for small brown and used to describe a small (demi-tasse) cup of coffee with a dash of milk.

kleiner Goldener (kli-nerr gold-a-nar) German for small gold and used to describe a small (demi-tasse) cup of Viennese coffee served with milk.

kleiner Schwarzer (kli-nerr sh-vart-zer) German for small black and used to describe a small (demi-tasse) cup of Viennese coffee served without milk.

kletski (kleet-skee) Russian for dumplings or quenelles.

Klevner (klev-ner) A red wine grape grown in Switzerland and blended with Pinot Noir. *See* Pinot Blanc.

klimp (klimp) Swedish for dumplings.

klip; klipfish (kleep) A Norwegian dish of salted cod smoked in the open air, cooked, and served with butter, sometimes flavored with parsley.

klipfisk (KLEEP-feesk) A Danish dish similar to klip.

Klopse (klop-sa) German meatballs; they usually contain two or three kinds of meat.

Klösse (KLEUS-eh) *See* Knödel.

Klosterkäse (klaus ter kaiz) A soft, ripened Romadur-style cheese made in Germany from whole cow's milk.

kluay budt chee (kloo-i boot che) A Thai dessert of bananas stewed in coconut milk and sugar, then sprinkled with chopped mung beans and served hot or cold.

klubnika (kloob-nee-kah) Russian for strawberry.

kluski (klue-skee) Light Polish dumplings or noodle strips, usually used to garnish soups.

kmaj (k'mahj) *See* mraqud.

knäckebröd (kneh-keh-brurd) A Swedish crispbread made from rye flour and rye meal.

Knackwurst (KNAAK-voost) A plump German sausage made from beef and pork and seasoned with garlic; the casing makes a cracking sound at first bite; also known as Knockwurst.

knafa; knafeh; knafee (kuh-nah-hah) A soft, uncooked wheat dough, similar to shredded wheat, used for pastries in Middle Eastern cuisines; also known as konafa, kadaifa, katafi and kataifi.

knaidel (knayd-dhul) *pl.* knaidlach. A Jewish dumpling sometimes flavored with schmaltz and usually served in beef or chicken soup garnished with carrots, onions and celery. *See* challah knaidel, kartoffel knaidel *and* matzoh knaidel.

knead 1. To work a dough by hand or in a mixer to distribute ingredients and develop gluten. 2. To press, rub or squeeze with the hands.

knedle (kneh-dleh) Polish for dumpling.

knedlíky (ned-lee-key) Czech for dumpling.

knelki (nell-key) Polish for quenelles.

knickerbocker glory A dessert consisting of layers of ice cream, jelly, fruit and cream served in a tall glass.

knife A sharp-edged instrument used to cut or spread food; it generally consists of a blade and handle.

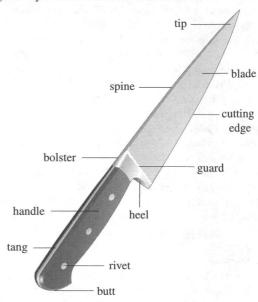

knife components

knife blade The part of a knife used to cut or spread; it is generally made of carbon steel, stainless steel or high-carbon stainless steel and consists of a tip (point), spine (back), cutting edge, bolster, heel, butt and tang.

knife blade, forged A knife blade that is made from metal heated and hammered into shape, creating a heavier, more front-weighted blade with a distinct bolster; this produces a knife with good balance, flexibility and handling quality.

knife blade, stamped A knife blade that is die cut in a press; it is lighter and less expensive than a forged blade and is back-heavy in the hand, requiring more forward pressure to cut.

knife block A hardwood block with slits into which knives are placed at an angle; the knives rest above the block's bottom to protect the tips and edges.

knife box A wooden or metal-encased wooden box with a hinged lid used to store knives and sometimes other flatware on a sideboard; the utensils are stored vertically in slots.

knife edge *See* cutting edge.

knife handle The part of the knife gripped by the user and that holds the blade's tang; it can be made of wood, horn, bone, metal, plastic-impregnated wood, plastic or other synthetic substances and can be two pieces attached to the tang by rivets or adhesives or a single piece in which the tang is embedded.

knife point The tip of a knife; it can be a spear, round spatula, sheep's foot (an outward arc from spine to flat cutting edge), cope (an abrupt forward angle from spine to flat cutting edge) or clip (a slightly concave arc from the midspine to the point; the secondary edge can be sharpened and called a swedge or left unsharpened and called a false edge).

knish (KAH-nish) A Jewish dish consisting of a dough made from mashed potatoes, egg, schmaltz and flour stuffed with a savory (e.g., potatoes and ground meats) or sweet (e.g., nuts and raisins) filling and baked.

kniv (kun-eev) Norwegian for knife.

knobbed whelk A variety of whelk found along the North American coast; it has a gray shell with a ring of knobs, a red-brown opening, an average length of 8 in. (19.6 cm), and lean, very tough, flavorful flesh; also known as the giant whelk.

Knoblauch (KNOP-lowsk) German for garlic.

Knochen (no-kan) German for bone.

Knockando The proprietary name of a single-malt Scotch whisky; it has a light, somewhat sweet flavor and a long aftertaste.

knockdowns Gift cartons packed separately from the product.

Knockwurst (KNOHK-vursht) *See* Knackwurst.

Knödel (KNUR-derl) Very light German and Austrian dumplings made from flour, potatoes, eggs and sometimes bread crumbs and often stuffed with meat, liver or a sweet filling; also known as Klösse.

Knöderl (KNUR-der'l) A small Knödel; often used to garnish soups.

knopfli (no-flee) Swiss button-shaped noodles.

knotroot *See* chorogi.

knotted majoram *See* marjoram.

knuckle 1. Anatomically, a joint where two bones meet or articulate. 2. A subprimal cut of the beef primal round; it usually contains the leg bone and is fairly tender and flavorful; it is sometimes fabricated into knuckle steaks. 3. On a veal or pork carcass, the lower part of the hind leg. 4. On a lamb carcass, the knee of the hind leg.

ko (koh) Japanese for flour.

Kobe beef (KOH-bay) Beef from cattle raised in Kobe, Japan; the cattle, massaged with sake and fed a diet that includes large amounts of beer, produce meat that is tender and full flavored.

Koch (corh) German for chef; also known as Küchenchef.

kocha *See* O-cha.

Köche (keuch-reh) A light, steamed or baked sweet or savory German pudding.

köchin (coe-chin) German for to cook.

kochujang (koe-shoe-young) A spicy Korean condiment made with soybean paste, ground red pepper and glutinous rice and used in stews, vegetable dressings and dipping sauces.

kød (kurhd) Danish for meat.

koeksister A South African snail-shaped doughnut deep-fried and brushed with a sweet syrup flavored with lemon and cinnamon and rolled in sugar.

kofe (ko-fyeh) Russian for coffee.

kofe s molokom (ko-fyeh s'moe-low-kom) Russian for coffee with milk.

kofta kebab (koff-tah ka-bohb) A Middle Eastern dish consisting of finely minced lamb flavored with onions, baharat, mint, parsley and pepper, skewered and grilled.

kofte (kaaf-tee) A Turkish dish of ground or minced meat (usually lamb) flavored with spices and herbs and mixed with rice, bulgur or bread crumbs, shaped into balls (and sometimes threaded onto skewers), and fried, grilled or simmered.

kofte-ekmek (kaaf-tee-ak-mak) A Turkish dish of cizbiz mixed with onion salad and served on a large roll; often sold by street vendors.

Kognak German for brandy.

Kognak *See* Branntwein.

kogt oksebryst (koegt oc'say-brist) A Danish smørrebrød dish of boiled brisket on black bread garnished with grated horseradish and vegetables in a mustard pickle.

kogt sild (koegt sleed) A Danish dish consisting of gutted (but not filleted) herring marinated and cooked in a brine made with vinegar, chopped onions and herbs; the fish is eaten cold.

kohado (koe-hah-doe) Japanese for gizzard shad. *See* shinko *and* konoshiro.

kohi (KOH-hee) Japanese for coffee.

ko-hitsuji (koh-HEE-tsoo-jee) Japanese for lamb.

Kohl (koal) German for cabbage.

kohlrabi (koal-RAH-bee) A vegetable created by cross-breeding cabbages and turnips (*Brassica oleracea* var. *gongylodes*); it has a pale green or pale purple bulbous stem and dark green leaves; the bulbous stem has a mild, sweet, turniplike flavor and is cooked like a root vegetable; also known as a cabbage turnip.

koi-kuchi shoya (koy-koo-chee shoe-yah) A dark Japanese soy sauce; it is thicker and heavier but less salty than light soy sauce.

koji (koh-gee) Grains or beans inoculated with the *Aspergillus* mold and used as a starter for most Japanese fermented foods, including miso, tamari, amazake, mirin and rice vinegar.

Kokei Cha (koh-KAY-ee chah) A Japanese green tea with a thin, needlelike leaf; the beverage has a fragrant aroma.

kokinistó (koh-key-nee-stow) A Greek dish of beef or veal braised in a tomato sauce.

Kokkineli (ko-key-na-lee) A Greek rosé wine flavored with pine resin. *See* Retsina.

kokorétsi (koh-koh-reh-tsee) A Greek sausage made from lamb offal and seasoned with marjoram and other herbs and spices.

kokos (ko-koss) Russian for coconut.

kokòshka (ko-kosh-kah) Bulgarian for chicken.

kokoska (ko-kos-kah) Serbo-Croat for chicken.

kokosnøtt (koo-koos-nuht) Norwegian for coconut.

Kokosnuss (koh-koh-nass) German for coconut.

kokwa (ko-koo-aw) Swahili for nut.

kolacky; kolachke (koh-LAH-chee) A small, sweet, flaky Polish pastry made with either a yeast dough or cream cheese dough, filled with poppy seeds, jam, nuts or crushed fruit.

kola nut *See* cola nut.

kolbas; kolbasa (kole-bah-sa) Russian for sausage.

kolbàsz (kohl-bash) Hungarian for sausage.

koldtbord (KOL-brurdh) Danish and Norwegian for cold table and used to describe cold hors d'oeuvres and open-faced sandwiches. *See* smørrebrød, smørbrød *and* smörgåsbord.

koldunai (kole-doon-ay) A Lithuanian dish consisting of dumplings with a meat filling boiled in stock.

kolduny (kohd-loo-nee) Polish noodles stuffed with meat; usually circular in shape.

koliflawa (koh-lee-flaw-wah) Swahili for cauliflower.

kolja (KOL-yah) Swedish for haddock.

kolokithakia (koh-low-key-tah-kee-ah) Greek for summer squash.

Kölsch A pale, golden ale with a delicate character, a light body and a fruity, winelike bouquet; served as an aperitif or digestif.

kombu; konbu (KOME-boo) Dark brown to grayish-black kelp that is sun-dried and folded into sheets; it is used in Japanese cuisine as a flavoring, stock base and for sushi.

kome (KOH-meh) Japanese for uncooked rice.

Komijne Kaas *See* Leiden.

komkommer (kawm-KAWM-ur) Dutch for cucumber.

kompot (kohm-poh't) A Jewish dish consisting of fruits mixed with sugar, fruit juice, wine or liqueur and served as is or baked.

Kompott (kom-pot) German for compote.

komugi (koh-MOO-ghee) Japanese for wheat.

komugiko (koh-MOO-ghee-kom) Japanese for wheat flour.

Kona Arabica coffee beans grown on Hawaii's Big Island; the beverage is highly aromatic with a smooth, mellow flavor.

konafa An Egyptian dessert of nuts, spices and butter.

kona sansho; kona-zansho (KOH-nah SAHN-sho) Japanese powdered pepper.

Konditorei (kon-dee-toe-rey) A German pastry shop where coffee and hot chocolate are offered with the pastries.

konfekt (kun-fekt) Norwegian for candy.

Konfekt (kohn-frek) German for candy.

konfeta (kahn-FYEH-ti) Russian for candy.

Konfitüre (kohn-fee-tou-ray) German for jam.

kongsincai (kong-sink-ee) An aquatic vegetable grown in southern China and related to the morning glory flower; it has long hollow stems and arrowhead-shaped leaves; also known as water spinach.

kong wan (kong whan) Thai for desserts; sweet foods.

Königenpastete (koh-nee-ghan-pah-sta-tah) A German pastry filled with meat and mushrooms or other savory fillings.

Königsberger Klopse (KUR-nig-berg-gehr KLOHP-seh) A German dish of meatballs in a savory sauce.

Königwurst (KUR-nig-vurst) A large German sausage made from chicken, partridge, truffles and mushrooms, seasoned with mace and white wine.

konijn (koh-NEYN) Dutch for rabbit.

konjakk (kon-yahk) Norwegian for brandy.

konnayaku *See* bean curd, black.

konnyaku (kon-NYA-koo) A Japanese pearly-toned gelatinous curd with a neutral flavor made from a vegetable tuber called devil's tongue; it is cut into strips and added to soups and braised dishes.

konokono (ko-now-ko-now) Swahili for snail.

konoshiro (koe-noh-she-row) An older gizzard shad (kohado); it should not be used for sushi or sashimi. *See* shinko.

kon'yak (kah-NYAHK) Russian for brandy.

kool (kuhl) Dutch for cabbage.

koosa (koe-say) Arabic for squash.

koosa ablama (koe-say ah-b'lah-ma) A Middle Eastern dish of summer squash stuffed with pine nuts and minced lamb and cooked in a yogurt sauce sprinkled with mint.

koosa mihshee (koe-say mih-shay-ah) A Middle Eastern dish of squash stuffed with hashwa.

Kopanisti (koh-pah-nee-stee) A soft, aged Greek blue cheese made from cow's milk; it has a sharp, peppery flavor.

kopcheniy (kop-ka-nee) Russian for smoked.

koper (koh-pehr) Polish for dill.

Kopfsalat (kopf-sah-lath) German for a lettuce salad.

Korean bean paste *See* dhwen-jang.

Korean cabbage pickle *See* kim chee.

Korean chile A long, slightly curved, tapering fresh chile with a bright green color, a thin flesh and a hot, green vegetal flavor.

Korean menudo *See* haejangkook.

Korean soybean paste *See* twoenjang.

kori (koh-reh) Japanese for ice.

kori dofu (koh-reh doo-foo) Japanese tofu that has been dehydrated by natural freezing and drying; also known as snow-dried tofu.

koriza (ko-re-tsah) Russian for cinnamon.

Korkenzeiher (kohr-ken-zell-er) German for corkscrew.

korketrekker (kore-ka-tra-kerr) Norwegian for corkscrew.

korma (kor-mah) 1. Hindi for braising, braised and to braise. 2. A spicy Indian and Pakistani dish of curried mutton, lamb or chicken cooked with onions and other vegetables.

Korn (corn) A German schnapps distilled from rye, wheat, buckwheat, oats or barley.

körte (kore-tay) Hungarian pear brandy.

korv (korv) Swedish for sausage.

korvel (kore-vell) Danish for chervil.

koryushki (koe-ree-oos-key) Russian for smelts.

kos (koosh) Albanian for sour milk; used principally as a sauce and flavoring.

kosa ma'liya (ko-saw mah-lee-hah) An Egyptian dish consisting of deep-fried zucchini served with a sauce made from garlic and vinegar.

koseliena (koh-sah-leh-an-ah) A Lithuanian dish consisting of the meat from pig's trotters and goose giblets and wings simmered with bay leaves, allspice, onions and peppercorns; the meat is left to jell and then garnished with parsley, dill pickles and hard-boiled eggs.

kosher 1. The Jewish dietary laws, as found in the Torah (the first five books of the Old Testament) and subsequent interpretations; these laws (1) identify kosher foods and ingredients and (2) define basic dietary principles; also known as kashrus (Yiddish). *See* fleischig, milchig, *and* pareve. 2. A menu or labeling term indicating that the product has been prepared or processed in accordance with Jewish dietary laws. 3. A food prepared in accordance with Jewish dietary laws.

kosher cheeses Cheeses made in conformity with Jewish dietary laws (typically, no animal rennet is used; the milk is curdled by natural souring or a vegetable acid starter is added); the cheeses are usually eaten fresh and are similar to cream cheese, cottage cheese and Limburger.

kosher dietary principles Simply stated, meat (fleischig) and dairy (milchig) cannot be cooked or eaten together; fruit, vegetables and grain (pareve or neutral foods) can be eaten with either meat or dairy.

kosher foods Those who keep kosher can only eat (1) meat from animals with hooves and that chew their cud (cattle, goats and some game; no hogs); (2) poultry that is not a bird of prey; (3) fish with gills and scales (no shellfish); (4) dairy products, provided the animal from which the milk comes is kosher; and (5) all fruits, vegetables and grains, provided animal fat is not used in processing.

kosher salt Purified coarse rock salt; approved for use on kosher meats.

kosher style 1. A menu or labeling term indicating that the product has been prepared or seasoned in a particular manner, usually one associated with Jewish cuisines from eastern Europe; the term has no religious significance. 2. A description of pure-beef sausage and corned beef that is seasoned with garlic and spices, imparting a flavor similar to comparable kosher products; the term is prohibited in several states.

kosher wine Wine made under rabbinical supervision and adhering to the Jewish dietary principles.

koshi-an *See* an.

kosho (koh-SHOH) Japanese for pepper.

kost' (kost) Russian for bone.

kosui A variety of nashi.

Kotelett (koh-ta-let) German for cutlet or chop.

kotlet (kot-let) Polish for cutlet.

kotlety; kotletki (koe-tla-tea) A Russian dish of salmon or chicken patties served with sour cream.

kotópita (koh-poh-pee-tah) A Greek dish of a phyllo dough chicken pie seasoned with fresh herbs.

kotópoulo (koh-toh-pooh-low) Greek for chicken.

kotópoulo me bamies (koh-toh-pooh-low mah bah-mees) A Greek dish of chicken cooked with okra.

kotópoulo pilaf (koh-toh-pooh-low pee-laff) A Greek dish of pilaf cooked with chicken, onions and tomato.

kött (khurt) Swedish for meat.

köttbullar (koht-boo-lahr) A Swedish smörgåsbord dish consisting of meatballs made from ground beef, bread crumbs, cream, parsley and eggs; the meatballs are fried in butter.

kottletten (kott-let-tin) Yiddish for ground meat patties.

koulourakia (koo-loo-rah-key-ah) Greek corkscrew-shaped Easter cookies flavored with brandy, brushed with egg wash, and sprinkled with sesame seeds.

koumiss; kumiss (KOO-mihs) A beverage made from fermented mare's, camel's or cow's milk by the nomadic tribes of central Asia; also known as kefir.

koumou (ko-moo) A whitish, irregularly shaped Chinese mushroom (*Tricholoma gambosan*) similar to an oyster mushroom.

kouneli (koo-neh-lee) Greek for rabbit.

kounoupidi; kounoupithi (koo-noo-pee-thee) Greek for cauliflower.

kourabiedes (koo-rah-bee-YAY-dehs) Crescent-shaped Greek cookies made with ground nuts and butter; they are rolled in confectioners' sugar after baking.

kousa (koo-sa) Arabic for marrow squash.

ko ushi no niko (koh oo-she no nee-coe) Japanese for veal.

koushry (koosh-ree) An Egyptian dish consisting of rice and lentils flavored with fried onions.

kovo A large-leafed vegetable with lightly textured leaves and a mild, sweet flavor; it is grown in Central Africa.

koya-doufu; kori-doufu (koh-yah-doo-foo; koh-ree-doo-foo) Lightweight cakes of frozen and dried Chinese-style tofu.

koyun pirzolasi (koh-yoon peer-soh-lah-sea) A Turkish dish of roasted mutton chops.

kozel (koh-zal) Russian for goat.

krab (krahb) Russian for crab.

krabbe (KRAHB-ber) Norwegian for crab.

Krabbe (krahb) German for crab.

krakelinge A figure eight–shaped South African cookie made of sweet dough flavored with cinnamon and brushed with beaten egg white mixed with sugar and ground almonds.

kransekage (krahns-cha-ga) A Danish ring cake made with flour, eggs, butter, confectioners' sugar and marzipan and shaped into rings that become progressively smaller; after baking, they are stacked and decorated in a zigzag pattern with a confectioners' sugar icing; they are often adorned with small flags or flowers or topped with a miniature bride and groom.

krap (krah'p) A Dutch cut of pork with the bone in.

Krapfen (krap-fan) Austrian deep-fried pastries similar to doughnuts.

krapiva (krah-pee-vah) A Russian soup made from beef, onions and young nettle sprouts garnished with diced beef and pearl barley.

krase (krah-seh) Danish for giblets.

krassato (krah-saw-toe) A Greek preparation method in which fish are cooked in wine.

kratiam (krah-tea-m) Thai for garlic.

K-ration Lightweight packaged foods developed for the U.S. Army in World War II.

kräuseln; kraeusen (kroy-sen) The large head of foam that forms on the wort's surface as fermentation peaks during beer brewing.

kräusening; kraeusening (kroy-sen-eng) The process of adding unfermented or partially fermented wort to fermented beer to increase natural carbonation through a secondary fermentation.

Krauter (krowt-er) German for herbs.

Krebs (krayps) Danish and German for crayfish.

kreem (cream) Hindi for cream.

krem (kraym) Norwegian for whipped cream.

krem (kram) Polish and Russian for cream.

kremidia (kreh-mee-thia) Greek for onions.

Kren *See* Meerrettich.

krentewegge (kran-ta-wah-ghe) A long, flat Dutch raisin roll made from a yeast dough and traditionally given to new mothers and their babies as a gift.

kreplach (KREHP-luhkh) Small Jewish noodle squares stuffed with chopped meat or cheese and usually used in soups.

krevetka (kra-vet-kah) Russian for shrimp.

kriek; krieken-lambic (kreek, KREEK-in-lam-bick) A lambic beer flavored with cherries.

Krimskoye (kream-skoh-ya) A sparkling Crimean wine available in white or the traditional red; it is made from Cabernet Sauvignon grapes as well as Sabernet, Saperavi and Matrassa grapes, which grow only near the Black Sea.

krimu (krem-moo) Swahili for cream.

kringle 1. A multilayered Christmas pastry filled with fruit or nuts; it is flat, wide and very flaky. 2. A buttery, lemon-flavored Christmas cookie.

kringler A Swedish yeast dough pastry, baked and drizzled with an almond-scented glaze; it is usually cut into diagonal slices and eaten for breakfast.

kristalklar (kris-tahl-clahr) A German labeling term indicating that the beer has been filtered.

kritharaki (kree-thaa-raa-kee) A fine barley kernel used in Greek cuisine for soup and casseroles.

Kroc, Ray (Am., 1902–1984) The founder of the McDonald's corporation; before McDonald's, most fast-food stands were found in big cities; Kroc was the first to target small towns.

Krokant (kroh-kant) A crunchy German nut brittle eaten as a candy or crushed and used to decorate cakes or pastries.

krolik (krah-leek) Russian for rabbit.

kruay (kroo-ah-ee) Thai for banana.

kruid (krohw) Dutch for herb.

kruiderijen (crew-hid-a-ree-yan) Dutch for spices.

kruidnagel (KTOHW-nahg-ah) Dutch for clove.

kruidnoot (crew-hid-no-hot) Dutch for nutmeg.

krumkake (kroom-kah-ka) A Norwegian Christmas cookie flavored with cardamom and made on a special iron; while warm, it is rolled into a cigarette or cone shape and often filled with whipped cream.

krumkake iron A utensil that consists of two 5-in.-diameter round engraved plates that are hinged; batter is placed in the center of one plate and the two are brought together and placed on a ring that sits over a stove burner; used to make krumkakes.

krung gaeng (kroeng kaeng) Curry pastes used in Thai cuisine; depending on their constituent herbs and spices, the pastes vary in flavor, intensity and color.

krung gaeng kare leung (kroeng keang ka-reh leh-ong) A yellow Thai curry paste with a mild flavor and colored with fresh turmeric root.

krung gaeng keo wan (kroeng keang keh-o wun) A green Thai curry paste with an extremely spicy flavor and colored with green chiles.

krung gaeng ped daeng (kroeng keang ped da-ung) A red Thai curry paste with a strong aroma and moderately spicy flavor.

krung gaeng som (kroeng kaeng sum) An orange Thai curry paste usually used in a sour-flavored curried shrimp soup.

krupnik (kroo-pee-neek) A Polish soup made with barley cooked in stock and garnished with meat scraps and mushrooms.

krupuk (ke-roo-pook) Hard, thin, dried wafers, often flavored with shrimp or fish, that are deep-fried and served as a snack or used as a garnish in Indonesian and Malaysian cuisines.

krush *See* mumbar.

krydder (krid-er) Norwegian for spice.

kryddersild (kree-dare-seald) A Danish smørrebrød dish of herring pickled in a sweet-and-sour marinade of herbs with crème fraîche, capers, chopped onions and dill served on black bread.

krydderurter (kree-dare-tour-ter) Norwegian for herbs.

krydret (kreed-rett) Norwegian for spicy.

k'sra (k'shrah) A Moroccan round loaf bread made with a sourdough-type starter and a mix of whole wheat, barley and unbleached flours and garnished with caraway seeds.

ktapódi krassato (tah-poh-dee krah-saw-toe) A Greek dish of octopus cooked in red wine and flavored with onions, garlic, bay leaf and tomatoes.

kuàizi (kwa-ee-tzee) Chinese for chopsticks.

kubécake (koo-bah-cah-ka) A Ghanaian snack consisting of fried balls of dough flavored with shredded coconut, ginger, rum and sugar.

kuchai *See* chives, garlic.

Küche (KOO-khe) German for kitchen.

kuchen (koo-chen) Yiddish for something baked and used to describe a yeast dough pastry studded with nuts and raisins and topped with streusel.

Küchen (KOO-khehn) 1. German for cake or pastry. 2. A yeast-leavened coffee cake topped with nuts or crumbs.

Küchenchef *See* Koch.

Kucker (TSUK-kerr) German for granulated sugar.

kudamono (KOO-dah-MOH-noh) Japanese for fruit.

kudzu A vine (*Pueraria lobata*) with a starchy, irregularly shaped root with white flesh and a mild, sweet flavor; a thin paste made from the ground root and a liquid is used in Japanese cuisine as a thickener or to coat foods before frying.

kugel (koo-gle; koo-gul) A Jewish puddinglike dish made from potatoes, noodles or a grain, eggs and flavorings (e.g., fresh or dried fruit, grebenes, soft cheeses or sautéed onions) and baked.

kugelhopf; gugelhopf (KOO-guhl-hof) A light yeast cake filled with raisins, nuts and candied fruit and baked in a special fluted mold; popular in Alsace, Germany, Poland and Austria, it is often served for breakfast or with afternoon tea.

kugelhopf mold A tall, round baking mold with deeply fluted sides and a narrow center tube; used for baking kugelhopf.

kuhnya (koo-nyah) Russian for kitchen.

kuiken (KIR-kuh) Dutch for chicken.

kukaanga (koo-kah-an-gah) Swahili for fried.

kugelhopf mold

kukata (koo-kah-tah) Swahili for to slice.

kukh (khookh) Arabic for peach.

kukicha (koo-kee-chah) A Japanese tea made from roasted tea twigs and stems.

kukki *See* bisket-to.

kuku (koo-koo) Swahili for chicken.

kukui A native Hawaiian nut with an ivory or gray color and an extremely high oil content.

kuku na nazi (koo-koo nah nah-zee) A Kenyan dish consisting of a chicken flavored with ginger, garlic, chiles, onions, curry powder, cumin and coriander cooked in coconut milk and coconut cream.

kukuruza (koo-koo-ROO-zah) Russian for corn.

kulcha (kool-cha) An Indian bread made from leavened white flour dough shaped into rounds and baked in a tandoor.

kulebiaka; koulibiaka (koo-lee-BYAH-kah) *See* coulibiac.

kulfi (KULL-fee) An east Indian ice cream made with full-cream milk and finely chopped almonds and pistachios, flavored with rose essence, and frozen in conical molds.

kulich (koo-LIHCH) A tall, cylindrical yeast-leavened Russian cake filled with candied fruit, raisins and spices; traditionally prepared for Easter celebrations.

kulikuli (koo-lee-koo-lee) A West African (especially Nigeria and Mali) dish consisting of balls of ground groundnuts or peanuts flavored with onions and pepper and deep-fried in groundnut oil.

kulolo (koo-loh-loh) A Hawaiian pudding of taro, brown sugar, honey and coconut milk; it is often served at a luau and is also known as taro pudding.

Kulturchampignon (kuhl-tuhr-cham-pee-nynon) German for the common store mushroom.

Kumamoto oyster A variety of Pacific oysters native to the waters off Japan and aquafarmed off the U.S. West Coast.

Kuminost; Kumminost (KOO-mihn-ohst) A firm Scandinavian spiced cheese made from whole or partly skimmed cow's milk; it has a pale yellow to orange interior and is flavored with cumin, caraway seeds or other spices and usually made in a large loaf; also known as Nökkelost.

kummathra (kumm-methra) Arabic for pear.

Kümmel (kimmel) 1. German for caraway. 2. A Dutch and German neutral spirit distilled from potatoes or grains and flavored with caraway and cumin seeds.

Kümmel Crystallize Kümmel containing crystallized sugar.

kummelweck A German–American caraway seed bun encrusted with coarse salt.

kumquat A small ovoid to spherical citrus fruit (*Fortunella margarita*) with a soft, thin, golden orange rind, an orange flesh with small seeds, and a tart flavor; the entire fruit is eaten fresh or used for preserves and pickles.

kumquats, crystallized Kumquats cooked in a sugar syrup and eaten as sweets or used in cakes or puddings in Chinese cuisines.

kumu A member of the goatfish family; this saltwater reef fish has a flaky white flesh and a delicate flavor.

kunde (koon-da) Swahili for beans.

kundzar An Alaskan dish made by Ten'a Indians; it consists of whitefish roe pounded with slightly unripened cranberries, mixed with snow and eaten frozen.

kung pao (gong bao) A Chinese stir-fry dish traditionally made with chicken (shrimp and vegetables are now also used) and great quantities of garlic, ginger, whole dried chiles and fried peanuts (formerly, corn kernels were used).

kungull me kos An Albanian dish of fritters made from zucchini and served with a cold sauce of thickened kos flavored with garlic.

kunsei no (koon-SAY-ee noh) Japanese for smoked; also known as sumoku.

kun-tu An Alaskan dish of boiled, fermented salmon roe.

kuoka motoni (koo-oh-kah moh-toe-nee) Swahili for to roast.

kupika (koo-pee-kah) Swahili for to cook.

kurakake (koo-rah-kah-key) A thin, savory Japanese omelet used for sushi.

kurayz (koo-raise) Arabic for cherry.

Kürbis (KEWR-biss) German for pumpkin and squash.

kurcze (koor-cheh) Polish for young chicken.

kure (que-ray) Czech for chicken.

kuri (koo-ree) Japanese for chestnut.

kurimu (koo-ree-moo) Japanese for cream.

kuri no kanro ni (koo-ree noh kahn-roh nee) A Japanese dish of cooked chestnuts in a sweet syrup.

kuritsa (koor-eet-sah) Russian for hen.

kurkka (kore-ka) Finnish for cucumber.

kuro goma (KOO-roh GOH-mah) *See* goma.

kuromaguro *See* maguro.

kuro-su (koo-roh-soo) A Japanese brown rice vinegar with a mellow flavor.

kurotake (KOO-roh-TAH-keh) A wild mushroom (*Boletopsis subsquamosa*) found in Japan; it has a slightly acrid flavor.

kuruma-ebi Japanese for a variety of delicately flavored and beautifully colored shrimp used for nigiri-zushi; also known as wheel shrimp.

kurumi (koo-RUH-mee) Japanese for walnuts.

kusa (koo-SAH) Japanese for herbs.

kushat' (koo-shot) Russian for to eat. *See* est'.

kushi (koo-shee) Japanese for a skewer or stick.

kushi-age (koo-shee-AH-gue) Japanese for morsels of food coated with Japanese-style bread crumbs (panko), skewered, and deep-fried.

kushi-gata (koo-shee-GAH-tah) 1. Japanese for comb-out and used to describe a decorative cut of food. 2. A portion of rice for nigiri-zushi shaped like a rounded, ornamental hair comb; also known as rikyu-gata.

kushi-yaki (koo-shee-YAH-kee) Japanese for assorted skewered and grilled foods prepared the same way as yakitori.

kuski (koos-key) Russian for slices.

kutokosa (koo-toe-koe-saw) Swahili for stew.

Kutteln (ku-teln) German for tripe.

kuwai *See* arrowhead.

kuzu (koo-zoo) Turkish for lamb.

kvass; quass (KBAH-ssoo) A weak Russian home-brewed beer made by pouring hot water over dark rye bread and allowing the mix to ferment.

kwark *See* quark.

kweilin gui hua jiu (kwe-lean goo-e wa gee-oo) An aromatic Chinese wine with a light, fragrant flavor; also known as cassia blossom wine.

kyabetsu (KYAH-beh-tsoo) Japanese for cabbage.

kyandé (KYAHN-day) Japanese for candy.

kyauk kyaw A Burmese fudgelike candy made of agar-agar, coconut milk and sugar and flavored with rosewater.

kyckling (TYEWK-ling) Swedish for chicken.

kydonia (kee-thoh-nhra) Greek for quince.

kyenam; kenan (key-n-nahm) A Ghanaian dish of deep-fried fish rubbed with a ginger and chile paste.

kyinkyinga (chin-chin-ga) A Mali snack of skewers of grilled meat and bell peppers sprinkled with groundnut powder.

kylling (KEW-leeng) Danish and Norwegian for chicken.

Kyoto (kee-yoh-toh) A cocktail made of gin, dry vermouth and melon liqueur.

Kyoto cucumber A variety of slicing cucumber developed in Japan; it is longer than typical and not always of a uniform shape.

kyufté (ki-oof-the) A Bulgarian dish consisting of ground mutton flavored with garlic and bound with eggs and bread crumbs.

kyuji (KYOO-jee) Japanese for waiter.

kyurdyuk (key-oor-dee-ook) Ground or melted lamb fat removed from under the tail; it is used as a cooking medium and flavoring in central Asian cuisines.

kyuri (KYOO-ree) Japanese for cucumber.

l *See* liter.

laab (law-ahb) A Thai cooked salad, usually of meat with onions and herbs.

laab nuea (law-ahb noo-a-ha) A Thai salad made from fried ground beef mixed with ground roasted sticky rice, fish sauce, galanga, shallots, green onions, chiles and mint leaves.

laal sharaab (lahl shah-rah-hab) Hindi for white wine.

laban (LAH'-um) Arabic for cultured milk or yogurt. *See* leben.

labanah mackbouseh (lah-bah-nah mahch-boo-sak) A Middle Eastern meza, snack or street food consisting of sun-dried balls of drained yogurt (labaneh); also known as jameed.

labaneh; labnah; labni (LA-ban-eh) A sour Middle Eastern goat's milk cream cheese–style cheese made from laban; it is sometimes shaped into balls and rubbed with olive oil and paprika or mint; ewe's milk and cow's milk varieties are also available.

label A placard on a container, wrapper or other packaging that identifies the product and its producer, manufacturer or retailer and provides information regarding authenticity, quantity, quality, nutrition, health or safety warnings, usage and directions and/or other topics; some label content is regulated by federal, state and local governments and trade associations.

laberdan Cod that is salted and packed in barrels immediately after it arrives at port; it has a more subtle flavor than salt cod; the name is a corruption of Aberdeen, where this process was first introduced. *See* salt cod.

lablab The edible pod and seeds of a twining vine (*Dolichos lablan*) native to the Mediterranean region; also known as hyacinth bean.

labor costs The amounts spent on employees (full-time and part-time), including benefits and taxes; these are fixed and/or variable costs associated with the production of goods and presentation of services.

Labrusca (lah-brews-kah) One of the principal grape species native to North America; it includes the Concord and Catawba varieties; the resulting wine is usually foxy and has a grapey aroma.

Labskaus (LAAPS-kowss) A northern coastal German dish consisting of a cake made from chunks of fish, mashed potatoes and onions, fried in bacon fat.

lacatan banana A banana variety; the fruit are particularly flavorful.

Lachssalm (larh-salm) German for salmon.

lacón (lah-kohn) Spanish for knuckle of pork.

lacón con grelos (law-kohn con gra-loss) A dish from Spain's Galicia region consisting of cured pork shoulder cooked with turnip tops.

La Côte Basque A cocktail made of gin, Forbidden Fruit, triple sec and orange bitters.

lacqua (lac-kah) A thick prune butter made from puréed cooked prunes and the grated peel and juice of lemons; it is used in Jewish cuisines.

lactaire délicieux (lac-tair day-lee-see-yuh) French for milky cap mushroom.

lactalbumin A milk protein used as a nutrient supplement; also known as milk albuminate.

lactario (lack-tah-ree-oh) Spanish for milky cap mushroom.

lactase An intestinal enzyme that breaks down lactose into monosaccharides during digestion.

lactase enzyme A food additive and enzyme derived from yeast and used to convert lactose into glucose and galactose.

lactase-treated milk Milk treated with the enzyme lactase, which breaks down the lactose into glucose and galactose; used by people who are lactose intolerant.

lactic A cheese-tasting term for a clean, wholesome, milky flavor.

lactic acid 1. Naturally occurring in several foods, a food additive used as an antimicrobial agent, flavor enhancer, flavoring agent, flavoring adjuvant and/or pH control agent in processed foods such as dairy products and frozen desserts; also known as 2-hydroxypropanoic acid. 2. An acid formed when lactose is fermented with *Streptococci lactis* bacteria, it occurs naturally when milk is soured and is partly responsible for the tart flavor of yogurt and cheese; also used as a preservative.

lactic starter Bacteria added to milk at the start of the cheese-making process; a culture usually containing *Streptococci* and *Lactobacilli;* ferments lactose into lactic acid and reduces the milk's pH to the proper range for rennet to facilitate the coagulation of the milk into curds and whey.

Lactobacillus acidophilus A bacteria found in some yogurts that may assist lactose digestion.

Lactobacillus bulgarius A bacteria found in some yogurts that assists lactose digestion.

lactoflavin *See* vitamin B$_2$.

lactose 1. A disaccharide occurring naturally in mammalian milk; it is the least sweet of the natural sugars, and many people cannot tolerate it in varying quantities; during digestion it is hydrolyzed into its component single sugars: glucose and galactose; also known as milk sugar. 2. A food additive used as a surface-finishing agent in processed foods such as baked goods. 3. Subject to FDA regulations, a filler in pharmaceutical products.

lactose intolerance An inability to digest milk because the enzyme lactase is absent.

lactovegetarian A vegetarian who does not eat meat, poultry, fish or eggs but does eat dairy products. *See* ovolactovegetarian *and* vegan.

lactylic esters of fatty acids Food additives used as plasticizers in processed foods such as bakery mixes and dehydrated fruits and vegetables and as emulsifiers in processed foods such as pudding mixes, frozen desserts, instant rice and shortenings.

la cuite (lah kweet) A thick, dark sugar syrup cooked until just before it burns and turns bitter; it is used in the American South as a candy, a topping for bread or in baked goods.

làde (lau-day) Chinese for spicy.

ladera (lah-da-rah) Greek for cooked vegetables. *See* briami.

laderes (lah-the-rees) Greek for foods braised in olive oil until done; they are usually served cold or lukewarm.

ladies' fingers *See* okra.

ladies' night A promotion made by bars offering women drinks at a reduced price to attract more women—and therefore more men—to the bar.

ladle *v.* To move portions of a food using a ladle. *n.* A utensil with a cuplike bowl and a long hooked or pierced handle and available in various sizes (the capacity is often stamped on the handle); used to pour sauces and liquids (e.g., soups) and to push sauces and other foods through a sieve.

ladoxido (lah-tho-xee-tho) Greek for salad dressing or vinaigrette.

lady apple A small, hard apple ranging in color from red to red-blushed yellow; it has a flavorful, delicate skin and a sweet–tart flavor; often used as a garnish.

ladles

Lady Baltimore cake A three-layer white cake made with egg whites, filled with raisins, nuts and dried fruit and covered with a fluffy white frosting such as boiled icing. *See* Lord Baltimore cake.

lady finger *See* Savoy cake.

ladyfinger; lady finger A flat, finger-shaped cookie made from a light, sponge cake batter; used as a petit four or to line a pan or mold for desserts.

ladyfish *See* bonefish.

lady locks *See* cream horn.

lady's smock *See* meadow cress.

Lafayette (lah-fehy-ette) *See* spot.

lagales (LAG-eiylz) A contraction of the words lager and ale and used to describe beers produced by blending the two beverages; term attributed to author H. Hillman.

Lage (LAH-guh) The German term for a vineyard site; similar to climat in Burgundy and cru in Bordeaux.

lage mat (lah-geh maht) Norwegian for to cook.

lager *v.* To store beer at low temperatures to condition it. *n.* A beer brewed with a bottom-fermenting yeast and stored in a refrigerated cellar for 1–3 months.

Lagerbier (LAH-ger-beer) German for lager.

lagmi (LAHG-mee) An Arabic fermented beverage made from palm sap.

lagosta (lah-gost-tah) Portuguese for crayfish.

lagôstim (lah-goush-TEEM) Portuguese for lobster or prawn.

lag phase A rest period (of 1–4 hours) for bacteria in a culture or colony during which little growth occurs; it usually follows the movement of the bacteria from one place to another and is the period during which the bacteria adjust to their new location. *See* log phase *and* decline phase.

La Grande Passion The proprietary name of a French passion fruit liqueur with an Armagnac base.

Laguiole (lah-YOLE or lie-YULL) A French unpasteurized cow's milk cheese; it has a dry, grayish-brown rind, a crumbly, straw-colored, moist interior and a sharp, complex flavor with a hint of grassiness; it is sold in fat barrel shapes with slightly swollen sides.

lahana (lah-haa-nah) Greek for cabbage.

lahanika (lah-haa-nee-kao) Greek for vegetables and also the separate vegetable course.

lahma bil ajeen (lah-mah bill a-ja-hen) A Middle Eastern pizzalike dish consisting of minced seasoned lamb baked on top of a pastry dough.

lahna (law-nah) Finnish for bream.

lahum; lahm (lah'um) Arabic for meat.

lahum adjoun (lah'um ahd-june) An Armenian meat pie (lamb or beef), usually flavored with lemon, thyme, parsley, yogurt and pine nuts.

lahum buqqar (lah'um boo'ck-garh) Arabic for beef.

lahum ijil (lah'um ein-jeel) Arabic for veal.

lahum khunzeer (lah'um k'hen-zeer) Arabic for pork.

lahum mishwee (lah'um mesh-wee) A Middle Eastern dish of grilled lamb chunks placed on skewers and flavored with mint and pepper.

lahum nee (lah'um nay) An Arabic dish consisting of raw ground lamb or beef flavored with onions, pepper and coriander; usually served as an appetizer.

lahvosh; lavash (LAH-vohsh) An Armenian cracker bread leavened with yeast and baked in round sheets that are thin, flat and crisp; they are used like other mildly flavored crackers or can be softened with water and rolled around sandwich fillings. *See* aram sandwich.

laim (law-him) Russian for lime.

laimun malih (lay-moon ma-lih) Arabic for lime.

lait (leh) French for milk.

lait cru (leh crew) French for raw milk.

laiterie; laitier (lay-tu-ree; lay-tee-ay) 1. French for dairy and dairyman, respectively. 2. A French cheese-labeling term indicating that the cheese was made in a creamery or factory.

lait perfumé An Algerian beverage of milk simmered with mint; served chilled.

laitue (lay-tew) French for lettuce.

là jiao (law gee-ah-oh) Chinese for chiles.

lake (lahk) Norwegian and Swedish for burbot.

Lake Erie North Shore A grape-growing and wine-producing region in Canada's Ontario province, located on a strip of land near Lake St. Clair; the principal grapes grown are Riesling, Maréchal Foch and Seyvel Blanc.

lake herring A fish found in the Great Lakes; it has an iridescent silvery skin, an average market weight of 0.5–1 lb. (225–450 g) and a high fat content and is often smoked; sometimes sold as whitefish and is also known as blueback and cisco.

lake perch *See* yellow perch.

lake pickerel *See* northern pike.

lakerda; lakertha (lah-kher-tha) A Greek dish of pickled fish, usually tuna or swordfish, commonly served as a meze.

lake sturgeon A fish found in the Columbia River as well as parts of the American Southeast; it has a grayish-green skin, a long pointed snout, an average market weight of 8–10 lb. (3.6–4.5 kg), and a firm flesh with a delicate flavor; also known as common sturgeon and shortnose sturgeon.

lake trout Any of several wild freshwater trout found in North American waters; skin colors vary, with shades of gray and olive predominating; the flesh ranges from pale ivory to deep pink and has a high fat content, a firm texture and a delicate flavor; average market weight is 2–4 lb. (0.9–1.8 kg); significant varieties include the Great Lakes trout and mackinaw; also known as char.

lake whitefish *See* whitefish.

lakh-lalo (lack-lah-low) A Mali stew made from dried salted fish (usually cod), onions, okra and tomatoes and flavored with netetou.

Lakka A Finnish liqueur made from the Arctic cloudberry.

laks (lahks) Danish and Norwegian for salmon.

laksa (luck-sa) 1. Filipino for 10,000 and used to describe a dish that contains various vegetables, shrimp, pork and bean flour vermicelli. 2. A Malaysian and Indonesian noodle dish with fish, shrimp or chicken in a creamy curry or tamarind sauce.

la kula (law koo-law) Swahili for to eat.

Lallah Rookh A cocktail made of light rum, Cognac and crème de vanilla or vanilla extract; served in a chilled wine glass and topped with whipped cream.

lal mirch (lahl meerch) Hindi for red pepper.

lam (lahm) Norwegian for lamb.

lamb The meat of a sheep slaughtered when less than 1 year old; it is generally tender and has a mild flavor; also known as a yearling. *See* baby lamb, spring lamb *and* mutton.

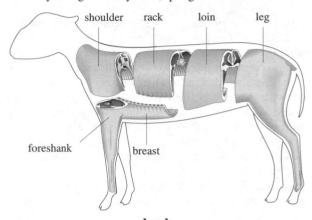

lamb
(American primals)

lamb, ground Lamb ground from muscles found in various primals but principally the shoulder and shank end of the leg.

lamb, Icelandic Small lamb raised in Iceland; the flesh has a finer texture and flavor than common lamb.

lambanog (lam-ba-nog) A Filipino alcoholic beverage made from distilled tuba.

lamb arm chops *See* lamb shoulder chop.

lambasteik (lahm-bass-tek) An Icelandic lamb dish.

lamb breast A subprimal cut of the lamb primal breast; it is neither particularly meaty nor flavorful and is available with or without bones.

lamb chop A fabricated cut of the lamb primal rack; it usually contains one rib (called a single chop) or two ribs (a double chop) and the flavorful, tender rib eye muscle.

lamb cushion shoulder roast A subprimal cut of the lamb primal shoulder; it is flavorful but somewhat tough.

Lambert cherry A large sweet cherry with a deep ruby red color, a firm, meaty flesh and a sweet flavor.

lambi *See* conch.

lambic (lahm-bic) A style of Belgian beer brewed with wild yeast and beer-souring bacteria.

lamb leg A subprimal cut of the lamb primal leg; available fully or partially deboned, it is quite tender and flavorful and is sometimes further fabricated into steaks.

lamb leg chop A fabricated cut of the lamb primal leg; it is somewhat tough.

lamb loin chop A fabricated cut of the lamb primal loin; it is a tender, flavorful chop.

lamb loin roast A subprimal cut of the lamb primal loin.

lamb medallions A fabricated cut of the lamb primal loin; the medallions are cut from the very tender and flavorful loin eye muscle.

lamb noisettes (nwah-ZET) A fabricated cut of the lamb primal loin; the noisettes are cut from the very tender and flavorful loin eye muscle.

lamb primals The five principal sections of the lamb carcass: the shoulder, rack, breast, loin and leg; each primal contains both bilateral halves.

lamb quality grades See USDA quality grades, prime, choice, good, utility and cull.

lamb riblets; lamb rib tips A fabricated cut of the lamb primal breast; they are the tips of the ribs (which are part of the primal rack); also known as Denver ribs.

lamb rib roast A subprimal cut of the lamb primal rack; it is one-half of the entire rack kept intact for roasting.

Lambrusco (lam-BROOS-co) 1. A red wine grape grown in Italy. 2. A lightly sparkling and somewhat sweet red wine made from this grape through the Charmat process; a dry version is also available.

lamb shoulder chop A fabricated cut of the lamb primal shoulder; it contains pieces of several muscles and is sometimes tough.

lamb's lettuce See mâche.

lamb square cut shoulder A subprimal cut of the lamb primal shoulder; it is an untrimmed roast.

lamb's quarters A wild, spinachlike green (Chenopodium album) with a mild flavor.

Lamb's Wool A drink made of heated sweetened, spiced beer to which the soft, fluffy pulp of baked apples is added; popular in England from the 16th to 19th centuries.

lamburgers Ground lamb shaped into patties.

lamb yield grades See USDA yield grades.

lamella pl. lamellae. A thin scale, plate, bone or tissue.

lamellate venus clam A variety of venus clam found in the western Pacific Ocean and Indian Ocean; it has a beige and violet shell that measures 1.5–2 in. (3.8–5.08 cm) across and a sweet meat.

laminated dough See rolled-in dough.

lamination The technique of layering fat and dough through a process of rolling and folding; this procedure is used to make puff pastry, croissant dough and Danish pastry dough. See rolled-in dough.

lamington An Australian dessert consisting of a square of sponge cake coated in chocolate and dried coconut; named for Lord Lamington, a governor of Queensland.

lamm (lahm) Swedish for lamb.

Lamm (lahm) German for lamb.

lammas (LAHM-mahss) Finnish for lamb or mutton.

lammellae See gills.

lamponi (lahm-POA-nee) Italian for raspberries.

lampreia (lamm-pra-yah) Portuguese for lamprey.

lamprey A long eel-shaped fish found in freshwater and saltwater of North America and Europe; it has black skin, very fatty flesh and a delicate flavor.

lampries (lump-rice) A festive Sri Lankan dish consisting of several foods wrapped in banana leaf parcels and baked.

lamsvlees (LAHMZ-vlays) Dutch for lamb.

Lanark Blue A semisoft to firm Scottish blue cheese made from unpasteurized ewe's milk; it has a rich, creamy white interior with blue-green veins and a strong, salty flavor.

Lancashire (LANG-kuh-sheer) A relatively moist, firm cheese made in Lancashire, England, from cow's milk; it has an ivory-white color and a mild flavor that becomes sharper as it ages; aged, it melts easily and is used for Welsh rarebit.

Lancashire hot pot A British hotchpotch.

Lancero A slim, elegant cigar with a 36 ring and a 7 1/2-in. length.

lancette (lahn-chay-tay) Italian for small spear and used to describe small spear-shaped pasta, usually used for soups.

land cress A plant (Barbarea verna) with small, slightly cupped dark green leaves and a mild peppery flavor similar to that of watercress; also known as American cress and winter cress.

Landwein (lahn'd-vine) A German quality designation within the Deutscher Tafelwein category for a dry to semi-dry wine.

Lane cake A white or yellow layer cake filled with a mixture of coconut, dried fruit and nuts and covered with a fluffy white frosting such as boiled icing; created by Alabama resident Emma Lane.

Langavulin The proprietary name of a single-malt Scotch whisky; it has a golden brown color and a robust, full, complex flavor; it is particularly suitable as a digestif.

Langhorne Creek A grape-growing and wine-producing area in South Australia; the principal grapes grown are Shiraz, Cabernet Sauvignon and, to a lesser extent, Merlot.

Langley Gage gooseberry A gooseberry variety; the fruit have a translucent whitish-green skin and a very sweet flavor.

langosta (lahn-goh-stah) Spanish for lobster.

langostino (lahn-goh-STEEN-oh) Spanish for prawn.

langouste (lahn-GOOST) French for spiny lobster.

langoustine (lahn-goo-STEEN) 1. A variety of small lobster found in the North Atlantic; it has a yellowish-pink shell, no claws, and a lean white flesh with a sweet flavor. 2. French for prawn.

Langra mango A rose-colored mango with a sweet, orange-yellow flesh; grown in India.

Langres (LAHNG-gruh) An unpasteurized cow's milk cheese from France's Champagne region; it has a concave top, a red-orange rind, and a blond-colored interior with a rich, soft texture and a spicy, intense flavor.

langue de boeuf (LAN-guh duh buff) French for ox tongue.

languedocienne, à la (lan-guh-doss-YEN, ah lah) A French preparation method associated with the cuisine of the Languedoc region; the dishes are characterized by a sauce flavored with garlic or a garnish of stuffed eggplants, minced cépes sautéed in oil, tomatoes and parsley and accompanied by pommes château.

langues de chat (lahngg duh sha) French for cat's tongue and used to describe a thin, finger-shaped biscuit or cookie.

lantern herb *See* winter cherry.

lanttu (LAHNT-too) Finnish for turnip or rutabaga.

lao (lah-oh) Chinese for pan-frying with little to no fat (e.g., cooking wheat flour cakes in a skillet without oil).

laos Malaysian for galanga.

Laotian rice Rice grown on the Laotian hillsides (as opposed to paddies); it is soaked before being steamed in a luang prabang.

lap (larp) A Laotian dish of finely ground raw meat, usually buffalo or venison, seasoned with chiles and herbs; served wrapped in a lettuce leaf.

lapereau (lah-peh-roa) French for young rabbit.

lapin (la-PEN) French for rabbit.

lapin du brasseur (la-PEN duh brahs-shur) A Belgian dish of rabbit braised in Lambic beer, flavored with juniper schnapps and smoked bacon and garnished with pearl onions.

Lapland A very hard Swedish Emmental-style cheese made by Laplanders from reindeer milk; it has an unusual shape: round and flat and formed so that a cross section resembles a dumbbell with angular rather than round ends.

Lapsang Souchong A Chinese black tea; the beverage has a tarry, smoky flavor and is best consumed without milk.

lapsha (lah'p-shah) Russian for noodles.

lapshkaus Norwegian for stew.

laptuca (lah-too-cah) Romanian for lettuce.

laranja (lah-RAHN-zhah) Portuguese for orange.

larb A northeastern Thai-style warm salad of grilled minced meat dressed with lime juice, dry chile and roasted rice powder; usually made with beef or chicken but can also be made with duck and freshwater fish.

larch gum A food additive used as a thickener in processed foods such as cake fillings.

lard (lahr) French for bacon.

lard *v.* To insert long, thin strips of fat into a dry cut of meat to increase its moistness and tenderness after cooking; also known as interlard. *n.* Rendered, clarified and purified pork fat; used as an ingredient and cooking medium; it is very rich. *See* leaf lard.

lard de poitrine fumé (lahr duh pwoh-treen foo-may) French for smoked bacon.

lard gras (lahr gra) French for the pork fat between the skin and the flesh of the chine.

larding needle A tool used for larding meat; it has a sharp, pointed tip with a hollow body that is used to hold the larding material.

lard maigre (lahr mah-gruh) French for the pork fat from the pig's belly, which is interspersed with lean pork.

larding needle

lardo (LAHR-doh) Italian for fatback.

lardon; lardoon (LAHR-don; lar-DOON) 1. A long thin strip of fat used to lard meat. 2. Diced, blanched and fried bacon used in French cuisine.

Large Cherry tomato A variety of red-skinned, flavorful cherry tomato.

large intestine Extending from the ileum to the anus, the large intestine contains the cecum, colon and rectum; the wall absorbs water from intestinal contents (mostly undigested wastes).

large T-bone A fabricated cut of the beef primal short loin; it is a porterhouse with a smaller tenderloin section.

largo chile A hot yellow chile used in Latin American cuisines.

La Rioja A grape-growing and wine-producing province in Argentina; the principal grape grown is the Torrontes Riojana.

lasagna (luh-ZAHN-yuh) 1. Wide, flat Italian pasta sheets with ruffled or smooth edges. 2. An Italian dish made with boiled lasagna layered with cheese (usually ricotta and mozzarella) and meats and/or vegetables and topped with a tomato, meat and/or béchamel and baked.

lasinietis (law-sea-niet-his) A Lithuanian white yeast bread made with whole peppercorns and crisp bacon rind; served with butter at meals or afternoon tea.

lassam (law-sahm) Hindi for garlic.

lassi (lah-see) An Indian cold beverage made of yogurt thinned with water, sweetened and flavored with rose essence or rosewater.

last call An announcement to bar patrons made just before closing time so that they can place their final drink orders.

late bottled vintage port A port of a specific vintage that has been aged in wooden pipes for 4–6 years; it must be labeled as such to avoid confusion with vintage port. *See* vintage port.

Late Cluster A variety of hops grown in the states of Idaho and Washington.

Late Harvest 1. A wine (usually from California) made from very ripe grapes or ones affected by the noble rot; generally a sweet white wine made from Johannisberg Riesling, Gewürztraminer, Sémillon, Sauvignon Blanc or Chenin Blanc grapes. 2. The benchmark of a labeling system for such wines based on the grape sugar content: Late Harvest (a minimum of 24° Brix or approximately 24% sugar), Select Late Harvest (a minimum of 28° Brix) and Special Select Late Harvest (a minimum of 35° Brix). *See* Early Harvest.

Latham raspberry A raspberry variety; the fruit are large and red.

latick (la-tick) A brown, curdlike substance left after coconut milk is heated until the oil separates; it is used as a topping for Filipino desserts or snack foods.

Latium (LAH-t'yum) A grape-growing and wine-producing area in central Italy; its white wines are made from a combination of Malvasia and Trebbiano grapes.

latke (LAHT-kuh) A Jewish potato pancake usually made from grated potatoes mixed with eggs, onions, matzo meal and seasonings; it is fried and served hot with applesauce.

lato (la-toh) A seaweed with grapelike clusters of tiny balls; it is used in Filipino cuisine.

la-tot *See* pepper leaves.

latte (LAHT-tay) Italian for milk.

lattice Strips of pastry dough arranged in a crisscross pattern, usually laid on top of a pie or tart.

lattice cutter 1. A plastic or metal stencil used to cut a diamond-shaped lattice pattern into rolled-out dough. 2. A rolling cutter with a 6-in.-wide axle holding several notched cutting wheels; used to cut a uniform lattice pattern in rolled-out dough; also known as lattice dough roller.

lattice cutter

lattice dough roller *See* lattice cutter.

latticello (lah-tee-tchae-low) Italian for buttermilk.

Lattich (LAH-tihk) German for lettuce.

lattuga (laht-TOO-gah) Italian for lettuce.

Lauch (lowkh) German for leek.

lau lau; laulau 1. A Hawaiian cooking method in which pork, chicken or fish is steamed in taro leaves tied with ti leaves. 2. A Hawaiian dish of such foods.

laung (lah-hoong) Hindi for clove.

laurel leaves Bay leaves from the laurel tree; those from the California laurel (*Umbellularia californica*) are edible and are used as a flavoring.

lauric acid A food additive derived from coconut oil and other vegetable fats; it is used as a lubricant, binder and defoaming agent.

laurier (lah-reh-ay) French for bay leaves.

lauter During beer brewing, to draw off the wort and separate it from the spent grains by sparging.

lauter tun A large vessel with a perforated false bottom used to strain the sweet wort from the draff or spent grain after mashing and during sparging in the beer-brewing process; also known as a mash tun.

Lavallière, à la 1. (lah-vah-lee-yair, ah lah) A French garnish for fowl and sweetbreads, consisting of sautéed truffles, lamb's sweetbreads larded with truffles and small steamed crayfish. 2. A French garnish for tournedos and noisettes, consisting of artichoke bottoms filled with asparagus tips, pommes château and sauce bordelaise.

Lavallière, sauce (lah-vah-lee-yair) A French compound sauce made from a demi-glaze flavored with game essence (extract), thickened with sour cream, and garnished with tarragon and truffles.

La Varenne, François Pierre (Fr., 1618–1678) Considered to be one of the founding fathers of French cuisine, his treatises, especially *Le Cuisinier Français* (1651), detail the early development, methods and manners of French cuisine; his analysis and recipes mark a departure from medieval cookery and a French cuisine heavily influenced by Italian traditions; as a chef he introduced the use of roux and bouquets garni.

lavender An herb (*Lavendula angustifolia*) with spikes of aromatic purple flowers and gray-green leaves, principally used for the strong fragrance of its essential oils; the flowers have a sweet, lemony flavor and are also used fresh in Middle Eastern and French cuisines or crystallized and used as a garnish, especially for baked goods.

lavender gem A citrus fruit that is a hybrid of a white grapefruit and a tangelo; the skin and flesh are a pale pink and the flesh has a sweet flavor; also known as wekiwas.

lavender honey A thick, deep golden–colored honey with a strong, perfumed flavor; principally made from lavender blossoms in France's Provence region.

lavender mulberry A variety of mulberry with a lavender-pink skin; the fruit are often dried.

laver (LAY-vuhr) Dried seaweed (genus *Porphyra*) sold in thin squares; it has a deep purple color and a tangy, sweet flavor; used in soups and breads and deep-fried as an appetizer in Great Britain and Japan; also known as purple laver. 2. An archiac term for a vessel, stone basin or trough.

laverbread A dense purée of laver; baked, it is used to flavor and thicken fish and shellfish sauces and as an ingredient in stuffings for fish.

lavraki (lah-nraa-kee) A Greek method for baking fish with butter, cream and lemon juice.

lax (lahks) Icelandic and Swedish for salmon.

Laxton A large and important group of apples similar to the Coxes but with a brighter color; they have a crisp texture and a light flavor.

Laxtonberry A hybrid berry similar to the raspberry.

Laxton's gage; Laxton's supreme plum A variety of plum with a reddish-yellow skin and a very sweet flavor.

Laxton's Giant currants A variety of black currants; they are relatively large and juicy.

layer *v.* 1. To stack one or more items, often with different items interleaved (e.g., a stack of crêpes separated by different fillings or two sheets of phyllo dough separated by melted butter). 2. To arrange items in an overlapping pattern (e.g., carrot slices laid out so that the top of one rests on the bottom half of the previous one). *n.* The single item being layered (e.g., a cake layer). *See* tiers.

layer cake Any cake with two or more layers of cake product joined with an icing or filling; the layers may be baked separately or as one large layer that is sliced horizontally into thinner layers after baking.

layer pack A storing or shipping unit containing cuts of meat layered in a single thickness and separated by a sheet or board.

laying away *See* storing.

laying down *See* storing.

laymun (lay-MOON) Arabic for lemon.

layos (laa-yoos) Greek for hare.

là yu (law you) Chinese for chile oil.

lazy-daisy cake A single-layer American yellow cake that is baked, topped with a brown sugar, butter and coconut mixture and finished under a hot broiler.

lazy Susan A rotating tray or platform placed in the center of a dining table from which diners can help themselves to food.

lazy tongs Tongs with a jointed extension framework operated by scissorlike handles; they are used for grasping an object at a distance.

lb. *See* pound.

LBV *See* late bottled vintage port.

LDL *See* low-density lipoproteins.

LDL cholesterol Cholesterol packaged in low-density lipoproteins; it transports cholesterol in the blood, and a high level of LDL cholesterol is associated with an increased risk of cardiovascular disease. *See* HDL cholesterol.

leach To cause water or other liquid to pass through a porous material such as food; in the process, substances such as nutrients may pass from the porous material into the liquid.

leaching The clarification and filtering process for distilled spirits, during which the spirits are filtered through finely ground and tamped-down charcoal.

leading sauces The foundation for the entire classic French repertoire of hot sauces; the five leading sauces (béchamel, velouté, espagnole [also known as brown], tomato and hollandaise) are distinguished by the liquids and thickeners used to make them; they can be seasoned and garnished to create a wide variety of small or compound sauces; also known as mother sauces. *See* small sauces.

leaf gelatin *See* gelatin, leaf.

leaf lard A high-quality lard made from the fat found around the hog's kidneys.

leaf lettuce *See* lettuce, leaf.

leaf stencil A tool used to create decorative leaf shapes from wafer-thin dough.

leaf vegetable; leafy vegetable A general term for any vegetable whose leaves are used for food, either cooked or raw.

leafy A wine-tasting term for a vegetal, leafy aroma (as opposed to an herbaceous one).

lean A food-labeling term approved by the FDA to describe meat, poultry, game, fish or shellfish that contains less than 10 g of fat, less than 4 g of saturated fat and less than 95 mg of cholesterol per serving or per 100 g.

lean dough A yeast dough that is low in fat and sugar (e.g., French bread and Cuban bread). *See* rich dough.

lear A traditional English sauce of flour, verjuice or vinegar and spices used for adding flavor and digestibility to gravies, meat pies and the like.

leather 1. An animal skin prepared for use by tanning or other process. 2. A description of a very tough, chewy food (usually unexpected or undesired). 3. Thin sheet of dried fruit purée. *See* fruit leather.

leatherwood honey An amber-colored, delicately flavored honey made in Australia from blossoms of the Tasmanian leatherwood tree.

leaven *v.* To increase the volume of a dough or batter by adding air or other gas. *n.* A leavening agent.

leavening agent; leavener; leaven 1. A substance used to leaven a dough or batter; it may be natural (e.g., air or steam), chemical (e.g., baking powder or baking soda) or biological (e.g., yeast). 2. A type of food additive used to produce or stimulate production of carbon dioxide in baked goods to impart a light texture.

Lebanon sausage A Pennsylvania Dutch reddish-brown, smoked, lean beef sausage flavored with black pepper and a little sugar; it is sliced thin and served with bread or cut into strips and combined with a cream sauce.

leben North African and Egyptian Arabic for laban.

Leber (LAY-beer) German for liver.

Leberkäse (LAY-buhr-kaiz) German for liver cheese and used to describe a smooth pâté made with pork liver, onions, garlic and eggs; it is formed into a tubular shape, sliced and steamed or sautéed.

Leberwurst (LAY-beer-voost) A German sausage made with pork liver and fat and seasoned with pepper and allspice.

Lebkuchen (LAYB-koo-kuhn) 1. A thick, cakelike German cookie made with honey, spices and ground nuts; the dough is usually cut into shapes or pressed into decorative molds; the baked cookies are decorated with a sugar glaze. 2. A Pennsylvania German Christmas pastry flavored with citrus and honey and leavened with yeast.

leblabi *See* balila.

leblebi (lehb-lehb-ee) An Indian snack or street food of cooked and dried or partially cooked and roasted chickpeas.

Le Brouere (luh broo-AIR) A pasteurized cow's milk cheese from France's Alsace region; it has a brushed chocolate-brown rind that bears a bas-relief design of trees and grouse, a creamy texture and a bright yellow interior with a buttery, nutty, sweet flavor.

leche (LEH-cheh) Spanish for milk.

lechebnie (la-cha-bnee-a) Russian for herbs.

lechecillas (lay-tcha-see-yahss) Spanish for sweetbreads.

leche cuajada (LEH-cheh kuh-hah-dah) Spanish for buttermilk.

leche flan A Filipino custard made with evaporated milk and flavored with lime zest.

leche frita (LEH-cheh free-tah) A Spanish custard flavored with lemon zest and cinnamon, baked, deep-fried and dusted with a mixture of cinnamon and confectioners' sugar; it has a crunchy exterior and a creamy interior.

lechefrite (lesch-freet) French for the pan placed underneath spit-roasted foods to catch the fat and juices.

lechon sarsa (le-chon sar-sah) A thick, slightly sweet Filipino sauce made from ground pork liver, brown sugar, vinegar and garlic; usually served with spit-roasted pork.

lechuga (leh-CHOO-gah) Spanish for lettuce.

lecithin 1. A fatty substance naturally occurring in animal tissue (especially liver and egg yolks) and plant tissue (especially legumes); it is both water soluble and fat soluble and is often used as an emulsifying agent. 2. A food additive used as a stabilizer, thickener, antioxidant and/or emulsifier in processed foods such as candies, mayonnaise, margarine and baked goods.

lecithinated soy flour Soy flour to which lecithin has been added; it is used as a pan release agent and emulsifier in baked goods.

leckerle; leckerli (LEH-kehr-lee) 1. A Swiss cookie made with honey, spices, candied citrus peel and ground almonds and covered with a sugar glaze after baking. 2. A Swiss cookie made with a mixture of egg whites, almonds and sugar that is dried, then baked briefly; also known as Zurich leckerli.

le concorde (luh kohn-cord) A French pastry composed of three layers of baked chocolate meringue filled and coated with chocolate mousse and covered with small sticks of baked chocolate meringue.

lecsó (leh-vish) A Hungarian dish of simmered green peppers, onions and tomatoes flavored with paprika and served with potatoes or rice.

led (lad) Russian for ice.

Lee cake A white layer cake flavored with lemon and orange; named for General Robert E. Lee (Am., 1807–1870) and popular in the American South.

leek A member of the lily family (*Allium porrum*); it has a thick, cylindrical, white stalk with a slightly bulbous root end and many flat, dull dark green leaves; the tender white stalk has a flavor that is sweeter and stronger than that of a scallion but milder than that of an onion and is used in salads and as a flavoring.

leeks

leen ngau *See* lotus root.

lees 1. The sediment a wine deposits while in a cask, barrel, tank or vat during fermentation, aging or storage; also known as dregs or bottoms. 2. The insoluble matter that settles from a liquid.

lees brandy Brandy distilled from the lees of a grape, citrus or other fruit wine; usually named for the appropriate fruit followed by the phrase lees brandy.

Leffe (lae-fae) The proprietary name of a dark, slightly sweet, top-fermented Belgian monastery beer.

lefse (LEFF-suh) Norwegian flatbread.

lefse rolling pin A 16.5-in.-long pin with a ribbed face used to score the surface of lefse.

lefse rolling pin

leg 1. A primal section of the veal carcass; it is the pos-terior portion of the carcass, containing both the legs and the sirloin; it contains portions of the backbone, hind shank and tail, hip, aitch and round bones and muscles such as top round, eye round, knuckle, sirloin, bottom round (which includes the sirloin) and butt tenderloin; used as is or fabricated into scallops and cutlets. 2. A primal section of the lamb carcass; it contains both legs and the sirloin; usually separated into the two legs, which are then partially or fully deboned and sometimes further fabricated into steaks.

leg of pork A British cut of the pork carcass; the leg without the foot, often further fabricated into the knuckle (similar to a shank) and fillet (butt end).

legs The streams of wine adhering to the inside of a glass that slowly descend to the wine in the body of the glass after the glass has been swirled; legs reflect the wine's viscosity and alcohol and glycerol contents (the higher the content, the slower the legs drain), not necessarily its quality; also known as tears and rivulets.

legumbres (leh-GOOM-bres) Spanish for root vegetables.

legumbres secos (leh-GOOM-bres SEH-kos) Spanish for dried vegetables.

legume (leg-umi) Portuguese for vegetables.

légumes (lay-GEWM) French for vegetables.

legumes A large group of plants that have double-seamed pods containing a single row of seeds; depending on the variety, the seeds, the pod and seeds together or the dried seeds are eaten. *See* beans, lentils, peas *and* pulses.

legumi (leh-GOO-mee) Italian for legumes.

légumier (lay-goo-mee-ay) At a food services operation following the brigade system, the person responsible for all vegetable and starch items; also known as the vegetable station chef.

leguminous plants Plants belonging to the family Leguminosae; they are generally flowering plants that have pods (legumes) as fruits (beans, peas and soybeans); there are three principal subgroups: *Caesalpiniaceae, Fabaceae* and *Mimosaceae;* they are imprecisely known as the pea family.

léh-sun (la-soon) Hindi for garlic.

Leicester (LESS-ter) A hard cheese made in Leicester, England, from cow's milk; it has a relatively high moisture content, a mellow flavor, a crumbly texture and an orange-red color (from annatto).

Leiden; Leyden (LY-dn) A semisoft Dutch cheese made from partly skimmed cow's milk and whole buttermilk that is flavored with caraway seeds and sometimes cumin, cloves and/or anise; it is produced in flat rounds with a sharp edge on one side; also known as Komijne Kaas.

leimoon (ley-mon) Hard, brown, dried limes or lemons; they are used whole or powdered to add a tart flavor to Arabic rice and other dishes; also known as loomi.

leimoon aswad; leimoon basra; leimoon omani Leimoon varieties from Egypt, Iraq and Oman, respectfully.

leipä (lay-pa) Finnish for bread and loaf.

leitao (lay-tah-oh) Portuguese for suckling pig.

leitao assado (lay-tah-oh ah-SAH-doo) A Portuguese dish of roast suckling pig flavored with herbs and spices.

leite (late) Portuguese for milk.

lekach (LEE-kasch) A Jewish honey–spice cake.

lekach (leh-kach) Yiddish for cake and used to describe a sponge cake or cakes in general.

lekvar (LEHK-vahr) 1. A thick, soft Hungarian spread of fruit cooked with sugar and used to fill pastries and cookies. 2. A thick prune butter used to flavor Jewish pastries.

lemon A citrus fruit (*Citrus limon*) with a bright yellow skin, an ovoid shape with a bulge at the blossom end, a juicy yellow flesh and a very tart, distinctive flavor.

lemonade *See* ade.

lemon-and-lime soda A sweetened carbonated soft drink with lemon and lime flavorings.

lemon balm A small perennial herb (*Melissa officinalis*) with slightly hairy, serrated leaves and a strong lemon flavor and fragrance; used in sweet and savory dishes and for tisanes.

Lemon Boy A variety of medium-sized tomato with a lemon yellow color, a deeply oblated shape and a tangy, lemony flavor.

lemon butter sauce An English butter sauce flavored with lemon juice and thickened with cornstarch; it is usually served with boiled pike.

lemon cucumber A slicing cucumber with a yellow skin and an ivory flesh.

lemon curd A soft, thick custard made from lemon juice, sugar, eggs and butter; used to fill tarts and cakes and as a spread for sweet breads and scones.

lemongrass A tropical grass (*Cymbopogon citratus*) with long, greenish stalks and serrated leaves; the white to pale green inner stalks have a strong lemonlike flavor and aroma and are used fresh in Southeast Asian cuisines; also known as citronella grass.

lemon grater A grater with a flat or slightly convex grating surface with fine teeth; used to remove the zest from citrus fruit.

lemoni (leh-moo-nee) Greek for lemon.

lemon juice The liquid constituent of a lemon; it has a tart, distinctive flavor, is used in sweet and savory dishes and is available fresh or frozen.

lemon grater

lemon meringue pie A dessert composed of a flaky pastry shell filled with a rich lemon custard and topped with a thick layer of soft meringue.

lemon oil The oil obtained from the lemon; it is used as a flavoring agent, especially in reconstituted lemon juice.

lemon sole A member of the flounder family found off the U.S. East Coast; it has a finely textured, white flesh, a sweet flavor and an average market weight of 2 lb. (900 g); also known as blackback flounder and winter flounder. *See* English sole.

lemon spout A spout screwed into the end of a lemon; when the lemon is squeezed, seed-free juice pours out.

lemon verbena An herb (*Lippia citriodora*) with light green pointed leaves and white or lilac blossoms; it has a strong lemonlike flavor and aroma and is used in tisanes and desserts; also known as verbena.

lemony A wine-tasting term for a wine, usually white, with excess acidity and a tart, acidic flavor.

Lendenschnitten (lan-dan-shnee-tan) German for filet of beef.

leng (lang) Chinese for cold.

length A wine-tasting term for the time a flavor lingers after tasting and swallowing or expectorating.

lengua (LEN-guah) Spanish for tongue.

lenguado (LEN-guah-doh) Spanish for flounder or sole.

lengua en salsa picante (len-guah en sal-saw pee-cahn-ta) A Chilean dish of beef tongue simmered in an aromatic stock and then served with a sauce flavored with the stock, vinegar and chiles.

lentejas (layn-TAY-khahss) Spanish for lentils.

lenticchie (layn-TEEK-kee-ay) Italian for lentils.

lentilhas (lehn-TEE-lee-ahs) Portuguese for lentils.

lentilles (lahng-tee) French for lentils.

lentils The small flat seeds of a variety of legumes (*Lens esculenta* or *L. culinaris*); sold shelled, dried or cooked.

lentils, Egyptian A smaller, rounder variety of lentils sold without the seed's outer covering; they have a reddish-orange color.

lentils, French A variety of lentils sold with the seed's outer covering intact; they have a grayish-brown exterior and a creamy yellow interior; also known as European lentils.

lentin (lahn-teen) French for shiitake.

Léopold (lay-oh-pold) A French beef consommé, thickened with semolina and garnished with sautéed sorrel and chervil.

lepre (LAI-pray) Italian for hare.

lesbian An ancient Greek sweet red wine.

les choesels (lay shoh-sail) A Belgian dish of oxtail, mutton, veal, sheep's trotters, ox kidney and sweetbreads simmered with herbs, cloves, nutmeg, onions and Madeira and garnished with fricandelles made with mushrooms.

lesco (less-cho) A Jewish and Hungarian dish consisting of roasted bell peppers simmered with cabbage, tomatoes and onions and flavored with garlic, sugar and vinegar.

leshch (lyehshch) Russian for bream.

lesnoy oreh (less-noh-e ork) Russian for hazelnuts.

less A food-labeling term approved by the FDA to describe a nutritionally altered food that contains at least 25% fewer calories than the regular or reference (i.e., FDA standard) food.

lesso (LEH-soh) Italian for boiled; it refers to both the method and the food that is boiled.

lesso rifato (LAYS-soa reh-fah-toh) An Italian dish of sliced cooked meat, usually beef, reheated with onions and garlic and flavored with lemon juice and parsley.

letas (lay-tahs) Swahili for lettuce.

let it down British slang for to thin or dilute.

lettuce Any of a variety of plants of the genus *Lactuca*, probably native to the Mediterranean and now grown worldwide; their leaves are generally consumed fresh in salads or used as a garnish; there are three principal types of lettuces: butterhead, crisp head and leaf.

lettuce, butterhead Any variety of lettuce (*Lactuca sativa*) with a small, spherical, loosely formed head of slightly cup-shaped leaves that have a sweet, buttery flavor and a soft, buttery texture; the outer leaves are pale to medium green and the inner ones tend to be yellow-green (e.g., Boston lettuce); red varieties (especially for baby lettuces) are also available; also known as butter lettuce and buttercrunch lettuce.

lettuce, crisp head Any variety of lettuce with a large, spherical head of densely packed, crisp, pale green, cup-shaped leaves that tend to be paler or a whitish-yellow toward the center; they have a rather bland flavor (e.g., iceberg).

lettuce, head A general name for any lettuce with leaves that grow in a moderately loose to dense rosette; the two principal categories of head lettuce are butterhead and crisp head.

lettuce, leaf Any variety of lettuce whose ruffle-edged leaves are loose rather than bunched in a head and have a mild flavor (e.g., green leaf lettuce and red leaf lettuce); also known as looseleaf lettuce.

leucine 1. An essential amino acid. 2. A food additive used as a nutrient source to significantly improve the biological quality of the total protein in a food containing the naturally occurring protein.

levadura (lay-vah-DUHR-rah) Spanish for yeast.

levain (le-VAN) A ripened, uncooked sourdough starter.

levedura (leh-veh-doo-rah) Portuguese for yeast.

Leveller gooseberry A gooseberry variety; the fruit have a yellowish-green skin and an intense flavor.

lever (LEH-vehr) Danish, Norwegian and Swedish for liver.

leveret (lah-vah-rah) French for a young hare.

leverpostej (la-var-pos-tay-ee) A Danish smørrebrød dish of liver pâté on black bread garnished with strips of aspic and pickled gherkins.

levrek (lah-vrack) Turkish for sea bass.

levulose *See* fructose.

levulose-bearing syrup *See* fructose corn syrup.

levure (luh-vurh) French for yeast.

li (lee) Chinese for nashi.

liability A debt or obligation owed by a business.

liaison (lee-yeh-zon) A mixture of egg yolks and heavy cream used to thicken and enrich sauces.

lian rong (lee-ahn rong) A Chinese flavoring paste made from cooked lotus seeds mashed with a little sugar.

liba (lee-bo) Hungarian for goose.

libation A beverage, usually alcoholic.

Liberty A variety of hops widely grown in the United States.

license state A state in which the government has little or no control over the distribution system for alcoholic beverages; also known as an open state. *See* control state.

lichee; lichi *See* litchi.

licor de café A beverage made in the Cape Verde Islands; pounded coffee beans and a sugar syrup are added to white rum and left to age for 3 weeks.

Licor 43 *See* Cuarenta y Tes.

licorice; liquorice 1. A feathery-leafed plant (*Glycyrrhiza glabra*) grown in Europe and Asia; its dried root and an extract taken from the root have a distinctive, sweet flavor similar to that of anise or fennel; used as a flavoring in candies, confections, baked goods and beverages. 2. A candy flavored with licorice extract, usually colored red or black.

licuado (lee-coo-ah-doe) Spanish for a fruit drink, especially citrus.

lid, self-sealing A two-part metal closure consisting of an enamel-lined metal lid with sealing compound and a threaded metal band or ring to hold the lid in place; when used as a manufacturer directs, it produces a vacuum seal that can be verified by the position of the lid after a jar's contents have cooled.

Liebfraumilch (LEEB-frow-milsh) German for milk of the Blessed Mother and used to describe a light, slightly sweet white wine made from a blend of grapes, which often includes Riesling, Silvaner and/or Müller-Thurgau.

liebre (LYAH-bray) Spanish for hare.

Liederkranz (LEE-der-krahnts) A semisoft cheese made in Ohio from cow's milk; it has an ivory interior, an edible pale yellow crust, and a mildly pungent, distinctive flavor and aroma; as it ages, the interior becomes a honey color, and the flavor and aroma become stronger.

liégeoise, à la (lea-zhwah, ah lah) A French and Belgian method of cooking using juniper berries, especially with veal kidneys, which are braised in butter with the berries and then flambéed with gin.

lievito (lee-YEA-vee-to) Italian for yeast.

lievito naturale; lievito madre (lee-VITO nat-u-ra-LAY; maa-DRAY) Italian for sourdough starter; usually made with flour, water and hops or grape skins.

lièvre (ly-ehvr) French for hare or rabbit.

lift (lift'h) Arabic for turnip.

light 1. A food-labeling term approved by the FDA to describe a nutritionally altered food with at least 33% fewer calories, 50% less fat or 50% less sodium than the regular or reference (i.e., FDA standard) food. 2. A wine-tasting term for a wine that is neither full bodied nor heavy.

light ale *See* pale ale.

light beef A beef carcass that averages 25% less fat or 25% fewer calories than standard beef.

light beer; lite beer A marketing term for a low-calorie American beer (usually in the Pilsner style) made by adding water to a beer that has been brewed from a barley mash and fermented dry.

light corn bread *See* corn bread, light.

light in sodium A food-labeling term approved by the FDA to describe a nutritionally altered food with 50% or less sodium than the regular or reference (i.e., FDA standard) food.

light malt vinegar *See* malt vinegar.

light meat The breast and wing flesh of a chicken or turkey; it has a light tannish-ivory color when cooked and less connective tissue and fat than dark meat; the lighter color is the result of a decreased myoglobin content in these infrequently used muscles.

light roast *See* roast, light.

light rosé *See* blush wine.

light rum A clear rum with a slight molasses flavor.

lights The lungs of an animal such as a calf or young hog.

light whiskey Whiskey distilled at 161–189 proof from a mash usually made from corn; it is aged in new or used uncharred oak barrels. *See* blended light whiskey.

light wine A labeling term approved by the FDA for a wine that has less than 14% alcohol by volume.

lignin A noncarbohydrate polysaccharide present in plants; it combines with cellulose to form the plant's woody materials and is sometimes classified as a dietary fiber.

liha (lee-ha) Finnish for meat.

li jiàng (lee gee-hang) Chinese for oyster sauce, a thick paste of oysters, salt and seasonings.

lilikoi Hawaiian for passion fruit.

Lillet (lee-LAY) A proprietary French aperitif made from wine, brandy, fruits and herbs; served over ice with a twist of orange; Lillet Blanc is made from white wine, and Lillet Rouge is made from red wine.

lily bud *See* tiger lily bud.

lily family *See* Allium.

lima (LEE-mah) Spanish for lime.

lima bean (LY-muh) A flat, kidney-shaped bean native to Peru; it has a pale green color that becomes creamy yellow as it matures and a waxy texture; available fresh, dried, canned or frozen; the mature bean is also known as the butter bean and calico bean.

limão (lee-MOW) Portuguese for lemon.

limau (lee-mah-who) Swahili for lemon.

limau kesturi (lee-mau kes-too-ree) A very small lime used in Filipino and Southeast Asian cuisines as a sour flavoring agent.

Limburger (LIHM-buhr-guhr) A semisoft, surface-ripened Belgian cheese made from cow's milk; it has a strong, distinctive flavor and aroma, a yellow to reddish-brown rind, and a yellow, pasty interior; also made in Germany and the United States.

Limburger vlaai (leam-boorct-her vlah-e) Small Dutch tortes made from a yeast dough and topped or filled with fruits or streusel.

lime 1. An ovoid citrus fruit (*Citrus aurantifolia*) with a thin, green skin; smaller than a lemon, it has a juicy, pale green pulp and a very tart flavor. 2. *See* calcium oxide.

lime *See* calcium oxide.

limeade *See* ade.

lime flower honey A rich, softly flavored honey with a green-gold color made in France and eastern Europe from linden tree blossoms; also known as linden honey.

lime juice The liquid constituent of a freshly squeezed lime; it has a tart, distinctive flavor and is used in sweet and savory dishes.

lime pickle A condiment made from limes, chiles, spices and vinegar.

limequat A hybrid of the lime and kumquat; a small citrus fruit with a pale yellow-green rind, a yellowish flesh and a sharp, fragrant flavor; the entire fruit is eaten or used in preserves.

Limerick ham An Irish ham smoked over oak shavings and juniper berries; usually boiled and served hot or cold with a parsley sauce.

lime solution A finely ground powder of calcium hydroxide mixed with water and used to add crispness to batters, for pickling and with fruits for desserts.

limestone lettuce *See* bibb lettuce.

limetta 1. A citrus fruit (*Citrus limetta*) that resembles a lemon with a nipple and a furrow at one end; it has a juicy yellow flesh and a sweet lemonade-like flavor; also known as a sweet lemon. 2. Italian for lime.

limited bottling A wine label term indicating that the producer made or has available for sale only a limited quantity of the particular wine; the term has no legal significance.

limón (lee-MON) A citrus fruit native to Mexico and the American Southwest; similar to a lemon, it is traditionally served (instead of limes) with tequila drinks.

limon (lee-MON) Hebrew and Russian for lemon.

limoncillo (lee-mohn-CHEH-loh) 1. An Italian liqueur made by steeping lemon peels in alcohol and adding a sugar syrup. 2. *See* genip.

limone (lee-MOA-nay) Italian for lemon.

Limone (lee-mon) German for lime.

limonene A food additive derived from orange, lemon and pineapple oils and used as an antioxidant and flavoring agent.

limonit (lee-mon-it) Hebrew for lime.

Limousin (lee-moo-zan) A forest in France whose oak trees are used to make barrels for aging wine; the wood is soft with a loose grain, allowing rapid extraction of tannin and flavor.

limousine, à la (lee-moo-zeen, ah lah) 1. A French method of cooking red cabbage in bouillon with bacon fat and garnishing it with braised chestnuts. 2. Meat or poultry garnished with such cabbage.

limpa; limpa bread (LIHM-puh) A moist Swedish rye bread flavored with anise and orange peel.

limpet Any of several varieties of gastropod mollusks found on rocks lining the coasts of temperate to tropical saltwaters; generally, they have a conical, hat-shaped shell and a tough, flavorful flesh; significant varieties include the common Mexican and tortoiseshell limpets.

limu Hawaiian for any of a wide variety of edible seaweed.

linalyl isobutyrate A food additive with a fruity aroma used as a flavoring agent.

Lincoln, Mrs. A. D. (Am., 1844–1921) The founder and original principal of the Boston Cooking School, secretary of her own baking powder company and culinary editor of the *American Kitchen* magazine. In 1884, she published *The Boston Cookbook,* the first of its kind to tabulate the ingredients at the start of each recipe and to offer a detailed table of weights and measures.

Lincoln County process The technique used for filtering Tennessee whiskey by passing it through at least 10 ft. of sugar maple charcoal before aging.

linden blossoms Blossoms of the small-leaved lime tree (*Tilia cordata*); when dried, they are used to make a tisane that, when sweetened and flavored with cinnamon, is believed by some to cure coughs and colds.

linden honey *See* lime flower honey.

linden tree *See* small-leaved lime tree.

ling *See* hake.

lingcod Not a true cod but a member of the greenling family found in the Pacific Ocean along the North American coast; this saltwater fish has a mottled brown to bluish-green skin with a cream-colored belly and brown, green or tan spots outlined in orange or light blue; it has very lean, green to bluish-green flesh that whitens when cooked, a delicate flavor, and an average market weight of 5–20 lb. (2.3–9 kg); also known as blue cod, buffalo cod, cultus cod and greenling.

lingering *See* finish.

ling gok (ling gok) Chinese for water caltrop.

lingkio (ling-key-oh) Chinese for water chestnut. *See* pi t'si.

lingonberry (LING-on-bear-ree) A member of the cranberry family (genus *Vaccinium*) grown in North America; it has a red skin and a tart flavor and is used for preserves and sauces.

lingua de vaca (LEEN-gwah deh vah-cah) Portuguese for calf's tongue.

lingua di bue (lean-guah dee boo-he) Italian for ox tongue.

linguado (leeng-WAH-doo) Portuguese for sole; it is usually served broiled or fried in butter.

linguica (lihng-GWEE-suh) A Portuguese and Brazilian sausage made from pork and seasoned with garlic.

linguine (lihn-GWEE-nee) Italian for small tongue and used to describe long, narrow, slightly flattened strands of pasta.

linolenic acid 1. An essential polyunsaturated fatty acid found in fish and plant oils; an omega-3 fatty acid. 2. A food additive used as a nutrient supplement as well as a flavoring agent and/or adjuvant.

linque di passeri (lean-guae dee pass-her-eeh) Italian for sparrow tongues and used to describe long flat pasta that is thicker than linguine.

Linsen (LIN-zern) German for lentils.

lin yun bao (lean yoon bah-oh) Chinese steamed lotus buns with a sweet bean paste filling.

Linzer cookie *See* Ischl tart.

Linzertorte (LIHN-zuhr-tort) A thin Austrian tart made with a rich, cookielike dough containing ground hazelnuts and spices, filled with raspberry jam and topped with a dough lattice.

lion's paw scallop A variety of scallop found in the Gulf of Mexico, Caribbean Sea and off Brazil; it has an irregularly shaped, reddish-brown shell with a diameter of 3–6 in. (7.6–15.2 cm) and a tender, sweet, white meat.

lipids A class of nutrients consisting of fats or fatlike substances insoluble in water but soluble in organic solvents such as alcohol; includes triglycerides (fats and oils), phospholipids and sterols.

lipoproteins A protein combined with a lipid component such as cholesterol or a triglyceride; the principal vehicle for lipids to travel through the body after processing in the intestines. *See* very-low-density lipoproteins (VLDL), low-density lipoproteins (LDL) *and* high-density lipoproteins (HDL).

Liptauer (LIHP-tower) A soft Hungarian cheese made from ewe's milk; typically seasoned with herbs, spices (particularly paprika, which turns it red), garlic, onions and sometimes capers, anchovies and other flavorings.

liqueur (lih-kuer) A strong sweet drink made from a distilled spirit base sweetened, flavored and sometimes colored with fruits and aromatics; it generally has a high alcohol content, is viscous and sticky and is sometimes aged; often consumed after a meal or used as an ingredient in a cocktail; also known as a cordial (especially in the United States).

liqueur, cold method A liqueur whose flavors are gained through the infusion or maceration of flavoring ingredients.

liqueur, hot method A liqueur whose flavors are gained by adding the flavoring ingredients during distillation.

liqueur de tirage (lih-kuer duh tee-raj) A solution of sugar in wine with a yeast culture; it is added to a still wine to produce a second fermentation in the bottle.

liqueur d'expedition *See* dosage.

Liqueur d'Or (lih-kuer dor) A liqueur flavored with lemon peel and herbs and containing gold flecks.

liqueur glass A stemmed, tubular glass ranging in size from 1 to 3 fl. oz.; used for serving liqueurs neat and layered cordial drinks.

liqueur rum A fine old rum, generally quite dry, with a mellow flavor and bouquet. *See* rum liqueur.

liqueur Scotch whisky A particularly old, fine Scotch with a mellow flavor acquired through proper aging and blending.

liqueur wine A sweet fortified wine to which wine spirits have been added.

liquid diet *See* clear liquid diet.

liquidize To reduce a food to a liquid in a blender or food processor.

liquid measuring cups *See* measuring cups, liquid.

liquid smoke A basting or flavoring ingredient with an artificial smoky flavor and aroma.

liquid tenderizer *See* tenderizer, liquid.

liquor 1. A potable liquid containing ethyl alcohol; generally used to refer only to distilled spirits. 2. In brewing beer, the liquid at any stage of the process. 3. The liquid or juice found in oysters. *See* juice.

Liquore Galliano (lee-coh-reh gal-LYAH-noh) A spicy, anise-flavored Italian liqueur with a yellow-orange color.

liquoreux (lee-co-ruh) A rich, sweet, white wine that has retained a high percentage of the natural grape sugar (e.g., Sauternes).

liquorice The British spelling of licorice. *See* licorice.

liquor license A permit issued by a state or local authority allowing the holder to sell and/or serve alcoholic beverages to the public at the stated location for the stated time period subject to state and local laws. *See* basic permit.

liquoroso (lee-kwoh-ROH-so) An Italian term for a sweet wine, usually a dessert wine, fortified with grape spirits and having a high alcohol content.

liquor sock A knitted sock used to carry a bottle of an alcoholic beverage into a restaurant that is prohibited from selling such beverages.

Lisbon lemon A variety of lemon; they have a smooth, thin skin and a slightly sweet flavor.

lisci (lee-show) Italian for smooth and used to describe any pasta with a smooth (not grooved or ridged) surface. *See* rigati.

lisichka (lee-sich-rah) Russian for chanterelle.

lista *See* carta.

lista dei vini (lee-stah they vee-knee) Italian for wine list.

lista de platos (lees-tah da plah-toss) Spanish for menu; also known as menú.

Listeria monocytogenes A species of bacteria that causes listeriosis (a common manifestation is meningitis); the bacteria are transmitted through ingestion of contaminated foods (especially milk) or water or by infected food handlers.

listofka (lees-tof-kah) A Russian liqueur made from black currants.

litchi; lychee; lichi; lichee (LEE-chee) A small tropical fruit (*Litchi sinensis*) native to China and Southeast Asia; it has a tough, knobby red skin (that often turns brown during shipping and is not used), a delicate white flesh, a single, large brown seed and a flavor reminiscent of muscat grapes; available fresh or canned.

lite A food-labeling term approved by the FDA to describe a nutritionally altered food with at least 33% fewer calories, 50% less fat or 50% less sodium than the regular or reference (i.e., FDA standard) food.

liter (l) The measure for volume (capacity) in the metric system; 1 l equals 1000 cubic centimeters of water at 20°C or 33.8 U.S. fl. oz. (1.06 qt.) at 68°F.

lithrini (lee-three-nee) Greek for sea bass.

lithuanienne, sauce (lee-to-ah-nyen) A French compound sauce made from a sauce Colbert, garnished with fresh bread crumbs sautéed in butter and minced herbs.

little A food-labeling term approved by the FDA to describe a food that can be eaten frequently without exceeding dietary guidelines for fat, saturated fat, cholesterol, sodium or calories.

Little Devil A cocktail made of gin, gold rum, triple sec and lemon juice.

Little Fingers eggplant A variety of long, very slender Asian eggplant.

littleneck clam; littleneck quahog An Atlantic hard-shell clam that is under 2 in. (5.08 cm) across the shell; the shells are tannish-gray and the chewy meat has a mild flavor; often served on the half shell.

Little Scarlet strawberry A strawberry variety used mostly for preserves; it is particularly well flavored.

liu (lee-who) Chinese for quickly stir-frying foods over low heat in an uncovered wok.

Livarot (lee-vah-roe) A soft cheese made in France's Normandy region from cow's milk; it has a strong, assertive flavor, a smooth yellow-gold interior, a brown crust colored with annatto and a pungent aroma.

lively A wine-tasting term for a wine, usually white, that is young, fresh, moderately acidic, fruity and sometimes spritzy.

liver 1. A large, multilobed organ that filters blood to remove and process the nutrients the blood absorbed from the intestines; it also manufactures proteins, secretes bile and destroys or stores toxins. 2. A variety meat; the livers of many varieties of birds (e.g., chicken and goose), fish (e.g., turbot and lote) and mammals (e.g., calf and hog) are edible; an oil extracted from cod and shark livers is used for home remedies.

liverwurst (LIHV-uhr-wurst; LIHV-uhr-vursht) Any of several varieties of seasoned sausages made from pork meat and pork liver; the texture can be semifirm to soft; available smoked or cooked in links, loaves and slices.

liyoujun (lee-yo-who-june) Chinese for chanterelle.

lizi (lee-zee) Chinese for pear.

llapingachos (yap-in-gachos) A South American dish of potatoes mashed with onions, cilantro and cheese, formed into patties and fried; sometimes topped with a fried egg and served with avocado, fried plantains and peanut sauce.

loaf 1. A shaped mass of bread (typically a yeast bread) baked in one piece. 2. A shaped, usually rounded or oblong, mass of food (e.g., a veal loaf), cooked or otherwise prepared in one piece. 3. A mass of otherwise shapeless or loosely shaped food cooked in a loaf pan (e.g., a quick bread).

loaf cake Any cake baked in a loaf pan; usually they are pound cakes or fruitcakes.

loaf cheese A cheese marketed in the shape of a loaf; usually a processed cheese but also some natural cheeses, such as Cheddar and Cheddar-style cheeses and cream cheese.

loaf pan A rectangular baking pan available in a variety of sizes; used for baking breads, cakes and meat loaves.

loaf sugar A traditional manner of keeping sugar; refined, crystallized sugar was moistened and compressed into hard cones called loaves; pieces were broken off or grated for table use.

loaf pan

lobed When referring to leaves, it describes a leaf that is divided (but not separated) toward the midrib, with each division rounded at its apex.

lobhia (low-be-ha) Hindi for black-eyed peas.

lobio (low-bee-oh) A puréed bean salad made in the Republic of Georgia.

lobo (loh-boh) Spanish for wolf fish.

lobster Any of several varieties of crustaceans found in saltwater areas worldwide; generally, they have a jointed body and limbs encased in a reddish-brown to blue-black shell, a large tail, large front claws, and a firm white flesh with a rich, sweet flavor; significant varieties include the Maine lobster, Norway lobster and spiny lobster.

lobster butter A compound butter made by heating ground lobster shells together with butter and straining the mixture into ice water to harden; used as a flavoring for sauces and soups and as a spread.

lobsterette A term used imprecisely for any of several varieties of small mature lobsters or clawless lobsters. *See* Norway lobster *and* prawn.

lobster fork A fork with two short, angled prongs and a long narrow shaft that allows access into the small recesses of a lobster, crab, snail or the like.

lobster Newburg A dish of lobster meat heated in a sauce of cream, egg yolks and sherry or Madeira.

lobster pick A long, narrow, pointed tool used to extract meat from hard-to-reach cavities of a lobster or crab.

lobster pincers A pair of spring-set pliers with 3.5-in.-long triangular blades with blunt tips and ridged edges used to crack a lobster's carapace; an oval opening below the hinge is used to crack the claws.

lobster pincers

lobster Thermidor (THUHR-mih-dohr) A dish of lobster meat bound with a béchamel flavored with white wine, shallots, tarragon and mustard and returned to the shells; it is sprinkled with Parmesan and broiled or covered with a Mornay sauce and glazed under the broiler.

locando (loh-KAHN-dah) A casual Italian country restaurant.

Lo Cha A Taiwanese oolong tea flavored with litchi flowers; the beverage has a faintly sweet flavor.

Lochan Ora A beverage made from Scotch whisky, honey and herbs.

loco moco A Hawaiian breakfast dish consisting of two scoops of rice and a hamburger patty topped with a thick brown gravy and a fried egg.

locro (loh-croh) A stewlike dish made throughout South America from meat, fish and/or shellfish, a grain and other ingredients.

locro de choclo (loh-croe day tcho-kloe) An Argentinean lorco made with green corn, tomatoes, squash, onions and garlic and garnished with parsley or cilantro.

locust The red or carmine locust, a member of the grasshopper family; it is fried and eaten in Middle Eastern cuisines; also known as jirad.

locust bean *See* carob.

locust bean gum A food additive derived from locust bean tree seeds and used as a stabilizer and/or thickener in processed foods such as ice creams, baked goods, baking mixes, beverages, cheeses, gelatins and jellies; also known as carob bean gum and carubin.

lodge 1. A Portuguese ground-level warehouse used to store port. 2. British term for a Portuguese port producer. 3. A rustic hotel, usually in the country.

Lodigiano (loa-dee-jee-AHN-oa) An Italian grana cheese made from cow's milk; it has a dark brown oiled rind, a yellow interior and a sharp, assertive and sometimes slightly bitter flavor that is not quite as strong as that of other granas; used for grating.

lody (loh-di) Polish for ice cream.

Löffel (loo-fell) German for spoon.

løg (lurg) Danish for onion.

loganberry A berry (*Rubus loganobaccus*) that is a hybrid of the raspberry and blackberry; shaped like an elongated raspberry, it turns purple-red when ripe and has a juicy flesh and a sweetly tart flavor; eaten fresh or used in preserves and baked goods.

loggerhead A long-handled tool with a ball or bulb at the end; after being heated in a fireplace, the loggerhead is plunged into beer or rum-based drinks to heat them.

logo; logogram A name or mark that identifies a product or business.

log phase A period during which bacteria in a culture or colony experience accelerated growth, usually following a lag phase and continuing until the bacteria begin to crowd others within their colony, creating competition for food, space and moisture. *See* lag phase *and* decline phase.

lohi (LOA-hi) Finnish for salmon.

lohki *See* dudi.

loin 1. A primal section of the veal carcass; it is posterior to the primal rib and contains two ribs and the very tender and flavorful loin eye muscle and tenderloin. 2. A primal section of the lamb carcass; located between the primal rack and leg, it contains one rib and the very tender and flavorful loin eye muscle and tenderloin and the less tender flank. 3. A primal section of the pork carcass; it is located above the belly and includes the entire rib section and loin and a portion of the sirloin and contains the very tender eye muscle and tenderloin; it is the only pork primal not typically smoked or cured.

loin chop A British cut of the pork carcass; it is a chop cut from the front end of the loin. *See* chump chop.

loin of lamb A British cut of the lamb carcass; the equivalent of the primal loin and the top portion of the primal leg to the tail; available with or without the bones.

loin pork chop A fabricated cut of the pork primal loin; a chop from the rear end of the loin that contains a section of the tenderloin.

loin tip A subprimal cut of the beef primal round; it is a lean, boneless cut from the top round and is further fabricated into a loin tip roast and loin tip steak; also known as a sirloin tip, triangle and top sirloin.

Loire Valley (l'whar) One of France's six principal grape-growing and wine-producing regions; located in eastern France, it produces a range of still and sparkling white wines, red wines and rosés; the upper Loire vineyards generally make crisp, herbaceous white wines from the Sauvignon Blanc grape; the western vineyards are known for their tangy white wine made from the Melon de Bourgogne grape; other grapes grown in the region include Gamay and Muscadet.

løk (lurk) Norwegian for onion.

lök (lurk) Swedish for onion.

lokhi *See* dudi.

lokma (lo-gh-mah) A Turkish pastry composed of small, sweet balls of deep-fried yeast dough dipped in sugar syrup flavored with honey or lemon; they are crisp on the outside with a hollow interior; known in Greece as loukoumáthes.

lokshen (lock-shen) Yiddish for noodles, usually made with white bread flour and eggs.

lokshen kugel (lock-shen koo-gle) A noodle kugel; it can be sweet (made with cheese, apples and raisins) or savory (made with onions and schmaltz).

loksinu su aguonais (lock-sea-nou sou ah-goo-oh-nah-is) A Lithuanian dish of egg noodles served with a sauce of poppy seeds, honey, brown sugar, blanched almonds, cream and butter.

loligo A variety of squid found off the U.S. East Coast; it has an ivory-white flesh, a firm, tender texture, a mild, sweet flavor and an average market weight of 2 oz. (56.7 g); also known as a winter squid.

l'ollada (low-ya-dah) A soup made in Spain's Catalonia region from dried beans, white cabbage, potatoes, onions and bacon, flavored with garlic and herbs and garnished with garlic, onions and parsley fried in bacon fat; the soup is traditionally made in an oulle.

lollipop A piece of hard sugar candy, variously shaped and flavored, attached to the end of a small wooden or paper stick; also known as a sucker.

lollo rosso A variety of head lettuce with curly, red-tipped, reddish-green leaves.

lombard, sauce (lohm-bar) A French compound sauce made from a hollandaise finished with mushrooms and parsley.

Lombardo A small Lodigiano.

lo mein 1. Fresh Chinese egg noodles. 2. A Chinese–American dish of poultry, shrimp and/or meat with vegetables such as bean sprouts, mushrooms, water chestnuts, bamboo shoots and green onions served over soft noodles.

lomi lomi; lomi lomi salmon A Hawaiian luau dish of salted shredded salmon mixed with tomatoes and onions.

lomo (loh-moh) Spanish for loin of pork.

lomo A South and Central American cut of the hog carcass; it is a pork loin.

lomo embuchado (loh-moh ehm-boo-cha-doh) A Spanish filet of pork marinated with herbs and spices and then dried in the skin; also known as caña de lomo.

lomo montado (loh-moh mon-tah-doh) A Bolivian dish consisting of a pan-fried steak with a fried egg on top.

lon (lon) Thai for cooked sauces; they are usually made with coconut milk and served with roasted or fried fish and raw vegetables.

lonac (low-nutz) 1. A Balkan stew of meat, whole vegetables (e.g., an onion with its skin still on) and spices simmered in a lonac. 2. A deep earthenware casserole used in the Balkans, especially Bosnia.

London broil A fabricated cut of the beef primal flank; it is a flank steak that is lean and somewhat tough; sometimes lean slabs of meat from the beef round and chuck primals are imprecisely called London broil.

London Dry gin 1. A gin made in or near London, England. 2. A style of American and British gin flavored with juniper berries and other botanicals.

London French 75 A cocktail made of gin, lemon juice, sugar syrup and sparkling wine; served in a chilled Collins glass.

Lone Tree A cocktail made of gin, dry vermouth, sweet vermouth and orange bitters; garnished with an olive.

longan (LONG-uhn) A plum-sized tropical fruit (*Euphoria longana*) native to India and China; it has an ovoid shape, a pink, red or yellow skin and a silvery white flesh surrounding a large black seed with a white eye-shaped marking; it has a very sweet flavor similar to that of a litchi but subtler; also known as a dragon's eye.

longaniza (lohn-gah-NEE-thah) A Spanish sausage made from fatty pork, seasoned with dried chiles and aniseed; it is partially smoked and dried.

long bean *See* yard-long bean.

longchamp (lohn-chomp) A French soup of shredded sorrel and vermicelli cooked in consommé; a purée of fresh green peas is stirred in just before service.

long drink A cocktail served in a larger-than-normal-sized glass (e.g., a highball glass), thus allowing a greater amount of mixer to be added; also known as a tall drink. *See* short drink.

long filler *See* filler, long.

long finish *See* finish.

longfin tuna *See* albacore tuna.

long-grain rice *See* rice, long-grain.

long green chile *See* Anaheim chile *and* New Mexico green chile, fresh.

Longhorn A Cheddar-style cheese made in Wisconsin; it has an orange color and a mild flavor; available in rectangles, cylinders and half-moons.

Long Island buck An American savory made with grated Cheddar cheese, beer, paprika, Worcestershire sauce and egg yolks spread on toast; it is baked in the oven until browned on top and served hot.

Long Island duck A variety of domesticated duck with white feathers; it has a large, rounded body and a dark flesh with a very rich flavor.

Long Island Iced Tea A cocktail made of one shot each of tequila, vodka, gin and rum and mixed with a cola-flavored soda; served over ice in a Collins glass.

longjaw rockfish *See* ocean perch.

Long Life melons Any of a group of melons cultivated for flavor and improved shelf life; they generally have an orange flesh and a smooth skin.

longneck A beer bottle with a long neck.

longneck clam An Atlantic soft-shell clam; the ovoid dark blue shell measures 2–5 in. (5.08–12.7 cm) and the meat is tender and sweet.

long panatela *See* panatela, long.

long rice Hawaiian–Chinese for rice sticks.

lóngxia (loong-siah) Chinese for lobster.

longxucai (long-shoe-cay) Chinese for asparagus.

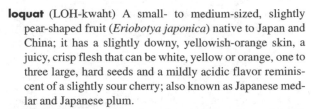

long neck

Lonsdale A well-sized cigar with a 42 ring and 6 to 7-in. length.

lontong An Indonesian dish of compressed rice (the rice is cooked tightly bound in a packet of banana leaves or a cloth bag); traditionally served cold with a spicy sauce.

lonza (LOHN-tzah) 1. Italian for loin, usually of pork. 2. An Italian dish of filet of pork cured like ham and flavored with spices, wine and garlic.

lonzo (LOHN-zoh) A Corsican dish consisting of a boned filet of pork, rubbed with salt, coated with saltpeter, then washed with garlic-flavored red wine, air-dried and dusted with paprika; it is sliced very thin and eaten raw.

loomi *See* leimoon.

looseleaf lettuce *See* lettuce, leaf.

loose meat sandwich *See* sloppy Joe.

loose side *See* open side.

lop chong; lop cheeng; lop cheong (lah-choong) A highly seasoned, smoked Chinese sausage made from pork and fat; it is slightly sweet, dry and rather hard; also known as Chinese sausage.

loquat (LOH-kwaht) A small- to medium-sized, slightly pear-shaped fruit (*Eriobotya japonica*) native to Japan and China; it has a slightly downy, yellowish-orange skin, a juicy, crisp flesh that can be white, yellow or orange, one to three large, hard seeds and a mildly acidic flavor reminiscent of a slightly sour cherry; also known as Japanese medlar and Japanese plum.

Lord Baltimore cake A three-layer yellow cake made with egg yolks, filled with a mixture of chopped nuts, candied cherries and crushed macaroons, and covered with a fluffy, white frosting such as boiled icing. *See* Lady Baltimore cake.

Lord Derby A cooking apple.

lorette (low-reht) 1. A French garnish consisting of chicken croquettes, asparagus tips and slices of truffles. 2. Chicken consommé with paprika, garnished with asparagus tips, truffle strips and chervil, with tiny balls of pommes lorette served separately. 3. Corn salad (mâche) accompanied by thin slices of cooked beetroot and thin slices of raw celery. 4. A French method of serving potatoes. *See* pommes lorette.

Lorraine (lohr-rain) A small, hard cheese made in France's Lorraine region from soured cow's milk; it is flavored with pepper, salt and pistachio nuts.

lorraine, à la (lohr-rain, ah lah) 1. A French garnish for meat consisting of red cabbage cooked in red wine and apples. 2. A French preparation method associated with the cuisine of Lorraine, a region in France; includes various egg-based dishes, all of which contain smoked bacon and Gruyère.

losos (low-soss) Russian for salmon.

loss leader An item offered for sale at or below cost to attract customers.

lot When referring to wine, it means wine of the same type bottled or transferred into retail containers on the same date and bottling line.

lotte (lot) French for burbot.

lotte de mer (lot duh mare) French for monkfish.

lotus eaters 1. In Greek mythology, one of the people described in the *Odyssey;* they fed on the lotus and lived in a drugged, indolent state. 2. Lazy people devoted to pleasure and luxury.

lotus leaves The large leaves of any of several varieties of water lilies and related plants (genus *Nymphaea*) used in Asian cuisines to wrap foods for steaming.

lotus nut; lotus seed The seed of the lotus plant (*Nelumbo nucifera*), a type of water lily; it has a flavor similar to that of an almond and is candied or puréed and used as a flavoring in Chinese and Thai cuisines; also known as med bua.

lotus packet A small bundle of food, usually a sticky rice with meat, chicken and/or vegetable garnishes; wrapped in a lotus (or similar) leaf and steamed; an Asian, especially Chinese, cooking method.

lotus root The long fleshy rhizome of a water lily (*Nelumbo nucifera*); it has a reddish-brown skin that must be peeled before use, a crisp, white flesh and a flavor reminiscent of coconut; used in Asian cuisines; also known as bhain, hasu, leen ngau and renkon.

lotus root starch A grayish, slightly granular starch ground from the lotus rhizome and used for making sweet dishes and soft-textured cakes and also as a thickener in Asian cuisines.

lotus seeds, crystallized Blanched lotus seeds crystallized in sugar and used in Chinese sweets and puddings.

loubieh (loob-yah) Arabic for green beans.

Loudspeaker A cocktail made of brandy, gin, lemon juice and Cointreau.

Louie sauce An American mayonnaise sauce made with heavy cream and a chile sauce, seasoned with cayenne and lemon juice and garnished with minced onions and green pepper.

Louisane, à la (lou-ee-san, ah lah) A French garnish for fowl or meat consisting of sweet corn fritters and rice darioles on sautéed sweet potatoes and rounds of fried banana.

louise-bonne (lou-eese-bun) A large pear grown in France; it has a yellow skin with a red blush and red spots, juicy white flesh and a sweet flavor.

Louis XVIII *See* belle du bois.

Louisiana soup Chicken broth seasoned with saffron and garnished with okra, crabmeat, rice, shrimp and sweet peppers.

Louisiana strawberry A small, sweet, red strawberry with a delicate, distinctive taste.

loukanika (loo-KAH-nih-kah) A fresh Greek sausage made from lamb and pork and seasoned with orange rind.

loukoumáthes (loo-koo-mah-thes) Greek for lokma.

lounge car A railroad car in which drinks and sometimes food are served; usually furnished with tables and swivel chairs; also known as a club car.

loup (loo) French for wolf fish.

loup de mer (loo duh mare) French for sea bass.

louquenka A small Basque sausage seasoned with garlic and pimiento; traditionally eaten grilled with oysters.

Lour (loor) A fresh Iraqi whey cheese made from ewe's milk; it has a white to ivory color and a mild flavor.

lou trebuc (loo trey-buc) A French dish of goose or pork cooked in its own fat and then covered with salt. *See* confit.

lovage An herb (*Levisticum officinale*) with tall stalks and large, dark green, celerylike leaves; the leaves, stalks and seeds (which are commonly known as celery seeds) have a strong celery flavor; the leaves and stalks are used in salads and stews, and the seeds are used for flavoring; also known as celeri bâtard (French for false celery), sea parsley, smallage, smellage and wild parsley.

lovage salt A mixture of crushed lovage seeds and salt; used as a flavoring, especially for meats and tomato dishes.

love and tangle A deep-fried doughnut; the dough is twisted and entwined before frying.

love in a cage *See* winter cherry.

love-in-disguise An old English dish made from calf's heart wrapped in fat pork or bacon and simmered; it is then coated with a veal forcemeat, rolled in bread crumbs and roasted; served with a gravy made from the pan juices.

Lovibond A scale used to measure the color of malt, wort and beer; the lower the number, the lighter the color.

lovi-lovi A small tropical fruit (*Flacourita inermis*) grown in Asia; it has a dark red skin and flesh and a sweet, astringent flavor; used for preserves.

low; low source of A food-labeling term approved by the FDA to describe a food that can be eaten frequently without exceeding dietary guidelines for fat, saturated fat, cholesterol, sodium or calories.

lowa A Tibetan dish consisting of a goat's or sheep's lung stuffed with butter flavored with garlic, cumin, turmeric and nutmeg, then boiled, sliced and fried.

lowball *See* on the rocks.

low calorie; low in calories A food-labeling term approved by the FDA to describe a food with 40 or fewer calories per serving or 0.9 kcalories per gram. *See* reduced calorie *and* diet.

low-carbohydrate diet A rapid (and, if unsupervised, potentially dangerous) reduction diet designed to create ketosis; low intake of carbohydrates causes the body to metabolize protein from lean muscles and lose water, the weight is easily regained.

low cholesterol A food-labeling term approved by the FDA to describe a food with 20 mg or less cholesterol per serving.

Low Country boil *See* Frogmore stew.

low-density lipoproteins (LDL) Lipoproteins that transport lipids from the liver to other tissues, such as muscles.

lower round A subprimal cut of the beef primal round; it is a roast from the bottom or eye of round.

low fat A food-labeling term approved by the FDA to describe a food with 3 g or less fat per serving.

lowfat milk Whole milk with a milkfat content reduced to 0.5–2%. *See* skim milk *and* two percent milk.

Lowland Scotch Scotch produced in the lowlands of southern Scotland; it generally has a light body and a mild, smoky flavor with hints of vanilla.

low salt A food-labeling term approved by the FDA to describe a food prepared with less salt than normal for the product.

low saturated fat A food-labeling term approved by the FDA to describe a food with 1 g or less saturated fat per serving and/or in which not more than 15% of a serving's calories are from saturated fat.

low sodium A food-labeling term approved by the FDA to describe a food with 140 mg or less salt per serving.

low-sodium diet A hospital diet in which the food is seasoned with pepper and other seasonings but no salt; portion size is carefully controlled and sugar is often excluded.

low-sodium salt A compound (potassium chloride) with a flavor very similar to that of salt but containing no sodium; potassium replaces the sodium; also known as a salt substitute.

low wine The vapor drawn off and condensed during the distillation of an alcoholic beverage; usually redistilled, which increases its alcohol content. *See* feints.

lowz (lowdz) Arabic for almonds.

lox Salmon that is brine cured and then typically cold smoked. *See* Nova *and* smoked salmon.

lozhka (lo-sh-kah) Russian for spoon.

lozi (low-zee) Swahili for almond.

lu (loo) Chinese for simmering a food slowly with soy sauce.

lua (loo-ah) Thai for blanch.

Luaka A Sri Lankan black tea with less caffeine and tannin than most Sri Lankan teas; the beverage has a mellow flavor.

luang prabang (loo-ang praa-bang) A round, handwoven Laotian basket with a tight-fitting lid used to cook and serve rice.

luau (LOO-ow) 1. Hawaiian for taro leaves. 2. A traditional Hawaiian feast, usually featuring a whole roasted pig.

lubee (loo-bee-ah) Arabic for green beans.

lubina (loo-bee-nah) Spanish for sea bass.

lubricant A type of incidental food additive that is applied to food-contact surfaces to prevent ingredients and finished products from sticking to them; also known as a release agent.

lucerne *See* alfalfa.

luckshen (look-hen) Yiddish for egg noodles; thin ones are usually used for soups, and medium to wide ones are used in noodle pudding or other dishes.

Lucullus, à la (loo-kuhl-us, ah lah) 1. A French garnish consisting of truffles cooked whole in Madeira and filled with quenelles of chicken forcemeat and chopped truffle centers; named for the Roman General Lucullus (106–56 B.C.). 2. A French velouté soup of chicken blended with purée of calves' brains, flavored with sherry and garnished with diced cucumber. 3. A French consommé of beef, garnished with diced carrots and turnips, cauliflowerets and quenelles.

lu dou ya (loo do who-ya) Chinese for mung bean sprouts.

lüfer (loo-fare) Turkish for bluefish.

luffa; loofa (loo-fah) An arched, cylindrical, edible squash with a dark green shell, a creamy white flesh and spongy seeds; used in Indian, Chinese and Southeast Asian cuisines.

lug A box, crate or basket in which produce is shipped to market; it usually holds 25–40 lb.

luganeghe (lou-ga-nee-ghee) A sausage from Italy's Romagna region made from pork, seasoned with sage and usually served with tomato sauce.

lug handle A handle that protrudes like an ear from a vessel.

luguan (loo-goo-ahn) Chinese for hotel.

Luján de Cuyo A grape-growing and wine-producing area in the Mendoza wine zone of Argentina.

luk (look) Russian for onion.

lukanka (look-ahn-kah) A Bulgarian sausage made from pork flavored with spices and lightly salted.

luk grawan (look gravan) Thai for cardamom.

luk-porei (look-poe-ray) Russian for leek.

luk taan *See* palm nut.

lula (loo-lah) Portuguese for calmar, a type of squid.

lulu avocado A large, pear-shaped avocado with a shiny, smooth, greenish-colored skin with yellow spots and a green-yellow flesh.

lumacha (loo-MAA-kay) Italian for snail and used to describe snail-shaped pasta.

lumachine (loo-MAA-cheh-neh) Small snail-shaped pasta.

lumacone (loo-MAA-koh-nay) Large snail-shaped pasta.

Lumberjack A cocktail made of gin, applejack, Southern Comfort and maple syrup.

lump A traditional measure of volume, especially for butter; it is approximately 2 tablespoons.

lumpfish A large fish found in the nothern Atlantic Ocean; it has a lumplike dorsal fin and is sought principally for its roe.

lumpfish caviar Roe harvested from the lumpfish; the small and very crisp pinkish eggs are generally dyed black, red or gold; also known as Danish caviar and German caviar and imprecisely known as caviar.

lumpia (LOOM-pee-ah) A Filipino dish consisting of a cornstarch or flour dough skin wrapped around raw or cooked meats and/or vegetables and deep-fried; sometimes the filling is served in a lettuce leaf (which is not deep-fried).

lumpia wrappers Thin round or square sheets of dough made from cornstarch and/or wheat flour and used to wrap foods in Filipino cuisine; also known as egg roll skins.

lump sugar Granulated sugar formed into 1/2-in. cubes; used in hot beverages; also known as sugar cubes.

lunch box; lunch pail A portable container for carrying one's lunch; it can be insulated and/or contain various other service or storage items such as a thermos; also known as a dinner pail and dinner bucket.

Luneberg (lou-nae-berg) A semisoft Austrian cheese made from cow's milk and colored with saffron; it has a mild, nutty flavor.

Lung Ching A Chinese green tea; the beverage has a mellow flavor and golden color and is considered to clear the mind without agitating the nerves.

lunsj (loonsh) Norwegian for lunch.

lush 1. A wine-tasting term for an aromatic, full-flavored wine. 2. A derogatory term for an alcoholic.

lute; lut A paste of flour and water used to seal lids to casseroles or terrines to keep the steam inside the cooking receptacle; the process is called luting.

lutefisk (LOO-teh-feeske) A Scandinavian dish of dried cod soaked in lye before cooking and traditionally served with a cream sauce or pork drippings at Christmas.

lychee *See* litchi.

lye water A solution of 42% potassium carbonate in 58% water; it is used in some noodles and pastries and for blanching or softening dried ingredients in Chinese cuisines.

Lyonerwurst (lee-oh-nar-voorst) A German ham sausage flavored with garlic.

lyonnaise, à la (ly-uh-NAYZ, ah lah; lee-oh-NEHZ) A French preparation method associated with the cuisine of Lyon, France; the dishes are garnished or prepared with onions.

lyonnaise, sauce A French compound sauce made from a demi-glaze flavored with white wine and sautéed onions; usually strained and served with meats and poultry.

lysine 1. An essential amino acid. 2. A food additive used as a nutrient source to significantly improve the biological quality of the total protein in a food containing the naturally occurring protein.

lyutenitsa (lee-who-ta-mee-tsah) A Bulgarian salad made from green vegetables dressed with garlic, chiles and vinegar.

m *See* meter.

maafe (maa-feh) A West African (especially Mali) stew consisting of chicken, groundnuts or peanuts, okra, sweet potatoes, corn and various greens and flavored with chiles and tomatoes.

ma'amoul (mah-MOOL) Arabic Easter cakes made with semolina.

maanz (mah-hanz) Hindi for meat.

maasa (mah-sah) A West African (especially Mali) dish consisting of brown rice flour and millet flour fritters flavored with sugar and cinnamon.

maatjes (mah-ah-teas) Dutch for young herring that have not yet spawned.

maatjessia (mah-ah-teas-see-ah) A Dutch salad made of herring fillets, cucumbers, apples and carrots and dressed with an herbed cream sauce.

mabo (mah-boh) Chinese for puffball mushroom.

maçá (mah-SAH) Portuguese for apple.

Macabeo (mah-cah-BEH-oh) A white wine grape grown in Spain (and also southern France); it is used for most of the white wines in Rioja, where it is known as Viura.

macabo A plant native to Asia; its small, brown, tuberous root is eaten boiled.

macadamia (mak-uh-DAY-mee-uh) The nut of an Australian evergreen tree (*Macadamia intergrifolia* and *M. tetraphylla*); shaped like a small marble, the nut has a very rich, buttery, slightly sweet flavor and a high fat content; because of the extremely hard shell, it is usually available shelled and raw or roasted; also known as Queensland nut.

macaroni 1. Dried pasta made from a dough of wheat flour and water. 2. In the United States, short, elbow-shaped tubes of pasta.

macaroni and cheese An American casserole dish of boiled macaroni layered with cheese and baked until the cheese melts and the top browns.

macaronischoteltje (mah-cah-row-nee-sho-tel-tea) A Dutch dish of macaroni, cheese and ham; it is topped with bread crumbs and butter and baked.

macaroon 1. A chewy cookie made with sugar, egg whites and almond paste or ground almonds; a variation is made with coconut. 2. A French confection made from two small almond or meringue cookies sandwiched together with jam or chocolate.

macaroon paste A mixture of almond and kernel pastes used to make macaroons.

macarrão (mah-kah-RROW) Portuguese for macaroni.

macca (MAH-kah) Italian for abundance and used to describe a soup made with fava beans, spaghetti, chiles, onions and tomatoes.

maccheroni (mah-keh-ROH-nee) Italian for macaroni and used to describe hollow or pierced pasta, such as semicircular tubes.

macdus (ma-doos) A Middle Eastern meza or flavoring consisting of eggplant stored in olive oil flavored with garlic, walnuts, chiles and shatta.

mace The lacy, reddish-orange outer covering (aril) of the nutmeg seed; it is used ground as a spice; it has a flavor and an aroma similar to those of nutmeg but is milder and more refined. *See* nutmeg.

macédoine (ma-say-DWAHN) A French term for a mixture of fruit or vegetables cut into small dice, cooked or raw, and served hot or cold.

macedonia di frutta (mah-seh-DOH-n'yah dee FROO-tah) An Italian salad consisting of chunks of various fruits dressed with sugar and Maraschino.

macerate (MAS-uh-rayt) To soak foods in a liquid, usually alcoholic, to soften them.

maceration (mas-uh-RAY-shun) *See* cuvage.

machaca (mah-cha-kah) A Mexican and Latin American dish of shredded meat usually flavored with chiles and onions.

machbous (mack-boos) A Middle Eastern dish consisting of rice flavored with saffron, baharat, tomatoes, loomi and parsley; it is usually served with lamb, fish, shellfish or chicken.

mâche (MAH-chee) A plant (*Valerianella olitoria*) with small, cupped, tender, dark green leaves and a delicate, slightly nutty flavor; used in salads or cooked like a green; also known as corn salad, field salad and lamb's lettuce.

machhlee (much-lee) Hindi for fish.

machi (mah-chee) Hindi for trout.

mâchon (mah-shon) A small meal in southwestern France consisting of a charcuterie item and a salad of potatoes, lentils or dandelion leaves and bacon.

mackerel A family of saltwater fish found worldwide; signifi-

mackerel

cant members include tuna, ono, Atlantic mackerel, king mackerel and Spanish mackerel.

mackinaw (MAK-uh-naw) *See* lake trout.

Mâconnais (mah-cawn-nay) 1. A grape-growing and wine-producing area in France's Burgundy region; the principal grape grown is Chardonnay. 2. A small square French cheese made from goat's milk.

mâconnaise, à la (mah-cawn-naiz, ah lah) A French preparation method associated with the cuisine of Mâcon, France; the dishes are cooked with Mâcon wine and garnished with brown glazed onions, fried mushrooms, croutons and shrimps.

Macoun apple (muh-KOON) An apple bred in North America from the McIntosh; it has a deep red color, a crisp, juicy flesh and a sweet–tart flavor; a good all-purpose apple, especially for eating out of hand.

macque choux; mocque chou (mock-choh) A Cajun dish of corn cut from the cob, cooked with tomatoes, onions and cream and flavored with cayenne and white pepper.

Macqueline (mock-clean) A soft, Camembert-style French cheese made in the same region as Camembert but from whole or partly skimmed cow's milk; its texture and flavor are inferior to those of Camembert.

macrobiotic diet A diet that is weighted toward cereals, grains, fish and vegetables (especially those grown with limited or no pesticides, herbicides and so forth); although fish may be eaten, animal proteins are generally avoided.

macronutrients Nutrients the body needs in large quantities: carbohydrates, fats, proteins and water. *See* micronutrients.

Maczola An Australian Gorgonzola-style cheese made from cow's milk.

Madagascar bean; Madagascar butter bean (mad-ee-GAS-kahr) A small, creamy-white, kidney-shaped European bean.

madai (mah-die) Japanese for red sea bream.

madako (mah-dah-ko) A variety of octopus used for sushi.

MADD (mad) Mothers Against Drunk Driving; an organization that promotes public awareness and knowledge regarding alcohol abuse and campaigns against driving while under the influence of alcoholic beverages.

made dish A dish compounded or made of several sorts of meats minced or cut in pieces; it is stewed or baked in pastry with wine and butter.

Madeira (muh-DEH-rah) A Portuguese fortified white wine similar to a sherry made from Malmsey, Boal, Sercial or Verdelho grapes; produced through the solera system and matured in an estufa, the wine is baked in its cask, imparting a caramelized flavor. *See* Malmsey, Sercial *and* Verdelho.

Madeira cake An 18th-century British pound cake flavored with lemon; traditionally eaten with a glass of Madeira in the morning.

madeleine (mad-ah-lynn) A French sponge cake baked in a small, shell-shaped mold and eaten as a cookie, especially with tea or coffee.

madeleine pan A flat rectangular plaque with several shallow, shell-shaped indentations for baking madeleines.

madeleine pan

made mustard An archaic term for wet mustard kept in a jar (as opposed to dry mustard or mustard seeds).

Madère, sauce; Madeira sauce A French compound sauce made from a demi-glaze flavored with sautéed shallots and Madeira and finished with butter; served as is or used as a base for other sauces.

maderisé (mad-DEHR-ee-zay) French for maderized.

maderized (MAD-uh-rized) A wine-tasting term, especially for a white or rosé wine that, through oxidation and heat, develops a brown tinge as well as an aroma and flavor reminiscent of Madeira. *See* oxidized.

madhu (mah-do) Hindi for honey.

madia (MAH-dee-ah) The Italian wooden trough or bowl used for kneading bread or pasta.

madnakosh (mahd-nah-kosh) A large, oval, semiflat Persian bread, scored in two directions to create squares on its surface.

madrilène (MAD-ruh-lehn) A clear Spanish consommé flavored with tomatoes and served hot, cold or jellied.

madrilène, à la (MAD-ruh-lehn, ah lah) French for in the style of Madrid and used to refer to foods cooked in or flavored with tomatoes or tomato juice.

ma-dun (ma-dan) A juicy, sour fruit (*Gardinia schombughiana*) native to Thailand and used in soups and curry dishes or made into pickles; also known as carcinia.

Madureira (ma-doo-RE-ruh) A cocktail made of equal parts Pilsner beer and Madeira wine and served in a tall chilled glass.

maduro (mah-doo-roh) Spanish and Portuguese for ripe.

maduro maduro (moh-dur-oh moh-dur-oh) A type of cigar wrapper; it has a nearly black color; an oily, shiny and slightly bumpy surface and a very rich, spicy flavor; also known as double maduro and oscuro.

maelezo ya upishi (ma-lah-zoh yah oo-pee-she) Swahili for recipe.

ma'el ward (mah-il wahrd) Arabic for rosewater.

maembe (mam-ba) Swahili for mango.

mafalde (mah-FAHL-day) Broad Italian pasta ribbons with ruffled ridges; they are wider than fettuccine and narrower than lasagna.

mafé (mah-fay) A Senegalese stew consisting of lamb and groundnuts or peanuts, onions and carrots, flavored with peanut oil, thyme, bay leaves and black pepper, and served over rice.

maftoul *See* maghrebiya.

mafuta (mah-foo-tah) Swahili for fat or oil.

maggiorana (mad-joar-RAA-nah) Italian for sweet marjoram.

maghrebiya (mah-grab-he-ah) The Middle Eastern Arabic name for the North African dish known as couscous (usually tomatoes are left out of the Middle Eastern version); also known as maftoul.

magisteres (mah-jzee-stair) French concentrated soups; they are extremely nourishing and are usually given to sick people.

maglietti (mah-glee-ET-tee) Italian for link and used to describe various types of short, slightly curved rods of pasta.

magnesium A major mineral principally used to facilitate certain enzyme reactions and to assist with regulating body temperature as well as building bones and proteins; found in many foods, significant sources include leafy green vegetables, legumes, whole grain cereals, nuts, cocoa, chocolate, fish and shellfish.

magnesium carbonate A food additive used as an anticaking agent, lubricant, pH control agent and/or flour aging and bleaching agent.

magnesium caseinate A food additive used as a nutrient supplement and color adjuvant.

magnesium chloride A food additive used as a nutrient supplement, flavoring agent and/or flavoring adjuvant.

magnesium hydroxide A food additive used as a nutrient supplement, pH control agent and/or processing aid.

magnesium laurate, magnesium myristate, magnesium oleate and magnesium palmitate Food additives used as binders, emulsifiers and anticaking agents.

magnesium oxide A food additive used as a nutrient supplement, pH control agent, anticaking agent, firming agent and/or lubricant.

magnesium phosphate A food additive used as a nutrient supplement and/or pH control agent.

magnesium silicate A food additive used as an anticaking agent.

magnesium stearate A food additive used as a nutrient supplement, lubricant and/or processing aid.

magnesium sulfate A food additive used as a nutrient supplement, flavor enhancer and/or processing aid.

magnetic knife holder A horizontal slat set with a magnetic bar; the slat is attached to a wall or other surface and knife blades are gripped by the magnet.

magnolia fig A large fig with an amber-colored skin and pinkish-yellow flesh; also known as a Brunswick fig.

magnolia grape A variety of Muscadine grape.

magnum (MAHG-num) An oversized still or sparkling wine bottle holding the equivalent of two 750-ml bottles or 1.5 liter (approximately 50 fl. oz.).

magras (mah-grass) Spanish for roast ham.

magret (ma-gray) A duck breast, usually taken from the fattened ducks that produce fois gras; it includes the skin but is usually boneless.

magri (mah-gree) Turkish for conger eel.

magro (MAH-groh) Italian for lean; it refers to either lean meat or a meatless dish.

maguey (mah-GAY) The Mexican name of the agave plant (known as the century plant in the United States) used in making tequila and mescal.

maguro (MAH-goo-roh) Japanese for tuna; also known as kuromaguro. *See* akami, chutoro *and* otoro.

magyar halleves (mah-jar hell-visch) A Hungarian fish soup garnished with sour cream, roe and noodles.

maharagwe (mah-ah-rah-goo-a) A Kenyan dish of beans flavored with chiles, cooked in coconut milk and served with rice.

mahi mahi (mah-hee mah-hee) *See* dolphinfish.

mahleb; mahaleb (MAAH-lahb) 1. A cherry with a dark red, almost black skin; also known as St. Lucy's cherry. 2. The highly fragrant, golden brown, lentil-sized seeds or pit of this cherry; used ground as a flavoring in Middle Eastern pastries, baked goods and savory dishes.

mahobho (mah-bow-bow) A spicy Tanzanian stew made with meat (usually beef), cabbage, turnips, onions, tomatoes and potatoes and flavored with honey, chiles and black peppers; also known as sadza ndiuraye.

Mahón (MA-hon) A Spanish cheese made from a mixture of cow's and goat's or ewe's milks; has a tough, brown rind, a supple, creamy interior and a slightly sour, sharp flavor; it is soaked in brine, then coated with olive oil.

mahonias *See* barberry.

mahshi (MAH-shee) Arabic for stuffed vegetables; the basic stuffing consists of ground lamb or beef and rice flavored with onions, garlic, parsley, baharat and pine nuts.

mah tai goh (mah tie go) A Chinese dim sum; it is a pan-fried square of sweet water chestnut pudding cake.

ma huang (mah who-ang) A Chinese herb containing the alkaloid ephedrine, which helps elevate the metabolism, boost energy and reduce appetite.

mai chiu (mah-ee key-oo) Chinese for beer.

maiale (MYE-ah-leh) Italian for pork.

maibock (may-bok) A bock beer that leaves the brewery by mid-May; it has a bronze color, a soft malt character and a less assertive flavor and aroma than other bock beers.

maida (mai-daa) A fine white wheat flour used in India for bread making, especially for naan.

maidenhair ferns Any of various ferns (genus *Adiantum*) with feathery fronds and edible, fan-shaped leaflets.

maidenhair nut *See* gingko nut.

maid of honor An individual tartlet filled with almond custard; usually served for afternoon tea in Great Britain.

mai fun; maifun; mi fun; my fun (mah foon) Chinese rice sticks.

Maigre (meh-gruh) *See* Fromage à la Pie.

Maigrèlet (may-kree-lay) A semisoft cheese made in Quebec, Canada, from skimmed cow's milk.

Maile (mah-yi-lee) A salty Crimean cheese made from ewe's milk and pickled in brine; Maile Pener is a richer version made with rennet added to the curds.

Maillard reaction (may-YARD ree-AEK-shen) A series of nonenzymatic reactions that occur between some carbohydrates and amino acids in foods; this reaction can occur at room temperature or during cooking and results in browning and the creation of caramel-like flavors.

Maillot, sauce (may-e-yoh) A French compound sauce made from a Madeira sauce seasoned with shallots and white wine and garnished with diced hard-cooked egg whites.

main course *See* entrée.

Maine lobster A variety of lobster found off New England; it has a brown to blue-black shell, large claws, and a firm white flesh with an exceptionally rich, sweet flavor; marketed as jumbo (more than 2 lb. [900 g]), large (1.5–2 lb. [680–900 g]), quarter (1.25–1.5 lb. [562–680 g]), chicken (1 lb. [450 g]) and chix (less than 1 lb. [450 g]); also known as American lobster and clawed lobster.

maini (mah-ee-nee) Swahili for liver.

Maintenon, sauce (men-tuh-NON) A French compound sauce made from a béchamel flavored with white onions, garlic and grated Parmesan and seasoned with cayenne.

Mainzer Hand (mine-sir hahnd) A small, aged German cheese made from soured cow's milk, kneaded by hand and sometimes aged with cumin.

Mainzer Handkäse (mine-sir hahnd-kaiz) An Austrian sour milk cheese; it has a reddish-brown or yellow wax rind, a yellow interior that becomes white in the center, a sharp, acidic flavor and a pungent aroma.

maionese (mahee-OA-nays) Italian for mayonnaise.

maioneza (mah-o-nae-tzah) Greek for mayonnaise.

Maipu (mah-e-poo) A grape-growing and wine-producing area in the Mendoza wine zone of Argentina; home to two of the world's largest wineries; the principal grapes grown include Malbec, Cabernet, Chardonnay and Chenin Blanc.

mais (mays) French for corn.

Maïs (mighss) German for corn.

mais Norwegian for corn.

maiskolbe (mys-kohl-beh) Norwegian for corn on the cob.

maison, à la (may-ZOHN, ah lah) French for of the house and used to describe a special dish or preparation method associated with the restaurant or its chef.

Mai Tai (my ty) Tahitian for out of this world and used to describe a cocktail made of light and dark rums, lime juice, curaçao, orgeat syrup and grenadine.

maito (MAH-toaah) Finnish for milk.

maître d' (may-truh DEE) *See* dining room manager.

maître d'hotel *See* dining room manager.

maître d'hôtel, beurre (MAY-truh doh-TELL, burr) Butter mixed with lemon juice and chopped parsley; served with grilled meats, either melted or in rounds or slices.

Maiwein (my-vine) A light, sweetened German white wine flavored with Waldmeister; served chilled and garnished with strawberries.

maíz (may'th) Spanish for corn.

maize (maaz) British for corn. *See* corn.

máj (murg) Hungarian for liver, especially goose liver.

maja blanca maiz (mah-ha blahn-kah-maze) A Filipino cake made of fresh coconut, corn kernels, milk and sugar and flavored with aniseeds; traditionally served with latick.

maji (mah-gee) Swahili for juice or water.

majolica (mah-joh-lee-cah) An Italian pottery coated with an opaque white tin oxide enamel and decorated with metallic colors.

Majoran (mah-yo-RAAN) German for marjoram.

Majorero (mah-hoh-RAE-roh) An aged goat's milk cheese from the Canary Islands; it has a pleasant, slightly nutty flavor.

major minerals A group of essential mineral nutrients found in the human body in amounts greater than 5 g; includes calcium, chlorine, magnesium, phosphorus, potassium, sodium and sulfur.

majroush (mah-he-roosh) A Middle Eastern meza dip of lentils and rice flavored with onions, cumin and samn.

makaee (mah-kah-ee) Hindi for corn.

makajiki (mah-kah-gee-key) Japanese for swordfish.

makapuno; macapuno (ma-ka-poo-noo) A type of coconut with soft, gelatinous meat that is sweetened and served as a dessert or used in ice cream in the Philippines.

makaron (mah-kah-ron) Polish for macaroni.

makaronada (mah-koh-roh-nah-dah) A Greek dish of macaroni with meat sauce.

makarondelach (mah-khah-roon-deh-lach) Yiddish for macaroons; because they are flourless, they are a typical Passover treat.

makboos (mah'k-booz) Any of a variety of Middle Eastern pickled vegetables, usually served as an appetizer or condiment; also known as mkhullal.

Maker's Mark Distillery One of the 12 remaining U.S. whiskey distilleries; located in Loretto, Kentucky, and founded in 1953 at the site of a small distillery originally built in 1805, it produces the wheated Maker's Mark whiskey, the best-selling bourbon in Kentucky.

makeua taet (makhua tet) Thai for tomato.

makhan (mak-khan) Hindi for butter.

makhlouta (mah-clue-tah) An Egyptian snack or meza of mixed roasted nuts (typically almonds, walnuts, pistachios, hazelnuts and cashews) and roasted salted watermelon, sunflower and/or pumpkin seeds.

makhrata (mah-kaah-tah) An Egyptian double-handled metal chopper.

maki (MAH-kee) Japanese for roll or rolled.

makisu (mah-key-soo) The small bamboo mat used to roll sushi.

maki-zushi (mah-key-zoo-shee) Japanese for rolled sushi and used to describe a type of sushi made by rolling zushi and other ingredients (e.g., raw or cooked fish, shellfish and vegetables) in nori; also known as wrapped sushi. *See* futo-maki *and* hoso-maki.

makkara (MAHK-kah-rah) Finnish for sausage.

makki ki roti (mah-key key row-tea) A thin, crispy-soft east Indian bread made from finely ground cornmeal.

makluba (mah-clue-bah) A Middle Eastern dish consisting of layers of chicken, rice, potatoes, eggplants and tomatoes flavored with cinnamon, nutmeg and pine nuts, cooked in a mold and inverted for service.

mako (MA-koh) *See* shark.

mákos (mah-KOSH) Hungarian for poppy seeds.

makowiec (mah-koh-ve-eck) A Polish poppy cake; it is a flat layer of dough filled with a mixture of poppy seeds, walnuts, honey, sugar and brandy and rolled into a cylinder before baking.

Makrele (mah-KRAY-ler) German for mackerel.

makrell (mahk-rill) Norwegian for mackerel.

makroud (mah-crood) Tunisian deep-fried pastries flavored with dates.

makrut *See* sambal.

maksa (MAHK-sah) Finnish for liver.

makwara (mah-koo-ah-raw) A tool used in the Middle East to core vegetables such as cusa so that they can be stuffed.

malác (mah-lot) Hungarian for pork.

Málaga (MAH-lah-gah) A fortified wine, usually sweet, produced in Spain's Andalusia region.

Málaga raisins Large, very sweet white raisins made from the Muscat grape.

malai (ma-laa-ee) 1. A rich milk product obtained by boiling milk until a skin forms and then reboiling until it is reduced to a firm, dry, creamy substance; used in Indian desserts and sweetmeats. 2. Hindi for cream.

malai kofta (mah-laa-ee koff-tah) An East Indian dish of meatballs simmered in creamy, buttery tomato sauce with spices.

malanga (mah-LAHNG-gah) A long, knobby, starchy tuber with a thin, shaggy, brown skin, a crisp flesh that may be beige, yellow or red and a sweet, nutty flavor; also known as cocoyam, tannia, tannier and yautia.

malaqueta (mah-lah-kee-tah) *See* bay rum seeds.

malassadas (mah-lass-saw-dass) Portuguese doughnuts made with a yeast dough, fried and rolled in sugar; they are traditionally served on Shrove Tuesday.

Malawian Arabica coffee beans grown in Malawi; the beverage is rich and pleasantly acidic and has a medium to full body.

Malbec (mahl-BEHK) A red wine grape grown principally in Bordeaux, France, where it is also known as Cot, and in Argentina; used as a blending grape with Cabernet Sauvignon and Merlot to contribute color and tannin to the resulting wine; also known as Auxerrois in the Cahors district of France.

Maldive coconut A variety of small, almost spherical coconut grown on the Maldive Islands.

Maldive fish Dried, salted tuna from the Maldive Islands southwest of Sri Lanka; used powdered or chipped as a flavoring and thickener for stews and curries.

malfatti (mahl-FAH-tee) Italian spinach and Ricotta gnocchi.

malfouf (mahl-FUHF) Arabic for cabbage.

mali (ma-li) Thai for jasmine (*Jasminum sambac*), whose flowers and essence are used in Thai dessert syrups and rice or added to finger bowls.

malic acid 1. A naturally occurring acid found in grapes, especially those grown in colder climates; it has a tart, astringent flavor. 2. A food additive used as a flavor enhancer, flavoring agent, flavoring adjuvant and/or pH control agent in processed foods such as beverages, confections, gelatins and fruit products.

malina (mah-lee-neh) Russian for raspberry.

malk (mal) Arabic for salt.

mallard A variety of wild duck found in North America; it has a greenish-black head and neck, a white collar, a chestnut breast and a brown back; it is fatty, with a flavorful flesh, especially if slaughtered during the autumn.

mall food 1. The foods available at a food court (generally fast food). *See* food court. 2. Slang for fast food other than burgers, pizza and chicken.

malloreddus (mahl-low-rae-duce) Tiny Italian dumplings flavored with saffron and served with meat sauce and grated Pecorino.

mallorquina (mahl-lohr-kwy-nan) 1. A fish soup from Majorca flavored with onions, tomatoes, garlic, parsley and white wine and garnished with slivers of fried bread. 2. A vegetable soup from Majorca consisting of simmered onions, cabbage, sweet peppers, garlic and tomatoes placed between layers of bread in a casserole, moistened with stock and baked.

mallow, common A biennial or perennial herb (*Malva sylvestris*) with a tall, straight stem, roundish, toothed and lobed leaves and purplish-rose flowers; the flowers and leaves are used medicinally, and fresh young leaves and shoots are used in salads and soups or cooked as a vegetable.

mallung A Sri Lankan vegetable dish cooked with coconut meat.

Malmsey (mah'm-zee) 1. A white wine grape grown on the island of Madeira and said to be identical to the Malvasia grape. 2. A Madeira wine made from this grape; the sweetest of the four Madeira styles.

malnutrition A disease condition caused by a deficiency of nutrients.

malossol; malosol (MAHL-oh-sahl) Russian for little salt and used to describe caviar that has had minimal salt added during processing; it has a truer, more delicate flavor.

Malpeque oyster An Atlantic oyster found in Malpeque Bay off Prince Edward Island, Canada; it has a narrow, curved shell.

malsouka (mahl-SOO-kah) Paper-thin semolina pastry from Tunisia and Morocco used to make brek and bastila.

malsouqua (mahl-soo-kwah) Very thin sheets of pastry made from semolina; used in African cuisines.

malt *v.* To soak, sprout and dry barley or other grains to develop enzymes. *n.* Barley or other grains that have been soaked, sprouted and dried to develop the proper enzyme content, rendering them suitable for making the mash used in brewing and distillation; the principal types are pale, crystal or caramel, and black.

maltagliato (mahl-tah-L'YAH-tee) Irregularly shaped flat ribbons of Italian pasta with the corners cut on the bias.

maltaise, á la (mahl-TEEZ, ah lah) A French preparation method for both sweet and savory dishes; characterized by the use of orange juice, particularly from the Maltese blood orange.

maltaise, sauce (mahl-TEEZ) A French compound sauce made from a hollandaise blended with Maltese orange juice and grated Maltese orange rind; used with vegetables, especially asparagus and green beans.

malt beverage *See* nonalcoholic malt beverage.

malted 1. A soda fountain drink made by combining malted milk powder, milk, ice cream and a flavoring such as chocolate or vanilla. 2. A description of barley or other grains that have been soaked, sprouted and dried.

malted barley *See* malt.

malted cereal syrup A food additive obtained from a combination of barley and other grains and used as a flavoring agent and nutrient in yeast fermentation; also known as extract of malted barley and corn.

malted milk A beverage made of milk and plain or chocolate-flavored malted milk powder. *See* milk shake.

malted milk powder A powder made from dried milk and malted cereals; sometimes flavored with chocolate.

malt enzymes Enzymes such as diastase developed from the malting of barley or other grains and used to assist the breakdown of grain starches into the sugars necessary for brewing beer and distilling spirits.

Maltese orange (mahl-TEEZ) A tart variety of medium-sized blood orange grown principally on the Island of Malta; used in the hollandaise sauce known as sauce maltaise.

malt extract A thick syrup made by removing the water from a sweet wort; used for brewing beer, it is sometimes flavored with hops.

malt flour The flour prepared from malt.

maltitol Sugar alcohol derived from fruits or produced from glucose.

malt liquor A malt beverage brewed like beer; it has a light to dark color and a high alcohol content.

maltodextrin A food additive used as a bodying agent and texturizer in crackers, puddings and candies.

maltol A food additive used as a flavor enhancer in fruit products and soft drinks.

maltose A disaccharide occurring naturally in sprouting (germinating) seeds and products made from them such as malt; during digestion it is hydrolyzed into its component single sugars (i.e., two glucose units); it has a significant role in the fermentation of alcohol (converting starch to sugar) and bread dough; also known as malt sugar.

maltranche *See* chataignier.

malt Scotch A Scotch whisky made from a mash of only malted barley and distilled by the pot still method; also known as a single-malt Scotch whisky.

malt shop A soda fountain not attached to a pharmacy.

malt sugar *See* maltose.

malt syrup The syrup obtained from barley by extraction and evaporation of worts.

malt vinegar A vinegar made from unhopped beer; naturally pale, it is sometimes labeled light malt vinegar; if caramel is added, it is labeled brown malt vinegar. *See* pickling vinegar.

malt whisky *See* single-malt Scotch whisky.

malty A beer-tasting term for the caramel-like flavor of germinated and roasted barley.

Malvasia; Malvoisie (mal-vah-ZEE-ah) 1. A white wine grape grown in Greece from ancient times and now grown in all Mediterranean countries and California; sometimes used as a blending grape in Chianti and Frascati. 2. A dry or sweet white wine made from this grape.

Malzbier (MAHLTS-beer) A dark, sweet, malty German beer with a low alcohol content.

mamaliga (mah-mah-lee-gah) A Jewish and Romanian dish consisting of cornmeal cooked with a liquid until it forms a soft mash and then boiled, fried, baked or grilled.

mame (mah-may) Japanese for beans.

Mamertine (mah-mer-tee-nay) A wine popular in ancient Rome.

mamey; mamey apple; mamee apple; mamey plum; mamwe plum (ma-MAY) A fruit (*Mammea americana*) native to the West Indies; the size of a large orange, it is spherical with slight points at the top and bottom and has a tough, matte-brown, bitter-flavored skin; the firm, golden flesh has a flavor reminiscent of an apricot.

mamia A Basque dessert of ewe's milk curds.

mamoncillo *See* genip.

ma'mool; maamoul (mah'mool) Small Middle Eastern cakes flavored with orange flower water and stuffed with nuts. *See* qalib.

manaita (ma-nay-e-ta) A rectangular chopping board used in Japan.

manakish (mah-nah-keesh) A Middle Eastern soft flat bread brushed with olive oil and zaatar before baking; it is often topped with ingredients.

manao; menao (mah-now) Thai for lime.

manapua (mah-nah-poo-ah) A Hawaiian dish consisting of steamed and baked Chinese buns or dumplings filled with roast pork.

manatee An herbivorous mammal found in tropical waters; an adult is approximately 10 ft. (3 m) long, with a thick black skin; the flesh has a sweet flavor reminiscent of pork, and the rendered fat is used like lard to make pastry; the flesh is also used in West Indian cuisine in much the same manner as bacon; also known as dugong or sea cow.

Manbollen *See* Edam.

mancha (mahn-t'shah) The highest grade of Spanish saffron. *See* rio *and* sierra.

Mancha, la (MAHN-t'shah, la) A grape-growing and wine-producing region in central Spain; the principal grape grown is the Airen; the resulting white wine has a neutral flavor, a low acid content and a high alcohol content.

manche (mensh) French for a chop or cutlet bone.

manche à gigot (mensh ah zhee-GOH) A tool used to hold a leg of lamb while carving; it has a flared cap with six internal teeth; the cap is placed over the shank end of the bone and tightened.

Manchego (mahn-CHAY-goh) A firm Spanish cheese made from ewe's milk; it has a golden color and a full, mellow flavor; two versions are generally available: Manchego Curado, which is aged for 3–4 months, and the longer-aged Manchego Viejo.

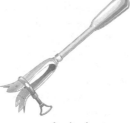

manche à gigot

Manchester lettuce *See* romaine lettuce.

manchet 1. The archaic name for a small, round, somewhat flat loaf of bread that is thicker in the middle than at the ends. 2. A bread made from the finest wheat flour and reserved for nobility during the Middle Ages.

manchette (mensh-ayt) The French paper frill or crown used to decorate the end of a chop or cutlet bone.

manchupa (mahn-choo-pah) A stewlike dish from the Cape Verde Islands consisting of pig's feet, corned spareribs, salt pork, samp, lima beans, yellow-eyed peas, onions, fresh spareribs and ham hocks; it is flavored with bay leaves, garlic, paprika, black pepper and chiles and garnished with calabaza and kale; also known as katchupa (West Africa).

mandarin (MAN-duh-rihn) 1. Any of several varieties of a small citrus fruit (*Citrus reticulata*) native to China, including the mandarin, dancy, tangerine, clementine and satsuma. 2. A citrus fruit; it generally has a somewhat flattened spherical shape, a loose yellow to reddish-orange rind, an orange flesh and a sweet flavor that is less acidic than that of an orange.

mandarine (man-duh-RIHN) French for tangerine.

Mandarine Napoleon A Belgian tangerine-flavored liqueur with a Cognac base.

mandarino (mahn-dah-REE-noa) Italian for tangerine.

Mandarino (mahn-dah-ree-noh) An Italian almond-flavored Marsala wine.

mandel (MAHN-dehl) Danish, Norwegian and Swedish for almond.

Mandel (MAHN-del) German for almond.

mandelbrot; mandelbroit (MAHN-duhl-broht) A crisp, twice-baked Jewish almond bread that is eaten as a cookie.

Mandelkren sauce (mahn-dell-carn) An Austrian cream sauce flavored with almond milk and garnished with horseradish.

mandelspan A Swedish arch-shaped lacy cookie lightly frosted and dusted with confectioners' sugar; often served on a round plate and arranged to resemble a crown.

Mandheling The best grade of Sumatra arabica coffee beans; the beverage is rich, full bodied and smooth.

mandilli de saêa (mahn-DEE-lee deh SAY'ah) Italian for silk handkerchiefs and used to describe very thin sheets of pasta dough; they are often served with pesto.

M & Ms Slang for "M & M's Plain Chocolate Candies," which are small disks of chocolate coated with colored sugar shells.

mandoline (MAHN-duh-lihn) A manually operated slicer with a narrow, rectangular body holding a blade and sits at a 45-degree angle; the food is passed and pressed against the blade to obtain uniform slices, matchstick shapes or waffle cuts.

mandoline

mandoo (mahn-doe) A Korean soup of pork- and tofu-filled dumplings in a clear flavorful broth.

mandorla (MAHN-doar-lay) Italian for almond.

mandu (mann-due) Korean meat- or vegetable-filled dumplings, similar to Chinese dumplings, served in soup, boiled, steamed or pan-fried.

manestra (mah-nes-trah) A Greek pasta with a small, grain-like shape.

man farang (mun fa-laang) Thai for potato.

manga (mun-gah) Portuguese for mango.

manganese A trace mineral principally used to facilitate many cell processes; significant sources include dairy products, meat, fish, poultry and whole grain cereals.

manganese chloride A food additive used as a nutrient supplement.

manganese citrate A food additive used as a nutrient supplement in processed foods such as baked goods, dairy products, fish products, meat products and beverages.

manganese gluconate A food additive used as a nutrient supplement in processed foods such as baked goods, dairy products, fish products, meat products and beverages.

manganese sulfate A food additive used as a nutrient supplement in processed foods such as baked goods, dairy products, fish products, meat products and beverages.

mangel-wurzel A version of the field beet used for animal fodder.

manger (mohn-zhaj) French for to eat.

mange-tout (monj-too) French for eat all and used to describe beans in which both the peas and the pods are eaten (e.g., snow peas and sugar peas).

mangguo (mang-guo) Chinese for mango.

mangiare (mann-gee-ah-rae) Italian for to eat.

mango (mann-go) A medium- to large-sized tropical fruit (*Mangifera indica*) native to India; it has a spherical to ovoid shape with a slight ridge on one side and a point at one end; the skin can be yellow or orange with a red blush, greenish-yellow, or golden yellow; the flesh, which is golden orange, encases a large, flat seed and has a sweet, resinous flavor.

mango

Mangobaum (mahn-go-bomb) German for mango.

mangosteen (MANG-uh-steen) A small tropical fruit (*Garcinia mangostana*) native to Malaysia and Indonesia; it has a slightly flattened spherical shape, a tough, thick, purple-red rind, an ivory-colored segmented flesh and a sweet–tart flavor.

mangue (mahn-gah) French for mango.

manguoa (mahn-goo-oh-ah) Arabic for marinades; the basic Middle Eastern marinade for meats consists of lemon juice, garlic, onions, pepper, cumin, paprika and oil.

Manhasset A cocktail made of whiskey, lemon juice, dry vermouth and sweet vermouth; garnished with a twist of lemon.

Manhattan A cocktail made of bourbon or blended whiskey, sweet vermouth and bitters, garnished with a maraschino cherry and served chilled in a cocktail glass; a perfect Manhattan contains equal parts dry and sweet vermouth; a dry Manhattan contains only dry vermouth.

manicotti (man-uh-KOT-tee) Italian for muffs and used to describe long, wide pasta tubes; they are usually boiled, stuffed with a meat or cheese mixture, covered with a sauce and baked.

manier (mahn-yay) French term for working a mixture by hand, such as kneading or mixing a fat with flour.

Manila clam A variety of Pacific clam with a brown and white shell that is less than 2 in. (5.08 cm) across; also known as a baby clam and Japanese littleneck clam.

manioc (mah-NEE-oahk) Spanish for tapioca or cassava.

manisan pala The candied fruit of the nutmeg tree; used in Indonesian and Caribbean cuisines.

manitas de credo rehogadas (mah-nee-tahs day kray-doh ray-hoe-gah-dahs) A Spanish dish of deboned pig's feet dipped in egg and bread crumbs and fried.

manjar blanco A South American milk pudding flavored with cinnamon and served as a dessert or used as a sweet spread or pastry filling.

mannish water A spicy Caribbean soup made from goat offal, green bananas and various vegetables (especially tubers).

mannitol 1. A sugar alcohol derived from fruits or produced from glucose. 2. A food additive used as an anticaking agent, lubricant, preservative, nutritive sweetener, flavor-ing agent, stabilizer and/or thickener in processed foods such as baked goods, frozen desserts and candies.

mano (mah-noh) A rectangular stone used to crush corn in a metate. *See* metate.

Manooria (mah-noo-ree-ah) A soft, white cheese made in Crete and Macedonia from goat's or ewe's milk.

mansef (mahn-seif) A Middle Eastern meal consisting of a communal platter lined with bread, on top of which is mounded rice and chunks of cooked lamb flavored with allspice, cardamom and pepper; it is garnished with a yogurt sauce and pine nuts.

mansikka (MAHN-sik-kaht) Finnish for strawberries.

manteca (mahn-TEH-kah) Spanish for lard.

Manteca (mahn-TEK-ah) A mozzarella or other pasta filata cheese molded around a lump of butter; the surface is sometimes smoked.

manteiga (mahn-TAY-gah) Portuguese for butter.

mantequilla (mahn-teh-KEE-yah) Spanish for butter.

manti (MAHN-teu) A Turkish pasta stuffed with ground beef, onions and yogurt.

mantis shrimp A variety of shrimp native to Japan; it grows to 6 in. (15 cm) in length and has a very sweet flavor.

mantle 1. The membrane embracing a mollusk and lining its shell; it secretes the shell-building materials. 2. A squid's body tube.

mantle scallop A variety of scallop found in the western Pacific Ocean and Indian Ocean; it has an orange to purple red-striped shell and a tender, sweet, white meat.

manufacturing cream; manufacturers' cream *See* cream, manufacturing.

manuka honey A clear, thick, deep golden–colored honey with a rich flavor; made in New Zealand from blossoms of the manuka or tea tree.

Manur (mahn-nurt) A Serbian cheese made from buttermilk and either cow's or ewe's milk; it has a slightly salty flavor.

Manx broth A thick soup from Great Britain's Isle of Man made with beef brisket, ham knuckle bone, barley, cabbage, turnip, carrots and leeks and flavored with thyme and parsley.

manzana (mahn-ZAH-nak) 1. Spanish for apple. 2. A medium-sized, bell-shaped fresh chile with a thick yellow-orange skin, black seeds and a medium to very hot, fruity flavor.

manzanilla (mahn-zah-NILL-lah) A type of sherry; it is very dry with a very slight bitter, almost salty flavor, very pale gold color and light body. *See* sherry.

manzanillo mango A variety of small, purple-skinned mango.

manzo (MAHN-dzoa) *See* bue.

manzo stufato (MAHN-dzoa stoo-FAH-toa) Italian for beef stew.

mao tai (mau toi) A Chinese spirit distilled from sorghum; it is clear and has a high alcohol content.

maotou quisan (mah-oh-too kwee-sohn) Chinese for shaggy mane mushroom.

MAP *See* modified American plan.

maple A tree native to North America (*Acer saccharinum*); its sap is used for natural maple syrup. Also known as sugar maple.

maple sugar A sweetener obtained by further concentrating the sap of the maple tree; it has a granular texture and is sweeter and denser than maple syrup.

maple syrup A reddish-brown, viscous liquid with a sweet distinctive flavor, it is made by reducing the sap of the North American maple tree.

maprao (mah-prah-oh) Thai for coconut.

maqloobee (mah-kah-lu-bah) A Middle Eastern dish consisting of layers of eggplant, rice and ground lamb or beef flavored with pine nuts and pepper.

maqualli (mah-call-lee) A Moroccan chicken tajine flavored with lemon peel, saffron, ginger and garlic and cooked with olives.

Maquée A soft Belgian cheese made from cow's milk.

maquereau (mah-ker-roa) French for mackerel.

mar Ethiopian for honey.

Maracaibo (mah-rah-kah-ee-boh) Arabica coffee beans grown in Venezuela; the beverage has a sweet, fine flavor and a light body.

maracujà (mah-rah-coo-jah) A yellow-skinned passion fruit grown in Brazil.

maranta *See* arrowroot.

marasca A variety of sour cherry grown in Italy; it has a sharp, bitter flavor.

Maraschino (mar-uh-SKEE-noh; mar-uh-SHEE-noh) An Italian marasca cherry–flavored liqueur.

maraschino cherry (mar-uh-SHEE-noh) 1. A cherry marinated in Maraschino liqueur and used for garnishing cocktails, desserts and baked goods. 2. A pitted cherry macerated in a flavored sugar syrup and dyed red or green; it is used for the same purposes as a maraschino cherry marinated in Maraschino liqueur.

marasme (mah-rah-s'may) French for fairy ring mushroom.

marazine filling A filling made with almond paste, eggs, butter and flour; used in many European pastries. *See* frangipane.

marble bagel; marbled bagel A bagel made with pumpernickel and plain dough twisted together.

marble cake A moist, buttery cake made by swirling vanilla and chocolate batters together to create a marblelike pattern.

marble slab A large, smooth piece of marble used for rolling out doughs and working with chocolate and sugar; it is useful because marble stays cool and does not absorb moisture.

marbling The whitish streaks of inter- and intramuscular fat found in muscles; it adds to the meat's flavor and tenderness and is a principal factor in determining its quality grade.

marc (mar) 1. French for pomace. 2. A clear, brandylike beverage with a high alcohol content distilled from the fermented juice of the pomace; also known as eau-de-vie de marc (French) and grappa (Italian). 3. The quantity of grapes required to load a Champagne press for a pressing (8000 lb. or 4000 kg).

marchand de vin, sauce (mah-shon duh vang) A French compound sauce made from a demi-glaze with shallots, red wine, butter, parsley and lemon juice; usually served with steak.

Marches (mar-kes) A hard cheese made in Italy's Tuscany region from ewe's milk.

marchew (mahr-hef-kee) Polish for carrots.

marchpane The traditional name for a paste of sugar and almonds or other nuts made into flat cakes or cookies or molded into ornamental forms; now usually referred to as marzipan.

maréchale, sauce (maahr-ay-shal) A French compound sauce made from an allemande garnished with diced mushrooms.

Maréchal Foch (MAH-ray-shahl FOSCH) A French grape hybrid that produces light, fruity red wines; now grown almost exclusively in Canada and the eastern United States.

marée (maahr-ay) The French collective name for all fish and shellfish sold in a fish market.

marengo, à la (mah-rehn-go, ah lah) A French dish of chicken braised with garlic, tomatoes, olives and white wine or brandy; garnished with crayfish and sometimes fried eggs.

Marengo, sauce A French sauce made with tomatoes, garlic, onions and mushrooms.

Marennes (mah-rehm) A variety of oysters found off Marennes, in France's Charente-Maritime district; it has a white and green shell, a greenish flesh and an exceptionally fine flavor.

mare's milk *See* milk, mare's.

Margaret River A grape-growing and wine-producing region in western Australia; the principal grapes grown include Chardonnay, Sauvignon Blanc, Sémillon, Rhine Riesling, Cabernet Sauvignon and Shiraz.

margarine A butter substitute made from animal or vegetable fats or a combination of such fats mixed with flavorings, colorings, emulsifiers, preservatives and vitamins and firmed through hydrogenation; like butter, it is approximately 80% fat and 16% water; also known as oleo.

margarine, whipped Margarine with air whipped into it, making it fluffy and easy to spread; the air can sometimes equal half the volume.

Margarita (mahr-gah-REE-tah) A cocktail made of tequila, lime juice and an orange-flavored liqueur (e.g., Triple Sec or Cointreau); traditionally served in a glass that has had its rim dipped in lime juice and then coated with salt.

Margarita, frozen A Margarita blended with crushed ice.

margarita glass A stemmed glass with a large, shallow bowl holding 12–17 fl. oz. (336–476 ml) and used for Margaritas and specialty drinks; also known as a fiesta grande.

Margherita 1. Italian for daisy; used to described a moderately narrow pasta ribbon with one ruffled edge, similar to fettucce riccie. 2. An Italian pizza that is topped with tomatoes, mozzarella and fresh basil.

margosa A slightly cylindrical, bumpy-skinned fruit (*Momordica balsamina*); it has a pale green skin (that turns yellow when ripe), a red flesh and a bitter flavor; used like a vegetable, it is cooked for use in salads or stuffed in Asian cuisines, especially Chinese; also known as a balsam apple.

Marguery, à la (mahr-gew-rey, ah lah) A French garnish for tournedos consisting of artichoke hearts filled with a salpicon of truffles, sautéed morels, cockscombs, and cocks' kidneys; the pan juices are boiled and reduced with port and cream.

Marguery, sauce (mahr-gew-rey) A French compound sauce made from a hollandaise flavored with oyster liqueur and diced poached oysters.

marides; marithes (mah-ree-thes) Small smelts native to the Mediterranean Sea near Greece; dredged in flour, deep-fried and served whole with lemon as a meze.

Marie-Jeanne, à la A French garnish for tournedos and noisettes consisting of small tarts filled with peas and tiny balls of carrot and turnip.

Marienhofer (mah-ree-en-hof-her) An Austrian limburger-style cheese made from cow's milk.

Marigny, sauce (mah-rehn-yay) A French compound sauce made from a demi-glaze, flavored with tomatoes and mushroom essence and garnished with sliced mushrooms and black olives.

marinade A seasoned liquid, usually containing an acid, herbs and/or spices, in which raw foods (typically meat, poultry, fish, shellfish or vegetables) are soaked or coated to absorb flavors and become tender before cooking or serving. *See* meat tenderizer.

marinara (mah-ree-NAIR-uh) An Italian pasta sauce made from tomatoes, garlic, onions and oregano.

marinata (mah-ree-nah-tah) A Greek preparation method in which fish are marinated in lemon juice, olive oil and herbs.

marinate To soak or coat a food in a marinade.

mariné (mah-reh-nay) French for marinated or pickled.

marine Pertaining to, existing in or produced from the sea.

marineret sild på fedtebørd (mah-re-na-rett sealed pah FED-ta-bored) A Danish smørrebrød dish of sweet-and-sour pickled herring with chopped red onion.

marinière, à la (mah-reen-YAIR, ah lah) French for mariner's style and used to describe seafood cooked in white wine and herbs and often garnished with mussels.

marinière, sauce; mariner's sauce A French compound sauce made from a sauce Bercy and mussel stock and garnished with poached mussels.

marinovannye (mah-re-no-vahn-ya-ee) Russian for marinated or pickled.

Marionberry A hybrid berry similar to the blackberry but with a more intense flavor.

mariscos (mah-REE-khos) Spanish for shellfish.

marjolaine (mahr-juh-layn) 1. A French pastry composed of rectangular layers of crisp almond or hazelnut meringue sandwiched together with chocolate, coffee and/or praline buttercream. 2. French for sweet marjoram.

marjoram (MAHR-juhr-uhm) An herb and member of the mint family (*Origanum marjorana*) native to the Mediterranean region; it has short, oval, pale green leaves, a sweet flavor reminiscent of thyme and oregano and a strong aroma; also known as sweet marjoram and knotted marjoram. *See* oregano *and* pot marjoram.

Mark (mahrk) German for bone marrow.

market *v.* 1. To attract a specific buyer population. 2. To purchase goods at a grocery or other store. *n.* 1. The number of people who have the ability and desire to purchase a business's goods or services. 2. A geographic area that includes a specific buyer population. 3. A grocery or similar store that sells foods and related items.

market basket competition A culinary contest in which participants are given various foods (unknown to them before the contest) and asked to create a dish or meal; the finished product is judged on flavor, skill and creativity.

market fit The likelihood that a new item or service will be purchased by the same customers who buy the business's existing goods and services.

marketing Activities designed to accelerate the movements of a business's goods and services to the consumer; includes advertising, merchandising, product planning, sales and warehousing.

market menu A menu based on product availability during a specific time period; written to use foods that are in season or readily available.

market mushroom *See* common store mushroom.

market plan; marketing plan A business's systematic plan for penetrating a market with its goods or services.

market share A business's percentage of the industry's total sales within a certain geographic area or time period.

Markgräflerland (mark-GRAYF-ler-lahnd) A grape-growing and wine-producing area along Germany's Rhine River; the principal grape grown is the Gutedel.

markup The amount added to the costs of goods to reflect overhead and provide a profit; the difference between the cost of the item and its selling price.

Marlborough The largest grape-growing and wine-producing region in New Zealand; it is a cool-climate area located on South Island; the principal grapes grown are Sauvignon Blanc and Chardonnay.

Marlborough pie An applesauce custard pie flavored with nutmeg and sherry.

marmalade (MAHR-mah-laid) A citrus jelly that also contains unpeeled slices of citrus fruit.

marmalade (mahr-mer-lahd) French for a jellylike purée of fruit or onions.

Marmalade A cocktail made of gin, lemon juice and orange marmalade.

marmalade box *See* genipap.

Marmelade (mahr-meh-LAA-der) German for jam.

marmellata (mahr-mayl-LAA-tah) Italian for jam.

marmite (mahr-MEET) A tall, straight-sided French metal or earthenware covered pot with a capacity of up to 14 gallons (51 l) used for cooking large quantities of foods, such as soups, cassoulet and pot-au-feu; larger ones are available with a spigot at the bottom.

marmot A rodent about the size of a cat; eaten in the French Alps and Pyrenees; it has a musky flavor.

Marnique An Australian liqueur made with brandy and tangerines.

Maroilles; Marolles (mah-wahee) A firm French cheese made from cow's milk; it has a soft yellow interior, a smooth, shiny, reddish-brown rind, a strong aroma and an assertive flavor.

Maronen (mah-RAH-nehn) German for chestnuts.

marqeh (marck-heh) Arabic for sauce.

marquise (mahr-keyz) 1. A French dessert consisting of a fruit ice into which whipped cream is folded. 2. A soft, mousselike chocolate cake. 3. A general term for any semi-soft, still-frozen dessert that is molded.

Marquise, sauce (mahr-keyz) A French compound sauce made from a hollandaise blended with caviar just before service.

marquq (mahrck-you'k) *See* khobaz arabee.

marron (ma-ROHN) French for chestnut.

marron glacé (ma-ROHN glah-SAY) French for chestnuts that are preserved or candied in a sweet syrup.

marrow The soft, fatty vascular substance found in the central cavity of a bone, particularly the shin and leg bones; it has an ivory color after it is cooked and a rich flavor; also known as bone marrow or marrowbone. *See* marrow bone.

marrow bean The largest and roundest of the white bean varieties; available fresh and dried. *See* white beans.

marrow bone A bone, usually from the thigh and upper legs of the beef primal round, with a high marrow content; it is usually cut into 2- to 3-in. (5.08- to 7.6-cm) lengths.

marrowfat pea A large dried bean with an ivory-tan color.

marrow spoon A long spoon with a long, narrow bowl used to extract marrow from a bone.

marrow squash 1. An elongated cylindrical summer squash with a green skin and flesh and a bland flavor; it is often stuffed with a meat mixture; also called a vegetable marrow squash. 2. In Great Britain, a general term for summer squash.

marrying 1. The process or concept of combining (serving or cooking) foods with complementary or contrasting flavors, aromas, textures, shapes and/or colors to achieve a more balanced or interesting flavor, dish or presentation. 2. The process or concept of combining (serving) foods with a specific wine to achieve a complementary or contrasting flavor combination. 3. The process or concept of mixing together different grape varieties in a must to obtain a better balance of body, aroma, acidity and flavor in the resulting wine. 4. The practice of combining opened containers of the same foods or beverages into one container (e.g., combining two bottles of ketchup).

Marsala (mar-SAH-lah) An Italian fortified white wine made from Catarratto, Grillo and Inzolia grapes; it has an amber to brown color and is available in three styles: fine (the sweetest), mosto cotto (with a caramelized flavor) and superiore (the driest, aged for at least 2 years in casks).

Marsanne (mahr-san) A white wine grape principally grown in France's northern Rhône River valley, Switzerland and Australia; the resulting wine is full bodied.

Marseillaise, à la (mahr-say-laze, ah lah) 1. A French garnish for tournedos and noisettes consisting of olives stuffed with anchovy fillets in hollowed tomatoes, large fried potato chips and sauce Provençal. 2. A mayonnaise mixed with a purée of sea urchin.

marshmallow 1. A perennial herb (*Althaea officinalis*) with a yellow, branched root, a leafy stem with toothed leaves and white or pinkish flowers; the leaves and flowers are used for medicinal, ornamental and culinary purposes; the root has a slightly sweet flavor and is cooked like a root vegetable; the mucilage from the roots was used to make the spongy sweets known as marshmallows. 2. A light, spongy confection made with egg whites, corn syrup and gum arabic or gelatin and formed into a small pillow-shaped candy.

marshmallow crème A thick whipped mixture made from the same ingredients as marshmallows and used in fudges, icings, cakes and candies.

marshmallow icing A boiled icing with a stabilizer, usually gelatin or confectioners' sugar.

marsh samphire (SAM-fy-uhr) A wild perennial herb (*Salicornia europaea*) with small succulent leaves used in salads or cooked like a vegetable; also known as glasswort and sea salicornia. *See* rock samphire.

Marsh's seedless grapefruit A common variety of white grapefruit; the flesh has a greenish tinge.

Martini A cocktail made of gin and dry vermouth, served straight-up or on the rocks, garnished with an olive or lemon twist; when made with vodka, it is known as a Vodka Martini.

martini glass A tall stemmed glass with a flared bowl and a capacity of 6–9 fl. oz. (177–266 ml); used for serving a Martini.

Martinique rhum A flavorful and full-bodied rum distilled on the island of Martinique from unfermented sugarcane sap, then shipped to Bordeaux, France, for aging in wood.

martrange *See* chataignier.

martynia A plant (*Martynia louisanica*) native to the American Southwest and Central America; its young pods are

martini glass

pickled in southwestern and Mexican cuisines; also known as devil's claw and unicorn plant.

maru (MAH-roo) Japanese for whole or round.

maruzze (mah-rou-tze) Italian for seashell and used to describe conch-shaped pasta available in several sizes; the larger sizes are usually stuffed.

Marvo A beverage made of eggs and Marsala.

maryann pan A round, shallow tart pan with fluted sides and a deep indentation around the circumference that causes the center of the pan's bottom to be raised; sponge cakes and tart shells are baked in the pan, then inverted and the indented center filled with cream or fruit; also known as an Obsttortenform.

Maryland stuffed ham A boiled ham stuffed with cabbage (or other greens) and onions, seasoned with mustard, chiles and other seasonings and served cold.

Marzenbier (mat-son-beer) A medium-strong, amber-colored German beer, usually brewed in March and consumed at Oktoberfest.

marzipan (MAHR-zih-pan) A sweet, pliable paste made of ground almonds, sugar and egg whites; often colored and shaped into three-dimensional decorations or used as a candy filling or cake coating. *See* marchpane.

marzipan tools A set of variously shaped, long, thin, plastic sticks used for forming and decorating marzipan designs.

masa (MAH-sah) 1. Spanish for dough. 2. A Mexican dough made of dried corn kernels that have been soaked and cooked in lime water.

masa harina (MAH-sah ah-REE-nah) 1. Spanish for dough flour. 2. Flour made by grinding dried masa dough; used in Mexican and U.S. cuisines for breads, tortillas, tamales and other foods.

masala (ma-SAH-la) Hindi for spice, spices, spice blend and blend of seasonings. *See* garam masala.

masala bhoonana (ma-SAH-la BHOO-na-nah) Hindi for roasting spices.

masala musulana (ma-SAH-la MUH-suh-leh-nah) Hindi for crushing spices.

masala peesana (PEE-sa-nah) Hindi for grinding spices.

masalédar (mah-sah-la-dahr) Hindi for spicy.

masamba A Malawi dish of pumpkin greens, spinach or kale simmered with tomatoes and onions and thickened with powdered groundnuts.

Mascarpone (mas-cahr-POHN-ay) A soft, double or triple cream cheese made in Switzerland and Italy's Lombardy and Tuscany regions from cow's milk; it has an ivory color and a sweet, slightly acidic flavor and is often blended with either sweet or savory flavorings.

mash *v.* 1. To crush a food into a smooth, evenly textured mixture for use in beer or spirits. 2. To make a grain mixture for use in beer or spirits. 3. To crush or pound; generally used in connection with cooked root vegetables, such as potatoes and turnips. *n.* 1. A soft, pulpy mass. 2. A thick mixture of crushed malted barley or other grains steeped in

hot water, which causes the malt enzymes to convert the grains' starches into the sugars necessary for making beer and distilled spirits. 3. Boiled grains and other foods used as fodder. 4. British for mashed potatoes.

mash, standard A mash made in a brewer's laboratory from specified quantities of water and malt; used in beer brewing to ensure consistent results.

mashamba (mah-shamm-bah) A green-fleshed, pumpkin-like melon grown in Zimbabwe.

mashawi (mah-shaw-we) A Middle Eastern cooking method in which foods are slowly grilled over a bed of embers.

mashbill The recipe or formula of grains used for making a whiskey.

mashshurum (mash-shoo-room) Japanese for mushrooms; also known as shiitake.

mash tun *See* lauter tun.

mask 1. To cover a food completely with a sauce or aspic. 2. To season a food to such a degree that the food's flavor becomes indistinct.

maslin A medievel European bread made from a mixture of rye and wheat flour.

maslina (mahs-LYEE-ni) Russian for olive.

maslo (MAH-sloh) Russian and Polish for oil or butter; also known as mazat.

Masnor (mas-nor) A whey cheese made in Greece and the Balkans from goat's milk; shaped like an elongated pear, it has a thin, smooth skin and a dense interior without any holes.

Mason jar A glass jar with a removable threaded lid and rubber gasket designed to keep the contents airtight and prevent spoilage; it is used for preserving foods.

masoor dal; masar dal A brown lentil, usually sold split and skinned; it becomes a somewhat translucent pink-orange-yellow color when cooked and is used in Indian cuisines.

MASP *See* minimum acceptable standard of performance.

massaged Meat that has been tenderized by tumbling it in a mechanical drum to break down connective tissues and fibers.

Mass cake A small sweet wafer not necessarily made for religious purposes but probably with a religious origin.

massepain (mah-sah-pahng) French for marzipan.

Master of Wine (MW) A title conferred by the Institute of Masters of Wine, a British organization founded in 1953; the Master must pass an examination emphasizing blind tastings, viticulture, viniculture, wine laws and marketing and is entitled to use the initials MW after his or her name.

master menu index A complete list of all foods and beverages that a food services facility sells, has sold or contemplates selling; used to develop menus.

Masthuhn (mast-who-en) German for pullet.

mastic A natural resin or gum with a faint licorice flavor; produced in Greece from the Acacia tree, it is used as a flavoring in the Middle East.

mastication The process of chewing food.

masticatory Any substance of vegetable origin chewed simply for pleasure; generally contains a flavoring substance and/or stimulant (e.g., betel nuts in Asia, chicle in Mexico and coca in South America).

Mastikha; Mastika (mah-stee-khaa) A Greek liqueur made from aniseed and the gum of the mastikha plant.

masu (mah-soo) Japanese for trout. *See* ayu.

mat (maht) Norwegian for food.

ma tai (mah tah-ee) The small, horseshoe-shaped tuber of an aquatic herb; used in Japanese cuisines, it has a crunchy texture and coconut-like flavor; sometimes imprecisely called a water chestnut.

ma tai; mah tai (mah tha-ee; mah tai) Chinese for water chestnuts.

matambre (ma-tam-barr-ay) Spanish for to kill hunger and used to describe an Argentinean dish consisting of a steak marinated with chiles and stuffed with chiles, spinach, carrots, onions, bacon and herbs, tied and simmered in the marinade and beef broth.

matar (mah-tar) Hindi for peas and chickpeas.

Matcha (mah-CHAH) A Japanese green tea made from powdered leaves beaten to a froth during the Japanese tea ceremony; the beverage is refreshing and astringent.

matchstick 1. A wine-tasting term for a wine with an undesirable aroma or flavor reminiscent of burned matches; it is caused by an excess of sulfur dioxide. 2. *See* allumette, batonnet *and* julienne.

maté (MAH-tay) A South American beverage with a low alcohol content made from the fermented dried leaves and shoots of an evergreen tree (*Ilex paraguayenis*) of the holly family; also known as Paraguay tea and yerba maté.

matelote (mah-tuh-lot) A French stew made with freshwater fish, especially eels, flavored with red or white wine and aromatics.

Matelote, sauce (mah-tuh-lot) A French compound sauce made from a demi-glaze flavored with red or white wine, fish stock or trimmings and cayenne and finished with butter.

matignon (mah-tee-yawng) 1. A vegetable fondue with or without bacon, used as a flavoring in various braised or fried dishes. 2. A French garnish for various cuts of meat, consisting of artichoke hearts stuffed with vegetable fondue, sprinkled with bread crumbs and browned. 3. An archaic term used to designate a coarsely chopped mirepoix containing ham.

Matjes herring (MAHT-yeh hay-ring) A Dutch dish made from a young herring skinned, filleted and cured in sugar, salt, vinegar and spices.

Matki Ser (maht-key sar) 1. Polish for mother's cheese and used to describe a farmer's cheese–style cheese made from cow's milk. 2. A caraway-seeded version made in Michigan.

matoke (mah-toh-kee) A variety of banana grown in Central and East Africa.

Matrassa *See* Krimskoye.

matsuba (maht-soo-bah) Japanese for pine needle and used to describe a decorative cut for foods.

matsutake (maht-soo-TAH-kee) A large mushroom (*Tricholoma matsutake*) that grows wild on pine trees in Japan; it has a reddish-brown color, a dense, meaty texture and a nutty flavor; usually available dried in the United States; also known as a pine mushroom.

mattha (maht-tah) An east Indian yogurt drink flavored with salt, roasted cumin and fresh mint leaves.

matunda (ma-toon-dah) Swahili for fruit.

mature A tasting term for a food (e.g., cheese) or beverage (e.g., wine) that has had its characteristic qualities fully developed.

maturing agent *See* aging agent.

maturo (mah-too-roh) Italian for ripe.

matutu *See* ikeleko.

matzo; matzoh (MAHT-suh) A thin, brittle, unleavened bread made with only water and flour and traditionally eaten during the Jewish Passover holiday; it can be ground into meal and used for matzo balls, pancakes and other dishes.

matzo ball *See* matzoh knaidel.

matzo brei (br-eye) A Jewish dish of matzo soaked in water, squeezed dry, dipped in beaten egg and fried; it is usually served with cinnamon sugar, maple syrup, honey or ketchup.

matzoh knaidel (mah-t'zoh knayd-dhul) A Jewish dumpling made from matzo meal and sometimes flavored schmaltz; it can range from light and fluffy to heavy and dense; also known as a matzo ball.

Mauby A western Indian beverage made from an extract of the bark from trees and shrubs of the buckthorn family (genus *Rhamnus*); it has a bittersweet flavor.

Maui onion A large onion with a golden yellow outer layer, a moist white flesh and a mild, sweet flavor; grown in the delimited area of Maui, Hawaii.

mauk (ma-euk) A variety of eggplant with an orange skin covered with fine, dark hairs and a bitter flavor; used in Thai cuisine raw in salads or minced in sauces; also known as hairy eggplant.

mauka A variety of macadamia grown in Hawaii; it has a particularly rich, buttery flavor.

Maultaschen (MAHUL-tea-schen) German for slap in the face and used to describe a southern German dish of large, square dumplings filled with meat (usually veal) and seasoned with parsley.

Mauritius peanut A variety of superior-quality peanut.

Mavrodaphne (mahv-ro-DAHF-nee) A red wine grape grown in Greece; the resulting wine is full bodied, sweet and reminiscent of port.

Maximilian, sauce A French compound sauce made from a hollandaise blended with anchovy essence.

Maya breadnut; Mayan breadnut *See* breadnut.

May apple A member of the barberry family (genus *Berberis*); this egg-shaped fruit is poisonous when green but safe after ripening; cherry-sized, it has a sweet, acidic flavor and is used for preserves.

Mayfair A cocktail made of Cognac, Dubonnet rouge, lime juice, sugar syrup and Angostura bitters; garnished with an orange twist.

mayhaw A hawthorn tree (*Crataegus aestivalis*) that grows in the American South; the acidic, juicy, red berry is used for making jellies and preserves.

mayhaw jelly *See* mayhaw.

mayonesa (mah-on-nay-sah) Spanish for mayonnaise.

mayonnaise (may-o-nayz) A cold, thick, creamy sauce consisting of oil and vinegar emulsified with egg yolks; used as a spread or base for a salad dressing or dip. *Note:* French mayonnaise sauces are listed alphabetically by their principal modifier (e.g., mayonnaise cressonière is listed cressonière, mayonnaise).

ma yu (mah yu) Chinese for sesame oil.

maza (meh-zah) *See* meza.

ma zaher (mah-eh za-ha-rah) Arabic for orange blossom water.

mazamorra morada (mah-sah-moe-rrah moe-rah-dah) A Peruvian gelatin-like dessert made from purple corn and cooked, dried fruits.

mazapan A Latin American marzipan-like substance made with peanuts, squash seeds and pumpkin seeds.

Mazarine (mah-zah-reen) The proprietary name of a French liqueur with a spicy, herbal flavor.

mazariso (mah-t'zah-REE-soh) A Sicilian cake made with ground pistachios, eggs, oranges and Marsala and iced with a saffron-flavored sugar glaze.

mazat (MAHS-lah) *See* maslo.

mazer A medieval English drinking bowl, usually with two handles and often footed, made of wood (typically, bird's-eye maple) with a silver base.

maziwa (mah-zee-wah) Swahili for milk.

Mazuelo *See* Carignan.

mazurek; mazarek (mah-zha-reck) A Polish Easter cake made with butter, flour, almonds and hard-cooked egg yolks, rolled thin and topped with a lattice that is filled with fruit jam and dusted with confectioners' sugar.

mazurka (mah-zoor-kah) A Russian meringuelike confection flavored with honey, lemon juice and finely ground nuts, baked in paper cups, garnished with whipped cream and dusted with nutmeg.

mazzard A wild sweet cherry native to Europe; the black-skinned fruit have a rich flavor and are often used for flavoring liqueurs in central Europe; the mazzard is a particularly hardy species and it is often used as a grafting stock; also known as a bird cherry or gean.

mbaazi (mbah-zee) Swahili for peas.

mbichi (mbee-key) Swahili for raw and fresh.

mbiru (mbee-roo) Swahili for ripe.

mboga (mbow-gah) Swahili for vegetables.

mboga ya maboga (m'boh-gah yah ma-boh-gah) A Tanzanian delicacy consisting of pumpkin flowers and leaves simmered with cream, flavored with turmeric, chiles, tomatoes and onions and served hot as an accompaniment to stews or ugali.

mboga za kukolezea chakula (mboh-gah za koo-koe-la-za-ah tcha-koo-law) Swahili for herbs.

McFarlin cranberry A cranberry variety; its red fruit are relatively large.

mcheler (mcha-lehr) Swahili for uncooked rice.

m'chermia (mkerr-me-ah) An Algerian dish consisting of cubed calf's liver fried with garlic, pepper and vinegar and served over rice.

mchicha (m'chi-chah) A spinachlike green grown in East Africa (especially Kenya and Tanzania); it has a slightly bitter flavor.

mchuzi (choo-zee) Swahili for sauce.

McIntosh apple A medium-sized apple with red-striped green or yellow skin, a soft, juicy flesh and a sweet–tart flavor; an all-purpose apple, it tends to fall apart when cooked.

mead A drink made from a fermented mixture of honey and water; also known as honey wine.

meadow cress A wild plant native to Europe (*Cardamine pratensis*); its young leaves have a biting, peppery flavor and are used for salads; also known as lady's smock.

meadow mushroom *See* common field mushroom.

meadow tea A Pennsylvania Dutch beverage (a tisane) made from meadow herbs such as peppermint and spearmint that are steeped in hot water.

meal 1. One of the regular occasions during the day when foods and beverages are consumed at a customary time. 2. The food served at such an occasion. 3. The coarsely ground seeds of any edible grain such as corn or oats. 4. Any dried, ground substance (e.g., bonemeal). 5. The quantity of milk given by a cow at a milking.

mealie-meal A South African dish consisting of a thick cornmeal porridge, sometimes flavored with chiles.

mealy Having a texture similar to meal: dry, grainy, crumbly, powdery and/or soft.

mealy potato *See* potato, mealy.

measuring cups, dry Vessels, usually made of plastic or metal, with a handle and a rim that is level with the top measurement specified; they are used to measure the volume of dry substances and are generally available in a set of 1/4-, 1/3-, 1/2-, and 1-cup capacities; metric measures are also available.

measuring cups, liquid Vessels, usually made of glass, plastic or metal, with a handle and a spout that is above the top line of measurement; specifically used to measure the volume of a liquid and generally available in 1-, 2- and 4-cup to 1-gallon capacities; metric measures are also available; also known as glass cup measures.

measuring spoons Plastic or metal spoons with a round or oval bowl and used to measure volume; they usually come in sets of four to measure 1/4, 1/2, and 1 teaspoon and 1 tablespoon.

meat 1. The flesh (muscles, fat and related tissues) of animals used for food. *See* skeletal meat. 2. The edible part of nuts. 3. The fleshy part of fruits and vegetables. *See* kernel.

meat and potatoes 1. Slang for a hearty meal, usually something plain and basic, for someone who is not an adventurous diner; also known as steak and potatoes. 2. Slang for someone who is not an adventurous eater.

meatballs; meat balls Small balls shaped from a mixture of minced or ground meats, usually flavored with onions, herbs and spices and bound with bread crumbs and/or egg; they are poached, pan-fried, threaded on skewers and grilled or broiled; served with or without a sauce in various cuisines worldwide.

meat by-products The edible and wholesome parts of a beef, veal, lamb or pork carcass other than skeletal meat. *See* variety meats.

meat carver *See* carving knife.

meat extender *See* textured plant protein.

meat glaze *See* glace de viande.

meat grinder; meat mincer A tool used to grind meat; the meat is placed in a hopper and forced through a rotating blade, then through a perforated disk (various sizes are available) and extruded; manual or electric, it can be fitted with attachments (e.g., one to hold sausage casings).

meat hammer *See* meat tenderizer.

meatloaf; meat loaf A loaf-shaped mixture of ground meat (beef, veal, lamb or pork) or poultry, seasonings and usually onions, bound with bread crumbs and/or eggs and baked; served hot or cold.

meat pounder; meat bat A metal tool used for flattening and tenderizing meat; it has a flat, broad face with a 5- × 4-in. striking surface and weighs 1.5–7 lb.

meat pounder

meat product; meat food product A labeling term recognized by the USDA for any food product containing more than 3% cattle, sheep, swine or goat meat.

meat replacement *See* textured plant protein.

meat tenderizer 1. A preparation of enzymes (principally the protease papain) applied to meat before cooking to help break down connective tissues; unlike a marinade, which can contain a meat tenderizer, it is not intended to add flavor. *See* mari-

meat tenderizer

nade. 2. A metal or wooden hammerlike tool used to tenderize meat; one striking face has a fine-toothed surface, and the other has a coarse-toothed surface; also known as a meat hammer.

meaty Heavily fleshed.

Meaux (moh) 1. A French prepared mustard made from yellow, brown and black seeds; it has a medium hot, spicy–fruity flavor and a grainy texture. 2. A French Brie; it has a tangier, fruitier flavor than that of ordinary Brie; also known as Brie de Meaux.

mebachi (ma-bah-tche) Japanese for bigeye tuna.

mechado (mah-gha-doe) Filipino for a beef roast, sometimes with pork fat or bacon inserted into it, then braised.

mechanical beverage control system An automated system programmed to record the number and size of drinks dispensed from a bottle.

méchoui (mah-shoo-ee) An Algerian dish consisting of a whole roasted lamb.

medallion A small, round or oval piece of meat (especially from the rib or loin of beef, veal, lamb or pork) or fish.

Medana tayberry A variety of particularly flavorful tayberry.

med bua *See* lotus nut.

mede (m'ye-dee) Russian for honey.

Medellin (mah-de-een) Arabica coffee beans grown in Colombia's Medellin region; the beverage is particularly well balanced with a good acidity.

medg; meadhg Irish for whey (especially when consumed as a beverage).

Médici, sauce A French compound sauce made from a béarnaise flavored with tomato purée and red wine.

medicinal 1. A tasting term for a food (particularly herbs and vegetables) or beverage with an unpleasant aroma or flavor associated with oral medications. 2. The use of a food or beverage (e.g., an herbal tisane) taken for health as opposed to culinary purposes.

medisterpølse (mad-ister-pull-seh) A Danish pork sausage that is lightly cooked and sometimes smoked.

medium A degree of doneness for meat; the meat should have a rosy pink to red center and be slightly firm and springy when pressed. *See* very rare, rare, medium rare, medium well *and* well done.

medium-dark roast *See* roast, Viennese.

medium dry *See* semidry.

medium-grain rice *See* rice, medium-grain.

medium rare A degree of doneness for meat; the meat should have a bright red center and be slightly springy when pressed. *See* very rare, rare, medium, medium well *and* well done.

medium roast *See* roast, medium.

medium sweet *See* semisweet.

medium well A degree of doneness for meat; the meat should have very little pink at the center (almost brown throughout) and be firm and springy when pressed. *See* very rare, rare, medium rare, medium *and* well done.

medlar (MEHD-lehr) A medium-sized fruit (*Mespilus germanica*) native to Iran; it has a yellowish-brown color and is picked when ripe and stored in moist bran or sawdust until it browns and softens; it has a slightly acidic, winy flavor.

medlar

Médoc (meh-doc) The largest and most important grape-growing and wine-producing district within Bordeaux, France, particularly known for its red wines; the principal grapes grown are Cabernet Sauvignon, Cabernet Franc and Merlot and, to a lesser extent, Petit Verdot and Malbec.

mee (me) Thai for thin noodles, including egg noodles (ba mee) and rice vermicelli (sen mee).

mee krob (mee krob) A Thai dish of deep-fried rice sticks, green onions, red bell peppers, chives, tofu, cilantro and a sweet-and-sour sauce.

Meerrettich (MAYR-reh-tish) German for horseradish; also known as Kren.

meetha (mee-thaa) Hindi for sweet.

meethe neam ke patte Hindi for kari leaves.

meeting seeds A term used by the Puritans for fennel seeds; they were chewed during Sunday church meetings to mask the smell of alcohol on one's breath.

mehallabiyeh (ma-ha-la-be-ah) A Middle Eastern pudding made with milk, sugar, cornstarch and rosewater.

Mehl (mayl) German for flour.

mehraz (ma-rahz) A heavy brass Moroccan mortar and pestle.

mehu (MAY-hoon) Finnish for juice.

meikancai (may-kahn-cah-ee) A variety of mustard grown in China; the tops of its leaves are bright red; it is either pickled or fermented, preserved in salt or sun-dried and generally used as a garnish; also known as red-in-the-snow.

Mei Kwei A Chinese black tea flavored with rosebuds; the beverage has a light, fragrant aroma; also known as rose tea.

mein (Cantonese); mian (Mandarin) (main) Chinese for noodles and often used to describe thin noodles made from wheat flour; usually preceded by another word or phrase indicating a type of noodle or noodle dish.

mein ga (ma-in gah) A Vietnamese chicken broth with chicken and clear noodles.

meiwei niugan (may-way new-gun) Chinese for bolete.

mejillón (mah-heh-hon) Spanish for mussel.

mejillónes (mah-heh-hon-nays) A Spanish tapas of mussels; they can be prepared in various ways and eaten hot or cold.

mejorana (meh-khoa-RAH-nah) Spanish for sweet marjoram.

Mekong whiskey (me-kong) A brown, raw-tasting distilled spirit found generally in Indochina.

mel (male) Norwegian for flour.

mel (mayl) Portuguese for honey.

méla (MAY-lah) Italian for apple.

melafefon avocado A small, cucumber-shaped, pitless avocado developed in Israel.

melagrana (may-lahg-RAH-nah) Italian for pomegranate.

Melange (ma-lahn-gue) A Viennese coffee that is equal parts coffee and milk; it is served with a crown of froth.

melanzane (may-lahn-TSAA-nay) Italian for eggplant.

melão (mah-LOWN) Portuguese for melon.

melão com presunto (mah-LOWN com pra-soon-toe) A Portuguese petisco dish of melon served with cured ham.

melba (MEHL-bah) A French garnish for small cuts of meat consisting of small tomatoes filled with a salpicon of chicken, truffles and mushrooms mixed with a velouté, sprinkled with bread crumbs and browned; it is often accompanied by braised lettuce.

Melba, sauce A French dessert sauce made with puréed raspberries, sugar, red currant jelly and cornstarch. *See* Peach Melba.

melba toast Very thin slices of white bread baked in a low oven until golden brown and very crisp.

melegueta pepper The berry of a plant (*Aframomum melegueta*) native to Africa; it has a spicy, peppery flavor.

meli (ma-lee) Greek for honey.

melilot A clover native to Europe; it is used as a flavoring, especially in cheeses.

melinjo (m'lean-jo) A tree (*Gnetum gnemon*) cultivated in Indonesia for its small red fruit; the fruit's kernel and skin are sun-dried and then fried and served as a snack or used as a garnish for soups and salads.

melisa (ma-lee-saw) Turkish for eggplant.

melitzanes (meh-lee-DZAH-nah) Greek for eggplant.

melitzanosalata (meh-lee-DZAH-noh-sah-lah-tah) A Greek appetizer of eggplant purée flavored with lemon juice, onion, garlic, parsley and olive oil and garnished with black olives.

melk (MEL-uk) Norwegian for milk.

mellet pak chee (mel-let pak chi) Thai for coriander seeds.

mellet yira (mellet jira) Thai for cumin, fennel and caraway seeds (no differentiation).

mellow 1. A coffee-tasting term used to describe a well-balanced coffee with low to medium acidity. 2. A wine-tasting term for a soft, ripe wine without rough edges; usually associated with a mature, well-aged wine.

melocotón (meh-lo-KOO-ton) Spanish for peach; also known as durazno.

melomel Mead blended with fruit juices other than apple juice.

melon A member of the gourd family Cucurbitaceae; grown on vines worldwide, these fruits generally have a thick, hard rind, many seeds and a sweet, juicy flesh; there are two principal types: muskmelons and watermelons. *See* muskmelon *and* watermelon.

melon (meh-lohn) French for melon.

melon baller A tool used to scoop smooth or fluted spheres or ovoids from melons, cucumbers or other foods; available with a single scoop on a handle or a handle with a scoop at either end, one larger than the other. *See* Parisian scoop.

mellon baller

melon cutter, V-shaped A tool with a V-shaped concave blade used to cut melons, creating a zigzag edge.

Melon de Bourgogne (meh-lohn duh boor-gwan-yuh) A white wine grape grown in France's Loire valley; the resulting wine is crisp and herbaceous; sometimes imprecisely known as Pinot Blanc in California.

melone (meh-LOHN-nay) Italian for melon.

Melone (may-LOA-ner) German for melon.

melónes (may-loh-ness) Spanish for melons.

melon pear *See* pepino.

meloukhia (ma-loo-key-ah) The deep-green leaf shoots of this plant (*Corchorus olitorius*) are used in North African cuisines (especially Egyptian and Tunisian); once cooked, they have a glutinous, slippery consistency.

melt The process by which certain foods, especially those high in fat, gradually soften and then liquefy when heated.

melting moments A British confection made of sweet dough shaped into balls, rolled in crushed cornflakes or dried, sweetened coconut and topped with a candied cherry or angelica before baking.

melts *See* spleen.

Melun (mehr-luhn) A French Brie; it has a firmer texture and a sharper flavor than most other Brie; also known as Brie de Melun.

membrillo (mem-bree-joe) Spanish for quince.

men (mehn) Chinese for braising a food over low heat; the ingredient is brushed with a coloring such as soy sauce or caramel, deep-fried or pan-fried, and then put in a pot with stock or water and simmered slowly until done.

ménagère, sauce (meh-nah-zher) A French compound sauce made from a demi-glaze flavored with onions, finished with lemon juice and garnished with chopped anchovies and parsley.

Mendip A hard English cheese made from goat's milk; it has a full, rich flavor after aging for 2–6 months.

Mendocino (mihn-doh-SEE-noh) A grape-growing and wine-producing region in northern California located along the Russian River and generally consisting of the Anderson Valley and Ukiah Valley; known for its red wines, the principal grapes grown are Zinfandel, French Colombard, Chardonnay, Cabernet Sauvignon, Sauvignon Blanc, Gewürztraminer and Johannisberg Riesling; Pinot Noir and Chardonnay grapes are also grown for sparkling wines made by the méthode champenoise.

Mendoza (mehn-doe-zah) A large grape-growing and wine-producing region located along the foothills of the Andes, near Buenos Aires, Argentina; the principal grapes grown are Cabernet Sauvignon, Malbec, Chardonnay, Gewürztraminer, Pinot Noir and Merlot.

menrui (men-ROO-ee) Japanese for noodles.

mensa (MEHN-sah) An Italian cafeteria-style dining room or restaurant, often associated with a school, office or factory.

menta (MAYN-teh) Italian for mint.

menthe (mahngt) French for mint.

menu A list of foods and beverages available for purchase. *See* cycle menu, hybrid menu, market menu *and* static menu.

menú *See* lista de platos.

menudo (meh-NOO-doh; meh-NOO-thoh) A spicy Mexican soup made from tripe, calf's feet, green chiles, hominy and seasonings and garnished with lime wedges, chopped chiles and onions.

menu format The grouping and categorizing of items offered for sale.

menu mix *See* sales mix.

menu objective A food service facility's statement of expectations based on its marketing plan and menu policy.

menu policy A food service facility's statement of the number and type of menu items that will be offered for sale.

menu pricing *See* à la carte, semi à la carte menu, combination menu *and* table d'hôte.

menyu (mehn-u) Japanese and Swahili for menu.

mercaptans 1. A class of organic substances, some of which are produced as by-products of putrefaction and are recognizable by their offensive, garlicky odor. *See* putrefaction. 2. Compounds formed in wine as a result of the breakdown of the sulfur dioxide used as a preservative, usually caused by poor wine making; they have an odor reminiscent of hydrogen sulfide or rotten eggs.

merchandising Planning and promoting a business's sale of goods and services; includes market research, product development, advertising and sales.

mercier A small, western European traditional apple with a red-blushed, mottled brown yellow skin and a crisp, slightly sour flesh.

mère de vinaigre (mare duh vee-NAH-gru) French for mother of vinegar.

merguez; mirqaz (mayr-GEZ) A North African and Spanish sausage made from beef and mutton, seasoned and colored with red chiles; sometimes used to garnish couscous.

Meridas (mah-ree-das) Arabica coffee beans grown in Venezuela; the beverage has a sweet, fine flavor and a light body.

meringue A mixture of stiffly beaten egg whites and sugar; depending on the ratio of sugar to egg whites, a meringue may be soft (used as a fluffy topping for pies or cakes) or hard (baked into crisp cookies, disks or shells for use in pastries and desserts). *See* common meringue, Italian meringue *and* Swiss meringue.

meringue powder A fine, white powder made with dried egg whites, sugar and gum; used to replace fresh egg whites when making icings and meringues.

Meritage (MER-i-tage) A marketing term used by some California wine makers for their red wines made from blends of traditional Bordeaux grape varieties (e.g., Cabernet Franc, Cabernet Sauvignon and Malbec); their wines have more complexity than the usual California varietals.

merlango (merr-LAN-goh) Spanish for whiting.

merlano (mayr-LAA-noa) Italian for whiting.

Merlot (mair-lo) 1. A red wine grape grown in France, Italy, California and other regions; it is often used as a blending grape with Cabernet to add softness, fruit and suppleness. 2. A red wine made from this grape; it is generally soft, with a dark, rich color and an earthy, fruity flavor.

merluza (mer-lou-zaw) Spanish for hake.

merluzzo (mayr-LOOT-tsoa) Italian for cod or haddock.

mermelada *See* confitura.

mero (mah-roh) Spanish for grouper.

meron (ma-rohn) Japanese for melon.

merrythought *See* wishbone.

Mersin (ma'r-sin) A clear Turkish liqueur made from oranges.

mersin baligi (mar-sin bah-lee-gee) Turkish for sturgeon.

Merton Pride A pear grown in England; it has a yellow skin, a soft, juicy flesh and a strong flavor.

mesa (may-sah) Portuguese and Spanish for table.

mesclun (MEHS-kluhn; MEHS-klahn) A mixture of several kinds of salad greens, especially baby lettuces; although there is no set standard, the mixture usually includes baby red romaine, endive, mâche, oak leaf, radicchio and rocket, among others.

mescouta (mess-coo-tah) A Moroccan cake leavened with baking powder and studded with dates, raisins and walnuts.

mesentery (mez-zen-tehr-ree) The membrane that attaches the intestines to the posterior wall of the abdomen.

meshwiya (mash-we-kah) A Tunisian dip made from tomatoes and bell peppers and flavored with cumin, garlic, lemon juice and olive oil.

Mesimara (MAY-si-MAHR-yah) A Finnish liqueur made from the wild Arctic bramble.

Mesitra (ma-sea-traw) A soft, unsalted Crimean cheese made from ewe's milk; it has a white color and mild flavor and is usually eaten fresh.

mesob (ma-sob) An Ethiopian decorated straw basket in which food is served.

mesocarp The fleshy portion or meat of a fleshy fruit, especially one from the genus *Prunus;* it is located beneath the skin. *See* endocarp *and* epicarp.

mesquite (meh-SKEET) A hardwood tree (genus *Prosopis*) native to the American Southwest and Mexico; when burned for cooking or smoking foods, it imparts a distinctive aroma and a slightly sweet flavor.

mess 1. Slang for an amount of food (e.g., he cooked up a mess of fish). 2. Archaic term for a serving of a soft, semi-

liquid food such as porridge. 3. A military term that refers to group dining.

Messer (mess-sah) German for knife.

metabolic accelerator A substance that speeds up the metabolic rate; sometimes used as part of or in lieu of a reduction diet.

metabolism All of the chemical reactions and physical processes that continually occur in living cells and organisms. *See* anabolism *and* catabolism.

metabolize To change a substance by chemical or physical process to release energy for the living cell or organism.

metallic A tasting term for an acrid, unpleasant flavor usually acquired through the product's contact with metal processing or storage containers.

metate (meh-TAH-teh) A concave stone used by Native Americans and others living in the American Southwest or Mexico to grind corn into cornmeal using a mano. *See* mano.

Metaxa (mch-TAX-suh) A sweet, dark-colored Greek brandy.

meteltek (muh-tel-tek) Fresh Hungarian noodles used in soups, main dishes and desserts.

Meteor cherry A variety of sour cherry; the fruit have a bright red skin and the flavor is less tart than that of most other sour cherries.

meter (m) The basic measure of length in the metric system; 1 m equals 39.37 in.

methacrylic acid–divinylbenzene copolymer A food additive used as a carrier of vitamin B_{12} in foods intended for special dietary uses.

methai *See* mithai.

methanol *See* methyl alcohol.

metheglin (ME-theg-lin) A Welsh drink made from fermented honey, water and aromatic spices.

methi (MEHT-hee) Hindi for fenugreek seeds or greens.

methionine 1. An essential amino acid. 2. A food additive used as a nutrient source to significantly improve the biological quality of the total protein in a food containing naturally occurring protein.

Méthode Cap Classique (meh-toh'd cap klass-eek) A South African wine industry term to describe the classic French method of making sparkling wines: méthode champenoise.

méthode carbonique (meh-toh'd kar-bohn-eek) French term for carbonic maceration.

méthode champenoise (meh-toh'd shahm-peh-n'wahz) The French term for the classic method of making Champagne or other sparkling wine; the process consists of (1) bottling a blend of still wines with sugar and yeast to create a second fermentation within the bottle; (2) the second fermentation creates carbon dioxide, which is trapped in the bottle and dissolved in the wine, thus producing the effervescence; (3) sediment is formed, however, which must be disgorged. *See* Charmat process *and* vinification.

méthode rurale A rarely used method of making a sparkling wine; the still wine is bottled before fermentation is complete; the trapped carbon dioxide creates a slight sparkle.

Methuselah; Methusalem (meh-THUS-eh-lah) An oversized Champagne or sparkling wine bottle holding eight 750-ml bottles (approximately 204 fl. oz.).

methyl alcohol A highly toxic type of alcohol; also known as methanol and wood alcohol.

methylcellulose A food additive used to control moisture in baked goods.

methyl compounds Food additives containing a methyl group and used as flavoring agents and/or adjuvants.

methylene chloride *See* direct contact method.

methyl ethyl cellulose A food additive used as an emulsifier, aerating agent and/or foaming agent.

methyl glucoside–coconut oil ester A food additive used as an aid in crystallizing sucrose and dextrose and as a surfactant in molasses.

methylparaben A food additive used as an antimicrobial agent.

methylxanthines *See* xanthines.

metodo classico (MEH-toh-do CLAH-see-co) The Italian term for the méthode champenoise.

metric system A measurement system developed by the French and used worldwide; a decimal system in which the gram, liter and meter are the basic units of weight, volume and length, respectively; larger or smaller units are formed by adding a prefix such as *centi-* (0.01, a centigram is 0.01 g), *deca-* (10, a decameter is 10 m), *deci-* (0.10), *hecto-* (100), *kilo-* (1000), *milli-* (0.001) and *quintal-* (100,000). *See* imperial system *and* U.S. system.

Mettwurst (MEHT-wurst; MEHT-vursht) A soft, fatty German sausage made from pork, seasoned with coriander and white pepper, cured and smoked; it has a bright red color; also known as Schmierwurst.

meunière (muhn-YAIR) French for miller's wife and used to describe a style of cooking in which the food (e.g., fish) is seasoned, lightly dusted with flour and sautéed in butter.

Mexican Any of a variety of arabica coffee beans grown in Mexico; the beverage, usually made from a blend of beans, is generally rich and sharp.

Mexican breadfruit *See* monstera.

Mexican Bull Shot A cocktail made of beef consommé, tequila, lime or lemon juice, Worcestershire sauce and celery salt or celery seed; served in a double old-fashioned glass and garnished with a lime wedge.

Mexican chocolate A sweetened chocolate flavored with almonds, cinnamon and vanilla; used in hot beverages.

Mexican coffee A cocktail made of tequila, Kahlua or sugar syrup and strong hot black coffee; served in a large mug and garnished with whipped cream.

Mexican garlic *See* Italian garlic.

Mexican green tomato; Mexican husk tomato *See* tomatillo.

Mexican lime *See* Key lime.

Mexican limpet A variety of large limpet found along the Pacific Ocean coasts from Mexico to Peru; it has an off-white, thick shell, an average length of 6–13.5 in. (15.2–34.2 cm), and a tough, flavorful, white-flecked black flesh.

Mexican potato *See* jícama.

Mexican saffron *See* safflower.

Mexican snapper *See* red snapper.

Mexican wedding cookies; Mexican wedding cakes Small, round, buttery cookies made with ground nuts and rolled in confectioners' sugar after baking; also known as Russian tea cakes.

méz (maz) Hindi for table.

meza; mezza; maza (mehz-zah) Arabic for hors d'oeuvre; it can be any of a wide variety of hot or cold salads, dips, fritters, pickles, savory pastries and the like.

meza Swahili for table.

mezcal; mescal (mehs-KAL) A colorless spirit made in Mexico from the fermented and distilled juice and pulp of an agave; it has a characteristic smoky flavor and is often sweetened and flavored with fruits, herbs and/or nuts; it is sometimes sold bottled with a blue agave root worm. *See* tequila.

meze (meh-ZAY) Greek and Turkish for hors d'oeuvre and used to describe both the social occasion preceding a meal during which they are served and the foods (e.g., feta cheese, olives, nuts and shellfish).

mezzaluna (mehz-zuh-LOO-nuh) A two-handled knife with one or more thick, crescent-shaped blades used to chop or mince vegetables; also known as a mincing knife.

mezzani (medz-DZAHN-nee) Italian for medium and used to describe medium-length maccheroni.

mfupa (mfoo-paw) Swahili for bone.

mezzaluna

mg *See* milligram.

mhammes (mah-mes) A large-grained couscous; it is used in Tunisian cuisine.

m'hanncha (mahn-tch-ah) A Moroccan confection of buttered phyllo dough wrapped around a filling of ground almonds, confectioners' sugar, cinnamon and melted butter, flavored with orange flower water or rosewater, baked and then sprinkled with cinnamon and confectioners' sugar.

miala (meh-ah-la) Greek for brains.

mian *See* mein.

miàn bao (meh-ahn bah-ho) Chinese for bread.

miànbaofang (meh-ahn-bah-oh-fahng) Chinese for bakery.

miànfen (mee-ahn-fan) Chinese for flour.

miàntiáo (meh-ahn-tea-ah-oh) Chinese for noodle.

miascia (mee-AH-sh'yah) A bread pudding with apples and pears and flavored with rosemary; a specialty from Italy's Lombard region.

Michel's Passion A cocktail made of gin, dry vermouth and La Grande Passion; garnished with a twist of orange.

michette (mee-KEH-tah) A round, crusty Milanese roll with five sides coming to a button on top.

mi chevre (me SHEV-ruh) A French cheese-labeling term indicating that the cheese is made from at least 25% goat's milk.

Mickey Finn; Mickey An alcoholic beverage that has been altered to induce diarrhea or unconsciousness.

microbrewery A brewery of small size and production.

microclimate The climatic and environmental conditions of a specific, and usually relatively small, area.

microflora Colonies of yeasts and bacteria.

micronutrients Nutrients the body needs in small quantities: vitamins and minerals. *See* macronutrients.

microorganisms Single-celled organisms and tiny plants and animals that can only be seen through a microscope, including bacteria, parasites, fungi and viruses; carried from one host to another by air, food, insects and other animals, and soil.

microparticulated protein product A fat substitute prepared from egg whites and/or milk proteins and used as a thickening agent or texturizer in dairy products, dressings and baked goods.

micro plane food rasp A long, coarse file with raised points and a wooden handle; used for grating nutmeg, cheese, citrus peel, ginger, bread crumbs and so on.

microwave cooking A heating method that uses radiation generated by a special oven to penetrate the food; the radiation agitates water molecules, creating friction and heat; this energy then spreads throughout the food by conduction (and by convection in liquids).

microwave oven An oven that cooks with microwaves; available with a revolving platform so that foods can cook more evenly.

middag (mi-dahg) Norwegian for dinner.

middleboard A 17th-century raised hexagonal or star-shaped, traylike structure of wood and wicker designed to display and serve pyramided fruits and sweetmeats in the center of a dessert or other serving table.

Middle Eastern green olive A small, tender olive sold in brine with hot peppers or mixed with olive oil.

middle neck A British cut of the veal or lamb carcass that comes from the forequarter between the head and best end of neck; it is bony but flavorful. *See* scrag end of neck *and* best end of neck.

middlings Coarse particles of wheat that contain the endosperm, bran and germ; a by-product of flour milling.

midia; mithia (mee-thia) Greek for mussels.

Midori (mih-DOOR-ee) A green Japanese liqueur with the flavor of honeydew melon.

midrib *See* chard.

midye (me-dee-ah) Turkish for mussel.

midye dolmasi (me-dee-ah dole-mah-sea) A Turkish hors d'oeuvre of stuffed mussels.

mie (mee) 1. French for the soft interior part of a loaf of bread. 2. French for fresh bread crumbs made from crustless white bread.

miel (mee-ale) Spanish for honey.

miel (myehl) French for honey.

miele (mee-AY-lay) Italian for honey.

mifan (mee-fan) Chinese for rice.

mi fen (mee fan) Chinese rice noodles (rice sticks).

migalhas (mee-gah-lyash) Portuguese for bread crumbs.

migas (MEE-gahth) 1. A Spanish dish consisting of small squares of bread soaked in milk and fried in oil. 2. Spanish for bread crumbs. *See* pan rallado.

mignonette (mee-nyohn-EHT) 1. A small, coin-shaped filet of meat; a medallion. 2. French for coarsely ground white pepper.

Mignonette, sauce A French sauce of red wine, white pepper and minced shallots; usually served cold with oysters on the half shell.

mignonne de Hollande *See* reinette de Caux.

Mignot (min-ynoh) A Livarot-style or Pont l'Eveque-style cheese made in France's Calvados region; there are two types: (1) Blanc, a fresh cheese made during the spring and summer and (2) Passe, a ripened cheese made during the rest of the year.

mihuanjun (meh-juan-june) Chinese for honey mushroom.

mikado (mee-KAH-doo) French for prepared in the style of Japan and used to describe foods characteristically seasoned with soy sauce and tangerine juice.

mikan (MEE-kahn) A citrus fruit grown in Japan; it is similar to a tangerine.

mi'l'aaq (me-laahq) Arabic for grilled.

milanaise, à la (mee-lah-NEEZ, ah lah) 1. A French preparation method associated with the cuisine of Milan, Italy; the principal foods are dipped in egg and bread crumbs mixed with Parmesan cheese and then fried in clarified butter. 2. A method of preparing macaroni; it is served in a sauce of butter with grated cheese and a tomato sauce. 3. A garnish for cuts of meat consisting of macaroni with cheese, coarsely shredded ham, pickled tongue, mushrooms and truffles all blended in a tomato sauce. 4. Dishes cooked au gratin with Parmesan. 5. A method of preparing risotto; it is scented with saffron.

milanaise, sauce A French compound sauce made from a demi-glaze flavored with tomatoes and garlic and garnished with mushrooms.

Milano (me-LAHN-noh) A soft Bel Paese–style cheese made in Lombardy, Italy, from cow's milk; also known as Bella Milano.

Milan white turnip A particularly flavorful variety of medium-sized turnip.

Milch (milkh) German for milk.

milchig (mill-chigg) Yiddish for dairy and dairy products; one of the three categories under Jewish dietary laws (kosher). *See* fleischig, kosher *and* pareve.

mild 1. A tasting term for a bland or unassuming flavor. 2. A coffee-tasting term used to describe a coffee with harmonious flavor components, none of which are particularly pronounced. 3. A Cheddar that is briefly aged.

mildew A disease of plants caused by any of a variety of fungi; it is characterized by a cottony, usually whitish, coating on the affected surface.

mileh (mell-hah) Arabic for salt.

mile-high cake; mile-high pie A tall, multilayer cake or a tall pie topped with several inches of ice cream or meringue.

milfoil (MIHL-foyl) *See* yarrow.

milho (MEEL-yoh) Portuguese for corn.

milk albuminate *See* lactalbumin.

milk *v.* To extract milk from a mammal. *n.* 1. The white or ivory liquid produced by adult, female mammals and used to nurture their young; it is composed of water, milkfat and milk solids; some milks are used for human consumption, either as is or processed into products such as cheese. 2. Whole cow's milk. 3. Any liquid resembling milk, such as the liquid in a coconut or the juice or sap of various plants.

milk, camel's Milk produced by a female camel; it has approximately 5.4% milkfat, 7.5% milk solids and 87.1% water.

milk, certified Milk produced from dairy herds recognized by local health departments as disease free; pasteurization has replaced the need for certification, but milk from certified herds is still available in a few areas.

milk, cow's Milk produced by a cow; it has approximately 3.5% milkfat, 8.5% milk solids and 88% water; used by humans as a beverage, for making dairy products and for cooking and baking; also known as milk, whole milk and whole cow's milk.

milk, evaporated A nonsweetened milk product made from whole milk from which 60% of the water has been evaporated; it is then sterilized and canned, resulting in a cooked flavor and darker color; it must contain at least 7.25% milkfat and 25.5% milk solids.

milk, evaporated skim A nonsweetened milk product made from skim milk from which 60% of the water has been evaporated; it is then sterilized and canned, resulting in a cooked flavor and darker color; it contains 0.5% milkfat.

milk, ewe's Milk produced by a female sheep; it has approximately 7.9% milkfat, 11.4% milk solids and 80.7% water; principally used by humans for cheese making.

milk, foamed *See* foamed milk.

milk, goat's Milk produced by a female goat; it has approximately 4.1% milkfat, 8.9% milk solids and 87% water; principally used by humans for cheese making.

milk, human's Milk produced by a lactating woman; it has approximately 3.7% milkfat, 8.7% milk solids and 87.6% water.

milk, mare's Milk produced by a female horse; it has approximately 1.1% milkfat, 8.4% milk solids and 90.5% water.

milk, raw Unpasteurized milk; used principally for cheese making.

milk, reindeer's Milk produced by a female reindeer; it has approximately 22.5% milkfat, 14.5% milk solids and 63% water.

milk, sweetened condensed A thick, sweet, slightly caramel-flavored milk product made from sweetened whole milk from which 60% of the water has been evaporated; usually sold canned, it cannot generally be substituted for whole or evaporated milk because of the sugar; also known as condensed milk.

milk, water buffalo's Milk produced by a female water buffalo; it has approximately 7.5% milkfat, 10.3% milk solids and 82.2% water; principally used by humans for cheese making.

milk bread A white wheat bread in which either all of the liquid is milk or it contains not less than 8.8 parts (by weight) of milk solids for each 100 parts of flour (by weight).

milk chocolate Sweetened chocolate containing not less than 12% milk solids and not less than 10% chocolate liquor; used for candies, creams and confections. *See* chocolate-making process.

milkfat The fat found in milk; a significant component in dairy products such as butter, cream and cheeses; the higher the milkfat content, the richer and creamier the product; also known as butterfat.

milk-fed veal *See* veal, milk-fed.

milkfish A large silvery fish found in the South Pacific and Indian Ocean; it has a moderately firm white flesh with a mild flavor.

milk grades A grading system developed by the USPHS for whole milk based on bacterial counts; grade A products have the lowest count; grades B and C, which have higher counts, are not generally available for retail or commercial use.

milk pot A tall, spouted, metal vessel used to froth milk for cappuccino and other coffee drinks.

milk powder Dry whole milk.

Milk Punch A punch made of liquor, sugar and milk; somewhat similar to eggnog, it is typically served at brunch.

milk shake A beverage made of milk, a flavored syrup and ice cream blended to a thick, slushy consistency and served chilled.

milk solids The proteins, milk sugar (lactose) and minerals (but not the milkfat) present in milk.

milk stout A stout with a creamy consistency, sweetened with lactose; the commercial use of the term is banned in England as misleading.

milk sugar *See* lactose.

milk toast Buttered toast, sometimes sprinkled with sugar and cinnamon, over which milk is poured; traditionally served to children and the infirm.

milkweed A wild plant (*Asclepias suriaca*) that yields a milky substance when cut; used by Native Americans as a flavoring and thickener.

milky cap mushroom A wild mushroom (*Lactarius deliciosus*) that exudes a milk when the flesh is broken; it has a firm texture, a reddish color and a pleasant flavor.

Milky Way The proprietary name for a popular candy bar composed of chocolate nougat and caramel coated with chocolate.

mill *v.* 1. To grind, pulverize or break down into smaller particles. *See* milling. 2. To agitate or stir until foamy. *n.* 1. A building equipped with machinery for grinding grain into flour or meal; the device that does so. 2. A device that reduces a solid or coarse substance into pulp or minute grains by crushing, grinding or pressing (e.g., a pepper mill). *See* grinder. 3. A device that releases the juice of fruits and vegetables by pressing or grinding (e.g., cider mill).

Milleens; Millsen (mih-LEENS) A soft Irish farm cheese made from unpasteurized cow's milk; it has a creamy texture and a strong flavor and aroma.

mille-feuille (meel-FWEE) 1. French for thousand leaves and used to describe any sweet or savory dish made with puff pastry. *See* feuilletage. 2. A French pastry composed of rectangular pieces of puff pastry layered with pastry cream, whipped cream and fruit or ganache; also known as a napoleon.

millesime (mee-lah-seh-meh) French for vintage (the year of production) of a wine.

millet A cereal grain (*Panicum milaiceum*) with a bland flavor and a white color; in the United States, it is used principally for animal feed, and in Asia, North Africa and southern Europe, it is usually ground into flour; also available as flakes.

milli- *See* metric system.

milligram (mg) A metric measure of weight; 1000 mg equal 1 g; 1 g equals 0.0353 oz.

milliliter (ml) A metric measure of volume; 1000 ml equal 1 l.

milling The mechanical process of changing the shape of grains or separating certain portions of the grains, such as the hull from the bran. *See* cracking, grinding, hulling *and* pearling.

Million Dollar A cocktail made of gin, sweet vermouth, pineapple juice, grenadine and egg white.

milt The gonads of a male fish; also known as soft roe. *See* roe.

Mimlotte (meem-lote) A firm French cheese made from cow's milk; it has a smooth, vivid orange–colored interior, a dark waxed rind, and a bland to mellow, faintly nutty flavor.

Mimosa (mih-MOH-suh) 1. A cocktail made of equal parts orange juice and sparkling wine, served cold. 2. A garnish of finely chopped hard-cooked egg yolk; so named because of its resemblance to the yellow mimosa flower.

mimosa salad A salad made from any of a variety of raw or cooked vegetables arranged in a bowl and sprinkled with chopped hard-boiled egg yolks.

Minas (mee-naz) A firm Brazilian cheese made from cow's milk; it has a dry, thin rind and a yellow-white interior with scattered eyes.

mince To cut or chop a food finely.

minced beef *See* beef, ground.

minced collop Archaic Scottish for a minced slice of meat or offal. *See* collop.

mincemeat A rich, finely chopped mixture of dried fruit, nuts, beef suet, spices and rum or brandy; used as a filling for pies, tarts and cookies; traditionally, lean meat was included in the mixture.

mincing knife *See* mezzaluna.

mindal'nyj (meen-dalh-n'ye-jh) Russian for almond.

minerals A class of nutrients composed of inorganic elements or compounds and used principally to regulate or assist body functions and form bones and teeth; occurring in nature, they cannot be synthesized by the body and must be obtained through the diet, generally by consuming plant foods from plants that have absorbed the nutrients from the soil or animal foods from animals that have consumed such plant foods.

mineral vann Norwegian for soft drink.

mineral water *See* water, mineral.

miner's lettuce A salad green with small, slightly cupped, triangular leaves with tiny flowers in the center and a fresh, mild spinach flavor; also known as claytonia.

minestra (mih-NAY-truh) Italian for soup and used to describe a moderately thick soup usually containing meat and vegetables. *See* minestrina *and* minestrone.

minestrina (mee-ness-TREE-nah) Italian for little soup and used to describe a broth sometimes garnished with pasta. *See* minestra *and* minestrone.

minestrone (mee-ness-TROH-nay) Italian for big soup and used to describe a vegetable soup flavored with herbs and sometimes garnished with pasta; there are variations made with rice, bacon, tomatoes, sage and cheese (in northern Italy), with navy beans (in Tuscany) and with beans, sauerkraut, potatoes, cumin seeds and garlic (in northeastern Italy). *See* minestra *and* minestrina.

Ming Dynasty eggs *See* hundred-year-old eggs.

miniature bottle *See* nip.

Minibel tomato A variety of small, spherical, red-skinned, flavorful tomato.

minimum acceptable standard of performance (MASP) The minimum amount of work an employee must do to keep his or her job.

minimum standards of quality Standards mandated by the FDA for color, tenderness and allowable freedom from defects for many canned vegetables and fruits.

Minneola (mehn-nee-oh-lah) A tangelo with a knob at the stem end, a dark orange rind and a rich, sharp flavor.

minnow A very small fish, usually used for bait, but ocassionally fried or cooked in a court bouillon and used to stuff omelets.

mint 1. A large family of herbs (genus *Mentha*) known for their aromatic

mint

foliage, many of which have flavors and/or aromas reminiscent of fruits (e.g., lemon) and other flavorings (e.g., chocolate). 2. A candy flavored with mint, often used as a breath freshener; it can be a hard candy or a soft patty with a hard candy or chocolate coating.

Mint Julep A cocktail made of bourbon, fresh mint, sugar and crushed ice; traditionally served in a silver mug.

mint sauce A sauce made from vinegar, water, sugar and salt mixed with finely chopped mint leaves, marinated for several hours and strained before service.

minute sirloin A fabricated cut of the beef primal short loin; it is a very thin steak.

minute steak A fabricated cut of the beef flank, chuck or round primals; it is a small, very thin, cubed steak.

Minze (min-zeh) German for mint.

miolos (mee-oh-loss) Portuguese for brains.

miolos de pevide (mee-oh-loss day peh-vee-dah) A Portuguese snack of pumpkin seeds, eaten either peeled or unpeeled.

miolos de pinhao (mee-oh-loss day pee-nyah-oh) A Portuguese snack of salted pine kernels.

Mirabeau, à la (meer-ah-bo, ah lah) A French garnish for grilled meats, consisting of anchovy fillets, stoned olives, chopped tarragon and anchovy butter.

Mirabeau, sauce A compound sauce made from allemande flavored with garlic and beaten with beurre maître d'hôtel.

mirabelle (mihr-uh-BEHL) 1. A small, round greengage grown in Great Britain and parts of continental Europe; its skin color ranges from golden yellow to red, and it is used principally for tarts and preserves; also known in Great Britain as a cherry plum. 2. A French eau-de-vie made from the mirabelle.

mirch (meer-chee) Hindi for pepper.

mirchi ka achar (meer-chee kah kah-akar) An east Indian dish of fresh red-hot chiles, slit, stuffed with spices and pickled in mustard oil.

mirepoix (meer-pwa) A mixture of coarsely chopped onions, carrots and celery used to flavor stocks, stews and other foods; generally, a mixture of 50% onions, 25% carrots and 25% celery, by weight, is used.

mirin (mee-REEN) A Japanese low-alcohol, sweet, syrupy, thin, golden-colored rice wine used to add sweetness and flavor to glazes, sauces and a variety of dishes.

mirliton (MIHR-lih-ton) 1. A puff pastry tart filled with almond cream and decorated with three almond halves arranged in a star pattern. 2. A crisp almond cookie flavored with orange flower water. 3. American name for the chayote.

mirtillo (mir-tee-low) Italian for blueberry.

miruku (MEE-roo-ku) Japanese for milk.

miscible Capable of being mixed.

mise en bouteille (meez ahn boo-tay) French for bottled.

mise en bouteilles au chateau; mise en bouteilles au domaine (meez ahn boo-tay oh shah-toe) A French wine-labeling term for a wine bottled at the designated estate.

mise en bouteilles dans nos caves (meez ahn boo-tay dahn no khav) A French wine-labeling term for a wine bottled in the specified cellars, often by a négociant.

mise en place (meez ahn plahs) French for putting in place and used to describe the preparation and assembly of all necessary ingredients and equipment for cooking. *See* batterie de cuisine.

mish me bamje (meesh ma bah-me-an) An Albanian dish of lamb or mutton stewed with onions, tomatoes and okra and served with rice.

mishmish (mesh-mesh) Arabic and Hebrew for apricot.

mishmishi Swahili for apricot.

misir Ethiopian for lentils.

miso (ME-so) A thick paste made by salting and fermenting soybeans and rice or barley and then inoculating the mixture with yeast; it is used in Japanese cuisines as a flavoring and thickener; the lighter the color, the sweeter the flavor. *See* hatcho-miso, inaka-miso *and* shinshu-miso.

miso shiru (ME-so SHEE-roo) A Japanese soup thickened with fermented bean paste.

Mission fig A fig with a purple-black skin; it was brought to California by Franciscan missionaries from Spain; also known as a black Mission fig.

Mission olive A ripe medium-sized green olive that has obtained its characteristic black color and flavor from lye curing and oxygenization.

Mississippi Mule A cocktail made of gin, crème de cassis and lemon juice.

Miss White American southern slang for the light, moist interior pieces of pork barbecue. *See* Mr. Brown.

mistelle (meese-tel) Grape juice to which alcohol has been added to stop fermentation; used in wine-based aperitifs such as vermouth.

misto (MEE-stoh) Italian for mixed (e.g., misto fruita means mixed fruit).

Mistra (mee-strah) An Italian anise-based liqueur.

miswa (mi-swa) Fine, white-colored wheat noodles used in Filipino cuisine.

mithai; methai (mi-thaa-ee) Sweetmeats, such as barfi, served at the end of an Indian meal.

mitindi (me-tin-dee) Swahili for buttermilk.

mitsu (mee-TSOO) Japanese for syrup.

mitsuba (mee-TSOO-bah) An herb grown in Japan; it is similar in shape and color to coriander and flat-leafed parsley, although its flavor is more delicate.

Mittagessen (mit-tok-ssen) German for lunch.

Mittelfrueh (mi-tel-FGHIE-ee) Noble Bavarian hops grown in Germany.

Mitzithra (me-zeeth-rah) A Greek cheese made from the whey remaining after feta has been made; it has a white color, a soft texture and a mild flavor.

mix *v.* 1. To combine ingredients in such a way that they are evenly dispersed throughout the mixture. 2. To create or form something by combining ingredients (e.g., a cocktail). *n.* 1. A mixture of ingredients that usually requires only the addition of water and/or yeast to produce a batter or dough. 2. A commercially packaged mixture of ingredients that usually requires only the addition of a liquid and/or a fresh product such as eggs, meat or fish and heating to produce a completed dish.

mix-and-measure bowl A bowl with a spout and liquid measurements on the exterior; it is used to mix ingredients.

mixed drink *See* cocktail.

mixed grill 1. A British dish consisting of assorted grilled or broiled meats (e.g., lamb chops, beefsteak, sausages, kidneys and liver) served with grilled tomatoes, watercress and mushrooms. 2. A dish consisting of assorted grilled or broiled meats, fish and/or poultry.

mixer 1. A kitchen appliance equipped with various beaters, dough hooks and other attachments and used for mixing, beating, kneading, whipping or creaming foods; it can be portable or stationary. 2. A nonalcoholic beverage such as a soft drink that is combined with an alcoholic beverage to make a cocktail.

mixing bowls Round, variously sized containers used for combining ingredients manually or mechanically.

mixing glass A large, tall glass holding approximately 16 fl. oz.; it is used either to serve tall mixed drinks, iced teas or soft drinks or to prepare hand-shaken mixed drinks (usually then fitted with a strainer or cap). *See* hand shaker.

mixiotes de conejo (me-xe-oh-tas da coh-na-ee-oh) A Mexican dish consisting of fried, spiced rabbit wrapped in maguey leaves and steamed.

mixologist *See* bartender.

mixology The art and science of following a formula to produce a standard and consistent cocktail or other drink.

mizu (mee-ZOO) Japanese for water.

mizu ame (mee-ZOO AH-may) *See* rice malt.

mizuna (mih-ZOO-nuh) A feathery Japanese salad green with a delicate flavor.

mizutake (mee-zoo-TAH-kay) Japanese for water simmered and used to describe a one-pot dish of chicken and vegetables simmered in water with seasonings and served with various condiments, such as green onions, ginger and ponzu sauce.

mkahawa (mkau-wah) Swahili for cafe or restaurant.

mkate (mkah-ta) Swahili for bread.

mkhullal (meh'kel-lehl) *See* makboos.

ml *See* milliliter.

mleko (mleh-koh) Polish for milk.

mlukheeyeh (muh'loh-kay-yah) An Egyptian soup made from molokhia and chicken flavored with lemon juice, vinegar, garlic, onions and allspice.

mlyako (mle-e-ah-koh) Bulgarian for milk.

moano; moana (moh-ah-noh) A member of the goatfish family found off Hawaii; this small reef fish has a white flesh, a high fat content, and a delicate, sweet, mild flavor.

mocha (moh-kah) A flavor created by combining coffee and chocolate, widely used in pastries and confections. *See* Moka.

mocha coffee A beverage made of strong, hot black coffee and hot chocolate; garnished with whipped cream, cinnamon, nutmeg and/or orange peel.

mochi (MOH-chee) A short-grain, sweet, gelatinous rice with a high starch content; used in Japanese cuisine to make rice cakes and confections.

mochiko (moh-chee-ko) A flour made from mochi.

mock apple pie A pie made with Ritz crackers and spices; popular during the Depression.

mock chicken leg Ground veal on a stick shaped to look like a chicken leg.

mock duck A fabricated cut from the lamb shoulder; it is partly boned, with the shank bone turned up and outward, and the whole roast is tied and decorated to resemble a duck.

mocktail A cocktail prepared without the customary alcoholic beverages; also known as a virgin drink.

mock tender *See* chuck tender.

mock turtle soup An English soup prepared by cooking a calf's head in water; the meat is served in the clear, brownish broth, which is usually spiced and thickened.

mocque chou *See* macque choux.

modeling chocolate A stiff dough made with melted chocolate and glucose or corn syrup; it is used for creating pastry decorations or garnishes.

moden (moe-dan) Norwegian for ripe.

moderate oven An oven set to a temperature of approximately 350°F (177°C). *See* hot oven *and* slow oven.

moderation In the nutrition context, it is the consumption of food and drink without excess. *See* adequacy *and* variety.

moderne, à la (mo-darin, ah lah) A French garnish for small cuts of meat consisting of individual dariole molds of layered carrot, turnip, green beans and peas, sealed with forcemeat, cooked in a bain marie and unmolded for service.

modified American plan (MAP) A daily hotel rate that includes any two meals and a room. *See* American plan.

modified food starch A food additive used as a stabilizer, thickener and/or texturizer.

modified hop extract A food additive used as a flavoring agent in beer brewing.

modified starch The product resulting from treating starch with various chemicals to modify its physical characteristics.

modular eating *See* grazing.

mo ehr Chinese for cloud ear mushroom.

moelas (ma-lass) A Portuguese petisco dish of well-spiced chicken stomachs.

moelle (mwahl) French for bone marrow.

Moelle, sauce (mwahl) A French compound sauce made from a bordelaise based on white wine instead of red wine, garnished with poached beef bone marrow.

moelleux (m'wah-luh) A French wine-tasting term for a rich, lush wine, usually white, that is neither sweet nor bone dry.

moghlie (mogh-lee-yeh) Arabic for rice pudding.

mogu (moe-goo) Chinese for the common store mushroom.

Mohawk pecan A variety of pecan; its very large nuts are easily cracked in half and are generally used for garnishing baked goods.

mohingha (mont-hin-gar) A Burmese dish consisting of fine egg noodles, vegetables and tender hearts of banana palms in a fish and coconut milk sauce.

moh loung ye baw (mont lone yeah baw) A Burmese dessert of small flour and coconut dumplings filled with jaggery and served floating in a coconut milk sauce.

moh sein buong A Burmese rice flour sponge cake flavored with palm sugar and steamed in a tall mold; after steaming the cake is sprinkled with grated coconut and crushed sesame seeds mixed with salt and served on a banana leaf.

moist-heat cooking methods Cooking methods, principally simmering, poaching, boiling and steaming, that use water or steam to transfer heat through convection; moist-heat cooking methods are used to emphasize the natural flavors of foods. *See* dry-heat cooking methods.

moisture-retention agent *See* humectant.

Mojito (moh-hee-toh) A cocktail made of light rum, lime juice, sugar and club soda; garnished with a mint sprig.

Moka; Mocha (moh-kah) Arabica coffee beans originally grown in Yemen but now also in Ethiopia and named for the Yemenite port city of Al Mukha; sometimes used as a blending bean with milder beans; the full-bodied, aromatic beverage, often brewed Turkish style, has a distinctive, winy and pungent flavor; also known as Ethiopian Mocha.

Moka Sanani (mo-kah sah-nah-nee) Arabica coffee beans grown in Saudi Arabia; the beverage is wild, pungent, spicy and winy.

mokhalafat (moe-kah-law-faht) Pickles, relishes, condiments, plates of fresh herbs, vegetables, cheese and yogurt and other side dishes served with an Iranian meal.

molasses 1. A thick, sweet, brownish-black liquid that is a by-product of sugar refining; used in breads, cookies and pastries for its distinctive, slightly bitter flavor and dark color. 2. A syrup made from boiling down sweet vegetable or fruit juices.

molasses, blackstrap A molasses removed after the third boiling of the sugarcane in the sugar-refining process; it is thick and dark and has a strong, distinctive flavor.

molasses, dark A molasses removed after the second boiling of the sugarcane in the sugar-refining process; darker, thicker and less sweet than light molasses, it is generally used as a flavoring.

molasses, light A molasses removed after the first boiling of the sugarcane in the sugar-refining process; it has a lighter body, color and flavor (although it is sweeter) than dark molasses and is usually used as a syrup.

molcajete y tejolote (mol-kah-HAY-tay ee tay-ho-LO-tay) A Mexican mortar and pestle.

mold *v.* To shape a food by using a vessel. *n.* 1. A vessel into which foods are placed to take on the container's shape; molds are available in a wide range of shapes and sizes,

many of which are associated with a particular dish. *See* timbale. 2. A food shaped by such a vessel. 3. Any of a large group of fungi that form long filaments or strands that sometimes extend into the air and appear as fuzzy masses; molds can grow at almost any temperature, moisture or pH level; a few that grow on food are desirable (e.g., those used in cheese making); most are not dangerous and merely affect the appearance of food, but some, called mycotoxicoses, produce toxins. 4. The fungi or their spores that contribute to the character of a cheese; they are generally absorbed during the ripening process either as a surface mold (which helps ripen the cheese from the surface inward) or internal mold (which helps ripen from the interior outward, such as those for blue cheeses).

molded cookie A type of cookie formed by pressing the dough into a decorative mold before baking.

molder A machine used to shape dough.

molding 1. The process of shaping gelatin-thickened foods in a decorative container. 2. The process of shaping foods, particularly grains and vegetables bound by sauces, into attractive, hard-edged shapes by using metal rings, circular cutters or other forms.

moldy 1. A food safety and sanitation term for a food that has decomposed to the point that mold or its characteristic odor is evident. 2. A cheese-tasting term for the characteristic flavor and aroma of mold; it can be desirable or not. 3. A wine-tasting term for a disagreeable aroma or flavor caused by using improperly cleaned casks.

mole; mole poblano de Guajolote (MOE-lay poe-BLAH-noh day goo-ah-hoe-loh-tay) A Mexican sauce usually served with poultry; it consists of onions, garlic, chiles, ground pumpkin or sesame seeds and Mexican chocolate.

môlho (MOHL-yoh) Portuguese for sauce.

molho cru (moh-lho croo) An Angolan sauce made of garlic, green onions, parsley, cumin and vinegar and used cold with fish or shellfish.

môlho malagueta (MOHL-yoh mahl-ah-gwee-tah) A Brazilian hot sauce made from dried or fresh malagueta chiles, vinegar and olive oil.

molinet (mo-li-NAY) A long-handled wooden tool with deep grooves and several loose wooden rings at one end; created in 16th-century Spain for blending chocolate beverages.

molleja (moh-ye-has) Spanish for sweetbreads.

mollusks One of the principal classes of shellfish; they are characterized by a soft, unsegmented body with no internal skeleton (many have hard outer shells); includes univalves (e.g., abalone), bivalves (e.g., clams) and cephalopods (e.g., octopus). *See* crustaceans.

mollusques (moh-lysk-kuh) French for mollusks.

molokhia; mlookheeyeh 1. A leafy plant resembling spinach or chard; it is glutinous, with a bland, slightly astringent flavor and is used in North African, Middle Eastern and Indian cuisines to flavor soups and vegetable stews; also known as Jew's mallow, Spanish jute, Spanish okra and Spanish sorrel. 2. A Middle Eastern soup, the principal ingredient of which is the plant.

moloko (mah-lah-KOH) Russian for milk.

molybdenum A trace mineral principally used to facilitate many cell processes; significant sources include legumes, cereals and organ meats.

mombin A small tropical fruit (*Spondias purpurea*) native to the Western Hemisphere; it has an ovoid or spherical shape, a deep red to yellow color, a juicy flesh and an acidic, spicy flavor; the large central core can be cracked and the seeds eaten like a nut; also known as a Spanish plum.

momem tofu (moh-mehn toh-fu) Japanese cotton bean curd.

momiji oroshi (moh-MEE-gee oh-ROH-shee) A Japanese condiment made with grated radish and chile.

momo (moh-moh) Japanese for peach.

momo A Tibetan steamed dumpling filled with ground beef or lamb flavored with cumin, nutmeg and ginger.

momone Dried, salted fish used as a flavoring in Ghanaian cuisine.

monastery product A product such as beer or cheese made by monks in a monastery, often with traditional recipes and methods.

Monastrell (mo-nass-trel) A red wine grape grown in Spain; it produces a strong, rich, rather pale wine or it can be used for liqueur wines.

monchong A deep-water fish found off Hawaii; it has a pink-tinged white flesh, a firm texture and a high fat content.

mondongo serrano Spanish for tripe, mountain style, and used to describe a Mexican dish of honeycomb tripe simmered and then sautéed with onions, bell peppers, tomatoes and olives and flavored with coriander and garlic.

Mondseer (mohnd-sehr) An Austrian Munster-style cheese made from either whole or partly skimmed cow's milk; has a supple, pale yellow interior dotted with small, irregular eyes and a somewhat sharp, acidic flavor; Mondseer Schachtelkäse is packed in boxes; Mondseer Schlosskäse is a richer and creamier variety.

Mongolian grill An Asian (northern Chinese) cooking method in which each diner cooks his or her own food on a hot grill in the center of the table; meat, usually lamb, is dipped in a marinade and placed on the grill, then eaten on a plain bun garnished with chopped scallions, mushrooms or watercress.

Mongolian hot pot An Asian (northern Chinese) cooking method in which each diner dips his or her own food into a pot of simmering stock to cook it; there are usually several condiments and sauces available.

moniatos (moh-nee-ah-tos) A variety of orange-colored sweet potato grown in Spain's Málaga region.

monkey bread A sweet yeast bread made by piling small balls of dough in a tube pan; raisins, nuts, sugar and cinnamon are usually added, and then the dough is allowed to rise; after baking, the mounds can be pulled apart for service. *See* baobab.

monkey nut A cashewlike nut grown in Brazil.

monkey puzzle A tree (*Araucaria araucana*) grown in South America; its seeds are eaten raw, roasted or boiled in Chile; also known as a Chile nut.

monkey rum A Southern spirit distilled from sorghum syrup.

monkfish A fish found in the Atlantic Ocean and Mediterranean Sea; only the tail flesh is edible and it is usually available as fillets; it is lean, with a pearly white color, a very firm texture and a rich, sweet flavor; also known as angler fish, bellyfish, devilfish, frogfish, goosefish, poor man's lobster, rapé and sea devil.

Monk's Head *See* Bellelay.

monocalcium phosphate A food additive used as an acidulant, leavening agent and nutritional supplement; also known as calcium phosphate monobasic and calcium biphosphate.

monoglyceride 1. A product of the digestion of lipids; composed of glycerol and one fatty acid. 2. A food additive used as an emulsifier in processed foods such as baked goods and ice creams.

monoglyceride citrate A food additive used to increase the solubility of antioxidants in fats.

monopotassium phosphate A food additive used as a pH control agent and sequestrant in low-sodium products, meat products and dairy products.

monosaccharide A carbohydrate such as glucose or fructose that is crystalline, sweet, very soluble and readily absorbed by the body to be used as an energy source; it is composed of a single sugar unit and will not hydrolyze; also known as a simple sugar or single sugar.

monosodium glutamate (MSG) A food additive derived from glutamic acid, an amino acid found in seaweed and certain vegetable proteins, and used as a flavor enhancer; widely used in Chinese and Japanese cuisines; also known as aji-no-moto and sold under the brand name Ac'cent. *See* Chinese restaurant syndrome.

monosodium phosphate A food additive used as an acidulant and sequestrant in cheese and beverages.

Monostorer (mono-stoh-rare) A washed rind cheese made in Romania's Transylvania region from ewe's milk.

monounsaturated fat A triglyceride composed of monounsaturated fatty acids; generally, it comes from plants (olive, peanut and cottonseed oils are high in monounsaturated fats) and is liquid (an oil) at room temperature.

monounsaturated fatty acid A fatty acid that can accommodate one more hydrogen atom along its carbon chain (i.e., it has one point of unsaturation).

monstera (mon-STAIR-uh) A tropical fruit (*Monstera deliciosa*) native to Central America; it has a thick, green skin covered in hexagonal scales that separate and loosen as the fruit ripens and a creamy, smooth, ivory flesh with a flavor reminiscent of pineapple, banana and mango; also known as ceriman, fruit salad fruit, Mexican breadfruit and Swiss cheese plant fruit.

Montasio (mon-tah-see-oh) A hard Italian grana cheese made from a mixture of cow's and goat's milks (in some areas, it is made from ewe's milk); white when fresh and yellow when aged, with a granular texture and sharp flavor; sometimes the rind is blackened with soot.

Montavoner (mon-tah-foh-ner) An Austrian cheese made from soured cow's milk and flavored with dried herbs.

montbéliard (mohn-bey-lee-ahr) A French smoked sausage made of three parts lean and one part fat pork; it is usually stewed, often with lentils.

Mont Blanc (mohn blon) A French dessert made with whipped cream and sweetened chestnut purée; the chestnut mixture is passed through a ricer to create small strands, which are piled into a fluffy mound.

Mont d'Or (mohn day-ohr) A soft cheese made near Lyon, France, from goat's milk or a mixture of goat's and cow's milks; it has a blue skin, a pale yellow interior, a fresh sweet–tart flavor and a strong odor; usually sold fresh.

monte bianco (MOHN-teh bee-AHN-koh) An Italian dessert of puréed chestnuts topped with whipped cream.

Monte Cristo sandwich A sandwich of bread, ham, chicken and Emmental or Emmental-style cheese dipped in beaten egg and fried.

monteith A scalloped basin traditionally used to cool glasses or wine bottles or to serve punch.

monter au beurre (mohn-tay ah burr) To finish a sauce by swirling or whisking in butter (raw or compound) until it is melted; it is used to give sauces shine, flavor and richness. *See* mount, to.

Monterey Jack A cooked and pressed cheese traditionally made in Monterey, California, from whole, skimmed or partly skimmed cow's milk; it has an ivory color, a semisoft texture and a rather bland flavor (varieties flavored with peppercorns, spices, herbs or jalapeños are available); it is high in moisture and melts easily; also known as Jack or California Jack, especially if not produced near Monterey.

monti (mon-tea) 1. Armenian stuffed noodles similar to ravioli. 2. Large Uzbek dumplings made from ground meat (usually lamb) wrapped in a sheet of a pastalike dough; they are usually served as is or in a soup flavored with tomatoes and spices.

montilla (mawn-YEE-yah) A sherrylike wine, sometimes fortified, produced from the Pedro Ximenez grape rather than the Palomino grape used for sherry.

Montmorency, à la (mon-moh-REHN-see, ah lah) French for made or served with cherries and used to describe both sweet and savory dishes.

Montmorency cherry (mon-moh-REHN-see) A sour cherry with a red skin, a creamy beige flesh and a mildly tart flavor.

montone (moan-TOA-nay) Italian for mutton.

Montrachet (mohn-truh-SHAY) A soft cheese made in France's Burgundy region from goat's milk; it has a creamy texture and a mild, tangy flavor; usually sold in white logs, sometimes covered with a gray, salted ash.

monzù (mohn-ZOO) An 18th-century term for a chef or cook in a well-to-do household of southern Italy; these chefs were often trained in France.

moo Thai for pork.

moo goo gai pan (moo goo gahi pan) A Chinese dish of boneless chicken stir-fried with mushrooms and flavored with garlic and ginger.

moolee (moo-lee) Hindi for in coconut sauce.

mooli (moo-lee) Chinese for daikon.

mool naengmyun (mool nang-my-an) A Korean dish consisting of cold noodles in a cold broth garnished with beef and vegetables.

moonfish *See* opah.

moong (moong) *See* mung bean.

moong badian (moong bah-dee-ahn) An east Indian dish of fried mung bean dumplings made with puréed yellow mung beans and spinach greens.

Moon Pie The proprietary name for a confection that consists of two large, round, flat cookies with a marshmallow filling and chocolate or other flavored coating.

moonshine Illegally distilled whiskey, usually made from corn mash; also known as white lightning.

Moorpark A hybrid apricot and plum.

Moosbeere (MOOZ-berry) German for cranberry.

Moose Milk An alcoholic beverage consisting of coffee, milk and rum; served hot or cold.

moo-shu; moo-shoo A Chinese stir-fried dish containing shredded pork, chicken or beef, scallions, tiger lily buds, wood ears, scrambled eggs and various seasonings; the mixture is rolled in a small, thin pancake, usually spread with plum sauce or hoisin sauce.

mopping sauce Liquids brushed on meat during barbecuing to add flavor and moisture; the sauce is usually applied with a small, moplike cotton utensil.

moquecas (moh-keh-kah) A Brazilian stew usually made with shrimp, crab or fish and flavored with coconut milk, dendê oil and chiles.

mora A dried jalapeño smoked over mesquite wood; it has a reddish-brown color and a moderately hot, smoky, mesquite wood flavor with strong tobacco and plum undertones.

mora; zarzamora (moh-rah; sa-sa-moh-rah) Spanish for blackberry.

mora di rovo (mo-rah dee row-voh) Italian for dewberry.

morango (moph-RAHN-goh) Portuguese for strawberry.

mora selvatica (mo-rah sell-va-tee-cah) Italian for blackberry.

Moravian cookies Ultrathin spicy ginger cookies.

Morbier (MOHR-byay) A semisoft French cheese made from cow's milk; it has a supple, smooth, ivory interior with a center streak of edible gray ash, a grayish-brown rind and a mild flavor.

morcela (more-SAH-law) A smoked, hard, heavily spiced Portuguese blood pudding made with pig's blood, lean meat, fat and bread.

Morchel (MOHT-chaund) German for morel.

morcilla (mohr-SEE-yah) A Spanish blood sausage seasoned with paprika and pepper.

morcilla blanca (mohr-SEE-yah blahn-kah) 1. A Spanish sausage made from chicken, hard-boiled egg and bacon and seasoned with black pepper and parsley. 2. A Spanish sausage made from pig's lights and tripe, fat and cereal.

morcilla negra (mohr-SEE-yah nay-graw) A Spanish black pudding made with pig's blood and pork fat, seasoned with onions, cayenne, black pepper and marjoram, stuffed into a pig's bladder and boiled.

morcón (mohr-cohn) A large Spanish sausage filled with coarsely chopped, marinated meat; it is usually served thinly sliced.

more (mo-ray) Italian for mulberries.

more A food-labeling term approved by the FDA to describe a food with at least 10% or more of the daily value for protein, vitamins, minerals, dietary fiber or potassium than the regular or reference (i.e., FDA standard) food.

morel (muh-REHL) A wild mushroom (*Morchella esculenta* and *M. vulgaris*) that grows during the spring in Europe, North America and Southeast Asia; it has a cream to buff-colored conical cap covered in irregular indentations, giving it a spongy, honeycombed appearance, a creamy white hollow stem and a smoky, earthy, nutty flavor; usually purchased dried; also known as sponge mushroom and spongie.

Morello cherry (muh-REHL-oh) A sour cherry with a dark red skin and flesh and a sharp, tart flavor; often used to flavor liqueurs and brandies; also known as an English Morello cherry. 2. An imprecisely used term for any of a variety of sour cherries.

Moreton Bay chestnut A poisonous nut grown in Australia; it is rendered edible after leaching and is eaten roasted by aborigines.

morgado (mor-gah-doe) A Portuguese sweet made with egg yolk, sugar, almonds and sometimes figs.

morilla (moe-ree-jya) Spanish for morel.

morille (mo-reey) French for morel.

morina (moe-ree-nah) Turkish for cod.

morkov' (mahr-kov) Russian for carrot.

Mornay, sauce (mor-nay) A French sauce made by adding grated cheese (Parmesan, Gruyère and/or Emmental) to a basic white sauce; served with fish, shellfish, vegetables and chicken.

Morning Kiss A cocktail made with orange juice, gin, apricot brandy and sparkling wine; served in a chilled wine glass.

Moroccan dry cured olive A black, wrinkled olive with an intense flavor; it is dry salt cured.

Moroccan olive A large, round, black olive; it is usually salt brine cured and packed with herbs.

moros (moh-rohs) Spanish (particularly in Mexico and Latin America) for black beans.

moros y christianos (moh-rohs e chres-teh-ah-nos) A Cuban dish of black beans and rice usually served with meat and fried plantains.

morozhena (moh-RO-jhah-nah) Russian for ice cream.

mortadela (mohr-tah-DEH-lah) A Spanish sausage made from lean pork, seasoned with brown sugar, saltpeter, garlic, herbs and brandy or other liquor.

mortadella (mohr-tuh-DELL-uh) 1. An Italian smoked sausage made with ground beef, pork and pork fat and flavored with coriander and white wine; it is air-dried and has a smooth, delicate flavor. 2. An American sausage made from bologna with pork fat and flavored with garlic.

mortar and pestle A tool, usually made of stone, wood or ceramic, used for grinding foods; the bat-shaped pestle presses and rotates the food against the sides of the bowl-shaped mortar.

mortar and pestle

mortella di palude (mor-tell-lah dee pah-lou-dae) Italian for cranberry.

morue (mo-RUE) French for salt cod.

Moscato (moss-CAH-to) A fortified wine made from Muscat grapes in various countries, such as Italy, Spain and Portugal.

moscovite, sauce (mahs-koh-veet) A French compound sauce made from a demi-glaze flavored with pepper and juniper berries or an infusion of juniper berries, garnished with sultanas and pine nuts and finished with Marsala or Málaga; served with game.

Moscow Mule A cocktail made of vodka and a squeeze of lemon juice, topped with ginger beer.

Mosel-Saar-Ruwer (MO-z'l-sahr-ROO-ver) A grape-growing and wine-producing region in Germany located near the Mosel, Saar and Ruwer Rivers and known for the light, fresh greenish-gold wines generally made from Riesling grapes.

mostaccioli (mos-tah-chee-OH-lee) Italian for little mustaches and used to describe medium-sized smooth pasta tubes with ends cut on a diagonal.

mostaccioli rigati Grooved mostaccioli.

mostarda (mohss-TAHR-dah) Portuguese for mustard.

mostaza (moas-TAH-thah) Spanish for mustard.

mostelle; mostele French for whiting.

mosto (MOH-stoh) An Italian grape concentrate used as a sweetener in the production of alcoholic beverages.

mostaccioli

mota Hindi for fat.

mote spoon A spoon with a long handle ending in a sharp point; the pointed handle is

mote spoon

used to push tea leaves from the teapot spout, and the pierced bowl is used as a strainer.

Mother An heirloom apple from Massachusetts (c. 1844); the spherical or ovoid fruit has a golden skin with a deep red blush, a creamy flesh and a rich, juicy, sweet flavor.

mother of vinegar A slimy, gummy substance consisting of various bacteria (especially *Mycoderma aceti*) that cause fermentation in a wine or cider, turning it into vinegar (it is removed once the vinegar-making process is completed).

mother sauces *See* leading sauces.

motto kiss A piece of candy in a wrapper inscribed with or enclosing a saying or verse.

Mou (moo) *See* Fromage à la Pie.

moule (mool) French for mussel.

moules à la poulette (mool ah lah poo-lay) A Belgian dish of mussels cooked with shallots, white wine, mushrooms and crème fraîche.

moules parquée (mool pahr-kee) A Belgian dish of raw mussels served with lemon and pepper or a mustard vinaigrette.

Mouli grater (moo-lee) A rotary grater; the food is held in a hopper above a grating cylinder that is rotated by turning a handle.

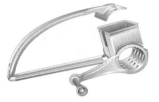

Mouli grater

Mounds Proprietary name for a two-piece candy bar composed of a creamy coconut filling coated with dark chocolate.

mount, to A cooking method in which small pieces of cold, unsalted butter are whisked into a sauce just before service to give it texture, flavor and a glossy appearance. *See* monter au beurre.

mountain A marketing term for certain California jug wines; it has no legal significance.

mountain apple A member of the myrtle family (genus *Myrtus*) grown in Hawaii, this fruit has a single seed, a light pink to red skin, a white to pink flesh and a perfumed, apple flavor.

mountain berry *See* cloudberry.

mountain cheeses Farm cheeses made from cow's, goat's and/or ewe's milk in mountainous areas; they are generally semisoft to firm with hardy, earthy flavors and aromas.

mountain cranberry *See* cowberry.

mountain dew Slang for illicit liquor.

mountain lettuce *See* saxifrage.

mountain oysters The testicles of an animal such as a lamb, calf or boar; they have little flavor and usually a coarse texture; also known as Rocky Mountain oysters and prairie oysters.

mountain spinach *See* orach.

mountain yam A type of Japanese yam with a gluey texture.

Mourteau (moor-toh) A lightly smoked French pork sausage; it is eaten cold or hot, usually served with beans, cabbage or sauerkraut.

Mourvèdre (moor-VEH-druh) A red wine grape grown in France and generally blended with Syrah, Grenache or Cinsaut.

moussaka; mousaka (moo-SOCK-kah) A Greek dish consisting of layers of eggplant and ground lamb or beef covered with a béchamel or cheese and baked; variations contain onions, artichokes, tomatoes and/or potatoes.

mousse (moos) 1. French for foam. 2. French for the head that forms on sparkling wine or beer. 3. A soft, creamy food, either sweet or savory, lightened by adding whipped cream, beaten egg whites or both.

mousse cake A dessert made by molding mousse on top of or between layers of sponge cake.

mousseline (moos-uh-leen) 1. A delicately flavored forcemeat based on white meat, fish or shellfish lightened with cream and egg whites. 2. A sauce or cream lightened by folding in whipped cream. 3. A tall cylinder of brioche bread, usually baked in a coffee can or similar mold.

Mousseline, sauce A French compound sauce made from a hollandaise mixed with stiffly whipped cream.

mousselines (moos-uh-leenz) *See* Chantilly.

mousseux (moo-suh) French sparkling wines made in regions other than Champagne; most are made by the méthode champenoise rather than the Charmat process.

moustarha, saltsa (moo-sah-kah, sawt-za) A Greek sauce made with garlic, olive oil, dry mustard and lemon juice; usually served with eggs or fish.

moutarde (MOO-tahrd) French for mustard.

moutarde à l'ancienne (MOO-tahrd ah lahn-see-en) French for traditional-style mustard. *See* mustard, whole grain.

mouth The cavity within the cheeks containing the tongue and teeth; the point at which ingestion of food occurs and digestion begins by mechanical (i.e., chewing) and chemical processes.

mouth feel The sensation, other than flavor, that a food or beverage has in the mouth; a function of the item's body, texture and, to a lesser extent, temperature.

mouton (moo-tohn) French for mutton.

moutwijn genever (moot-win gha-nah-verr) A Dutch gin that has been twice redistilled through various botanicals, especially juniper berries.

mouvette (moo-veht) French for a wooden spoon used to stir sauces.

moyashi (mo-YAH-shee) Japanese for bean sprouts.

moyo de poulet fumé A dish from Benin consisting of smoked chicken simmered with tomatoes, onions, peanut oil and chiles and served over rice.

mo yuan chi (moe juan tchee) A Chinese brown bean sauce made from ground fermented soybeans, wheat flour, salt and water.

mozzarella (maht-suh-REHL-lah) 1. A southern Italian pasta filata cheese, originally made from water buffalo's milk but now also from cow's milk; it has a white color and a mild, delicate flavor; used mostly for cooking. 2. An American version usually made from cow's milk; it is drier and stringier than the fresh water buffalo's milk variety and becomes very elastic when melted; also known as pizza cheese.

mozzarella affumicata Smoked mozzarella.

mpishi (pee-she) Swahili for chef.

mraqud (mah'rah-cood) Middle Eastern pita bread; also known as kmaj.

Mr. Brown American southern slang for the dark, smoky exterior pieces of pork barbecue. *See* Miss White.

MS Master Sommelier.

MSG *See* monosodium glutamate.

msir (me-ser) Salted lemons preserved in jars and used as a flavoring in tajine.

Mt. Hood A variety of hops grown in the United States.

mtori (m'tory) A Tanzanian soup made from plantains and beef and flavored with tomatoes and onions.

mtumishi mezani (too-me-she ma-zah-nee) Swahili for waiter.

muajeenot (moo-ah-ja-not) Arabic for savory pastries; generally, they are made from a thin, flaky and crunchy crust and are filled with meat and nut mixtures, creamed chicken, cheese, cooked vegetables, zaatar paste or the like; they can be crescent shaped, triangular, round, oval or rectangular, with the filling open or enclosed.

muamba de galinha (moo-ahm-bah da gah-lean-yah) An Angolan and Central African stew consisting of chicken, tomatoes, onions and calabaza flavored with palm oil, garlic, lemon juice and chiles.

mücver (mooc-var) A Turkish hors d'oeuvre of zucchini fritters flavored with mint and dill.

muddle *v.* To crush and mix ingredients in the bottom of a bowl or glass (e.g., crushing and mixing sugar and mint leaves with a spoon when making a Mint Julep); to mix something up. *n.* An American southern fish stew made with potatoes, tomatoes and onions and flavored with thyme, bay leaves and cloves.

muddler A rod or stick with a flattened end used for mashing or crushing ingredients for cocktails.

mud hake *See* hake.

mud pie A dessert that consists of a chocolate cookie crust filled with chocolate, vanilla and coffee ice cream and drizzled with chocolate sauce.

Muenster (MUHN-stuhr) Munster cheese produced in the United States or other areas outside France's Alsace region; it has a light yellow interior, an orange rind and a bland flavor. *See* Munster.

muesli *See* musli.

muffa nobile (MOO-fah NOH-bee-leh) 1. Italian for the noble rot. 2. A dessert wine produced in Italy's Umbria region.

muffin *v.* To give someone a gift basket containing muffins and/or other baked goods. *n.* 1. A tender quick bread baked in small, cup-shaped pans; the batter is often flavored with nuts or fruit. 2. An English muffin. 3. In Great Britain, a small yeast-leavened product baked on a griddle.

muffineer British for a sugar dredger (it was originally used to sprinkle sugar on muffins).

muffin method A mixing method used to make quick bread batters; it involves combining liquid fat with other liquid ingredients before adding them to the dry ingredients.

muffin pan; muffin tin A rectangular baking pan with cup-shaped depressions for holding muffin batter.

muffin ring A small ring, usually of tinned iron, used to make muffins such as English muffins.

muffuletta; muffaletta (muhf-fuh-LEHT-tuh) A New Orleans hero-style sandwich consisting of a round loaf of Italian bread that is split and filled with layers of provolone, salami and ham and topped with a mixture of chopped green olives, pimientos, celery, garlic, capers, oregano, olive oil and red wine vinegar.

muffin pan

mug A flat-bottomed vessel, usually glass or ceramic, with a single handle and generally ranging in size from 8 to 14 fl. oz.; often used to serve hot beverages or beer.

muggie *See* haggamuggie.

mughal garam masala A classic Indian blend of highly fragrant and mild-tasting spices used for flavoring dishes of Moghul origin.

mugi cha (moo-GHEE chah) A Japanese beverage made from roasted barley; also known as barley tea.

mugwort A perennial plant native to Europe (*Artemisia vulgaris*); its aromatic leaves have a faintly bitter flavor and are used as a seasoning in stews, stuffings and sweets.

muhallebi (moo-hah-lah-BEE-yah) A category of Turkish desserts that are flavored with almonds, pistachios, mastic, scented rosewater and vanilla beans; they can be baked or steamed or burned like crème caramel.

muhallebili baklava (moo-hah-la-bee-lee bahk-lah-vah) A Turkish baklava with a sweet, milky cream filling in a sweet syrup.

muhammara (mo-ha-mra) A Turkish spread made from walnuts, garlic, bread crumbs, pomegranate syrup and cumin; usually served on a flat bread.

muhindi (moo-hin-dee) Swahili for corn.

mui quai lu (moo-ee kwa-ee lou) A Chinese liqueur made from fermented rose petals.

mujaddarah (MO-judd-dara) Arabic for lentil stew.

muka (moo-kah) Russian for flour.

mukassaraat (moo-kass-ahr-ah-aht) An Egyptian flavoring paste or condiment made from ground nuts (typically roasted or unroasted almonds, pecans, hazelnuts, cashews and/or peanuts) mixed with rosewater. *See* makhlouta.

mukhalalat (moo-kall-al-aht) A category of Middle Eastern meza; they are pickled vegetables such as eggplants, carrots, green tomatoes, garlic, chiles, beets, onions and cucumbers.

mukhalal filfil (moo-kau-al feel-feel) A Middle Eastern meza or flavoring consisting of chiles pickled in vinegar and salt.

mukhalal toum (moo-kall-al toom) A Middle Eastern meza or flavoring consisting of garlic pickled in vinegar and salt.

muk nge (mook ngha) Chinese for cloud ear mushroom.

mulato (moo-LAH-toh) A long, tapering dried poblano chile with a dark chocolate brown color and a mild to medium hot flavor.

mulberry A berry (genus *Morus*) similar to a blackberry in size and shape with a rather bland, sweet–sour flavor; there are three principal varieties: black, red and white; eaten raw or used for preserves, baked goods or mulberry wine.

mulberry, black A variety of mulberry native to western Asia; it is similar to a loganberry and has a dark red to purplish-black skin and a good flavor.

mulberry, red A variety of mulberry native to North America; it has a bright red to dark purplish-red skin and an excellent flavor.

mulberry, white A variety of mulberry with a pinkish-white skin and a bland flavor.

Mule's Hind Leg A cocktail made of gin, apple brandy, Benedictine, apricot brandy and maple syrup.

mulfoof (mel-foof) Arabic for cabbage.

mulgoa (mool-goh-ah) A variety of mango grown in India; it is particularly flavorful.

muli (moo-lee) Chinese for oyster.

muligapuri (moo-lee-ga-poo-ree) An Indian condiment mix of fenugreek seeds and powdered roasted red chiles; usually served with breads.

mull To heat a beverage such as wine, cider or beer with herbs, spices, fruit and sugar and serve it hot.

mullagatanni (mool-ah-ga-TAH-nee) Hindi for mullaga (black pepper) and tanni (water or broth), the origin of mulligatawny soup.

mulled cider A beverage made of hot apple cider, brown sugar, allspice berries, cloves, cinnamon and dried apple rings.

mulled wine A heated mixture of red wine, sugar, lemon or orange peels and spices such as cloves, cinnamon and nutmeg.

Müller-Thurgau (MEW-luhr-TOOR-gow) 1. A white wine grape principally grown in Germany; it produces a fairly neutral white wine. 2. A white wine grape planted in New Zealand, England, Italy and Austria; it produces a floral-scented wine.

mullet A variety of fish found in the Atlantic Ocean off the southern U.S. East Coast, the Gulf of Mexico and the Pacific Ocean off California; generally, it has a dark-

mullet

bluish striped skin on top that becomes silvery on the sides, an average market weight of 2–3 lb. (0.9 g–1.36 kg), a moderate to high fat content, and a firm, tender flesh with

a mild, nutlike flavor; significant varieties include black mullet, Florida mullet, silver mullet and striped mullet; also known as gray mullet.

mulligan stew (MUHL-ee-gahn) A stew of various meats, potatoes and vegetables.

mulligatawny soup (muhl-ih-guh-TAW-nee) A spicy soup from southern India consisting of meat or vegetable broth flavored with curry and garnished with chicken, meats, rice, eggs, coconut shreds and cream.

mumbar (moom-bahr) A Middle Eastern sausage made from lamb flavored with garlic, onions, baharat and parsley; also known as farareg and krush.

muna (MOO-nah) Finnish for egg.

munakas (moo-nah-kass) Finnish for omelette.

Münchener (muench-ner) A malty, lightly hopped, bottom-fermented beer produced in Munich, Germany; both light and dark versions are made.

munchies 1. Slang for snack foods. 2. Slang for a food craving.

mungaude ki bhaji (mung-gaw-RAY kee BHA-jee) An east Indian dish of moong badian simmered with tomatoes, seasonings, and spices.

mung bean A small dried bean (*Phaseolus lunatus*) with a green or sometimes yellow or black skin, a tender yellow flesh and a slightly sweet flavor; used to grow bean sprouts and in Chinese and Indian cuisines as a bean and ground for flour; also known as green gram and moong.

Munster A semisoft cheese made in France's Alsace region from cow's milk; it has a smooth, yellow interior with small holes, a red or orange rind and a flavor that ranges from mild when young to assertive when old. *See* Muenster.

Munster Géromé *See* Géromé.

mupunda (moo-poon-dah) The medium-sized, plumlike fruit of an African shrub; it has a brown or grayish skin.

mûr (myr) French for ripe.

murabba (MO-rudd-ba) Arabic for jam.

murabbaa (moo-rahb-bah) Hindi for jam.

Mürbeteig A rich, buttery German short crust pastry dough used for tart shells and cookies.

mûre (mewr) French for blackberry.

Mûre (mewr) An eau-de-vie made from the blackberry or mulberry.

mûre de la baie (mewr duh lah bay) French for dewberry.

murgh; murghi (moorg; mur-gee) Hindi for chicken.

murgh musallam (moorg moo-saw-lahm) A traditional east Indian dish of whole chicken cooked in a rich spiced yogurt; now often made with chicken pieces.

murphy Slang for potato.

musakhan (muh-sah-khann) Arabic for she has a fever and used to describe a Middle Eastern dish consisting of chicken flavored with onions, cinnamon, nutmeg, sumac, pine nuts, lemon juice and olive oil and served on a platter lined with thin bread.

muscade (moos-kahd) French for nutmeg.

muscadelle (mus-cah-del) A pear with a musky flavor grown in France.

Muscadelle (mus-cah-del) An aromatic white wine grape grown in Europe and generally used for blending.

Muscadet (mus-cah-day) A dry, light white wine, usually with a high acid content, produced in France's Loire Valley; it matures early and has a trace of muskiness.

Muscadine (MUHS-kah-dine) 1. A grape variety native to the southern United States; it has a thick purple skin and a strong musky flavor; used principally for eating out of hand and for jams and jellies; also known as southern fox grape. 2. A red wine, generally sweet, made from this grape; similar to a light cordial.

Muscat (mus-cat) 1. A grape grown throughout the Mediterranean region, California and Australia and used for eating out of hand, raisins and wine making. 2. A wine made from this grape; it can range from pale, delicate, fruity and low in alcohol to dark amber, sweet and fortified.

Muscat de Beaumes-de-Venise (mews-KAH duh bohm-duh-vuh-NEEZ) A sweet, fortified white wine made from the Muscat grape near the village of Beaumes-de-Venise, France.

Muscatel (muhs-kuh-TEHL) 1. A rich, sweet, fortified dessert wine made from Muscat grapes; the color can range from golden to pale amber-red. 2. Raisins made from Muscat grapes.

Muscatel oil *See* clary sage.

Muscat Hamburg grape A variety of large Muscat grape with a greenish-amber skin and a strong aroma.

Muscat Ottonel grape A variety of large Muscat grape with an amber skin and strong aroma.

Muschel (MU-sherl) German for mussel.

muscle endurance A muscle's ability to contract repeatedly within a set time without exhaustion.

muscles Animal tissue consisting of bundles of cells or fibers that can contract and expand; they are the portions of a carcass usually consumed.

muscovado sugar (muhs-coh-vah-doh) A raw, unrefined sugar that is dark or light and has a strong molasses flavor.

muscovy duck; musk duck (mus-kove-ee) A domesticated duck; young birds have a rich flavor and tender texture; older ones have a tougher texture and a strong aroma.

muscular A wine-tasting term for a full-bodied, flavorful, heavy and unrefined wine, usually red.

muselet (moo-suh-lay) The wire cage used to secure a domed cork or plastic stopper to the rim of a sparkling wine bottle; also known as a wire hood.

mush A thick porridge or cereal made by cooking cornmeal with water or milk; served for breakfast with milk or maple syrup or cooled, cut into squares, fried and served with gravy as a side dish.

mushi (moo-SHEE) Japanese for steamed.

mushi-ki (moo-shee-ki) Japanese wood steamers with bamboo latticework bases; they are used in tiers over simmering water.

mushimono (moo-SHEE-moh-noh) Japanese for steamed foods.

mushroom Any of many species of cultivated or wild fleshy fungus (class Basidiomycota; edible ones are generally members of the genus *Agaricus*), usually consisting of a stem, cap (which may have gills) and mycelium; available fresh or dried and eaten raw, reconstituted or cooked.

mushroomy A cheese-tasting term for a cheese, usually surface ripened, that has developed the pleasant aroma of mushrooms.

mu-shu *See* moo-shu.

musk 1. Any of several plants, particularly fruits, that produce a musky odor (e.g., musk apple). 2. A food additive used to fix, stabilize or enhance flavorings and aromas; it is derived from a glandular secretion of the male musk deer.

Muskat-Silvaner *See* Sauvignon Blanc.

musk cucumber *See* cassabanana.

muskellunge; muskie A freshwater fish of the pike family found in the northern United States and Canada; it has a light skin with dark patterning, an average market weight of 10–30 lb. (4.5–13.5 kg), a low fat content and a firm flesh with many small bones.

musk lime A variety of calamondin with a greenish-yellow skin and a very bitter flavor; also known as a Kalamansi calamondin.

muskmelon A category of melons (*Cucumis melo*) characterized by a dense, fragrant flesh, a central fibrous seed cavity, a hard rind that can be netted (e.g., cantaloupe and Persian) or smooth (e.g., casaba and honeydew), rind colors that include ivory, yellow, orange and green, and flesh colors that include ivory, yellow, lime green and salmon; also known as sweet melon. *See* watermelon.

musky A wine-tasting term for a spicy, earthy characteristic.

musli; muesli (MYOOS-lee) A breakfast cereal made from raw or toasted cereals (e.g., oats, wheat, barley and millet), dried fruits, nuts, bran, wheat germ, sugar and dried milk solids and usually eaten with milk or yogurt; sometimes imprecisely known as granola.

muslin (MUHS-lehn) A thin, loosely woven cotton cloth; used to line a sieve or wrap a bouquet garni.

mussels Any of several varieties of bivalve mollusks found in the shallow waters of the Atlantic and Pacific Oceans and Mediterranean Sea; they generally have a dark blue shell with a violet interior, an average length of 2–3 in. (5.08–7.6 cm) and tough meat with a slightly sweet flavor; significant varieties include blue mussels and greenshell mussels.

must Unfermented grape juice or crushed grapes ready to be made into wine or in the process of being fermented.

mustard Any of several species of a plant that is a member of the cabbage family (*Brassica nigra* and *B. juncea*); the seeds are used for a spice and the leaves are eaten as vegetables.

mustard, American A smooth, somewhat runny prepared mustard made from white or yellow mustard seeds, sugar, vinegar and turmeric; it has a mild, slightly sharp flavor and a bright yellow color; also known as ballpark mustard.

mustard, Chinese A smooth prepared mustard made from mustard seeds, flour and water; it has a dull to bright yellow color and an extremely hot, pungent flavor.

mustard, English A smooth prepared mustard made from brown and yellow or white mustard seeds blended with wheat flour and flavored with turmeric; it has a very hot, pungent flavor; also available dried.

mustard, French *See* Bordeaux, Dijon *and* Meaux.

mustard, German A somewhat coarse prepared mustard made from brown or black mustard seeds; it has a pungent, medium hot, sweet–sour flavor.

mustard, ground A blend of finely ground mustard seeds; it has a bright yellow color; also known as powdered mustard and dry mustard.

mustard, prepared A condiment made from one or more kinds of powdered mustard seeds mixed with flavorings, a liquid such as water, wine or vinegar and sometimes a thickener such as wheat flour.

mustard, whole grain A coarse prepared mustard made from ground and slightly crushed whole mustard seeds (the husks are not removed); it has a hot, earthy, nutty flavor.

mustard flour Ground mustard seeds; it is generally used in sauces and as a condiment.

mustard greens The large, dark green leaves of the mustard plant; they have a peppery, pungent flavor.

mustard greens, salted A bitter mustard plant preserved in brine, sometimes with wine added; it has a salty, sour, tangy flavor and is used in Chinese cuisines.

mustard oil 1. A cooking oil infused with mustard flavor and aroma. 2. An oil obtained by pressing mustard seeds; it is used as a flavoring and in certain cosmetics and soaps. 3. *See* allyl isothiocyanate.

mustard pot A small covered bowl used for serving mustard; the lid is notched so that a spoon can stay in the pot.

mustard pot

mustard seeds The seeds of three different varieties of mustard plants; all are small, hard spheres with a bitter flavor and no aroma; white and yellow seeds have the mildest flavor, and black seeds have the strongest flavor; brown seeds are moderately hot and generally have their husks attached; fine to coarsely ground mustard seeds are used for the condiment prepared mustard or as a spice.

mustard spatula A 4.5-in.-long (11.4-cm-long) spatula.

mustard spoon A small spoon with a rounded bowl with a capacity of 1/4 teaspoon.

must weight The measurable or otherwise quantifiable amount of sugar in ripe grapes or a must.

mustard spoon

musty A wine-tasting term for a disagreeable aroma or flavor caused by using improperly cleaned casks.

mutabbal *See* baba ghanoush.

mut dua (mook doa) Vietnamese candied coconut.

Mutsu (MOO-tsu) A large apple of Japanese origin, now grown in Great Britain under the name Crispin; developed from the Golden Delicious, it has a moderately acidic, full flavor.

mutton The meat of a sheep slaughtered after its first year; the meat is generally tougher and more strongly flavored than lamb. *See* baby lamb, lamb *and* spring lamb.

mutton fat The rendered fat of a lamb or sheep; it has a creamy white color, a hard texture and a strong, distinctive flavor and is used in Middle Eastern cuisines.

muttonfish A variety of abalone found near Australia; it has an ivory flesh with a chewy texture and a mild flavor.

mutton snapper A fish found in tropical Atlantic Ocean waters, including those off Florida; it has an olive green skin with red flanks and brick red fins.

mutual supplementation The dietary practice (especially among vegetarians) of combining two or more plant foods that lack different essential amino acids (i.e., complementary proteins) so that when consumed together, all essential amino acids will be provided (e.g., lentils and wheat or rice; beans and corn).

muz (moze) Arabic and Ethiopian for banana.

mvinyo nyekundu (vi-nho nhe-koon-doo) Swahili for red wine.

mvinyo nyeupe (vi-nho nhe-coo-peh) Swahili for white wine.

MW *See* Master of Wine.

mwambe (moo-ahm-bah) A Congolese and Central African stew consisting of beef, onions and tomatoes flavored with lemon juice, peanut oil and chiles.

my (maa'ah) Arabic for water.

myaso (my-AH-ssah) Russian for meat.

myato Russian for mint.

mycelium (mi-SEE-lee-um) The fine, threadlike structures at the base of a fungus that act like roots to gather nutrients.

Mycella (me-sae-law) A semisoft Danish blue cheese made from cow's milk; it has a creamy yellow interior streaked with greenish veins and a rather mild flavor.

mycology (mi-KAHL-ee-jee) The study of fungi, including mushrooms.

mycophagist A connoisseur of mushrooms.

mycotoxicoses *See* mold.

mynte (mean-tah) Norwegian for mint.

myoga (mewo-gah) Japanese for ginger bud.

myoglobin The iron-containing pigment in muscle tissue that makes oxygen available for muscle contraction; also known as myohemoglobin.

myohemoglobin *See* myoglobin.

myrcene A food additive used as a flavoring agent.

myristic acid A food additive derived from coconut oil and other fats; it is used as a lubricant, binder and defoaming agent.

myrobalan *See* plum, cherry.

myrtille (mer-tey) French for blueberry.

Myrtille (mer-tey) An eau-de-vie made from the whortle-berry, hurtleberry or bilberry; also known as Airelle.

myrtle (meer-teyl) A shrub (*Myrtus communis*) native to the Mediterranean region; its blue berries have a sweet, acidic flavor and its leaves have a flavor reminiscent of juniper and rosemary.

myrtle jam A purple-red jam made from small, brownish-red myrtle berries.

Mysore Arabica coffee beans grown in India and often blended with Moka; the beverage is full flavored.

Mysost (MEWS-oost) A Scandinavian cheese made from boiled cow's milk whey and consisting principally of caramelized lactose; it has a light brown color, a buttery con-sistency and a mild, sweetish flavor; a variety flavored with cinnamon, cloves, cumin and brown sugar is available.

mystery cake A layer cake made with spices, raisins and canned condensed tomato soup.

mystery meat Slang for a difficult-to-recognize cut of meat served in an institutional dining room such as a school cafeteria.

mzeituni (za-ee-too-nee) Swahili for olive.

naan (nah'-han) An Indian flatbread made with white wheat flour and sourdough starter, traditionally baked on the wall of a tandoor oven; it is slightly puffy with a chewy texture and is often flavored with garlic, onions and other seasonings.

naan-bae (nah-han-bah-ee) Hindi for bakery.

naartjie (nah-ahr-tea-a) A tangerine grown in South Africa; it has a slightly tart flavor and is often used in condiments or as a flavoring for a liqueur known as Van der Hum.

naashpatee (na-ash-pah-ee) Hindi for pear.

naashtaa (na-ash-taa) Hindi for breakfast.

nab Slang abbreviation for no-alcohol beer.

nabal avocado A large, spherical avocado with a thick skin and a pale green flesh; it has a particularly sweet flavor.

nabe (NAH-beh) Japanese for pot.

nabemono (nah-beh-MOH-noh) Japanese for communal one-pot meals that are served family style or cooked by the individual diner at the table; they are accompanied by various condiments and sauces.

nabeta A small fish found in the Pacific Ocean from Hawaii to Japan; it has a gray skin, moist, white flesh and mild flavor; also known as a sheepshead.

nabiças (nah-bee-sas) Portuguese for young turnip leaves; they are usually steamed.

nabos (NAH-bohss) Portuguese for small white turnips; they are used in soups and stews and mixed with potatoes for a purée.

Nabulsia (nah-bool-see-ah) A very salty Middle Eastern cheese; it is usually fried as a meza or snack.

nachos (NAH-choh) A Mexican and American Southwest snack of a crisp tortilla or tortilla chips topped with melted cheese and chiles, sometimes with salsa, sour cream, refried beans or other garnishes.

Nachtisch (NAAKH-teesh) German for dessert.

Nadaba (nee-da-bah) The ancient Babylonian goddess of beer.

nadzienie (nah-dzyeh-ñyeh) Polish for stuffing.

naeng myun (nang me-hoon) Thin, long, brown Korean noodles made from buckwheat flour and potato starch, usually served cold in broth with garnishes.

naflion A dark green, crisp, cracked olive cured in salt brine and packed in olive oil.

nagashi-bako (na-ga-shee-bak-ko) A small square pan used as a mold when jelling ingredients for Japanese desserts.

nage, à la (nahj, ah lah) A French preparation method, especially for shellfish; the principal items are cooked in a court bouillon flavored with herbs and are then served with the bouillon, either hot or cold.

Nagelkaas (na-ghel-kass) A Dutch cheese made from skimmed cow's milk, flavored with cloves and cumin seeds and eaten fresh; marketed as a large flat wheel.

nahit (nah-hit) A Jewish dish consisting of dried, soaked chickpeas; sometimes rice, onions and/or brisket of beef are added.

naifu (NAH-ee-foo) Japanese for knife.

nailao (nah-ee-lah-oh) Chinese for cheese.

naipkin (nah-hip-keen) Hindi for napkin.

nairagi (NAH-ee-rah-ghee) A migratory fish of the marlin family found off Hawaii during the winter and spring; it has a striped skin and a pink to orange-red flesh, weighs 40–130 lb. (18–58.5 kg) and is considered the most flavorful of all marlin; its darker flesh is used for sashimi.

naiyóu (nah-ee-yo-ooh) Chinese for cream.

nakari-bōtchō (nah-KEE-ree-BOH-cho) A Japanese knife used to cut produce; it has an elongated rectangular blade with a blunt tip and a straight 8-in.-long cutting edge.

nakari-bōtchō

nakazumi See shinko.

naked frying A cooking method in which foods, usually small items, without any flour or batter coating are deep-fried in moderately hot oil.

nalim (nah-leem) Russian for burbot.

nalisniki (nah-lees-nee-kee) A Russian dish consisting of pancakes rolled around tvorog (cottage cheese) and butter, dipped in melted butter and deep-fried.

nalivka (nah-leave-kah) A Russian liqueur made with vodka flavored with berries.

nam (num) Thai for water.

Nama See Commandaria.

namagashi (nah-mah-gah-shee) A classification of wagashi; these Japanese confections are made from various sweet raw pastes filled with an; they are intended as a sweet counterpart to the bitter tea-ceremony tea (matcha). See han namagashi and higashi.

namak (nah-mack) Hindi for salt.

nama no (NAH-mah no) Japanese for raw.

nama wuni (nah-mah wu-nee) Japanese for the bright orange-red roe of sea urchins; they are used as a garnish for fish and shellfish dishes.

nam cha (num chah) Thai for tea.

ñame *See* yam.

nameko (nah-MEE-koh) Mushrooms native to Japan; they are firm and round, with an orange or gold color, a rich, earthy flavor and a slippery, almost slimy, coating.

nam jim (num jim) A spicy peanut Thai dipping sauce made of ground roasted peanuts, coconut milk, curry paste, fish sauce and sugar; it is usually served with satay.

nam jim kratiem (num jim kray-tee-hem) A Thai sweet-and-sour sauce served with grilled or sliced cold meats.

nam kaeng (nam kang) Thai for ice.

namkin (nam-keen) A general term used in Hindi for all salty, savory snacks.

nammura (namm-moo-raw) A Middle Eastern confection of cream of wheat mixed with yogurt, baking powder and a lemon-flavored syrup and garnished with blanched almonds; after baking, it is soaked in a sweet, lemon-flavored syrup.

na mool (na mool) A Korean term for marinated vegetables or cooked dishes served cold, usually as accompaniments.

NAMP/IMPS The Institutional Meat Purchasing Specifications (IMPS) published by the USDA; the IMPS are illustrated and described in *The Meat Buyer's Guide* published by the National Association of Meat Purveyors (NAMP).

nam pla (num PLAH) A salty condiment made from fermented fish and used in Southeast Asian cuisines.

nam pla raa (num plaa raa) An aromatic Thai sauce made by boiling fermented fish with crushed lemongrass and kaffir lime leaves.

nam prik (num preek) A spicy Thai sauce made by pounding together salted fish, garlic, chiles, nam pla, fresh lime juice, light soy sauce and palm sugar.

nam prik num (num preek noom) A thick green vegetable curry from northern Thailand, usually eaten with sticky rice.

nam prik pao (nam phreek pha-o) A very spicy Thai sauce made from dried roasted red chiles and traditionally served with rice, vegetables and salads; also known as roasted chili paste and roasted curry paste.

nam tan (num tun) Thai for sugar.

na'na (nah-nah) Arabic for mint.

Nanaimo bar (nah-naa-moh) A Canadian multicolored pastry with three layers; the bottom layer is made of chocolate, butter, sugar, dried coconut, graham crackers and walnuts, the middle layer is buttercream flavored with vanilla or Grand Marnier, and the top layer is dark chocolate; the pastry is chilled and cut into bars or squares for serving.

nanas goreng (nah-nass go-rang) Indonesian pineapple fritters, served warm with coffee or tea.

nanasi (nah-nah-see) Swahili for pineapple.

nanking feng gang jiu (nun-king phang gahne gee-you) An aromatic, sweet Chinese wine made from rice.

Nantua, sauce (nan-TOO-uh) A French compound sauce made from a béchamel flavored with cream and crayfish butter and garnished with crayfish tails; it is served with fish, shellfish and egg dishes.

napa cabbage A member of the cabbage family with a stout, elongated head of relatively tightly packed, firm, crinkly, pale yellow-green leaves with a thick white center vein and a mild, delicate flavor; also known as chard cabbage, Chinese cabbage and snow cabbage.

Napa Valley A grape-growing and wine-producing region located in Napa County, near San Francisco, that incorporates nearly the entire county; the principal grapes grown are Cabernet Sauvignon and Chardonnay and, to a lesser extent, Merlot, Pinot Noir, Sauvignon Blanc, Johannisberg Riesling, Zinfandel and Chenin Blanc.

napery Table linens.

napitok (nah-pea-tock) Russian for beverage.

napkin A piece of cloth or absorbent paper used at the table to protect the clothes or wipe the lips or fingers.

Naples biscuit A large (8 × 3 × 1 in.) sponge cake or cookie used for the base of trifles; similar to a lady finger.

napoleon (nuh-POH-lee-uhn) A French pastry made with rectangular sheets of puff pastry layered with pastry cream, whipped cream and fruit or chocolate ganache; the top is then dusted with powdered sugar or coated with fondant glaze; also known as mille-feuille.

Napoleon A label term on bottles of Armagnac and Cognac; it indicates that the youngest brandy in the blend is at least 5½ years old.

napoletana, alla (nah-poa-lay-TAA-nah, al-ah) An Italian method of preparing and garnishing foods associated with Naples, Italy; the foods (e.g., pasta, grilled dishes and pizza) are often topped with a pizzaiola sauce.

nappe (nap) *v.* To coat a food with sauce. *n.* 1. The consistency of a liquid, usually a sauce, that will coat the back of a spoon. 2. French for tablecloth.

nappy An earthenware or glass dish with sloping sides; used for serving sauces.

napukin (NAH-poo-keen) Japanese for napkin.

narangi (nah-ran-gee) Hindi for orange.

naranja (nah-RAHN-jah) Spanish for orange.

naranjilla (nah-RAHN-hee-lah) A small fruit (*Solanum quitoense*) native to South America; it has an orange skin, a yellowish-green segmented flesh, many tiny, flat seeds and a sweet–sour flavor reminiscent of a pineapple and lemon.

nargisi kofta (nar-ghee-see kof-tah) An Indian dish of meatballs stuffed with whole egg, fried, cut in half to expose the egg, and simmered in onion gravy.

NARGUS *See* National Association of Retail Grocers of the United States.

narial; nariyal (nah-ree-al; naa-ri-yal) Hindi for coconut.

narsharab (nahr-sha-raab) A tart syrup made from pomegranate juice.

naseberry *See* sapodilla.

nashi (NAH-shee) A Japanese pearlike fruit (*Pirus serotina*); it is medium sized, with a white- or brown-spotted golden-green skin, a juicy, crunchy, firm, granular white flesh, and a sweet flavor and almondlike aroma; also known as a 20th-century pear.

nashpate (naash-paa-tee) Hindi for pear.

nasi goreng; nassi goreng (nahg-SEE goh-REHNG) An Indonesian dish consisting of rice cooked with foods such as shrimp or other shellfish, meat, chicken, eggs, onions, chiles, garlic, cucumber, peanuts and seasonings.

Nassau grouper A variety of Atlantic grouper.

nastoika (nass-toy-kah) A Russian liqueur made with vodka flavored with herbs.

nastrini (naught-tree-knee) Italian for ribbon or tape and used to describe small pasta bows with a zigzag edge all around. *See* farfalle.

nasturtium An annual or perennial herb (genus *Tropaeolum*); the leaves have a peppery flavor and can be used like watercress; the yellow- to rust-colored flowers also have a peppery flavor and can be used in salads, as a flavoring or garnish, and the immature flower buds can be pickled and used like capers; also known as Indian cress.

nasu (NAH-soo) Japanese for eggplant.

nata (nah-tah) Portuguese and Spanish for cream.

nata (na-ta) A thick, white, translucent gelatinous surface coating (believed to be dextran) sometimes found on fruits such as pineapple, coconut or sugarcane; it attracts acid-forming bacteria and, after washing and boiling, is used as a flavoring in Filipino, Indonesian and other Southeast Asian desserts.

natal plum *See* carissa.

natamycin A food additive used to inhibit the growth of mold on cheese; also known as pimaricin.

natillas (nah-TEE-yah) A soft, runny Spanish custard usually made from ewe's milk and flavored with spices.

National Association of Meat Purveyors *See* NAMP/IMPS.

National Association of Retail Grocers of the United States (NARGUS) An organization of American retail grocers; NARGUS, along with the USDA, designed and implemented a system for sanitation and food safety in retail food stores.

national cuisine The characteristic cuisine of a nation.

National Institutes of Health A collection of various institutes established and funded by the federal government; each is devoted to a specific aspect of health, including nutrition, and basic biological research.

National Sanitation Foundation *See* NSF International.

native Pacific oyster *See* western oyster.

na-tloda An Alaskan dish consisting of bear fat, moose tallow, and sometimes seal oil heated and melted together;

snow or a mixture of minced dried fish or berries is added, and the whole mixture is frozen before eating.

natsume-yashi no mi (nah-tsoo-meh-yah-shee noh meh) Japanese for dates.

natto (NAH-toh) Steamed, fermented, and mashed soybeans used as a condiment and flavoring in Japanese cuisine; the resulting product has a strong cheeselike flavor and a glutinous texture.

natto-maki (naht-toh-mah-kee) Rolled sushi made with fermented soybeans; usually strips of one or more vegetables are added for texture and flavor.

nattsu (NAHT-tsu) Japanese for nut.

natural beef Beef from cattle raised on a natural diet and not given supplements.

natural food 1. A food altered as little as possible from its original farm-grown or ranch-raised state. *See* processed food. 2. A popular and often misleading label term not approved by the FDA and used for a food that does not contain any additives and/or has been minimally processed; its use is intended to suggest that consuming such food will promote health.

natural rind A rind that develops naturally on a cheese's exterior during ripening without the aid of ripening agents (bacteria) or washing; most firm or hard cheeses have natural rinds that range from thin (e.g., Cheddar) to thick and tough (e.g., Parmesan).

natural rindless loaf cheese A cheese that does not form a rind; either before or after aging it is packaged in a transparent, flexible wrapper to minimize or eliminate moisture loss.

natural sweetener Any natural (as opposed to artificial) sweetener other than refined sucrose (e.g., honey).

natural vitamins Vitamin supplements that contain vitamin extracts from food and are not completely synthetic.

natural water *See* water, natural.

natural wine A wine made without additives or preservatives that could alter or influence the wine's aroma, flavor or alcohol content.

natural wrapper *See* claro.

nature (nah-toor) 1. A French term for a wine to which nothing has been added, especially sugar. 2. A sparkling wine (other than Champagne) labeling term indicating that the wine was made without dosage or other sweetening and is drier than a brut; also known as brut nature.

natuto (na-tu-to) A cylindrical-shaped kamaboko marked with a swirling design picked out in red.

Navaho blackberry A blackberry variety; the fruit are relatively small and intensely flavored.

navalheira (nah-vahl-ye-e-raw) Portuguese for a small type of crabs; also known as caraguejo.

naval rum A spirit blended from various West Indian rums.

navarin (nah-veh-rahng) A French stew made from lamb or mutton, onions, turnips, potatoes and other vegetables and flavored with a bouquet garni and garlic.

Navarra (nah-VAHR-rah) A grape-growing and wine-producing region in northern Spain; source of some of the world's finest rosados (rosé wines).

navel orange A variety of large orange with a thick, bright orange rind, an orange meaty flesh, a sweet, citrusy flavor and few if any seeds.

navet (nah-VEH) French for turnip.

navette (nah-veht) 1. A variety of turnip grown in France with a long, tapering shape and a pale white-tan skin. 2. A dry French boat-shaped cake flavored with orange flower water.

navy bean A variety of kidney bean; small and ovoid with a white skin and flesh; a staple of the U.S. Navy since the 1880s, it is also known as the beautiful bean, Boston bean and Yankee bean. *See* white beans.

Navy Grog A cocktail made of lime juice, orange juice, pineapple juice, Falernum and rum; served in a large old-fashioned glass with shaved ice.

nazi (nah-zee) Swahili for coconut.

nbeeth (n'beet'hah) Arabic for wine.

ndimu (ndee-moo) Swahili for lime.

ndizi (ndee-zee) 1. Swahili for banana. 2. A Kenyan dish of sliced plantains seasoned with chiles and cilantro and fried.

Neapolitan (nee-uh-PAHL-uh-tuhn) An imprecisely used term for any molded dessert composed of three layers.

Neapolitan flip A three-tiered coffeemaker; water is heated in the bottom container and coffee grounds are held in the middle container; after the water is heated, the device is turned upside down and the brewed coffee is collected in the third container, now on the bottom.

Neapolitan ice cream Three layers of ice cream, usually chocolate, vanilla and strawberry, molded together, then sliced for service.

near beer A beerlike malt beverage made from cereals and brewed to have no to a low alcohol content; it was introduced during Prohibition. *See* nonalcoholic malt beverage.

neat 1. A drink of liquor consumed without water, ice or mixers. 2. An old English name for an ox, bullock, cow or heifer; also known as neet.

neat's tongue; neat's hoof An archaic name for the tongue or hoof of a cow, bullock, ox or the like.

Nebbiolo (neb-B'YOH-low) A red wine grape grown in Italy's Piedmont region; the resulting wine is generally sturdy and full bodied and has fairly high alcohol and tannin contents.

Nebraska currant *See* buffalo berry.

Nebuchadnezzar (nehb-uh-kuh-NEHZ-ahr) An oversized sparkling wine bottle holding 20 750-ml bottles (approximately 570 fl. oz.).

neck A British cut of beef, veal, lamb and pork carcasses; it extends from the neck, through the shoulder, and into the rib cage. *See* scrag end of neck, middle neck *and* best end of neck.

neck fillet A fabricated cut of the beef primal chuck; popular in Great Britain.

neck of beef A subprimal cut of the beef primal chuck that is located above the first rib blade bone and arm bone.

nectar 1. In Greek and Roman mythology, the drink of the gods. 2. A sugary liquid secreted by many flowers and attractive to bees. 3. In the United States, undiluted fruit juice or a mixture of fruit juices. 4. In France, the diluted, sweetened juice of peaches, apricots, guavas, black currants or other fruits, the juice of which would be too thick or too tart to drink straight.

nectarine A medium-sized stone fruit (*Prunus persica*) with a smooth red and yellow skin, a firm yellowish-pink flesh and a peachy flavor with undertones of almond; available as freestone and clingstone.

nectarine, white A clingstone nectarine with a white flesh.

nectarine

needle coconut A variety of conical-shaped coconut grown in Indonesia.

needled beer A near beer, often containing distilled spirits.

needlefish *See* gar.

needling A process used to tenderize meat; the meat is penetrated by closely spaced, thin blades with sharp points, the muscle fibers are thus cut into shorter lengths; also known as pinning.

neep; nep (neph) Scottish or Old English for a root vegetable, especially turnips.

neet *See* neat.

nèfle (nay-flay) French for medlar.

negative growth phase *See* decline phase.

negative reservation A reservation accepted by a restaurant for a table only when a regular customer calls to relinquish his or her standing reservation.

négi; naganégi (NAY-ghee; NAH-gah-NAY-ghee) Japanese for leek.

negimaki (NAH-ghee-MAH-kee) A Japanese–American dish of sliced beef wrapped around a scallion, broiled with a soy-based sauce and served with a thicker soy-based sauce.

négociant (neh-go-see-ahn) The French term for a person in the wine trade who buys wines and sells them to wholesalers and exporters.

négociant-éleveur (neh-go-see-ahn-eh-leh-VUHR) The French term for a person in the wine trade who buys wines before they are ready for resale; he or she usually cellars the wines during aging, bottles the wines and sells them primarily to exporters.

négociant-embouteilleur (neh-go-see-ahn-ahm-boh-teh-yur) The French term for a person in the wine trade who bottles and stores wines.

négociant-expéditeur (neh-go-see-ahn-ex-pey-dee-tuhr) The French term for a person in the wine trade who ships wines.

négresse (nay-grehss) A French dessert consisting of chocolate mousse topped with whipped cream.

Négresse potato A variety of small, long, thin potato with a purple-black skin, a purple-and-white mottled flesh, and a delicate, rich flavor; also known as Truffe de Chine.

negro *See* chilaca.

Negroni A cocktail made of Campari, gin, sweet vermouth, a splash of seltzer and a twist of lemon.

Negus (nee-GAHS) An old English drink made of port, lemon, sugar, nutmeg and hot water; served warm, usually before bedtime.

neige (nehzh) 1. French for snow and used to describe egg whites whisked until they form stiff peaks. 2. A type of sorbet or grated ice used in the presentation of certain French dishes.

neige de Florence (nehz duh flow-rhance) A very fine, light, flakelike white French pasta used to garnish consommés.

Nelkenschwindling (nek-ken-swine-leng) German for fairy ring mushroom.

nem (nam) A Thai raw cured sausage fermented with large quantities of garlic, chiles and rice.

nematode Any of a variety of roundworms or threadworms, many of which are parasitic in humans and other animals.

nem nuong (nam noo-ong) Vietnamese grilled meatballs.

Nemours, à la (nuh-moor, ah lah) 1. A French garnish for entrées consisting of green peas, carrots and pommes duchesse. 2. A French garnish for meats consisting of sautéed mushrooms and tournée potatoes. 3. A French dish of poached fillet of sole coated with shrimp sauce, topped with a sliced truffle and garnished with quenelles and small mushrooms in a sauce normande.

Neopolitan medlar *See* azaroles.

Nerello Mascalese (neh-REH-loh mah-skah-LEH-seh) A red wine grape grown in Sicily; it is used to make Faro.

nerol and nerolidol Food additives used as flavoring agents.

néroli bigarade (neh-row-li be-gahr-rahd) A bitter orange tree (*Citrus aurantium* var. *bergamia*); its fruit and flowers yield a highly aromatic oil.

neroli oil The aromatic oil produced from the neroli bigarade; it is used to flavor soft drinks and desserts.

nerveux (nair-vuh) A French wine-tasting term for a lively, well-balanced wine with a well-defined character; it is a fine and vigorous wine.

Nesselrode pudding A pudding mixed with chestnut purée, candied fruit, raisins and Maraschino liqueur and then topped with whipped cream; often frozen or used to fill a pie shell.

net An elastic or twine netting used to secure a pieced or rolled roast.

net cost A food's total cost after subtracting the value of the trim and cutting loss.

netetou (na-ta-too) A small yellowish- or reddish-green fruit grown in West Africa; it has a crisp flesh and a tart flavor and is used as a flavoring.

net income; net profit The total revenue from sales and other income less total expenses.

net protein utilization (NPU) A measure of protein quality based on a comparison of the amounts of protein ingested and retained.

netted melon A type of muskmelon with a raised, weblike surface pattern; there are two principal varieties: cantaloupes and Persian melons.

nettle, common A perennial herb (*Urtica dioica*) with long, pointed, coarsely serrated leaves; the young shoots are added to salads, cooked as a vegetable or used to make nettle beer; also known as a stinging nettle.

net weight The weight of a package's contents; the container and packaging (tare) are not included. *See* gross weight.

neua (nua; nuer) Thai for meat or flesh (as in beef).

Neufchâtel (noo-shuh-TELL) 1. A soft, unripened cheese made in France's Normandy region from cow's milk (the milkfat content varies); it has a white color and a slightly salty flavor that becomes more pungent as it ages; sold as small cylinders, rectangles or hearts. 2. An American cheese made from pasteurized milk or a mixture of pasteurized milk and cream; similar to cream cheese and smoother than its French inspiration.

neutral 1. A tasting term for a food or beverage that lacks character or distinguishing features. 2. A wine-tasting term for a wine that lacks a distinctive character but is otherwise flawless.

neutral brandy Brandy produced with a proof of greater than 170.

neutral spirits Virtually colorless and flavorless spirits distilled from grain at a proof of 190 or greater; later reduced in proof, they are used in blended whiskeys and for making vodka, gin and other liquors.

neutral wine A wine, either red or white, of little distinction and often with a relatively low alcohol content; generally used as a blending wine or as an ingredient in alcoholic beverages such as wine coolers.

New American mulberry A variety of black mulberry with long, sweet, black-skinned fruit.

New Brunswick stew A Canadian casserole of roasted lamb or beef, smoked ham, string beans, wax beans, new potatoes, onions, green peas and carrots cooked in the oven.

Newburg A dish consisting of cooked shellfish (lobster, shrimp or crab) in a rich sauce of cream and egg yolks flavored with sherry; usually served over toast points.

New England boiled dinner An American dish of various meats (originally salted beef but now also corned beef, ham, salt pork or chicken) cooked with root vegetables, cabbages and onions and served with horseradish or mustard.

New England chowder A fish, clam or corn chowder containing salt pork, potatoes and onions.

New Mexico green chile, dried A dried New Mexico green chile; it has an olive to dark green color and a sweet, light, smoky flavor with hints of citrus and dried apple; also known as the dried California chile.

New Mexico green chile, fresh A very long, thin, tapering chile with a pale to medium green color, a moderately thick flesh, and a medium to hot, sweet, earthy flavor; also known as the long green chile.

New Mexico red chile, dried A dried New Mexico red chile; it has a dark red to brown color and a medium hot to hot flavor; available as crushed flakes or powder; also known as chile Colorado and dried California chile.

New Mexico red chile, fresh A ripened New Mexico green chile; it has a dark red color, a thick flesh and a medium to medium hot, sweet flavor.

New Orleans coffee *See* Creole coffee.

New Orleans roast *See* roast, French.

Newport rib roast A fabricated cut of the beef primal rib; it is a semiboned roast.

new potato 1. A small, immature red potato. 2. An imprecisely used term for any variety of small young potato.

new sugar giant tomatillo A variety of large tomatillo with a yellow or green skin.

Newton pippin apple An all-purpose apple with a yellowish-green skin, a crisp, juicy flesh, and a slightly tart flavor; also known as pippin and yellow pippin apple.

New Valentine rhubarb A variety of rhubarb; its stalks are dark red.

New York chowder A clam chowder that contains aromatic vegetables and clams in a tomato broth.

New York steak; New York strip steak *See* strip loin steak.

New York–style round A subprimal of the beef primal round; it is the round with the sirloin tip removed.

New York–style steak A fabricated cut of the beef primal round; it is a fully trimmed, center-cut steak.

New Zealand spinach A climbing plant native to New Zealand and Australia (*Tetragonia tetragonioides*); it has dark green, spear-shaped leaves with a slightly acidic flavor; also known as patent spinach and summer spinach.

ngano (n'gah-noh) Swahili for wheat.

ngan pya ye chet (ngan pyar yeah chat) A strongly flavored Burmese sauce of onions, lemongrass, garlic, fish sauce and chili powder.

ngapi htaung (nga-pi taung) A pungent Burmese dipping sauce made with onions, garlic, fermented fish paste and finely ground dried shrimp.

ngau yuk siu mai (ngah-who yook see-you may) A Chinese steamed minced-beef dumpling wrapped in a won ton skin.

Ngunjum (n'goon-jum) A green tea from China's Canton province; the beverage has a light color; also known as silver needle.

nhorm lahong (nyorm law-hong) A Cambodian pork, shrimp and shredded green papaya salad in a lime dressing.

ni (nee) Japanese for braised or simmered food.

niacin *See* vitamin B$_3$.

niacinamide A food additive used as a nutrient (vitamin B$_3$) supplement; also known as nicotinamide. *See* vitamin B$_3$.

Niagara grape A spherical to ovoid table grape grown in the eastern United States; it has a pale greenish-white color and a sweet, foxy flavor.

Niagara Peninsula A grape-growing and wine-producing region in Canada's Ontario province, located along the shore of Lake Ontario; many of Canada's leading producers are located in this region and both red and white wines, especially icewines, are produced here.

niboshi (nee-BOH-shee) Japanese dried sardines that are used for making soup stock, eaten as a snack or used as a flavoring ingredient.

nibs Cleaned, roasted cocoa kernels that are ready for processing. *See* chocolate-making process.

Nicaraguan Arabica coffee beans grown in Nicaragua; the beverage has a clean, lively flavor with a light to medium body.

niche marketing Targeting sales of a business's goods or services to a narrowly defined and selected segment of a larger market.

nickel 1. A trace element used for various biological functions and as a protein component; found in many foods. 2. A food additive used as a catalyst in the hydrogenation of fats.

niçoise (nee-SWAHZ) A tiny black olive native to the Mediterranean region.

niçoise, à la (nee-SWAHZ, ah lah) A French preparation method associated with the cuisine of Nice, France; the dishes are characterized by the use of tomatoes, garlic, black olives, green beans and anchovies.

niçoise, salad (nee-SWAHZ) A salad from Nice, France, consisting of tomatoes, green beans, black olives, tuna, hard-cooked eggs and herbs, dressed with olive oil and garlic.

niçoise galette (nee-SWAHZ gah-lyet) A round, thin French pastry made with a base of sablée dough and a filling of rum frangipane and topped with shortbread cookie dough.

nicotinamide–ascorbic acid complex A food additive used as a source of ascorbic acid and nicotinamide in multivitamin preparations.

nicotinic acid and nicotinamide *See* vitamin B$_3$ *and* niacinamide.

Nieheimer (nee-hih-mer) A German cheese made from soured cow's milk; it has a smooth interior with no eyes; it is packed in casks with hops for a period and then broken up and mixed with caraway seeds, milk or beer for further aging.

nier (neer) Dutch for kidney.

Niere (NEE-rer) German for kidney.

nieru (neh-ee-roo) Japanese for to boil.

nigari (nee-gah-ree) A Japanese tofu coagulant extracted from evaporated seawater.

nigella; nigella seeds (nee-gell-a) A spice that is the seeds of an annual herb (*Nigella sativa*); the black seeds have a mild peppery flavor and are used in Indian and Middle Eastern cuisines in baked goods and sweet dishes; also known as black cumin (no relationship) and fennel flower (no relationship).

niger oil A highly flavored yellow oil extracted from the black seeds of a plant (*Guizotia abyssinica*) grown in Africa and India; used in Indian vegetarian dishes for its nutty flavor.

nightcap 1. During the 18th and 19th centuries, a drink taken on going to bed to warm the person and induce sleep. 2. The last drink of the evening.

nightshade Any plant of the Solanaceae family (e.g., tomato, pepino and eggplant).

nigiri (nee-ghee-ree) Japanese for to compress or compact.

nigiri-zushi (nee-gui-ree-zoo-shi) Japanese for squeezed sushi and used to describe a type of sushi made by placing tane (the topping, which can be raw, marinated or cooked fish or shellfish or other food) on a bed of pressed zushi; also known as Edomae-zushi.

nigiri-zushi shapes *See* funa-gata, hako-gata, kushi-gata, ogi-gata *and* tawara gata.

NIH *See* National Institutes of Health.

nijisseiki (nee-gee-say-ee-kee) A variety of nashi.

nikiri (nee-key-ree) A Japanese condiment; it is a reduction of soy sauce and mirin.

niku (nee-KOO) Japanese for meat or for a dish using beef.

Niligiri A black tea from the Niligiri region in southern India, sometimes used for blends; the beverage has a pleasant, somewhat neutral flavor.

nimboo; nimbu (nim-boo) Hindi for lemon.

nimono (nee-MOH-noh) Japanese for foods such as meat, fish and vegetables that are simmered in a seasoned broth.

nineteenth hole The bar or lounge of a golf course or clubhouse.

nine varieties *See* guchul pan.

ninfa (ninn-fah) Spanish for fairy ring mushroom.

ningbo nian gao (neeng-bow nee-ahn gah-oh) Chinese rice cakes made from a mixture of long-grain and glutinous rice flours.

ning fun (neeng foon) Chinese cellophane noodles.

ningméng (neeng-mang) Chinese for lemon.

ninjin (NEEN-jeen) Japanese for carrot.

nin'niku (nee-nee-kuh) Japanese for garlic.

nioi (nee-OH-ee) A Hawaiian flavoring made with chiles, water and salt.

nip *v.* To consume a small amount of an alcoholic beverage. *n.* 1. A small bottle of an alcoholic beverage; also known as a miniature bottle or airline bottle. *See* split. 2. A small amount of an alcoholic beverage (usually a distilled spirit).

Nisa (nee-sah) A semihard Portuguese ewe's milk cheese; it is curdled with cardo, a thistle.

nisin preparation A food additive derived from certain bacteria and used as an antimicrobial agent.

nispero (neh-spay-roh) Spanish for medlar.

nitrates Food additives such as potassium nitrite and sodium nitrite used to stabilize the pink color associated with cured meats and as antioxidants.

nitrites Food additives such as sodium nitrite and potassium nitrite that are used as curing agents, color stabilizers and/or preservatives in processed foods such as meat products; converted in the stomach into carcinogenic substances called nitrosamines.

nit'r k'ibé *See* nitter kibbeh.

nitrogen 1. A colorless, odorless, tasteless gaseous element found free in the atmosphere and as a component of all proteins. 2. A food additive used to displace oxygen to retard spoilage and as a propellant and aerating agent.

nitrogen balance A comparison of the amount of nitrogen consumed and the amount excreted during a set time period.

nitrosamines *See* nitrites.

nitrous oxide A food additive used as a propellant and/or aerating agent in processed foods such as dairy products.

nitsuke (nee-tzu-kee) A Japanese cooking method in which foods are simmered in a clear liquid or a thin sauce.

nitter kibbeh; nit'r k'ibé (nitter key-bah) A golden yellow, clarified butter flavored with onions, garlic, ginger, turmeric, cardamom seeds, cinnamon, cloves and nutmeg and used as a flavoring in Ethiopian cuisine.

niúnai (nee-who-nah-ee) Chinese for milk.

niúnai de kéfèi (nee-who-nah-ee da ka-fay) Chinese for coffee with milk.

niúpái (nee-oh-pie) Chinese for beef steak.

niuròu (niu-row) Chinese for beef.

Niva (nee-vah) A Roquefort-style cheese made in Russia and eastern Europe from cow's or ewe's milk.

niwatori *See* hiyoko.

nixtamal (knics-tah-mal) Mexican and Latin American dried, soaked corn treated with slaked lime and used to make masa.

njure (NYEW-rer) Swedish for kidney.

njvgu (njee-v-goo) Swahili for peanut.

nkate (nkah-ta) A Ghanaian dish consisting of boiled fresh groundnuts or peanuts.

nkatenkwan (nkah-ten-koo-ahn) A Ghanaian groundnut soup made with chicken, groundnuts, chiles, tomatoes and onions; it can also be prepared with fish.

no A food-labeling term approved by the FDA to describe a food containing no or only physiologically inconsequential amounts of fat, saturated fat, cholesterol, sodium, sugars or calories.

Noah's ark *See* ark shells.

no-alcohol beer A beer from which almost all alcohol has been removed; contains less than 0.5% alcohol by volume.

noble 1. A wine-tasting term for a wine that has the proper balance of elegance, body, maturity, breed, structure and character. 2. Certain grape varieties, such as Cabernet Sauvignon, Pinot Noir, Chardonnay and Sauvignon Blanc. 3. A designation for a vineyard or winery that is far superior to its neighbors.

noble experiment Slang for Prohibition in the United States. *See* Prohibition.

noble hops Hops with a relatively low alpha acid content used to impart aroma and flavor, but not necessarily bitterness, to a beer; they are grown in Belgium and Germany; also known as aromatic hops.

noble rot The desirable deterioration of ripened white wine grapes affected by the mold *Botrytis cinerea*; the mold forms on the grape's skin, reducing liquid content and concentrating sugars; this is responsible for the characteristic sweetness of wines such as Sauternes, Beerenauslese and Tokay Aszú. *See* gray rot.

noble scallop A variety of scallops found in Japanese waters; it has a violet, salmon and yellow symmetrical shell and a tender, sweet, white meat.

nocciola (noat-CHO-lay) Italian for hazelnut.

noce (no-tchae) Italian for nut or walnut.

noce di cocco (no-tchae dee cock-ko) Italian for coconut.

Nocello (noh-CHEH-loh) An Italian walnut-flavored, straw-colored liqueur used to flavor desserts, pastries and confections.

Nocino (noh-CHEE-noh) An Italian liqueur made from green walnuts, spices and lemon rind.

Nockerl (NOK-uhrl) 1. Austrian and German dumplings made with flour and used in soups and stews. 2. Austrian dumplings made with stiffly beaten egg whites and used in fruit soups and desserts.

Nodulator (nod-u-lah-tohr) A cocktail made of Frangelico, Irish cream and peppermint schnapps.

no-eyed pea *See* pigeon pea.

nog 1. Generic term for eggnog or any other drink made with beaten egg, milk and spirits. 2. A traditional English term for strong ale.

noggin An English measure for beer, equal to 0.25 pt. or 5 fl. oz.

no-host bar *See* cash bar.

nohu A variety of rock cod fish found off Hawaii; it has a lean, large-flaked, white flesh and an average weight of 2–3 lb. (0.907–1.35 kg).

Noilly Prat (noi-yeh pra) A French vermouth made from dry white wine and mistelle.

noisette (nwah-ZEHT) 1. French for hazelnut. 2. A small, tender, round slice of meat taken from the rib or loin of lamb, veal or beef.

noisette butter *See* beurre noisette.

noix (nwah) 1. French for nut or walnut. 2. A French cut of the veal carcass; a lengthwise cut from the upper part of the filet end of a veal leg. 3. A French cut of the veal carcass; it is the eye muscle of a cutlet. *See* cuisseau.

noix de coco (nwah duh ko-ko) French for coconut.

noix de pacane (nwah duh pah-can-nae) French for pecan.

nojime (noh-gee-mah) Japanese for fish that are kept alive until shortly before service. *See* ikijime.

Nökkelost (NUR-ker-loost) *See* Kuminost.

nom (nom) Thai for milk.

nomimono (noh-mee-moh-noh) Japanese for beverage.

nonalcoholic malt beverage A fermented beverage product made from malted grains and containing less than 0.5% alcohol by volume; it cannot be labeled as beer, ale, stout, and so on but can be labeled as near beer, malt beverage or cereal beer.

nonanal A food additive with a strong orange and rose aroma used as a flavoring agent.

noncontrollable costs *See* fixed costs.

nondairy creamer A product used to lighten and dilute coffee and tea; made from a hydrogenated oil or saturated fat such as coconut or palm oil, sweeteners, preservatives and emulsifiers; it is available in powdered, liquid or frozen form; also known as coffee whitener.

nonessential amino acids Amino acids that can be synthesized by the body and are not required in the diet; generally recognized as nonessential for a normal adult are alanine, aspartic acid, arginine, citrulline, glutamic acid, glutamine, glycine, hydroxyglutamic acid, hydroxyproline, norleucine, proline and serine.

nonfat dried milk; nonfat dry milk powder *See* dried milk, nonfat.

nonfat milk *See* skim milk.

nonna, della (NOH-nah, DEH-lah) Italian for grandmother's style and used to describe a homestyle or traditional dish.

nonnutritious; nonnutritive Not providing any or only physiologically inconsequential amounts of nutrients.

nonnutritive sweetener 1. Any sweet substance used as a sweetener that has less than 2% of the caloric value of sucrose per equivalent of sweetening capacity. 2. A category of nonnutritive food additives used as a sweetener (e.g., saccharin). *See* nutritive sweetener.

Nonpareil almond The leading commercial variety of almond tree.

nonpareille, sauce (nuhn-pah-reel) A French compound sauce made from a hollandaise flavored with crayfish butter and garnished with diced crayfish tails, mushrooms and truffles.

nonpareils (non-puh-REHLZ) 1. Tiny sugar pellets used to decorate cakes and confections. 2. Small chocolate disks coated with these pellets. 3. French for without equal and used to describe small capers from France's Provence region.

nonperishable Foods and beverages that do not quickly spoil or deteriorate, especially if stored under appropriate conditions.

nonperishable processed food Any processed food not subject to rapid decay or deterioration that would render it unfit for consumption (e.g., flour, sugar and crackers).

nonreactive A term used to describe cooking and serving utensils made of materials that do not react with acids and brine (a salt and water solution) to discolor foods or form toxic substances; nonreactive saucepans and pots include all of those with undamaged nonstick interiors, plus pots and pans made from flameproof glass, glass ceramic, stainless steel, enameled steel and enameled iron; uncoated iron and copper form toxic substances when used for cooking high-acid foods; uncoated aluminum darkens some fruits and may become pitted if salty mixtures are left standing in them.

nonrefundable A specified condition of a sale or a promise of a sale whereby the seller can retain part or all of the sales price received or limit the purchaser to a credit or replacement.

nonstick plastic; nonstick coating; nonstick finish A polymer such as polytetrafluoroethylene (PTFE) that is applied to the surface of some cookware; it provides a slippery, nonreactive finish that prevents foods from sticking and allows the use of less fat; easily scratched.

nonvintage 1. A wine (usually a table wine) without a vintage date on the label. 2. A wine made from grapes harvested from more than one year or blended from such wines. 3. A sparkling wine whose cuvée contains one or more wines from one or more previous vintages.

Nonya cuisine The cooking style of Chinese–Malay families who settled in Malacca, Penang, and Singapore; it combines Chinese ingredients and local herbs and seasonings such as galanga, turmeric roots, pandanus, ginger, tamarind and chiles.

nonyl acetate and nonyl alcohol Food additives used as flavoring agents and/or adjuvants.

noodles 1. Ribbons of various lengths, widths and thicknesses made from a dough of wheat flour, water and eggs (or egg yolks) and generally boiled; also known as egg noodles. *See* pasta. 2. A generic term for ribbons of boiled dough (whether made with eggs or wheat flour) of various lengths, widths and thicknesses; used principally to describe Asian products. 3. British for fettuccini and similar pasta shapes.

noodle squash *See* spaghetti squash.

nopales (noh-PAH-lays) The pads of the nopal cactus (genus *Nopalea*) native to Mexico; they have a flat, irregular oval shape, short stinging needles, a pale to dark green color and a delicate, tart flavor reminiscent of green beans.

nopalitos (no-pah-LEE-toes) Nopales diced or cut into strips and pickled or canned in water.

noques (nohks) Small flour dumplings from France's Alsace region, flavored with nutmeg and eggs.

nori (NOH-ree) Dark green, purple or black paper-thin sheets of dried seaweed with a sweet, salty ocean flavor; used in Japanese cuisine to wrap sushi or as a garnish or flavoring. *See* yakinori *and* afifsuke-nori.

nori-maki (NOH-ree-mah-kee) A category of Japanese sushi; a core of principal ingredients (e.g., raw fish and sprouts) are rolled in zushi and the whole is wrapped in nori; the roll is then cut into bite-sized slices.

nori nest (NOH-ree) A nest made of nori and used for serving quick-fried vegetables in Japanese cuisine.

nor mai (nor mah-e) A Chinese steamed lotus packet of sticky rice, chicken, sausage, pork and black mushrooms.

normal flora Microorganisms usually present in an environment, including the human body, under normal or nondisease circumstances.

normande, à la (nohr-MAHND, ah lah) A French preparation method associated with the cuisine of Normandy; the dishes are characterized by the use of typical Norman products such as butter, fresh cream, seafood, apples, cider and Calvados.

normande, sauce A French compound sauce made from a fish velouté with mushroom stock and oyster liquor, thickened with a liasion, and finished with butter.

Normandy Cocktail (NOHR-man-dee) A cocktail made of gin, apricot brandy and Calvados or applejack.

normandy sauce *See* normande, sauce.

no roll A beef carcass or cut that has not been officially graded.

Northern Brewer A variety of hops grown in Kent, England, and in the states of Oregon and Washington.

northern Pacific halibut *See* Pacific halibut.

northern pike A freshwater fish found in North America; it has a dark skin with light spots, an average market weight of 0.5–1.5 lb. (225–680 g) and a lean, firm, flaky flesh; also known as a grass pike and lake pickerel.

northern pike

northern red snapper *See* red snapper.

Northern Spy apple A large apple native to North America; it has a red and yellow striped skin and a sweet–tart flavor; also known as a Spy apple.

Northland blueberry A blueberry variety; the fruit have a particularly fine flavor.

North Star cherry A variety of sour cherry; the fruit have a mahogany red skin.

Northwest Greening apple *See* Rhode Island Greening apple.

Norwalk virus A virus that causes gastroenteritis; common sources are contaminated food handlers, human feces, contaminated water and vegetables fertilized with manure.

Norway lobster A variety of lobster found in the northern Atlantic Ocean; it has an elongated tail and claws, a brick to salmon red shell, a maximum length of 9 in. (22.5 cm), a tender flesh and a sweet, delicate flavor; also known as Icelandic lobster and lobsterette.

nose 1. A wine-tasting term for a wine's bouquet or aroma. 2. A tasting term for a person with a highly developed and discerning sense of smell.

nostrale; nostrano (noh-STRA-lee; noh-STRAH-noh) Italian for homemade and used to describe local products, such as cheeses, wines or sausages.

no-time dough A bread dough made with a large quantity of yeast; except for a short rest after mixing, no time is set aside for fermentation.

nøtt (nuhtt) Norwegian for nut.

Nottingham medlar An exceptionally flavorful variety of medlar.

nouet (noo-ay) A muslin bag containing herbs, spices or other flavorings and tied with a string; used in French cuisine to impart flavors to a liquid without leaving solid particles behind. *See* bouquet garni *and* sachet.

nougat (noo-guht) A French confection made with a cooked sugar or honey syrup mixed with roasted nuts and candied fruit; sometimes the confection is made with egg whites, which produce a white, chewy, taffylike candy.

nougatine (noo-gah-teen) A crisp French nut brittle made with caramelized sugar and almonds or hazelnuts; before it cools, nougatine can be cut into pieces or shaped into cups or containers for creams or other pastries; once it hardens, nougatine can be crushed and used to flavor ice cream, pastries or other confections.

nouilles (noo-yuh) French for noodles.

nourishment 1. The process of providing a plant or animal with sustenance to maintain life functions. 2. The particular item that provides such sustenance.

nourriture (noo-ree-tuhr) French for food.

nouveau (noo-vo) French for new; used to describe wines, except for Beaujolais Nouveau, of the most recent vintage year (the vintage year ends on August 31).

nouvelle cuisine (noo-vehl kwee-zeen) French for new cooking and used to describe a mid-20th-century movement away from many classic cuisine principles and toward a lighter cuisine based on natural flavors, shortened cooking times and innovative combinations.

Nova Salmon that is brine cured and then typically cold smoked; it is less salty than lox. *See* smoked salmon.

noviho (noh-vee-ho) Portuguese for a young cow weighing no more than 650 lb. (300 kg) and no older than 30 months when slaughtered.

noyaux (nwah-YOH) *See* crème de noyaux.

noz (nosh) Portuguese for nut.

nozh' (no-sh) Russian for knife.

NPU *See* net protein utilization.

NSF International An organization that promulgates standards for the design, construction and installation of kitchen tools, cookware and equipment and certifies products that meet these standards; formerly known as the National Sanitation Foundation.

nsima; nshima (n'sea-mah) A Zambian dish consisting of a thick cornmeal porridge, similar to foofoo, sometimes flavored with chiles.

ntomo krako (ntoe-moe kraw-koe) A Ghanaian dish consisting of yam or sweet potato slices dipped in a bread crumb batter and fried in peanut oil.

nua (noo-ah) Thai for beef.

nua pad prik (noo-ah pahd preek) A Thai dish consisting of slices of beef fried in a sauce of garlic, chiles, fish sauce, sugar and cilantro.

Nudel (noo-derln) German for noodle.

nudler (nood-lahr) Norwegian for noodle.

nudoru (NOO-doh-roo) Japanese for noodle.

nuez (new-ez) *pl.* nueces. Spanish for nut or walnut.

nuez de coco (new-ez day ko-ko) Spanish for coconut.

nuka (noo-KAH) A Japanese rice bran powder used primarily as a pickling agent.

nuka-zuke (NOO-kah-ZU-keh) Japanese rice bran pickles.

numb A beer- and wine-tasting term for a product that has been so chilled that little flavor can be detected.

number of portions Number of servings.

numname (nuhm-nah-mee) Arabic for basil; also known as hubaq.

nun's toast Archaic slang for French toast.

nuoc cham (noo-AHK CHAHM) An all-purpose Vietnamese condiment made of chiles, nuoc mam, sugar and lime juice.

nuoc dua tuoi (nee-AHK yoo-a tuoi) Vietnamese for coconut water.

nuoc mam (noo-AHK MAHM) Vietnamese for a salty condiment made from fermented fish.

nuoc mau (noo-AHK maw) A caramelized sugar used to add color and gloss to Vietnamese cooked dishes and foods to be grilled.

nuo mi fen (noo-oh me fan) Chinese rice flour made from glutinous rice.

nuong (noo-ong) Vietnamese for charcoal-grilled foods.

Nuragus The most popular variety of white wine grape grown in Sardinia; it produces a dry, crisp, clean wine.

Nürnberger Wurst (nuren-barg-er verst) A sausage traditionally made in Nuremberg, Germany, from pork meat and fat, seasoned with Kirsch, thyme, marjoram, nutmeg and pepper.

Nüss (NEW-sser) German for nut or walnut.

nut 1. The edible single-seed kernel (the meat) of a fruit surrounded by a hard shell (e.g., hazelnut); it has high protein and fat contents and is used for snacking or to provide flavor and texture to foods. 2. A term used imprecisely to describe any edible seed or fruit with an edible kernel surrounded by a hard shell (e.g., walnut).

nutcracker A utensil used to crack nuts; it consists of two pivoted 7-in. (17.8-cm) lengths with small and large arc inserts with ridges to grip the nut.

nutcracker

Nutella The proprietary name for a paste made from hazelnuts, cocoa and sugar; it is used as a spread for bread or toast and as a flavoring for pastries and confections.

nut flour A flour made of finely ground nuts and used in certain cakes and other pastries.

nutlet 1. A small nut. 2. The stone or pit of certain fruits such as a peach or cherry, respectively.

nut meat; nutmeat The edible kernel of a nut.

nutmeg The hard seed of a yellow fruit from a tree (*Myristica fragrans*) native to the East Indies; it has an oval shape, a smooth texture and a strong, sweet aroma and flavor; used ground (grated) in sweet and savory dishes. *See* mace.

nutmeg grater A grater used for reducing a whole nutmeg to a powder; the grating surface can be flat or convex.

nutmeg melon *See* cantaloupe, American.

nut mill A tool used to produce a nut flour; shelled nuts are put into the hopper and pressed against the grating drum by a rotating hand crank.

nutmeg grater

nut oil Any oil extracted from a nut; typically labeled as pure, it generally has the strong aroma and flavor of the nut from which it was processed.

nut pick; nutpick A small, sharp-pointed tool used for digging the meat from nuts.

NutraSweet *See* aspartame.

nutrient additive A mineral, chemical compound, vitamin or other organic matter added to a food to improve its nutritive value; added to a processed food, its use is subject to FDA regulations. *See* enriched *and* fortified.

nutrient density The measure of nutrients per calorie of food; a nutrient-dense food has more nutrients per calorie than a low-density one; useful for selecting foods on a reduction diet.

nutrients The components of food (i.e., carbohydrates, lipids [fats], proteins, vitamins, minerals and water) that provide the energy and raw materials for the growth, maintenance and repair of the body.

nutrient supplements *See* supplements.

nutrition 1. All of the processes by which living cells and organisms ingest, digest, absorb and assimilate food. 2. The study of these processes.

nutritionally inferior A term approved by the FDA to describe a food with a reduction in one or more essential vitamins, minerals or proteins equal to 10% or more of the U.S. (RDA).

nutrition facts Nutritional information mandated by the FDA that must appear on the label of most processed foods. *See* calories, calories from fat, calories per gram, daily values, percent daily value, recommended daily intake, serving size *and* servings per container.

nutritionist A person who has specialized in the study of nutrition or related fields and, generally, has an advanced degree; a nutritionist may also be a registered dietitian. *See* dietitian.

nutritious; nutritive Providing one or more nutrients in a physiologically significant quantity.

nutritive sweetener 1. A sweetener such as sucrose, corn syrup, honey or molasses that contributes calories and nutrients to the diet. 2. A type of food additive used as a sweetener and that has more than 2% of the caloric value of sucrose per equivalent of sweetening capacity. *See* nonnutritive sweetener.

nutshell The hard covering surrounding the nut meat.

nutty 1. A food containing an abundance of nuts or having the pronounced flavor of nuts. 2. A cheese-tasting term for a cheese with a flavor reminiscent of nuts, especially hazelnuts or walnuts. 3. A wine-tasting term for the characteristic nutlike aroma and flavor of Madeira, Marsala, sherry, Vin Santo or wines that have oxidized.

Nuwara Eliya A Sri Lankan black tea; the beverage has a delicate, light flavor and is often served after dinner.

NV A label term for a nonvintage wine (often applied to Champagne).

nwo-nwo (no-oo no-oo) A Nigerian peppersoup made with goat or mutton.

nyama (NYAH-mah) Swahili for meat.

nyama ya kondoo (NYAH yah kon-doh) Swahili for lamb.

nyama ya mbuzi (NYAH yah boo-zee) Swahili for goat.

nyama ya ndama (NYAH yah dah-mah) Swahili for veal.

nyama ya ng'ombe (NYAH yah in'gom-ba) Swahili for beef.

nyama ya nguruwa (NYAH yah ngoo-roo-wah) Swahili for pork.

nyama ya nguruwe (NYAH yah ngoo-roo-ooa) Swahili for bacon.

nyiur-gading *See* dwarf coconut.

Nyon (nee-ohn) A small, wrinkly, greenish-black olive from the Nyon region of France; it has an intense, somewhat bitter flavor and is dry salt cured and rubbed with oil or used for oil.

nyovhi (ne-oh-ve) A plant with small narrow green leaves grown in Zimbabwe; it has a mild, slightly bitter flavor and is used in stews.

nyre (NEW-re) Danish and Norwegian for kidney.

O *See* old.

oak fired Food prepared in an oak wood–fired oven (the wood produces a fire with high heat); the fire and smoke give foods a deep, smoky flavor with a resin aroma.

oak leaf lettuce A leaf lettuce with red-tinged green leaves similar in shape to an oak tree's leaves.

oaky A wine-tasting term for the characteristic toasty or spicy, vanilla-like aroma and flavor of a wine that has been aged in oak barrels; a moderate amount is desirable, an excessive amount is not.

oast (oost) A kiln used to dry the hops, barley or other grains used for brewing or distilling.

oat bran The oat kernel's bran; used as a high-fiber nutrient supplement.

oatcake A large, round disk of dough made of oatmeal, salt, bacon fat and warm water; cut into segments, it is sprinkled with oatmeal and cooked in an iron skillet until the edges curl upward; it is served hot or cold with unsalted butter or cottage cheese.

oat flour Finely ground oats with the hull removed.

oat groat The oat kernel with the husk removed; it is the portion most often consumed as a cereal or in baked goods.

oatmeal Coarsely ground oats that are cooked as a hot cereal and used in baking.

oatmeal stout A dark, rich, flavorful stout made by adding oatmeal to the roasted malt used for brewing.

oats A cereal grass (*Avena sativa*) with a highly nutritious grain kernel.

oats, instant Rolled oats that have been partially cooked and then dried before rolling.

oats, quick-cooking Rolled oats cut into smaller pieces to reduce cooking time.

oats, rolled Steamed oat groats rolled into flat flakes; also known as old-fashioned oats.

oats, steel-cut Toasted oat groats cut into two or three pieces per grain; they require a longer cooking time than that for rolled oats; also known as Irish oats and Scotch oats.

Oaxaca (wah-ha-kaa) *See* Asadero.

Oban The proprietary name of a single-malt Scotch whisky; it has a mellow, smoky malt flavor with a hint of sweetness and a pleasant aftertaste.

ob chuy (ob choo-ee) Thai for cinnamon.

obed (o-bead) Russian for dinner.

obese Having an excessively abnormal amount of fat on the body (generally, being 20% or more above the appropriate weight for height). *See* overweight.

Oblaten (ohb-LAH-ten) A plate-sized, paper-thin waffle biscuit (cookie) given to patients at the Karlsbad spa (Czech Republic); the large size gives the feeling of eating something substantial.

obligate anaerobic bacteria; obligate anaerobes *See* bacteria, obligate anaerobic.

oblique cuts Small pieces of food, usually vegetables, with two angle-cut sides; also known as roll cuts.

oboro (o-BOU-row) A type of Japanese tofu; the unpressed soft curds of coagulated soy milk; also known as soy milk curds.

O'Brien potatoes A dish of diced potatoes (sometimes precooked) fried with onions and red and green sweet peppers.

Obst (ohbst) German for fruit; also known as Frucht.

Obstler (obs-tlaer) German schnapps made from apples or pears or a combination of both.

Obsttorte (ohbst-tor-ta) A fruit tart made with a maryann pan.

Obsttortenform (ohbst-torten-form) German for a maryann pan.

oca (OH-cah) 1. Italian and Spanish for goose. 2. The egg-sized tuber of a sorrel grown principally in Peru; it has a yellow to red-brown skin, a white flesh and a very sweet flavor.

occhi di lupo (OH-kee de loo-poh) Italian for wolf's eyes and used to describe large tubes of pasta.

occhi di passeri (OH-kee de PAH-she-reh) Italian for sparrow eyes and used to describe tiny circles of pasta, usually used for soups.

occhio di bue (OH-k'yoh dee BOO-eh) Italian for eye of the ox and used to describe a fried egg.

occhi di lupo

Occupational Safety and Health Act (OSHA) Federal legislation designed to reduce hazards in the workplace, thereby reducing accidents and injuries; the Act and regulations promulgated under the Act cover a broad range of safety matters, requiring careful compliance by the employer.

ocean perch A member of the rockfish family found in the Atlantic Ocean from New England to Labrador and in the Pacific Ocean from California to Alaska; it usually has an orange to bright red skin (brownish-red varieties are available), a firm, lean, white flesh and an average market weight of 0.5–2 lb. (225–900 g); also known as deep-sea perch, longjaw rockfish, red perch, redfish and rosefish.

O-cha (oh-chah) A Japanese green-colored liqueur with the flavor and aroma of fresh green tea.

ocha Japanese green tea.

ochoko (oh-tcho-koe) A small porcelain handleless cup traditionally used for serving sake in Japan; also known as sakazuki.

Ochsenmaulsalat (AHK-sern-maw-zah-laa-ter) A German cold meat salad.

octanoic acid *See* caprylic acid.

octopus Any of several varieties of cephalopod mollusks found in the Atlantic and Pacific Oceans and the Mediterranean Sea; generally, they have a large head and tentacles but no cuttlebone; the skin is gray when raw and turns purple when cooked and the lean, white flesh has a firm, somewhat rubbery texture and a mild flavor; also known as devilfish.

octyl acetate A food additive with an orange and jasmine aroma used as a flavoring agent.

octyl alcohol A food additive with a sharp fatty aroma used as a flavoring agent in beverages, candies and baked goods.

Odd McIntyre A cocktail made of brandy, Lillet Blanc, lemon juice and Cointreau or Triple Sec.

odor A quality of something that affects the sense of smell.

odori (oh-DOH-ree) Italian term for aromatic vegetables, usually the combination of carrots, onions and celery.

odori-ebi (oh-DOH-ree-a-bee) Japanese for dancing shrimp and used to describe shrimp served live.

Oechsle (uh'k-sleh) The German and Swiss equivalent of Brix.

oeil de perdrix (uh'y duh pair-dree) French for eye of the partridge and used as a wine-tasting term to describe a wine with a slightly pink or bronze color.

oenologist *See* wine maker.

oenology *See* enology.

oenophile *See* enophile.

oester (OOS-turs) Dutch for oyster.

oeuf (ouf) French for egg.

oeuf de coq (ouf duh kohk) A plant grown in Africa; its yellow, egg-shaped fruit have a slightly bitter flavor.

oeuf en gelée (ouf ahn ghee-leh) A French dish consisting of a poached or boiled egg in aspic.

oeufs à la neige (OUF ah lah nehzh) French for snow eggs and used to describe the dessert known in the United States as floating island.

oeufs en gelée mold (ouf ahn ghee-leh) A small oval metal mold used for preparing oeufs en gelée.

oeufs meulemeester (ouf mew-lam-mee-stare) A Belgian dish consisting of hard-boiled eggs mixed with prawns, topped with cream flavored with chervil, parsley, butter, mustard and pepper, garnished with grated cheese and browned.

off; off-aroma; off-flavor A tasting term for a food or beverage with an unusual, undesirable aroma, flavor or other attribute not typically displayed by the product.

offal (OWF-fuhl) *See* variety meats.

off-premise outlet A retail establishment specializing in the sale of alcoholic beverages; usually, a package store in which alcoholic beverages are sold in bottles or cans to be consumed elsewhere.

offset spatula A tool with a flat, unsharpened stainless steel blade with a bend or step near the handle, forming a Z shape; the end of the blade is rounded and blunt;

offset spatula

available in a variety of lengths and widths; used for spreading batter, filling and frosting cakes and pastries and moving items from one place to another; depending on the size of the blade, an offset spatula may also be referred to as a grill spatula or a cake spatula.

ofiziant (oh-ee-sianht) Russian for waiter.

ogen A variety of small cantaloupe grown in Israel; it has a rough yellow skin with green stripes and a green flesh.

ogi-gata (oh-ghee-gah-tah) A portion of rice for nigiri-zushi shaped like a fan.

ogurez (ahg-urtz) Russian for cucumber.

ohagi (oh-hah-gee) Japanese sweet rice cakes made by wrapping egg-shaped short-grain rice in a paste of beans, sugar and salt; they are sometimes rolled in toasted sesame seeds.

ohashi *See* hashi.

ohelo berry A berry native to Hawaii; it has a tart flavor.

Ohio squash *See* Hubbard squash.

ohra (oah-rah) Finnish for barley.

ohraleipä (oh-raw-lay-pah) A Finnish bread made with barley and wheat flour.

oidium (oh-EE-d'yum) A fungus that attacks the fruit, leaves, shoots and tendrils of grape vines; it can be prevented by spraying with sulfur; also known as powdery mildew.

oie (wah) French for goose.

oignon (ohn-nawng) French for onion.

oignon brûlée (ohn-nawng brew-lay) French for burned onion and used to describe charred onion halves that are used to flavor and color stocks and sauces.

oignon pique (ohn-nawng pee-k) French for pricked onion and used to describe a peeled onion with a bay leaf tacked with a clove to its side; used to flavor sauces and soups.

oil can Slang for a 32-fl. oz. can of beer.

oiler Slang for a person who drinks alcoholic beverages excessively.

oil of rue A food additive derived from various plants of the genus *Ruta* and used as a flavoring agent in baked goods and mixes.

oil of vitriol *See* sulfuric acid.

oils Fats (generally derived from plants) that are liquid at room temperature.

oilstone *See* whetstone.

oily A tasting term used to describe the greasy surface of some foods, created by excessive use of oil in their preparation or the presence of natural oils (e.g., hard cheeses).

oinochoe (oh-ne-NOW-cha) An ancient Greek pitcherlike vessel with a three-lobed rim; used for dipping wine from the bowl and pouring it into the drinking cup.

oison (wah-zyon) French for a goose up to 6 months old.

Ojen (oh-hen) A Spanish anise-flavored liqueur.

ojinguh bokum (ogoing o-po-kum) A Korean dish consisting of pan-fried squid and vegetables with spicy seasonings.

Ojo de Liebre (oho day lee-ay-bray) Spanish for Tempranillo grapes.

oka 1. A Nigerian porridge made from yam flour; it is frequently used as a base for many soups or stews; also known as amala. 2. A Benin dish consisting of a cassava meal porridge flavored with palm oil; also known as funge (Angola).

Oka (o-KAH) A Port du Salut–style cheese made from cow's milk in the Trappist monastery at Oka, Canada.

Okanagan Valley A grape-growing and wine-producing region in Canada's British Columbia province; the principal grapes grown are Pinot Noir and Chardonnay; the region is home to several organic wineries.

okara (oh-kah-rah) The moist, white, high-protein pulp of ground soybeans that remains after the liquid is drained off to make bean curd; used in Japanese cuisine in soups, vegetable dishes and salads.

okayu (o-KAI-yoo) Japanese for porridge.

okhotnichya (och-hat-nee-chay-ya) An eastern European and Russian vodka flavored with herbs; it has an aroma reminiscent of heather honey.

oklava (ohk-lava) A long, relatively slender Turkish rolling pin used to prepare borek and manti.

okolehao (oh-koh-leh-HAH-oh) An alcoholic beverage distilled in the Hawaiian Islands from a mash of cooked ti leaves.

okome (oh-KOH-may) Japanese for raw hulled rice.

okra The seed pod of a tropical plant (*Abelmoschus esculentus*) of the hollyhock family native to Africa; the oblong, tapering pod has ridged green skin and a flavor reminiscent of asparagus and is used like a vegetable in African and southern U.S. cuisines; because it develops a gelatinous texture if cooked for long periods, it is also used as a thickener; also known as gombo and ladies' fingers.

ok-rong (ok-rong) A pale yellow mango used in a variety of sweet Thai dishes.

oksekjott (oks-eh-shut) Norwegian for beef.

Oktoberfest (ohk-TOE-ber-fehst) An annual beer festival held in late September and early October; it originated in Munich, Germany, in 1810 as a celebration of the marriage of Prince Ludwig and Princess Theresa and is now celebrated worldwide.

okun (ahk-un) Russian for perch.

Öl (eul) German for oil.

øl (url) Danish and Norwegian for beer.

olallieberry; olallie berry A berry that is a hybrid of a youngberry and a loganberry; it resembles an elongated blackberry in shape and color and has a sweet, distinctive flavor.

old 1. A food or beverage (especially wine) past its prime. 2. A labeling term for Cognac, Armagnac and other brandies indicating that it is a well-aged product; sometimes written as O.

Old Bay Seasoning The proprietary name of a spice blend containing celery salt, dry mustard, paprika and other flavorings; used in shellfish preparations.

old cocoyam *See* taro.

Old Fashioned A cocktail made of bourbon, water, bitters and a sugar cube or sugar syrup served over ice in a squat glass called an old-fashioned glass and garnished with a maraschino cherry and orange slice.

old-fashioned glass A short, cylindrical glass with a heavy, faceted base and ranging in size from 3 to 10 fl. oz.; used for short drinks on the rocks.

old-fashioned glass

old-fashioned oats *See* oats, rolled.

old greengage *See* greengage.

Old Heidelberg A soft Liederkranz-style cheese made in Illinois from cow's milk.

Old Peculier The proprietary name of a strong, dark English ale with a sweet, heavy flavor.

Old Tom Gin An English sweetened gin.

oleic acid (oh-LAY-ic) A monounsaturated fatty acid that is one of the principal fatty acids present in foods.

oleic acid derived from tall oil fatty acids A food additive used as a lubricant, binder, defoaming agent and/or component in the manufacture of other food additives.

olenina (ah-leen-een-ya) Russian for game venison.

oleo *See* margarine.

oleoresins The extracts from spices that contain the volatile and nonvolatile flavor components.

Olestra (OH-less-trah) A molecularly restructured fat (a sucrose polyester) that passes through the human body without being absorbed, thus adding no calories or cholesterol to the food in which it is used; available for use only in commercial food processing.

oliebollen (O-le-bawl-luh) A Dutch pastry consisting of a ball of yeast dough with or without a sweetener and with various fillings; it is fried in hot oil or lard.

Olifantsrivier; Olifants River Valley A grape-growing and wine-producing region of South Africa known primarily for producing bulk wine for distilling into grape spirits and brandy.

olio (oh-lee-oh) A heavily spiced Spanish stew of meats, vegetables and chickpeas.

olio (OL-yoa) Italian for oil.

olio di sansa d'oliva (oh-le-oh dee san-sah doh-lee-vah) Italian for olive pomace oil; the main ingredient is pomace oil extracted using solvents from the pulp remaining after pressing.

olipodrigo (oh-lee-poe-dree-go) A Dutch one-pot meal of meats and vegetables.

oliva (o-LEE-vay) Italian for olive.

olivada (oh-lee-VAH-dah) An Italian spread that consists of black olives, olive oil and black pepper.

olive The small fruit of a tree (*Olea europaea*) native to the Mediterranean region; it has a single pit, a high oil content, a green color before ripening and a green or black color after ripening and an inedibly bitter flavor when raw; it is eaten on its own after washing, soaking and pickling or pressed for oil; available in a range of sizes, including (from smallest to largest) medium, colossal, supercolossal and jumbo.

olive (o-leev) French for olive.

Olive (o-LEE-veh) German for olive.

oliven (ohl-eev-er) Norwegian for olive.

olive oil An oil obtained by pressing tree-ripened olives; it has a distinctive fruity, olive flavor and is graded according to its degree of acidity; used as a cooking medium, flavoring and ingredient.

olive oil, extra virgin Olive oil produced from the first cold pressing, the finest and fruitiest; it has a pale straw to bright green color and not more than 1% acid.

olive oil, light An olive oil resulting from the last pressing; it has a very mild flavor, light color, high smoke point and up to 3% acid.

olive oil, pure An olive oil that has been cleaned, filtered and stripped of much of its flavor and color by using heat and mechanical devices during the refining process; it has up to 3% acid.

olive oil, virgin Olive oil with 2% acid; it has a less fruity flavor than extra virgin olive oil and a pale yellow to medium yellow-green color.

olives cassées Cracked green olives soaked in salt water flavored with fennel; made in France's Provence region, they are eaten as is or used in cooking.

Olivet (oh-lee-veh) A soft French cow's milk cheese available in three forms: (1) unripened, fresh cream cheese–style cheese made from whole milk, sometimes with cream added; (2) half-ripened or blue (surface, not interior, mold), made from whole or partly skimmed milk and known as Olivet Bleu; and (3) ripened, also made from whole or partly skimmed milk.

olivette glacate (oh-lee-VEH-teh GLAH-kah-teh) An Italian dish consisting of a veal roll stuffed with chopped ham, parsley and Parmesan, and braised in white wine, stock and tomato purée.

Olivier de Serres A pear grown in France; it has a dull greenish-brown skin and a squat shape.

olje (OL-yah) Norwegian for oil.

olla (ohl-lah) A round earthenware pot with a globular body, a wide mouth and handles; it is used to heat or hold water and to cook stews in Spain and South and Central America.

olla podrida (ohl-lah poh-DREE-dah) A traditional Spanish soup or stew.

oloroso (o-lo-RO-so) A type of sherry (no flor forms during aging); it is full bodied, semisweet and dark amber to walnut in color.

olsuppe (ohl-suh-pe) A Norwegian soup made from milk, rice, lemon peel and mild beer flavored with sugar.

oluteza (OA-loot-zah) Finnish for beer.

Olympia oyster; Olympia flat oyster A small Pacific flat oyster native to the northwest U.S. coast; it has a grayish-white shell and an extremely delicate flavor.

omar (oh-mahr) Russian for lobster.

omble *See* Arctic char.

omble chevalier (ombl she-vahl-yay) French for Arctic char.

omble de fontaine (ombl duh fohn-tain) French for brook trout.

omega fatty acids Named for the position of the endmost double bond in a fatty acid, it is a group of essential fatty acids, occurring naturally in fish oils and certain vegetable oils, believed to be particularly beneficial to coronary health; includes omega-6 (linoleic acid and arachidonic acid) and omega-3 (linolenic acid).

omelet; omelette (AHM-leht) A dish made from beaten eggs, seasonings and sometimes milk or water, cooked in butter until firm; it can be plain or filled with sweet or savory fillings and served flat or folded.

omeleta (oh-mu-leh-tah) Portuguese for omelette.

omelet pan A shallow pan with gently curved sides, a flat bottom and a single long handle; available with a nonstick surface and in 6- to 10-in. diameters.

omelet pan

omellatta *See* tortilha.

omenat (OH-mah-nah) Finnish for apple.

omnivore An animal that eats both plant and animal foods.

omum *See* ajowan seeds.

onaga (oh-nah-gah) Hawaiian for red snapper.

oncom (on-com) A fermented paste made from the residue of soybeans that have been used to make bean curd; it is usually eaten fried.

onde-onde (on-da on-da) Indonesian sweet rice balls that are poached and rolled in shredded coconut.

ondulati (OHN-duh-lah-teh) Italian for wavy and used to describe wavy pasta.

one mix A cake-mixing method in which all of the ingredients are combined and beaten at one time.

one-pot meal A dish in which all of the foods (the meat, vegetables and starches) are cooked in one pot (e.g., New England boiled dinner).

one-stage method A cookie-mixing method in which all of the ingredients are added to the bowl at once.

one-two-three-four cake A simple American yellow cake with a recipe that is easy to remember: 1 cup shortening, 2 cups sugar, 3 cups flour and 4 eggs plus flavoring and leavening.

onglet (on-GLAY) A French cut of the beef carcass; it consists of two small muscles joined by the elastic membrane that supports the diaphragm.

onigiri (oh-nah-GHEE-ree) A Japanese dish consisting of rice formed into a ball or triangle around a small morsel of strong-tasting food such as a pickled plum or salted cod roe.

onion 1. Any of a variety of strongly aromatic and flavored bulbous vegetables of the lily family (genus *Allium*) and native to central Asia; flavors range from relatively sweet to strongly pungent, the color of the outer papery layer ranges from white to yellow to red, the shape ranges from spherical to ovoid and sizes vary depending on the variety (larger onions tend to be sweeter and milder); an onion can be eaten raw, cooked like a vegetable or used as a flavoring. 2. Commonly, a medium-sized to large spherical to slightly ovoid onion (*Allium cepa*) with a bright golden yellow outer layer, crisp white flesh and strong, pungent flavor; also known as a yellow onion.

onion flakes Onions that have been dried and cut into flakes.

onion powder Dehydrated grated onions.

onion salt A mixture of dried powdered onions and salt.

onion sauce An English sauce made from onions cooked in butter and cream; it is usually served with shoulder of lamb.

ono A saltwater fish of the mackerel family found off Hawaii; it has flaky, firm, lean flesh that whitens when cooked, a mild flavor and an average market weight of 20–40 lb. (9–18 kg); it is used for sashimi; also known as wahoo.

on-off sales The sale of alcoholic beverages by an appropriately licensed commercial establishment to customers for both on-site and off-premises consumption.

on-premise outlets Commercial establishments such as bars, taverns, restaurants and the like where alcoholic beverages are sold for consumption on the premises.

on scholarship Slang for a bartender who spends too much time talking to customers while his or her colleagues do most of the work.

on tap A marketing term for an alcoholic beverage (usually beer) available in and dispensed from a keg, container or other system and not served in individually sized containers.

Ontario apple A large, North American traditional apple with a yellow-green skin and a delicate white flesh.

ontbijtje (ont-bee-tea-ah) A Dutch breakfast of cheese, herring, bread and beer.

on the half shell Raw shellfish served in their bottom shell, usually on a bed of crushed ice with lemon juice, cocktail sauce, horseradish, ketchup or other condiments.

on the house Slang for when an item for which there would otherwise be a charge is given to the customer for free.

on the rocks An alcoholic beverage served over ice without water or a mixer; also called a lowball.

on the yeast The period during a wine's second fermentation when it is allowed to remain in contact with the yeast; this sometimes contributes a yeasty aroma to the wine.

oobalana (who-baa-laa-naa) Hindi for boil.

oolong tea One of the three principal types of tea; the leaves are partially fermented to combine characteristics of black and green teas; particularly popular in China and Japan, the beverage is generally a pale color with a mild, fragrant flavor. *See* black tea *and* green tea.

ooyala A variety of yam.

OP *See* oven prepared.

opah A saltwater fish found off Hawaii; it has a large-flaked, fatty, pinkish flesh and a market weight of 60–200 lb. (27.1–90.0 kg); also known as a moonfish.

opakapaka; opaka-paka (oh-pah-kah-pah-kah) A variety of snapper found off Hawaii; it has pink skin, a moist, light pink flesh that whitens when cooked, a delicate flavor and a market weight of 1–12 lb. (0.45–5.4 kg).

opal basil A variety of basil with purple crinkled leaves and a slightly milder flavor than sweet basil; available fresh and dried.

opaque 1. Not transparent. 2. A beer- and wine-tasting term for a product such as a stout or a dark red wine through which light does not penetrate.

open; opened 1. A wine-tasting term for a wine that is ready to drink. *See* closed. 2. A cheese-tasting term used to describe an interior with large or small holes, ranging from a dense pattern of uniform sizes to a random scattering of irregular shapes.

open bar A social function at which guests receive both their alcoholic and nonalcoholic beverages free; also known as a host bar, host's bar, hosted bar and sponsored bar.

open container law A law regulating the consumption of alcoholic beverages in public areas by prohibiting open containers of alcoholic beverages.

open cup mushroom A stage in the growth of a cultivated mushroom when the brownish-pink gills are visible and the cap is darkened and speckled.

open date A date stamped by a manufacturer, distributor or retailer on a food product's label so that the consumer can determine its freshness; the date is usually preceded by the phrase "use by" or "best if used by"; also known as freshness date. *See* closed date.

open-faced sandwich A slice of bread topped with foods such as cheese, cucumbers, sliced meats and so on; served cold or hot (it is usually heated by pouring hot gravy over it).

opening cash *See* cashier's bank.

opening inventory The value of the goods on hand at the beginning of a given period.

open pit A barbecue cooking pit or style of cooking in which the meat is placed directly over hardwood coals. *See* closed pit.

open side The left side of a beef carcass; also known as the loose side. *See* closed side.

open state *See* license state.

Opera A cocktail made of gin, Dubonnet rouge and Maraschino liqueur; garnished with a twist of lemon. *See* gâteau l'opera.

opihi A small mollusk found along the Hawaiian coast; it has a black shell, a flavor similar to that of an oyster, and a chewy, snail-like texture.

Oporto (OH-pour-toe) *See* Porto.

oppskrnift (ohp-skrift) Norwegian for recipe.

oppvarter (ohp-var-ter) Norwegian for waiter.

Opus One A red wine made principally from Cabernet Sauvignon grapes and produced in Napa Valley, California, as a joint venture between the Baron de Rothschild of Château Mouton-Rothschild in Bordeaux and Robert Mondavi.

orach A plant native to Asia and Siberia; A salad green with arrow-shaped leaves and a mild spinach flavor; also known as mountain spinach.

orange Any of a variety of citrus (*Citrus sinensis*) with juicy, orange-colored segmented flesh, a thin to moderately thick orange-colored rind and a flavor ranging from bitter to tart to sweet; depending on the variety, an orange can be eaten fresh, cooked in sweet or savory dishes, juiced or used as a flavoring or aromatic.

orange French for orange.

Orange (o-rahnja) German for orange.

orangeade *See* ade.

orange and port wine sauce An English sauce made from orange juice and port, thickened with cornstarch; it is usually served with fried or grilled poultry.

orange bitters Bittersweet, orange-flavored bitters.

Orange Blossom A cocktail made of gin and orange juice; garnished with an orange slice.

orange blossom honey A clear liquid honey with a pale reddish-gold color and a delicate flavor; made principally from orange blossoms in Florida and California.

orange crush *See* ade.

orange fannings Relatively large particles of broken tea leaves. *See* fannings *and* dust.

orange flower water A clear, fragrant liquid distilled from bitter orange flowers; used to flavor baked goods, confections (especially in Middle Eastern cuisine) and beverages.

orange juice The juice of an orange.

orange oil The oil expressed from the fruit's fresh peel.

orange peel The rind of an orange; it is used for flavorings or is candied; also known as zest.

orange pekoe (PEE-koh) The smallest size grade of whole black tea leaves, generally the ones picked from the top of the plant.

orangequat An orange and kumquat citrus hybrid.

Orangeriver A grape-growing and wine-producing region of South Africa in the hot, arid northern Cape; various dry white wines, dessert wines and sultana raisins are produced there.

orange rockfish A member of the rockfish family found off the U.S. West Coast; it has a light olive-gray skin with prominent orange-red colorations, three yellow-orange stripes across the head, reddish-orange streaks along its body, an average market length of 30 in. (76 cm), firm, white flesh and a mild flavor.

orange roughy A fish found off New Zealand and Australia; it has a bright orange skin, a firm, pearly white flesh, a low fat content, a bland flavor and an average market weight of 3.5 lb. (1.6 kg).

orange sauce *See* bigarade, sauce.

orange syrup A sweet orange-flavored syrup used as a flavoring, especially in beverages.

orata (oa-RAA-tah) Italian for the daurade of Provence.

orchid bulbs Bulbs of certain orchids of the *Orchis* genus; they are dried and then ground and used to make salep.

Orchid Island chevre A cheese made from goat's milk on the Big Island of Hawaii; it has a mild flavor and a creamy texture; also known as Puna goat cheese.

order form A form used to record all goods (specifying quantity and price) ordered from a purveyor and to verify that they were later received.

ordinary A tasting term for a food or beverage (especially wine) that is sound but lacks distinction and finesse.

orecchiette (oh-rayk-kee-EHT-tay) Italian for little ears and used to describe pasta that are formed from a twist of the fingertips.

orécchio di guida (oh-rayk-kee-oh dee gwee-who-da) Italian for cloud ear mushroom.

orecchióne gelone (oh-rayk-kee-oh geh-lon-ae) Italian for oyster mushroom.

oregano (oh-REHG-uh-noh) An herb (*Origanum vulgare*) and the wild form of marjoram; it has a woody stalk with clumps of tiny, dark green leaves that have a pungent, peppery flavor and are used, fresh or dried, principally in Italian and Greek cuisines; also known as wild marjoram. *See* marjoram.

oregano

Oregon grape *See* barberry.

Oregon tea A beverage made from boiling water and yerba buena.

oreh Russian for pine nut.

oreille de judas (oh-rehy duh juh-dah) French for cloud ear mushroom.

oreillette (oh-reh-yet) French for oyster mushroom.

oreja de judas (oh-ray-hah day hoo-dahs) Spanish for cloud ear mushroom.

orekh (oh-rack) Russian for nut.

orelheira (oh-ra-ya-raw) Trimmed, smoked pig's ear; an important ingredient in Portuguese stews.

OREO Proprietary name for a cookie composed of two round, flat, crisp chocolate cookies sandwiched together with a creamy white filling.

organ A part of the body having a special function; often found in pairs.

organic 1. Traditionally used to describe the class of compounds found in or derived from plants or animals; now also included are all other carbon compounds. 2. Foods, usually plant foods sold fresh or minimally processed, that are grown without chemicals or other incidental food additives such as pesticides.

organically grown wine A wine made from organically grown grapes and naturally vinified, with minimal amounts of sulfites added.

organic farming A method of farming that does not rely on synthetic pesticides, fungicides, herbicides or fertilizers.

organic food 1. A food grown without the use of chemical fertilizers, pesticides or other such substances. 2. A labeling term approved by the FDA for a processed food product, 95% of which (exclusive of water and salt) is grown according to federal organic farming standards.

organ meats Edible organs and glands such as the heart, kidneys, liver and sweetbreads. *See* variety meats.

organoleptic (or-guh-nl-EHP-tihk) The analysis and evaluation of any beverage by using the senses of sight, smell, taste and touch.

orgeat (OHR-zhat) 1. A sweet syrup made from almonds, sugar and rosewater or orange flower water; its strong almond flavor is used as a flavoring for cocktails and baked goods. 2. A barley–almond mixture, similar to English barley water. *See* almond syrup.

oribu (oh-ree-boo) Japanese for olive.

oriental eggplant *See* eggplant, Asian.

oriental garlic *See* chives, garlic.

oriental sesame oil An oil obtained from roasted sesame seeds; it is darker and more strongly flavored than sesame oil and is used as an accent oil.

origan (ko-ree-gahng) French for oregano.

origano (oa-REE-gah-noa) Italian for wild marjoram.

original specific gravity In beer making, the specific gravity of the wort before fermentation; also known as starting specific gravity.

orkinos (ore-key-noss) Turkish for tuna.

Orkney A firm to hard cheese made in the Orkney Islands, Scotland, from cow's milk; it has a white color, sometimes tinted orange and a mild flavor; also available smoked.

Orléans, sauce A French compound sauce made from a fish velouté flavored with white wine and mushrooms, seasoned with cayenne and finished with crayfish butter.

Orleans sugar An archaic term for brown sugar or molasses.

orlistat A compound that reduces the absorption of fat in the intestines.

ormer (OHR-mehr) A variety of medium-sized abalone found in the Atlantic Ocean from England to Senegal; it has a flat shell with spiral stripes, brown or pink speckles, slight marbling, and an ivory flesh with a chewy texture and mild flavor.

ornamental kale *See* kale, ornamental.

orodha ya vyakula (oh-row-dah yah vee-ah-kah-lah) *See* menyu.

oroshi-gane (oh-BOH-shee-GAH-may) A Japanese grater.

ørred (URR-erdh) Danish for trout.

ørret (URR-eht) Norwegian for trout.

orris root The fragrant rootstock of *Iris germanica*, formerly used to restore the perfume to Bordeaux wines destroyed by mixing or blending.

ortanique (or-tah-knee-kay) A member of the orange family grown in Jamaica; it is a seedless hybrid of the satsuma and ugli and has a loose skin and sweet flesh.

Orval (or-val) The proprietary name of a Belgian monastery beer that is orange in color and full of flavor, with a slightly bitter aftertaste.

Orvieto (ohr-v'yay-toh) A crisp, straw-colored white wine made from the Procanico grape in Italy's Umbria region; available as secco and abbocato.

orzechy (oh-sheh-hi) Polish for nuts.

orzo (OHR-zoh) Italian for barley and used to describe rice-shaped pasta.

os (oss) French for bone.

Oscar; Oskar (OS-kuhr) A dish that consists of the main ingredient (e.g., veal cutlets) sautéed, topped with crab or crayfish meat and béarnaise and garnished with spears of asparagus.

oseille (oh-zehj) French for sorrel.

osetra A very flavorful caviar; the medium-sized crispy eggs are golden yellow to brown and quite oily.

osetrina (ah-see-tree-nah) Russian for sturgeon.

osetrina varjonaja (oh-sah-tree-nah vah-ree-oh-nah-yah) A Russian dish of sturgeon poached in Champagne flavored with butter and lemon.

OSHA *See* Occupational Safety and Health Act.

oshibori (oh-shee-BOH-ree) Japanese for the small wet cloth offered to diners before a meal to freshen up.

oshifima (oh-she-FEE-mah) A Namibian dish consisting of a thick cornmeal porridge, sometimes flavored with chiles.

oshi-zushi (owe-shi-zoo-shi) Sushi pressed into a wooden box mold, covered with toppings, then unmolded and cut into squares.

oshongali (oh-shawn-gah-lee) A Namibian dish of black-eyed peas flavored with chiles.

osmanthus (ohs-mahn-toos) A fragrant Chinese liqueur.

osmanthus flowers Tiny, sweet-scented white flowers grown in China and used to make a fragrant liqueur or as a garnish (either fresh, candied or preserved in a spirit with sugar).

osmosis The tendency of a solution to pass through a semipermeable membrane from an area where it is more highly concentrated into one where it is less concentrated, in an effort to equalize the concentrations.

ossenhaas (AWS-suh-hahs) A Dutch cut of the beef carcass; it is the tenderloin.

osso (AW-soh) Italian for bone.

osso (oh-soo) Portuguese for bone.

osso buco; ossobuco (AW-soh BOO-koh) An Italian dish consisting of veal shanks braised in olive oil, white wine, stock, onions, tomatoes, garlic, carrots, celery and lemon peel, garnished with gremolada and served with risotto.

ost (oost) Scandinavian for cheese.

osteomalacia An adult disease caused by a deficiency of vitamin D; symptoms include softening of the bones.

osteria (oh-steh-REE-ah) 1. An Italian neighborhood wine shop or tavern. 2. A simple Italian inn or restaurant.

østers (URSS-tersh) Norwegian for oyster.

ostia (ohs-tee-ah) Italian wafer paper made from wheat starch and used to line molds and baking pans for pastries, desserts and confections such as panforte and torrone.

ostkaka (host-kah-kah) A Swedish cheesecake flavored with currants.

ostra (OS-trahss) Portuguese and Spanish for oyster.

ostraka (os-trah-kah) Greek for crustaceans fried in oil.

ostreon (os-tra-on) Greek for oysters.

ostrica (o-STREE-kah) Italian for oyster.

ostrich A large flightless bird native to Africa; its meat is lean and purple, turning brown when cooked, and has a flavor similar to that of lean beef. *See* emu *and* rhea.

ostrich fern *See* fiddlehead fern.

ostriy (os-tree) Russian for spicy.

osushi (oh-SOO-shee) The honorific form for Japanese vinegared-rice dishes. *See* sushi.

ot (eu) Vietnamese for chile pepper.

otaheite Tahitian for ambarella.

otaheite apple *See* ambarella.

otaheite gooseberry A medium-sized fruit (*Phyllanthus acidus*) grown in Southeast Asia and Central America; it has a ribbed, light yellow skin and tart flavor and is often pickled or used as a filling for baked goods.

Othello A British pastry named for the Moor in Shakespeare's *Othello;* made with two round cookies or biscuits sandwiched together with chocolate buttercream, then coated completely with chocolate fondant.

otoro (oh-toh-roh) Japanese for the fatty flesh found at the belly near the body cavity of a tuna (maguro); it is used for sushi and sashimi. *See* akami *and* chutoro.

O-toso (OH-toh-soh) A Japanese medicinal drink made by infusing herbs in mirin.

otsumami (OH-tsoo-MAH-mee) Japanese for tidbits and the small plates of food usually eaten while drinking sake or other alcoholic drinks.

OTW On the way; slang for a customer who has made a reservation and has called to say that he or she will be late and requested that the reservation be held.

ou Romanian for egg.

ouanachie (oo-ahn-ah-chee) A Canadian land-locked freshwater salmon; it is generally small with a mild flavor.

oulle (oh-oo-jyay) A Spanish earthenware pot.

ounce beverage control system An automated system that records and analyzes beverage sales by number and type of drinks dispensed.

Our Home A cocktail made of gin, peach brandy, dry vermouth, lemon juice and egg white.

ouriço (oh-ree-soo) Portuguese for sea urchin.

oursin (oor-zinh) French for sea urchin.

outside round *See* bottom round.

ouvido beira la mego (oo-vee-doe ba-e-rah law mah-go) Boned, dried and smoked pig's head; it is used in Portuguese stews.

ouzo (OO-zoh) A Greek brandy with a strong anise flavor; it is clear, turning cloudy when water is added.

oval dariole *See* aspic mold.

Ovaltine The proprietary name for a powder made from malt extract, dried milk and eggs; the beverage, made by adding hot or cold milk to the powder, is considered a nourishing food and a nonalcoholic nightcap.

Ovelheira *See* Queijo de Ovelha.

oven An enclosed space used for baking and roasting.

oven-dried tomato A tomato that has been dried in an oven; it has a dark red color, a chewy texture and a flavor that is not quite as strong as that of a sun-dried tomato; available dried or packed in oil (including flavored oils). *See* sun-dried tomato.

oven frying A method of frying without turning; the food, usually meat, is dredged in flour, rolled in melted fat, placed on a baking sheet and baked in a hot oven; also known as ovenizing.

ovenizing *See* oven frying.

oven prepared (OP) A food that, when purchased, needs no further preparation other than cooking.

ovenproof A description for a baking dish or other item of cookware, usually made of glass, pottery or ceramics, that can withstand an oven's high temperatures.

oven ready A food ready for cooking; it can be a commercially processed food product or one made on-site at a food services facility.

oven spring The rapid rise of yeast goods in a hot oven, resulting from the production and expansion of trapped gases.

ovenware Heat-resistant dishes of glass, pottery or ceramics used for baking and serving foods.

overaged A wine-tasting term for a wine that has been aged longer than necessary; the wine's color usually browns and flavor is usually lost.

over egg An egg that is flipped once during frying; the yolk is often broken during the process. *See* sunny-side-up egg.

overfining A hazy condition in beer or wine caused by excessive use of a fining agent.

overhead costs A term used in the food services industry to refer to all costs except food and labor costs.

overpouring Pouring a quantity of an alcoholic beverage in excess of a standardized recipe.

overproduction The production of a quantity in excess of normal needs or demands.

overproof *v.* To allow a yeast dough to rise (ferment) too long. *n.* Alcoholic beverages with an alcohol content greater than 50% or 100 proof.

overripe A wine-tasting term for the raisinlike aroma and flavor of a wine made from overly ripened grapes; the wine usually has a high alcohol content.

overrun The increase in volume of ice cream or similar frozen products caused by incorporation of air during the freezing process.

overweight Having an abnormal amount of fat on the body (generally, being 10–20% above the appropriate weight for height). *See* obese.

ovine Pertaining to sheep.

ovn (oven) Norwegian for oven.

ovo (AH-voh) Portuguese for egg.

ovoid A three-dimensional shape with an oval cross section.

ovolactovegetarian A vegetarian who does not eat meat, poultry or fish but does eat eggs and dairy products. *See* lactovegetarian *and* vegan.

ovoli (oa-VAWL-lee) Italian for egg shaped and used to describe very small forms of mozzarella.

ovoschi (oh-voh-she) Russian for vegetables.

ovos moles (oh-voss moe-loss) A mixture of egg yolks, sugar and sometimes rice used to make Portuguese sweets; it is available in various shapes or sold plain in painted wooden boxes.

ovos moles d'averio (oh-voss moe-loss dahv-e-ree-oh) A Portuguese egg custard–like dessert made from rice flour or cooked puréed rice, sugar and egg yolks and used as a topping for cakes, as a filling for tarts, cakes or marzipan candies and as a dessert sauce.

oxalic acid An acid found in certain plants (e.g., rhubarb, spinach and sorrel); it inhibits the absorption of calcium and iron and is poisonous in large amounts.

oxalis (AHKS-ah-lis) French for oca.

ox bile extract A food additive derived from ox bile and used as a surfactant.

Oxford pudding A British dessert consisting of an apricot tart topped with meringue.

Oxford sauce A British sauce of red currant jelly dissolved with port and flavored with shallots, orange zest and mustard; usually served with game.

oxidation 1. A chemical reaction between a substance and oxygen; it changes the nature of the substance, usually to its detriment. 2. An energy-releasing metabolic process during which a nutrient breaks down and its components combine with oxygen.

oxidized A wine-tasting term, especially for a white or rosé wine that, through exposure to oxygen, develops a brown tinge as well as an aroma and flavor reminiscent of Madeira. *See* maderized.

oxidized polyethylene A food additive used as a protective coating on many fresh fruits and vegetables.

oxidizing agent A type of food additive used to oxidize a food component to produce a more stable product; also known as a reducing agent.

oxkött (OOKS-tyurt) Swedish for beef.

oxtail A fabricated cut of the beef primal round or veal primal leg; it is a portion of the tail and contains many bones but is quite flavorful.

ox tongue mushroom *See* beefsteak mushroom.

oxygen A colorless, odorless, tasteless gaseous element found free in the atmosphere and essential for respiration; it is also a component of organic matter.

oxystearin A food additive used as a crystallization inhibitor, sequestrant and/or release agent in processed foods such as vegetable oils and shortenings.

oyako nabe (oh-YAH-koh NAH-bay) A Japanese chicken and egg dish.

oyster A member of a large family of bivalve mollusks found in saltwater regions worldwide; generally, they have a rough gray shell (the top shell is flat and the bottom is somewhat convex) and a grayish tan flesh with a soft texture and briny flavor; they are eaten raw or cooked; there are four principal types of domestic oysters: Atlantic oysters, European flat oysters, Olympia oysters and Pacific oysters.

oyster crab A variety of crab that lives in the gill of an oyster and shares the food ingested by the host.

oyster cracker A small, round, slightly hard cracker; it is traditionally served with oyster stew.

oyster knife A knife used to pry open oyster shells; it has a fat, 3-in.-long, pointed, arrow-shaped blade and usually a protective flange for the hand; also known as a shucking knife.

oyster knife

oysterleaf An herb (*Mertensia maritima*) with fleshy, pale yellow-green leaves and a flavor reminiscent of oysters.

oyster meat In poultry, it consists of the two succulent ovals of meat along either side of the backbone, level with the thigh.

oyster mushroom A wild, fan-shaped mushroom (*Pleurotus ostreatus*) that grows in clusters on dead logs and tree stumps and is now cultivated in limited quantities; it has a gray to dark-brownish-gray cap, a grayish-white stem and a slightly peppery, oysterlike flavor that becomes milder when cooked; also known as a tree oyster mushroom, phoenix mushroom and sovereign mushroom.

oyster plant *See* salsify.

oyster sauce A thick brown concentrated sauce made from oysters, brine and soy sauce; used as a flavoring in Asian cuisines.

oysters Bienville (bee-en-vell) An American dish of oysters covered with a béchamel, green peppers, onions, cheese and bread crumbs and baked.

oysters, cupped A category of oysters characterized by two concave, somewhat circular valves and a flattened spherical flesh.

oysters, flat A category of oysters characterized by two shallow concave, somewhat elongated valves and a flattened ovoid flesh.

oyster shell A nutrient supplement derived from powdered oyster shells and intended to supply calcium.

oysters Rockefeller (OEHY-stur rock-ee-fehl-lehr) An American dish of oysters served hot on the half shell with a topping of spinach, bread crumbs and seasonings.

Ozark Beauty strawberry A variety of ever-bearing strawberry; the fruit are large (up to 4 in.) and well flavored.

Ozark pudding A baked pudding made with chopped apples, walnuts and vanilla and served with rum-flavored whipped cream.

Ozette A variety of small, long potato with a yellow skin and flesh.

ozone A naturally occurring gas used as an antimicrobial agent in bottled waters.

ozoni (oh-ZOH-nee) A Japanese chicken and vegetable soup served in deep bowls over rice cakes; also known as zoni.

ozor (oh-zor) Polish for tongue.

P *See* pale.

pa amb tomaquetá (pah aam toh-mah-kae-tah) Bread toasted with olive oil and garlic and then rubbed with ripe tomatoes; it is a specialty of Spain's Catalonia region.

paan (pahn) Hindi for leaves of the betel pepper plant; also the digestive preparation made with betel leaf, lime paste and betel nut.

paani (pah-neh) Hindi for water.

Paarl One of the premier grape-growing and wine-producing regions of South Africa; it includes the wards of Franschloek and Wellington and produces a large variety of wines, from dry whites to rich reds as well as sherries, ports, brandies and sparkling wines (using the Méthode Cap Classique).

pabellòn criollo (pah-bay-jyon cree-oh-jyoh) A Venezuelan dish of simmered, shredded flank steak served with sautéed bananas, rice and black beans.

pa boeuk *See* trey reach.

paca (pot-sah) Serbo-Croat for duckling.

pachadi (pah-cha-dee) An Indian yogurt salad made with raw vegetables and flavored with fried black mustard seeds.

Pacific barracuda A fish found in the tropical waters of the Pacific Ocean; it has a silvery skin, an average market weight of 4–8 lb. (1.8–3.6 kg), a white flesh with a firm texture, a moderately high fat content and a slightly sweet flavor.

Pacific clams Any of several varieties of clams found along the U.S. West Coast; they generally have hard shells; significant varieties include the butter clam, geoduck clam, Manila clam and pismo clam.

Pacific cod *See* cod, Pacific.

Pacific halibut A variety of halibut found in the Pacific Ocean from California to Canada; it has lean white flesh with a sweet, mild flavor and firm texture; also known as Alaskan halibut, northern Pacific halibut and western halibut.

Pacific oysters; Pacific cupped oysters; Pacific king oysters Any of several varieties of oysters native to the China Sea, the waters off Japan and other areas of the Pacific rim and now aquafarmed along the U.S. West Coast; they generally have a high domed, compact shell that can grow as large as 1 ft. (30.4 cm) in diameter and silvery-gray to gold to almost white flesh; also known as Japanese oysters.

Pacific pink scallop A variety of scallop found in the Pacific Ocean from Alaska to California; it has a rounded pink to pale yellow to white shell and tender, sweet, white meat.

Pacific pollock *See* pollock, Alaskan.

Pacific sea herring *See* sardine, Pacific.

Pacific venus clam, large A variety of venus clam found in tropical waters of the Pacific Ocean; it has an ivory to brown shell that measures 3 in. (7.6 cm) in diameter.

package goods Liquor sold in packages rather than by the drink.

package store A store licensed to sell alcoholic beverages in closed containers; the beverages cannot be consumed on the premises.

pack date A date stamped by a manufacturer or distributor on a food product's label, indicating when the food was processed, manufactured or packaged.

packed under federal inspection The voluntary inspection program of the USDC for fish and shellfish; it signifies that fish and shellfish are safe and wholesome, properly labeled, have reasonably good flavor and odor and have been produced under inspection in an official establishment; also known as PUFI (puffy).

packer brand name *See* brand name.

paczki (poonch-key) A round puffball-like Polish doughnut filled with raspberry preserves, custard, or strawberry, poppy seed, or prune filling.

pad (pahd) Thai for stir-fry.

padang (pah-dang) A term for very spicy dishes from Sumatra.

padaria (pah-dah-tee-ah) Portuguese for bakery; also known as confeitaria.

paddock (pah-dok) In Australia, a specific vineyard.

paddy-straw mushroom; padi-straw mushroom *See* straw mushroom.

padek (pah-dek) A Laotian fish sauce and flavoring made from fish preserved in brine and rice bran.

pad thai (pahd tah-ee) A Thai stir-fried dish of cooked rice noodles, tofu, shrimp, crushed peanuts, nam pla, bean sprouts, eggs, garlic and chiles.

paella (pah-AY-lyah) A rustic Spanish dish of rice, vegetables, sausages, poultry, fish and shellfish seasoned with saffron.

paella pan A wide, shallow pan with slightly sloping sides and two handles; often made of metal or earthenware, it is used for cooking paella. *See* sarten.

paella pan

pære (PAER-err) Norwegian for pear.

Paglia (pahg-LE-ah) A Gorgonzola-style cheese made in Switzerland from cow's milk; it has a semisoft body and a mellow flavor.

paglia e fieno (PAL-ya ee FYE-noh) Italian for straw and hay and used to describe long, thin, flat ribbons of yellow and green pasta.

Paglia-style cheeses A general term for soft-ripened Italian cow's milk cheeses sold under various proprietary names; they have a white, bloomy rind that becomes beige-mottled when ripe and a straw-colored interior with a mushroom–garlic aroma and flavor.

pagma A Tibetan tomato sauce flavored with fenugreek, garlic, onions, chiles, turmeric and soy sauce.

pagophagia The practice of eating large quantities of ice.

paid bar An event in which the guest pays for his or her own drinks, usually by purchasing tickets in advance.

païdakia (pah-ee-tha-khia) Greek for lamb chops.

pai gwat (pah-e goo-at) Chinese pork spareribs served with barbecue sauce or sour plum sauce.

paillarde (pahy-lahrd) A scallop of meat or poultry pounded until thin; usually grilled.

paille (pi-yay) French for potatoes that are cut in thin, straw-like shreds; also known as straw potatoes.

pain (pahn) French for bread.

pain à la bière (pahn ah lah bee-yair) French for beer loaf and used to describe a robust wheat bread made with beer.

pain à la grecque (pahn ah lah grah-kew) A Belgian bread that is rolled in sugar before baking; the heart-shaped version is known as coeur de Bruxelles.

painappuree (PAH-een-AH-poo-roo) Japanese for pineapple.

pain au chocolat (pahn oh shok-kol-lah) A French pastry consisting of a rectangle of croissant dough rolled around dark chocolate.

pain au fromage blanc (pahn oh froh-MAJH blahn) French for bread with farmer cheese and used to describe wheat bread dough enriched with farmer cheese.

pain au son (pahn oh sohn) French for bran loaf and used to describe wheat bread containing 20% bran.

pain boulot (pahn booh-low) *See* pain rond.

pain complet (pahn kohm-pleh) French for whole wheat bread.

pain de mie (pahn duh me) French for white wheat sandwich bread.

pain d'épice (pahn d'eh-spehs) A rich, spicy, breadlike French cake, similar to gingerbread.

Pain de Pyrenees (pahn duh peer-rey-ney) *See* Doux de Montagne.

pain ordinaire (pahn or-dinn-AIR) French for an ordinary or daily bread and used to describe a bread made with only white wheat flour, yeast, water and salt.

pain perdu (pahn pehr-DOO) French for lost bread and used to describe French toast.

pain rond (pahn rohn) French for round loaf and used to describe a flat, round loaf of bread that can weigh up to 4 lb. (2 kg); also known as pain boulot.

painted pony A small brown bean with a white eye.

paio (pah-EE-oo) Portuguese smoked ham or pork filet meat; it is very lean and eaten raw.

paiola (pah-ee-oh-lah) A Portuguese sausage made with pork and fat and seasoned with paprika, pepper and garlic.

paiolo (pye-OH-loh) An Italian deep, rounded copper pan used for making polenta.

pak Thai for vegetables.

pakana (paa-kaa-naa) Hindi for to cook.

pak bung (pak boong) Thai for swamp cabbage.

pak chee farang (pak chi falaang) Thai for parsley.

pak choi (bahk-CHOY) *See* bok choy.

pakna (paak-naa) Hindi for ripe.

pakoras (pah-KO-rah) Indian fritters of vegetables, meat, fish or nuts held together with besan and deep-fried; also known as bhajias.

paksiw (pak-siw) A Filipino term referring to fish or meat pickled with vinegar and salt and sometimes ginger and sugar, simmered until done and usually served cold with the pickling liquid.

palabok (pa-la-bok) Filipino (Tagalog) for the ingredients used to garnish dishes (e.g., flaked dried fish, pork cracklings, hard-cooked eggs, diced bean curd, scallions and dried shrimp).

palacsinta (POL-lo-cheen-to) A Hungarian dish of pancakes spread with minced ham and mushrooms, topped with grated cheese, sour milk or yogurt and heated.

palak (paa-lak) Hindi for spinach.

palamut (pah-law-moot) Turkish for bonito.

palatschinken (pah-law-shin-can) Austrian and Hungarian paper-thin sweet crêpes served either stacked with alternating layers of jam or cottage cheese and cut into wedges or wrapped around the filling and dusted with confectioners' sugar.

palava (pah-lah-vah) A Ghanaian stew of smoked fish, dried shrimp, fresh fish, meat (usually beef) and spinach flavored with tomatoes, chiles and egusi and served with gari, rice, yams or plantains.

palaver sauce; palava sauce A West African sauce made with greens, chiles, palm oil, fish, egusi and sometimes beef, tripe, pig's feet and/or chicken; it is served with foofoo.

palayok (pah-la-yok) An unglazed clay cooking pot used in the Philippines for cooking curries, rice, dried peas and dried beans.

pale 1. A labeling term for pale-colored brandies, Cognac and Armagnac; sometimes written as P. 2. A beer-tasting term for the color of some ales.

pale ale A full-bodied, amber-colored ale with a bitter flavor; also known as light ale.

pale malt Malted barley that is air-dried (as opposed to kiln-dried) to minimize color development.

palermitaine, sauce (pah-lehr-me-tain) A French compound sauce made from a demi-glaze flavored with shallots and a hearty Italian red wine, finished with shallot butter and garnished with orange zest.

paleron (pal-ROHN) A French cut of the beef carcass; similar to a chuck roast, it is cut from an area somewhat closer to the neck.

palette knife The British term for a spatula.

palillo (pah-lee-jyoh) A Peruvian herb used as a yellow food coloring.

palillos chinos (pah-lee-jyo chee-nohs) Spanish for chopsticks.

pálinka Hungarian fruit brandies with high alcohol contents.

pallet A low stand on which supplies are stacked to keep them off the floor; usually made of wood and designed so that it can be easily lifted and moved by a forklift, dolly or cart.

Palmcham (pahlm-chahm) A carbonated wine made in Ghana from the juice of the adoka tree.

palm dates *See* honey dates.

palmenta *See* pompano.

palm hearts *See* hearts of palm.

palmier (pahlm-YAY) A thin, crisp French cookie made with puff pastry dough rolled in granulated sugar; also known as an elephant ear.

palmitic acid One of the principal fatty acids present in foods.

palm-kernel oil An oil obtained from the nut (kernel) of various palms; it has a yellowish-white color, a mild flavor and a high saturated fat content; it is used in margarine and cosmetics and interchangeably with coconut oil.

palm nut; palmyra palm nut The fruit of the palmyra palm (*Borrasus flabellifer*) grown in India and Southeast Asia; the gelatinous opaque sap extracted from the nut has a mildly nutty flavor and is used in desserts; also known as siwalan (Indonesia), atap chee (Malaysia and Singapore), kaong (Philippines) and luk taan (Thailand).

palm oil An oil obtained from the pulp of the African palm's fruit (*Elaeis guineensis*); it has a red-orange color and a very high saturated fat content; used in West African and Brazilian cooking or decolored and deodorized and used for generic processed fat and oil products.

palm sugar *See* jaggery.

palm syrup A very dark, sticky syrup made from the concentrated sap of various species of palm tree; used in Middle Eastern, Indian and Asian cuisines.

palm tree cabbage *See* borecole.

palm vinegar A mild, greenish-white vinegar made from palm sap and used in adobo sauces and other Filipino dishes.

palm wine An alcoholic beverage made from the sap of the palm tree, usually a coconut or date palm.

palochkidlya edi (pah-low-key-d'lee-yah ah-dee) Russian for chopsticks.

palo cortado (PAH-lo cor-TAH-do) A rare type of sherry similar to a light oloroso but with the bouquet of an amontillado.

Paloise, sauce (pahl-wahz) A French compound sauce made from a hollandaise flavored with fresh mint; it is served with lamb or mutton; also known as sauce pau.

Palomino (pah-lo-mee-no) A white wine grape grown in Spain (where it is used principally to make sherry), Australia, South Africa and California; also known as Golden Chasselas (especially in California).

palten (pahl-tyen) A Russian black pudding flavored with nutmeg and marjoram and covered with browned butter after cooking.

pampano A small dolphinfish with an average market weight of 5 lb. (2.7 kg).

Pampelmuse (PAHM-perl-moo-zwe) German for grapefruit.

pamplemousse (pahng-pler-moos) French for grapefruit.

pan 1. Any of various metal vessels of different sizes and shapes in which foods are cooked or stored; generally, they have flat bottoms and low straight or sloped sides. 2. A pot with a single long handle and low straight or sloped sides.

pan (pahn) Japanese and Spanish for bread.

Panaché (pa-na-shay) A cocktail made with equal parts beer and lemonade; also known as a shandy. *See* shandy.

panada; panade (pah-nahd) 1. Something other than fat added to a forcemeat to enhance smoothness, aid emulsification or both; it is often béchamel, rice or crustless white bread soaked in milk. 2. A mixture for binding stuffings and dumplings, notably quenelles; it is often choux pastry, bread crumbs, fangipane, puréed potatoes or rice.

pana de pepita (pah-nah de pae-pee-tah) A large, spherical fruit of a tropical tree in the fig family; it has green, bumpy skin, a cream-colored flesh, a texture similar to that of fresh bread and a bland flavor; it can be cooked for sweet or savory dishes; also known as a panapan.

panadería (paa-naa-day-ree-ah) Spanish for bakery.

panaeng (pah-nang) A dry red Thai curry paste, usually used with beef and always cooked with coconut milk.

panage (pah-nahj) French for coating a food with bread crumbs before frying or grilling.

panais (pah-neh) French for parsnip.

Panama A cocktail made of gin, cream and a chocolate liqueur.

Panamanian Arabica coffee beans grown in Panama; the beverage has a clean, lively flavor with a light to medium body.

panapan *See* pana de pepita.

pan-broiling A dry-heat cooking method that uses conduction to transfer heat to food resting directly on a cooking surface; no fat is used and the food remains uncovered.

pancake A flat, round, leavened bread cooked on a griddle and served with butter and sweet syrup, especially for breakfast; also known as griddle cake and flapjack.

pancake syrup A sweet sauce made from corn syrup and flavored with maple; used as a topping for pancakes and waffles.

pancetta (pan-CHEH-tuh) An Italian pork belly bacon cured with salt, pepper and other spices (it is not smoked); available rolled into a cylinder and used to flavor items such as pasta dishes, sauces and forcemeats.

panch (pahunch) *See* punch.

pancit (PAHN-ceet) Filipino for noodle.

pancit bihoon (PAHN-ceet bee-hoon) Filipino rice noodles.

pancit guisado (PAHN-ceet gwee-sah-doh) Filipino pan-fried noodles.

pancit lug lug (PAHN-ceet loog loog) Filipino spaghetti-like rice noodles topped with a wide assortment of ingredients including smoked fish.

pancit sotanghon Filipino bean thread noodles.

pancreas A gland that secretes hormones (e.g., insulin used in carbohydrate metabolism) and pancreatic juice, which is composed of various enzymes and is used to digest food and neutralize stomach acids.

pancreatic duct The passage through which pancreatic juice travels from the pancreas to the duodenum.

Panda A cocktail made of gin, Slivovitz, orange juice and Calvados or applejack.

pandanus (pan-DAY-nahs) A bush (*Pandanus amaryllifolius*) native to Asia; its young, pointed leaves are used as a green food coloring and/or pungent flavoring in Asian cuisines; also known as a screw pine.

pandoro (pahn-DOH-roh) An Italian Christmas bread from Verona; similar to panettone and baked in a star-shaped mold; the eggs and butter give it a golden color.

pandoro mold A star-shaped mold used for baking pandoro.

pandowdy A deep-dish dessert made with apples or other fruit mixed with molasses or brown sugar, spices and butter, then topped with a biscuitlike dough and baked.

pandoro mold

pan-dressed A market form for fish in which the viscera, gills and scales are removed and the fins and tail are trimmed.

pan drippings *See* drippings.

pan dulces (pahn dool-chays) Mexican and Latin American sweet breads eaten for breakfast.

pane (PAA-ney) Italian for bread.

pané (pah-nay) French for to coat in bread crumbs.

pane alla salvia (pah-nay ah-lah sal-vee-ah) A sage bread made by kneading white wine and sage into a yeast dough; a specialty of Italy's Tuscany region.

pane casareccio (pah-nay cah-saw-ray-tchee-oh) 1. An Italian bread baked on the premises. 2. A round, very light loaf of bread with a light, crisp crust; a specialty of Italy's Apulia region.

pane cotto; pancotto (pahn-KOH-toh) Italian for cooked bread and used to describe a dish of stewed tomatoes, garlic and olive oil with bread.

pane di segale (pah-nay dee say-gah-lay) Italian for rye bread.

paneer *See* surati.

panela An unrefined dark brown cane sugar sold in cakes or cones and eaten plain as candies or used to make syrups for desserts in Latin American cuisines.

pane nero (pah-nay nay-row) Italian black bread made from a mixture of rye and wheat flour.

pané station A kitchen area that is organized and set aside for breading foods.

panetière, à la (pan-eh-tyayr, ah lah) A French cooking method in which foods are put into round scooped-out loaves of bread and finished in the oven.

panetteria (pah-nett-aer-eh-ah) Italian for bakery, especially for bread.

panettone (PAH-neh-TOH-nay) A sweet Italian yeast bread filled with raisins, candied citrus peel and pine nuts; traditionally baked in a rounded cylindrical mold and served as a breakfast bread or dessert.

panfish Refers to almost any small freshwater fish big enough to eat and usually pan-fried.

panforte (pahn-FOHR-tay) A dense, rich Italian fruitcake-like pastry made with honey, nuts, candied fruit and spices, baked in a flat round or square shape, then heavily dusted with confectioners' sugar; also known as a Siena cake.

pan-frying A dry-heat cooking method in which the food is placed in a moderate amount of hot fat.

panggang (pang-gang) An Indonesian cooking technique referring to foods, usually seasoned with spices, that are roasted over a fire.

pan gravy A sauce made by deglazing pan drippings from roasted meat or poultry.

pángxiè (pong-sieh) Chinese for crab.

pani An Indian dish of thin semolina puffs resembling ping-pong balls; they are filled with diced potatos and beans, flavored with tamiarind chutney and served with a watery mint sauce.

paniala A small fruit (genus *Flacorirta*) native to India and Indonesia; it has a maroon or purple skin, a whitish-yellow flesh and an acidic flavor.

panier (pah-neer) A basket traditionally used to gather grapes in France's wine regions.

panino (pah-NEE-noa) Italian for roll, biscuit or sandwich.

panko (PONG-ko) Large-flaked, unseasoned Japanese bread crumbs.

panna (PAHN-nah) Italian for cream (especially in southern Italy). *See* crema.

panna cotta (PAHN-nah COTT-ta) An Italian dessert consisting of a simple molded custard made with gelatin, usually served with fresh fruit or chocolate sauce.

pannekoeken (pahn-neck-coe-ken) Dutch for pancakes; they are made plain or with ingredients such as apples (appelpannekoek) or bacon (spekpannekoek) and served with a light brown syrup (stroop) derived from sugar beets.

pannequet (pahn-nuhr-kahy) French for pancake.

Pannerone; Pannarone (pan-nayr-O-nay) *See* Gorgonzola Bianco.

pannikin (PAN-i-kin) British for a small metal vessel, usually used for drinking.

Pannonia (pah-NO-nee-ah) A Hungarian cheese made from whole cow's milk; it has a smooth, dry rind, a golden yellow interior with a few evenly distributed holes and a slight nutty, sweet flavor.

panocha (pah-NOO-choh) 1. Dark brown raw sugar, usually sold in cone-shaped pieces. 2. A fudgelike Mexican candy made with brown sugar, milk, butter and sometimes nuts; also known as penuche. 3. A U.S. southwestern pudding made with harina enraizada, brown sugar or molasses, vanilla and cream.

panorato alla romana (pa-no-rah-tow ah-lah ro-ma-nah) An Italian dish consisting of bread soaked in milk and then in beaten egg, fried, and sprinkled with lemon juice and either vanilla sugar or ground cinnamon.

pan rallado (pahn raa-jyaa-doh) Spanish for bread crumbs; also known as migas.

pan sciocco (pahn SHOH-koh) Unsalted bread from Italy's Tuscany region.

pansies A wide variety of edible flowers (genera *Achimenes* and *Viola*) with a flavor reminiscent of grapes and used as a garnish.

pansit (pan-sit) *See* pancit.

pansôti (pahn-SOH-tee) An Italian dish of ravioli filled with Ricotta, egg, Parmesan and herbs and served with a sage butter sauce.

pansotti (pan-SOHT-tee) Italian for pot bellied and used to describe triangular-shaped stuffed pasta with zigzag edges.

pantin (pohn-tahn) 1. A French crescent-shaped mold used for making certain pâtés. 2. A French pork pâté, sometimes mixed with truffles, made in a small rectangular mold.

pantothenic acid (pan-too-THIN-ik) *See* vitamin B$_5$.

pantry; pantry chef *See* garde manger.

panucho (pah-NOO-choh) Mexican and Latin American Yucatecan-style antojito; a fried tortilla with black beans, turkey meat and crumbled hard cheese.

pan-ya (pahn-yah) Japanese for bakery.

panzanella alla marinna (pahn-tsah-NAYL-lah ah-la may-reh-neh) An Italian salad made from bread cubes mixed with capers, anchovies, tomatoes, cucumbers and other ingredients dressed with olive oil.

panzarotti (pahn-zah-ROH-tee) Italian for little bellies and used to describe filled pastry or pasta half-moons that are deep-fried or boiled.

panzi (pahn-zee) Chinese for plate.

p'ao (pah-oh) Chinese for cooking a food, usually meat, very quickly in very hot oil.

pão (pao) Portuguese for bread.

pap *See* putu.

papa (PAH-pah) Spanish for potato; also known as patata.

papa a la Huancaina (pah-pah ah lah wuan-kai-nah) A Peruvian dish of potatoes served with a sauce of cheese, onions and chiles; often served with corn.

papadzules (pah-PAW dzoo-less) A Mexican dish consisting of tacos stuffed with hard-boiled eggs in a pumpkin seed sauce.

papaia (pa-pa-ya) Italian for papaya.

papain (pah-PAI-un) 1. A protein-splitting enzyme. 2. A food additive enzyme derived from papaya and used as a texturizer and/or tenderizer in processed foods such as meat products and meat tenderizer preparations; also known as papaya enzyme. 3. An enzyme obtained from the juice of a papaya; it breaks down the protein in meat and is used as a natural tenderizer.

papanash (pah-pah-nash) A Bulgarian dish of balls of cottage cheese mixed with eggs, semolina, flour and butter, boiled, rolled in sour cream or bread crumbs and fried in butter; sometimes served with sugar as a dessert.

pa-pao-fan (pah-pao-phahn) A traditional Chinese dessert of rice pudding decorated with eight different dried or candied fruits or nuts; also known as eight treasures and eight-precious pudding.

papas Arequipena (pah-pahs ah-ray-kee-pay-nah) A Peruvian dish of potatoes served in a sauce of peanuts, cheese and chiles and garnished with olives and hard-boiled eggs.

papas Chorreadas (pah-pas chyo-ree-ah-das) A Colombian dish of boiled potatoes topped with a sauce of onions, tomatoes, hot chiles, cream and cheese.

papa seca (pah-PAH sek-ko) Dried, ground potatoes used in Peruvian cuisine.

papaw (PA-paw) A slightly elongated and curved medium-sized fruit (*Asimina triloba*) native to North America; it has a smooth yellowish skin, a pale yellow flesh, a custardlike texture, many seeds and a flavor and aroma reminiscent of a banana and pear.

papaya A large pear-shaped tropical fruit (*Carica papaya*); it has a yellowish skin, a juicy orange flesh (that contains papain) and a central mass of black seeds encased in a gelatinous coating; the peppery seeds are edible, and the flesh has a sweet, astringent flavor; also known as a pawpaw.

papaya enzyme *See* papain.

papaye French for papaya.

papayou French for voatang.

papaz yahnisi (pah-pahs yah-nee-see) A Turkish mutton stew cooked with onions and flavored with garlic, cinnamon and vinegar.

papeda A variety of hybrid grapefruit grown in Asia and India.

papeeta (pah-pee-tah) Hindi for papaya.

papengaye A long, thin, green-skinned, ribbed vegetable native to India; best just before it ripens; it is eaten peeled and cooked; also known as pipengaille, torui and tourch gourd.

paper *See* parchment paper, silicone paper *and* wax paper.

paper bread *See* piki bread.

paper candy cups Small fluted paper cups, 1.5 in. in diameter and 5/8 in. high, used to hold finished candies, truffles or other small confections; the cups are usually dark brown, with other colors and decorations (especially seasonal ones) available; also known as petit four cases.

paper cases Accordion-pleated paper cups used to present sweets or line muffin tins.

papermouth *See* crappie.

papero (PAH-peh-roh) Italian for duckling.

paper pastry cone A triangular piece of parchment paper rolled into a cone and used instead of a pastry bag for decorating, especially when piping chocolate or royal icing.

Papilionaceae The former name of the leguminous plant family now known as Fabaceae.

papillote, en (pa-pee-yoht, ahn) A food (e.g., fish with a vegetable garnish) enclosed in parchment paper or a greased paper wrapper and baked; the paper envelope is usually slit open table side so that the diner can enjoy the escaping aroma.

papio A small white ulua; it has an average market weight of 10 lb. (4.5 kg).

papos de anjo (pah-poss da ah-nyo) Portuguese for angels' stomachs and used to describe sweets made with egg yolk and sugar dough, covered with syrup or jam.

papoutsakia (pah-poo-tsah-khia) A Greek dish consisting of eggplant stuffed with a mixture of minced meat, onions and tomato juice, covered with a béchamel and grated Kasseri and baked.

pappadam (PAH-pah-duhm) A wafer-thin Indian flatbread made with lentil flour; it may be grilled or deep-fried and flavored with various herbs and spices; it is eaten before or after a meal.

pappardelle (pahp-PAHR-dehl-leh) Italian for broad noodles and used to describe broad, flat strips of pasta; usually served with a game sauce.

paprika (pa-PREE-kuh; PAP-ree-kuh) A blend of dried red-skinned chiles; the flavor can range from slightly sweet and mild to pungent and moderately hot and the color can range from bright red-orange to deep blood red; used in central European and Spanish cuisines as a spice and garnish; also known as Hungarian sweet pepper.

paprika oleoresin A food additive made from concentrated red pepper extract and used as a red coloring agent.

paprikás csirke (PAH-pree-kash CHEER-kah) A Hungarian dish of chicken (meat or fish is sometimes used) and onions braised in chicken stock and flavored with bacon drippings, paprika and other seasonings; the braising liquid is mixed with sour cream for a sauce.

Papua New Guinean Arabica coffee beans grown in Papua New Guinea; the beverage is rich, pungent and tangy and has a medium body.

paquette (pah-kett) French for an egg-carrying hen lobster.

para *See* Brazil nut.

paraath (pa-RAHDH) A large high-rimmed Indian platter used for mixing and kneading dough, cleaning dal or basmati rice and preparing and cutting vegetables.

parabens A group of food additives used as antimicrobials, especially in meat and poultry products.

para cress A green leafy vegetable, similar to spinach, with a peppery flavor; used raw or cooked in Madagascan cuisine.

paraffin The wax coating applied to the rinds of some cheeses to protect the cheeses during transport and increase shelf life; generally the paraffin is red, black, yellow or clear.

Paraguay tea *See* maté.

paralytic shellfish poisoning *See* Gonyaulax.

paranut (pah-rah-noot) *See* Brazil nuts.

parasites Any of numerous organisms that live within, on or at the expense of another organism (known as the host); parasites include the protozoa and worms living within the host's body, especially in the digestive tract and body cavities.

parasol mushroom A large wild mushroom (*Lepiota procera*) that grows during the summer and autumn; it has a distinctive musky flavor.

paratha (pah-RAH-tah) A flat, unleavened Indian bread made with whole wheat flour and fried on a griddle.

parboiled rice *See* converted rice.

parboiling Partially cooking a food in a boiling or simmering liquid; similar to blanching, but the cooking time is longer.

parch A term meaning to dry or roast a food, usually grain or coffee, over an open fire or on the stove top.

parched corn *See* chicos.

parchment paper Heavy grease-resistant paper used to line cake pans or baking sheets, to wrap foods for baking en papillote and to make disposable piping bags.

parcooking Partially cooking a food by any cooking method.

pare To remove the thin outer layer of foods such as fruits (e.g., apple) and vegetables (e.g., potato) with a small, short-bladed knife known as a paring knife or with a vegetable peeler.

Parellada (pah-RAH-yah-dah) A white wine grape grown in Spain; it is used to add fruitiness and refinement to Cava and dry white wines.

pareve; parve (PAHR-vuh) One of the principal categories of food under the Jewish dietary laws (kosher); referred to as neutral foods, they include fruits, vegetables and grains, and, provided they are not processed with animal products, they can be eaten with either meat or dairy; they are sometimes designated with *U* in a circle or *K* in a circle. *See* fleischig, kosher *and* milchig.

parfait (pahr-FAY) 1. A dessert composed of layers of ice cream, sauce and whipped cream served in a tall, narrow glass. 2. A French frozen custard or water ice usually flavored with fruit.

parfait amour (pahr-FAY ah-moor) A red- to purple-colored French liqueur made from lemon, citron and coriander.

parfait glass A footed glass that is bulbous at the bottom and becomes more cylindrical at the top, sometimes with a flared rim and ranges in size from 4 to 8 fl. oz.; used for blended or frozen cocktails, tropical drinks and specialty drinks.

parfum (pa-fum) French for scent or aroma.

pargo (pahr-go) Portuguese for sea bream.

parihuela (pahr-ee-WAY-lah) A Peruvian seafood soup.

paring knife A small knife used for trimming and peeling produce or detail work; it has a 2- to 4-in.-long rigid blade. *See* bird's beak knife.

paring knife

paring knife, sheep's foot A small paring knife with a semiflexible blade and a curved tip.

paring knife, sheep's foot

Paris-Brest (pah-ree-BREHST) A French pastry made with pâte à choux shaped into a ring and sprinkled with sliced almonds; after baking it is split and filled with pastry cream or buttercream (traditionally praline flavored); the dessert takes its name from a bicycle race run between the cities of Paris and Brest in 1891.

Paris brown mushroom *See* common store mushroom.

Parisian cream *See* crème Parisienne.

Parisian scoop The smaller scoop on a two-scoop melon baller.

Parisienne, sauce; Parisian sauce A French sauce made by blending cream cheese, olive oil, lemon juice, chervil and sometimes paprika; used to top cold asparagus.

Paris sticks Soft, finger-shaped shortbread cookies with one or both ends dipped in chocolate.

park A pond for aquafarming oysters.

Parker House croutons Croutons made from bread toasted on one side only, spread on the untoasted side with a mixture of grated Parmesan, butter and egg yolk and baked.

Parker House rolls A white flour yeast roll shaped by folding each individual round of dough in half along an off-center crease before baking; named for the Parker House Hotel in Boston.

parkia (par-kee-ee-ah) The edible bright green, ridged seed pods from a tree (*Parkia speciosa*) cultivated in Thailand and used to give a characteristic flavor and aroma to regional dishes; also known as sa-taw. *See* peteh.

parkin A British gingerbread made with oatmeal and treacle and baked as cookies or a loaf.

Parma ham (PAHR-muh) Ham from Parma, Italy; it is seasoned, salt cured and air-dried but not smoked and has a rosy-brown color and a firm, dense texture; known as prosciutto in the United States.

Parmentier (pahr-mahng-tee) A French term generally used to describe dishes that include potatoes in some form.

Parmesan (PAHR-muh-zahn) 1. A Parmigiano-Reggiano–style cheese made from cow's milk in places other than Italy. 2. An imprecisely used term to describe any grana or grana-style grating cheese. 3. A dish whose main ingredient (e.g., veal cutlet) is dipped in an egg mixture and then bread crumbs, Parmesan and seasonings, sautéed, and covered with a tomato sauce; sometimes a slice of mozzarella is melted on top before adding the tomato sauce.

Parmesane, à la (pahr-mee-zan, ah lah) A term that refers to a dish prepared with Parmesan, usually gratins.

Parmesan knife A knife with a leaf-shaped 5-in.-long blade and a sharp or somewhat rounded tip; after piercing the cheese, the blade is twisted, causing the cheese to come apart.

Parmigiano *See* Parmigiano-Reggiano.

Parmigiano-Reggiano
Parmesan knives
(pahr-muh-ZHAH-noh-reh-zhee-AH-noh) A hard grana cheese made in Italy's Parma region from cow's milk; it has a golden yellow interior, a hard, oily rind and a spicy, rich, sharp flavor; aged for 2–3 years, it is used for grating; also known as Genuine Parmigiano and Parmigiano.

parotid glands (pah-RAHT-id) The salivary glands located in the neck under the floor of the mouth.

parrilladas (par-REE-lyah-dohs) Restaurants in Argentina and Uruguay that specialize in grilled meats.

parsley An herb (*Petroselium crispum*) with long, slender stalks, small, curly, dark green leaves and a slightly peppery, tangy fresh flavor (the flavor is stronger in the stalks, which are used in a bouquet garni); generally used fresh as a flavoring or garnish; also known as curly parsley. *See* Italian parsley.

parsley family A large family Umbelliferae (Apiaceae) of aromatic herbs; it includes vegetables (e.g., carrots, celery and parsnips), herbs (e.g., dill and parsley) and spices (e.g., anise, coriander and cumin).

parsley

parsley mincer A tool with four rows of sharpened teeth at the bottom of a hopper; it minces the herbs held in the hopper when the crank is turned.

parsley root A member of the parsley family; its beige, carrotlike root has a flavor reminiscent of a carrot and celery; also known as Hamburg parsley and turnip-rooted parsley.

parsnip A root vegetable (*Pastinaca sativa*) with bright green, feathery leaves; the long, tapering root has a creamy-white skin and flesh and a slightly sweet flavor reminiscent of a carrot.

parson's nose *See* pope's nose.

parstock; par The amount of stock necessary to cover operating needs between deliveries.

partan (PAHR-uns) Scottish for crab.

partial veil A sheet of tissue stretching under a mushroom cap from the edge of the cap to the stem; it protects the gills until the spores mature. *See* annulus.

particle cork *See* agglomerated cork.

particle matter The minute pieces of grape skins, dead yeast cells, grain fragments, proteins and so on in suspension in a liquid such as beer or wine; generally removed through fining.

partitioned food A food composed or consisting of a part of a whole food (e.g., olive oil from olives).

Partom A sweet, red, port-type Israeli wine.

partridge Any of several varieties of game birds; generally, the bird has an average weight of 1 lb. (450 g), a dark flesh, a somewhat tough texture and an earthy flavor; significant varieties include the Hungarian partridge and chukar partridge.

parts 1. Traditional cooking term for a nonspecific unit of measure (e.g., two parts water to one part sugar). 2. A portion of a whole; any of several equal units into which something can be divided or separated (e.g., "take three parts beef").

pasa (pah-sah) Spanish for raisin.

pasa makarouna (pah-sah mah-kah-roo-nah) A Greek dish of meat, pasta and cheese.

Pascal celery *See* celery.

Pasha (pah-shaw) A Turkish coffee-flavored liqueur.

pasilla (pah-SEE-yah) A name used incorrectly for the fresh poblano and its dried forms, the ancho and mulato. *See* chilaca.

paska (pahs-ka) A Russian cream and cheese dish.

paskha (PAHS-khuh) A Russian Easter dessert made with pot cheese or cottage cheese, sugar, sour cream, almonds and candied fruit; it is molded into a four-sided pyramid and decorated with almonds to form the letters *XB* (Christ is risen).

passa (pah-sah) Portuguese for raisin.

passatelli (pah-sah-TELL-lee) Very thin Italian pasta ribbons.

passato (pah-sah-toh) Italian for purée.

passe-crasanne; passacrassana A large pear grown in southern Europe; it has a dull, greenish-brown skin and a coarse texture.

passed hors d'oeuvre *See* butler service.

Passe-tout-grains (pahss-too-gran) A red wine from France's Burgundy region made from one-third Pinot grapes and two-thirds Gamay grapes fermented together.

Passionfrucht (pah-see-ohn-frut) German for passion fruit.

passion fruit A small ovoid tropical fruit (*Passiflora edulis*); it has a wrinkled, purple skin, a soft, golden flesh with tiny edible seeds and a tropical sweet–tart flavor; often used as a flavoring for sauces and beverages; also imprecisely known as granadilla.

passion fruit liqueur A liqueur made from the fruit of the passion flower and other tropical fruits; it has a slightly acidic, fragrant flavor.

Passito (pah-see-toe) An Italian dessert wine made from partially dried grapes, generally Moscato and Malvasia.

Passover Wine A sweet, heavy kosher wine made partly from Concord grapes and served for the Jewish festival of Passover.

pasta (PAHS-tah) 1. Italian for dough or pastry. 2. An unleavened dough formed from a liquid (eggs and/or water) mixed with a flour (wheat, buckwheat, rice or other grains or a combination of grains) and cut or extruded into tubes, ribbons and other shapes; flavorings such as herbs, spices and vegetables (e.g., tomatoes and spinach) can be added to the dough; pasta is usually boiled and served with a sauce. *See* noodles. 3. The second course of an Italian meal, served after the antipasto.

pasta, commercial Pasta typically made from a dough of semolina and water and, sometimes, flavoring ingredients such as spinach, tomatoes, herbs and/or spices; sold dried and packaged. *See* macaroni.

pasta alla chitarra (PAHS-tah al-lah kee-TAH-rah) Italian pasta ribbons cut by a chitarra; also known as spaghetti alla chitarra and tonnarelli.

pasta e fagioli (PAHS-tah ay fah-JOA-lee) Italian for pasta and beans and used to describe a thick soup of pasta and red or white beans.

pasta fazool (PAHS-tah fah-zool) American slang for the Italian dish pasta e fagioli.

pasta filata (fe-LAH-toa) 1. An Italian term describing the curds resulting from a special cheese-making process during which the fermented curds are heated until they are plastic, allowing them to be stretched into ropes, kneaded and shaped; the resulting cheeses are free of holes and whey and can be eaten fresh or, after aging, used for cooking; also known as plastic curds or spun curds. 2. A description of the cheeses (e.g., mozzarella and Provolone) made by this process.

pasta fork A long, scooplike fork with 1-in.-long blunt-tipped prongs with slots between; used to lift and drain pasta and portion single servings of already sauced pasta; also known as a spaghetti fork or spaghetti rake.

pasta fresca (PAHS-tah FRES-kah) Italian for fresh pasta or pasta dough.

pasta fresca all'uovo (PAHS-tah FRES-kah ahl'oo-OH-voh) Italian for fresh pasta dough made with eggs.

pasta fork

pasta frolla (PAHS-tah FROH-lah) A rich, sweet Italian pastry dough; used for many tart- and pie-type pastries.

pasta grattugiata (PAHS-tah grah-tou-gee-ah-tah) Grated or minced fresh pasta, usually used in soups.

pastahane (pas-tah-ha-nay) A Turkish patisserie where cakes and pastries as well as sweetmeats are sold. *See* tathci.

pasta ke faki (pah-stah keh fah-kee) A Greek dish from Rhodes consisting of cooked noodles and lentils fried in butter and garnished with fried onion rings.

pasta machine, extrusion-type An electrical appliance that mixes pasta dough and forces it through plates or dies of various sizes and shapes to form and cut tubes, shapes and/or ribbons of pasta.

pasta machine, roller-type An electrical or manual tool with a series of smooth rollers that roll, flatten and thin pasta dough; the dough is then passed through notched rollers, which cut it into ribbons.

pasta pot A tall pot with a capacity of 6–8 qt.; it has a perforated basket insert that holds the pasta and, removed from the water, acts as a strainer.

pasta primavera (PAHS-tah pree-mah-VEH-rah) An American dish of pasta with a sauce of sautéed vegetables.

pasta rolling pin A long, thin, lightweight wooden pin used for rolling kneaded pasta dough.

pasta sfogliata (PAHS-tah sfog-lee-AHT-tah) Italian for puff pastry.

pasta verde (PAHS-tah vayr-DAY) Italian for green pasta, usually made with spinach.

paste 1. The interior portion of a cheese, especially a surface-ripened one. 2. A smooth mixture of a starch (such as flour) and a liquid.

paste-board baking pan A traditional homemade baking sheet of cardboard covered with parchment paper.

pastechi; pastelilo *See* patty.

pastéis de cenoura (pass-ta-ess da she-noo-raw) A Portuguese pastry filled with carrots, eggs, sugar and sometimes nuts.

pastéis de feijao (pass-ta-ess da fay-zhah-o) A small Portuguese cake made with white beans and sometimes almonds.

pastéis de grao (pass-ta-ess da gra-oh) A small Portuguese cake made with chickpea flour.

pastéis de laranja (pas-sta-ess da lah-rahn-zhah) A Portuguese pastry with an egg and sugar filling flavored with orange.

pastel (pahs-TAYL) 1. A South American method of garnishing a casserole with a crust of eggs and puréed corn. 2. Spanish for a pie, pastry, cupcakes or filled roll.

pastél (pahs-TEL) A Portuguese sweet or savory dish in which pastry is used.

pastel de carne y durazno o albaricoque (pas-tell day cahr-nay ee doo-ras-noh oh al-bah-ree-koh-kay) An Argentinean dish of sliced beef and onions flavored with oregano, cinnamon, cloves, allspice, bay leaf and sugar, placed in a pastry shell, garnished with peaches or apricots, covered with a crust and topped with meringue.

pastel de choclo (pass-tell da tcho-cloe) A Chilean casserole of ground beef and onions seasoned with chiles, cumin, oregano and paprika, topped with puréed corn and baked.

pastel de choclo con relleno de pollo (pass-tell da tcho-cloe con relle-noh de po-yo) A Bolivian casserole of chicken and vegetables with a crust of puréed corn and eggs.

pastel de nata (pas-tell da nya-tah) A Portuguese sweet consisting of a pastry case filled with a pudding of eggs, cream and sugar.

pastelitos (pah-stehl-EE-tohs) 1. Colombian empanadas; the fillings frequently include potatoes. 2. Mexican little cakes or cookies.

pastenco (pas-ten-koh) Spanish for Easter lamb; one usually slaughtered when older than 8 weeks. *See* cordero lechal.

pastèque (pah-stehk) French for watermelon.

Pastete (pas-TAT-teh) A German puff pastry shell filled with meat.

Pasteur, Louis (Fr., 1822–1895) A chemist and bacteriologist who discovered the sterilization method known as pasteurization and is credited with conducting the first scientific study of fermentation.

pasteurization The process of heating milk to a high temperature (usually 161°F [72°C]) for approximately 15 seconds to kill pathogenic bacteria and destroy enzymes that cause spoilage, thus increasing shelf life; by law, all grade A milk must be pasteurized before sale.

pasteurization, ultra The pasteurization process during which milk is heated to a higher temperature (275°F [135°C]) for a shorter period of time (2–4 seconds); often used for whipping cream.

pasteurization, ultrahigh-temperature (UHT) A form of ultrapasteurization in which milk is held at a temperature of 280–300°F (138–150°C) for 2–6 seconds; packed in sterile containers and aseptically sealed to prevent bacteria from entering; the product can be stored (unopened) without refrigeration for at least 3 months; also known as ultrahigh-temperature processing.

pasteurize To sterilize a food, especially milk, by heating it to a temperature of 140–180°F (60–82.2°C) for a short period to kill bacteria.

pasticceria (pah-stee-t'cheh-REE-ah) An Italian pastry shop; breads are usually not sold there.

pasticciata (pass-tee-tchee-ah-tah) A northern Italian meat stew with herbs and vegetables.

pastilla *See* b'steeya.

pastillage (phast-tee-ahz) A paste made of sugar, cornstarch and gelatin; it may be cut or molded into decorative shapes.

pastillas de leche A chewy, fudgelike Filipino candy made of milk cooked with sugar, spread on a sugared board and cut into pieces that are rolled in sugar and wrapped in brightly colored paper; traditionally made for holiday celebrations.

pastille (pas-TEEL) French for a small, lozenge-shaped hard candy made with sugar, water and flavorings.

Pastinake (pass-teen-ah-keh) German for parsnip.

pastini (pahs-STEE-nah) Italian for little pasta and used to describe several shapes of very small pasta usually used for broth-based soups; includes alfabeto, amorini, astri, avena, funghini, pulcini and stivaletti.

pastirma A Turkish dish of slices of air-dried beef coated with a paste of garlic, cumin, red pepper and fenugreek.

pastis (pas-TEES) 1. A category of anise-based, licorice-flavored French aperitifs, including Pernod and Ricard; when mixed with water, the aperitif turns white and cloudy. 2. A variety of yeast-leavened pastries found in southwestern France and flavored with brandy and orange flower water.

pastitsada kerkireikia (pas-tea-tsah-dah kerr-key-rey-ket-ah) A Greek dish from Corfu consisting of veal cooked with onions, tomatoes and herbs; the meat is served separately, and the sauce is served with pasta.

pastitsi (pass-tea-tsee) A Greek dish of pasta filled with ground meat and covered with a cheese sauce.

pastitsio (pah-STEE-tshis-oh) A Greek casserole dish consisting of pasta, ground beef or lamb, grated cheese, tomatoes and béchamel flavored with cinnamon.

pastourma (pah-stoo-rmah) A Greek black-rinded, smoked bacon highly flavored with garlic and served as a meze.

pastrami (puh-STRAH-mee) A cut of beef (usually from the plate, brisket or round), rubbed with salt and a seasoning paste containing garlic, peppercorns, red pepper flakes, cinnamon, cloves and coriander seeds, then dry cured, smoked and cooked.

pastry 1. A dough made with flour and shortening and used for the crust of pies, tarts and the like. 2. A food made with such a dough. 3. A term used broadly and imprecisely for all fancy sweet baked goods, including cakes, sweet rolls and cookies.

pastry bag A cone-shaped bag with two open ends, the smaller of which can be fitted with a plastic or metal tip; the bag is filled with icing, cream, dough or batter, which is squeezed through the tip in decorative patterns or designs; available in a range of sizes and variety of materials; also known as a piping bag.

pastry blender A tool with several U-shaped metal wires attached to a wooden or plastic handle; used to cut cold fat into flour.

pastry bag, coupler and tips

pastry brush A small brush used for applying glaze, egg wash and the like to doughs, buttering pans and brushing excess flour from dough; available in a variety of sizes, with either a round or flat head and natural or nylon bristles.

pastry chef See pâtissier.

pastry cloth A large piece of canvas or plastic-coated cotton used as a non-stick surface for rolling out dough.

pastry blender

pastry comb See cake comb.

pastry cream A rich, thick custard made with milk, eggs, sugar and flour or cornstarch, and cooked on the stove top; used to fill éclairs, tarts, cakes and other pastries; also known as crème pâtissière.

pastry cutters A nested set of tinned steel cutters; one edge is rolled and the other is sharp for cutting through doughs; they can be plain or fluted and are available in various shapes (e.g., rounds, hearts and stars). See dough cutter.

pastry flour A weak flour made primarily from low-gluten soft wheat with a high starch content and used to produce tender, crumbly baked goods such as pastries.

pastry tip A small cone-shaped metal or plastic insert for a pastry bag; the small end of each tip is cut, bent or perforated so that the mixture forced through it will form various designs or patterns; used for piping creams, fillings, frostings and other soft mixtures into decorative shapes and patterns.

pastry tips

pastry wheel A small tool with a thin, sharp wheel (plain or fluted) attached to a short handle; used for cutting doughs. See jagging wheel.

pàsturma (pass-toor-mah) 1. A dry Bulgarian sausage flavored with garlic. 2. A

pastry wheel

Turkish dish of lean beef rubbed with a paste of paprika, allspice, cumin, pepper, garlic and salt and then air-dried; it is cut into paper-thin strips and served with Raki, as a filling for börek, in stews or fried with eggs.

pasty (PAS-tee) A British short crust pastry filled with a meat (beef, lamb, veal or pork) and potato mixture; traditionally, this savory filling was at one end and a sweet filling at the other; also known as a Cornish pasty.

pasztet (pah-sh-teht) Polish for a pâté made from goose liver, salt pork, onions, peppercorns and truffles.

pata (PAH-tah) Spanish for duck.

patacones (pah-tah-coe-ness) A Colombian snack or antojito of deep-fried green plantain slices.

Patagras (pah-tah-grahs) A hard cheese made in Latin America (particularly Argentina and Cuba) from pasteurized whole or slightly skimmed cow's milk; it has a pale yellow interior, a smooth texture, a mild, nutty flavor and a red wax coating.

patapaisti (pa-tah-pie-stee) A Finnish dish consisting of a veal or beef pot roast garnished with vegetables, such as peas, carrots and onions, and served with a sauce made from the stock thickened with cream.

patata (pah-TAH-tah) Spanish, Italian and Greek for potato.

patates piyazi (pah-tah-tess pee-yah-ze) A Turkish hors d'oeuvre of potato and onion salad.

pâte (paht) French for dough, paste or batter.

pâté (pah-TAY) 1. French for pie. 2. Traditionally, a fine savory meat filling wrapped in pastry, baked and served hot or cold. 3. A pork, veal, lamb, beef, game, fish, shellfish, poultry and/or vegetable forcemeat that is seasoned and baked; it is served hot or cold.

pâte à choux (paht uh SHOO) French for cream puff dough or choux pastry.

pâte à foncer (paht ah fose) French for a buttery pastry dough made with very little sugar; used for making tart and pie shells.

pâte au pâté (paht oh pah-tay) A specifically formulated pastry dough used for wrapping pâté when making pâté en croûte.

pâte brisée (paht bree-ZAY) French for a rich, flaky short dough used as a crust for sweet or savory dishes.

pâte d'amandes (paht dah-mahngd) French for almond paste or marzipan.

pâté de campagne (pah-tay duh cam-pah-gnae) French for country pâté; it is made with pig's liver, pork shoulder and fat bacon and usually flavored with herbs, shallots, garlic, salt, pepper and Armagnac.

pâté de foie gras (pah-tay duh fwah gwah) A pâté made with 80% goose liver (foie gras) and usually flavored with truffles.

pateela (pah-tee-lah) An Indian handleless saucepan used for general cooking.

pâté en croûte (pah-tay awn croot) A pâté baked in a pastry dough such as pâté au pâté.

pâté en croûte mold, oval fluted An oval metal mold with hinged sides embossed with a fluted pattern; the sides lock in place along the rim of the bottom plate and are easily removed when the pâté is finished; traditionally used for meat and game pâtés en croûte.

pâté en croûte mold

pâté en croûte mold, rectangular A metal mold with two L-shaped side pieces that are connected by pins and fit into a rim on the bottom; the sides are often embossed with a herringbone design that imprints on the sides of the pâté; available in 1- to 2-qt. capacity and 10–14 in. long.

pâte feuilletée (paht fuh-yuh-tay) A rolled-in dough used for pastries, cookies and savory products; it produces a rich and buttery but not sweet baked product with hundreds of light, flaky layers; also known as puff pastry.

pâte levée (paht leh-vay) French for a leavened dough.

patent flour A fine grade of wheat flour milled from the interior of the wheat kernel.

patent spinach *See* New Zealand spinach.

patent still A continuous still able to produce purer distilled spirits at a faster rate and in greater quantities than traditional stills.

pâte sablée (paht SOB-lee) French for a delicate, sweet, short dough used for tarts, tartlets and cookies; also known as sandy dough.

pâté spice A blend of herbs and spices used to season forcemeats; generally includes cloves, dried ginger, nutmeg, paprika, dried basil, black pepper, white pepper, bay leaf, dried thyme, dried marjoram and salt.

pâte sucrée (paht soo-CRAY) French for a sturdy, rich, sweet dough made with butter and egg yolks; used for pies, tarts and as a base for other pastries; also known as sweet dough.

pathogen A microorganism that can cause disease.

pathogenic bacteria In the food safety context, bacteria that are harmful when consumed by humans. *See* infection, intoxication *and* toxin-mediated infection.

patience *See* perpetual spinach.

patis (pah-teese) A very salty Filipino sauce made from fermented fish; it has an amber color and thin consistency.

pâtisserie (pah-tees-uh-ree) 1. French for the general category of all sweet baked goods and confections. 2. French for the art of pastry making. 3. French for a shop where pastries are made and sold.

pâtissier; pâtissiére (pah-tes-SYAY) 1. French (masculine and feminine, respectively) for pastry cook or pastry chef. 2. At a food services operation following the brigade system, the person responsible for all baked goods, including breads, pastries and desserts; also known as a pastry chef.

patitas de cerdo Spanish for pig's feet.

patitas de cerdo con chile poblano (pah-tee-tass da craydoh con ghee-lee poh-blah-noe) A Mexican dish of pig's feet served with a sauce flavored with poblano chile.

patlagele vinete (pat-law-gah-lah vee-nata) A Romanian eggplant salad.

patla jhol (pat-law jole) Hindi for stew.

patlican (paht-lee-jahn) Turkish for eggplant.

patlican salatasi (pah-tlee-chan saw-law-taw-see) A Turkish salad of eggplants and tomatoes dressed with olive oil, garlic, chiles and sometimes yogurt and garnished with parsley.

patlican tursusu (pah-tlee-chan toor-soo-soo) A Turkish dish of small eggplant pickles stuffed with cabbage, sweet red peppers, garlic and dill.

Patna rice An Indian rice with a very long grain.

pato (PAH-toh) Portuguese and Spanish for duck.

patricieni (pah-tree-chee-ah-nee) Spicy Romanian pork sausages.

Patriot blueberry A variety of high-bush blueberry; the fruit are relatively large and intensely flavored.

patrons Customers, especially repeat customers.

patsas (pah-tsas) A Greek soup made from tripe and pig's feet, flavored with garlic, lemon peel and avgolémono sauce.

patty 1. A small thin round of ground or finely chopped foods such as meat, fish or vegetables. 2. A round flat piece of candy (e.g., peppermint patty). 3. A West Indies crescent-shaped pie with a flaky pastry shell and a highly spiced minced meat filling; also known as a pastechi and pastelilo.

patty melt A dish that consists of a ground beef patty on a slice of bread, garnished with grilled onions and cheese, topped with another slice of bread and grilled until the cheese melts.

pattypan squash A medium-sized spherical, somewhat flat summer squash with a deeply fluted shell, a pale green, smooth to slightly bumpy shell and a pale green flesh; also known as a cymling squash, custard squash and scalloped squash.

patty shell A small, baked, cup-shaped shell, usually made of puff pastry, used to hold individual servings of creamed preparations.

patum peperium A Victorian English spread for toast consisting of pounded anchovies, butter, cereal, spices and salt; also known as Gentleman's Relish.

paua A variety of abalone found near New Zealand; it has an ivory flesh with a chewy texture and a mild flavor.

paunch and pluck The principal ingredients for haggis: the paunch is the lamb or sheep's stomach used as the casing, and the pluck is the heart, liver and lights used for the filling.

paupiette (poh-PYEHT) A thin slice of meat, usually beef or veal, rolled around a filling of finely ground meat or vegetables and then fried, baked or braised in wine or stock; also known as a roulade.

pau, sauce *See* paloise, sauce.

pauzinhos (pow-zeen-nyush) Portuguese for chopsticks.

pavé (pah-VAY) French for paving stone and used to describe any square or rectangular cake or pastry, especially one made with multiple layers of sponge cake and buttercream.

pavezky (pah-vase-key) Czech croutons made from thin slices of bread moistened with milk, dipped in beaten egg and bread crumbs and fried.

Pavlova (pav-LOH-vuh) An Australian dessert named for the Russian ballerina Anna Pavlova; it consists of a crisp meringue shell filled with whipped cream and fresh fruit, usually passion fruit, kiwi and pineapple.

pavo (PAH-bhoa) Spanish for turkey.

pavot, graines de (pah-vo, gran duh) French for poppy seeds.

pawpaw *See* papaya.

pa-y-all (pah-ee-al) A dish from Spain's Catalonia region consisting of fresh bread, sometimes fried in olive oil or pork fat, rubbed with garlic and sprinkled with salt and olive oil.

payasam (pah-yah-sahm) An Indian pudding made with yellow mung beans, split peas and coconut milk, a specialty of the southern regions.

paysanne (pahy-sahn) 1. Foods cut into flat squares of approximately 0.5 × 0.5 in. and 0.25 in. thick (12 × 12 × 6 mm). *See* brunoise. 2. Foods garnished with vegetables cut to this size.

paysanne, à la (pahy-sahn, ah lah) 1. French for peasant style and used to describe dishes prepared with a mixture of vegetables, especially potatoes, carrots and turnips, cut into small squares and used for soups or to garnish meat, fish or omelets. 2. Various braised dishes cooked with softened vegetables. 3. Potatoes cut into rounds and simmered in an herb-flavored stock.

payusnaya (pah-yah-oos-nah-yah) A coarse, pressed form of caviar.

pe (pay) Portuguese for lees.

pea bean The smallest of the dried white beans. *See* white beans.

Peaberry Arabica coffee beans grown in Kenya; the beverage has a full flavor and fine acidity.

peach A medium-sized stone fruit (*Prunus persica*) native to China; it has a fuzzy, yellow-red skin, a pale orange, yellow or white juicy flesh surrounding a hard stone and a sweet flavor; available as clingstone and freestone. *See* Persian apple.

Peach Blow Fizz A cocktail made of gin, lemon juice, heavy cream, sugar syrup, club soda and mashed peaches; served in a chilled highball glass.

Peach Fuzz A cocktail made of peach brandy, heavy cream and white crème de cacao; topped with a float of apple schnapps.

Peach Melba A dessert made with poached peach halves, vanilla ice cream and raspberry sauce; created by the French chef Auguste Escoffier for the opera singer Nellie Melba. *See* Melba sauce.

peach nut *See* pewa.

Peach Tree Street A cocktail made of cranberry juice, orange juice, vodka and peach schnapps; served in a chilled wine glass and garnished with a peach slice.

peachy A ciderlike beverage made from peaches; popular in colonial America.

peak gai yang (pik gah-e young) A Thai dish consisting of chicken wings marinated in lemongrass, garlic, pepper, cilantro and turmeric and then barbecued.

peanut A legume and not a true nut (*Arachis hypogea*); it is the plant's nutlike seed that grows underground; the hard seed has a papery brown skin and is encased in a thin, netted tan pod; the seed is used for snacking and for making peanut butter and oil; also known as a groundnut, earthnut, goober (from the African word nguba) and goober pea. *See* bambara.

peanut butter A paste made of ground peanuts, vegetable oil (usually hydrogenated) and salt; available in smooth and chunky styles.

peanut butter, natural A peanut butter made from only peanuts and peanut oil.

peanut butter pie A baked dessert from the American South consisting of a flaky pie crust and filling made by folding beaten egg whites and whipped cream in a mixture of peanut butter, butter and cream.

peanut oil A clear oil obtained by pressing peanuts; it has a delicate flavor and a high smoke point and is used as an all-purpose culinary oil.

peanut sauce A Southeast Asian (particularly Indonesian) sauce made from peanut oil, garlic, onions, chiles, soy sauce and peanut butter.

pear A spherical to bell-shaped pome fruit (*Pyrus communis*), generally with a juicy, tender, crisp, off-white flesh, a moderately thin skin that can range in color from celadon green to golden yellow to tawny red and a flavor that can be sweet to spicy; pears can be eaten out of hand or cooked and are grown in temperate regions worldwide.

peardrop A pear-shaped candy flavored with pentyl acetate, whose characteristic fruity aroma has made it a standard term for describing aromas, especially in wine.

pearl ash A gray-colored leavener made from wood ash; used as a rudimentary baking powder (with sour milk); commonly known as potash.

pearl barley *See* barley.

pearling A milling process in which all or part of the hull, bran and germ are removed from grains.

pearl onion A small onion with a white to yellow outer layer, a white flesh and a mild flavor; it is usually cooked like a vegetable or used in stews and soups.

pearl oyster Not a true oyster but a bivalve mollusk related to the mussel and found in the Pacific Ocean; it has a shell with a winglike extension on one side and can grow as large as 8 in. (19.8 cm) in diameter; the smooth, iridescent interior of the shell is mother of pearl, and the pearl is composed of aragonite; the flesh has little culinary significance; also known as a wing oyster.

pearl plum A variety of plum; the fruit has yellow skin and flesh and a particularly rich, sweet flavor.

pearl sugar A coarse granulated sugar used for decorating pastries and confections; also known as sanding sugar and crystal sugar.

pearl tapioca *See* tapioca.

pear tomato A small pear-shaped tomato with a bright red or golden yellow color; eaten raw or used as a garnish.

pear whelk *See* channeled whelk.

peas 1. The edible seeds contained within the pods of various vines of the family Leguminosae (Fabaceae); the seeds are generally shelled and the pod discarded; although available fresh, peas are usually marketed canned or frozen. *See* beans. 2. A term used imprecisely as synonymous with beans.

peasant breads A general category for coarse, rough-textured breads; often produced on small farms, especially in Europe.

pease pudding A British dish of dried, soaked, cooked and puréed split peas.

pea shoot; pea tendril The growing tip of the pea plant; it has soft, tender green leaves and is used in Hong Kong cuisine; also known as dao minu.

peat Partially carbonized plant matter (principally sphagnum moss) decomposed in water and used for smoking foods such as the barley used to distill Scotch whisky.

peat reek The dark, oily smoke that comes from burning the peat used to smoke the barley used for making Scotch whisky; the smoke creates the characteristic flavor and aroma of Scotch whisky.

peberrod (PEH-ooer-roadh) Danish for horseradish.

pebre (pe-bray) A Chilean sauce made from olive oil, vinegar, fresh aji chiles, garlic, onion, cilantro and oregano; also known as Chilean hot sauce.

pebronata (peh-bro-nah-tah) A Corsican dish consisting of beef or wild boar braised with juniper berries.

pecan (pih-KAHN; PEE-kan) The nut of a tree of the hickory family (*Carya oliviformis*) native to North America; it has a smooth, thin, hard, tan shell enclosing a bilobed, golden brown kernel with a beige flesh and a high fat content. *See* hickory nut.

pecan pie A dessert from the American South made with a single flaky crust filled with a very sweet, rich mixture of butter, eggs, brown sugar and pecans, then baked until firm.

pecan rice *See* wild pecan rice.

pêche (pehsh) French for peach.

pechen' (pah-can) Russian for liver.

pechenoe (pah-can-ho-ah) Russian for bakery.

pech'ka (peck-kam) Russian for oven.

pecho de ternera (PAY-choo day tehr-NAY-rah) A Spanish cut of the veal carcass; the breast.

peck A unit of volume measurement equal to 1/4 bushel; in the U.S. system, it is equal to approximately 538 cu. in. or 8 dry quarts; in the imperial system, it is equal to approximately 555 cu. in.

pecorino (peh-kuh-REE-noh) An Italian term referring to any cheese made from only ewe's milk; most are aged, have a white to pale yellow color and a sharp, pungent flavor and are classified as grana.

Pecorino Incanestrato *See* Incanestrato.

Pecorino Romano (peh-kuh-REE-noh roh-MAH-noh) A ewe's milk Romano.

Pecorino Sardo (peh-kuh-REE-noh sahr-doa) *See* Fiore Sardo.

pectin 1. A polysaccharide present in plant cell walls. 2. A gummy, water-soluble dietary fiber that can lower blood cholesterol levels by modest amounts. 3. A food additive used as a thickener in foods such as jams and jellies.

pectin, low-methoxyl A gum derived from pectinic acid and used to assist gelling, especially in low-fat products.

ped (phet) Thai for pungent, peppery and spicy.

pedicel The short stem on the grape that connects it to the bunch.

pedo de lobo (pe-doh day loh-boh) Spanish for puffball mushroom.

Pedro Ximenez (PEH-dro hee-MEH-nez) 1. A white wine grape grown principally in Spain. 2. A very sweet fortified blending wine for sherries made from this grape and often referred to as PX. 3. A dry white wine made from this grape, especially in areas other than Spain's Jerez–Xérès–Scherris district.

peel *v.* To remove rind or skin. *n.* 1. A wooden or metal tool with a long handle and large blade used to transfer pizzas and yeast breads to and from a baking stone or baking

peel

sheet in the oven; also known as a baker's peel or pizza paddle. 2. The rind or skin of a fruit or vegetable.

peeled 1. A fruit or vegetable from which the skin or rind has been removed. 2. *See* denuded.

peeler crab A hard-shell blue crab that has a fully formed soft shell beneath its hard outer shell. *See* buckram *and* crab, soft-shell.

peento A variety of peach with a flat, spherical shape, a very crisp, juicy flesh and a honeylike flavor.

Peg 1. English term for a jigger. 2. An English cocktail made with brandy or whiskey and soda water.

Pegu Club A cocktail made of gin, orange curaçao, lime juice, Angostura bitters and orange bitters.

peixe (pay-shay) Portuguese for fish.

peixe-galo (pay-shay-gah-low) Portuguese for John Dory.

Peking cabbage *See* po tsai.

Peking doily A thin, round pancake on which moo shu pork is served.

Peking duck A Mandarin Chinese dish consisting of a duck whose skin is separated from the meat by means of an air pump; the duck cavity is stuffed with a mixture of soy sauce, garlic, leeks, brown sugar and ginger, trussed and hung, coated with flour and honey and then roasted.

Peking sauce *See* hoisin.

pekmèz (pek-mez) Serbo-Croat for jam.

pekoe (PEE-koh) The medium-size grade of whole black tea leaves; generally coarse.

pelau (pae-law-oo) A Caribbean dish of meat or chicken, peas and rice, flavored with coconut milk.

peli-peli *See* peri-peri.

pellagra (pa-LAA-grah) A disease caused by a deficiency of vitamin B_3; symptoms include diarrhea, weakness, irritability, loss of appetite, skin rash and mental confusion.

pelle rouge (pehl roojg) French for salamander; also known as fer à glacer and salamandre.

Pellkartoffeln (PEHL-kahr-tof-ferln) A German dish of potatoes cooked in their skins.

pelmeni (pell-m'ye-nee) A Russian dish of noodles stuffed with meat or cabbage and often served with rendered pork fat and sour cream.

pelota (pah-loh-tah) Spanish for meatball.

pelte (peh-lteh) An Albanian and Greek dish made from cornstarch, molasses, sugar and water boiled until syrupy, flavored with almonds and lemon juice and baked.

pelure d'oignon (peh-loor doh-n'yahn) French for onion skin and used as a wine-tasting term for the pale, orange-brown color or tawny tinge of some light red wines and rosés as well as certain red wines that acquire this tint as they age.

pemmican (PEM-eh-kan) A mixture of buffalo or venison, melted fat, berries and sometimes marrow; it is compressed into a small cake and dried; used in Native American cuisine.

pen *See* cephalopods.

penchenè (peen-chye-niyeh) Russian tea cakes or cookies.

Pendennis Club A cocktail made of gin, apricot brandy, lime juice, sugar syrup and Peychaud's bitters.

Penedé (pay-NAY-dahss) A grape-growing and wine-producing region along Spain's Mediterranean coast near Barcelona; known for its cavas and for quality white wines and smooth red wines.

p'eng (pang) Chinese for splashing, as when seasonings are scattered over food.

Penicillium The principal genus of fungi used to develop molds on cheeses during ripening; *P. canidum* is used for surface-ripened cheeses such as Brie; *P. glaucum* and *P. roqueforti* are used for blue cheeses.

penne (PEN-nay) Italian for pen or quill and used to describe short- to medium-length straight tubes (ridged or smooth) of pasta with diagonally cut ends.

pennette (pen-net-tay) Very short penne.

pennine (pen-nee-nay) Short penne.

penny bun British for bolete.

pension (pawn-SEE-ohn) A French boarding house; three meals a day are included.

pensióne (pen-see-oh-nee) An Italian boarding house; three meals a day are included.

pentagone *See* api étoile.

penteola (pen-teh-oh-lah) Portuguese for scallop.

pentyl acetate A food additive with a distinctive fruity aroma; used as a flavoring agent in candies. *See* peardrop.

penuche (pah-NOO-chee) *See* panocha.

peoci (pae-oh-tchee) Italian (especially in Venice) for mussels.

Pepato (peh-PA-toh) A southern Italian incanestrato-style spiced cheese made from ewe's milk; its peppery flavor is the result of either aging the cheese between layers of pepper or mixing the pepper into the curds.

pépe (PAY-pay) Italian for pepper.

peperonata (pehp-uh-roh-NAH-tah) An Italian dish of sweet peppers, tomatoes, onions and garlic cooked in olive oil; served as an antipasto or a condiment.

peperoncini (peh-peh-rohn-CHEE-neh) Italian small, sweet, green or red peppers, usually pickled.

peperoncino (peh-peh-rohn-CHEE-noh) Italian for chile pepper.

peperoni (peh-peh-ROH-nee) Italian for sweet peppers.

Pépin, Jacques (Fr., 1935–) Former chef to three French heads of state, including Charles de Gaulle; now a well-known cooking teacher, newspaper columnist and author of numerous English-language cookbooks, including *La Technique, La Methode* and *The Art of Cooking,* Volumes 1 and 2.

pepin de Bourgueil (pa-pen day bour-ghay) A small, western European traditional apple with a yellow-orange skin and white flesh.

pepinex A variety of slicing cucumber; it has a moderately strong, astringent flavor.

pepino (pay-pee-noh) Portuguese for cucumber.

pepino (puh-PEE-noh) 1. A medium- to large-sized subtropical fruit (*Solanum muricatum*) native to Peru; it has a smooth, glossy, violet-streaked golden skin, a golden yellow, a juicy flesh, a fragrant aroma and a flavor reminiscent of a pear with undertones of vanilla; also known as a melon pear. 2. Spanish for cucumber.

pepino de comer (puh-pee-noh day koh-mehr) A smaller pepino with a white skin and a cucumber-like flavor; eaten raw or pickled in vinegar in South American cuisines.

pepitas (peh-PEE-tah) Hulled and roasted pumpkinseeds; used in Mexican cuisine as a snack and thickener.

pepitoria (peh-PEE-toh-ree-ah) Toasted squash seeds ground to a powder and used as a thickener in Mexican and Guatemalan cuisines.

pepo The fruit of any of a variety of related plants such as squash and melons; the fruit generally have a leathery or hard rind, a fleshy interior and many flattened seeds.

peppar (PAH-pahr) Swedish for pepper.

pepper 1. The fruit of various members of the *Capsicum* genus; native to the Western Hemisphere, a pepper has a hollow body with placental ribs (internal white veins) to which tiny seeds are attached (seeds are also attached to the stem end of the interior); a pepper can be white, yellow, green, brown, purple or red and can have a flavor ranging from delicately sweet to fiery hot; the genus includes sweet peppers and hot peppers. *See* chile *and* sweet pepper. 2. Peppercorns, whole or ground.

peppercorn The berry of the pepper plant (*Piper nigrum*), a climbing vine native to India and Indonesia; it has a brown color when fully ripened and is available in three principal varieties: black, green and white. *See* pink peppercorn.

peppercorn, black A peppercorn picked when green and dried in the sun until it turns black; it has a slightly hot flavor with a hint of sweetness; whole or ground, it is the most commonly available peppercorn.

peppercorn, decorticated A black peppercorn that has had its skin removed by a mechanical process so that it has the appearance of a white peppercorn.

peppercorn, green An unripened peppercorn that is either freeze-dried or pickled in brine or vinegar; it has a soft texture and a fresh, sour flavor similar to that of capers.

peppercorn, pink *See* pink peppercorn.

peppercorn, Tellicherry A fine black peppercorn from southwest India.

peppercorn, white A peppercorn allowed to ripen on the vine; the berry is then fermented and its red-brown skin removed; it has a light white-tan color and milder flavor and aroma than those of a black peppercorn; available whole or ground.

pepper dulse A red seaweed; dried, it is used as a seasoning in Scottish cuisine.

pepper grinder; pepper mill A grinder used to crush peppercorns; many can be adjusted to produce fine to coarse granules.

pepper leaves The roundish, crinkly leaves from a bush related to the plant that produces peppercorns; used as wrappers for marinated meats, fish and shellfish and in soups and vegetable dishes in Thai and Vietnamese cuisines; also known as la-lot.

peppermint An herb and member of the mint family (*Mentha piperita*); it has thin, stiff, pointed, bright green, purple-tinged leaves and a pungent, menthol flavor; used as a flavoring and garnish.

peppermint oil The essential oil of peppermint; it has a sharp, menthol flavor and is used as a flavoring for sweet dishes.

peppermint schnapps A mint-flavored distilled spirit; it has a lighter body than crème de menthe.

pepperoncini (pehp-per-awn-CHEE-nee) 1. A short, tapered dried chile with an orange-red color, thin flesh and a medium hot, slightly sweet flavor. 2. Small, short pickled green peppers used as a garnish and salad ingredient.

pepperoni (pehp-puh-ROH-nee) A slender, firm, air-dried Italian sausage made from beef or pork, seasoned with chiles and red and black pepper.

pepperpot; pepper pot 1. A West Indian stew made with poultry, game or other meats, chiles and vegetables and thickened and flavored with cassareep. 2. A colonial American soup of tripe, meat, vegetables, black peppercorns and other seasonings; also known as Philadelphia pepperpot.

pepperrot (PEHPP-ehr-root) Norwegian for horseradish.

pepper sauce *See* poivrade, sauce.

peppersoup A spicy Nigerian soup flavored with garlic, dried bird chiles, dried smoked shrimp, mint, anise, coriander, cumin, allspice, ginger, fennel and tamarind; it can be made with chicken, goat, fish, mutton or organ meats.

pepper steak 1. Beef steak coated with coarsely ground black peppercorns; it is sautéed in butter and served with a sauce made from the drippings, stock, wine and cream; sometimes flamed with brandy or Cognac. 2. A Chinese stir-fry dish consisting of beef, green pepper and onions cooked with soy sauce and other seasonings.

peppery A wine-tasting term for a pungent aroma and flavor reminiscent of black peppercorns or other spices; sometimes caused by tannins and a high alcohol content, it can dissipate with age.

peppery furrow shell A bivalve mollusk found in warm waters of the Atlantic Ocean and in the Mediterranean Sea; it has a somewhat ovoid whitish-gray shell with thick growth lines, an average length of 1.5–2.5 in. (3.8–6.3 cm) and a tough, chewy flesh.

peptide (PEP-tid) A strand of two or more amino acids; a product of the digestion of proteins.

peptones (PEP-tones) A variable mixture of polypeptides, oligopeptides and amino acids derived from animal tissues that, as food additives, are used as nutrient supplements and/or processing aids.

pequeno almoço (puh-keh-noo al-moh-soo) Portuguese for breakfast.

pequín; piquin (pee-kihn) A small, conical dried chile with an orange-red color, a thin flesh and a sweet, smoky flavor.

PER *See* protein efficiency ratio.

pera (PAY-rah) Italian and Spanish for pear.

pêra (PAY-rah) Portuguese for pear.

perceived cost; perceived value A customer's idea of how much a product should cost as opposed to the seller's idea; also known as price–value relationship.

percentage of alcohol by volume *See* alcohol by volume.

percent daily value A nutrition facts term approved by the FDA describing how a food fits into the daily diet; it identifies the grams per serving of total fat, saturated fat, cholesterol, sodium, total carbohydrates, dietary fiber, sugars and protein and gives the percentage of the daily recommended amount of each nutrient (based on a 2000-calorie diet) that one serving provides.

perception The process of receiving information through one of the senses, comparing the information with past experiences, evaluating the comparisons, identifying the information and then storing it for future reference.

perch Any of various freshwater fish found in North America and Europe; they generally have an olive skin that becomes yellow on the sides, dark vertical bands, red-orange fins, and firm flesh with a delicate, mild flavor; the most significant variety in the United States is the yellow perch, and in Europe it is the pike perch.

perch

perche (pehrsh) French for perch.

perciatelli (per-chaa-TEHL-lee) Italian for small pierced and used to describe very thin, short, straight, hollow pasta.

perciatelloni (per-tcha-tel-low-nee) Wide perciatelli.

percolation (per-koh-lay-shun) A method of obtaining a liquid extract of a food such as coffee; a liquid is heated in the bottom of a container and then pumped to the top, where it is sprayed over the material to be extracted, dripping back to the bottom to be repercolated repeatedly until the desired flavor has been extracted.

percolator An electric coffeepot in which boiling water rising through a tube is deflected downward through a perforated basket containing coffee grounds.

perdiz (per-diss) Spanish and Portuguese for partridge.

perdrix (pehr-dree) French for partridge.

Peregrine peach A variety of peach; the fruit have an orange-flushed, golden skin, a yellowish-white flesh and an excellent flavor.

perejil (PEHR-eh-jeel) Spanish for parsley.

Père Joseph (PAIR jo-SEFF) A Belgian Trappist-style cow's milk cheese with a painted black rind and a mild, distinctive flavor.

peremende (pah-rah-men-dah) Swahili for candy.

peren (pee-AHR-en) Dutch for pears.

perennial A plant that lives for more than 2 years and usually flowers each year.

perez (pah-raz) Russian for pepper.

Perfection apricot A variety of apricot; the fruit are very large and have a firm texture and a fine flavor.

perforated spoon A spoon with a low-rimmed, honeycombed bowl that is generally 4 in. long and 3/8 in. deep; used to lift and drain small amounts of delicately textured foods.

perfume A wine-tasting term for the aroma of a young wine as opposed to the bouquet that a wine acquires with maturity.

pergulakan *See* chobek.

Perigord (perre-gohr) *See* truffle, black.

périgourdine, à la (pay-ree-gour-DEEN, ah lah) A French preparation method associated with Perigord, a region in France famous for black truffles; dishes are garnished or flavored with truffles and sometimes foie gras.

Périgueux, sauce (pay-ree-GOUH) A French compound sauce made from a demi-glaze flavored with Madeira and truffles.

perilla A member of the mint family grown in Hawaii; it has red and green leaves and is aromatic.

peri-peri; peli-peli South, Central and East African for a variety of red chiles.

perishable Foods and beverages that can spoil or deteriorate rapidly, even under appropriate storage conditions.

peristalsis (per-ah-STAL-sis) A progressive, wavelike movement occurring in the hollow tubes of the body (e.g., esophagus and intestines) and used to move food.

periwinkle A univalve mollusk found in freshwater and saltwater; it has a small, conical, spiral-shaped shell with a gray to dark olive surface and reddish-brown bands; it is eaten in various European cuisines after being boiled in its shell and has a chewy texture and yellow-ivory color; also known as a winkle or sea snail.

perlage (pehr-lahj) The bubbles in a glass of sparkling wine and the length of time they will last.

perlant (pehr-lahn) *See* cremant *and* spritzig.

Perle A variety of hops grown in Germany and Oregon.

Perlette grapes A variety of small table grapes with a light green skin, a crisp flesh and a very sweet flavor.

perlwein (PAIR'l-vine) The German equivalent of a slightly sparkling wine described as petillant. *See* spritzig.

pernice (pair-NEE-tchay) Italian for partridge.

Pernod (pair-noh) A French licorice-flavored pastis; similar to absinthe but made without oil of wormwood.

Pernod Cocktail A cocktail made of Pernod, water, sugar syrup and Angostura bitters.

peroo (peh-roo) Hindi for turkey.

perpetual inventory A system used to record all goods entering and leaving a storeroom.

perpetual spinach A plant with edible leaves similar to spinach or sorrel; also known as patience.

Perrier (peh-reh-ay) The proprietary name of a French mineral water.

perry A mildly alcoholic ciderlike beverage made from the fermented juice of pears; it can be still or sparkling and was popular in colonial America.

perry pears Any of a variety of small pears characterized by their bitter, astringent flavor; generally used for juice.

persetorsk (per-seh-tor-shk) Norwegian salted, boiled and pressed cod.

Persian apple A traditional name for the peach; native to China, the fruit originally came to Europe and the Western Hemisphere via Persia.

Persian herb *See* spinach.

Persian lime The most common market variety of lime (*Citrus latifolia*).

Persian melon A melon with a subtly netted yellowish-green skin and a dense, fragrant flesh.

Persian walnut *See* English walnut.

Persico A peach liqueur with overtones of almond and other fruits and flavorings.

persik (p'yer-seek) Russian for peach.

persil (pair-SEE) French for parsley.

persilja (POER-silyah) Swedish for parsley.

persillade (payr-se-yad) 1. A food served with or containing parsley. 2. A mixture of bread crumbs, parsley and garlic used to coat meats, usually lamb.

persille (pear-SILL-eh) Danish and Norwegian for parsley.

persimmon A spherical fruit with a glossy yellow to bright red skin, an orange-red flesh, a jelly-like texture and a sweet flavor when ripe; also imprecisely known as kaki and Sharon fruit.

persimmon

persimmon, American A small- to medium-sized persimmon (*Diospyros virginiana*) with a yellowish-pink or orange to red color and a very sweet flavor when ripe.

persimmon, Japanese A slightly elongated persimmon (*Diospyros kaki*) with red-orange skin and flesh, a soft, creamy texture and a tangy, sweet flavor; two types are available: hachiya (with a pointed base) and fuyu (smaller and more spherical).

persistence A beer- and wine-tasting term referring to the length of time a product's flavor remains in the mouth after swallowing or expectorating.

Pertsovka (pert-sov-kah) A dark brown Russian vodka flavored with capsicum and cayenne; it has a pleasant aroma and a burning, peppery flavor.

peru (pay-roo) Portuguese for turkey.

peruna (PAY-roo-nah) Finnish for potato.

Peruvian cress *See* capuchin.

Péruvienne, à la (pay-roo-vee-ahn, ah lah) A French garnish for meat consisting of stuffed oca and a sauce allemande.

pesca (PEH-skah) Italian for peach.

pescada (pesh-cah-dah) Portuguese for hake.

pescado (pays-KAH-dhoa) Spanish for fish.

pescado a la Veracruzana A Mexican dish of fish prepared in the style of Veracruz; the fish (usually a firm, white fish such as snapper) is seasoned with lemon or lime juice and pepper and then added to a sauté of onions, garlic, olives and tomatoes flavored with capers, chiles and pepper; it is served garnished with potatoes.

pescatora, alla (peh-skah-TOH-rah, AH-lah) Italian for the fisherman's style and used to describe a dish containing fish or shellfish.

pescatrice (pass-ka-tree-tchae) Italian for monkfish.

pesce (PAY-shay) Italian for fish.

pêssego (PAY-say-goh) Portuguese for peach.

pesticides Any of a group of synthetic or naturally occurring substances used to kill insects (insecticides), plants (herbicides), fungi (fungicides) or rodents (rodenticides); used to protect a food crop or as pest management, a pesticide can become an incidental food additive.

pestiños al anis (pess-tee-nyos al ah-ness) Spanish pastries made from a sweet pastry dough mixed with white wine and flavored with lemon zest and aniseeds, deep-fried, dipped into honey syrup and dusted with confectioners' sugar.

pestle (PES-tahl) *See* mortar and pestle.

pest management In the food safety context, the process of controlling and eliminating pests by (1) building them out of the facility; (2) creating an environment in which they cannot find food, water or shelter; and (3) exterminating those that do find such conditions.

pesto (PEH-stoh) 1. An Italian pasta sauce made from basil, garlic, olive oil, pine nuts and Parmesan or Pecorino. 2. In the United States, a term imprecisely used to describe a sauce or spread made principally from one herb (e.g., basil or cilantro) mixed with olive oil and a sharp, hard cheese, with pine nuts sometimes added.

pests In the food safety context, insects (e.g., roaches and flies) and rodents (e.g., mice and rats) that carry harmful bacteria or other microorganisms and therefore contaminate or potentially contaminate any surface with which they come in contact.

petanga *See* pitanga.

peteh; pete cina The edible bright green, ridged seed pods from a tree (*Parkia speciosa*) cultivated in Indonesia and used to give a characteristic flavor and aroma; the pods are also eaten as a vegetable and the seeds as a snack; also known as sindootan. *See* parkia.

petel (pah-tell) Hebrew for raspberry.

Peter Herring A Danish cherry-flavored liqueur made from the juice and pits of Danish cherries and aged in oak vats; formerly known as Cherry Herring.

Petersilie (pay-terr-ZEE-lier) German for parsley.

petillant (peh-tee-yahn) *See* cremant, frizzante *and* perlwein.

petiscos (peh-TISS-cohs) Small Portuguese delicacies similar to tapas; they are usually served in publike establishments with a glass of wine.

petit (peh-tee) French for small.

petita A variety of slicing cucumber; it is small, with a slightly wrinkled skin.

petit beurre (peh-tee burr) French for a small sweet biscuit or cookie made with a buttery dough, traditionally oblong with a fluted or scalloped edge.

petit déjeuner (peh-tee day-zhoo-NAY) French for breakfast.

petite marmite (peh-tee mar-meet) 1. French for a rich consommé garnished with beef and vegetables and served in the small earthenware pot in which it is cooked. 2. A miniature marmite used for serving single portions of soups, stews and the like.

petite steak A fabricated cut of the beef primal chuck; it is a small, tender steak.

Petite Syrah; Petite Sirah (peh-teete sih-RAH) 1. A red wine grape planted in California; derived from the Durif variety grown in France's Rhône Valley, it is sometimes used as a blending grape. 2. A red wine made from this grape; it generally has a full body, an intense, spicy aroma and a light to deep red color.

petit four (peh-tee FOOR) 1. A French term for any bite-sized cake, pastry, cookie or confection served after a meal or with coffee or tea. 2. A French confection consisting of a small piece of filled sponge cake coated with fondant icing and elaborately decorated.

petit four cases *See* paper candy cups.

petit four glacé (peh-tee FOOR glahs-say) An iced or cream-filled petit four.

petit fours sec (peh-tee FOOR seck) French term for small, dry, crisp cookies often served with coffee or tea or as an accompaniment to ice cream or sorbet.

petit-gris (peh-tee-gree) *See* escargot petit-gris.

petit poussin (peh-tee poo-SAHN) *See* poussin.

petit sale (peh-tee sal) French for the salted belly or flank of pork.

petits-pieds (peh-tee pee-ay) French for small birds such as blackbirds, thrushes, larks and finches that have culinary significance.

petits pois (peh-tee PWAH) French for green garden peas.

Petit Suisse (peh-tee SWEES) A small unripened French cheese made from fresh cow's milk and cream; it has the consistency of cream cheese and a delicate, sweetly tangy flavor.

petmèz (peht-mez) A sweet syrup made in the Balkans by boiling grape juice and sugar.

petrale sole (peh-TRAH-lee) A member of the flounder family found off the U.S. West Coast; it has an olive brown skin, a lean, white flesh, a fine texture, an excellent flavor and an average weight of 2.5 lb. (1.14 kg); also known as a brill sole.

petrolatum A food additive used as a release agent for processed foods such as baked goods and dehydrated fruits and vegetables and/or as a protective coating on raw fruits and vegetables.

petroleum naphtha A food additive used as a solvent in protective coatings on fresh citrus fruit; it may contain antioxidants.

petroleum wax A food additive refined from petroleum and used as a chewing gum base or protective coating on cheese and raw fruits and vegetables.

petrushka (pet-rue-scha) Russian for parsley.

pe-tsai (pa-tza-ee) A form of cabbage native to China; similar in appearance to romaine lettuce but with yellow-green leaves; it is eaten raw or cooked.

petticoats The shoots, rings or layers of an oyster shell, which help establish its age.

petticoat tail British for a pie-shaped wedge of shortbread cut from a large round; said to resemble a 12th-century woman's petticoat.

petti di pollo (PEHT-tee dee POAL-loa) Italian for chicken breasts.

petty cash A small amount of cash kept for minor or incidental expenses that do not warrant a formal purchase order.

pewa The large datelike fruit of a tree native to Central America; usually cooked in salt water, it has a flavor reminiscent of chestnuts; also known as a peach nut.

Peychaud Bitters An aromatic, anise-flavored New Orleans bitters used for a Sazerac.

peynir (pan-ir) Turkish for cheese.

pézinho do porco (pah-zee-nyo doh por-koh) Portuguese for smoked pig's feet.

Pfannkuchen (PFAN-eh-kook-hern) German for pancake.

Pfeffer (PFEH-ferr) German for pepper.

Pfeffernüesse (FEF-ferr-noos) A hard, round, spicy German Christmas cookie flavored with honey and black pepper.

Pfeffer-Potthast (pfer-ferr-PO-tahast) A German stew consisting of beef, onions, bay leaves and other herbs; it is thickened with bread crumbs and highly seasoned with pepper.

Pfifferling (PFIF-ferr-leng) German for chanterelle.

Pfirsich (PFEER-zikh) German for peach.

Pflaume (PFLOW-may) German for plum.

pH Abbreviation for potential of hydrogen, a measure of the acidity or alkalinity of a substance; maximum acidity is a pH of 0, maximum alkalinity is 14 and 7 is the neutral point, with a tenfold difference between each number.

phal (fahl) Hindi for fruit.

phalsa; pharsa The small, red berries of a shrub native to India; they have a tart flavor and are usually used for flavoring syrups and sorbets.

pH control agent A type of food additive used to change or maintain a food's acidity or alkalinity; includes buffers, acids, alkalies and neutralizing agents.

pheasant A game bird with a light to medium dark flesh, a tender texture, a sweet flavor and an average dressed market weight of 1.5–2.2 lb. (0.3–1 kg); also farm raised.

phenylacetaldehyde Food additive used as a flavoring agent and/or adjuvant.

phenylalanine 1. An essential amino acid. 2. A food additive used as a nutrient source to significantly improve the biological quality of the total protein in a food containing naturally occurring protein.

phenylethylamine (PEA) An organic substance found in chocolate that may release endorphins in the brain.

phenylethyl anthranilate A food additive with a grape or orange blossom aroma used as a flavoring agent in beverages, candies, baked goods and ice creams.

phenylketonuria (PKU) An inherited intolerance of the amino acid phenylalanine; it can cause retardation if dietary intake of phenylalanine is not restricted.

phenylpropanolamine (FEN-ill-pro-pah-NOLE-ahmeen) A drug approved by the FDA that suppresses the appetite; it is the principal active ingredient in most over-the-counter diet pills and may cause adverse side effects in some people.

Philadelphia cheese steak *See* cheese steak.

Philadelphia pepperpot *See* pepperpot.

Philippine spinach A variety of purslane used like spinach.

phlegm (flem) *See* humors.

pho (fo) A northern Vietnamese beef noodle soup; when made with chicken it is known as pho ga.

pho ga *See* pho.

Phoebe Snow A cocktail made of Cognac, Dubonnet rouge and Pernod.

phoenix mushroom *See* oyster mushroom.

pholiotte (foe-lee-oh-tay) A mushroom (*Agrocybe aegerita*) originally cultivated by the ancient Greeks and Romans on poplar wood; it has a long, slender stem and a smooth, round, yellow cap.

phool badi (pool bah-dee) Indian tapioca or sago wafers; rice wafers.

phool go-bhee (pool go-bee) Hindi for cauliflower.

phosphated flour Flour to which monocalcium phosphate has been added.

phosphates A group of food additives used as pH control agents and/or flavor (tartness) enhancers in processed foods such as tart beverages and gelatins.

phospholipids Any of a group of lipids, similar to triglycerides, composed of two fatty acids, a phosphorus-containing acid and glycerol (e.g., lecithin); often found as a constituent of cell walls.

phosphoric acid A food additive used as a flavor enhancer (tartness) and/or pH control agent in processed foods such as soft drinks and desserts.

phosphorus A major mineral used principally to form bones and teeth, assist the conversion of glycogen to glucose and as a part of a buffering system that maintains the acid–base balance; it is found in many foods and significant sources include liver, dairy products, legumes, grains, beef, poultry, fish, cabbage, celery and carrots.

photosynthesis The chlorophyll-assisted process by which plants utilize the sun's energy to combine carbon dioxide and water to form carbohydrates.

phulka (pool-kah) An Indian whole wheat puffed bread.

phyllo; filo Pastry dough made with very thin sheets of a flour-and-water mixture; several sheets are often layered with melted butter and used in sweet or savory preparations.

phylloquinone *See* vitamin K.

Phylloxera vastatrix A genus of plant lice (aphid); the lice attack the leaves and roots of grapevines; native to America, the lice were introduced into Europe and almost destroyed all the vineyards of France and other wine-producing countries in the late 19th century.

physical contaminant; physical hazard *See* hazard, physical.

physical inventory The actual counting of all goods in stock at the end of an accounting period.

phytates Compounds found in plant foods such as whole grains and beans; they prevent the absorption of zinc.

phytochemical A chemical found in plants believed to help prevent some cancers and promote others.

piadina (pee-ah-DEE-nah) Italian for little plate and used to describe a thin round of bread grilled in an earthenware pan and topped with a slice of prosciutto, salami or cheese and then folded over.

piano-wire whisk *See* sauce whisk.

piànr (pee-ahnr) Chinese for slices.

piatto (peh-ah-toh) Italian for plate.

piatto del giorno (pee-at-tow dale gee-or-no) Italian menu term for the day's special.

pibil (pee-bill) A Mexican and Latin American method of pit cooking foods; replaced today by wrapping food in a banana leaf and steaming it.

pica (PIE-ka) An appetite for nonfood substances, such as clay, ashes, plaster and laundry starch.

picada (pee-cah-dah) A Spanish flavoring paste made of garlic, parsley and saffron ground with almonds or pine nuts.

picadillo (pee-kah-DEE-yoh) Spanish for hash and used to describe a Central American and Caribbean dish of ground pork and beef or veal, onions, garlic and tomatoes used as a stuffing (in Mexico) or sauce (for beans in Cuba).

picadinho de porco (pee-kah-deen-nyu duh pohr-koo) A Central and South American dish of ground pork, onions, tomatoes and chiles, seasoned with sage and lemon juice and used as a filling for empanadas, a stuffing for vegetables or as is, garnished with hard-boiled eggs and olives.

picante (pee-KAHN-tay) Spanish and Portuguese for spicy.

piccalilli (PIHK-uh-lih-lee) An English relish of pickled tomatoes, sweet peppers, onions, zucchini, cucumber, cauliflower and cabbage, flavored with brown sugar, allspice and cider vinegar.

piccante (pick-CON-tay) Italian for spicy.

piccante, salsa A piquant Italian cold sauce made from red wine, olive oil, wine vinegar, onions, garlic, red pepper seeds and rosemary; used for cold meats or as a basting agent.

piccata (pih-CAH-tuh) An Italian dish of thinly sliced chicken or veal, lightly floured, sautéed in butter and sprinkled with lemon juice.

Picheisteiner (PIK-herl-shtigh-nerr) A German meat and vegetable casserole.

pichet (pee-shay) A small earthenware jug or pitcher used in France to serve wine at the table.

pichi (pe-che) Swahili for peach.

picholine (pee-show-leen) A large green olive grown in France.

pichón (pe-CHON) Spanish for squab.

picked Crab or lobster meat removed from the shell with a fine, needlelike tool called a pick.

pickerel A freshwater fish and member of the pike family; it has an average market weight of 2–3 lb. (0.09–1.35 kg), a low fat content and a finely textured flesh with a moderately strong flavor.

pickle v. To preserve food in a brine or vinegar solution. n. Food that has been preserved in a seasoned brine or vinegar.

pickle castor A covered glass jar, about 6 in. high, set in a metal frame; the frame has a base and tall handles; tongs hanging from it are used to retrieve the pickles.

pickled cheeses Cheeses to which considerable salt has been added as a preservative; typically made in Mediterranean countries, they are usually soft, white cheeses steeped in brine (e.g., feta, Damietta and Brandza).

pickle castor

pickled eggs Shelled hard-boiled eggs immersed in vinegar and peppercorns; often served as bar food.

pickled herring Herring marinated in vinegar and spices and then bottled in either a sour cream or wine sauce.

pickled onions Small onions pickled in vinegar, sugar and pickling spices.

pickled pork Pork pickled in salt, sugar, saltpeter and water; after pickling it is usually boiled with root vegetables.

pickled walnuts Green (young) walnuts pickled in vinegar, caramel, black pepper and other spices; they turn black and are eaten with cold cuts and cheese.

pickling *See* curing.

pickling agent *See* curing agent.

pickling lime A fine white powder (calcium hydroxide) that reacts with acidic ingredients such as cucumbers, tomatoes and melons to make them crisp.

pickling onion A small, tender onion with a golden yellow outer layer, white flesh and mild flavor; usually pickled, boiled or used for sauces.

pickling salt A fine-grained salt without additives.

pickling spices A spice blend used to flavor the solution used to pickle foods or as a seasoning; generally the blend contains whole or coarsely broken allspice, red chile flakes, bay leaves, peppercorns, mustard seeds, cardamom seeds, coriander seeds, cloves and ginger.

pickling vinegar A malt vinegar flavored with black and white peppercorns, allspice, cloves and small hot chiles.

Pick Me Up Any beverage designed to allay the effects of an overindulgence in alcoholic beverages.

pickup station A section at a bar where servers place drink orders, receive the drinks, deposit cash and return empty glasses.

picnic 1. Traditionally, a meal eaten inside or outside to which each guest brought a dish. 2. A meal, usually midday, eaten outside; although hot and cold foods can be served, if foods are cooked, it is usually referred to as a barbecue.

picnic ham; picnic shoulder A subprimal cut of the pork primal shoulder; cut from the foreleg, it is usually deboned and smoked; also known as a California ham, cala and pork shoulder.

picnic noodles *See* yee fu mein.

pico de gallo (PEE-koh day GI-yoh) Spanish for rooster's beak and used to describe a relish of finely chopped jicama, onions, bell pepper, oranges, jalapeños and cucumbers.

pico de pajaro (PEE-koh day PAH-ha-roh) A small dried chile shaped like a bird's beak; it has a thin, deep orange-red skin and a mild, fruity flavor.

Picodon de la Drome (pee-koh-DAW duh lah DROHM) A goat's milk cheese from France's Provence region; it has an off-white, slightly wrinkled exterior, a soft, creamy, white interior and a very sweet, mild flavor; it is often aged in eau-de-vie, brandy or wine and has a dark golden exterior and a buff-colored interior with a strong nutty flavor; available herbed, peppered with garlic or packed in jars with olive oil and herbs.

picolit (PEE-koh-leet) A semisweet to sweet golden wine from Italy's Fruili region; it is made from Picolot grapes.

Pícon (pee-kohn) 1. A bitter French cordial; often mixed with sparkling water and sometimes sweetened with grenadine. 2. A cocktail made of Amer Pícon and sweet vermouth.

Picón (pe-KOHN) A Spanish blue-veined goat cheese; also known as Cabrales.

pide (pid) A Turkish flatbread with a soft crust and a chewy interior; it is sometimes glazed and sprinkled with sesame or nigella seeds and is eaten plain, filled or with the filling on top.

pie 1. A pastry consisting of a sweet filling in a pastry crust baked in a slope-sided pan, it may have a bottom crust only or a top and bottom crust. 2. A savory meat- or vegetable-filled turnover or pastry. 3. A sweet fruit mixture baked in a deep dish with only a top crust (e.g., cobbler).

pie bird A small, hollow figurine available in various shapes, but typically a bird, that is placed in the middle of a double-crusted pie and acts as a vent to release the steam that builds up during baking.

pièce de boeuf (pee-es duh buff) *See* aiguillette.

pièce de résistance (pee-ace duh rae-see-stans) A French term traditionally reserved for the most important or impressive dish served at a meal and now also used for the main course.

pièces montée (pee-es mohn-tay) The elaborate, lavish table decorations (both inedible and edible) popular at French grande cuisine banquets.

pie cheese Any cheese, such as bakers' or cottage cheese, used to make cheesecake, cheese pie or other baked goods.

pied de mouton (pee-ay duh moo-tohn) French for hedgehog mushroom.

Piedmont; Piemonte (PYAY-mahnt; pee-eh-MOHN-teh) One of Italy's principal grape-growing and wine-producing regions, located in northwest Italy, bordered by France on the west and Switzerland on the north; the region's predominant grape is the Nebbiolo.

piédmont butter A compound butter made with Parmesan, lemon zest and nutmeg.

piédmontese See truffle, white.

pieds de porc (pee-ay duh por) French for pig's feet.

pie jagger See jagging wheel.

piel de sapo (peh-el de sah-poh) A variety of honeydew melon.

piémontaise, à la (pyay-mohntez, ah lah) A French garnish for poultry and meat consisting of risotto with shredded truffles; prepared in a timbale or as a border around the dish.

piémontaise, sauce à la; piédmont sauce (pyay-mohntez, sos ah lah) A French compound sauce made from a cream sauce flavored with chicken glaze, lemon juice, onions and garlic, garnished with truffles and pine nuts and finished with garlic butter.

pien (pee-hen) Chinese for quickly stir-frying foods without oil or sauce.

piens (pee-ahns) Latvian for milk.

pie pan; pie plate A round, 1- to 2-in.-deep glass or metal pan with sloped sides used for baking pies.

pie plant; pieplant See rhubarb.

pierna de cordero (PYEHR-nah day koar-DAY-roa) A Spanish dish consisting of leg of lamb.

pierogi (peer-OH-gee) A Polish dish consisting of dumplings or noodles stuffed with mixtures such as pork, onions and cottage cheese or cabbage, mushrooms, potatoes and rice and boiled, baked or fried.

pierre rouge (pee-err rooj) A small, western European traditional apple with a yellow and red-blushed skin and a very juicy, white flesh.

Piesport (PEEZ-port) A wine-producing village along the Moselle River in Germany; its white wines are delicate, fragrant and fruity.

pie veal A British cut of the veal carcass, usually diced meat from the less desirable cuts such as the scrag or middle neck.

pie weights Ceramic or aluminum pellets used to weigh down a pie crust that is baked without a filling. See bake blind.

pig The young swine of either sex weighing less than 120 lb. (54 kg). See boar and sow.

pig, suckling A pig slaughtered when it is 6–8 weeks old; the meat has a light-colored flesh with a succulent flavor and a tender texture.

pigeon 1. One of the principal kinds of poultry recognized by the USDA; domesticated pigeon has dark meat and an earthy, gamy flavor. 2. A mature pigeon slaughtered when older than 4 weeks has a coarse skin, a moderately tough flesh and an average market weight of 1–2 lb. (0.45–1 kg). 3. French for squab.

pigeon classes Significant pigeon classes are the squab and pigeon.

pigeon grape A North American grape variety; the early-ripening grapes have a black skin; also known as bunch grape and summer grape.

pigeon pea A small, slightly flattened pea (*Cajanus cajan*) native to Africa; it grows in a long, twisted, fuzzy pod, has a grayish-yellow color and is usually available dried and split into two disks and used in African and Caribbean cuisines; also known as arhar dhal, channa, dhal, goongoo, congo pea, gungo pea, red gram, cajan, no-eyed pea and tropical green pea.

pighvar (PIG-varr) Norwegian and Swedish for turbot.

pigment A substance that contributes color to a food or processed food; either naturally occurring (e.g., the yellow-orange beta-carotene pigment found in carrots) or a chemical additive. See coloring agent.

pigne (pin-yee) French for pine nut.

pig out Slang for overeating, usually without discrimination.

pig peas See cu-san.

pig pickin' American southern (especially North Carolina) slang for a social gathering at which pulled pork is cooked and served.

pig's feet A pig's ankles and feet; available fresh, pickled or smoked, they contain many small bones and connective tissue and are rich in pectin; also known as trotters (especially in Great Britain).

pigs in blankets 1. Sausages (usually small cocktail sausages) wrapped in pie or bread dough. 2. Breakfast sausages wrapped in pancakes.

pig's knuckles A fabricated cut of the pork carcass; part of the pig's feet and available fresh and pickled.

pigwa (pee-goo-ah) Polish for quince.

piijiu (pee-jew) Chinese for beer.

piimä (PEE-may) Finnish for clotted milk. See viilipiimä.

pikant (pee-KAHN't) German for spicy; also known as würzig.

pike Any of various freshwater fish found worldwide; they generally have a greenish skin that becomes white on the belly, red fins, an average market weight of 4–10 lb. (1.8–4.5 kg), a low fat content and a firm flesh with a mild flavor and many small bones; significant varieties include the muskellunge and pickerel.

pikelet 1. In England, a small, flat crumpet. 2. In Australia and New Zealand, a small drop scone.

pike perch A freshwater fish found in Europe; it has an average market weight of 40 lb. (18 kg) and a white flesh with a delicate flavor; also known as walleyed pike.

Pike's Peak A fabricated cut of the beef primal round; it is a peak-shaped roast cut from the top and heel of the round.

piki bread (pee-kee) A traditional Hopi bread made with blue cornmeal and ashes; the batter is baked in very thin sheets on a hot stone, then rolled into a cylinder; also known as paper bread.

pikkelsagurk (peak-kal-saw-goork) Norwegian for gherkin.

pikkulämpimät (peack-kool-lahm-pimo) Finnish for hot hors d'ouevre. *See* voileipäpyötä.

pilaf (PEE-lahf) A cooking method for grains; the grains are lightly sautéed in hot fat and then a hot liquid (usually stock) is added; the mixture is simmered without stirring until the liquid is absorbed.

pilafi (pea-law-fee) A Greek dish of Turkish origin consisting of rice cooked by the pilaf method and garnished with any of a variety of items.

pilau; pilav (PEE-lahf) A Turkish dish consisting of grains, usually rice, cooked as salma (the grains are boiled in stock until all stock is absorbed), suzme (strained method—the grains are boiled in salted water and fat is poured over them) and kavurma (fried method—the grains are sautéed and then cooked in stock).

pilau; purloo (pi-loe; puhr-loo) A rice dish from the Low Country of the American South consisting of long-grain rice cooked in an aromatic broth until almost dry; meat, fish or shellfish is usually added and the whole is garnished with minced parsley.

pilaw turecki (pee-lat too-reh-ts-kee) A Polish pilaf flavored with tomato purée and paprika.

pilchard (PIHL-chuhrd) A small fish found in the Atlantic Ocean from Scandinavia to Portugal; it is similar to a sardine and has a high fat content.

pīles (pee-less) Latvian for duck.

pileus *See* cap.

pilgrim's squash *See* Hercules' bludgeon gourd.

pili The nut of a tree (*Canarium ovatum* and *C. luzonicum*) native to the Philippines; similar to an almond in texture, flavor and use and with an extremely high oil content; also imprecisely known as a Chinese olive or Java almond.

pili pili A West African condiment; the basic sauce consists of tomatoes, onions, garlic, chiles and horseradish, with other ingredients added to complement the dish with which it will be served.

Pi Lo Chun Chinese for green snail spring and used to describe a Chinese green tea; the tender young leaves are hand rolled into tiny spirals from which the tea takes its name; the beverage has an aroma reminiscent of the peach, apricot and plum trees planted among the tea bushes.

piloncillo (pee-loan-che-yoh) Mexican brown sugar packaged in pyramid-shaped pieces.

pilot cracker A form of hardtack, but usually sweetened.

pilpili manga (peel-pee-lee mahn-gah) Swahili for pepper.

Pilsner; Pilsener; Pils (pilz-nur) 1. Traditionally, a fine, light lager beer with a strong hop finish of a style associated with Pilsen, Czech Republic. 2. Today, any pale, light lager beer.

Pilsner glass A tall, slender, V-shaped, footed glass with a 7- to 10-fl. oz. capacity used for serving draft or bottled beer, especially lager beer.

Pilsner glass

Pilsner Urquell (pilz-nur ur-KELL) The original and most famous Pilsner beer; made in the town of Pilsen, Czech Republic.

Pilze (pilt-ser) German for mushroom.

pimaricin *See* natamycin.

pimenta (pee-MEN-tah) Portuguese for pepper.

piment basquais (pee-ment bass-kway) A spicy brick red pepper used in Spain's Basque cuisine.

pimento (pee-MEHN-toh) Another name for allspice, the dried aromatic berry of the tree *Pimenta officinalis;* also known as Jamaican pepper and pimenta.

Pimento Dram A spicy Jamaican liqueur made from the flower buds of the pimento tree.

pimentón (pee-mayn-TON) Spanish for paprika and cayenne pepper.

piment pays *See* cubebs.

pimet *See* pymet.

pimienta (pee-MYEHN-tah) Spanish for pepper.

pimiento A large, heart-shaped pepper with a red skin and a sweet flavor; used in paprika and to stuff olives.

pimiento cheese Any cheese (typically cheese spreads, Neufchâtel-style cheese and cream cheese) to which chopped pimientos have been added.

pimientos assados (pee-me-n-toss assa-dos) A Portuguese petisco dish of broiled peppers served with vinegar, oil, garlic, salt and paprika.

Pimm's Cup; Pimm's No. 1 Cup A gin-based British beverage made from a secret recipe; it has a refreshing, slightly herbal flavor; it can be drunk neat but is usually mixed with lemonade, soda water or ginger ale and garnished with orange, lemon or cucumber slices; other versions were discontinued in 1974: No. 2 (whiskey base), No. 3 (brandy base) and No. 4 (rum base).

piña (PEE-nayh) Spanish for pineapple.

pinaatti (PEE-natt-tee) Finnish for spinach.

Piña Colada (PEEN-yuh koh-LAH-duh) A cocktail made of rum, pineapple juice and cream of coconut served over ice and garnished with a pineapple chunk.

pinakbet (pe-nahk-bet) A Filipino braised mixed vegetable dish that always includes eggplant.

pinaksiw (pee-nak-siw) A Filipino pickling method for sardines; the fish are layered in large pots with banana leaves, salt and coconut vinegar and simmered over a wood fire.

pinard (pee-nahr) French slang for an inexpensive red wine.

pinatsu (pee-nah-tsoo) Japanese for peanut.

pinbone sirloin A fabricated cut of the beef carcass; a small sirloin steak containing the pinbone cut from the loin end.

pincer (PIN-sehr) To heat meats and vegetables to release and caramelize their juices before braising.

pinch A traditional measure of volume; refers to the amount of a seasoning or other food one can hold between the thumb and forefinger, approximately 1/16 teaspoon.

pinched noodles *See* csipetke.

pinchito (pen-CHEE-toh) Spanish for kabob.

pineapple 1. A tropical fruit (*Ananas comosus*) with a spiny, diamond-patterned, greenish-brown skin and swordlike leaves; the juicy yellow flesh surrounds a hard core and has a sweet–tart flavor. 2. *See* bromelin.

pineapple cheese 1. A Cheddar-style cheese made in the United States from cow's milk; it has a rosy color and pineapple-like shape. 2. Cream cheese combined with crushed pineapple and used as a sandwich spread or filling.

pineapple corer A tall tool with two concentric rings with serrated teeth; as the corer is pressed down over the pineapple, one ring separates the flesh from the skin and the other separates the core from the flesh.

pineapple guava *See* feijoa.

pineapple melon A melon with a netted orange skin and flesh; it has an aroma reminiscent of a pineapple.

Pineau des Charentes (pee-no day shah-rahn't) A French aperitif made from young Cognac and unfermented grape juice.

pine kernel *See* pine nut.

pine mushroom *See* matsutake.

pine nut The nut of various pine trees (genus *Pinus*); it has a shell that covers ivory-colored meat, a rich distinctive flavor and a high fat content; also known as a pine kernel and Indian nut.

pine nut, Chinese A squat, triangular-shaped pine nut.

pine nut, Italian An elongated ovoid pine nut; also known as pinolo.

pine nut oil An oil obtained by pressing pine nuts; it has a light brown color and a rich, nutty, full flavor; used for salads or in place of butter.

pinggou (PING-guo) Chinese for apple.

pinhoadas (pee-nyo-ah-dass) A Portuguese sweet of pine nuts bound with honey, sugar and butter.

Pinienuss (pee-yohn-nuss) German for pine nut.

pinion (PIN-yahn) 1. The terminal segment of a bird's wing; used in soups, fricassees and braised dishes; also known as the tip. 2. The raybone in a fish fin.

pinipig (pee-nee-pig) A toasted, flattened glutinous rice used in Filipino baked goods, puddings and dessert toppings.

pink abalone A variety of abalone found in the Pacific Ocean off California and Mexico; it has a large, round, corrugated shell with a pinkish interior and an ivory flesh with a chewy texture and mild flavor; also known as corrugated abalone.

pink bean A smooth reddish-brown dried bean, similar to the pinto bean.

pink champagne, California A sparkling rosé made in California by the Charmat process using a pink or rosé wine.

Pink Gin A cocktail made of gin (usually Plymouth) and a dash of Angostura bitters.

Pink Lady A cocktail made of grenadine, lemon juice, apple brandy, gin, egg white and cream, shaken with ice and strained into a stemmed cocktail glass.

pink peppercorn The dried berry of a South American rose plant; it has a rose color and a bitter, pinelike flavor and is available dried or pickled in vinegar. *See* peppercorn.

pink rose apple A pink variety of rose apple with a striped skin; it is eaten raw in salads or desserts; also known as chompoo (Thailand).

Pink Rye A cocktail made of rye and Angostura bitters.

pink salmon A variety of salmon found in the Pacific Ocean from California to Alaska; it has a bluish-green skin with numerous black blotches, a lean, soft, pink flesh and a mild flavor and is generally used for canning; also known as a humpback salmon.

Pink Squirrel A cocktail made of crème de noyaux, white crème de cacao and cream.

Pinklewürst (pinka-voorst) A sausage traditionally made in Bremen, Germany, from groats and smoked pork; also known as Grütswurst.

pinning *See* needling.

pinol Dry toasted corn kernels ground to a powder and used to thicken sauces for poultry dishes in Central American cuisines.

pinole; panola (pah-NOH-lah) A Mexican and American Southwestern pudding made from ground dried corn, spices and a sweetener.

pinoli (pee-NOH-lee) Italian for pine nuts.

piñon (PIHN-yuhn) Spanish for pine nut.

Pinot, true Any of several closely related varieties of grapes derived from the Pinot Noir grape.

Pinotage (pee-noh-TAHJ) A red wine grape originating in South Africa; it is a cross between a Pinot Noir and a Hermitage (Cinsaut).

Pinot Bianco *See* Pinot Blanc.

Pinot Blanc (PEE-noh BLAHN) 1. A white wine grape considered to be a true Pinot and planted in France (Alsace), Germany, Austria, Italy and California; also known as Weissburgunder (in Germany and Austria) and Pinot Bianco (in Italy). *See* Melon de Bourgogne. 2. A white wine made from this grape; dry and crisp but with less flavor than a Chardonnay; because of its high acidity, it is suitable for making sparkling wine.

Pinot Chardonnay *See* Chardonnay.

Pinot Grigio *See* Pinot Gris.

Pinot Gris (pee-noh gree) A white wine grape grown in Italy, Germany, France and parts of central Europe; the resulting wine is generally full bodied; also known as Pinot Grigio (Italy), Tokay d'Alsace (Alsace) and Rülander (Germany).

Pinot Meunier (pee-noh muh-n'yay) A red wine grape closely related to the Pinot Noir; it is often used as a blending grape with Chardonnay or Pinot Noir to add fruitiness to the resulting wine.

Pinot Nero *See* Pinot Noir.

Pinot Noir (PEE-noh n'wahr) 1. A red wine grape grown worldwide, including France's Champagne and Burgundy regions, Germany, Italy, central Europe, California and Oregon; also known as Spätburgunder (in Germany) and Pinot Nero (in Italy). 2. A red wine made from this grape; it has a medium to deep ruby red color and a minty or black cherry aroma; also used to make a rosé wine and sparkling wines.

pinpoint bubbles *See* beads.

pint 1. A unit of volume measurement; in the U.S. system, it is equal to 16 fl. oz., and in the imperial system, it is equal to 20 fl. oz. 2. British slang for a beer.

pintada (pang-tah-da) Spanish for guinea fowl.

pintade (pen-TAD) French for guinea fowl.

pinto bean A medium-sized pale pink bean with reddish-brown streaks; available dried; also known as a crabeye bean and a red Mexican bean.

pinworm *See* threadworm.

pip A seed of a fleshy fruit that has many seeds, such as an orange, apple or pear; also known as a carpel.

piparjuuri (pee-par-yoo-ari) Finnish for horseradish.

pipe A large wooden barrel with sharply tapered ends, used to mature and ship port and Madeira; a standard port pipe is 522.5 l, or 138 U.S. gallons; a standard Madeira pipe is 418 l, or 110 gallons.

pipengaille *See* papengaye.

pipérade (pee-pay-RAHD) A Basque stewlike dish of tomatoes and sweet peppers seasoned with onions and garlic and cooked in olive oil or goose fat and then mixed with beaten eggs.

piperies (pee-peh-rhies) Greek for sweet peppers.

piperitenone A food additive with a peppery flavor used as a flavoring agent and/or adjuvant.

piperonyl acetate A food additive with a berry aroma used as a flavoring agent in baked goods, beverages, ice creams and candies.

piperonyl isobutyrate A food additive with a fruity aroma used as a flavoring agent in baked goods, beverages, ice creams and candies.

pipette (pi-pet) *See* thief.

pipiân (pee-PYHAN) A Mexican spicy stew with a nut- or seed-thickened sauce.

pipikaula; pipi kaula (PEE-pee-kah-OO-lah) A Hawaiian dish of sun-dried beef jerky sometimes brushed with teriyaki sauce before drying; it is usually eaten as is or in salads.

piping Forcing a material, such as icing, chocolate, buttercream or choux pastry, from a pastry bag in a steady and even manner to form specific shapes or decorative designs.

piping bag *See* pastry bag.

piping chocolate Melted chocolate mixed with water, a simple syrup or other liquid to make it fluid enough for piping.

piping gel A sweet but flavorless, colored transparent substance made from sugar, corn syrup and vegetable gum; used for decorating cakes and pastries.

pipis de frango (pee-pes day frahn-go) A Portuguese petisco dish of fried chicken offal served warm with garlic and piri-piri.

pipkin (PIP-kin) A small metal or earthenware pot or pan with a single long handle.

Pipo Crem' A soft French cheese made from cow's milk; it has a thin, whitish rind, an ivory interior with blue veins and a rich, salty flavor.

pippin 1. A generic name given to an apple from a tree raised from seed. 2. Any of a variety of roundish or ovoid apples. *See* Newton pippin apple.

piquant (pee-kant) 1. French for spicy. 2. An agreeably pungent, sharp or tart aroma or flavor. 3. A wine-tasting term for a tart, lively, acidic white wine.

piquante, sauce A French compound sauce made from a demi-glaze flavored with shallots, wine and vinegar and garnished with herbs and gherkins.

piquette (pee-ket) 1. A wine product made by adding water to the pomace after the principal wine has been made and then refermenting it. 2. A wine-tasting term for a poor, thin, acidic wine.

piquillos (pee-kee-yos) Long, red, tapering, triangular Spanish peppers.

piquín (pe-KEEN) *See* pequín.

piri-piri (pee-ree-pee-ree) Portuguese for small, very hot, red chiles.

piroshki; pirozhki (pih-ROSH-kee) Russian or Polish turnovers made of choux pastry, puff pastry or a yeast dough filled with a savory mixture of meat, fish, cheese or mushrooms, baked or deep-fried.

pirouettes (pir-oh-ET) Thin wafer cookies that are curled tightly around a dowel while still hot; the ends are often dipped in melted chocolate.

pirozhnoye (pih-roshz-nan-ye) Russian for pastry.

pirurutung (pee-roo-roo-tong) A dark, purple-colored rice used in Filipino cuisine.

pisang goreng (pee-sung goh-REHNG) A Dutch–Indonesian dish of bananas sprinkled with lemon juice and butter and baked; served with nasi goreng.

Pisco (PIHS-koh) A Peruvian grape brandy made from Muscat wine pomace; aged in paraffin-coated containers rather than oak to avoid the absorption of flavors and color.

Pisco Sour A cocktail made of Pisco, lemon juice, sugar syrup, egg white and Angostura bitters.

piselli (pee-SEHL-lee) Italian for green peas.

pismo clam A variety of Pacific clam with a hard shell that measures more than 5 in. (12.7 cm); it has a tender, sweet flesh.

pissaladiere (pee-sah-lah-DYAIR) A savory southern French tart consisting of a crust topped with onions, anchovies, black olives and sometimes tomatoes.

pissalat; pissala (pee-sah-lah) A condiment from France's Nice region made from anchovy purée flavored with cloves, thyme, bay leaf and pepper mixed with olive oil.

pissed Slang for intoxicated.

pissenlit (pee-sehn-lee) French for dandelion.

pistacchio (pe-STACH-cheo) Italian for pistachio.

pistaches (pee-stash) French for pistachios.

pistachio (pih-STASH-ee-oh) A pale green nut (*Pistacia vera*) encased in a hard, tan shell that is sometimes dyed red with food coloring or blanched until white; it has a delicate, subtle flavor.

pisto (PEES-toh) A Spanish dish of cooked tomatoes, red and green peppers, onions, garlic, mushrooms, eggplant and other vegetables; sometimes ham or other meat is added.

pistolet (pees-TOO-lay) A Belgian roll; it is generally eaten with sausages, cheese and eggs.

pisto manchego (pees-TOH mahn-TCHE-goh) A Spanish dish consisting of stewed zucchini, green peppers and tomatoes garnished with chopped parsley.

pistou (pees-TOO) 1. A condiment from France's Provence region made from fresh basil crushed with garlic and olive oil; sometimes Parmesan and tomatoes are added. 2. A French soup made with white beans, green beans, onions and tomatoes and seasoned with pistou.

pisztráng (piz-trag) Hungarian for trout.

pit *v.* To remove the pit or stone from a fruit. *n.* The seed or stone of a fruit, such as a cherry, peach or apricot.

pita; pita bread; pitta; pitah (PEE-tah brehd) An oval- or round-shaped, hollow Middle Eastern flatbread leavened with yeast; it is often split open or cut crosswise to form a pocket, then filled with a stuffing; also known as pocket bread. *See* khobaz.

píta Greek pastry pies made with phyllo dough.

pitahaya; pitaya (pee-tah-ha-yah; pee-ta-ee-ah) The medium-sized ovoid fruit of a cactus (*Hylocereus undatus*) native to Central and South America; there are two principal varieties: one with a red skin and pink flesh, the other with a yellow skin and white flesh; both have a soft, juicy flesh with numerous black seeds and a bland flavor; also known as a strawberry pear.

pitanga; petanga (pee-than-gah; pae-than-gaw) A cherry-sized fruit of a tree (*Eugenia uniflora*) native to Central America; it has a bright red skin marked by deep furrows, one or more seeds and a pleasant, slightly sour flavor and is usually made into jams; also known as Surinam cherry.

pitch To add yeast to a cooled wort.

pitcher A relatively large vessel with a handle and a wide mouth; used for storing and serving liquids.

pith The bitter, white membrane found in citrus fruit between the rind (zest) and the pulp.

Pithiviers (pee-tee-vee-a) A round, thin French pastry made with two circles of puff pastry dough enclosing a frangipane (almond) filling; a spiral or rosette pattern is etched on the top before baking; a speciality of the town of Pithiviers in France's Loire region.

piti A spicy Azerbaijan lamb stew flavored with tomatoes.

pitmaster A cook responsible for turning meat into barbecue.

Pitmaston Pine Apple A small apple grown in England; it has a conical shape and a rich flavor.

pito (PEE-to) A Nigerian beer made from malted sorghum.

pi t'si (pe tsi) The small, horseshoe-shaped tuber of an aquatic herb; it has a crunchy texture and a coconut-like flavor and is used in Chinese cuisines; sometimes imprecisely called a water chestnut.

pitted A fruit such as a plum or apricot that has had its pit removed.

pitter A tool used to remove stones from cherries and olives; it has two handles: the top one has a metal shaft and the bottom one is ring shaped and holds the fruit; when squeezed together, the shaft pushes the pit through the fruit and out the hole; also known as a stoner.

pitter

pittu A steamed flour or rice flour pastry used in Sri Lankan cuisines as a substitute for bread or rice.

pitu (pee-tu) Portuguese for baked prawns, left in the shell.

pivo (PEE-vah) Russian for beer.

pivoulade (pee-voo-lade) French for honey mushroom.

piwo Polish for beer.

pizza (PEET-tzah) An Italian dish consisting of a flat pie or tart made from bread dough topped with any of a variety of foods, but principally tomato sauce and cheese (often mozzarella) and baked.

pizza, deep-dish An American pizza style with a thick, chewy dough; it is baked in a 1- to 2-in.-deep pan, allowing the dough to rise and remain compact; also known as a Chicago deep-dish pizza.

pizza, designer Slang for American pizzas made with nontraditional toppings such as Peking duck, peanut sauce, goat cheese and the like.

pizza, New York–style An American pizza style that uses a thin, moderately soft (as opposed to crispy) dough.

pizza, thin crust An American pizza style that uses a thin, usually crispy dough.

pizza, white An American variation on a pizza; made without any tomato sauce.

pizza alla napolitana (peet-tzah ah-lah nah-poe-lee-tah-nah) An Italian pizza made with tomatoes, mozzarella, anchovies, oregano and olive oil.

pizza alla romana (pee-tzah ah-lah row-mah-nah) A classic Italian pizza topped with tomatoes, mozzarella, oregano and anchovies.

pizza alla siciliana (pee-tzah ah-lah see-tchee-lee-ah-nah) An Italian pizza topped with tomatoes, mozzarella, mushrooms, salami and red, green and yellow peppers fried in olive oil.

pizza alle vongole (pee-tzah ah-lay vohn-goh-lay) An Italian pizza topped with tomatoes, oregano, clams, parsley and garlic.

pizza al prosciutto (pee-tzah al pro-shoo-toh) An Italian pizza topped with tomatoes, mozzarella and cooked ham.

pizza calabrese (pee-tzah cah-lah-bree-see) An Italian pizza topped with tomatoes, tuna, anchovies, olives, capers and lard instead of olive oil.

pizza cheese A pasta filata cheese made in the United States from pasteurized milk; similar to mozzarella, it is used to make pizzas.

pizza con funghi (pee-tzah con phoon-ghee) An Italian pizza topped with tomatoes, mozzarella, sliced mushrooms, parsley and garlic.

pizza dough A yeast dough used as the crust for pizzas; it may be thick and bready or thin and crisp.

pizzaiola, alla (peat-zee-OHL-ah, ah-lah) An Italian method of garnishing a dish with a sauce of tomatoes, garlic and oregano.

pizza paddle *See* peel.

pizza pan A large round metal pan with a shallow, rounded, raised rim used to bake pizza; available with a perforated bottom that allows steam to escape and helps brown the crust.

pizza pugliese (pee-tzah poo-yay-say) An Italian pizza topped with finely chopped onions, oregano, grated Pecorino and olive oil.

pizza quattro stagioni (pee-tzah kwa-trow stah-gee-oh-nee) Italian for pizza four seasons; it is topped first with tomatoes and mozzarella, and, each covering a quarter of the pizza, mushrooms, cooked ham, finely chopped artichokes and olives.

pizza spinaci (pee-tzah spee-nah-tchee) An Italian pizza topped with spinach and garlic.

pizza stone *See* baking stone.

pizza wheel; pizza cutter A tool with a sharp-edged revolving wheel; the wheel is dragged across the pizza to cut it.

pizzelle (peets-TSEH-leh) A large, crisp, round Italian cookie made from a rich batter of butter, eggs, sugar, flour and vanilla; the batter is cooked on a pizzelle iron.

pizzelle iron Similar to a waffle iron, it is a tool with two embossed or intricately carved 5-in.-wide disks hinged together and attached to a long handle and used to make pizelle; the iron is heated on the stove top, the batter is poured in and it is all returned to the stove to bake; the pattern imprints onto the cookies.

pizzelle iron

pizzeria (pee-tsay-REE-ah) An establishment where pizza is made, sold (whole or by the slice) and often consumed.

pizzette (peet-zay-tay) A miniature pizza made with very thin dough.

pizzoccheri (pee-tzo-kae-ree) Thick, dark-colored Italian pasta strips made from buckwheat flour.

pla Thai for fish.

placebo bottle A liquor bottle filled with colored or plain water and used by the bartender to make a drink for himself or herself if a patron insists on buying the bartender a drink.

place card A small card with a diner's name placed at a table setting to show the guest where the host has seated him or her.

placemat A small, usually rectangular, paper, plastic, fabric or woven mat placed on a table on which a place setting is laid.

placement The art and science of creating seating arrangements.

place setting 1. The selection of china, glasses, flatware and napery necessary for the meal. 2. A set of various pieces of china and flatware necessary for one person for any meal (e.g., a five-piece place setting).

plaetchen (plah-et-ken) A square Jewish noodle used in soups.

plafond (plah-fon) A French tinned-copper baking sheet.

plaice, American (plas) A member of the flounder family found in the northern Atlantic Ocean; it has a reddish to gray-brown skin, a lean, pearly white flesh, a sweet flavor and an average market weight of 2–3 lb. (0.9–1.4 kg); also known as a dab or sanddab.

plaice, European A member of the flounder family found in the Atlantic Ocean off Europe; it has a brown skin with orange-red spots, a pearly flesh, a delicate milky flavor and an average market weight of 2 lb. (900 g).

plain water icing *See* flat icing.

plaki (plaa-kee) A Greek preparation method of baking or braising fish with vegetables.

plank; planked A method of cooking and serving meat or fish on a seasoned board; some of the wood flavor is imparted to the food.

plantain; plantain banana (plahn-TAYNE) A starchy banana (*Musa paradisiaca*) with a green skin, a fairly firm, pinkish flesh, a fatter, longer shape than an eating banana and a squashlike flavor; used for cooking much like a squash; also known as a cooking banana.

plantain flour Dried and ground plantains; suitable for baking but used principally as a thickener for sauces.

Planter's Punch A cocktail made of Jamaican rum, lime juice and sugar, served in a tall glass over cracked ice.

plastered Slang for intoxicated.

plastering A wine-making procedure intended to change the acidity of the resulting wine; acidity is increased if calcium sulfate or gypsum is added to the must before fermentation, and acidity is decreased if potassium tartrate or calcium carbonate is added.

plaster of paris *See* calcium sulfate.

plastic curds *See* pasta filata.

plasticizer *See* softener.

plastic wrap A thin sheet of clear polymers such as polyvinyl chloride; it clings to surfaces and is used to wrap foods for storage.

plastron The ventral part of the turtle shell that, together with the dorsal part, is used for making turtle soup.

plata Labeling term used to indicate a clear, white or silver mezcal or Tequila that is not aged.

plátano (plah-tah-noss) *See* banana.

platanos a salteados (plah-tah-noss ah sal-tae-ah-doss) A South American dish of plantains sautéed in chile butter until browned and served with a drizzle of sour cream.

plat de côtes (plah duh COAT) 1. A French cut of the beef carcass; it is the equivalent of American short ribs. 2. A French cut of the pork carcass; it is a whole forequarter flank.

plat de ménage (pla duh meh-NAHJ) A large platter or plateau holding casters, bottles and baskets for the necessities of the table.

plat du jour (pla duh zjur) French menu term for the speciality of the day.

plate *v.* To place foods on a plate; it can be done with extreme care to create an appealing visual impression. *n.* 1. A smooth, thin, relatively flat dish, usually china or pottery, on which food is served to each individual. 2. The contents of a dish (e.g., a plate of sausages). 3. Service and food for one person at a meal. 4. Serviceware, dinnerware, flatware and the like covered with a thin coating of a precious metal, such as gold or silver. 5. A cut of the beef carcass that combines the beef short plate and brisket (without the shank) primals.

plateau A footed, mirrored tray designed to display figurines, candlesticks and occasionally foods, as a centerpiece; popular during the 18th and 19th centuries.

plate lunch 1. A Hawaiian meal consisting of two scoops of rice, a mayonnaise-bound macaroni or potato salad and an entrée such as beef stew, fried fish, teriyaki chicken, meatloaf or barbecued short ribs; it is often sold from a plate lunch wagon. 2. *See* blue plate special.

plate rack A tiered metal or wooden frame used to hold plates, for either storage, service or decoration; the stand can be conical in shape (thereby limiting each successive tier to a smaller plate) or columnar (with each tier accommodating plates of the same size).

plate rack, hanging A wooden or metal rack hung on a wall to hold dinnerware; plates are held vertically in slots or flush against the back, being retained by a small lip on the shelf; bowls and cups rest on a shelf.

plate short ribs *See* short ribs.

platija (plah-tee-hah) Spanish for plaice.

platine (pla-teen) A shallow French baking tin.

plato (plah-toh) Spanish for plate.

Plato (play-toe) A saccharometer (hydrometer) used to measure the percentage of fermentable sugars in a mash used for fermentation or distillation; its scale is a refinement of the Balling scale.

plättar (PLAH-tar) Small Swedish pancakes, traditionally served with lingonberries.

Platte (plat-tah) German for plate.

plèt (plet) Hindi for plate.

plett pan A flat cast-iron pan with seven round, shallow, 3-in.-wide indentions; used to make plättar.

pleuroto ostreado (ple-oo-roh-toh os-tray-ah-doh) Spanish for oyster mushroom.

pleurotte en huître (pluhr-AHT ahn weetr) French for oyster mushroom.

plett pan

pljeskavica (pless-kah-vee-sah) A Balkan sausage made from mutton, pork and veal, seasoned with herbs, spices and hot red chiles.

plombières (PLOOM-bee-ay) 1. A French ice cream made with a custard base and blended with whipped cream and candied fruits and frozen in a square mold. 2. A French custard blended with whipped egg whites and fresh or candied fruits.

plomme (ploom) Norwegian for plum.

plonk (plohnk) British and Australian slang for a very ordinary vin ordinaire.

plov (plahv) A Russian and central Asian pilaf; it can be sweet but is usually savory and flavored with lamb and garnished with carrots, chickpeas and raisins.

plover A small migratory game bird that is farm raised in the United States or imported from Europe; it has a delicate flavor.

pluck *v.* To remove the feathers from poultry and gamebirds. *n.* 1. The lungs, heart and other entrails of a mammal. 2. *See* paunch and pluck *and* game.

plum A small- to medium-sized ovoid or spherical stone fruit (genus *Prunus*) that grows in clusters; it has a smooth skin that can be yellow, green, red, purple or indigo blue, a juicy flesh, a large pit and a sweet flavor. *See* prune.

plum, American beach Any of a variety of plums (*Prunus maritima*) grown in the United States; the small fruit have a red, yellow or purple skin and a sweet flavor; they are used principally for preserves.

plum

plum, cherry Any of a variety of plums (*Prunus cerasifera*) grown in the Middle East and Europe; the spherical fruit are relatively small with a red, yellow or purple skin, a juicy flesh and a sweet flavor; also known as myrobalan.

plum, damson Any of a variety of plums (*Prunus institia*); the ovoid fruit are medium sized with a bluish-black skin, a bluish-red flesh and a sweet, spicy flavor; principally used for pies and preserves.

plum, greengage An imprecisely used term for the greengage.

plum, Japanese Any of a variety of plums (*Prunus salicina* and *P. triflora*) that flourish in warm climates; the conical fruit are relatively large with an orange-red or golden skin and a mild, sweet flavor.

plum, wild Any of a variety of plums (*Prunus americana*) growing wild in North America; the very small fruit have a red or yellow skin and a tart flavor; also known as a goose plum, hog plum or yellow plum.

plum duff A traditional English boiled suet pudding flavored with raisins or currants.

plum grape *See* fox grape.

plump, to A cooking technique in which dried fruit is soaked in a liquid until the fruit softens and swells slightly from absorbing the liquid.

plum pudding A steamed breadlike British dessert containing spices, prunes and other dried fruit; usually served warm, flamed with rum or brandy and accompanied by hard sauce.

plum sauce A spicy, fruity sauce made from plums, chiles, vinegar and sugar; used in Chinese cuisine as a dip and flavoring; also known as duck sauce.

plum tomato A medium-sized ovoid tomato with a meaty flesh and a red skin (a yellow variety is also available); also known as an Italian tomato or Roma tomato.

plunger coffeepot *See* cafetiére.

pluot An apricot and plum hybrid; it has a smooth, yellow-spotted russet skin with a juicy flesh.

pluvier (ploo-vay) French for plover.

Plymouth gin A gin that is heavier and more strongly flavored than London dry gin.

PO *See* purchase order.

poacher's relish An English relish of vegetables in a sweet-and-sour marinade.

poaching A moist-heat cooking method that uses convection to transfer heat from a hot (approximately 160–180°F [71–82°C]) liquid to the food submerged in it.

poblano (poh-BLAH-noh) A long, tapering fresh chile with thick flesh, a medium to hot flavor and a dark green color tinged with purple or black; sometimes known imprecisely as pasilla. *See* ancho *and* mulato.

po'boy; poor boy *See* hero.

po cai mian (poe cah-e me-ahn) Chinese noodles flavored with spinach.

pochero (poe-ka-roe) A Filipino dish of boiled beef, chicken, dumplings and vegetables.

pochki (pahch-kee) Russian for kidneys.

pocket bread *See* pita.

pod The outer covering of certain seeds such as peas and beans.

podere (poh-DEH-reh) A small Italian wine estate.

podina (poh-DEE-nah) Hindi for mint.

podlvàsa (pohd-vah-sah) Bulgarian for the culture used to turn fresh milk into yogurt.

poe A South Pacific Island (Tahiti) dessert of puréed tropical fruits flavored with brown sugar and vanilla, thickened with arrowroot, baked and served chilled with coconut cream.

poêle chinoise (pwehl sheen-wahz) French for wok.

poêler (pweh-lay) French for to roast in a covered pot with butter and sometimes aromatic vegetables; the closest English translation of this very specific French culinary term is pot-roasting. *See* casserole braising.

poelon (pweh-lohn) A small uncovered French earthenware or metal casserole with a short, stubby handle and a pouring lip.

Pofesen (poo-fee-son) An Austrian dish consisting of bread soaked in milk, dipped in egg and fried; served with sugar and a fruit syrup.

poffert (pof-fert) A small Dutch raisin cake served with butter balls, crushed candied sugar and syrup.

poha (poh-ha) Hawaiian for cape gooseberry.

pohole (poh-ho-lay) Hawaiian for fiddlehead fern.

poi (POH-ee) A Hawaiian dish consisting of fermented pounded taro root; eaten mixed with milk or used as a condiment for meat or fish.

point *See* knife point.

Point, Fernand (Fr., 1897–1955) The chef-owner of La Pyramide, located near Lyon, France; his cuisine was based on high-quality foods enhanced by preparation; he disdained dominating sauces and distracting accompaniments and garnishes and believed that each dish should have a single dominant ingredient, flavor or theme; he refined and modernized the classic cuisine of Escoffier and is credited with laying the foundation for nouvelle cuisine.

pointe (pwan't) French for punt.

pointe de culotte (pwan't duh que-lot) *See* aiguillette.

pointe de filet (pwan't duh fee-lay) A French cut of the pork carcass; it is cut from the posterior of the pork loin.

point of purchase (POP) A display or other in-house advertising such as a table tent or menu board that is intended to encourage impulse sales.

point-of-sales system (POS) A computerized system for recording sales and cash information at a food services operation; located in the dining room, it transmits orders to the bar and kitchen.

point of unsaturation A place in a molecule where the bonding will allow a hydrogen atom to be added easily.

poire (pwahr) French for pear.

poireau (pwah-roa) French for leek.

poire Belle-Helene (pwahr bel-ay-LEN) A French dessert consisting of a pear poached in vanilla syrup served on top of vanilla ice cream with warm chocolate sauce.

poires au vin rouge (pwahr oh van rooje) A French dessert of pears poached in red wine.

Poire William A French eau-de-vie made from Williams pears; some versions are marketed with a pear in the bottle.

pois (pwah) French for pea.

pois chiche (pwah chee-che) French for chickpea.

pois rouges maconne (pwahr rooj mae-kohn-ay) A Guadeloupe dish of kidney beans and rice flavored with hot peppers and bacon and thickened with cassava powder.

poisson (pwah-sawng) French for fish.

poissonier (pwah-sawng-yay) At a food services operation following the brigade system, the person responsible for all fish and shellfish items and their sauces; also known as the fish station chef.

poi supper A Hawaiian term for luau food served on wooden trays in a sit-down format; it is usually at home and is more formal than the casual outdoor luau.

poitrine (pwah-TREEN) A French cut of the veal carcass; it is the breast, available with or without bones; also known as flanchet.

poivrade, sauce (pwahv-rahd) Any of various French sauces in which peppercorns provide the dominant or characteristic flavor.

poivre (pwahv-rahd) French for pepper.

poivre de la Jamaïque (pwahv duh lah jah-mah-eek) French for allspice.

pojarski (pah-jar-skee) 1. A Russian dish of veal chopped and mixed with butter, bread soaked in milk, seasoned, reformed on the bone and fried in butter. 2. A cutlet of chicken or salmon, covered with flour or bread crumbs and sautéed in butter.

poke (poh-kay) A Hawaiian dish consisting of bite-sized bits of raw fish traditionally seasoned with salt, limu and inamona; today soy sauce, ginger, garlic, sesame oil, sesame seeds, green onion and chile peppers are also used.

poke; pokeweed A wild field green (*Phytolacca americana*) native to North America; the young shoots are cooked like asparagus, and the leaves are used in salads.

pokekas (poh-keh-kush) Brazilian ragoûts of fish and shellfish combined with oil and seasonings; traditionally wrapped in banana leaves and roasted.

Pökelfleisch (per-kul-flash) 1. German for pickled pork. 2. German for brawn.

poker beer Beer heated with a red-hot poker and usually served during the winter as a warming drink.

pokerounce An English dish popular in the Middle Ages consisting of spiced toast spread with warm honey (flavored with fir sap) and sprinkled with pine nuts.

pole bean A variety of bean that is cultivated on poles rather than allowed to grow freely on the ground.

polédwica (poe-lah-doh-e-cam) A Polish cut of the beef carcass; it is a filet or tenderloin.

polenta (poh-LEHN-tah) 1. Italian for cornmeal. 2. An Italian dish made by cooking cornmeal with a liquid until it forms a soft mass; it is eaten hot or cooled, cut into squares and grilled or fried.

polenta base A piece of polenta used to support or as a base for an elaborate presentation of food on a plate.

pole unit A display piece supported by a cardboard pole; the pole can be freestanding or attached to the display.

polévka (poh-lev-kah) Czech for soup.

Polignac, sauce (poh-lee-nyak) A French white wine sauce finished with heavy cream and garnished with julienne of mushrooms.

polished rice *See* white rice.

Polish ham A boneless ham covered with a layer of fat and skin; smoked and then cooked.

Polish sausage *See* kielbasa.

Polish Sidecar A cocktail made of gin, lemon juice, blackberry liqueur or blackberry brandy and fresh blackberries; garnished with blackberries.

pollastra; pollastro (poll-LASS-traw; poll-LASS-trow) Italian for pullet.

Polled Hereford An American breed of hornless beef cattle developed by an Iowa rancher.

pollo (POH-yoh) Italian and Spanish for chicken.

pollo alla diavola (POH-loh AH-lah dee-AH-voh-lah) A dish from Italy's Tuscany region consisting of broiled chicken heavily seasoned with black pepper and served with fresh lemon.

pollo alla scarpariello (POH-loh AH-lah skahr-pah-ree-EH-loh) Italian for the shoemaker's style and used to describe an Italian–American dish of small, bone-in chicken pieces cooked in a spicy sauce with garlic, sausage slices, mushrooms and white wine.

pollock, Alaskan A fish similar to the American pollock and found off Alaska; it has a light gray, flaky flesh, a mild flavor and an average market weight of 2 lb. (900 g); it is used principally to make imitation shellfish products; also known as Pacific pollock, snow cod and walleye pollock.

pollock

pollock, American A fish related to cod and found in the Atlantic Ocean from Nova Scotia to Virginia; it has a deep olive skin on top that pales to a yellow or smoky gray, a lean flesh, a slightly sweet flavor and an average market weight of 4–12 lb. (1.8–5.4 kg); used in gefilte fish, salted, smoked or to make imitation shellfish products; also known as Boston bluefish and blue cod.

polonaise, à la (pohl-loh-NEHZ, ah lah) A French preparation method associated with the cuisine of Poland; the dishes, especially cauliflower and asparagus, are boiled, then sprinkled with chopped hard-boiled egg yolk, parsley, bread crumbs and melted butter.

Polonaise, sauce (pohl-loh-NEHZ) 1. A French compound sauce made with veal velouté mixed with sour cream, horseradish and chopped fennel. 2. A French compound sauce made with a demi-glaze flavored with reduced red wine, sugar and vinegar and garnished with raisins and sliced almonds.

polpette (pohl-PEH-the) Italian for meatballs; also known as polpettine and purpetti.

polpetti (poal-PAYT-tay) An Italian soup made from Parmesan mixed with beef broth and garnished with pasta.

polpettine *See* polpette.

polpo (POAL-poa) Italian for octopus.

pølse (PURLSS-err) Norwegian for sausage.

poludennik (poh-loo-dahn-nik) Russian for lunch.

polvo (pohl-voo) Portuguese for octopus.

polweka (poh-let-kah) A thin Polish porridge made from rye flour and flavored with cream.

polydextrose A food additive used as a formulation aid, humectant, bulking agent and/or texturizer in processed foods such as baked goods and baking mixes, confections, candies, dressings and frozen dairy products.

polyethylene glycol A food additive used as a flavor adjuvant and/or bodying agent for nonnutritive sweeteners.

polyglyceryl esters of fatty acids Food additives derived from vegetable oils and used as emulsifiers.

polygonum (pol-leh-goh-num) An herb (*Polygonum* sp.) with purple-tinged stems, long, slender, deep green leaves and a flavor similar to that of basil and mint; used in Malaysian fish and noodle dishes.

polyoxyethylene sorbitan fatty acid esters *See* polysorbates.

polypeptide A chain of linked amino acids.

polypodium A fern; its young, unopened leaves have a smoky flavor.

polysaccharide A complex carbohydrate such as starch, dextrin, cellulose or glycogen that has little to no flavor and varying levels of solubility and digestibility; composed of chains of monosaccharides or disaccharides.

polysorbates Food additives used primarily as emulsifiers in chocolate products, baked goods and baking mixes, icing mixes, shortenings and frozen desserts; also used as dough conditioners and dispersing agents in gelatins.

polytetrafluoroethylene (PTFE) *See* nonstick plastic.

polyunsaturated fat A triglyceride composed of polyunsaturated fatty acids; generally, it comes from plants (cottonseed, safflower, soybean, corn and sesame oils are high in polyunsaturated fats) and is liquid (an oil) at room temperature.

polyunsaturated fatty acid A fatty acid that can accommodate more than one additional hydrogen atom along its carbon chain (i.e., it has more than one point of unsaturation).

pomace (PAH-muss) Grape pressings; the crushed skins, pips, stems and seeds left in the press after the juice has been extracted from the grapes.

pombe (pom-ba) Swahili for beer.

pombe ya dawa (pom-ba yah dah-wah) Swahili for alcohol; also known as spititi.

pomegranate (POM-uh-gran-uht) A medium-sized fruit (*Punica granatum*) with a thin, red to pink-blushed yellow, leathery skin and many seeds encased in a pinkish, translucent flesh separated by an ivory-colored, bitter membrane; the flesh has a sweet–tart flavor and the seeds are crunchy.

pomegranate syrup A thick sweet–sour syrup made by boiling the juice of sour pomegranates; also known as grenadine molasses.

pomelit A fruit grown in Israel that is a hybrid of a grapefruit and pomelo; it has a yellowish-green to green rind, juicy segmented flesh and a flavor similar to that of a grapefruit but sweeter.

pomelo; pommelo; pummelo (pom-EH-loh) The largest citrus (*Citrus maxima*); it has a thick, coarse, yellow to pink rind and yellow to pink segmented flesh with a tart grapefruitlike flavor; also known as shaddock.

pomelo (pohm-EH-loh) Spanish for grapefruit. *See* toronja.

Pomerol (paw-meh-rawl) A grape-growing and wine-producing area within France's Bordeaux region; known for its red wines made from Merlot and Cabernet Franc grapes.

pomes Members of the family Rosaceae; these fruits (e.g., apples, pears and quince) grow on trees in temperate and cooler climates worldwide; they generally have a thin skin and moderately firm to firm juicy flesh surrounding a central core containing many small seeds (called pips) and a tart to sweet flavor.

pomfret (POHM-freht) 1. A fish found in the north Atlantic Ocean, Pacific Ocean and Mediterranean Sea; it has a brown-gray skin and a lean, delicate flesh. 2. A term used imprecisely in Europe for members of the butterfish family.

pomidor (pah-mee-dor) Russian for tomato.

pomidory (poh-mee-doh-ri) Polish for tomato.

Pommard (po-mar) A grape-growing and wine-producing commune in Burgundy's Côte de Beaune.

pomme (pom) French for apple.

pomme cythère (pom see-tear) French for ambarella.

pomme d'amour (pom dah-moor) Archaic French for tomato.

pomme d'api (pom dah-pee) French for lady apple.

pomme de lait (pom duh lay) A small fruit with a thin, greenish-violet skin and an easily bruised, crisp white flesh; eaten fresh or used for a syrup.

pomme d'étoile *See* api étoile.

Pomme Grise (pom gree) An heirloom apple from Montreal and the St. Lawrence Valley, Canada (c. 1650); the small, spherical fruit has a gray to russet skin and a yellowish, crisp, firm, juicy flesh.

pommes (pomz) *See* pommes de terre.

pommes à la bordelaise (pomz ah lah bore-day-laze) A French dish consisting of cubed potatoes sautéed in butter with a little garlic.

pommes à la vapeur (pomz ah lah vah-pehr) French for steamed potatoes.

pommes Anna (pomz ahn-nah) A French dish of thinly sliced potatoes that are layered with butter, cooked in a lidded dish and then inverted and cut into wedges for service.

pommes Anna pan A round, tin-lined copper pan used to make pommes Anna; it has a 6.5- to 9.5-in. diameter, a 3-in. depth and a lid that cuffs nearly 1.5 in. over the pan's sides to compact the potatoes.

pommes Anna pan

pommes Annette Pommes Anna made with potatoes cut into slivers.

pommes au four (pomz oh for) A French dish consisting of potatoes baked in their skin.

pommes bonne femme (pomz bun fam) A French dish consisting of potatoes cooked in stock with small whole braised onions.

pommes château (pomz sha-toe) A French dish of potatoes cut into 1.5-in-long pieces, tournéed and sautéed in butter until browned; traditionally used as a garnish for châteaubriand.

pommes cocotte (pomz ko-kot) Small pommes château.

pommes dauphine (pomz doa-fawng) A French dish of potatoes mashed with butter and egg yolk, blended with choux pastry, shaped into balls and fried; served with grilled or roasted meat or game.

pommes dauphinoise (pomz doa-feen-wahz) A French dish of potatoes cut in thick round slices and layered with cream in a gratin dish rubbed with garlic and butter (or a mixture of eggs, milk and cream is poured over the potatoes), sprinkled with grated cheese and baked.

pommes de terre (pomz duh tehr) French for potatoes (often shortened to pommes).

pommes de terre à l'anglaise (pomz duh tehr ah lahn-glaas) French for boiled potatoes.

pommes de terre en papillote (pomz du tehr ahn pah-pee-yoh-tay) French for potatoes baked in aluminum foil.

pommes de terre sautées (pomz duh tehr sah-tay) French for fried potatoes.

pommes duchesse (pomz doo-shess) A French garnish or dish of mashed potatoes mixed with raw eggs, piped (especially if a garnish) or shaped into patties and oven browned.

pommes en robe des champs (pomz ahn rohb day tcham) French for potatoes boiled in their skins.

pommes fondantes (pomz fohn-dant) A French dish of tournéed potatoes (larger than château) cooked in butter in a covered pan.

pommes frites (pomz FREET) French for French-fried potatoes.

pommes lorette (pomz low-reht) A French dish of pommes dauphine shaped into small crescents and deep-fried.

pommes Lyonnaise (pomz lee-oh-nez) A French dish of sliced boiled potatoes browned in butter with onions and sprinkled with parsley.

pommes noisette (pomz nwah-ZEHT) Potatoes cut into small hazelnut-shaped balls and sautéed in butter.

pommes nouvelles (pomz noo-vell) French for new potatoes.

pommes rissolées (pomz ree-soh-lay) A French dish of pommes château cooked until dark brown.

pommes soufflées (pomz soo-flay) A French dish of thinly sliced potatoes puffed into little pillows through a double-frying process.

pommes tian (pomz tee-ahn) A French dish of potatoes prepared in a tian and made of alternating layers of sliced potatoes, onions and tomatoes, flavored with thyme and pepper, covered with grated cheese and olive oil.

pommes vapeur A utensil with a bulbous bottom and a V-shaped top used to steam potatoes; the bottom is filled with water and the potatoes are placed on a perforated insert; the condensation collects on the domed lid and is directed to the sides and falls to the bottom, thus preventing sogginess; also known as a potato steamer.

pommes vapeur

pomodoro (poam-oa-DAW-roa) Italian for tomato.

Pompadour, sauce (poam-pah-dohr) A French white wine sauce finished with crayfish butter and garnished with sliced truffles, diced crayfish tails, tarragon and chervil.

pompano (pahm-pah-noh) A fish found off Florida; it has a metallic blue skin on top that becomes silvery on the belly, an average market weight of 1.5–4 lb. (0.68–1.8 kg) and a firm, white flesh with a moderate amount of fat; also known as cobblerfish and palmenta.

pompèlmo (poam-PAYL-moa) Italian for grapefruit.

pompe ya n'dizi (pom-pay yah n'dee-zi) A Tanzanian winelike beverage made from fermented bananas or plantains.

ponderous A wine-tasting term for a wine that is heavy and tiring to drink.

pond pudding A sweet suet pudding with a central cavity containing sugar, butter and lemon juice; when cut, the melted butter and lemon juice run out, creating a pond around the pudding; also known as well pudding.

pone (pohn) A word of American Indian origin meaning baked.

ponentine A small, slender, purple-black olive from Italy; it is salt brine cured and packed in vinegar.

ponki (pohn-kee) Swahili for pumpkin.

pönnukökur (poe-new-koe-kuhr) Large, very thin Icelandic pancakes served with jelly and whipped cream.

pontefract cake A small, flat, round British cake flavored with licorice.

Pont l'Évêque (pon lay-VEHK) A surface-ripened French cheese made from cow's milk; it has a creamy, pale yellow interior, a golden brown skin, a sharp, tangy flavor and a strong odor.

pont neuf (pon nuf) French for a cut of potato that is 1/2 × 1/2 × 3 in. (1.27 × 1.27 × 7.6 cm); also known as steak fries.

pont-neuf batter (pon-nuf) A French pastry dough made with equal parts of pastry cream and pâte à choux flavored with Kirsch.

pont-neuf tart (pon-nuf) A French pastry made by layering apple compote, apple slices and pont-neuf batter onto a base of puff pastry.

pony A small drink of straight liquor.

pony glass A short glass used for cordials or measuring 1 fl. oz. of liquid.

pony keg A small beer barrel that holds one-fourth of a keg.

ponzu (PON-zoo) A Japanese dipping sauce made with lemon juice or rice vinegar, soy sauce, mirin or sake, kombu and dried bonito flakes.

poo (pu) Thai for crab.

poolish (poo-LEESH) A semiliquid starter dough, usually yeast leavened, that has fermented for at least 6 hours before being used to make bread.

pool party A party that takes place near the pool; food served can be snacks, picnic food or barbecued food.

poor knight's pudding An English dessert of bread soaked in milk and beaten eggs and then fried in butter, spread with jam or fruit and sandwiched together.

poor man's lobster *See* monkfish.

pootu (poo-tu) A hot cereal made of coarsely ground rice steamed in bamboo; popular in southwestern India.

POP *See* point of purchase.

pop Slang, particularly in the American Midwest, for any nonalcoholic, flavored and colored, carbonated drink; also known as a soft drink and soda pop. *See* soda.

popcorn 1. A variety of corn that explodes when it is exposed to dry heat (the moisture and air inside the kernel expands, forms steam, splits the hull and turns the kernel inside out); available as unpopped seeds and fully popped, plain or flavored. 2. Small pieces of battered and deep-fried shrimp, chicken, clams and the like.

popcorn cheese Large-curd cottage cheese.

pope's nose Slang for the stubby tail protuberance of a dressed fowl; used as a demeaning term for Catholics in 17th-century England; also known as a parson's nose.

popover A batter quick bread baked in a muffin shape; the crust is crisp and brown and the interior moist and almost hollow.

popover pan A heavy baking pan used for making popovers and Yorkshire pudding; similar to a muffin pan but with deeper, tapered indentions that are spaced farther apart.

popover pan

poppy, common An annual herb (*Papaver rhoeas*) with a slender, branched stem, toothed, lobed leaves and a single red flower; the flower petals are used

medicinally and the leaves are eaten as a vegetable; also known as corn poppy.

poppy seed The tiny, round, hard, blue-gray seed of the poppy (genus *Papaver*); it has a sweet, nutty flavor and is used in baked goods or processed for oil.

poppy seed, white Similar in flavor to the blue-gray seed; it is toasted, ground and used as a thickener in Indian cuisines.

poppy seed oil Oil made from poppy seeds; it has a pale color and a pleasant, delicate flavor and is used principally as an ingredient or flavoring.

Popsicle The trademarked name for a colored, flavored ice confection with one or two sticks for a handle; it is often incorrectly written as popsicle.

Pop-Tarts The proprietary name for a packaged breakfast pastry made with various fruit or chocolate fillings encased in a sweet, thin, rectangular crust; they are sold fully cooked but are usually heated in a toaster.

Populo (poh-poo-low) A 17th-century Italian liqueur made from brandy, musk, sugar, amber, aniseed and the essence of cinnamon.

pop wine Slang for a sweet, fruit-flavored wine, usually inexpensive and with a low alcohol content.

porc (por) French for pork.

porcelain A hard, fine-grained, nonporous ceramic that is fired at a high temperature and used for bakeware, dinnerware and service items.

porcelain quiche dish *See* shallow porcelain baker.

porcelet (por-suh-lay) French for suckling pig.

porchetta (poar-KAYT-tah) 1. Italian for suckling pig. 2. An Italian dish of roast suckling pig cooked with rosemary tucked inside and basted with white wine.

porcine (por-seen) Pertaining to swine.

porcini (poar-CHEE-nee) Italian for bolete.

porgand (pore-gahnd) Estonian for carrot.

porgy (POHR-gee) A saltwater fish and member of the perch family native to the Atlantic Ocean from New England to the Carolinas; it has a dull silver skin with dusky spots that becomes white with dusky spots on the belly, an average market weight of 1–2 lb. (450–900 g), a tender texture, a low fat content and a delicate, mild flavor; also known as bream, scup and sea bream.

poricha (pore-key-ah) A Korean beverage made from roasted barley; also known as barley tea.

pork The flesh of hogs, usually slaughtered under the age of 1 year.

pork and apple pie An English dish consisting of pork, apples and onions covered with potato purée and baked.

pork belly *See* belly.

pork ciste An Irish dish consisting of roast pork with a crispy skin.

pork cutlet A fabricated cut of the pork primal fresh ham; a small boneless cut from the shank.

porker A pig slaughtered at 6–12 months.

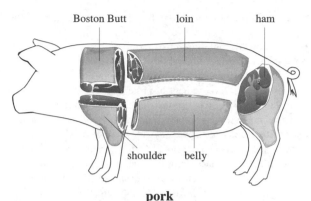

Boston Butt   loin   ham

shoulder   belly

pork
(American primals)

porkkana (POARK-kah-nah) Finnish for carrot.

porklet A fabricated cut of the pork primal shoulder; it is cubed meat.

pork loin roast, full A subprimal cut of the pork primal loin; it is a roast taken from either end of the loin or can be the entire trimmed loin.

pork loin roast, rolled A subprimal cut of the pork primal loin; it is a tender, boned, rolled roast.

pörkölt (PURR-kurlt) A Hungarian stew made from meat or poultry fried with onions and then simmered with paprika, tomato purée, marjoram, caraway seeds and vinegar; if veal is used, sour cream is added.

pork primals The five principal sections of the pork carcass: the Boston butt, shoulder, loin, belly and fresh ham; each side of pork contains one of each primal.

pork quality grades The USDA quality grades for pork are no. 1 (the highest quality), no. 2, no. 3 and utility. *See* USDA quality grades *and* utility.

pork sausage Any of several varieties of fresh sausage made from ground pork and pork fat, typically seasoned with pepper and sage; sold as links, patties or in bulk and also available smoked.

pork shoulder *See* picnic ham.

pork tenderloin A subprimal cut of the pork primal loin; it is the tender, lean tenderloin muscle and can be used as is or further fabricated into medallions.

porotos (por-roh-tohs) Spanish for beans (especially in Chile).

porotos granados (por-roh-tohs gran-doss) A Chilean stew of beans (porotos), beef, tomatoes, winter squash and corn, flavored with onions, aji, garlic, basil, oregano and thyme and usually served with pebre.

porridge A thick, puddinglike dish made from any of various cereals or grains cooked in water or milk; usually eaten hot for breakfast with sugar and cream or milk.

porringer A low, round ceramic or metal bowl with one handle; often used to feed children.

porringer

porro (POA-ro) Italian for leek.

porron (poh-rone) A double-spouted Spanish glass or ceramic vessel used for drinking wine; the wine streams out of one narrow spout (the vessel should not touch the drinker's lips) while the other spout lets air in.

porrusalda A Basque leek soup.

porsaansorkat (poor-shan-soar-kaht) Finnish for pig's feet.

port A sweet fortified wine made in northern Portugal from red and white wine grapes such as Tinta Roriz, Tinta Francisca, Tinta Cao, Touriga Nacional, Mourisco and Shite Malvasia; traditionally served with dessert or after a meal. *See* Porto, ruby port, twany port *and* vintage port.

portabella (pohr-tah-bel-lah) A very large crimini; the mushroom has a dense texture and a rich, meaty flavor.

portable bar *See* rolling bar.

Port du Salut; Port Salut (por suh-LOO) A semisoft French cheese made from cow's milk by Trappist monks; it has an edible orange rind, a pale yellow interior, a smooth, satiny texture and a mild flavor. *See* Saint-Paulin.

porter Originally brewed in London, it is a dark, fruity, dry beer made with top-fermenting yeast.

Porter An heirloom apple from Massachusetts (c. 1800); the spherical fruit has a yellow skin marked with red and a juicy, crisp, flavorful, yellow flesh.

porterhouse steak A fabricated cut of the beef primal short loin; this tender cut contains a distinctive T-shaped portion of the backbone and large portions (on either side of the center bone) of the loin eye muscle and tenderloin; also known as a king steak. *See* club steak *and* T-bone steak.

porterhouse tails A fabricated cut of the beef primal short loin; they are small, tender portions of the flank muscle trimmed from the short loins; also known as steak tails.

port glass *See* dock glass.

portion *v.* To divide or separate a food into specific amounts or individual servings; can be divided by weight, count or volume. *n.* An individual serving of food or drink.

portion control cut A fabricated cut of meat such as a steak or chop that has been cut to a specified weight and thickness.

portion control measurements The use of measuring devices such as automatic pours, shot glasses and the like to ensure that all beverages will be the standard size.

portion controls Methods to ensure that a portion of food or drink is of the appropriate (standard) size.

portion cost The ingredient costs for a given portion of a standardized recipe; calculated by dividing the total recipe cost by the number of portions produced by that recipe.

portion scale Small spring scale used to measure the weight of an ingredient or portion. *See* electronic scale *and* spring scale.

portion scoop A utensil similar to an ice cream scoop with a lever-operated blade for releasing contents held in its bowl; used for portioning soft foods such as salads and batters, it is available in several standardized sizes (the number stamped on it indicates the number of level scoopfuls per quart); also known as a disher.

portion size The amount, measured by weight, volume or count, of a portion.

portion size conversion The adjustment of ingredient quantities to reflect a desired change in a recipe yield. *See* conversion factor.

Porto (por-toe) The official designation for all Portuguese ports shipped to the United States; used to distinguish the authentic Portuguese product, which is shipped from the city of Oporto, Portugal, from ports made elsewhere.

portugaise, à la (pohr-tay-gaez, ah lah) A French garnish for meat consisting of small stuffed tomatoes and pommes château with sauce Portugaise.

Portugaise, sauce (pohr-tay-gaez) A French compound sauce made from a demi-glaze flavored with tomato purée, onion and garlic.

Portuguese cupped oyster A variety of oysters found off western Europe; it has a slate gray to brown shell, a grayish-violet flesh and a strong flavor.

Portuguese sweet bread A rich yeast dough bread made with sugar, eggs and butter and baked in long loaves.

port wine sauce 1. A sauce made from the drippings of roasted mutton or venison, red currant jelly, port and lemon juice. 2. A compound sauce made with demi-glaze flavored with port.

POS *See* point-of-sales system.

posnet A metal pot or skillet with three feet and a long straight handle.

posole; pozole (poh-SOH-leh) A Mexican soup of pork and broth, hominy and onions, flavored with garlic, chiles and cilantro and garnished with lettuce, onions, cheese and cilantro.

posset (POS-iht) A hot drink made of milk curdled with ale or wine, sweetened and spiced.

posterior At or toward the rear of an object or place. *See* anterior.

post off A wholesaler's discounted price for a quantity of alcoholic beverages.

postre (POHS-treh) Spanish for dessert.

Postum The proprietary name for a coffee substitute made of cereal.

pot A cylindrical vessel with straight sides, two loop handles and usually a flat or fitted lid; used for steaming, simmering and boiling foods.

potable (POH-tuh-bil) Any liquid suitable for drinking; used principally to describe water.

potable spirit Any distilled spirit fit for human consumption.

potage (poh-TAHZH) French for soup and used to describe a puréed soup that can be thickened with cream or egg yolks. *See* consommé *and* soupe.

potager (poh-tah-zaj) At a food services operation following the brigade system, the person responsible for all stocks and soups; also known as the soup station chef.

potage Saint Germain (po-tahzh san zhair-man) A French purée soup made with dried peas, fresh peas, greens, onion, salt pork, chervil and sometimes cream.

potash Common name for potassium carbonate, especially when derived from wood ashes; also known as pearl ash.

potash lye *See* potassium hydroxide.

potassium A major mineral principally used as an electrolyte to assist the transmission of nerve impulses, contraction of muscles and development of protein and to facilitate many reactions; significant sources include bananas and other fruits, green leafy vegetables, grains, legumes and potatoes.

potassium acid tartrate 1. A by-product of wine making with a pleasant acidic taste. 2. A food additive used as an anticaking agent, antimicrobial agent, humectant, leavening agent, pH control agent, stabilizer and/or thickener in foods such as confections, baked goods, gelatins, jams and jellies; also known as potassium bitartrate and cream of tartar.

potassium alginate A food additive derived from certain brown kelp; used as a stabilizer and/or thickener in processed foods such as frozen desserts.

potassium bicarbonate A food additive used as a nutrient supplement, pH control agent and/or processing aid.

potassium bisulfite and potassium metabisulfite Food additives used as preservatives.

potassium bitartrate *See* potassium acid tartrate.

potassium bromate A food additive used in the malting of barley for the production of fermented malt beverages and distilled spirits and as an aging agent for flour.

potassium bromide A food additive used in the washing and lye peeling of fruits and vegetables and as a thickener in baked goods.

potassium carbonate A food additive used as a flavoring agent, flavoring adjuvant, nutrient supplement and/or pH control agent.

potassium chloride A food additive used as a flavoring agent, flavoring adjuvant, nutrient supplement and/or pH control agent; also used as a salt substitute (the potassium replaces the sodium atom).

potassium citrate, monohydrate A food additive used as a processing aid in low-sodium foods.

potassium hydroxide A food additive used as a stabilizer, thickener, processing aid and/or pH control agent; also known as caustic potash and potash lye.

potassium iodate A food additive used as a dough strengthener.

potassium iodide A food additive used as a nutrient supplement (iodine) in salt.

potassium lactate A food additive used as a flavor enhancer, flavoring agent, flavoring adjuvant, humectant and/or pH control agent.

potassium metabisulfite A food additive used as a preservative.

potassium metaphosphate A food additive used as a fermentation nutrient.

potassium nitrate A food additive used as a curing agent, especially in the processing of cod roe, and/or coloring agent; some evidence suggests that it may be carcinogenic.

potassium nitrite A food additive used as an antibacterial agent and/or color stabilizer, especially in cured and/or smoked fish and meats; some evidence suggests that it may be carcinogenic.

potassium propionate and potassium sorbate Food additives used as preservatives.

potassium sorbate A food additive used as a preservative in cheese, bread, margarine, beverages and other products.

potassium sulfate A food additive used as a flavoring agent and/or adjuvant.

potatis (poh-taht-is) Swedish for potato.

potato The starchy tuber of a succulent, nonwoody annual plant (*Solanum tuberosum*) native to the Andes Mountains; it is cooked liked a vegetable, made into flour, processed for chips and used for distillation mash.

potato, mealy Any of a variety of potatoes (e.g., russet) with a high starch content, low sugar content, low moisture content and thick skin; used principally for baking, deep-frying and making into whipped or puréed potato dishes; also known as a baker or starchy potato.

potato, waxy Any of a variety of potatoes (e.g., red potato) with a low starch content, high moisture content, high sugar content and thin skin; used principally for boiling; also known as a boiling potato.

potato alcohol Alcohol distilled from a potato mash.

potato buds A form of dehydrated mashed potatoes; the granules or nuggets require some stirring for reconstitution.

potato chips Very thinly sliced, deep-fried potatoes, usually salted; also called Saratoga chips because they were first made in Saratoga Springs, New York; also known as potato crisps.

potato crisps *See* potato chips.

potato flour An ultrafine, soft, white powder that is the pure starch obtained by either soaking grated potatoes in water or grinding cooked, dried potatoes; used as a thickener or for baking (alone or blended with wheat flour); also called potato starch.

potato masher A utensil with an inflexible zigzag wire and a wooden or metal handle; it is used to reduce high-starch vegetables such as potatoes or parsnips to a soft, fluffy mass.

potato masher

potato nail A nail-shaped utensil with a sharp tip and large head that is inserted into a raw potato; it is used to conduct heat through the potato so that it bakes quickly and uniformly.

potato nails

potato nest A dish consisting of shredded potatoes deep-fried in hot fat in a potato nest basket; it is used as a container for serving certain foods.

potato nest basket An assemblage of two wire baskets, one smaller than the other; shredded potatoes are placed in the larger basket, and the smaller basket is placed on top of the potatoes; the assemblage is submerged in hot fat and cooked; available in various sizes.

potato nest basket

potato ricer *See* ricer.

potato salad A dish of cooked, sliced or diced potatoes bound with mayonnaise and flavored with ingredients such as onions, green peppers, cooked eggs, herbs and spices; usually served chilled.

potato salad, German A dish of cooked, sliced or diced potatoes bound with a vinegar dressing, flavored with bacon, bacon fat and onions and served warm.

potato starch *See* potato flour.

potato steamer *See* pommes vapeur.

pot au feu (paw toh fuh) French for pot on the fire and used to describe a thick French soup of meat and vegetables; the broth is often served separately before the meat and vegetables.

pot barley Barley with the hull removed; it is not polished to the same extent as pearl barley and has a nuttier flavor.

pot cheese A soft, fresh, white cheese made from cow's milk; similar to cottage cheese but drier because its whey is allowed to drain away for a longer period of time.

pot de crème (poa duh kreme) 1. A French dessert consisting of a rich, baked custard, usually chocolate. 2. A small porcelain pot with a lid, one or two handles, a capacity of 2.5–8 oz. and used for serving pot de crème.

pote (poh-tay) 1. A Spanish stew made with white beans and beef in a pote. 2. A Spanish earthenware pot.

potée (POO-tay) 1. A French term traditionally indicating that a dish was cooked in an earthenware pot. 2. French for a rich meat and vegetable stew.

poteen; potheen (po-cheen) Irish slang for illegally distilled Irish whiskey; originally, any strong liquor distilled at home.

potential cost In the food services industry, the price of foods and/or beverages bought under ideal conditions and used as a standard for comparing actual costs.

potentially hazardous foods Foods on which bacteria thrive and that should be handled with care to avoid transmitting an infection, intoxication or toxin-mediated infection; includes foods high in protein, such as meat, fish, shellfish, grains and some vegetables as well as dairy products, eggs and products containing eggs, such as custards.

potet (poo-TEY) Norwegian for potato.

potherb 1. A term used from the 16th to the 19th century for any plant with stalks and leaves that could be boiled as greens. 2. Culinary herbs, as opposed to medicinal herbs.

potica (po-teet-sa) A Bohemian–Slovenian dessert made with a thinly stretched yeast dough filled with ground walnuts and cooked in honey and milk.

potiron (poh-tee-rohn) French for pumpkin.

pot liquor; potlikker The liquid remaining after cooking greens or other vegetables; served in the American South with cornbread.

potluck; potluck supper 1. A meal offered to a guest without the host having made any special preparations; sometimes consisting of dishes brought by the guests or foods delivered from restaurants. 2. *See* covered-dish supper.

pot marigold *See* calendula.

pot marjoram A species of marjoram with a stronger (and slightly more bitter) flavor than sweet marjoram, which is also slightly bitter.

potpie; pot pie A casserole dish of meat or poultry and vegetables in a rich sauce topped with a crust and baked.

potrawka (poh-trah-fkah) Polish for foods baked in a casserole.

pot roast *v.* To cook a piece of meat by first browning it in hot fat and then braising it in a covered pot. *n.* 1. A subprimal cut of the beef chuck or round primals; it is usually tough and flavorful. 2. *See* Yankee pot roast

potrokha (paht-ruhk-hah) Russian for giblets.

po tsai (poe tsah-e) A vegetable with pale green, tightly wrapped, crinkly, serrated leaves with crisp, broad-based white stems and a mild, delicate flavor reminiscent of cabbage; there are two principal varieties: one long and pointed and the other short with a barrel-shaped head; also known as Chinese leaf and Peking cabbage.

pot stickers Small Chinese dumplings made of won ton wrappers with a meat, fish, shellfish and/or vegetable filling, either fried or browned and then cooked in a broth or steamed; usually served with dipping sauces; also generally known as Chinese dumplings.

pot still A still consisting of a large, broad-based copper pot topped by a long column; it produces only single batches and must be refilled; used principally to distill high-quality Irish grain whiskeys and single-malt Scotch whiskys.

potted A preservation method in which foods (particularly meat and shrimp) are seasoned, cooked, stored in a container with a layer of fat on top and chilled.

potted pork An English dish consisting of diced pork slowly cooked in a covered saucepan, then mashed and shredded and made into a spread; it is eaten cold with toast.

pouders; poudres Old English for powders or powdered spices such as ginger, cinnamon and nutmeg.

pouding (poo-deng) French for pudding.

Pouilly Fuissé (pooy-yee fwee-say) A white wine from Burgundy, made with Chardonnay grapes; it is dry, fresh and fruity.

Pouilly Fumé (pooy-yee fu-may) A white wine made from Sauvignon Blanc grapes, produced in the village of Pouilly-sur-Loire, France; it is dry and has a smoky quality.

poularde (poo-LAHRD) French for a neutered, fattened hen.

poule (pull) French for boiling fowl.

poulet (poo-LAY) French for a young, tender spring chicken.

Poulette, sauce (poo-let) A French compound sauce made from an allemande flavored with mushroom essence and lemon juice and garnished with parsley.

poultry Any domesticated bird used for food; the USDA recognizes six kinds of poultry: chicken, duck, goose, guinea, pigeon and turkey; each includes various classes. *See* fowl.

poultry by-products The edible and wholesome parts of a domesticated bird other than flesh and sex glands.

poultry lacer A large needle used to pierce the skin of fowl and lace the cavity closed with twine.

poultry meat; poultry flesh The white and dark meat portions of deboned poultry, excluding fat, skin and other edible poultry parts.

poultry product; poultry food product A labeling term recognized by the USDA for any food product containing more than 2% poultry flesh.

poultry quality grades USDA quality grades; grade A poultry has thick flesh and a well-developed fat layer and is free of pinfeathers, deformities, tears, broken bones and discoloration; if frozen, it is free from storage and freezing defects; grades B and C are of lesser quality and used in processed poultry products.

poultry seasoning A commercial blend of herbs and spices, usually sage, parsley, majoram and thyme, used to season poultry stuffing.

poultry shears A pair of strong scissors with slightly curved blades (one blade has a notched and serrated edge) used to cut through poultry flesh and bones. *See* kitchen shears.

poultry shears

pound *v.* To beat a food with a heavy object to break down its texture and make it tender. *n.* A basic measure of weight in the U.S. system; 16 oz. equal 1 lb. and 1 lb. equals 453.6 g, or 0.4536 kg.

pound cake A dense, rich cake originally made with 1 lb. each of butter, flour, sugar and eggs.

pounder *See* drum sieve.

pound of eggs A traditional measure of eggs; approximately 1 dozen large eggs.

pound of flour A traditional measure of weight for flour; depending on the type of flour, it can have a volume of 3–4½ cups.

pounds per square inch (psi) A measure of pressure.

poured sugar Sugar cooked to the hard-crack stage and poured into a shallow template; when hard, pieces can be glued together with royal icing or hard-crack sugar to form three-dimensional shapes.

pourer A plastic or metal device that fits on the neck of a bottle and permits the pouring of a free or predetermined amount of alcohol.

pourpier (poor-pee-yay) French for purslane.

pourriture grise (pooh-ree-toh-rae grees) French term for the gray rot.

pousse-café (pooze-ka-fay) 1. A drink made by layering cordials in a tall cordial glass or a pousse-café glass according to their specific densities (the heaviest on the bottom, the lightest on the top). 2. French slang for a digestif such as brandy or a cordial.

pousse-café glass A footed, tubular glass holding approximately 2 fl. oz.; used for the drink of the same name.

poussin (poo-SAHN) French for a squab chicken; also known as petit poussin.

powdered baking ammonia *See* ammonium bicarbonate.

powdered bone A nutrient supplement derived from bones and intended to supply calcium and other minerals.

powdered eggs Dehydrated whole eggs; used in commercial food production.

powdered garlic *See* garlic powder.

powdered mustard *See* mustard, ground.

powdered sugar *See* confectioners' sugar.

powder squash *See* Hercules' bludgeon gourd.

powdery mildew *See* oidium.

powerful 1. A wine-tasting term for a full-bodied, mouth-filling, flavorful red wine with high alcohol and extracts contents. 2. A wine-tasting term for a white wine that has been fermented or aged in oak barrels.

pozole *See* posole.

practically free of fat A cut of meat on which there is practically no trimmable fat present.

Prague ham *See* Prazská sunka.

prahok; prahoc (prah-hock) A paste made from fish pressed under banana leaves, mixed with coarse salt, sundried and then pounded to a paste and left to ferment; it is used as a condiment and sauce in Cambodian cuisine.

prairie buffalo fish *See* buffalo fish.

prairie dog *See* woodchuck.

prairie oysters *See* mountain oysters.

Prairie Spy apple A variety of cider apple; the fruit are particularly sweet.

prakkes (prack-keys) A Jewish dish of stuffed vegetables, usually cabbage; also known as holishkes and golubtses.

praline (PRAY-leen) A rich, fudgelike candy made with cream, brown sugar and pecans, shaped into small flat patties; popular in Louisiana and Texas.

praline (prah-leen) 1. French hard candy made with caramelized sugar and nuts, usually almonds or hazelnuts; eaten as a candy or crushed and used as a flavoring, filling or decoration for pastries and confections. 2. A 17th-century French term for roasted almonds.

praline paste A thick, bittersweet paste similar to peanut butter made by grinding caramelized almonds or hazelnuts; used to flavor pastries, creams and candies.

pranzo (PRAHN-zoh) Italian for lunch or dinner, depending on the region.

prasa (prah-saw) Turkish and Greek for leek.

Prästost (PREHST-oost) A Swedish cheese made from cow's milk and similar to Gouda except that a distilled spirit is added to the curds and is also used to wash the ripening cheese; also known as Saaland Pfarr.

prataiolo coltivato (prah-tah-eeoh-low kol-tee-vah-toh) Italian for the common store mushroom.

pratha *See* roti.

pratinho (prah-tin-nyo) Portuguese for a small plate of petiscos.

prato (PRAH-too) Portuguese for plate.

praty (PRAHT-tee) Traditional Anglo-Irish slang for a potato.

prawn 1. An anadromous shrimplike crustacean with a narrower body and longer legs than a shrimp; it has an average market length of 3–4 in. (7.6–10.1 cm), firm, pearly white flesh and a sweet, delicate flavor. *See* shrimp. 2. A term used imprecisely to describe any large shrimp (i.e., a shrimp that weighs more than 1 oz. [15 or fewer per pound]). 3. A term used imprecisely to describe a small lobster that has an average market length of 6–8 in. (15.2–19.3 cm); also known as a Caribbean lobsterette, Danish lobster, Dublin Bay prawn and Florida lobsterette.

prawn crackers *See* shrimp chips.

praz (prazz) Romanian for leek.

prazone (prah-shoh-neh) A Polish stew made with potatoes, onions, kielbasa and butter cooked over a wood fire.

Prazská sunka (prash-kah soon-kah) Prague ham; a very delicately smoked ham from the Czech Republic; first salted, placed in a mild brine, smoked over beechwood ashes and then aged.

Prebkohlsuppe (prep-kohl-soup-phet) An Austrian soup of beef broth and stuffed cabbage.

Pre Catelan A cocktail made of gin, parfait amour and lemon juice.

precook To cook a food partially or completely before using it to complete a dish.

precursor *See* provitamin.

pregado (preh-GAH-doo) Portuguese for turbot.

pregelatinized starch Starch that has been processed to permit swelling in cold water; used as a base or food additive for instant puddings, cake mixes and soup mixes; also known as gelatinized wheat starch.

preheat To bring an oven, broiler or pan to the desired temperature before putting in the food.

premier cru (preh-m'yay crew) French for first growth and used as a designation of the best vineyards in France's Bordeaux region and the better (not best) vineyards in Burgundy. *See* cru *and* grand cru.

premium A marketing term suggesting the superior quality of a top-of-the-line beer, wine, distilled spirit, coffee, ice cream or other product; it has no legal significance.

premium brand; premium pour A high-quality, expensive brand of a specific alcoholic beverage and usually recognized as such by the consumer.

premium well A premium brand that a bar uses as its house brand.

premix soda system A commercial system for dispensing carbonated beverages in which all the ingredients (water, syrups and carbon dioxide) have been mixed at a fixed ratio before being purchased.

prep and schlep Slang for supplying catered food to an off-site location.

prepared and bottled by A wine-labeling term indicating that although the producer or bottler may have treated the wine in some fashion, it has not altered the class or type of the wine.

prepared pan A pan thinly coated with fat and perhaps dusted with flour so that foods baked in it will not stick to the insides.

preportioned foods Foods divided into portions before or during their preparation as opposed to after preparation and right before service.

preprepared foods Foods for which some or all of the preparation is done before the foods are needed for further preparation or service; it can be done by the purveyor or on-site by the food services facility.

Presbyterian A cocktail made of bourbon, ginger ale and club soda.

presentation pan A pan, usually copper, that is used for flaming foods table side or for bringing food to the table for service.

presentation shot glass A shot glass with a heavy, faceted base ranging in size from 1 to 3 fl. oz.; used for liquor neat, layered cordial drinks, slammers and chilled shooter drinks.

presentoir (preh-san-twar) French for the dish on which a tureen stands.

preservative A food additive used to increase the shelf life of processed foods by retarding decomposition, fermentation, microbial growth, oxidation and/or other processes that spoil food.

preserve *v.* To extend the shelf life of a food by subjecting it to a process such as irradiation, canning, vacuum packing, drying or freezing and/or by adding preservatives. *n.* A fruit gel that contains large pieces of whole fruits.

preserved lemons Lemon slices or chunks cured in a salt–lemon juice mixture; used as an ingredient or flavoring, especially in Moroccan cuisine.

preserved sweet melon *See* tea melon, pickled.

preserving pan A wide, low, unlined copper pan with two handles and slightly sloping sides; used for making jams and jellies; also known as a confiture pan.

president (pre-zee-dahnt) A French pastry made with two disks of baked almond meringue sandwiched together with praline mousse.

Presidente Cocktail A cocktail made of light rum, dry vermouth, curaçao and grenadine; garnished with a lemon twist.

presifted flour Flour that is sifted before packaging.

pressed A food from which liquids have been extracted under pressure.

pressed beef A cut of beef, usually from the primal flank, cooked with calves' feet, onions and seasonings, then pressed flat and served cold.

pressed cheese *See* farmer cheese.

pressed cookies Small, dainty cookies formed by pressing dough through a cookie press or pastry bag fitted with a decorative tip.

pressed duck 1. A Chinese dish consisting of a steamed, boned duck that is pressed and steamed and flattened again; quartered and fried. 2. *See* canard à la presse.

pressed sushi *See* oshi-zushi.

press juice The juice squeezed from grape skins and pulp by pressure after the free-run juice has drained off; it has more aroma, flavor, color, extracts, tannins and other components than a free-run juice and is sometimes blended with free-run juice to add character and structure to a wine. *See* free-run juice.

pressure cooker A pot with a locking lid and a valve for escaping steam, usually available in 4- to 10-qt. capacities and sometimes with a wire basket insert; food is quickly cooked and tenderized under the high heat of steam pressure.

pressure cooker

pressure cooking A method of cooking food in a pressure cooker at specific levels of pressure; the higher the pressure, the higher the temperature at which water boils; by cooking food in a liquid under pressure, the trapped steam cooks the food in less time than conventional methods of steaming.

pressurized whipping cream *See* cream, pressurized whipping.

press wine Wine made exclusively from press juice; it is sometimes used as a blending wine to add character and structure.

presunto (pray-ZOON-toh) A Portuguese cured and smoked ham, often sliced thin and eaten raw.

pretendered; pretenderized Meat made tender by mechanical means or the use of enzymes such as papain.

pretzel A hard, crisp snack food made from a slender rope of leavened dough that is coated with salt and baked into a loose knot or stick.

prezzémolo (preht-TSAY-moa-loa) Italian for parsley.

prezzo fisso (PREH-t'zoh FEE-sho) Italian for a fixed price meal, similar to the French prix fixe.

price leader An item offered for sale with an especially low price, often temporarily; intended to attract customers who will buy other goods at regular prices (e.g., an inexpensive shrimp cocktail).

price margin The amount by which the sales price of an item exceeds the amount the seller paid for it.

price-off A temporary price reduction used as a sales promotion.

pricer A sign designed to display a featured price.

price–value relationship *See* perceived cost.

pricing policy In the food services industry, the method of establishing the amount of money to be charged to customers for each menu item.

prick To make small holes in the surface of a food, especially an unfilled pie crust.

prickly pear The small barrel- or somewhat pear-shaped fruit of a species of cactus (*Opuntia fiscuindica*); studded with small sharp pins and stinging fibers, it has a green to purplish-red skin, a soft yellow-green to deep pink flesh with numerous black seeds, a melon-like aroma and a sweet, bland flavor; also known as barbary fig, barbary pear, cactus pear, Indian fig, Indian pear and tuna fig.

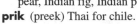
prickly pear

prik (preek) Thai for chile.

prik chee far (phrik chee far) Thai cayenne peppers.

prik dong (preek dong) A Thai bottled chile sauce made from chiles, onions, apricots, lemon, garlic and vinegar.

prik pon (preek pohn) Thai for red Chile powder.

prik yuak (phrik you-ak) Medium to large, light green to red Thai chiles; they are usually stuffed and fried.

prima colazione (pree-mah koh-la-tzee-on-ae) Italian for breakfast.

primal; primal cut The primary divisions of muscle, bone and connective tissue produced by the initial butchering of a mammal's carcass; primals are further broken down into smaller, more manageable cuts that are called subprimals or fabricated cuts; also known as a wholesale cut.

primal side pork *See* belly.

primary fermentation In beer brewing and wine making, the first stage of fermentation, during which most fermentable sugars are converted to alcohol and carbon dioxide.

primavera, alla (pree-mah-VAY-rah, ah-lah) Italian for springtime and used to describe dishes garnished with fresh vegetables.

prime *v.* To add sugar to a finished beer or wine before bottling to induce another fermentation and create carbonation or effervescence. *n.* The highest USDA quality grade for beef, lamb and veal; the meat is well aged, is well marbled, with thick external fat, has a rich flavor and is produced in limited quantities.

prime cost In the food services industry, the combination of food costs and direct labor (i.e., the labor actually required for an item's production).

prime cost pricing Establishing the price of a menu item based on the prime cost.

prime rib roast; prime rib of beef *See* rib roast.

primero (pree-mah-roh) A marketing designation for Spanish rice with a maximum of 7% broken grains. *See* extra.

primeur (pree-muh'r) French for a wine meant to be consumed when very young.

primo piatto (PREE-moh pee-AH-toh) An appetizer course in an Italian meal, usually following the antipasto.

primrose A plant grown in Europe and North America (*Primula vulgaris*); its flowers can be candied or used to make wine.

princesse, à la (pran-ses, ah lah) 1. A French garnish for poultry, salmon and vol-au-vents characterized by sliced truffles and asparagus tips in a cream sauce. 2. A French garnish of asparagus tips stuffed in artichoke bottoms.

princesse, sauce (pran-ses) A French compound sauce made from a béchamel blended with chicken glaze and mushroom essence.

Princess Mary's Pride A cocktail made of Calvados, Dubonnet rouge and dry vermouth.

Princeton A cocktail made of gin, port and orange bitters; garnished with a twist of lemon.

principal ingredient The food whose volume, texture, flavor and/or aroma dominates a dish.

prinsefisk (prin-seh-fisk) A Norwegian dish made from cod topped with an egg sauce.

printaniére, à la (prin-tan-yair, ah lah) French for garnished with spring vegetables.

printaniére, sauce (prin-tan-yey) A French compound sauce made from a velouté finished with herb butter and garnished with diced spring vegetables (e.g., asparagus, carrots and green peas); also known as sauce Spring.

Printen (preen-tan) A variation of German gingerbread flavored with candied brown sugar and candied orange and lemon peels; it is cut into thin strips and coated with a chocolate glaze.

private label A marketing term for a line of foods, beverages or sundries that carry the name of the retailer on the label.

private reserve *See* reserve.

prixe com molho de amendoim (pree-sha com moh-yo da ah-mehn-doh-him) A Brazilian dish consisting of a fish sautéed with onions and then simmered with coriander seeds, ginger and ground peanuts and served with rice and fried bananas.

prix fixe (pree feks) *See* table d'hôte.

Procanico (pro-cah-knee-coe) A white wine grape grown in Italy; it is closely related to the Trebbiano grape.

processed American cheese *See* American cheese, processed.

processed blended cheese A processed cheese made with cream cheese and without an emulsifying agent; herbs, spices, fruits, vegetables, meats, fish and/or other flavorings can be added.

processed cheese A cheese made from one or more cheeses of the same or different varieties; the cheeses are finely ground, mixed together with an emulsifying agent and sometimes flavoring ingredients (e.g., spices or liquid smoke), heated and molded. *See* cold-pack cheese.

processed cheese food A processed cheese made from cheese and other dairy products such as cream, milk, skim milk and cheese whey; oils or milk solids are often added to make it soft and spreadable; at least 51% of the final weight must be cheese.

processed cheese spread Processed cheese food with additional moisture and less fat; it must be spreadable at 70°F (21.1°C); herbs, spices, fruits, vegetables, meats, fish or other flavorings can be added.

processed food Food that has been subjected to any artificial form of modification, such as enriching, bleaching, milling or cooking. *See* natural food.

processing aid A general term for any food additive used during processing to enhance the appeal or utility of a food or food component.

produce Agricultural products such as fruits and vegetables but usually not herbs or grains.

produced and bottled by A wine-labeling term indicating that the producer or bottler has made at least 75% of the wine (i.e., at least 75% of the grapes must have been crushed and fermented at the winery) or has treated the wine in such a way as to change its classifacation.

product mix *See* sales mix.

professional cooking 1. A system of cooking based on a knowledge of and appreciation for ingredients and procedures. 2. To engage in cooking as an occupation for pay.

profit *See* net income.

profiterole (pro-FEHT-uh-rohl) 1. A miniature cream puff filled with either a sweet or savory cream or custard. 2. A French dessert consisting of small cream puffs filled with pastry cream, ice cream or Chantilly cream, usually mounded into a low pyramid and topped with chocolate sauce.

Prohibition The period of January 16, 1920, to December 5, 1933, when the manufacture, sale, transport, import and export (but not consumption) of intoxicating liquors (defined as any beverage containing a minimum of 0.5–1% alcohol) was illegal in the United States under the Eighteenth Amendment to the U.S. Constitution (introduced in Congress as the Volstead Act).

proline 1. An amino acid. 2. A food additive used as a nutrient source to significantly improve the biological quality of the total protein in a food containing naturally occurring protein.

pronghorn A horned ruminant found in the western United States and Mexico; its flesh is similar to that of antelope but less juicy and is prepared like venison.

pronounced A tasting term for an obvious, forceful aroma or flavor.

proof *v.* To allow shaped yeast dough products to rise a final time before baking. *See* fermentation. *n.* 1. A technique used to determine whether yeast is viable: the yeast is dissolved in a warm liquid with a small amount of sugar, then allowed to rest in a warm place for 5–10 minutes; if the mixture swells and becomes bubbly, the yeast is active and the mixture can be used to leaven dough. 2. A system for measuring the alcohol content of alcoholic beverages; in the United States, one degree of proof equals 0.5% alcohol by volume at a temperature of 60°F (15°C) (e.g., a 70 proof beverage contains 35% alcohol by volume). *See* Gay-Lussac *and* Sikes.

proof box A cabinet or room in which heat and humidity are controlled to create the correct environment for proofing yeast doughs.

proofing The rise given shaped yeast products just before baking.

pro-oxidant A substance that promotes oxidation.

propane A food additive used as a propellant and aerating agent.

propellant A food additive in the form of a gas used to supply force to expel a product from a container or to reduce the amount of oxygen in contact with the food in its packaging; also known as aerating agent and aerating gas.

propionic acid A food additive with a slightly pungent, rancid odor, used as an antimicrobial agent.

propriétaire-récoltant (proh-pree-ay-TEHR-ray-coh-tahn) French for a vineyard owner who also makes wines.

proprietary name A name or brand created by a food or beverage manufacturer, distributor or the like for its exclusive use; often this name is more familiar than the producer's name (e.g., Blue Nun and Old Bay Seasoning).

proprietor's reserve *See* reserve.

propylene glycol A food additive used as an anticaking agent, antioxidant, dough strengthener, emulsifier, humectant, processing aid, solvent, thickener and/or stabilizer in processed foods such as baked goods, confections, shredded coconut and icings.

propylene glycol alginate A food additive derived from certain brown kelp; used as a stabilizer in frozen dairy desserts and jams and as an emulsifier and/or thickener in processed foods such as cheeses, fats, gelatins, sweet sauces and condiments.

propylene glycol mono- and diesters Food additives used as emulsifiers.

propylene glycol monostearate A food additive used as an emulsifier, aeration aid and stabilizer.

propyl gallate A food additive used as an antioxidant.

propylparaben A food additive used as an antimicrobial agent.

prosciutto (proh-SHOO-toh) Italian for ham and used to describe a seasoned, salt cured, air-dried product that is not smoked. *See* Parma ham.

prosciutto cotto (proh-SHOO-toh koh-toh) Cooked prosciutto.

prosciutto crudo (proh-SHOO-toh KROO-doa) Cured, uncooked prosciutto; it can be eaten without cooking because it is fully cured.

Prosecco (pro-SEH-co) 1. An Italian white wine grape grown in the Veneto region. 2. The wine made from this grape can be still, frizzante or spumante; all three can be dry or amabile.

prostokvasha (prah-stahk-vash-ah) Russian for yogurt.

protease A protein-splitting enzyme.

protein efficiency ratio (PER) A measure of protein quality based on a determination of how well a protein supports weight gain in a laboratory animal.

proteins A class of nutrients containing hydrogen, oxygen, carbon and nitrogen arranged as strands of amino acids (some amino acids also contain sulfur); they occur naturally in animals and plants (significantly in grains) and are essential for the growth and repair of animal tissue.

protose steak Processed vegetable protein flavored and shaped like a steak.

Provatura (proh-vah-too-rah) A soft, fresh southern Italian pasta filata cheese traditionally made from water buffalo's milk but now from cow's milk.

provençale, à la (pro-vohn-sahl, ah lah) 1. French for dishes cooked in the style of Provence, France, usually with garlic and olive oil. 2. French for entrées that are garnished with small grilled tomatoes, stuffed mushroom caps and sauce Provençale.

Provençale, sauce (proh-vohn-SAHL) A French compound sauce made with demi-glaze and flavored with garlic, tomatoes, olive oil, onions, olives, anchovies and eggplant.

provence squash (pro-VAHNS) A variety of medium-sized, ribbed squash with a dark green skin.

provitamin An inactive organic substance the body can convert into a vitamin; also known as a precursor.

Provolone (proh-voh-LOH-nee) An Italian pasta filata cheese traditionally made from water buffalo's milk but now also cow's milk; it has a light ivory color, a mild, mellow flavor and a smooth texture that cuts without crumbling; shapes include a sausage, squat pear and piglet.

Provolone Dolce (proh-voh-LOH-nee dol-shay) Provolone aged for only 2 months; it has a very mild flavor and smooth texture.

Provolone Piccante (proh-voh-LOH-nee pee-KAHN-tay) Provolone aged for 6 months; it has a stronger flavor and stringier or flakier texture.

prsut (prr-shot) A Balkan smoked and air-dried ham; usually served raw in thin slices with olives and gherkins.

prugna (PROO-nyah) Italian for plum.

prugna secca; pruna (PROO-nyah seh-cah) Italian for prune.

prugnolo gaska (proo-noh-loh ghas-kah) Italian for blewit.

prune 1. A dried red or purple plum. 2. A variety of plum grown in Italy. 3. French for plum.

pruneau (pro-noo) French for prune.

prunelle (proo-nehl) French for sloeberry.

Prunelle A French brandy-based liqueur flavored with sloeberries.

Prunelle Alexander A cocktail made of gin, Prunelle, heavy cream and cinnamon; served in a chilled cocktail glass and sprinkled with cinnamon.

Prunus *See* drupes.

pryanosti (pree-ah-nos-tea) Russian for spice.

psári (psah-ree) Greek for fish.

psari plaki (psah-ree plah-kee) A Greek preparation method in which fish are baked in the oven.

psi *See* pounds per square inch.

psitó (psee-toe) A Greek preparation method in which fish are fried.

psomi (psoh-me) Greek for bread.

PTFE *See* nonstick plastic.

ptomaines (toh-main) A class of organic substances produced during putrefaction; some are very poisonous and are usually easily detected in decomposing food by their very bad odor. *See* putrefaction.

puak (poo-ahk) Thai for taro.

pub 1. A commercial establishment in Great Britain licensed to sell alcoholic beverages; also known as a public house. 2. An American bar, especially one emphasizing the sale and consumption of beer or one having a British decorative or culinary theme.

pub crawl British slang for visiting several pubs in one night; similar to the American expression barhopping.

publican (PUB-li-kahn) The bartender in an English pub.

public house *See* pub.

puchero (poo-CHEH-roa) A Spanish stew of beef and ham or chicken with chickpeas, chorizo and seasonings; garnished with dumplings made with chopped ham, bacon, eggs, bread crumbs and garlic and fried in butter.

pudding 1. A soft, creamy cooked dessert made with eggs, milk, sugar and flavorings and thickened with flour or another starch. 2. The dessert course of a British meal.

pudding basin A deep British mixing bowl.

pudding mold, steamed A bucket-shaped mold with plain or fluted sides and a central tube; the lid is clamped in place and has a handle on top; used for steaming puddings.

pudim (poo-dim) Portuguese for pudding, usually a rich egg custard.

pudim de amênodoa (poo-dim day ah-mah-no-doh-ah) A Portuguese almond pudding.

pudding mold

pudim de bacalhau (poo-din du bah-kah-lye-ow) A Brazilian dish of salt cod flavored with parsley and cooked with eggs for a soufflélike consistency.

pudim de leite (poo-dim day la-eta) A Portuguese dessert of a rich egg custard with caramelized sugar; it is sometimes flavored with lemon.

pudim do abade de priscos (poo-dim doh ah-bah day prees-kos) A Portuguese pudding with smoked bacon, cinnamon, lemon peel and port.

pudim flan (poo-dim flahn) A Portuguese dessert of a rich egg custard served with a caramel sauce.

pudim molotoff (poo-dim mohl-low-toof) A Portuguese dessert of a rich egg custard thickened with cornstarch and baked; when cool, it is removed from the mold and decorated with toasted almonds and served with a sweet egg sauce.

pudin de choclo y tomate (poo-dinn day chyoh-cloh ee toh-mah-tay) An Ecuadoran soufflélike dish of corn, cheese, eggs and tomatoes, flavored with cilantro.

puerco (PWAYR-koh) Spanish for pork.

puerro (PWAYR-roa) Spanish for leek.

Puerto Banus A cocktail made of gin, Grand Marnier and fino sherry or dry vermouth.

Puerto Rican rum A very dry, brandylike rum.

Puerto Rican rum, golden or amber A Puerto Rican rum that is deeper in color and more strongly flavored than a white or silver rum.

Puerto Rican rum, white or silver A clear, light-bodied and delicately flavored Puerto Rican rum.

Puff A cocktail made of equal parts distilled spirits and milk and topped with club soda; usually served in an old-fashioned glass.

puffball mushroom A round white mushroom (genus *Lycoperdales*) found in various sizes; it has a mild, blandly nutty flavor and a firm texture.

Puffbohnen German for lima beans.

puffed grain Grain, often rice or wheat, that has been heated until it expands and becomes light and fluffy; usually packaged as breakfast cereal.

puffert (poof-ert) A Dutch leavened pancake fried in a frying pan.

puff pastry A rich flaky pastry made by enclosing fat, usually butter, in a sheet of dough, rolling the dough out, and continuing to fold and roll the dough until many thin layers of fat and dough are created; as it bakes, the layers rise and separate slightly, due to the steam released by the fat; it is used in many preparations, both sweet and savory (e.g., napoleons, palmiers, tart shells, vol-au-vents and fleurons); also known as pasta sfogliata and pâte feuilletée. *See* feuilletage *and* mille-feuille.

PUFI (puffy) *See* packed under federal inspection.

pui (poo-ee) Romanian for chicken.

pulasan A variety of litchi native to Asia (*Nephelium mutabile*); it has a dark red shell with short hairs, a large seed, minimal flesh and a delicate, sweet flavor.

pulcini (pool-tchee-knee) Italian for little chicken and used to describe pastina in the shape of small chickens.

pule (paa-leh) Albanian for chicken.

pulegone A food additive used as a flavoring agent.

pullao (poo-LAW-oo) An Indian pilaf; basmati rice cooked in ghee or oil with spices, meat, chicken or vegetables.

pull date A date stamped on a product by the manufacturer, distributor or retailer indicating the date by which the product should be removed from the shelf; after that date, the product will begin to deteriorate.

pulled meat Shredded cooked meat, usually barbecued or roasted beef or pork, torn from a larger cooked cut such as a shoulder; it is typically used for sandwiches.

pulled sugar Sugar cooked to the hard-crack stage, then kneaded and pulled by hand until it is soft and pliable enough to shape into flowers, ribbons, fruits and other decorative shapes; these decorations are assembled into elaborate centerpieces or displays or used to garnish pastries, especially fancy cakes.

pullet A young hen, less than 1 year old (more particularly, one between the age of the first laying of eggs and the first molting); it has a tender texture.

pulling sauces The practice of pulling a knife or toothpick through one or more differently colored sauces, usually dessert sauces, to create an interesting pattern.

pullman loaf A yeast bread that is proofed and baked in a lidded rectangular pan; this keeps the loaf flat and even textured.

pullman pan A lidded rectangular loaf pan used to proof and bake yeast bread into an even rectangular loaf.

pullman pan

pulp The flesh of a fruit.

pulpo (POOL-poa) Spanish for octopus.

pulque (POOL-keh) An ancient Mexican alcoholic beverage made from the fermented sap of various agave plants; it has a milky consistency and color.

pulses The dried edible seeds of any of a variety of legumes, such as beans, peas and lentils.

pulverize To reduce a food to a powder or dust, usually by processing, grinding, pounding or crushing.

pulverized A food that has been reduced to a powder or very fine grind.

pulverized grind *See* grind, powdered.

pummelo (PUHM-mehl-loh) *See* pomelo.

pumped meat *See* injected meat.

pumpernickel (PUHM-puhr-nik-uhl) 1. Coarsely ground rye flour. 2. A coarse, dark German-style bread with a slightly sour flavor; it is made with dark rye flour and molasses; also known as Westphalian rye bread.

pumpkin A spherical winter squash with a flattened top and base; can range in size from small to very large and has a fluted orange shell (yellow and green varieties are also available), a yellow to orange flesh with a mild sweet flavor and numerous flat, edible seeds.

pumpkin pie A baked custard dessert made with a single flaky crust and a smooth filling of puréed pumpkin, sugar, eggs, milk and spices; traditionally served at Thanksgiving dinner.

pumpkinseed oil A thick oil made in Austria from pumpkinseeds; it has a dark brown color and a slightly toasted flavor with a hint of pumpkin.

pumpkinseeds *See* pepitas.

Puna goat cheese A common name for Orchid Island chevre, which is produced in the Puna district of Hawaii; it is a superior, mild, creamy goat cheese made in the French style.

punch A hot or cold drink blended from various ingredients, usually with a fruit or fruit juice base and often with sparkling wine or one or more liquors (although it does not have to contain any alcohol); punch is derived from the Hindi panch (five), referring to the original recipe's five ingredients: lime, sugar, spices, water and arak; made in a large bowl and served to a number of people; individually made punches are called cups.

punch bowl A large, decorative metal, ceramic or glass bowl from which punch is ladled into cups or small glasses.

punch down A folding and pressing technique used to deflate fermented yeast dough to expel and redistribute pockets of carbon dioxide and to relax the gluten. *See* breadmaking process.

punch-phoron (poonch-for-on) An Indian spice blend used for flavoring vegetables.

pungent 1. A sharp, biting, sometimes acrid or bitter aroma or flavor. 2. A wine-tasting term for a heavy, penetrating, strong aroma, usually indicating a high degree of volatile acids.

punnet A British berry basket.

Punschtorte An Austrian dessert composed of a genoise split into three layers and soaked in a rum-flavored syrup, then filled with apricot jam and frosted with pink fondant icing.

punt The indention in the bottom of a still or sparkling wine bottle; it provides the bottle with additional strength and helps steady sediment when the wine is poured.

Punt e Mes (poohnt a mess) A sweet Italian vermouth flavored with quinine.

Punt e Mes Negroni (poohnt a mess nay-gro-nee) A cocktail made of gin or vodka, Punt e Mes and sweet vermouth; served in a chilled cocktail glass and garnished with a twist of orange.

Punxatawny Phil A cocktail made of gin, light rum, lemon juice, grenadine and ginger ale; served in a chilled highball glass.

pupitre (poo-pee-truh) French term for a riddling rack.

pupu; pu pu (POO-poo) Hawaiian for any hot or cold hors d'oeuvre.

pupu platter; pu pu platter A tray with a selection of hot and/or cold hors d'oeuvre; it is available at many Chinese and other Asian restaurants in the United States.

pupusa A Central American dish consisting of a corn tortilla layered with pork, rice, cheese and/or beans and then topped with another tortilla; it is served with a pickled cabbage salsa.

purchase order (PO) A written order form from the buyer specifying the goods to be bought from the purveyor.

purchase requisition A form used by a department asking a purchasing agent to order certain goods.

purchase specifications Detailed descriptions of items to be purchased from purveyors; usually includes information regarding quality, appearance, weight, condition, size and instructions for special processing; also known as standard purchase specifications and specification.

purchasing The acquisition of goods and services through a purchase order and by payment of money or other valuable consideration.

pure alcohol *See* ethyl alcohol.

pure bar A beverage facility that serves only nonalcoholic beverages.

pure de inhame A dish from the Cape Verde Islands consisting of baked mashed yams dusted with nutmeg.

purée (pur-ray) *v.* To process food to achieve a smooth pulp. *n.* A food that has been processed by mashing, straining or fine chopping to achieve a smooth pulp.

purée soup A soup usually made from starchy vegetables or legumes; after the main ingredient is simmered in a liquid, the mixture, or a portion of it, is puréed.

purgatives *See* cathartics.

purge The juices remaining in a package after fresh, cooked or cured meat is removed.

purging The elimination of food before its full digestion or absorption in the body through self-destructive methods such as self-induced vomiting or laxative and enema abuse.

puri; poori (POO-ree) *See* roti.

purified water *See* water, purified.

purloo *See* pilau.

purpetti *See* polpette.

purple laver *See* laver.

purple onion *See* red onion.

Purple Passion A cocktail made of grape juice, vodka and ginger ale or club soda.

Purple Peruvian A South American fingerling potato with a deep purple skin and flesh.

purple potato A moderately long, slightly spherical potato with a thick purple skin and bright purple, mealy flesh; similar to a russet potato; also known as a blue potato.

purple scallop A variety of scallops found in the Pacific Ocean off Chile and Peru; it has a red and white flecked shell and a tender, sweet, white meat.

purrer (poo-rare) Norwegian for leeks.

purslane (PURSC-leen) A small plant (*Portulaca oleracea*) with stiff, reddish stems and fleshy, rounded leaves with a mild flavor and crisp texture; it can be eaten raw or cooked.

purveyor A vendor supplying goods or services to a buyer at the wholesale or retail level.

Pusser's British Navy Rum A blend of full-bodied Caribbean rums with a high alcohol content; it has been standard issue to sailors of the British Royal Navy since 1655.

pútáo (poo-tao) Chinese for grapes.

putaogar (pooh-tao-gahr) Chinese for raisin.

puto A South African dish consisting of a thick cornmeal porridge, sometimes flavored with chiles.

putrefaction (pyoo-trah-FAK-shun) The decomposition, rotting or breakdown of organic matter; this decay, often accompanied by an obnoxious odor and poisonous by-products such as ptomaines, mercaptans and hydrogen sulfide, is caused by certain kinds of bacteria and fungi.

putrefactives; putrefactive bacteria Bacteria that spoil food without rendering it unfit for human consumption.

puttanesca (poot-tah-NEHS-kah) An Italian sauce that consists of tomatoes, onions, capers, black olives, anchovies, oregano and garlic cooked in olive oil and is usually served with pasta; the name is a derivation of puttana, which is Italian for whore.

putt-i-panna (pewt-ee-PAHN-nah) A Swedish potato and cold meat hash garnished with poached or fried eggs and served with pickled beetroot.

putu (poo-too) A thick South African porridge usually made of cornmeal or sometimes sorghum; also known as pap (Afrikaans).

PX *See* Pedro Ximenez.

pyaaz (pee-ahz) Hindi for onion.

pymet; pimet 1. Mead made with grape juice. 2. A grape wine flavored with spice and honey.

pyramid Any cone- or pyramid-shaped object or formation used to display or present foods, especially items such as fruits or sweetmeats.

pyramide (phi-rah-MEED) Any French goat's milk cheese shaped like a truncated pyramid, often coated in a dark gray vegetable ash; its texture can range from soft to slightly crumbly.

pyridoxine *See* vitamin B_6.

pyridoxine hydrochloride A food additive used as a nutrient supplement in cereals, milk products, beverages, plant products and meat products.

pyroligneous acid extract A food additive used as a flavoring agent for smoked meat products.

pyruvic acid A food additive used to assist the fermentation process.

qahweh (kwah-wah) Arabic for coffee.

qahweh bel habahan (kah-va bell hah-bah-han) An Egyptian beverage consisting of thick coffee flavored with cardamom and sugar.

qalib (koo-lib) A small wooden mold with deep engravings used to make impressions on the dough when making ma'mool.

qamar el-deen (kah-mar el-deen) Arabic for dried apricot leather.

qater (kah-tar) The honey or sugar syrup poured over various Middle Eastern pastries.

qawwrama (kah-n'rah-mah) A Middle Eastern (particularly Lebanese) dish consisting of mutton preserved in its own fat; it is used for stews or fried.

QbA *See* Qualitätswein bestimmter Anbaugebiete.

qiaokeli (chiao-ke-lee) Chinese for chocolate.

qibe (key-bah) Ethiopian for butter.

qiézi (chieh-dzi) Chinese for eggplant.

qíncài (ching-tsai) Chinese for celery.

QmP *See* Qualitätswein mit Prädikat.

qouzi (koo-ree) A Middle Eastern dish consisting of a whole lamb stuffed with rice, garlic, onions, almonds, pistachios, pine nuts and cashews and flavored with baharat, turmeric, saffron, lemon juice and rosewater; a special occasion dish, it is usually roasted outdoors on a spit.

qt. *See* quart.

quadrettini (kua-drae-tee-knee) Italian for small square and used to describe small, flat, square pasta.

quadruped A four-legged animal, especially a mammal.

quaff (kwaf) To drink deeply.

quàglia (KWAH-l'yah) Italian for quail.

quahogs (KWAH-hahgs) *See* Atlantic hard-shell clams.

quaich; quaigh A Scottish two-handled drinking cup.

quail, American A small nonmigratory game bird related to the partridge family; it has 1–2 oz. (30–60 g) of breast flesh, a light, lean flesh, a delicate texture and a sweet, nutty flavor; varieties include the bobwhite, blue quail and Gambel.

quail, European A small migratory game bird related to the partridge family; it has 1–2 oz. (30–60 g) of breast flesh, a medium-dark, lean flesh, a tender texture and a sweet, nutty flavor.

quaking custard A soft New England cream custard dessert, usually garnished with meringue.

Qualitätswein bestimmter Anbaugebiete (QbA) (kval-ee-TAT'S-vine behr-SHTIHMT-tuhr ahn-BOW-geh-beet) Under the 1971 German wine laws, this denotes a good-quality wine meeting minimum alcohol and natural grape sugar contents, produced in the specified region from the specified grape variety.

Qualitätswein mit Prädikat (QmP) (kval-ee-TATE'S-vine mit PRAY-dee-kat) Under the 1971 German wine laws, this denotes a good-quality wine with distinction; the label must identify the wine as (from driest to sweetest) Kabinett, Spätlese, Auslese, Beerenauslese, Eiswein or Trockenbeerenauslese, the amount of natural grape sugar and that it was produced in the specified region from the specified grape variety; the regulations are more stringent for these finer wines than for those labeled QbA.

quality control A system for ensuring the maintenance of proper production standards; it is often achieved by inspection or testing.

quality grades *See* USDA quality grades.

quantity discount A discount provided by the seller to the buyer for purchases made in large amounts; also known as a volume discount.

quantity purchasing *See* bulk buying.

quark; quarg; kvarg (qwark) A soft central European cottage cheese–style cheese made from skimmed or partially skimmed cow's milk; it has a white color, mild flavor and runny consistency; also known as kwark.

quarnabeet (ga-run-beat) Arabic for cauliflower.

quart (qt.) A measure of volume in the U.S. system; 32 fl. oz. equal 1 qt., and 4 qt. equal 1 gallon.

quarter *v.* To cut into four equal pieces. *n.* 1. A one-fourth portion of something (e.g., a quarter of a pound). 2. One leg plus attached parts of a four-legged animal (e.g., a hind quarter). 3. A marketing term for a 1 1/8- to 1 1/4-lb. (510- to 567-g) lobster. *See* chicken lobster, deuce, heavy chicken, heavy select, jumbo, select *and* small jumbo.

Quart House The oldest retail liquor store in the United States; located in Marion County, Kentucky, neighbors would bring quart jars to be filled from the miller's barrels.

quasi (kah-ZEE) A French cut of the veal carcass; taken from the rump end of the loin, it is similar to a loin steak cut; also known as a cul.

quass *See* kvass.

quaternary ammonium chloride combination A food additive used as an antimicrobial agent during the processing of sugarcane.

quatre-épices (KAH-tray-PEES) French for four spices and used to describe a blend of black peppercorns with lesser amounts of nutmeg, cloves and dried ginger (and sometimes cinnamon or allspice).

quatre-quarts (ka-truh-kar) A French pound cake, originally made with 1 lb. each of butter, flour, sugar and eggs.

Queen cake 1. A round white loaf cake usually iced with hard white icing; it was popular during the 18th century. 2. A small diamond- or heart-shaped currant cake; it is sometimes iced.

queen crab *See* snow crab.

queen of puddings A British dessert made with custard and bread crumbs layered with strawberry jam, topped with meringue and lightly browned.

Queen of Sheba cake *See* Reine de Saba.

queen olive A large edible variety of green olive not used for oil.

Queen's biscuit A small diamond- or heart-shaped currant cake; it is sometimes iced. *See* Queen cake.

queen scallop A variety of scallops found in the Atlantic Ocean from Norway to North Africa and in the Mediterranean Sea; it has a reddish-brown shell with a slightly marbled surface, an average diameter of 3 in. (7.6 cm) and tender, sweet, white meat.

Queensland nut *See* macadamia.

Queensware Light-bodied earthenware with lead glaze introduced by Josiah Wedgewood in Staffordshire, England, in 1750 and named in honor of Queen Charlotte, wife of George III.

queijadas (qua-he-ha-das) A small Portuguese cake made with fresh cheese and egg yolk, sometimes flavored with chopped almonds, coconut and cinnamon.

queijo (KAY-zhoh) Portuguese for cheese.

Queijo Amarelo da Beira Baixa (kwa-yo ah-mah-ra-lo da beh-e-raw bah-e-shaw) A Portuguese ewe's milk cheese; it is dark yellow and has a mild buttery flavor.

Queijo da Ilha (kwa-yo da e-ya) A Portuguese pressed, crumbly cow's milk cheese, cylindrical in shape, with either a very spicy or mild flavor; generally used for grating; also known as Sao Jorge.

Queijo da Serra Estrela; Queijo Serra (kwa-yo da see-ah-raw es-tray-law; kwa-yo ser-raw) A Portuguese ewe's milk cheese with a fine, creamy, buttery texture and a mild spicy, acidic flavor; it is held together with linen and eaten with a spoon.

Queijo de Ovelha (kwa-yo da oh-va-ya) A Portuguese ewe's milk cheese with a hard rind and a spicy flavor; generally used for grating; also known as Ovelheira.

Queijo Prato (kwe-yo prah-toh) A hard Brazilian cheese made from pasteurized whole cow's milk; it has a pale yellow interior, a smooth texture and a mild, nutty flavor.

quenelle (kuh-NEHL) A small ovoid dumpling made of seasoned ground fish, chicken, veal or game, bound with panada or egg and poached in stock; usually served with a rich sauce or in a soup.

quenelles de brochet (kuh-nell duh bro-shay) A French dish of dumplings made from a pike forcemeat.

quente (kent) Portuguese for hot.

quesadilla (keh-sah-DEE-yah) A Mexican and American Southwestern dish of a flour tortilla filled with cheese and sometimes meat, chicken, refried beans or the like, folded in half and grilled; usually served with salsa and sour cream.

queso (KEH-soh) Spanish for cheese.

Queso Añejo (KEH-soh ahn-YEA-ho) An aged white Mexican cheese made from skimmed cow's milk; it has a rather dry, crumbly texture and a salty flavor; also available covered with chile powder and marketed as Queso Enchilado.

Queso Blanco (KEH-soh BLAHN-ko) A soft Latin American cheese made from whole, partly skimmed or skimmed cow's milk; it has an ivory-white color and a mild flavor and can be eaten fresh without pressing or after pressing but not aged.

Queso de Bola (KEH-soh day boh-loh) An Edam-style cheese made in Mexico from whole cow's milk.

Queso de Cabra (KEH-soh day kah-brah) A farmhouse cheese made in Chile from raw goat's milk; it has a strong, sharp, goaty flavor and a dry rind without mold or bloom.

Queso de Cincho (KEH-soh day ceen-choh) A Venezuelan cheese made from soured cow's milk; it has a spherical shape and is wrapped in palm leaves.

Queso de Crema (KEH-soh day kreh-mah) A semifirm, rich Central American (principally Costa Rican) and South American cream cheese–style cheese made from whole cow's milk and enriched with cream.

Queso de Hoja (KEH-soh day oh-hah) A Puerto Rican cheese made from cow's milk; it has a slightly salty flavor and is composed of layers of curds.

Queso del Pais (KEH-soh dell paz) A semisoft Puerto Rican cheese made from cow's milk; it has a white color and a mild flavor.

Queso de Mano (KEH-soh day mah-noh) A Venezuelan cooked cheese made from soured cow's milk.

Queso de Puna (KEH-soh day poo-nah) A fresh Puerto Rican cottage cheese–style cheese; it is usually molded in forms.

queso de tuna (KEH-soh day too-nah) A paste formed from fermented prickly pear juice; it has a sweet flavor and is used in Mexican confections.

Queso Enchilado *See* Queso Añejo.

Queso Fresco A rather dry cottage cheese–style cheese made in Spain and Latin American countries from goat's milk.

quetsch; quetsche (ketch) A plum grown in France's Alsace region; it has a mauve skin and yellow flesh and is used in baked goods, preserves and brandy.

Quetsch (ketch) A brandy made in France's Alsace region from small, highly aromatic plums.

quiche (keesh) A French dish consisting of a pastry crust filled with a savory custard made with eggs and cream and garnished with ingredients such as cheese, bacon, ham, onions, broccoli, mushrooms and/or shellfish.

quiche dish A fluted porcelain dish that is 1.5 in. high and 5–12 in. in diameter.

quiche Lorraine (keesh loh-rain) A quiche garnished with bacon and cheese (usually Gruyère).

quiche dish

quick breads A general category of breads and other baked goods made with quick-acting chemical leavening agents, such as baking powder and baking soda; these products are tender and require no kneading or fermentation (e.g., biscuits, scones, muffins and coffee cakes). *See* yeast breads.

quick-cooking oats *See* oats, quick-cooking.

quick-cooking rice *See* instant rice.

quick frozen (QF) A general term to describe a product that was rapidly frozen by any of several processes in an attempt to retain flavors, nutritional values and/or other properties.

quicklime *See* calcium oxide.

quick-read thermometer *See* thermometer, internal.

quill A toothpick made from the hollow stemlike portion of a bird's feather (a quill).

Quinalt A variety of ever-bearing strawberries; the fruit are very large and well flavored.

quince (kwenc) A spherical or pear-shaped fruit (*Cydonia vulgaris* or *C. oblonga*) with a downy yellow skin, hard, yellowish-white flesh and astringent, tart flavor reminiscent of a pear and apple; always used cooked.

quindin A Brazilian dessert of a cupcake-sized macaroon with a jellylike sugar and egg topping, baked in a water bath.

quinine A bitter alkaloid obtained from the bark of the *Cinchona* tree, which is native to the Andes Mountains and also grown in Southeast Asia and India; it is used to flavor tonic water and other beverages.

quinine water *See* tonic.

quinoa (KEEN-wah) A grain that was a staple of the ancient Incas; it has a high protein content (contains all essential amino acids), a small beadlike shape, an ivory color and a delicate, almost bland flavor; it is now prepared like rice.

Quinquina (kin-kee-nah) A Spanish aperitif wine with a quinine flavor.

quinta (KEEN-tah) Portuguese for farm or vineyard estate.

quintal; quintale (KWINT-l) A measure of weight in the metric system; 1 quintal equals 100 kg, or 220.46 lb.

Quitte (KVIT-ter) German for quince.

qumeh (komh-hah) Arabic for whole wheat.

quofte (khoh-fteh) Albanian meat balls, usually made from minced mutton.

rå (roh) Norwegian for raw.

raaee (raae) Hindi for mustard.

raat kaa khaanaa (raht kah kah-nah) Hindi for dinner.

Rabaçal (rah-bah-SAHL) A firm Portuguese cheese made from ewe's or goat's milk; it has a rustic flavor.

rabadi (RA-bhree) An East Indian beverage of thickened or reduced milk.

rabanadas (rah-bah-nah-dass) A Portuguese sweet consisting of fried rolls or bread slices dipped in milk, eggs, sugar, honey, lemon peel and wine.

rabàrbaro (rah-BAR-bar-oh) Italian for rhubarb.

Rabàrbaro An Italian aperitif made from rhubarb.

rabarber (rah-BAHR-berr) Danish, Dutch and Swedish for rhubarb.

rabbit, domesticated Any of a variety of small burrowing mammals with long ears; farm raised, it has a lean flesh with an ivory color, a relatively tender texture and a mild, delicate flavor; the average market weight for a young rabbit is 2.2 lb. (1 kg), and for a mature rabbit it is 3–5 lb. (1.4–2.3 kg).

rabbit, wild Any of several varieties of rabbits that have not been domesticated; generally, it has a lean flesh with a tannish color and a tougher texture and gamier flavor than that of a domesticated rabbit. *See* hare.

rabbiteye blueberry Any of a variety of blueberries favoring a warmer climate.

rabbit food Slang for vegetables, particularly carrots, celery and salad greens.

rabo de toro (rah-voh day toh-roh) Spanish for oxtail.

Rachel, sauce (rah-shell) A French compound sauce made from a béarnaise flavored with a demi-glaze and garnished with diced tomatoes.

rack A primal section of the lamb carcass; it contains both bilateral portions of eight ribs along with the tender, flavorful rib eye muscle and is usually split in half along the backbone and used as is or further fabricated into chops; also known as a hotel rack and, when split into bilateral halves, as a split rack.

rackhouse The building in which whiskey is aged.

racking *v.* To transfer a clear liquid (e.g., wine, beer or wort) from one container to another, leaving the solids behind. *n.* A means of aerating wine.

Râclette (rah-KLEHT) 1. A firm Emmental-style cheese or group of cheeses made in Switzerland from cow's milk; it

has a mellow, nutty flavor. 2. A dish of Râclette heated, usually by an open fire, and scraped off as it melts; served with boiled potatoes, dark bread and cornichons.

Radener (rod-de-ner) A hard, aged northern German cheese made from skimmed cow's milk; also known as Rundkäse.

radiation cooking A heating process that does not require physical contact between the heat source and the food being cooked; instead, energy is transferred by waves of heat or light striking the food; two kinds of radiant heat used in the kitchen are infrared and microwave.

radiatóri (raw-dee-ah-toe-ree) Italian for radiator and used to describe wide, spiral tubes of pasta.

radicchio (rah-DEE-kee-oh) A variety of chicory native to Italy; the purple and white cup-shaped leaves have a bitter flavor and can be used in salads, as garnish or cooked like a vegetable; also known as red-leaf chicory.

radicchio di Treviso (ra-DEE-key-oh dee trae-VEE-soh) A variety of radicchio that has a tight, tapered head of narrow pointed leaves with a pink to dark red color.

radicchio di Verona A variety of radicchio that has a small, looseleaf head of burgundy red leaves with white ribs.

radici (rah-DEE-chee) Italian for radishes; sometimes known as ravanélli.

Radieschen (rah-DEES-khern) German for radish.

radis (rah-DEE) French for radish.

radish A member of the mustard family grown for its root (*Raphanus sativus*); generally, the crisp white flesh has a mild to peppery flavor and is usually eaten raw.

radish, black A medium-sized slightly spherical radish with a dark brown-black skin.

radish, green oriental A long, large radish with a green skin and flesh.

radish, red A small spherical radish with a bright red skin, a white flesh and a mild, peppery flavor; its irregularly shaped medium green leaves have a pungent, spicy flavor and are used in salads.

radish, white A medium-sized conical radish with a dull white-tan skin, a white flesh and a peppery flavor. *See* daikon.

rådjurskött (roh-yoor-shut) Swedish for venison.

raekjur (rae-key-oor) Icelandic for shrimp or prawn.

rafano (raf-FAH-noh) Italian for horseradish.

raffinade (ra-fee-nahd) French for refined sugar.

raft A clump of clearmeat and impurities from the stock formed during clarification; it rises to the top of the simmering stock and releases additional flavors.

råg (rohg) Swedish for rye.

ragoût (rah-goo) 1. Traditionally, a well-seasoned, rich French stew containing meat and vegetables and flavored with wine. 2. Any stewlike dish, whether containing meats, poultry, vegetables and/or fruits.

ragù (rah-GOO) *See* Bolognese.

Rahm (rahm) German for cream.

Rahm Brie A German Brie-style cheese.

Rahm Camembert A German Camembert-style cheese.

rai (rah-ee) Hindi for rye.

raidir (ray-deer) French term for sealing or searing foods quickly in butter.

raifort (rai-for) French for horseradish.

rail 1. The recessed portion of a bar closest to the bartender; it is the surface the bartender usually uses to pour, mix or otherwise prepare drinks. 2. The metal pipe at the base of the front of the bar; it is used by patrons as a footrest.

raimu (RAH-ee-moo) Japanese for lime.

raimugi (RAH-ee-moo-ghee) Japanese for rye.

rainbow smelt A variety of smelt found along the U.S. East Coast; it has a silvery, iridescent skin, an average market length of 7–8 in. (18–20 cm), a high fat content and a rich, mild flavor; also known as icefish and frostfish.

rainbow trout A freshwater trout found throughout North America; some are anadromous; it has a broad reddish band or rainbow along its side that blends into its dark olive skin, which

rainbow trout

becomes silvery on the belly, a pink to red flaky flesh, a delicate flavor and an average market weight of 5–10 oz. (140–280 g). *See* steelhead trout.

Rainier cherry (ray-NER) A heart-shaped sweet cherry with a light red-blushed yellow skin, a yellowish-pink flesh and a sweet flavor.

Rainwater A moderately sweet Madeira; the wine is subjected to a fining process to create a golden color.

raised In the United States, refers to a cake, muffin or other baked good made with yeast or other leavening agent added to the dough.

raised pie A British double-crusted savory pie; the crust rises during baking and aspic is poured into it.

raisin 1. A sweet dried grape. 2. French for grape.

raisin and celery sauce A thickened English sauce made with chopped celery and raisins and flavored with dry cider; it is usually served with freshly boiled ham.

raisin sec (reh-zang sehk) French for raisin (dried grape).

raisin wine A sweet wine made from dried grapes.

raisu (RAH-ee-soo) Japanese for cooked rice served in a bowl.

raita (RI-tah) An eastern Indian yogurt salad that consists of yogurt and various chopped vegetables (e.g., cucumbers, eggplant, potatoes or spinach) or fruits (e.g., bananas) and flavored variously with garam masala, black mustard seeds and herbs.

raja (RAH-hah) Spanish for slice and used in Mexico to describe strips of food such as chiles or tortillas.

rajma (RA-jeh-mah) Hindi for red kidney beans.

rak (rahk) Russian for crayfish.

rakam A variety of sweet salak grown in Bali; the fruit is eaten fresh or preserved, and its seeds are ground and used as a flavoring or thickener.

Raki (ray-KEE) 1. A Turkish liqueur made from fermented raisins, figs or dates and flavored with aniseed; it resembles Pernod and turns milky when mixed with water. 2. A generic term for spirits in the Balkans.

Rakiya *See* Tsikoudia.

räkor (RAI-kor) Swedish for shrimp.

rakørret (RAH-ker-ret) A Norwegian dish of trout partially fermented in salt and sugar.

rakott palacsinta (raw-kott pah-lahk-seen-tah) A Hungarian layered cake of crêpelike pancakes stacked alternately with a filling and either topped with a meringue and baked or sprinkled with sugar and dotted with butter and baked, then cut into wedges for service.

ramadaniya (rah-mah-dahn-ee-yah) A Middle Eastern compote of dried apricots, figs and plums, almonds, pistachios and pine nuts flavored with orange blossom water and apricot paste.

raman (roh-mahn) Arabic for pomegranate.

rambai; rambeh A tree native to Malaysia and Indonesia (*Baccaurea motleyana*); its small, ovoid fruits grow in long clusters and have a thin, velvety, pale brown skin, a whitish flesh, a few flat brown seeds and a mild, sweet flavor.

rambutan (ram-BOO-ten) A variety of litchi (*Nephelium lappaceum*) native to Malaysia; it has a thick red shell covered with hooked hairs, a large stone with a flavor reminiscent of almonds and a pale aromatic flesh with a more acidic flavor than that of the common litchi.

ramekin; ramequin (RAM-ih-kihn) 1. A small ceramic soufflé dish with a 4-oz. capacity. 2. A small baked pastry filled with a creamy cheese filling.

ramekin

ramen (RAH-mehn) 1. A Japanese dish of noodles in broth garnished with small pieces of meat and vegetables. 2. Packets of such instant noodles and dehydrated broth.

ramontchi A plum-sized fruit (*Flacourtia indica*) native to India; it has a red skin, a yellowish-white juicy flesh and an acidic, tart flavor; used for preserves; also known as botoko and Governor's plum.

Ramos Gin Fizz A cocktail made of gin, lime juice, lemon juice, sugar syrup, heavy cream and a dash of orange flower water; served in a Collins glass.

ramp A wild onion that resembles a scallion with broad leaves; also known as a wild leek.

ram's head mushroom *See* hen of the wood mushroom.

ranch beans A dish of dry pinto beans cooked in water and flavored with onions, garlic and bacon.

ranchero (rahn-cheh-roh) A Spanish term for a dish prepared country style, usually containing tomatoes, peppers, onions and garlic.

rancid A tasting term to describe a product with a fetid or tainted character.

rancio (rahn-CHEH-oh) 1. Spanish for rancid. 2. A Spanish wine-tasting term for the pleasant flavor in a well-matured wine or the nutty flavor in a fortified wine such as sherry or Madeira.

range An appliance with surface burners on which foods are cooked.

ran-giri (RAHN-ghee-ree) Japanese for oblique cut.

rangoon bean A type of lima bean.

Rangoon sauce A sauce, popular in Florida, made from tropical fruits, butter, parsley and lemon juice and served over fish.

Ranhofer, Charles (Am., 1836–1899) The first internationally renowned chef of an American restaurant, Delmonico's in New York City; in 1893 he published his Franco-American encyclopedia of cooking, *The Epicurean,* which contains more than 3500 recipes.

Ranina (raw-knee-nah) A sweet, strong dessert wine made in the Balkans from late-gathered grapes.

rapa (RA-pah) Italian for turnip.

raparperi (RAH-pahr-payri) Finnish for rhubarb.

rape (rayp) A vegetable (*Brassica napus*) related to the cabbage and turnip families; it has a tall, leafy, green stalk with scattered clusters of tiny broccoli-like florets and a pungent, bitter flavor; also known as broccoli rabe, brocoletti di rape and rapini.

rape (RA-pah) Italian for turnip.

râpé (rah-pay) French term for cheeses suitable for grating.

rapé (RAH-pay) Spanish for monkfish.

rapeseed oil *See* rapeseeds.

rapeseeds Seeds of the rape; they are used to make a cooking oil marketed as canola oil. *See* canola oil.

rapini (rah-PEE-nee) *See* rape.

rare A degree of doneness for meat; the meat should have a large, deep red center and provide a slight resistance and be spongy when pressed. *See* very rare, medium rare, medium, medium well *and* well done.

ras (rass) Hindi for juice.

ras al-hanout (rass al-ha-noot) A spice blend generally including cloves, cinnamon and black pepper and used in North African (especially Moroccan and Tunisian) cuisines.

rasam (ra-sam) A spicy southern Indian lentil broth flavored with tamarind, a specialty of southern India.

ras gulla *See* roshgulla.

rasher (RAH-sher) 1. A thin slice of bacon. 2. A serving of two or three thin slices of bacon or ham.

ras kharouf (rass kah-roof) A Middle Eastern dish consisting of a sheep's head simmered with onions, garlic, lemon juice, carrots, cardamom, peppercorns, loomi and bay leaves; after cooking the meat is removed from the bone, sliced and served.

ras malai (rass mah-lay) An eastern Indian dessert of cheese balls or patties simmered in a syrup until puffed, then served cold with a thick cream sauce, garnished with almonds and pistachios.

rasoi (raw-so-ee) Hindi for kitchen.

rasol (rah-sol) A Balkan sauerkraut juice used as a flavoring.

raspberry A small ovoid or conical berry (*Rubus idaeus*) composed of many connecting drupelets (tiny individual sections of fruit, each with its own seed) surrounding a central core; it has a sweet, slightly acidic flavor; the three principal varieties are black, golden and red.

raspberry sauce A thick pourable mixture of puréed fresh or frozen raspberries blended with sugar and often flavored with Chambord, Kirschwasser or framboise; used for desserts.

rasphead *See* red rockfish.

raspings Bread crumbs made from dried bread crusts.

rassolnik (rahs-soul-neck) A Russian soup of fish and meat cooked with salted cucumbers.

rasstegay (rahs-styegh-aye) A Russian dish of yeast dough patties filled with salmon, rice, boiled egg, butter and parsley and baked.

Rasteau (rahss-toe) A village in France's Rhône district known for a sweet, fortified wine similar to a white port (a port made from white grapes).

Ratafia (rah-tah-FEE-ah) 1. A sweet French aperitif made from brandy and unfermented grape juice. 2. A sweet cordial made from an infusion of fruit kernels and alcohol.

Ratafia drop 1. A cookie flavored with Ratafia. 2. A cookie made with almond paste and served with the drink.

ratatouille (ra-tuh-TOO-ee; ra-tuh-TWEE) A vegetable ragoût made in France's Provence region from tomatoes, eggplant, zucchini, onions, garlic, sweet peppers and herbs simmered in olive oil.

rat cheese Slang for unprocessed American cheese, usually a yellow Cheddar-style cheese.

ratchet effect The vicious cycle of weight loss with subsequent rebound to a higher weight; also known as the yo-yo effect and yo-yo dieting.

ration 1. The food allowance for one person for one day. 2. The fixed daily food allowance for a soldier or sailor.

rattail tang *See* tang.

Ratte potato A variety of long, thin potato with a brown skin and a yellow flesh.

rattle A traditional name for a beef shank or brisket.

rattlesnake A snake found in the United States; its flesh has a bland flavor and chewy texture.

Rauchbier (ghawk-beegh) An amber or brown bottom-fermented beer produced in Bambery, Germany; it has a distinctive smoky flavor caused by drying the malts over an open beechwood fire.

Rauchfleisch (rhoh-flaish) German for smoked beef.

rauginti kopustai (raw-who-gin-tea koe-pooh-stah-E) Lithuanian for sauerkraut.

rau la tia to (row la tea tall) The spicy, pungent, round, green and purple leaves of a caraway plant; they are used in salads in Vietnam; also known as caraway mint.

rau ram (row ram) An herb (*Polygonum* sp.) with purple-tinged stems, long, slender, deep green leaves and a flavor similar to that of basil and mint; used in Vietnamese fish and noodle dishes.

ravaillac A small, western European traditional apple with a red skin; used principally for cider and jellied fruit.

ravanélli *See* radici.

ravanie; revani (raw-vah-nee) A Greek nut cake soaked with a honey syrup flavored with lemon or orange juice and zest or orange flower water.

ravier (rah-v'yay) A flat, boat-shaped china plate used in France for serving hors d'oeuvre.

Ravigiolo; Raviggiolo (rah-veg-jge-oh-lah) A soft cheese made in Italy's Tuscany and Umbria regions from ewe's milk; it has a creamy texture and a slightly sweet flavor.

Ravigote, sauce (rah-vee-GOT) 1. A cold French sauce made from a vinaigrette garnished with capers, chopped onions and herbs. 2. A French compound sauce made from a velouté flavored with white wine, vinegar and shallots and finished with herbs; usually served with calf's head, brains and boiled fowl.

ravioli (rav-ee-OH-lee; ra-VYOH-lee) Italian for little wraps and used to describe small squares or rounds of pasta stuffed with meat, cheese or vegetables. *See* agnolotti.

ravioli alla Genovese (raw-vee-Oh-lee ah-lah jay-now-vay-say) An Italian dish of ravioli stuffed with calves' udders, brains and sweetbreads flavored with Parmesan, borage and spinach.

ravioli mold A metal tray with fluted-edge indentions; the pasta dough is laid on the tray, filled, and another sheet of dough is placed on top; a rolling pin is then used to seal and cut the layered pasta.

ravut (rav-oot) Finnish for crayfish.

raw food costs *See* food costs.

raw milk *See* milk, raw.

raw sugar Sugar in the initial stages of refining; according to the U.S. Department of Agriculture (USDA), true raw sugar is unfit for direct use as a food ingredient.

raw sugar, washed A raw sugar with a larger crystal.

ray *See* skate.

razor shell clams Any of several varieties of clams found in tropical saltwaters; they have long, narrow, straight or slightly curved shells; also known as jackknife clams.

RDA *See* recommended daily allowance.

RDI *See* recommended daily intake.

rè (ra) Chinese for hot.

RE Retinol equivalent; the unit of measure for vitamin A.

reach-in A refrigerator or freezer in which foods are stored on shelves and are accessible by opening a door and reaching in; it can be a freestanding unit or located under or above a counter. *See* walk-in.

ready to cook (RTC) A processed food product that is ready to cook (usually heat); all of the preparation has been done by the manufacturer or on-site at the food services facility.

ready to eat (RTE) A processed food product that is fully prepared and ready for service to the customer; the preparation can be done by a manufacturer or on-site at the food services facility.

real ale Draft ale that has been conditioned naturally in its cask and dispensed from the cask without external pressure; also known as cask-conditioned ale.

reamer A cone-shaped wooden utensil with a ridged surface; used for extracting juice from fruit, particularly citrus. *See* juicer.

reamer

reba (REH-bah) Japanese for liver.

rebanada (ray-bah-nah-dah) Spanish for slice, especially bread.

Reblochon (reh-bluh-SHON) A soft French and Swiss cheese made from cow's milk; it has a creamy texture, a dark golden rind, a light yellow interior and a delicate flavor that becomes bitter when overripened.

recado (reh-cah-doh) Mexican and Latin American seasoning pastes made of ground chiles and/or other spices.

receita (reh-say-tah) Portuguese for recipe.

receiving The act of accepting goods that have been ordered, checking them against an invoice or other description and recording their receipt.

receiving report A form completed periodically that summarizes purchases of all goods.

receta (reh-se-tah) Spanish for recipe.

recette (ruh-set) French for recipe.

réchaud (rah-choh) French for reheat and used to describe a chafing dish.

rechauffé (reu-choh-fay) French for reheated and used to describe any dish made with previously cooked meats or poultry.

recheio (ra-chay-you) Portuguese for the filling used for empadas and pastéis.

Recioto (reh-t'CHO-toe) A generally sweet red wine made in Italy's Valpolicella district from partially dehydrated and specially ripened grapes.

recipe A set of written instructions for producing a specific food or beverage; also known as a formula (especially with regards to baked goods). *See* standardized recipe.

recipe conversion The adjustment of ingredient quantities to reflect a desired change in a recipe yield. *See* conversion factor.

recipe costing Calculating the exact cost of every ingredient in a recipe to determine total recipe cost and portion cost.

recipe costing form A form used by a food services operation to determine and record the costs associated with a standardized recipe; generally includes the as-purchased, yield percentage, edible portion and quantity of the ingredients, the total recipe costs, yield, portion size and cost, food cost percentage and selling price.

recipe forecasting The practice of estimating, before sales, how many portions a standardized recipe will yield.

recipe yield The amount of an item a standardized recipe will produce; it can be expressed in volume, weight or servings.

recirculate To filter cloudy runoff by pouring it through the grain bed in the lauter tun during beer brewing.

recommended daily allowance (RDA) Published by the Food and Nutrition Board; it identifies the amount of protein and several vitamins and minerals that should be consumed on a daily basis to avoid clinical nutrient deficiencies; the recommendations are tailored by gender, age, size and other factors.

recommended daily intake (RDI) A Nutrition Facts term approved by the U.S. Food and Drug Administration (FDA) that represents the percentage of the daily recommended intake of vitamin A, vitamin C, calcium and iron per serving based on the balanced diet of a standard adult; formerly known as the U.S. RDA.

reconstitute To build up again by adding back the part or parts that have been subtracted, such as adding back the appropriate amount of water to dry milk solids.

recovery time The length of time it takes hot fat to return to the desired cooking temperature after food is submerged in it.

rectification Purification, especially of spirits, through repeated or fractional distillation, sometimes with the addition of flavorings.

rectum The lower portion of the large intestine; stores waste before elimination.

red abalone A variety of abalone found off the U.S. West Coast; it has an extremely large shell with a white, tan or reddish-brown exterior, a white mother of pearl interior and a black flesh with a chewy texture and mild flavor.

Red Astrachan An apple grown in Russia; it has a red skin and a sweet, acidic, full flavor.

red banana A short, squat banana; it has a red skin, sometimes with a green stripe, pink-tinged creamy white flesh and a sweeter flavor than that of a common yellow banana.

red Bartlett pear *See* Bartlett pear.

red bass *See* redfish.

red bean A medium-sized, kidney-shaped bean (*Phaseolus vulgaris*) with a dark red skin and flesh; available dried.

red bean curd cheese *See* Chinese red cheese.

red beans and rice An American Southern dish of red beans cooked with ham and served over white rice.

red beet *See* beet.

red beet eggs A Pennsylvania Dutch dish consisting of eggs steeped in the liquid remaining from beets pickled in vinegar, water and brown sugar.

redbreast sunfish A member of the sunfish family found in eastern North American lakes and rivers; it has a long black ear flap, a bright orange-red belly, an average market weight of 0.5–2 lb. (225–900 g) and a mild flavor; also known as robin, sun perch and yellow belly sunfish.

red cabbage *See* cabbage, red.

Red Cap Chimay *See* Chimay.

red chile pepper paste A spicy purée of hot chiles, blended with oil and used as a condiment or flavoring.

red clover A perennial herb (*Trifolium pratense*) with dark green leaves and reddish-purple flowers; the leaves are used fresh in a salad or cooked like a vegetable, and the flowers are used in tisanes.

red cooking A Chinese cooking method in which the food is browned in soy sauce, changing its color to a deep red. *See* shao.

red currant syrup A sweetened syrup made from red currants and used as a flavoring agent in beverages and desserts; also known as sirop de groseilles.

red date *See* Chinese date.

Red Delicious apple A large native North American apple; it has a brilliant red skin, an elongated body with five projections at the base, a juicy, crisp texture that becomes mealy when stored and a sweet flavor that lacks acidity; good for eating out of hand.

Red Diamond plum A variety of small plum with a reddish-purple skin, a juicy reddish flesh and a sweet flavor.

red drum *See* redfish.

red durum wheat Wheat obtained from the durum wheat kernel; it is used for processed pastas.

redear (RED-ir) A member of the sunfish family found in southeastern North American lakes and rivers; it has a red or orange outline around its ear flap, an average market weight of 0.5–4 lb. (0.225–1.8 kg) and a firm white flesh with a rich flavor; also known as shellcracker.

red endive A variety of endive, similar to witloof, with red tips.

redeye bass *See* rock bass.

redeye gravy; red-eye gravy; red ham gravy A thin gravy made from ham drippings and water, often flavored with coffee; also known as frog-eye gravy.

redfin A small freshwater fish of the carp family found in lakes throughout the United States; it has distinctive red fins; also known as a shiner.

redfish A member of the drum family found in the southern Atlantic Ocean and Gulf of Mexico; it has a reddish-bronze skin with a black-spotted tail, an average market weight of 2–8 lb. (0.9–3.6 kg) and a firm, ivory flesh with a mild flavor; also known as channel bass, red drum and red bass. *See* ocean perch.

red flame seedless grapes *See* flame seedless grapes.

red flannel hash A dish from the New England region of the United States; it consists of fried beets, potatoes, onions and bacon; usually served with cornbread.

Red Gold nectarine A variety of nectarine; the fruit have a red-blushed yellow skin and a good flavor.

red gram *See* pigeon pea.

red grouper *See* grouper, red.

red herring A herring that has been cleaned but not split and then heavily salted; the skin retains its original color, but the eyes turn red.

red huckleberry A red-skinned huckleberry variety.

red ink Slang for red wine sold in New York City's Italian delicatessens during Prohibition.

red-in-the-snow *See* meikancai.

red kidney bean *See* kidney bean.

Red Lake currants A variety of dark red currants; they are particularly flavorful.

red leafed chicory *See* radicchio.

red leaf lettuce A variety of leaf lettuce with dark red-tinged green leaves that have ruffled edges, a tender texture and a mild flavor.

Red Lion A cocktail made of gin, Grand Marnier, orange juice and lemon juice.

red mayonnaise An English and American mayonnaise sauce blended with lobster coral and beetroot juice; usually served with lobster salad.

red Mexican bean *See* pinto bean.

red miso *See* inaka-miso.

red mullet A fish found in the Mediterranean Sea; not a true mullet, it is a member of the goatfish family; it has a reddish-pink skin, an average market weight of 0.5–2 lb. (225–900 g) and a lean, firm flesh.

red nos. 3 and 40 *See* coloring agent.

red onion A medium to large onion with a maroon-colored outer layer, a light pinkish-white flesh and a slightly sweet, mild flavor; also known as a purple onion.

red onion, Italian A medium to large ovoid red onion.

redox agent A substance that acts as an antioxidant under some circumstances and as a pro-oxidant under other circumstances.

red pepper 1. A generic name for any of various red chiles with a hot flavor; generally dried and available whole, flaked or powdered. 2. *See* cayenne; cayenne pepper.

red perch *See* ocean perch.

red porgy A fish found in the Atlantic Ocean from New York to Argentina and in the Mediterranean Sea; it has a reddish-silver skin with many tiny yellow spots that create a striped pattern on the upper half of the body, an average market weight of 2.5 lb. (1.2 kg) and a mild flavor.

red potato A small spherical potato with a thin red skin, a white waxy flesh, a small to medium size, a high moisture content and a low starch content; also known as a boiling potato.

red rice 1. An American Southern dish of rice cooked with tomatoes; often served with shrimp. 2. A glutinous variety of rice grown in China and the Camargue region of France; it has a dull, pale red color and a flavor similar to that of brown rice.

red rockfish; red rock A member of the rockfish family found in the Pacific Ocean from California to Alaska; it has a deep red skin that becomes lighter at the belly, whitish streaks along its side and black spots around its head and an average market length of 3 ft. (90 cm); sometimes marketed as red snapper even though it is unrelated to the Atlantic red snapper; also known as rasphead.

red salmon *See* sockeye salmon.

red sangre A red-skinned, white-fleshed waxy potato developed in Colorado.

red sauce In the United States, any of several varieties of Italian-style tomato sauces, some with meat.

Redskin peach A variety of freestone peach with a red-blushed yellow skin and a yellowish-white flesh.

red snapper A fish found along the U.S. East Coast and in the Gulf of Mexico; it has red eyes, a rosy skin fading to pink and then white at the belly, a lean, flaky, pink flesh that whitens

red snapper

when cooked, a delicate, sweet flavor and an average market weight of 2–8 lb. (0.9–3.6 kg); also known as the American snapper, American red snapper, Mexican snapper and northern red snapper.

red sorrel *See* Jamaican sorrel.

Redstar apple A medium-sized apple with a dark red or burgundy skin, a firm, yellow flesh and a sweet flavor.

reduce To cook a liquid mixture, often a sauce, until the quantity decreases through evaporation; typically done to concentrate flavors and thicken liquids.

reduced calorie; reduced in calories A food-labeling term approved by the U.S. Food and Drug Administration (FDA) to describe a nutritionally altered food that contains at least 25% fewer calories than the regular or reference (i.e., FDA standard) food. *See* low calorie *and* diet.

reduced sodium A food-labeling term approved by the U.S. Food and Drug Administration (FDA) to describe a nutritionally altered food with 75% less sodium than the regular or reference (i.e., FDA standard) food.

reducing The process of lowering the alcohol content of an alcoholic beverage by adding distilled water during production.

reducing agent *See* oxidizing agent.

reducing sugar A food additive such as dextrose or fructose used to help create the brown crust on baked goods.

reduction A sauce or other liquid that has been reduced.

red vegetable sauce *See* hoisin.

red velvet cake An American cake composed of three or four layers of a rich chocolate cake dyed bright red with food coloring and filled and frosted with white cream cheese icing.

red vermouth *See* vermouth, sweet.

red vinegar A clear, pale red liquid with a delicate, tart, slightly salty flavor; used in northern Chinese cuisine as a condiment.

redware 1. Pottery made in the eastern United States from red clay; one of the first types of pottery produced commercially; used extensively. 2. Unglazed earthenware.

red watermelon *See* watermelon.

red whortleberry *See* cowberry.

red wine *See* wine, red.

red wine sauce A sauce made from a reduction of red wine flavored with shallots, garlic and bay leaves and beaten with butter until incorporated. *See* marchand de vin, sauce.

red wine vinegar *See* wine vinegar, red.

reference protein *See* biological value of proteins (BV).

refined A food freed of inedible or undesirable components through processing (e.g., refined cereals consist of the starchy endosperm after the chaff, bran and germ are removed).

refined fusel oil A food additive derived from a by-product of fermenting grains and used as a flavoring agent and/or adjuvant.

réforme, sauce; reform sauce A French and English pepper sauce garnished with julienne of hard-cooked egg whites, mushrooms, ox tongue and gherkins and served with lamb or venison cutlets; it was created by Alexis Soyer.

refractometric index (RI) A measure of a fruit's sugar content.

refrescos (reh-frehs-cohs) Spanish for soft drinks.

refreshing 1. The process of adding a newer wine, distilled spirit or other beverage to the existing one to give the old product a new liveliness. 2. Submerging a food (usually a vegetable) in cold water to cool it quickly and prevent further cooking; also known as shocking. 3. The pleasantly fresh flavor of a food or beverage.

refreshment bar; refreshment stand A food services facility that offers a limited menu of simple foods and beverages that can be consumed while standing or seated on stools; usually located in an area of high pedestrian traffic.

refreshments Foods and beverages taken to revive one's spirits or vigor; usually a snack or light meal.

refried beans A Mexican–American dish of cooked and mashed pinto beans; served as a side dish or filling. *See* frijoles refritos.

refrigerator An insulated cabinet (reach-in) or room (walk-in) used to store foods at low temperatures created by mechanical or chemical refrigeration. *See* freezer.

refrigerator cookie *See* icebox cookie.

Régence, sauce; Regency sauce (ray-ZHANSS) 1. A French compound sauce made from a demi-glaze flavored with a Rhine wine, mirepoix and truffle peelings. 2. A French compound sauce made from a suprême flavored with mushrooms, truffle peelings and a Rhine wine.

Regensburger Braten (RAY-gerns-bur-gerr BRA-ten) A German and Austrian meat loaf made with beef and pork, suet and bread crumbs, flavored with garlic, marjoram and other seasonings and basted with gravy and sour cream.

Reggiano (reh-zhee-AH-noh) A hard grana cheese made in Italy's Reggio region from cow's milk; it has a golden yellow interior, a hard, oily rind and a spicy, rich, sharp flavor; once aged, it is used for grating. *See* Parmigiano-Reggiano.

regional cuisine A set of recipes based on local ingredients, traditions and practices; within a larger geographic, political, cultural or social unit, regional cuisines are often variations of each other that blend together to create a national cuisine.

regional wine Generally, a blended wine named for the area from which one or more of the blending wines are made (e.g., Sonoma Valley Red).

regular diet *See* house diet.

regular roast *See* roast, city.

regular steak A fabricated cut of the beef primal round; it is a steak cut from the top of the round.

Rehoboam (rea-ah-BOH-um) An oversized still and sparkling wine bottle holding six 750-ml bottles (approximately 156 fl. oz.).

Rehrücken (RAY-rew-kern) 1. German for saddle of venison. 2. An Austrian pastry composed of a chocolate–almond cake baked in a saddleback pan, then glazed with chocolate and studded with almond slivers; the cake's shape represents a saddle of venison, and the riblike pattern is used as a cutting guide.

rehrücken mold *See* saddleback pan.

rehydrate To restore the water lost during a drying process (usually by cooking, storing or freeze-drying).

reif (rife) German for ripe.

reindeer cheese An aged cheese made in Norway and Sweden from reindeer milk; it has a rich, slightly salty flavor.

reine, sauce (ren) A French compound sauce made from a suprême blended with whipped cream and garnished with strips of poached chicken breast.

Reine Claude (rehn clawd) French for the greengage plum (named for the wife of François I). *See* greengage.

Reine de Saba (rehn da SAW-bah) A dense, rich, single-layer French cake made with almonds and chocolate and topped with a poured chocolate glaze; also known as a Queen of Sheba cake.

Reine des Reinettes A medium-sized apple with a red-blushed, yellow skin and a sharp flavor.

reine des vallées A variety of cultivated strawberry that resembles a wild strawberry in flavor and size.

Reinette (reh-neh) Any of several varieties of apples grown in France that ripen late and have a dull green skin that is sometimes russeted and a firm, slightly dry flesh and sharp flavor.

reinette blanche de la Creuse A small, western European traditional apple with a bright yellow-gold skin and a very sweet, juicy flesh.

reinette bure A small, tannish-gold western European traditional apple; traditionally dried and used to flavor mulled wine.

reinette de Caux A medium-sized western European traditional apple with a wrinkly, yellow-orange-red skin, a crisp flesh and a sweet–tart flavor; also known as mignonne de Hollande.

reinette des danois *See* belle du bois.

reinette du Mans A medium-sized, western European traditional apple with brown- and white-spotted yellow skin and a white flesh with a flavor reminiscent of vanilla; traditionally used for tarte Tatin; also known as reinette jaune.

reinette grise de Saintonge A medium-sized, western European traditional apple with a yellow-spotted brown skin and a white flesh with an aniselike aroma.

reinette jaune *See* reinette du Mans.

Reinheitsgebot (ryne-heights-geh-boat) A German law stating that only water, malted grains, hops and yeast can be used to brew beer; also known as German beer purity law.

reintier de cochon (reen-tee-ay day coh-shon) A Cajun dish consisting of a hog's backbone cut into pieces, browned and cooked with vegetables, with a brown roux added; usually served over rice.

Reis (righss) German for rice.

Reisauflauf (righss-OWF-lowf) German for rice pudding.

Reizker (rites-ker) German for milky cap mushroom.

reje (RICH-err) Danish for shrimp.

rejesalat (ra-ye-sah-latt) A Danish smørrebrød dish of cooked shrimp on white bread spread with mayonnaise and garnished with hard-boiled egg, dill and lemon.

réjouissance (reh-joo-ee-shans) French for the bones that are weighed in a joint of meat (the proportion of bones to flesh is set by French law).

reke (RAY-kerr) Norwegian for shrimp.

release agent *See* lubricant.

Reliance grapes A popular variety of table grapes; the fruit have a pinkish-red skin, a crisp flesh and a sweet flavor.

religieuse (reh-leh-geh-oose) French for nun and used to describe a pastry or large cake resembling a nun in her habit; it is composed of two choux pastry puffs filled with chocolate, vanilla or coffee pastry cream and frosted with chocolate or coffee icing.

relish A cooked or pickled sauce usually made with vegetables or fruits and often used as a condiment; it can be smooth or chunky, sweet or savory and hot or mild.

relish fork A small, narrow fork with a long handle and two or three tines; used to spear olives or onions to be used in cocktails or to serve or take foods from a relish tray.

relish tray; relish plate A small dish of olives, pickles, carrot sticks, cherry tomatoes, celery stalks and the like served as an appetizer; there is usually one dish per table and diners help themselves, usually while waiting for and enjoying their drinks.

relleno (rreh-YEH-noh) 1. Spanish for stuffing or forcemeat. 2. Any of several Mexican dishes consisting of an item such as a chile stuffed with cheese and usually dipped in batter and fried.

remon (REH-mohn) Japanese for lemon.

remouillage (rhur-moo-yahj) French for rewetting and used to describe a stock produced by reusing the bones from another stock.

rémoulade (ray-muh-LAHD) A French mayonnaise-based sauce flavored with mustard, capers, chopped gherkins, herbs and anchovies; usually served with cold shellfish, fish or meat.

remove *v.* To take away a dish or dishes from a table during a meal so that additional items may be served. *n.* A dish thus removed or brought in place of one removed.

rempah (r'm-pah) A flavoring paste made from ingredients such as lemongrass, fresh or dried chiles, onions, garlic, coriander, ginger and shrimp paste; used in Malaysian and Indonesian curry dishes and to season meat for satays.

Remsen Cooler A cocktail made of Scotch, sugar syrup and club soda; served in a chilled Collins glass with a twist of lemon.

rémuage (reh-mu-ahj) French term for riddling.

Renault wine tonic A wine containing 22% alcohol made by the Renault Winery in New Jersey during Prohibition and sold legally (as a medication) in drugstores.

rendang (ren-dung) An Indonesian coconut milk–based currylike dish, flavored with spices and rempah, cooked until the liquid is absorbed by the meat.

render 1. To melt and clarify fat. 2. To cook meats and poultry to remove the fat.

rengha (rhe-nka) A Greek dish consisting of dried, smoked, boned herring in olive oil and lemon juice; served as a meze.

renkon (LEHNG-kong) Japanese for lotus root; also known as hasu.

rennet 1. A substance found in the mucous membranes of a calf's stomach; it contains rennin, an acid-producing enzyme that aids in coagulating milk and is used in cheese making. 2. A term imprecisely used to describe any substance used to facilitate the separation of curds and whey during cheese making.

rennin The naturally occurring enzyme used to coagulate milk.

reorder point The time when goods must be ordered, allowing sufficient time for their receipt so that business will not be interrupted because of shortages.

repanakia (reh-pah-nah-khia) Greek for radishes.

repollo (ray-POAL-yoa) Spanish for cabbage.

reposado tequila (reh-poh-sah-doh teh-KEE-luh) A tequila aged for 2–12 months in an oak barrel or tank.

repounsous *See* black bryony.

representative; rep A person or company authorized to represent a supplier for the sale of its goods or services.

requisition form A form used to request that an item be withdrawn from a storeroom for use.

resale at wholesale A sale made by a manufacturer, distributor or supplier to another distributor or supplier.

reserva (reh-ZEHR-vah) Spanish labeling term indicating that a red wine was aged for at least 3 years, with at least 1 year in a wooden cask, or that a white or rosé wine was aged for at least 2 years, with 6 months in wood.

reservation A table, room, seat or the like held at a customer's request for the customer's later use at a specified time.

reserve A wine-marketing term (particularly for California wines) indicating that the producer considers the product finer and longer lived than the regular bottling of the same variety; it has no legal significance; also known as private reserve and proprietor's reserve.

reserve wine A wine from a previous vintage added to a cuvée of nonvintage wines to produce wines of consistent quality and style.

residual chemicals In the food safety context, chemicals such as pesticides, herbicides, fungicides, fertilizers and the like that are used for beneficial purposes in the production of food but that, if they remain on or in the food, pose or may pose a danger when ingested.

residual sugar The natural grape sugar intentionally left in the wine after fermentation; this sweetness should be balanced by the wine's acidity.

rest 1. The period during which a bottle of wine is allowed to lay undisturbed, usually for several days after purchase, before consuming. 2. The period during which a food (e.g., bread or a roasted turkey) is allowed to lay undisturbed immediately after cooking and before slicing or carving.

restaran (res-tah-ran) Russian for restaurant.

restaurang (rest-aur-ang) Norwegian for restaurant.

restaurant A food services operation offering customers foods and beverages from a menu, usually for consumption on the premises. *See* cafe.

restaurant bacon *See* bacon, thin sliced.

restaurante (res-toh-rann-tay) Spanish and Portuguese for restaurant.

restaurant row A block or street known for its extensive number of restaurants.

retail The sale of goods and the price charged by a business selling goods or services to members of the general public. *See* wholesale.

retard To refrigerate a yeast dough to slow fermentation.

retasu (REH-tah-soo) Japanese for lettuce.

retinol (RET-n-ahl) The mammalian form of vitamin A.

retinol equivalent *See* RE.

Retsina (ret-SEE-nah) A dry, white Greek wine flavored with pine resin. *See* Kokkineli.

rettiche *See* daikon.

Reuben; Reuben sandwich A sandwich of corned beef, an Emmental-style cheese and sauerkraut on rye bread and fried in butter.

revenue The money received by a business from the sale of goods or services to its customers.

revenuers Members of the U.S. Internal Revenue Service's Alcohol Tax Unit; they enforce taxation of alcoholic beverages.

Reverend W. Wilks A cooking apple that disintegrates to a yellow froth when cooked.

reverse osmosis A water filtration method that uses pressure to force water through a fine membrane to remove inorganic contaminants.

revithia (reh-vee-thua) Greek for chickpeas.

revival chestnut A variety of chestnut tree grown in the United States; its nuts are very large and sweet.

revolving cashier's bank Money used by a cashier to make change for guests; each shift receives the same amount from the prior shift.

rex sole A small member of the flounder family found off the U.S. West Coast; it has a white flesh and a mild flavor.

rezat' na kusochki (ra-zaht na koo-sow-key) Russian for to slice.

rezept (ra-zept) Russian for recipe.

Rezept (rae-zept) German for recipe.

Rhabarber (rah-BAHR-berr) German for rhubarb.

rhea A large flightless bird native to South America; smaller than an ostrich, its meat is similar: lean and purple, turning brown when cooked, and with a flavor similar to that of lean beef. *See* emu *and* ostrich.

Rheingau (RINE-gao) A grape-growing and wine-producing region in Germany along the Rhine River; its fine ripe, full-bodied white wines are generally made from the Riesling grape and, to a lesser extent, the Silvaner.

Rhein-Riesling *See* Riesling.

Rhenish (rine-esh) An old British term for Rhine wine. *See* hock.

Rhine Riesling *See* Riesling.

Rhine wine (rine) 1. A white wine from the Rhine Valley in Germany; generally made from the Riesling grape. 2. In the United States, any semisweet white wine (regardless of the grape variety used) with an alcohol content of less than 14% can be labeled Rhine wine.

Rhine Wine Spritzer A cocktail made of Rhine or Riesling wine and club soda; served in a chilled wine glass and garnished with a lemon twist.

rhizome A creeping, usually horizontal, underground storage system (a branch or stem) that sends up leafy shoots each year.

Rhizopus-derived enzymes Enzymes derived from the fungus genus *Rhizopus* and, as food additives, used as processing aids.

Rhode Island Greening apple An apple used principally for commercial food preparation; it has a pale green skin, a crisp texture and a sharp flavor that holds up well to cooking; also known as a Northwest Greening apple.

rhubarb A perennial plant (*Rheum rhaponticum*) with long, pink to red, celerylike stalks and large green leaves that are toxic; the stalks have an extremely tart flavor and are used in baked goods; also known as pie plant.

rhubarb chard A variety of chard with bright ruby red stalks and leaf veins and dark green-purple leaves; it has a stronger flavor than chard.

rhubarbe (ru-bar-bae) French for rhubarb.

rhubarb sauce An English sauce made from rhubarb (without sugar) and flavored with dry cider and lemon juice; it is usually served with mackerel.

rhum (ruhm) French and Italian for rum.

RI *See* refractometric index.

rib 1. A primal section of the beef carcass; it consists of ribs 6–12 and a portion of the backbone; it includes such subprimal or fabricated cuts as the blade, rib roast, short ribs, rib eye roast and rib eye steaks. 2. A primal section of the veal carcass; it consists of both bilateral portions of seven ribs and includes such subprimal or fabricated cuts as a veal hotel rack and chops; also known as a double rack. 3. A single stalk of a vegetable such as celery.

riba (ree-bah) Serbo-Croat for fish.

ribbenssteg med rødkål (rib-ben-stæg med road-kahl) A Danish smørrebrød dish of sliced roast pork on black bread, served with boiled red cabbage, sweet-and-sour pickled gherkins and prunes.

ribbon 1. A term used to describe the consistency of a batter or mixture, especially a mixture of beaten eggs and sugar; when the beater or whisk is lifted, the mixture will fall slowly back onto its surface in a ribbonlike pattern. 2. A long strip or strand of pasta.

Ribera (reh-behr-rah) A full-bodied red wine made in northwest Spain.

Ribera del Duero (ree-BEHR-ah dell DWAY-roh) A grape-growing and wine-producing region in northwest Spain, known for its quality red wines made from Tempranillo and Bordeaux varietals.

ribes rosso (REE-bays roh-soh) Italian for red currant.

rib eye roast A subprimal cut of the tender eye muscle of the beef primal rib; boneless, it is sometimes known erroneously as a prime rib roast.

rib eye roll A lean subprimal cut of the rib eye muscle from the beef primal rib.

rib eye steak A fabricated cut of the tender eye muscle of the beef primal rib.

rib fingers *See* finger meat.

Ribier grape A large grape with a tough blue-black skin, a juicy flesh and few seeds; used for eating and generally not for wine.

rib lifter meat *See* blade meat.

riboflavin 1. A food additive used as a nutrient supplement and/or yellow coloring agent in processed foods such as flour, pasta and breakfast cereals. 2. *See* vitamin B_2.

rib roast A large subprimal of the beef primal rib containing the tender eye and other muscles, a large amount of marbling and available with or without the bones; also known as prime rib roast and prime rib of beef. *See* rolled rib roast *and* standing rib roast.

rib roast, full A subprimal cut of the pork primal loin; the entire trimmed rib section.

rib steak A fabricated cut of the beef primal rib; it has eye muscle meat attached to a portion of a rib bone; also available boneless.

ricci (REE-chee) Italian for curly and used to describe various widths of otherwise flat pasta strips that have one or both edges wavy or rippled.

riccio di mare (REE-chee-oh de MAH-ray) Italian for sea urchins.

ricciolini (ree-tchee-oh-lee-nee) Italian for little curls and used to describe little wavy strips or curls of pasta.

rice The starchy seed of a semiaquatic grass (*Oryza sativa*), probably originating in Southeast Asia and now part of most cuisines; there are three classifications based on seed size—long grain, medium grain and short grain—each of which is available in different processed forms such as white rice and brown rice.

rice, coated Rice that has been coated with talc and sometimes glucose to retard spoilage.

rice, long-grain Rice with a length four to five times its width; when cooked, it produces firm, fluffy grains that separate easily.

rice, medium-grain Rice that is shorter than long-grain rice and less starchy than short-grain rice; when cooked, it produces relatively moist, tender grains that begin to stick together as the rice cools.

rice, short-grain Rice with a fat, almost round, grain and a high starch content; when cooked, it produces moist, tender grains that tend to stick together.

rice bran oil An oil made from rice bran and used in salad dressings, cooking oils and hydrogenated shortenings.

rice bran wax A food additive refined from rice bran and used as a coating for candies and fresh produce.

rice cooker An electric utensil, usually round with a lid, used for steaming rice; when the rice is done, it shuts off automatically; it can also be used to steam vegetables.

rice flour Finely ground white or brown rice; used as a thickener for baking and in cosmetics.

rice flour noodles *See* rice noodles.

Rice Krispies The proprietary name of a puffed rice boxed breakfast cereal.

Rice Krispie Treats A confection of Rice Krispies, butter and marshmallows mixed together and put into a buttered dish; when cool, it is typically cut into squares.

rice malt A natural, high-quality sweetener made in Japan from malted barley or koji, rice and water; also known as mizu ame.

rice milk *See* amazake.

rice noodles Very thin noodles made from finely ground rice and water and used in many Asian cuisines; when deep-fried they expand greatly in size and become crispy, when stir-fried they remain soft; also known as rice flour noodles and rice vermicelli.

rice paper 1. An edible paper made from water and the pithy root of the rice paper plant, an Asian shrub (sometimes rice flour is also used). 2. A thin, dry, almost translucent sheet made from a dough of rice flour and water and used as wrappers in Vietnamese and Thai spring rolls.

rice powder Long-grain rice, pan roasted until golden brown and ground to a powder; used in Vietnamese cuisine as a garnish for salads and plain rice and as a binder in fillings.

rice pudding A creamy, custardlike dessert made with milk, sugar, eggs and rice, often flavored with spices and garnished with raisins or currants.

ricer A tool used to reduce a cooked food, such as a potato, into ricelike pieces; the food is placed in a hopper and pushed through a die by a plunger; also known as a potato ricer.

rice sticks Generally broad, ribbonlike Asian noodles made from a rice flour dough; they are brittle, dry and hard when made and white, somewhat opaque, shiny and smooth when cooked and are available dried and fresh; also known as thin sticks.

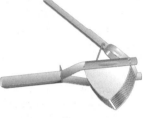

ricer

ricetta (ree-tchae-tah) Italian for recipe.

rice vermicelli (ver-mih-chehl-ee) A fine, creamy-white noodle made from a dough of finely ground rice and water. *See* rice noodles.

rice vinegar; rice wine vinegar A type of vinegar made from rice wine; it is generally clear with a straw color; Chinese rice vinegars are sharp and sour, whereas Japanese ones are mellow and almost sweet.

rice vinegar, black A Chinese vinegar made from glutinous sweet rice; it has a dark color and a rich, mild flavor and is used for braising.

rice vinegar, red A Chinese vinegar made from rice; it is pink, with a sweet–tart, salty flavor, and is used in dipping sauces.

rice vinegar, sweet A Chinese vinegar made from rice; it is brownish-black and caramelized and has a slight licorice flavor.

rice vinegar, white A Chinese vinegar made from rice; it is clear and has a slightly starchy flavor; it is used for sweet-and-sour dishes and also sold sweetened and spiced.

rice wine *See* sake.

rich 1. A tasting term for a food that has a large complement of fat or fatty substances; it usually gives a heavy, sleek mouth feel. 2. A beer- and wine-tasting term for a product that is full bodied, aromatic, flavorful, appropriately acidic and mouth filling.

rich dough A yeast dough that contains a high ratio of fat, eggs or sugar (e.g., challah, brioche and Danish pastry dough). *See* lean dough.

Riche, sauce (reesh) A French compound sauce made from a sauce normande flavored with lobster butter and gar-

nished with diced lobster and truffles; also known as sauce diplomat.

Richelieu, à la (reesh-ul-LOU, ah lah) 1. A French garnish for meat, consisting of stuffed tomatoes and mushrooms, braised lettuce and pommes château. 2. A French dish of fish dipped in melted butter and white bread crumbs, fried, then topped with maître d'hôtel butter.

Richelieu, sauce (reesh-ul-LOU) 1. A French compound sauce made from a tomato sauce flavored with a meat glaze. 2. A French compound sauce made from a demi-glaze flavored with white wine, chicken stock and truffle essence and finished with Madeira wine. 3. A French compound sauce made from an allemande flavored with onions and chicken stock, finished with chicken glaze and butter and garnished with chervil.

rickets A childhood disease caused by a deficiency of vitamin D; symptoms include abnormal bone shapes and structures.

Rickey A cocktail made of lime juice, soda water and usually gin, although bourbon, blended whisky or applejack is also used.

Ricotta (rih-COH-tah) 1. A rich fresh Italian cheese made from the whey remaining after other cow's milk cheeses have been made; it has a white color, a moist, somewhat grainy texture and a slightly sweet flavor and is used in both savory and sweet dishes; sometimes allowed to age until firm enough for grating; also known as Brocotta. 2. In the United States, the whey is usually mixed with whole or skimmed cow's milk and the cheese is similar to cottage cheese; also known as whey cheese and albumin cheese.

Ricotta Salata (ree-COH-tah sah-LAH-tah) An Italian ewe's milk whey or whey and whole milk cheese sold in plastic-wrapped wheels; it has a firm, yet tender, smooth texture, a pure white interior and a mild, usually sweet, nutty, milky flavor.

riddle A sieve with large holes; used in the kitchen for separating husks from grains.

riddling A step during the making of sparkling wines by méthode champenoise or bottle fermentation; the bottles are shaken and turned a little each day to loosen sediment until the bottle is resting upside down and the sediment is lodged against the cork, ready for disgorgement; also known as rémuage (French for shaken).

riddling rack A two-sided A-framed wooden rack used to hold bottles of sparkling wine during riddling; also known as a pupitre. *See* gyropalette.

Riesling (reece-ling) 1. The principal white wine grape grown in Germany's Rhine region, France's Alsace region and various areas of North America and, to a lesser extent, Italy, Australia, Austria and New Zealand; also known as Rhine Riesling (especially in Australia and New Zealand); Rhein-Riesling (in Austria), Johannisberg Riesling (in California), White Riesling (also in California) and Riesling Renano (in Italy). 2. The rich, sweet wine made from such grapes affected with the noble rot. 3. The flowery, fragrant, acidic white wine with a fruity flavor made from such grapes unaffected by the noble rot.

Riesling Renano *See* Riesling.

rifaki (ree-faa-ki) Greek for kid.

riganáto (ree-yah-nah-toh) Greek term designating a dish seasoned with marjoram.

rigani (ree-yah-nee) Greek for wild marjoram.

Rigatello *See* Incanestrato.

rigati (ree-gahtee) Italian for grooved and used to describe pasta that has a grooved or ridged (not smooth) surface. *See* lisci.

rigatoni (ree-gah-TOE-nee) Italian for large groove and used to describe large, grooved, slightly curved pasta tubes.

rigatoni

rigió jancsi (ree-joe yahnk-see) A Hungarian pastry consisting of two layers of chocolate cake with a whipped rum- or orange-flavored ganache center and topped with a chocolate glaze.

Rigotte (ree-got-tay) A group of small, soft French cheeses made from cow's and/or goat's milks; flavors range from mildly sour to strong and nutty, depending on the milk used; some are aged for 2 weeks, sometimes in oil or wine.

rijst (rayst) Belgian and Dutch for rice.

rijsttafel (RAY-stah-fuhl; RIHS-tah-fuhl) Dutch for rice table and used to describe an Indonesian-inspired dish of spiced rice surrounded by small dishes of foods such as hot curried, steamed or fried fish, shellfish and/or vegetables and served with chutneys.

rijst-vlaai (wrist-vlah-ee) A small Dutch torte filled with a sweet, creamy rice pudding.

rikyu-gata *See* kushi-gata.

rillette (rih-YEHT; ree-yeht) A French dish of meat, poultry or fish slowly cooked, mashed and preserved in its own fat, packed in small pots and served cold, usually spread on toast.

rillettes pot A porcelain pot with slightly bowed sides and a raised rim lid; available with an 8- to 12-oz. capacity and used to pack, store and serve pork pâté.

rillons (ree-yahng) A French dish made by salting pieces of pork belly or pork shoulder and then cooking them in lard; served hot or cold.

rillettes pot

rim 1. The edge of the glass that is touched by the lips; generally, the thinner the rim, the better the quality of glass. 2. The edge of a wine (usually red) when viewed against a white surface while the glass is tipped to a 45-degree angle; a brick red color usually indicates a mature wine, whereas a brown color indicates a deteriorated one. 3. Portuguese for kidney.

rimming The process by which the rim of a glass is coated with sugar or salt for certain cocktails.

rind 1. A relatively thick, firm coat, skin or covering found on certain foods such as fruits, vegetables and cheeses. 2. The outer surface of a cheese, produced naturally or by adding mold during curing; some rinds are eatable and all rinds vary in texture, thickness and color. *See* natural rind.

Rind (rint) German for beef.

Rindfleischwurst (rind-flysh-voorst) A fresh German sausage made from beef and pork fat, seasoned with garlic and cloves.

rind-ripened cheese *See* surface-ripened cheese.

Rindsgulasch (reends-goo-lash) An Austrian beef goulash seasoned with vinegar and thickened with tomato sauce.

ringed perch *See* yellow perch.

ringo (REEN-goh) Japanese for apple.

riñones (ree-YNOS-nayss) Spanish for kidneys.

rio *See* belle du bois.

rio The middle grade of Spanish saffron; it is determined by the time of harvest and the care with which it is picked. *See* mancha *and* sierra.

Rioja (ree-oh-ha) A grape-growing and wine-producing region of Spain near the French border; known for its red wines, which are generally soft, with a low alcohol content and light body.

rioler (re-yoh-lee) A French term meaning to decorate with strips of dough; used principally for decorating tarts with strips of dough placed over the surface in a diagonal pattern.

ripasso (ree-PAH-so) A process used by some producers of Italian Valpolicella wine to make a richer, fuller wine; after the wine has been fermented, it is passed over the skins of the dried grapes used for making Amarone, thus acquiring more color, tannin and flavor.

ripe 1. Fully grown and developed fruit; the fruit's flavor, texture and appearance are at their peak and the fruit is ready to eat. 2. A tasting term for a food (e.g., cheese) or beverage (e.g., wine) that is fully aged; it is mature and has the appropriate flavor. 3. An unpleasant odor indicating that a food, especially meat, poultry, fish or shellfish, may be past its prime.

ripening 1. The period during which the bacteria and mold present in a green cheese change the cheese's texture and flavor; a cheese can ripen from the surface inward by the application of microorganisms to the cheese (called surface-ripened cheese), from the interior outward by the injection of microorganisms into the cheese (used for certain blue-veined cheeses) or all through the cheese by the microorganisms already present; also known imprecisely as aging and curing. 2. The period during which fruits mature.

ripening agent *See* aging agent.

ripiéni (ree-PAY-nee) Italian for foods that are stuffed.

ripiéno (ree-PYAP-no) Italian for stuffing or forcemeat, especially when used for tomatoes, sweet peppers, poultry and meat.

Rippchen (RIP-chern) A German cut of the pork carcass; it consists of pork chops or cutlets from the short rib.

ripped Slang for intoxicated.

ris (recess) Danish, Norwegian and Swedish for rice.

ris (ree) French for sweetbreads.

ris (rees) Russian for rice.

ris d'agneau (ree dahn-yoh) French for lambs' sweetbreads.

ris de veau (ree duh voh) French for calves' (veal) sweetbreads.

riserva (ree-ZAIR-vah) An Italian wine-labeling term indicating that the wine has been aged longer than a regular bottling of the same variety (usually 3 years, but it can vary).

risi-bisi (ree-see-bee-see) A Polish casserole of peas and rice.

risi e bisi (REE-see eh BEE-see) An Italian Venetian dish consisting of green peas and rice; served with a bowl of Parmesan.

riso (REE-soh) 1. Italian for rice. 2. Rice-shaped pasta, similar to orzo.

risotto (rih-zot-toh; ree-ZAW-toh) 1. A cooking method for grains (especially rice) in which the grains are lightly sautéed in butter and then a liquid is gradually added; the mixture is simmered with nearly constant stirring until the still-firm grains merge with the cooking liquid. 2. A Northern Italian rice dish prepared in this fashion.

risotto Milanese (ree-ZAW-toh me-lay-nay-say) An Italian risotto flavored with saffron.

rissóis (rees-soh-is) Half-moon–shaped, deep-fried Portuguese choux pastries filled with crabmeat.

rissole (rih-SOHL; ree-SOHL) 1. A sweet- or savory-filled turnover-shaped pastry; it can be baked or fried. 2. A small, partially cooked potato ball that is browned in butter until crisp.

rissolé (RIHS-uh-lee; ree-saw-LAY) French for a food that has been fried until crisp and brown.

ristet saltsild (rees-tat salt-sealed) A Danish dish consisting of herring broiled over an open fire until the skin is crispy and a dark golden color.

ristorante (rees-toh-RAN-tay) Italian for restaurant.

ristras (rees-trass) A Spanish sausage shape; the filled sausage is tied off at intervals and then shaped into large loops. *See* sarta *and* vela.

rivel Small beads of a flour and egg dough dropped into boiling broth or water.

riverbank grape 1. A North American grape variety; the fruit have an amber or purplish-black skin and a tart flavor. 2. A vine that grows wild in the United States; it produces a very sour black berry that is used in baked goods and preserves.

Riverside navel orange A common market variety of navel orange.

Rivesaltes (ree-vah-sal-taae) A French aperitif made of wine whose fermentation is completed by adding brandy or fortified wine, so that the natural sugar is preserved.

rivulets (RIV-you-litz) *See* legs.

riz (ree) French for rice.

riz à la conde (ree a lah KON-da) A cold French rice pudding, molded with gelatin and served in a pool of fruit purée.

riz a l'imperatrice (REE ahl-ahm-pair-ah-tres) A very rich French rice pudding made with vanilla custard, whipped cream and candied fruit.

rizi (ree-zee) Greek for rice.

rizoto (ree-jhot) Serbo-Croat for risotto; often flavored with shellfish or squid.

road house Traditional slang used for a bar or tavern located alongside a roadway.

roast 1. The large joint of meat or game (with or without the bones) that has been roasted or is intended for roasting. *See* roasting. 2. The entrée course served after the sorbet and before the entremets during a French grande cuisine meal. 3. The entrée course, consisting of roasted meats, following the soup, fish and poultry or game courses during a 19th-century British meal.

roast, Brazilian A roasting style for coffee beans; the beans are darker than city roasted beans and have a hint of dark roast flavor; the roasting style has no relationship to Brazilian coffee beans.

roast, cinnamon A roasting style for coffee beans; the coffee beans are lightly roasted and do not provide much flavor, body or complexity to the beverage; also known as institutional roast.

roast, city The most widely used roasting style for coffee beans in the United States; the beans are medium roasted, resulting in a moderately flavorful, acidic beverage that may lack brilliance or be a bit flat; also known as American roast, brown roast and regular roast.

roast, espresso A roasting style for coffee beans; the beans are roasted until they are virtually burned and have a shiny, oily surface; also known as continental roast and Italian roast.

roast, European A blend of two-thirds dark roasted coffee beans and one-third medium roasted beans.

roast, French A roasting style for coffee beans; the beans are dark roasted to a degree approaching an espresso roast but without sacrificing smoothness; they should be the color of semisweet chocolate, with apparent oiliness on the surface; they yield a beverage with a spicy, pungent, caramel-like flavor; also known as dark roast, full roast and New Orleans roast.

roast, light A roasting style for coffee beans; the beans are roasted just long enough to bring out a full but delicate flavor; often popular for a breakfast coffee.

roast, medium A roasting style for coffee beans; the beans are roasted longer than a light roast to create a stronger flavor and aroma; the beans should be a medium brown color and look dry.

roast, Viennese A roasting style for coffee beans; the coffee beans are darker roasted than city roast but not as dark as French roast; also known as medium-dark roast.

roast, yellow A roasting style for coffee beans; the coffee beans are roasted very briefly, even more briefly than in cinnamon roast.

roast beef hash *See* hash.

roasted chile paste; roasted curry paste *See* nam prik pao.

roasted malt Malted barley roasted to a chocolate brown–black color and often used to color beer.

roaster; roaster chicken *See* chicken, roaster.

roaster duck; roaster duckling *See* duck, roaster.

roasting A dry-heat cooking method that heats food by surrounding it with hot, dry air in a closed environment or on a spit over an open fire; the term is usually applied to meats, poultry, game and vegetables. *See* baking.

roasting bag A paper or plastic bag able to withstand high temperatures and used to hold foods during roasting; tightly sealed, it will prevent juices from escaping and help keep the foods moist.

roasting pan A deep or shallow, oval or rectangular, metal or ceramic pan with two handles.

roasting rack A slightly raised flat or V-shaped rack used to keep a roast or poultry above the pan during roasting to prevent it from cooking in its drippings. *See* vertical roaster.

roast station chef *See* rotisseur.

robalo (roh-bah-loh) Portuguese for sea bass.

robata yaki (roh-BAH-tah YAH-kee) Japanese for open-hearth cooking.

Robert, sauce (roh-bare) A French compound sauce made from a demi-glaze flavored with onions, white wine and vinegar and finished with a Dijon-style mustard.

Robertson A grape-growing and wine-producing region of South Africa; formerly known for producing sweet dessert wines and bulk wine for distilling into brandy, it now produces some of South Africa's finest Chardonnays.

Robillard A large, western European traditional apple with an orange-blushed yellow-orange skin and a very juicy flesh.

robin *See* redbreast sunfish.

robin saus (roe-bean sass) A Norwegian sauce made from apples cooked with cider or vinegar and puréed; mayonnaise or horseradish is added before service; generally used for game.

Robiola Lombardia (roh-bee-OH-lah lom-bar-DEE-ah) A general term for a group of cow's milk cheeses from Italy's Lombardy region; they have a rough, reddish-brown, occasionally moist rind, an off-white to faintly yellow interior and a meaty, nutty, slightly salty flavor with hints of fruit.

Robiola Piemonte (roh-bee-OH-lah pyeh-MAWN-teh) A general term for a variety of fresh, rindless ewe's, goat's or cow's milk cheeses from Italy's Piedmont region to which cream has been added; they are white, with a soft, moist, creamy interior and a slightly tart, mild, sweet flavor and fruity aroma.

Rob Roy A cocktail made of Scotch whisky, sweet vermouth and bitters; also known as a Scotch Manhattan.

robust 1. A tasting term for an alcoholic or nonalcoholic beverage that is full bodied, flavorful and mouth filling. 2. A wine-tasting term for such a wine, but not necessarily a fine one. 3. A cheese-tasting term for an earthy, full-flavored cheese.

robusta coffee beans (ro-BUS-tah) A species of coffee beans grown around the world in low-altitude tropical and subtropical regions; although they do not produce as flavorful a beverage as that made from arabica beans, they are becoming increasingly important commercially, particularly because the trees are heartier and more fertile than arabica coffee trees. *See* arabica coffee beans.

Rocamadour; Rocamadur (roh-kah-mah-door) A small, soft, southern French cheese made from ewe's or goat's milk; often wrapped in leaves.

rocambole (ROK-uhm-bohl) A leeklike plant that grows wild in Europe; the bulb has a mild garlicky flavor and is used as a flavoring; also known as a sand leek, giant garlic and giant leek.

rocambole de batata (roe-cam-bow-lay day bah-tah-tah) A Brazilian dish consisting of a shrimp, onion, red bell pepper and parsley mixture encased like a jelly roll in a mixture of potatoes, eggs and cheese flavored with parsley and cilantro.

Rocca (roh-coh) An Italian aperitif with a bittersweet flavor similar to that of vermouth and bitters.

Rochambeau, à la (rho-shahm-bow, ah lah) A French garnish for meat that consists of braised carrots, stuffed lettuce, boiled cauliflower, pommes Anna and demi-glaze.

Rochefort (roosh-for) The proprietary name of a fruity, top-fermented Belgian monastery beer.

Rock and Rum A liqueur made from rum, rock candy syrup and sometimes fruit.

Rock and Rye A liqueur made from a blended whiskey base, rock candy syrup and sometimes fruit.

rock bass A member of the sunfish family found in eastern North American lakes and rivers; it has a dark olive skin with brassy brown blotches, bright red eyes, an average market weight of 0.5–4 lb. (0.23–1.8 kg) and a delicate flavor; also known as redeye bass and goggle-eye bass.

rock cake; rock bun British for a small cake or cookie filled with chopped dried and candied fruits and baked in a mound that resembles a rock.

rock candy A hard candy made by crystallizing a concentrated sugar syrup around a small wooden stick or a piece of string.

Rock Cornish game hen; Rock Cornish hen A young or immature progeny of a Cornish chicken and White Rock chicken slaughtered when 4–6 weeks old; it has an average market weight of 2 lb. (900 g), white and dark meat, relatively little fat and a fine flavor.

rocket *See* arugula.

rockfish A large family of fish found in the Pacific Ocean from California to Alaska; generally, their skin ranges from black or olive to bright orange or crimson and is sometimes spotted or striped; they have a firm, white flesh with a mild flavor; significant varieties include bocaccio, ocean perch, orange rockfish, red rockfish and yellowtail rockfish. *See* striped bass.

rock lobster *See* spiny lobster.

rocks Ice cubes.

rock salt A large, coarse salt that is less refined than table salt; it has a grayish cast and is generally not used for consumption but rather as a bed for shellfish or in hand-cranked ice cream makers; also known as bay salt and ice cream salt.

rock samphire A perennial herb (*Crithmum maritimum*) that grows along the cliffs of European seacoasts; the crisp, fleshy leaves have a salty, fishy flavor and are used as a flavoring, cooked like a vegetable or pickled. *See* marsh samphire.

rock sea bass *See* black sea bass.

rocks glass A short glass with straight sides, ranging in size from 5 to 12 fl. oz.; used to serve liquor or liqueur over ice.

rock shrimp A variety of shrimp found off Florida; it has a tough, ridged exoskeleton, a firm and chewy texture, and a rich, sweet flavor and comes 20–25 per pound.

rock sole A small member of the flounder family found off the U.S. West Coast; it has a white flesh and a mild flavor.

Rocky Mountain juniper A variety of juniper that produces particularly flavorful berries.

Rocky Mountain oysters *See* mountain oysters.

Rocky Mountain raspberry A raspberry variety; the fruit are relatively large and flavorful.

rocky road A flavoring combination of chocolate, marshmallows and nuts; used as a candy and in ice creams, pies, cakes and other desserts.

rocotillo; rocoto A small, squat chile with an orange-yellow to deep red color, a thin flesh and a very hot, somewhat fruity flavor.

rodaballo (roh-dah-bah-yoh) Spanish for turbot.

rodaja (roh-dah-hah) Spanish for slice.

rödbetor (ruhd-bett-or) Swedish for beetroot.

rödbetsallad (ruhd-bet-sal-ladd) A Swedish smörgåsbord salad consisting of small pieces of red beets, apple and gherkins and dressed with horseradish and sour cream.

rodellón (roh-day-jyon) Spanish for bolete.

rodenticide A synthetic or naturally occurring substance used to kill rodents such as mice; if used to protect a food crop or as part of a pest management program it can become an incidental food additive.

rödkål (ruhd-kawl) Danish and Norwegian for red cabbage.

rodovalho (roe-doh-valh-yoh) Portuguese for turbot.

rødvin (road-vihn) Norwegian for red wine.

roe A collective term for the spawn of female fish (also known as hard roe), the milt of male fish (also known as soft roe) or the eggs contained within the fish's or shellfish's (e.g., lobster's) ovarian membrane.

roebuck A small European deer, prepared the same as vension.

Roero (roh-AIR-oh) The sturdy, dry red wine of Italy's Piedmont region made from the Nebbiolo grape.

Roffignac (rho-fee-nyak) 1. A cocktail made of whiskey, grenadine and soda water. 2. An oyster dish made with mushrooms, red wine, shrimp and scallions.

rogan josh (row-gan josh) An Indian dish of lamb braised in yogurt, cream and spices; a Kashmiri specialty.

røget (roe-get) Danish for smoked, particularly fish.

røget ål med roræg (roe-get al med roe-rag) A Danish smørrebrød dish of slices of smoked eel on black bread garnished with scrambled eggs and chives.

røget laks (roe-get lacks) A Danish smørrebrød dish of smoked salmon on white bread garnished with slices of lemon and freshly ground black pepper.

røget sild (roe-get sealed) A Danish smørrebrød dish of a fillet of smoked herring on black bread garnished with an egg yolk in an onion ring, chopped radish and chives.

roggebrood (RAWHK-uh-broht) An unleavened Dutch rye bread made with potatoes and molasses.

roggelach (rho'g-geh-lach) Crescent-shaped Jewish pastries filled with cream cheese, walnuts and raisins and flavored with cinnamon.

Roggen (RO-gehn) German for rye.

rognon (ron-nyon) French for kidney.

rognoni (roa-NYOA-nee) Italian for kidneys.

rognons de veau flambes (rohn-yohn duh voh flahm-bay) A French dish of calf's kidneys flamed in brandy; usually prepared table side.

rognosa (roh-N'YOH-sah) An Italian frittata made with Parmesan and salami.

rognures (ronyr) French for trimmings or scrapes, specifically of puff pastry; these trimmings can be used in other preparations, such as Napoleons or cookies.

rogonnade (roh-guhn-ahd) A French cut of the veal carcass; it is taken from the loin and has the kidney attached.

roh (ro) German for raw.

Roiano (roh-ee-ah-noh) The proprietary name of an Italian liqueur made from various herbs; it has an anise, vanilla and spice flavor.

rojas (roh-has) Mexican for a fresh chile cut into strips.

rökt (rurkt) Swedish and Norwegian for smoked.

röktlax (rurkt-tlahcs) Swedish for smoked salmon.

roll A small bread made with yeast dough; it can be variously shaped and flavored. *See* bread-making process.

roll cuts *See* oblique cuts.

roll cutting A method of diagonal cutting; a diagonal cut is made about 1 5/8 in. (4 cm) from one end of the vegetable, the vegetable is rolled a quarter of a turn, a second cut is made the same distance along and rolling and cutting are continued to the end; usually used for root vegetables.

rolled A general term for any of several boneless cuts of meat (beef, veal, lamb or pork), usually consisting of more than one set of connected muscles, rolled or folded together and tied; usually used as a roast.

rolled Boston butt A subprimal cut of the pork primal Boston butt; it is a boneless, rolled roast.

rolled cookie A cookie made by rolling out a firm dough to an even thickness, then cutting it into various shapes with a knife or cookie cutter.

rolled cross rib A subprimal cut of the beef primal chuck; it is a trimmed, rolled roast.

rolled double lamb loin A subprimal cut of the lamb primal loin; it is the undivided primal loin, deboned, rolled together and tied.

rolled fondant An icing with the consistency of a dough; made from confectioners' sugar, corn syrup, gelatin and glycerin, it is rolled out with a rolling pin and draped over a cake to create a perfectly smooth, plasterlike surface for decorating; naturally pure white, it can be colored with food dyes; also known as Australian icing.

rolled fresh ham A subprimal cut of the pork primal fresh ham; it is a rolled roast cut from the leg.

rolled-in dough A dough in which a fat is incorporated in many layers by using a rolling and folding procedure; it is used for flaky baked goods such as croissants, puff pastry and Danish; also known as laminated dough. *See* lamination.

rolled oats *See* oats, rolled.

rolled plate A subprimal cut of the beef primal short plate; somewhat tough, it is usually available rolled.

rolled rib roast A rib roast that has been boned and tied.

rolled rump A subprimal cut of the beef primal round; a lean roast from the hip end of the round.

rolled sushi *See* maki-zushi.

rolling bar A mobile bar equipped with ice bins and a limited selection of popular call brands of alcoholic and non-alcoholic beverages; usually used at a resort or other facility in banquet rooms, by the pool or in other such areas; also known as a portable bar.

rolling boil A boil that cannot be dissipated by stirring.

rolling mincer A tool with five or more circular blades set in a handled housing; used to mince herbs, garlic, onions and the like by rolling the tool back and forth over the foods.

rolling out The process of flattening dough with a rolling pin into a thin, flat, even layer.

rolling pin A heavy, thick, smooth cylinder of hardwood, marble, glass or other material; used to roll out doughs.

rollmops Fillets of Bismarck herring wrapped around a pickle slice, secured with a wooden pick and preserved in vinegar and spices.

Rolls Royce A cocktail made of gin, dry vermouth, sweet vermouth and Benedictine.

roly-poly A British pudding made with a suet pastry dough covered with jam or dried fruit, rolled up in a spiral, tied in a towel and steamed or boiled.

Romadour; Romadur (rho-mah-duer) A soft Limburger-style cheese made in Germany's Bavaria region from whole or partly skimmed cow's milk; it has a mildly pungent aroma.

romaine, sauce à la; Roman sauce (RO-mahn) A French compound sauce made from a demi-glaze flavored with sugar, white wine vinegar and game stock and garnished with sultanas, dried currants and pine nuts; it is usually served with tongue, light meats and game.

romaine lettuce (roh-MAYN) A lettuce with an elongated head of loosely packed crisp leaves that are dark green and become paler toward the center; the leaves have a slightly bitter flavor and a crunchy stem; also known as cos lettuce and Manchester lettuce.

Romanée-Conti (roh-mah-nay cohn-tee) A grand cru vineyard in the village of Vosne-Romanée in Burgundy; produces a celebrated red Burgundy wine.

Romanello (roh-MAH-nehl-loh) A very hard Italian Romano-style cheese made from partly skimmed or skimmed cow's milk; it has a sharp flavor and is used for grating.

Romanesca cauliflower; Romanesco (roh-mah-NEHS-kah) An Italian cauliflower that is pale lime green with a delicate flavor; it has flowerettes that form a pyramid of pointed, spiraling cones.

Romano (roh-MAH-noh) A hard grana cheese made in southern and central Italy; it has a brittle texture, a pale yellow-white color and a sharp flavor; generally used for grating after aging for 1 year. *See* Pecorino Romano, Vacchino Romano *and* Caprino Romano.

Romanoff; Romanov (rho-mahn-off) 1. A French garnish for meat associated with the Imperial family of Russia; it consists of cucumbers stuffed with duxelles and duchesse potato cases filled with a salpicon of celeriac and mushrooms in a velouté seasoned with horseradish. 2. *See* strawberries Romanoff.

Roman punch A drink made of lemons, spirits and water, sometimes with frozen sherbet added; it was used between courses of formal Victorian dinners to clear the palate.

romarin (roa-mah-rang) French for rosemary.

Roma tomato *See* plum tomato.

romazava; roumazava (roh-mah-zah-vah) A Madagascan stew of beef, pork shoulder, chicken, tomatoes, onions and spinach flavored with garlic, ginger, black pepper and peanut oil.

Rome Beauty apple An apple native to North America; it has a deep red skin, an ivory-white flesh that can be mealy or tender and a bland sweet–tart flavor; especially good baked.

Romer; Roemer (ruh-mer) A traditional German wineglass, usually green, with a long stem and a round bowl ranging in size from 7 to 8 fl. oz.

romesco (roh-MEHS-koh) A Spanish sauce that consists of a finely ground mixture of tomatoes, red bell peppers, onions, garlic, almonds and olive oil; usually served with grilled fish or poultry.

rømme (rohm-meh) Norwegian for sour cream.

Romer

ron (ron) Spanish for rum.

Roncal (roan-KAHL) A ewe's milk cheese from Spain's Navarre region; it has a hard, beige to gray rind, a beige interior and a rich, olivelike, nutty flavor.

rondeau (rohn-doh) A shallow, wide, straight-sided pot with loop handles.

rondelles (ron-dells) Disk-shaped slices of cylindrical vegetables or fruits; also known as rounds.

rondena (rohn-dae-nah) A well-seasoned blood sausage from Spain's Andalusia region.

rondeau

rooibeet slaai (roo-e-ba-et slah-e) A South African salad of sliced beets and onions dressed with red wine vinegar, salt and sugar.

room (rohm) Dutch for cream.

Roomi (roo-me) A Middle Eastern cow's milk cheese flavored with black pepper; it has a white color, a mild flavor and a crumbly texture.

room service Food supplied directly from a hotel's kitchen to the guest's room.

room temperature 1. Generally, 72°F (22.2°C). 2. When referring to the proper temperature for serving red wine, it is 65–68°F (18–20°C).

rooster The male of the domestic fowl, especially the chicken; generally too tough to eat but used for stocks; also known as a cock. *See* capon.

root *See* taproot.

root beer 1. Traditionally, a low-alcohol-content, naturally effervescent beverage made by fermenting yeast and sugar with various herbs and roots, such as sassafras, sarsaparilla, ginger and wintergreen. 2. A nonalcoholic sweetened, carbonated beverage flavored with extracts of various roots and herbs.

rooter buffalo fish *See* buffalo fish.

root vegetables A general category of vegetables that are used principally for their taproots (e.g., carrots, celery roots and parsnips) or tubers (e.g., potatoes).

ropa vieja (roh-pah vee-ay-hah) Spanish for old clothes and used to describe a Central and South American dish consisting of flank steak braised with onions, carrots and celery, flavored with parsley, garlic, peppercorns and bay leaf and served with a sauce made from tomatoes and onions sautéed with chiles and parsley.

Roquefort (ROHK-fuhr) A semisoft to hard French cheese made from ewe's milk; it has a creamy white interior with blue veins and a pungent, somewhat salty flavor; considered the prototype of blue cheeses, true Roquefort, produced only in Roquefort, France, is authenticated by a red sheep on the wrapper and contains approximately 45% milkfat.

Roquefort dressing A salad dressing made with Roquefort, heavy cream or sour cream, lemon juice, chives, Worcestershire sauce and Tabasco sauce. *See* blue cheese dressing.

Roquencourt (row-can-koort) A particularly flavorful variety of French wax bean.

rosa bianca (roh-sah bee-ahn-kah) A variety of Italian eggplant with a light pink skin and a mild flavor.

Rosaceae *See* pomes.

Rosalinda (ROZ-a-lynn-dah) A small pastry named for a character in Shakespeare's *As You Like It.*

rosato (roh-ZAH-toe) Italian and Spanish for rosé.

roschette (roh-SKEH-teh) Crisp baked dough rings made by Sephardic Jews in Livorno, Italy.

rosé; rosé wine (ro-zay) *See* wine, rosé.

rose apple A tropical fruit (*Syzygium malaccensis*) grown in Thailand, Sri Lanka, Malaysia and Indonesia; it has the size and shape of a small pear, a rosy red, waxy skin, a crisp or mealy flesh and a flavor reminiscent of an apple.

rosebay willowherb A perennial herb (*Epilobium angustifolium*) with a creeping rhizome and a tall, unbranched stem with long narrow leaves and rose-purple flowers; the leaves are used medicinally, and the rhizome, leaves and tender young shoots are cooked like vegetables; also known as fireweed because it thrives on ground that has been cleared by fire.

rose de Benauge A medium-sized, western European traditional apple with a yellow, red-blushed skin; used principally for baking.

rose de Touraine A very small, western European traditional apple with a very dark skin and a pinkish flesh.

rosefish *See* ocean perch.

rose geranium A plant (*Pelagonium graveolens*) whose flowers and fragrant leaves are used as a flavoring in tisanes and some baked goods.

rose hip The berrylike portion of the rose (genus *Rosa*) that contains its seeds; it has a red-orange color and a tart flavor; usually available dried and ground and used for syrups, tisanes and preserves.

roselle; rozelle *See* Jamaican sorrel.

rosemary An herb (*Rosmarinus officinalis*) with silver-green, needle-shaped leaves, a strong flavor reminiscent of lemon and pine and a strong, sharp, camphorlike aroma; available fresh and dried.

rosemary honey A pale yellow, clear honey with a full, fragrant flavor; principally made in France and Spain from rosemary flowers.

rose paprika A piquant and very pungent Hungarian paprika with a medium-fine texture.

rose petals The petals of a rose flower (genus *Rosa*); they are used fresh as an ingredient in North African, Middle Eastern and Asian cuisines for their floral aroma.

rosemary

rose petals, dried A flavoring ingredient for sugar and confections, especially in Chinese cuisine.

Rose Pouchong A Chinese black tea that is mixed with rose petals; the beverage is very delicate, with a fragrant, floral flavor, and is served without milk or lemon.

Rose's Lime Juice A reconstituted, nonalcoholic sweetened lime juice made in England from West Indian limes; used principally as an ingredient in cocktails.

rose tea *See* Mei Kwei.

rosetta (roh-ZEH-tah) A very crisp hollow roll resembling a rose; a Venetian specialty.

rosette (roh-ZEHT) 1. A flowerlike design made with icing, whipped cream or the like using a piping bag fitted with a star-shaped tip. 2. A deep-fried pastry made by dipping a rosette iron into a thin, rich batter, then into hot fat; when crisp and brown, the rosette is removed from the fat and dusted with confectioners' sugar or cinnamon sugar. 3. A French sausage made from pork; its casing, which is thick and fat, helps keep the meat moist; smoked and eaten raw.

rosette bok choy *See* tatsoi.

rosette iron A long, L-shaped metal rod with a heat-proof handle at one end and various interchangeble decorative metal forms attached to the other end; used for making rosettes.

Roseval potato A variety of potato with a somewhat conical shape, an orange-red skin and a yellow flesh; generally grown in western Europe.

rosewater An intensely perfumed flavoring distilled from rose petals; widely used in Asian and Middle Eastern pastries and confections.

roshgulla (rosh-goo-law) An East Indian pastry made with chenna mixed with flour, formed into small balls that are cooked in a sweet syrup flavored with rosewater and then served in the cooking syrup; also known as ras gulla.

rosie (row-see-ah) Romanian for tomato.

rosin (row-seen) Norwegian for raisin.

Rosinen (ro-ZEE-nern) German for raisins.

rosmarino (roaz-mah-REE-noa) Italian for rosemary.

rosolio (roh-so-leh-o) 1. An Italian liqueur made from brandy, sugar and cherry or mulberry juice. 2. A cordial made from rose petals and honey in Italy's Calabria and Sicily regions; used as a flavoring rather than as a beverage.

rossel (ross-ell) Soured beet juice used as a flavoring and ingredient in Jewish cuisine.

Rossini, à la (roh-SEE-nee, ah lah) A French garnish for meat named for the Italian operatic composer Gioacchino Rossini; it consists of a fried steak placed on a crouton and topped with a slice of foie gras, truffles and a Madeira sauce made with pan drippings and demi-glaze.

Rostbraten (ROAST-broa-tern) German for roast beef.

rostélyos (roost-laush) Hungarian for steak.

rösten (rus-ten) German for to grill or grilled.

rösti; roesti (RAW-stee; ROOSH-tee) A large cake made from sliced or shredded potatoes fried until golden brown.

rotary egg beater A tool with two flat-bladed beaters connected to a gear-driven wheel with a hand crank located near the handle; used to whip cream, eggs and the like.

rotary grater *See* Mouli grater.

rotating stock *See* FIFO.

Rote Grutze (roh-tah GRUT-zeh) A German fruit pudding made with heavy cream and farina or tapicoa.

Rote Johannisbeere (roh-tah jo-hanss-beera) German for red currant.

roteka tukra (ro-tee-ka tuk-raa) Hindi for bread crumbs.

rotelle (roh-tell-lae) Italian for small wheel and used to describe pasta shaped like a wheel with spokes.

Rötelritterling (rue-tal-rit-tel-ling) German for blewit.

Rothschilds (roh-chilled) French cookies made with fingers of baked almond meringue coated on the flat side with tempered chocolate.

rôti (roe-TEE) French for to roast and used to describe a dish of roasted meat and the course during which it is served.

roti (RO-tee) 1. A Caribbean stew flavored with curry powder, jira and Scotch bonnet pepper and served over puri. 2. Hindi for the collective name for breads, including chapati (an unleavened whole wheat griddle-baked bread), naan (a yeast-leavened baked flatbread cooked against the walls of the tandoor), paratha (a flaky, unleavened whole wheat flatbread), puri (or poori, a deep-fried whole wheat bread) and kulcha (an oval yeast-leavened tandoor-baked or deep-fried white bread often containing onions).

roti jala (ro-tee ja-la) A lacy-patterned Malaysian fry bread made of wheat flour, eggs and coconut milk.

roti jala cup (ro-tee ja-la) A tin cup with four funnel spouts, each with a fine hole in the base; it is used to dispense batter onto an oiled hot plate to form roti jala.

rotisserie (row-TIS-ahr-ee) 1. Cooking equipment that slowly rotates food (usually meat or poultry) in front of or above a heat source. 2. A restaurant or shop that specializes in roasted meats. 3. The area in a large restaurant kitchen where roasting is done.

rotisseur (roh-tess-uhr) At a food services operation following the brigade system, the person responsible for all roasted items and jus or related sauces; also known as the roast station chef.

Rotkohl; Rotkraut (ROAT-koal) *See* Blaukraut.

rotmos (ROAT-moess) A Swedish dish of mashed turnips and potatoes, sometimes flavored with pork stock.

rotten-egg odor The unmistakable odor of hydrogen sulfide; added to natural gas.

Rotwein (rot-vine) German for red wine.

ròu (row) Chinese for meat.

rouelle (roo-ell) A French cut of the veal carcass; it is the thick part of the leg between the rump and knuckle and includes the cuisseau or noix.

rouennaise, sauce (roo-an-NEZ) A French compound sauce made from a bordelaise flavored with cayenne, lemon juice and puréed duck livers; usually served with duck.

rough A wine-tasting term for an astringent, harsh wine with a high tannin content.

roughage *See* dietary fiber.

rouille (roo-EE; roo-YUH) A rust-colored spicy French paste made from hot chiles, garlic, fresh bread crumbs, olive oil and stock; it is served as a sauce or garnish with fish stews.

roulade (roo-lahd) 1. A slice of meat, poultry or fish rolled around a stuffing. 2. A filled and rolled sponge cake. 3. *See* paupiette.

rouleau (roo-low) French for rolling pin.

rouló (roo-leh) A Greek dish consisting of meat loaf served with noodles.

round 1. A primal section of the beef carcass; it is the animal's hind leg and contains the round, aitch, shank and tail bones; it produces fairly tender and flavorful subprimal and fabricated cuts such as the top round, eye round, bottom round, knuckle and shank. 2. A wine-tasting term for a wine that is well balanced and complete without a major defect, but not necessarily a fine wine.

round bone shank A fabricated cut of the beef primal brisket and shank; it is cut from the foreshank.

rounded out A wine-tasting term for a mature, soft red wine.

roundel A circular wooden trencher used during Elizabethan times; it was usually painted or otherwise decorated and often inscribed with verses.

round fish A general category of fish characterized by round, oval or compressed bodies with eyes on either side of their heads; they swim in a vertical position and are found in freshwater and saltwater regions worldwide (e.g., catfish, cod and salmon). *See* flatfish *and* whole fish.

rounding The process of shaping yeast dough into smooth, round balls to stretch the outside layer of gluten into a smooth coating. *See* bread-making process.

rounding out The maturing process for a red wine during which the harsh tannins precipitate out and the wine softens.

rounds *See* rondelles.

roundsman *See* tournant.

round spatula *See* knife point.

round steak A fabricated cut of the beef primal round; it is a steak cut from the top, bottom and/or eye section and is available with or without the bone. *See* topside.

round tip A fabricated cut of the beef primal round; a roast or steak cut from the top, bottom and/or eye section.

roundworm A nematode, many of which are parasitic in humans and other animals.

roupa velha (row-pah vay-lyah) Portuguese for old clothes and used to describe a South American dish of shredded meat mixed with onions, tomatoes, garlic and jalapeños and flavored with oregano and cumin.

rousing The process of vigorously stirring a beer or wine, usually in the tank or barrel after a fining agent has been added, to disturb the sediment so that it can be fined.

Roussanne (roo-sahn) A white wine grape grown in France's Rhône Valley; it is usually blended with other grapes to add refinement to the wine.

roux (roo) A cooked mixture of equal parts flour and fat, by weight, used as a thickener for sauces, soups and other dishes; cooking the flour in fat coats the starch granules with the fat and prevents them from forming lumps when introduced into a liquid.

roux whisk *See* flat whisk.

rova (ROO-vah) Swedish for turnip.

rowanberry The small berry of the mountain ash tree or rowan tree (*Sorbus aucuparia*); it has a bright red skin, grows in clusters and has a sour, astringent flavor; used to make syrups, preserves and liqueurs.

Roxbury Russet The oldest American heirloom apple, from Massachusetts (c. 1630); the large spherical fruit has a green to yellow skin and a coarse, flavorful flesh.

royal A labeling term for Armagnac or Cognac indicating that the youngest brandy used was at least 5 1/2 years old.

Royal Ann cherry A heart-shaped sweet cherry with a golden-pink skin and flesh and a sweet flavor; it is eaten fresh, canned or used to make maraschino cherries.

Royal Brabant A small Limburger-style cheese made in Belgium from whole cow's milk.

royale (rwah-yal) A custard cooked in a dariole mold, cut into shapes and used as garnish for clear soups in French cuisine.

Royal Gin Fizz A cocktail made of gin, lemon juice, Grand Marnier, sugar syrup, egg and club soda; garnished with a maraschino cherry.

royal glaze; glacé royale A French compound sauce made from béchamel, hollandaise and unsweetened whipped cream folded together, spread over various dishes and then glazed under the broiler.

royal icing A decorative icing made with confectioners' sugar, egg whites and lemon juice; pure white and very hard when dry; it is used for fine-line piping and making durable decorations such as flowers.

Royalp *See* Tilsit.

Royal Smile A cocktail made of applejack, gin, lemon juice and grenadine.

Royalty raspberry A raspberry variety; the fruit are purplish-black and intensely flavored.

røyktlaks (ruykt-lox) Norwegian for smoked salmon.

røykttorsk (ruykt-tor-snk) Norwegian for smoked cod.

roz (roz) Arabic for rice.

rozh' (rosh) Russian for rye.

rozijnen (roh-ZI-en) Dutch for raisin.

rozl (row'zil) A fermented beet liquor with a deep red color and somewhat sour flavor; it is used as a flavoring in Jewish cuisine, especially for soups of the same name.

rozlfleisch (row'zil-fly'sch) A sweet-and-sour Jewish pot roast flavored with rozl and sugar and garnished with onions and potatoes.

RTC *See* ready to cook.

RTE *See* ready to eat.

rubbed A coarsely ground dried herb.

rubbery A tasting term for an overly chewy or elastic product.

rubets (rue-betz) Russian for tripe.

rubs Dry seasonings massaged into meat before it is cooked.

ruby port A young, deep red, fruity port that has been aged in wooden pipes for only 3 years. *See* tawny port.

rucola (roo-CHOA-lah) *See* arugula.

rue (roo) An herb (*Ruta graveolens*) that grows to a small shrub; it has blue-green serrated leaves and greenish-yellow flowers; its extremely bitter leaves are used medicinally and in salads.

Rueda (roo-AY-dah) A grape-growing and wine-producing region in northwest Spain; known for its quality white wines.

rugalach (RUHG-uh-luhkh) Bite-size crescent-shaped Jewish cookies made with a cream cheese dough rolled around various fillings, such as nuts, chocolate, poppy seed paste or fruit jam; also known as kipfel.

Rugen A variety of Alpine strawberry.

rughetta (rou-get-tah) A plant grown in Italy; it is a salad green similar to lamb's lettuce and has a slightly peppery flavor.

rugula *See* arugula.

Rührei (ruhr-i) German for scrambled eggs.

ruibarbo (rwee-BHANK-boa) Spanish for rhubarb.

ruis (roo-is) Finnish for rye.

rukak (roo-kahk) A thin, unleavened Middle Eastern bread; it is typically used for layering foods or torn into shreds and used for eating chicken or lamb dishes.

rukam A small fruit grown in Madagascar and southern Asia; it has an almost black skin, a yellowish-white juicy flesh and an acidic flavor; used to make preserves.

Rülander (ruhr-land-er) *See* Pinot Gris.

rullepølse (rule-le-pol-sa) A Danish smørrebrød dish of sausage roulade on black bread garnished with strips of aspic and onion rings.

rum A spirit distilled from fermented sugarcane juice, sugarcane molasses, sugarcane syrup or other sugarcane by-products; generally made in the Caribbean, it is aged in wooden barrels; its color can range from clear to gold to amber (dark) and its flavor from delicate to heavy.

rumaki (ruh-MAH-kee) 1. A hot hors d'oeuvre consisting of a slice of water chestnut and piece of chicken liver skewered and wrapped in bacon, marinated in soy sauce, ginger and garlic and grilled or broiled. 2. An imprecisely used name for any hors d'oeuvre consisting of a crunchy item (e.g., almond) on a skewer surrounded by a softer, chewier one (e.g., date) and served hot or cold.

rum balls A confection made with a mixture of cake or cookie crumbs, rum and ground nuts shaped into small balls and rolled in melted chocolate or chocolate jimmies.

rumbledethumps A Scottish dish made from boiled potatoes and cabbage mashed with pepper and sometimes onions.

rumbullion A 17th-century British term for West Indian rum.

Rum Collins A cocktail made of light or gold rum, sugar syrup, lime juice and club soda.

rum ether A food additive used as a flavoring agent; also known as ethyl oxyhydrate.

ruminant Any hoofed, cud-chewing quadruped mammal such as cattle, bison and deer; their multiple stomachs can digest cellulose.

rum liqueur A liqueur for which rum is used as the exclusive distilled spirit base; the resulting liqueur has a predominant rum flavor. *See* liqueur rum.

rummer A glass or other vessel used for toasting someone or something.

rummy Slang for a person who drinks too many alcoholic beverages.

Rum Old Fashioned A cocktail made of gold or dark rum, sugar syrup, Angostura bitters and water; garnished with lemon and orange twists.

rump An imprecisely used term to describe the rear portion of a beef, veal, lamb or pork carcass.

rump roast A subprimal cut of the beef primal round; it is the round's upper part, next to the primal sirloin, and is a lean, boned, rolled roast. *See* culotte de boeuf.

Rum Punch A punch made of rum, fruit syrup, lime juice and water.

Rum Sour A cocktail made of light or dark rum, sugar syrup, orange juice and lime juice; garnished with an orange slice and maraschino cherry.

rum tum tiddy A New England dish of tomato soup, Cheddar cheese and egg, flavored with dry mustard and served on buttered toast.

runcible (ruhn-see-bl) A utensil that is curved like a spoon and has three broad prongs, one of which has a sharp edge; used for pickles and other condiments.

Rundkäse *See* Radener.

run-down A Jamaican dish of salted mackerel, shad or cod boiled to a custard with peppers, onions and scallions.

rundvlees (ROONT-vlays) Dutch for beef.

runner bean A fresh bean with a long green pod containing medium-sized, red-streaked beige-colored seeds, available fresh, dried and canned; also known as scarlet runner bean and stick bean.

running tab A guest check system; drinks are served but no moneys are collected until the guest is ready to leave the premises.

runoff The sweet wort drained from the lauter tun and recirculated before sparging during beer brewing.

runza A baked German–Russian sandwich, popular in the American Midwest; it consists of a sweetened bread dough enclosing a filling of ground beef, shredded cabbage and chopped onions, sometimes with cheese and mustard added.

ruota; ruota de carro (RWAW-tay; rwaw-tay day KAHR-rohl) Italian for cartwheel and used to describe small, spoked, wheel-shaped pasta.

rural method An old and difficult process of making sparkling wine; the must is filtered, the wine is bottled before fermentation is complete, the bottle is emptied under pressure and the sparkling wine is filtered to remove sediment thrown off during fermentation and then rebottled.

rusk A slice of a slightly sweet yeast bread baked until dry, crisp and golden brown; also known as Zwieback.

russe, à la (roose, ah lah) A French preparation of shellfish coated in aspic, covered with chaud-froid or thick mayonnaise and served with a Russian salad.

Russe, mayonnaise à la *See* Russian mayonnaise.

Russe, sauce (roose) A French compound sauce made from a velouté flavored with tarragon vinegar, finished with sour cream and garnished with grated horseradish.

russet apples Any of a variety of apples ranging in size from tiny to very large and with a crisp flesh, a flavor reminiscent of pears and a rough golden brown skin, often red spotted or with a faint red blush.

russet potato A long, flattened ovoid potato with a rough, thick brown skin, a mealy white flesh, numerous large eyes, a low moisture content and a high starch content; principally used for baking and frying.

Russian Coffee A cocktail made of coffee liqueur, heavy cream and vodka; served in a chilled brandy snifter.

Russian dressing A salad dressing made from mayonnaise, chile sauce, pimiento, green peppers and chives.

Russian mayonnaise A French mayonnaise sauce flavored with a Dijon-style mustard and tomalley and garnished with Beluga.

Russian River Valley A grape-growing and wine-producing region in northern California with a relatively cool climate; best known for its still and sparkling wines made from Pinot Noir and Chardonnay grapes as well as wines made from Sauvignon Blanc, Gewürztraminer, Cabernet Sauvignon and Zinfandel grapes.

Russian Rob Roy A cocktail made of vodka, dry vermouth and Scotch; garnished with a lemon twist.

Russian Rose A cocktail made of vodka, grenadine and orange bitters.

Russian salad A French salad of a macédoine of vegetables bound with mayonnaise and garnished with capers, beets and hard-boiled eggs.

Russian service A style of service in which a waiter serves the entrée, vegetables and starches from a platter onto the diner's plate.

Russian stout 1. A high-alcohol-content stout beer brewed in England; it is nonpasteurized and matured in casks for 2 months, then bottle aged for a full year. 2. A strong stout beer brewed in Britain between 1780 and World War I for export to St. Petersburg, Russia.

Russian tea 1. A black tea from the Republic of Georgia in the former Soviet Union; the beverage has a full-bodied flavor and should be served strong with lemon rather than milk or cream; traditionally served in a glass with a separate holder and consumed with a sugar cube held in the teeth. 2. A hot spiced tea punch made with lemon and orange rinds and lemon, orange and pineapple juices.

Russian tea cakes *See* Mexican wedding cookies.

Russisk salat (russ-isk saw-latt) A Danish smørrebrød dish of herring salad Russian style (with onions, red beets and a purée of sweet-and-sour pickled herring) with a hard-boiled egg on top.

rustic 1. A tasting term for a food, beverage or cooking style that is somewhat coarse, simple and does not necessarily reflect professional skills; often associated with regional cooking. 2. A cheese-tasting term for a cheese, usually a farmhouse cheese, that has a hearty, earthy flavor and an assertive barnyardy aroma.

rusty dab *See* yellowtail flounder.

Rusty Nail A cocktail made of equal parts Scotch whisky and Drambuie, served over ice.

rutabaga (roo-tuh-BAY-guh) A member of the cabbage family (*Brassica napobrassica*); the medium-sized, somewhat spherical root has a thin, pale yellow skin, sometimes with a purple blush, a firm, pale yellow flesh and a slightly sweet flavor; also known as a swede or Swedish turnip.

Rutherford Bench A section of California's Napa Valley that runs from north of Rutherford to south of Oakville; best known for its wines made from Cabernet Sauvignon grapes.

rutin A bioflavonoid.

Rutte (ruhr-tah) German for burbot.

Ruwer (ROO-ver) A grape-growing and wine-producing area along this tributary of the Moselle River east of Trier in Germany; the delicate, flowery white wines produced in this area from Riesling grapes are labeled Mosel-Saar-Ruwer.

ruz (rooz) Ethiopian for rice.

ryadovka fiolyetovaya (rya-dov-kah fee-ote-yet-ov-ah-ya) Russian for blewit.

ryba (RI-boo) Czech and Polish for fish.

rybá (RI-boo) Russian for fish.

rye A cereal grass (*Secale cereale*) similar to wheat; its seed is milled into flour or used to make whiskey in the United States, Holland gin in the Netherlands and kvass in Russia.

rye blend A mixture of rye flour and hard wheat flour.

rye bran The outer casing of the rye seed.

rye flour A flour milled from rye seeds; it has a dark color and low gluten-forming potential; it is often combined with wheat flour for baking.

rye whiskey; rye A U.S. whiskey distilled from a mash made with a minimum of 51% rye and then aged in barrels for at least 1 year. *See* straight rye *and* blended rye.

ryori (ree-OH-ree) Japanese for food.

ryori suru (ree-OH-ree su-roo) Japanese for to cook.

ryoriten (ree-OH-ree-tehn) Japanese for restaurant.

ryumochki (r'ya-un-osh-kee) A Russian shot glass used for vodka straight.

ryz (rish) Polish for rice.

ryze (ree-zah) Czech for rice.

rzewien (sheh-vyeñ) Polish for rhubarb.

saag (sahng) Hindi for leafy greens (e.g., spinach, mustard, collard, beet and escarole); they are usually cooked.

saai-lupuputski *See* black drink.

Saaland Pfarr *See* Prästost.

Saar (sahr) A grape-growing and wine-producing area along this tributary of the Moselle River west of Trier in Germany; the dry, steely white wines with delicate bouquets produced from the Riesling grape in this district are labeled Mosel-Saar-Ruwer.

Saaz (tsots) A variety of hops grown in the Czech Republic and Oregon and traditionally used for flavoring Pilsner-type beers.

saba (sah-BAH) Japanese for mackerel.

sabanigh (sah-bah-nech) Arabic for spinach.

sabat moong (sah-baht moong) Hindi for green whole mung beans.

sabayon (sah-by-on) A foamy, stirred French custard sauce made by whisking eggs, sugar and wine over low heat; known in Italian as zabaglione.

sablée (SAH-blay) A French cookie with a delicate, crumbly texture, often flavored with citrus zest or almonds.

sablefish A fish found in the northern Pacific Ocean; it has a compressed body with a slate black to green skin on top that lightens at the belly, a soft, white flesh, a mild flavor and an average market weight of 8 lb. (3.6 kg); it is often smoked; also known as Alaska cod and black cod, even though it is not a true cod.

sabler (sahb-lay) French for to break up and used to describe the dough preparation technique in which butter and flour are worked together with the fingertips to break the mixture into little beads or chunks.

Sabra (SAH-brah) An Israeli liqueur flavored with chocolate and oranges.

sabzi (sah-bzee) Hindi for vegetables.

sacacorcho (soh-kah-korr-chyoh) Spanish for corkscrew.

saca-rolha (sah-kah-roh-lyah) Portuguese for corkscrew.

saccharides The scientific name for sugars.

saccharin 1. Discovered in the late 1800s, it is a nonnutritive (1/8 calorie per teaspoon) artificial sweetener about 300 to 500 times as sweet as sugar; it may leave a bitter aftertaste, especially if heated. 2. A food additive used as a sweetener, especially in processed foods such as beverages and candies; sometimes used as a salt form (eg., ammonium sac-

charin, calcium saccharin or sodium saccharin); some believe saccharin may be carcinogenic.

saccharometer A hydrometer used to measure the sugar content of a must, wort, wine, distilled spirit or the like. *See* Balling, Baumé, Brix *and* Plato.

Saccharomyces The genus of yeasts used for fermentation.

Saccharomyces carlsbergensis The first pure yeast culture used for brewing beer.

Saccharomyces cerevisiae The principal yeast strain used to ferment grapes into wine.

Sachertorte; Sacher torte (ZAH-kuhr-tohrt) A Viennese pastry composed of three layers of a very dense, rich chocolate cake filled with apricot jam and coated with a poured chocolate glaze.

sachet; sachet d'épices (sah-say; sah-say day-pea-sah) A French seasoning blend of aromatic ingredients tied in a cheesecloth bag and used to flavor stocks, sauces, soups and stews; a standard sachet consists of parsley stems, cracked peppercorns, dried thyme, cloves and sometimes garlic. *See* bouquet garni *and* nouet.

sack An Elizabethan English term for any sweet, fortified wine (although usually sherry).

sàco (sah-coe) Spanish for elderberry.

sacramental wine Red or white wine used during the Christian Mass; the church regulates its purity and alcohol content.

sacristain (sahc-chrees-stahng) A small French pastry or cookie made from a stick of puff pastry coated with granulated sugar and chopped almonds before baking.

sad cake An American Southern dessert made with raisins, coconut and pecans; it sinks in the middle after baking, giving it a sad appearance.

saddle 1. A cut of the lamb, mutton and venison carcasses; it is the unseparated loin (from rib to leg) from both sides of the animal. 2. A cut of the hare or rabbit carcass; it is the main body cavity without the hind legs and forelegs.

saddleback pan A trough-shaped cake pan with deep, curved crosswise ridges; the shape is intended to be a trompe l'oeil representation of a saddle of venison and

saddleback pan

is used in preparing the Austrian pastry known as Rehrücken; also used for quick breads and cakes; also known as a deerback pan and a rehrücken mold. *See* Rehrücken.

sadzai (sahd-sah-e) A Zimbabwean dish consisting of a thick cornmeal porridge, sometimes flavored with chiles.

sadza ndiuraye *See* mahobho.

saetina (sah-ah-tee-nah) Italian for ground chiles.

SAFE *See* Sanitary Assessment of the Food Environment.

safed sharaab (sah-fed, sha-rabb) Hindi for red wine.

safety index A numerical indicator of the safety of high doses of a nutrient, usually to be consumed as a supplement (e.g., a safety factor of 3 means that doses up to three times the U.S. RDA are considered safe).

safety stock The amount of stock a food services establishment needs to function for a shift or a day.

safflower A plant (*Carthamus tinctorius*) with a flower that looks like a saffron crocus; its flavorless threads have a deep burnt orange color and are used as a food coloring; also known as bastard saffron, false saffron, haspir, Mexican saffron and saffron thistle.

safflower oil A viscous oil obtained from the seeds of the safflower; higher in polyunsaturated fats than any other oil; it has a strong flavor, a rich yellow color and a high smoke point and does not solidify when chilled.

saffran (saff-rhan) Swedish for saffron.

saffron (SAF-ruhn) A spice that is the dried yellow-orange stigma of a crocus's purple flower (*Crocus sativus*); native to the Middle East, it has a slightly bitter, honeylike flavor and a strong, pungent aroma; used as a flavoring and yellow coloring agent.

saffron thistle *See* safflower.

safio *See* congro.

safra (saw-frah) An Arabic semolina cake filled with a date mixture flavored with cinnamon and cloves; it is baked, then soaked in a hot syrup of sugar, honey, water and lemon juice; traditionally served as a snack.

safran (sahf-rahng) French for saffron.

safrole-free extract of sassafras A food additive derived from the root bark of the *Sassafras albidium* tree and used as a flavoring agent.

saft (sahft) Norwegian for juice.

Saft (zahft) German for juice.

safu The fruit of a tree native to West Africa; it is a large, violet-skinned drupe with a bitter flavor when raw; usually eaten cooked.

saganaki (sah-gah-NAH-kee) A Greek appetizer of kasseri fried in butter or oil and sprinkled with lemon juice; it is sometimes soaked in brandy and flamed.

sage An herb (*Salvia officinalis*) native to the Mediterranean region; it has soft, slender, slightly

sage

furry, gray-green leaves and a pungent, slightly bitter, musty mint flavor; used for medicinal and culinary purposes; available fresh or dried and chopped, whole or rubbed.

sage cheese A firm American spiced cheese made from cow's milk; sage extract creates a mottled green appearance.

Sage Derby *See* Derby.

sago (SAY-goh) A starch extracted from the pith of the sago palm (genus *Cycas*) and various other tropical palms; it is processed into flour, meal and sago pearl and is used for baking, desserts and as a thickener.

sago pearl Small balls of sago.

saguaro; sahuaro A very large cactus with upward-pointing arms native to the American Southwest and Mexico; its red fruit have a bland flavor.

sahani (sa-haa-nee) Swahili for plate.

sah goh *See* jícama.

sahlab (SAH-lab) Arabic for corn flour.

saidi A common variety of date.

saifun (SAH-ee-foon) Small, very thin, Japanese noodles made from yams.

saignant (sah-nyahng) French for bloody and used to describe meat, game and duck cooked very rare or underdone.

saijo (saw-he-ho) A variety of Japanese persimmon; it is small, conical and very sweet.

sailor's biscuit *See* hardtack.

saimin A Hawaiian dish consisting of Chinese noodles in a Japanese broth topped with kamaboko, slivers of roast pork and green onions.

Saingorlon (sawng-gor-lawhn) A semisoft Gorgonzola-style cheese made in France from cow's milk; it has a rich, sharp flavor and a creamy white interior speckled with green mold.

Saint-Andre (san't-ahn-dree) A French triple cream cheese made from cow's milk; it has a yellow-ivory paste and a rich flavor that lacks character.

Saint Arnou; Saint Arnou le Lorrain (san't ahr-noh; son't ahr-noh luh lohr-rahn) The patron saint of brewers.

Saint-Benoit (san't-behn-nwah) A soft Olivet-style cheese made in France from cow's milk; the rind is rubbed with charcoal.

Sainte-Maure (san-mo-reh) A soft French cheese made from goat's milk; it has a pinkish rind, a smooth white paste, a goaty aroma and a full, slightly piquant flavor; sold as a cylinder with a long straw through the center.

Saint-Émilion (san't-ay-mell-yonh) *See* Trebbiano.

Saint George A Chesapeake Bay oyster with a smooth, dark, symmetrical shell and sweet, tender meat.

Saint-Germain (san-zhehr-MAHN) A French garnish consisting of green peas or a pea purée.

Saint-Marcellin (san-marh-sel-lin) A small French cheese made from goat's milk with either ewe's or cow's milk sometimes added; it has a soft, creamy texture and a fresh, mildly piquant flavor; because blue mold is cultivated on the cheese's surface but not the interior it is not classified as bleu.

Saint-Nectaire (san-nek-tayr) A semisoft French cheese made from cow's milk; it has a grayish rind and a slightly nutty, tangy flavor.

Saint-Paulin (san-poo-lin) A Port du Salut–style cow's milk cheese made in France by cheese makers other than Trappist monks; it has a mild flavor and a semisoft texture.

Saint-Raphaël (san-rah-fel) A French aperitif made of must and wine and flavored with quinine.

saison (sae-son) A sharply refreshing, amber-colored Belgian ale with a faintly sour flavor.

saj (saw-he) A woklike pot used in Middle Eastern cuisines.

saji (SAH-jee) Japanese for spoon.

sajt (soy-yet) Hungarian for cheese.

saka-mushi (sah-kah-mu-shee) A Japanese cooking method in which foods are marinated in sake and then steamed over water and sake.

sakana (sah-KAH-nah) Japanese for fish.

sakazuki See ochoko.

sake (SAH-keh) Japanese for salmon.

sake; saké (sah-KEE) A clear Japanese wine made from fermented rice and served hot or cold; because of its grain base, it is sometimes categorized as a beer; also known as rice wine.

Saketini A cocktail made of gin and sake; served in a chilled cocktail glass and garnished with a green olive or lemon twist.

sakhar (sahk-hahr) Russian for granulated sugar.

saku (sah-koo) Thai for sago.

sakurambo (sah-koo-RAHM-boh) Japanese for cherry.

sal (sahl) Portuguese and Spanish for salt.

salaad (sah-lahd) Hindi for lettuce or salad.

salad A single food or a mix of different foods accompanied or bound by a dressing; it can be served as an appetizer, a second course after an appetizer, an entrée or a course following the entrée or dessert and can contain almost any food.

salad, composed A salad whose ingredients (greens, garnishes and dressing) are arranged carefully and artfully on the plate.

salad, tossed A salad whose ingredients (greens, garnishes and dressing) are placed in a bowl and tossed to combine.

salada (sa-LAH-da) Portuguese for salad.

salada de bacalhau (sah-lah-dah day bah-cahl-ah-oo) A Portuguese petisco dish of dried cod in vinegar and oil.

salada de feijao frade (sah-lah-dah day fay-zha-ah-oh frah-da) A Portuguese petisco dish of small white beans with onions, eggs, parsley, vinegar and oil.

salada de orelha (sah-lah-dah day oh-rah-yah) A Portuguese petisco dish of diced pigs' ears in a vinaigrette.

salada de polvo (sah-lah-dah day pole-voe) A Portuguese petisco dish of diced octopus in a vinaigrette.

salad bowl lettuce A general term for a variety of common lettuces used for green salads (e.g., iceberg and romaine).

salad burnet (BUR-niht) See burnet.

salad dressing A sauce for a salad; most are cold and are based on a vinaigrette, mayonnaise or other emulsified product.

salade (sah-lahd) French for salad.

salad fork A short, broad fork with four tines and used for salads and desserts; also known as a cake fork and dessert fork.

salad greens Any of a variety of leafy green vegetables that are usually eaten raw.

saladi (saa-laa-dee) Swahili for salad.

salad oil 1. A highly refined blend of vegetable oils. 2. Any oil used as a cooking medium or ingredient. See cooking oil.

salad relish A relish of cabbage and green tomatoes that is flavored with brown sugar, mustard seeds, celery seeds, cloves and cinnamon and cooked in vinegar.

salad shredder A tool used to shred salad greens and other produce; the food is placed in a hopper and sliced by various-sized disks.

salad spinner A tool used to remove moisture from the surface of salad greens; the produce is held in a perforated bowl sitting inside a container; the inner container is spun, displacing the water through centrifugal forces and through the perforations into the outer container.

salak A pear-shaped fruit (*Zalaccia edulis*) grown in Malaysia; it grows in clusters on a small, stemless palm and has a shiny brown, scaly skin, a white segmented flesh, a dry, waxy texture and a slightly acidic flavor.

salamander 1. A small overhead broiler used primarily to finish or top-brown foods. 2. A tool with a heavy iron head attached to a metal shaft with a wooden handle; heated over a burner and held closely over a dish to brown the food.

salamander

salamander tree See bignay.

salamandre (sah-lah-mahndr) 1. French for salamander. 2. A French garnish of bread crumbs fried in butter until golden.

salambô (sah-lahm-boh) A French pastry consisting of a choux pastry puff filled with Kirsch-flavored pastry cream; the top is dipped in hot caramel or iced with a green fondant and sprinkled with shaved chocolate.

salami (suh-LAH-mee) 1. A style of Italian sausages made from pork and beef, highly seasoned with garlic and spices; rarely smoked, they are cured and air-dried and vary in size, shape and seasonings (e.g., Genoa and cotto). 2. Used in English as the singular; in Italian, the singular is *salame*.

salami di Felino (suh-LAH-mee dee fay-LE-noh) Italian salami made from pork and pork belly, lightly salted and flavored with pepper and garlic pressed in white wine.

salami di Milano (suh-LAH-mee dee meh-LAH-noh) A large Milanese salami made from lean, finely ground pork or pork and beef and aged 3–6 months.

salami di Napoli (suh-LAH-mee dee na-POE-lee) Lightly smoked and air-dried southern Italian salami made from pork and beef and flavored with garlic and peppers.

salami di Varzi (suh-LAH-mee dee vaar-TZEE) A long Italian salami made from coarsely ground pork and bacon and flavored with white wine, garlic and nutmeg.

salami d'oca (suh-LAH-mee D'OH-cah) Italian salami made from lean pork, pork belly and goose.

salami gentile (suh-LAH-mee jan-TEE-lay) Salami from Italy's Emilia-Romagna region; it is made from lean pork and bacon and has a thick casing.

salami nostrano veneto (suh-LAH-mee noss-TRAH-noh vehn-AY-toh) Coarse Venetian salami made from lean and fatty pork and crushed peppercorns; sometimes garlic is added.

salangane *See* bird's nest soup.

salat (sah-lahdt) Russian for salad and used to describe a variety of cold appetizers, usually fish, eggs, meat and/or vegetables bound with mayonnaise or sour cream.

salat (sall-att) Danish and Norwegian for salad.

Salat (za-LAHT) German for salad or lettuce.

salata (sah-LAH-tehss) Greek and Turkish for salad.

salata (sah-la-tah) Arabic for salad.

salatalik tursusu (saw-law-taw-leek toor-soo-soo) A Turkish hors d'oeuvre of pickled gherkins.

salatit fasulya khadra (saw-lah-teet fah-jool-lee-ah kah-drah) An Egyptian salad of onions and blanched string beans dressed with lemon juice and olive oil.

salayish (saw-law-ish) An Ethiopian shredded beef stew.

salchicha (sahl-CHEE-chah) A fresh Spanish sausage made from pork meat and fat, lightly seasoned with paprika.

salchichón (sal-chee-chon) A Spanish smoked sausage made from lean pork and fat, salt and pepper.

sale An exchange of goods or services for an agreed-upon sum of money or other valuable consideration.

sale (SAA-la) Italian for salt.

salé (sal-ay) French for salted.

salées au fromage (sah-layz oh fro-maz) French for cheesecake.

salep (saw-lap) A Middle Eastern and Greek drink made from dried, ground orchid bulbs mixed with water, honey, milk and dried figs.

saleratus (sal-ah-RAT-us) Bicarbonate of potash; it was a rudimentary baking powder that replaced pearl ash.

sales brochure A brochure that details upcoming events or products or advertises existing facilities.

sales history In the food services industry, a daily record of all menu items sold; also known as a scatter sheet.

sales income The amount of money received from customers for goods sold and services rendered.

sales mix The combination of a business's goods or services and the total individual sales of each good or service; also known as product mix; in the foods services industry, also known as a menu mix.

salfetka (sah-felt-kah) Russian for napkin.

salgados (sal-gha-dohs) Salty Portuguese pastries of choux or puff pastry and a spicy filling of meat, fish, sausage or shellfish mixed with potatoes and vegetables seasoned with herbs; the pastries are sometimes battered first and then baked or deep-fried.

Salgurke (sahtz-gur-ka) German for pickled cucumber (gherkins).

salicornia A North American variety of marsh samphire.

salicylaldehyde A food additive with an almondlike flavor and aroma and used as a flavoring agent.

salim (sa-lim) Slim noodles.

salino (sah-LEE-noh) An Italian yeast roll made with rock salt on the crust.

Salisbury steak (SAWLZ-beh-ree) A beef patty seasoned with parsley, broiled or fried with onions and served with a gravy made from the pan drippings.

saliva The mildly alkaline secretion that begins the digestive process by moistening food, assisting mastication, lubricating the mouth and initiating the breakdown of starches.

salivary glands Glands whose secretions form saliva; they are located beneath the ears and in the lips, cheeks and floor of the mouth.

sallow thorn The small, orange-skinned bitter berries of this plant (genus *Salix*), which is grown in northern Europe and Russia, are used as a flavoring or distilled into a beverage.

Sally Lunn A rich, slightly sweet British yeast bread flavored with lemon and nutmeg and served for afternoon tea.

salma *See* pilau.

salmagundi; salmagundy (sal-mah-GON-de) A saladlike dish of chopped meat, hard-boiled eggs, anchovies, onions and vinegar; it is usually served over lettuce leaves.

Salmanazar (SAHL-mah-nah-zur) An oversized sparkling wine bottle holding 10–12 750-ml bottles (approximately 270–312 fl. oz.).

salmão (sal-MEOWN) Portuguese for salmon.

salmis (sahl-mee) 1. A cooking method for wild or domesticated birds; the bird is partially roasted and the meat is then removed and finished in a sauce made from the carcass. 2. A French game stew made from any variety of game left over from a previous service; it is usually reheated in a sauce.

Salmis, sauce (sahl-mee) A French compound sauce made from a demi-glaze prepared from a game stock and wine.

salmon A large family of anadromous fish found in the northern Atlantic and Pacific Oceans; generally, they have a silver to gray skin, a pink-red flesh, a

salmon

firm texture and a rich flavor; principal varieties include the Atlantic salmon, chinook salmon and coho salmon.

salmón (sahl-mohn) Spanish for salmon.

salmonberry 1. A plump red-orange berry (*Rubus chamae-morus*) native to the American Northwest; related to wild raspberries but less flavorable, it grows in clusters that look like salmon eggs. 2. A variety of Japanese wineberry; the fruit are small, with a yellow-orange color and a tart flavor.

salmon caviar Roe harvested from chum and silver salmon; the large eggs have an orange color and a good flavor.

salmóne (sahl-MOA-nay) Italian for salmon.

Salmonella A genus of bacteria that cause food poisoning (called salmonellosis); the bacteria are commonly transmitted through poultry, eggs, milk, meats and fecal matter.

salmoneta (sal-moe-nah-tah) Portuguese for red mullet.

salmon trout *See* steelhead trout.

saloon 1. A somewhat antiquated term for any establishment serving alcoholic beverages. 2. An old western bar.

salotas (sah-law-tass) Lithuanian for salad.

salpiçao (sal-pee-sah-o) A Portuguese smoked sausage made with pork that has been marinated in white wine, garlic and spices.

salpicon (sal-pee-kon) Diced foods bound together by a sauce, syrup or other liquid.

salpicon, savory (sal-pee-kon) Diced ingredients bound with a sauce and used to fill barquettes, vol-au-vents and canapés, to make croquettes or to garnish other foods.

salpicon, sweet (sal-pee-kon) Diced ingredients bound with a syrup or cream and used to garnish pastries and desserts.

sal prunella A curing agent and form of saltpeter (it contains some potassium nitrites); it accelerates the salting process in foods.

salsa (SAHL-sah) 1. Spanish for sauce. 2. Traditionally, a Mexican cold sauce made from tomatoes flavored with cilantro, chiles and onions. 3. Generally, a cold chunky mixture of fresh herbs, spices, fruits and/or vegetables used as a sauce or dip. 4. In Italian usage, a general term for pasta sauces. 5. Portuguese for parsley.

salsa criolla (SAHL-sah cree-oh-law) A Caribbean salsa of chopped onions, tomatoes, jalapeños, garlic, parsley and vinegar; traditionally served with matambre.

salsa de maní (SAHL-sah da mah-nee) A Caribbean salsa of chopped onions, jalapeños, tomatoes and roasted peanuts; traditionally served with llapingachos.

salsa para asados (SAHL-sah pah-rah ah-saw-dos) A South American barbecue sauce flavored with vinegar, paprika, thyme, garlic and oregano and mixed with olive oil.

salsa piccante (sal-sah peak-kan-tae) Italian for chutney.

salsicce (sal-SEE-chay) Italian fresh sausages, usually made from pork and pork fat coarsely ground and highly spiced, sometimes with whole peppercorns and coriander or fennel seeds embedded in them.

salsicha (sahl-SEE-shash) A Portuguese sausage, usually smoked.

salsichao (sal-sea-tchah-oh) A salami-like Portuguese pork sausage seasoned with peppercorns.

salsify A long, thick root vegetable (*Tragopogon porrigolius*) with a white flesh, numerous offshoots and a delicate flavor reminiscent of oysters; also known as an oyster plant and vegetable oyster. *See* scorzonero.

salt 1. A substance resulting from the chemical interaction of an acid and a base, usually sodium and chloride. 2. A white granular substance (sodium chloride) used to season foods.

Salta A grape-growing and wine-producing province in Argentina; the principal grapes grown are Chardonnay, Malbec, Cabernet and Torrontes.

salt and pepper shakers Small containers with perforated lids used to dispense salt and ground pepper, usually at the table; they can be made of metal, plastic, glass, wood or ceramic and are available in a wide selection of shapes. *See* saltcellar.

salt beef A British dish consisting of salted, spiced beef similar to corned beef.

salt bush Any of several saltwater-tolerant plants (genus *Atriplex*) used in Asian cuisines as greens or garnish.

saltcellar A bowl filled with salt; the bowl, which can be metal, glass, ceramic or wood and range from the simple to the very elaborate, is set on the table and diners take a pinch of salt with their fingers or use a salt spoon; sometimes a second cellar filled with ground black pepper is set beside it.

salt cod Cod that is salted and dried.

salt curing The process of surrounding a food with salt or a mixture of salt, sugar, nitrite-based curing salt, herbs and spices; salt curing dehydrates the food, inhibits bacterial growth and adds flavor.

salted *See* dry-cured.

salted butter *See* butter, salted.

salted plums Dried, heavily salted Chinese plums with a sweet–sour flavor; served as a confection, appetite stimulant or breath freshener.

salted white radish White radish strips speckled with salt (they turn a brownish-white); used to flavor soups, braised dishes and vegetables in Chinese cuisine.

salted wine A wine or wine product with not less than 1.5 g of salt per 100 ml of wine; intended as a cooking wine, not as a beverage.

salteñas (sahl-TAY-nyah) Bolivian empanadas; usually filled with beef, potatoes, raisins, olives, hard-boiled eggs and aji.

saltfiskur (sahlt-fiss-kure) Icelandic for cured fish.

saltimbocca (salt-eem-BOHK-ka) An Italian dish of veal scallops sautéed in butter, topped with thin slices of prosciutto and braised in white wine.

saltine A thin, crisp cracker sprinkled with coarse salt.

salt lick A block of salt or an artificial medicated saline preparation set out for cattle, sheep, deer or other animals to lick.

salt mill A handheld tool used to grind granules of sea salt.

saltpeter A common name for potassium nitrate, which is used to preserve food.

salt pork Very fatty pork, usually from the hog's sides and belly, cured in salt and used principally as a cooking fat or flavoring; also known as corned belly bacon and white bacon. *See* fatback.

salt potato A new potato soaked or boiled in brine.

salt-rising bread A bread leavened with a fermented mixture of flour, cornmeal, water and salt instead of yeast.

salts of fatty acids Food additives used as emulsifiers, binders and/or anticaking agents.

salt spoon A tiny spoon used to remove salt from a saltcellar and sprinkle it on food.

saltspoonful A traditional measure of volume; it is approximately 1/4 teaspoon.

saltsteg sild (salt-stag seald) A Danish dish consisting of fried salted herring served with bread and pan drippings, red beets and mustard.

salt substitute *See* low-sodium salt.

saltwater taffy A taffy made with a small amount of saltwater; popular in Atlantic City, New Jersey, during the late 1800s.

salty black beans *See* fermented black beans.

Salty Dog A cocktail made of vodka, grapefruit juice, granulated sugar and salt; garnished with a lime wedge.

salumi (sah-LOO-mee) The general Italian term for cured meats such as salami, prosciutto, coppa and other pork products; they are typically eaten cold and sliced.

salver A tray, usually of metal, available in various shapes and sizes and used to serve food and/or beverages.

salvia (SAL-vyah) Italian for sage.

salvia pineapple The velvety leaves of this plant (*Salvia rutilans*), which is native to North America, have a mild flavor and a pineapple-like aroma; they are used in salads and tisanes.

Salz (zahlts) German for salt.

Salzburger nockerl (zahlt-BOOR-gehr nokh-rehl) An Austrian dessert consisting of a sweet, lemon soufflé traditionally baked in three mounds in an oblong dish.

samak (sum-mack) Arabic for fish.

samaki (sah-MAH-kee) Swahili for fish.

saman (sah-mahn) Hindi for salmon.

sambaar (sahm-bar) An East Indian vegetable and lentil stew with tamarind, flavored with spices.

sambaar podi (sahm-bar poe-dee) An Indian blend of hot spices used for flavoring sambaar.

sambal A small citrus fruit with a thick, wrinkly green skin; its skin is grated as a sweet lime flavoring in Southeast Asian cuisines; also known as combava and makrut.

sambal bajak (sahm-bahl bah-jak) A hot, cooked chile sauce mellowed with sugar and ground nuts or coconut milk and served with the Indonesian fried rice dish nasi goreng.

sambal kacang (sahm-bahl kah-cahng) An Indonesian bottled sauce made from ground peanuts, chiles, tamarind, sugar and soy sauce and used for satay and other grilled meats.

sambal kacang kedele (sahm-bahl kah-cahng ka-da-la) An Indonesian relish made from dried soybeans, chiles, onions, garlic and lime juice.

sambal kecap (sahm-bahl ka-chap) An Indonesian sauce made from soy sauce flavored with onions, garlic and lime juice and used for grilled vegetables.

sambals; sambols Any of several very spicy mixtures or relishes based on chiles; used in Indian and Southeast Asian cuisines as a flavoring and condiment.

sambal terasi (sahm-bahl ta-rah-see) A Javanese spicy relish made from bird chiles with cooked shrimp paste, garlic, onion and lime juice.

sambal ulek; sambal oelek (sahm-bahl who-lek; sahm-bahl a-lak) An Indonesian flavoring paste made from ground bird chiles, salt, oil and vinegar.

sambar masala (sam-bar ma-saa-laa) A tart spice mixture used in southern India to season a thin vegetable curry that is the traditional accompaniment to dosa.

sambousik; sambusik (sahm-BOO-sek) Arabian half-moon–shaped pastries filled with a nut paste, baked and glazed with a lemon-flavored honey syrup.

Sambuca (sam-BOO-kuh) A clear anise-flavored, semi-sweet Italian liqueur often served flaming and with three coffee beans floating on top. *See* tre mosche.

sambuco (sam-BOO-koh) Italian for elderberry.

sambusa (sahm-boo-sah) An Ethiopian pastry turnover filled with meat or lentils and hot chiles.

sambusilk (sahm-boo-silk) A Middle Eastern pastry made from a circle of sweet dough filled with walnuts and sugar, folded in half to form a half-moon and baked; after baking, it is dipped into a cool honey syrup flavored with lemon and rosewater.

sambutes; salbutos (sahm-boo-tess) A Mexican antojito dish consisting of a small tortilla stuffed with ground pork, onions and tomatoes.

samek (sah-mek) Arabic for fish.

samek makli (sah-mah mah-klee) A Middle Eastern dish consisting of fried fish, usually rubbed with a mixture of garlic, baharat, turmeric, lemon juice and pepper.

samek masgouf (sah-mah m'sah-goof) A Middle Eastern dish consisting of chunks of a firm white fish threaded on a skewer and grilled.

samek mashawi (sah-mah mah-shaw-we) A Middle Eastern dish consisting of grilled fish; the whole fish is usually rubbed with oil, garlic, pepper, powdered chiles and cumin.

samfaina (sahm-fah-ee-nah) A Spanish dish consisting of summer vegetables such as eggplant, green and red peppers and tomatoes flavored with garlic and olive oil.

samin (sam-nah) Arabic for butter.

samit (sah-mitt) A hard Egyptian bread similar to a pretzel.

sammak (SUM-mack) Arabic for sumac.

samn; samneh (samn'h; SAHM-neh) Arabic for clarified butter, a popular shortening.

samoki was nazi (sah-moh-key oo-as nah-zee) A Tanzanian dish consisting of fish simmered in coconut milk flavored with chiles, curry powder, onions and lemon juice.

samosa (sah-MOH-sah) East Indian snacks consisting of triangular pastries filled with meat and/or vegetables and deep-fried; they are often served with a dipping sauce.

samovar (SAM-ah-vahr) A Russian metal urn with a spigot at the base and a central tube for holding charcoal or an alcohol lamp; water is kept heated in the space between the urn's outer surface and the inner metal tube; a small teapot fits on top of the metal tube, and the thick, strong tea brewed in it is diluted with the hot water held in the samovar; used to boil water for tea.

samp Broken or coarsely ground hominy.

samphire (sahm-FEHR) *See* marsh samphire *and* rock samphire.

Samsø (SAHM-sur) A Danish Emmental-style cheese made from cow's milk; it has a yellow interior with small holes and a mild, nutty, slightly sweet flavor.

samui (sah-mu-ee) Japanese for cold.

sanbusik (sen-boo-sik) A Lebanese meat pie (lamb or beef), usually flavored with yogurt and pine nuts and made open faced or closed.

Sancerre (sahn-sair) A grape-growing and wine-producing area in France's Loire Valley known for its dry white wine made from the Sauvignon Blanc grape; the wine has a fresh, lively acidity and an herbaceous flavor with hints of black currant.

sancocho (sahn-COH-cho) 1. A Central and South American stew; it usually consists of slow cooked meats (chicken, beef, lamb, goat or pork) with potatoes, sweet potatoes, corn, tomatoes and/or squash and flavored with either chiles or herbs. 2. An unfermented grape juice concentrate (reduced to one-third its original volume) added to sherry for color and sweetness. *See* arrope.

sancocho de gallina (sahn-COH-cho da gah-ee-nah) A Venezuelan stew of chicken, carrots, tomatoes and turnips flavored with coriander.

sandalwood The dried bark of a tree (*Santalum album*) native to southern India; distilled to yield an essential oil containing sanatol that is used in cosmetics, confectionery and baked goods.

sand cherry The small, sweet, purple-black berry of a small tree native to the Midwest.

sanddab *See* dab *and* plaice, American.

Sandersasha A speckled gray mango with a sweet, orange-yellow flesh.

sandia (sahn-DEE-ah) Spanish for watermelon.

sanding sugar *See* crystal sugar.

sandkage (sahnd-kah-gah) A Danish cake made with potato flour and flavored with brandy; usually baked in a loaf shape and dusted with confectioners' sugar.

sandkaka (sahnd-kah-kah) A Swedish version of sandkage.

sand leek *See* rocambole.

sandoitchi (sahnd-WEE-chee) Japanese for sandwich.

sand pike *See* pike perch.

sand pot *See* sar bo.

sandre (sahn-drah) French for pike perch.

sand shark *See* shark.

sanduiche (sun-doo-ee-shee) Portuguese for sandwich.

sandwich Slices of bread separated by any of a wide variety of fillings such as meats, poultry, fish, shellfish, cheeses, preserves, vegetables and/or condiments; served hot or cold. *See* wrap.

sandwich cake *See* Victoria sandwich.

sandwich grilling iron A tool consisting of two hinged metal plates with handles; the plates usually have shell-shaped or other indentions; a sandwich (e.g., ham and cheese) is placed between the plates and browned on the stove top.

sandwich spreader A short, spatula-like tool with one dull and one serrated edge; the dull edge is used to scoop and spread, and the serrated edge is used to cut.

sandwich spreader

sandwich steak A fabricated cut of the beef sirloin, round or chuck primals; it is a very thin steak.

sandy dough *See* pâte sablée.

Sangaree A drink made from whiskey, gin, rum or brandy with port floated on top; sprinkled with nutmeg.

sangionaccio (sahn-gwon-NAH-ch'yoh) A large blood sausage from Italy's Tuscany region; seasoned with pine nuts, raisins, candied fruit, cinnamon, coriander and nutmeg.

Sangiovese (san-joh-VAY-zeh) The dominant red wine grape grown in Italy's Tuscany region and the principal variety used for Chianti.

sanglier (sahng-glyay) French for wild boar.

sangrante (san-gran-tay) Spanish for underdone or rare meat, particularly steak.

Sangria (sahn-GREE-ah) A Spanish punch usually made of red wine, lemon and orange slices, sugar and sometimes soda water.

Sangrita (sahn-gah-REE-tah) A cocktail made of tequila or gin, tomato juice, orange juice, lime juice, finely minced onion, Tabasco sauce, Worcestershire sauce, white pepper and celery salt.

sanguinaccio (sahn-gwee-NAH-ch'yoh) An Italian blood pudding or blood sausage.

sanguinante (sahn-gwee-nan-tae) Italian for underdone or rare meat, particularly steak.

Sanitary Assessment of the Food Environment (SAFE) A system adopted by the National Restaurant Association to promote and ensure food safety; similar to the Hazard Analysis Critical Control Points system.

sanitation 1. The design, implementation and application of practices that will establish conditions favorable to health, especially public health. 2. In the food safety context, the design, implementation and application of practices that will prevent food contamination and food-borne illnesses.

sanitize In a food safety context, to reduce pathogenic organisms on an object or in an environment to a safe level. *See* clean *and* sterilize.

sanitizing solutions Chemical solutions used to sanitize or sterilize food-contact surfaces; they are recognized as indirect food additives.

San Marzano tomato A variety of fleshy plum tomato; it has a slightly pointed shape.

sanmingzhi (sahn-meang-zhe) Chinese for sandwich.

sanriku maguro (sahn-ree-koo mah-goo-roh) A variety of tuna particularly prized for sashimi and sushi.

sansho (SAHN-sho) A Japanese fragrant pepper; the green berry of the prickly ash tree (genus *Zanthoxylum*), crushed to a fine powder to make an aromatic spice.

San Simón (SAN see-MOHN) A tall, conical, semifirm Spanish cow's milk cheese with a burnished, walnut brown rind and a light yellow to golden interior with a creamy, smoky flavor.

Santa Claus melon A member of the muskmelon family; it has a long ovoid shape, a splotchy green and yellow skin, a yellow-green flesh and a flavor similar to that of honeydew melon; also known as a Christmas melon, because its peak season is December.

Santa Fe grande A broad-shouldered, long chile with a pale yellow color (which turns orange-red when ripe), a thick flesh and a medium hot flavor with a slightly sweet, melonlike undertone.

santalol A food additive with a sandalwood aroma used as a flavoring agent. *See* sandalwood.

santaré (san-ta-ree) Hindi for orange.

Santa Rosa plum An ovoid plum with a dark red skin and juicy flesh with a flavor reminiscent of oranges.

Santo Domingo Arabica coffee beans grown in the Dominican Republic; when made from the best grades, the beverage is strong and full bodied.

santol A fruit tree (*Sandoricum koetjape*) that grows in Malaysia and Indochina; it occurs in two main forms, one with sweet fruit and leaves that wither to yellow, the other with sour fruit and leaves that turn red (the latter is often called kechapi); both have round fruits with a tough, yellowish-brown skin enclosing five segments of white pulp and have the aroma of peach; they are eaten fresh, dried, pickled or candied.

santola (san-toe-lah) Portuguese for spider crab.

Santos (SAHN-toos) Arabica coffee beans grown in Brazil; the beverage is smooth and slightly sweet.

santuko A Japanese-style knife with a sheep's foot blade; used for chopping vegetables.

santuko

sanwin makin A Burmese cake or pudding made of semolina flour, coconut milk, ghee and sesame seeds and flavored with cardamom and raisins.

Sao Jorge *See* Queijo da Ilha.

sap The watery fluid of a plant.

sapho; saphou A plant (*Canarium sapho*) with a small, violet fruit containing a nut covered in a purple-blue skin; the nut is similar to a very fragrant chestnut.

sapin-sapin (sah-pin-sah-pin) A Filipino layered dessert made from steamed galapong, coconut milk and sugar.

sapodilla A small spherical fruit (*Manilkara zapota*) native to Central America; it has a yellow skin covered by brown fuzz, flat, black seeds and a yellow-brown juicy flesh with a flavor reminiscent of brown sugar; also known as chikkus and naseberry.

sapote (sah-PO-tay) A medium- to large-sized ovoid tropical fruit (*Pouteria sapota*) native to the Caribbean; it has a rough, russet-colored skin, a salmon-colored flesh and a sweet flavor; used for preserves.

saprophyte (SAP-roh-fyte) An organism that lives on dead or decaying organic matter (e.g., fungi or bacteria).

Sapsago (sap-SAY-goh) A small, hard Swiss cheese made from cow's milk; it has a sharp, pungent flavor, a pleasing aroma and a light green color, all resulting from the melilot (clover) leaves added to the curd; used for grating.

sapucaya (sah-poo-sah-yah) A variety of superior-quality Brazil nuts.

sara (SAH-rah) Japanese for plate.

saracen corn *See* buckwheat.

sarada (SAH-rah-dah) Japanese for salad.

Sarah Bernhardt An individual-sized British pastry consisting of an almond macaroon topped with a cone of rich chocolate ganache, then coated with dark chocolate glaze; named for the popular 19th-century actress.

saramura (sah-rah-moo-rah) A Romanian broth of vinegar, salt and garlic, garnished with meat or fish.

sarapatel (sah-rah-pah-TELL) A Portuguese dish of fried liver and bacon.

sarashi-an (sa-rah-shee-ahn) A flour of ground adzuki used in Japanese desserts.

Saratoga chips *See* potato chips.

Saratoga chop A fabricated cut of the lamb primal shoulder; it is a boneless shoulder chop.

Saratoga water A mineral water from a spring in the Adirondack Mountains of New York state.

sar bo (sar bo) A Chinese cooking pot made from light, sandy, porous clay usually unglazed on the outside and sometimes glazed on the inside; also known as a sand pot.

sardayle (sahr-dah-lee-ah) Turkish for sardine.

sarde, à la (sard, ah lah) A French garnish for meats, especially steak, consisting of grilled or fried tomatoes, stuffed cucumber or zucchini and croquettes of saffron-flavored rice.

sardina (sahr-dee-nah) Italian and Spanish for sardine. *See* agoni.

sardine 1. A generic name for any of several small, soft-boned, saltwater fish, such as the pilchard, sprat, herring and alewife; generally not available fresh outside the area in which they are caught and usually available smoked, salted, pickled, cured in brine or packed in tomato sauce, mustard sauce or oil. 2. A young herring.

sardine, Atlantic A young herring from the northern Atlantic Ocean; it has an elongated body, a greenish-blue skin with a silvery cast and an average market length of 3–4 in. (7.5–10 cm).

sardine, Norwegian A sardine found off the coast of Norway; it is particularly tender and flavorful; also known imprecisely as a brisling.

sardine, Pacific A small fish found in the Pacific Ocean from California to Alaska; generally used for fish meal, oil or bait; also known as a Pacific sea herring.

sardinhas (sar-DEEN-yash) Portuguese for sardine.

Sardo *See* Fiore Sardo.

sargasso (sahr-GAS-o) Spanish for seaweed.

sariette (sari-yeht) French for savory.

sarma (sahr-mah) A Balkan dish of cabbage leaves rolled around a stuffing of meat, rice and seasonings and sometimes served with yogurt or sour cream.

sarmades (sah-rmah-thes) A Greek dish of cabbage leaves stuffed with beef, pork, onions and rice, flavored with lemon slices, baked in a casserole and served with a sauce avgolémono.

sarmale (sahr-mah-la) Romanian stuffed cabbage rolls.

sarrasin; sarrazin (sah-rah-zen) French for buckwheat; also known as blé noir. *See* buckwheat.

sarsaparilla 1. The dried roots of a number of American woody vines (genus *Smilax*) of the lily family; formerly used for medicinal purposes. 2. A sweetened, carbonated beverage similar to root beer made from an extract of these roots; today, sarsaparilla products generally use artificial flavorings.

sarsoon (saar-soon) Hindi for mustard greens.

sarta (sahr-tah) A horseshoe shape used for raw or cooked Spanish sausages. *See* ristras *and* vela.

sarten (sahr-tan) A flat, heavy, two-handled Spanish pot used for cooking paella; sometimes the pot itself is known as a paella. *See* paella pan.

sartizzu (sahr-TEE-t'zoo) Smoked pork sausage from Sardinia, flavored with cinnamon, fennel and pepper.

sarume (sah-roo-meh) Seasoned and roasted cuttlefish.

sås (soass) Swedish for sauce.

sasagaki (sah-sah-GAH-kee) Japanese for whittle and used to describe a decorative food cut.

sasage mame (sah-SAH-gay MAH-may) Small dried red beans; used in Japanese cuisine as a starch cooked with rice or made into a sweet bean jam for stuffing rice flour cakes.

sashimi (sah-SHEE-mee) A Japanese dish of sliced raw fish served with condiments such as soy sauce, daikon, wasabi or ginger. *See* sushi.

sassafras An aromatic, native American tree (*Sassafras albidum*) belonging to the laurel family; the bark of the root is dried and used as a flavoring for root beer, and the leaves are pounded to make filé powder.

sa-taw *See* parkia.

saté; satay (sah-TAY) A Southeast Asian dish consisting of small cubes or strips of meat, fish or poultry threaded on skewers and grilled or broiled; usually served with a spicy peanut sauce.

sateh (saw-tay) A Dutch–Indonesian dish of marinated meat or poultry prepared on skewers.

satiety The feeling of being full or satisfied after eating; consuming fats provides a greater degree of satiety than does consuming carbohydrates or protein.

sato imo (sah-TOE ee-moh) Potatoes grown in Japan; they have a dark brown, hairy skin and a pale gray interior; also known as taro potatoes.

satsuma (saht-SOO-mah) A member of the mandarin orange family native to Japan; the fruit has a small, squat shape, an orange rind, a pale orange flesh and a sweet flavor; usually available in the United States as canned mandarin oranges.

satsuma imo (SAH-soo-mah ee-moh) A variety of sweet potatoes grown in Japan; the fruit have a reddish skin, a golden yellow interior and a slightly sweet flavor.

satuk (sah-took) A Tibetan soup made from nettle leaves and flavored with black pepper and ginger.

saturated fat A triglyceride composed of saturated fatty acids and implicated in raising blood cholesterol levels; generally, it is solid at room temperature and comes from a few plants (e.g., coconut and palm) and most animals, except fish (e.g., butter, lard and suet).

saturated fatty acid A fatty acid with the maximum number of hydrogen atoms attached to its carbon chain.

sauce *v.* To add a sauce; to flavor or season a food with a sauce. *n.* 1. A thickened liquid or semiliquid preparation used to flavor and enhance other foods. *See* leading sauces *and* small sauces. 2. Slang for an alcoholic beverage (to hit the sauce).

sauce French for sauce. *Note:* French sauces are listed alphabetically by the principal modifier (e.g., sauce printanière is listed as printanière, sauce).

sauceboat *See* gravy boat.

sauce de la Reine A drink of milk, eggs, sugar and vanilla, heated and served in a silver cup to the Queen of Mardi Gras to help her wind down after a day of excitement.

sauce mère French for mother sauce.

sauce mop *See* basting mop.

saucepan A round metal cooking vessel with one long handle and straight or sloped sides; generally smaller and shallower than a pot, it is available in

saucepan

a range of sizes, from 1 pt. to 4 qt., and sometimes with a fitted lid.

saucepan, flare-sided A thick, heavy saucepan with flared sides and a long handle; it has a wide surface area and is used for rapid evaporation; also known as a Windsor saucepan.

saucepot A large saucepan with a lid and two handles; available in sizes from 4 to 14 qt.

saucer A small shallow dish with a slight indention for holding a cup.

saucer; saucer glass *See* Champagne saucer.

sauce whisk An elongated whisk; its nine fairly rigid looped wires create a pear-shaped outline; also known as a piano-wire whisk.

sauce whisk

saucier (saw-see-yay) At a food services operation following the brigade system, the person responsible for all sautéed items and most sauces; also known as a sauté station chef.

saucisse (soh-CEESE) French for a small sausage.

saucisse de foie (soh-CEESE duh fwah) An air-dried French sausage containing chopped liver and bacon.

saucisse de Paris; saucisson de Paris (soh-CEESE duh pah-ree) *See* cervelas.

saucisse de Toulouse (soh-CEESE duh too-loos) A fresh French sausage made from pork and used in cassoulet.

saucisse sèche (soh-CEESE sae-shay) A hard, medium-coarse French sausage made from raw, salted pork stuffed into long natural skins and air-dried in long twisting loops; a specialty of the south of France.

saucisson (soh-SEES-sohn) French for a large sausage.

saucisson à la cendre (soh-SEES-sohn ah lah cen-drae) A French pork sausage rolled in ashes; it has a subtle smoky flavor.

saucisson d'Arles (soh-SEES-sohn darl) A sausage made in the south of France from lean pork and beef, flavored with peppercorns, garlic, paprika, saltpeter and red wine; smoked for a month or so and eaten raw or in soups and stews.

saucisson de Lyon nature (soh-SEES-sohn duh lee-on nah-tur-rae) A stout, raw French sausage made from lean and fat pork; it is boiled and eaten with potatoes and sauerkraut or used in stews.

saucisson de porc (soh-SEES-sohn duh por) A French salami-like sausage of finely diced fat and lean pork with a flour coating to prevent the fat from melting.

saucisson de sanglier (soh-SEES-sohn duh san-glee-ay) An air-dried, salami-like French sausage made from wild boar meat, sometimes with lean and fat pork.

saucisson sec (soh-SEES-sohn seck) Any of several varieties of regional French dried, salami-like sausages.

Sauerampfer (sow-uhr-ahmf-er) German for sorrel.

Sauerbraten (ZOW-er-brah-t'n) German for sour roast and used to describe a beef roast marinated in a sour–sweet

marinade and then braised; it is usually served with dumplings, boiled potatoes or noodles.

sauerkraut (SOW-uhr-krowt) A German dish of shredded, salted, fermented green cabbage, sometimes flavored with juniper berries.

sauge (soazh) French for sage.

sauger *See* pike perch.

Saumeise (sah-who-my-she) An Austrian snack of ground meat wrapped in pig's caul, smoked and boiled; it is served with Heurigen.

Saumer *See* Anjou.

saumon (soa-mawng) French for salmon.

saunf (saw-oonf) Hindi for fennel; anise.

saupiquet (soh-pee-kay) A medieval French sauce made from wine flavored with cinnamon and ginger and thickened with grilled bread.

Saure Blunzen (ZOY-re bloon-zen) An Austrian snack of sliced blood sausage marinated in vinegar.

Saure Sahne (ZOY-re zah-neh) German for sour cream.

saus (sows) Norwegian for sauce.

sausage A forcemeat stuffed into a casing; the principal ingredients, seasonings, shape, size, casing type, curing technique and degree of drying vary.

sausages, cooked A style of sausages made from uncured meats; they are cooked but not smoked.

sausages, cooked and smoked A style of sausages made from cured meats; they are lightly smoked, then cooked, and do not require further cooking.

sausages, dried A style of sausages made from cured meats and air-dried; they may or may not be smoked or cooked; also known as hard sausages, summer sausages and seminary sausages.

sausages, fresh A style of sausages made from meats that are neither smoked nor cured; they require cooking before service.

sausages, smoked A style of sausages made from cooked or cured meats and smoked; they are cooked before serving.

saussiska; sassiska (sahz-sees-ka) A Russian smoked pork sausage.

sauté de poulet au coco (soh-tay duh poo-lay oh ko-ko) A Caribbean dish of chicken simmered in coconut milk with onions, garlic, chiles and mushrooms and served over rice.

sautéing (saw-tay-ing) A dry-heat cooking method that uses conduction to transfer heat from a hot pan to food with the aid of a small amount of hot fat; cooking is usually done quickly over high temperatures.

sauté pan *See* sauteuse *and* sautoir.

Sauternes (saw-tairn) 1. A grape-growing and wine-producing district in France's Bordeaux region known for the white wine of the same name. 2. A wine made from overly ripe grapes (usually Sauvignon Blanc or Sémillon) affected by the noble rot; it is sweet, complex and honeyed.

sauté station chef *See* saucier.

sauteuse (saw-toose) The basic sauté pan with sloping sides and a single long handle.

sautoir (saw-twahr) A sauté pan with straight sides and a single long handle (if very large, it may have a loop handle on the other side); used to fry foods quickly in a limited amount of fat.

sauteuse

sautoir

sauvage (soh-vazh) French for wild; a wine-labeling term used to indicate wine that is made with wild yeasts.

Sauvignon Blanc (so-vee-n'yohn blahn) 1. A white wine grape grown extensively in France's Bordeaux and Loire regions, California, Australia and New Zealand; also known as Blanc Fume (especially in the Loire Valley) and Muskat-Silvaner (in Germany and Austria). 2. A white wine made from this grape, generally known for its acidity and grassy or herbaceous aroma and semisweet character. 3. *See* Fumé Blanc.

savarin (SAV-uh-rahn) A rich French yeast cake baked in a ring mold, soaked with rum syrup and filled with pastry cream, crème Chantilly and fresh fruit. *See* baba.

savarin mold A plain, shallow ring mold, usually metal, used for baking savarins or for molding gelatins, aspics or Bavarians.

savoiardi (sah-voy-AHR-dee) Ladyfingers from the Valle d'Aosta; also known as biscotti di Savoia.

Savor A Long Life melon.

savóre (sah-voh-rah) A Greek preparation method in which fish are pickled.

savory 1. A food that is not sweet. 2. An herb of the mint family.

savory, summer An herb (*Satureja hortensis*) with small, narrow, gray-green leaves and a similar but milder flavor than that of winter savory; available fresh and dried.

savory, winter An herb (*Satureja montana*) with small, narrow, gray-green leaves and a bitter, pungent flavor reminiscent of thyme and rosemary; available fresh and dried.

savory nut *See* Brazil nut.

Savory Tango A cocktail made of apple brandy and sloe gin.

savoury 1. Traditionally, foods served at a British meal after dessert to cleanse and refresh the palate after the sweets and in anticipation of port or liqueurs. 2. Today, also foods served as spicy appetizers at a British meal.

savoy (sah-voy) *See* kale, ornamental.

savoyarde, à la (sahv-wah-yahd, ah lah) 1. A French dish of gratin potatoes made with milk and cheese. 2. Any of a variety of egg dishes, including omelettes stuffed with potatoes and Gruyère.

savoy cabbage A member of the cabbage family with a spherical, relatively loose head of curly, wrinkled leaves in variegated shades of green and purple; it has a milder flavor than that of red or green cabbage.

Savoy cake; Savoy drop An oval- or finger-shaped sponge cookie dusted with sugar and popular during the 19th century; also known as a ladyfinger.

savoyed A description for any leaf vegetable with bumpy, wavy, crinkly and/or wrinkly leaves.

saw cutting A method of finely slicing meat with a slow and gentle sawing action; any fat and/or bone is removed, the meat is frozen or chilled until firm, then cut into paper-thin slices by using one hand to hold the meat and the other hand to hold the knife and slice in a sawing motion.

saxifrage (SAK-sah-frij) A lettucelike leafy green vegetable (genus *Saxifraga*) that grows wild in the crevices of rocks along the U.S. East Coast; it is used like a vegetable in American Southern cuisine; also known as branch lettuce and mountain lettuce.

saxitoxin A potent neurotoxin produced by certain organisms consumed by shellfish; it can cause food poisoning in humans who eat the tainted shellfish.

saxon An old English beer.

saya endo (SAH-yah EHN-doe) Japanese for snow peas.

sayurs (sa-your) Indonesian dishes with crisp-cooked vegetables in a thin coconut milk sauce.

Sazerac (SAZ-uh-rak) A cocktail made of whiskey, sugar syrup, Peychaud Bitters and an anise-flavored liqueur.

sbitien (sbee-teh-en) A Russian hot drink made from honey and spices such as ginger, cloves, nutmeg, cinnamon and caraway seeds.

Sbrinz (zbrihnz) A hard Swiss and Italian Alpine cheese made from whole cow's milk; it has a dark yellow interior, a brownish-yellow rind and a savory, mellow flavor, it is aged for 2–3 years and used for grating; if aged for less than 2–3 years, it is known as Spalen.

scaachi (SKAH-kee) A Jewish Italian torta made with matzo and beef and served during Passover.

scald To heat a liquid, usually milk, to just below the boiling point.

scale *v.* 1. To remove the scales from a fish, usually by scraping. 2. To measure ingredients by weight. *n.* One of the many small hard plates, either flat or with small, teethlike projections, that form the covering of a fish.

scales Equipment used to measure the weight of an object. *See* balance scale, beam balance scale, electronic scale, portion scale *and* spring scale.

scaling The act of measuring ingredients, especially those for a bread formula. *See* bread-making process.

scallions 1. The immature green stalks of a bulb onion. 2. A variety of onion with a small white bulb and long, straight, hollow green leaves. 3. A bulbless onion with these green stalks; also known as green onions, spring onions and bunch onions.

scallop *v.* 1. To cook a food (e.g., potatoes) by layering it with cream or a sauce and usually topping it with crumbs before baking. 2. To form a raised, decorative rim on a pie crust. *n.* A thin, boneless round or oval slice of meat or fish.

scalloped squash *See* pattypan squash.

scallop roe The orange or red egg sacs next to the adductor muscle found in some scallops; the eggs have a crunchy texture and salty flavor.

scallops A family of bivalve mollusks found in saltwater regions worldwide; they have rounded, fan-shaped shells with small ears or wings at the hinge; the adductor muscle generally has an ivory or pinkish-beige color that becomes white when cooked, a tender texture and a sweet flavor; most scallops are shucked aboard ship; significant domestic varieties include the bay scallop, calico scallop, Pacific pink scallop and sea scallop.

scalogno (skah-LOH-n'yoh) Italian for a scallion or shallot.

scaloppina (skah-luh-PEE-nah) An Italian term for a thin scallop of meat, usually veal; often dredged in flour and sautéed.

scaloppine alla marsala (skol-a-PEE-nee ah-lah mar-SAH-lah) An Italian dish whose main ingredient (e.g., veal scallop) is sautéed and served with a Marsala wine sauce.

scaloppine di maiale al marsala (ska-lop-PEE-nay dee mah-AH-lay al mar-SAH-lah) An Italian dish consisting of a pork cutlet in Marsala wine.

Scamorze (ska-MOHRT-zuh) *See* Fior di Latte.

scampi (SKAHM-pee) 1. Italian for a small lobster. *See* prawn. 2. An American dish of large shrimp cooked in butter, seasoned with lemon juice, garlic and white wine; also known as shrimp scampi.

scampi fritti (SKAHM-pee FREE-tee) An Italian dish of shrimps or prawns sautéed in olive oil and usually served with a sauce of olive oil, garlic and parsley.

scant A traditional measuring term for just barely (e.g., 1 scant teaspoon).

scarlet runner bean *See* runner bean.

Scarlet Virginian strawberry A variety of June-bearing strawberries whose fruit have a particularly intense, rich flavor; most modern strawberries are a hybrid of Scarlet Virginian and Chilean Pine strawberries. *See* Chilean Pine strawberry.

scarola (skah-ROH-lah) Italian for escarole.

scarole (skah-rohl) French for smooth endive.

scarpazzone (skahr-pay-T'ZOH-neh) A dish from Italy's Emilia-Romagna region consisting of an egg custard made with spinach, onions and Parmigiano-Reggiano.

scattered sushi *See* chirashi-zushi.

scatter sheet *See* sales history.

scelta, al (SHEHL-tah, ahl) Italian for your choice and used on Italian menus to indicate that the customer may choose from several items.

scent A tasting term for the pleasant odor or smell of a food (particularly fresh fruits, vegetables and cheeses) or beverage (e.g., wine, beer or distilled spirit).

schab (s'hap) A Polish cut of the pork carcass; it is the loin of pork with the filet left in.

Schabzieger (SHAHB-tsee-ger) A small, hard Sapsago-style cheese made in the United States from cow's milk; it has a sharp, pungent flavor, a pleasing aroma and a light green color, all resulting from the melilot (clover) leaves added to the curd; used for grating.

schaleth (shaw-let) A Jewish dish consisting of a bottom layer of noodle dough filled with apple purée, raisins, sultanas and currants flavored with orange and lemon peels and Malága wine, topped by a layer of noodle dough and baked.

Schalotten (sha-LO-tern) German for shallots.

Schaum torte; Schaumtorten (SHOWM tohrt) An Austrian dessert composed of baked meringue filled or topped with whipped cream and fresh fruit.

Schaumwein (SHOW'm-vine) The lowest category of German sparkling wines.

schav (schah'v) A Jewish soup made from fresh sorrel flavored with sugar and lemon juice and garnished with sour cream; it is served cold.

Scheiben (SHI-beh) German for slices; also known as Schnitte.

Scheidling (shi-ding) German for straw mushroom.

schiacciata (skee-ah-CH'YAH-tah) A large flatbread usually brushed with olive oil and sprinkled with coarse salt; a specialty of Italy's Tuscany region.

schiacciata alla florentina (skee-ah-CH'YAH-tah ah-lah floo-rehn-tee-nah) A flatbread flavored with orange; a specialty of Italy's Tuscany region.

schienale (skee-eh-NAH-leh) Italian for spinal cord, which is often prepared like sweetbreads.

Schinken (SHING-kehn) German for ham.

Schinkenfleckerln (shenk-en-fleck-krl'n) A variety of very small, square German and Austrian noodles made with sour cream and minced ham.

Schlag; Schlagober (sh'-lahag) German and Austrian for whipped cream.

Schloss (sh'loss) German for castle and, as a wine term, the equivalent of the French term *château*.

Schlosskäse (sh'loss-kaiz) A mild Limburger-style cheese made in Germany and Austria from cow's milk.

schmaltz Yiddish for rendered fat, usually chicken fat, used in Jewish cuisines as a cooking medium, ingredient and spread. *See* grebenes.

schmaltz herring A fatty herring that is pickled and preserved in brine.

Schmierkäse (SHMEER-kaiz) 1. German for any white spreadable cheese, especially cream cheese–style cheeses; they can be flavored with herbs. 2. Pennsylvania Dutch for cottage cheese.

Schmierwurst (SHMEER-vurst) *See* Mettwurst.

Schmoren (shmor-en) German for stew.

Schnapps (shnahps) A group of Dutch or German strong, colorless alcoholic spirits distilled from grains or potatoes; they are often flavored (e.g., peach schnapps and peppermint schnapps).

Schnaps (shnahps) German for whiskey.

Schnecke (sh'-nenk) 1. German for snail. 2. A small German sweet cake shaped to resemble a snail.

Schnitte (schnit) German for slice.

Schnittkäse (schnit-kaiz) Any German or Austrian semihard cheese.

Schnittlauch (SCHNIT-lowkh) German for chives.

schnitz and knepp (shneetz and kae-nep) A Pennsylvania Dutch dish of dried apples simmered with ham; spoonfuls of batter are added to the cooking liquid to make dumplings.

Schnitzel (SHNIHT-suhl) German for cutlet and used to describe a thin slice of meat, typically veal, that is dipped in egg, breaded and fried.

Schokolade (sho-ko-LAH-deh) German for chocolate.

scholles (sho-lae) A Belgian dish of sun-dried plaice.

schooner A large glass commonly used for beer; it holds a pint or more.

Schopftintling (shopf-tint-ling) German for shaggy mane mushroom.

Schottenziger (shot-en-zee-ger) *See* Ziger.

Schwarzenberger (SHVART-zen-behr-gehr) A Limburger-style cheese made in Germany, Hungary and Austria; it is a popular beer cheese.

Schwarzwalder Kirschtorte (SHVART-val-der KEERSH-tohrt) German for a Black Forest cherry torte.

Schwarzwurst (SHVARTS-voorst) A German blood sausage.

Schwein (shvine) German for pork.

schweinerei (SHVINE-eh-ree) An American Jewish dish of cottage cheese, strawberry preserves and chopped cold vegetables.

Schweinerippchen (SHVINE-eh-rip-khern) German for spareribs.

scimitar (SIM-ah-tahr) *See* butcher knife.

scone (skohn; scahn) 1. A traditional Scottish quick bread originally made with oats and cooked on a griddle. 2. A rich, delicate quick bread similar to a biscuit; it is sometimes studded with raisins or other dried or fresh fruit and is usually served with jam, butter or clotted cream.

scoop and plop Slang for banquet food.

score To make shallow cuts in meat or fish, usually in a diamond pattern; done for decorative purposes, to assist in absorbing flavors and to tenderize the product.

Scorpion A cocktail made of light rum, orange juice, lemon juice, brandy and orgeat syrup; garnished with a gardenia.

scorzetta candita (skohr-T'ZEH-tah kahn-DEE-tah) Italian candied citrus peel eaten as a candy.

scorzonero (skor-tho-NAY-rah) A variety of salsify (*Scorzonera hispanica*); unlike true salsify, it is darker, longer, tapering and does not have offshoots; also known as black salsify.

Scotch; Scotch whisky A whisky distilled in Scotland from a mash made from sprouted barley that has been dried over

a peat fire (which gives the spirit its distinctive flavor); aged for at least 3 years in casks of American oak or used sherry casks. *See* blended Scotch *and* single-malt Scotch whisky.

Scotch ale A Scottish full-bodied, malty ale.

Scotch bonnet chile A short, conical, fresh chile with a pale yellow-green, orange or red color and a very hot, smoky flavor with a fruity undertone.

Scotch broth A Scottish soup made with lamb or mutton, barley and various vegetables; also known as barley broth.

Scotch egg A British dish of a hard-cooked egg coated with sausage, dipped into beaten egg, rolled in bread crumbs and deep-fried; served halved, hot or cold.

Scotch Manhattan *See* Rob Roy.

Scotch oats *See* oats, steel-cut.

Scotch sauce *See* écossaise, sauce.

Scotch tender *See* chuck tender.

Scotch woodcock A British dish of toast spread with anchovy paste and topped with eggs scrambled with cream.

Scoville heat units A subjective rating for measuring a chile's heat.

scrag British for the bony end of the neck of a veal carcass.

scrag end of neck; scrag A British cut of the neck of beef, veal, lamb and pork carcasses; it is used for soups. *See* middle neck *and* best end of neck.

scramble To mix a food or foods until well blended.

scrape down To remove batter or dough from the sides of a mixing bowl with a spatula; the material gathered is typically added to the bulk of dough or batter in the bowl.

scraper *See* bowl scraper.

scrapple A Pennsylvania Dutch dish of boneless pork simmered with cornmeal flavored with sage, packed in a loaf pan and chilled, then sliced and fried in bacon fat; usually served at breakfast.

scratch *See* from scratch.

Screwdriver A cocktail made of orange juice and vodka; garnished with an orange slice.

screw pine *See* pandanus.

scripture cake A colonial American cake made with ingredients mentioned in certain verses of the Bible.

scrod A marketing term for Atlantic cod or haddock weighing less than 2.5 lb. (1.1 kg); it has a very mild flavor.

scruple A traditional apothecary's measure of weight; it is approximately 1/4 teaspoon.

scuddy A wine-tasting term for a wine that is cloudy and thickened by disturbed sediment.

scullery 1. Traditionally, the part of a household in charge of the dishes and cooking utensils. 2. A room near the kitchen for cleaning and storing utensils, cleaning vegetables and similar work.

scum The froth that forms on the top of boiling liquids; it usually contains impurities and other undesirable items and is removed with a skimmer.

scungilli (shukn-GEE-lee) Italian for whelk.

scungilli marinara (shukn-GEE-lee mahr-ah-NAHR-rah) An Italian dish of whelk in a tomato sauce flavored with garlic, basil, oregano and hot pepper seeds.

scup *See* porgy.

Scuppernong (SKUHO-pehr-nong) 1. A native American grape, cultivated in the southeastern United States. 2. A white wine made from this grape since colonial times; it is pungent, aromatic and sweet (sugar is usually added to assist fermentation).

scurvy A disease caused by a deficiency of vitamin C; symptoms include anemia, depression, frequent infections, bleeding gums, loosened teeth, muscle degeneration and pain, bone fragility and failure of wounds to heal.

scurvy grass *See* sea kale.

sdoba (s'doh-bah) Russian for bakery.

sea anemone A flowerlike saltwater invertebrate of various bright colors; its tentacles are generally not consumed, but its somewhat chewy body cavity is sliced, battered and fried.

sea ant A crustacean found in the Persian Gulf; it has a tail that looks like that of a lobster and a head like that of a giant ant; it grows to 5–6 in. (12–15 cm), and its tender, white tail meat has a sweet flavor.

sea bass *See* giant sea bass *and* grouper, Pacific.

sea beef Scottish for the flesh of a young whale.

sea biscuit *See* hardtack.

sea bream An imprecisely used term to describe various members of the perch family native to waters off Southeast Asia; they generally have a market weight of 1–2 lb. (450–900 g), a lean flesh, a coarse texture and a delicate flavor. *See* bream *and* porgy.

sea cat Slang for a catfish.

sea clam *See* surf clam.

sea cow *See* manatee.

sea crawfish; sea crayfish *See* spiny lobster.

sea cuckoo *See* gurnard.

sea cucumber An invertebrate saltwater animal; it has an elongated cylindrical shape with a leathery, velvety or slimy body tube and a mouth surrounded by short tentacles; the body is generally boiled, sun-dried and then smoked and used in Japanese and Chinese cuisines as a flavoring; also known as a sea slug.

sea devil *See* monkfish.

sea eagle Slang for a skate.

seafoam frosting *See* seven-minute frosting.

seafood 1. Shellfish. 2. Shellfish and other small, edible marine creatures. 3. Saltwater shellfish. 4. Saltwater shellfish and fish. 5. All shellfish and fish, saltwater and freshwater.

sea grape *See* marsh samphire.

sea holly A European evergreen herb with bluish, slightly salty leaves and small blue or purple flowers. *See* eryngo.

sea kale; sea kale chard A wild seashore plant (*Crambe maritima*); its white, stemmed, cabbagelike leaves are cooked like a vegetable; also known as scurvy grass.

seal A large carnivorous marine mammal; its dark flesh and its brain, heart and liver are used in Eskimo cuisine.

sea lettuce A bright green, cellophane-like seaweed (*Ulva lactuca*) that grows on rocky shores; it has a tough texture and a good flavor.

seal sausage An Eskimo sausage made from seal variety meats.

sea parsley *See* lovage.

sear To brown a food quickly over high heat; usually done as a preparatory step for combination cooking methods.

searce An archaic form of a sieve, used to remove lumps from pounded loaf sugar or impurities from flour.

sea rocket A plant (genus *Cakile*) grown in North American marshes; its small, bulbous, pointed fruit, budlike leaves, young shoots and small violet flowers are edible; they have a salty flavor.

sea run A term used for anadromous fish when they are in saltwater.

sea salicornia *See* marsh samphire.

sea salt Salt recovered through the evaporation of seawaters; it is available in fine and coarse crystals and is used for cooking and preserving.

sea scallop A variety of scallop found off the east coasts of the United States and Canada; it has a light brown shell and a tender, sweet meat with an average diameter of 1.5 in. (3.8 cm) and a pale beige to creamy-pink color; also known as the Atlantic deep sea scallop, giant scallop and smooth scallop.

sea slug *See* sea cucumber.

sea snail *See* periwinkle.

season 1. Traditionally, to enhance a food's flavor by adding salt. 2. More commonly, to enhance a food's flavor by adding salt and/or ground pepper as well as herbs and other spices; other than adding salt and pepper, seasoning is usually done by the chef and not by the diner. 3. To mature and bring a food (usually beef or game) to a proper condition by aging or special preparation. 4. To prepare a pot, pan or other cooking surface to reduce or to prevent sticking.

seasonal menu A menu featuring (1) dishes that rely on foods that are generally available only during a particular season (e.g., fresh produce during the late spring), and/or (2) dishes whose overall qualities complement a season (e.g., a hearty beef stew for winter or a poached salmon salad for summer).

seasoned salt A seasoning blend; its primary ingredient is salt, with flavorings such as celery, garlic or onion added.

seasoning; seasoner 1. Traditionally, an item added to enhance the natural flavors of a food without changing its flavor dramatically; salt is the most common seasoning. 2. More commonly, salt as well as all herbs and spices; other than salt and ground black pepper, seasonings are usually added to the dish by the chef. *See* condiment.

sea squirt An invertebrate saltwater animal; it has an elongated and flattened cylindrical body that is red, brown or white and a thick, gelatinous or leathery covering; eaten fresh.

seating plan; seating chart A document indicating placement for an event, usually a dinner party or banquet.

sea trout A fish of the drum family found along the U.S. East Coast; it has an iridescent dark olive skin with black, dark green or bronze spots, an average market weight of 0.5–3.5 lb. (0.25–1.6 kg) and a tender flesh with a mild flavor; also known as a gray sea trout, speckled trout, squeteagues, summer trout and weakfish.

seat turnover The number of guests served in a given period divided by the number of seats available.

sea turtle *See* green turtle.

sea urchin An invertebrate saltwater animal; its ovaries and gonads are used in Japanese cuisine.

sea urchin scissors A pair of scissors with sharp-pointed, narrow, tapered blades and handles three times the blades' length; they are used to expose sea urchins so they can be extracted from their shells.

sea urchin scissors

seaweed A general name for a large group of primitive sea plants belonging to the algae family; seaweed can be flat, stringy or green bean shaped and dark green, brown or bluish and generally has a salty, earthy flavor; it is used as a flavoring, stabilizer and thickener.

sea wolf British for sea bass.

séb (sab) Hindi for apple.

sébille (say-bee'y) A French wooden bowl used for beating eggs or mixing chopped ingredients.

sec (sek) 1. French for dry and used to describe a dry (not sweet) wine. 2. A medium-sweet Champagne or sparkling wine; it has 1.7–3.5% sugar. *See* brut, demi-sec *and* extra dry.

secco (SECK-o) 1. Italian for dry. 2. When referring to an Italian wine, sweeter than asciutto (very dry) and drier than abboccato (semidry) and dolce (sweet).

séché (seh-shay) French for dried and used as a wine-tasting term for a wine that has lost its freshness and fruit through prolonged barrel aging.

Seckel pear A small all-purpose pear with a russet skin, a firm flesh and a sweet, spicy flavor.

séco (seh-co) Portuguese and Spanish for dry.

secondary fermentation The second and slower fermentation of a beer or sparkling wine; usually done in a bottle or cask and initiated by priming and/or adding yeast.

secondary sales In the food services industry, sales of additional items such as an appetizer, dessert or beverage, along with the entrée.

second chef *See* sous-chef.

secondi piatti (sah-CON-dee pee-AH-tee) An entrée course in an Italian meal.

second wine *See* false wine.

sectioned and formed A meat product consisting of entire muscles or muscle systems that are closely trimmed, massaged and formed into the desired shape. *See* ham, sectioned and formed.

sèdano (SEH-dah-noa) Italian for celery.

sediment Particles, primarily tannins and pigments, that settle to the bottom of a wine (usually a red); depending on when the sediment forms, it is referred to as crust, deposit or lees.

see byan (si py-an) A Burmese term for the stage in curry making when the cooking oil and oils from the ingredients begin to float to the surface; this indicates that the water has evaporated and the dish has the proper flavor.

seed cake An English tea cake flavored with caraway seeds.

seek kabab (seek kaa-baab) An Indian dish consisting of a thin, sausage-shaped kabob of broiled ground meat and fresh herbs.

seeni sambol A sambol flavored with chiles, onions, Maldive fish and sugar.

seet gnee (seent nee) Chinese for white fungus.

seffa (sah-fah) A Moroccan dessert of couscous cooked with butter and flavored with cinnamon, sugar and orange flower water; it is usually served mounded on a platter.

segale (se-gah-lae) Italian for rye.

sehriye çorbasi; tavuk suyuyla sehriye çorbasi (sha-rieh shoo-bash-ee tah-vook sue-you-e-law) A Turkish chicken soup flavored with lemon juice, garnished with vermicelli and finished with egg yolks.

seigle (saag-lah) French for rye.

seigo (say-goh) Japanese for a small sea bass (suzuki); it should not be used for sushi or sashimi. *See* fukko.

seitan (SAY-tan) A protein-rich food made from wheat gluten; it has a firm, chewy texture and a bland flavor and is used in many vegetarian dishes.

sekerpare (sah-ker-paw-rah) A Turkish sweet pastry made from semolina and almonds.

Sekt (zekt) A German sparkling wine; generally produced by the Charmat method, the wine tends to be fruitier and not as dry as a French or Spanish sparkling wine.

sel (sehl) French for salt.

selaree Hindi for celery.

selasih (se-la-seeh) A variety of basil that grows wild in Indonesia.

selderey (sell-dah-ray) Russian for celery.

select 1. A marketing term indicating that an item has certain qualities or attributes setting it apart from others; the term has no legal significance. 2. A midlevel U.S. Department of Agriculture (USDA) quality grade for beef; the meat lacks the flavor and marbling of the higher grades. 3. A marketing term for a 1 1/4- to 1 3/4-lb. (567- to 793-g) lobster. *See* chicken lobster, deuce, heavy chicken, heavy select, jumbo, quarter *and* small jumbo.

select harvest A marketing term indicating that the wine was made from grapes taken during a specially conducted harvest; the term has no legal significance.

Select Late Harvest *See* Late Harvest.

seledka (seh-leed-kha) Russian for herring.

selenium A trace mineral principally used as a component in an enzyme that acts as an antioxidant; significant sources include fish, shellfish, meats and grains.

selery (seh-leh-ri) Polish for celery.

self-rising flour An all-purpose white wheat flour to which salt and baking powder have been added.

self whisky A Scottish term for a straight Scotch malt whisky.

selinon (seh-lee-non) Greek for celery and celeric.

sell-by date A date stamped by a manufacturer, distributor or retailer on a food product's label indicating the last day the product should be sold; the date is usually preceded by the phrase "sell by" or "pull by."

selle d'agneau (sell dan-yoh) French for saddle of lamb.

selleri (SAH-lea-REE) Norwegian for celery.

Sellerie (ZE-leh-ree) German for celery.

Selles-sur-Cher (SELL-sir-SHAIR) A goat's milk cheese from France's Loire Valley; it has a black ashed exterior, a firm, soft, moist, white interior and a sweet, nutty flavor with a light goaty aroma.

seltzer; seltzer water 1. A mineral water from the town of Nieder Selters in Germany's Weisbaden region. 2. A flavorless water with induced carbonation consumed plain or used as a mixer for alcoholic drinks and soda fountain confections; also known as club soda and soda water.

selvaggo (sehl-VAH-j'yoh) Italian for wild and used to describe either meat from game animals or mushrooms.

semelle (she-MEH-leh) Small crusty yeast bread rolls with a ridge or cleft in the top; a speciality of Italy's Tuscany region.

semi à la carte menu A menu on which some foods (typically appetizers and desserts) and beverages are priced and ordered separately, while the entrée is accompanied by and priced to include other items, such as a salad, starch or vegetable.

semi-completo (sae-mee-kom-plae-toh) A Spanish marketing designation for rice that is lightly threshed; it has characteristics of both whole grain and refined rice.

semi di finocchio (sami dee fee-no-key-oh) Italian for fennel seeds.

semidry A wine-tasting term for a wine that is less dry than sweet. *See* dry, semisweet *and* sweet.

semifirm cheeses; semihard cheeses *See* cheeses, firm.

semifreddo (seh-mee-FRAYD-doh) A chilled dessert made with frozen mousse, custard or cream into which large amounts of whipped cream or meringue are folded to incorporate air; layers of sponge cake and/or fruit may be added for flavor and texture (e.g., frozen soufflées, marquis, mousses and neapolitans); also known as a still-frozen dessert.

Sémillon (seh-mee-yohn) 1. A white wine grape principally grown in southwestern France, Australia, Chile and California; it is the primary variety used for Sauternes and is also used as a blending grape; also known as Chevrier (especially in California). 2. A white wine with low acidity made from this grape.

seminary sausages *See* sausages, dried.

semiperishable A food or beverage that is canned, dried or otherwise processed so that it can be kept unrefrigerated without spoiling for a relatively long period of time.

semisoft cheeses *See* cheeses, semisoft.

semisweet A wine-tasting term for a wine that is less sweet than dry. *See* dry, semidry *and* sweet.

semisweet chocolate A type of chocolate containing moderate amounts of sugar and from 15 to 35% chocolate liquor; usually sold in bars or chips and eaten as a candy or used for baking. *See* chocolate-making process.

semmel (ZEH-merl) A Pennsylvania Dutch yeast roll, usually served for breakfast.

Semmel (ZEM-mel) A German yeast roll made with white wheat flour dough.

Semmelstoppelpilz (sam-mel-stop-pel-peeltz) German for hedgehog mushroom.

semneh (sam-neh) Arabic for clarified butter.

semolina (seh-muh-LEE-nuh) A grainy, pale yellow flour coarsely ground from wheat (usually durum or other hard wheats) with a high protein content and gluten-forming potential; used principally for pasta dough.

semoule (suh-moole) French for semolina.

sènape (SAY-nah-pay) Italian for mustard.

Senate bean soup A soup served in the U.S. Senate dining room; made from white beans cooked with smoked ham hocks, mashed potatoes, onions and garlic.

Sencha (SEHN-cha) A Japanese green tea; the beverage has a yellow color and vegetal flavor and is often consumed with meals.

sendai-miso *See* inaka-miso.

send it up An archaic service term referring to the order to bring food from a kitchen, wherever it was located, to the dining table.

sendwichi (send-we-chee) Swahili for sandwich.

Senegalaise (say-nay-gah-lez) A French soup of creamed and curried chicken stock, served cold and thick.

Senf (zehnf) German for mustard.

sen-giri (SEHN-ghee-ree) A Japanese decorative cut of food similar to julienne.

sengong (san-gong) A Tibetan dish consisting of cooked tsampa dough served with pagma.

sen mee Thai for thin rice noodle.

sennep (SEHN-erp) Danish and Norwegian for mustard.

sen-nuki (sehn-noo-kee) Japanese for corkscrew.

sequestrant A type of food additive that helps to remove trace metals such as iron and copper that could cause a food to discolor.

ser (sehr) Polish for cheese.

Serbian butter *See* Kajmak.

Sercial (sair-s'yahl) 1. A white wine grape grown on the island of Madeira. 2. A Madeira wine made from this grape; it is the driest of the four Madeira styles.

Serena (say-ray-nah) A handmade Spanish ewe's milk cheese; it is pressed and salted by hand, matured for 1 month and available only during the spring.

serikaya dengan agar agar (sa-re-ka-ya dahn-gahn ah-gahr ah-gahr) A Malaysian jellylike candy made with coconut milk, agar-agar, sugar and water and flavored with cardamom.

serine 1. An amino acid. 2. A food additive used as a nutrient source to significantly improve the biological quality of the total protein in a food containing the naturally occurring protein.

serori (SEH-roh-ree) Japanese for celery.

serotonin A substance in the brain that helps regulate food intake, sleep, pain and mood.

serpentaria *See* dragoncello.

Serra da Estrella (SEHR-rah dur es-strahl-lah) A soft Portuguese cheese usually made from ewe's milk but also from a mixture of goat's and ewe's milks; it has a pleasing, acidic flavor, a smooth, yellow rind and a light yellow-ivory interior.

serrano (seh-RRAH-noh) A short, tapered fresh chile with a green or orange-red color, a thick flesh and a very hot flavor.

serrated edge The cutting edge of a knife; generally used for slicing items with a hard exterior and a soft interior (e.g., crusty bread or tomato); the blade has a series of tiny, sharp V-shaped teeth that saw the food. *See* wave cut edge.

serrano

server A person who takes a customer's orders for food and/or beverages and serves them to the customer; also known as a waiter or waitress.

service 1. The act or style of providing beverages and/or food to customers as requested. 2. A place setting. 3. A set of dishes, serviceware and/or utensils used for serving and consuming a particular food or course (e.g., tea service).

service bar An area of the bar or a separate bar in the kitchen or other area that provides servers with drinks ordered by seated patrons.

serviceberry; service berries 1. Small red or purplish berries from a tree native to the Mediterranean region (*Sorbus domestica*); the berries can be eaten raw or used to make wine; also known as Juneberry and sorb apple. 2. *See* shad bush.

service plate *See* charger.

service tree *See* sorb tree.

serviceware The china, flatware, glassware, trays, tools and other items used to serve food. *See* dinnerware.

serviette (serv-aytt) Norwegian for napkin.

serviette (ser-vey-yet) French and British for napkin.

Serviette (ser-vey-yet-a) German for napkin.

servilleta (ser-vee-jyeh-tah) Spanish for napkin.

serving *See* portion.

serving size A Nutrition Facts term approved by the U.S. Food and Drug Administration (FDA) to identify the FDA-defined serving size for a food; reflecting the amount that people generally consume, it is intended to make it easier for consumers to compare the nutritional contents of different brands.

servings per container A Nutrition Facts term approved by the U.S. Food and Drug Administration (FDA) to identify the number of FDA-defined servings in a container.

servir tres frais (sahr-veei tray fray) *See* frais.

servizio compreso (sehr-VEE-t'zee-yoh kohm-PREH-soh) Italian for service included and used on Italian menus to indicate that the waiter's tip will be included in the bill.

servizio non compreso (sehr-VEE-t'zee-yoh non kohm-PREH-soh) Italian for service not included and used on Italian menus to indicate that the waiter's tip will not be included in the bill and that the patron should leave one.

sesame balls A Chinese dessert or pastry made with a dough of glutinous rice powder and water, shaped into a ball, filled with sweet bean paste, rolled in sesame seeds and deep-fried.

sesame chile oil A hot and flavorful oil made by frying red chiles in sesame oil until the oil turns red; usually used as a condiment or seasoning in Asian cuisines.

sesame oil; sesame seed oil An oil obtained from sesame seeds; it has a light brown color and a rich, nutty flavor and is used for dressings and cooking. *See* oriental sesame oil.

sesame paste A thick, somewhat dry paste made from toasted white sesame seeds and used as a flavoring in many Southeast Asian cuisines.

sesame rings *See* simit.

sesame seeds The tiny, flat seeds of a plant (*Sesamum indicum*) native to India; they have a nutty, slightly sweet flavor and are available with a red, brown, black or grayish-ivory color; also known as benne seeds.

sesos (SAY-sohs) Spanish for brains.

set 1. To allow a mixture to thicken or congeal, usually by chilling (e.g., gelatin). 2. To place on a table the napery, flatware, glassware and dinnerware necessary for dining.

setampo *See* ikeleko.

setas (SAY-tahss) Spanish for mushrooms.

setine (sah-TEE-nay) An ancient Roman wine.

seto fuumi (seh-toh foo-oo-mee) A Japanese seasoning compound made from dried seaweed, tuna, sesame seeds and monosodium glutamate.

set-point theory The theory that the body tends to maintain a certain weight through internal controls; it is a theoretical explanation for why people return to a certain weight after periods of weight loss or gain.

setting agents *See* thickening agents.

settling 1. The process of matter suspended in a liquid falling out of suspension and dropping to the bottom. 2. A traditional white wine–making process of delaying fermentation by maintaining the grape juice at a low temperature while impurities (stems, skins and seeds) fall to the tank's bottom.

settling agent *See* fining agent.

setups The nonalcoholic mixers, garnishes, ice and glasses provided to customers who bring in or purchase on-site bottled alcoholic beverages.

Seven & Seven; 7 & 7 A cocktail made of 7-Up soda and Seagram's 7 Crown blended whiskey.

seven-bone A subprimal cut from the beef primal chuck; after extensive trimming, somewhat tough steaks and roasts can be fabricated from it.

seven food groups Before 1956 and the introduction of the four food groups, the U.S. Department of Agriculture (USDA) divided foods into seven categories for dietary considerations: (1) meats, eggs, dried peas and beans; (2) milk, cheese and ice cream; (3) potatoes and other vegetables and fruits; (4) green leafy and yellow vegetables; (5) citrus fruits and tomatoes; (6) breads and flour; and (7) butter and fortified margarine.

seven-minute frosting A fluffy meringue frosting made by beating egg whites, sugar and corn syrup together in a double boiler until stiff peaks form; also known as seafoam frosting and foam frosting.

seven-spice powder A spice blend generally consisting of ground anise pepper, sesame seeds, flax seeds, rapeseeds, poppy seeds, nori and dried tangerine (or orange) peel; used in Japanese cuisine.

seviche; ceviche; cebiche (seh-VEE-chee; seh-VEESH) A Latin American dish of raw fish marinated in citrus juice, onions, tomatoes and chiles and sometimes flavored with cilantro.

Sévillane, sauce (sey-vee-yahn) A French compound sauce made from a velouté flavored with tomato purée and red bell pepper purée.

Seville A cocktail made of gin, fino sherry, orange juice, lemon juice and sugar syrup.

Seville orange An orange (*Citrus aurantium*) grown principally in Spain with a thick, rough orange skin, a bitter, tart flesh and many seeds; used for marmalades and flavoring liqueurs; also known as bitter orange and sour orange.

sevruga (sehv-ROO-guh) Caviar harvested from a small species of sturgeon; the tiny eggs are a light to dark gray color and tend to clump together.

Sewickley Hunt Stirrup Cup A cocktail made of orange juice, grapefruit juice, vodka and sloe gin; served in a silver stirrup cup or a double old-fashioned glass.

Seyval Blanc (say-vahl BLAHN) A white wine grape grown in New York, Canada and England; the resulting wine is generally highly acidic and dry.

sfeeha (s'fee-hah) Middle Eastern meat pies made open faced or closed.

sfogato (sh'foh-yha-to) A Greek dish from Rhodes consisting of a meat and vegetable custard or souffle served with fresh tomato sauce.

sfoglia (sfo-glee-ah) Italian for a thin, flat sheet of pasta dough that can be cut into ribbons, circles, squares or other shapes.

sfogliatelle (sfo-LYAH-tah-la) Shell-shaped Italian pastries made with a flaky dough filled with a sweet mixture of ricotta, semolina and candied citrus peel.

sfogli in saor (SFOL-yee een SOUR) An Italian dish from Venice consisting of sole (flounder) fried or sautéed and served with a sauce made from wine vinegar, onions, sultanas and pine nuts.

sformato (sfor-MAH-toa) An Italian dish consisting of a custard or soufflé made from meats, poultry, cheese or vegetables (especially spinach, beans or peas).

shabril (shaw-brill) A Tibetan dish consisting of beef or lamb balls flavored with fenugreek, ginger and garlic and cooked with radishes and mushrooms in sour cream.

shabu-shabu (SHAH-boo-SHAH-boo) A Japanese dish consisting of raw meat and vegetables cooked in a pot of hot broth by each diner and served with various sauces; noodles are added to the broth and served as soup.

shad, American A member of the herring family found in North American rivers and along coasts; it has a shiny greenish skin that becomes silvery on the sides, dark spots, an average market weight of 3–4 lb. (1.4–1.8 kg) and a bony flesh; also known as white shad.

shad bush; shadbush A small tree (genus *Amelanchier*) native to North America; its red, purplish or blue-black berries are used for pies and preserves; also known as Juneberry and serviceberry.

shaddock *See* pomelo.

shad roe The roe of the American shad; the eggs are large and bright red.

shaft fruit A hybrid of black currants and gooseberries.

shaggy mane mushroom A small wild mushroom (*Coprinus comatus*) with a thin-edged cap; it has a crunchy, firm texture and a delicate flavor.

sha kampo (shaw kahm-poe) Tibetan dried meats, usually beef or lamb.

sha katsa (shaw kaht-saw) A Tibetan dish consisting of grilled lamb or beef served with pagma.

shaking A method of mixing ingredients by placing them in a covered container and shaking the container.

shako (shaw-koh) Japanese for mantis shrimp.

shalà (shaw-law) Chinese for salad.

shallot (SHAL-uht; shuh-LOT) A member of the onion family (*Allium ascalonicum*) native to the Middle East and formed like garlic, with a head composed of several cloves covered in a thin papery skin; the outer covering can be pale brown, bronze, pale gray or rose; it has a pink-tinged ivory-colored flesh and a flavor that is more subtle than that of onion and less harsh than that of garlic.

shallot butter *See* Bercy butter.

shallow poaching A moist-heat cooking method that combines poaching and steaming; the food (usually fish) is placed on a vegetable bed and partially covered with a liquid (cuisson) and simmered.

shallow porcelain baker A shallow porcelain baking dish with fluted edges used for baking and serving custards with or without a pastry top, baked fruits and desserts such as clafouti; imprecisely known as a porcelain quiche dish.

shamdur (sham-duhr) A Tibetan sauce made with dried meat (beef or lamb) and tomatoes and flavored with chiles, garlic, fenugreek, onions and soy sauce; it is served with rice or bread.

shammam (sham-MEHM) Arabic for melon.

shamme kabab (shaam-meh kaa-baab) An East Indian dish of ground meat and yellow split peas, flavored with mint, gingerroot and spices, shaped into small patties and fried.

shandy; shandygaff A British drink made of beer and lemonade or ginger beer; also known as Alsterwasser and Panaché.

Shanghai hairy crab A small, square-bodied crab with long, hairlike growths covering its legs and upper shell; found in the waters near Shanghai, it has a sweet meat and its yellow yolk is considered a delicacy. *See* drunken crabs.

Shanghai noodles Thick, round, fresh egg noodles used in southeastern Chinese cuisine; usually served with a brown sauce flavored with white pepper.

shank 1. The lower portion (below the knee) of a quadruped's limb. *See* foreshank *and* hindshank. 2. A subprimal cut of the beef primal round; it has a large amount of connective tissue and flavorful meat; also known as the hindshank.

shankalis (shahn-kah-liss) A Middle Eastern dish consisting of a cheese ball of thickened laban rolled in zaatar.

shank end The lower part of the leg of a lamb or pork carcass. *See* shin.

shanku (shahn-koo) Chinese for shiitake.

shanyáng (shahn-yeng) Chinese for goat.

shao (shah) Chinese for fry-stewing food (usually meat, poultry or fish); the food is fried, steamed or boiled and then simmered in a soy sauce–based sauce; also known as red cooking.

shao bing (shah-oh beeng) Chinese for northern-style flaky, hollow, sesame seed–topped buns.

shaohsing; shaoxing (show-sing) An amber-colored wine made in China from glutinous rice, millet and a yeast mold and aged for 10–100 years; also known as yellow rice wine.

shao-mai (shah-mae) Canton Chinese steamed pork dumplings consisting of wonton wrappers filled with ground pork, celery and bamboo shoots and flavored with rice wine and soy sauce.

shapalé (shaw-pah-lay) A Tibetan dish of lamb or beef flavored with onions, cumin, nutmeg and ginger folded into a dough and baked or fried.

sharaab (sha-raaw'b) Hindi for alcohol.

sharbat A thick, sweet beverage from India flavored with fruit juice or flower petals and sometimes eaten with a spoon.

sharbat (shahr-bat) Arabic for various nonalcoholic beverages whose principal ingredient is fruit juice.

shari *See* zushi.

Sharir A semidry, golden, sherry-type Israeli wine.

shark Any of a variety of marine invertebrates found in tropical to temperate saltwater areas worldwide; they generally have a lean red- or pink-tinged white flesh that becomes off-white when cooked, a firm texture and a mild flavor; usually available as wheels, loins or smaller cuts; varieties with culinary significance include the mako (which is often sold as swordfish), sand shark (also known as the dogfish), dusky shark, sharpnose shark, bonnethead shark, blacktip shark, angel shark and thresher shark.

shark's fin The fins and cartilaginous segments of the tail of the dogfish; believed by some to be an aphrodisiac, it provides a protein-rich gelatin used in Chinese cuisine, especially shark's fin soup.

Shark's Tooth A cocktail made of rum, lemon juice, lime juice, grenadine, rock candy syrup and club soda; served in a large Pilsner glass and garnished with the shell of a half lime.

Sharon fruit *See* persimmon.

sharp A tasting term for a biting, pungent flavor.

sharpening stone *See* whetstone.

sharpnose shark *See* shark.

shashlik (shahsh-LIHK; SHAHSH-lihk) *See* shish kebab.

shashlyk (shash-lik) A Russian dish consisting of pork, lamb or mutton; the meat is marinated with onions and sometimes yogurt and then threaded on skewers and grilled.

shataavar (shah-tah-vahr) Hindi for asparagus.

shatta (shaw-tah) A very spicy Middle Eastern flavoring or condiment made with the fiery piri-piri chile, cumin, coriander, olive oil and tomatoes and used in African and Middle Eastern cuisines to add flavor to soups, stews and bland grains. *See* bisbas *and* harissa.

shave ice A Hawaiian confection of finely shaved ice topped with one or more fruit-flavored syrups and served in a conical paper cup; sometimes ice cream is put in the bottom of the cup.

shawarma (shaw-whar-mah) A Middle Eastern cooking method for lamb or chicken; a large amount of thinly sliced lamb or chicken (usually flavored with baharat, garlic, vinegar and herbs) is placed on a vertical skewer that rotates before a flame running along a vertical shaft; bits of meat are sliced vertically from the mass and served on flatbread and garnished with yogurt, cucumbers, tomatoes and the like.

Shawnee blackberry A blackberry variety; the fruit are relatively large, firm and flavorful.

shchi (schch-ee) A Russian soup consisting of cabbage simmered with onions, carrots, celeriac, parsley root and leeks in a beef or pork broth.

shea A tropical tree (*Butyrospermum parkii*) native to Africa; its fruit contains oily seeds that are crushed to form a butterlike fat called shea butter, which is used for cooking in several African countries.

shears *See* fish shears, kitchen shears *and* poultry shears.

she-crab soup An American Southern soup made with fresh crabmeat and roe, flavored with sherry.

sheep's foot *See* knife point.

sheepshead 1. A saltwater fish found in the Gulf of Mexico and the Atlantic Ocean off the southeast U.S. coast; it has several dark vertical stripes on the side, an average market weight of 0.75–8 lb. (0.34–3.6 kg) and a tender white flesh with a flaky texture and a mild flavor. 2. A freshwater fish found in the Great Lakes and midwestern rivers; it has a silvery skin, an average market weight of 0.25–5 lb. (0.11–2.3 kg) and a lean white flesh; also known as a gasperou, gray bass, freshwater drum and white perch. *See* nabeta.

sheeter A machine used in professional kitchens for rolling out large pieces of dough, especially puff pastry and Danish pastry doughs.

sheet gelatin *See* gelatin, leaf.

sheet pan extender A 2- to 4-in.-high semiflexible rectangular frame that is placed inside a sheet pan to extend the height of the pan's sides; it is used for baking cake batter and assembling and molding multilayer pastries.

shef (SHEH-fa´) Japanese for chef.

sheikh il mihshee (she-k el mee-shee) *See* bantinjan bil saneeyee.

shekar (shae-kahr) 1. Hebrew for an alcoholic beverage (the source for the word cider). 2. Hebrew for being or becoming inebriated.

shelf date A date stamped by a manufacturer, distributor or retailer on a food product's label indicating the date the product was placed on the retailer's shelf.

shelf life The period that a product such as a processed food or medicine remains suitable or useful for consumption.

shelf stable Pertaining to a product that can be stored at room temperature for an extended period; used especially with regard to canned goods.

shelf talker A small display that attaches to a shelf and promotes the product; it can include refund slips.

shell *v.* To remove the edible part of a food from its natural container (e.g., clam meat from its shell, a pea from its pod or a corn kernel from its ear). *n.* 1. A glass shaped like a tall, tapered, plain cylinder; it is used for beer or cocktails. 2. The hard outer covering of a mollusk, crustacean, tortoise, egg, nut or the like. 3. The lower pastry crust of a pie, tart or the like, usually baked before the filling is added. 4. A small, delicate pastry or chocolate container used to hold a sweet preparation; it can be shaped like a shell or other object. 5. A pasta shaped like an open clamshell.

shell bean; shellout *See* cranberry bean.

shell beans Any of various beans cultivated for their edible seeds rather than their pods.

shellcracker *See* redear.

shellfish Any of many species of aquatic invertebrates with shells or carapaces found in saltwater and freshwater regions worldwide; most are edible; shellfish are categorized as crustaceans and mollusks. *See* crustacean, mollusks *and* fish.

shellfish quality grades U.S. Department of Commerce (USDC) grades for common shellfish packed under federal inspection; each species has its own grading criteria; grade A products are top quality with good flavor and odor and practically free of blemishes, grade B products are good quality and grade C products are fairly good quality and usually canned or processed.

shell loin A fabricated cut of the beef primal short loin; a bone-in strip loin; it can be fabricated into shell steaks.

shell steak A fabricated cut of the beef primal short loin; it is a club steak without the tail ends.

sheng (shang) Chinese for raw.

sheng cài (shang cah-ee) Chinese for lettuce.

sheperd's pie An old English dish of ground meat, usually lamb or mutton, and sometimes vegetables such as corn or peas, bound with a gravy, topped with mashed potatoes and baked.

Sheperd's Suffering Bastard A cocktail made of Angostura bitters, gin, brandy, Rose's lime juice and ginger beer; garnished with a mint sprig, cucumber slice and orange or lemon slice.

sherbet A frozen dessert made with fruit juice, sugar and water; it can also contain milk, cream and egg whites. *See* sorbet.

sherry A fortified wine made principally from the Palomino grape in a delimited district in southern Spain centering around the city of Jerez de la Frontera; a sherry can range from pale gold and bone dry to dark brown and very sweet; its distinctive flavor and aroma are partly the result of a flor forming during the solera. *See* amontillado, brown sherry, cream sherry, fino, manzanilla *and* oloroso.

sherry glass A stemmed, conical glass ranging in size from 2 to 5 fl. oz.; used for sherry, port, Madeira, aperitifs neat, liqueurs neat and layered cordials. *See* copita.

sherry vinegar A nutty brown–colored vinegar with a full, round flavor made from sherry and aged in wooden barrels in a process similar to that used to make sherry.

shibo (shee-boh) Japanese for fat.

shichimencho (shee-chee-MEN-cho) Japanese for turkey.

shichimi togarashi (she-CHEE-mee toh-gah-RAH-shee) A Japanese spice blend generally consisting of dried chiles, rape, sesame seeds, mustard and dried sea vegetation.

shichu-ryori (SHEE-chu-ree-OH-ree) Japanese for stew.

Shiedam gin *See* Genever.

shift schedule *See* stacked schedule.

Shigella (shi-GEL-ah) A genus of bacteria that causes diarrhea or dysentery (called shigellosis); the bacteria are transmitted through ingestion of contaminated foods or water.

shiitake (shee-TAH-kay) A mushroom (*Lentinus edodes*) native to Japan and now cultivated in the United States; it has a tough stem that is usually not eaten and a dark brown cap that has a velvety texture and a meaty, smoky flavor; available fresh and dried; also known as black forest mushroom, flower mushroom, winter mushroom, doubloon and golden oak.

Shiitakepilz (she-taka-pilz) German for shiitake.

shika (shee-kah) Japanese for venison or game.

shikkereh babka (shihk-ker'h bahb-kah) Yiddish for drunken babka and used to describe a babka soaked in rum, brandy or a distilled spirit.

shimbra (shimm-brah) Ethiopian for chickpea.

shimeji (shee-MAY-gee) Japanese for oyster mushroom.

shimeyane (shee-mei-ya-nei) A South African alcoholic beverage made from brown sugar, brown bread and malted corn.

shimofuri (shee-moh-foo-ree) Japanese for blanching.

shin (shen) The lower part of the leg of a beef or veal carcass. *See* shank.

shiner *See* redfin.

shining noodles *See* cellophane noodles.

shinko (sheen-koh) A small, young gizzard shad (kohado); it is used for sushi and sashimi; also known as nakazumi. *See* konoshiro.

shinmai (shan-mah-i) A Japanese rice harvested during the fall; it has moist, tender, sweet grains.

shin of beef A British cut of the beef carcass; it is the foreshank.

shinsen na (SHEEN-sen nah) Japanese for fresh.

shinshu-miso (shin-shoo-mee-so) A smooth, salty, yellow miso usually made with a rice-based mold.

shinsui (SHEEN-soo-ee) A variety of nashi.

shio (shee-oh) Japanese for salt.

shiogame (shee-oh-ga-me) A heavy, earthenware Japanese platter; it is usually used, thickly coated with coarse salt, to broil chicken, fish or shellfish.

shio-yaki (shee-oh-YAH-kee) Japanese for salt broiled, meaning that food is dry marinated in salt and then grilled.

shio-zuke (shee-oh-ZOO-kay) Salty Japanese pickles.

shirataki (shi-rah-tah-kee) Extruded Japanese noodles made from a konnyaku and water paste; also known as snowed black bean curd.

Shiraz (shee-rahz) *See* Syrah.

Shirley Temple A child's mocktail made of lemon–lime soda and grenadine syrup; garnished with a maraschino cherry.

shiro goma (SHEE-roh GOH-mah) *See* goma.

shiro kikurage (shi-row ke-koor-ah-gue) Japanese for white fungus.

shiromi (shee-roh-mee) Japanese for white meat, usually referring to fish.

shiro miso (SHEE-roh MEE-soh) A white or light-colored Japanese bean paste.

shiro uri (SHEE-roh OOH-ree) A zucchini-like vegetable grown in Japan.

shiro wot (she-row what) An Ethiopian stew made with groundnuts and vegetables flavored with berberé.

shirr To cook something, especially by baking, in a ramekin.

shirred eggs Eggs covered with milk or cream and sometimes bread crumbs and baked in a small dish until the whites are firm.

shiru; shirumono (she-roo; she-rou-moh-noh) Japanese for soup.

shish kebab (SHIHSH kuh-bob) 1. A Mediterranean dish of marinated meats (usually lamb or beef) and vegetables threaded on a skewer and grilled or broiled; also known as shashlik. 2. A term used imprecisely to describe a grilled or broiled skewer of meats, poultry, shellfish, firm fish, vegetables and/or fruits; the foods are often marinated.

shiso *See* beefsteak plant.

shiso (SHEE-so) Japanese for perilla.

shitor din (CHEE-tor dean) A spicy Ghanaian sauce made from chiles, dried shrimp, ginger and onions and used for grain porridges.

shmear A Yiddish word used in delicatessens to describe a dab of something, usually a condiment such as cream cheese, to be spread on a bagel or bread.

sho Tibetan yogurt.

shocking *See* refreshing.

shoestring potatoes Very slender, short French fries.

shoga (SHO-gah) Japanese for fresh ginger.

shokoladnyj (shoh-kahl-ad-n'yej) Russian for chocolate.

shoku beni (SHO-koo BEH-nee) Japanese for red food coloring.

shokubutsu no (SHO-koo-BOO-tsu no) Japanese for vegetables; also known as yasai.

shokuryo (sho-KOO-ree-oh) Japanese for food; also known as tabemono.

shokutaku (SHO-koo-TAH-koo) Japanese for table; also known as teburu.

sholeh zard (SHO-lay zahrd) An Iranian rice pudding flavored with saffron, almonds, pistachios and cinnamon.

Sho May Chinese for eyes of longevity and used to describe a green tea from Canton province; the beverage has a pale color and a mild flavor.

shoofly pie A Pennsylvania German dessert consisting of a flaky pastry shell filled with a spicy molasses and brown sugar custard.

shooter Slang for a shot of liquor taken neat; also called a neat.

Shopshire Blue (SHOP-shur bloo) A cow's milk cheese from England's Shopshire region; it has a rough, brown rind, a crumbly yet firm and creamy texture, an orange, blue-veined interior and a sharp, rustic, slightly tannic flavor.

shorba (shor-baa) Hindi for soup.

shorbat adas (showr-baht ah-das) A Middle Eastern soup made from lentils flavored with onions, cumin and lemon juice and garnished with lemon wedges and onion slices.

shore dinner A large dinner of fresh fish and/or shellfish caught in nearby waters.

short 1. A wine-tasting term for a wine lacking in persistence. 2. A term used to describe a pastry dough that contains a high ratio of fat; the fat creates a tender, crisp product.

shortage The amount by which the quantity supplied or on hand is less than the quantity ordered or needed at the existing price. *See* surplus.

shortbread A rich, crumbly British butter cookie; the dough is traditionally formed into a circle and cut into pie-shaped wedges called petticoat tails. *See* highlanders.

shortbread mold A round or square ceramic plate, similar to a pie plate, marked in wedges or squares, usually with decorative designs that imprint the shortbread.

shortcake A dessert made with a sweet biscuit split in half and filled with fresh fruit, especially strawberries, and whipped cream; angel food cake or sponge cake is sometimes used instead of a biscuit.

short crust; short pastry A dough made with a high fat content, such as a pie crust.

short drink A cocktail served in a glass smaller than that usually used, thus allowing only a small amount of mixer to be added; also known as a burned drink. *See* long drink.

shortening 1. A white, flavorless, solid fat formulated for baking or deep-frying. 2. Any fat used in baking to tenderize the product by shortening gluten strands.

short finish *See* finish.

short-grain rice *See* rice, short-grain.

short hip A subprimal cut of the beef sirloin; it is usually fabricated into sirloin steaks.

short loin A primal section of the beef carcass; the front portion of the beef loin, just behind the rib; it contains one rib and a portion of the backbone, the very tender loin eye muscle (a continuation from the rib eye muscle) and the short tenderloin and produces fabricated cuts such as club steaks, T-bone steaks and porterhouse steaks. *See* tenderloin.

shortnose sturgeon *See* lake sturgeon.

short-order cook At a food services operation, the person responsible for preparing foods quickly; he or she works the grill, griddles and deep-fryer and makes sandwiches and some sautéed items.

short-order section One of the principal work sections of a food services facility; it typically contains a griddle station, fry station and broiler station.

short plate A primal section of the beef carcass; it is under the primal rib and contains a large amount of connective tissue; includes such meaty subprimal or fabricated cuts as short ribs and skirt steak.

short ribs 1. A fabricated cut of the beef primal short plate consisting of not more than five ribs (numbers 6–10); it is meaty and has a high percentage of connective tissue; also known as plate short ribs and beef ribs. 2. A fabricated cut of the beef primal chuck; they are rectangular chunks of meat, typically 2–3 in. (5.08–7.6 cm) long, with layers of fat, meat, bone and connective tissue.

short shot A small amount of any beverage.

short sirloin A fabricated cut of the beef primal sirloin; it is a small steak from the center of the sirloin.

short tenderloin The smaller portion of the tenderloin found in the beef primal short loin; it is used to fabricate filet mignon, tournedos and tenderloin tips. *See* butt tenderloin.

short texture A tasting term for a baked good with a high percentage of fat and a crumbly texture.

shorva (shor-vah) Hindi for soup.

shot *See* jigger.

shot and a beer A quickly consumed drink of liquor with a beer chaser.

shot glass A short, squat, thick-bottomed glass holding approximately 1 fl. oz.; it has an etched line marking the 5/8 fl. oz. fill and is used for liquor neat and for measuring liquids; also known as cheater, because a full fluid ounce is not always poured.

shottsuru (SHOH-tsu-roo) A salty condiment made from fermented fish and used in Japanese cuisine.

shot glass

shoulder 1. A primal section of the veal carcass; it consists of the animal's shoulder and contains the often tough muscles along a portion of the backbone, four rib bones and the bladebone and arm bones and a large amount of connective tissue; its meat is usually ground, cubed or fabricated into shoulder chops and steaks. 2. A primal section of the lamb carcass; it consists of the animal's shoulder, four ribs and many small, tough muscles; it is usually diced, ground or fabricated into chops or boned for roasts. 3. A subprimal cut of the beef primal chuck; somewhat tough but flavorful, it is often fabricated into steaks and roasts. 4. A primal section of the pork carcass; it consists of the hog's lower foreleg and contains the arm and shank bones; relatively tough, lean and flavorful, it is often fabricated into steaks or diced. 5. *See* bolster.

shoulder butt *See* Boston butt.

shoulder clod *See* clod.

shoulder steak; shoulder butt steak A fabricated cut of the pork primal shoulder; it is a relatively tough steak with a bone.

shouraba; shorbat (show-ra-bah) Arabic for soup.

shouting Australian slang for buying a round of drinks.

shoyu (SHOH-yoo) A sweet Japanese soy sauce.

shpik (sch'peek) Russian for bacon.

shpinat (shpee-natt) Russian for spinach.

shraab (sah-ruhb) A Middle Eastern beverage of reduced, sweetened fruit juices.

shraak (shrah-hack) A thin, crispy unleavened Middle Eastern bread; it is typically used for layering foods or torn into shreds and used for eating chicken or lamb dishes.

shred To shave, grate, cut or otherwise reduce a food to relatively long, narrow pieces.

Shrewsbury cake A flat, round, crisp sugar cookie flavored with cinnamon, nutmeg or cardamom and caraway seeds.

shrimp Any of several varieties of crustaceans found worldwide, particularly in the Atlantic and Pacific Oceans and Gulf of Mexico; generally, they have 10 legs, a shell that can be light brown, pink, red, grayish-white, yellow, gray-green or dark green, a lean, white flesh and a rich, sweet flavor; usually sold according to count (number per pound) and categorized as colossal (10 or less per pound) jumbo (11–15), extra large (16–20), large (21–30), medium (31–35), small (36–45), miniature (about 100) and titi (about 400); significant varieties, which are generally distinguished by shell color, include brown, pink, white, Caribbean white, sea bob and royal red shrimps. *See* prawn *and* rock shrimp.

shrimp, dried Small, pinkish-orange, dried shrimp, usually rehydrated before being used as a flavoring in many Asian and Latin American dishes.

shrimp and grits An American Southeastern dish of shrimp sautéed with onions and green pepper, simmered in chicken or shrimp broth and served over grits; usually served at breakfast.

shrimp boil *See* crab boil.

shrimp chips Dried wafers of shrimp and tapioca; deep-fried and eaten as snacks in China and Southeast Asia; also known as prawn crackers.

shrimps de Jonghe An American dish of shrimps flavored with garlic, sherry, parsley, cayenne and paprika, topped with buttered bread crumbs and baked.

shrimp deveiner A tool with a handle and a curved blade with a serrated tip; the tool follows the arc of the shrimp's shell; as it is pushed from the head to the tail, the ridged edge removes the intestinal vein while the upper edge cuts the shell.

shrimp deveiner

shrimp roe, dried *See* dried shrimp roe.

shrimp scampi (SKAM-pee) *See* scampi.

shrinkage 1. Loss of weight or volume during storage or preparation of a food; it is usually caused by a loss of moisture. 2. Loss of merchandise or supplies because of theft.

shrink wrap *v.* To use a plastic, self-adhering wrapping material to cover a food; the wrap conforms to the shape of the food or its container and helps prevent contamination and moisture loss. *n.* The self-adhering wrapping.

Shrub 1. A drink popular in colonial America; it is made of rum or brandy, sugar and orange or lemon juice, aged in a glass, crockery or wooden container and then strained and served over ice, sometimes diluted with water or soda water. 2. A drink made by adding acidulated fruit juice to water.

shtopor (sh-toh-pore) Russian for corkscrew.

shu (shoe) Chinese for ripe (fruit).

shubbak al habayb (shoe-back ahl ah-bah-hib) Arabic for lovers' windows and used to describe small, sweet fried waffles dusted with confectioners' sugar.

shucài (shoe-cah-ee) Chinese for vegetables.

shuck *v.* To remove the edible part of a food (e.g., clam meat, a pea or ear of corn) from its shell, pod or husk. *n.* A shell, pod or husk.

shucking knife *See* oyster knife.

shui (shoe-ee) Chinese for water.

shui dòufù (shoe-ee doo-foo) Chinese silk bean curd.

shui duan fen (shui hian fen) A paste of cornstarch and water used as a thickener in most Chinese dishes that have a sauce.

shuiguo (shoe-ee-goo-oh) Chinese for fruit.

shuiguo zhi (shoe-ee-goo dzih) Chinese for juice.

shui mo fen (shoe-ee moh fahn) Chinese water-ground rice flour (both long-grain and glutinous rice).

shuk-ti (shook-tee) Hindi for oyster.

shun (shoon) A Japanese term for any food in season and at the peak of freshness, quality and usually abundance.

shungiku (SHUNG-ghee-koo) Japanese for chrysanthemum or dandelion leaves.

shunkleesh (shuun-klee'shah) A Syrian cow's milk cottage cheese–style cheese.

shutome A broadbill swordfish found off Hawaii; it has a pinkish flesh, a high fat content and a mild flavor and weighs 10–600 lb. (4.5–27.5 kg).

shy (shay'ah) Arabic for tea.

shy ma'qirfee (shay'ah mah-kwer-fah) A Middle Eastern drink of tea flavored with cinnamon.

siagi (sea-ah-gee) Swahili for butter.

Siamese gourd A variety of squash with a striped, white-spotted green skin and a stringy, cinnamon-flavored flesh; often used to make jam; also known as angel's hair squash.

sianliha (si-ahn-LI-haa) Finnish for pork.

Siberia Slang for the area of a restaurant, bar, nightclub or the like that is considered by some to offer a socially undesirable location or poor seating; also known as the doghouse.

Siberian cherry *See* cornelian cherry.

Sicilian-style Californian olive A firm, green olive packed in vinegar brine with hot peppers.

sicilienne, sauce (see-see-l'yehn) A French compound sauce made from a demi-glaze flavored with game glaze or game stock, finished with Marsala and garnished with fried onion rings.

Sidamo Arabica coffee beans grown in Ethiopia; the beverage is sweet and has a floral aroma.

side Either bilateral half of a beef or pork carcass.

sideboard A serving table in a dining room, sometimes with a marble top and often having one or two narrow drawers in the apron.

Sidecar A cocktail made of brandy, an orange-flavored liqueur and lemon juice; shaken and strained into a cocktail glass.

side dish The name given to a dish such as a starch or vegetable that accompanies the main dish or entrée; usually served in a separate dish.

side masking The technique of coating only the sides of a cake with garnish.

sidemeats *See* variety meats.

side order An à la carte menu item intended to be ordered as part of or an accompaniment to an entrée or main dish.

sidra (see-draw) Spanish for cider.

sieden (see-den) German for bringing to a boil and then simmering.

Siena cake *See* panforte.

sienet (SIAY-nayt) Finnish for mushrooms.

sierra (see-air-rah) The lowest grade of Spanish saffron; it contains numerous yellow strands mixed with the red strands. *See* mancha *and* rio.

Sierra Ibores *See* Ibores.

sieve *v.* 1. To strain a liquid from a food through the fine mesh or perforated holes of a strainer or sieve. 2. To rub or press food through a sieve or strainer with a utensil such as the back of a spoon. *n.* A utensil with perforated holes or fine mesh wire used for straining a liquid from a food. *See* wire mesh strainer.

sift To pass dry ingredients, such as flour and baking powder, through a sieve or sifter to remove lumps and blend and aerate the ingredients.

sifter A handheld utensil used to sift dry ingredients, especially flour; it consists of a cylinder with four curved rods connected to a hand crank; the rods brush the contents through a fine mesh screen; battery-powered models are available; also known as a flour sifter.

sifter

siga (see-gah) Ethiopian for meat.

signature item A unique or typical food or beverage item prepared in an atypical fashion for which an establishment or person is known (e.g., a signature drink or signature dessert); also known as a speciality item.

sikai (sea-ky) Hindi for to roast.

sikana *See* cassabanana.

sikar (sue-carh) Arabic for sugar.

Sikes A system for measuring the alcohol content of beverages; in Great Britain, 1 degree of proof equals 0.57% alcohol (e.g., a 70 proof beverage contains 40% alcohol by volume); a beverage intended for export to the United States is marked with the American proof system. *See* proof.

siki (see-key) Swahili for vinegar.

sikotakia (shee-koo-tah-khia) Greek for liver.

siksikosh (seek-sea-kosh) An Ethiopian beef stew made with ribs.

sild (seel) Danish and Norwegian for herring.

silgochu (sil-go-choo) Fine threads of dried red chile used in many Korean dishes.

silica aerogel A food additive used as an antifoaming agent.

silicon A trace element used for various biological functions; found in many foods.

silicon dioxide A food additive used as an anticaking agent in processed foods such as table salt and coffee whiteners.

silicone baking mat A thin, flexible sheet of reusable siliconized plastic with a nonstick surface; it is heat resistant and used to line sheet pans.

silicone paper Paper coated on both sides with a nonstick surface of silicone able to withstand very high temperatures; it is used for lining baking pans.

silk tofu *See* kinugoshi.

silky A wine-tasting term for a soft, lush, velvety, finely textured wine.

sill (seel) Swedish for herring.

silli (SEE-li) Finnish for herring.

silq (silk) Arabic for Swiss chard.

silungur (sill-ung-ar) Icelandic for trout.

Silvaner (sil-VAH-ner) German for Sylvaner.

Silver Bullet 1. An extremely cold, dry Vodka Martini. 2. Slang for Coors Light beer, which is packaged in silver-colored cans.

silver ears A mushroom similar to cloud ears but with a lighter, off-white color.

silver eel *See* eel, American.

Silver Fizz A gin fizz with egg white added.

silver fungus *See* white fungus.

silver hake *See* whiting.

silver kale A variety of kale with pale greenish-white, broad stalks and pale green leaves with a silvery bloom.

silver leaf The pure metal beaten into a gossamer-thin square and sold in packages interleaved with tissue paper; it is edible in small quantities and is used to decorate rice dishes in East Indian cuisines as well as desserts, confections and candies; also known as vark.

silver mullet *See* mullet.

silver needle *See* Ngunjum.

silver noodles *See* cellophane noodles.

silver onion; silver-skin onion A very small onion with a silvery skin and white flesh; it is generally pickled.

silver perch *See* whiting.

silver pin noodles Noodles made by rubbing small balls of wheat starch dough across an oiled board to form the long, nail-shaped noodles; used in Asian cuisines.

silver salmon *See* coho salmon.

silverside 1. A British cut of the beef carcass; it is a lean, tough outside thigh muscle. 2. A piece of lean salt beef.

silverskin *See* elastin.

silver sprouts Mung bean sprouts with the roots and seed pods removed; they are usually used as a garnish.

silverware Eating utensils such as forks, knives and spoons, made from or plated with silver. *See* flatware.

Similkameen A grape-growing and wine-producing region in the southern interior of Canada's British Columbia province; a wide variety of grapes are grown, including Chardonnay, Pinot Blanc, Merlot, Cabernet Franc and Pinot Noir.

simit (see-mit) A Turkish yeast dough in the shape of a ring; it is dipped in molasses water or pekmez and sesame seeds and baked; also then known as sesame rings.

simla mirch *See* hari murch.

simmering 1. A moist-heat cooking method that uses convection to transfer heat from a hot (approximately. 185–205°F [85–96°C]) liquid to the food submerged in it. 2. Maintaining the temperature of a liquid just below the boiling point.

simnel cake (SEHM-nul) 1. A rich, lavishly decorated British spice cake made with dried and candied fruit and layers of almond paste. 2. A light biscuitlike bread made from flour that was boiled and then baked; popular during the Middle Ages.

simple buttercream *See* buttercream.

simple carbohydrates A group of sweet, soluble and digestible carbohydrates that includes single sugars (monosaccharides) such as glucose and fructose and double sugars (disaccharides) such as sucrose, lactose and maltose.

Simplesse The proprietary name of a fat substitute made from egg and milk proteins and used in processed foods.

simple sugar *See* monosaccharide.

simple syrup A syrup made by mixing equal parts of sugar and water and then boiling until the sugar dissolves; it is used for glazing and moistening cakes and pastries and in beverages and sorbets; also known as bar syrup. *See* sugar syrup.

simsim (seem-seem) Swahili for sesame seed.

simsimiya (seem-sea-me-ah) A Middle Eastern confection, similar to a brittle, made with sesame seeds and honey.

simsum (seem-tzum) Arabic for sesame seed.

sin crianza (seen cree-AHN-zah) *See* crianza.

sindootan *See* peteh.

Singapore Sling A cocktail made of gin, cherry brandy, Cointreau, Benedictine and citrus juices; it is served in a cocktail glass with ice and garnished with a pineapple wedge and maraschino cherry.

singe 1. To remove excess feathers when cleaning fowl by scorching the skin. 2. To burn slightly or superficially.

singer To add flour to the pan used for browning meat before any liquid is added; it is a process often used when thickening meat stews.

singhara (sing-ha-ra) Hindi for water caltrop.

singing hinny A northern English griddle cake made with flour, ground rice, lard, currants and milk.

single-acting baking powder *See* baking powder, single-acting.

single cream *See* cream, single.

single-malt Scotch whisky A whisky produced from malt whisky alone (no grain whisky is added) and made by a single distillery; it has a very full body and flavor; also known as all-malt whisky.

single sugar *See* monosaccharide.

sinigang (see-nee-gang) A tart Filipino souplike meat or fish dish; fruits such as green or ripe guavas, tamarind, belimbing and kalamansi are added as sour flavoring agents.

siphon A thick fleshy tube found in certain varieties of clams (especially Pacific clams) that cannot be retracted and through which the clam takes in and expels water.

siphon squash *See* Hercules' bludgeon gourd.

sippets; sipets (SEHP-pehtz) 1. Traditionally, toasted bread soaked in gravy, sauce or wine; also known as sops. 2. A soup containing such bread. 3. Triangular pieces of toast served with melted cheese or minced beef dishes in 19th-century England.

Siraz A semisoft Serbian cheese usually made from whole cow's milk and ripened in a wooden container; it has a mellow flavor and compact body.

sirih *See* betel quid.

sirkaa (shir-kah) Hindi for vinegar.

sirloin A primal section of the beef carcass; it is located between the short loin and round and contains a portion of the backbone and hip bone and a portion of the tenderloin muscle; other than the tenderloin, the meat is less tender than that of the strip loin; it is used to produce fabricated cuts such as the sirloin butt and strip loin steak.

sirloin butt A subprimal cut of the beef primal sirloin; this moderately tough cut consists of several muscles from the posterior end of the backbone and is used to fabricate roasts and steaks.

sirloin pork chop A fabricated cut of the pork primal loin; it is a chop cut from the posterior end of the loin.

sirloin steak *See* culotte de boeuf.

sirloin tip *See* loin tip.

sirop (see-rho) French for syrup.

sirop d'amandes (see-rho da-mahnd) *See* almond syrup.

sirop de cassis (see-rho day cah'ss) *See* black currant syrup.

sirop de citron (see-rho day see-trohn) A syrup made from lemons; it has a mild, lemony zestiness and a low acid content and is used for cocktails and cooking.

sirop de groseilles (see-rho duh gro-zay-yuh) *See* red currant syrup.

siroper (see-rho'p) French for to soak in syrup and used to describe the addition of a flavored syrup to an item such as a genoise to moisten or flavor it.

sitron (si-TROON) Norwegian for lemon.

sitsaron (sit-sa-ron) A crisp, dry Filipino snack made from pig skins or intestines.

siu loon bau (see-who loon bah-who) A Shanghai (Chinese) dumpling filled with a soupy mixture of minced pork and shrimp and served with finely shredded young ginger and a red vinegar dipping sauce.

siu mai (see-you mah-ee) Chinese steamed open-faced dumplings shaped with a waist near the top; filled with minced pork or shrimp and pork.

siwalan *See* palm nut.

six-pack A market form of six cans or bottles of a beverage (usually beer or a soft drink) sold together, linked by a plastic grip or in a cardboard carrier.

sixpenny piece A British measuring scoop used for dry ingredients (especially baking soda); equal to 1/2 teaspoon.

sizzle The hissing sound characteristic of frying fat.

sizzling platter A Chinese–American presentation method in which cooked foods are placed on a heated metal platter at table side; when the moist foods come in contact with the hot metal, they sizzle.

sizzling rice soup A Chinese broth with chicken or pork and vegetables served in bowls over deep-fried rice cakes; the cakes sizzle and pop when the broth is added.

sjalottløk (shal-ott-luhk) Norwegian for shallot.

sjokolade (shoo-kall-alad) Norwegian for chocolate.

skabu kapostu supa (skah-boo kahpos-too sue-paw) A Latvian soup made with sauerkraut, pork, onions and pearl barley and garnished with sour cream.

skarp saus (skahrp sohs) A Norwegian sauce similar to Worcestershire sauce.

skate A kite-shaped saltwater fish found worldwide; the winglike pectoral fins have a firm, white flesh with a mild, sweet flavor; also known as a ray.

skatole A food additive with a strong, meaty flavor and aroma; used as a flavoring agent.

skeletal meat Flesh taken from the muscles attached to an animal's bone structure.

skembe (skeh-mpeh) Greek for tripe.

skewer *v.* To impale small pieces of meat or other food on a skewer. *n.* 1. A long, narrow, sharp-pointed metal or wooden pin that is put through the center of a large piece of food (particularly meat) or several small pieces of meat in order for them to be cooked together. 2. A small, slender metal pin that is used to hold meat together when it is stuffed. 3. A spit.

skewings Confetti-like pieces of pure gold leaf that can be sprinkled onto pastries and confections.

skillet *See* frying pan.

skim To remove the upper part of a liquid while leaving the rest intact (e.g., removing fat from a liquid or scum from a soup or stew).

skimmed milk cheese *See* Holsteiner Maigerkäse.

skimmer A long-handled tool with a shallow mesh or perforated bowl; used for skimming stocks and removing food from a liquid.

skimmer clam *See* surf clam.

skimmer

skim milk Whole milk with its milkfat content reduced to 0.5%; also known as nonfat milk. *See* lowfat milk *and* two percent milk.

skim milk, canned Concentrated skim milk with at least 18% milk solids and no more than 0.2–0.3% milkfat; sold in cans.

skim milk, evaporated *See* milk, evaporated skim.

skin *v.* To remove the skin, peel or outer layer from a food, such as poultry, fish, fruits or vegetables, before or after cooking. *n.* 1. The membranous tissue forming the outer covering of an animal; in vertebrates, it consists of the epidermis and dermis. 2. An animal pelt. 3. A usually thin outer covering of a whole food (particularly produce and cheese) or a prepared food (e.g., sausage skin). 4. A container for liquids, often wine, made of animal skin.

skin contact A red wine–making procedure in which the grape juice is kept in contact with the skins to extract flavor, aroma, tannin and other elements that affect the character and balance of the wine.

skink 1. An Irish or Scottish stew or soup made from any meat and a variety of green or root vegetables and seasonings. 2. An archaic British term for essence or extract.

skinka (SKIN-kah) Swedish for ham.

skinke (SKEEN-ker) Danish and Norwegian for ham.

skinke med Italiensk salat (skin-ka mad ita-lee-ansk saw-latt) A Danish smørrebrød dish of cooked ham with a salad of carrots and peas in mayonnaise (called salad Italian style) on white bread.

skinless-shankless ham *See* ham, skinless-shankless.

skinny Slang for a coffee drink made with nonfat milk.

skipjack tuna A variety of tuna found in the Pacific Ocean from Chile to California; it has a dark blue skin that becomes silvery on the belly and black to dusky stripes on the lower sides, an ivory-pink flesh and an average market weight of 4–24 lb. (1.8–10.8 kg); often used for canning; also known as a striped tuna.

skirts and bodices An Irish dish of pork trimmings and pickled spareribs cooked with pork kidneys, root vegetables and herbs; usually served with potatoes boiled in their skins and mashed turnips.

skirt steak 1. A fabricated cut of the beef primal short plate; the lean flat cut has a tough, stringy texture and a good flavor. 2. A British cut of the beef carcass; it is cut from the flank.

skive (sheh-ve) Norwegian for slices.

skiver pan A pan used for making round, fried, doughnut-like cakes; it has seven rounded indentations, which are greased before the cake batter is added. *See* aebleskiver.

skje (sh-oye) Norwegian for spoon.

skorthalia; skordalia (score-tah-lee-ah) A Greek sauce generally made from garlic, lemon and nuts such as walnuts, almonds and pignoli.

skudahkharis (skoo-daw-kah-rees) A Somali dish consisting of lamb and rice flavored with onions, tomatoes, garlic, parsley, cumin, cloves, cinnamon and cardamom.

skunk egg Cowboy slang for an onion.

skunk grape *See* fox grape.

skunky A beer-tasting term for an unpleasant odor detected in beer that has been left for a long period in direct sunlight or a keg of unpasteurized beer that has been left unrefrigerated.

sky juice A Jamaican beverage of tropical fruit–flavored syrup poured over shaved ice.

skyr (sker) An Icelandic dish made from soured skimmed milk; similar to a thin cottage cheese or yogurt, it is served with sugar, cream and bilberries as a dessert.

Skyr (skeer) A Scandinavian cow's milk product with characteristics of both cheese and yogurt; often thinned with milk, whipped to a creamy consistency and sprinkled with sugar.

sla (slah) Dutch for lettuce or salad.

slab An imprecisely used term to describe a large, thick slice of a food (e.g., bread, bacon, spareribs, pie or cheese).

slab bacon Unsliced bacon, usually cut from the hog's belly.

slack dough A yeast dough that contains more water than it should; the excess water impairs handling.

sladkiy (slahd-key) Russian for sweet.

slake To mix cornstarch or arrowroot with water so that it can be used as a thickener.

slaked lime *See* calcium hydrate and calcium hydroxide.

slata fel fel (slah-tah fell fell) A Moroccan salad of grilled bell peppers dressed with lemon juice, olive oil, cumin, parsley and black pepper.

slatko (slut-koh) A Balkan preserve made from raspberries, strawberries or watermelon rind.

slaw *See* coleslaw.

sleeve-fish British for calamari.

slice *v.* To cut a food into relatively broad, thin pieces. *n.* 1. The cut pieces of the food. 2. A triangular spatula used for lifting, especially cakes and fish.

slicer A knife with a long, thin flexible or rigid blade used primarily for slicing cooked meats; the tip can be round or pointed.

slicer

slicer, electric A tool used to cut meats, cheeses, vegetables and other items into uniform slices; the food is placed on a carrier and passed against a high-speed circular blade; the slices are then gathered on the opposite side of the blade.

slicer, serrated A knife with a long, thin flexible or rigid blade used primarily for slicing bread or pastry items; the blade has a serrated edge and its tip is round or pointed.

slicing tomato *See* beefsteak tomato.

slider A small, sometimes square, hamburger topped with chopped, grilled onions; popular in the American Midwest.

slimaki (sy-lee-mah-kee) Polish for snails.

Sling 1. A long drink, typically gin, diluted with water and lemon juice and sweetened with sugar or sugar syrup. 2. A warm cocktail made of two-thirds strong beer, sweetened with sugar, molasses or dried pumpkin, topped with rum, stirred with a loggerhead and served in a mug.

Slipcoat; Slipcote A soft cream cheese–style cheese made in England from cow's milk; it is aged briefly between cabbage leaves; when ripe, the surface softens and has a tendency to slip off.

slipper lobster A variety of small lobster found off Hawaii; it has a relatively large tail and small claws, a brownish shell and a white flesh with a rich, sweet flavor.

slippery jack Related to the bolete, this large meaty mushroom (*Suillus luteus*) has a slimy cap and a distinctive musty flavor; often used to augment boletes (cepes); also known as a forest mushroom.

sliva (slee-vah) Russian for plum.

sliver *v.* To cut into long, narrow strips. *n.* A long, thin piece of food such as cheese or meat or a small piece of pie.

sliver cutting A method of cutting in which the ingredient is sliced into slabs 3/16 in. (5 cm) thick and the pieces are stacked together and then cut into strips of the same width.

slivki (SLIHV-key) Russian for buttermilk and cream.

Slivovitz (SLIHV-uh-vihts) A dry, slightly bitter plum brandy made in the Balkans.

Slivovitz Fizz A cocktail made of lime juice, sugar syrup, club soda and Slivovitz or plum brandy; garnished with a plum slice.

sloeberry; sloe The wild plum that is the fruit of the blackthorn (*Prunus spinosa*); it is purple skinned and has a tart, yellow flesh; also known as blackthorn plum.

sloe gin A sloeberry-flavored liqueur.

Sloe Gin Fizz A cocktail made of sloe gin, lemon juice, sugar and soda water.

sloppy Joe A dish of ground beef, onions and green peppers, flavored with ketchup and other seasonings and served on a hamburger bun; also known as loose meat sandwich and tavern.

slow food A term used in Italy and other parts of Europe to describe a restaurant that uses traditional preparation and cooking methods as well as quality ingredients.

slow oven An oven set to a temperature of 300–325°F (148.8–162.8°C). *See* hot oven *and* moderate oven.

slumgullion (sluhm-GUHL-yuhn) Slang from California's Gold Rush days for a weak alcoholic beverage or a meat stew made from leftovers.

slump A baked cobbler-type dessert made with fresh fruit and a biscuit or dumpling dough topping.

slurry A mixture of raw starch and a cold liquid used for thickening.

smaiskeh (smee-keh) Arabic for filet of lamb.

småkaker (smaw-kah-ker) Norwegian for cookies.

small A wine-tasting term for a wine without distinction or body; it can nonetheless be agreeable and enjoyable.

smallage; smellage *See* lovage.

small beer An English term for low-alcohol-content beer.

small intestine Divided into three sections (the duodenum, jejunum and ileum), the wall is lined with minute fingerlike projections (called villi) through which the products of digestion, such as monosaccharides, fatty acids and amino acids, are absorbed into the bloodstream.

small jumbo A marketing term for a 2 1/4- to 2 1/2-lb. (1- to 1.2-kg) lobster. *See* chicken lobster, deuce, heavy chicken, heavy select, jumbo, quarter *and* select.

small-leaved lime tree A tall deciduous tree (*Tilis cordata*) with fragrant yellow-white flowers called linden blossoms; the blossoms are used to make a tisane; also known as a linden tree.

smallmouth buffalo fish *See* buffalo fish.

small sauces Any of a large variety of French sauces made by adding one or more ingredients to a leading sauce; they are grouped together into families based on their leading sauce; some small sauces have a variety of uses, and others are traditional accompaniments to specific foods; also known as compound sauces. *See* leading sauces.

small sugar pumpkin A pumpkin variety used principally for pie filling.

small T-bone A fabricated cut of the beef primal short loin; it is one of the first steaks cut from the small end of the primal.

Smash A cocktail made of liquor, muddled sugar and ice cubes; served in an old-fashioned glass.

smashed Slang for intoxicated.

smeed (shmead) Arabic for semolina.

smell *v.* To perceive an odor through the nose by means of the olfactory nerves. *n.* An odor or scent.

smellage *See* lovage.

smelt A variety of anadromous fish; they generally have a slender body, a silvery skin, large, fanglike teeth, an average market length of 4–7 in. (10–17.5 cm), a high fat content and a rich, mild flavor; significant varieties include the eulachon, rainbow smelt and whitebait.

smen; smenn; smeun (sa-men) Clarified butter made from ewe's milk; it is used in Arabic and Maghrebi cuisines; stored in earthenware pots, it develops a flavor reminiscent of almonds as it ages.

smetana; smitane (smyee-TAH-n'ya) Russian for sour cream.

Smithfield ham A country-cured ham from the Smithfield, Virginia, area; it comes from hogs raised on hickory nuts, peanuts and acorns and is processed by dry curing, seasoning, hickory smoking and aging for 6–12 months; the lean flesh has a dark color and a rich, salty flavor.

Smjör (sm-uhr) An Icelandic cream cheese–style cheese made from cow's milk.

smoke curing *See* smoking.

smoked butt A subprimal cut of the pork primal Boston butt; it is a smoked roast.

smoked cheese A cheese (usually one of the American cheeses) characterized by a smoky flavor and aroma imparted by (1) adding a chemical or liquid smoke to the curds, (2) adding smoked salt to the curds or (3) smoking the cheese.

smoked ham *See* ham, smoked.

smoked salmon Salmon cured by either hot smoking or cold smoking; often, the origin of the salmon is added to the name (e.g., Irish smoked salmon). *See* kippered salmon, lox *and* Nova.

smoke flavoring A food additive made synthetically or derived from burning hardwoods; it is used as a smoke flavoring in bacon, ham and sausages.

smoke point The temperature at which a fat begins to break down, releasing an acrid blue gas and giving a burned flavor to foods.

smoking A method of preserving and flavoring foods by exposing them to smoke; this includes (1) cold smoking, in which the foods are not fully cooked, and (2) hot smoking, in which the foods are cooked; also known as smoke curing. *See* cold smoking *and* hot smoking.

smoky 1. A tasting term for a food that has been exposed to wood smoke. 2. A beer- and wine-tasting term for an aroma or flavor reminiscent of smoke; generally caused by aging the products in charred oak casks. 3. A tasting term for such an aroma or flavor in Scotch whisky caused by roasting the grains over peat.

smolt A salmon that is 2 years old and leaving the freshwater spawning grounds for the sea. *See* grilse.

smooth *v.* To make a surface even, level or unwrinkled. *adj.* 1. Free of surface projections (e.g., a smooth frosting). 2. Of a fine texture or even consistency (e.g., a smooth pudding). 3. A wine-tasting term for a soft, silky wine with a well-rounded texture; the opposite of astringent.

smooth cayenne pineapple A cylindrical pineapple with a golden, moderately unbumpy skin and a pale yellow flesh.

smooth ear shell abalone A variety of abalone found off Australia; it has a large, smooth, greenish-white ovoid shell and an ivory flesh with a chewy texture and mild flavor; also known as a green lip abalone.

smooth endive *See* endive, smooth.

smoothie A beverage made by puréeing fruits or vegetables with juice, yogurt, milk and/or ice cream to a thick consistency; nutrient supplements are sometimes added; served chilled.

smooth scallop *See* sea scallop.

smooth venus clams *See* brown venus clams.

smør (smurr) Norwegian for butter.

smör (smurr) Swedish for butter.

smørbrød (SMURR-brur) Norwegian for open-faced sandwich. *See* koldtbord.

smorchok (schmor-chohk) Russian for morel.

s'mores Confections made by sandwiching milk chocolate and marshmallows between graham crackers and heating the sandwich, often over an open fire, until the chocolate melts.

smörgåsbord (SMOHR-guhs-bohrd) Swedish for bread-and-butter table and used to describe a Swedish buffet of salads, open-faced sandwiches, cooked vegetables, pickled or marinated fish, sliced meats and cheeses. *See* koldtbord.

smorgasbord (smore-gas-bord) In the United States, a buffet of various hot and cold dishes.

smørrebrød (smoe-rae-bored) 1. A Danish buffet table of salads, open-faced sandwiches, cheeses and marinated fish. 2. An imprecisely used term for Danish open-faced sandwiches. *See* koldtbord.

smother A cooking method in which one food is completely covered with another food or sauce while baking or braising in a covered container.

smothered steak *See* Swiss steak.

Smyrna quince A variety of quince; the pear-shaped fruit has a golden yellow skin, a tender flesh and a rich flavor.

snack A small amount of food that is served or eaten informally, usually between meals.

snack foods A general category of foods intended for between meal eating; some are not particularly nutritious, and many are processed products with a high salt and/or fat content.

snail cup A small earthenware cup with a 2-oz. capacity used for baking a single snail, usually with a bit of garlic butter.

snail fork *See* escargot fork.

snail plate *See* escargot plate.

snails Univalve land animals found in warm to temperate climates worldwide; significant varieties include escargot de Bourgogne and escargot petit-gris.

snail tongs *See* escargot tongs.

Snakebite A drink made from equal amounts of cider and a pale beer (usually pale ale).

snake-head whiskey Cowboy slang for cheap whiskey.

snakeroot *See* bistort, common.

snap bean *See* green bean.

snaps Scandinavian for schnapps, referring to aquavit (akvavit).

Sneaky Pete A cocktail made of tequila, white crème de menthe, pineapple juice and lime or lemon juice; garnished with a lime slice.

snegle (sneh-gle) Norwegian for snail.

Snert (snaert) A Dutch pea soup made with dried peas, smoked sausages, bacon and pickled pork shank or pork chops and flavored with celery and leeks.

snickerdoodle A cookie with a crackly surface; usually flavored with cinnamon and nutmeg and coated in sugar before baking.

Snickers The proprietary name for a candy bar consisting of peanut butter nougat, caramel and peanuts coated with milk chocolate.

snifter A footed glass with a large balloon-shaped bowl that is larger at the bottom, tapering toward the top; used for fine brandy and also known as a brandy glass or brandy snifter.

snip *v.* 1. To cut foods (e.g., chives) into uniform lengths using kitchen shears. 2. To remove a leaf, bud, sprig or the like from a plant (often an herb) using a small pair of scissors. *n.* The item so cut.

snifter

snipe A large family of small game birds found worldwide; they generally have an average dressed weight of 2–10 oz. (56.7–283.5 g) and an excellent flavor; significant varieties include the common snipe, dowitcher, great snipe, jack snipe and red-breasted snipe.

snittebønner (snit-BEHRN-nehr) Norwegian for green beans.

snoober (sah-noo-bahr) Arabic for pine nuts.

snow ball A dessert consisting of a scoop of ice cream rolled in shredded coconut and topped with chocolate syrup.

snow cabbage *See* napa cabbage.

snow cod *See* pollock, Alaskan.

snow cone Scraped ice drizzled with a flavored syrup and served in a cone-shaped paper cup.

snow crab A variety of crab found in the Pacific Ocean from Alaska to Oregon; it has long, slender legs, a white flesh with vivid red markings, a delicate, succulent flavor and a tender texture; also known as queen crab, spider crab and tanner crab.

snow cream A snack made with freshly fallen snow that is quickly mixed with vanilla and sugar.

snow-dried tofu *See* kori dofu.

snowed black bean curd *See* shirataki.

snow eggs *See* oeufs à la neige.

snow fungus *See* white fungus.

snow pea A bean (*Pisum sativum* var. *macrocarpon*) with a bright green pod and small, paler green seeds; the thin, crisp pod and the tender, sweet seeds are eaten cooked or raw; also known as the Chinese snow pea and sugar pea.

soaked-curd cheese *See* washed-curd cheese.

soap 1. Any of a group of cleaning agents prepared by treating a fat with an alkali such as sodium or potassium hydroxide. *See* detergent. 2. A term used imprecisely for any cleaning agent.

soapy 1. A tasting term for a food or beverage that has an unpleasant flavor reminiscent of soap. 2. A wine-tasting term for a flat, unappetizing wine with a low acid content.

Soave (S'WAH-veh) A dry white wine made in Italy's Veneto region from a blend of Garganega and Trebbiano Toscano grapes; it has a pale, straw color and a light, clean, fresh flavor.

soba; soba noodles (so-BAH) Japanese noodles made from buckwheat and wheat flour; they are thin, flat and grayish-brown in color.

sobreasada; sobreassada (soh-bray-ah-sah-dah) A highly seasoned, soft Spanish sausage made from chorizo and pork fat, seasoned with sweet pepper.

sobrebarriga (soh-bray-bahr-ree-gah) A South and Central American cut of the beef carcass; it is a flank steak.

sobremesa (soh-breh-meh-za) Portuguese for dessert.

socarat (soh-cah-rah) The Catalonian Spanish term for the lumps of rice sticking to the bottom of a paella pan; they are considered a delicacy.

socca (soh-kah) Pancakes from Nice, France; they are thick and coarse and made from chickpea flour.

sochu; shochu (SHO-choo) A triple-distilled Japanese spirit made from a mash of barley, corn, wheat, sugarcane and/or sweet potatoes; aged in white oak barrels; it is clear with a slightly sweet, smooth, distinctive aroma and flavor.

socker (sok-KERR) Swedish for sugar.

sockeye salmon A variety of salmon found in the Pacific Ocean from Washington to Alaska; it has a greenish-blue skin with silvery sides and belly, no spots, a deep red flesh, a high fat content, a rich flavor and an average market weight of 3–12 lb. (1.4–5.4 kg); generally used for canning; also known as blueback salmon and red salmon.

sock mai jai (suk mai jai) Chinese for corn.

soda 1. Slang for any nonalcoholic, flavored and/or colored, carbonated drink; used principally in the American Northeast; also known as soft drink and soda pop. *See* pop. 2. Another name for baking soda. 3. A fountain drink made with scoops of ice cream topped with a flavored soft drink or soda water and a flavored syrup.

soda bread *See* Irish soda bread.

soda fountain 1. The equipment necessary for preparing and serving sundaes, sodas, ice cream and the like. 2. The counter, sometimes part of a pharmacy or other store, from which such concoctions are served.

soda jerk A person who prepares sodas, ice cream items and other concoctions behind a soda fountain.

soda out To finish a cocktail by topping it with soda.

soda pop *See* soda.

soda water *See* seltzer.

sodium A major mineral principally used as an electrolyte and to assist transmitting nerve impulses; significant sources include salt, soy sauce and many processed foods. *See* salt.

sodium acetate A food additive used as a flavoring agent, flavoring adjuvant and/or pH control agent in processed foods such as breakfast cereals, grain products, snack foods, fats, candies, jams and jellies.

sodium acid pyrophosphate A food additive used as a leavening agent and preservative in doughnuts and biscuits.

sodium alginate A food additive derived from certain brown kelp; used as a stabilizer and/or thickener, especially in products containing chocolate.

sodium aluminosilicate A food additive used as an anticaking agent.

sodium aluminum phosphate, acidic A food additive used as a leavening agent in cake and pancake mixes.

sodium aluminum sulfate A food additive used as a leavening agent in baked goods; it needs heat for activation.

sodium ascorbate *See* ascorbic acid.

sodium benzoate A food additive used as an antimicrobial agent, flavoring agent and/or adjuvant in acidic processed foods such as fruit juices.

sodium bicarbonate A food additive used as a leavening agent; also known as baking soda.

sodium calcium aluminosilicate A food additive used as an anticaking agent.

sodium carbonate A food additive used as an antioxidant, curing and pickling agent, flavoring agent, flavoring adjuvant and/or pH control agent.

sodium caseinate A food additive used as a protein source and as an emulsifier and whiting agent in coffee whiteners, nondairy whipped products, processed meats and desserts.

sodium citrate A food additive used as a pH control agent, especially in tart-flavored foods.

sodium diacetate A food additive used as an antimicrobial agent, pH control agent, flavoring agent and/or adjuvant in processed foods such as baked goods, snack foods, fats, candies, soups, meat products and gravies.

sodium erythorbate *See* ascorbic acid.

sodium hydroxide A food additive used as a processing aid and/or pH control agent.

sodium lactate A food additive used as an emulsifier, flavor enhancer, flavoring agent, flavoring adjuvant, humectant and/or pH control agent.

sodium lauryl sulfate A food additive used as an emulsifier in or with egg whites, a wetting agent in fats, a surfactant in beverages and a whipping agent for confections.

sodium mono- and dimethyl naphthalene sulfonates Food additives used to reduce hardness and aid sedimentation in potable water systems, to assist in the washing and lye peeling of fruits and vegetables and as anticaking agents in sodium nitrite.

sodium nitrate A food additive used as a preservative, curing agent and/or color stabilizer, especially in cured and/or smoked fish and meats; often used with sodium nitrite; some evidence suggests that it may be carcinogenic.

sodium nitrite A food additive used as an antibacterial agent and/or color stabilizer, especially in cured and/or smoked fish and meats; often used with sodium nitrate; some evidence suggests that it may be carcinogenic.

sodium propionate A food additive used as an antimicrobial agent, flavoring agent and/or adjuvant.

sodium saccharin *See* saccharin.

sodium sesquicarbonate A food additive used as a pH control agent.

sodium silicoaluminate A food additive used as an anticaking and conditioning agent in salt, cake mixes, sugar, nondairy creamers and dry mixes; also known as sodium aluminosilicate.

sodium sorbate A food additive used as a preservative.

sodium stearyl fumarate A food additive used as a dough conditioner in yeast-leavened products, a stabilizer in non-yeast-leavened products and a conditioning agent for starch-thickened products and dehydrated potato products.

sodium stearyl lactylate A food additive used as a dough strengthener in baked goods and as an emulsifier and/or stabilizer in processed foods such as nondairy creamers, snack dips, cheese substitutes and gravies.

sodium sulfite, sodium bisulfite and sodium metabisulfite Food additives used as preservatives.

sodium tartrate and sodium potassium tartrate Food additives used as pH control agents and/or emulsifiers.

sodium thiosulfate A food additive used as a formulation aid in table salt and beverages.

soep (soop) Dutch for soup.

sofrito; sofritto (so-FREE-toe) 1. Spanish for fried. 2. A Caribbean and Central American sauce made from salt pork, annatto oil, onions, garlic, green peppers and tomatoes cooked in oil and flavored with cilantro and oregano. *See* battuto. 3. A Greek dish of a steak cooked in a garlic sauce.

soft 1. A tasting term for a food that is mild, bland and usually smooth. 2. A coffee-tasting term used to describe a coffee with a low acidity level. 3. A wine-tasting term for a mild or even dull wine that is neither harsh nor green; softness can be appealing, provided that it does not result in a flat wine. 4. A food that is easily molded, cut or worked; it yields to pressure.

soft-ball stage A test for the density of sugar syrup: the point at which a drop of boiling sugar will form a soft, sticky ball when dropped in cold water; equivalent to approximately 234–240°F (112–115°C) on a candy thermometer.

soft-boiled egg; soft-cooked egg An egg simmered in its shell, at least until some of the white has solidified, usually 3–5 minutes. *See* hard-boiled egg.

soft cheeses *See* cheeses, soft.

soft copy *See* dupe.

soft-crack stage A test for the density of sugar syrup: the point at which a drop of boiling sugar will separate into firm but bendable strands when dropped in cold water; equivalent to approximately 270–290°F (132–143°C) on a candy thermometer.

soft diet A hospital diet in which the food is seasoned with salt and pepper but no other seasonings, portion size is carefully controlled and many of the foods are puréed.

soft drink A beverage that does not contain alcohol; it is usually carbonated, flavored, sweetened and/or colored. *See* carbonated beverage.

soften To prepare a food, usually butter, by leaving it at room temperature until it becomes pliable but not runny.

softener A type of food additive used for its hydroscopic properties; also known as a plasticizer.

soft peak A mixture of eggs and sugar whipped to the point at which it forms a peak that is wet and has a tendency to fold over; also known as wet peak.

soft-ripened cheese *See* surface-ripened cheese.

soft roe *See* milt *and* roe.

soft-shell turtle A variety of turtle found in North America, Africa and Asia; the carapace and plastron are covered with a soft skin and the tannish-green flesh has a chewy texture and excellent flavor.

soft soybean curds *See* tofu pudding.

soft tofu *See* kinugoshi.

soft water *See* water, soft.

sogan dolma (soh-gahn dol-mah) A Balkan dish of onions stuffed with meat and rice and then braised.

sogan piyazi (soh-gahn pee-yah-zee) A Turkish salad of salted sliced onions flavored with parsley and sumac and served with kebabs or kofte.

sògliola (SAW-lyoa-lah) Italian for sole.

soguk mantar bugulama (soo-gook mahn-tor boo-goo-law-mah) A Turkish hors d'oeuvre of pickled mushrooms.

sohleb (so-leb) A Tunisian dish consisting of a millet porridge flavored with confectioners' sugar, ginger and orange flower water; it is a traditional Ramadan dish.

soi *See* soybean.

soja *See* soybean.

sok (sohk) Russian for juice.

sol (sohl) Russian for salt.

sola (so-lah) Polish for sole.

sole A family of saltwater flatfish related to the flounder family; they generally have a white belly, a brown to gray skin on top, a finely textured, pearly white flesh and a sweet, distinctive flavor; the most significant variety is Dover sole; many flounder harvested in American waters are also marketed as sole (e.g., petrale sole and English sole). *See* flounder.

sole, Dover 1. A flatfish found in the English Channel and North Sea; it has an average market weight of 1–2 lb. (450–900 g), a firm, white flesh and a pleasant flavor; also known as black sole (especially in Ireland) and true Dover sole. 2. A flatfish found in the Pacific Ocean from California to Alaska; it has a slender body covered with a heavy slime, an average market weight of 2–6 lb. (0.9–2.7 kg), a white flesh and a flavor inferior to that of true Dover sole.

sole bonne femme (bohn FEHM) A French dish of poached sole served with a white wine sauce and lemon juice and garnished with small onions and mushrooms.

sole Marguery (mar-geh-ree) A French dish of sole poached in white wine and fish stock, garnished with mussels, shrimps and a white sauce and browned.

solera (soh-LEH-rah) A system for blending and maturing sherry; over several years, the sherry passes through five or six butts, with younger wines added to maintain consistent style and quality.

sole Thermidor (THUHR-mih-dohr) A French dish of sole poached in white wine and fish fumet and served with a sauce made from the cooking liquid seasoned with mustard.

sole Véronique (vay-roh-neek) A French dish of baked sole topped with a cream sauce, garnished with seedless white grapes and browned.

solid A wine-tasting term for a sound, firm, long-lasting wine that has the ability to improve with age.

solid molding A chocolate or candy molding technique using a two-part hinged mold; the mold is closed and filled with the candy mixture or melted chocolate; after it sets, the mold is opened, yielding a single, solid unit. *See* hollow molding.

solid pack Canned fruits, vegetables, fish or other products with little or no water added.

solid shortening Shortening that remains firm at room temperature. *See* shortening.

solid spoon *See* spoon, solid.

solöga (soh-loh-gah) Swedish for sun's eye and used to describe a chilled smörgåsbord dish consisting of chopped anchovies placed in the center of a shallow plate and surrounded by concentric circles of chopped onion, chopped beets, chopped parsley and cubed potatoes; a raw egg yolk is placed in the center.

solomillo (soh-loh-mee-yoh) Spanish for sirloin.

Solomon's seal A member of the lily family (*Polygonatum officinale*); its young shoots are eaten in the same way as asparagus.

soltetees; soltys A cake with a surprise filling; popular at banquets during the Middle Ages.

solubility The quality or property of a substance to be dissolved in a solution.

solute The substance dissolved in a solution.

solution A gas, liquid or solid in which another gas, liquid or solid is uniformly disbursed (dissolved) without chemical change (e.g., a solution of salt and water).

solvent A substance used to extract or dissolve another substance; also known as a vehicle.

solyanka (so-lee-ahn-kah) A Russian soup with three variations, one made with meat, another with fish and a third with mushrooms; all are flavored with tomato and garnished with sour cream.

som (som) Thai for orange.

som (some) Turkish for salmon.

somen (SO-mehn) Fine, glossy, white, Japanese noodles made from wheat flour; usually sold dried; various colors and flavors are available, including yellow (made with egg yolk), pink (flavored with strawberries), green (flavored with green tea) and gold (flavored with citrus).

som khay (som kay) A Laotian dish made from the creamy, gray-pink roe of the pa boeuk, a Mekong River fish.

sommelier (suhm-uhl-YAY) The person at a restaurant in charge of the wine cellar (and sometimes all other beverages, alcoholic or not); he or she generally assists patrons in selecting wine and then serves it; also known as the wine steward or wine captain. *See* tastevin.

Sommer Garden The proprietary name of a Danish liqueur sweetened with saccharin.

som tam A Thai salad of shredded unripe papaya topped with dry shrimp and roasted peanuts and an exceptionally hot lime chile dressing.

songaya (sang-kha-yaa) A traditional Thai dessert consisting of egg custard flavored with jasmine or orange flower water; it is baked inside the shell of a young coconut.

songxon (song-snon) Chinese for matsutake.

Sonoma Coast An area in Sonoma County, California; it includes the cooler locations such as Russian River Valley, Green Valley, Chalk Hill, Bennet Valley and the Carneros districts of Sonoma Valley.

Sonoma County A grape-growing and wine-producing region in California (north of San Francisco and west of Napa Valley); subdivided into Sonoma Coast, Sonoma Mountain and Sonoma Valley; the principal grapes grown are Chardonnay and Cabernet Sauvignon as well as Pinot Noir, Sauvignon Blanc, Johannisberg Riesling, Gewürztraminer, Merlot, Zinfandel and Cabernet Franc.

Sonoma Jack A Monterey Jack cheese made in Sonoma County, California, sometimes flavored with spices and other ingredients, such as jalapeño; available semisoft or dry.

Sonoma Mountain An area within Sonoma County; located on the eastern face of the Sonoma Mountains, above the valley; the principal grape grown is Cabernet Sauvignon, but Zinfandel and Sauvignon Blanc grapes are also grown.

Sonoma Valley An area within Sonoma County; it is the valley between the Sonoma Mountains and the Mayacamas Mountains; the principal grapes grown are Cabernet Sauvignon and Sauvignon Blanc.

sonth (sawnt) *See* adrak.

sookhaa (soo-kah) Hindi for dry.

sookha dhania (soo-kah dah-nee-ah) Hindi for coriander seeds.

soomsoom mah assal (soom-soom mah ah-sal) A Middle Eastern confection of honey and lemon syrup with toasted sesame seeds and chopped walnuts or coconut; it is cooled and cut into squares.

soon dae (soon day) A Korean-style blood sausage.

soon doo boo (soon doo boo) A Korean soup of soft tofu, oysters and vegetables.

so o-yosopy (soh oh-yo-soh-pee) A Paraguayan soup made from ground beef, flavored with onions, chiles and oregano and thickened with rice; usually served with sopa Paraguaya.

sopa (SOA-pah) Portuguese and Spanish for soup.

sopa de albóndigas (soh-pah de ahl-bohn-dee-gaas) A Mexican and Spanish beef broth soup with meatballs and vegetables.

sopa de berza (soh-pah de behr-sah) A Chilean soup made from cabbage, potatoes, onions and chicken stock and flavored with nutmeg and allspice; grated cheese is added just before service.

sopa de chayote (soh-pah day cha-yoh-tay) A Central and South American soup made from chayotes and flavored with garlic and pepper.

sopa de flor de calabaza (soh-pay day floor day cah-lah-bah-zah) A Central and South American soup made from squash blossoms and flavored with epazote, pepper and onions.

sopa de jtomate (soh-pah day toh-mah-teh) A Central and South American soup made from tomatoes and flavored with onions, garlic and pepper.

sopa de lima (soh-pah de lee-mah) A Mexican soup of chicken broth garnished with fried tortilla pieces.

sopa de maní (soh-pah de mah-nee) A Bolivian soup of chicken broth and peanut dumplings, garnished with cilantro.

sopa de milho com camarão (soh-pah duh mee-lyu kon kah-mah-reown) A Brazilian soup made from corn and shrimp; it is flavored with onions and paprika and garnished with avocado.

sopa de palmito e de leite de coco (soh-pah duh pahl-mee-two ee duh lay-tuh duh koh-koh) A Brazilian cream soup made from hearts of palm and coconut milk; it is flavored with nutmeg and garnished with chopped peanuts.

sopa de pedra (soh-pah day pa-draw) Portuguese for stone soup and used to describe a soup made from pig's ears, bacon, chouriço, beans, potatoes, carrots and turnips and flavored with garlic, bay leaves and cilantro.

sopaipilla (soh-pah-PEE-yuh) A crisp deep-fried Mexican pastry or bread that is puffy with a hollow center; usually served with honey or a cinnamon-flavored syrup.

sopa Paraguaya (soh-pah pah-rah-goo-ah-yah) A Paraguayan cornbread made from fresh puréed corn and cornmeal.

sopari (soo-PAH-ree) Hindi for betel nut.

sopa seca (SOH-pah SEH-kuh) A Mexican dish of rice, vermicelli or dry tortilla strips combined with tomatoes, onions and garlic and cooked in a broth until the liquid is entirely absorbed.

sope (SO-pay) A Mexican appetizer or first course consisting of a small round of tortilla dough that is fried, then filled with a savory stuffing.

sopp (sopp) Norwegian for mushrooms.

soppa (SO-ppah) Swedish for soup.

soppresso (sop-PRESS-soh) A northern Italian pork and beef salami.

sops; soppets *See* sippets.

sor (zohr) Hungarian for beer.

sorb apple; sorbapple The small, ovoid, red-skinned fruit of the white bean tree; it has a pale flesh with a crunchy texture. *See* serviceberry.

sorbet (sor-BEY) A soft, smooth frozen dish made with puréed fruit or fruit juice and sugar and sometimes flavored with liqueur, wine or coffee; served as a dessert or a palate cleanser between courses. *See* sherbet.

sorbétière (sor-bah-teh-yay) A three-part ceramic assemblage used on a dessert table, often in pairs or quartets, to keep frozen desserts cold; the bottom contains crushed ice, the middle holds fruit ice, sherbet or ice cream and the cover has a shallow cylinder that holds more crushed ice; also known as a glacier, glacière and ice pail.

sorbetto (sor-BET-toe) Italian for sorbet.

sorbic acid A food additive used as a preservative, especially in cheeses and dried fruits.

sorbitan monostearate A food additive used as a flavoring agent and/or emulsifier in processed foods such as cake mixes, whipped oil toppings, frozen desserts, candy coatings, cake icings and fillings and dairy substitutes for coffee.

sorbitol 1. A sugar alcohol derived from fruits or produced from glucose. 2. A food additive used principally as a nutritive sweetener and/or humectant in candies as well as an anticaking agent, emulsifier, firming agent, flavoring agent, flavoring adjuvant, lubricant, stabilizer and/or thickener in processed foods such as baked goods and frozen desserts.

sorb tree A tree (genus *Sorbus*) grown in the Mediterranean region; its golden yellow, pear-shaped, berrylike fruit are used for preserves; also known as a service tree.

sorghum A grass (*Holcus sorghum*) cultivated as a grain and forage; a relative of millet; it is used for flour in parts of the Middle East, Africa and Northern China; also known as juwar.

sorghum oil An oil derived from sorghum; it is similar to corn oil.

sorghum syrup A syrup made by reducing the juice extracted from the cereal grass sorghum; it has a medium brown color and a sweet flavor; similar to molasses but thinner and less sweet than a molasses made from sugarcane.

soro de leite coalhado Portuguese for buttermilk.

sorrel Any of a variety of members of the buckwheat family (genus *Rumex*); they have spear-shaped, dull, gray-green leaves with a tart, sour flavor and are eaten raw or cooked; also known as sour dock, sour grass, spinach dock and herb patience dock.

sorvête (sohr-VAY-tay) Portuguese for ice cream.

sosaties (soe-sah-teas) A South African dish consisting of lamb marinated with cooked onions, vinegar, dried apricots, curry powder, turmeric, sugar and black pepper; the meat is threaded on skewers and then grilled; chicken, fish or shrimp is also used for this popular braai (barbecue) dish.

sosej (soh-say) Swahili for sausage.

soseji (so-SAY-jee) Japanese for sausage.

sosiski (soh-shee-kee) Polish for sausages.

Sosse (sohs-sah) German for sauce.

sosu (SO-soo) Japanese for sauce.

søtt (surt) Norwegian for sweet.

søtunge; tunge (SUR-toon-ger) Danish for sole.

soubise (soo-BEEZ) 1. An onion purée, usually thickened with rice and served as an accompaniment to meats. 2. Dishes (e.g., oeufs à la soubise) that are topped or accompanied by a creamy onion sauce.

soubise, sauce (soo-BEEZ) A French compound sauce made by adding puréed cooked onions to béchamel sauce.

Souchet, sauce; souchett, sauce (soo-shay soo-cheht) A French compound sauce made from a white wine sauce garnished with julienne of potatoes, carrots, leeks and celery cooked in fish stock.

souchong (soo-chohng) The largest size grade of whole black tea leaves.

soudzoukákia (soo-dzoo-kah-key-ah) A sausage traditionally made in Smyrna, Turkey, from veal or pork, garlic, eggs, parsley, cumin seeds and bread crumbs; served with tomato sauce.

soufflé (soo-FLAY) A sweet or savory French dish made with a custard base lightened with whipped egg whites and then baked; the whipped egg whites cause the dish to puff.

soufflé mold A round, porcelain mold with a ridged exterior and a straight, smooth interior; available in 2- to 3.5-qt. capacities.

soul food Traditional African-American cuisine, especially as developed in the American

soufflé mold

South; characterized by such foods as yams, collard greens, black-eyed peas, corn bread, chitterlings and ham hocks.

sound A wine-tasting term for a well-made wine without defects but not necessarily a fine wine or one with great distinction.

soup A combination of meats, poultry, fish, shellfish, vegetables and/or fruits cooked in a liquid; it can be garnished with any of an extremely wide range of garnishes, can be hot or cold, sweet or savory, thin or thick and served as a first course or main dish.

soupa (soo-pah) Greek for soup.

soup bones Bones from the foreshanks and/or hindshanks of a beef or veal carcass; rich with marrow, they are used for stocks and soups.

soup bowl A deep bowl, usually without a rim, used for soups, stews or other foods with a liquid component.

soupe (soop) French for soup and used to describe a thick, hearty soup with chunks of garnish. *See* consommé *and* potage.

soupe à l'oignon (soup ah lo-nyohn) French for onion soup.

soupikanya (soo-peak-ahn-e-ah) A Senegalese stewlike dish consisting of fish, okra, eggplant and onions flavored with garlic, guedge and yete; the dish is served with a float of palm oil.

soup kitchens Facilities organized by charitable groups during the Great Depression to feed the needy.

soup meat A fabricated cut of the beef primal round and breast and shank; the meat, usually diced and with a large amount of connective tissue, is from the foreshanks and hindshanks.

soup plate A shallow dish with a wide rim and used for serving soup or foods with a liquid component or sauce.

soup spoon A spoon with a large rounded or slightly pointed bowl used for eating soup.

soup station chef *See* potager.

sour *v.* 1. To ferment. 2. To spoil or become rancid. *n.* 1. An acidic, tart, possibly unpleasant flavor. 2. A wine-tasting term for a wine that has spoiled and become vinegary. 3. A cocktail made of liquor, sugar and citrus juice shaken with cracked ice and served in

soup spoon

a sour glass with a maraschino cherry and orange slice.

sour cherry *See* cherry, sour.

sour cream Pasteurized, homogenized light cream (containing not less than 18% milkfat) fermented by the bacteria *Streptococcus lactis;* it has a tangy flavor, a gel-like body and a white color; used as a condiment and for baking and cooking.

sour dock *See* sorrel.

sourdough A bread dough leavened with a fermented starter; this gives the bread a tangy, slightly sour flavor. *See* starter.

sour glass A short, squat glass holding approximately 6 fl. oz.; used for sours.

sour grass *See* sorrel.

sour mash bourbon Bourbon made through a sour mash process.

sour mash process A whiskey-making process (primarily for bourbon) in which stillage or spent beer from a previous distillation is added to fresh mash; the mixture is allowed to ferment and is then distilled; also known as the yeasting back process. *See* sweet mash process.

sour glass

sour orange *See* Seville orange.

soursop A very large fruit of a tree (*Annona muricata*) native to the Caribbean and northern South America; it has an irregular ovoid shape, a thin, tender, leathery skin with soft spines and a yellow color when ripe, a white, soft, juicy, segmented flesh with few seeds and an aroma and flavor reminiscent of a pineapple; also known as guanabana.

sous (saw's) Russian for sauce.

sous-chef (SOO-chef) 1. French for underchef. 2. At a food services operation following the brigade system, the chef's principal assistant and the one responsible for scheduling personnel, acting as the aboyeur and replacing the chef and station chefs as necessary; also known as the second chef.

souse (sahus) *v.* To pickle a food in brine or vinegar. *n.* Sour pork in aspic, now sold commercially as luncheon meat.

soused Slang for intoxicated.

soused herring A British dish made of a herring pickled in vinegar, white wine and spices.

sous-vide (soo-VEED) A food-packaging technique; fresh ingredients are combined into various dishes, vacuum-packed in individual-portion pouches, cooked under a vacuum and chilled for storage.

South American squid A variety of very large squid found off South America and usually sold as steaks; it has an ivory white color, a firm, tender texture and a mild, sweet flavor.

southern (China) cheese *See* Chinese red cheese.

Southern Comfort A cordial made from fresh peaches and bourbon.

southern fox grape *See* Muscadine.

southern green abalone A variety of abalone found in the Pacific Ocean off California and Mexico; it has a large reddish-brown to greenish-opal brown-speckled shell with a dark-green to violet interior and an ivory flesh with a chewy texture and mild flavor.

Southside A cocktail made of bourbon, sugar syrup, lemon juice, spring water and mint leaves.

soutirage (soo-tee-rahj) French for racking.

souvlaki; souvlakia (soo-VLAH-kee; soo-VLAH-kee-uh) A Greek dish consisting of lamb chunks marinated in olive oil, lemon juice, oregano and other seasonings, then skewered (sometimes with vegetables such as green peppers and onions) and grilled.

Souwaroff, sauce (soo-wha-roff) A French compound sauce made from a béarnaise flavored with meat glaze and garnished with julienne of truffles.

sovereign mushroom See oyster mushroom.

sow (sov) Sweetened buttermilk; it is used as a flavoring and beverage in West African (especially Senegalese and Malian) cuisines.

sow The adult female swine. See boar and pig.

soya (SOI-ah) British spelling for soy.

soy added A food-labeling term indicating that soy protein has been added to the processed food.

soybean; soyabean; soy pea A versatile legume (*Glycine max*) whose beans are used to make a variety of products, including curds, milk and soy sauce; the pods are tan to black with a tawny to gray fuzz, and the beans, which range from pea to cherry sized, can be red, yellow, green, brown or black and have a bland flavor; also known as soi and soya.

soybean curd See tofu.

soybean pudding See tofu pudding.

soybean sprouts Sprouted soybean seeds; used in Southeast Asian cuisines.

Soyer, Alexis (Fr., 1809–1858) A French chef who spent most of his career in England; he was a restaurant owner (introducing the cocktail bar to England), a chef at the Reform Club, an inventor (e.g., a portable stove for the military), an entrepreneur (he bottled and sold his own sauce and condiments), a social activist and the author of *The Modern Housewife* (1849) and *A Schilling Cookery for the People* (1855).

soy flour; soybean flour A fine, light beige flour made from soybeans; although it does not have glutenin and gliaden, it is high in other proteins and is usually added to wheat flour for baking.

soy jam A soybean paste; it is more viscous and flavorful than soy sauce and less salty.

soy milk A pale yellow liquid made by pressing ground, cooked soybeans; it has a slightly bitter flavor and is used for people with milk allergies and in infant formulas and cooking; available plain or flavored with honey or carob.

soy milk curds See oboro.

soy oil A colorless, all-purpose oil obtained from soybeans; it is inexpensive and has little flavor.

soy paste (fermented) See miso.

soy powder; soya powder A soybean product made from finely ground cooked soybeans; it is used to make a drink or added to wheat flour for baking.

soy protein A product made from processed soybeans; it has a very high protein content and is used as a nutrient supplement and meat extender; also known as vegetable protein.

soy sauce A sauce made from fermented boiled soybeans and roasted wheat or barley; its color ranges from light to dark brown and its flavor is generally rich and salty (a low-sodium version is available); used extensively in Asian cuisines (especially Chinese and Japanese) as a flavoring, condiment and sometimes a cooking medium.

spacer A nonalcoholic beer (or other beverage) consumed between regular beers (or other alcoholic beverages) to regulate alcohol intake over the course of an evening.

spa cuisine An American preparation method for foods; it emphasizes fresh, low-fat, low-sodium ingredients prepared without added fat.

spada; pesce spada (spah-dah) Italian for swordfish.

Spaetzle; Spätzle (SHPEHT-slee) Irregular-shaped Austrian and German noodles made from a dough of flour, water and sometimes eggs and formed by rubbing the dough through a colander or special sieve directly into boiling water or broth.

Spa Food The trademarked name of dishes created at New York's Four Seasons Restaurant by chef Seppi Renggli; they are low in calories, fat, cholesterol and sodium.

spagheto (spa-ghe-toh) Greek for spaghetti.

spaghetti (spah-GEHT-tee) 1. Italian for a length of cord or string and used to describe long, thin, solid rods of pasta with a circular cross section. See capellini and fedelini. 2. In the United States, a term used imprecisely to describe any of several types of long, solid strands of pasta with varying widths and either oval, rectangular or circular cross sections.

spaghetti alla chitarra See pasta alla chitarra.

spaghetti con carne (kon KAHR-nee) Italian for spaghetti with meat sauce.

spaghetti fork; spaghetti rake See pasta fork.

spaghettini (spagh-eht-TEE-nee) Very thin spaghetti.

spaghetti squash A large watermelon-shaped winter squash (*Cucurbita pepo*) with a creamy yellow shell and a slightly nutty-flavored flesh that separates into yellow-gold spaghetti-like strands when cooked; also known as noodle squash and vegetable spaghetti.

spaghettoni (spagh-eht-TOHN-ee) Fat spaghetti.

Spalen See Sbrinz.

Spalt (shpehlt) A variety of hops grown in Germany.

Spalt Select A variety of hops grown in the United States.

Spam The proprietary name of a canned ground pork shoulder and ham product; a staple during World War II.

spanakopita (span-uh-KOH-pih-tuh) A Greek dish consisting of phyllo dough baked with a stuffing of feta cheese and spinach bound with an egg.

Spanferkel (SHPAAN-fehr-kerl) An Austrian dish of suckling pig roasted with lemon slices and served with a cream and caper sauce.

Spanish cream An American dessert made with milk, egg yolks and sugar, thickened with gelatin and lightened with whipped egg whites; it is shaped in a decorative mold and garnished with fresh fruit and whipped cream.

Spanish fly See cantharides.

Spanish jute; Spanish okra; Spanish sorrel See molokhia.

Spanish lime *See* genipap.

Spanish mackerel A member of the mackerel family found in the Atlantic Ocean from Brazil to New England and in the Pacific Ocean from California to the Galápagos Islands; it has a dark blue skin that pales to silver on the belly and many small yellow or olive spots, a high fat content, a firm, flavorful flesh and an average market weight of 1.5–4 lb. (0.68–1.8 kg).

Spanish mayonnaise *See* espagnole, mayonnaise à l'.

Spanish melon A large ovoid member of the muskmelon family; it has a ribbed, green skin, a pale green flesh and a sweet, succulent flavor.

Spanish olive A green olive that is picked young, soaked in lye and then fermented for 6–12 months; packed in a weak brine and sold with the pit, pitted or stuffed with other flavorings such as a pimiento, almond or pearl onion.

Spanish onion A white- or yellow-skinned onion with a mild flavor.

Spanish oyster plant *See* golden thistle.

Spanish plum *See* mombin.

Spanish potato A large, reddish-brown variety of sweet potato used in Spain for both sweet and savory dishes.

Spanish sauce *See* brown sauce.

Spanish wind torte An Austrian confection of a meringue shell decorated with piped shell shapes, rosettes and crystallized violets, filled with fresh berries and whipped cream and topped with a decorated meringue disk; in Austria a meringue is called Spanish wind.

spareribs A fabricated cut of the pork primal belly; it is a long, narrow cut containing the lower portion of the ribs and breastbone.

Spargel (SHPAAR-gerl) German for asparagus.

sparging 1. The process of spraying the mash with hot water to extract residual sugars during beer brewing. 2. The process of obtaining clear sweet wort from the mash.

sparklets Small capsules holding carbon dioxide; soluble in liquids, they are used to carbonate certain nonalcoholic beverages.

sparkling The bubbly characteristic of a wine whose effervescence is induced by the méthode champenoise or Charmat process.

sparkling burgundy A somewhat sweet sparkling red wine made by the Charmat process in New York and California.

sparkling Muscat A sparkling white wine made in California from the Muscat of Alexandria grape; it has a strong Muscat bouquet; generally sold as Moscato Champagne or Spumante.

sparkling water *See* water, sparkling.

sparkling wine *See* wine, sparkling.

sparzha (spahr-skaw) Russian for asparagus.

spat An oyster younger than 1 year.

Spätburgunder (SH'PATE-boor-gun-der) *See* Pinot Noir.

Spätlese (sh'PAY't-lay-zuh) A German wine-labeling term for late picking; the wine is generally richer, fuller and sweeter than a wine made from an early picking. *See* Qualitätswein mit Prädikat.

spatula A utensil with a handle and a broad or narrow, long or short, flexible or rigid flat blade.

spatula, cake *See* offset spatula.

spatula

spatula, metal 1. A spatula with a narrow flexible metal blade; used to spread foods such as icings. 2. A spatula with a broader, less flexible metal blade; used to turn foods while cooking or to remove them from a heat source or cookware; also known as a grill spatula.

spatula, rubber A spatula with a beveled and slightly curved rectangular rubber blade; available with blades ranging from 1×2 to 3×5 in.; used to press and smooth foods, remove foods from bowls and fold and stir ingredients.

spatula, wooden A spatula with a wooden blade; used to mix foods when high heats are present or to turn food or remove it from a heat source or cookware.

spawn *v.* To produce or deposit eggs, sperm or young. *n.* 1. Eggs of certain aquatic animals. 2. Fertilized fish eggs. 3. A mycelium produced in order to cultivate a mushroom.

SPE *See* sucrose polyester.

speakeasy A commercial establishment where alcoholic beverages were sold illegally during Prohibition.

spear *See* knife point.

spearfish A large fish found throughout the Pacific Ocean; generally caught for sport. *See* hebi.

spearmint An herb (*Menta spicata*) and member of the mint family; it has soft, bright green leaves and a tart menthol flavor and aroma that is milder than that of peppermint; used as a flavoring, garnish and tisane.

special inventory The physical counting of all stock on hand at irregular periods of time or because of extraordinary circumstances.

special natural wines A category of wines made from grapes and other fruits to which natural fruit flavors have been added; generally sweet, they can be fortified or relatively low in alcohol.

Special Select Late Harvest *See* Late Harvest.

specialty item *See* signature item.

species A botanical and zoological term used to describe the basic unit of classification, which is a group of individual organisms with similar characteristics that can interbreed and cannot or do not breed with other species; related species are grouped into a genus; the species is denoted by the second word(s) in the scientific name.

specification A detailed and accurate description of a product to be supplied to a business. *See* purchase specifications.

specification form A form used to describe precisely to suppliers what a purchaser desires; it generally includes information regarding the item's quality or grade, weight or size, packaging and delivery conditions.

specific gravity The weight of a liquid compared with the weight of an equal volume of water; measured by a hydrometer.

Speck (shpehk) German for bacon.

speckled perch *See* crappie.

speckled trout *See* brook trout, crappie *and* sea trout.

specs *See* purchase specifications.

speculaa (spae-coo-la-ah) A crisp, spicy Dutch gingerbread cookie traditionally made by pressing the dough into elaborately carved wooden molds.

speculaus (spay-que-low) A Belgian cookie containing rock candy, cinnamon, cloves, nutmeg, ginger and other spices; available in various shapes and sizes, it is particularly popular in the shape of St. Nicholas.

speed *See* amphetamines.

speed pour A device inserted into the neck of a bottle of distilled spirits that aids in dispensing the liquid quickly.

speed rack 1. A stainless steel trough below the bar and directly in front of the bartender, usually at the cocktail station, holding bottles of frequently ordered distilled spirits, mixes or wines sold by the glass. 2. Slang for a baker's rack.

Speise (spiez-za) German for food.

Speisekarte (spiez-karta) German for menu.

spek (speck) 1. Dutch for bacon. 2. Cured pig fat; it has a hard texture and a rich, strong flavor and is used in Dutch cuisine for larding meats or as a flavoring in stews.

spekpannekoek *See* pannekoeken.

speliy (spa-lee) Russian for ripe.

spelt A hard wheat kernel with the husk attached; used as a thickener in soups or served as a side dish.

spenat (speh-NAAT) Swedish for spinach.

Spencer 1. A fabricated cut of the beef primal chuck; it is a center-cut filet. 2. A fabricated cut of the beef primal rib; it is a boneless rib roast or steak.

Spencer roll A fabricated cut of the beef primal rib; it is a trimmed, boneless, rolled rib roast.

spetsiótiko (speh-tsee-oh-tee-koh) A Greek preparation method in which fish are baked with wine, garlic and parsley.

spèzie (SPE-tsye) Italian for spices.

spezzatino di vitello (spay-tsah-TEE-noa de vee-tehl-loa) An Italian veal stew.

spherical A three-dimensional shape with a round cross section.

spice cake A cake flavored with cinnamon and nutmeg and studded with dried and candied fruits.

spiced beef Salt beef rubbed with spices; used during the Middle Ages to preserve beef and still part of Irish cuisine.

spiced cheese A cheese to which one or more spices or herbs (e.g., anise, caraway seeds, chives, cloves, cumin seeds, pepper or sage) or spice extracts are added to the curds during the cheese-making process.

spiced red bean curd *See* Chinese red cheese.

spice mill A tool similar to a meat grinder with a clamp to fix it to the work surface; electric grinders are also available.

Spice Parisienne (pa-ree-ZYEHN) A spice and herb blend that includes white pepper, allspice, mace, nutmeg, rosemary, sage, bay leaves, cloves, cinnamon and marjoram.

spices Any of a large group of aromatic plants whose bark, roots, seeds, buds or berries are used as a flavoring; usually available dried, either whole or ground. *See* herbs.

Spickgans (SPEEK-gahns) A German dish consisting of a cured, smoked goose breast.

spicy 1. A tasting term for a food with a predominant flavor from one or more spices; although the flavors can range from very mild to very hot, the term is more often used to describe hot, pungent foods. 2. A wine-tasting term for a wine with a bouquet and/or flavor reminiscent of black peppercorns, cinnamon and other spices. 3. A cheese-tasting term for a flavor reminiscent of pepper or other spice; usually not applied to cheeses that are flavored with spices or herbs. 4. A coffee-tasting term used to describe an aroma or flavor reminiscent of a particular spice or group of spices.

spider 1. A hand tool with a long handle attached to a mesh disk used for skimming stocks or removing foods from liquids, especially hot fat. 2. A cast-iron frying pan with a long handle and three legs that stands over a bed of coals in the hearth.

spider crab *See* snow crab.

spiedini (spee-ay-DEE-neh) Italian skewers used to hold foods for grilling.

spièdo, allo (SPAY-doh, ah-loh) An Italian term for a food roasted on a spit or skewered and grilled.

spiegeleier (spee-ghel-eyer) Dutch for fried egg.

spigot (spee-gut) A metal or wooden tap used to drain liquids from a barrel or tank.

spike To add an alcoholic beverage, often surreptitiously, to a nonalcoholic or low-alcohol-content drink.

spile (spil) A barrel stopper or bung.

spillage allowance The amount of a given volume (e.g., a bottle) of an alcoholic beverage assumed to be lost through bartender mishaps or overpours; deducted from the number of drinks to be expected from that volume.

spina, alla (SPEE-nah, AH-la) Italian for on tap, referring to draught beer.

spinach A vegetable (*Spinacea oleracea*) with dark green, spear-shaped leaves that can be curled or smooth and are attached to thin stems; the leaves have a slightly bitter flavor and are eaten raw or cooked; also known as Persian herb.

spinach beet; spinach green A beet whose leaves resemble a coarse form of spinach and are used like spinach; also known as beetgreen.

spinach dock *See* sorrel.

spinaci (spee-NAA-chee) Italian for spinach.

Spinat (shpee-NAAT) German for spinach.

spinat (spee-nat) Norwegian for spinach.

spinazie (spee-NAH-zee) Dutch for spinach.

spine The thick, unsharpened (top) edge of a knife blade; also known as the back. *See* backbone.

spinner A wine bottle capsule that rotates because it was not set properly.

spiny lobster A variety of lobster found in temperate and tropical saltwater areas worldwide; it has a mottled brown, orange and blue shell, small claws, a large meaty tail, a lean, snow-white flesh with a sweet flavor and an average market weight of 2–5 lb. (0.9–2.3 kg); usually sold as a frozen tail; also known as rock lobster, sea crawfish and sea crayfish. *See* cold-water tails *and* warm-water tails.

spirilla *See* bacteria.

spirits *See* distilled spirits *and* ethyl alcohol.

spirits of wine *See* ethyl alcohol.

spirit vinegar A liquid (often molasses or sugar beet alcohol) that is distilled before all the alcohol has been converted to acetic acid; it is colorless and used primarily for pickling purposes; also known as grain vinegar and distilled vinegar.

spirochetes (SPI-row-kets) *See* bacteria.

spirt Russian for alcohol.

spise (spee-seh) Norwegian for to eat.

spisekart (spee-seh-khart) Norwegian for menu.

spisepinner (spee-sah-pin-nar) Norwegian for chopsticks.

spit A thin metal bar on which meat, poultry or game is placed to be roasted before an open fire. *See* skewer.

spititi *See* pombe ya dawa.

Spitzenwein (sh'pitz-en-vine) German wine-tasting term for an outstanding or exceptional wine.

Spitzkäse (sh'pitz-kaiz) A small Limburger-style spiced cheese made in Germany and Belgium from skimmed cow's milk; it has caraway seeds.

splash 1. An imprecise measure of volume for a liquid; usually a small amount. 2. A small amount of a liquid ingredient added to a drink or other food item.

splatter screen A disk with small perforations and a handle placed over a frying pan to reduce grease splatters while allowing vapors to escape.

spleen A variety meat, especially from cows; it has a brown color and a spongy texture and is used in mixed offal dishes; also known as melts.

splice the main brace Old navy and maritime slang for to drink whiskey.

split A small bottle of wine or sparkling wine; one-fourth the size of a regular bottle, it contains approximately 6 fl. oz., or 185 ml.

split pea *See* field pea.

split rack *See* rack.

spoilage Food loss attributed to poor food handling or planning.

spoiled A product that has decayed because of bacterial contamination or improper processing, storing or handling.

sponge 1. A soupy mixture of flour, liquid and yeast used as the first stage in making certain breads; the sponge is allowed to ferment, then the remaining ingredients are incorporated and the bread is finished; a sponge gives the bread a slightly tangy flavor and a denser texture. 2. A light

dessert made with whipped gelatin, beaten egg whites and whipped cream.

sponge cake; spongecake A light, airy cake leavened primarily by air whipped into egg whites, which are then folded into the remaining batter ingredients; it can be flavored and shaped in a wide variety of ways. *See* genoise.

sponge mushroom; spongie *See* morel.

sponsored bar *See* open bar.

spoom A type of French sherbet made with fruit juice or wine; when partially frozen, an Italian meringue is folded in, making the mixture frothy or foamy.

spoon A metal, plastic, ceramic or wooden utensil used for eating or cooking; it consists of a round or oval bowl and a handle.

spoon, metal A metal spoon with an oval bowl that has a pointed end.

spoon, solid A spoon that is 11.75–15.5 in. long with an oval bowl that has a 4-in.-long face, a 3-tablespoon capacity and a tapered tip; used for stirring, removing impurities from the surface of foods, transferring foods and basting.

spoon, wooden A spoon with a flat surface and almost no bowl; because wood does not conduct heat, it can be used for prolonged stirring.

spoon bread; spoonbread A puddinglike cornbread baked in a casserole and served as a side dish; also known as egg bread.

spore 1. A reproductive body, usually unicellular and thick walled, produced by some plants and protozoa. 2. A thick-walled structure formed by certain bacilli bacteria in which the bacterium remains in a dormant state under adverse conditions; many spores are resistant to normal cooking and sanitation techniques. 3. The often microscopic, seed-like reproductive unit of a fungus.

sports bar A bar designed with a sports theme and often offering patrons a selection of televised sporting events.

sports drink A beverage containing carbohydrates, minerals (including salt), vitamins and/or other supplements consumed to help replenish fluids and nutrients lost during vigorous activities and exercise.

spot A member of the drum family found off the U.S. East Coast and in the Gulf of Mexico; it has 12–15 yellowish bars above the lateral line, a yellowish-black spot behind the gills and a lean, flaky flesh; also known as a goody and Lafayette.

spotted cabrilla (cah-bree-yay) A variety of Pacific grouper.

spotted dick; spotted dog A British steamed pudding made with suet and raisins.

spouted saucepan *See* butter melter.

sprat (spraht) A small saltwater fish, similar to a herring, found in the Atlantic Ocean off Europe; it has a fatty flesh and an average length of 6 in. (15.2 cm). *See* brisling.

spread *v.* 1. To distribute a food (e.g., a condiment or icing) evenly over the surface of another. 2. To prepare a table for dining or to arrange platters of food on it. *n.* 1. The butter, cream cheese, mayonnaise or the like used on bread, crackers, canapé bases or similar items, often before one or more garnishes or sandwich fillings are added. 2. An abundant meal laid out on a table. 3. A tablecloth or other fabric used on a table.

spreader Any of several utensils used to distribute a soft food over the surface of another food (e.g., a butter knife or spatula).

sprig A small branch of a leafy substance such as thyme or rosemary.

sprightly A beer- and wine-tasting term for a lively, flavorful product.

spring sauce *See* printaniére, sauce.

Springerle (SPRING-uhr-lee) German Christmas cookies flavored with anise; the dough is molded or imprinted with a decorative design before baking.

springerle rolling pin A rolling pin with 16 shallow designs carved into the lightweight barrel; used to emboss springerle.

springform pan A circular baking pan with a separate bottom and a side wall held together with a clamp that is released to free the baked product; used primarily for baking cheesecakes.

springform pan

spring greens Cabbages that do not form a heart; available year-round.

spring lamb The meat of a sheep slaughtered when it is 3–5 months old and between March and early October; the pink meat is quite tender and has a mild flavor. *See* baby lamb, lamb *and* mutton.

spring onions *See* scallions.

spring roll A smaller, more delicate version of the egg roll; it is wrapped in rice paper and traditionally eaten on the first day of spring.

spring scale A scale that weighs objects according to the degree that an internal spring is depressed when the object is placed on a tray above the spring; the weight is indicated by a needle on a dial that can be calibrated in the metric, U.S. or imperial system; a spring scale is often used as a portion scale. *See* electronic scale.

spring water *See* water, spring.

springy A tasting term for the resilient texture of a food; it is one that springs back when gently pressed.

sprinkle To scatter small amounts of a dry substance or drops of liquid over the surface of a food.

sprinkles *See* hundreds and thousands.

spritz A wine-tasting term for the light sparkle or prickling sensation on the tongue provided by some wines; the sparkle is caused by a second fermentation in the bottle or the addition of carbon dioxide. *See* crackling.

spritz cookie A small buttery cookie formed by forcing the dough through a cookie press or pastry bag; also known as bagged cookie.

Spritzer A cocktail traditionally made of Rhine wine and soda water; it now refers to any combination of wine and soda.

spritzig (SPRITS-igh) The German equivalent of a slightly sparkling wine described as perlant. *See* perlwein.

sprouting broccoli *See* calabrese.

sprouts The very young shoots emerging from germinated seeds; generally, they have a soft texture, a white or yellow stem, a green leaf bud and a delicate, sometimes nutty flavor.

spruce beer An alcoholic beverage made from spruce twigs and leaves boiled with molasses and then fermented.

sprue (spru) Thin or young asparagus shoots.

spruitjes (SPRIR-tyus) Dutch for Brussels sprouts.

spud Slang for potato.

spugnola rotonda (spoo-nho-lah rho-ton-dah) Italian for morel.

spuma (SPOO-mah) Italian for spoom.

spumante (spoo-MAHN-teh) A slightly sparkling wine made in Italy by the metodo classico.

spumoni; spumone (spuh-MOH-nee) An Italian dessert made with variously flavored layers of ice cream and whipped cream, often containing candied fruit.

spun curds *See* pasta filata.

spun sugar A sugar syrup cooked to the hard-crack stage (310°F [153°C]), then drawn out into fine, golden threads with a fork or whisk; these threads are used to decorate desserts and pastries.

spurtle A wooden stick traditionally used in Scotland for stirring porridge; also known as a theevil.

Spy apple *See* Northern Spy apple.

squab An immature pigeon, slaughtered when 4 weeks old or younger; it has a tender flesh, a small amount of fat, an average market weight of 0.75–1.5 lb. (0.3–0.7 kg) and an earthy, gamy flavor.

squab chicken A chicken slaughtered when 4–6 weeks old; it has an average market weight of 1.5 lb. (625 g), a tender texture and a mild flavor.

squall glass A large, footed, pear-shaped glass holding approximately 15 fl. oz.; used for blended or frozen cocktails, tropical drinks and speciality drinks.

squash 1. The edible fleshy fruit of various members of the gourd (*Cucurbitaceae*) family; generally divided into two categories based on peak season and skin type: summer and winter. 2. A British beverage made by diluting a sweetened citrus concentrate, usually with soda water.

squash, summer Any of several varieties of squashes with edible thin skins, soft seeds, a moist flesh and a mild flavor; they have a peak season of April through September and can be eaten raw or grilled, sautéed, steamed or baked. *See* marrow squash.

squash, turban A category of winter squash characterized by a hard bumpy shell and a turbanlike formation at the blossom end; they have an elongated, plump, pearlike shape, with a yellow, orange or green shell, and a firm, dry, sweet flesh that is a deep orange color; they are often used as decorations.

squash, winter Any of several varieties of squashes with hard skins (called shells) and hard seeds, neither of which are generally eaten; the flesh, which is usually not eaten raw, tends to be sweeter and more strongly flavored than the flesh of summer squashes; winter squashes have a peak season between October and March and can be baked, steamed, sautéed or puréed for soups and pie fillings.

squash blossoms The edible blossoms of both winter and summer squashes; usually stuffed and fried, they have a slight squash flavor.

squashed-fly biscuit An English butter cookie studded with currants.

squat lobster A term used imprecisely for any of several varieties of clawless lobsters.

squaw candy Strips of salmon flesh cured in a salt–sugar brine and hot smoked by Native Americans in the Northwest.

squeezed sushi *See* nigiri-zushi.

squeeze out To extract the juice from fruits (e.g., lemons) or vegetables (e.g., mushrooms) or excess liquid from a food by applying pressure.

squeezin's Slang for the final product or tails of a distillation.

squeteagues *See* sea trout.

squid Any of several varieties of cephalopod mollusks found in the Atlantic and Pacific Oceans; generally, they have a long, slender body, an elongated head and tentacles, an ivory-white flesh, a firm, tender texture and a mild, sweet flavor; they vary greatly in size and are available whole or in steaks; also known as inkfish.

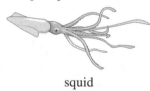

squid

squilla Small, burrowing crustaceans (*Squilla mantis*) found along the eastern Atlantic and Mediterranean coasts; used in soups and chowders.

Squirt A cocktail made with liquor or wine, fresh fruit or fruit syrup and sweetened seltzer or club soda.

sriacha (sree-ah-chah) A Thai sauce made from chiles, salt, sugar and vinegar.

St. *See* Saint, Saint- *and* Sainte-.

stabilizers; stabilizing agents A type of food additive used to produce viscous solutions or dispersions, impart body, improve consistency, improve texture and/or stabilize emulsions; it includes thickeners, suspending agents, bodying agents, setting agents, jellying agents and bulking agents.

stabilizing Any of a group of processes intended to keep processed foods and beverages stable and thus retard deterioration; for beverages this includes adding ascorbic acid, sorbic acid or sulfur dioxide as well as cold stabilization, filtering, fining, pasteurization and refrigeration.

Stachelbeere (STAH-kherl-bay-re) German for gooseberry.

stack cake A cake consisting of seven thin layers of baked cake batter; each layer is spread with a spiced dried apple filling and the top layer is garnished with confectioners' sugar.

stacked schedule A staffing schedule in which employees within a department begin and end work at the same time; also known as a shift schedule. *See* staggered schedule.

staffing schedule A list designed for a specific period showing when different employees will begin and end work and sometimes what stations or tasks they will be assigned. *See* stacked schedule *and* staggered schedule.

staggered schedule A staffing schedule in which employees within a department begin and end their shifts at different times. *See* stacked schedule.

stags Male cattle castrated after maturity; principally used for animal food. *See* steers.

stainless steel An alloy of steel, usually with chromium; it is strong and will not rust or corrode; when used for a knife blade, it is difficult to sharpen but holds its edge; when used for cookware, it does not react with acids but is a poor heat conductor, so it is sometimes sandwiched with cooper. *See* carbon steel, high-carbon stainless steel *and* tinned steel.

sta kavouna (stah kah-voo-nah) A Greek preparation method in which fish are cooked on a charcoal grill.

stale 1. A tasting term for a food or beverage that has lost its freshness because of age, moisture loss or improper storage. 2. A beer- and wine-tasting term for a product that has lost its lively, fresh, youthful character and has become flat, dull, musty and flavorless; often the result of a beverage being kept too long.

staling A change in the distribution and location of water molecules within baked products; stale products are firmer, drier and more crumbly than fresh baked goods; also known as starch retrogradation.

stalky (STAHL-kee) *See* green.

stamp and go A Caribbean fritter made from a heavy batter and salty cod, flavored with annatto, onions and chiles.

stamped knife blade *See* knife blade, stamped.

stamppot (stahm-pot) A Dutch cabbage stew made with pork shoulder, cabbage and potatoes.

standard 1. A midlevel U.S. Department of Agriculture (USDA) quality grade for beef and the second-lowest quality grade for veal; the meat lacks the flavor and marbling of the higher grades. 2. A norm of quantity and/or quality against which comparisons are made.

standard beverage costs *See* beverage cost.

standard breading procedure The procedure for coating foods with crumbs or meal by passing the food through flour, then an egg wash and then the crumbs; this process gives food a relatively thick, crisp coating when deep-fried or pan-fried.

standard drink list A list of the alcoholic beverages most often ordered in a retail, on-premise establishment such as a bar or restaurant.

standard food costs *See* food costs.

standard glassware The specific size, quality and shape of the glassware used for a specific drink.

standardized drink A drink made from a standardized recipe.

standardized menu *See* static menu.

standardized portion; standard portion The predetermined size (quantity) of a single portion of a product made from a standardized recipe; also known imprecisely as a portion.

standardized recipe A set of written instructions for producing a known quantity and quality of a specific food or beverage for a specific food services operation. *See* recipe.

standardized recipe form A form used by a food services operation to record a standardized recipe; it generally includes product name, yield, portion size, presentation or garnish information, ingredient quality and quantity, preparation notes, cooking time and temperatures and holding instructions as well as cost information and sometimes a photograph.

standard of performance Objective criteria by which a product's or worker's performance is measured.

standard purchase specifications *See* purchase specifications.

standard-sized bottle A bottle with a capacity of 750 ml, or 25.4 fl. oz.

standards of composition Set by the U.S. Department of Agriculture (USDA), each standard is the minimum percentage of meat or poultry that a product labeled as such must contain.

standards of fill Standards set by the Bureau of Alcohol, Tobacco, and Firearms (BATF) regarding the exact quantity of an alcoholic beverage that a particular-sized bottle must contain.

standards of fill of containers Set by the U.S. Food and Drug Administration (FDA), each standard is the minimum amount of food that a package of a given size must contain.

standards of identity Standards mandated by the U.S. Food and Drug Administration (FDA) for processed food recipes that manufacturers must follow if they want to use the common name for the product (e.g., ketchup); these standards encompass approximately 300 foods, and adherence to the standard allows the manufacturer to omit listing the ingredients on the label.

standard yield The number of portions produced by a standardized recipe.

standing dish A dish that appears on the table each day or at each meal.

standing order An arrangement with a supplier to provide a predetermined quantity of specific goods on a daily or other basis without the buyer having to contact the supplier each time.

standing pie A meat pie with a hard cylindrical crust that maintains an upright position without support.

standing rib roast A rib roast that includes the last three ribs and is roasted resting on the rack of rib bones.

stannous chloride A food additive used as an antioxidant.

Staphylococcus aureus (staf'a-lo-KAA-kes ah-RE-us) Bacteria that cause food poisoning; common sources are contaminated starchy foods, cold meats, baked goods, dairy products and food handlers with infected wounds; commonly called staph.

staples 1. Certain foods regularly used throughout the kitchen (e.g., cooking oil, flour and salt). 2. Certain foods, usually starches, that help form the basis for a regional or national cuisine and are principal components in a diet.

star anise The dried, dark brown, star-shaped fruit of the Chinese magnolia (*Illicium verum*); its seeds have a pungent, bitter licorice flavor and are available whole or ground; the fruit is used in Chinese cuisine and as an ingredient in Chinese five-spice powder; also known as badian and Chinese anise.

star apple A fruit (*Chrysophyllum cainito*) native to South America and the Caribbean region; it has a purple skin, a flesh that changes from purple near the skin to white toward the center, a mild, sweet flavor and, when cut open, transparent seeds in a star pattern; also known as a cainito.

starch 1. A polysaccharide hydrolyzed into glucose for energy; it has little or no flavor and occurs naturally as a minute, white granule in seeds, tubers and other parts of plants, especially vegetables. 2. A rice, grain, pasta or potato accompaniment to a meal.

starch retrogradation *See* staling.

starchy potato *See* potato, mealy.

Star Daisy A cocktail made of gin, apple brandy, lemon juice, sugar syrup and curaçao; served in a chilled wine glass.

star fruit *See* carambola.

Starka Vodka aged for 10 years in oak casks that were previously used for maturing wine; the aging process imparts flavor and an amber color to the vodka.

Starkimson apple A medium-sized apple with a dark red or burgundy skin with small yellow spots, a moderately firm flesh and a sweet flavor.

Stark Tilton apricot An apricot variety; the medium-sized fruit have a yellow-orange skin, a whitish-yellow flesh and a sweet flavor.

starry flounder A member of the flounder family; it has an alternating pattern of orange, white and black bars on the fins, a dark brown to black mottled skin on top, a pearly white flesh, a good flavor and an average market weight of 5–10 lb. (2.3–5.4 kg).

starter 1. A foamy, pungent mixture of flour, liquid and yeast (either commercial or wild) that is allowed to ferment; a portion of the starter is used to leaven bread dough, and the starter is then replenished with additional flour and liquid and reserved for later use. *See* sourdough. 2. Fermenting yeast started in a small amount of sterile wort and, after growth, added to the wort to activate fermentation for the beer-brewing process. 3. The first course or appetizer of a meal.

starter, lactic *See* lactic starter.

starting specific gravity *See* original specific gravity.

static menu A menu that lists the same foods and beverages for sale for the same meal period day after day; usually used in a fast-food operation, ethnic restaurant or institutional setting; also known as a standardized menu.

station 1. An area of a buffet dedicated to a particular type of food (e.g., carved meats or desserts) or preparation (e.g., omelettes). 2. *See* workstations.

station chefs At a food services operation following the brigade system, the individuals who produce the menu items and are under the supervision of the chef and sous-chef; generally, each station chef is assigned a specific task based on either cooking method and equipment (e.g., fry station chef) or category of items to be produced (e.g., garde-manger); also known as chefs de partie.

Stäubling (staub-ling) German for puffball mushroom.

Stayman apple An all-purpose apple with a dull, red-striped skin, an off-white, moderately firm flesh and a tart flavor.

Stayman Winesap apple An all-purpose apple native to North America; the medium-sized fruit has an elongated shape, a yellow-streaked skin, a firm, aromatic flesh and a tangy flavor.

St. Cecelia Society Punch A punch made of sparkling wine, Cognac, peach brandy, club soda, iced tea, dark Jamaican rum, sugar, curaçao, sliced limes, sliced lemons and chunked pineapple.

steady boil *See* boil, steady.

steak 1. A cross-sectional slice of a round fish with a small section of the bone attached. 2. A fabricated cut of meat, with or without the bone.

steak and kidney pie A British dish of chopped beef, kidneys, mushrooms, onions and beef stock (potatoes, hard-cooked eggs and/or oysters are sometimes added), topped with a pastry crust and baked.

steak and potatoes *See* meat and potatoes.

steak au poivre (oh PWAHV-rh) A French dish consisting of a steak covered with crushed peppercorns before being broiled or sautéed.

steak fries Large flat or wedge-shaped French fries.

steak knife 1. A small, slender, slightly bowed knife with a very sharp blade used in place settings. 2. A large, broad-bladed knife with a large handle used in place settings.

steak tails *See* porterhouse tails.

Steam Beer A hybrid of lager and ale, it is a style of beer brewed with bottom-fermenting yeast in traditional shallow vessels at 60–70°F (15.5–21.1°C).

Steamboat Gin A cocktail made of gin, Southern Comfort, grapefruit juice and lemon juice.

steamed bread A moist, tender bread leavened with baking powder or baking soda; it is placed in a covered container and steamed for several hours.

steamed buns Soft, round yeast rolls cooked in a bamboo steamer; created in regions of China where wheat was plentiful and now a standard dim sum dish.

steamed milk Milk that is heated with steam to approximately 150–170°F (65–76°C); used in coffee drinks.

steamed pudding A sweet, dense, breadlike dessert made by steaming batter in a covered container; the batter is often made with bread crumbs, spices and dried fruit (e.g., plum pudding).

steamer 1. An appliance used to steam foods in a closed compartment; the steam is generated by a built-in heat source. 2. An assemblage of two pots and a lid used on a stove top to steam foods; the bottom pot holds the water, and the upper pot, which rests on or in the bottom pot and has a perforated bottom, holds the food; also known as a vegetable steamer. *See* asparagus steamer *and* bamboo steamer. 3. A perforated metal or bamboo insert placed in a pot and used to steam foods. 4. A type of soft-shell clam from the U.S. East Coast.

steamer basket A collapsible basket with three or four short legs and numerous overlapping petals that open to a circle with an 8- to 10-in. diameter; the basket sits in a pot of boiling liquid holding the food above the liquid; the petals are perforated to allow the rising steam to cook the foods; also known as an expandable steamer basket.

steamer clam A small Atlantic soft-shell clam; it has a sweet, tender meat.

steaming A moist-heat cooking method in which heat is transferred by direct contact from steam to the food being cooked; the food to be steamed is placed in a basket or rack above a boiling liquid in a covered pan.

steam kettle; steam-jacketed kettle An appliance similar to a stockpot except that it is heated from the bottom and sides by steam (generated internally or from an outside source) circulating between layers of stainless steel; available in sizes from a 2-gallon table model to a 100-gallon floor model.

steamship round A subprimal cut of the beef primal round; it is a round rump with the shank partially removed.

steam table A large hollow table with a heat source and a grid top that accommodates various-sized hotel pans; water is added to the table and the steam that is created keeps the food warm for service.

steam table pan *See* hotel pan.

stearic acid 1. One of the principal fatty acids present in foods. 2. A food additive used as a flavoring agent and/or adjuvant.

stearoyl lactylate A food additive used as a dough conditioner in breads, an emulsifier in puddings and low-fat margarine and a whipping agent in egg products and vegetable fat toppings.

stearoyl propylene glycol hydrogen succinate *See* succistearin.

stearyl citrate A food additive used as an antioxidant in vegetable oils and margarine.

stearyl monoglyceridyl citrate A food additive used as an emulsion stabilizer in or with shortenings containing emulsifiers.

steccherino dorato (steh-cheh-reh-noh doh-rah-toh) Italian for hedgehog mushroom.

steel 1. Any of various artificially produced modified forms of the element iron; strength, hardness and elasticity vary depending on its exact composition. 2. A textured rod of steel or ceramic used to hone or straighten a knife blade immediately after and between sharpenings; also known as a butcher's steel and a straightening steel. *See* whetstone.

steel-cut oats *See* oats, steel-cut.

steelhead trout An anadromous rainbow trout found off the U.S. West Coast; after it returns to the saltwater from spawning, it acquires a grayish skin and loses its rainbow-striped olive to silver skin color; it has a pink to red flaky flesh and a mild flavor; also known as a salmon trout.

steely A wine-tasting term for a wine that is tart or austere without being harsh or green or has a mineral-like aroma or flavor.

Steen (steen) *See* Chenin Blanc.

steep To soak a food or seasoning in a hot liquid to extract flavors or impurities or to soften the item's texture.

steers Male cattle castrated before they mature and principally raised for beef. *See* stags.

stein (stine) An earthenware mug, originally German, sometimes with a lid; it has 1-pt. to 1-qt. capacity; often used for serving beer.

Steinhager (sh'tine-hay-ger) A German gin made exclusively from juniper berries that are crushed, fermented, distilled and then redistilled with grain neutral spirits; also known as Wacholder.

Steinpilz (sh'tine-pilz) German for bolete.

Steinwein (sh'tine-vine) An obsolete generic name for Franconian wines traditionally sold in a Bocksbeutel; the term now applies only to wines from the Stein vineyard in Würzburg (i.e., Würzburger Stein).

stek (stak) Swahili for beef steak.

steke (steh-ke) Norwegian for to roast.

stekt (styakt) Norwegian for fried.

stelk An Irish mashed potato dish flavored and colored with green onions and often served with bacon; also known as thump.

Stella cherry A variety of sweet cherry; the fruit have a bright to dark red skin and a sweet flavor.

Stellenbosch A grape-growing and wine-producing region of South Africa with the largest number of wine estates of any region in South Africa; the principal grapes grown are Cabernet Sauvignon, Pinot Noir, Chardonnay and Sauvignon Blanc; many other grapes are also grown and often used for blending; it produces both still and sparkling wines (using the Méthode Cap Classique).

stem 1. The slender, vertical part of a goblet, wineglass or other glass between the bowl and the base. 2. The handle of a spoon. 3. The part of a plant that produces and supports secondary branches, leaves and flowers. 4. The stalk of a mushroom, supporting the cap; also known as a stipe.

stemmer A machine that removes the stems from wine grapes before crushing and fermentation.

stemmy A wine-tasting term for a wine with a green disagreeable flavor reminiscent of damp twigs; it is often caused by fermenting the grapes with their stems.

stem thermometer; stem-type thermometer *See* thermometer.

sterculia gum *See* karaya gum.

sterilize In a food safety context, to destroy all living microorganisms on an object or in an environment. *See* clean *and* sanitize.

Sterno The proprietary name for canned solid fuel often used with chafing dishes or other serviceware to keep foods warm.

sterols Any of a group of lipids found in plants and animals.

Steuben grapes A variety of Concord table grapes; the large fruit have a purple-black skin and a sweet–tangy flavor.

stew *v.* To cook by stewing. *n.* Any dish prepared by stewing, usually containing meat and vegetables.

steward The person in charge of the storeroom where alcoholic beverages are kept.

stewed A wine-tasting term for a wine that is dull and has a vegetal, old tealike aroma.

stewing A combination cooking method similar to braising but generally involving smaller pieces of meat that are first blanched and then served with a sauce and various garnishes.

stewing beef *See* beef, stewing.

stewing hen *See* chicken, stewing.

St. Honoré (san-toh-naw-RAY) *See* gâteau St. Honoré.

stick bean *See* runner bean.

sticky bun A sweet yeast roll flavored with cinnamon and brown sugar; usually shaped into a pinwheel and baked atop a layer of butter and sugar, which caramelizes and becomes sticky.

sticky rice *See* glutinous rice.

stiff but not dry A culinary term for egg whites that are beaten until they hold firm peaks and are still glossy; they are moist and not too finely grained.

stikkelsbaer (stick-ells-bayr) Norwegian for gooseberry.

still An apparatus generally consisting of an evaporator, condenser and heat source; by applying heat to the still filled with a liquid, the alcohol in the liquid can be separated out and recovered. *See* distillation, pot still, Coffey still, patent still *and* double column still.

stillage The mash residue left in the still after distillation; it is often used for animal food.

still frozen A term used to refer to creamy or liquid items that are frozen without churning (e.g., marquise).

still-frozen desserts *See* semifreddo.

still house *See* distillery.

still water *See* water, still.

still wine *See* wine, still.

Stilton (STIHL-tn) A hard cheese made in England's Leicester, Derbyshire and Nottinghamshire areas from cow's milk; it has a pale yellow interior with blue-green veins, a wrinkled, melonlike rind, a rich, creamy, yet crumbly texture and a pungent, tangy flavor.

Stilton, White A young Stilton marketed before the veins develop; it has a white color and a mild, slightly sour flavor.

stimulant A substance such as alcohol or caffeine that temporarily increases some vital process or functional activity.

Stinger A cocktail made of equal parts white crème de menthe and either brandy, Cognac or other distilled spirits.

stinging nettle *See* nettle, common.

stingo A strong, dark, bitter beer named for the sharpness of its flavor.

stinkweed *See* epazote.

stipe *See* stem.

stiphado; stefado (stee-fah-doh; sta-pha-doh) A thick Greek stew of beef and onions, flavored with garlic, bay leaf, tomato purée and red or white wine.

stir-fry 1. A dry-heat cooking method similar to sautéing in which foods are cooked over very high heat with little fat while stirring constantly and briskly; usually done in a wok. 2. Any dish that is prepared by the stir-fry method.

stirred-curd cheese *See* granular cheese.

stirrer *See* swizzle stick.

stirring A mixing method in which ingredients are gently mixed until blended using a spoon, whisk or rubber spatula.

Stirrup *See* Hot Bricks.

stirrup cup A cup used to serve the last drink to a departing guest; named because of the old custom of serving the guest after he had mounted his horse and had his feet in the stirrups.

sti skara (stee skah-rah) A Greek preparation method in which fish are cooked on a grill.

stivaletti (stee-vah-lae-tea) Italian for little boots and used to describe pastina in the shape of small boots.

St. John's bread *See* carob.

St. Lawrence dressing A Canadian dressing made from olive oil, green olives, lemon juice, orange juice, paprika, onions, Worcestershire sauce, parsley and mustard.

St. Lucy's cherry *See* mahleb.

stock 1. A clear, unthickened liquid flavored by soluble substances extracted from meat, poultry or fish and their bones as well as from a mirepoix, other vegetables and seasonings; used for soups and sauces. 2. A plant or stem onto which a graft is made. 3. Total merchandise on hand.

stockfish Air-dried Norwegian cod.

stockless purchase The purchase of large quantities of goods that are stored by the seller and transported to the buyer as needed or desired; this practice is unethical or illegal in a few states.

stockpot A large pot that is taller than it is wide, with two handles, a flat lid, a capacity of 8–20 qt. and sometimes a spigot at the bottom to release liquid contents; used for making stocks or soups or boiling large amounts of water for pasta.

stockpot

stoemp (stemp) A Belgian dish of potatoes mashed with vegetables such as carrots, leeks, spinach, chicory or endive, flavored with nutmeg and served with sausages or sliced bacon.

sto foúrno (stoh foor-noh) A Greek preparation method in which fish are cooked in an oven.

stol (stohl) Russian for table.

stollen (STOH-luhn) A sweet German yeast bread filled with dried fruit, shaped like a folded oval and topped with a confectioners' sugar icing and candied cherries.

stolovaya (stah-LOH-vi-yah) A Russian cafeteria-style dining room or restaurant; often associated with a school, office or factory.

stomach A saclike distensible enlargement of the alimentary canal located between the esophagus and small intestine; it stores food, adds gastric juices, begins the breakdown of proteins and churns food into a liquid mass.

stone boiling A method of cooking used by Native Americans such as the Pueblos; foods are placed in a basket and hot stones are added.

stone crab A variety of crab found in the Atlantic Ocean from the Carolinas to Florida; it has a purple or reddish-brown mottled shell, large claws with black tips and firm, white claw meat with a sweet flavor similar to that of lobster; only the claws can be marketed; they have an average weight of 2.5–5.5 oz. (75–155 g).

stoned Slang for intoxicated.

Stone Fence; Stonewall A drink popular in the United States during the early 19th century; it is made of apple cider or applejack and a liquor such as rum.

stone fruits *See* drupes.

stoneground A method of preparing cornmeal or whole wheat flour by grinding the grist between two slowly moving stone wheels; the end product is generally coarse and contains all of the components of the grain.

stone-ground flour Flour produced by grinding the grain between two slowly moving stones; the grain is crushed without separating the germ or generating excess heat.

stone pine *See* umbrella pine.

stoner *See* pitter.

stones Seeds.

stoneware A hard, opaque ceramic fired at a very high temperature; usually fully glazed, nonporous and chip resistant; used for bakeware, cookware, dinnerware and serviceware.

Stonsdorfer (stohns-dor-fer) The proprietary name of a German bitters served as a digestif.

stoof 1. An enclosed chamber for drying foods. 2. A foot warmer that is also used to keep foods warm. 3. A chafing dish.

stoofsla (stoof-slah) A Dutch dish of boiled lettuce topped with bread crumbs and braised.

store cheese A term used in Canada and the Northeast United States for regional Cheddars and related cheeses.

storeroom purchases Goods received by a business and placed in a storeroom; they are released from the storeroom only on presentation of a requisition form.

storing 1. The activity of purchasing items in advance of their use and maintaining them until needed. 2. The process of aging barrels or bottles of wine or other items for future use; also known as laying away or laying down.

storione (stoh-reh-oh-neh) Italian for sturgeon.

storioni (stoh-ree-oh-nee) Greek for sturgeon.

stout A dark, bittersweet and heavy-bodied beer made with roasted malt and a relatively high hops content; it is fermented with a top-fermenting yeast.

stove-top grill A cast-iron grill with a ridged cooking surface (similar to both a frying pan and a griddle), often coated with a nonstick finish; it uses the stove top as a heat source.

stovies (stoh-veez) Scottish for boiled potatoes.

St. Peter's fish *See* John Dory.

St. Peter's mark *See* haddock.

Stracchino (strah-KEE-no) A group of several Italian cheeses made from cow's milk; they have a mild and delicate lactic flavor similar to that of cream cheese, a white, smooth interior and no rind; generally sold in slabs or loaves.

stracciatella (strah-chee-TEL-lah) A central Italian soup made from beef or chicken broth and semolina; eggs are mixed into the heated liquid to form strands and the soup is garnished with Parmesan.

Stragotte, sauce (stra-gut) A French compound sauce made from a demi-glaze flavored with a game stock and trimmings, herbs, tomato purée and red or white wine, finished with butter and Madeira wine and garnished with mushrooms.

straight A beverage, usually alcoholic, served without any other ingredients except ice.

straight bourbon *See* bourbon.

straight cut A cutting method in which the food is cut perpendicular to the cutting surface with one smooth downward stroke; also known as guillotine cut.

straight dough method A technique for mixing yeast breads in which all ingredients are combined at once.

Straight 8 cucumber A variety of slicing cucumber.

straightening steel *See* steel.

straight flour Wheat flour milled from all parts of the wheat kernel except the bran and germ.

straightforward A wine-tasting term for a wine that is direct, honest and simple, without pretense.

straight rye A straight whiskey made with a mash containing at least 51% rye.

straight-up A cocktail served without ice; also known as up.

straight whiskey A whiskey (e.g., bourbon, rye or Tennessee whiskey) distilled at 160 proof or less from a mash made with a minimum of 51% of a single grain and aged at least 2 years in new charred white oak barrels; at bottling, it must have a proof no lower than 80; a straight whiskey can be mixed provided that the spirits are from the same distillation period at a single distillery. *See* blended whiskey.

strain To pour foods through a sieve, mesh strainer or cheesecloth to separate or remove the liquid component from solids.

strainer *See* wire mesh strainer.

Strasbourg goose A French goose bred for its liver.

strattù (strah-TOO) An Italian sauce made from sun-dried tomatoes.

Stravecchio (strah-veh-chee-oh) A 3-year-old Parmesan.

Stravecchionel (strah-veh-chee-oh-nee'l) A Parmesan that is 4 years or older.

straw A wine-tasting term for the color of a young white wine; it can range from pale yellow to green-gold.

strawberries Romanoff; Romanov (roh-mahn-off) A dessert consisting of strawberries soaked in orange-flavored liqueur, then topped with whipped cream.

strawberry A low-growing plant (genus *Fragaria*) with a conical berry that has tiny seeds on the outside of its red skin; the berry has a red to white juicy flesh and a sweet flavor.

strawberry, ever-bearing Any of a variety of cultivated strawberries that bear fruit continuously through the autumn.

strawberry, June-bearing Any of a variety of cultivated strawberries that bear fruit during the late spring or early summer; June-bearing varieties are considered more consistently flavorful than ever-bearing ones.

strawberry, modern Any of a variety of cultivated strawberries, including June-bearing and ever-bearing ones; most modern strawberries are a hybrid of the Chilean Pine and Scarlet Virginian strawberries.

strawberry bass *See* crappie.

strawberry guava A variety of small, particularly sweet guava.

strawberry huller A pair of tweezers with gripping surfaces on each rounded end used to grasp a picked strawberry's leaves; the leaves are twisted and pulled, removing them and the berry's core.

strawberry huller

strawberry pear *See* pitahaya.

strawberry shortcake *See* shortcake.

strawberry tomato *See* ground-cherry.

strawberry tree A shrub (*Arbutus unedo*) native to Korea and Japan and grown in Europe; its large red, strawberry-like fruit have a bland flavor; also known as cane fruit.

straw mushroom A mushroom (*Volvariella volvacea*) with a long, conical cap over a bulbous stem; it has a gray-brown color, a silky texture and a mild flavor and is usually available canned; also known as a paddy-straw mushroom.

straw potatoes Long, thin French fries.

straw wine *See* vin de paille.

streak o'lean; streak-of-lean Slang for bacon.

streaky bacon Smoked bacon from the hog's belly.

street food Hot and cold snacks prepared and sold by street vendors.

Strega (STRAY-guh) A yellow Italian liqueur flavored with oranges and herbs.

Streickwurst (strike-voorst) A German sausage made to be used as a spread; it is usually smoked.

strength 1. The quality or state of being strong or powerful. 2. The muscles' ability to work against resistance. 3. The concentration or potency of a liquor or flavor.

Streptococcus lactis Bacteria found in some buttermilk and that helps digest lactose.

Streptococcus pyogenes Bacteria that cause a severe sore throat (called streptococcal pharangitis, or strep throat) or scarlet fever; the bacteria are transmitted through ingestion of contaminated foods (especially milk) or water or by infected food handlers.

stress eating Inappropriate eating in response to anxiety or stress.

streusel (STROO-zuhl) A crumbly mixture of fat, flour, sugar and sometimes nuts and spices; used to top baked goods.

strike temperature The water temperature when the grist is added to begin the beer-brewing process.

string bean *See* green bean.

string cheese A mozzarella-style cheese made in the United States from cow's milk; the cheese is formed into ropes that can be pulled apart and eaten.

string hopper *See* appa.

striped bass 1. A true bass, this anadromous fish is rarely available commercially. 2. A hybrid of the striped bass and white bass or white perch aquafarmed along both coasts of the United States and marketed as striped bass; it has a silvery skin with horizontal dark gray stripes, a firm, slightly fatty, flaky white flesh, a rich, sweet flavor and an average market weight of 1–15 lb. (0.5–6.8 kg); mistakenly known as rockfish.

striped mullet *See* mullet.

striped perch *See* yellow perch.

striped tuna *See* skipjack tuna.

strip loin steak; strip steak A fabricated cut of the beef primal short loin; it is the flavorful, tender, usually boneless top loin or eye muscle; also known as a Delmonico steak, Kansas City strip steak and New York steak.

stripper A tool with a short flat blade with a U-shaped indention

stripper

used to cut thin strips of citrus zest or to peel vegetables in a decorative pattern; also known as canelle knife and citrus stripper.

strip stamp A U.S. Internal Revenue Service (IRS) tax stamp affixed over the closure of bottles of distilled spirits; green stamps are used for bottled-in-bond distilled spirits, and red stamps are used for most other distilled spirits.

strisciule (strees-shoe-lay) A Corsican stew made with sun-dried goat's meat and onions, flavored with herbs.

stroganoff (STROH-guh-noff) A Russian dish of beef, onions and mushrooms in a sour cream sauce; usually served over noodles.

stromboli (strohm-bow-lee) A Philadelphia speciality sandwich of pizza dough wrapped over fillings such as mozzarella and pepperoni and baked. *See* calzone.

strong 1. A tasting term for a flavor, aroma or other attribute that is particularly pronounced in a food or beverage. 2. A tasting term for a beer, wine or distilled spirit in which the high alcohol content is detectable as a harsh, burning aroma and flavor. 3. A wine-tasting term for a wine that is flavorful and full bodied, with relatively high levels of acid, extracts and alcohol.

strong flour *See* flour, strong.

stroop A light brown syrup used in the Netherlands for pancakes.

stroopwafel (stroop-vah-fell) A Dutch cookie consisting of two thin, crisp, sweet wafers flavored with cinnamon and nutmeg and imprinted with a crosshatch pattern, sandwiched together with molasses or a caramel-flavored syrup.

structure A wine-tasting term referring to the interaction of the wine's essential components, such as tannin, acid and alcohol, which create the wine's body, flavor and aroma.

strudel (STROO-duhl) A long rectangular German pastry made with many layers of a very thin dough rolled around a sweet or savory filling and baked until crisp and golden.

struffoli (STROO-foh-leh) Small deep-fried rounds of dough coated in caramel and traditionally piled together in a pyramid shape; a Christmas dessert from Naples, Italy.

stucchevole (stoo-kae-voh-lae) Italian for cloying.

Stück (shtook) A German cask used to hold wines, especially Rhine wines; it has a capacity of 1200 liters.

stuck fermentation *See* stuck wine.

stuck wine A must that fails to ferment because either excessively high temperatures kill the yeast or the juice does not contain sufficient nutrients for the yeast to function.

stud To insert a decoration or flavor-enhancing edible substance into the surface of food (e.g., cloves into a ham).

stufato (stu-FAH-toa) Italian for stew.

stuff To fill a cavity in a food with another food.

stuffed flank steak A beef flank steak into which a pocket has been cut; it is then filled with a stuffing.

stuffing 1. A seasoned mixture of foods used to fill a natural or created cavity in poultry, meats, fish and vegetables or around which a strip of poultry, meat, shellfish, fish or vegetables may be rolled. 2. *See* dressing.

stump knocker *See* warmouth.

sturdy A wine-tasting term for a wine that is solid, substantial and capable of aging well.

sturgeon An anadromous fish found in the Black Sea, Caspian Sea, the Pacific Ocean off the northwest U.S. coast and in the southern Atlantic Ocean; it has a pale gray skin, an average market weight of 60 lb. (27 kg), a high fat content and a firm flesh with a rich, delicate flavor. *See* caviar *and* isinglass.

sturgeon

style 1. A particular, distinctive or characteristic mode of cooking, garnishing and/or presenting foods and/or beverages. 2. The sum of flavors and other sensory characteristics used to compare foods and beverages; foods and beverages of the same style tend to have the same general flavor profile.

styrene A food additive with a pleasantly sharp, penetrating aroma and flavor; used as a flavor enhancer.

styrofoam A lightweight plastic material used to make insulating containers such as cups and ice chests.

su (soo) Japanese for rice vinegar.

su-age (sue-ah-guh) A Japanese cooking method in which foods, usually small items without any flour or batter coating, are deep-fried in moderately hot oil.

suàn (swen) Chinese for garlic.

suanmei (soo-ahn-may) Plums pickled in brine; they are brown and soft and used as a flavoring in Chinese meat and fish dishes.

suan niúnai; suan nai (soo-ahn nee-oon-ah-ee; soo-ahn na-ee) Chinese for yogurt.

suar kaa maans (soo-ar kah mahns) Hindi for pork.

subah kaa naashtaa (soo-bah kah nassh-tah) Hindi for breakfast.

subcutaneous fat The fat layer between the hide and muscles of a carcass; it appears on the outer edges of certain fabricated cuts; also known as exterior fat.

sub gum The base of many Chinese dishes; it consists of bamboo shoots, water chestnuts and fresh mushrooms.

submarine sandwich; sub *See* hero.

submersion poaching A poaching method in which the food is completely covered with the poaching liquid.

subprimal cuts The basic cuts of meat (with or without bones) produced from each primal; relatively large, they are sometimes further reduced into fabricated cuts.

subtle A tasting term for a food or beverage that has delicate flavor nuances not easily detected.

subtlety An archaic term for a highly ornamented device wholly or chiefly made of sugar and gum; it was sometimes eaten but generally used as a table decoration.

subye (soo-bee-ah) A mixture of rice and water used as a basis for Turkish milk desserts.

succès (sou-say) A French pastry made with layers of baked almond meringue and praline buttercream.

succinic acid A food additive used as a flavor enhancer and/or pH control agent; also known as amber acid and ethylenesuccinic acid.

succinic derivatives A group of food additives used as a protective coating on some fruits and tubers.

succinylated monoglycerides A food additive used as an emulsifier in shortenings and as a dough conditioner.

succistearin A food additive used as an emulsifier in or with shortenings and edible oils intended for use in cakes and cake fillings, toppings and icings; also known as stearoyl propylene glycol hydrogen succinate.

succo (SOOK-ko) Italian for juice.

succory (SOOK-ko-ree) A variety of chicory; its root is roasted and ground and used as a coffee substitute or blended with coffee to add aroma and body. *See* Creole coffee.

succotash (SUHK-uh-tash) An American Southern dish of corn, lima beans and sometimes red and green peppers.

suck cream A British beverage from the Cornwall region made from cream, egg yolk, white wine, sugar and grated lemon peel; served cold with dry toast.

sucker *See* lollipop.

suckermouth buffalo fish *See* buffalo fish.

sucket; succade; succate An archaic term for fruit, fruit rind and nuts preserved in sugar, either candied or in a syrup; sweetmeats of candied fruits.

sucket fork A metal (usually silver) utensil with a fork (tines) at one end and a spoon (a bowl) at the other; used for eating preserved fruit: the fruit is held by the fork and the juice by the spoon.

suco (SOO-koh) Portuguese for juice.

sucré (sewkr) French for sugar.

sucrine 1. A small, firm-headed lettuce with a sweet flavor; grown in France. 2. A variety of medium-sized, pear-shaped squash with a dark green skin.

sucrose A disaccharide derived from sugarcane, sugar beet, sorghum and other sources; available as white or brown sugar, molasses or powdered sugar; sweeter than glucose but not as sweet as fructose; during digestion it is hydrolyzed into its component single sugars: glucose and fructose; also known as table sugar and sugar.

sucrose fatty acid esters Food additives used as emulsifiers in baked goods, dairy substitutes and frozen desserts, as texturizers in bakery mixes and as components of protective coatings for fruit.

sucrose polyester (SPE) An artificial fat used instead of oil or butter; indigestible, it contributes no calories to the diet.

sucrosity The sensation or taste of sweetness, with or without the presence of sugar.

sucs The savory juices released by meats and fish during cooking; generally, they are the caramelized juices left on the bottom of a sauté or roasting pan before deglazing.

sudak (sue-dack) Russian for pike perch.

sudaré (soo-dah-reh) The Japanese slatted mat used for rolling foods.

suds; bucket of suds American slang for beer.

suédoise, mayonnaise; Swedish mayonnaise (soo-dwahz) A French mayonnaise sauce blended with apple purée that has been cooked with white wine; it is garnished with horseradish.

suéhiro (soo-ha-he-row) Japanese for fan and used to describe a decorative cut of food.

suero de leche (soo-roh da lee-chee) Spanish for whey.

suet The hard, crisp, white fat found around the kidneys of cattle, sheep and other animals; used as an ingredient, flavoring and cooking medium.

suey gow (soo-hei go) Flat rounds of dough used to wrap foods in Chinese cuisines.

suf *See* tabouli.

sufu *See* dòufù-ru.

sugar 1. A group of carbohydrates containing one (monosaccharide) or two (disaccharide) sugar units; occurring naturally principally in fruits and honey, it is sweet, soluble and readily absorbed to be used as an energy source. 2. A sweet, water-soluble crystalline carbohydrate; used as a sweetener and preservative for foods. *See* confectioners' sugar, crystal sugar, molasses, raw sugar, sucrose, sugar beet, sugarcane, superfine sugar *and* turbinado sugar.

sugar, raw A natural sugar that has been washed to remove the impurities; it has a light golden color and a large crystal.

sugar alcohol Any of a group of caloric sweeteners derived from fruits or produced from glucose; chemically related to sugar (sucrose), they are absorbed more slowly or metabolized differently than sugar.

sugar apple *See* cherimoya.

sugar beet A variety of beet (*Beta vulgaris*) with a white flesh and a white, yellow or black skin; it has an extremely high sugar content and is used to produce table sugar.

sugar beet extract flavor base A food additive used as a flavoring agent.

sugar bloom A white crust of sugar crystals that forms on the surface of chocolate or other candies; sugar is drawn out of the candies and dissolves in the surface moisture; when the moisture evaporates, the sugar crystals remain.

sugar boiler *See* sugar pan.

sugar bowl A small covered bowl used to serve and store sugar; the lid sometimes has a notch to accommodate a spoon's handle.

sugarcane; sugar cane A very thick, tall, perennial grass (*Saccharum officinarum*) grown in tropical and subtropical areas; its sap has an extremely high sugar content and is used to produce table sugar.

Sugar Cherry tomato A variety of extremely small (pea-sized), red-skinned cherry tomato.

sugarcoat To cover a food with sugar.

sugar cube *See* lump sugar.

sugar cured Pertaining to a food preserved with a preparation of sugar, salt and nitrates (e.g., a sugar-cured ham).

sugar dredger A container with a perforated lid used for coating a food with sugar.

sugar-free; sugarless Food-labeling terms approved by the U.S. Food and Drug Administration (FDA) to describe a food containing no saccharide sweetener such as sucrose; the product may contain sugar alcohols, even though they provide similar calories.

sugar grove; sugar orchard A grove of maples used as a source of maple sugar or syrup.

sugaring The process of adding sugar to the must to increase the wine's alcohol content. *See* chaptalization.

sugar loaf A large, conical loaf of pure, concentrated sugar; it was the form in which sugar was traditionally purchased.

sugar maple *See* maple.

sugar pan; sugar boiler A deep, straight-sided, flat-bottomed, unlined, heavy-gauge copper pan with a hollow handle and a pour spout; used to melt sugar, make sugar syrup and cook sugar mixtures; also known as a sugar boiler.

sugar pea *See* snow pea.

sugar plate A traditional name for a confection or sweetmeat made in a flat cake; it was sometimes formed with a decorative flat wooden mold.

sugarplum A small sugary candy made with dried fruits and fondant.

sugar snap pea A sweet pea that is a hybrid of the English pea and snow pea; the bright green, crisp pod and the paler green, tender seeds are both edible.

sugar substitute *See* artificial sweetener.

sugar syrup 1. A syrup made from sugar and water heated gently until the sugar is dissolved; also known as a simple syrup. 2. Melted sugar cooked until it reaches a specific temperature.

sugata-zuke (soo-gah-tah-zoo-she) Japanese for a very small whole fish that is the topping for a nigiri-zushi.

sugo (SOO-goa) 1. Italian for the juice from a fruit or vegetable. 2. Italian for sauce or gravy, generally used to describe meat sauces. *See* bolognese.

suhoy Russian for dry.

sui-doufu (soo-ee-doo-foo) Chinese for kinugoshi.

sui maai (soo-ee mah-ha-ee) Chinese wrappers similar to won tons.

su-joyu (soo-joe-you) Japanese for a mixture of vinegar and soy sauce.

suju (su-ju) An alcoholic beverage distilled in Korea from grain or potatoes.

sukari (soo-kah-ree) Swahili for granulated sugar.

sukhar' (soo-kahr) Russian for bread crumbs.

sukiyaki (soo-kee-YAH-kee) A Japanese dish of sliced beef or chicken cooked with soy sauce and often garnished with bamboo shoots, soybean curd, onions and other vegetables.

sukiyakinabe (soo-kee-jah-kee-na-be) A shallow, cast-iron pan used in Japan for making sukiyaki.

sukker (sou-kerr) Norwegian for sugar.

sukkertøy Norwegian for candy.

sukuma wiki (soo-koo-mah we-key) A Kenyan dish consisting of diced cooked beef, spinach, tomatoes, bell peppers and onions flavored with chiles and served over rice.

Sulawesi Arabica coffee beans grown on the island of Celebes in Indonesia; the beverage has a smooth, buttery flavor and a rich aroma.

sulfated butyl oleate A food additive used to dehydrate grapes to produce raisins.

sulfites Sulfur-containing agents used as preservatives for fresh and frozen fruits and vegetables; they can cause allergy symptoms in sensitive individuals.

sulfur A major mineral principally used as a component of biotin, thiamine, insulin and certain amino acids and to assist the body's detoxification process; it is found in all protein-containing foods.

sulfur dioxide A food additive used as a preservative.

sulfuric acid A food additive used as a pH control agent in alcoholic beverages and cheeses; also known as oil of vitriol.

Sultana The Australian name for Thompson Seedless grapes; used for raisins, table grapes or to make a neutral wine used in blending inexpensive white wines.

sultanas See golden raisins.

Sumac; sumaq (soo-mak) A shrub (genus *Rhus*) native to Turkey; its fleshy petals and berries are dried and reduced to a purple powder that has an acidic flavor, and its leaves are steeped in water and have a sour, slightly peppery flavor; both are used as flavorings in Middle Eastern cuisines.

suman (su-man) A Filipino dish made with glutinous rice and coconut milk, wrapped in coconut or banana leaves and boiled.

Sumatran (soo-MA-trahn) Arabica coffee beans grown on the island of Sumatra in Indonesia; the beverage is sweet, mellow, earthy, rich and full bodied.

Su-Mi-Re (soo-MEE-ray) A smooth, full-bodied Japanese cordial the color of violets made from a citron and fruit base and flavored with spices, herbs, almonds, oranges and vanilla.

summer coating A mixture of sugar, vegetable fat, flavorings and colorings used as a candy coating (it does not contain cocoa butter); also known as confectionery coating.

summer flounder See fluke.

summer grape See pigeon grape.

summer pudding A British dessert consisting of slices of white bread and sweetened fresh berries, usually red currants, molded in a casserole dish and served with whipped cream.

summer sausages See sausages, dry.

summer savory See savory, summer.

summer spinach See New Zealand spinach.

summer squash See squash, summer.

summer trout See sea trout.

sumoku (su-MOH-koo) See kunsei no.

sun (suen) Chinese for bamboo shoots.

sunchoke See Jerusalem artichoke.

sundae A dessert made with one or more scoops of ice cream topped with one or more sweet sauces and garnished with whipped cream and chopped nuts.

Sunderland pudding A light, spongy custard flavored with nutmeg and served with a sauce of sugar and wine.

sundowner British and British colonial slang for a cocktail party.

sun-dried tomato A tomato that has been dried in the sun; it has a dark, ruby red color, a chewy texture and an intense flavor; available dried or packed in oil (including flavored oils). See oven-dried tomato.

sunfish A large family of small to moderately large freshwater fish; generally known for vivid skin colors and a subtle, sweet flavor; significant varieties include the bluegill, crappie, rock bass and warmouth.

sunflower oil; sunflower seed oil An oil obtained from sunflower seeds; it has a pale yellow color and virtually no flavor and is high in polyunsaturated fats and low in saturated fats; used for cooking and in dressings.

sunflower seeds The seeds of the sunflower plant; they have a hard black-and-white-striped shell that is removed before eating; usually eaten dried or roasted, with or without salt.

sungkaya (song-kah-yah) A Thai custard made with coconut milk, eggs and sugar steamed in a bowl or half coconut and chilled before serving.

Sunglo nectarine A variety of nectarine; the yellow and red fruit have a particularly sweet flavor.

Sungold tomato A variety of relatively small, spherical, orange-skinned, flavorful tomato.

sung rugu (soon'g roo-goo) Chinese for milky cap mushroom.

sun mian (soon mah-in) Chinese vermicelli-style noodles made of soft wheat.

sunny-side-up egg An egg that is not flipped during frying; its yolk should remain intact. See over egg.

sunomono (SOO-noh-moh-noh) Japanese for vinegared foods, used to describe salads of raw or cooked vegetables that are coated with vinegar, sometimes sweetened with sugar and flavored with various seasonings.

sun perch See redbreast sunfish.

sunset yellow FCF See FD&C Yellow #6.

sunshine snapper See tilapia.

sup (soop) Russian for soup.

superfine sugar A finely granulated form of refined sugar; used in beverages and frostings because of the speed with which it will dissolve; also known as castor (caster) sugar.

superiore (soo-pair-y'OH-reh) Italian for superior and used as a labeling term for a wine that was made from riper than normal grapes and then aged.

supermarket A departmentalized self-service market selling foods, household items and convenience goods arranged in open displays.

Super Roma tomato A variety of fleshy plum tomato; it has a slightly pointed shape.

super-Tuscans High-quality red and white wines produced in Italy's Tuscany region using methods, varietals or compositions not approved by the DOC/DOCG.

supp (soop) Estonian for soup.

supparot (soo-pah-rott) Thai for pineapple.

suppe (suh-peh) Danish and Norwegian for soup.

Suppe (ZUP-per) German for soup.

supper 1. Traditionally, a light meal served in the evening. *See* dinner. 2. Now, the main meal of the day in the United States, served in the evening; also known as dinner.

supple 1. A wine-tasting term for a well-balanced, smooth, soft, agreeable wine that is not too tannic. 2. A cheese-tasting term for the resilient or pliable texture of a cheese, usually a semisoft cheese; the cheese should be bendable but not rubbery.

supplements Preparations such as pills, powders or liquids containing one or more specific nutrients and consumed to augment a real or perceived dietary deficiency; some supplements are unsafe food additives as defined by the U.S. Food and Drug Administration (FDA); also known as nutrient supplements and food supplements.

suppli (SOO-plee) An Italian dish consisting of leftover risotto bound with an egg and shaped into balls, sometimes with a meat or cheese stuffing, rolled in bread crumbs and deep-fried.

suprême A boneless, skinless chicken breast with the first wing segment attached.

suprême, sauce (soo-prem) A French sauce made by adding cream to a velouté made from chicken stock; it is used to make several compound sauces of the velouté family.

suprême de volaille (soo-prem duh vo-lye) A French dish consisting of a chicken breast served with a cream sauce.

supu (SOO-poo) Japanese and Swahili for soup.

supuya papai (soo-poo-yah pah-pie) A hot or cold Tanzanian soup made from papaya, cream and onions.

Surati (SU-rah-te) A soft Indian cheese made from water buffalo's milk; it has a pale ivory-white color and sharp flavor; it is kept in whey while it ages; also known as paneer.

Surbraten (suhr-brah-tan) A general description for Austrian dishes of pickled meats that are then cooked and served warm.

sur commande (suhr com-mahn'd) French for on order; used on menus to describe foods that will be cooked to order (as opposed to being prepared in advance).

surdo (soor-doe) A mixture of unfermented grape juice and alcohol; used to sweeten Madeira.

sureau (suhr-roe) French for elderberry.

Sureau (suhr-roe) A French eau-de-vie made from elderberries.

surface-finishing agent A type of food additive used to maintain or add gloss and/or inhibit surface discoloration of a food; it includes protective coatings, polishes, waxes and glazes.

surface-ripened cheese A category of cheeses that have ripened from the rind inward as a result of the application of mold, yeast or bacteria to the surface; after ripening, the paste should be soft and creamy; there are two types of surface-ripened cheeses: bloomy rind and washed rind; also known as rind-ripened cheese and soft-ripened cheese.

surf clam Any of several clams found in deep waters off the east coasts of the United States and Canada; they have white, ovoid shells and a somewhat chewy, pinkish-tan flesh; often used for canning; also known as bar, beach, hen, sea and skimmer clams.

surf-n-turf Meat and seafood served on the same plate (usually a steak and lobster).

surgelato (soor-jeh-LAH-toh) Italian for frozen, as in frozen food.

Surhaxe (suhr-hah-xan) A Bavarian dish of ham hocks baked with sauerkraut and mashed potatoes.

suribachi (SOO-ree-BAH-chee) An unglazed earthenware or plastic Japanese mortar with a moderately low concave face with a ridged surface and available with 5- to 10-in. diameters; used for crushing seeds and grinding chopped foods such as shrimp into a paste. *See* surikogi.

surikogi (SOO-ree-KOH-ghee) A 10-in.-long Japanese pestle used with a suribachi. *See* suribachi.

surimi (soo-REE-mee) A Japanese processed food made from a mild white-fleshed fish such as Alaskan pollock, shaped, flavored and colored to resemble various types of shellfish, such as crab and shrimp.

Surinam cherry *See* pitanga.

sur lie (soo'r lee) 1. The process of leaving wine in contact with its lees to add complexity. 2. The period a bottle-fermented sparkling wine spends on the lees before being disgorged.

surplus The amount by which the quantity supplied or on hand exceeds the quantity needed at the existing price. *See* shortage.

surrounding beverage cost The cost of all items accompanying a drink (e.g., lime wedge with a gin and tonic).

surrounding dish cost The cost of all items accompanying an entrée (e.g., salad and bread) or the main ingredient of a dish (e.g., cocktail sauce with a shrimp cocktail).

surtout; surtout de table (suhr-tou; suhr-tou duh tahbl) A decorative and useful object, usually of silver or silver and glass, holding oil bottles, sugar shakers, fruit and/or pickles and sweetmeats that remains in the center of the table during the entire meal.

sushi (SOO-shee) 1. A Japanese dish of cooked seasoned rice (zushi) garnished with a variety of cooked or raw ingredients such as fish, shellfish and vegetables; there are four principal types of sushi: chirashi-zushi, maki-zushi, nigiri-zushi and oshi-zushi. 2. An imprecisely used term for nigiri-zushi. 3. An incorrectly used term for sashimi. *See* sashimi.

sushi, pressed *See* oshi-zushi.

sushi, rolled *See* maki-zushi.

sushi, scattered *See* chirashi-zushi.

sushi, squeezed *See* nigiri-zushi.

sushi bar A restaurant or an area within a restaurant featuring sushi and sashimi (although other Japanese foods are often available); typically, diners are seated at a counter so that they can watch the chefs prepare the food.

sushi meshi (SOO-shee MEH-shee) Japanese for the vinegared rice used in sushi dishes.

sushi oke (SOO-shee OH-keh) The Japanese wooden tub used to season rice for sushi.

sushi su (SOO-shee soo) Japanese for seasoned vinegar.

susina (soo-ZEE-nee) Italian for plum.

suspending agents *See* thickening agents.

Sussigkeit (soo-seae-kite) German for candy.

Süssreserve (soo'ss-reh-zer-veh) Unfermented grape juice rich in natural sugar that is added to a wine just before bottling to increase sweetness.

Sutton's Perfection asparagus A variety of particularly flavorful asparagus.

sutzukakia (sue-tzoo-kah-kea-ah) A Greek dish of grilled meat sausages served with tomato, onion and feta.

suwar ka gosht (soo-vahr kah gosht) Hindi for ham.

suya (soo-yah) A Nigerian dish consisting of chicken marinated in garlic, ginger, paprika, minced peanuts, dried onions and peanut oil and then threaded on skewers and grilled; beef or lamb is also used.

Suze (sooz) A dry French aperitif derived from gentian root; it has a yellow color and a bitter flavor; usually served with ice and soda.

suzine *See* pilau.

suzuki (soo-zoo-kee) Japanese for sea bass. *See* seigo *and* fukko.

svamp (svahmp) Danish and Swedish for mushrooms.

svekla (svehk-la) Russian for beetroot.

svezhiy (sva-zhe-hee) Russian for fresh.

svid (sveed) An Icelandic dish made from simmered meat pulled from a lamb's head and served, hot or cold, with mashed turnips.

svinekjøtt (svee-neh-shut) Norwegian for pork.

svinekod (svee-neh-kood) Danish for pork.

svinina (sveh-nee-nah) Russian for pork.

svinjsko meso (sveen-sko meh-soh) Serbo-Croat for pork.

sviske (SVISS-kerr) Norwegian for prune.

Swaledale A firm English cheese made from unpasteurized cow's milk; it has a creamy white interior, a dark yellow rind and a mild flavor.

swamp blueberry *See* blueberry, high-bush.

swamp cabbage *See* hearts of palm.

Swan River Valley A grape-growing and wine-producing region in western Australia, north of Perth; it is known for its fortified wines.

Swartland A small and relatively new grape-growing and wine-producing region of South Africa best known for Pinotage and other full-bodied red wines, including ports.

swatow mustard *See* gai choy.

sweating Cooking a food (typically vegetables) in a small amount of fat, usually covered, over low heat without browning until the food softens and releases moisture; sweating allows the food to release its flavor more quickly when it is later cooked with other foods. *See* butter steam.

swede; Swedish turnip *See* rutabaga.

swedge *See* knife point.

Swedish Brown A bean with a light brown color and a white eye.

Swedish meatballs A dish of ground beef mixed with onions, bread crumbs soaked in milk, eggs and seasonings, shaped into small balls and fried or broiled and then served in a brown gravy made from the pan drippings and cream.

Swedish Punsch; Swedish Punch A Swedish liqueur with a sweet, spicy flavor; its principal flavoring is Batavia arak; also known as Arak Punsch and Caloric Punsch.

sweet 1. One of the basic taste sensations. 2. Something having a flavor of or like sugar. 3. A candy or other small sweetly flavored treat. 4. A wine-tasting term for a wine that retains some detectable amount of sugar after fermentation; it is generally quite noticeable on the palate (e.g., Sauternes). *See* dry, semidry *and* semisweet. 5. A coffee-tasting term used to describe a smooth and palatable coffee.

sweet almond *See* almond.

sweet-and-sour Any of a variety of dishes that combines sweet and sour flavors, usually sugar and a vinegar-based ingredient.

sweet anise *See* fennel, Florence.

sweet basil *See* basil.

sweet beer A combination of beer and fruit juice (usually lemon or lime); it often has a higher alcohol content than lager beer.

sweet bell pepper *See* bell pepper.

sweetbreads The thymus gland of a calf, lamb or young hog; it consists of two principal parts, the elongated throat bread and the more spherical heart bread; both have a mild, delicate flavor.

sweet calabash A medium-sized fruit (*Passiflora maliformis*) grown in South America and the West Indies; it has a thin yellow-brown skin, a gray or orange-yellow juicy flesh and a pleasant flavor.

sweet cherry *See* cherry, sweet.

sweet cicely An herb from a bushy perennial plant (*Myrrhis odorata*) with hairy, thin, fernlike leaves that have a sweet scent and a flavor reminiscent of anise.

sweet cider Freshly pressed apple juice that has not been fermented.

sweet corn *See* corn.

sweet cream butter *See* butter, sweet cream.

sweet cucumber *See* tea melon.

sweet-curd cheese Cheese made by the cheddaring process, except that the curd is cut, heated and drained to reduce acidity; similar to a Cheddar-style cheese but with more moisture and a less compact body (e.g., brick, Edam and Gouda).

sweet dough *See* pâte sucrée.

sweetened condensed milk *See* milk, sweetened condensed.

sweetener Anything used to add a sweet flavor to foods (e.g., sugar, molasses, saccharin and honey).

sweet fennel *See* fennel, Florence.

Sweet Heart Seedless watermelon A watermelon variety; it is relatively small and flavorful.

sweet lemon *See* limetta.

sweet lightnin' Moonshine sweetened with honey, maple syrup or other sweetener to make it more palatable.

sweet lime A variety of lime with a sweet (not sour) flavor.

sweet marjoram *See* marjoram.

Sweet Martini A cocktail made of gin, sweet vermouth and orange bitters and garnished with a twist or orange peel.

sweet mash process A whiskey-making process (primarily for bourbon) in which only fresh yeast is used for the mash (i.e., no spent beer or stillage is used); also known as yeast mash process. *See* sour mash process.

sweetmeal biscuit *See* digestive biscuit.

sweetmeat Any small piece of sweet candy or pastry, especially candied fruit.

sweetmeat glass A broad bell-shaped bowl with a tall stem and foot, used for holding dry sweetmeats on a dessert table or on the top of a pyramid of salvers.

sweetmeat pole An English term for a glass épergne consisting of a center pole with horizontal arms holding baskets for dry sweetmeats or pickles.

sweet melon *See* muskmelon.

sweet milk A term used imprecisely for whole cow's milk.

Sweet Million tomato A variety of red-skinned, flavorful cherry tomato.

Sweet 100 tomato A variety of relatively small, spherical, red-skinned, flavorful tomato.

sweet pepper 1. The fruit of various plants of the genus *Capsicum;* it has a mild, sweet flavor with undertones of various fruits and spices; a fresh sweet pepper can be white, yellow, orange, green, red, brown or purple, and its shape is generally conical to nearly spherical; sweet peppers are rarely used dried. *See* bell pepper, chile *and* pepper. 2. A term used imprecisely for a bell pepper.

sweet pepper

sweet potato The starchy tuber of a morning glory plant (*Ipomoea Batatas*) native to South America; it is unrelated to the potato plant and yam and has a sweet flavor.

sweet potato, red A variety of sweet potato with a thick, dark orange skin and an orange flesh that remains moist when cooked; sometimes erroneously called a yam.

sweet potato, white A variety of sweet potato with a thick, light yellow skin, a pale yellow, mealy flesh that becomes dry and fluffy when cooked and a flavor that is less sweet than that of a sweet potato; also known as a batata dulce, boniato, camote and Cuban sweet potato.

sweet potato pie A baked custard dessert made with a single flaky crust and a smooth filling of puréed sweet potatoes, sugar, eggs, milk and spices.

sweet potato squash *See* delicata squash.

sweet rice *See* glutinous rice.

sweet rice flour A flour obtained from a low-starch, high-sugar rice; generally used as a food additive in frozen products; also known as waxy rice flour.

sweet shrimp *See* ama-ebi.

sweetsop A medium-sized, irregularly shaped fruit (*Annona squamosa*) grown in Central America; it has a bumpy, scaly, yellowish-green skin, a white flesh, a clovelike flavor and large black seeds; eaten fresh or used for beverages and sherbets; also known as a sugar apple. *See* cherimoya.

Sweet Success cucumber A variety of seedless slicing cucumber.

sweet tea Tea that has been sweetened before service; popular in the American South.

sweet tea pickle *See* tea melon, pickled.

sweet tooth Having a fondness or craving for sweets.

sweet vermouth *See* vermouth, sweet.

sweet vinegar A brown-black, slightly thick rice vinegar processed with sugar, cassia and star anise and used in Chinese braised dishes.

sweet woodruff *See* woodruff.

sweet wort In beer brewing, the solution of grain sugars strained from the mash.

Swei Shien Hwa (soo-ay shin hoo-ah) Chinese for water nymph and used to describe a green tea from Canton province; the beverage has a pale color and is usually served midmorning.

swine The domestic hog.

swing cook *See* tournant.

Swiss; Swiss cheese A term used imprecisely to describe any of several large, firm, pressed-curd cheeses with an elastic body, many large holes and a mild, nutty, slightly sweet flavor. *See* Emmental.

Swiss chard *See* chard.

Swiss cheese plant fruit *See* monstera.

Swiss Dessert A soft Swiss double cream cheese made from cow's milk; it has a white, moldy crust, a creamy interior and a rich flavor.

Swiss meringue A mixture of stiffly beaten egg whites and sugar made by combining the ingredients, heating them over simmering water to approximately 140°F (60°C), then whipping until light, fluffy and cool.

Swiss roll A thin sponge cake spread with jam and rolled in a spiral so that slices resemble a pinwheel.

Swiss steak A thick piece of beef, usually round or chuck, coated with flour and browned, then braised, baked or simmered with tomatoes, onions, carrots, celery, beef broth and seasonings; also known as smothered steak (especially in England).

Swiss water method A chemical-free method of removing caffeine from coffee beans by first steaming the beans and then mechanically scraping away the outer layer of caffeine; the process can weaken the flavor of the beverage made from such beans. *See* direct contact method.

switchel A drink of molasses, vinegar, water and usually brandy, cider or rum that was popular in colonial America; also known as haymakers' punch.

Swizzle A cocktail made of almost any liquor mixed with citrus juices, bitters, sugar and ice in a pitcher until frothy, then strained and served.

swizzle stick A thin round or flat stick, with or without prongs, used to stir cocktails or other drinks and served with the drink, sometimes with garnishes attached; also known as a stirrer.

Swong Yuck (swon ee-ook) A tisane from China's Hangchow province made from young mulberry leaves.

swordfish A fish found in the tropical oceans off the Americas; it has a long upper jaw and snout that forms a flat, sharp, double-edged sword, a dark, purplish skin that fades to white on the sides

swordfish

and belly, a moderately lean, gray, off-white or pink flesh that whitens when cooked, a very firm texture, a sweet, mild flavor and an average market weight of 100–200 lb. (45–90 kg); usually sold as wheels or smaller cuts.

syllabub (SIHL-uh-buhb) An old English thick, frothy drink made of milk and wine.

syllabub glass An 18th-century glass used to serve syllabub; it is footed and has a lily-shaped bowl, the top part of which spreads outward to hold the froth.

syltetøj (sil-teh-toy) Danish for jam.

syltetøy (sealta-toy) Norwegian for jam.

Sylvaner; Silvaner (sil-VAH-ner) 1. A white wine grape grown in California, Italy, Austria, France (Alsace), Germany and Switzerland; also known as Johannisberger (especially in Switzerland). 2. A white wine made from this grape; it is generally fresh, fruity and semidry.

synthetic isoparaffinic petroleum hydrocarbons Food additives used as coating components for fruits, vegetables and eggshells.

synthetic paraffin A food additive used as a protective coating on some fruits and tubers.

synthetic petroleum wax A food additive used as a chewing gum base or protective coating on cheese and raw fruits and vegetables.

synthetic sweetener *See* artificial sweetener.

syr (se-air) Russian for cheese.

Syrah (see-RAH) 1. A red wine grape grown in France (northern Rhône Valley), California, South Africa and Australia; also known as Shiraz or Hermitage (especially in South Africa and Australia). 2. A red wine made from this grape; slow to mature and long-lived, it has a deep red color, a high tannin content and a spicy, peppery aroma.

syrniki (sihr-NEE-kee) A Russian dish consisting of fried cakes made from pot cheese or farmer cheese, flour and eggs; it can be sweet (sprinkled with confectioners' sugar and sour cream) or savory (topped with sour cream and herbs).

syroy (sea-roy) Russian for raw.

syrup 1. A thick, sweet, sticky liquid consisting of sugar dissolved in a liquid, usually water; it is often flavored with spices or citrus zest. 2. The juice of a fruit or plant boiled with sugar until thick and sticky; it is usually used as a topping or sweetener.

syrup pack Cans of fruits with a light, medium or heavy syrup added.

syrupy A wine-tasting term for a very rich, sweet wine that is low in total acidity.

Szamorodni (soh-moh-ROD-nee) A style of Hungarian Tokay wine that can be sweet (labeled edes) or dry (labeled szaraz), depending on the proportion of overripe Aszú grapes used.

szaraz *See* Szamorodni.

Szechwan; Szechuan; Sichwan Sichuan (SAY-chwan) A province in south-central China; its cuisine is characterized by its spiciness and the use of chile paste.

Szechwan chile sauce A sauce or paste made from chiles, oil, salt and garlic and used as a flavoring in Chinese Szechwan cooking; also known as chile paste or chile paste with garlic.

Szechwan pepper; Szechuan pepper The dried berry and husk of a type of ash tree (*Xasthoxylum piperitum*); it has a hot, peppery, spicy flavor and is used as an ingredient in Chinese five-spice powder and in the cuisines of China's Szechwan and Hunan provinces; also known as anise pepper and Chinese pepper.

szilvaslepeny (seal-vash-lap-een) A Hungarian plum pie usually eaten warm with cream.

szparag (sh'pah-rahk) Polish for asparagus.

szpinak (sh-pee-mahk) Polish for spinach.

szynka (shin-kah) Polish for ham.

T. *See* tablespoon.

t. *See* teaspoon.

taai-taai (tah-ee-tah-ee) A chewy Dutch version of the German Lebukuchen; molded in carved wooden boards and unmolded before baking.

Tabasco (tah-BAHS-koh) A small, tapering chile with an orange-red color, a thin flesh and a very hot flavor with celery and onion undertones; named for the Mexican state of Tabasco, it is used principally to make Tabasco Sauce.

Tabasco Sauce The proprietary name for a hot pepper sauce made in Louisiana; Tabasco peppers are mashed and fermented with salt and vinegar in barrels for 3 years.

tabbouli (tah-BOO-lee) A fine grind of bulgur.

tabemono (TAH-bay-MOH-noh) *See* shokuryo.

taberu (TAH-bay-roo) Japanese for to eat.

table *v.* To put an item on a table. *n.* 1. A piece of furniture that consists of a flat slab usually wood, glass or stone fixed to legs. 2. A selection of foods and beverages offered to guests (as in, she sets a fine table). 3. The diners and social intercourse at a particular table (as in, I sat at a bad table). *adj.* In the culinary context, a term often used to describe a product (e.g., wine or cheese) of modest quality, served routinely with a meal or a product (e.g., fruit) served without any further preparation.

table (tahblu) French for table.

table cheese An imprecisely used term to describe a cheese that is generally consumed during a meal as a condiment or accompaniment.

tablecloth A cloth spread over the table before it is set with dinnerware.

tablecloth restaurant; tableclother Slang for a full-service restaurant, with tables usually set with tablecloths; it offers a variety of foods and some level of formality; also known as a white tablecloth restaurant.

table cream *See* cream, light.

table d'hôte (tah-buhl DOHT) A menu offering a complete meal for a set price; also known as prix fixe.

table grapes Any variety of grape eaten out of hand (as opposed to being used principally for wine making).

table hopping Moving from table to table in a restaurant or club to greet friends and change company, if only for a few minutes.

table linens Napery (tablecloth, napkins, placemats and the like).

tablering A commonly used method for tempering chocolate by hand; melted chocolate is spread out and stirred on a marble slab to cool it to the proper temperature. *See* tempered chocolate.

table salt Finely ground and refined rock salt; it usually contains anticaking agents and other additives.

tablespoon 1. A spoon with a large, slightly pointed bowl used to serve foods at the table. 2. A measure of volume in the U.S. system; 1 tablespoon (T.) equals 3 teaspoons or 0.05 fl. oz.

table sugar *See* sucrose *and* granulated sugar.

table tent A folded flyer placed on a table to promote specific menu items, brand name products or specials.

table wine 1. In the United States, a red, white or rosé wine that is naturally fermented; it contains 7–14% alcohol and is generally consumed with a meal. 2. In Europe, a wine without a quality designation.

tabouli; tabbouleh; tabuli (tuh-BOO-luh) A Middle Eastern dish consisting of bulgur wheat mixed with tomatoes and onions, flavored with parsley, mint, olive oil and lemon juice; served cold; also known as suf.

tacchino (tahk-KEE-no) Italian for turkey.

taco (tah-COH) A Mexican dish consisting of a small folded corn or flour tortilla filled with beef, pork, chicken, chorizo and/or refried beans and garnished with tomatoes, lettuce, cheese, onions, guacamole, sour cream and/or salsa; it can be crisp (deep-fried into a U-shaped holder) or soft.

taeng kwa (tang kwah) Thai for cucumber.

tafah (too-fair-ah) Arabic for apples.

Tafelspitz (TAH-fell-speetz) An Austrian dish consisting of boiled beef rump, sliced thin and served with a little beef broth ladled over it and garnished with chives.

Tafelwein (TAH-fel-vine) German for table wine; also known as Tischwein. *See* Deutscher Tafelwein.

taffy A soft, chewy candy made with cooked sugar, butter and flavorings; the mixture is pulled repeatedly into long ropes and twisted as it cools; this incorporates air and creates a shiny, opaque color; the ropes of taffy are then cut into bite-sized pieces. *See* saltwater taffy.

tagetes Food additive derived from Aztec marigolds and used as a yellow coloring agent.

tagliarini (tahl-yah-REE-nee) Long, thin, flat strips of pasta approximately 0.15 in. wide.

tagliatelle (tahl-yuh-TEHL-ee) Long, thin, flat strips of pasta approximately 0.75 in. wide.

tagliati (tahl-ya-tee) Italian for cut and used to describe a shortened form of certain pastas.

tagliere (tah-L'YEH-reh) Italian for a cutting board.

tagliolette (tah-yoh-LAY-tay) Long, thin, flat strips of pasta approximately 0.5 in. wide.

tagliolini (tah-yoh-LEE-nee) Long, thin, flat strips of pasta approximately 0.25 in. wide.

tahari (tah-ha-ree) A spicy Indian dish of rice and peas flavored with turmeric and herbs.

taheeni (TA-hee-nee) Arabic for sesame oil.

tahini (tah-HEE-nee) A thick, oily paste made from crushed sesame seeds and used in Middle Eastern cuisines as a flavoring.

taho (TAH-ho) Filipino bean curd.

tai (tah-he) Japanese for sea bream.

tail 1. The largest edible part of shellfish such as shrimp, prawns, crayfish and lobsters. 2. The rear appendage of certain mammals; it is bony, and its tough, flavorful meat is generally used for stocks and stews.

tailgate picnic; tailgate party An outdoor meal served from the folded-down rear door or tailgate of a station wagon or the trunk of a car, often before a sporting event.

Taillevent (Fr., c. 1312–1395) Born Guillaume Tirel, Taillevent was the master chef for Charles V of France; sometime around 1375 he wrote *Le Viandier*, the oldest known French cookbook, which describes a cooking style that relies on pounding, puréeing, saucing and spicing most foods so that the finished dish bears little resemblance in shape, texture or flavor to the original principal ingredients.

tails The last elements to boil and vaporize during the distillation process.

tajada (tah-HAH-dah) Spanish for slice.

tajine; tajin (TAH-jin) *pl.* touajen. 1. A deep, earthenware dish with a tight-fitting conical lid that fits flush with the dish; used in North African cuisines. 2. Any of several meat and vegetable stews made in such a dish.

takaro (tah-kah-ro) Japanese for codfish roe; they have a mild fishy flavor and a creamy, grainy texture and are used in simmered dishes.

take-away *See* takeout.

takenoko (tah-KAY-no-KO) Japanese for bamboo shoots.

tajine

takeout; take home Foods ordered from a restaurant or other food services facility and eaten off premises, usually at home; also known as take-away (especially in England), carryout and to go.

tako (tah-koh) Japanese for octopus.

takrai (tah-kry) Thai for lemongrass.

takuan (tah-koo-ahn) A Japanese pickle made from daikon; it is yellow, firm, crunchy and of medium saltiness.

tala (tah-lah) Hindi for deep-fried.

talc-coated rice White rice with a coating of talc and glucose; the coating is intended as a preservative, and the rice should be washed before use.

Taleggio (tahl-EH-zhee-oh) A soft, surface-ripened cheese made in Italy's Lombardy region from whole cow's milk; it has a pale yellow color when young that deepens as it ages, a moldy surface, a runny texture and a rich, slightly piquant flavor; also known as Talfino.

Talfino *See* Taleggio.

talharim (tah-lya-rin) Portuguese for noodle.

Talisker The proprietary name of a single-malt Scotch whisky; it has a moderately strong malt flavor, a smoky, peat aroma and a prolonged, warm aftertaste.

Talisman (TAE-lis-men) A variety of hops grown in the state of Washington.

tallarín (tahl-lah-REEN) Spanish for noodle.

tall boy Slang for a 16-fl. oz. can of beer.

tall drink *See* long drink.

tallerken (tah-ler-ken) Norwegian for plate.

tallow An animal fat (principally mutton and beef) used as a source of fat in cake mixes, shortening and cooking oils.

Tallyrand, sauce (tal-lee-rahn) A French compound sauce made from a chicken velouté flavored with white wine and shallots, finished with cream and Madeira wine and garnished with brunoise of celery, carrot, onion, truffle and pickled tongue; usually served with braised poultry, sautéed and fried meat, and large roasted or braised joints.

Tallyrand-Perigord, Charles Maurice (Fr., 1745–1838) A French statesman who was a celebrated host and connoisseur of fine food, in part because he employed the great chef Carême; Tallyrand's dinner menus regularly consisted of two soups, two removes (a change of dishes during the meal), one of which was fish, two roasts, four sweets and dessert; this menu became the rule for all the best tables; his name is associated with numerous food preparations.

talna (tahl-nah) Hindi for deep-frying.

taloa (tah-loh-ah) A Basque corn bread leavened with yeast and shaped like an English muffin; used for sandwiches.

talong (TAH-long) Filipino for eggplant.

tamago (TAH-mah-goh) Japanese for egg.

tamago-su (TAH-mah-goh-soo) A Japanese medicinal tonic made by dissolving an egg in rice vinegar.

tamago yaki (TAH-mah-goh YAH-kee) A Japanese-style omelet cooked in a thin sheet and rolled to form a loaf; it is served in sushi bars. *See* gyoku *and* kurakake.

tamale (tuh-MAH-lee) A Mexican dish consisting of chopped meat or vegetables coated with a masa dough, wrapped in a softened corn husk and steamed (the husk is not eaten); sweet tamales are filled with fruit.

tamanegi (TAH-mah-NAY-ghee) Japanese for onion.

tamara (TAH-mah-rah) Portuguese for dates.

tamari (tuh-MAH-ree) A Japanese sauce made from soybeans; it is usually aged, making it thicker, darker and more mellow than soy sauce; used as a condiment, sauce and baster.

tamarillo (tam-uh-RIHL-oh; tam-uh-REE-oh) A small- to medium-sized ovoid fruit (*Cyphomandra betacea*) native to South America; it has a tough, smooth skin that can be red, purple, amber or yellow, a red or yellow flesh, black seeds and a rich, sweet, slightly tart flavor; also known as a tree tomato.

tamarind (TAM-uh-rihnd) The fruit of a tree (*Tamarindus indica*) native to Asia and northern Africa; the long pods contain small seeds and a sweet–sour pulp that is dried and used as a flavoring agent in Indian and Middle Eastern cuisines as well as in Worcestershire sauce; also known as an Indian date.

tamarind liquid A South African and Asian flavoring made from soaking tamarind pulp in water.

tamatar (tah-maa-tar) Hindi for tomato.

tamatem (tah-mah-tem) Arabic for tomato.

tamboril (tam-roh-ril) Portuguese for angler fish.

tamer (tah-mar) Arabic for dates.

Tamie A Reblochon-style cow's milk cheese made by Trappist monks in France's Savoy region.

tamis (TAM-ee) *See* drum sieve.

tammycloth A cloth used to strain liquids.

tamu (tah-moo) Swahili for sweet.

tandoor; tandoor oven An Indian barrel-shaped clay oven fueled by hot coals whose temperatures reach up to 800°F (425°C); the tandoor sears meat in seconds and bakes flatbread in minutes.

tandoori A menu term for foods cooked in a tandoor oven; correctly spelled tandur.

tandoori masala A red spice mixture used to prepare meats, poultry, fish and shellfish for cooking in a tandoor.

tane (tah-nay) Japanese for the ingredients used to top nigirizushi. *See* zushi.

tang (tahne) Chinese for soup.

tang The unsharpened rear extension of a knife blade that is attached to or embedded in the handle; a full tang runs the entire length of the handle; a three-quarter tang extends partially into the handle, and a rattail tang is a rod that runs down the handle's length.

táng (tahng) Chinese for sugar and candy.

tangawizi (tahn-gah-wee-zee) Swahili for ginger.

tangelo (tan-JEHL-oh) A small- to medium-sized citrus; a hybrid of a mandarin orange or tangerine and pomelo; it has a loose, yellow-orange to dark orange, smooth or rough rind, few seeds, a juicy, orange flesh and a sweet flavor.

tangerine A small- to medium-sized citrus (*Citrus reticulata*); it has a thick, loose, orange rind, a dark orange, juicy flesh and a sweet flavor; named after the city of Tangier, Morocco.

tangerine oil, expressed A food additive derived from the peels of the Dancy tangerine and related varieties; it has a citrus aroma and is used as a flavoring agent.

tangerine peel, dried The hard, dried peel of tangerines; used as a flavoring for both sweet and savory dishes, especially in Chinese cuisines; available in powdered form.

Tangier A cocktail made of gin, Triple Sec and Napoleon Mandarine; served in a chilled cocktail glass and garnished with orange peel.

tang myon (tahng me-ohn) Korean buckwheat vermicelli.

tango (tahn-goh) Swahili for cucumber.

tangor An orange and tangerine citrus hybrid.

tangy 1. A tasting term used to describe a pleasantly tart flavor. 2. A cheese-tasting term for a cheese, typically a goat's milk or blue cheese, with a pleasing acidity or tartness.

tank 1. A large container used for fermenting or storing wine, beer or distilled spirits; it can be made from wood (usually in the form of an upright cylinder), stainless steel (an upright or horizontal cylinder) or concrete (cubical). 2. A usually artificial pool or cistern used to store water or to raise fish or shellfish.

tankard A tall, one-handled drinking vessel with a lid; it is used for serving and drinking beer and usually made of pewter, silver or ceramic.

tank fermentation *See* Charmat process.

tanner crab *See* snow crab.

tannia; tannier *See* malanga.

tannic A wine-tasting term for an astringent, mouth-puckering wine.

tannic acid 1. An astringent-tasting food additive used as a flavoring agent and/or adjuvant in processed foods such as baked goods, alcoholic and nonalcoholic beverages, candies and meat products; also known as hydrolyzable gallotannin. 2. An astringent acid usually added to must or wine to increase the wine's longevity by slowing down the aging process.

tannier *See* malanga.

tannin A group of organic compounds found in plants; a wine acquires tannin from grape seeds, skins and stems as well as from being aged or stored in oak barrels; tannin imparts structure, flavor, texture and complexity and, as an antioxidant, helps the wine to age.

tannisage (tahn-nee-sahj) The process of adding tannin to a must to correct a deficiency or to assist fining.

tansy (TAN-zee) An herb (*Tanacetum vulgare*) with an extremely bitter flavor and a dank musty smell; it is rarely used culinarily but is used for medicinal purposes.

tant pour tant (TPT) (tahn poor tahn) French for as much as and used in pastry making to refer to a mixture containing equal amounts of powdered nuts, usually blanched almonds, and confectioners' sugar.

tanuri (tah-noo-ree) Swahili for bakery.

Tanzanian 1. Any of various teas grown in Tanzania, many of which are used for blending. 2. Arabica coffee beans grown in Tanzania; the beverage has a brisk, clean flavor.

tao hou (taho hoo) Thai for bean curd.

Taos lightning A distilled spirit made near Taos, New Mexico, and enjoyed by the early trappers; the Spanish called it aguardiente.

taozi (tah-oh-zee) Chinese for peach.

tap *v.* To draw a liquid from a vessel, container or tree. *n.* 1. The faucet used to draw beer from a keg or draft beer system. 2. The faucet, spigot or cock used to dispense beverages, primarily alcoholic ones, from a cask or other container. 3. A beverage dispensed through such a system.

tapas (tah-pahs) Spanish appetizers that can be hot or cold, simple or complex. *See* antojito.

tapas bar An establishment specializing in tapas; diners usually graze.

tap beer *See* draft beer.

tapenade (TA-puh-nahd; ta-pen-AHD) A thick paste made from capers, anchovies, olives, olive oil, lemon juice and seasonings in France's Provence region; used as a condiment, garnish and sauce.

taphouse A British inn or tavern where liquor is kept on tap for sales.

tapioca 1. A starch extracted from the root of the cassava plant and used for thickening. 2. A milk pudding made with processed pellets of tapioca, known as pearl tapioca.

tapioca pudding *See* tapioca.

tapioca shreds *See* hu tieu uot.

tapman A British bartender.

tappit-hen 1. A Scottish term for an oversized wine bottle holding three 750-ml bottles. 2. An oversized drinking vessel with a handle and a lid with a knob.

taproom A British bar.

taproot The single root of a plant (e.g., carrot); it extends deep into the soil to supply the aboveground plant with nutrients; also known as a root.

tapuah (tah-pooh-ah) Hebrew for apple.

tapuz (tah-pooz) Hebrew for orange.

tap water Drinking water obtained from a standard indoor plumbing faucet.

tarak (tah-rack) Turkish for scallops.

taralli (tah-RAH-lee) Round unsweetened Italian semolina cookies that are boiled and then baked; they are sometimes flavored with fennel seeds, peppercorns or chiles.

tarama (tah-rah-mah) Greek and Turkish for pale orange carp roe.

taramasalata (tah-rah-mah-sah-LAH-tah) A Greek dish consisting of tarama, lemon juice, milk-soaked bread crumbs, olive oil and seasonings; served as a creamy dip.

Tarator sauce; Tartator sauce (tah-rah-tor) A Turkish sauce made from toasted almonds or pine nuts, garlic and white bread soaked in milk; the ingredients are pounded to a paste, seasoned with salt and vinegar or lemon juice and beaten with oil.

taratour (tahr-rah-TOR) Arabic for sesame sauce.

taratouri (tah-raw-too-ree) A cold Greek soup made from cucumber and goat's milk yogurt; it is garnished with mint leaves and paprika.

tarelka (tah-ral-kah) Russian for plate.

tare weight The weight of a container or package, without the contents.

tarhonya (tore-ahn-yah) A Hungarian dish consisting of tiny flour dough balls browned in lard and then simmered in water.

tari (TAAR-ree) 1. An East Indian alcoholic beverage made from the fermented sap or juice of a palm tree. 2. Hindi for gravy.

tarkari (tar-ka-ree) An East Indian dish consisting of vegetables fried in ghee and then simmered in their own juices.

Tarla A hardwood rolling pin with short knob handles and a thin sheet of copper covering the cylinder; used for rolling out doughs with a high fat content or hot sugar mixtures such as nougatine.

taro The large tuber of the tropical taro plant (*Colocasia esculenta*); it has a brown skin, a starchy, gray-white flesh and an acidic flavor when raw that becomes somewhat nutty when cooked; also known as Caribbean cabbage, colasse and old cocoyam.

taro leaves The large, dark green leaves of the taro plant; they have a delicate flavor and are used to wrap foods for cooking in Hawaiian cuisine.

taro potatoes *See* sato imo.

taro pudding *See* kulolo.

tarragon An herb (*Artemisia dracunculus*) native to Siberia with narrow, pointed, dark green leaves, tiny gray flowers, a distinctive aniselike flavor with undertones of sage and a strong aroma; available fresh and dried.

tarragon sauce *See* estragon, sauce à l'.

tarragon vinegar A red or white wine vinegar in which tarragon has been steeped.

Tarrazu (tah-rah-zoo) Arabica coffee beans grown in Costa Rica's Tarrazu region; the beverage has a rich flavor and sharp acidity.

tarry A wine-tasting term for a thick, tarlike flavor; usually associated with bottle-aged red wines made from very ripe grapes.

tart *n.* A shallow-sided pastry dough crust filled with a sweet or savory mixture; the tart may or may not have a top crust. *adj.* 1. A sharp, piquant, often acidic or sometimes sour flavor. 2. A wine-tasting term for a wine that is either highly acidic but not necessarily unpleasant or one that is disagreeably sharp.

tarta (TAHR-tah) Spanish for cake.

tartare An imprecisely used term for any dish featuring a raw ingredient (e.g., salmon tartare).

tartare steak *See* beef tartare.

Tartarian cherry (tar-TAIR-ee-uhn) A large sweet cherry with a dark purple, almost black skin and a juicy flesh.

tartaric acid 1. The principal acid in wine; it throws off tasteless potassium bitartrate crystals (cream of tartar), which are insoluble in wine and are sometimes mistaken for sugar crystals. 2. An odorless and acidic-tasting food additive used as a firming agent, flavoring agent and/or pH control agent.

tartar sauce; tartare, sauce A mayonnaise-based sauce made with dill pickles, capers, onions, lemon juice or vinegar and traditionally served with fried fish.

tart cherry *See* cherry, sour.

tarte au suif (tahrt-tah oh soo-if) A Canadian tart or pie consisting of a suet crust filled with chopped nuts, beaten eggs and maple syrup; it is baked and served cold.

tarte Tatin (tahrt tah-TAN) A French apple tart in which layers of butter, sugar and sliced apples are placed in a sauté pan and topped with puff pastry or sweet dough; after baking, the dish is inverted so that the caramelized apples become the topping for service.

tartine (tar-teen) French and Italian for a slice of bread spread with butter, jam, honey or the like.

tartlet A small, single-serving tart.

tartlet pan A small pan, 2 to 4 in. in diameter and 0.75 to 1.5 in. high, available in many shapes including round, oval, rectangular and square, with plain or fluted straight or sloping sides; it is used for baking tartlets and usually made of tinned or black steel and generally without a removable bottom.

tart pan A pan, 4.5 to 12.5 in. in diameter and 0.75 to 1.25 in. high, usually round, square or rectangular, with fluted, slightly sloping sides; it is used for baking tarts and usually made of tinned or black steel with a removable bottom.

tartrazine *See* FD&C Yellow #5.

tartufo (tahr-TOO-foh) Italian for truffle; tartufo bianco is a white truffle.

tas (tass) A Greek earthenware pot.

tasajo (tah-sah-ho) South American salt-cured, sun-dried beef.

tasala (tah-sha-laa) An unglazed clay cooking pot used in Nepal for cooking curries, rice and dried peas and beans.

tas kebab (tass ka-bhab) A Greek stew made with small pieces of meat, usually lamb, and cooked in a tas.

task procedure A detailed, step-by-step description, often written, of how a specific job or task is to be done.

tasse (tas) French for cup.

tasso; tasso ham (TAH-soh; TA-soh) A Cajun sausage made from cured pork or beef, seasoned with red pepper, garlic, filé powder and various herbs and spices and then smoked; principally used as a flavoring ingredient.

taste *v.* 1. To test the flavor of something by placing it in the mouth or on the tongue. 2. To sample a food or beverage. *See* flavor. *n.* One of the five senses; concerned with perceiving and distinguishing the flavors (e.g., sweet, sour, umami, salty and bitter) of foods and beverages.

tastevin (taht-van) A shallow, saucerlike silver wine taster's cup with dimpled sides and bottom; the dimpled areas refract light, which assists in evaluating color and clarity; used in Burgundy to sample wine out of the barrel; it is also part of a sommelier's traditional equipment.

tastevin

tasting menu *See* dégustation menu.

tatar med garniture (tah-tarr mad gar-nee-tou-ray) A Danish smørrebrød dish of raw ground beef on black bread garnished with egg yolk, chopped onion, red beet, capers and grated horseradish.

tate de amêndoa (tah-ta day ah-mahn-doh-ah) A small Portuguese tart covered with almond pieces.

tate-jio (tah-te-jee-ow) A Japanese preparation method in which food is soaked in a mild brine solution to which kombu has been added.

tathci (tah-ta-he) A Turkish confectionery where sweetmeats and desserts are sold. *See* pastahane.

tatsoi A salad green with thick, dark green, rounded leaves and a rich mustard flavor; also known as rosette bok choy.

tattari (tah-tar-ee) Finnish for buckwheat.

Taupinière (toh-pee-nyehr) A firm cheese made in France's Loire region from goat's milk; it has a dome shape, a moist, smooth, firm texture that gets drier with age, a black-and-white bloomy rind, a white interior and a tangy, musty flavor.

Taursai (tau-RAH-zee) A DOC red wine made from Aglianico grapes in Italy's Campania region.

Tavel (tah-vel) A rosé wine produced in southern France from Grenache grapes; it is dry and has a pink-orange color.

tavern 1. A commercial establishment where alcoholic beverages are sold and consumed on premises. 2. Traditionally, an inn where guests were given food and lodging. 3. *See* sloppy Joe.

taverna (TAH-ver-nah) Italian and Greek for tavern.

tavola (tah-voh-lah) Italian for table.

tavuk (tah-vook) Turkish for chicken.

tawa (ta-vaa) A circular and slightly concave iron disc used to cook various unleavened Indian breads.

tawara-gata (ta-wah-rah-gah-tah) A portion of rice for nigiri-zushi shaped like a rectangular box with rounded edges and corners.

tawny port A mature, golden red port; aged in wooden pipes for more than 3 years; it has a softer, rounder flavor than a ruby port. *See* ruby port.

tayberry A large berry developed in Scotland that is a hybrid of the blackberry and raspberry; it has a bright purple color, an elongated conical shape and a flavor similar to that of a ripe blackberry.

tayglach; taiglach (tie-glack) A Jewish confection made of honey-sweetened dough cut into 1-in. pieces and baked, then poached in a ginger-flavored sugar and honey syrup; after poaching, they are rolled into balls and the balls are rolled in chopped nuts or coconut.

taza (tah-zah) Hindi for fresh and raw.

tazuna (tah-zoo-nah) Japanese for braid and used to describe a decorative cut for food.

TBHQ *See* tertiary butylhydroquinone.

T-bone steak A fabricated cut of the beef primal short loin; this tender cut contains a distinctive T-shaped portion of the backbone and on either side of the center bone, a large portion of the loin eye muscle and a smaller portion of the tenderloin. *See* club steak *and* porterhouse steak.

té (tai) Spanish for tea.

te Norwegian for tea.

tè Italian for tea.

tea 1. An aromatic beverage made by infusing water with the cured leaves of the shrub *Camellia sinensis;* a mild stimulant due to caffeine, a tea is generally named for its leaf type and size or region of origin. 2. The leaves used to make the beverage. *See* black tea, green tea, oolong tea *and* white tea. 3. An imprecisely used term for a beverage made from steeping the leaves of shrubs, herbs or other plants in water. *See* tisane. 4. An imprecisely used term for a very thin, runny sauce, usually one flavored with vegetables, herbs or spices.

tea, afternoon 1. A light British meal or refreshment of bread and butter, cucumber or other delicate sandwiches, cookies, scones and Devonshire cream and the like served with a pot of tea during the late afternoon. 2. A formal social occasion or reception at which tea and other refreshments are served.

tea, high A late afternoon or early evening British meal, usually quite substantial and consisting of meat and/or fish dishes, biscuits and jam, an array of cakes and pastries and a pot of tea.

tea bag A cloth or filter paper bag containing a premeasured portion of loose tea leaves; used to make tea in a cup or pot.

tea ball A perforated metal ball that holds loose tea leaves; used for making tea in a cup or pot.

teaberry *See* wintergreen.

tea biscuit British expression for any of a variety of cookies or crackers served with afternoon tea; also known as a tea cake.

tea bowl A handleless cup used for tea, especially in Asia.

Tea Breeze A French liqueur with a tealike flavor.

tea caddy A metal canister used to store tea.

tea caddy spoon A short-handled silver spoon used for scooping tea from the caddy; the spoon's bowl is often shaped to resemble a shell, grape leaf, eagle or other motif.

tea cake *See* tea biscuit.

tea cart A small, wheeled table used for holding a tea service

tea ball

tea caddy spoon

or from which tea or other beverages are served; also known as a tea wagon.

tea cozy A cloth cover for a tea pot used to insulate the pot and retain the heat while the tea is steeping.

teacupful A traditional measure of volume; approximately 3/4 cup.

tea egg A hard-cooked egg; its shell is cracked and the egg is simmered in strong tea, creating a marblelike effect; an appetizer in Chinese cuisine.

tea garden An outdoor area where tea and light refreshments are served.

teahouse An Asian restaurant serving tea and other light refreshments.

teakettle A utensil used for boiling water for teas, tisanes, filtered coffee and so on; it has a broad base, a high-set handle, an often rounded or tapered top with a tightly fitting lid and sometimes a whistle on the spout to indicate when the contents have produced steam.

teakettle broth Any of several British porridges.

teakettle

teal A small wild duck with dark blue-green coloring and a very flavorful flesh; often grilled or roasted and served with a port sauce.

tea leaves *See* Camellia sinensis.

tea maker A perforated covered spoon that holds loose tea leaves; used to brew tea in a cup.

tea masala A spice blend used in Central Africa (especially Kenya) for flavoring teas; it consists of jaggery, ginger, cinnamon, cloves, cardamom and peppercorns.

tea melon A small cucumber-shaped fruit with a yellow skin, crisp texture and mild flavor; also known as a Chinese cucumber, Chinese melon and sweet cucumber.

tea melon, pickled A tea melon pickled in honey and spices or soy sauce and used in Chinese cuisine; also known as a Chinese pickle, Chinese pickled cucumber, preserved sweet melon and sweet tea pickle.

tea party 1. An afternoon social gathering feturing tea and light refreshments. 2. Slang for a cocktail party or other event featuring alcoholic beverages in an area or country where alcoholic beverages are frowned on or prohibited.

teapot A pot with a handle, spout and lid; used for brewing tea in hot water; available in a wide variety of shapes, sizes and materials; some contain a central perforated container to hold the loose tea.

teapoy A small, decorative, three-legged table used for serving tea.

tear (taher) To pull a food apart and into pieces, usually of different, uneven shapes and sizes.

tea rolls Small sweet buns, usually served with tea.

tears (teers) *See* legs.

tea server *See* dessert server.

tea service; tea set A set of silver or china pieces used for serving tea; usually includes a teapot, creamer, sugar bowl and tray.

teaspoon 1. A small spoon with a slightly pointed bowl used to stir tea or coffee. 2. A measure of volume in the U.S. system; 1 teaspoon equals 1/3 or 0.17 fl. oz.

tea strainer A small perforated bowl placed over a cup to strain the leaves when the tea is poured into the cup.

tea table A small side table used for holding a tea service and serving tea. *See* teapoy.

tea towel A small towel, usually of linen or cotton, used to dry dishes; also known as a dishtowel or dish cloth.

tea wagon *See* tea cart.

teburu *See* shokutaku.

Tee (tay) German for tea.

teedum barrel A barrel or other storage vessel in which moonshiners kept their liquor.

teemateem (tea-mah-team) Ethiopian for tomatoes.

teen (teen) Arabic for figs.

teetotaler Slang for a person who abstains from all alcoholic beverages.

t'ef *See* teff.

teff A North African high-protein, high-carbohydrate grain with a mild nutty flavor; sometimes spelled t'ef.

Teflon The proprietary name of a synthetic coating used on cooking utensils to prevent food from sticking.

tefteli; teftely (tyef-tel-ee) Russian meatballs, usually served with boiled rice, kasha or potatoes.

teishoku sakura denbu (te-i-show-koo sah-koo-rah den-boo) A bright pink, crystalline substance made from ground, dried codfish, sugar and food coloring; it has a slight fishy flavor and is used as a garnish in Japanese cuisine.

tej patta (ta-e pah-tah) Hindi for bay leaf.

tekka (tek-kah) Japanese for raw tuna.

tekka-maki (tek-kah-mah-key) A nori-maki made with raw tuna.

tekoua (ta-ko-do-ah) A North African dessert consisting of a paste of toasted sesame seeds and sugar, shaped into balls and rolled in confectioners' sugar.

Te Kwan Yin A black tea from China's Fukien province, it grows on steep cliffs and is gathered by monkeys; called iron goddess of mercy, the beverage is quite thin and served in small cups.

tél (tell) Hindi for oil.

telba (tell-bah) Ethiopian for flax seeds.

Teleme (TEHL-uh-may) 1. A feta-style cheese made in Bulgaria, Greece and Turkey from goat's or ewe's milk, pickled in brine. 2. A soft cheese made from cow's milk in California; it has a pliant texture and a mild flavor.

Telemea A Romanian cheese made from pasteurized ewe's milk; it has a pure white, glazed surface and a white interior and is sometimes flavored with cumin seeds.

Teleme Jack A soft to semisoft cheese made in northern California from cow's milk; it has a creamy texture, an ivory color and a tangy flavor; used for cooking; also known as Teleme, Cream Jack and High-Moisture Jack.

tel kadayif (tell kah-daw-if) A Turkish confection of vermicelli soaked in syrup and sprinkled with pistachios and other chopped nuts.

telyatina (tyel-yah-tee-nah) Russian for veal.

temaki-zushi (teh-mah-kee-soo-she) Sushi ingredients (the principal ingredients are zushi and nori) rolled into a cone.

Temecula (teh-MEH-kyoo-luh) A grape-growing and wine-producing region in southern California, north of San Diego; the principal grape varieties are Chardonnay, Chenin Blanc and Sauvignon Blanc.

tempe; tempeh (TEHM-pay) A fermented soybean cake with a yeasty, nutty flavor used in Asian and vegetarian cuisines.

temper To bring something to the proper temperature or texture by mixing, stirring, heating or cooling (e.g., to temper eggs by slowly whisking in hot milk to avoid curdling).

temperature danger zone The broad range of temperatures between 40 and 140°F (4 and 60°C) in which bacteria thrive and reproduce; by keeping foods out of this temperature range, the chances of an infection, intoxication or toxin-mediated infection are decreased. *See* time-and-temperature principle.

tempered chocolate Chocolate treated with a heating and cooling process to stablize the cocoa butter crystals; tempered chocolate is shiny, smooth and unblemished by bloom.

tempering 1. Heating gently and gradually. 2. The process of slowly adding a hot liquid to eggs or other foods to raise their temperature without causing them to curdle.

tempering machine An electric machine designed for melting and tempering chocolate, then holding it at the correct temperature for use in making candy or decorations.

tempi (tam-pe) Japanese for oven.

temple orange A medium-sized ovoid orange that is a hybrid of an orange and a tangerine; it has a rough, thick, deep orange rind, a dark orange flesh, many seeds and a sweet–tart flavor.

Tempranillo (tem-prah-NEE-yo) 1. A red wine grape widely planted in Spain's Rioja region. 2. A well-balanced, deep-colored red wine made from this grape.

tempura (TEM-poo-ra) A Japanese dish of battered and deep-fried pieces of fish and vegetables, usually accompanied by a sauce.

tempura ko (TEM-poo-rah ko) A Japanese low-gluten wheat flour used for making tempura.

tende (tan-day) Swahili for date.

tender 1. A fabricated cut of the beef primal sirloin; it is a trimmed, boneless steak. 2. A strip of flesh found on the inside of the chicken breast next to the bone. 3. A wine-tasting term for a young, light-bodied wine that is easy to drink.

tenderette A fabricated cut of the beef primal round; it is a small cubed steak.

tenderize To soften and/or break down tough muscle fibers in meat by cubing, needling, pounding, marinating in acidic ingredients, adding enzymes and/or cooking in moist heat.

tenderized steak *See* cubed steak.

tenderizer An additive or substance used to soften and/or break down tough meat fibers; includes enzymes (e.g., papain) and acidic marinades (e.g., a red wine marinade).

tenderizer, liquid A solution containing an enzymatic tenderizer.

tenderloin A flavorful and very tender muscle that runs through the beef short loin and sirloin primals; it is part of T-bone and porterhouse steaks or can be cut into châteaubriand, filet mignon and tournedos. *See* butt tenderloin *and* short tenderloin.

tenderloin tips A fabricated cut of the beef primal short loin; they are small pieces of the short tenderloin.

tenedor (teh-nay-dohr) Spanish for fork.

ten-flavored sauce *See* hoisin.

Tennessee jam cake *See* Kentucky jam cake.

Tennessee whiskey A straight whiskey made in Tennessee by the sour mash process; the mash has a minimum of 51% of a single grain, usually corn; after distillation, it is filtered through finely ground sugar maple charcoal and aged in charred oak barrels for at least 4 years.

tent A traditional British term for any sweet red wine from Spain.

tentsuyu (TEHN-tsoo-yoo) Japanese dipping sauce for tempura.

tenuta (teh-NOO-tah) An Italian estate that produces and bottles its own wine.

10 X sugar *See* confectioners' sugar

tepary bean (the-PAHR-ray) A bean grown in the hot, arid conditions of the American Southwest; it is similar to a pinto bean.

tepín A small ovoid or spherical fresh chile with a thin flesh and a very hot flavor; also known as chíltepin or chíltecpin.

teppan (tep-PAHN) Japanese for griddle.

teppan-yaki (tep-PAHN-YAH-kee) A Japanese style of cooking done on a large grill in front of diners.

tequila (tuh-KEE-luh) A spirit made in Mexico from the fermented and distilled sap and pulp of the maguey plant (it must contain at least 51% maguey sugars); it has a high alcohol content, colorless to straw color and somewhat herbaceous flavor; it is often sold as either blanco (white) or plata (silver). *See* blue agave tequila, mezcal *and* reposado tequila.

Tequila Maria A cocktail made of tomato juice, tequila, grated horseradish, Worcestershire sauce, Tabasco sauce, white pepper, celery salt or celery seed, tarragon, oregano, dill and lime juice.

Tequila Sunrise A cocktail made of orange juice, tequila, grenadine and lime juice; garnished with a lime slice.

teri (TAY-ree) Japanese for glaze.

teriyaki (tayr-ee-YAH-kee) 1. A Japanese dish of beef, chicken or pork marinated in soy sauce, ginger, sugar and seasonings, skewered and grilled or broiled. 2. A Japanese marinade or sauce made from soy sauce, ginger, sugar and seasonings.

Terizzo (teh-REE-t'zoh) A red wine made from Sangiovese and Cabernet Sauvignon grapes in Liguria, Italy.

terminal specific gravity *See* final specific gravity.

tern A wild bird found along the northern Atlantic coasts; its small eggs are eaten hard boiled.

ternera (tehr-NEH-rah) Spanish for veal.

ternera en pipián verde (tehr-neh-rah en pee-pian varday) A Mexican pipián made with veal, flavored with chiles, onions, tomatoes and cilantro and thickened with pepitas.

terrapin (TEHR-ah-pen) A variety of turtle found in fresh or brackish water; it is 7–8 in. (17.7–20.2 cm) in length, and its tenderized flesh has a rich, earthy flavor.

terrine 1. Traditionally, coarsely ground and highly seasoned meats baked without a crust in an earthenware mold and served cold. 2. A coarsely or finely ground and highly 

terrine

seasoned meat, fish, shellfish, poultry and/or vegetable forcemeat baked without a crust in an earthenware mold, usually lined with pork fat, and served hot or cold. *See* pâté. 3. The earthenware, metal or glass mold used for such preparations; usually a long, narrow rectangular loaf pan with a flared edge to hold the cover.

terroir (teh-RWAHR) French for soil and used to refer to the entire grape-growing environment, including soil, site and climate.

tertiary butylhydroquinone (TBHQ) A food additive used as an antioxidant, especially in processed oils and foods containing oils.

testes (tas-tes) French for a bird's kidneys.

teswin An ancient Mexican beverage made from dried corn and finely ground roasted wheat and flavored with anise, cloves and cinnamon.

tête (tet) French for head.

tête de cuvée (tet duh coo-vay) 1. A term formerly used to denote the best vineyards in Burgundy, France. 2. An unofficial designation for a vintner's best bottling of Champagne.

Tête de Moine (tet duh mwone) *See* Bellelay.

Tetilla (teh-TEE-yah) A squat, cone-shaped cow's milk cheese from Spain; it has a greenish-beige rind, a soft, white interior and a mild, tangy flavor similar to that of Monterey Jack.

tetrahydrofurfuryl acetate A food additive with a slightly fruity aroma used as a flavoring agent in candies and baked goods.

tetrahydrofurfuryl propionate A food additive with a chocolate aroma used as a flavoring agent in candies and baked goods.

Tettnang (TEHT-nang) A variety of hops grown in Germany and in the states of Washington, Idaho and Oregon.

te-uchi (tay-OO-chee) Handmade Japanese noodles.

Texas almond A variety of almond that is particularly flavorful.

Texas sheet cake A large, rich single-layer chocolate cake.

Texas toast A very thick slice of white bread that is toasted and brushed with butter; often served with steaks.

Texmati rice An aromatic U.S. white or brown rice that is a cross between long-grain rice and basmati.

Tex-Mex A term used for food that is based on the combined cultures of Texas and Mexico; these foods include burritos, nachos and tacos, and the principal flavorings include tomatoes and chiles.

texture A tasting term for the fabric or feel of a food or beverage as it enters the mouth and is sensed on the palate; it can be smooth, grainy, creamy, flaky, dense, crumbly, brittle, hard, soft, firm, springy and so on.

textured plant protein; textured vegetable protein Isolated, flavored and processed proteins from plants such as soybeans, peanuts and wheat; used to create high-protein, nutritious ersatz foods or to extend other food products nutritiously; also known as meat extender and meat replacements.

textured soy flour Soy flour processed and extruded to form products with specific shapes and textures such as meatlike nuggets; the products are crunchy when dry and moist and chewy when hydrated.

texturizer A type of food additive used to improve the appearance or feel of a food.

Thai chile A short, thin, elongated and pointed chile with a green to red color, a thick flesh and a very hot flavor.

Thai coffee Coffee mixed with sweetened condensed milk.

Thai curry paste A paste of aromatic herbs, spices and vegetables used in Thai cuisine as a flavoring; yellow paste is the mildest, red can vary in heat and green is the hottest.

Thai green eggplant A variety of Asian eggplant with a green skin and a mild flavor.

thai sai (thal sah-ee) A bitter Chinese cabbage with oval, dark green leaves and white stems.

Thai tea A Thai–American beverage of strong black tea mixed with cream and sugar and served chilled over ice.

thal (tahll) An Indian metal platter used for serving food.

thala guli (tha-law goo-lee) A Sri Lankan candy made of sesame seeds and palm sugar and formed into balls; the balls are wrapped in waxed paper, and the ends of the paper are twisted and cut into a fringe; served as a dessert (especially after a meal with a curry dish) or as a snack.

than daa (than dah-ah) Hindi for cold.

thareed (thaw-reed) A Middle Eastern dish consisting of a soup of meat, potatoes and other vegetables poured over bread and left to soak before service; sometimes a layer of rice, puréed chickpeas and/or yogurt is spread on the bread before the soup is added. *See* fatta.

Thassos olive A small, wrinkled, dry-cured Greek olive with a strong flavor.

thé (tay) French for tea.

theevil *See* spurtle.

theme restaurants Restaurants carefully designed and marketed to reflect a certain cultural (e.g., rock and roll), ethnic or other concept, often to the detriment of the food.

thé naa naa marocaine (ta nah nah mah-row-kah-nay) Moroccan mint tea.

theobromine A bitter crystalline compound found in cacao beans and to a lesser extent in cola nuts and tea leaves; closely related to caffeine and with a similar stimulating affect on the central nervous system.

thermidor (THERM-ee-dohr) A dish prepared by poaching or roasting the main ingredient (e.g., lobster or fish) and making a sauce by reducing the juices, white wine and fish fumet and adding this concentrate to a béchamel sauce seasoned with mustard.

thermogenesis The production of heat and a reflection of energy use, especially by the body.

thermometer A device designed to measure temperatures; it can be calibrated in Fahrenheit and/or Celsius and can be a column of mercury with temperatures indicated on a glass tube or a stem-type thermometer in which temperatures are noted by an arrow on a dial or a digital readout.

thermometer, dairy A thermometer used to check the temperature of milk when making cheese or yogurt; its range is 10–230°F (−12 to 110°C).

thermometer, density A thermometer used to test brines and sugar syrups; a salometer is used for brines, and a saccarometer is used for sugar syrups. *See* hydrometer.

thermometer, freezer A thermometer used to check the temperature of a refrigerator or freezer; it should register temperatures as high as 40°F (5°C).

thermometer, instant-read A thermometer used to measure the internal temperature of foods; the stem is inserted into the food, producing an instant temperature readout.

thermometer, internal A stem-type thermometer inserted into a food for

thermometer, instant read

1–2 minutes while it is being cooked; generally it is more accurate than an instant-read thermometer and registers temperatures of 0–220°F (−18 to 104°C); also known as a quick-read thermometer.

thermometer, meat A thermometer inserted into the meat to read the internal temperature; the top of the thermometer usually has a scale indicating the temperatures of doneness for certain meats.

thermometer, oven A thermometer used to test the accuracy of an oven's thermostat; it must be able to withstand temperatures as high as 500°F (260°C).

thermometer, sugar/fat A thermometer used to test sugar syrup or hot fat; it must be able to withstand temperatures as high as 500°F (260°C).

thermos An insulated vacuum bottle used to keep food hot or cold.

thesrib (thas-reer) An Iraqi dish consisting of layers of bread and a rich lamb soup; the final layer of meat is spread with samn and yogurt and sprinkled with chopped garlic.

thiamine *See* vitamin B_1.

thiamine hydrochloride A food additive used as a nutrient supplement, flavoring agent and/or adjuvant.

thiamine mononitrate A food additive used as a nutrient supplement.

thick agé (ah-gue) Deep-fried tofu; sold in cakes, slices, small triangles and cubes.

thicken The process of making a liquid substance dense by adding a thickening agent (e.g., flour or gelatin) or by cooking to evaporate some of the liquid.

thickening agents; thickeners 1. Ingredients used to thicken sauces, including starches (flour, cornstarch and arrowroot), gelatin and liaisons. 2. A type of food additive used to produce viscous solutions or dispersions, impart body and/or improve texture or consistency; includes stabilizers, suspending agents, bodying agents, setting agents, jellying agents and bulking agents.

thick flank A British cut of the beef carcass; it is a somewhat tough roast cut from a muscle at the front of the thigh; also known as a top rump.

thiebou dienn sous verre; tiebou dienn sous verre (tea-a-boh-who de-ann soa va-rey) A Senegalese dish consisting of a fish stew made with a white fish, calabaza, cassava, turnips, cabbage, sweet potatoes, eggplants, carrots and okra flavored with onions, guedge, yete, tomatoes, parsley, garlic, chiles and scallions and served over rice.

thief A glass or metal tube used to sample wine through the bunghole of a barrel; also known as a wine thief or pipette.

thimbleberry Any of a variety of thimble-shaped raspberries, especially the black raspberry, grown in the United States.

thin *v.* To dilute mixtures by adding more liquid. *adj.* A tasting term for a product that is watery or lacks body.

thin flank A British cut of the beef carcass; used for stews, it is a fatty cut of muscles found toward the rear of the belly.

thinh (think) Toasted, ground rice used in Vietnamese cuisine (especially in ground pork dishes) for its distinctive aroma, flavor and texture.

thin sticks *See* rice sticks.

thiodipropionic acid A food additive used as a preservative.

thira (theer-rah) Arabic for corn.

thirst The sensation resulting from a lack of or need for water or other fluid.

13th thermal bath of Karlsbad *See* Becherovka.

thit bo nuong (teet hoe noo-ang) Vietnamese grilled barbecued beef.

thit nuong (teet noo-ang) Vietnamese grilled pork.

Thomas Black walnut A variety of black walnut; the nuts are large and have thin shells.

Thompson Seedless The most widely planted grape in California; used for raisins, table grapes or to make a neutral wine used in blends of inexpensive jug white wines. *See* Sultana.

thon (ton) French for tuna fish; also known as tunny.

thong muan (tong moo-ahn) A Thai dessert made of flour, coconut milk, eggs, sugar and lime juice mixed to form a thin batter that is cooked on a utensil similar to a krumkake iron, then rolled into a tight cigarette shape.

Thousand Island dressing A salad dressing or sandwich spread made from mayonnaise, cream and chile sauce garnished with pickles, green peppers, olives and hard-cooked eggs.

thousand-year eggs *See* hundred-year-old eggs.

thread cut *See* alto-zukuri.

thread stage A test for the density of sugar syrup; the point at which a drop of boiling sugar will form a thin thread when dropped in cold water; equivalent to approximately 230–234°F (110–112°C) on a candy thermometer.

threadworm A nematode, many of which are parasitic in humans and other animals; also known as a pinworm.

three-compartment sink An assembly of three adjacent sinks used for sanitizing dishes and equipment; the item to be sanitized is first scraped and sprayed and then washed in the first sink, rinsed in the second, sanitized in the third and left to air-dry.

Three Musketeers The proprietary name for a candy bar composed of a fluffy chocolate nougat center coated with chocolate.

three sheets in (to) the wind Slang for drunk; derived from a sailor's use of a rope called a sheet to tack sails; if three sheets were free, the sail was not under control.

threonine (THRE-ah-nen) 1. An essential amino acid. 2. A food additive used as a nutrient source to significantly improve the biological quality of the total protein in a food containing the naturally occurring protein.

thresher shark *See* shark.

throat bread *See* sweetbreads.

thume (tohm) Arabic for garlic.

thump *See* stelk.

Thuringer (THOOR-ihn-juhr) A style of German sausages made from chopped pork and/or beef, seasoned with herbs, spices and other flavorings such as garlic, coriander or mustard; they are preserved by curing, drying and smoking and have a semidry to moist, soft texture.

thym (tim) French for thyme.

thyme (time) A low-growing herb (*Thymus vulgaris*) with small purple flowers and tiny, gray-green leaves; the leaves have a strong, slightly lemony flavor and aroma; used fresh and dried.

thymol A food additive with a pungent flavor and aroma; used as a flavoring agent.

thymus gland A glandular body or ductless gland of uncertain purpose and generally located at the base of the brain in vertebrate animals. *See* sweetbreads.

thyroxine A thyroid hormone that regulates the metabolism; in large doses, it can act as a metabolic accelerator.

tiakri (tea-ah-cree) A Senegalese dessert consisting of steamed balls of millet flour mixed with sow and sugar.

Tia Maria (TEE-uh muh-REE-uh) A dark brown, coffee-flavored Jamaican liqueur made from rum.

tián (tea-ahn) Chinese for sweet.

tian (tyahn) A square or rectangular earthenware dish with slightly raised edges and used in France's Provence region to prepare gratin dishes, which are also called tians.

tian mian jiang (tyen myen jung) A Chinese sweet bean sauce that is less sweet than hoisin.

tianshi (tyen-she) Chinese for dessert.

Tibet A hard cheese made in the Himalayas from yak's milk; it is hung like large beads on a string to dry and then used for grating.

Tiddy A liqueur made from Canadian whisky.

tie To roll or piece together a boneless roast and then wrap it with twine or twine net.

tied-house A law prohibiting a manufacturer, importer or wholesaler of alcoholic beverages from owning an interest in a retail operation.

tiella (tee-EH-lah) An Italian baked casserole-type dish made with layers of potatoes, onions, rice, fish, shellfish and other ingredients.

tientsin pear A large pear with a spherical shape and a curving stalk; it has a pale yellow, slightly rough skin, a firm, juicy, crisp, grainy texture and a sweet flavor.

tiere (tea-a-ray) A couscous made from millet and used in West African (especially Senegalese and Malian) cuisines.

tiered candy dish *See* dessert server.

tiere sow (tea-a-ray sov) A Senegalese dessert consisting of chilled, cooked tiere mixed with sow and sugar.

tiers The different levels in an assemblage of items, one stacked on top of another (e.g., a wedding cake). *See* layer.

tiffin (ti-fen) An Indian lunch or midmorning snack, usually consisting of rice or bread, curry and dal, delivered in tiered aluminum or enameled containers.

tiganita (tea-gah-nee-tah) A Greek preparation method in which fish are coated with flour or batter and deep-fried in oil.

tiganites (tea-gah-nee-tess) A Greek confection of small cakes fried in oil; usually flavored with orange.

tigeladas (tea-zha-lah-das) A Portuguese sweet that is a light, fluffy, thick, pancakelike pudding made with milk, eggs and sugar baked in a clay dish.

tiger lily bud The dried bud of the tiger lily (*Lilium lancifolium*); it has an elongated shape, a golden color and a del-icate and musky-sweet flavor and is used as a garnish and in stir-fry dishes in Chinese and other Asian cuisines; also known as golden needle and lily bud.

tiger nut A small wrinkled tuber of a plant (*Cyerus esculentus* var. *sativus*); it has a crisp white flesh and a sweet, nutty flavor somewhat similar to that of an almond; also known as chufa and earth almond.

tigiega mimlica (tee-gee-ah-gah meem-LEE-cah) A Maltese dish consisting of a roasted chicken stuffed with minced beef and pork, hard-boiled eggs and bread crumbs.

tikiti (tee-kee-tee) Swahili for melon.

tikka (teek-kah) Hindi for cutlet or pieces.

tikva (teak-vah) Bulgarian for pumpkin.

tilapia (tuh-LAH-pee-uh) 1. A generic name for several species of freshwater fish aquafarmed worldwide; they generally have a gray skin, a lean white flesh, a firm texture, a sweet, mild flavor and an average market weight of 3 lb. (1.3 kg); sometimes marketed as cherry snapper or sunshine snapper, even though not members of the snapper family; also known as mudfish. 2. One such fish, native to Africa and aquafarmed in the United States, with an average market weight of 1–1.5 lb. (450–700 g).

ti leaves (tee) The long, narrow leaves of the ti plant (*Cordyline terminalis*); they are used to wrap foods for cooking in Pacific Island cuisines.

tilefish A fish found in the Atlantic Ocean from the mid-Atlantic states to New England; it has a multicolored skin with distinctive yellow dots, a lean flesh, a firm texture and an average market weight of 4–7 lb. (1.8–3.2 kg).

Tillamook (TIHL-uh-mook) A firm Cheddar-style cheese made from cow's milk in Oregon; it has a yellow color and ranges from mild to sharp in flavor.

tilleul A tisane made from sprigs of the linden tree, picked as they bloom; it has a mild, faintly fruity flavor.

tilliliha (till-ill-eeha) A Finnish dish of mutton with dill sauce.

Tilsit (TIHL-siht) A firm cheese made in Switzerland's Thurgau area from cow's milk; it has a yellow color, a firm, supple texture, few holes and a buttery flavor with a spicy aftertaste; also known as Royalp.

Tilsiter (TIHL-ziht-er) A firm cheese made in Germany and central Europe from cow's milk; it has a slightly yellow interior, sometimes with small round eyes, and a medium-sharp, piquant flavor; caraway seeds are often added.

tilting kettle A large, flat-bottomed, freestanding pan about 6 in. deep with an internal heating element below the pan's bottom; used as a stockpot, fry pan, griddle or steam table; it usually has a hand-crank mechanism to turn or tilt the pan to pour out the contents.

timbale 1. A dish, usually a custard base mixed with vegetables, meats or fish, baked in this mold. 2. A pastry shell made with a timbale iron; it can be filled with a sweet or savory mixture.

timbale iron An iron used for making timbales; it consists of a long handle and a flat head that is available in various shapes and sizes, such as hearts and stars; the head is dipped into a batter and then into hot oil.

timbale mold A 1½ in. (3.8 cm) deep, flair-sided, round, stainless steel mold with a capacity of 4 oz. (113.4 g); it is used for single servings of foods such as eggs in aspic. *See* aspic mold.

timbale mold

timballo (teem-BAH-loh) An Italian dish, usually pasta or rice, made in a form and unmolded.

tim choy (team cheong) A thick, sweet, black soy sauce used in Malaysian cuisine.

time-and-temperature principle Keep hot foods hot and cold foods cold; by keeping potentially hazardous foods outside the temperature danger zone, the chances of an infection, intoxication or toxin-mediated infection are decreased.

time-share ownership An ownership interest in a resort, hotel or the like; each participant owns the right to occupy a particular unit for a specific time period, with all owners sharing pro rata maintenance costs and other expenses; also known as interval ownership and vacation ownership.

timian (TEE-mi-ahn) Norwegian for thyme.

timo (TEE-moh) Italian for thyme.

tin 1. A soft silver-white, malleable metal used as an alloy and in making tinfoil, utensils and the like. 2. A trace element used for various biological functions and found in many foods. 3. A pan used for baking (e.g., pie tin, loaf tin and flan tin). 4. A can or comparable metal container, especially in Great Britain.

tindoori A small squash and member of the cucumber family grown in India; it has a green-striped skin, a moist, crisp, pale green flesh with many seeds and a strong cucumber flavor.

tinga (tinn-gah) A Mexican and Latin American dish of seasoned braised meat flavored with chipotle, poblano or other chiles.

tini (tee-nee) Swahili for fig.

tin kitchen A type of reflector oven.

tinned 1. Pertaining to an object coated or plated with tin. 2. Food that is in or came from a can.

tinned steel Steel coated with tin and used for baking tins and molds; it is tough, durable and does not warp over high heat but does rust.

Tinta (TEEN-tah) A family of red wine grapes grown in Spain and Portugal; some subvarieties are also known as Grenache and Tempranillo.

tioro A Basque stew made from onions and fish cooked in fish stock.

tip *See* knife point and pinion.

Tipperary A cocktail made of Irish whiskey, sweet vermouth and green Chartreuse.

tips An acronym for To Insure Prompt Service and used to describe gratuities given to someone for performing a service; also known as gratuity.

tipsy pudding; tipsy parson A British dessert similar to trifle made with several layers of whipped cream, custard and wine-soaked sponge cake.

tiquira (te-kee-rah) A Brazilian spirit distilled from fermented tapioca roots; it has a very high alcohol content.

tirage (tee-raj) 1. French for the process of bottling wines. 2. In France's Champagne region, it refers to the bottling of a still wine with a mixture of sugar and yeast to induce a second fermentation in the bottle. *See* liqueur de tirage.

Tiramisù; tirami sù (tih-ruh-mee-SOO) Italian for pick me up and used to describe a dessert made with layers of liqueur-soaked ladyfingers or sponge cake, sweetened mascarpone cheese and zabaglione, usually garnished with whipped cream and shaved chocolate.

t'ire (tea-ray) Ethiopian for raw.

tirebouchon (teer-boo-shonh) French for corkscrew.

tired 1. A wine-tasting term for a wine that is showing signs of age; it may be slightly oxidized and beginning to lose its fruity aroma and flavor. 2. A tasting term for a food or beverage that lacks freshness and zest. 3. A critical term for a restaurant that needs to change its menu, freshen its decor or otherwise invigorate its operations. 4. A critical term for a menu or dish that has become boring or dull because of overexposure.

Tirel, Guillaume *See* Taillevent.

Tiroler Knödlsuppe (tee-rol-ler ka-nudel-shup-pa) A soup made in Austria's Tyrol region from beef broth garnished with Knödel.

tirópita (tee-rop-PEE-tah) A Greek dish made with phyllo dough, cheese and eggs, baked as a pie or folded into rolls or small triangles and served as a meze.

tisane (teh-ZAHN) An infusion of herbs, flowers, spices and other plant matter, usually consumed hot for refreshment, medicinal, calming or rejuvenating purposes; also known as herb tea or herbal tea and known imprecisely as tea.

Tisch (tish) German for table.

Tischwein (tish-vine) *See* Tafelwein.

tiswin A fermented beverage made by Apaches from corn, water, brown sugar and flavored with spices such as cinnamon and orange peel.

titanium dioxide A food additive used as a white coloring agent.

titi *See* shrimp.

toadback *See* calabaza.

toad-in-the-hole A British dish of Yorkshire pudding baked with small link sausages.

toadstool An inedible or poisonous fungus with an umbrella-shaped body.

toast *v.* To make an item (usually baked goods) crisp and hot. *n.* 1. A piece of bread grilled or broiled on both sides. 2. A speech made or a phrase stated before drinking a beverage in a person's or thing's honor. 3. The beverage consumed in honor of someone or something. 4. Slang for an item that has been greatly overcooked.

toaster An electrical appliance that toasts bread, bagels, and so on to a preset degree of doneness automatically.

toaster oven A small electrical appliance used on the countertop for toasting, baking or broiling foods.

toast points Triangular pieces of toast, usually without the crusts, used as a base for cream sauce dishes or canapés.

toasty A wine-tasting term for an aroma reminiscent of grilled bread; often caused by aging the wine in charred wooden barrels.

tobacco plant *See* corona.

tobiko The roe of the flying fish; it has an orange-red color, mild flavor and slight crunch; used in Hawaiian cuisine.

Tocai Friulano (toh-KYE free-oo-LAY-noh) A popular white wine grape grown principally in Friuli, Italy.

tocco (TOH-koh) A term used in the region of Genoa, Italy, for any of a variety of sauces served on rice or pasta.

tocino (toa-THEE-noa) Spanish for bacon.

tocopherol (toe-KAHF-er-ol) A food additive used as an antioxidant and/or nutrient supplement (vitamin E) in processed foods such as baked goods, dairy products and breakfast cereals. *See* vitamin E.

tod (todd) Thai for deep-fry.

toddy A warming drink made of whiskey, sugar and hot water; the word is derived from the Hindi tari.

toddy; tody (tod-dee) A sweet alcoholic Indian beverage made from the fermented sap of coconut or other palms.

toffee; toffy 1. A firm but chewy candy made with brown sugar or molasses and butter; Danish and English versions are hard and brittle instead of chewy. 2. The British spelling of taffy.

tofu (TOH-foo) A custardlike product made from curdled soy milk from which some of the water has been removed by pressure; it has a white color and a slightly nutty, bland flavor that absorbs other flavors; available dried and fresh (usually packed in water) and used in Asian cuisines in soups or cooked; also known as soybean curd and bean curd. *See* bean curd.

tofu, cotton A common variety of tofu; it has a firm texture, an irregular surface pattern (caused by the weave of the cotton fabric used during pressing) and a low moisture content.

tofu, silk A common variety of tofu; it has a smooth, soft texture, a smooth surface pattern (the silk fabric used during the pressing does not leave any patterns) and a high moisture content.

tofu custard *See* kinugoshi.

tofu pudding Soft curds of soy milk, generally unpressed or lightly pressed; also known as soybean pudding and soft soybean curds.

tofutti A frozen mixture of sweeteners, flavoring agents and tofu products; intended to resemble ice cream in flavor and texture but not calories.

togarashi (to-gah-RAH-shee) Japanese for dried chiles used as a seasoning or garnish.

to go *See* takeout.

togue Slang in the New England region of the United States for a large lake trout.

Tokay; Tokay Aszú; Tokaji Aszú (toh-kay; toh-kay ah-SOO; toh-kai ah-SOO) 1. A sweet Hungarian white wine made principally from the Furmint grape; the wine is made by adding mashed grapes affected by the noble rot to a dry wine and cask aging the mix for 5–7 years. 2. The Australian name for the Muscadelle grape.

Tokay; Tokay-Hegyalja A grape-growing and wine-producing region of Hungary known for Tokaji.

Tokay d'Alsace (toh-kai dal-zase) The Alsatian name for the Pinot Gris grape.

tolee molee (toh-le mo-li) The condiments served with a Burmese meal; they usually include at least one pungent fish- or shrimp-based sauce.

Toll House cookie A drop cookie made with brown sugar and chocolate chips; sometimes nuts are added.

tom 1. A male turkey. 2. Thai for to boil.

tomaat (toa-MAAD) Dutch for tomato.

tomalley (TOM-al-ee; toh-MAL-ee) 1. The olive green liver of a lobster; it is often used to flavor sauces and other items. 2. The rich, yellow, fatty yolk of crab eggs.

Tom and Jerry A cocktail made of eggs, sugar, brandy and either bourbon or rum and mixed with hot milk or boiling water; served in a large mug with a sprinkling of grated nutmeg.

tomate (toh-MAH-tay) Portuguese for tomato.

tomate (to-maht) French for tomato.

tomate, sauce *See* tomato sauce.

Tomaten (tom-MAA-tern) German for tomatoes.

tomater (tom-ah-terr) Norwegian for tomatoes.

tomates (toa-MAH-tayss) Spanish for tomatoes.

tomatillo (tohm-ah-TEE-oh) A plant (*Physalis ixocarpa*) native to Mexico whose fruit resembles a small tomato with a papery tannish-green husk; the fruit has a thin, bright green skin (yellow and purple varieties are also available) and a firm, crisp, pale yellow flesh with a tart, lemony–herb flavor; used like a vegetable in American Southwestern and Mexican cuisines; also known as jamberry, Mexican green tomato, Mexican husk tomato and husk tomato.

tomato The fleshy fruit of the *Lycopersicon esculentum,* a vine native to South America and a member of the nightshade family; used like a vegetable, tomatoes are available in a range of sizes, from tiny spheres (currant tomatoes) to large squat ones (beefsteak tomatoes), and colors from green (unripe) to golden yellow to ruby red.

tomato concassée *See* concassée.

tomato concentrate *See* tomato paste.

tomato figs Sun-dried tomatoes.

tomato juice The thick liquid produced by blending the pulp and juice of a tomato.

tomato knife A knife used to slice tomatoes, sausages and hard cheeses; it has a 5-in.-long, ridged, wave cut blade with two prongs on the end for transferring slices to a plate; also known as a European tomato knife.

tomato knife

tomato paste A thick, slightly coarse paste made from tomatoes that have been cooked for several hours, strained and reduced to form a richly flavored concentrate used as a flavoring and thickener; also known as tomato concentrate.

tomato press A tool that presses tomatoes through a stainless steel cone, the juice and pulp going through one chute and the skins and seeds through another.

tomato purée A thick liquid made from cooked and strained tomatoes; often used as a thickener for sauces.

tomato sauce 1. A French mother or leading sauce made by sautéing mirepoix and tomatoes; white stock is added, and the sauce is then thickened with a roux; also known as sauce tomate. 2. A pasta sauce made from skinned, cooked, deseeded tomatoes; it can be thick or thin, seasoned with a variety of herbs and spices and garnished with meat, mushrooms, onions or the like. 3. A slightly thinned tomato purée, often seasoned, used as a base for sauces or as a flavoring or topping ingredient.

tombo Hawaiian for albacore tuna.

Tom Collins A cocktail made of gin, lemon juice, sugar syrup and club soda; served in a Collins glass and garnished with a maraschino cherry.

Tomerl (toh-merl) An Austrian pancake made from cornmeal, eggs and milk and flavored with onions.

tomillo (to-my-yo) Spanish for thyme.

tom kha kai A Thai chicken and coconut milk soup flavored with kha, chile and lemongrass.

tomme (tohm) A group of mountain cheeses made in France's Pyrenees or Savoy regions from ewe's, goat's and/or cow's milk; generally, they are semisoft to firm and of rather simple, hearty character.

tomoro-koshi (toh-moh-roh-KOH-shee) Japanese for corn.

tong (tawng) Dutch for sole.

tonghao cai (tongue-tchao cah-ee) Chinese for chrysanthemum greens.

tongs A utensil with two long handles attached at the top; there are two types: those with a heavy wire scissor action and those with a spring; both are made in either stainless steel or chromed steel and are used as a retrieval tool.

tongue A variety meat (typically from a cow, although tongues from other animals are also available); generally it is skinned before service; it has a pink color and a tough, chewy texture and is available fresh, pickled, salted, smoked and corned.

tongue press A hinged metal plate and bowl used for pressing tongue; it keeps the meat flat as it cools.

tongue sausage A sausage made from tongue and other meats, sometimes flavored with pistachio nuts.

ton hom (ton homm) Thai for green onions.

tonic; tonic water Quinine-flavored water infused with carbon dioxide to create effervescence; also known as quinine water.

tonkatsu (ton-kah-tzu) A Japanese dish of breaded deep-fried pork tenderloin, served sliced on finely shredded lettuce garnished with lemon and served with tonkatsu sauce.

tonkatsu sauce (ton-kah-tzu) A dipping sauce for tonkatsu; similar to a barbecue sauce, it is made with ketchup, dark soy sauce, sake, Worcestershire sauce and mustard.

tonnarelli (ton-nah-RAL-lee) Very thin Italian pasta ribbons; also known as pasta alla chitarra.

tonnato (tohn-NAH-toh) An Italian dish that contains or is accompanied by tuna.

tonne (tun) French for a large cask or tun.

tonno (TOH-noh) Italian for tuna.

tonnos (ton-noss) Greek for tuna.

tonno stufato (TOH-noh stoo-FAH-toh) An Italian dish of braised tuna flavored with onion, garlic and rosemary.

tonsil plant Slang for whiskey; used in movies about the old west.

tonyu (TOHN-yoo) Japanese for soy milk.

tooa (thua) Thai for peas, beans or peanuts.

toogbei (toog-bay) A Ghanaian dish consisting of loops of deep-fried dough flavored with sugar, nutmeg and orange rind; they are sometimes brightly colored.

toor dal (tour dahl) Hindi for red lentils.

Tootsie Roll The proprietary name for candy in the form of chewy chocolate logs; the same chocolate mixture is used as the filling for fruit-flavored lollipops known as Tootsie Pops.

Topaz A sweet, golden, Tokay-type Israeli wine.

top-brown To brown a food (often one with a bread crumb, grated cheese or other topping) under an overhead heat source.

top butt A fabricated cut of the beef primal sirloin; it is a tender, boneless center cut used for a roast or further fabricated into steaks.

Topfen (TOHP-fehrn) A German word that, when used as a prefix, indicates that a dish contains curds or cottage cheese.

top-fermented beer *See* ale.

top-fermenting yeast A yeast used in brewing beers such as ale; it converts sugars to alcohol and carbon dioxide at 50–70°F (10–21.1°C), flocculates early in fermentation and is carried up into the kräusen by carbon dioxide.

Topfkäse (tohp-kaiz) A German cooked cheese made from soured cow's milk.

topinambour (toe-pe-nam-ber) French for Jerusalem artichoke.

topneck clam; topneck quahog An Atlantic hard-shell clam that is under 4 in. (10.1 cm) across the shell; the shells are a dark tannish-gray, and the chewy meat has a mild flavor.

top off; top up To add enough liquid to fill a container to the top or near the top.

top of Iowa A fabricated cut of the beef primal sirloin; it is a fully trimmed steak.

topping; topping off; topping up 1. Refilling a wine barrel to ensure that no air space has been created between the wine and the stopper through evaporation. 2. Adding a bit more liquid to a glass that is already somewhat full.

top round A subprimal cut of the beef primal round; it is the muscle along the leg bone on the inside portion of the animal's leg; it is fairly tender and flavorful and sometimes fabricated into round steaks; also known as the inside round.

top rump *See* thick flank.

topside 1. A British cut of the beef carcass; it is a lean, boneless joint from the top of the inside hind leg; also known as a buttock steak or round steak. 2. A British cut of the veal carcass; it is the small, lean, cushion-shaped muscle from the anterior from which scallops are cut; also known as cushion of veal.

top sirloin *See* loin tip.

top sirloin butt steak A fabricated cut of the beef primal sirloin; it contains muscles from the top of the hip area and is slightly tough but flavorful.

toque (toke) The tall, white, pleated hat worn by a chef.

Torgiano (tohr-J'YAH-noh) A DOC wine-making zone in Italy's Umbria region that produces red and white wines from a variety of grapes, including Trebbiano, Sangiovese and Canaiolo.

torigai (toh-ree-gha-ee) Japanese for cockle.

toro (toh-roh) Japanese for tuna belly; it is the fatty cut of raw prime tuna used for sashimi.

toronja (to-RON-ha) Spanish for grapefruit.

tørr (tohrr) Norwegian for dry.

torrone (tor-ROHN-nay) An Italian nougat of honey and nuts.

Torrontes A highly aromatic red or white wine grape grown exclusively in Argentina.

torsk (torshk) Danish, Norwegian and Swedish for cod.

torsketunge (tore-ska-toon-gah) A Norwegian dish consisting of boiled fresh cod's tongues served with melted butter or a white sauce flavored with curry.

tort (tohr-ta) Polish and Russian for cake.

torta (TOHR-tah) Italian, Portuguese and Spanish for a pie, tart, light round cake, sandwich cookie or a dish containing pastry.

torta delizia (THOR-tah dee-leet-tsee-ah) An Italian cake consisting of layers of sponge cake filled with jam or pastry cream; the outside of the cake is completely covered with almond macaroon paste, baked briefly and then brushed with a sweet, shiny glaze.

torta di mandorle (TOHR-tah dee mahn-dohr-lah) 1. An almond tart traditionally made in Venice, Italy; found in a variety of shapes and sizes, it is composed of a sweet pastry shell filled with creamy frangipane and covered with unblanched whole almonds; after baking, it is heavily dusted with confectioners' sugar. 2. In other areas, this torta also contains chocolate and Strega.

tortas de carne (TOHR-tah de car-nae) Spanish for meat patties.

Törtchen (TUHR-chehn) German for a tartlet or small tart with a sweet filling.

Torte (TOR-ta) 1. German for cake. 2. German for a cake made with ground nuts or bread crumbs instead of flour; some versions are single layered, and others are multilayered and filled with whipped cream, jam or buttercream.

tortellini (tohr-te-LEEN-ee) Italian for small twists and used to describe small stuffed pasta shaped like a ring.

tortelloni (tohr-te-LONE-ee) Large tortellini.

tortilha (tor-TEE-lya) Portuguese for an open-faced (unfolded) omelette; also known as omellatta.

tortilla (tohr-TEE-yuh) A round, thin, unleavened Mexican bread made from masa or wheat flour and lard and baked on a griddle (depending on its use, it could then be deep-fried), it is eaten plain or wrapped around or garnished with various fillings.

tortilla-basket fryer A tool used to shape and hold tortillas for deep-frying; it consists of two wire U-shaped baskets that hold the tortilla.

tortilla chips Corn or flour tortillas cut into wedges and deep-fried or baked; eaten as a snack, usually with a dip or salsa.

tortilla press A metal utensil used to flatten tortilla dough; it consists of two hinged disks: the top disk has a handle and is lowered over the ball of dough resting on the lower disk.

tortini (toar-TEE-nee) Italian for small round cakes or croquettes of food, usually savory.

tortoiseshell limpet A variety of limpet found along the Pacific coast from Canada to California; it has a brown-striped reddish-brown shell slightly ovoid in shape, an average length of 1.5 in. (3.8 cm) and a tough, flavorful flesh.

tortoni (tohr-TOH-nee) A rich frozen Italian dessert made with whipped cream or ice cream, flavored with rum and coated with macaroon crumbs or ground almonds.

tortue (tor-too) 1. French for turtle. 2. Mock turtle soup made from beef consommé and turtle herbs.

tortue, sauce à la (tor-too, saus ah lah) A French compound sauce made from a demi-glaze flavored with white wine, turtle herbs, truffle essence, cayenne and Madeira.

torui *See* papengaye.

tosa soy sauce (to-sa) A Japanese soy sauce flavored with dried bonito; it is a traditional accompaniment to sashimi.

Toscanello (tohs-cah-NELL-loa) A very hard Italian grana cheese made from ewe's milk; it has a smooth white to pale yellow rind, a dense white interior with a few scattered holes and a muted, mild to slightly sharp flavor.

toscatårta (tos-kah-tahr-tah) A Swedish sponge-type cake that is baked, topped with a cooked mixture of butter, sugar, flour, milk and almonds and placed under the broiler to brown the topping.

toss To flip or shake foods to combine them.

tostada (toh-STAH-duh) A Mexican dish of a crisp-fried tortilla topped with refried beans and garnished with meat, cheese, lettuce, tomatoes, sour cream, guacamole and/or salsa.

tot A small amount of any beverage.

total costs The sum of fixed and variable costs.

total recipe cost The total cost of ingredients for a particular recipe; it does not reflect overhead, labor, fixed expenses or profit.

totopos (toh-TOH-pohs) 1. A corn tortilla cut into wedges and fried until crisp; essentially, tortilla chips. 2. A Mexican snack or antojito consisting of masa harina dough flavored with chiles and mashed beans and then fried and topped with guacamole or other garnish.

totori muk (toh-toh-ree mook) Slabs of gelatinous curd made from acorns; the curd has a bland flavor and is used in Korean cuisine; also known as acorn curd.

Touareg (too-ah-rag) A hard, dry, unsalted cheese made by the Touareg nomads of North Africa; it is coagulated with the leaves of the Korourou tree and dried in the sun.

touch A small amount of any beverage.

toucinho (toe-seen-nyo) Portuguese for bacon.

toucinho do céu (too-see-nyo doh sah-oo) Portuguese for heavenly bacon and used to describe a sweet made of eggs, almonds, pumpkin and butter.

touffe (touf) French for a bundle of herbs and/or vegetables with their stalks, tied in a bundle.

toulousaine, sauce (too-loo-zhan) A French compound sauce made from an allemande flavored with mushroom and truffle essences.

Toulouse sausage (too-loos) A small French sausage made from pork, seasoned with garlic and wine.

toupin (too-pahn) *See* daubière.

touraine A variety of medium-sized, spherical squash with a pale green flesh covered with darker green spots and streaks.

tourch gourd *See* papengaye.

Touriga (too-REE-gah) A red wine grape grown in Portugal and used for making port and table wines.

tourist class *See* economy class.

tourist noodles *See* yee fu mein.

tournant (toor-nahn) At a food services operation following the brigade system, the person who works wherever needed; also known as the roundsman or swing cook.

tournedo (tour-nah-doe) A fabricated cut of the beef primal short loin; cut from the short tenderloin, it is very lean, tender and flavorful and smaller than a filet mignon.

tournedos Rossini (toor-nuh-doh roas-see-nee) A French dish of tournedos sautéed in butter, placed on a crouton, garnished with foie gras and truffles and served with a brown sauce flavored with Madeira.

tournée (toor-nay) *See* bird's beak knife.

tournéed An English version of the French verb used to describe a vegetable that is cut into a football shape with seven equal sides and blunt ends.

tourner (toor-nay) French for to trim or to turn and used to describe the act of cutting foods, usually vegetables, into football-shaped pieces with seven equal sides and blunt ends.

toursi (toor-sea) Greek for pickled, especially with regard to fruits and vegetables.

tourte (toor-teh) A French open-faced savory pastry tart.

tourtière (tour-tea-yay) 1. French for the pie dish used to make a tourte. 2. A Canadian pie made with pork, veal and onions, flavored with allspice and baked in a pastry shell; it is eaten hot or cold.

tovagliolo (toh-vah-yo-loh) Italian for napkin.

toxic metals Metals such as lead, mercury, copper, zinc and antimony that may be dispersed in food or water; they are poisonous if ingested.

toxin A chemical produced by a living organism that is poisonous to humans or other animals.

toxin-mediated infection A type of bacterial illness sharing characteristics of intoxications and infections; it is caused by ingesting pathogenic bacteria; the bacteria establish colonies in human and animal intestinal tracts, where they produce toxins.

TPT *See* tant pour tant.

trace minerals; trace elements A group of essential mineral nutrients found in the human body in amounts less than 5 g; includes chromium, cobalt, copper, fluorine, iodine, iron, manganese, molybdenum, nickel, selenium, silicon, tin, vanadium and zinc.

trade buyer Any wholesaler or retailer of goods such as distilled spirits or produce.

trademark A registered word, name, symbol and/or device used by a manufacturer or merchant to identify and distinguish goods.

trade whiskey 1. Whiskey traded to Native Americans during the 19th century; also known as Indian whiskey. 2. Slang for any cheap, inferior distilled spirit.

traditional apple An imprecisely used term to denote any variety of apple generally in existence before 1914.

tragacanth (TRAHG-ah-kahnth) A food additive used as an emulsifier or thickener in sauces, ice cream and candy.

trahana (trah-hah-nah) Greek noodles made with a sour dough and resembling rice; used in soups and stews.

trail The intestines of small game birds.

Traminer (tra-MEE-ner) The former German name for the Gewürztraminer grape.

trammel (TRAM-ahl) A long pothook for a fireplace crane that can be raised and lowered.

tranbär (trahn-bahr) Swedish for cranberry.

tranche (tranch) 1. French for a slice. 2. A slice (usually of fish) that is cut on the diagonal to increase the apparent size of the item.

trancher (trahn-shey) French for to slice.

trans-fatty acids Unusually shaped fatty acids that can arise when polyunsaturated oils are hydrogenated.

transfer method A sparkling wine–making technique in which the second fermentation takes place in bottles, but riddling and disgorging are eliminated by emptying the wine and sediment into a tank under pressure, filtering the wine, adding the dosage and then rebottling; wine produced by this method may be labeled fermented in the bottle.

transfers to bar A request from the bar to the kitchen for foods to be used by the bar to prepare or garnish drinks (e.g., strawberries for a strawberry daiquiri); items transferred from the kitchen are charged to beverage costs.

transfers to kitchen A request from the kitchen to the bar for beverages and other bar items to be used by the kitchen to prepare menu items (e.g., rum to flavor a dessert); items transferred from the bar are charged to food costs.

translucent noodles *See* cellophane noodles.

Transparent gage A variety of greengage with a red-spotted golden skin, a yellow flesh and a sweet flavor reminiscent of honey.

transparent noodles Chinese and Japanese noodles that are made from mung bean paste, soybean starch and wheat flour; they have a silvery, somewhat translucent appearance.

transparent pudding *See* bakewell tart.

Trappist (trap-pehst) A group of cheeses developed by Trappist monks; some recipes date to the Middle Ages; generally, they are semisoft to firm with a mild to moderately pungent flavor and aroma; they include Port du Salut (France), Bellelay (Switzerland) and Oka (Canada).

Trappist beer Any of several beers brewed by Trappist monks at one of six remaining brewing abbeys in Belgium and the Netherlands; most are strong, golden to amber in color and high in alcohol; they are fruity and bittersweet.

trash fish Fisherman's slang for fish with no culinary value; typically, fish used for animal fodder.

traub (troob) The sediment that precipitates out of the wort during the boiling and cooling stages of the beer-making process.

Traube (trau-buh) German for grape.

Traveler's Joy A cocktail made of gin, cherry liqueur and lemon juice.

tray *v.* To place foods and the like on a tray. *n.* An open, variously shaped receptacle with a flat bottom and low sides that is used to hold or carry articles (e.g., glasses) or food.

treacle (TRE-kehl) 1. British for molasses. 2. A sweet syrup or ingredient made from molasses and corn syrup; also known as golden syrup.

treacle berry The small red berries of the herbaceous garden plant *Smilacina racemosa;* also known as false Solomon's seal.

treadles Archaic term for chalazae; they were thought to be rooster sperm.

Trebbiano (treh-bee-AH-no) 1. A white wine grape principally grown in Italy and often used as a blending grape (with Malvasia or as a component of Frascati and Soave); also known as Ugni Blanc (especially in France's Cognac region) and Saint-Émilion (especially in California). 2. A rather neutral white wine made from this grape and generally used for blending or as a table wine.

tree ear mushroom *See* cloud ear mushroom.

tree oyster mushroom *See* oyster mushroom.

tree strawberry *See* arbutus.

tree sweetin' A traditional term for maple syrup.

tree tomato *See* tamarillo.

treipen (tray-pen) A dish from Luxembourg consisting of black pudding, sausages and mashed potatoes; served hot with horseradish sauce.

tremella (tree-mel-la) *See* white fungus.

tre mosche (TREH MOH-skeh) Italian for three flies and used to describe the three coffee beans traditionally served in a glass of Sambuca.

trencher 1. A slice of stale bread used as a platter or plate; such a use has been recorded since the Middle Ages. 2. A flat piece of round or square wood on which meat is served. 3. A wooden, metal or ceramic plate.

trenette (treh-NEHT-tay) Narrow, thick ribbons of Italian pasta.

Tres Rios Arabica coffee beans grown in Costa Rica; the beverage is lively, with a tangy flavor and a fragrant aroma.

trey reach (tray reech) A large freshwater fish from the Mekong River in Cambodia that grows to 6 ft. (2 m) and has a roe weighing more than 20 lb. (10 kg); eaten fresh or used to make fermented fish sauces; also known as pa boeuk (Laos).

triacetin A food additive used as a flavoring agent, flavoring adjuvant, humectant and/or solvent in processed foods such as baked goods and mixes, beverages, confections, frozen desserts and gelatins.

triangle *See* loin tip.

Trianon, mayonnaise (tree-yay-nohn) A French mayonnaise sauce blended with tomato purée and white onion purée and garnished with diced gherkins and red sweet pepper.

Tribune strawberry A variety of ever-bearing strawberries; the fruit have a somewhat tart flavor.

tributyrin A food additive used as a flavoring agent or flavoring adjuvant in processed foods such as baked goods, alcoholic beverages, fats, frozen desserts, gelatins and candies.

tricalcium silicate A food additive used as an anticaking agent.

Trichinella spiralis A type of nematode worm that is parasitic in humans; its ingestion, typically through undercooked meat, especially pork, causes trichinosis.

trichinosis A disease caused by ingesting larvae of *Trichinella spiralis;* symptoms include fever, muscle weakness and pain, vomiting and diarrhea.

tricholome chaussé (tree-show-lom sho-sey) French for matsutake.

tricholome pied-bleu (tree-show-lom pee-a-bluh) French for blewit.

Trick or Treat pumpkin A pumpkin variety; its seeds lack hulls and are ideal for roasting and snacking.

tricoloma (tree-coh-loh-mah) Spanish for blewit.

trie (tree) French for sorting or selecting and refers to the harvesting of grapes by repeated partial pickings of only the ripest bunches or individual grapes.

trifle (TRI-fuhl) A deep-dish British layered dessert made with sponge cake, sherry, custard, jam or fruit and whipped cream.

trifoliate (try-foe-leh-ate) A leaf with three lobes or three leaves attached to one stem.

triggerfish A fish found in the Atlantic Ocean off North America; brightly colored, it has a firm, white flesh with a rich flavor.

triglycerides The major class of lipids, including fats and oils; each triglyceride consists of one glycerol unit and three fatty acid units.

trigo (tree-goo) Portuguese and Spanish for wheat.

trim *v.* To remove undesirable portions of a food item (e.g., external fat from a cut of beef or stems from grapes) before further preparation or service. *n.* The portion of the item removed.

trim loss The amount of a product removed when preparing it for consumption.

trimmed whisk A utensil made by cutting the wires of a whisk so that only a few inches remain attached to the handle; used for spun sugar.

trimono (tree-moh-noh) A Tibetan whole wheat bread; the dough is rolled and folded into a flower shape and then baked with a coating of oil and turmeric; it is eaten with curries or sauces.

triolein One of the three principal fats present in foods.

Triomphe de Farcy A particularly flavorful variety of French green beans.

tripa (tre-pah) A Corsican dish consisting of a boiled sheep's belly stuffed with beetroot, spinach, herbs and sheep's blood.

tripalmitin One of the three principal fats present in foods.

tripe The first and second stomachs of ruminants such as cattle, oxen and sheep; it has a tender texture and a subtle flavor.

tripe, honeycomb A part of the lining of a ruminant's second stomach; the inner side has a honeycomb pattern and a very delicate flavor.

tripe, pocket A portion of a ruminant's second stomach; cut so that it forms a pocket with the honeycomb-patterned side inside the pocket.

triple cream; triple crème A description of a cow's milk cheese enriched with cream and having a minimum milk-fat content of 72–75% (e.g., Boursin); the flavor is mild and very rich.

triple distilled A whiskey-making process (especially for Irish whiskey); the wash is distilled in a large pot (wash still), yielding low wines that are then distilled in a smaller pot still to produce strong and weak feints, which are collected separately; the strongest feints are then distilled in a third pot still to produce the finished product, which is then aged.

Triple Sec A clear, strong, orange-flavored liqueur used principally to make cocktails.

trippa (trip-pah) Italian for tripe; generally referring to tripe from a calf.

Tristar strawberry A variety of ever-bearing strawberries; the fruit are particularly sweet.

tristearin One of the three principal fats present in foods.

tritato misto (tree-tah-toh mees-toh) Italian for mixed grill.

triticale (triht-ih-KAY-lee) A cereal grain that is a hybrid of wheat and rye; it contains more protein and has less gluten-forming potential than wheat and has a nutty, sweet flavor; available in whole berries, as flour and in flakes.

trivet 1. A three-legged stand used to hold a kettle near a fire. 2. An ornamental stand (either flat or with short feet) placed under a hot dish at the table.

trocken (TRAW-ken) German for dry.

Trockenbeerenauslese (TRAW-ken-BEAR-en-OUSE-lay-zuh) A German wine-labeling term for extremely sweet wines made from selected dried, raisinlike grapes or from Riesling grapes that have been affected by the noble rot. *See* Qualitätswein mit Prädikat.

trompette (throm-pay) French for horn of plenty mushroom.

Tronchón (trone-CHONE) A ewe's or goat's milk cheese from Spain's Aragón, Catalonia and Valencia regions; it has a dome shape with a deep indention on top, a buff-colored rind, a bone-colored interior with many small holes, a mild herb flavor and a firm yet melting texture.

tronçon (trohn-sohn) French for chunk and used to describe a piece of food cut so that its length is greater than its width.

tronçon de milieu (trohn-sohn duh me-l'yuh) A French cut of a fish; it is usually from a midsection.

tropical green pea *See* pigeon pea.

tròta (TRAW-tah) Italian for trout.

trotters *See* pig's feet.

trough shell clams Any of a variety of clams found worldwide but particularly in Europe; they have ovoid, triangular or elliptical chalky gray shells and an average length of 1–2 in. (2.5–5 cm).

trout Any of various fish belonging to the salmon family, some of which are anadromous and many of which are aquafarmed; they generally have a firm, white, orange or pink, flaky flesh, a low to moderate fat content and an average market weight of 8–10 oz. (225–280 g); important varieties include lake trout, rainbow trout, brook trout, brown trout and steelhead trout.

Trouville (troo-veel) A soft, ripened French cheese made from whole cow's milk.

trucha (TROO-chah) Spanish for trout.

true Dover sole *See* sole, Dover.

true lime *See* Key lime.

trufa (TROO-fah) Spanish for truffle.

truffe (truff-lah) French for truffle.

Truffe de Chine *See* Négresse potato.

Trüffel (TREWF-fehl) German for truffle.

truffle 1. A fungus (genus *Tuber*) that grows underground near the roots of certain trees, usually oaks; generally spherical and of various small sizes, with a thick, rough, wrinkled skin; there are two principal varieties: black and white. 2. A rich, creamy chocolate candy made with chocolate, butter, cream and flavorings, formed into small rough balls and coated with cocoa powder or melted chocolate.

truffle, black A truffle grown in France with a dark brown to black skin with white striations and a pungent aroma and rich flavor; also known as a Perigord.

truffle, white A truffle grown in Italy with an off-white to grayish-tan skin and an earthy, garlicky flavor; also known as a piédmontese.

truffle dipper *See* chocolate dipping fork.

truffle slicer A small tool used to shave slivers or slices from a truffle; it consists of an adjustable blade mounted at a 45-degree angle on a frame; the truffle is pressed down and across the blade.

truffles sous la cendre (truff soo lah sahn-dra) A French dish of truffles seasoned with salt and Champagne and wrapped in pork belly and covered with hot ashes; after baking, they are arranged on a napkin and served with butter.

trufle (troo-fleh) Polish for truffle.

truite (tre-WEET) French for trout.

truite au bleu (tre-wee toh bluh) A French dish of freshly killed trout

truffle slicer

poached in court bouillon and served with hollandaise or melted butter and garnished with parsley.

trumpet of death mushroom *See* horn of plenty mushroom.

truss To secure poultry or other food with string, skewers or pins so that it maintains its shape during cooking.

trussing needle A 4- to 10-in.-long metal needle used to truss foods with butcher's twine.

truta (TROO-tah) Portuguese for trout.

Truthahn (troo-tah-han) German for turkey.

try out To cook solid fat or fatty meat cut into small pieces in order to render fat from it.

tryptophan (TRIP-toh-fahn) 1. An essential amino acid used to form vitamin B₃. 2. A food additive used as a nutrient source to significantly improve the biological quality of the total protein in a food containing the naturally occurring protein.

tsai goo choi (tsah-ee goo cho-ee) A member of the cabbage family; it resembles a stunted, flattened bok choy and has ivory stems and soft, slightly coarse, dark green leaves; also known as Chinese flat cabbage.

tsampa (sahm-paw) A Tibetan flour made from ground, toasted barley; a wheat version is also used.

tsamtuk (sahm-toon) A Tibetan soup made of tsampa and chura.

tsao gu (tsah-oh goo) Chinese for straw mushroom.

tsatsiki (tzah-tzee-key) A Greek salad consisting of cucumber dressed with goat's milk yogurt and garnished with mint leaves and paprika.

tsee goo *See* arrowhead.

Tsikoudia (tsee-koo-dee-ah) A Greek digestif made from grape skins; also known as Rakiya.

Tsípouro (tsee-poo-row) A Greek digestif distilled from grape skins or grapes.

tsoonth *See* séb.

tsp. *See* teaspoon.

tsubushi-an *See* an.

tsukémono (tzu-ke-mow-no) The pickles that accompany most Japanese meals.

tsume (too-ma) A Japanese coating often used for eel and hirame; it is a thick boiled mixture of soy sauce, sugar and stock.

tsuyu (TSOO-yoo) Japanese for a seasoned liquid or clear sauce.

tsvetnaja kapusta (tshvet-na-jah kah-pu-stah) Russian for cauliflower.

tsypljenok (tsee-plee-ah-nok) Russian for chicken.

tua Thai for bean or nut.

Tuaca A sweet, citrus-flavored Italian liqueur.

tub *See* tun.

tuba (tu-ba) The milky sap obtained from the young, flowering coconut palm; it is distilled in the Philippines to make lambanog.

tube pan A deep round pan with a hollow tube in the center; used for baking cakes, especially angel food, chiffon and pound cakes. *See* Bundt pan.

tuber The swollen, fleshy part of a plant's underground stem.

tubetti (too-beht-TEE) Italian for little tubes and used to describe small and slightly bent tubes of pasta; also known as elbow macaroni.

tube pan

tuck *See* chavetta.

tudou (too-do) Chinese for potato.

tufaa (too-fah-ah) Swahili for apple.

tuffah (toof-fah) Arabic for apple.

tufoli (too-FOE-lee) Large Italian pasta tubes usually stuffed with meat, poultry, cheese or vegetable mixtures; they are smaller than manicotti and cannelloni.

tuile (twee) French for tile and used to describe a thin, crisp wafer cookie traditionally shaped while still hot around a curved object such as a rolling pin.

tuile cookie mold A 12- × 14-in. tinned steel mold with six smooth, narrow, curved troughs used to create the cookie's curved tile shape.

tukra (too-krah) Hindi for slice or piece.

Tulbagh A grape-growing and wine-producing region of South Africa that produces very dry white wines, sherries and Bordeaux-style reds.

tulip *See* Champagne tulip.

tulipe (too-LEEP) A thin, crisp French wafer cookie that is formed into a ruffled, cuplike shape while still hot and used as an edible container for ice cream, fruit, mousse and other desserts.

tulumba tatlisi (too-loom-bah tah-tlee-see) A Turkish confection of piped batter fried in oil and dipped in a sugar syrup.

Tulum Peyniri (too-loom pay-nee-ree) A crumbly, salted Turkish cheese made from ewe's or goat's milk.

tumbler A short, cylindrical glass ranging in size from 3 to 10 fl. oz.; used for short drinks on the rocks.

tumblerful A traditional measure of volume; it is approximately 2 cups.

tun (ton) 1. Any large vessel used in brewing beer; often mistakenly called a tub in the United States. 2. Chinese for stewing meat or poultry in a covered pot.

tuna Any of several varieties of saltwater fish of the mackerel family found in tropical and subtropical waters worldwide; they generally are available as loins or smaller cuts and have a low to moderate fat content, a dark pink, flaky flesh that becomes light gray when cooked, a firm texture and a distinctive rich flavor; significant varieties include albacore tuna, bluefin tuna, bonito, skipjack tuna and yellowfin tuna.

tuna fig See prickly pear.

tunas (too-nahs) Spanish for prickly pear fruit.

tuna salad A salad of tuna (usually canned) typically garnished with celery and onions, bound with mayonnaise and often flavored with celery salt.

Tung Ting A Chinese oolong tea; the beverage has a green tea–like flavor with the richness of black tea.

tungule (toon-goo-lay) Swahili for tomato.

Tunisian five-spice powder A Tunisian spice blend consisting of cinnamon, cloves, grains of paradise, nutmeg and pepper.

tunneling A condition in quick breads caused by overmixing and characterized by elongated holes.

tunny See thon.

tunny-fish British for tuna.

tuo (too-oh) A staple of Niger cuisine; it is a thick cornmeal porridge, sometimes flavored with chiles.

tuong (too-ong) A thick, strongly flavored Vietnamese sauce made of fermented soybeans, sugar and salt and used in dips and marinades for roasted meats.

turban (thur-bahn) 1. A French preparation method for certain foods, especially forcemeats, cooked in a circular border mold. 2. A French presentation method for foods arranged in a circular pattern on a plate.

turban shells A family of univalve shellfish; they have a thick, conical shell with rounded whorls and edged with small knobs; the flesh is generally tough and chewy, with a mild flavor.

turban squash See squash, turban.

turbante (toor-BAHN-te) An Italian baked puff pastry shell or case, similar to a vol-au-vent.

turbinado sugar Raw sugar that has been cleaned with steam to make it edible; it is light brown and coarse, with a molasses flavor.

turbot (thur-bow) 1. A diamond-shaped flatfish found in the Atlantic Ocean off Europe and in the Mediterranean Sea; it has a silvery-brown skin, a firm, white flesh, a delicate flavor and weighs up to 30 lb. (13.5 kg). 2. A marketing name given to several Pacific Ocean flatfish of no culinary significance.

turbot

turbotière (thur-bow-tee-yay) French for turbot poacher.

turbot poacher A large diamond-shaped pan designed to poach a whole turbot; it is 25 in. long and 6 in. deep, with an inset rack.

turbot poacher

tureen A deep dish, usually with two handles and a notch in the lid for a ladle; used to serve soups, stews and the like. See presentoir.

turfjes met bessensap (tour-fees met essen-sahn) A Dutch bread pudding served cold with raspberry sauce and whipped cream.

turion A thick, fleshy emerging shoot or sucker, such as an asparagus stem.

turkey One of the principal kinds of poultry recognized by the U.S. Department of Agriculture (USDA); it has light and dark meat and a relatively small amount of fat.

turkey, fryer-roaster An immature turkey slaughtered when 16 weeks or younger; it has a smooth skin, a very tender flesh, a flexible breastbone and an average market weight of 4–9 lb. (2–4 kg).

turkey, mature An older turkey slaughtered when 15 months or older; it has a coarse skin, a tough flesh and an average market weight of 10–30 lb. (4.5–13 kg).

turkey, wild A variety of turkey that has not been domesticated; generally, its flesh is darker than that of a domesticated turkey and has a denser texture and a nuttier, gamier flavor reminiscent of duck.

turkey, yearling A fully mature turkey slaughtered when 12–15 months old; it has a slightly coarse skin, a reasonably tender flesh and an average market weight of 10–30 lb. (4.5–13 kg).

turkey, young A turkey slaughtered when 8 months old or younger; it has a smooth skin, a tender flesh, a somewhat flexible breastbone and an average market weight of 8–22 lb. (3.5–10 kg).

turkey classes Significant turkey classes are the fryer-roaster turkey, young turkey, yearling turkey and mature turkey.

Turkish coffee A very strong coffee made by boiling finely ground coffee, sugar and water three times, cooling the mixture briefly between boilings; made in an ibrik and served in small cups immediately following the third boil; also known as Greek coffee.

Turkish delight A chewy, rubbery Middle Eastern candy made with cornstarch or gelatin, honey and fruit juice, often flavored with nuts; the candy is cut into small squares and coated with powdered sugar.

Turkish vinegar A strong, sharp vinegar with a touch of sweetness.

Türk kahvesi (tork ghahsi) Turkish for Turkish coffee.

Turk's head mold A tube pan with fluted indentions and a cover; used for steaming pudding.

turlu (toor-loo) A Turkish stew of mutton, onions, garlic, tomatoes, pumpkin, red peppers, eggplant and green beans.

turmeric (tehr-MEHR-rik) A dried, powdery spice produced from the rhizome of a tropical plant related to ginger (*Curcuma longa*); it has a strong, spicy flavor and yellow color and is used in Indian and Middle Eastern cuisines and as a yellow coloring agent; also known as Indian saffron.

turn To shape a vegetable or fruit with a paring knife. *See* tourner.

turn-bone sirloin A fabricated cut of the beef primal sirloin; it is a steak with portions of several bones of varying sizes.

turn-down service A hotel service, usually done in the evening, when towels are changed, the bed is turned down and a sweet, usually chocolate, is left on the pillow.

turned cornmeal A Bermudan dish consisting of a thick cornmeal porridge, sometimes flavored with chiles.

turner (offset) A utensil used to turn food or transfer food from cookware; it has a handle and a broad, flat metal blade that can be solid or perforated (to help drain liquids) with a round or straight edge; available in sizes from 2.5 × 2.5 in. (6.3 × 6.3 cm) to 5 × 3 in. (12.7 × 7.6 cm).

turner

turnip The rounded, conical root of the turnip plant (*Brassica rapa*); it has a white skin with a purple-tinged top, a delicate, slightly sweet flavor that becomes stronger as it ages and a coarse texture.

turnip greens The crinkly green leaves of the turnip plant; they have a sweet, peppery flavor when young that becomes more bitter with age.

turnip-rooted parsley *See* parsley root.

turnover 1. A square piece of pastry dough folded in half over a sweet or savory filling to create a triangle. 2. The frequency with which stock is sold and replenished during a given period.

turns Slang for the number of times a food services facility will seat customers at a particular table during the course of a specific period, such as dinner; a high number indicates a short customer stay.

turnspit The child or animal (usually a dog) who turned a spit by walking a treadmill.

turntable A lazy Susan with a sturdy cast-iron pedestal and a rotating flat, metal plate; used for assembling and decorating cakes and pastries and sometimes for serving food.

turo-turo (too-roe-too-roe) Filipino for a small restaurant selling plates of rice with various toppings from a steam table.

turshiya (tour-she-ha) Bulgarian mixed pickles.

tursusu (toor-soo-soo) A Turkish hors d'oeuvre of pickled vegetables such as carrots, pimientos, eggplants, beans or cucumbers.

turtle 1. Any of several varieties of land, freshwater or saltwater reptiles; they generally have a domed shell on top (called a carapace) and a flat shell below (called a plastron); the most significant variety for culinary purposes is the green turtle. 2. A round, flat, caramel and pecan candy coated with chocolate.

turtle bean *See* black bean.

turtle herbs A spice blend consisting of basil, thyme and marjoram; used to flavor soups, such as mock turtle soup.

Tuscany (tus-kay-nee) A grape-growing and wine-producing region in northern Italy; it is known for its Chianti, and the principal red wine grape variety is Sangiovese.

tuskudani (TOOS-koo-DAH-nee) A sweet and salty Japanese relish made from flaked dried tuna, shrimp, soy sauce and sugar.

Tutové (too-tohv) A French rolling pin with deep, horizontal ridges in the cylinder; used to distribute fat evenly in layers of dough, as when making puff pastry or croissant dough.

Tutové

tut sadeh (toot saw-deh) Hebrew for strawberry.

tutti-frutti 1. Italian for all fruit or mixed fruit. 2. In the United States, a sweet fruity flavoring used for gum, candy, ice cream and the like.

Tutti-Frutti A cocktail made of gin, diced apples, diced pears, maraschino liqueur and amaretto; served in a chilled highball glass.

tuyo (tu-yoh) A Filipino dish of salted and dried small fish that are fried or grilled and usually served with sliced tomatoes.

tùzi (too-zee) Chinese for rabbit.

tvorog (tvah-rohgh) A Russian cottage cheese–style cheese made from cow's milk.

Twelfth-Night cake A rich British spice cake made with candied fruits, almonds and almond paste; traditionally served on January 6, the twelfth day after Christmas.

twentieth-century pear *See* nashi.

twice-baked An expression used to refer to a product that is baked, then reworked and baked a second time (e.g., twice-baked potatoes or biscotti).

Twinkies The proprietary name for a confection of small oblong sponge cakes filled with vanilla cream.

twirl stick *See* baton lele.

twist A strip of citrus peel used as a garnish for certain cocktails.

twists Napoletani *See* gemelli.

twoenjang (twan-young) A salty, hot, brown paste of fermented soybeans used as a soup base and sauce flavoring in Korean cuisine; also known as Korean soybean paste.

2-hydroxypropanoic acid *See* lactic acid.

200 pan *See* hotel pan.

two percent milk; 2% milk Whole milk with a milkfat content reduced to 2%. *See* skim milk *and* lowfat milk.

2 pounder *See* deuce.

two-pronged fork A fork with two long tines; used to turn large pieces of meat or to hold meat or poultry while carving. *See* carving fork.

two-stage method *See* high ratio.

two-top Restaurant slang for a table for two; also known as a deuce.

two-pronged forks

txistorra (sme-sto-raw) A heavily spiced Basque pork sausage.

txitxili (she-sme-lee) A Basque dish consisting of minced cooked pork marinated in paprika and salt.

Tybo (TY-boh) A hard Danish cow's milk cheese; it has an ivory interior dotted with small holes, a yellow rind and a mild flavor; sometimes caraway seeds are added.

tykva (t'yet-vah) Russian for pumpkin.

Tyler pie; Tyler pudding pie A pie named for President John Tyler and popular throughout the American South; it is made with brown sugar, butter, cream and eggs and topped with grated coconut.

tyramine A chemical found in foods such as aged cheeses that causes migraines in some people.

tyrolienne, à la (tee-roll-YEN, ah lah) 1. A French preparation for fish; it is fried, served on tomato concassée and garnished with fried onion rings. 2. A French preparation for meat; it is pan-fried, served on tomatoes, garnished with onion rings and topped with a sauce Tyrolienne.

Tyrolienne, sauce (tee-roll-YEN) A French compound sauce made from a sauce béarnaise prepared with olive oil instead of butter.

Tyrolienne mayonnaise (tee-roll-YEN) A French mayonnaise sauce lightly flavored with tomato purée and used for cold fish or meat.

tyrophile A connoisseur and lover of cheese.

tyrosine 1. An amino acid most nutritionists consider essential; used to form the nerve tissue chemical epinephrine, melanin skin pigment and a thyroid hormone. 2. A food additive used as a nutrient source to significantly improve the biological quality of the total protein in a food containing the naturally occurring protein.

tzallaten (t'zhall-ah-tin) Yiddish for salads.

tzimmes (TSIHM-ihs) A Jewish dish of root vegetables (e.g., sweet potatoes, potatoes or carrots), dried fruit (e.g., raisins) or fresh fruit (e.g., apples) and sometimes meat, such as beef brisket, flavored with honey and cinnamon.

tzimmes; tzimmes mit mehren und pastermakken (t'zim-mis mit mayh-rhen und pass-ther-mahk-kin) A Jewish dish consisting of carrots and parsnips flavored with honey.

tzimshterner kichelach (t'zim-shter-nehr kick-hel-ach) Yiddish for cookies for the stars and used to describe gingerbread-like cookies.

ubales (oo-baa-lees) Swahili for slices.

ube A bright purple tuber with a bland, starchy flavor used to make puddings and jams in Filipino cuisine.

ublaa-huaa (oo-bla-hoo-ah) Hindi for to boil.

ubod (oo-bod) The creamy-white, fibrous pith from the center core of the coconut palm; used in Filipino cuisine, especially in egg rolls.

uccèlletti (oot-CHEHL-leh-tah) Italian for all kinds of small edible birds, generally grilled or roasted.

Uco Valley A grape-growing and wine-producing area in the Mendoza wine zone of Argentina.

udder A cow's mammary gland; used in French and Italian cuisines.

udder fat A smooth fat deposit found in the udder region of heifers and cows.

udon; udong (oo-DOHN) Wide, flat, ribbonlike Japanese noodles made from wheat flour (or sometimes corn flour); available in a variety of widths, either dried, fresh or precooked.

ugali (oo-gah-lee) A Kenyan and Tanzanian dish consisting of a thick cornmeal porridge, sometimes flavored with chiles.

Ugandan Arabica coffee beans grown in Uganda; the beverage is rich and pleasantly acidic, with a medium to full body.

ugli; usli (OO-gli) A large hybrid citrus fruit that is a cross between a grapefruit, orange and tangerine; it is grown in Jamaica and has a very thick, yellow-green, loose skin, a yellow-orange flesh and a flavor reminiscent of a mandarin with overtones of honey and pineapple.

Ugni Blanc (oo-n'yee blahn) The grape used to make the base wine for Cognac and many brandies. *See* Trebbiano.

ugnsomelett (uhgns-dhm-ell-ett) A Swedish baked omelette usually filled with mushrooms, shrimp, chicken or the like.

UHT *See* pasteurization, ultrahigh-temperature.

Uisgebaugh; uisgebeatha (whis-geh-BAW) Irish and Scottish words, respectively, for water of life and used to describe whisky.

uisuki (oo-EE-skee) Japanese for whiskey.

uitsmijter (OUT-smi-ter) A Dutch sandwich consisting of meat (typically ham) on a slice of buttered or fried bread, topped with a fried egg and garnished with a dill pickle.

ujeqe (oo-ye-quay) A South African steamed whole wheat and cornmeal dumpling.

ujjah (uhj-jah) A Middle Eastern dish consisting of a thick frittata-like egg item often studded with meat, fish, chicken, potatoes and/or vegetables and flavored with herbs.

uj-wee (uh-jhuh-wee) A Middle Eastern confection of dates stuffed with almonds and rolled in sugar.

ukha (who-kah) A Russian soup made with a fish stock flavored with onions, parsley, peppercorns and bay leaf; the stock is poured over fish fillets that have been cooked in the stock and garnished with dill and parsley.

Ukiah Valley *See* Mendocino.

ukoy (oo-koy) A Filipino fritter of ground rice or flour, diced scallion and small peeled shrimp; it is fried and served with vinegar and minced garlic as a snack.

ukrop (uch-crop) Russian for fennel.

uksus (uch-suus) Russian for vinegar.

uku A fish with a pale pink flesh, a firm texture, a delicate flavor and an average weight of 4–18 lb. (1.8–8.1 kg); also known as a gray snapper and jobfish.

Ulanda A cocktail made of gin, Cointreau and Pernod.

Uld Man's Milk Scottish for old man's milk and used to describe a cocktail made with milk, cream, sugar, whisky and egg yolks folded into beaten egg whites and sprinkled with nutmeg.

ulekan (oo-lee-kan) A small, deep, stone bowl with a stone pestle made from granite or volcanic rock and used in Indonesia to grind spices.

ulitka (oo-lit-kah) Russian for snail.

ullage (UHL-lahg) The amount of space not occupied by a liquid in a cask, barrel or bottle.

ultrahigh-temperature pasteurization; ultrahigh-temperature processing *See* pasteurization, ultrahigh-temperature.

ultrapasteurization *See* pasteurization, ultra.

ulu (oo-lu) Hawaiian for breadfruit.

ulua (oo-lu-ah) A fish found off Hawaii; a member of the jack family; it has an average market weight of 10–40 lb. (4.5–18 kg), a firm flesh with minimal red muscle and a mild flavor; there are two principal varieties: black ulua and white ulua; also known as jackfish. *See* papio.

uma (who-mah) Swahili for fork.

umami (u-MOM-ee) One of the five primary sensations comprising the sense of taste; it refers to the savory taste of protein.

umbles (UM-buls) The edible entrails of a deer. *See* humble pie.

umbrella pine The source for most varieties of pine nuts; also known as a stone pine.

Umbria (OOM-bree-ah) A grape-growing and wine-producing region in central Italy best known for the wines made in the area around the town of Orvieto; the principal grapes grown are Trebbiano, Procanico, Sangiovese and Canaiolo.

umbu *See* imbu.

ume (OO-meh) Japanese for plum.

ume-boshi (OO-meh-boh-shee) Japanese pickled plums; they have a dusty pink color and a tart, salty flavor.

umeshu (oo-meh-shoo) A Japanese liqueur made from unripened apricots.

umm Ali (whom ah-lee) Arabic for mother of Ali and used to describe a creamy bread pudding made with bread and samn and studded with a variety of nuts and dried fruits.

umngqusho (hoon-koo-sho) A South African samp and cowpea stew.

unbalanced A wine-tasting term for a wine whose components have not combined in a desirable fashion or a wine with too much alcohol in comparison to its body and weight. *See* balanced.

unbleached flour Wheat flour that has not been treated with a whitening agent.

unbolted An unsifted, coarsely ground grain (including the bran); it generally refers to cornmeal or wheat flour.

underbar The area of a bar that houses equipment used to make cocktails, such as blenders, ice bins, bottle wells, speed racks and other supplies.

Underberg (un-der-bairg) The proprietary name of a German beverage used to remedy hangovers and upset stomachs.

under chef *See* sous-chef.

undercut A British cut of the beef carcass; it is the tenderloin; also known as filet of beef.

underdeveloped A wine-tasting term for a wine that needs further barrel or bottle aging.

underground cherry *See* carrot.

underproof A distilled spirit of less than 100 proof.

under-the-table Slang for intoxicated.

underweight Having less than a normal amount of fat on the body (generally, being 10% or more below the appropriate weight for height).

unga (oon-gah) Swahili for flour.

ung choy (hung tchoee) A vegetable with soft green, arrowhead-shaped leaves and firm, hollow stems used in Chinese cuisines; also known as Chinese water spinach.

uni (oo-nee)1. Japanese for sea urchin. 2. An imprecisely used term for sea urchin roe.

unicorn plant *See* martynia.

unicum (oo-nee-coom) A bitter Hungarian brandy made from a secret herbal recipe.

unit An individual item within a group of similar items (e.g., 1 of 12 eggs) or a smaller amount of a larger quantity (1 oz.

of flour from a 5-lb. sack); may be expressed in count, weight or volume.

unit cost; unit price The amount paid to acquire one of the units specified.

United States Department of Agriculture *See* USDA.

United States Department of Commerce *See* USDC.

univalves A general category of mollusks characterized by a single shell and a single muscle; significant varieties include abalone, limpet, periwinkle, snails and whelks; also known as gastropods.

Universal Product Code A code consisting of numbers and linear symbols printed on packaged items; it identifies the product, manufacturer, distributor, contents and price and can be scanned directly into a cash register for sales and inventory purposes; also known as a bar code.

unmold To remove food from the container (usually a decorative dish) in which it was prepared; it is usually done by inverting it over a serving plate.

unripened cheeses *See* cheeses, fresh.

unsalted A food-labeling term approved by the U.S. Food and Drug Administration (FDA) to describe a food prepared without the salt ordinarily used in the processed food product.

unsaturated fat A triglyceride composed of monounsaturated or polyunsaturated fatty acids and believed to help reduce the amount of cholesterol in the blood; generally, it comes from plants and is liquid (an oil) at room temperature. *See* monounsaturated fat *and* polyunsaturated fat.

unsaturated fatty acid A fatty acid that can accommodate one (monounsaturated) or more (polyunsaturated) additional hydrogen atoms along its carbon chain (i.e., it has one or more points of unsaturation).

unsweetened chocolate Chocolate liquor or mass, without added sugar or flavorings; used in baking. *See* chocolate-making process.

unsweetened cocoa *See* cocoa powder.

uovo (WAW-voh) Italian for egg.

uovo di bufalo (WAW-voh dee boo-phah-low) Italian for buffalo egg and used to describe an egg-shaped mozzarella.

up *See* straight-up.

upside-down cake A dessert made by lining the bottom of a baking pan with butter, sugar and fruit (typically pineapple), then adding a light cake batter; after baking, the cake is inverted so that the glazed fruit becomes the top surface.

usable portion The part of a product that has value; the amount being used in a recipe, or trim, fat or bones that have resale value.

usagi (oo-sah-gee) Japanese for rabbit.

USDA (U.S. Department of Agriculture) A cabinet-level department of the executive branch of the federal government; one of its principal responsibilities is to make sure that individual foods are safe, wholesome and accurately labeled, and it attempts to meet these responsibilities through inspection and grading procedures; it also provides

U
V

services for food producers and publishes nutrition information.

USDA inspections A mandatory U.S. Department of Agriculture (USDA) program of inspecting slaughterhouses and other processing facilities to ensure that all meat and poultry are processed under strict sanitary guidelines and are wholesome and fit for human consumption. *See* establishment number *and* inspection mark of meat products.

USDA quality grades 1. A voluntary U.S. Department of Agriculture (USDA) system of grading beef, lamb, pork and veal based on the animal's age and the meat's color, texture and degree of marbling; grading is intended to provide a guide to the meat's tenderness, juiciness and flavor. *See* beef quality grades, lamb quality grades, pork quality grades *and* veal quality grades. 2. The USDA's voluntary system of grading poultry based on overall quality; it has little bearing on the product's tenderness or flavor. *See* poultry quality grades.

USDA yield grades A voluntary U.S. Department of Agriculture (USDA) system based on conformation and finish and used to measure the amount of usable meat (as opposed to fat and bone) on a beef or lamb carcass and providing a uniform method of identifying cutability differences among carcasses; the grades run from 1 to 5, with 1 representing the greatest yield.

USDC (U.S. Department of Commerce) A cabinet-level department of the executive branch of the federal government; one of its responsibilities is to inspect fish and shellfish as well as related facilities and vessels under a voluntary food-safety compliance program.

USDC inspections A voluntary U.S. Department of Commerce (USDC) inspection program for fish and shellfish as well as vessels, warehouses and processing facilities. *See* packed under federal inspection.

USDC quality grades *See* fish quality grades *and* shellfish quality grades.

uskumru (oos-koom-roo) Turkish for mackerel.

uskumru dolmasi (oos-koom-roo dol-mah-see) A Turkish dish of mackerel stuffed with onions, pine nuts, currants and bread crumbs, flavored with cinnamon, cloves, allspice, parsley and dill and deep-fried.

usli *See* ugli.

usli ghee (oos-lee ghi) Hindi for clarified butter.

U.S. RDA *See* recommended daily intake (RDI).

U.S. system A measurement system used principally in the United States; it uses ounces and pounds for weight and cups for volume. *See* imperial system *and* metric system.

ustriza (oos-tree-kah) Russian for oyster.

usturoi (oos-too-roh-e) Romanian for garlic.

usui hito-kire (oo-SOO-ee HEE-tah-KEE-ray) Japanese for a slice.

usukuchi shoyu (oo-soo-KOO-chee SHOH-yoo) A Japanese thin or light soy sauce.

usuku kiru (oo-SOO-koo KEE-roo) Japanese for to slice.

usu-zukuri (oo-su-zoo-koo-ri) A Japanese slicing technique for cutting thin, diagonal slices from firm fish fillets.

uszka (oosh-kah) Polish for little ears and used to describe a stuffed pasta similar to tortellini.

utility The lowest U.S. Department of Agriculture (USDA) quality grade for pork and one of the lowest for beef, lamb and veal; the meat is usually used for ground, canned or otherwise processed products.

utility knife An all-purpose knife used for cutting produce and carving poultry; it has a rigid 6- to 8-in.-long blade shaped like a chef's knife but narrower.

utility knife

utka (uht-kah) Russian for duck.

uva (oo-bhah) Spanish for grape.

uva (OO-vah) Italian and Portuguese for grape.

Uva A black tea from the highlands of Sri Lanka; the beverage has a deep, rich color, strong full flavor and strong aroma; it is excellent for breakfast and usually served with milk.

uva passa (OOH-va PAHS-sa) Italian for raisin.

uvas pasas (oo-vah pah-sahs) Spanish for raisins.

uva spina (OO-vah SPRR-nah) Italian for gooseberry.

uyoga (oo-yoh-gah) Swahili for mushrooms.

Uzès, sauce (eu-zehz) A French compound sauce made from hollandaise flavored with anchovy paste and Madeira wine.

uzhin Russian for dinner.

vaca (VAH-kah) Portuguese for beef.

vacation ownership *See* time-share ownership.

vacchino (vah-chee-noh) Italian term for cow's milk cheese.

Vacchino Romano (vah-chee-noh roh-mah-noh) A cow's milk Romano.

vacherin (vasher-ANN) A French dessert consisting of a crisp baked meringue container filled with ice cream or Chantilly cream and fruit.

Vacherin (vasher-ANN) A group of rich, creamy cow's milk cheeses made in France and Switzerland; they usually contain 45–50% milkfat.

Vacherin à la Main (vasher-ANN ah lah ma'n) A Vacherin made in Switzerland and France; it has a hard rind and a soft interior.

Vacherin du Haut-Doubs (vasher-ANN duh oh-DOO) An unpasteurized cow's milk cheese from France's Franche-Comte region; it has a wavy, reddish-brown, velvety washed rind, a supple texture with a woodsy, nutty, fruity flavor and a strong aroma.

Vacherin Fondú (vasher-ANN fohn-do) An Emmental-style cheese that is melted after curing so that spices and other flavorings can be added.

Vacherin Fribourgeois (vasher-ANN FREE-boor-zhwah) A semisoft Vacherin made in Switzerland; it has a grayish-yellow rind, a pale yellow interior and a slightly nutty flavor.

Vacherin Mont d'Or (vasher-ANN moan DOR) A cow's milk cheese from Switzerland; it is very similar to Vacherin du Haut-Doubs.

vacuum-distilled gin A gin distilled in a glass-lined vacuum still at a low temperature; this preserves the light, volatile flavors and aromas of the gin without adding any bitterness.

vacuum packaging A food preservation method in which fresh or cooked food is placed in an airtight container (usually plastic); virtually all air is removed through a vacuum process, thus sealing the container and eliminating the environment necessary to sustain the growth of certain microorganisms that would otherwise spoil the food. *See* sous-vide.

vafler (VAHF-fehl) Norwegian for waffles.

vainilla (vee-ee-nee-yah) Spanish for vanilla.

Val d'Arbia (VAHL DAHR-bee-yah) A DOC wine-making zone in Italy's Tuscany region that produces a dry white wine from Malvasia and Trebbiano grapes.

Valdepeñas (bahl-deh-PEH-nyahss) A grape-growing and wine-producing region in the central plateau of Spain; known for both its red and white table wines.

Valencay (vah-lahn-say) A French goat's milk cheese shaped like a squat pyramid; the farm variety has a blue-gray rind dusted with wood ash, a chalky white interior, a light goaty smell and a mild flavor; the factory version is coarser and stronger, with a white bloom on the rind.

Valencia A cocktail made of apricot brandy, orange juice, orange bitters and sparkling wine.

Valencia orange A sweet, juicy, almost seedless orange; it is spherical and has a thin skin.

Valencia peanut A variety of peanut with up to four kernels.

Valencia rice A short- to medium-grain rice that does not become creamy when cooked; it has a nutlike flavor and is used principally for paella.

valine (VAL-en) 1. An essential amino acid important for normal growth in children and nitrogen balance in adults. 2. A food additive used as a nutrient source to significantly improve the biological quality of the total protein in a food containing the naturally occurring protein.

Valle d'Aosta (VAHL DOH-stah) A region in northern Italy renowned for its cheeses, including Fontina, Toma and Robiola.

valley tan Slang for whiskey made by the Mormons of Salt Lake Valley.

Valpolicella (vahl-poh-lee-t'CHELL-ah) A red wine made in Italy's Veneto region from grapes such as Corvina and Molinara; it has a fragrant aroma, a fruity flavor, a light body and a relatively low alcohol content.

Vampiros A Mexican cocktail; it is a Bloody Mary made with tequila instead of vodka.

vanadium A trace element used for various biological functions; found in many foods.

vanaspati ghee (vah-nass-pah-tee ghee) Hindi for vegetable shortening.

Van cherry A variety of sweet cherry; the fruit have a dark red skin, a firm flesh and a sweet flavor.

Vancouver Island A grape-growing and wine-producing region in Canada's British Columbia province.

Van der Hum A South African brandy-based tangerine liqueur.

Vandermint A Dutch liqueur flavored with mint and chocolate.

Vandyke *v.* 1. To embellish a decorative feature of a dish. 2. To cut an orange or lemon so that it has zigzag edges (a Vandyked citrus is used as a decorative garnish). *n.* An old English presentation method for foods; the dish was circled with a border of toast, pastry or potato cut into pointed shapes or triangles reminiscent of the pointed Van Dyke beard.

vanguard lettuce A variety of crisp head lettuce similar to iceberg.

vaniglia (vah-NEE-l'yah) Italian for vanilla.

vanila (vah-nee-lah) Swahili for vanilla.

vanilin (vah-nel-ee) Russian for vanilla.

vanilje (vah-NEEL-yer) Norwegian for vanilla.

vanilla, imitation A vanilla-flavored product composed entirely of artificial ingredients.

vanilla bean; vanilla pod The dried, cured podlike fruit of an orchid plant (*Vanilla planifolia*) grown in tropical regions; the pod contains numerous tiny black seeds; both the pod and the seeds are used for flavoring.

vanilla custard sauce A stirred custard made with egg yolks, sugar and milk or half-and-half and flavored with vanilla; served with or used in dessert preparations; also known as crème anglaise.

vanilla extract A vanilla-flavored product made by macerating chopped vanilla beans in a water–alcohol solution to extract the flavor; its strength is measured in folds.

vanilla extract, pure Vanilla extract made with 13.35 oz. of vanilla beans per gallon during extraction and 35% alcohol.

vanilla flavoring A combination of pure vanilla extract and imitation vanilla.

vanilla pod *See* vanilla bean.

vanilla sugar Granulated sugar infused with the flavor of vanilla and made by burying vanilla beans in a container of sugar for a brief time; used in baked goods, creams and with fruit.

vanilla wafers Small, round, golden-colored crisp cookies with a strong vanilla flavor.

vanille (vah-neey) French for vanilla.

Vanille (vah-NIL-ler) German for vanilla.

vanillin (vah-NIL-lahn) 1. A fragrant, crystalline substance produced by vanilla beans or made synthetically; used for flavoring and in perfumes. 2. Synthetic vanilla flavoring.

vanillin acetate A food additive with a vanilla aroma; used as a flavoring agent in beverages, ice creams, desserts and baked goods.

vann (vahn) Norwegian for water.

vapeur (vah-purr) French for steam.

varak *See* gold leaf.

varen'em (vah-ren-yern) Russian for jam.

vareniki (vah-ren-ne-ke) A Russian dish consisting of noodle dough stuffed with meat, cottage cheese, cabbage and the like, topped with melted butter and sour cream.

Varenne *See* La Varenne, François Pierre.

vareschaga (vah-resch-ah-gah) A Russian dish consisting of pork cooked with pickled beetroot juice, onions and pepper and thickened with rye bread crumbs.

variable costs Costs that increase or decrease in direct relationship with the volume of business (e.g., inventory and salaries); generally within the operation's control; also known as controllable costs. *See* fixed costs.

variegated scallop A variety of scallops found in the Atlantic Ocean from Norway to West Africa and in the western Mediterranean Sea; it has a domed shell in a variety of colors with an average diameter of 2.5 in. (6.3 cm) and a tender, sweet, white meat.

varietal; varietal designation The name of the dominant grape used to make a wine; that variety must account for at least 75% of the grapes used to make the wine.

varietal character A wine-tasting term for the generally recognizable, specific combination of flavors, aromas and other characteristics that are directly attributable to the variety of grape used to make a wine.

varietal wine A wine named for the primary grape used in its making; American wines tend to be varietal wines, whereas European ones tend to be named for the region, village or other location in which they are made.

variety 1. A plant produced by the fertilization of one member of a species by another; the two plants are similar genetically but have different qualities or characteristics, and the resulting plant has features of both. *See* hybrid. 2. A term imprecisely used to describe a commercial variant or market name of a particular whole food. 3. In the nutrition context, the consumption, over the course of a day and at each meal, of foods from various sections of the food pyramid as well as different foods within each section. *See* adequacy *and* moderation.

variety meats The edible organs and other portions of a mammal; includes the brain, heart, kidneys, liver, pancreas, thymus (sweetbreads), tongue, stomach wall (tripe), hog intestines (chitterlings), testicles (fries), spleen, oxtail and pig's feet; also known as offal (especially in Great Britain). *See* meat by-products.

vark Indian gold and silver foil.

varkenscarbonaden (VAR-ken-kar-boh-nah-den) Dutch for pork chops.

varkensvlees (VAHR-kuns-vlays) Dutch for pork.

varmt (varm) Norwegian for hot.

västkustsallad (vest-kuhst-sah-lahd) A Swedish salad of fish and vegetables garnished with hard-boiled egg slices.

vat 1. A large container used for storing or holding liquids. 2. A large metal, wooden or cement container used for fermenting, blending or storing wine.

vatapa (vah-tah-pah) A Brazilian stew consisting of fish, shrimp, chicken and/or meat combined with dried shrimp, coconut milk, peanuts, dende oil and other ingredients.

vatkattu karpalohyytelo (vat-kah-too kar-phlow-he-tah-low) A Finnish whipped jelly made with cranberries or other berries.

vatting 1. The process of flavoring, blending and aging whiskys to produce a more balanced, uniform product. 2. The process of leaving grape skins in contact with the must for a prolonged period of time to extract additional tannins, color and flavors.

VCM *See* vertical cutter/mixer.

veado (vay-AH-doo) Portuguese for venison.

veal Meat from calves slaughtered when younger than 9 months (usually at 8–16 weeks); it has a lean, light pink flesh, a delicate flavor and a tender, firm texture. *See* beef, bob veal *and* calf.

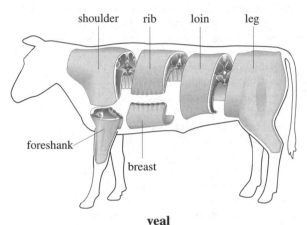

shoulder   rib   loin   leg

foreshank

breast

veal
(American primals)

veal, free-range The meat of calves that are allowed to roam freely and eat grasses and other natural foods; the meat is pinker and more strongly flavored than that of milk-fed calves.

veal, ground Veal ground from muscles found in various primals but principally the shoulder.

veal, milk-fed The meat of calves that are kept in pens and fed milk-based formulas; the meat is pale pink and very delicately flavored; also known as formula-fed veal.

veal back A portion of the veal carcass that contains an undivided rib primal and loin primal.

veal bottom round A subprimal cut of the veal primal leg; it is used as a roast or further fabricated into scallops and cutlets.

veal choplet A fabricated cut of veal; it is cubed veal shaped like a chop.

veal hindshank A subprimal cut of the veal primal leg; it contains a large amount of connective tissue.

veal holstein *See* Holsteiner Schnitzel.

veal hotel rack A subprimal cut of the veal primal rib; it consists of one bilateral half of the seven rib bones with the tender rib eye muscle; it is used as is or fabricated into chops.

veal leg A subprimal cut of the veal primal leg; it contains only the leg (the sirloin is removed); available with the entire bone, the bone without the shank or boneless.

veal loin chop A fabricated cut of the veal primal loin; it is very tender and flavorful and available with or without the bone.

veal loin roast A fabricated cut of the veal primal loin; a tender roast.

veal medallions A fabricated cut of the veal primal loin; they are cut from the very tender and flavorful tenderloin.

veal Orloff A dish of braised loin of veal carved into even horizontal slices, each spread with a thin layer of puréed sautéed mushrooms and onions, stacked back in place and tied to reform the loin; this is covered with additional mushroom mixture, topped with béchamel sauce and grated Parmesan and browned in the oven.

veal Oscar Sautéed veal cutlets served with béarnaise and garnished with asparagus tips and crab.

veal patties Ground veal shaped into patties.

veal primals The five principal bilateral sections of the veal carcass: the shoulder, foreshank and breast, rib, loin and leg.

veal quality grades *See* USDA quality grades, prime, choice, good, standard, utility *and* cull.

veal rib chop A fabricated cut of the veal primal rib; it usually contains one rib and the flavorful, tender rib eye muscle.

veal rib eye roast A subprimal cut of the tender eye muscle of the veal primal rib; it is usually available without the bones.

veal Scotch tender A cut fabricated from the veal primal shoulder; it is a large filet from the center of the shoulder.

veal shoulder clod A subprimal cut of the veal primal shoulder; it contains the large outside muscle system above the elbow and is lean, tough and flavorful.

veal side One bilateral half of the veal carcass; it contains half of each veal primal.

veal tenderloin A fabricated cut of the veal primal loin; it is very tender and flavorful and sometimes further fabricated into the butt and short tenderloins as well as medallions.

veal tonnato *See* vitello tonnato.

veal top round A subprimal cut of the veal primal leg; it is used as a roast or further fabricated into scallops and cutlets.

veau (voh) French for veal.

vecchio (vay-KEY-oh) Italian for old and used to describe a wine that has been aged for a longer period than normal.

vegan (VEE-gun; VAY-gun) A vegetarian who does not eat any animal products. *See* lactovegetarian *and* ovolactovegetarian.

Vegemite A salty, dense vegetable paste made in Great Britain; popular in Australia.

vegetable coloring Commercial dye preparations derived from vegetable sources and used to color foodstuffs such as Easter eggs and icings.

vegetable gums Gums obtained from plants.

vegetable marrow *See* avocado.

vegetable marrow squash *See* marrow squash.

vegetable oil 1. A category of specific oils obtained from plants. 2. A general term describing blends of different

vegetable oils such as corn, safflower, rapeseed, cottonseed and/or soybean oils; these blends are generally intended to have little flavor and aroma and to be used as all-purpose oils.

vegetable oyster *See* salsify.

vegetable pear *See* chayote *and* marrow squash.

vegetable peeler A knifelike utensil whose stationary or swiveling blade has two slits; used for thinly stripping the peel from produce.

vegetable protein *See* soy protein.

vegetables The edible parts of plants, including the leaves, stalks, roots, tubers and flowers (and in certain cases the fruit); they are generally savory rather than sweet and often salted or otherwise dressed; some are always consumed cooked, others always raw (fresh) and some can be consumed either cooked or raw; sometimes associated with meat, fish, shellfish and poultry as part of a meal or ingredient; vegetables are mostly water (approximately 80%) and usually contain vitamins, minerals, carbohydrates, protein and fats. *See* fruits.

vegetable spaghetti *See* spaghetti squash.

vegetable stamp A brass stamp in the shape of a fish, dragon, plum blossom or other design used to cut vegetables used as garnish.

vegetable station chef *See* légumier.

vegetable steamer *See* steamer.

vegetal A wine-tasting term for either the undesirable aroma of stems or unripened grapes or a more desirable herbaceous or grassy aroma or flavor.

vegetal snake The very long (more than 3 ft.), slender green- and white-streaked fruit of the *Trichosanthes anguina,* native to India; it is usually served sliced and boiled.

vegetarian A person who eats primarily or exclusively plant foods. *See* lactovegetarian, ovolactovegetarian, vegan *and* fruitarian.

veggies Slang for vegetables.

vehicle *See* solvent.

vein steak A fabricated cut of the beef sirloin or strip loin primals; it contains a distinctive crescent-shaped piece of connective tissue.

Veitchberry A hybrid of the blackberry and raspberry.

vela (veh-lah) A Spanish sausage shape; the straight sausage usually contains large pieces of meat and is sliced thin and served raw as tapas. *See* ristras *and* sarta.

velouté, sauce (veh-loo-TAY) A French leading sauce made by thickening a veal stock, chicken stock or fish fumet with a white or golden roux; also known as a blond sauce.

velveting A Chinese preparation method for fish; the fish is marinated in egg white, cornstarch and rice wine and fried.

Velvet Hammer A cocktail made of Tia Maria, heavy cream, brandy and either Cointreau or Triple Sec, shaken with ice and strained into a cocktail glass.

velvet stem mushroom *See* enoki.

velvety A tasting term for a lush, silky, smooth texture.

Venaco (veh-NAH-coh) A Corsican cheese made from goat's or ewe's milk.

venado (veh-NAH-doh) Spanish for venison.

venaison (vee-nay-sohn) French for venison.

vendange (vahn-dawnj) French for vintage or grape harvest; it refers to a particular year's harvest, not to a vintage year.

vendange tardive (vahn-dawnj tahr-deev) French term for late harvest; principally used to describe relatively rich, full-bodied, sweet wines made in France's Alsace region.

vendee The firm or person to whom something is sold; the buyer.

vendemmia (vayn-DAYM-myah) Italian for vintage; it refers to a particular year's harvest and not to a vintage year.

vendimia (ven-DEE-mee-ah) Spanish for vintage; it refers to a particular year's harvest and not to a vintage year.

vendor (VEN-dahr) A firm or person who sells; the seller.

venencia (veh-NEN-see-ah) A tool used to take sherry samples from a cask through the bunghole; it has a long, flexible handle (traditionally made of whalebone) with a silver cup at one end and a silver hook at the other; the sample is poured into a glass from a height of 12–18 in.

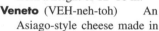

venencia

Veneto (VEH-neh-toh) An Asiago-style cheese made in Italy's Veneto region from cow's milk; it has an oiled, dark-colored exterior, a greenish-yellow interior and a sharp, sometimes bitter flavor; also known as Venezza.

Venezuelan Arabica coffee beans grown in Venezuela; the beverage has a slightly sweet flavor and light body.

Venezza (veh-neez-ee) *See* Veneto.

venison The flesh of any member of the deer family, including the antelope, caribou, elk, moose, reindeer, red-tailed deer, white-tailed deer and mule deer; it typically has a dark red color with very little intramuscular fat or marbling, a firm, dense, velvety texture, a mild aroma and a sweet, herbal, nutty flavor; significant cuts include the loin, leg, rack and saddle.

vent *v.* 1. To allow the circulation or escape of a liquid or gas. 2. To cool a pot of hot liquid by setting the pot on blocks in a cold water bath and allowing cold water to circulate around it. *n.* An exhaust fan, usually vented outdoors, that is mounted above or near a stove; used to eliminate odors while cooking; also known as a hood and hood vent.

ventaglini (vehn-tah-L'YEE-nee) An Italian butterfly-shaped puff pastry cookie, similar to a palmier.

ventresca (ven-TRAY-ska) A Sardinian dish of tuna fish stomach brushed with oil and grilled.

venus shell clams Any of several varieties of clams with an elongated, compressed, smooth, thin, glossy shell that ranges from dull pink to bluish purple; they have an average length of 5–7 in. (12.5–17.5 cm) and a very sweet, relatively tender meat.

Veracruz (ver-ah-KROOZ) A Mexican preparation method associated with the state of Veracruz; the principal ingredient, usually fish or shellfish, is cooked in a sauce of tomatoes, chiles, onion and garlic, flavored with oregano and lime juice and usually served over rice.

verbena *See* lemon verbena.

Verdelho (vair-DAY'L-yo) 1. A white wine grape grown on the island of Madeira. 2. A Madeira wine made from this grape; of the four Madeira styles, it is medium dry.

Verdi, sauce; Verdi mayonnaise (verh-dee) A French mayonnaise sauce made with chopped spinach, gherkins, chives and sour cream.

verdura (vehr-doo-rah) Spanish for green vegetables.

verdure (vehr-DOO-reh) Italian for green vegetables.

verenika (vah-ray-nee-kah) A Jewish crescent-shaped dumpling with a sweet filling.

veripalttu (vah-ree-pal-tou) A Finnish black pudding.

verjus; verjuice (vair-jue) The unfermented juice of unripened grapes; it has a very high acid content and is sometimes used as a substitute for vinegar.

vermicelli (ver-mih-CHEHL-ee) 1. Italian for little worms and used to describe very thin spaghetti; available in straight rods or twisted into a cluster. 2. A general term for any long, very thin rods of pasta or noodles.

Vermont Vigor A cocktail made of gin, lemon juice and maple syrup.

vermouth A neutral white wine flavored with various herbs, spices and fruits and fortified to a minimum of 16% alcohol; used as an aperitif and cocktail ingredient.

vermouth, dry A type of vermouth; it is pale and contains 2–4% sugar; also known as French vermouth and white vermouth.

vermouth, sweet A type of vermouth made from wine; it is caramel colored and has a minimum of 14% sugar; also known as Italian vermouth and red vermouth.

Vernaccia di Oristano (vair-NATCH-ah dee aw-riss-TAH-no) A sherrylike wine produced on the island of Sardinia; deliberately oxidized, it ranges from dry to sweet.

Verne's Lawyer A cocktail made of gin, lime juice and apple brandy or Calvados.

Verona A cocktail made of gin, amaretto, sweet vermouth and lemon juice and garnished with an orange slice.

Véronique (vay-roh-NEEK) A French term describing dishes garnished with seedless white grapes.

verte, mayonnaise (vehrt) A French mayonnaise sauce flavored with tarragon, parsley, watercress and basil.

vertebra *See* backbone.

verte de cambrai (vehrt day kahm-bray) A French variety of mâche.

verte d'Espagne (vehrt des-pain-ya) A variety of slightly elongated spherical squash with a light green skin and dark green streaks.

vertical cutter/mixer (VCM) An appliance that operates like a very large, powerful blender; usually floor mounted and with a capacity of 15–80 qt.

vertical roaster A towerlike cross-braced metal stand used for roasting poultry; generally 9.5 in. high with a 6-in. base, it prevents the poultry from cooking in its drippings. *See* roasting rack.

vervain (VUR-van) An herb (*Verbena officinalis*) and member of the same family as lemon verbena; used to flavor liqueurs and infusions.

Verveine de Velay (veer-vyn duh veh-lay) A French herbal liqueur made from verbena.

vertical roaster

very-low-density lipoproteins (VLDL) Lipoproteins made in the intestines and liver; they transport lipids to other organs.

very low sodium A food-labeling term approved by the U.S. Food and Drug Administration (FDA) to describe a food with 35 mg or less of salt per serving.

very rare A degree of doneness for meat; the meat should have a very red, raw-looking center, the center should be cool to the touch and the meat should provide almost no resistance when pressed; also known as bleu. *See* rare, medium rare, medium, medium well *and* well done.

very superior A label term on bottles of Armagnac and Cognac indicating that the youngest brandy in the blend is at least 4.5 years old, although many of the brandies used in the blend are 5–9 years old; often written as VS.

very superior old 1. A label term on bottles of Armagnac and Cognac indicating that the youngest brandy in the blend is at least 4.5 years old, although many of the brandies used in the blend are 12–17 years old; often written as VSO. 2. A label term on bottles of brandy indicating that the brandy has aged for 12–17 years in a wooden cask; often written as VSO.

very superior old pale A label term on bottles of Armagnac and Cognac indicating that the youngest brandy in the blend is at least 4.5 years old, although many of the brandies used in the blend are 12–20 years old; often written as VSOP.

very very superior old pale A label term on bottles of Armagnac and Cognac indicating that the youngest brandy in the blend is at least 5.5 years old, although many of the brandies used in the blend are 20–40 years old; often written as VVSOP.

verza (VEHR-dzah) Italian for savoy or crinkly leafed cabbage.

vescia (va-SHE-ah) Italian for puffball mushroom.

vesiga The marrow from a sturgeon's backbone; it is sold dried as a flavoring and thickener.

vesse-de-loup (vess-duh-loo) French for puffball mushroom.

vetar (vee-tahr) Hindi for waiter.

vetchina (vee-chyee-NAH) Russian for ham.

vetelängd (va-ta-lahngd) A Swedish braided bun made of yeast dough and garnished with sliced almonds, sugar or confectioners' sugar icing; usually served with coffee in the afternoon.

viande (vee-YAWND) French for meat.

viazi (vee-ah-zee) Swahili for potato.

Vibrio cholerae Bacteria that cause cholera; the bacteria are transmitted through ingestion of contaminated food or water.

Vichy (VEE-shee) A French mineral water from the town of Vichy.

Vichy, à la (VEE-shee, ah lah) A French garnish for meat consisting of carottes à la Vichy and pommes château.

Vichy, carottes à la (VEE-shee, kah-rote ah lah) A French dish of carrots cooked in Vichy water.

vichyssoise (vee-shee-swahz) A French soup made from puréed onions or leeks, potatoes, cream, chicken stock and seasonings, garnished with chives and usually served cold.

Victoria, sauce A French white wine sauce seasoned with cayenne, finished with lobster butter and garnished with truffles and diced lobster.

Victoria pineapple A small, round pineapple with a yellow skin and a deep yellow flesh.

Victoria plum A variety of plum; the large, ovoid fruit have a yellow skin heavily flushed with scarlet, a golden yellow flesh and a sweet flavor.

Victoria sandwich; Victoria sponge A British dessert consisting of two layers of sponge cake filled with raspberry jam and whipped cream or buttercream; usually served for afternoon tea; also known as sandwich cake.

Vidalia onion A large onion with a pale yellow outer layer and a sweet, juicy white flesh; grown in a delimited area around Vidalia, Georgia.

videlle (vee-dell) 1. A wheel-shaped French pastry cutter. 2. A small French tool used to remove stones from fruits.

vieille reserve (v'yay rah-serv) A labeling term for brandy, Cognac and Armagnac indicating that the youngest brandy used in the blend is at least 5.5 years old.

Vielle Cure (vee-yay quer) A French liqueur with an herbal flavor; made from more than 50 ingredients and available in yellow and green.

Vienna beer A style of amber-colored, medium-bodied beer with a pronounced malty flavor; traditionally made in Vienna.

Vienna bread A hearth bread with a heavy, crisp crust, sometimes with a seed topping.

Vienna roll See kaiser roll.

Vienna sausage 1. An Austrian sausage similar to a frankfurter. 2. A small sausage with a mild flavor; often available canned with gelatin.

Vienna steaks A dish consisting of small patties of ground beefsteak mixed with onions, flavored with parsley, marjoram and ketchup, fried and served with crisp rolls of bacon and fried or braised onions.

Viennese coffee Strong, hot coffee sweetened to taste and topped with whipped cream; served in a tall glass.

Viennese roast See roast, Viennese.

viennoise, à la (veen-NWAHZ, ah lah) 1. A French preparation and presentation method for escallops of veal, chicken or fish; they are rolled in egg and bread crumbs, pan-fried and garnished with hard-boiled eggs, capers, olives, parsley, beurre noir and lemon slices. 2. A Viennese preparation in which the meat, fish or poultry is breaded, pan-fried and garnished only with lemon slices.

Vierge, sauce (vee-erge) A French compound sauce made from a béchamel blended with artichoke purée and finished with whipped unsweetened cream.

vieux lambic (vo LAM-beek) Old lambic beer, defined as one aged for 3 years in a cask and 1 year in the bottle.

vigna (VEE-nyah) Italian for vineyard.

vigneron (vee-nyrh-ROHN) French for a grape grower (but not necessarily a wine maker).

vignoble (vee-NYOHBL) French for vineyard; it can refer to a single plot or an entire region.

vigorous A wine-tasting term for a young, lively wine with good acidity and balance.

viilipiimä; piimä (vee-lee-pill-mah; pill-mah) A thick Finnish beverage of clotted milk made from fresh milk and sour cream or sour milk; sometimes served with sugar, cinnamon and ginger; also used as a sauce for fish or potatoes.

vildfägel (villd-fawg-ell) Swedish for feathered game.

vildt (villt) Danish for game.

vilka (veel-kah) Russian for fork.

Villafranca lemon A variety of medium-sized lemon.

villand (vill-ahnd) Norwegian for wild duck.

villeroi, sauce; villeroy sauce (vee-loh-wah) A French compound sauce made from an allemande flavored with ham and truffle peelings or essence.

vilt (villt) Norwegian for game.

vin (van) French for wine.

vinagre (vee-NAH-gray) Portuguese and Spanish for vinegar.

vinaigre (van-AY-greh) French for vinegar.

vinaigre à la framboise (van-AY-greh ah lah frahm-bwahz) French for raspberry vinegar.

vinaigre à l'estragon (van-AY-greh ah les-trah-GON) French for tarragon vinegar.

vinaigre de Banyuls (van-AY-greh duh bahn-yulz) A French vinegar made from the sweet Banyuls liqueur.

vinaigre de vin blanc (van-AY-greh duh van blahn) French for white wine vinegar.

vinaigre de vin rouge (van-AY-greh duh van rouj) French for red wine vinegar.

vinaigrette (vihn-uh-GREHT) A temporary emulsion of oil and vinegar (usually three parts oil to one part vinegar) seasoned with herbs, spices, salt and pepper; used as a salad dressing or sauce. See French dressing.

vinasse The residue left in a still after distillation.

vin blanc (van blahn) French for white wine.

vin blanc, sauce *See* white wine sauce.

vindaloo (VEN-deh-loo) A spicy Indian dish consisting of meat or chicken flavored with tamarind juice, lemon juice and a masala of cayenne pepper, cumin, ginger, turmeric, cinnamon and oil, usually served over rice.

vin de carafe French term for a young, inexpensive wine of limited quality; usually served in a carafe.

vin de coupage (van duh coo-pahj) French for a blending wine.

vin de garde (van duh gahr'd) French for a wine made to be aged.

vin de l'année (van duh lah-nay) French for a wine of the most recent vintage.

vin de liqueur A sweet French white wine fortified by adding alcohol to the must before or after fermentation, thereby also preserving the natural grape sugar; usually served as a dessert wine.

vin de paille (van duh pah'y) A French white wine made from dehydrated grapes; the wine is rich and sweet and has a golden color.

vin de pays (van duh peh-yee) The French AOC designation for wines of third-tier quality; their origins must be noted on the label in specific although very broadly defined areas; formerly known as Appellation d'Origin Simple.

vin de table (van doo tahb'l) French for table wine and usually used to describe a blended wine of low quality labeled with only the shipper's name or a propriety brand name; these wines account for half of the French wines shipped to the United States; formerly known as Vins de Consommation Courante; also known as zip code wines. *See* vin ordinaire.

vin doux naturel (van do nat-u-rehl) A naturally sweet French wine.

vindtørret sild (vin-tore-at seeld) A Danish dish consisting of dried salted herring fried in a skillet and served with mustard.

vin du pays (van doo peh-YEE) French for a country or regional wine and used to describe a local wine of any quality; it has no legal significance.

vine 1. A weak-stemmed plant that derives support from climbing, twining or creeping along a surface. 2. A grapevine or a group of grapevines (e.g., a product of the vine).

vinedresser One who cultivates and prunes grapevines.

vinegar From the French vin aigre (sour wine); a weak solution of acetic acid made from a fermented liquid such as cider, wine or beer, subjected to certain bacterial activity; generally clear, the liquid can be tinted various shades depending on the base liquid and can reflect the flavor of the base liquid or be flavored by the introduction of other ingredients.

vinegar eel; vinegar worm A minute nematode that feeds on the organisms that ferment vinegar.

vinegar pie A sweet dessert made with a mixture of eggs, sugar, flour, vinegar and nutmeg baked in a flaky pie shell.

vinegar salts *See* calcium acetate.

vine leaves *See* grape leaves.

vinery *See* vineyard.

vinestock The rootstock to which a new vine (e.g., grapevine) is grafted.

vinete (vee-na-ta) Romanian for eggplant.

vineyard Land dedicated to the cultivation of grapevines; the term is sometimes used imprecisely to describe a winery; also known as a vinery.

vin gris (van gree) A very pale French rosé wine usually made from the Pinot Noir grape in Burgundy and Alsace; some are almost white with a slight pink or bronze color.

vinho branco (VEEN-yoh brahn-ku) Portuguese for white wine.

vinho verde (VEEN-yoh VAIR-day) A sprightly, light-bodied red or white Portuguese wine; the wine is generally young, immature and intended for drinking soon after bottling.

vinho vermelho (VEEN-yoh vehr-may-lyoo) Portuguese for red wine.

viniculture The art, science and practice of wine making, from growing the grapes to marketing the wine. *See* viticulture.

vinifera (vin-IF-er-ah) *See* vitis vinifera.

vinification The process of transforming grape juice into a still wine: generally (1) grapes are gently crushed to release their juice; (2) the crushed grapes and juice (collectively, the must) are put in a vat to ferment (if the wine will be a white one, the grape skins are removed and only the juice is allowed to ferment); (3) the juice is removed and the residue is pressed to extract more juice (for red wines only); (4) the fermented product, now called wine, is transferred to containers (often barrels) for aging (a process called racking); (5) after this preliminary aging, the wine is transferred to bottles for further aging and distribution; also known as the wine-making process. *See* Charmat process *and* méthode champenoise.

vin jaune (van jhon) *See* Château Chalon.

vino beloe (VEE-noh bah-low-ah) Russian for white wine.

vino bianco (vee-no b'yahn-co) Italian for white wine.

vino blanco (vee-noh blahn-koh) Spanish for white wine.

vino da tavola (vee-noh dah TAH-voh-lah) Italian for table wine.

vino de crianza (vee-noh day cree-AHN-zah) *See* crianza.

vino de mesa (VEE-no duh MEH-sah) Spanish for table wine.

vinograd (vee-noh-grad) Russian for grape.

vino joven (vee-noh hoh-ven) A Spanish wine intended to be consumed young.

vino krasnoe (VEE-noe krash-no-ah) Russian for red wine.

vinometer (vih-NAHM-ih-ter) An instrument used to measure the approximate alcohol content of dry wines; it is used primarily by home wine makers and is not very accurate.

Vino Nobile di Montepulciano (veen-no NOH-bee-leh dee MOHN-teh-pool-CH'YAH-noh) A long-lived, powerful, intense red wine made from Prugnolo Gentile,

Canaiolo, Trebbiano, and Malvasia grapes in the Tuscany region of Italy; it must be aged a minimum of 2 years in wood.

vino novello (VEE-no noh-VELL-o) Italian for new wine; similar to the French Beaujolais Nouveau, it is a light, fruity, usually red wine, bottled and marketed within weeks of the harvest.

vin ordinaire (van or-dee-nair) French for ordinary wine and used to describe a common wine for everyday use, usually of unknown or unstated origin; also known as table wine. *See* vin de table.

vino rosso (vee-noh ROSS-oh) 1. Italian for red wine. 2. In the United States, a marketing term for an inexpensive, not necessarily dry, red table wine.

vinosity (vi-NAHS-ih-tee) A wine-tasting term referring to the winelike aroma or flavor of a wine caused by its alcohol content.

vino tinto (vee-noh TEEN-toe) Spanish for red wine.

vin rouge (van rooj) French for red wine.

vin santo (van SAHN-toe) An Italian white wine made from dried Trebbiano and Malvasia grapes fermented in partially filled barrels that are sealed for 2–3 years; the golden wine is rich and sweet, with a slightly oxidized flavor similar to sherry.

Vins de Consommation Courante (van duh kohn-so-mah-shun coor-rahnt) *See* vin de table.

Vins Délimités de Qualité Supérieure The AOC designation for French wines of second-tier quality.

vintage; vintage wine The gathering of grapes and the wine made from those grapes; a vintage wine is one made in a specific year from grapes harvested during that year; the term does not imply an old wine. *See* nonvintage.

vintage port A port made from grapes from a single harvest, bottled after 2 years of aging in wooden pipes and left on its side to bottle age for 10–20 years; has the deepest red color, the fruitiest bouquet and the fullest body of all ports. *See* late bottled vintage port.

vintner 1. A person who makes wine (regardless of whether he or she also grows the grapes used to make the wine); in the commercial context, this may include a person who blends and sells wines; also known as a wine producer. *See* wine maker. 2. In Great Britain, a person who sells wine; also known as a wine merchant.

Vintners Quality Alliance (VQA) Designation awarded to wines produced in either of the Canadian provinces of Quebec or British Columbia; it indicates that the wine is made from 100% provincially grown grapes, the wine has passed a tasting panel and all other VQA production standards have been met.

vinum Latin for wine.

Viognier; Vionnier (vee-oh-n'yay) 1. A white wine grape grown in France's Rhône Valley; it is sometimes blended with Syrah to add bouquet and acidity. 2. A white wine made from this grape; its bouquet contains hints of peach or apricot.

violas (vi-OH-lahz) Edible flowers (genus *Viola*) similar to violets with a flavor reminiscent of grapes; used as a garnish.

virgin brandy *See* álcool blanc.

virgin cream A traditional term for a mixture of cream, sugar and egg whites.

virgin drink *See* mocktail.

Virginia ham *See* Smithfield ham.

Virgin Mary A Bloody Mary without the alcohol.

virus The smallest known form of life; although it can survive on its own, a virus is parasitic in that it is completely dependent on nutrients inside a host's cells for its metabolic and reproductive needs; some viruses are food-borne and can cause an illness or disease.

vis (vis) Dutch for fish, especially freshwater fish.

viscera Internal organs.

visciola (vee-she-oh-lah) Italian for wild cherry.

viscous The quality of being thick and syrupy.

viskee (vees-key) Hindi for whiskey.

viski (vees-kee) Russian for whiskey.

vital gluten Dried gluten that has retained its elastic properties.

vitamin A class of nutrients composed of noncaloric complex organic substances necessary for proper body functions and health maintenance; with the exceptions of vitamins A, D and K, they are essential nutrients occurring naturally in animals and plants and can be categorized as fat soluble (vitamins A, D, E and K) or water soluble (the B vitamins and vitamin C).

vitamin A A fat-soluble vitamin essential for vision, growth and skin maintenance and synthesized in the body from the provitamins alpha-, beta- and gamma-carotene; not destroyed by ordinary cooking temperatures; significant dietary sources include dairy products, eggs, liver, dark green leafy vegetables and orange-colored fruits and vegetables; also known by its active form, retinol.

vitamin A$_1$ and vitamin A$_2$ Forms of vitamin A found in fish liver oils.

vitamina de abacate (vee-tah-mee-nah day ah-bah-cah-tay) A South American (especially Brazilian) beverage made by blending avocado, cold milk, sugar and vanilla.

vitamin B$_1$ A water-soluble vitamin essential for metabolizing carbohydrates and the proper functioning of the appetite and nervous system; not readily destroyed at normal cooking temperatures; it occurs in moderate amounts in nearly all foods, but significant sources include pork, liver, whole grain cereal, wheat germ, legumes and nuts; also known as thiamine.

vitamin B$_2$ A water-soluble vitamin essential for forming cells and enzymes and maintaining vision and tissues; not destroyed during ordinary cooking; significant sources include dairy products, eggs, leafy green vegetables, brewer's yeast, liver and whole grain or enriched breads and cereals; also known as riboflavin, lactoflavin and vitamin G.

vitamin B$_3$ A water-soluble vitamin essential for hydrolyzing sugars, aiding fat synthesis and proper functioning of the skin, nervous system and digestive system; not destroyed during ordinary cooking; significant sources include liver, poultry, lean meat, fish, yeast, legumes, whole grain cereals, nuts and enriched foods; also known as niacin; its active forms are nicotinic acid, nicotinamide and niacinamide.

vitamin B₅ A water-soluble vitamin essential for metabolizing sugars and fats; found in most foods, but significant sources include yeast, liver, heart, grains and legumes; also known as pantothenic acid.

vitamin B₆ A water-soluble vitamin essential for forming enzymes and normal metabolism; significant sources include liver, fish, poultry and whole grain cereals; also known as pyridoxine; its active forms are pyridoxal and pyridoxamine.

vitamin B₁₂ A water-soluble vitamin essential for metabolizing fats and carbohydrates, forming new cells and maintaining the nervous system; it is unstable in hot acidic or alkaline solutions; significant sources include liver, lean meats and dairy products; also known as cyanocobalamin and cobalamin.

vitamin B complex A group of water-soluble vitamins, including vitamins B₁, B₂, B₃, B₅, B₆ and B₁₂, biotin and folacin.

vitamin C A water-soluble vitamin essential for forming collagen, healing wounds and bone fractures and preventing scurvy; easily leached from foods during cooking; significant sources include fruits, green leafy vegetables, cantaloupe, strawberries, tomatoes and potatoes; also known as ascorbic acid.

vitamin D A fat-soluble vitamin essential for forming bones and regulating calcium and phosphorus absorption; it is synthesized in the body by exposure to sunlight; significant dietary sources include fortified dairy products, eggs and fish oils; also known by its active forms, calciferol and cholecalciferol.

vitamin E A fat-soluble vitamin essential as an antioxidant for unsaturated fatty acids; significant sources include plant oils, green leafy vegetables, wheat germ, whole grain products and nuts; its active forms include tocopherol and alphatocopherol.

vitamin G *See* vitamin B₂.

vitamin H *See* biotin.

vitamin K A fat-soluble vitamin essential for normal blood clotting; derived from bacterial synthesis in the intestinal tract; significant dietary sources include green leafy vegetables, root vegetables, fruits and alfalfa; its active forms include phylloquinone.

vitamin P *See* bioflavonoids.

vitamins, fat-soluble Vitamins A, D, E and K; after absorption from the intestinal tract, they are not easily excreted and are stored in the liver and fatty tissues.

vitamins, water-soluble The B vitamins and vitamin C; after absorption from the intestinal tract, any excess is generally excreted in the urine.

vitela (vee-TEL) Portuguese for veal.

vitello (vee-TEL-loa) Italian for veal.

vitellone (vee-TEL-loa-nay) Italian for heifer or young cow.

vitello tonnato (vee-TEL-loa toan-NAA-toa) An Italian dish consisting of veal served with sauce flavored with tuna fish.

Viticultural Area; American Viticultural Area A delimited grape-growing region with recognized boundaries defined by the Bureau of Alcohol, Tobacco, and Firearms (BATF) based on geographic features, climate and historical precedent; the equivalent of the French Appellation d'Origine.

viticulture The art, science and practice of growing grapes. *See* viniculture.

vitis labrusca (vee-tihs luh-bruhs-kuh) The native North American species of grape, some varieties of which are used for wine making.

vitis vinifera (VEE-tihs vihn-IHF-uh-ruh) Latin for wine bearer and used to describe the native European species of grape responsible for producing most of the world's wine; there are hundreds of known varieties.

vitunguu (vee-toon-goo-oo) Swahili for onion.

vitunguu saumu (vee-toon-goo-oo saw-who-moo) Swahili for garlic.

Viura *See* Macabeo.

Vizé (vee-ZAY) A small, hard Romano-style cheese made in Greece from ewe's milk; it is used for grating.

VLDL *See* very-low-density lipoproteins.

vlees (vlays) Dutch for meat.

voatang A long, melonlike fruit with a green-spotted yellow skin and a pale flesh; grown in African coastal regions.

voda (voh-dah) Russian for water.

vodka (VAHD-kah) A distilled spirit made from potatoes and various grains, principally corn, with some wheat added; it is distilled at proofs ranging from 80 to 100 and is sometimes flavored.

Vodka Gimlet A cocktail made of vodka and Rose's lime juice.

Vodka Grand Marnier A cocktail made of vodka, Grand Marnier and lime juice; garnished with a maraschino cherry.

Vodka Martini *See* Martini.

Vodka Sour A cocktail made of vodka, lemon juice and sugar syrup; garnished with a lemon slice and maraschino cherry.

Vodka Stinger A cocktail made of vodka and white crème de menthe.

Vodkatini A contraction of Vodka Martini; a martini made with vodka instead of gin.

void; voyd To clear a table of dishes, remains of food and the like after a meal.

voide; viodee; voydee A small repast consisting of wine and comfits eaten before bedtime or before guests depart, usually following a feast; a parting dish.

voider; voyder 1. To place dirty dishes, remains of food or the like into a basket or on a tray when clearing the table or during a meal. 2. To hold, carry or pass around a tray, a basket or a large plate with sweetmeats.

voileipäpyötä (VOY-LAY-pa-PUH-ew-toh) Finnish for cold hors d'ouevre. *See* pikkulämpimät.

volaille (vohl-yay) French for chicken, fowl or poultry.

volatile Rapidly evaporating or vaporizing.

volatile acidity The development or presence of acetic acid in a wine; the result of bacterial spoilage.

volatile oil An oil that evaporates or vaporizes easily; such oils provide distinctive odors and flavors to plants.

vol-au-vent (vawl-oh-VAHN) A large, deep puff pastry shell often filled with a savory mixture and topped with a pastry lid.

vol-au-vent cutter A tinned steel tool for cutting vol-au-vents from puff pastry; it looks like a double cookie cutter with an inside cutter about 1 in. smaller and slightly shorter than the other.

vol-au-vent cutter

Volstead Act *See* Prohibition.

volume 1. The space occupied by a substance. 2. The measurement typically used to measure liquids; volume measurements are commonly expressed as liters, teaspoons, tablespoons, cups, pints, gallons, fluid ounces and bushels. 3. A quantity of something, either tangible or intangible (e.g., a volume of goods or business).

volume discount *See* quantity discount.

volvaire (vuhl-vair) French for straw mushroom.

vongole (vong-goa-lay) Italian for clams.

Vorarlberg (foe-rah-rl-berg) A hard Austrian cheese made from soured cow's milk; it is generally low in fat and has a moist surface and a pronounced flavor and aroma.

vörtbroöd (vuhrt-bruhd) A spicy Swedish bread made with rye flour and barley wort.

Votre sante! (vote-tra sahn-tay) A French toast meaning to your health.

Vouvray (voo-vray) A white wine produced in Vouvray in France's Loire Valley from Chenin Blanc grapes; it can be fruity and dry, soft, semidry and moelleux, or rich and sweet; a sparkling version is produced in limited quantities.

VQA *See* Vintners Quality Alliance.

VS *See* very superior.

V-shaped ice chisel A metal ice-carving tool with a handle and a 0.5- to 1.2-in.-wide V-shaped blade.

VSO *See* very superior old.

VSOP *See* very superior old pale.

VVSOP *See* very very superior old pale.

Wachau A grape-growing and wine-producing region of Austria, located north of Vienna along the Danube river; the principal grapes grown are Riesling and Grüner Veltliner.

Wacholder *See* Steinhager.

Wachtel (vact-tel) German for quail.

wafer A very thin, crisp cookie or cracker; it can be sweet or savory.

wafer iron A cast-iron device heated on the hearth and brought to the table to cook batter into thin wafers.

waffle A thin, crisp, light cake with a honeycomb surface; it is baked in a waffle iron and served with sweet or savory toppings.

waffled Slang for intoxicated.

waffle iron An appliance used for making waffles; there are two types: a stove-top waffle iron, which consists of two hinged honeycomb-patterned forms with handles (the forms are heated on the stove, the batter is poured in and cooked on one side then turned to cook the other side), and an electric waffle iron with a built-in heat source.

wagashi (wah-gah-shee) Japanese confections, cakes, cookies and candies; design is often more important than flavor; there are three principal classifications: namagashi, han namagashi and higashi.

wahoo *See* ono.

wain (oo-a-in) Japanese for white wine.

waist to hip ratio A measurement of the distribution of body fat; a high ratio reflects the excess accumulation of fat above the waist, which is associated with an increased risk of heart disease, cancer, diabetes and other disorders.

waiter; waitress The person responsible for taking orders and serving food at a restaurant. *See* back waiter, captain, front waiter, headwaiter *and* server.

waiter's wine opener A tool with a coiled wire worm, perpendicular handle, hinged arm, and two small knife blades set at opposite ends; it measures about 4 1/2 in. long and 5/16 in. wide; used for removing the cork from a wine bottle or the cap from a beverage.

waiter's wine opener

wakame (WAH-kah-meh) A dark green seaweed with a mild flavor and a soft texture; it is sold dried or pickled and can be eaten as is or cooked like greens in Japanese cuisine.

wakégi (wah-KAHY-ghee) Japanese for scallions.

Waldmeister (VALT-mye-stehr) German for woodruff.

Waldorf A cocktail made of bourbon, Pernod, sweet vermouth and Angostura bitters.

Waldorf salad A salad of apples, celery and sometimes walnuts in a mayonnaise dressing.

waldorf sweetbreads A dish of blanched sweetbreads sautéed in butter, placed on artichoke bottoms and covered with a sauce allemande.

Walewska; Waleska (vah-LEF-skah) A French dish in which the main ingredient (e.g., poached sole) is garnished with lobster and truffles, coated with Mornay sauce and browned.

Walflete oyster *See* Colchester oyster.

wali (wah-lee) Swahili for cooked rice.

walk-in A large insulated box or room used to store foods on adjustable shelves at appropriately low temperatures; it is large enough to enter; a separate walk-in freezer is sometimes attached. *See* reach-in.

walleyed pike *See* pike perch.

walleye pollock; walleyed pollock *See* pollock, Alaskan.

wallop Australian and British slang for a beer or ale.

walnut *See* English walnut.

walnut oil An oil obtained by pressing walnuts; it is high in polyunsaturated fatty acids, has a nutty flavor and aroma and is used in salad dressings, sauces and baked goods.

Wälschkorn (velch-kohn) A German pickle made from small, young, unripened corncobs flavored with bay leaf, peppercorns and vinegar.

wampee A small fruit (*Clausenia lansium*) native to China; it has a yellow-green skin and an aromatic, mildly acidic flesh.

wandòu (juan-doo) Chinese for peas.

wanfan (juan-fan) Chinese for dinner.

wapiti (WAHP-aht-ee) A deer found principally in Canada; its meat is prepared like any other venison.

warabi (wah-RAH-bee) Japanese and Hawaiian for fiddlehead ferns.

waraq al gar (wahr-rak el gahr) Arabic for bay leaf.

waraq inib mihshee (wahr-rak ein-neb mah-shee) A Middle Eastern dish of grape leaves stuffed with hashwa or a mixture of chickpeas, cracked wheat and parsley and flavored with lemon juice.

war cake *See* depression cake.

war bread A bread popular in the New England region of the United States for almost 200 years; most of the white wheat flour (which would be scare in wartime) is replaced with a mixture of oats, cornmeal and whole wheat.

Warday's A cocktail made of gin, sweet vermouth, yellow Chartreuse and Calvados or applejack.

warden A cooking pear grown in England.

ware (wer) An oyster older than 3 years.

waribashi (wah-ree-bah-shi) Japanese disposable chopsticks.

wari shio (wah-ree shi-o) A mixture of salt, cornstarch and aji-no-moto; used in Japanese cuisine as a seasoned coating for fried foods.

warishita (wa-ree-shi-ta) A mixture of dashi stock, soy sauce and mirin used to cook sukiyaki.

warka (vahr-kah) A round, thin, translucent pastry leaf used in Moroccan cuisine; it is similar to phyllo.

warm To bring a food slowly to a slightly higher temperature.

Warmbier (VERM-beer) A German soup made with raw eggs beaten into warm beer flavored with lemon.

warming beer A beer with a high alcohol content, such as Doppelbock.

warming case A three-sided case of Plexiglas with a wooden bottom and top; the case holds a heat lamp that is used to keep sugar warm and pliable while it is being pulled or blown.

warming oven An oven used to maintain cooked foods at a proper temperature or to gently warm cooked foods to the proper temperature; it usually has a limited temperature range, with the highest setting at 200–250°F (93–121°C).

warmouth A freshwater fish of the sunfish family found in the eastern United States; it has a dark olive skin with bluish lines radiating from its red eyes and a soft flesh with a muddy flavor; also known as a stump knocker.

warm-water tails Tails harvested from spiny lobsters caught off Florida and Brazil and in the Caribbean Sea; available frozen, their flavor is inferior to that of cold-water tails.

warty venus clam A variety of venus clam found off western Europe and West Africa and in the Mediterranean Sea; it has a brownish-red, slightly ovoid bumpy shell measuring 1–3 in. (2.54–7.6 cm) and sweet meat.

wasabi; wasabe (wah-SAH-bee) The root of an Asian plant (genus *Armoracia*) similar to horseradish; it is ground and, when mixed with water, becomes a green-colored condiment with a sharp, pungent, fiery flavor used in Japanese cuisines.

wash *v.*1. To apply a liquid to the surface of an object to remove dirt; a cleansing agent is often added to the liquid; the process may not kill microorganisms. 2. To apply a liquid to the surface of a food. *n.*1. A liquid such as water, milk or eggs applied to the surface of a food, usually before bak-

ing. 2. A solution of thickening agent (such as flour) in a cool liquid. 3. The liquid obtained from fermenting wort with yeast; the raw material for the first distillation in the pot still and the only distillation in the patent still. 4. A Caribbean beverage made of brown sugar, water and lime juice or sour orange juice. *See* beer.

washed-curd cheese A semisoft to firm cheese made by the cheddaring process except that the curds are washed with water before salting, thus increasing the moisture content and decreasing the lactose content, final acidity and firmness; soaked-curd cheese is washed for a longer period than is washed-curd cheese.

washed-rind cheese A surface-ripened cheese whose surface is washed with a liquid (sometimes brine, beer or wine) to promote the growth of mold during aging; it gives the cheese a smooth, somewhat shiny appearance that is often tinged a red-orange and also contributes flavor and aroma. *See* brushing.

washings The water used to rinse uncooked rice; in some Asian cuisines (e.g., Filipino), it is used as a flavoring and thickening agent.

Washington navel A particularly flavorful, pulpy variety of navel orange; virtually seedless, it is generally grown in the United States.

Washington plum A variety of plum with a reddish-yellow skin and a very sweet flavor.

Washington tomato A variety of red-skinned, flavorful cherry tomato.

wash still A type of still used for the primary distillation of a wash.

wassail (WAHS-uhl) An archaic British toast meaning "be whole or be well."

Wassail Bowl A punch made of brown sugar, Cognac or gold rum, nutmeg, ginger, mace, allspice, cloves, eggs, cinnamon, baked apples and Madeira, sherry, port or Marsala and served in a large wassil bowl (similar to a punch bowl) garnished with small roasted apples.

Wasser (VAH-sserr) German for water.

Wasserkatze (VAH-sserr-kact-seh) German for wolffish.

Wassermelone (VAH-sserr-meh-lon-a) German for watermelon.

waste The portion of a food that is neither usable nor edible.

water 1. A tasteless, odorless, colorless liquid; each water molecule consists of two hydrogen atoms and one oxygen atom (H_2O). 2. The principal chemical constituent of the body; essential for life, it provides the medium in which metabolic activities take place and also acts as a transportation medium, lubricant and body-temperature regulator. 3. A beverage.

water, acidulated A mildly acidic solution of water and lemon juice or vinegar that is used to prevent cut fruits and vegetables from darkening.

water, artesian well Water obtained from an underground source; the water rises to the surface under pressure.

water, bottled Any water, usually a still or sparkling natural water, that is bottled and sold; generally consumed as an alternative to a soft drink or other nonalcoholic beverage.

water, carbonated Water that has absorbed carbon dioxide; the carbon dioxide produces an effervescence and increases mouth feel.

water, deionized Water that has had cations and anions removed by passing it over a bed of ion-exchange resins. *See* ion.

water, demineralized Water that has had all the minerals removed by passing it over a bed of ion-exchange resins.

water, distilled Water that has had all the minerals and impurities removed through distillation; generally used for pharmaceutical purposes.

water, drinking Water that comes from a government-approved source and has undergone some treatment and filtration; it can be bottled or available on tap and is used for drinking and general culinary purposes.

water, fluoridated Water that is either naturally fluoridated or treated with a fluorine-containing compound; intended to promote healthy teeth by preventing tooth decay.

water, hard Water with relatively high calcium and magnesium concentrations.

water, mineral Drinking water that comes from a protected underground water source and contains at least 250 parts per million of total dissolved solids such as calcium.

water, natural Bottled drinking water not derived from a municipal water supply; it can be mineral, spring, well or artesian well water.

water, purified Bottled water produced by distillation, reverse osmosis, deionization or other suitable processes that meet federal standards.

water, soft Water with a relatively high sodium concentration.

water, sparkling Water that has absorbed carbon dioxide, either naturally or artificially; the carbon dioxide produces effervescence and increases mouth feel.

water, spring Water obtained from an underground source that flows naturally to the earth's surface.

water, still Water without carbonation.

water, tap Water obtained from a standard indoor plumbing faucet; it can be from a water treatment center or well.

water, well Water obtained from a hole bored into the ground to tap an aquifer.

water activity A measure of the amount of moisture bacteria need to grow; often written as Aw; water has an Aw of 1.0, and any food with an Aw of 0.85 or greater is considered potentially hazardous.

water added The U.S. Department of Agriculture (USDA) labeling term indicating that a processed meat product has been injected with a curing solution in excess of the amount of natural fluids lost during curing and smoking.

water-added ham *See* ham, water-added.

water bagel *See* bagel, water.

water bath *See* bain marie.

water biscuit A bland, thin, crisp cracker, often served with cheese and wine.

waterblommetjie A plant (genus *Nymphaea*) related to the water lily and native to South Africa; its seedpods have a flavor reminiscent of asparagus and artichokes.

water buffalo; water ox An Old World buffalo with large, flattened curved horns; used principally for its milk.

water buffalo's milk *See* milk, water buffalo's.

water caltrop A two-horned nut (*Trapis bicornis*) with a shiny black skin, a crisp, white flesh and a flavor similar to that of a water chestnut; used in Chinese and Indian cuisines.

water chestnut The fruit of a water plant (genus *Trapa*) native to Southeast Asia; it has a brownish-black skin, an ivory to tan flesh, a crisp texture and a slightly sweet, nutty flavor; used in various Asian cuisines; also known as water caltrop.

water chestnut powder; water chestnut flour A powdered starch made from ground dried water chestnuts; used as a thickener in Asian cuisines.

water chestnuts, crystallized Small, round water chestnuts cooked in a sugar syrup and eaten as snack or used in puddings and cakes in Chinese cuisines.

watercress A plant (*Nasturtium aquaticum*) with small, dark green leaves and a pungent, peppery, slightly bitter flavor; used as an herb, a garnish and in soups, salads and sandwiches.

water ice A frozen dessert of sugar and water flavored with fruit juice, coffee, liquor or another beverage; made without fat or egg whites.

watering hole Slang for a bar.

water lemon A short, ovoid fruit (*Passiflora laurifolia*) native to South America with a yellow or orange color and a sweet juicy flesh; also known as yellow granadilla and Jamaican honeysuckle.

waterless cooker Any of several cooking utensils made of heavy metal, with tight-fitting covers, in which foods are cooked in their own juices (e.g., pressure cooking).

watermelon 1. A category of melons (*Citrullus vulgaris*) native to Africa; they are characterized by a very thick rind, a very juicy granular flesh with seeds generally disbursed throughout the flesh and a sweet flavor. *See* muskmelon. 2. A large to very large ovoid to spherical melon with green striped or pale to dark green rind and a pink to red flesh; a seedless variety is available; also known as a red watermelon.

watermelon, American A variety of watermelon with an ovoid shape.

watermelon, Mediterranean A variety of watermelon with a spherical shape.

watermelon, Thai A yellow-skinned watermelon cultivated in Thailand.

watermelon, yellow A very large melon with green striped or pale green rind and a golden yellow flesh; also known as a gold or golden watermelon.

water miscible Pertaining to fat-soluble compounds that mix readily with water and can be absorbed without fat.

water pack Canned fruits, vegetables or fish with water or other liquid (e.g., juice) added.

water-soluble vitamins *See* vitamins, water-soluble.

water spinach *See* kongsincai.

waterzooi (VAH-tuhr-zoh-ee) A Belgian (Flemish) dish of freshwater fish and eel (chicken is sometimes substituted) cooked in a court bouillon with herbs; after vegetables are added, it is finished with butter and cream and sometimes thickened with bread crumbs.

wave cut edge The cutting edge of a knife; generally used for slicing items with a hard exterior and a soft interior; the blade has a series of small V-shaped teeth arranged along a slightly scalloped edge. *See* serrated edge.

wax bean A yellow version of the green bean; it has a slightly waxier pod.

wax gourd A plant native to Java (*Benincasa cerifera*); its long, slightly ovoid, cylindrical fruit have a waxy green skin, a pale flesh and a bland flavor; used fresh in salads or cooked.

wax paper; waxed paper Semitransparent paper with a waterproof coating on both sides and used to line baking pans and cover foods for storage; also known as grease-proof paper. *See* silicone paper *and* parchment paper.

waxy corn *See* corn, waxy.

waxy potato *See* potato, waxy.

waxy rice flour *See* sweet rice flour.

waxy starch; waxy maize starch The starch portion of a waxy corn; sometimes used as a food additive to thicken puddings and sauces; also known as amioca.

wayfaring tree The reddish-black fruit of this tree (*Viburnum lantana*) have a plumlike flavor and are eaten raw when fully ripened.

weakfish *See* sea trout.

weak flour *See* flour, weak.

Wealthy apple 1. A large apple grown in America; it has a bright red skin, a pinkish flesh and a sharp flavor. 2. A variety of cider apple; the fruit have a sweet, strawberry-like flavor.

Wedding Belle A cocktail made of gin, Dubonnet rouge, orange juice and cherry brandy.

wedding cake An elaborately tiered and decorated cake that is the centerpiece of a wedding meal or celebration.

wedge bone A fabricated cut of the beef primal sirloin; a small, end-cut steak with a large bone.

wedge meat *See* blade meat.

wedlina (veh-nd-lee-nah) A Polish dish consisting of cold cooked meats or sausage.

wee dram A small amount of any beverage.

weedy A wine-tasting term for a wine with a harsh, green disagreeable flavor reminiscent of damp twigs; often caused by fermenting the grapes with their stems.

weenie American slang for a frankfurter or hot dog.

weeper A wine bottle showing seepage around the cork; if there is no loss of wine, the wine is still likely to be in a good condition.

weeping A cheese-tasting term for holes that are shiny with butterfat; usually a sign of maturity in Emmental-style cheeses.

Wehani rice An American russet colored aromatic rice that splits slightly when cooked; it has an aroma similar to that of popcorn.

wei (way) *See* dun.

Weichkäse (vie-kaiz) A group of soft German cheeses with a high moisture content; they have a bloomy, thin rind or are covered with a white rind flora, a close-textured interior (sometimes with small holes) and a fresh, delicate flavor.

weight The mass or heaviness of a substance; weight measurements are commonly expressed as grams (metric), ounces and pounds (U.S. and imperial).

Wein (vine) German for wine.

Weinberg (VINE-bairg) German for vineyard.

Weingut (VINE-goot) German for vineyard estate, including the vines and the cellar.

Weinkellerei (vine-KEL-er-rye) German for wine cellar; a wine-labeling term that does not necessarily mean that the grapes used for the wine come from the producer's own vineyards.

weishiji (weh-he-she-gee) Chinese for whiskey.

Weissburgunder (VICE-boor-gun-der) *See* Pinot Blanc.

Weisse (vice) A northern German wheat beer; it has an acidic, tart and lightly fruity flavor and usually an unfiltered, cloudy appearance.

Weisse Bohnen (vice BOA-nern) German for white or navy beans.

Weisse Rübe (vice REW-ber) German for turnip.

Weisslacker (vice-lah-ka) A semisoft cheese made from cow's milk in Bavaria, Germany; it has a mild flavor, a thin, whitish, glossy rind and a smooth white interior with few holes; as it ages, the flavor becomes more pungent, and the cheese is often called Bierkäse (beer cheese) or Weisslacker Bierkäse.

Weisslacker Bierkäse *See* Weisslacker.

Weisswein (vice-vine) German for white wine.

Weisswurst (VICE-voorst; vice-vurscht) A German sausage with a delicate flavor; it is made from veal, cream and eggs and served with sweet mustard and rye bread.

Weizen (vi-zen) German for wheat.

Weizenbier (vi-zen-beer) A southern German (Bavarian) wheat beer with a banana- and clovelike aroma; usually served as a summer beverage, either filtered (kristalklar) or unfiltered (hefe-weizen).

wekiwas *See* lavender gem.

Welcome gooseberry A gooseberry variety; the tart-flavored fruit have a light green skin that turns pinkish-red.

well-and-tree platter A serving platter with a depressed design of a tree with branches and a trough at the bottom of the tree; these indentations allow meat juices to drain away and collect in the trough.

well-balanced *See* balanced.

well brand The house brand of a distilled spirit; usually of relative low price and quality and without consumer brand recognition; used when a customer does not specify a particular product.

well done A degree of doneness for meat; the meat should have no red (and be brown throughout), be quite firm and spring back when pressed. *See* very rare, rare, medium rare, medium *and* medium well.

well drink; from the well A drink made from an inexpensive house brand of liquor when a brand is not specified.

Wellfleet oyster An Atlantic oyster found off Wellfleet, Cape Cod; it has an oval shell and plump flesh with a firm texture and moderately salty flavor.

Wellington mulberry A variety of black mulberry with long, sweet, black-skinned fruit.

Wellington XXX currants A cultivated variety of black currants; they are relatively large and juicy.

well pudding *See* pond pudding.

well water *See* water, well.

Welschriesling (VELSH-reez-ling) A white wine grape grown in Austria, Italy and central Europe.

Welsh cawl A Welsh soup made from mutton, root vegetables, onions and leeks; sometimes the meat is served separately.

Welsh onion A variety of onion (*Allium cepa perutile*) with a bunching, leeklike, interleaved bulb and tubular leaves.

Welsh rarebit; Welsh rabbit (RARE-beht) A British dish of cheese melted with beer, poured on toast and broiled. *See* golden buck.

Wensleydale, Blue (WEHNS-slee-dale) A firm English cheese made from cow's milk; it has a white, blue-veined interior, a smooth rind and a strong, sharp flavor.

Wensleydale, White A firm English cheese made from cow's milk; it has a white interior, a flaky texture and a mild flavor.

wentelteefjes (ven-tul-tays-yus) A Dutch dish consisting of bread soaked in milk and eggs and fried.

West African spice mixture A spice mixture used throughout West Africa; it generally consists of ground ginger, grains of paradise, dried chiles, cubebs, black and white peppercorns and allspice.

Westcott Bay oyster A variety of Pacific oyster found off Westcott Bay, in the U.S. Northwest.

Western eggplant *See* eggplant, Western.

western halibut *See* Pacific halibut.

western lettuce A variety of crisp head lettuce similar to iceberg.

western omelet An omelet made with green peppers, onions and diced ham; also known as a Denver omelet.

western oyster An oyster native to the Pacific Ocean off the U.S. West Coast; it has a round shell, grows up to 2 in.

(5 cm) across and has an extremely delicate flavor; also known as an Olympia oyster, Olympia flat oyster and native Pacific oyster.

western sandwich A sandwich of eggs scrambled with green peppers, onions and diced ham served on white bread or toast; also known as a Denver sandwich.

West Indian cherry *See* acerola.

West Indian pumpkin *See* calabaza.

West Indian turkey wing A bivalve mollusk found in the tropical Atlantic Ocean and the Caribbean Sea; it has an irregularly shaped shell with brown and white stripes and radiating ribs, a length of 3.5 in. (8.87 cm) and a chewy flesh with a mild flavor.

West Indies lime *See* Key lime.

Westphalian ham (wehst-FAIL-ee-uhn) A German-style boneless ham that is dry cured (sometimes with juniper berries added to the salt mixture) and smoked over a beechwood fire to which juniper twigs and berries have been added.

Westphalian rye bread *See* pumpernickel.

west Texas strawberries Cowboy slang for pinto beans.

we't Ethiopian for spiced stew.

wet aging The process of storing vacuum-packaged meats under refrigeration for up to 6 weeks to increase tenderness and flavor. *See* dry aging.

wet bar A small bar (a sink, refrigerator and cabinet and counter space) equipped to make cocktails or other drinks; it may be in a home, hotel room or office.

wet county A county that permits the sale of alcoholic beverages on premises, off premises or by package only. *See* dry county.

wet peak *See* soft peak.

wet sugar A deep brown, moist granular sugar made by boiling cane juice until it crystallizes; unlike refined sugar, it contains the nutrients found in cane juice.

wheat A cereal grass (genus *Triticum*, especially *T. aestivum*) grown worldwide; there are three principal varieties: durum, hard and soft; in many climates, there can be as many as three planting cycles per year; crops are sometimes identified by the planting season as winter, spring or summer wheat.

wheat, durum *See* durum wheat.

wheat, hard A wheat berry with a high protein content; flour ground from hard wheat has a high gluten-forming potential and is used for yeast breads.

wheat, hard red spring A wheat with a high protein content and gluten-forming potential; excellent for making bread.

wheat, hard red winter A wheat with a thinner kernel than hard red spring wheat; good for making bread.

wheat, soft A wheat with a low protein content; flour ground from soft wheat has a low gluten-forming potential and is used for baking tender products such as cakes.

wheat, soft red winter A wheat that is starchier than hard red winter wheat; used primarily for baking.

wheat berry The whole, unprocessed wheat kernel; it consists of the bran, germ and endosperm.

wheat bran The wheat berry's rough outer covering; it is high in fiber and is used as a cereal and nutrient supplement.

wheat bread A bread made from a mixture of white and whole wheat flours.

wheated bourbon A bourbon made with wheat instead of rye grain.

wheat endosperm The largest part of the wheat berry; it contains certain vitamins and minerals and is usually ground into flour.

wheat germ The embryo of the wheat berry; it is very oily and rich in vitamins, proteins and minerals, has a nutty flavor and is generally used as a nutritional supplement.

wheat starch A finely textured, white, gluten-free starch (it is the residue after protein is extracted from wheat); used in Chinese cuisine as a thickener and in dough used for dumpling wrappers.

wheel 1. A cut from a large roundfish (e.g., swordfish and tuna); the fish is cut in a thick slice perpendicular to the backbone and then fabricated into steaks; also known as a center cut. 2. A cylindrical cheese. 3. A citrus fruit sliced in the shape of a wheel and used as a garnish.

wheel shrimp *See* kuruma-ebi.

whelks A group of gastropod mollusks found in saltwater areas worldwide; they have an ovoid, spherical, pear-shaped or spiral shell and a flavorful, lean and very tough adductor muscle; significant varieties include the channeled whelk and knobbed whelk. *See* scungilli.

whetstone A dense-grained stone used to put an edge on a dull knife; also known as a sharpening stone or oilstone. *See* steel.

whey The liquid portion of coagulated milk (curds are the semisolid portion); used for whey cheese, processed foods (e.g., crackers) and principally livestock feed.

whey butter *See* butter, whey.

whey cheese A fresh cheese made from the whey remaining after a cow's milk cheese has been made; it has a white color, a somewhat grainy or granular texture and a mild, slightly sweet flavor; also known as albumin cheese. *See* Ricotta *and* boiled-whey cheese.

whey solids The dry form of whey; used as a replacement for milk solids and as a nutrient and flavor supplement in baked goods, ice creams, dry mixes and beverages.

whig; wig A kind of square or triangular bun or small cake made of yeast-risen dough and flavored with currants.

whim-wham A Scottish dessert consisting of whipped cream mixed with white wine and grated lemon peel, layered with sponge cake and red currant jelly, topped with more cream and garnished with candied lemon peel.

whip *See* whisk.

whipped butter *See* butter, whipped.

whipping A mixing method in which foods are vigorously beaten to incorporate air; a whisk or an electric mixer with its whip attachment is used.

whipping cream *See* cream, heavy whipping; *and* cream, light whipping.

whisk A utensil consisting of several wire loops joined at a handle; the loops generally create a round or teardrop-shaped outline and range in sizes from 8 to 18 in. (20.3 to 45.7 cm); used to incorporate air into foods such as eggs, cream or sauces; also known as a whip. *See* balloon whisk, flat whisk, sauce whisk *and* trimmed whisk.

whisks
(balloon, sauce and flat)

whiskey 1. An alcoholic beverage distilled from a fermented mash of grains such as corn, rye and barley; whiskys vary depending on factors such as the type and processing of the grain and water as well as the length and type of aging process. *See* bourbon, rye whiskey *and* Scotch. 2. The American, English and Irish spelling for this spirit; used to identify these countries' products; in Scotland and Canada it is spelled whisky.

whiskey, grain A straight unblended whiskey made from grains that have not been malted.

Whiskey Daisy A cocktail made of whiskey or bourbon, lemon juice, red currant syrup or grenadine, yellow Chartreuse and club soda; garnished with a lemon slice.

Whiskey Fuzz A cocktail made of whiskey, sugar syrup, Angostura bitters and club soda.

whiskey liqueur A liqueur for which whiskey is used as the exclusive distilled spirit base; the resulting liqueur has a predominant whiskey flavor.

Whiskey Mac A cocktail made of equal parts whiskey and ginger wine.

whiskey-making process The process for making whiskey: generally, (1) ground grain (corn, rye and/or wheat) is cooked to release starch from the tough cellular coating; (2) malt is added to convert the starches into fermentable sugars; (3) this mix is soaked in water to form the wort; (4) yeast is added to the wort, which goes into fermenting vats to ferment; (5) the fermented mix, now called beer, is distilled and then called whiskey; (6) the whiskey is then aged (usually in charred white oak barrels) and sometimes (7) blended.

whiskey mill Slang for a frontier saloon in the U.S. old west.

Whiskey Punch An Irish drink made by placing a lemon slice studded with cloves, brown sugar and Irish whiskey into a glass and adding boiling water; it is garnished with a lemon slice and a cocktail cherry and served hot.

whisky 1. Canadian and Scottish spelling of whiskey. 2. In the United States, the spelling approved by the federal government; whiskey, however, is still generally used for all products.

whisky, all-malt A straight unblended malt whisky.

white A description for a clear and colorless, straw-yellow- or golden-colored wine, distilled spirit or nonalcoholic beverage.

white asparagus *See* asparagus, white.

White Baby A cocktail made of gin, heavy cream and Cointreau or Triple Sec.

white bacon Salt pork, especially in the U.S. South. *See* salt pork.

whitebait A variety of smelt found worldwide; it has a silvery body, an average market length of 8–12 in. (20–30 cm), a high fat content and a rich flavor.

white beans A generic term used for a variety of ovoid or kidney-shaped beans with an ivory-white skin and flesh and a delicate to bland flavor; the four principal varieties are the marrow bean, great Northern bean, navy bean and pea bean.

white beer A cloudy Belgian-style wheat beer flavored with dried curaçao orange peel and coriander seeds.

white buffalo's milk *See* milk, water buffalo's.

white button mushroom *See* common store mushroom.

White Cap Chimay *See* Chimay.

White Cargo A cocktail made of gin, maraschino liqueur, dry white wine and vanilla ice cream; served in a chilled wine glass.

white chocolate 1. A candy made from cocoa butter, sugar, milk solids and flavorings; because it contains no chocolate liquor it is usually labeled white confectionary bar or coating; it can be eaten as a candy or used in confections and pastries. 2. *See* chocolate-making process.

white corvina; white corbina (kohr-VEE-nah) *See* white sea bass.

white crappie *See* crappie.

white deadnettle A perennial herb (*Lamium album*) with a creeping rhizome and an erect, leafy stem; its white flowers are used for a tisane, and the tender, thin young leaves are cooked like greens; also known as archangel.

whitefish A member of the salmon family found in North American freshwater lakes and streams; it has a silver skin, a moderately high fat content, a flaky white flesh, a sweet flavor and an average market weight of 2–6 lb. (0.9–2.7 kg); significant varieties include lake whitefish, eastern whitefish and inland whitefish. *See* chub *and* lake herring.

white fungus A silvery white, crinkly, edible fungus (*Tremella fuciformis*) that resembles a natural sponge when dried; used in Asian cuisines, especially in soups and vegetarian dishes; also known as silver fungus, snow fungus and tremella.

white goods A liquor industry term describing clear or light-colored distilled spirits such as vodka, gin and tequila. *See* brown goods.

White Gorgonzola (gohr-guhn-ZOH-lah) *See* Gorgonzola Bianco.

white hake *See* hake.

White Ischia fig A particularly flavorful and meaty variety of fig; it has a green skin.

White Joaneting An apple grown in England; it has a yellow skin with a red flush, a juicy flesh and a good flavor.

white kidney bean A medium-sized, kidney-shaped bean with a creamy-white skin, cream-colored firm flesh and a flavor similar to that of the red kidney bean but not as robust; also known as cannellini. *See* kidney bean.

White Lady 1. A cocktail traditionally made of equal parts lemon juice, white crème de menthe and Cointreau, shaken over ice and strained into a cocktail glass; today, gin has replaced the crème de menthe and sometimes egg white is added. 2. Australian slang for an inexpensive blend of methylated spirits and powdered milk.

white lightning *See* moonshine.

White Marseilles fig A variety of pale-skinned fig.

white mineral oil A food additive refined from petroleum and used as a release agent for processed foods such as baked goods, dehydrated fruits and vegetables, egg white solids, confections and yeast, as a dust control agent for wheat and other grains and as a protective coating on raw fruits and vegetables.

white mustard An annual herb (*Sinapis alba*) whose seeds are used whole in pickling spices or ground to make prepared mustards.

white mustard cabbage *See* bok choy.

white peppercorn *See* peppercorn, white.

white perch *See* sheepshead.

white pizza An American pizza topped with roasted garlic, basil, oregano, mozzarella and olive oil.

white port A port made from white wine grapes; its flavor ranges from dry and slightly tangy to medium sweet.

white potato, long A long, slightly rounded potato with thin, pale gray-brown skin, tiny eyes and a tender, waxy yellow or white flesh; used principally for boiling or sautéing; also known as California long white potato, white rose potato and Yukon gold potato.

white potato, round A medium-sized, spherical potato with thin, freckled, pale gray-brown skin and a tender, waxy yellow or white flesh; used principally for boiling or sautéing; also known as chef potato, all-purpose potato and boiling potato.

white raisins *See* golden raisins.

white rice Rice that has been pearled to remove the husk and bran; it has a mild flavor and aroma; also known as polished rice.

White Riesling *See* Johannisberg Riesling.

white rose potato *See* white potato, long.

White Russian A cocktail made of vodka, a coffee-flavored liqueur such as Kahlua and cream, served over ice.

White Russian Bear A cocktail made of vodka, gin and white crème de cacao.

whites Slang for the white jackets traditionally worn by kitchen staff.

white sapote (sah-PO-tee) A small fruit that grows wild in Central America (*Casimiroa edulis*); it has pale yellow skin and a flavor reminiscent of a pear.

white sauce *See* béchamel sauce.

white sausage A type of sausage made with poultry, veal, pork or rabbit, often mixed with bread crumbs.

white sea bass Not a true bass but a member of the drum family found in the Pacific Ocean from Alaska to Chile; it has a gray to blue skin that becomes silvery on the sides and white on the belly, a firm white flesh, a mild flavor and an average market weight of 10 lb. (4.5 kg); also known as a white corvina.

white shad *See* shad, American.

white sorrel A variety of roselle with a greenish calyx.

white stew *See* fricassée *and* blanquette.

White Stilton *See* Stilton, White.

white stock A light-colored stock made from chicken, veal, beef or fish bones simmered in water with vegetables and seasonings.

white tablecloth restaurant *See* tablecloth restaurant.

white tea A type of tea for which the leaves are simply steamed and dried; the beverage is generally light and fragrant.

White Tie and Tails *See* Cuff and Buttons.

White Transparent A cooking apple native to Scandinavia and Russia; it has a pale, almost transparent skin and a mild flavor.

white vermouth *See* vermouth, dry.

White Versailles currants A variety of white currants; they are particularly flavorful.

white walnut A native American nut (*Juglans cinera*) with a brownish-gray shell and a rich oily meat; generally used for baked goods; also known as a butternut. *See* black walnut.

whitewash A thin mixture or slurry of flour and cold water used like cornstarch for thickening.

white wine *See* wine, white.

white wine sauce 1. A French compound sauce made from a velouté flavored with a fish fumet or chicken stock and white wine and beaten with butter until emulsified. 2. A French sauce made from a fish fumet or chicken stock and white wine reduced to a glaze and beaten with butter; also known as sauce vin blanc.

white wine vinegar *See* wine vinegar, white.

White Zinfandel A California blush wine made from Zinfandel grapes that are harvested earlier than those used for the red wine; it has a pale salmon to pink color, a low alcohol content and an acidic flavor.

whiting A fish found in the Atlantic Ocean from New England to Virginia and along the European coast; it has grayish-silver skin and an average market weight of 0.5–5 lb. (0.25–2.3 kg); also known as silver hake and silver perch.

Whitstable oyster A variety of European flat oyster found off England.

whole-berry fermentation *See* carbonic maceration.

whole cow's milk *See* milk, cow's.

whole fish A market form for fish; the fish is in the condition in which it was caught; intact; also known as round fish.

whole fish protein concentrate A dry protein supplement derived from whole (i.e., heads, viscera, fins and the like attached) fish, usually hake and hakelike fish, herring and anchovies.

whole food Food that has not been partitioned (e.g., whole milk or a squash).

wholemeal 1. Flour that contains a certain proportion of bran. 2. A flour made from a blend of rye and wheat flours.

whole milk *See* milk, cow's.

wholesale The sale of goods and the price charged by a manufacturer, distributor or supplier to another distributor or supplier or to a business selling the goods to the general public. *See* retail.

wholesale cut *See* primal.

wholesomeness The condition of a food that is free from pathogenic microorganisms.

whole wheat A flour that is either milled from the entire hulled kernel or has had some of the components restored after milling.

whoopie pie A Pennsylvania German confection similar to a cupcake; usually made with leftover chocolate cake batter and white icing.

whortleberry *See* huckleberry.

wiamanola (why-amm-ann-ho-lah) A variety of macadamia grown in Hawaii; the nuts have a particularly rich, buttery flavor.

widgeon (wij-un) A small wild duck found in Europe, Asia and North America.

Widow's Kiss A cocktail made of applejack, Benedictine, yellow Chartreuse and Angostura bitters; garnished with a strawberry.

wiener *See* frankfurter.

Wiener Schnitzel (VEE-nuhr SHNIHT-shul) German for Viennese cutlet and used to describe veal scallops that are breaded, sautéed and served with lemon slices and sometimes hard-cooked eggs, capers and anchovies.

Wilcox hickory A variety of American hickory; the nuts are flavorful and easily cracked.

wild A coffee-tasting term used to describe an unusual, racy flavor.

Wild (vilt) German for game meat.

wild asparagus An ancestor of cultivated asparagus; it grows wild in western Europe and has long, slender shoots.

wild beer A beer fermented with wild, airborne yeasts.

wild boar A close relative of the domesticated hog found in Europe, North America, Asia and North Africa; the lean, dark red flesh of the mature animal (usually 1–2 years old) has a firm texture and a rich, sweet, nutty flavor that is stronger than that of pork; generally available during the autumn; also known as boar. *See* baby boar.

Wildbret (VILT-bret) German for venison.

wild duck *See* duck, wild.

Wildente (vilt-en-te) German for wild duck.

wild leek *See* ramp.

wild mango *See* duika.

wild marjoram *See* oregano.

wild parsley *See* lovage.

wild pecan rice A unique long-grain rice grown only in the bayous of southern Louisiana; it has a strong nutty flavor and an exceptionally rich aroma; also known as pecan rice.

wild plum *See* plum, wild.

wild rice The grain of a reedlike aquatic plant (*Zizania aquatica*) unrelated to rice; grown in the United States and Canada, the grains are long, slender and black, with a distinctive earthy, nutty flavor; available in three grades: giant (a very long grain and the best quality), fancy (a medium grain and of lesser quality) and select (a short grain).

Wildschwein (vilt-schvine) German for wild boar.

wild strawberry Any of a variety of strawberries growing wild in Europe and North America; the fruit are generally small, with a tapered, conical shape, a yellowish-red to bright red skin and an intense flavor. *See* Alpine strawberry.

wild turkey *See* turkey, wild.

Wild Turkey Distillery One of the 12 remaining U.S. whiskey distilleries; located in Lawrenceburg, Kentucky, and founded c. 1869, it produces the Wild Turkey line of bourbon and rye whiskeys.

wild yeast A yeast indigenous to a particular area used to make the local foods (e.g., cheeses and breads) or beverages (e.g., wine and beer).

Willamette Valley A grape-growing and wine-producing region in western Oregon known for its fine Pinot Noir wines.

William banana A variety of medium-sized, slightly stubby banana.

Williams pear *See* Bartlett pear.

Wiltshire A hard, English, Derby-style cheese made from cow's milk.

Windsor saucepan *See* saucepan, flare-sided.

Windsor soup A British beef consommé slightly thickened with arrowroot, flavored with turtle herbs and sherry and garnished with strips of calf's foot.

wine The fermented juice of a fruit, typically freshly gathered ripe grapes.

wine, red A wine made from black grapes and that derives its color from the contact between the juice and the grape skins during fermentation; the color can range from pink or rosé to a dark red.

wine, rosé (ro-zay) A wine made from black grapes whose skins are left in contact with the fermenting juice just long enough to add the desired amount of color; the color can range from pale salmon to pink.

wine, sparkling A wine bottled with dissolved carbon dioxide; generally made by either the méthode champenoise or the Charmat process. *See* Champagne.

wine, still A nonsparkling wine; the term is generally used to distinguish a wine from a sparkling wine.

wine, white A wine made from white (and occasionally red) grapes; there is minimal if any contact between the juice and the skins; its color can vary from pale to almost amber.

wine ball; wine cube A type of compressed brewer's yeast used in Chinese wine making.

wine bar A bar specializing in serving a selection of wines by the glass or bottle.

winebibbing Slang for drinking too much wine.

wine bottle, oversized A large bottle used for still or sparkling wines. *See* Balthazar, demijohn, double magnum, Imperial, Jeroboam, magnum, Methuselah, Nebuchadnezzar, Rehoboam *and* Salmanazar.

wine bottle, standard A bottle used for still or sparkling wines; it usually holds 750 ml (25.4 fl. oz., roughly the equivalent of a fifth). *See* bordeaux bottle, burgundy bottle *and* flute bottle.

wine brick Pressed, dehydrated grapes added to water to make ersatz wine; popular during Prohibition.

wine bucket *See* ice bucket.

wine captain *See* sommelier.

wine cellar *See* cellar.

wine cooler A beverage with a relatively low alcohol content made from a neutral wine, water, sugar, carbon dioxide gas and fruit flavors.

wine cooperative A winery or cellar owned and operated jointly by a number of small wine producers.

wine cradle A metal, wicker or straw holder used to carry a sedimented bottle of wine from the cellar to the table; by keeping the bottle almost horizontal during opening and decanting, the sediment that formed on the bottle's side will not be disturbed.

wineglass, all-purpose A stemmed, clear crystal glass with a moderately large bowl that is slightly curved inward or tapered toward the rim; it ranges in size from 6.5 to 10 fl. oz. (8.5 to 10 oz. is preferable).

wineglass, balloon A wineglass with a very large bowl ranging in size from 10 to 16 fl. oz.; traditionally used for red Burgundy wines.

wineglass, balloon

wineglass, red A glass with a shorter stem and a larger, more spherical bowl.

wineglass, white A long-stemmed glass with a medium-sized, slightly elongated bowl.

wineglassful A traditional measure of volume; it is approximately 1/4 cup.

wine grower An improperly used term for a person who grows grapes and produces wine.

wineglass, white

wine list A menu identifying the wines available for purchase at a restaurant, bar or the like; each entry is usually described or categorized by its place of origin and/or grape varietal and is accompanied by its price and bin number; it sometimes includes a list of wines that are available by the glass.

wine maker In the United States, the person responsible for the production of wine in a winery.

wine-making process *See* vinification.

wine merchant A person who sells but does not necessarily make wine.

wine pail An urn-shaped or cylindrical vessel designed to sit on a table and hold a wine bottle in water or ice.

wine palm Any of a variety of palms (family Palmae or Arecaeae) having sap or juice from which a wine is made.

wine pouch A soft-sided container used to carry wine; it usually has a long neck and a flat body and is made of goatskin.

wine press; winepress A device used to extract juice from grapes; grapes are pressed after crushing and before fermentation.

wine producer *See* vintner.

wine product A wine processed with additives such as salt and generally used for cooking and not as a beverage; also known as cooking wine.

wine rack A structure with individual openings for storing and displaying wine bottles in the horizontal position.

winery 1. A building housing the apparatuses used to make, store and age wine. 2. The establishment making the wine.

Winesap apple An all-purpose apple native to North America; the medium-sized fruit has an elongated shape, a yellow-streaked red skin, a firm aromatic flesh and a tangy flavor.

wine-sediment paste A red seasoning made from fermented rice and rice wine sediments and used in Chinese chicken and shellfish dishes.

wine steward The person responsible for a restaurant's wine service, including purchasing wines, assisting guests in selecting wines and then serving the wine; also known as the chef de vin and sommelier.

wine taster 1. One who evaluates the quality of wine by tasting it, especially on a professional basis. 2. A small bowl used to hold wine for tasting.

wine thief *See* thief.

wine vinegar A vinegar made from any wine; it has an acidity of approximately 6.5%.

wine vinegar, red A vinegar made from any red wine; it has a dark red color and a mellow, acidic flavor.

wine vinegar, white A vinegar made from any white wine; it can be colorless to a pale straw color and has a tart, acidic flavor.

wine waiter *See* wine steward *and* sommelier.

winged bean A tropical legume (*Psophocarpus tetragonolobus*) with four ruffled wings running the length of the pod; the pod can be green, purple or various shades of red; the bean seeds have a flavor similar to that of cranberry beans and the texture of starchy green beans; also known as asparagus pea, drumstick and goa.

wing oyster *See* pearl oyster.

winkle *See* periwinkle.

winnowing Separating the chaff from grains by means of air pressure; it is usually accomplished by placing grains in a flat basket and bouncing and tossing the contents. *See* fanner basket.

wino Slang for a person addicted to alcoholic beverages (usually cheap, sweet, fortified wine).

winter cherry 1. A cherry-sized fruit (*Phylsalis alkekengi*) native to Europe; it has a bright red skin and is enclosed in a loose, papery, lantern-shaped red husk; usually cooked with sugar to make a syrup; also known as apple of love, bladder cherry, Chinese lantern, love in a cage and lantern herb. 2. An imprecise name for the closely related cape gooseberry.

winter cress *See* land cress.

winter flounder *See* blackback flounder *and* lemon sole.

winter grape *See* frost grape.

wintergreen An evergreen plant (*Gultheria procumbens*) with small red berries that produce a pungent oil used in jellies or to flavor candies and medicines; also known as checkerberry and teaberry.

winter greens Kale and turnip tops.

winter melon A large muskmelon with a pale green rind, a white flesh and a flavor reminiscent of zucchini; used in Asian cuisines in sweet and savory dishes.

winter melon, crystallized Winter melon cooked in a sugar syrup and eaten as a snack or used in Chinese cuisines to sweeten meat dishes or in cakes and puddings; available in either transparent white lumps or in slices covered in crystallized sugar.

winter mushroom *See* enoki *and* shiitake.

Winter Nelis A small pear with a russet and green skin, a spicy flavor and a grainy texture.

winter radish *See* daikon.

winter savory *See* savory, winter.

winter squash *See* squash, winter.

winter squid *See* loligo.

winy; winey 1. A wine-tasting term referring to the winelike aroma or flavor of a wine; caused by its alcohol content. 2. A coffee-tasting term used to describe a coffee's fruitlike acidity and/or smooth body.

Winzergenossenschaft (vin-zer-geh-NAW-sen-shahft) German for wine cooperative.

wire hood *See* muselet.

wire mesh strainer A tool with a mesh bowl, sometimes reinforced with narrow crossbands and a handle; available in various sizes and thicknesses of mesh; it is used to strain liquids from solids or to sift dry ingredients; also known as a strainer. *See* sieve.

wishbone 1. The forked bone found between the neck and breast of a chicken or turkey. 2. The cut of chicken containing the wishbone.

Wishniak; Wisniak (vee-sh-ñyahk) A Polish wild cherry liqueur.

wiski (we-skee) Swahili for whiskey.

Wisniowka (VEES-ne-oh-kam) A liqueur from Russia, the Czech Republic and Slovakia made from wild cherries.

witch flounder *See* gray sole.

Withania A Southeast Asian (principally Indonesian) cheese made from cow's milk coagulated with berries from the Withania plant; it has a pleasant flavor that becomes acrid as the cheese ages.

without A food-labeling term approved by the U.S. Food and Drug Administration (FDA) to describe a food containing no or only physiologically inconsequential amounts of fat, saturated fat, cholesterol, sodium, sugars or calories.

witloof *See* Belgian endive.

witte bonen (VIT-tuh BOH-nuh) Dutch for dried white beans.

Wladimir, sauce *See* ivoire, sauce.

wok Cookware with a rounded bottom and curved sides that diffuses heat and makes it easy to toss or stir contents; it usually has a domed lid and two handles, although a single long-handled version is available; used originally in Asian cuisines.

wok

wok spatula A wide, flat, square-shaped spatula with the working edge curved to fit the wok.

wolffish; wolf fish A fish found in the northern Pacific and Atlantic Oceans; it has a bluish-brown skin, weighs up to 40 lb. (18.0 kg) and has a firm, white flesh.

won ton; won-ton (WAHN tahn) A small Chinese dumpling made from a thin dough filled with a mixture of finely minced meats, poultry, fish, shellfish and/or vegetables; it can be steamed, fried or boiled and eaten as dumplings, in soups and as appetizers.

won ton skins Wafer-thin sheets of dough made from flour, eggs and salt and used to wrap fillings; available in squares or circles.

won ton soup A Chinese soup consisting of chicken broth garnished with won tons, green onions, pork or chicken and/or vegetables.

wood aging The maturing of wine or spirits in wooden casks or barrels; this permits minute amounts of air to interact with the components of the liquid and permits the liquid to absorb certain flavor and aroma characteristics from the wood.

wood alcohol *See* methyl alcohol.

wood apple A medium-sized, spherical fruit (*Feronia limonia*) native to India; it has a hard gray shell and a brown flesh and is used in chutneys and preserves; also called an elephant apple.

woodblewit *See* blewit.

woodchuck An herbivorous rodent found in North America; it has an average weight of 6–10 lb. (2.6–4.5 kg) and an earthy flavor; also known as groundhog and prairie dog.

woodcock A small wild game bird related to the snipe; its darkish flesh has a rich flavor, and its trail is a great delicacy.

wood ear mushroom *See* cloud ear mushroom.

wooden spoon *See* spoon, wooden.

wood hedgehog mushroom *See* hedgehog mushroom.

woodruff An aromatic herb (genus *Asperula*) native to Europe and used as a flavoring in May wine; also called sweet woodruff.

woody A wine-tasting term for a woodlike flavor or aroma caused by extended storage or aging in a wooden barrel or cask.

woo gok A Chinese dim sum; it is an egg-shaped deep-fried croquette of mashed taro root stuffed with a minced mixture of pork, shrimp, mushrooms and bamboo shoots.

woo lo gwa *See* dudi.

Woo Lung (who loong) A black tea from China's Chinkiang province; the beverage has a smoky flavor and is generally served at public teahouses.

Worcester A grape-growing and wine-producing region in the Breede River Valley of South Africa; it is best known for its white wines.

Worcesterberry A gooseberry variety; the fruit, which resemble black currants, are relatively small and have a purplish-black skin; it is cultivated in the United States.

Worcester Pearmain An apple grown in England; it has a firm, sweet flesh and a flavor reminiscent of a strawberry.

Worcestershire sauce (WOOS-tuhr-shuhr; WOOS-tuhr-sheer) A thin, dark brown sauce developed in India for British colonials and first bottled in Worcester, England; it consists of soy sauce, tamarind, garlic, onions, molasses, lime, anchovies, vinegar and other seasonings.

work sections The general divisions of kitchen responsibilities and space at a food services facility; each work section is composed of one or more workstations. *See* hot-foods section, garde-manger section, bakery section, short-order section *and* beverage section.

workstations The various preparation areas within a food services facility's kitchen, usually defined by the equipment used or foods produced.

worm The spiral part of the corkscrew that is inserted into the cork.

wormweed *See* epazote.

wormwood A bitter, aromatic herb (*Artemisia mayoris* and *A. vulgaris*), the oil of which is used in distilling absinthe.

wort (wert) The solution of grain sugars, proteins and other substances that are produced by mashing and straining the mash; the substance from which beer and certain distilled spirits (e.g., whiskey) is ultimately produced.

wot´ (what) Ethiopian for stew; usually one made with meat or vegetables and legumes.

wrap An American sandwich consisting of a filling and spread rolled in a soft flour tortilla (unlike a classic Mexican tortilla, the one used for a wrap can be flavored with herbs, spices or the like). *See* burrito.

wrap cooking A method of cooking foods in steam.

wrapped sushi *See* maki-zushi.

Wright apple An heirloom apple from Vermont (c. 1875); the spherical fruit has a lemon yellow skin with a pinkish-red blush, a tender white flesh and a musty, aromatic, vinous flavor.

wufan (woo-fen) Chinese for lunch.

wuhuaguo (who-juan-goo-oh) Chinese for fig.

wun sen (hoon san) Thai for vermicelli or clear noodle.

Wurst (voorst) German for sausage.

Würste von Kalbsgekröse (voorst vahn kahl-qheur-row-sah) A German sausage made from a calf's mesentery, seasoned with nutmeg, eggs and cream and cooked in a pork casing.

Wurstkraut (voorst-kraut) German for herbs such as sweet marjoram and savory; commonly used to flavor Wurst.

Wurth hickory A variety of American hickory; the nuts are flavorful and easily cracked.

Würzburg (VURTZ-boorg) The principal city in Franconia; known for its wine and beer, both called Würzburger.

Würze (vurt-sa) German for spice or seasoning.

würzig *See* pikant.

Würzkraüter (vurtz-kah-oo-terr) German for herbs with a pungent aroma.

Würztunke (vurtz-toon-ka) German for chutney.

wu xiang fen (woo shang fen) Chinese for five-spice powder; it generally consists of some combination of star anise, fennel seeds, cloves, cinnamon, Szechwan peppercorns, ginger and nutmeg.

xanthan gum A food additive produced from corn syrup; used as a thickener, emulsifier and stabilizer.

Xanthia A cocktail made of gin, cherry brandy and yellow Chartreuse.

xanthines A group of alkaloid drugs occurring in more than 60 plant species; examples include the caffeine in coffee beans, cocoa beans, cola nuts and tea leaves and the theobromine in cocoa beans; also known as methylxanthines.

xarope (shah-ROU-puh) Portuguese for syrup.

Xérès (sair-ress) 1. Former name of the Spanish city Jerez de la Frontera and the wine now called sherry. 2. French for sherry.

Xérès, sauce au (sair-ress) A French compound sauce made from a demi-glaze flavored with dry or medium-dry sherry.

xia (shah) Chinese for shrimp.

xia mi (shah me) Chinese for dried shrimp.

xiang cai (shang cahee) Chinese for coriander.

xiangcaojing (shang-cah-oh-jing) Chinese for vanilla.

xiangchang (shang-chahng) Chinese for sausage.

xiangjiao (shang-gee-ah-oh) Chinese for banana.

xiang jun (shang june) Chinese for dried black mushrooms.

xianròu (shan-roo) Chinese for bacon.

xiaodianxin (shano-deean-shin) Chinese for cookies.

xiaomai (shah-oh-mah-ee) Chinese for wheat.

xiaoniurou (shah-oh-mew-roo) Chinese for veal.

xiaoshaor (shah-oh-shah-or) Chinese for spoon.

xihongshi (she-hong-she) Chinese for tomato.

xi mi fen (she me fan) Chinese for tapioca flour.

xingzi (sing-dze) Chinese for apricot.

xin xiande (shin shan-day) Chinese for fresh.

xin-xin de galinha (shin-shin da gah-lean-nya) A Brazilian dish of chicken, dried shrimp, dende oil and peanuts; it is garnished with parsley or mint and served with rice.

xiphios (xee-fee-oss) Greek for swordfish.

xithum (sae-toom) An Egyptian beer made from barley.

XO *See* extra old.

xocolatl (sho-con-lah-tea) Ancient Aztec for chocolate.

xoi gat (soy-gah) A bright orange powder made from a fruit and used to color rice in festive dishes in Vietnamese cuisine; also known as carrot powder.

xouba (chou-bah) A small sardinelike fish found near Spain.

xue cai (shoe cah-ee) Chinese for red-in-the-snow pickled cabbage.

xun (shoon) A Chinese cooking method in which an ingredient, usually raw, is smoked with wood shavings (pine or poplar), tea leaves, sugarcane pulp and brown sugar and then steamed or deep-fried; the ingredient may be steamed or deep-fried before being smoked.

x x x 1. An ancient Egyptian symbol denoting purity; used by distillers to indicate the number of times a product was distilled (i.e., x x x meant a triple-distilled product). 2. A label symbol adopted by some brew masters during the 19th century; it has no brewing or legal significance.

XXX; XXXX Labeling symbols that indicate the fineness of confectioners' sugar: the more Xs, the finer the sugar was pulverized.

xylitol (ZI-lah-tohl) A sugar alcohol derived from fruits or produced from glucose.

𝒴

ya (yah) Chinese for duck.

yabloko *See* jablok.

yagi (YAH-gee) Japanese for goat.

yahni (yah-neh) 1. A Greek preparation method; the food is braised with onions in olive oil, then a little water or tomatoes are added and all are simmered. 2. A Turkish stew usually made with mutton, lamb or hare.

yai (yah-ee) Swahili for egg.

yaitsa po-minski (yah-it-saw poh-min-skee) A Russian dish consisting of hard-boiled eggs whose whites are stuffed with a mixture of egg yolks mixed with mayonnaise, cream and herbs and topped with anchovy strips, grated cheese and bread crumbs and browned in the oven; also known as eggs Minsk.

yaizo (yah-he-tzo) Russian for egg.

yak bap (yahk bahp) A Korean confection of glutinous rice, dates, chestnuts, pine nuts and honey; traditionally served on the 15th day of the first lunar month.

yakhni (YAHF-nee) Arabic for stew, especially one with potatoes. *See* yukhnee.

yakhni baza *See* fesanjune.

yak-hwe (yahk-oo-a) A Korean dish of minced raw beef served with condiments and lettuce to use as an edible wrapper.

yaki (YAH-kee) Japanese for grill or broil.

Yakima Valley A grape-growing and wine-producing area in the Columbia Valley, 200 miles southeast of Seattle and east of the Cascade Mountains in Washington state; the principal grape varieties are Cabernet Sauvignon, Chenin Blanc, Chardonnay, Merlot, Riesling, Sauvignon Blanc and Sémillon.

yaki-mono (YAH-kee-MOH-noh) Japanese for grilled or broiled foods.

yaki-niku (YAH-kee-NEE-koo) Japanese for soy-marinated grilled beef.

yakinori (YAH-kee-NOH-ree) Toasted sheets of nori.

yaki-onigiri (YAH-kee-oh-nee-GHEE-ree) Japanese for grilled rice balls.

yaki soba (YAH-kee soh-bah) Japanese instant noodle soup.

yakitori (yah-kih-TOH-ree) A Japanese dish of chicken marinated in soy sauce, sugar and sake, placed on skewers and broiled or grilled.

yakni (yaa-kh-nee) *See* garhi yakhni.

yakumi (yah-koo-mee) Japanese for spice.

Yale A cocktail made of gin, dry vermouth, orange bitters and maraschino liqueur.

yam (yum) A Thai salad, whether composed of vegetables, meats and/or fruits; also known as ñame.

yam The thick, starchy tuber of various tropical vines native to Asia (genus *Dioscorea*) and unrelated to the potato and sweet potato; it has an off-white to dark brown skin and flesh that can range from creamy white to deep red; it is less sweet than a sweet potato.

yama-gata (YAH-ma-GAH-tah) Japanese for mountain shaped; used to describe a decorative cut of food.

yama imo (yah-MAH EE-mo) Glutinous yams grown in Japan; they have a hairy, beige skin with a white, slightly sticky interior and are often grated and eaten raw.

yam bean *See* jícama.

ya moto (yah moh-toh) Swahili for hot.

yampie A small tuber with a white flesh and delicate flavor; often served boiled in Caribbean cuisines.

yán (ee-ahn) Chinese for salt.

yanagi-ba-bōtchō (yah-NAH-ghee-bah-BOH-cho) A Japanese knife used to make sushi; it has a 10- to 14-in.-long slender blade ground on one side.

yanagi-ba-bōtchō

yangcong (ee-ahn-cong) Chinese for onion.

yangdujun (ee-hang-doo-june) Chinese for morel.

Yankee bean *See* navy bean.

Yankee pot roast A pot roast to which vegetables have been added during braising. *See* pot roast.

yansoon (yahn-soon) Arabic for anise.

yao horn (yao horn) A Cambodian dish in which thinly sliced beef, chicken, fish and shellfish are poached at the table in a charcoal-heated chafing dish and then dipped in raw egg and peanut sauce before eating.

yaourt (yah-oort) French for yogurt.

yard-long bean A very thin, exceptionally long legume; it resembles a green bean with a more pliable pod and a similar but less sweet flavor; also known as long bean and asparagus bean.

yard of ale An elongated glass that measures approximately 36 in. and contains 42 fl. oz.

yard of flannel A drink (and purported cold remedy) made from ale, eggs, brown sugar and nutmeg and served warm.

Yarg A cheese made in Cornwall, England, from cow's milk; it has a white color and a mild flavor.

yarng (yaang) Thai for roasted.

Yarra Valley A grape-growing and wine-producing region in the Australian state of Victoria; the principal grapes grown are Pinot Noir and Cabernet Sauvignon.

yarrow A perennial herb (*Achillea millefolium*) with dark green leaves, downy stems and a compact flower head; the leaves have a slightly bitter, peppery flavor and are used in salads; also known as milfoil.

yasai (yah-SAH-ee) *See* shokubutsu no.

Yashmak A cocktail made of rye, dry vermouth, Pernod, Angostura bitters and sugar syrup.

yassa au poulet (yah-saw oh poo-let) A Senegalese dish consisting of chicken marinated in lemon juice, onions, black pepper, peanut oil and chiles, briefly grilled and then simmered with the marinade; it is served over rice.

yatakleta kilkil (yah-tah-kla-tah kill-kill) An Ethiopian dish of potatoes, carrots and/or other vegetables sautéed with nitir qibe.

yaupon *See* black drink.

yautia *See* malanga.

yayin (yah-yin) Biblical Hebrew for wine.

yayla çorbasi (yah-yah sore-baw-see) A Turkish soup made from yogurt, stock and rice or pounded grains (e.g., hulled wheat) and flavored with mint or cilantro.

yaytsa; jajtza *See* jajtsa.

ye'abesha gomen (ya-ah-besh-ah goh-man) An Ethiopian dish consisting of any green leafy and slightly bitter vegetable (e.g., spinach or collard greens) simmered and then fried with garlic, onions, ginger and chiles.

yearling *See* lamb.

yearling turkey *See* turkey, yearling.

yeast A microscopic fungus (genus *Saccharomyces,* especially *S. cerevisiae*) that converts its food (carbohydrates) into carbon dioxide and alcohol through a metabolic process known as fermentation; yeast is necessary for making beer, wine, cheese and some breads. *See* brewer's yeast, compressed yeast *and* active dry yeast.

yeast breads A general category of breads that use yeast as a leavening agent; these breads have a wide variety of textures and shapes but all require kneading to develop gluten (e.g., French bread, sourdough bread, croissant and challah). *See* quick breads.

yeast extract A seasoning made from the liquid separated from fresh yeast, reduced and mixed with a vegetable extract.

yeasting back process *See* sour mash process.

yeast-malt sprout extract A food additive used as a flavor enhancer.

yeast mash process *See* sweet mash process.

yeasty A wine-tasting term for a wine, usually a young one still in the cask, that retains fermentation odors; these usu-ally disappear after the wine is racked; in most bottled wines, this odor is deemed a flaw.

yee fu mein (ya foo main) Instant, dehydrated Chinese noodles that are twisted or coiled in a block and packaged with a seasoning packet; also called tourist noodles and picnic noodles.

yegomen kitfo (yoh-goh-man kit-foe) An Ethiopian dish consisting of cheese flavored with nitir qibe and served with greens (spinach, kale or the like) cooked with ginger, garlic, cinnamon and nitir qibe.

Yellow A cheese made in North Carolina from fresh cow's milk and eggs.

Yellow Baby A watermelon variety; the fruit are small and have a golden yellow flesh.

yellow bean sauce A sauce made from salted and preserved yellow soybeans, sometimes flavored with chiles; used in Chinese and Thai cuisines.

yellow belly sunfish *See* redbreast sunfish.

yellow berry *See* cloudberry.

yellow bile *See* humors.

yellow cake A cake made from a batter containing egg yolks.

yellow-eyed pea The seed of a member of the pea family native to China; it is small and beige with a yellow circular eye on the inside curved edge; used in American southern cuisine. *See* black-eyed pea.

yellowfin flounder *See* flounder.

yellowfin grouper A variety of Atlantic grouper.

yellow Finn potato *See* Finnish yellow potato.

yellowfin tuna A variety of tuna found in the Pacific Ocean from Chile to California; it has a yellowish skin, an ivory-pink flesh and a weight of 30–150 lb. (13.5–68 kg); often used for canning.

yellow granadilla A variety of passion fruit grown in the Caribbean region; it has a yellow skin and an ovoid shape; also known as water lemon.

yellow ligament *See* backstrap.

yellowmouth grouper A variety of Atlantic grouper.

yellow no. 5 *See* coloring agent.

yellow onion *See* onion.

yellow perch A fish found in North American lakes and streams; it has a dark-banded golden yellow skin that becomes white on the belly, an average market weight of 4–12 oz. (110–340 g) and a lean, white flesh with a firm texture and mild flavor; also known as coon perch, lake perch, ringed perch and striped perch.

yellow pippin apple *See* Newton pippin apple.

yellow plum *See* plum, wild.

yellow prussiate of soda A food additive used as an anti-caking agent, especially in table salt and bakery mixes.

yellow rice *See* arroz marillo.

yellow rice wine *See* shaohsing.

yellow roast *See* roast, yellow.

yellow squash *See* crookneck squash.

Y
Z

yellowtail A game fish related to the pompano and found in the Pacific Ocean; it weighs up to 100 lb. (45 kg) and has a distinctive yellow tail fin, a firm flesh that whitens when cooked and a rich flavor.

yellowtail flounder A member of the flounder family found in the Atlantic Ocean from the mid-Atlantic states to Canada; it has a grayish-olive to reddish-brown skin on top with rust-colored spots, a yellow tail fin, a very lean, pearly white flesh, a mild flavor and an average market weight of 1 lb. (450 g); also known as rusty dab.

yellowtail rockfish A member of the rockfish family found in the Pacific Ocean from California to Vancouver; it has a grayish-brown skin streaked with dark brown and green, a distinctive yellow tail fin, an average market length of 26 in. (65 cm) and a firm, white flesh with a mild flavor.

yellowtail snapper A fish found in the Atlantic Ocean from Florida to Brazil; it has a bright yellow horizontal stripe, a finely flaked, white flesh with a sweet flavor and an average market weight of 1.5 lb. (680 kg).

yemissis (yeh-meh-sis) Greek for stuffing.

yemista (yeh-meh-stah) A Greek dish consisting of vegetables stuffed with minced meat and rice and steamed or baked.

yemistó (yeh-mes-toh) A Greek preparation method in which fish are stuffed.

yen (he-an) Thai for cold.

yengeç (yah-jess) Turkish for crab.

yenji (ien-gee) A Chinese cooking method in which a marinated ingredient is wrapped in layers of greaseproof paper and roasted in a pot of preheated salt.

yerba buena (yehr-bah bwan-nah) Spanish for mint.

yerba maté (yehr-bah MAH-ta) *See* maté.

Yergacheffe Arabica coffee beans grown in Ethiopia; the beverage is medium bodied and has a sweet flavor and aroma.

yermades (yur-mah-des) A particularly flavorful peach grown in Greece.

yerra (YEH-reh) *See* jheengari.

yeshimbra asa (yah-shimm-bra ah-saw) An Ethiopian dish consisting of a chickpea flour dough flavored with onions and berberé; it is shaped to resemble fish and fried.

yete (yah-tah) A dried smoked mollusk used as a flavoring in West African (especially Senegalese) cuisine.

yew tree The bright red arils surrounding this tree's (genus *Taxus*) seeds have a mild, slightly sweet flavor.

yezi (yeh-dze) Chinese for coconut.

yield 1. The total amount of a food item created or remaining after trimming or fabrication; the edible portion of the as-purchased unit. 2. The total amount of a product made from a specific recipe.

yield factor; yield percentage The ratio of the edible portion to the amount purchased.

yield grades *See* USDA yield grades.

yield test An analysis conducted during the butchering and fabrication of meat, fish or poultry or during the cleaning and preparation of produce to determine the usable amount of the product (the yield) remaining after preparation.

yi fu; efu; yi (he foo; a-foo; he) Yellow egg noodles used in Chinese soups and stir-fried dishes.

yi fu mian (hee foo me-ahn) Puffy Chinese yi fu noodles sold already fried, then dried.

yiner (yin-er) Chinese for white fungus.

ying-táo (hing-tah-oh) Chinese for cherries.

yin liao (hin lee-ah-oh) Chinese for beverage.

ylang-ylang (E-lahn-E-lahn) A large tree native to the Philippines (*Cananga odorata*); the oil made from its flowers has a strong, flowerlike aroma and bitter flavor and is used in soft drinks, ice cream, confectionery and baked goods.

Yoder hickory A variety of American hickory; the nuts are flavorful and easily cracked.

yoe A Tibetan snack of toasted barley, wheat kernels, corn, millet or soybeans.

yoghurt (YOGH-oort) Norwegian for yogurt.

yogur (YOA-goor) Spanish for yogurt.

yogurt; yoghurt (YOH-gert) A thick, tart, custardlike fermented dairy product made from cow's milk to which bacteria cultures (e.g., *Streptococcus thermophilus, Thermobacterium bulgaricum* and *T. jogurt*) have been added; it has the same percentage of milkfat as the milk from which it is made.

yogurt, flavored Yogurt with a sweetener and natural and/or artificial flavorings (usually fruit) added; low-fat and nonfat products are available.

yogurt, frozen A soft frozen confection made from a sweetened yogurt base and various natural and/or artificial flavorings; low-fat and nonfat products are available.

yogurt, low-fat Yogurt made from low-fat milk.

yogurt, nonfat Yogurt made from nonfat or skim milk.

yogurt, plain Yogurt without any flavoring ingredients added; low-fat and nonfat products are available.

yogurt, Swiss-style flavored Flavored yogurt with the fruit flavorings blended into the product.

yogurt cheese A soft cheese made in Mediterranean countries from milk and the bacteria used for yogurt; it has a white, creamy interior and a sharp, tart flavor.

yogurt tatlisi (yoh-goort tah-tlee-see) Turkish yogurt cake soaked in a sugar syrup and garnished with chopped pistachios.

yoguruto (YAH-goo-roo-toh) Japanese for yogurt.

yoich (yoy'ch) Yiddish for stock.

yokan (yoh-kahn) A Japanese sweet of agar gelatin with sweetened bean paste and other flavorings.

yolk The yellow portion of the egg; it contains all of the egg's fat and most of its calories, minerals, vitamins (except riboflavin) and lecithin.

yookgae jang (yook-he jong) A Korean soup of boiled, shredded beef with hot seasonings.

York A soft English cheese made from whole cow's milk; it has a salty, fresh flavor and should be eaten fresh.

York ham An English ham from Yorkshire pigs; it is cured with salt, saltpeter and brown sugar for at least 3 weeks before being smoked and then cooked.

York Imperial apple A medium to large apple with yellow-streaked red skin, off-white, moderately firm flesh and a tartly sweet flavor; excellent for cooking.

Yorkshire liqueur *See* Bronte.

Yorkshire pudding A British bread made of popover batter (eggs, flour and milk) baked in hot beef drippings; the finished product is puffy, crisp, hollow and golden brown and is traditionally served with roast beef.

Yorkshire Stilton *See* Cotherstone.

Yorsh A cocktail made of beer and vodka; served in a beer mug.

yóu (yo-who) Chinese for oil.

young; youthful A wine-tasting term for a wine that has not yet reached its peak and is still improving.

youngberry A hybrid blackberry with a dark red color and a sweet, juicy flesh.

young dough Underfermented yeast dough.

young tobacco Tobacco that has been insufficiently cured, fermented and aged; also known as green tobacco.

youth hostel *See* hostel.

you tiau (yau ja) Long, doughnutlike, deep-fried Chinese pastries served with congee and other soups or as a snack.

youvarlakia (yo-oo-vahr-law-kee-ah) A Greek dish of egg–lemon soup with ground meat and rice dumplings.

yo-yo effect; yo-yo dieting *See* ratchet effect.

ysa (eas-ah) Icelandic for fresh haddock.

yú (yoo) Chinese for fish.

yuan shai chi (ee-oo-ahn sha-ee tchee) A Chinese sauce made from whole fermented soybeans and wheat flour; used as a flavoring.

yuba A film made from dehydrated soybean milk and used in Japanese cuisine; also known as bean curd sheets.

yubileyneya osobaya (u-be-lay-nay-ya ahs-sah-bay-ya) A Russian vodka flavored with brandy, honey and other ingredients.

yuca (jhew-kah) Spanish for cassava root or tapioca; a staple throughout South and Central America and the Caribbean region.

yuca con mojo (jhew-kah kohn moh-hoh) A Cuban dish of boiled yuca with a sauce of minced fried garlic.

yue bing (ee-who a-bing) Chinese for moon cakes and used to describe a short pastry with a decorative design enclosing various sweet fillings made of bean paste, nuts or fruits surrounding a piece of salted duck egg yolk.

yufka (yoof-kah) Very thin, Turkish pastry dough; similar to phyllo dough and used to make sweet and savory pastries.

yu jao (yu jiao) Chinese stuffed balls or ovals of deep-fried, mashed, steamed taro filled with pork, shrimp and mushrooms.

yukhnee; yakhni (yuh'k-h'nee) A Middle Eastern lamb and potato stew flavored with tomatoes, onions and pepper.

Yukon gold potato *See* white potato, long.

Yukon Jack The proprietary name of a semisweet liqueur made from herbs, orange peels and Canadian whisky.

yule log English for Bûche de Noël.

yum (yum) Thai for a salad or composed dish.

yumi (you-me) Chinese for corn.

yung dau fu (ee-ung da-oh foo) A Chinese dim sum consisting of fresh tofu stuffed with shrimp.

yung nge (ee-ung ngha) Chinese for cloud ear mushroom.

Yungueño (hun-gha-nyo) A cocktail made of Pisco, orange juice and confectioners' sugar served over cracked ice.

Yunnan (YOO-nahn) 1. A black tea grown in China's Yunnan province; the beverage has a deep golden color with a sweet delicate flavor and aroma. 2. A rustic cheese made in China's Yunnan province from goat's milk.

yunomi (oo-noh-me) A thick-walled, handleless Japanese cup used for drinking tea, especially in sushi bars.

yu to (yue to) A Chinese delicacy consisting of a dried, cleaned and fried fish maw.

yuyo (iyu-iyo) A Spanish sauce flavored with herbs or greens such as spinach.

yuzu (yoo-zoo) A small citrus fruit (*Citrus aurantium*) native to Tibet and China; it has a thick, bumpy, yellowish-green rind, pale yellowish-green flesh with a slightly acidic flavor and many seeds.

Z

zaatar; zatar (ZAH-tahr) A Middle Eastern flavoring blend consisting of dried thyme, dried wild marjoram (oregano), sumac and toasted sesame seeds; it can be mixed with oil or left dry.

zabaglione (zah-bahl-YOH-nay) An Italian foamy dessert custard made by whipping together egg yolks, sugar and wine (usually Marsala). *See* sabayon.

zabaglione pot (zah-bahl-YOH-nay) A round-bottomed unlined copper pot with a long handle; designed to allow easy whisking while being held over simmering water; used to make zabaglione.

zabaglione pot

zabibu (zah-bee-boo) Swahili for grapes.

zabibu kavu (zah-bee-boo kah-voo) Swahili for raisin.

zacierka (zah-chy-ehr-kah) A very dry Polish dough grated into soups as a garnish.

zafferano (dzahf-feh-RAA-noa) Italian for saffron.

zaffran (ZAH-frohn) *See* kesar.

zahra (zah-ha-rah) Arabic for cauliflower.

zaitoon (zah-ee-toon) Hindi for olive.

zakuski (zah-KOOS-kee) Russian for hors d'oeuvre.

zaletti (zah-LET-tea) Buttery Italian cornmeal cookies flavored with raisins, lemon zest and vanilla.

zalivnoe (zah-leev-noe-e) A Russian dish consisting of a jelly made from fish, meat, poultry, game or eggs, sometimes with aspic added; it is garnished with vegetables.

Zambian Arabica coffee beans grown in Zambia; the beverage is rich and pleasantly acidic, with a medium to full body.

zambo chile A medium-length, broad, red Central American chile with a moderately hot flavor; it is usually sold dried.

Zamorano (zah-moh-RAH-noh) A hard Spanish cheese made from ewe's milk; it has a distinctive flavor.

zampa (tzam-pah) Italian for the leg of an animal.

zampone di Modena (dzahm-POH-nay day moh-DE-nah) An Italian sausage made from pork rind and meat, seasoned with nutmeg, cloves and pepper and stuffed into a hog's foreleg complete with the trotter.

zanahorias (thah-nah-OA-ryahs) Spanish for carrots.

Zander (zahn-der) German for pike perch.

Zante grape A small purple grape used as a garnish or dried (and known as a currant).

zaofan (sa-oh-phan) Chinese for breakfast.

zaozi (dzao-dze) Chinese for dates.

zapallo (zah-PAHL-loh) *See* calabaza.

zapekanka (zah-pek-ank-ka) A Russian dish consisting of potatoes mashed with milk, eggs and butter, layered in a casserole with fried onions, topped with butter or sour cream, baked and served with a mushroom sauce.

zarame (zah-RAH-may) Japanese for granulated sugar.

zardalu (zard-aa-lu) Hindi for apricot.

zaru (ZAH-roo) A Japanese woven tray, strainer or colander.

zarzamora (thaht-thah-MOA-rahss) Spanish for blackberry or dewberry.

zavtrak (zahv-trak) Russian for breakfast.

zayatz (zah-yahtz) Russian for rabbit.

zayt (zaayt) Arabic for oil.

zaytun (zaay-toon) A Middle Eastern meza or flavoring consisting of olives pickled in vinegar and salt or stored in olive oil flavored with lemon, salt, chiles and carob leaves.

zbeeb (zeh-beeb) Arabic for raisins.

zebrine (za-bree-na) A variety of eggplant grown in France; it has violet and white stripes.

Zeeland oysters A variety of oysters found off Holland's Zeeland province.

zein A food additive derived from corn proteins and used as a coating and glaze for confections and baked goods.

zelbo gomen (tza-lbow goh-man) An Ethiopian dish consisting of kale simmered with garlic, ginger and chiles.

zelen fasul (za-lan fah-sool) Bulgarian for string bean.

zeleniy luk (zah-lah-nee look) Russian for shallot.

zeli (zha-le) Czech for cabbage.

Zeller Schwarze Katze (zeller schwahts kat-za) A wine from the lower Moselle River Valley of Germany; the label has a black cat on a barrel.

zenmai (zehn-mah-ee) Japanese for bracken.

zenryu-fu (zan-roo-yoo-foo) A Chinese product made from wheat gluten; it has a bland flavor and a rubbery texture.

zènzero (DZEHN-dzeh-roa) Italian for ginger.

zephyr A sweet or savory dish served hot or cold and characterized by a light and frothy consistency; used to describe quenelles, mousses and the like.

zerde (zar-dah) An Azerbaijani pudding made with milk, sugar and butter, flavored with rosewater and saffron and dusted with cinnamon.

zerno (zar-noh) Russian for wheat.

zero A food-labeling term approved by the U.S. Food and Drug Administration (FDA) to describe a food containing no or only physiologically inconsequential amounts of fat, saturated fat, cholesterol, sodium, sugars or calories.

zest *v.* To remove strips of rind from a citrus fruit. *n.* The colored, outermost layer of citrus rind; used for flavoring creams, custards and baked goods; it can be candied and used as a confection or decoration. *See* albedo.

zeste (zehst) French for zest.

zester A tool used to cut slivers of zest from citrus; its short, flat blade has five small holes with sharp edges.

zester

zhan mi fen (han me fan) A Chinese rice flour made from long-grain rice.

zharenniy (sha-rah-nee-ee) Russian for fried.

zharit' (sha-ritt) Russian for to roast.

zhau gu (shau goo) Chinese for shiitake.

zhenzi (shan-zee) Chinese for hazelnuts.

zhi (she) Chinese for sauce.

zhi ma jiang (she ma gee-hang) A Chinese sesame seed paste.

zhir (shir) Russian for fat.

zhú (dzoo) Chinese for pork.

zhuozi (shoo-oh-zee) Chinese for table.

Zibarten (tzee-bahr-tan) German for schnapps distilled from plums of the same name.

Ziege (zee-gah) German for goat.

Ziegelkäse (zee-gehl-kaiz) An Austrian cheese made from whole cow's milk with as much as 15% cream added.

Ziegenkäse (zee-gan-kaiz) Austrian and German for goat's milk cheese.

Ziger (zee-ga) A German whey cheese made from cow's milk; also known as Schottenziger.

zigni (zeeg-nee) Ethiopian for ground beef stew.

Zimbabwean Arabica coffee beans grown in Zimbabwe; the beverage is rich, pungent and well balanced and has a spicy aftertaste.

Zimt (tsimt) German for cinnamon.

Zimtsterne (zeemt-star-nay) German Christmas cookies known as cinnamon stars and made from finely ground almonds and cinnamon-flavored meringue; before baking, they are spread with a thin meringue icing flavored with lemon juice or Kirsch and often sprinkled with colored sugar crystals.

zinc A trace mineral principally used as an enzyme and hormone component and to assist protein development, building of genetic materials, functioning of the immune system and taste perception; significant sources include meat, liver, poultry, eggs, fish and shellfish.

Zinfandel (ZIHN-fuhn-dehl) 1. A red wine grape widely planted in California. 2. A red wine made from this grape; it has an easily recognizable character often described as berrylike or spicy and can range from light and fruity to medium bodied, with more character and structure, to a ripe, rich, tannic, intensely flavored wine. *See* White Zinfandel.

zingara, à la (zihn-GAH-rah, ah lah) French for gypsy style and used to describe dishes that are garnished with chopped ham, tongue, mushrooms and truffles combined with tomato sauce, tarragon and sometimes Madeira; usually served with meat, poultry and eggs.

zingerone A food additive used as a flavoring agent.

zinjibil (zeen-gee-bill) Ethiopian for ginger.

zinne di monara (ZEE-neh dee MOH-nah-rah) Italian for nun's tits and used to describe small round cakes topped with icing and a candied or maraschino cherry.

zip code wines American slang for inexpensive French wines (vin de table); they are blended wines with no specific appellation d'origine; the producer's address is identified only by a number that is the equivalent of a French zip code.

ziste (zest) French for the acrid white pith found between the flesh and peel of citrus fruit.

zite (zay-tah) Arabic for oil.

zite il zitoon (zay-tah el zah-toon) Arabic for olive oil.

ziti (TSEET-tee) Italian for bridegrooms and used to describe large, slightly curved tubes of pasta, similar to rigatoni.

zitoni (TSEET-toh-neh) Large, grooved ziti.

zitoon (zah-toon) Arabic for olives.

Zitronat-Zitrone (zee-TROA-nat-zee-TROA-nee) German for citron.

Zitrone (tsi-TROA-ne) German for lemon.

ziti

zogghiu (ZOH-g'yoo) A Sicilian pesto made with parsley and mint.

Zombie A cocktail made of dark and light rum, curaçao, lemon juice, orange juice, pineapple juice, papaya or guava juice, orgeat syrup, grenadine and Pernod; served in a Collins glass with a pineapple chunk and mint sprig.

Zomma (zoh-mah) A Turkish pasta filata cheese; it has at least a 30% milkfat content.

zoni (zoe-nee) A Japanese New Year's soup consisting of rice cakes, kamaboko, chicken and vegetables in a dashi broth garnished with yuzu peel. *See* ozoni.

zonked Slang for intoxicated.

zouave, sauce (zwhav) A French compound sauce made from a demi-glaze mixed with tomato purée, flavored with mustard and garlic and garnished with tarragon.

zrazy (z'rah-zyah) A Polish and Russian dish consisting of meat or fish stuffed with bread crumbs or kasha, fried onions, mushrooms and bacon, flavored with herbs, covered with stock and baked; the stock is thickened with sour cream.

Zubrowka; Zubrovka (zoo-broh-fkah) A Polish vodka flavored with European buffalo grass; it has a slight yellow color and an aromatic bouquet.

zucca (ZOO-ka) 1. Italian for pumpkin. 2. Italian for all manner of squashes and gourds.

zucchero (TSOOK-kay-roh) Italian for sugar.

zucchero candito (TSOOK-kay-roh kan-dee-toh) Italian for candy.

zucchini (zoo-KEE-nee) A moderately long, cylindrical summer squash with smooth, dark green skin and a slightly bumpy surface, a creamy white-green flesh and a mild flavor; also known as courgette (especially in Europe).

zucchini blossoms The long, pale yellow blossoms of the zucchini; they are sometimes battered and fried.

zucchini corer A utensil with a long, pointed, trough-shaped blade that is inserted into the zucchini and rotated, thus removing the core and leaving a space for stuffing.

zuccotto (zoo-KOHT-oh) A dome-shaped Italian dessert made by lining a bowl with liquor-soaked ladyfingers or sponge cake; it is then filled with sweetened whipped cream, chopped chocolate and toasted hazelnuts and topped with additional cake slices; it is chilled, then unmolded and dusted with cocoa powder and confectioners' sugar for service.

Zücher Geschnetzeltes (zoo-kerr ghash-na-tza-less) A Swiss dish known as Zurich diced veal; it consists of onions, mushrooms and veal cooked in a creamy wine sauce; it is usually accompanied by rösti.

Zucker (TSUK-kerr) German for sugar.

Zugor Kirschtorte See Kirschtorte.

zuke (ZOO-keh) Japanese for pickled foods.

zumo (zoo-moe) Spanish for juice.

Zunge (TSUN-ger) German for tongue.

Zungenwurst (ZUHNG-uhn-voorst) A German blood sausage containing chunks of pickled tongue.

zunyu (tzun-you) Chinese for trout.

zuóhiào (soo-noh-yah-oh) Chinese for herbs.

zuóliào (tzoo-lee-ah-oh) Chinese for spices.

zuppa (ZOO-pah) Italian for soup.

zuppa Inglese (ZOO-pah in-GLAY-zay) Italian for English soup and used to describe a refrigerated dessert similar to English trifle; it is made by layering rum-soaked slices of sponge cake in a deep bowl with custard, whipped cream, candied fruit and nuts.

zuppa romana (ZOO-pah roh-mah-nah) An Italian dessert of sponge cake layered with vanilla cream and candied and preserved fruit.

Zurich leckerli (LEH-kehr-lee) See leckerle.

zuring (zoo-ring) Dutch for sorrel.

zushi (zhoo-she) The seasoned rice used for sushi; also known as shari. See gohan and tane.

zuurkool (ZEWR-kohl) Dutch for sauerkraut.

zwezerik (zua-za-rick) Dutch for sweetbreads.

Zwieback (ZWY-bak) German for twice-baked and used to describe bread that is baked, sliced and returned to the oven and baked until dry and crisp. See rusk.

Zwiebel (TSVEE-bel) German for onion.

zymase (zay-meis) The enzyme secreted by yeasts that promotes fermentation by breaking down glucose and other carbohydrates into alcohol and carbon dioxide.

zymurgy (ZI-mahr-jee) The art and science of fermentation, especially as applied to the production of beer and wine.

zythos; zitos (DZEE-tohs) Greek for beer.

Zytnia (zi-tee-ñyah) A Polish vodka.

Appendices

COMMON EQUIVALENTS IN THE U.S SYSTEM

⅛ teaspoon	=	dash
½ teaspoon	=	30 drops
1 teaspoon	=	⅓ tablespoon or 60 drops
3 teaspoons	=	1 tablespoon or ½ fluid ounce
½ tablespoon	=	1½ teaspoons
1 tablespoon	=	3 teaspoons or ½ fluid ounce
2 tablespoons	=	1 fluid ounce
3 tablespoons	=	1½ fluid ounces or 1 jigger
4 tablespoons	=	¼ cup or 2 fluid ounces
5⅓ tablespoons	=	⅓ cup or 5 tablespoons + 1 teaspoon
8 tablespoons	=	½ cup or 4 fluid ounces
10⅔ tablespoons	=	⅔ cup or 10 tablespoons + 2 teaspoons
12 tablespoons	=	¾ cup or 6 fluid ounces
16 tablespoons	=	1 cup or 8 fluid ounces or ½ pint
⅛ cup	=	2 tablespoons or 1 fluid ounce
¼ cup	=	4 tablespoons or 2 fluid ounces
⅓ cup	=	5 tablespoons + 1 teaspoon
⅜ cup	=	¼ cup + 2 tablespoons
½ cup	=	8 tablespoons or 4 fluid ounces or 1 gill
⅝ cup	=	½ cup + 2 tablespoons
¾ cup	=	12 tablespoons or 6 fluid ounces
⅞ cup	=	¾ cup + 2 tablespoons
1 cup	=	16 tablespoons or ½ pint or 8 fluid ounces
2 cups	=	1 pint or 16 fluid ounces
1 pint	=	2 cups or 16 fluid ounces
1 quart	=	2 pints or 4 cups or 32 fluid ounces
1 gallon	=	4 quarts or 8 pints or 16 cups or 128 fluid ounces
2 gallons	=	1 peck
4 pecks	=	1 bushel

PRECISE METRIC EQUIVALENTS

VOLUME:			
	¼ teaspoon	=	1.23 milliliters
	½ teaspoon	=	2.46 milliliters
	¾ teaspoon	=	3.7 milliliters
	1 teaspoon	=	4.93 milliliters
	1¼ teaspoons	=	6.16 milliliters
	1½ teaspoons	=	7.39 milliliters
	1¾ teaspoons	=	8.63 milliliters
	2 teaspoons	=	9.86 milliliters
	1 tablespoon	=	14.79 milliliters
	1 fluid ounce	=	29.57 milliliters
	2 tablespoons	=	29.57 milliliters
	¼ cup	=	59.15 milliliters
	½ cup	=	118.3 milliliters
	1 cup	=	236.59 milliliters
	2 cups *or* 1 pint	=	473.18 milliliters
	3 cups	=	709.77 milliliters
	4 cups *or* 1 quart	=	946.36 milliliters
	4 quarts *or* 1 gallon	=	3.785 liters
WEIGHT:	1 ounce	=	28.35 grams
	8 ounces *or* ½ pound	=	226.8 grams
	16 ounces *or* 1 pound	=	453.6 grams
	2 pounds	=	910 grams
	2 pounds + 3 ounces	=	1 kilogram *or* 1000 grams

TEMPERATURE EQUIVALENTS

FAHRENHEIT	CELSIUS
32° F	0°C (water freezes)
40°	4.4°
50°	10°
60°	15.6°
70°	21.1°
80°	26.7°
90°	32.2°
100°	37.8°
110°	43.3°
120°	48.9°
130°	54.4°
140°	60°
150°	65.6°
160°	71.1°
170°	76.7°
180°	82.2°
190°	87.8°
200°	93.3°
212°	100°(water boils)
250°	121°
300°	149°
350°	177°
400°	205°
450°	233°
500°	260°

CONVERTING TO METRIC

WHEN THIS IS KNOWN	MULTIPLY IT BY	TO GET
teaspoons	4.93	milliliters
tablespoons	14.79	milliliters
fluid ounces	29.57	milliliters
cups	236.59	milliliters
cups	0.236	liters
pints	473.18	milliliters
pints	0.473	liters
quarts	946.36	milliliters
quarts	0.946	liters
gallons	3.785	liters
ounces	28.35	grams
pounds	0.454	kilograms
inches	2.54	centimeters
Fahrenheit	subtract 32 multiply by 5 divide by 9	Celsius (centigrade)

CONVERTING FROM METRIC

WHEN THIS IS KNOWN	DIVIDE IT BY	TO GET
milliliters	4.93	teaspoons
milliliters	14.79	tablespoons
milliliters	29.57	fluid ounces
milliliters	236.59	cups
liters	0.236	cups
milliliters	473.18	pints
liters	0.473	pints
milliliters	946.36	quarts
liters	0.946	quarts
liters	3.785	gallons
grams	28.35	ounces
kilograms	0.454	pounds
centimeters	2.54	inches
Celsius (centigrade)	multiply by 9 divide by 5 add 32	Fahrenheit

STAGES OF COOKED SUGAR

STAGE	TEMPERATURE	WHEN A SMALL AMOUNT OF SUGAR SYRUP IS DROPPED INTO ICE WATER IT:
Thread	230° to 234° F (110° to 112° C)	Spins a soft 2-inch thread
Soft ball	234° to 240° F (112° to 116° C)	Forms a soft, flat ball
Firm ball	244° to 248° F (118° to 120° C)	Forms a firm but pliable ball
Hard ball	250° to 265° F (121° to 129° C)	Forms a hard, compact ball
Soft crack	270° to 290° F (132° to 143° C)	Separates into hard but not brittle threads
Hard crack	300° to 310° F (149° to 154° C)	Forms hard, brittle threads
Caramel	320° to 338° F (160° to 170° C)	Forms hard, brittle threads and the liquid turns brown

ROUNDED MEASURES FOR QUICK REFERENCE

1 oz.		= 30 g
4 oz.		= 120 g
8 oz.		= 125 g
16 oz.	= 1 lb.	= 450 g
32 oz.	= 2 lb.	= 900 g
36 oz.	= 2¼ lb.	= 1000 g (1 kg)
1/4 tsp.	= 1/24 oz.	= 1 ml
1/2 tsp.	= 1/12 oz.	= 2 ml
1 tsp.	= 1/6 oz.	= 5 ml
1 Tbsp.	= 1/2 oz.	= 15 ml
1 c.	= 8 oz.	= 250 ml
2 c. (1 pt.)	= 16 oz.	= 500 ml
4 c. (1 qt.)	= 32 oz.	= 1 liter
4 qt. (1 gallon)	= 128 oz.	= 3.75 liter
32°F	= 0°C	
122°F	= 50°C	
212°F	= 100°C	

LADLE SIZES

SIZE	PORTION OF A CUP	NUMBER PER QUART	NUMBER PER LITER
1 oz.	1/8	32	34
2 oz.	1/4	16	17
2⅔ oz.	1/3	12	13
4 oz.	1/2	8	8.6
6 oz.	3/4	5⅓	5.7

CANNED GOOD SIZES

SIZE	NUMBER OF CANS PER CASE	AVERAGE WEIGHT	AVERAGE NUMBER OF CUPS PER CAN
No. 1/2	8	8 oz.	1
No. 1 tall (also known as 303)	2 or 4 dozen	16 oz.	2
No. 2	2 dozen	20 oz.	2½
No. 2½	2 dozen	28 oz.	3½
No. 3	2 dozen	33 oz.	4
No. 3 cylinder	1 dozen	46 oz.	5⅔
No. 5	1 dozen	3 lb. 8 oz.	5½
No. 10	6	6 lb. 10 oz.	13

CONVERSION GUIDELINES

1 gallon	=	4 qt.
		8 pt.
		16 c. (8 oz.)
		128 fl. oz.
1 fifth bottle	=	Approximately 1½ pt. or exactly 26.5 fl. oz.
1 measuring cup	=	8 fl. oz. (a coffee cup is generally 6 fl. oz.)
1 large egg white	=	1 oz. (average)
1 lemon	=	1–1¼ fl. oz. of juice
1 orange	=	3–3½ fl. oz. of juice

OVEN TEMPERATURES

°F	°C	GAS NUMBER	OVEN HEAT
225°F	110°C	1/4	Very cool
250°F	130°C	1/2	Very cool
275°F	140°C	1	Cool
300°F	150°C	2	Slow
325°F	170°C	3	Moderately slow
350°F	180°C	4	Moderate
375°F	190°C	5	Moderately hot
400°F	200°C	6	Moderately hot
425°F	220°C	7	Hot
450°F	230°C	8	Hot
475°F	245°C	9	Very hot
500°F	260°C	10	Very hot

OVERSIZED WINE BOTTLES

NAME	NUMBER OF 750-ml BOTTLES	NUMBER OF LITERS	NUMBER OF FLUID OUNCES
Magnum	2	1.5	50.7
Double magnum	4	3.0	101.4
Jeroboam	4	3.0	101.4
Rehoboam (champagne)	6	4.5	156
Methuselah (champagne)	8	6.0	204.8
Imperial	8	6.0	204.8
Salmanazar	12	9.0	307.2
Balthazar	16	12.0	416
Nebuchadnezzar	20	15.0	570

CIGAR SIZES

CIGAR	RING[a]	LENGTH IN INCHES
Ascot	30–36	3–5
Belicoso	48	6
Belicoso, petite	40	5
Belvedere	30–36	3–5
Churchill	47–48	6–8
Corona	42	5½
Corona, double	49–52	7½–8
Corona, petite	40–42	4½–5
Corona extra; corona royale	44–46	5¾
Corona grandes	44–46	6–6½
Demitasse	30–36	3-5
Director	52–64	8–10
Gigante	52–64	8–10
Immensa	52–64	8–10
Lancero	36	7½
Lonsdale	42	6–7
Panatela	34–39	6–6½
Panatela, long	36	7½
Perfecto	Varies[b]	5½
Presidente	52–64	8–10
Pyramid	52/42[c]	6–7
Robusto	50	4½
Rothschild	50	4½

[a]A ring is the unit for measuring the diameter of a cigar; 1 ring equals 1/4 in. (e.g., a 32-ring cigar has a 1/2 -in. diameter).

[b]The perfecto has a pointed head and end and bulge in the center.

[c]A pyramid cigar has a conical shape with a 52-ring tip tapering to a 42-ring head.

ENGLISH	CHINESE	HINDI	JAPAN	PORTUG	RUSSIAN	FRENCH	GERMAN	ITALIAN	NORWGN	SPANISH	SWAHILI
alcohol	jiŭjīng	sharaab	arukoru	álcool	spirt	álcool	Alkohol	alcool	alkohol	alcohol	1. pombe ya dawa 2. spititi
almond		badaam		amêndoa	mindal'nyj	amande	Mandel	mandorla	mandel	almendra	lozi
apple	píngguŏ	séb	ringo	maçã	1. yabloko 2. jablok	pomme	Apfel	mela	eple	manzana	tufaa
apricot	xīngzi	zardalu	anzu	damasco	abrikos	abricot	Aprikose	albicocca	aprikots	albaricoque	mishmishi
asparagus	lóngxūcài	shataavar	asparagus	aspargo	sparzha	asperges	Spargel	asparago	asparges	espárrago	asparagus
bacon	xiánròu		bekon	toicinho	shpik	lard	Speck	pancetta	bacon	tocino	nyama ya nguruwe
bakery	miànbāofáng	naan-bae	pan-ya	1. padaria 2. confeitaria	1. sdoba 2. pechenoe	boulangerie	Bäckerei	panetteria	bakeri	panadería	tanuri
banana	xiāngjiāo	kela	banana	banana	banan	banane	Banane	banane	banan	1. plátano 2. banana	ndizi
beans	biān dòu		mame	feijão	1. fasol 2. bobi	haricots	Bohnen	fagioli	bonner	frijoles	kunde
beef steak	niúpái		bifuteki	steak da carne	bifstek	bifteck	Beef steak	bistecca	biff	bistec	stek
beef	niúròu	gaaykaa gosht	gyuniku	1. carne 2. vaca	govyadina	boeuf	Rindfleisch	1. manzo 2. bue	oksekjøtt	carne de res	nyama ya ng'ombe
beer	1. píjiŭ 2. mài chiu	biyar	biru	cerveja	pivo	bière	Bier	birra	øl	cerveza	pombe
beverage	yĭn liào	1. paani (water) 2. daru (alcoholic)	nomimono	bebida	napitok	boisson	Getränk	bevanda	drikkevarer	bebida	kinywaji
boil, (to)	shāo kāishuĭ	ublaa-huaa	nieru	ferver	kipyatit'	bouillir	sieden	bollire	å koke	1. hervir 2. cocer	chemsha
bone	gŭtou	haddee	hone	osso	kost'	os	1. Bein 2. Gräte (fish) 3. Knochen	osso	bein	hueso	mfupa
brandy	báilándì	daru	burande	conhaque	kon'yak	cognac	1. Kognak 2. Branntwein	cognác	konjakk	coñac	brandi
bread	miàn bao	roti	pan	pão	khleb	pain	Brot	pane	brød	pan	mkate
breadcrumbs		roteka tukra	panko	migalhas	1. sukhar' 2. khlebnie kroshki	chapelure	Brotkrume	briciole	brødsmuler	1. migas 2. pan rallado	
breakfast	zăofàn	naashtaa	1. choshoku 2. asagohan	pequeno almoço	zavtrak	petit déjeuner	Frühstück	prima colazione	frokost	desayuno	chakula cha asubuhi
butter	huángyóu	makhan	bata	manteiga	maslo	beurre	Butter	burro	smør	mantequilla	siagi
buttermilk		ghee		1. leitelho 2. soro de leite coalhado	slivki	babeurre	Buttermilch	latticello	kjerne melken	leche cuajada	mitindi
cabbage	bái cài	band gobhee	kyabetsu	couve	kapusta	chou	Kohl	cavolo	kål	col	kebeji

ENGLISH	CHINESE	HINDI	JAPAN	PORTUG	RUSSIAN	FRENCH	GERMAN	ITALIAN	NORWGN	SPANISH	SWAHILI
cafe	kafeiguanr	kafi	kissaten	café	kafé	café	Cafe	caffè	café	café	mkahawa
cake	dàn-gao	kék	keki	bolo	1. keks 2. tort	gâteau	1. Küchen 2. Torte	torta	kake	1. tarta 2. pastel	keki
candy	táng	barfi	kyande	docu	konfeta	confiserie	1. Konfekt 2. Süssigkeit	zucchero candito	1. konfekt 2. sukkertøy	caramelo	peremende
capers				alcaparras	kapartsy	câpres	Kaper	capperi	kapers	alcaparras	
carrot	húluóbò	gaa-jar	ninjin	cenoura	morkov'	carotte	Karotte	carota	gulrøtt	zanahoria	karoti
cauliflower	càihua	phool go-bhee	karifurawa	couve-flor	tsvetnaya kapusta	chou-fleur	Blumenkohl	cavolfiore	blomkål	coliflor	koliflawa
celery	qíncài	selaree	serori	aipo	selderey	céleri	Sellerie	sèdano	selleri	apio	jibini
cheese	nailao	paneer	chizu	queijo	syr	fromage	Käse	formaggio	ost	queso	mpishi
chef	chúshi	khansama	shef	cozinheiro(a)-chefe	shef	chef	Koch	1. cuoco 2. capocuoco	1. kjøkkensjef 2. chef	cocinero	
cherry	ying-táo		sakurambo	cereja	chereshnya	cerise	Kirsche	ciliegia	kirsebær	cereza	
chicken	ji	murghi	1. hiyoko 2. niwatori	galinha	tsypljenok	poulet	Geflügel	pollo	kylling	pollo	kuku
chocolate	qiaokeli	chaclét	chokoreto	chocolate	shokoladnyj	chocolat	Schokolade	cioccolata	sjokolade	chocolate	chakleti
chopsticks	kuàizi		hashi	pauzinhos	palochki-dlya edi	baguettes	Esstäbchen	bastoncini	spisepinner	palillos chinos	
chutney		charni		conserva picante		condiment	Würztunke	salsa piccante		chutney	chatini
cinnamon	guìpí	dahchini		canela	koriza	cannelle	Zimt	cannella	kanel	canela	dalasini
coconut	yezi	narial		coco	kokos	noix de coco	Kokosnuss	noce di cocco	kokosnøtt	nuez de coco	nazi
coffee, with milk	niúnai de kéfei	kahfe dudhke saath		café com leite	kofe s molokom	café au lait	Kaffee mit Milch	caffè latte	kaffe med melk	café con leche	kahawa yenye maziwa
coffee	kéfei	kahfe	kohi	café	kofe	café	Kaffee	caffè	kaffe	café	kahawa
cold	leng	than daa	1. samui 2. hiyashi	frio	kholodnye	froid	kalt	freddo	kaldt	frío	baridi
cook (v)		pakana	ryori suru	cozer	gotovit	cuire	köchen	cucinare	lage mat	a cocinar	kupika
cookies	xiaodianxin		1. bisket-to 2. kukki	bolacha	1. biskviti 2. pechenê	biscuits	Kekse	biscotti	småkaker	galletas	biskuti
corkscrew	kai ruanmùsai de jiuqizi	kaag-pénch	sen-nuki	saca-rolhas	shtopor	tire-bouchon	Korken-zieher	cavatappi	korke-trekker	sacacorcho	kizibuo
corn	yùmi	makaee	tomoro-koshi	milho	kukuruza	mais	Maïs	granturco	maïs	maíz	muhindi
crab	pángxiè	kekada	kani	caranguejo	krab	crabe	Krabbe	granchio	krabbe	1. cangrejo 2. jaiba	kaa

English	Chinese	Hindi	Japanese	Portuguese	Russian	French	German	Italian	Norwegian	Spanish	Swahili
cream	naiyóu	1. kreem 2. malai	kurimu	nata	1. krem 2. slivki	crème	Creme	1. crema 2. panna	krem	1. nata (on boiled milk) 2. crema (whipped)	krimu
cucumber	huánggua	kheera	kyuri	pepino	ogurez	concombre	Gurken	cetriolo	agurk	pepino	tango
curry	gali	jhol	kare	caril	kari	curry	Curry	curry	karri	cari	bizari
date	zaozi	kajur	natsume-yashi no mi	tâmara	finiki	datte	Dattel	dattero	dadler	dátil	tende
dessert	tiánshi	mithai	dezato	sobremesa	dessert	dessert	Nachtisch	dolci	dessert	postre	
dinner	wanfan	raat kaa khaanaa	bansan	jantar	1. obed 2. uzhin	dîner	Abendessen	cena	middag	cena	chakula cha jioni
dry	gan	sookhaa	kawaita	séco	suhoy	sec	trocken	secco	tørr	seco	-kavu
duck	ya	battak	ahiru	pato	utka	canard	Ente	anitra	and	pata	bata
(to) eat	chi	khaanaa	taberu	comer	1. est 2. kushat	manger	essen	mangiare	spise	comer	la kula
egg	dan	andé	tamago	ovo	1. yaizo 2. jajtsa	oeuf	Eier	uovo	egg	huevo	yai
eggplant	qiézi	baingan	nasu	berinjela	baklazhan	aubergine	Aubergine	melanzane	eggplante	berenjena	biringani
fat	féi	mota	shibo	gordo	zhir	graisse	Fett	grasso	feit	grasa	mafuta
fennel	huíxiang	saunf		fennel	ukrop	fenouil	Fenchel	finocchio	fennikel	hinojo	
fig	wuhuuaguo	anjeer	ichijiku	figo	figa	figue	Feige	fico	fiken	higo	tini
fish	yú	machhlee	sakana	peixe	rybá	poisson	Fisch	pesce	fisk	pescado	samaki
flour	miànfen	maida	ko	farinha	muka	farine	Mehl	farina	mel	harina	unga
food	fàn	khaanaa	1. tabemono 2. shokuryo 3. ryori	comida	eda	nourriture	Speise	cibo	mat	comida	chakula
fork	chazi	kanta	foku	garfo	vilka	fourchette	Gabel	forchetta	gaffel	tenedor	uma
fresh	xin xiande	taza	shinsen na	fresco	svezhiy	frais	frisch	fresco	frisk	fresca	mbichi
fried	chao	1. talna (deep-fried) 2. bhona	agemono	fritada	zharenniy	frit	fritiert	fritto	stekt	frito	kukaanga
fruit	shuiguo	phal	kudamono	fruta	frukt	fruit	1. Frucht 2. Obst	frutta	frukt	fruta	matunda
garlic	suàn	lassam	nin'niku	alho	chesnok	ail	Knoblauch	aglio	hvitløk	ajo	vitunguu saumu
ginger	jiang	1. adrak 2. sonth	shoga	gengibre	imbir	gingembre	Ingwer	zènzero	ingefær	jengibre	tangawizi
goat	shanyáng	1. chagal 2. bakara	yagi	cabra	kozel	chèvre	Ziege	capra	geit	cabrito (baby)	nyama ya mbuzi
goose	é		gacho	ganso	gus	oie	Gans	oca	gås	1. oca 2. ganzo	bata wa bukini
grapes	pútáo	angoor	budo	uva	vinograd	raisins	Trauben	uvas	druer	uvas	zabibu

COMMONLY USED INTERNATIONAL TERMS—CONTINUED

ENGLISH	CHINESE	HINDI	JAPAN	PORTUG	RUSSIAN	FRENCH	GERMAN	ITALIAN	NORWGN	SPANISH	SWAHILI
ham	huo tui	suwar ka gosht	hamu	presunto	vetchina	jambon	Schinken	prosciutto	skinke	jamón	
hazelnut	zh'nzi	badaam		avela	lesnoy oreh	noisette	Haselnüsse	nocciola	hasselnøtter	avellana	
herb	zuóliào	bheshaj	kusa	erva	lechebnie	herbe	Kräuter	erba	krydderurter	hierba	mboga za kukolezea chakula
honey	fengmi	madhu	hachimitsu	mel	mede	miel	Honig	miele	honning	miel	asali ya nyuki
hot	rè	garam	atsui	quente	goryachee	chaud	heiss	caldo	varmt	caliente	ya moto
hotel	luguan	hoTel	hoteru	hotel	gostinitza	hôtel	Hotel	albergo	hotell	hotel	hoteli
ice cream	bingqiling		aisu-kur-imu	sorvête	morozhena	1. glace 2. crème glacée	Eis	gelato	iskrem	helado	ayskrimu
ice	bing	baraf	kori	gelo	led	glace	Eis	ghiaccio	is	hielo	barafu
jam	guojiàng	murabbaa	jamu	geléia	varen'em	confiture	1. Konfitüre 2. Marmelade	marmellata	syltetøy	1. confitura 2. mermelada	jamu
juice (n)	shuiguo zhi	ras	1. juse 2. frutsu jus	suco	sok	jus	Saft	succo	saft	1. jugo 2. zumo	maji
kitchen	chúfáng	rasoi	1. daidokoro 2. kitchin	cozinha	kuhnya	cuisine	Küche	cucina	kjøkken	cocina	jikoni
knife	daozi	1. chhooree 2. chakko	naifu	faca	nozh'	couteau	Messer	coltello	kniv	cuchillo	kisu
lamb	deng	1. bher 2. katch	ko-hitsuji	cardeiro	barashek	agneau	Lamm	agnello	lam	cordero	nyama ya kondoo
leek			negi	alho-poró	luk-porei	poireau	Lauch	porro	purrer	puerro	
lemon	ningméng	nimboo	remon	limão	limon	citron	Zitrone	limone	sitron	limón	limau
lettuce	sheng cài	salaad	retasu	alface	salat	laitue	1. Salat 2. Lattich	lattuga	lettuce	lechuga	letas
lime			raimu	limão	limon	citron vert	Limone	limetta	kalk	1. lima 2. limón	1. ndimu 2. limau
liver	gan	kaléje	reba	fígado	pechen'	foie	Leber	fegato (calves)	lever	hígado	maini
lobster	lóngxia	1. jheengari 2. yerra	ise-ebi	lagôstim	omar	homard	Hummer	aragosta	hummer	langosta	kamba mkubwa
lunch	wufan	dopahar kaa khaanaa	chushoku	almoço	poludennik	déjeuner	Mittagessen	colazione	lunsj	almuerzo	chakula cha mchana
mango	mangguo	aam		manga	mango	mangue	Mangobaum	mango	mango	mango	maembe
meat	ròu	maanz	niku	carne	myaso	viande	Fleisch	carne	kjøtt	carne	nyama
melon		kharbuja	meron	melão	dynya	melon	Melone	melone	melon	melón	tikiti

1. orodha ya vyakula 2. menyu	1. menú 2. lista de platos	spisekart	1. lista 2. carta	Speisekarte	carte	menu	ementa	menyu		càidānr	menu
maziwa	leche	melk	latte	Milch	lait	moloko	leite	miruku	doodh	niún ai	milk
	hierbabuena	mynte	mente	Minze	menthe	myato	hortela	hakka	podina	bōhétáng	mint
uyoga	1. seta 2. champiñon	sopp	fungo	1. Champignon 2. Pilze	champignon	gribi	cogumelo	mashshurum	khumee	1. dong gu 2. mogu	mushroom
hardalis	mostaza	sennep	sènape	Senf	moutarde	gorchitsa	mostarda	karashi	raaee	jièmo	mustard
kitambaa	servilleta	serviette	tovagliolo	Serviette	serviette	salfetka	guardanapo	napukin	naipkin	canjin	napkin
	tallarines	nudler	taglierini	Nudel	nouilles	lapsha	talharim	1. nudoru 2. menrui		miàntiáo	noodle
kokwa	nuez	nøtt	noce	Nüss	noix	orekh	noz	nattsu	badaam		nut
mafuta	aceite	olje	olio	Öl	huile	1. maslo 2. mazat	azeite	abura	tél	yóu	oil
mzeituni	aceituna	oliven	oliva	Olive	olive	maslina	azeitona	oribu	zaitoon	gánlan	olive
vitunguu	cebolla	løk	cipolla	Zwiebel	oignon	luk	cebola	tamanegi	pyaaz	yángcong	onion
chungwa	naranja	appelsin	arancia	Orange	orange	apel'sin	laranja	mikan	santaré	ganzi	orange
jiko la kuokea	horno	ovn	forno	Backofen	four	1. pech'ka 2. pech	forno	tempi		kaoxiang	oven
chaza	ostra	østers	ostrica	Auster	huître	ustritsa	ostra	kaki	shuk-ti	muli	oyster
	perejil	persille	prezzé-molo	Petersillie	persil	petrushka	salsa		ajmodaa		parsley
pichi	1. melocotón 2. durazno	fersken	pesca	Pfirsich	pêche	persik	pêssego	momo	aru	taozi	peach
njvgu	cacahuate	jordnøtter	arachide	Erdnuss	cacahuète	arakhis	amendolm	pinatsu		hua sheng	peanut
	pera	pære	pera	Birne	poire	grusha	pêra	nashi	naashpaatee	lizi	pear
mbaazi	1. guisantes 2. echicharos	erter	piselli	Erbsen	pois	gorokh	ervilha	endo-mame	matar	wandòu	peas
pilpili manga	pimienta	pepper	pépe	Pfeffer	poivre	perez	pimenta	kosho	mirch	hújiao	pepper
	piñon	gran kongle	pinolo	Pinienuss	pigne	oreh	pinheiro	crenata			pine nut
nanasi	piña	ananas	ananas	Ananas	ananas	ananas	1. abacaxi 2. ananás	painappuree	anaaras	boluó	pineapple
sahani	plato	tallerken	piatto	Platte	assiette	tarelka	prato	sara	plét	pánzi	plate
nyama ya nguruwa	1. cerdo 2. puerco	1. gris 2. svinekjøtt	maiale	Schwein	porc	svinina	carne de porco	buta	su-ar kaa maans	zhū	pork
viazi	1. patata 2. papa	potet	patata	Kartoffel	1. pommes 2. pommes de terre	kartofel	batata	jagaimo	aloo	tudòu	potato
boga	calabaza	gresskar	zucca	Kürbis	potiron	tykva	abóbora	kabocha	kaddoo		pumpkin
isungura	conejo	kanin	coniglio	1. Kaninchen (rabbit) 2. Hase (hare)	1. lapin 2. lievre	1. zayatz 2. krolik	coelho	usagi	khar-gosh	tùzi	rabbit

COMMONLY USED INTERNATIONAL TERMS—CONTINUED

ENGLISH	CHINESE	HINDI	JAPAN	PORTUG	RUSSIAN	FRENCH	GERMAN	ITALIAN	NORWGN	SPANISH	SWAHILI
raisin	putaogar	kish-mish	hoshi-budo	passa	izyum	raisin sec	Rosine	uva passa	rosin	pasa	zabibu kavu
raspberry			ki-ichigo	framboesa	malina	framboise	Himbeere	lampone	bringebær	frambuesa	fursadi
raw	sheng	1. taza 2. kacha	nama no	cru	syroy	cru	roh	crudo	rå	crudo	mbichi
recipe	hupu		choriho	receita	rezept	recette	Rezept	ricetta	oppskrmift	receta	maelezo ya upishi
restaurant	fanguan		ryoriten	restaurante	restaran	restaurant	Gaststätte	ristorante	restaurang	restaurante	hoteli ya kula
rice	mifan	chawal	kome	arroz	ris	riz	Reis	riso	ris	arróz	1. wali (cooked) 2. mcheler (uncooked)
ripe	shu (fruit)	pakna	juku shta	1. maduro (adj) 2. amadureur (n)	speliy	mûr	reif	maturo	moden	maduro	mbiru
roast (v)	kao	sikai	1. aburu 2. iri	assar	zharit'	rôti	braten	arrosto	steke	asado	kuoka motoni
rye	h'imài	rai	raimugi	centeio	rozh'	seigle	Roggen	segale	rye	centeno	
salad	shalà	salaad	sarada	salada	salat	salade	Salat	insalata	salat	ensalada	saladi
salmon	dà mahayu	saaman	sake	salmão	losos	saumon	Lachssalm	salmóne	laks	salmón	samaki (fish)
salt	yán	namak	shio	sal	sol	sel	Salz	sale	salt	sal	chumvi
sandwich	sanmíngzhì		sandoitchi	sanduíche	buterbrod	sandwich	Belegtes brot (open-faced)	panino	smørbrød	bocadillo	sendwichi
sauce	zhi		sosu	môlho	sous	sauce	Sosse	salsa	saus	salsa	mchuzi
sausage	xiangchang		sos'ji	salsicha	kolbas	saucisse	Wurst	salame	pølse	salchicha	sosej
shallot		chota piaz		cebolinha	zeleniy luk	échalote	Schalotte	scalogno	sjalottløk	chalote	
shrimp	xia	chingri	ebi	camarão	krevetka	crevettes	Garnele	gambero	reke	1. camarónes 2. gambas	kamba
slice (v)		kaatna	usuku kiru	cortar em fatias	rezat' na kusochki	trancher	schneiden	affetare	å skiver	cortar	kukata
slices (of)	piànr	tukra	usui hito-kire	fatias	kuski	tranche	1. Scheiben 2. Schnitte	fetta	skive	1. tajada (meat) 2. rodaja (vegetable) 3. rebanada (bread)	ubale
smoked			1. kunsei no 2. sumoku	defumado	kopcheniy	fumé	geräuchert	affumicato	rökt	ahumado	chomwa
snail				caracol	ulitka	escargot	Schnecke	1. chiocciola 2. lumaca	snegl	caracol	konokono

English	Chinese	Hindi	Japanese	Portuguese	Russian	French	German	Italian	Norwegian	Spanish	Swahili
soup	tang	shorva	1. supu 2. jiru	sopa	sup	1. soupe 2. potage	Suppe	zuppa	suppe	sopa	supu
spice	zuóliào	masala	yakumi	especiaria	pryanosti	épice	1. Gewürze 2. Würze	spèzia	krydder	especia	
spicy	làde	masalédar	karai	picante	ostriy	piquant	1. würzig 2. pikant	piccante	krydret	1. picante (pepper) 2. condementada	
spinach	bócài	palak ka-saag	horen-so	espinafre	shpinat	épinard	Spinat	spinaci	spinat	espinacas	mchicha
spoon	xiaosháor	chammach	saji	colher	lozhka	cuillère	Löffel	cucchiaio	skje	cuchara	kijiko
stew	dùn	patla jhol	shichu-ryori	guisado	sup	ragoût	Schmoren	stufato	1. frikasse 2. lapshkaus	estofado	kutokosa
strawberry	cao-mei		ichigo	morango	klubnika	fraise	Erdbeere	fragola	jordbær	fresas	
stuffed		bhara	tsumeru	enchido	farshirovanniy	farci	gefüllt	farcito	fylt	relleno	
sugar, granulated	táng	cheenee	zarame	açúcar	sakhar	sucré	Zucker	zucchero	1. farin sukker 2. sukker	azúcar	sukari
sweet	tián	meetha	amai	doce	sladkiy	sucré	süss	dolce	søtt	dulce	tamu
table	zhuozi	méz	1. teburu 2. shokutaku	mesa	stol	table	Tisch	tavolo	bord	mesa	meza
tarragon				estragao	estragon	estragon	Estragon	1. dragoncello 2. serpentaria	estragon	estragón	
tea	chá	chaay	ocha	chá	chai	thé	Tee	tè	te	té	chai
tomato	xihóngshi	tamatar	tomato	tomate	pomidor	tomate	Tomate	pomodoro	tomat	tomate	tungule
trout	zunyu	machi	1. masu 2. ayu	truta	forel	truite	Forelle	trota	ørret	trucha	samaki (fish)
turkey	huoji	peroo	shichimencho	peru	indeyka	1. dindon (m) 2. dinde (f)	Truthahn	tacchino	kalkun	pavo	bata mzinga
vanilla	xiangcaojing		banira	baunilha	vanilin	vanille	Vanille	vaniglia	vanilje	vainilla	vanila
veal	xiaoniúròu		ko-ushi no niku	vitela	telyatina	veau	Kalb	vitello	kalv	ternera	nyama ya ndama
vegetables	shucài	sabzi	yasai	legumes	ovoschi	légumes	Gemüse	contorni	grønnsaker	verduras	mboga
venison, game		hirankaa gosht	shika	veado	olenina	chevreuil	Wildbret	cèrvo	dyrekjøtt	venado	
vinegar	cù	sirkaa	su	vinagre	uksus	vinaigre	Essig	aceto	eddik	vinagre	siki
waiter	fuwuyuan	vetar	kyuji	empregado	ofiziant	garçon	Kellner	cameriere	1. oppvarter 2. kelner	camarero	mtumishi mezani
water	shui	paani	mizu	água	voda	eau	Wasser	acqua	vann	agua	maji
wheat	xiaomài	gehoon	komugi	trigo	zerno	blé	Weizen	grano	1. hrete 2. hvete	trigo	ngano

COMMONLY USED INTERNATIONAL TERMS—CONTINUED

ENGLISH	CHINESE	HINDI	JAPAN	PORTUG	RUSSIAN	FRENCH	GERMAN	ITALIAN	NORWGN	SPANISH	SWAHILI
whiskey	weishìjì	viskee	uisuki	whisky	viski	whisky	Schnaps	whisky	whisky	whisky	wiski
wine, red	hóng pútáojiu	safed sharaab	budoshu	vinho vermelho	vino krasnoe	vin rouge	Rotwein	vino rosso	rødvin	vino tinto	mvinyo nyekundu
wine, white	bái pútáojiu	laal sharaab	wain	vinho branco	vino beloe	vin blanc	Weisswein	vino bianco	hvitvin	vino blanco	mvinyo nyeupe
yeast			isuto	levedura	drozhzhi	levure	Hefe	lievito	gjoer	levadura	hamira
yogurt	1. suan niúnai 2. suan nai	dahee	yoguruto	iogurte	prostok-vasha	yaourt	Joghurt	iogurt	yoghurt	yogur	